THE GUINNESS BOOK OF RECORDS 1992

EDITOR

Donald McFarlan

FOUNDING EDITOR

Norris D. McWhirter

EXECUTIVE EDITOR, U.S. EDITION

Michelle Dunkley McCarthy

EDITOR, U.S. EDITION (NEW YORK)

Mark Young

Facts On File
New York • Oxford

COPYRIGHT

ISBN 0-8160-2643-2

ISSN 0300-1679

"Guinness International" is a registered trademark of Guinness Publishing Ltd.
Text design by Guinness Publishing Ltd, Enfield
Jacket design by Amanda Ward and Catherine Hyman
Composition by Guinness Publishing Ltd, Enfield
Manufactured by R.R. Donnelley & Sons
Printed in the United States of America

This book is printed on acid-free paper.

ACKNOWLEDGEMENTS

The Guinness Book of Records
wishes to thank:

DEPUTY EDITORS
Sheila Goldsmith
Nicholas Heath-Brown
Maria Morgan
Stewart Newport

SPORTS EDITOR
Peter J. Matthews

CORRESPONDENCE EDITOR
Martin Day

COPY EDITORS
Virginia Rubens
Joseph Reilly
Joseph P. McCarthy

DESIGN MANAGER
David L. Roberts
Jo Stein

LAYOUT DESIGNER
Amanda Ward

PAGE MAKE-UP
Amanda Sedge

PICTURE EDITOR
Alex P. Goldberg

**INFORMATION
SYSTEMS MANAGER**
Alex E. Reid

PRODUCTION MANAGER
Chris Lingard
Olivia Westlin McKean

PRODUCTION ASSISTANT
Kevin Duffy

EDITORIAL ASSISTANTS
Aña Pachéco
Linda A. McClean
John W. Hansen

SECRETARIAL SUPPORT
Debbie Bigmore
Sallie Collins
Muriel Ling

PRESS OFFICER
Cathy Brooks

INDEX
Marjorie B. Bank

Acknowledgements

The editors would like to thank the many people contacted by our research staff who have provided us with the information needed to produce an accurate account of the world and its records.

Norris McWhirter

Regrettably, space prevents us from mentioning everyone. However, we would like to give special thanks to Norris McWhirter, whose advice and expertise have been invaluable in expanding this year's edition; and to the editor and staff of the *Facts On File World News Digest*, whose resources, talents and consideration have greatly added to the success of this edition.

Michelle D. McCarthy, Enfield, England
Mark Young, New York City

The History of The Guinness Book of Records

On Saturday, 10 Nov 1951, Sir Hugh Beaver (1891–1967) was out shooting on The North Slob, by the river Slanery in County Wexford in the southeast of Ireland. Some golden plover flew by so fast that they were missed by the shooting party. That evening at Castlebridge House, the company concluded that it was not possible to confirm in reference books whether or not the golden plover was Europe's fastest game bird.

Then, in August 1954, argument arose again, this time as to whether grouse were even faster than golden plover. Sir Hugh, Managing Director of Guinness plc, thought that there must be many other such questions debated nightly, but there was no book with which to settle the arguments about records.

On 12 Sep 1954, Sir Hugh challenged Norris and Ross McWhirter, who ran a fact and figure agency in London, England, to compile a book of records. An office was set up at 107 Fleet Street, London, and work began on the initial 198-page edition. The first copy was bound by the printers on 27 Aug 1955. Before Christmas, *The Guinness Book of Records* was No. 1 on the British best-seller lists, and it has remained there every year since, except for 1957 and 1959 when it was not published.

The Guinness Book of Records began its worldwide expansion in 1956, when the first United States edition was published in New York City. This successful venture was followed by editions in French (1962) and German (1963). In 1967 there were first editions in Japanese, Spanish, Danish and Norwegian, and in subsequent years editions were published in Portuguese (1974), Czechoslovakian (1976), Hebrew, Serbo-Croat and Icelandic (all in 1977) and Slovene (1978). In the 1980s there were translations into Greek, Indonesian, Chinese, Turkish, Hindi, Malay, Polish, Arabic, Tamil, Thai, Telugu, Malayalam, Kannada and Hungarian. The first Russian edition was printed in 1990, bringing the total to 182 editions in 36 languages.

In November 1974 *The Guinness Book of Records* itself earned a place in The Book by becoming the top-selling copyrighted book in publishing history, with sales of 23.9 million. By 1989, global sales had risen to more than 60 million, which is equivalent to more than 163 stacks each as high as Mt Everest, or 3,260 stacks each as high as the Sears Tower, or 526,635 stacks each as high as Robert Wadlow, the world's tallest man.

On 31 Mar 1986, having edited The Book for 31 years (22 of them with his twin brother Ross), Norris McWhirter relinquished his position as Editor, but remains as Editor Advisor to *The Guinness Book of Records*.

This 1992 edition marks the thirtieth published in the United States overall and the second by Facts On File, Inc. The editors have updated world and United States records and have included new records never previously published. It is their hope that they have continued to fulfill Sir Hugh's mandate to produce an entertaining reference book that provides accurate, authenticated and easily accessible answers to questions on the world, its inhabitants and its records. (The answer to Sir Hugh's question as to Europe's fastest game bird appears on page 38.)

■ **Arthur Guinness**
A portrait of the founder of the Guinness Dublin Brewery (Ireland) in 1759. (Photo: Arthur Guinness and Sons Plc)

Policy

The Guinness Book of Records is the authoritative source for facts, feats and exploits of the world and its inhabitants. This collection of records covers all fields of human, and nonhuman, endeavor; however, it is not a compendium of every record set, but rather a subjective selection of those that the editors find to be the most significant. Records in our sense have to be both measurable and comparable. Novel events, unique occurrences and fascinating idiosyncrasies are not necessarily records. We are likely to publish only those records that improve upon previously published records. We reserve the right to determine at our sole discretion the records to be published.

Guidance regarding the breaking of records is available from this office upon written application and receipt of a business-size self-addressed stamped envelope, and should be sought at least one month before completing plans for a record attempt.

Send your application to:
Guinness Book of Records
Facts On File, Inc.
460 Park Avenue South
New York, NY 10016

CONTENTS

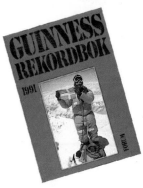

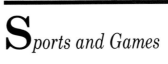

The Earth and Space

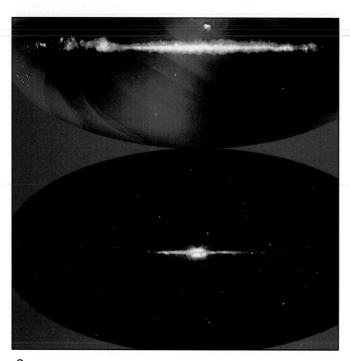

The Universe

ASTRONOMICAL UNIT—the distance from the center of the Earth to the center of the Sun as defined in 1938, equivalent to 92,955,807 miles. LIGHT-YEAR—the distance traveled by light (speed 186,282.397 miles/sec) in one tropical year (365.24219878 mean solar days at January 0.12 hours Ephemeris time in A.D. 1900). This is equivalent to 5,878,499,814,000 miles. The unit was first used in March 1888. MAGNITUDE—a measure of stellar brightness such that the light of a star of any magnitude bears a ratio of 2.511886 to that of a star of the next magnitude. Thus a fifth-magnitude star is 2.511886 brighter than a sixth-magnitude star, while a first-magnitude star is 100 (or 2.511886^5) times brighter. Magnitude is expressed as a negative quantity for exceptionally bright bodies such as the Sun (apparent magnitude −26.78). PARSEC—the true measure of stellar distance, being the reciprocal of half of the angle in seconds of arc subtended when the position of a star is measured on both sides of the Earth's orbit (parallactic displacement against a background of "fixed" stars) and equivalent to 206,264.806 astronomical units, 19,173,511,000,000 miles or 3.261633 light-years.

Large structures in the Universe
Our own Milky Way galaxy is only one of 10 billion galaxies. It is part of the so-called Local Group of galaxies moving at a speed of 370 miles/sec with respect to the cosmological frame in the general direction of a dense concentration of galaxy clusters known as the "Great Attractor" (a term coined by Alan Dressler [USA]). In November 1989 Margaret Geller and John Huchra (USA) announced the discovery of a "Great Wall" in space, a concentration of galaxies in the form of a "crumpled membrane" with a minimum extent of 280×800 million light-years (1.6×10^{21} miles $\times 4.7 \times 10^{21}$ miles) and a depth of up to 20 million light-years (9.6×10^{19} miles). In July 1990 Juan M. Uson, Stephen P. Boughn and Jeffrey R. Kuhn (USA) announced the discovery of the largest galaxy—the central galaxy of the Abell 2,029 galaxy cluster, 1,070 million light-years distant in Virgo. It has a major diameter of 5,500,000 million light-years (4.6×10^{19} miles), which is eight times the diameter of our own galaxy (see below) and has a light output equivalent to 2 trillion (2×10^{12}) Suns.

Age of the Universe For the age of the Universe a consensus value of 14 ± 3 eons or gigayears (an eon or gigayear being 1 billion years) is obtained from various cosmological techniques. The equivalent value of the Hubble constant based on a Friedman model of the Universe without cosmological constant is Mpc43 ± 9 m/s. In 1973 an *ex nihilo* creation was postulated by Edward P. Tryon (USA). Modified versions of the Inflationary Model, originally introduced by Alan Guth (USA) in 1981, now complement the Big Bang theory of creation.

Remotest object Both the interpretation of the very large red shifts exhibited by quasars and the estimation of equivalent distances remain controversial. The record red shift of $z = 4.73$ for quasar PC 1158 + 4635 was announced by Donald Schneider, Maarten Schmidt and James Gunn in August 1989 from spectroscopic and photometric observations made between February 1988 and March 1989 using the Hale Telescope at Palomar Observatory, CA. If it is assumed that there is an "observable horizon," where the speed of recession is equal to the speed of light, i.e., at 14 billion light-years or 82.3 million trillion miles, then this quasar would be 13.2 billion light-years distant.

Farthest visible object The remotest heavenly body visible with the naked eye is the Great Galaxy in *Andromeda* (mag. 3.47), known as Messier 31. It was first noted from Germany by Simon Marius (1570–1624). It is a rotating nebula in spiral form at a distance from the Earth of about 2,309,000 light-years, or 1.36×10^{19} miles (13 million trillion miles), and is moving towards us. It is just possible that under ideal conditions for observations, Messier 33, the Spiral in Triangulum (mag. 5.79), can be glimpsed by the naked eye by sharp-eyed people at a distance of 2,509,000 light-years.

Quasars An occultation of 3C-273, observed from Australia on 5 Aug 1962, enabled the existence of quasi-stellar radio sources ("quasars" or QSOs) to be announced by Maarten Schmidt (Netherlands b. 1929). The red shift proved to be $z = 0.158$.

Quasars have immensely high luminosity for bodies so distant and of such small diameter. It was announced in May 1983 that the quasar S5 0014 + 81 had a visual luminosity 1.1 quadrillion times greater than that of the Sun.

The first double quasar (0957 + 56) among 1,500 known quasars was announced in May 1980.

The most violent outburst observed in a quasar was recorded on 13 Nov 1989 by a joint US-Japanese team which noted that the energy output of the quasar PKS 0558-504 (which is about 2 billion light-years distant) increased by two-thirds in three minutes, equivalent to the total energy released by the Sun in 340,000 years.

STARS

Nearest Except for the special case of our own Sun, the nearest star is the very faint *Proxima Centauri*, discovered in 1915, which is 4.225 light-years (25 trillion miles) away.

The nearest star visible to the naked eye is the southern hemisphere binary *Alpha Centauri*, or *Rigel Kentaurus* (4.35 light-years distant), with an apparent magnitude of −0.29. It was discovered by Nicolas L. de Lacaille (1713–62) in *c.* 1752. In A.D. 29,700 this binary will reach a minimum distance from the Earth of 2.84 light-years and should then be the second brightest star, with an apparent magnitude of −1.20.

Farthest The Solar System, with its Sun's nine principal planets, 61 satellites, asteroids and comets, is located in the outer regions of our Milky Way galaxy, orbiting the center of the galaxy at a mean distance of 29,700 light-years and with an orbital eccentricity of 0.07. The present distance from the center is 27,700 light-years and it will reach the minimum distance of 27,600 light-years (perigalacticon) in about 15 million years, on the last day of the year.

The Milky Way galaxy has a diameter of about 70,000 light-years, so the most distant star will be at 66,700 light-years when the Solar System is farthest from the center (apogalacticon). At present the most distant stars are at 62,700 light-years.

The present orbital velocity of the Sun and a large number of nearby stars has been averaged to 492,000 mph (the "Local Standard of Rest"), which would lead to an orbital period of 237 million years.

However, the Sun's actual velocity is 60,400 mph faster than this average.

Largest, heaviest and most luminous The largest star is the M-class supergiant *Betelgeux* (Alpha Orionis—the top left star of Orion), which is 310 light-years distant. It has a diameter of 400 million miles, which is about 500 times greater than that of the Sun. In 1978 it was found to be surrounded not only by a dust "shell" but also by an outer tenuous gas halo up to 5.3×10^{11} miles in diameter or over 1,100 times the diameter of the star.

The heaviest star is the variable *Eta*

Carinae, 9,100 light-years distant in the Carinae Nebula in our own galaxy, with a mass 200 times greater than that of our own Sun. If all the stars could be viewed at the same distance it would also be the most luminous star, with a total luminosity 6,500,000 times that of the Sun. However, the visually brightest star is the hypergiant Cygnus OB2 No.12, which is 5,900 light-years distant. It has an absolute visual magnitude of -9.9 and is therefore visually 810,000 time brighter than the Sun. This brightness may be matched by the supergiant IV b 59 in the nearby galaxy Messier 101. During 1843 the absolute luminosity and absolute visual brightness of *Eta Carinae* temporarily increased to values 60 and 70 million times the corresponding values for the Sun.

Smallest, lightest and dimmest A mass of 0.014 that of the Sun is estimated for RG 0058.8-2807, which was discovered by I. Neill Reid and Gerard Gilmore using the UK Schmidt telescope (announced in April 1983). It is also the faintest star detected, with a total luminosity only 0.0021 that of the Sun and an absolute visual magnitude of 20.2 so the visual brightness is less than one millionth that of the Sun. The smallest star appears to be the white dwarf L362-81 with an estimated diameter of 3,500 miles or only 0.0040 that of the Sun.

Brightest (as seen from Earth) *Sirius A* (*Alpha Canis Majoris*), also known as the Dog Star, is the brightest star of the 5,776 stars visible to the naked eye. It has an apparent magnitude of -1.46 but because of the relative motions of this star and the Sun this should rise to a maximum value of -1.67 by *c.* A.D. 61000. *Sirius* is 8.64 light-years distant and has a luminosity 26 times greater than that of the Sun. It has a diameter of 1.45 million miles and a mass 2.14 times that of the Sun. The faint white dwarf companion *Sirius B* has a diameter of only 6,000 miles, which is less than that of the Earth, but its mass is slightly greater than that of the Sun. *Sirius* is in the constellation *Canis Major* and is visible in the winter months of the northern hemisphere, being due south at midnight on the last day of the year.

Pulsars The earliest observation of a pulsating radio source, or "pulsar," CP 1919 (now PSR 1919 + 21), by Dr Jocelyn Burnell (nee Bell, b. 1943) was announced from the Mullard Radio Astronomy Observatory, Cambridgeshire, Great Britain on 24 Feb 1968. It had been detected on 28 Nov 1967.

For pulsars whose spin rates have been accurately measured, the fastest-spinning is PSR 1937 + 214, which was discovered by a group led by Donald C. Backer in November 1982. It is in the minor constellation *Vulpecula* (the Little Fox), 16,000 light-years distant, and has a pulse period of 1.557806449 millisec, which is equivalent to a spin rate of 641.9282708 revolutions per sec.

The pulsar that has the slowest spin-down rate and is therefore the most

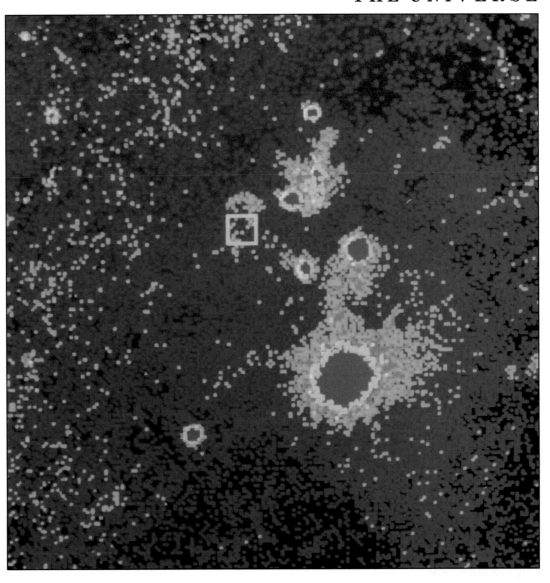

accurate stellar clock is PSR 1855 + 09 at only 2.1×10^{-20} sec per sec.

Brightest and latest supernova The brightest supernova ever seen in historic times is believed to be SN 1006, noted in April 1006 near *Beta Lupi*. It flared for two years and attained a magnitude of -9 to -10. The remnant is believed to be the radio source G.327.6 + 14.5, nearly 3,000 light-years distant.

Others have occurred in 1054, 1604, 1885, and most recently on 23 Feb 1987, when Ian Shelton sighted the one designated $-69,202$ in the Large Magellanic Cloud 170,000 light-years distant. This supernova was visible to the naked eye when at its brightest in May 1987. A claim to have detected a fast-spinning pulsar at the center of the supernova debris was withdrawn in February 1990.

Black holes The concept of superdense bodies was first proposed by the Marquis de LaPlace (1749–1827). This term for a star that has undergone complete gravitational collapse was first used by Prof John Archibald Wheeler at an Institute for Space Studies meeting in New York City on 29 Dec 1967.

The first tentative identification of a

black hole was announced in December 1972 in the binary-star X-ray source Cygnus X–1.

The best candidate is LMC X–3 of 10 solar masses at 180,000 light-years distant reported in January 1983. The critical size has been estimated to be as low as a diameter of 3.7 miles. One at the center of the Seyfert galaxy, NGC 4151 in *Canes Venatici*, was estimated by Michael Preston (Great Britain) in October 1983 to be of between 50–100 million solar masses, or up to 2.205 $\times 10^{35}$ tons.

Stellar planets All claims to have discovered planetary systems around other stars must be treated with suspicion. There appears to be a confusion with small dim stellar companions known as "brown dwarfs" that are failed stars since they are too cool to trigger the fusion of hydrogen.

Of the nine possible candidates announced by Bruce Campbell, Gordon Walker and Stephenson Yang of the University of Victoria, British Columbia, Canada, in August 1988, the most promising appears to be the inferred existence of a planet one and a

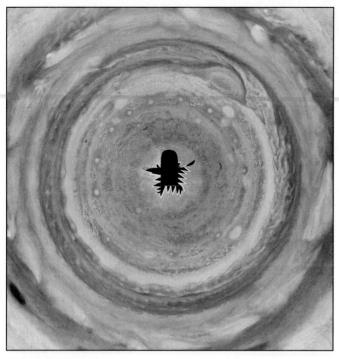

■ Largest planet— Jupiter

Jupiter is the largest of the nine major planets (including the Earth). This view shows the southern hemisphere from above the pole. It is a composite of pictures taken from Voyager I. (Photo: NASA)

half times the mass of Jupiter orbiting the bright star *36 Ursae Majoris A* with an orbital period of three years.

Constellations The largest of the 89 constellations is *Hydra* (the Sea Serpent), which covers 1302.844 $\deg^{02}$ or 6.3 percent of the hemisphere and contains at least 68 stars visible to the naked eye (to 5.5 mag).

The constellation *Centaurus* (Centaur), ranking ninth in area, however, embraces at least 94 such stars.

The smallest constellation is *Crux Australis* (Southern Cross) with an area of only 0.16 percent of the sky, or 68.477 $\deg^2$ compared with the 41,252.96 $\deg^2$ of the whole sky.

Longest name *Torcularis Septentrionalis* is the name applied to the star *Omicron Piscium* in the constellation *Pisces*.

THE SUN

Distance extremes The true distance of the Earth from the Sun is 1.00000102 astronomical units or 93 million miles. The orbit is elliptical and the distance of the Sun varies between a minimum (perihelion) of 91.5 million miles and a maximum (aphelion) of 94.5 million miles. Based on an orbital circumference of 58.4 million miles and an orbital period (sidereal year) of 365.256366 days, the average orbital velocity is 66,620 mph, but this varies between a minimum of 65,500 mph at aphelion and a maximum of 67,750 mph at perihelion.

Temperature and dimensions The Sun has a stellar classification of a *yellow dwarf* type G2, although its mass at 2 octillion tons is 332,946.04 times that of the Earth and represents over 99 percent of the total mass of the Solar System. The solar diameter at 865,040 miles leads to a density of 1.408 times that of water.

The Sun has a central temperature of about 15,400,000 K and a core pressure of 1.65 billion tons. It uses up about 4.4 million tons of hydrogen per sec, equal to an energy output of 3.85×10^{26} watts, although it will take 10 billion years to exhaust its energy supply (about 5 billion years from the present).

The luminous intensity of the Sun is 2.7 octillion candela, which is equal to a luminance of 290,000 candela/in^2.

Sunspots To be visible to the *protected* naked eye, a sunspot must cover about one two-thousandth part of the Sun's disc and thus have an area of about 0.5 billion miles^2. The largest sunspot ever noted was in the Sun's southern hemisphere on 8 Apr 1947. Its area was about 7 billion with an extreme longitude of 187,000 miles and an extreme latitude of 90,000 miles. Sunspots appear darker because they are more than 2,732 ° F cooler than the rest of the Sun's surface temperature of 9,945 ° F.

In October 1957 a smoothed sunspot count showed 263, the highest recorded index since records started in 1755 (the previous record was 239 in May 1778). In 1943 one sunspot lasted for 200 days, from June to December.

PLANETS

Largest The nine major planets (including the Earth) are bodies within the Solar System and revolve round the Sun in definite orbits.

Jupiter, with an equatorial diameter of 88,846 miles and a polar diameter of 83,082 miles, is the largest of the nine major planets, with a mass 317.828 times, and a volume 1,323.3 times, that of the Earth. It also has the shortest period of rotation, resulting in a Jovian day of only 9 hr 50 min 30.003 sec in the equatorial zone.

Smallest, coldest and outermost Pluto was first recorded by Clyde William Tombaugh (b. 4 Feb 1906) at Lowell Observatory, Flagstaff, AZ on 18 Feb 1930 from photographs he took on 23 and 29 January. His find was announced on 13 March.

Pluto's companion Charon was announced on 22 Jun 1978 from the US Naval Observatory, Flagstaff, AZ. Pluto, with a mass about 1/500th of that of the Earth, has a diameter of 1,429 miles, while Charon has a diameter of 737 miles. Their mean distance from the Sun is 3,674,488,000 miles, with a period of revolution of 248.54 years. Because of their orbital eccentricity they will be temporarily closer to the Sun than Neptune in the period from 23 Jan 1979 to 15 Mar 1999. The lowest observed surface temperature of any natural body in the Solar System is 391° F in the case of Neptune's large moon *Triton*, although the true surface temperature of Pluto and Charon remain to be measured.

Fastest Mercury, which orbits the Sun at an average distance of 0.4 million miles, has a period of revolution of 87.9686 days, thus registering the highest average speed in orbit of 107,030 mph.

Hottest For Venus a surface temperature of 864 ° F has been estimated from measurements made from the USSR *Venera* and US *Pioneer* surface probes.

Nearest The fellow planet closest to the Earth is Venus, which is, at times, only 26 million miles inside the Earth's orbit, compared with Mars' closest approach of 35 million miles outside the Earth's orbit.

Mars, known since 1965 to be cratered, has temperatures ranging from 85° F to −190° F.

Surface features By far the highest and most spectacular is *Olympus Mons* (formerly *Nix Olympica*) in the Tharsis region of Mars, with a diameter of 310–370 miles and a height of 75,450–95,150 ft above the surrounding plain.

Venus has a canyon some 1,000 miles south of the Venusian equator that is 21,000 ft deep and 250 miles long.

The ice cliff on the Uranian moon Miranda is 3.23 miles high.

Brightest and faintest Viewed from the Earth, by far the brightest of the five planets visible to the naked eye is Venus, with a maximum magnitude of −4.4.

Uranus, the first to be discovered by telescope when it was sighted by Sir William Herschel from his garden at 19 New King St, Bath, Great Britain on 13 Mar 1781, is only marginally visible, with a magnitude 5.5.

The faintest planet is Pluto, with a magnitude of 15.0.

Densest and least dense Earth is the densest planet, with an average figure of 5.515 times that of water, while Saturn has an average density only about one-eighth of this value or 0.685 times that of water.

Conjunctions The most dramatic recorded conjunction (coming together) of the other seven principal members of the Solar System (Sun, Moon, Mercury, Venus, Mars, Jupiter and Saturn) occurred on 5 Feb 1962, when 16° covered all seven during an eclipse in the Pacific area. It is possible that the sevenfold conjunction that occurred in September 1186 spanned only 12°.

The next notable conjunction will take place on 5 May 2000.

Largest scale model The largest scale model of the Solar System was inaugurated by the Futures' Museum, Falun, Sweden on 29 Nov 1986. A model of the Earth with a diameter of ½ in was placed in the museum. The Sun (diameter 5 ft), and the planets (with diameters ranging from 0.13 in to 5 ½ in) were positioned in the nearby city of Borlange some 10 miles away. *Proxima Centauri* was sited in the Museum of Victoria, Melbourne, Australia.

SATELLITES

Most and least The Solar System has a total of 61 satellites, with Saturn having the most at 18 while Earth and Pluto have only one satellite each and Mercury and Venus none. The most

THE MOST DISTANT MEASURED HEAVENLY BODIES

The possible existence of galaxies external to our own Milky Way system was suggested in 1789 by Sir William Herschel (1738–1822). These extra-galactic nebulae were first termed "island universes." Sir John Herschel (1792–1871) opined as early as 1835 that some might be more than 250 quadrillion miles distant. The first direct measurement of any body outside our Solar System was in 1838. Distances in the table below assume that the edge of the observable Universe is at a distance of 14 billion light-years.

Estimated Distance in Light-years[1]	Object	Method	Astronomers	Observatory	Date
about 6 (now 11.08)	61 Cygni	Parallax	F. Bessel	Königsberg, Germany	1838
>20 (now 26)	Vega	Parallax	F. G. W. Struve	Dorpat (now Tartu), Estonia	1840
c. 200	Limit	Parallax			by 1900
900,000 (now 2.31 million)[2]	Galaxy M31	Cepheid variable	E. P. Hubble (1889–1953)	Mt Wilson, CA	1924

Millions of Light-years	Recession Speed % of c	Object	Red Shift[3]	Astronomers	Observatory	Date
c.200	1.4	NGC 7619		M. L. Humason	Mt. Wilson, CA	early 1928
>2,100	>15.0	Ursa Major No. 2		Humason & E. P. Hubble	Mt. Wilson, CA	by 1936[4]
4,600	32.6	Cluster 1448	0.403		Palomar, CA	1956
5,100	36.2	3C 295 in Boötes	0.461	R. Minkowski	Palomar, CA	Jun 1960
5,700	41.0	QSO 3C 147	0.545	M. Schmidt & T. A. Matthews	Palomar, CA	Feb 1964[5]
11,200	80.1	QSO 3C 9	2.01	M. Schmidt	Palomar, CA	Apr 1965
11,400	81.3	QSO 0106 +01	2.11	E. M. Burbridge et al	Palomar, CA	Dec 1965
11,400	81.4	QSO 1116 +12	2.12	C. R. Lynds & A. N. Stockton	Steward, AZ	Mar 1966
				M. Schmidt	Palomar, CA	Mar 1966
11,500	82.4	QSO Pks 0237 −23	2.22	H. C. Arp et al	Palomar, CA	Dec 1966
11,700	83.7	QSO 4C 25.05	2.36	E. T. Olsen & M. Schmidt	Palomar, CA	Dec 1967[6]
12,300	87.5	QSO 4C 05.34	2.88	R. Lynds & D. Wills	Kitt Peak, AZ	Mar 1970
12,600	90.2	QSO OH 471	3.40	R. F. Carswell & P. A. Strittmatter	Steward, AZ	Mar 1973
12,700	90.7	QSO OQ 172	3.53	E. J. Wampler et al	Lick, CA	May 1973
12,800	91.6	QSO Pks 2000 −330	3.78	B. A. Peterson et al	Siding Spring, Australia	Apr 1982[7]
12,800	91.7	QSO Pks 1208 +1011	3.80	C. Hazard et al	Siding Spring, Australia	Feb 1986[8]
12,900	92.3	QSO 0046 −293	4.01	S. J.Warren et al	Siding Spring, Australia	Sept 1986[8]
12,900	92.4	QSO PC0910 +5625	4.04	M. Schmidt et al	Palomar, CA	June 1987
13,000	92.6	QSO 0000 −2620	4.11	C. Hazard et al	Siding Spring, Australia	Aug 1987[8]
13,100	93.4	QSO 0051 −279	4.43	S. J. Warren et al	Siding Spring, Australia	Nov 1987[8]
13,200	94.1	QSO PC 1158 +4635	4.73	D. P. Schneider et al	Palomar, CA	Aug 1989

Note: c is the notation for the speed of light. (see page 8). [1] *Term first utilized in March 1888.* [2] *Re-estimate by M. Rowan-Robinson in March 1988.* [3] *Discovered by Vesto Slipher (1875–1969) from Flagstaff, AZ, 1920. Red shift, denoted by z, is the measure of the speed of recession indicated by the ratio resulting from the subtraction of the rest wavelength of an emission line from the observed wavelength divided by the rest wavelength.* [4] *In 1934 Hubble opined that the observable horizon would be 3 billion light-years.* [5] *In Dec 1963 Dr I. S. Shklovsky's (USSR) suggestion that QS0 3C2 was more distant was subsequently confirmed with a value of 0.612 c.* [6] *In Oct 1968 Dr Margaret Burbidge published a tentative red shift of 2.38 for QSO 5C 2.56.* [7] *Anglo-Australian telescope.* [8] *Great Britain, Schmidt telescope.*

recently discovered, announced on 16 Jul 1990 by Mark R. Showalter (USA), is the Saturnian satellite temporarily designated 1981 S13 which was found on eleven *Voyager 2* photographs taken during the close approach in August 1981. It has a diameter of only about 12 miles and orbits within the 200-mile Encke gap in the A ring. E.A. Marouf and G.L. Tyler have predicted the existence of two further Saturnian satellites in the Cassini Division between the A and B rings.

Distance extremes The distance of satellites from their parent planets varies from the 5,827 miles of *Phobos* from the center of Mars to the 14,700,000 miles of Jupiter's outer satellite *Sinope*.

Largest and smallest The largest and heaviest satellite is *Ganymede* (Jupiter III), which is 2.017 times heavier than the Earth's Moon and has a diameter of 3,273 miles. Of satellites whose diameters have been measured the smallest is *Deimos*, the outermost moon of Mars. Although irregularly shaped, it has an average diameter of 7.8 miles. The diameter of *Leda* (Jupiter XIII) is estimated to be less than 9 miles.

ASTEROIDS

Number and distance extremes
There are estimated to be about 45,000 asteroids, but only the orbits of just over 5,000 have been accurately computed. While most orbit between Mars and Jupiter, average distances from the Sun vary between 72,200,000 miles (just outside of Venus's orbit) for the Aten asteroid 1954XA (discovered 5 Dec 1954 but currently lost) and 1,269 million miles for the remote 2060 *Chiron* (discovered 18 Oct 1977), which orbits between Saturn and Uranus. There is increasing evidence that this body has a cometary rather than asteroidal nature. Because of its large orbital eccentricity the closest approach to the Sun is by the Apollo asteroid 3200 *Phaethon* (discovered 11 Oct 1983) to within 12,980,000 miles at perihelion, while the known closest approach to the Earth by an asteroid is 105,700 miles on 18 Jan 1991 by 1991BA (the day after its discovery).

Largest and smallest The largest and first discovered (by G. Piazzi in Palermo, Sicily on 1 Jan 1801) is *1 Ceres*, with a diameter of 582 miles. Most asteroids' measurements are estimated to the nearest yard in diameter, the smallest reported value being 30 ft for the closest Earth-approaching asteroid, 1991BA. The only asteroid visible to the naked eye is 4 *Vesta* (discovered 29 Mar 1807) which is 323 miles in diameter and has a maximum apparent magnitude as viewed from the Earth of 5.0.

THE MOON
The Earth's closest neighbor in space and its only natural satellite is the Moon, which has an average diameter of 2,159.3 miles and a mass of 8.1×10^{19} tons, or 0.0123 Earth masses, so the density is 3.344 times that of water.

The Moon orbits at a mean distance from the Earth of 238,854.5 miles center-to-center, although the center of mass is displaced from the center of figure by 1.1 miles towards the Earth so that the distance surface-to-surface is 233,813 miles. In the present century the closest approach (smallest perigee) was 221,441 miles center-to-center on 4 Jan 1912 and the farthest distance (largest apogee) was 252,718 miles on 2 Mar 1984.

The orbital period (sidereal month) is 27.321661 days, giving an average orbital velocity of 2,289 mph.

The currently accepted "giant impact" theory of the lunar origin suggests that the Moon was formed just outside the Earth's Roche Limit (about 11,500 miles from the Earth's center) from the debris resulting from a glancing collision between the Earth and a Mars-size planetesimal. That this event must have occurred in the early history of the Solar System is indicated by the fact that the oldest lunar rocks and soils brought back to Earth by the Apollo program crews are of a similar age to the oldest known meteorites (about 4.5 billion years).

The first direct hit on the Moon was achieved at 2 min 24 sec after midnight (Moscow time) on 14 Sep 1959, by the Soviet space probe *Lunar II* near the *Mare Serenitatis*.

The first photographic images of the hidden side of the Moon were collected by the USSR *Lunar III* from 6:30 A.M. on 7 Oct 1959 from a range of up to 43,750 miles, and transmitted to the Earth from a distance of 292,000 miles.

Crater Only 59 percent of the Moon's surface is directly visible from the Earth because it is in "captured rotation," i.e., the period of rotation is equal to the period of orbit. The largest wholly visible crater is the walled plain Bailly, towards the Moon's South Pole, which is 183 miles across, with walls rising to 14,000 ft. The Orientale Basin, partly on the averted side, measures more than 600 miles in diameter.

The deepest crater is the Newton Crater, with a floor estimated to be between 23,000 and 29,000 ft below its rim and 14,000 ft below the level of the plain outside. The brightest directly visible spot on the Moon is Aristarchus.

Highest mountains In the absence of a sea level, lunar altitudes are measured relative to an adopted reference sphere of radius 1,079.943 miles. The greatest elevation attained on this basis by any of the 12 US astronauts who have landed on the moon has been 25,688 ft on the Descartes Highlands by Capt. John Watts Young (USN) and Major Charles M. Duke, Jr. on 27 Apr 1972.

Temperature extremes When the Sun is overhead the temperature on the lunar equator reaches 243° F (31° F above the boiling point of water). By sunset the temperature is 58° F, but after nightfall it sinks to −261° F.

ECLIPSES

Earliest recorded For the Middle East, lunar eclipses have been extrapolated to 3450 B.C. and solar ones to 4200 B.C.

The oldest record of a total solar eclipse is on a clay tablet found in 1948 among the ruins of the ancient city of Ugarit (now in Syria).

A reassessment in 1989 suggests that this records the eclipse of 5 Mar 1223 B.C.

Longest duration The maximum *possible* duration of an eclipse of the Sun is 7 min 31 sec.

The longest actually *measured* was on 20 Jun 1955 (7 min 8 sec), seen from the Philippines. An eclipse of 7 min 29 sec should occur in the mid-Atlantic Ocean on 16 Jul 2186, which will then be the longest for 1,469 years.

Most and least frequent The highest number of eclipses possible in a year is seven, as in 1935, when there were five solar and two lunar eclipses. In 1982 there were four solar and three lunar eclipses.

The lowest possible number in a year is two, both of which must be solar, as in 1944 and 1969.

AURORAE

Most frequent Polar lights, known since 1560 as aurora borealis or northern lights in the northern hemisphere, and since 1773 as aurora australis in the southern, are caused by electrical solar discharges in the upper atmosphere and occur most frequently in high latitudes. Aurorae are visible at some time on *every* clear dark night in the polar areas within 20 degrees of the magnetic poles.

The extreme height of aurorae has been measured at 620 miles, while the lowest may descend to 45 miles.

Lowest latitudes Extreme cases of displays in very low latitudes were recorded at Cuzco, Peru (2 Aug 1744) Honolulu, HI (1 Sep 1859), and questionably, Singapore (25 Sep 1909).

Noctilucent clouds These remain sunlit long after sunset owing to their great altitude, and are thought to consist of ice crystals or meteoric dust. Regular observations (at heights of *c.* 52 miles) in Western Europe date only from 1964; since that year the record high and low number of nights on which these phenomena have been observed have been 43 (1979) and 15 (1970).

COMETS

Earliest recorded Records date from the 7th century B.C. The speeds of the estimated 2 million comets vary from 700 mph in outer space to 1.25 million mph when near the Sun. The successive appearances of Halley's Comet have been traced back to 467 B.C. It was first depicted in the Nuremberg Chronicle of A.D. 684.

The first prediction of its return by Edmund Halley (1656–1742) proved true on Christmas Day 1758, 16 years after his death. On 13–14 Mar 1986, the European satellite *Giotto* (launched 2 Jul 1985) penetrated to within 335 miles of the nucleus of Halley's Comet. It was established that it was 9.3 miles in length and velvet black in color.

Closest approach On 1 Jul 1770, Lexell's Comet, traveling at a speed of 23.9 miles/sec (relative to the Sun), came to within 745,000 miles of the Earth. However, the Earth is believed to

have passed through the tail of Halley's Comet, most recently on 19 May 1910.

Largest The tail of the brightest of all comets, the Great Comet of 1843, trailed for 205,000,000 miles.

The bow shock of Holmes Comet of 1892 once measured 1.5 million miles in diameter.

Shortest period Of all the recorded periodic comets (that are members of the Solar System), the one which most frequently returns is Encke's Comet, first identified in 1786. Its period of 1,206 days (3.3 years) is the shortest established. Only one of its 53 returns has been missed by astronomers; this was in 1944. Now increasingly faint, it is expected to die by February 1994.

The most frequently observed comets are Schwassmann-Wachmann I, Kopff and Oterma, which can be observed every year between Mars and Jupiter.

Longest period At the other extreme is Delavan's Comet of 1914, whose path was not accurately determined. It is not expected to return for perhaps 24 million years.

METEOROIDS

Meteoroids are of cometary or asteroidal origin. A meteor is the light phenomenon caused by the entry of a meteoroid into the Earth's atmosphere.

Meteor "shower" The greatest shower on record occurred on the night of 16–17 Nov 1966, when the Leonid meteors (which recur every 33¼ years) were visible between western North America and eastern USSR. It was calculated that meteors passed over Arizona at a rate of 2,300 per min for a period of 20 min from 5 A.M. on 17 Nov 1966.

METEORITES

Meteorites When a *meteoroid* (consisting of broken fragments of cometary or asteroidal origin and ranging in size from fine dust to bodies several miles in diameter) penetrates to the Earth's surface, the remnant, which may be either aerolite (stony) or siderite (metallic), is described as a *meteorite*. Such events occur about 150 times per year over the whole land surface of the Earth.

In historic times, the only recorded person injured by a meteorite was Mrs Ann Hodges of Sylacauga, AL. On 30 Nov 1954 a 9-lb stone, some 7 in in length, crashed through the roof of her home, hitting Mrs Hodges on the arm and bruising her hip. The physician who examined her, Dr Moody D. Jacobs, declared her fit but she was subsequently hospitalized as a result of the publicity. The most anxious time of day for meteorophobes should be 3 P.M.

Oldest A revision by T. Kirsten in 1981 of the age estimates of meteorites which have remained essentially undisturbed after their formation suggests that the oldest accurately dated is the Krahenberg meteorite at 4600 ± 20 million years, which predates the Solar System by about 70 million years.

■ **Meteor shower**
The Leonid shower which was the greatest on record occurred 16–17 Nov 1966. The meteors (shooting stars) are the straight vertical lines which thicken and brighten as the meteoroids burn up in the Earth's atmosphere.
(Photo: Science Photo Library)

It was reported in August 1978 that dust grains in the Murchison meteorite which fell in Australia in September 1969 may also be older than the Solar System.

Largest There was a mysterious explosion of 12½ megatons at Lat. 60° 55′ N, Long. 101° 57′ E, in the basin of the Podkamennaya Tunguska River, 40 miles north of Vanavar, in Siberia, USSR, at 00 hrs 17 min 11 sec UT (Universal Time) on 30 Jun 1908. The cause was variously attributed to a meteorite (1927), a comet (1930), a nuclear explosion (1961), and antimatter (1965). The explosion devastated an area of about 1,500 miles² and the shock was felt as far away as 600 miles. The theory now favored is that it was the terminal flare of stony debris from a comet, possibly Encke's comet, at an altitude of 20,000 ft or less.

The largest known meteorite was found in 1920 at Hoba West, near Grootfontein in Namibia, and is a block 9 ft long by 8 ft broad, estimated to weigh 65 tons.

The largest meteorite exhibited by any museum is the "Tent" meteorite, weighing 68,085 lb, found in 1897 near Cape York, on the west coast of Greenland, by the expedition of Commander Robert Edwin Peary (USA; 1856–1920). It was known to the Inuits as the Abnighito and is now exhibited in the Hayden Planetarium in New York City.

The largest piece of stony meteorite recovered is a piece weighing 3,902 lb, part of a 4.4-ton shower which struck Jilin (formerly Kirin), China on 8 Mar 1976.

Craters It has been estimated that some 2,000 asteroid–Earth collisions have occurred in the last 600 million years. One hundred and two collision sites or astroblemes have been identified.

A crater 150 miles in diameter and ½ mile deep was attributed to a meteorite in 1962 in Wilkes Land, Antarctica. Such a crater could have been caused by a meteorite weighing 14,329,900,000 tons striking at 44,000 mph. Soviet scientists reported in December 1970 an astrobleme with a diameter of 60 miles and a maximum depth of 1,300 ft in the basin of the River Popigai.

There is a crater-like formation or astrobleme 275 miles in diameter on the eastern shore of Hudson Bay, Canada, where the Nastapoka Islands are just off the coast.

One of the largest and best-preserved craters is the Coon Butte or Barringer Crater, discovered in 1891 near Canyon Diablo, Winslow, AZ. It is 4,150 ft in diameter and now about 575 ft deep, with a parapet rising 130–155 ft above the surrounding plain. It has been estimated that an iron-nickel mass of some 2,204,600 tons and a diameter of 200–260 ft gouged this crater in *c.* 25,000 B.C.

The New Quebec (formerly the Chubb) Crater, first sighted on 20 Jun 1943 in northern Ungava, Canada, is 1,325 ft deep and measures 6.8 miles around its rim.

Tektites The largest tektite (a class of small natural glassy objects of uncertain origin found only in certain areas of the Earth's surface) of which details have been published weighed 7.04 lb and was found in 1932 at Muong Nong, Saravane Province, Laos. It is now in the Louvre Museum, Paris, France. Eight SNC meteorites (named after their find sites at Shergotty in India, Nakla in Egypt and Chassigny in France), are believed to have emanated from Mars.

Fireball The brightest ever photographically recorded was by Dr Zdenek Ceplecha over Sumava, Czechoslovakia on 4 Dec 1974 with a momentary magnitude of − 22 or 10,000 times brighter than a full Moon.

The Earth

The Earth is not a true sphere, but is flattened at the poles and hence an oblate spheroid. The polar diameter of the Earth, which is 7,899.806 miles, is 26.575 miles less than the equatorial diameter (7,926.381 miles). The Earth has a pear-shaped asymmetry, with the north polar radius being 148 ft longer than the south polar radius. There is also a slight ellipticity of the equator, since its long axis (about longitude 37° W) is 522 ft greater than its short axis. The greatest departures from the reference ellipsoid are a protuberance of 240 ft in the area of Papua New Guinea and a depression of 344 ft south of Sri Lanka, in the Indian Ocean.

The greatest circumference of the Earth, at the equator, is 24,901.46 miles, compared with 24,859.73 miles at the meridian.

The area of the surface is estimated to be 196,937,400, miles².

The period of axial rotation, i.e., the true sidereal day, is 23 hr 56 min 4.0996 sec, mean time.

The mass of the Earth was first assessed by Dr Nevil Maskelyne (1732–1811) in Perthshire, Great Britain in 1774. The modern value is 6.6 sextillion tons and its density is 5.515 times that of water.

The volume is an estimated 0.26 trillion miles³.

The Earth picks up cosmic dust, but estimates of the amount vary widely, with 36,375,000 tons a year being the upper limit. Modern theory is that the Earth has an outer shell or lithosphere 50 miles thick, then an outer and inner rock layer or mantle extending 1,745 miles deep, beneath which there is an iron-rich core of radius 2,164 miles. If the iron-rich core theory is correct, iron would be the most abundant element in the Earth. At the center of the core, the estimated density is 0.4729 lb/in³, the temperature 8,132° F and the pressure 364 GPa or 26,432 tons f/in².

Structure and Dimensions

OCEANS

The area of the Earth covered by water

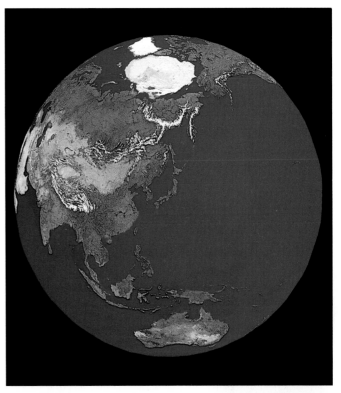

(the hydrosphere) is estimated to be 139,781,000 miles² or 70.98 percent of the total surface.

The mean depth of the hydrosphere was once estimated to be 12,450 ft, but recent surveys suggest a lower estimate of 11,660 ft.

The total weight of the water is estimated to be 1.45 quintillion tons, or 0.022 percent of the Earth's total weight.

The volume of the oceans is estimated to be 323.9 million miles³ compared to 8.4 million miles³ of fresh water.

Largest The largest ocean in the world is the Pacific. Excluding adjacent seas, it represents 45.9 percent of the world's oceans and covers 64.2 million miles² in area. The average depth is 13,740 ft.

The shortest navigable transpacific distance, from Guayaquil, Ecuador to Bangkok, Thailand, is 10,905 miles.

Deepest The deepest part of the ocean was first pinpointed in 1951 by the British Survey Ship *Challenger* in the Mariana Trench in the Pacific Ocean. The depth was measured by wide-band sounding at 35,639 ft. Subsequent visits have resulted in slightly deeper measurements. A survey by the Soviet research ship *Vityaz* in 1957 produced a depth that was later refined to 36,200 ft, and on 23 Jan 1960 the US Navy bathyscaphe *Trieste* descended to the bottom at 35,813 ft. A more recent visit produced a figure of 35,839 ft ± 33 ft, from data obtained by the survey vessel *Takuyo* of the Hydrographic Department, Japan Maritime Safety Agency in 1984, using a narrow multi-beam echo sounder.

A metal object, for example a 2.2-lb ball of steel, dropped into water above this trench would take nearly 64 min to fall

■ **Largest archipelago and largest sea**
This composite of the whole earth, created from thousands of separate satellite images, clearly shows both the largest of the world's seas (the South China Sea, with an area of 1,148,500 miles²) and the greatest archipelago (the crescent of more than 13,000 islands, 3,500 miles long, which forms Indonesia). (Photo: Science Photo Library)

to the seabed, where hydrostatic pressure is over 18,000 lb/in[2].

United States Defining US waters as within 200 nautical miles of any US territory (Economic Exclusive Zone [EEZ]), the deepest point in American waters is Challenger D in the Mariana Trench in the Pacific Ocean. Challenger D is 5,973 fathoms (35,838 ft) deep, 170 nautical miles SW of Guam at 11° 22.4 N, 142° 35.5 E.

The deepest point from an American state is the Vega Basin in the Aleutian Trench, which is 4,198 fathoms (25,188 ft) deep at 50° 51 N, 177° 11 E, 60 nautical miles south of the Aleutian Islands, AK.

Largest sea The largest of the world's seas is the South China Sea, with an area of 1.1 million miles[2].

Largest gulf The largest gulf in the world is the Gulf of Mexico, with an area of 580,000 miles[2] and a shoreline of 3,100 miles from Cape Sable, FL, to Cabo Catoche, Mexico.

Largest bay The largest bay in the world measured by shoreline length is Hudson Bay, northern Canada, with a shoreline of 7,623 miles and with an area of 317,500 miles[2]. The area of the Bay of Bengal, in the Indian Ocean, is larger, at 839,000 miles[2].

Longest fjord The world's longest fjord is the Nordvest Fjord arm of the Scoresby Sound in eastern Greenland, which extends inland 195 miles from the sea.

Highest seamount The highest known submarine mountain, or seamount, is one discovered in 1953 near the Tonga Trench, between Samoa and New Zealand in the South Pacific. It rises 28,500 ft from the seabed, with its summit 1,200 ft below the surface.

Remotest spot from land The world's most distant point from land is a spot in the South Pacific, approximately 48° 30′ S, 125° 30′ W, which is about 1,660 miles from the nearest points of land, namely Pitcairn Island, Ducie Island and Cape Dart, Antarctica. Centered on this spot is a circle of water with an area of about 8.6 million

miles[2]—about 7,000 miles[2] larger than the USSR, the world's largest country.

Most southerly The most southerly part of the oceans is 85° 34′ S, 154° W, at the snout of the Robert Scott Glacier, 305 miles from the South Pole.

Temperature The normal Red Sea temperature is 71.6° F. The temperature of the water at the surface of the sea varies from 28.5° F in the White Sea to 96° F in the shallow areas of the Persian Gulf in summer.

The highest temperature recorded in the ocean is 759° F, for a spring measured by an American research submarine some 300 miles off the west coast of the United States, in an expedition under the direction of Prof. Jack Diamond of Oregon State University in 1985. Remote probes measured the temperature of the spring, which was kept from vaporizing by the weight of water above it.

Clearest The Weddell Sea, 71° S, 15° W off Antarctica, has the clearest water of any sea. A Secchi disc was visible to a depth of 262 ft on 13 Oct 1986, as measured by Dutch researchers at the German Alfred-Wegener Institute. Such clarity corresponds to what scientists consider attainable in distilled water.

STRAITS

Longest The longest straits in the world are the Tatarskiy Proliv or Tartar Straits between Sakhalin Island and the USSR mainland, running from the Sea of Japan to Sakhalinsky Zaliv—497 miles, thus marginally longer than the Malacca Straits, between Malaysia and Sumatra.

Broadest The broadest *named* straits in the world are the Davis Straits between Greenland and Baffin Island, Canada, with a minimum width of 210 miles.

The Drake Passage between the Diego Ramirez Islands, Chile and the South Shetland Islands is 710 miles across.

Narrowest The narrowest navigable straits are those between the Aegean island of Euboea and the mainland of Greece. The gap is only 131 ft wide at Khalkis.

WAVES

Highest The highest officially recorded sea wave was calculated at 112 ft from trough to crest; it was measured by Lt Frederic Margraff, USN from the USS *Ramapo* proceeding from Manila, Philippines to San Diego, CA on the night of 6–7 Feb 1933, during a 68 knot hurricane.

The highest instrumentally measured wave was one 86 ft high, recorded by the British ship *Weather Reporter*, in the North Atlantic on 30 Dec 1972 at Lat. 59° N, Long. 19° W. It has been calculated on the statistics of the Stationary Random Theory that one wave in more than 300,000 may exceed the average by a factor of four.

On 9 Jul 1958 a landslip caused a 100 mph wave to wash 1,720 ft high along the fjord-like Lituya Bay in Alaska.

Highest seismic The highest estimated height of a *tsunami* (often called a tidal wave in layman terms) was one of 278 ft, which appeared off Ishigaki Island, Ryukyu Chain on 24 Apr 1771. It tossed a 826.7-ton block of coral more than 1.3 miles. Tsunami (a Japanese word: *nami*, a wave; *tsu*, overflowing) have been observed to travel at 490 mph, and are usually caused by a submarine earthquake.

Evidence for a 1,000-ft ocean wave having occurred about 100,000 years ago was reported on 4 Dec 1984. This is believed to have broken on the southern shore of Lanai, Hawaiian Islands and was due to a meteorite, a volcanic eruption or a submarine landslide.

CURRENTS

Greatest The greatest current in the oceans is the Antarctic Circumpolar Current or West Wind Drift Current. On the basis of four measurements taken in 1982 in the Drake Passage, between South America and Antarctica, it was found to be flowing at a rate of 4.3 billion ft[3] per sec. Results from computer modeling in 1990 estimate a higher figure of 6.9 billion ft[3] per sec. Its width ranges from 185–1,240 miles and it has a proven surface flow rate of 4/10 of a knot.

Strongest The world's strongest currents are the Nakwakto Rapids, Slingsby Channel, British Columbia, Canada (Lat. 51° 05′ N, Long. 127° 30′ W), where the flow rate may reach 16 knots.

TIDES

Extreme tides are due to lunar and solar gravitational forces affected by their perigee, perihelion and syzygies. Barometric and wind effects can superimpose an added "surge" element. Coastal and sea-floor configurations can accentuate these forces. The normal interval between tides is 12 hr 25 min.

Greatest The greatest tides occur in the Bay of Fundy, which divides the peninsula of Nova Scotia, Canada from Maine and the Canadian province of New Brunswick.

Burncoat Head in the Minas Basin, Nova Scotia, has the greatest mean spring range, with 47 ft 6 in.

A range of 54 ft 6 in was recorded at springs in Leaf Basin, in Ungava Bay, Quebec, Canada in 1953.

Tahiti experiences virtually no tide.

ICEBERGS

Largest and tallest The largest iceberg on record was an antarctic tabular iceberg of over 12,000 miles[2], 208 miles long and 60 miles wide (and thus larger than Belgium), sighted 150 miles west of Scott Island, in the South Pacific Ocean, by the USS *Glacier* on 12 Nov 1956.

The tallest iceberg measured was one of 550 ft reported off western Greenland by the US icebreaker *East Wind* in 1958.

Most southerly arctic The most southerly arctic iceberg was sighted in

■ Greatest tides
The greatest tides occur in the Bay of Fundy, which divides the peninsula of Nova Scotia, Canada from Maine and the Canadian province of New Brunswick. Burncoat Head in the Minas Basin, Nova Scotia, has the greatest mean spring range with 47 ft 6 in.
(Photos: Spectrum)

UNITED STATES EXTREME POINTS

Geographic Center	Butte County, SD (west of Castle Rock)
(50 states)	Lat. 44 ° 58' N, Long. 103 ° 46' W
Geographic Center	Smith County, KS (near Lebanon)
(48 coterminous states)	Lat. 39 ° 50' N, Long. 98 ° 35' W
Northernmost Point	Point Barrow, AK
	Lat. 71 ° 23' N, Long. 156 ° 29' W
Easternmost Point	West Quoddy Head, ME
	Lat. 44 ° 49' N, Long. 66 ° 57' W
Southernmost Point	Ka Lae (South Cape), HI
	Lat. 18 ° 55' N, Long. 155 ° 41' W
Westernmost Point	Pochnoi, AK (Semisopochonoi Island)
	Lat. 51 ° 17'N, Long. 172 ° 09' E

the Atlantic by a USN weather patrol at Lat. 28° 44' N, Long. 48° 42' W, in April 1935.

Most northerly antarctic The most northerly antarctic iceberg was a remnant sighted in the Atlantic by the ship *Dochra* at Lat. 26° 30' S, Long. 25° 40' W, on 30 Apr 1894.

LAND

There is satisfactory evidence that at one time the Earth's land surface comprised a single primeval continent of 80 million miles^2, now termed Pangaea, and that this split about 190 million years ago, during the Jurassic period, into two supercontinents, which are called Laurasia (Eurasia, Greenland and North America) and Gondwanaland (Africa, Arabia, India, South America, Oceania and Antarctica), named after Gondwana, India, which itself split 120 million years ago. The South Pole was apparently in the area of the Sahara as recently as the Ordovician period of *c.* 450 million years ago.

Largest state The largest state in land area is Alaska, with 570,833 miles^2. The largest in the 48 coterminous states is Texas, with 262,017 miles^2 of land.

Smallest state The smallest state is Rhode Island, with 1,055 miles^2.

Coastline According to the measurements of the National Oceanic and Atmospheric Administration (NOAA), the entire coastline of the United States, including Hawaii Alaska and the Great Lakes states, is 94,112 miles. Excluding Hawaii and Alaska, the coastline equals 59,156 miles. The state with the longest coastline is Alaska; it measures 33,904 miles.

ROCKS

The age of the Earth is generally considered to be within the range of 4,500 ± 70 million years, based on the lead isotope systematics. However, no rocks of this great age have yet been found on the Earth since geological processes have presumably destroyed them.

Oldest The greatest reported age for any scientifically dated rock is 3,962 million years in the case of Acasta Gneisses found in May 1984. The rocks were discovered approximately

200 miles north of Yellowknife, Northwest Territories, Canada by Dr Samuel Bowring as part of an ongoing Canadian geology survey mapping project. When the samples were analyzed in June 1989, Dr Bowring and scientists from the Australian National University in Canberra established their age, using a machine called SHRIMP (Sensitive High-mass Resolution Ion MicroProbe). Older minerals have been identified that are not rocks. Some zircon crystals discovered by Bob Pidgeon and Simon Wilde in the Jack Hills, 435 miles north of Perth, Western Australia in August 1984 were found to be 4,276 million years old, again using SHRIMP. These are the oldest fragments of the Earth's crust discovered so far.

United States The oldest rocks in the United States are the Morton Gneisses, found in 1935 by G.A. Phiel and C.E. Dutton scattered over an area of 50 miles from New Ulm, Brown Co. to Renville Co. in Minnesota. In 1980 these rocks were dated at 3.6 billion years old by Sam Goldrich of the US Geological Survey in Denver, CO, using the Uranium-Lead Dating method.

Largest The largest monolith in the world is Ayers Rock, which rises 1,143 ft above the surrounding desert plain in Northern Territory, Australia. It is 1.5 miles long and 1 mile wide. The nearest major town is Alice Springs, which is 250 miles to the northeast.

It was estimated in 1940 that La Gran Piedra, a volcanic plug located in the Sierra Maestra, Cuba, weighs 67,632 tons.

CONTINENTS

Largest Of the Earth's surface, 41.25 percent, or 81.2 million miles^2, is covered by continental masses of which only about two-thirds or 29.02 percent (57.2 million miles^2) is land above water, with a mean height of 2,480 ft above sea level. The Eurasian landmass is the largest, with an area (including islands) of 20.7 million miles^2. The Afro-Eurasian landmass, separated artificially only by the Suez Canal, covers an area of 32.7 million miles^2 or 57.2 percent of the Earth's landmass.

Smallest The smallest continent is the Australian mainland, with an area of 2.9 million miles^2, which, together with Tasmania, New Zealand, Papua New Guinea and the Pacific Islands, is sometimes described as Oceania.

Land remotest from the sea The point of land remotest from the sea is at Lat. 46° 16.8' N, Long. 86° 40.2' E in the Dzungarian Basin, which is in the Xinjiang Uighur Autonomous Region (Xinjiang Uygur Zu zhi ju), China's most northwesterly province. It was visited by Nicholas Crane and Dr Richard Crane (both Great Britain) on 27 Jun 1986 and is at a straight-line distance of 1,645 miles from the nearest open sea—Baydaratskaya Guba to the north (Arctic Ocean), Feni Point to the south (Indian Ocean) and Bo Hai Wun to the east (Yellow Sea).

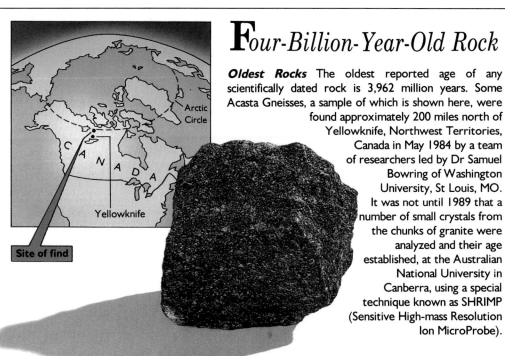

Four-Billion-Year-Old Rock

Oldest Rocks The oldest reported age of any scientifically dated rock is 3,962 million years. Some Acasta Gneisses, a sample of which is shown here, were found approximately 200 miles north of Yellowknife, Northwest Territories, Canada in May 1984 by a team of researchers led by Dr Samuel Bowring of Washington University, St Louis, MO. It was not until 1989 that a number of small crystals from the chunks of granite were analyzed and their age established, at the Australian National University in Canberra, using a special technique known as SHRIMP (Sensitive High-mass Resolution Ion MicroProbe).

Peninsula The world's largest peninsula is Arabia, with an area of about 1.25 million miles[2].

ISLANDS

Largest Discounting Australia, which is usually regarded as a continental land-mass, the largest island in the world is Greenland (now officially known as Kalaallit Nunaat), with an area of about 840,000 miles[2]. There is evidence that Greenland is in fact several islands overlaid by an ice cap, without which it would have an area of 650,000 miles[2].

The largest sand island in the world is Fraser Island, Queensland, Australia with a sand dune 75 miles long.

The largest island in North America is Newfoundland, Canada, with an area of 42,030 miles[2].

Freshwater The largest island surrounded by fresh water (18,500 miles[2]) is the Ilha de Marajó in the mouth of the River Amazon, Brazil.

The world's largest inland island (i.e., land surrounded by rivers) is Ilha do Bananal, Brazil (7,000 miles[2]).

The largest island in a lake is Manitoulin Island (1,068 miles[2]) in the Canadian section of Lake Huron.

Remotest The remotest island in the world is Bouvet Island (Bouvetøya), discovered in the South Atlantic by J. B. C. Bouvet de Lozier on 1 Jan 1739, and first landed on by Capt George Norris on 16 Dec 1825. Its position is 54° 26′ S, 3° 24′ E. This uninhabited Norwegian dependency is about 1,050 miles from the nearest land—the uninhabited Queen Maud Land coast of eastern Antarctica.

The remotest inhabited island in the world is Tristan da Cunha, discovered in the South Atlantic by Tristão da Cunha, a Portuguese admiral, in March 1506. It has an area of 38 miles[2] and a habitable area of 12 miles[2]. The first permanent inhabitant was Thomas Currie, who landed in 1810. The island was annexed by Great Britain on 14 Aug 1816. After evacuation in 1961 (due to volcanic activity), 198 islanders returned in November 1963. The nearest inhabited land to the group is the island of St Helena, 1,320 miles to the northeast. The nearest continent, Africa, is 1,700 miles away.

Greatest archipelago The world's greatest archipelago is the crescent of more than 13,000 islands, 3,500 miles long, which forms Indonesia.

Highest rock pinnacle The world's highest rock pinnacle is Ball's Pyramid near Lord Howe Island in the Pacific, which is 1,843 ft high, but has a base axis of only 660 ft. It was first scaled in 1965.

Northernmost land On 26 Jul 1978 Uffe Petersen of the Danish Geodetic Institute observed the islet of Oodaq Ø, 100 ft across, 0.8 miles north of Kaffeklubben Ø off Pearyland, Greenland at Lat. 83° 40′ 32.5″ N, Long. 30° 40′ 10.1″ W. It is 438.9 miles from the North Pole.

Southernmost land The South Pole, unlike the North Pole, is on land. The Amundsen–Scott south polar station was built there at an altitude of 9,370 ft in 1957.

DEEPEST CAVES BY COUNTRIES

Depth (ft)		
5,256	Réseau Jean Bernard	France
4,947	Shakta Pantjukhina	USSR
4,728	Sistema del Trave	Spain
4,547	Cueva Cave	Mexico
3,999	Schwersystem	Austria
3,970	Abisso Olivifer	Italy
3,930	Veliko Fbrego	Yugoslavia
3,802	Anou Ifflis	Algeria
3,346	Siebenhengste System	Switzerland
1,565	Carlsbad Caverns	United States

It is drifting bodily with the ice cap 27–30 ft per year in the direction 43° W and was replaced by a new structure in 1975.

Newest The world's newest island is the lava islet of Fukuto Kuokanoba, near Iwo Jima in the Pacific, reported in January 1986. It measures 2,132 × 1,476 ft and is 40 ft above sea level.

Largest atoll The largest atoll in the world is Kwajalein in the Marshall Islands, in the central Pacific Ocean. Its slender coral reef 176 miles long encloses a lagoon of 1,100 miles².

The atoll with the largest land area is Christmas Atoll, in the Line Islands in the central Pacific Ocean. It has an area of 248 miles², of which 125 miles² is land. Its principal settlement, London, is only 2½ miles distant from another settlement, Paris.

Longest reef The Great Barrier Reef off Queensland, northeastern Australia is 1,260 statute miles in length. Between 1959 and 1971 a large section between Cooktown and Townsville was destroyed by the crown-of-thorns starfish (*Acanthaster planci*).

DEPRESSIONS

Deepest The deepest depression so far discovered is the bedrock in the Bentley subglacial trench, Antarctica at 8,326 ft below sea level.

The greatest submarine depression is an area of the northwest Pacific floor that has an average depth of 15,000 ft.

The deepest exposed depression on land is the shore surrounding the Dead Sea, now 1,312 ft below sea level. The deepest point on the bed of this saltiest of all lakes is 2,388 ft below sea level. The rate of fall in the lake surface since 1948 has been 13.78 in per year.

The deepest part of the bed of Lake Baikal in Siberia, USSR is 4,872 ft below sea level.

United States The lowest-lying area in the United States is in Death Valley, CA at 282 ft below sea level.

Largest The largest exposed depression in the world is the Caspian Sea basin in the Azerbaijan, Russian, Kazakh and Turkmen Republics of the USSR and northern Iran. It is more than 200,000 miles², of which 143,550 miles² is lake area. The preponderant land area of the depression is the Prikaspiyskaya Nizmennost, lying around the northern third of the lake and stretching inland for a distance of up to 280 miles.

CAVES

Longest The most extensive cave system in the world is that under the Mammoth Cave National Park, KY, first entered in 1799. Explorations by many groups of cavers have revealed the interconnected cave passages beneath the Flint, Mammoth Cave and Toohey Ridges to make a system with a total mapped length that is now 348 miles.

Largest The world's largest cave chamber is the Sarawak Chamber, Lubang Nasib Bagus, in the Gunung Mulu National Park, Sarawak, Malaysia, discovered and surveyed by the 1980 British-Malaysian Mulu Expedition. Its length is 2,300 ft; its average width is 980 ft; and it is nowhere less than 230 ft high. It would be large enough to garage 7,500 buses.

Underwater cave The longest explored underwater cave is the Nohoch Na Chich cave system in Quintana Roo, Mexico, with 43,600 ft of mapped passages. Exploration of the system, which began in November 1987, has been carried out by the CEDAM Cave Diving Team under the leadership of Mike Madden.

Greatest descent The world depth record was set by the Groupe Vulcain in the Gouffre Jean Bernard, France at 5,256 ft in 1989.

However, this cave, explored via multiple entrances, has never been entirely descended, so the "sporting" record for the greatest descent into a cave is recognized as 4,947 ft in the Shakta Pantjukhina in the Russian Caucasus Mountains by a team of Ukrainian cavers in 1988.

Longest stalactite The longest known stalactite in the world is a wall-supported column extending 195 ft from roof to floor in the Cueva de Nerja, near Málaga, in Spain.

The longest freehanging stalactite in the world is one of 21 ft 6 in, in the Poll an Ionain cave in County Clare, Ireland.

Tallest stalagmite The tallest known stalagmite in the world is one in the Krásnohorska cave in Czechoslovakia, which is generally accepted as being about 105 ft tall.

The tallest cave column is considered to be the Flying Dragon Pillar, 128 ft high, in Nine Dragons Cave (Daji Dong), Guizhou, China.

Deepest The deepest cave in the United States is Lechuguilla Cave in Carlsbad Caverns, Carlsbad, NM, which currently measures 1,565 ft.

MOUNTAINS

Highest An eastern Himalayan peak of 29,028 ft above sea level on the Tibet–Nepal border (in an area first designated Chu-mu-lang-ma on a map of 1717) was discovered to be the world's highest mountain in 1852 by the Survey Department of the Government of India, from

US HIGHEST ALTITUDES		
State	**Highest Point**	**Elevation (feet)**
Alaska	Mt McKinley	20,320
California	Mt Whitney	14,494
Colorado	Mt Elbert	14,433
Washington	Mt Rainer	14,410
Wyoming	Gannett Peak	13,804
Hawaii	Mauna Kea	13,796
Utah	Kings Peak	13,528
New Mexico	Wheeler Park	13,161
Nevada	Boundary Peak	13,140
Montana	Granite Peak	12,799
Idaho	Borah Peak	12,662
Arizona	Humphrey's Peak	12,633
Oregon	Mt Hood	11,239
Texas	Guadalupe Peak	8,749
South Dakota	Harney Peak	7,242
North Carolina	Mt Mitchell	6,684
Tennessee	Clingmans Dome	6,643
New Hampshire	Mt Washington	6,288
Virginia	Mt Rogers	5,729
Nebraska	Johnson Township	5,426
New York	Mt Marcy	5,344
Maine	Mt Katahdin	5,267
Oklahoma	Black Mesa	4,973
West Virginia	Spruce Knob	4,861
Georgia	Brasstown Bald	4,784
Vermont	Mt Mansfield	4,393
Kentucky	Black Mountain	4,139
Kansas	Mt Sunflower	4,039
South Carolina	Sassafras Mountain	3,560
North Dakota	White Butte	3,506
Massachusetts	Mt Greylock	3,487
Maryland	Blackbone Mountain	3,360
Pennsylvania	Mt Davis	3,213
Arkansas	Magazine Mountain	2,753
Alabama	Cheaha Mountain	2,405
Connecticut	Mt Frissell	2,380
Minnesota	Eagle Mountain	2,301
Michigan	Mt Arvon	1,979
Wisconsin	Timms Hill	1,951
New Jersey	High Point	1,803
Missouri	Taum Sauk Mt	1,772
Iowa	Sec. 29, T 100N, R 41W	1,670
Ohio	Campbell Hill	1,549
Indiana	Franklin Township	1,257
Illinois	Charles Mound	1,235
Rhode Island	Jerimoth Hill	812
Mississippi	Woodall Mountain	806
Louisiana	Driskill Mountain	535
Delaware	Ebright Road	442
Florida	Sec. 30, T 6N, R 20W	345

HIGHEST MOUNTAINS

Everest	Nepal/China	29,028
K2	Kashmir	28,250
Kanchenjunga	Nepal/India	28,208
Lhotse I	Nepal/China	27,923
Makalu I	Nepal/China	27,824
Lhotse II	Nepal/China	27,560
Dhaulagiri	Nepal	26,810
Manaslu I	Nepal	26,760
Cho Oyu	Nepal/China	26,750
Nanga Parbat	Kashmir	26,660

NORTH AMERICAN MOUNTAINS

Mt McKinley	Alaska	20,320
Mt Logan	Yukon	19,850
Citlaltepetl	Vera Cruz, Mex.	18,700
Mt Saint Elias	Alaska/Yukon	18,008
Popocatepetl *	Mexico City	17,887

* Volcano

theodolite readings taken in 1849 and 1850. In 1860 its height was computed to be 29,002 ft. On 25 Jul 1973 the Chinese announced a height of 29,029 ft 3 in. It was named Mt Everest after Col. Sir George Everest (1790–1866), formerly surveyor-general of India.

Everest's status as the world's highest mountain, maintained for 135 years (1852–1987), was most recently challenged by K2 (formerly Godwin Austen), also known as Chogori, in the disputed Kashmiri northern areas of Pakistan, in an announcement on 6 Mar 1987 by the US K2 Expedition. Their satellite transit surveyor yielded altitudes of between 29,064 and 29,228 ft as against the hitherto official 19th-century figure of 28,250 ft, and the 20th-century proposed height of 28,740 ft. However, on 13 Aug 1987 China reaffirmed their heights of 29,029 ft 3 in for Everest and 28,250 ft for K2. The Research Council in Rome, Italy announced on 23 Oct 1987 that new satellite measurements restored Everest to primacy at 29,078 ft, and put K2 down to 28,238 ft. It was on 31 Jul 1954 that K2 was first climbed, by A. Compagnoni and L. Lacedelli (Italy), 14 months after the summit of Everest had been reached. (For details of Everest ascents, see Mountaineering, Chapter 11.)

The mountain whose summit is farthest from the Earth's center is the Andean peak of Chimborazo (20,561 ft), 98 miles south of the equator in Ecuador, South America. Its summit is 7,057 ft further from the Earth's center than the summit of Mt Everest.

The highest mountain on the equator is Volcán Cayambe (19,285 ft), Ecuador, in Long. 77° 58′ W. A mountaineer on the summit would be moving at 1,038 mph relative to the Earth's center, due to the Earth's rotation.

The highest insular mountain (of, relating to, or resembling an island) in the world is Puncak Jaya (formerly Puncak Sukarno, formerly Carstensz Pyramide) in Irian Jaya, Indonesia. A survey by the Australian Universities' Expedition in 1973 yielded a height of 16,023 ft. Ngga Pulu (also in Irian Jaya), which is now 15,950 ft, was in 1936 possibly 16,110 ft before the melting of its snow cap.

United States The highest mountain in the United States is Mt McKinley in Alaska, with a highest point of 20,320 ft. McKinley, so named in 1896, was called

Denali (Great One) in the Athabascan language of North American Indians. The highest mountain in the 48 contiguous states is Mt Whitney in California with a highest point of 14,494 ft.

Unclimbed The highest unclimbed summit is Lhotse Middle Peak (27,605 ft) in the Khumbu district of the Nepal Himalaya. It is the tenth highest individually recognized summit in the world, Lhotse being the fourth highest mountain.

The highest unclimbed mountain is Namcha Barwa (25,531 ft), in the Great Bend of the Tsangpo (Brahmaputra), China.

Tallest The world's tallest mountain measured from its submarine base (3,280 fathoms) in the Hawaiian Trough to its peak is Mauna Kea (Mountain White) on the island of Hawaii, with a combined height of 33,476 ft, of which 13,796 ft are above sea level.

Another mountain whose dimensions, but not height, exceed those of Mt Everest is the volcanic Hawaiian peak of Mauna Loa (Mountain Long) at 13,680 ft. The axes of its elliptical base, 16,322 ft below sea level, have been estimated at 74 miles and 53 miles.

It should be noted that Cerro Aconcagua (22,834 ft) is more than 38,800 ft above the Pacific abyssal plain (16,000 ft deep) or 42,834 ft above the Peru–Chile Trench, which is 180 miles distant in the South Pacific.

Greatest ranges The greatest of all mountain ranges is the submarine Mid-Ocean Ridge, extending 40,000 miles from the Arctic Ocean to the Atlantic Ocean, round Africa, Asia and Australia, and under the Pacific Ocean to the west coast of North America. It has a greatest height of 13,800 ft above the base ocean depth.

The world's greatest land mountain range is the Himalaya-Karakoram, which contains 96 of the world's 109 peaks of over 24,000 ft. *Himalaya* derives from the Sanskrit *him*, snow; *alaya*, home.

Longest lines of sight Vatnajökull (6,952 ft), Iceland has been seen by refracted light from the Faeroe Islands 340 miles distant. In Alaska, Mt McKinley (20,320 ft) has been sighted from Mt Sanford (16,237 ft), a distance of 230 miles.

Greatest plateau The most extensive high plateau in the world is the Tibetan Plateau in Central Asia. The average altitude is 16,000 ft and the area is 77,000 miles^2.

Sheerest wall Mt Rakaposhi (25,498 ft) rises 3.72 miles from the Hunza Valley, Pakistan in 6.21 miles with an overall gradient of 31°.

The 3,200-ft-wide northwest face of Half Dome, Yosemite, CA is 2,200 ft high but nowhere departs more than 7° from the vertical. It was first climbed (Class VI) in 1957 by Royal Robbins, Jerry Gallwas and Mike Sherrick.

Highest halites Along the northern shores of the Gulf of Mexico for 725 miles

there exist 330 subterranean "mountains" of salt, some of which rise more than 60,000 ft from bedrock and appear as the low salt domes first discovered in 1862.

WATERFALLS

Highest The highest waterfall (as opposed to vaporized "bridal-veil fall") in the world is the Salto Angel (Angel Falls) in Venezuela, on a branch of the River Carrao, an upper tributary of the Caroni, with a total drop of 3,212 ft—the longest single drop is 2,648 ft. The Angel Falls were named after the American pilot Jimmy Angel (d. 8 Dec 1956), who recorded them in his log book on 14 Nov 1933. The falls, known by the Indians as Cherun-Meru, were first reported by Ernesto Sanchez La Cruz in 1910.

United States The tallest continuous waterfall in the United States is Ribbon Falls in Yosemite National Park in California, with a drop of 1,612 ft. This is a seasonal waterfall and is generally dry from late July to early September.

Yosemite Falls, also in Yosemite National Park, has the greatest *total* drop at 2,425 ft, but actually consists of three distinct waterfalls. These are the Upper (1,430 ft), Middle (675 ft) and Lower falls (320 ft).

Greatest On the basis of the average annual flow, the greatest waterfalls in the world are the Boyoma (formerly Stanley) Falls in Zaïre with 600,000 cusec.

The flow of the Guaíra (Salto das Sete Quedas) on the Alto Paraná river between Brazil and Paraguay has at times attained a peak rate of 1.75 million cusec.

It has been calculated that a waterfall 26 times greater than the Guaíra and perhaps 2,625 ft high was formed, when some 5.5 million years ago the Mediterranean basins began to be filled from the Atlantic through the Straits of Gibraltar.

Widest The widest waterfalls in the world are the Khône Falls (50–70 ft high) in Laos, with a width of 6.7 miles and a flood flow of 1.5 million cusec.

RIVERS

Longest The two longest rivers in the world are the Nile (*Bahr el-Nil*), flowing into the Mediterranean, and the Amazon (*Amazonas*), flowing into the South Atlantic. Which is the longer is more a matter of definition than of simple measurement.

The length of the Nile watercourse, as surveyed by M. Devroey (Belgium) before the loss of a few miles of meanders due to the formation of Lake Nasser, behind the Aswan High Dam, was 4,145 miles. This course is unitary from a hydrological standpoint and runs from the source in Burundi of the Luvironza branch of the Kagera feeder of the Victoria Nyanza via the White Nile (*Bahr el-Jebel*) to the delta in the Mediterranean.

The true source of the Amazon was discovered in 1953 to be a stream named Huaraco, deriving from the Misuie Glacier (17,715 ft) in the Arequipa Andes of Peru. This stream progressively becomes the Toro, then the Santiago, then the Apurimac, which in turn is known as the Ene and then the Tambo before its confluence with the Amazon prime tributary, the Ucayali. The length of the Amazon from this source to the South Atlantic via the Canal do Norte was measured in 1969 and found to be 4,007 miles (usually quoted to the rounded-off figure of 4,000 miles).

If, however, a vessel navigating down the river follows the "arm" (carrying 10 percent of the river's water) to the south of Ilha de Marajó through the Furo Tajapuru and Furo dos Macacos into the Pará, the total length of the watercourse becomes 4,195 miles. The Rio Pará is *not*, however, a tributary of the Amazon, being hydrologically part of the basin of the Tocantins, which itself flows into the Bahía de Marajó and out into the South Atlantic.

United States The longest river in the United States is the Mississippi, with a length of 2,348 miles. It flows from its source at Lake Itasca, MN through 10 states before reaching the Gulf of Mexico. The entire Mississippi River System, including the eastern and western tributaries, flows through 25 states in all.

Shortest As with the longest river, two rivers could also be considered to be the shortest river with a name. The Roe River, near Great Falls, MT, has two forks fed by a large fresh water spring. These relatively constant forks measure 201 ft (East Fork Roe River) and 58 ft (North Fork Roe River) respectively. The Roe River flows into the larger Missouri River. The D River, located at Lincoln City, OR, connects Devil's Lake to the Pacific Ocean. Its length is officially quoted as 120 ± 5 ft.

Largest basin The largest river basin in the world is that drained by the Amazon (4,007 miles), which covers about 2,720,000 miles^2. It has about 15,000 tributaries and sub-tributaries, of which four are more than 1,000 miles long. These include the Madeira, the longest of all tributaries, with a length of 2,100 miles, which is surpassed by only 14 rivers in the world.

Longest sub-tributary The world's longest sub-tributary is the Pilcomayo (1,000 miles) in South America. It is a tributary of the Paraguay (1,500 miles long), which itself is a tributary of the Paraná (2,500 miles).

Longest estuary The world's longest estuary is that of the often frozen Ob, in the northern USSR, at 550 miles. It is up to 50 miles wide.

Largest delta The world's largest delta is that created by the Ganges (Ganga) and Brahmaputra in Bangladesh and West Bengal, India. It covers an area of 30,000 miles^2.

Greatest flow The greatest flow of any river in the world is that of the Amazon, which discharges an average of 4.2 million cusec into the Atlantic Ocean, increasing to more than 7 million cusec in full flood. The lowest 900 miles of the Amazon average 300 ft in depth.

Submarine In 1952 a submarine river 250 miles wide, known as the Cromwell Current, was discovered flowing eastward 300 ft below the surface of the Pacific for 3,500 miles along the equator. Its volume is 1,000 times that of the Mississippi.

Subterranean In August 1958 a crypto-river, tracked by radio isotopes, was discovered flowing under the Nile with six times its mean annual flow or 20 trillion ft^3.

Largest swamp The world's largest tract of swamp is in the basin of the Pripyat River — a tributary of the Dnieper in the USSR. These swamps cover an estimated area of 18,125 miles^2.

Largest marsh The Everglades is a vast plateau of subtropical saw-grass marsh in southern Florida, covering 2,185 miles^2. Fed by water from Lake Okeechobee, the third largest freshwater lake in the United States, the Everglades is the largest subtropical wilderness in the continental United States.

RIVER BORES

The bore on the Qiantong Jiang (Hangzhou He) in eastern China is the most remarkable of the 60 in the world. At spring tides the wave attains a height of up to 25 ft and a speed of 13–15 knots. It is heard advancing at a range of 14 miles.

The annual downstream flood wave on the Mekong, in southeast Asia, sometimes reaches a height of 46 ft.

The greatest volume of any tidal bore is that of the Canal do Norte (10 miles wide) in the mouth of the Amazon.

LAKES AND INLAND SEAS

Largest The largest inland sea or lake in the world is the Kaspiyskoye More (Caspian Sea) in the southern USSR and Iran. It is 760 miles long and its total area is 143,550 miles^2. Of the total area, some 55,280 miles^2 (38.5 percent) are in Iran, where it is named the Darya-ye-Khazar. Its maximum depth is 3,360 ft and the surface is 93 ft below sea level. Its estimated volume is 21,500 miles^3 of saline water. Its surface has varied between 105 ft (11th century) and 72 ft (early 19th century) below sea level.

United States The largest lake in the United States is Lake Michigan, with a water surface area of 22,300 miles^2, a length of 307 miles, a breadth of 118 miles and a maximum depth of 923 ft. Both Lake Superior and Lake Huron have larger areas, but these straddle the Canadian/American border.

Excluding the Great Lakes, the largest natural lake wholly within the United States is the Great Salt Lake, UT, which has a water surface area of 1,361 miles^2.

Deepest The deepest lake in the world is Lake Baikal in central Siberia, USSR. It is 385 miles long and between 20–46 miles wide. In 1957 the lake's Olkhon Crevice was measured and found to be 6,365 ft deep and hence 4,872 ft below sea level.

United States The deepest lake in the United States is 6-mile-long Crater Lake, in Crater Lake National Park in the Cascade Mountains of Oregon. Its surface is 6,176 ft above sea level and its extreme depth is 1,932 ft, with an average depth of 1,500 ft. The lake has neither inlets nor outlets; instead it is filled and maintained solely by precipitation.

Highest The highest navigable lake in the world is Lake Titicaca (maximum depth 1,214 ft, with an area of about 3,200 miles^2) in South America (1,850 miles^2 in Peru and 1,350 miles^2 in Bolivia). It is 130 miles long and is 12,506 ft above sea level.

There are higher lakes in the Himalayas, but most are glacial and of a temporary nature only. A survey of the area carried out in 1984 showed a lake at a height of 17,762 ft, named Panch Pokhri, which was 1 mile long.

Freshwater The freshwater lake with the greatest surface area is Lake Superior, one of the Great Lakes of

■ **Highest lake**
The highest navigable lake in the world is Lake Titicaca, in South America, which is 130 miles long and is situated 12,506 ft above sea level.
(Photo: Images)

■ Largest gorge
The largest land gorge in the world is the Grand Canyon, in Arizona. It extends over a distance of 217 miles, varying in width from 4–13 miles. It is some 5,300 ft deep.
(Photo: Spectrum)

North America. The total area is 31,800 miles[2], of which 20,700 miles[2] are in Minnesota, Wisconsin and Michigan and 11,100 miles[2] in Ontario, Canada. It is 600 ft above sea level. The freshwater lake with the greatest volume is Lake Baikal in Siberia, USSR, with an estimated volume of 5,520 miles[3].

Lake in a lake The largest lake in a lake is Manitou Lake (41.09 miles[2]) on the world's largest lake island, Manitoulin Island (1,068 miles[2]), in the Canadian part of Lake Huron. The lake itself contains a number of islands.

Underground The world's largest underground lake is believed to be that in the Drachenhauchloch cave in Namibia, discovered in 1986. Its surface has an area of 5¼ acres, and lies 200 ft underground, over water 300 ft deep.

United States Reputedly the United States' largest underground lake is the Lost Sea, 300 ft subterranean in the Craighead Caverns, Sweetwater, TN, measuring 4½ acres and discovered in 1905.

Largest lagoon Lagoa dos Patos in southernmost Brazil is 158 miles long and extends over 4,110 miles[2].

OTHER FEATURES

Desert Nearly an eighth of the world's land surface is arid, with a rainfall of less than 9.8 in per year. The Sahara in North Africa is the largest desert in the world. At its greatest length it is 3,200 miles from east to west. From north to south it is between 800 and 1,400 miles. The area covered by the desert is about 3.25 million miles[2]. The land level varies from 436 ft below sea level in the Qattâra Depression, Egypt to the mountain Emi Koussi (11,204 ft) in Chad. The daytime temperature range in the western Sahara may be more than 80° F.

United States The largest desert in the United States is the Mojave Desert in southeast California. It covers an area of 115,000 miles[2] and has an average rainfall of 5 in.

Sand dunes The world's highest measured sand dunes are those in the Saharan sand sea of Isaouane-N-Tifernine of east-central Algeria at Lat. 26° 42′ N, Long. 6° 43′ E. They have a wavelength of 3.1 miles and attain a height of 1,410 ft.

Largest mirage The largest mirage on record was that sighted in the Arctic at 83° N 103° W by Donald B. MacMillan in 1913. This type of mirage, known as the Fata Morgana, appeared as the same "hills, valleys, snow-capped peaks extending through at least 120 degrees of the horizon" that Peary had misidentified as Crocker Land six years earlier.

On 17 Jul 1939 a mirage of Snaefells Jokull (4,715 ft) on Iceland was seen from the sea at a distance of 335–350 miles.

Largest gorge The largest land gorge in the world is the Grand Canyon on the Colorado River in north-central Arizona. It extends from Marble Gorge to the Grand Wash Cliffs, over a distance of 217 miles. It varies in width from 4–13 miles and is some 5,300 ft deep.

The submarine Labrador Basin canyon is c. 2,150 miles long.

Deepest canyon The deepest canyon is El Cañón de Colca, Peru, reported in 1929, which is 10,574 ft deep. It was first traversed by the Polish Expedition CANOANDES' 79 kayak team from 12 May–14 Jun 1981.

A stretch of the Kali River in central Nepal flows 18,000 ft below its flanking summits of the Dhaulagiri and Annapurna mountain groups.

The deepest submarine canyon yet discovered is one 25 miles south of Esperance, Western Australia, which is 6,000 ft deep and 20 miles wide.

United States The deepest canyon in the United States is Kings Canyon, East Fresno, CA, which runs through Sierra and Sequoia National Forests. The deepest point, which measures 8,200 ft, is in the Sierra National Park Forest section of the canyon.

The deepest canyon in low relief territory is Hell's Canyon, dividing Oregon and Idaho. It plunges 7,900 ft from the Devil Mountain down to the Snake River.

Cliffs The highest sea cliffs yet pinpointed anywhere in the world are those on the north coast of east Moloka'i, HI near Umilehi Point, which descend 3,300 ft to the sea at an average gradient of more than 55°.

Natural arches The longest natural arch in the world is the Landscape Arch in the Arches National Park, 25 miles north of Moab in Utah. This natural sandstone arch spans 291 ft and is set about 100 ft above the canyon floor. In one place erosion has narrowed its section to 6 ft.

Larger, however, is the Rainbow Bridge, UT, discovered on 14 Aug 1909, which although only 278 ft long, is more than 22 ft wide.

Longest glaciers It is estimated that 6.02 million miles[2], or 10.5 percent of the Earth's land surface, is permanently glaciated. The world's longest known glacier is the Lambert Glacier, discovered by an Australian aircraft crew in Australian Antarctic Territory in 1956–57. It is up to 40 miles wide and, with its upper section, known as the Mellor Glacier, it measures at least 250 miles in length. With the Fisher Glacier limb, the Lambert forms a continuous ice passage about 320 miles long.

The longest Himalayan glacier is the Siachen (47 miles) in the Karakoram range, though the Hispar and Biafo combine to form an ice passage 76 miles long.

The fastest-moving major glacier is the Quarayaq in Greenland, flowing 65–80 ft per day.

United States The largest glacier in the United States is the Malaspina glacier, 30 miles north of Yakutut, AK. It measures 850 miles[2] and is part of the 2,000-mile[2] Malaspina Glacier Complex.

Thickest ice The greatest recorded thickness of ice is 2.97 miles, measured by radio echo soundings from a US Antarctic research aircraft at 69° 9′ 38″ S, 135° 20′ 25″ E 250 miles from the coast of Wilkes Land on 4 Jan 1975.

Deepest permafrost The deepest recorded permafrost is more than 4,500 ft, reported from the upper reaches of the Viluy River, Siberia, USSR in February 1982.

Natural Phenomena

EARTHQUAKES

(Seismologists record all dates with the year *first*, based not on local time but on Universal Time/Greenwich Mean Time).

Greatest It is estimated that each year there are some 500,000 detectable seismic or microseismic disturbances, of which 100,000 can be felt and 1,000 cause damage. The deepest recorded hypocenters are of 447 miles in Indonesia in 1933, 1934 and 1943.

The scale most commonly used to measure the size of earthquakes is Rich-

WORLD'S STRONGEST EARTHQUAKES

Kanamori Scale Magnitudes M_w	Richter Scale Magnitude M_s	Location	Date
8.8	8.6	Ecuador	1906 Jan 31
9.0	8.25	Kamchatka, USSR	1952 Nov 4
9.1	7.75	Andreanof Islands, Aleutian Islands, AK	1957 Mar 9
9.2	8.4	Alaska	1964 Mar 27
9.5	8.3	Chile	1960 May 22

$\log E = 1.5M + 4.8$ (joules)

WORLD'S MOST DEADLY EARTHQUAKES

Richter Scale Magnitude M_s	Estimated Deaths	Location	Date
Unknown	1,100,000	Near East and eastern Mediterranean	1201 c. July
Unknown	830,000	Shanxi, China	1556 Jan 23
Unknown	300,000	Calcutta, India	1737 Oct 11
Unknown	250,000	Antioch, Syria (now Turkey)	A.D. 526 May 20
8.2*	242,000	Tangshan, China	1976 Jul 28

* As many as 750,000 people were killed in Tangshan and its surrounding region.

ter's magnitude scale (1954). It is named after Dr Charles Richter (1900–85) and the most commonly used form is M_s, based on amplitudes of surface waves, usually at a period of 20 sec. The largest reported magnitudes on this scale are about 8.9, but the scale does not properly represent the size of the very largest earthquakes, above M_s about 8, for which it is better to use the concept of seismic moment, M_o, devised by K. Aki in 1966. Moment can be used to derive a "moment magnitude," M_w, first used by Hiroo Kanamori in 1977. The largest recorded earthquake on the M_w scale is the Chilean shock of 1960 May 22, which had $M_w = 9.5$, but only 8.3 on the M_s scale. For the largest events, such as the Chilean shock of 1960, the energy released is more than 10^{19} joules.

United States The strongest earthquake in American history was near Prince William Sound, AK (80 miles east of Anchorage) on 1964 Mar 27, which measured 8.4 on the Richter Scale, killed 117 people and caused an estimated $750 million in damage. It caused a tsunami 50 feet high that traveled 8,445 miles at 450 mph. The town of Kodiak was destroyed, and tremors were felt in California, Hawaii and Japan.

Worst death toll The greatest chronicled loss of life occurred in the earthquake that rocked every city of the Near East and eastern Mediterranean c. July 1201. Contemporary accounts estimate the loss of life at 1.1 million.

Less uncertain is the figure of 830,000 fatalities in a prolonged earthquake (*ti chen*) in the Sheanxi, Shanxi and Henan provinces of China, of 1556 Feb 2 (new style; January 23 old style).

The highest death toll in modern times has been in the Tangshan earthquake (Mag. $M_s = 7.9$) in eastern China on 1976 Jul 27 (local time was 3 A.M. Jul 28). The first figure published on 4 Jan 1977 revealed 655,237 killed, later adjusted to 750,000. On 22 Nov 1979 the New China News Agency inexplicably reduced the death toll to 242,000.

United States The highest death toll for the United States is 700 in the Great San Francisco Earthquake of 1906 Apr 8, which measured an estimated 8.3 on the Richter Scale. Accurate records were not kept at this time, and some experts believe the 700 deaths to be a low calculation. There was also no Richter Scale, and this measurement, although it is the consensus, is debated.

Material damage The greatest physical devastation was in the earthquake on the Kanto plain, Japan, of 1923 Sep 1 (Mag. $M_s = 8.2$, epicenter at Lat. 35° 15′ N, Long. 139° 30′ E); in Sagami Bay the sea bottom in one area sank 1,310 ft. The official total of persons killed and missing in this *shinsai* or great quake and the resultant fires was 142,807. In Tokyo and Yokohama 575,000 dwellings were destroyed.

VOLCANOES

The total number of known active volcanoes in the world is 1,343, of which many are submarine. The greatest active concentration is in Indonesia, with some 200 volcanoes. The word *volcano* derives from the now-dormant Vulcano Island (from the Roman god of fire *Vulcanus*) in the Mediterranean.

Greatest explosion The greatest explosion in historic times (possibly since Santoriní in the Aegean Sea, 60 miles north of Crete, in 1628 B.C.) occurred at c. 10 A.M. (local time), or 3:00 A.M. GMT, on 27 Aug 1883, with an eruption of Krakatoa, an island (then 18 miles[2]) in the Sunda Strait, between Sumatra and Java, in Indonesia. One hundred and sixty-three villages were wiped out, and 36,380 people killed by the wave it caused. Pumice was thrown 34 miles high and dust fell 3,313 miles away 10 days later. The explosion was recorded four hours later on the island of Rodrigues, 2,968 miles away, as "the roar of heavy guns," and was heard over one-thirteenth of the surface of the globe. This explosion, estimated to have had about 26 times the power of the greatest H-bomb test (by the USSR; for details of thermo-nuclear explosions, see Bombs, Chapter 4), was still only a fifth of the Santoriní cataclysm.

Greatest eruption The total volume of matter discharged in the eruption of Tambora, a volcano on the island of Sumbawa, in Indonesia, 5–7 Apr 1815, was 36–43 miles[3]. The energy of this 1,395 mph eruption, which lowered the height of the island by 4,100 ft from 13,450 ft to 9,350 ft, was 8.4×10^{19} joules. A crater 7 miles in diameter was formed. More than 90,000 were killed or died as a result of the subsequent famine. This compares with a probable 14–16 miles[3] ejected by Santoriní (see above) and 5 miles[3] ejected by Krakatoa (see above). The internal pressure at Tambora has been estimated at 20.76 tons/in[2].

The ejecta in the Taupo eruption in New Zealand c. A.D. 130 has been estimated at 33 billion tons of pumice moving at one time at 400 mph. It flattened 6,180 miles[2] (over 26 times the devastated area of Mount St Helens, which erupted in Washington State on 18 May 1980). Less than 20 percent of the 15.4 billion tons of pumice ejected in this most violent of all documented volcanic events fell within 125 miles of the vent.

Longest lava flow The longest lava flow in historic times is a mixture of *pahoehoe*, ropey lava (twisted cordlike solidifications) and *aa*, blocky lava, resulting from the eruption of Laki in 1783 in southeast Iceland, which flowed 40½–43½ miles. The largest-known prehistoric flow is the Roza basalt flow in North America c. 15 million years ago, which had an unsurpassed length (185 miles), area (15,400 miles[2]) and volume (300 miles[3]).

Largest active Mauna Loa in Hawaii has a dome 75 miles long and 31 miles wide (above sea level), with lava flows which occupy more than 1,980 miles[2] of the island. Its pit crater, Mokuaweoweo, measures 4 miles[2] and is 500–600 ft deep. It rises 13,677 ft and has averaged one eruption every 3½ years since 1832, although none since 1984.

Highest active The highest volcano regarded as active is Ojos del Salado (which has fumaroles), at a height of 22,595 ft, on the frontier between Chile and Argentina.

Highest potentially active The highest potentially active volcano is Volcán Llullaillaco (22,057 ft), also on the frontier between Chile and Argentina.

Northernmost and southernmost The northernmost volcano is Beeren Berg (7,470 ft) on the island of Jan Mayen (71° 05′ N) in the Greenland Sea. It erupted on 20 Sep 1970 and the island's

Lightning, most times struck

The only man in the world to be struck by lightning seven times is ex-park ranger Roy C. Sullivan (USA), the human lightning conductor of Virginia. His attraction for lightning began in 1942 (lost big toenail), and was resumed in July 1969 (lost eyebrows), in July 1970 (left shoulder seared), on 16 Apr 1972 (hair set on fire), on 7 Aug 1973 (new hair refired and legs seared), on 5 Jun 1976 (ankle injured), and he was sent to Waynesboro Hospital with chest and stomach burns on 25 Jun 1977 after being struck while fishing. In September 1983 he died by his own hand, reportedly rejected in love.

39 inhabitants (all male) had to be evacuated. It was possibly discovered by Henry Hudson, the English navigator and explorer (d. 1611), in 1607 or 1608, but was definitely visited by Jan Jacobsz Mayen (Netherlands) in 1614. It was annexed by Norway on 8 May 1929. The Ostenso seamount (5,825 ft), 346 miles from the North Pole at Lat. 85° 10′ N, Long. 133° W, was volcanic. The most southerly known active volcano is Mt Erebus (12,450 ft), on Ross Island (77° 35′ S) in Antarctica. It was discovered on 28 Jan 1841 by the expedition of Capt. (later Rear-Admiral Sir) James Clark Ross of the British Navy (1800–62), and first climbed at 10 A.M. on 10 Mar 1908 by a British party of five, led by Prof. Tannatt William Edgeworth David (1858–1934).

Largest crater The world's largest *caldera* or volcano crater is that of Toba, north-central Sumatra, Indonesia, covering 685 miles².

AVALANCHES

Greatest The greatest natural avalanches, though rarely observed, occur in the Himalayas, but no estimates of their volume have been published. It was estimated that 120 million ft³ of snow fell in an avalanche in the Italian Alps in 1885.

The 250-mph avalanche triggered by the Mount St Helens eruption in Washington State on 18 May 1980 was estimated to measure 96 billion ft³ (see Accidents and Disasters).

GEYSERS

Tallest The Waimangu (Maori "black water") geyser, in New Zealand, erupted to a height in excess of 1,500 ft in 1904, but has not been active since it erupted violently at 6:20 A.M. on 1 Apr 1917 and killed four people.

Currently the world's tallest active geyser is the National Park Service's Steamboat Geyser, in Yellowstone National Park, WY. During the 1980s it erupted at intervals ranging from 19 days to more than four years, although there were occasions in the 1960s when it erupted as frequently as every 4–10 days. The maximum height ranges from 195–380 ft.

The greatest measured water discharge was an estimated 740,000–1,000,000 gallons by the Giant Geyser, also in Yellowstone National Park. However, this estimate, made in the 1950s, was only a rough calculation.

The *Geysir* ("gusher") near Mt Hekla in south-central Iceland, from which all others have been named, spurts on occasions to 180 ft, while the adjacent Strokkur, reactivated by drilling in 1963, spurts at 10–15 min intervals.

Weather

The meteorological records given below necessarily relate largely to the last 140–160 years, since data before that time are both sparse and often unreliable. Reliable registering thermometers were introduced as recently as c. 1820. The longest continuous observations have been maintained at the Radcliffe Observatory, Oxford, Great Britain since 1815, though discontinuous records have enabled the Chinese to assert that 903 B.C. was a very bad winter.

It is believed that 1.2 million years ago the world's air temperature averaged 95° F.

Most equable temperature The location with the most equable recorded temperature over a short period is Garapan, on Saipan in the Mariana Islands, Pacific Ocean. During the nine years from 1927–35, inclusive, the lowest temperature recorded was 67.3° F on 30 Jan 1934 and the highest was 88.5° F on 9 Sep 1931, giving an extreme range of 21.2° F.

Between 1911 and 1966 the Brazilian offshore island of Fernando de Noronha had a minimum temperature of 65.5° F on 17 Nov 1913 and a maximum of 89.6° F on 2 Mar 1965, an extreme range of 24.1° F.

Greatest temperature ranges The greatest recorded temperature ranges in the world are around the Siberian "cold pole" in the eastern USSR. Temperatures in Verkhoyansk (67° 33′ N, 133° 23′ E) have ranged 188° F, from −90° F to 98° F.

The greatest temperature variation recorded in a day is 100° F (a fall from 44° F to −56° F) at Browning, MT on 23–24 Jan 1916.

The most freakish rise was 49° F in 2 min at Spearfish, SD, from −4° F at 7:30 A.M. to 45° F at 7:32 A.M. on 22 Jan 1943.

Upper atmosphere The lowest temperature ever recorded in the atmosphere is −225.4° F at an altitude of about 50–60 miles, during noctilucent cloud research above Kronogård, Sweden from 27 Jul to 7 Aug 1963.

Most intense rainfall Difficulties attend rainfall readings for very short periods, but the figure of 1½ in in one min at Barst, Guadeloupe on 26 Nov 1970 is regarded as the most intense recorded in modern times.

Humidity and discomfort Human comfort or discomfort depends not merely on temperature but on the combination of temperature, humidity, radiation and wind speed. The United States Weather Bureau uses a Temperature-Humidity Index (THI), which equals two-fifths of the sum of the dry and wet bulb thermometer readings plus 15. A THI of 98.2 has been twice recorded in Death Valley, CA—on 27 Jul 1966 (119° F and 31 percent) and on 12 Aug 1970 (117° F and 37 percent). A person driving at 45 mph in a car without a windshield in a temperature of −45° F would, by the chill factor, experience the equivalent of −125° F, i.e., within 3.6° F of the world record.

Hurricanes The most commonly used scale to measure the size of a hurricane is the Saffir-Simpson Scale, which rates hurricanes on a scale of one to five, five being the most severe.

The most damaging hurricane in the United States was Hurricane Hugo, which hit the mainland 21–22 Sep 1989 after devastating a number of islands in the Caribbean. The storm made landfall at Sullivan Island, northeast of Charleston, SC. On crossing the mainland, Hugo measured four on the Saffir-Simpson Scale. Winds measured 135 mph and 28 people were killed.

The greatest number of fatalities from an American hurricane is an estimated 6,000 deaths on 8 Sep 1900 in Galveston Island, TX. The second highest death toll was 1,836 people killed by a hurricane that hit Lake Okeechobee, FL on 17 Sep 1928. Both hurricanes measured four on the Saffir–Simpson Scale.

Lightning The visible length of lightning strokes varies greatly. In mountainous regions, when clouds are very low, the flash may be less than 300 ft long. In flat country with very high clouds, a cloud-to-Earth flash may measure 4 miles, though in the most extreme cases such flashes have been measured at 20 miles. The intensely bright central core of the lightning channel is extremely narrow. Some authorities suggest that its diameter is as little as ½ in. This core is surrounded by a "corona envelope" (glow discharge), which may measure 10–20 ft in diameter.

EXTREME TEMPERATURES
(Progressive recordings)

HIGH

127.4°F	Ouargla, Algeria	27 Aug 1884
130°F	Amos, CA	17 Aug 1885
130°F	Mammoth Tank, CA	17 Aug 1885
134°F	Death Valley, CA	10 Jul 1913
136.4°F	Al'Aziziyah, Libya *	13 Sep 1922

* Obtained by the US National Geographical Society but not officially recognized by the Libyan Ministry of Communications.

A reading of 140° F at Delta, Mexico, in August 1953 is not now accepted because of overexposure to roof radiation. The official Mexican record of 136.4° F at San Luis, Sonora on 11 Aug 1933 is not internationally accepted.

A freak heat flash reported from Coimbra, Portugal, in September 1933 said to have caused the temperature to rise to 158° F for 120 sec is apocryphal.

LOW

−73°F	Floeberg Bay, Canada	[1] 1852
−90.4°F	Verkhoyansk, Siberia	3 Jan 1885
−90.4°F	Verkhoyansk, Siberia	5 Feb 1892
−90.4°F	Verkhoyansk, Siberia	7 Feb 1892
−90.4°F	Oymyakon, Siberia[2]	6 Feb 1933
−100.4°F	South Pole, Ant*	11 May 1957
−102.1°F	South Pole, Ant	17 Sep 1957
−109.1°F	Sovietskaya, Ant	2 May 1958
−113.3°F	Vostok, Ant	15 Jun 1958
−114.1°F	Sovietskaya, Ant	19 Jun 1958
−117.4°F	Sovietskaya, Ant	25 Jun 1958
−122.4°F	Vostok, Ant	7/8 Aug 1958
−124.1°F	Sovietskaya, Ant	9 Aug 1958
−125.3°F	Sovietskaya, Ant	25 Aug 1958
−126.9°F	Vostok, Ant	24 Aug 1960
−128.6°F	Vostok, Ant	21 Jul 1983

*Antartica

[1] The earliest recorded occasion that mercury froze (at −40° F) was by M. V. Lomonosov, near Moscow c. 1750.

[2] Population in 1986 reported to be 4,000— the world's coldest inhabited place.

■ **Minimum sunshine**
At the South Pole there is no sunshine for 182 days every year. Work continues, however, frequently with the aid of floodlights, as is the case here at the Halley Station on Antarctica. (Photo: Science Photo Library)

The speed of a discharge varies from 100–1,000 miles/sec for the downward leader track, and reaches up to 87,000 miles/sec (nearly half the speed of light) for the powerful return stroke.

Every few million strokes there is a giant discharge, in which the cloud-to-Earth and return strokes flash from and to the top of the thunderclouds. In these "positive giants" energy of up to 3 billion joules (3×10^{16} ergs) has been recorded. The temperature reaches about 54,032° F, which is more than that of the surface of the Sun.

Highest waterspout The highest waterspout of which there is a reliable record was one observed on 16 May 1898 off Eden, New South Wales, Australia. A theodolite reading from the shore gave its height as 5,014 ft. It was about 10 ft in diameter.

Cloud extremes The highest standard cloud form is cirrus, averaging 27,000 ft and above, but the rare nacreous, or mother-of-pearl formation sometimes reaches nearly 80,000 ft (see also Noctilucent clouds). A cirrus cloud is composed almost entirely of ice crystals at temperatures of −40° F or below. The lowest is stratus, below 3,500 ft. The cloud

form with the greatest vertical range is cumulonimbus, which has been observed to reach a height of nearly 68,000 ft in the tropics.

Highest shade temperature The highest shade temperature ever recorded is 136.4° F at Al'Azīzīyah, Libya (alt. 367 ft) on 13 Sep 1922.

United States The highest temperature in the United States was 134° F at Greenland Ranch, Death Valley, CA on 10 Jul 1913.

Lowest screen temperature A record low of −128.6° F was registered at Vostok, Antarctica (alt. 11,220 ft) on 21 Jul 1983.

The coldest permanently inhabited place is the Siberian village of Oymyakon (pop. 4,000), 63° 16′ N, 143° 15′ E (2,300 ft), in the USSR, where the temperature reached −90.0° F in 1933.

United States The lowest temperature in the United States was −79.8° F on 23 Jan 1971 in Prospect Creek, AK.

The lowest temperature in the continental United States was −69.7° F in Rogers Pass, MT on 20 Jan 1954.

Greatest rainfall A record 73.62 in of rain fell in 24 hours in Cilaos (alt.

3,937 ft), La Réunion, Indian Ocean on 15 and 16 Mar 1952. This is equal to 8,327 tons of rain per acre.

For a calendar month, the record is 366.14 in, at Cherrapunji, Meghalaya, India in July 1861.

The 12-month record was also at Cherrapunji, with 1,041.78 in between 1 Aug 1860 and 31 Jul 1861.

United States In the United States, the 24-hour record is 19 inches at Alvin, TX, on 25–26 Jul 1979. Over a 12-month period, 739 inches fell at Kukui, Maui, HI from December 1981–December 1982.

Wettest place By average annual rainfall, the wettest place in the world is Tutunendo, in Colombia, with 463.4 in per year.

Most rainy days Mt Wai-'ale-'ale (5,148 ft), Kauai, HI has up to 350 rainy days per year.

Greatest snowfall 1,224½ in of snow fell over a 12-month period from 19 Feb 1971 to 18 Feb 1972 at Paradise, Mt Rainier, in Washington State.

The record for a single snowstorm is 189 in at Mt Shasta Ski Bowl, CA from 13–19 Feb 1959, and for a 24-hr period the record

■ **Longest drought**
Desierto de Atacama, near Calama, Chile experienced a drought for some 400 years up to 1971. With its annual rainfall being effectively zero, water is piped 60 miles from a water collection and storage site in the mountains to this town in the desert.
(Photo: Science Photo Library)

snowfall is 76 in at Silver Lake, CO on 14–15 Apr 1921.

The greatest depth of snow on the ground was 37 ft 7 in at Tamarack, CA in March 1911.

The highest average snowfall in the United States for 1989 was 240.8 inches in Blue Canyon, CA.

Maximum sunshine The annual average at Yuma, AZ is 90 percent (over 4,000 hr).

St Petersburg, FL recorded 768 consecutive sunny days from 9 Feb 1967 to 17 Mar 1969.

Minimum sunshine At the South Pole there is zero sunshine for 182 days every year, and at the North Pole the figure is zero for 176 days.

Barometric pressure The highest barometric pressure ever recorded was 32 in at Agata, Siberia, USSR (alt. 862 ft) on 31 Dec 1968.

The lowest sea-level pressure was 25.69 in in Typhoon Tip, 300 miles west of Guam, Pacific Ocean, at Lat. 16° 44′ N, Long. 137° 46′ E, on 12 Oct 1979.

Highest surface wind speed A surface wind speed of 231 mph was recorded

at Mt Washington (6,288 ft), NH on 12 Apr 1934.

The fastest speed at low level was registered on 8 Mar 1972 at the USAF base at Thule, Greenland (145 ft), when a peak speed of 207 mph was recorded.

The fastest speed measured to date in a tornado is 280 mph at Wichita Falls, TX on 2 Apr 1958.

Thunder-days In Tororo, Uganda an average of 251 days of thunder per year was recorded for the 10-year period 1967–76.

Between Lat. 35° N and 35° S there are some 3,200 thunderstorms each 12 night-time hours, some of which can be heard at a range of 18 miles.

Hottest place On an annual mean basis, with readings taken over a six-year period from 1960 to 1966, the temperature at Dallol, in Ethiopia, was 94° F.

In Death Valley, CA, maximum temperatures of over 120° F were recorded on 43 consecutive days, between 6 Jul and 17 Aug 1917.

At Marble Bar, Western Australia (maximum 121° F), 162 consecutive days with maximum temperatures of over 100° F were recorded between 30 Oct 1923 and 8 Apr 1924.

At Wyndham, also in Western Australia, the temperature reached 90° F or more on 333 days in 1946.

Coldest place Polus Nedostupnosti (Pole of Cold), Antarctica at 78° S, 96° E, is the coldest place in the world, with an extrapolated annual mean of − 72 ° F.

The coldest measured mean is − 70 ° F, at Plateau Station, Antarctica.

Driest place The annual rainfall in the Desierto de Atacama, near Calama, Chile is effectively zero.

Longest drought Desierto de Atacama, in Chile, experienced a drought for some 400 years up to 1971.

Heaviest hailstones The heaviest hailstones on record, weighing 2¼ lb, are reported to have killed 92 people in the Gopalganj district of Bangladesh on 14 Apr 1986.

Longest sea-level fogs Sea-level fogs—with visibility less than 3,000 ft—persist for weeks on the Grand Banks, Newfoundland, Canada, with the average being more than 120 days per year.

Windiest place The Commonwealth Bay, George V Coast, Antarctica, where gales reach 200 mph, is the world's windiest place.

Gems, Jewels and Precious Stones

DIAMOND

Largest. 3,106 carats. This was found on 25 Jan 1905 in the Premier Mine, Pretoria, South Africa and named *The Cullinan* after the mine's discoverer, Sir Thomas Cullinan. Presented to Britain's King Edward VII in 1907. Currently the largest uncut stone is of 599 carats, found near Pretoria, South Africa in July 1986, although its existence was only announced by De Beers on 11 Mar 1988. It is expected to yield a 350-carat cut stone.

Largest cut. 530.2 carats. A 74-facet pear-shaped gem named *The Star of Africa*, it was cleaved from *The Cullinan* by Jak Asscher and polished by Henri Koe in Amsterdam, Netherlands in 1908. It is now in the Royal Sceptre, Great Britain.

Largest natural intense fancy blue. 136.25 carats. The "Queen of Holland" cushion-shaped brilliant-cut diamond was found in 1904. It was cut by F. Freedman & Co. in Amsterdam, Netherlands, and was exhibited at the Paris Exhibition in 1925. It was then sold to an Indian maharaja, but its current owner is unknown.

Largest natural intense fancy green. 41 carats. This is located in the Green Vaults in Dresden, Germany.

Smallest. 0.0001022 carat. D. Drukker & Zn NV of Amsterdam, Netherlands has produced a 57-facet brilliant with a diameter of 0.009 in.

Rarest color. Blood red. The largest is a 5.05-carat flawless stone found in Tichtenburg, South Africa in 1927 and now in a private collection in the United States.

Highest-priced. $12,760,000. A superb 11-sided pear-shaped mixed-cut diamond of 101.84 carats was sold to Robert Mouawad at Sotheby's, Geneva, Switzerland on 14 Nov 1990. The record per carat is $975,068 for a 0.95-carat purplish-red stone sold at Christie's, New York in April 1988. A record price of $10 million was paid for a rough uncut diamond by Chow Tai Fook of Hong Kong on 4 Mar 1989.

RUBY

Largest star. 2,475 carats. The *Rajarathna* ruby from India, owned by G. Vidyaraj, Bangalore, India, displays an animated star of six lines and is cut as a cabochon.

Largest double star. 1,370 carats. A cabochon cut gem, *Neelanjali*, also owned by G. Vidyaraj, displays 12 star lines and measures 3 in in height and 2 in in diameter.

Largest. 8,500 carats. In July 1985 jeweler James Kazanjian of Beverly Hills, CA displayed a 5¹⁄₂-in-tall red corundum (Al_2O_3) carved to resemble the Liberty Bell.

Highest priced. $4,620,000. This ruby and diamond ring made by Chaumet, in Paris, France weighs 32.08 carats and was sold at Sotheby's, New York on 26 Oct 1989. The record per carat is $227,300 for a ruby ring with a stone weighing

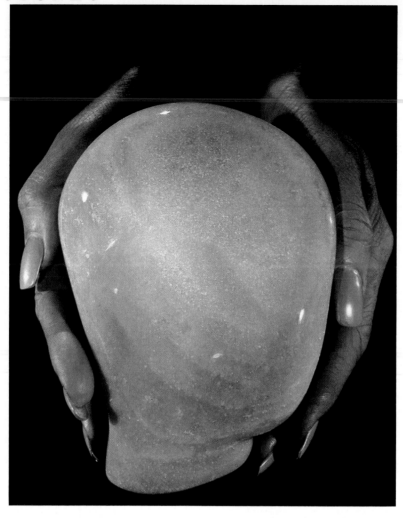

15.97 carats, which was sold at Sotheby's, New York on 18 Oct 1988.

EMERALD

Largest cut. 86,136 carats. This natural beryl was found in Carnaiba, Brazil in August 1974. It was carved by Richard Chan in Hong Kong and valued at £718,000 ($1,120,080) in 1982.

Largest single crystal. 7,025 carats. The largest single emerald crystal of gem quality was found in 1969 at the Cruces Mine, near Gachala, Colombia, and is owned by a private mining concern. Larger Brazilian and Russian stones do exist, but they are of low quality.

Highest-priced. $3,080,000. (Single lot of emeralds). This emerald and diamond necklace made by Cartier, London, Great Britain in 1937 (a total of 12 stones weighing 108.74 carats) was sold at Sotheby's, New York on 26 Oct 1989. The highest price for a single emerald is $2,126,646, for a 19.77-carat emerald and diamond ring made by Cartier in 1958, which was sold at Sotheby's, Geneva, Switzerland on 2 Apr 1987. This also represented the record price per carat for an emerald, at $107,569.

SAPPHIRE

Largest carved. 2,302 carats. Found at

Anakie, Queensland, Australia in *c.* 1935, this corundum (Al_2O_3) was carved into a 1,318-carat head of Abraham Lincoln and is now in the custody of the Kazanjian Foundation of Los Angeles, CA.

Largest star sapphire. 9,719.50 carats. This stone, cut in London, Great Britain in November 1989, has been named *The Lone Star* and is owned by Harold Roper.

Highest-priced. $2,791,723. A step-cut stone of 62.02 carats was sold as a sapphire and diamond ring at Sotheby's, St Moritz, Switzerland on 20 Feb 1988.

CRYSTAL BALL

Largest. 106.75 lb. The world's largest flawless rock crystal ball is 13 in in diameter, and was cut in China from Burmese rough material. It is now in the Smithsonian Institution in Washington, DC.

OPAL

Largest. 26,350 carats. The largest single piece of gem-quality white opal was found in July 1989 at the Jupiter Field at Coober Pedy in South Australia. It has been named *Jupiter-Five* and is in private ownership.

Largest polished opal. 3,749 carats. The largest free-form cabochon cut precious opal has been named "Galaxy," and measures $5 \frac{1}{2} \times 4 \times 1 \frac{5}{8}$ in. It was excavated in Brazil in

1976 and was displayed by Steven Sodokoff at the Tucson Gem Show at Tucson, AZ in February 1991.

Largest black opal. 1,520 carats. A stone found on 4 Feb 1972 at Lightning Ridge in Australia produced this finished gem, called the *Empress of Glengarry*. It measures $4 \frac{3}{4} \times 3 \frac{1}{8} \times \frac{5}{8}$ in, and is owned by Peter Gray.

Largest rough black opal. 2,020 carats. The largest gem-quality uncut black opal was also found at Lightning Ridge, on 3 Nov 1986. After cleaning, it weighs 2,020 carats and measures $4 \times 2 \frac{5}{8} \times 2 \frac{1}{2}$ in. It has been named *Halley's Comet* and is owned by a team of opal miners known as The Lunatic Hill Syndicate.

PEARL

Largest. 14 lb 1 oz. The *Pearl of Lao-tze* (also known as the *Pearl of Allah*) was found at Palawan, Philippines on 7 May 1934 in the shell of a giant clam. The property of Wilburn Dowell Cobb until his death, this 9 1/2-in long by 5 1/2-in diameter molluscan concretion was bought at auction on 15 May 1980 in San Francisco, CA by Peter Hoffman and Victor Barbish for $200,000. An appraisal by the San Francisco Gem Laboratory in May 1984 suggested a value of $40–42 million.

Largest cultured pearl. 138.25 carats. A 1 1/2-in round cultured pearl weighing 1 oz was found near Samui Island, off Thailand, in January 1988. The stone is owned by the Mikimoto Pearl Island Company, Japan.

Highest-priced. $864,280. *La Régente*, an egg-shaped pearl weighing 302.68 grains and formerly part of the French crown jewels, was sold at Christie's, Geneva, Switzerland on 12 May 1988.

TOPAZ

Largest. 22,892.5 carats. The rectangular, cushion-cut *American Golden Topaz* with 172 facets and 5 7/8 in in overall width has been on display at the Smithsonian Institution, Washington, DC since 4 May 1988.

JADE

Largest. 291 tons. A single boulder of nephrite jade was found in northeast China in Mar 1990. It measured $23 \times 20 \times 16$ ft.

AMBER

Largest. 33 lb 10 oz. The "Burma Amber" is located in the Natural History Museum, London, Great Britain. Amber is a fossil resin derived from extinct coniferous trees, and often contains trapped insects.

GOLD

Largest nugget. 7,560 oz. The *Holtermann Nugget* found on 19 Oct 1872 in the Beyers & Holtermann Star of Hope mine, Hill End, New South Wales, Australia contained some 220 lb of gold in a 630-lb slab of slate.

Largest pure nugget. The *Welcome Stranger* found at Moliagul, Victoria, Australia in 1869 yielded 2,248 troy oz of pure gold from 2,280 1/4 oz.

The Living World

Animal Kingdom

GENERAL RECORDS

Noisiest The noisiest land animals in the world are the howling monkeys (*Alouatta*) of Central and South America. The males have an enlarged bony structure at the top of the windpipe that enables the sound to reverberate, and their fearsome screams have been described as a cross between the bark of a dog and the bray of a donkey increased a thousandfold. Once they are in full voice they can be clearly heard for distances up to 10 miles.

Most fertile It has been calculated that a single cabbage aphid (*Brevicoryne brassica*) can give rise in a year to a mass of descendants weighing 906 million tons, more than three times the total weight of the world's human population. Fortunately the mortality rate is tremendous!

Strongest In proportion to their size, the strongest animals are the larger beetles of the family Scarabaeidae, which are found mainly in the tropics. In tests carried out on a rhinoceros beetle (*Dynastinae*) it was able to support 850 times its own weight on its back (compared with 25 percent of its body weight for an adult elephant). A dor beetle (*Geotrupes stercorosus*) shifted a load weighing 2.82 oz or 400 times its own body weight from one point to another and also managed to lift 3 ½ oz.

Strongest bite Experiments carried out with a Snodgrass gnathodynamometer (shark-bite meter) at the Lerner Marine Laboratory in Bimini, Bahamas revealed that a 6-ft-6¾-in-long dusky shark (*Carcharhinus obscurus*) could exert a force of 132 lb between its jaws. This is equivalent to a pressure of 22 tons/in^2 or 22 tons at the tips of the teeth.

Suspended animation In 1846 two specimens of the desert snail *Eremina desertorum* were presented to the British Museum (Natural History) in London as dead exhibits. They were glued to a small tablet and placed on display. Four years later, in March 1850, the museum staff, suspecting that one of the snails was still alive, removed it from the tablet and placed it in tepid water. The snail moved and later began to feed. This hardy little creature lived for another two years before it fell into a torpor and then died.

Regeneration The sponge (Porifera) has the most remarkable powers of regeneration of lost parts of any animal, as it can regrow its entire body from a tiny fragment of itself. If a sponge is squeezed through a fine-meshed silk gauze, each piece of separated tissue will live as an individual.

Most dangerous The world's most dangerous animals (excluding human beings) are the malarial parasites of the genus *Plasmodium* carried by mosquitoes of the genus *Anopheles*, which, if we exclude wars and accidents, have probably been responsible directly or indirectly for 50 percent of all human deaths since the Stone Age. Even today, despite major campaigns to eradicate malaria, at least 200 million people are afflicted by the disease each year, and more than one million babies and children die annually from it in Africa alone.

Largest colonies The black-tailed prairie dog (*Cynomys ludovicianus*), a rodent of the family Sciuridae found in the western United States and northern Mexico, builds the largest colonies. One single "town" discovered in 1901 contained about 400 million individuals and was estimated to cover 24,000 miles^2.

Greatest concentration The greatest concentration of animals ever recorded was an unbelievably huge swarm of Rocky Mountain locusts (*Melanoplus spretus*) that passed over Nebraska on 15–25 Aug 1875. According to one local scientist who watched their movements for five days, these locusts covered an area of 198,600 miles^2 as they flew over the state. If he overestimated the size of the swarm by 50 percent, it still covered 99,300 miles^2, which is approximately the area of Colorado or Oregon. It has been calculated that this swarm of locusts contained at least 12.5 trillion (10^{12}) insects, weighing 27.5 million tons. For unexplained reasons, this pest mysteriously disappeared in 1902 and has not been seen since.

Most prodigious eater The larva of the Polyphemus moth (*Antheraea polyphemus*) of North America consumes an amount equal to 86,000 times its own birth weight in the first 56 days of its life. In human terms, this would be equivalent to a 7-lb baby taking in 301 tons of nourishment!

Champion dieter During the 7-month lactation period, a 132-ton female blue whale (*Balaenoptera musculus*) can lose up to 25 percent of her body weight nursing her calf.

Most valuable The most valuable animals in cash terms are thoroughbred racehorses. The most ever paid for a yearling was $13.1 million on 23 Jul 1985 at Keeneland, KY by Robert Sangster and partners for Seattle Dancer. (See Horse Racing.)

Size difference Although many differences exist in the animal world between the males and females of species, the most striking difference in size can be seen in the marine worm *Bonellia viridis*. The females of this species are 3.9–39 in long compared with just 0.039–0.12 in for the male, making the females millions of times heavier than the males.

Slowest growth The slowest growth in the animal kingdom is that of the deep-sea clam *Tindaria callistisormis* of the North Atlantic, which takes c. 100 years to reach a length of 0.31 in.

Mammals Mammalia

Largest and heaviest The longest and heaviest mammal in the world, and the largest animal ever recorded, is the blue or sulphur-bottom whale (*Balaenoptera musculus*), also called Sibbald's rorqual. The longest specimen ever recorded was a female landed in 1909 at Grytviken, South Georgia in the South Atlantic; it measured 110 ft 2½ in in length. Another female measuring 90 ft 6 in, caught in the Southern Ocean by the Soviet Slava whaling fleet on 20 Mar 1947, weighed 209 tons. Its tongue and heart weighed 4.7 tons and 1,540 lb respectively.

Blue whales inhabit the colder seas and migrate to warmer waters in the winter for breeding. Observations made in the Antarctic in 1947–48 showed that a blue whale can maintain a speed of 20 knots for 10 minutes when frightened. It has been calculated that a 90-ft blue whale traveling at 20 knots would produce 520 hp. Newborn calves measure 21 ft 3½ in–28½ ft in length and weigh up to 6,614 lbs.

The barely visible ovum of the blue whale calf, weighing a fraction of a milligram, grows to a weight of c. 29 tons in 22¾ months, made up of 10¾ months' gestation and the first 12 months of life. This is equivalent to an increase of 30 billion.

The low-frequency pulses made by blue whales when communicating with each other have been measured up to 188 decibels, making them the loudest sounds emitted by any living source. They have been detected 530 miles away.

It has been estimated that, as a result of over-hunting, there are only about 10,000–12,000 blue whales roaming the world's oceans today. This compares

with a peak estimate of *c.* 220,000 at the turn of the century. The species has been protected by law since 1967, although nonmember countries of the International Whaling Commission, e.g., Panama, Taiwan, South Korea and the Philippines, are not bound by this agreement. An indefinite worldwide ban on commercial whaling came into force at the start of the 1985/86 season, but Japan, Norway and Iceland are still slaughtering minke, fin and sei whales (*Balaenoptera acutorostrata*, *B. physalus* and *B. borealis*) under the guise of "research whaling." In 1988 Iceland caught 68 fin whales and 10 sei whales, and 300 minke whales were captured by Japanese whalers in the Southern Ocean. The ban on commercial whaling was reassessed in July 1990.

Deepest dive On 14 Oct 1955 a 47-ft bull sperm whale (*Physeter catodon = macrocephalus*) was found at a depth of 3,720 ft, its jaw entangled with a submarine cable running between Santa Elena, Ecuador and Chorillos, Peru. At this depth the whale withstood a pressure of 1,680 lb/in^2 of body surface. In 1970 American scientists, by triangulating the location clicks of sperm whales, calculated that the *maximum* depth reached by this species was 8,202 ft. However, on 25 Aug 1969 another bull sperm whale was killed 100 miles south of Durban, South Africa after it had surfaced from a dive lasting 1 hr 52 min, and inside its stomach were found two small sharks that had been swallowed about an hour earlier. These were later identified as *Scymnodon sp.*, a type of dogfish found only on the seafloor. At this point from land the depth of water exceeds 9,876 ft for a radius of 30–40 miles, which suggests that the sperm whale sometimes descends to a depth of over 9,840 ft when seeking food and is limited by pressure of time rather than by water pressure.

Largest land The largest living land animal is the African bush elephant (*Loxodonta africana*). The average adult bull stands 10 ft 6 in at the shoulder and weighs 6.3 tons. The largest specimen ever recorded was a bull shot in Mucusso, Angola on 7 Nov 1974. Lying on its side this elephant measured 13 ft 8 in in a projected line from the highest point of the shoulder to the base of the forefoot, indicating that its standing height must have been about 13 ft. Other measurements included an overall length of 35 ft (tip of extended trunk to tip of extended tail) and a forefoot circumference of 5 ft 11 in. The weight was computed to be 13.5 tons.

The endangered desert elephant of Damaraland in Namibia (reduced to 84 in August 1981) is the tallest species in the world because it has proportionately longer legs than other elephants. The tallest elephant ever recorded was a bull shot near Sesfontein in Damaraland, Namibia on 4 Apr 1978 after it had reportedly killed 11 people and caused widespread crop damage. Lying on its side, this mountain of flesh measured 14½ ft in a projected line from the shoulder to the base of the forefoot,

indicating a standing height of about 13 ft 10 in. Other measurements included an overall length of 34 ft 1 in, and a forefoot circumference of 5 ft 2 in. This particular animal weighed an estimated 8.8 tons.

Largest marine The largest toothed mammal ever recorded is the sperm whale (*Physeter catodon*), also called the cachalot. In the summer of 1950 a record-sized bull measuring 67 ft 11 in was captured off the Kurile Islands in the Pacific by a Soviet whaling fleet, but much larger bulls were reported in the early days of whaling. The 16-ft-4¾-in-long lower jaw of a sperm whale exhibited in the British Museum (Natural History) in London belonged to a bull measuring nearly 84 ft, and similar lengths have been reported for other outsized individuals killed.

Tallest land The giraffe (*Giraffa camelopardalis*), which is now found only in the dry savannah and semidesert areas of Africa south of the Sahara, is the tallest living animal. The tallest ever recorded was a Masai bull (*G. camelopardalis tippelskirchi*) named George, received at Chester Zoo, Great Britain on 8 Jan 1959 from Kenya. His "horns" almost grazed the roof of the 20-ft-high Giraffe House when he was nine years old. George died on 22 Jul 1969. Less-credible heights of up to 23 ft (measured between pegs) have been claimed for bulls shot in the field.

Smallest land The endangered Kitti's hog-nosed bat (*Craseonycteristhonglongyai*), also called the bumblebee bat, is confined to about 21 limestone caves (population more than 2,000) on the Kwae Noi River, Kanchanaburi, Thailand. Mature specimens of both sexes have a wingspan of *c.* 6.29 in and weigh 0.062–0.071 oz.

Mature specimens of Savi's white-toothed pygmy shrew (*Suncus etruscus*), also called the Etruscan shrew, which is found along the coast of the Mediterranean and southwards to Cape Province, South Africa, have a head and body length of 1.32–2.04 in, a tail length of 0.94–1.14 in and weigh 0.052–0.09 oz. (See Insectivores.)

Smallest marine In terms of weight, the smallest totally marine mammal is probably Commerson's dolphin (*Cephalorhynchus commersonii*), also known as Le Jacobite, which is found off the tip of South America. The weights of a group of six adult specimens ranged from 50.7 lb to 77.1 lb. The sea otter (*Enhydra lutris*) of the North Pacific is of comparable size (55–81.4 lb), but this species sometimes comes ashore during storms.

Rarest land A number of mammals are known only from a single or type specimen. One of these is the small-toothed fruit bat (*Neopteryx frosti*), collected from Tamalanti, Sulawesi (Celebes), Indonesia in 1938.

The thylacine or tasmanian wolf or tiger (*Thylacinus cynocephalus*), feared extinct since the last captive specimen died in Beaumaris Zoo, Tasmanina, Australia on 7 Sep 1936, was possibly identi-

fied in July 1982 when a wildlife ranger claimed he saw one of these predatory marsupials in the spotlight of his parked car. Since then, however, there have been no more positive sightings.

The red wolf (*Canis rufus*) of the southeast United States became extinct in the wild in the early 1970s, but there are now over 125 individuals (not all of them genetically pure) held by the US Fish and Wildlife Service. In June 1988 it was announced that two pairs released in North Carolina by the captive breeding program had produced cubs.

The black-footed ferret (*Mustela nigripes*) of the northern United States is also extinct in the wild, but in 1988 the captive population of 25, housed in a special center in Cheyenne, WY, more than doubled when the second breeding season produced 38 pups. There are now at least 300 individuals in captivity and the ferret will be reintroduced in Wyoming in the early 1990s.

Rarest marine Longman's beaked whale (*Indopacetus pacificus*) is known only from two skulls. The type specimen was discovered on a beach near MacKay, Queensland, Australia in 1922, and the second near Muqdisho, Somalia in 1955.

The vaquita or gulf porpoise (*Phocoena sinus*) has not been sighted since 1980, and may now be extinct. Many hundreds of thousands have been accidentally killed by gillnet fishing in the last 45 years.

Fastest land Over a short distance (i.e., up to 1,800 ft) the cheetah or hunting leopard (*Acinonyx jubatus*) of the open plains of East Africa, Iran, Turkmenia and Afghanistan has a probable maximum speed of 60–63 mph on level ground. Speeds of 71, 84 and 90 mph have been claimed for this animal, but these figures must be considered exaggerated. Tests in London, Great Britain in 1937 showed that on an oval greyhound track over 1,035 ft a female cheetah's average speed over three runs was 43.4 mph, compared with 44.91 mph for the fastest race horse (see Chapter 11), but this specimen was not running flat out and had great difficulty negotiating the bends.

The fastest land animal over a sustained distance (i.e., 3,000 ft or more) is the

pronghorn antelope (*Antilocapra americana*) of the western United States.
Specimens have been observed to travel
at 35 mph for 4 miles, at 42 mph for 1
mile, and at 55 mph for ½ mile.

Fastest marine On 12 Oct 1958 a bull
killer whale (*Orcinus orca*), measuring an
estimated 20–25 ft in length, was timed at
34.5 mph in the east Pacific. Similar
speeds have also been reported for Dall's
porpoise (*Phocoenoides dalli*) in short
bursts.

Slowest The ai or three-toed sloth
(*Bradypus tridactylus*) of tropical South
America has an average ground speed of
6–8 ft per minute (0.068–0.098 mph), but
in the trees it can "accelerate" to 15 ft
per minute (0.17 mph). (Compare these
figures with the 0.03 mph of the common
garden snail and the 0.17 mph of the
giant tortoise.)

Sleepiest Some armadillos (Dasypo-
didae), opossums (Didelphidae) and
sloths (Bradypodidae) spend up to 80
percent of their lives sleeping or dozing,
while it is claimed that Dall's porpoise
(*Phocoenoides dalli*) never sleeps at all.

Longest hibernation The barrow
ground squirrel (*Spermophilus parryi
barrowensis*) of Point Barrow, AK hiber-
nates for nine months of the year.
During the remaining three months it
feeds, breeds and collects food for storage in its burrow.

Oldest No other mammal can match the
extreme proven age of 120 years attained
by humans (*Homo sapiens*; see Chapter
3). It is probable that the closest
approach is made by the Asiatic elephant (*Elephas maximus*). The greatest age that has been verified with
absolute certainty is 78 years in the case
of a cow named Modoc, who died at
Santa Clara, CA on 17 Jul 1975. She was
imported into the United States from
Germany in 1898 at the age of two.

Nepal's royal elephant Prem Prasad was
reportedly 81 when he died at Kasra,
Chitwan on 27 Feb 1985, but his actual
age was believed to have been 65–70
years. Sri Lanka's famous bull elephant
Rajah, who had led the annual Perahera
procession through Kandi carrying the

Sacred Tooth of the Buddha since 1931,
died on 16 Jul 1988, reportedly at the age
of 81 years.

Highest-living The yak (*Bos grun-
niens*), of Tibet and the Sichuanese Alps,
China, occasionally climbs to an
altitude of 20,000 ft when foraging.

Largest herds The largest herds on
record were those of the springbok
(*Antidorcas marsupialis*) during migration across the plains of the western
parts of southern Africa in the 19th
century. In 1849 John Fraser observed a
herd that took three days to pass
through the settlement of Beaufort
West, Cape Province, South Africa.
Another herd seen moving near Nels
Poortje, Cape Province in 1888 was estimated to contain 100 million head,
although 10 million is probably a more
realistic figure. A herd estimated to be
15 miles wide and more than 100 miles
long was reported from Karree Kloof,
Orange River, South Africa in July 1896.

Longest gestation period The Asiatic elephant (*Elephas maximus*) has an
average gestation period of 609 days
(over 20 months) and a maximum of 760
days—more than two and a half times
that of a human. By 1981 only about
35,000 survived.

Shortest gestation period The gestation periods of the American opossum
(*Didelphis marsupialis*), also called the
Virginian opossum, the rare water opossum or yapok (*Chironectes minimus*) of
central and northern South America,
and the eastern native cat (*Dasyurus
viverrinus*) of Australia are all normally
12–13 days but can be as short as eight
days.

Largest litter The greatest number of
young born to a *wild* mammal at a single
birth is 31 (30 of which survived) in the
case of the tailless tenrec (*Tenrec ecau-
datus*) found in Madagascar and the
Comoro Islands. The normal litter size is
12–15, although females can suckle up
to 24.

Youngest breeder The streaked
tenrec (*Hemicentetes semispinosus*) of
Madagascar is weaned after only five
days, and females can breed 3–4 weeks
after their birth.

CARNIVORES

Largest on land The average adult
male Kodiak bear (*Ursus arctos midden-
dorffi*), native to Kodiak Island and the
adjacent Afognak and Shuyak islands in
the Gulf of Alaska, has a nose-to-tail
length of 8 ft, with the tail measuring
about 4 in. It stands 52 in at the shoulder
and weighs 1,050–1,175 lb. In 1894 a
weight of 1,656 lb was recorded for a
male shot at English Bay, Kodiak Island,
whose *stretched* skin measured 13½ ft
from nose to tail. This weight was
exceeded by a "cage-fat" male in the
Cheyenne Mountain Zoological Park,
Colorado Springs, CO, which weighed
1,670 lb at the time of its death on 22 Sep
1955.

In 1981 an unconfirmed weight of over
2,000 lb was reported for a peninsula
giant bear (*Ursus a. gyas*) from Alaska

on exhibition at the Space Farms Zoological Park in Beemerville, NJ.

Weights exceeding 2,000 lb have also
been reported for the polar bear (*Ursus
maritimus*), but the average adult male
weighs 850–900 lb and measures 7 ft 9 in
from nose to tail. In 1960 a polar bear
reportedly weighing 2,210 lb was shot at
the polar entrance to Kotzebue Sound,
AK. In April 1962 the 11-ft-1¼-in-tall
mounted specimen was put on display at
the Seattle World's Fair.

Smallest The smallest living member
of the order Carnivora is the least weasel
(*Mustela rixosa*), also called the dwarf
weasel, which is circumpolar in distribution. Four races are recognized, the
smallest of which is *Mustela r. pygmaea*
of Siberia, USSR. Mature specimens
have an overall length of 6.96–8.14 in
and weigh 1¼–2½ oz.

Largest feline The largest member of
the cat family (Felidae) is the protected
long-furred Siberian tiger (*Panthera
tigris altaica*), also called the Amur or
Manchurian tiger. Adult males average
10 ft 4 in in length from the nose to the
tip of the extended tail, stand 39–42 in at
the shoulder and weigh about 585 lb. In
1950 a male weighing 846.5 lb was shot in
the Sikhote Alin Mountains, Maritime
Territory, USSR.

An outsized Indian tiger (*Panthera
tigris tigris*) shot in northern Uttar
Pradesh in November 1967 measured
10 ft 7 in between pegs (11 ft 1 in over the
curves) and weighed 857 lb (compared
with 9 ft 3 in and 420 lb for an average
adult male). Its stuffed body is now on
display in the Museum of Natural
History at the Smithsonian Institution,
Washington, D.C.

The largest tiger ever held in captivity,
and the heaviest "big cat" on record, is a
nine-year-old Siberian male named
Jaipur, owned by animal trainer Joan
Byron-Marasek of Clarksburg, NJ. This
specimen measured 10 ft 11 in in total
length and weighed 932 lb in October
1986.

The average adult African lion (*Panthera leo*) measures 9 ft overall, stands
36–38 in at the shoulder and weighs
400–410 lb. The heaviest wild specimen
on record weighed 690 lb and was shot
near Hectorspruit, Transvaal, South
Africa in 1936.

In July 1970 a weight of 826 lb was
reported for a black-maned lion named
Simba (b. Dublin Zoo, Ireland, 1959) at
Colchester Zoo, Essex, Great Britain.
He died on 16 Jan 1973 at the now-
defunct Knaresborough Zoo, North
Yorkshire, Great Britain and his stuffed
body was put on display there.

An adult male litigon (a hybrid of an
Indian lion and a tigon—itself the offspring of a tiger and a lioness) named
Cubanacan at Alipore Zoological Gardens, Calcutta, India is also believed to
weigh at least 800 lb. This animal stands
52 in at the shoulder (compared with
44 in for the lion Simba) and measures a
record 11½ ft in total length. This
animal, the first and only one of its kind,

was reported to have died on 12 Apr 1991.

Smallest feline The smallest member of the cat family is the rusty-spotted cat (*Felis rubiginosa*) of southern India and Sri Lanka. The average adult male has an overall length of 25–28 in (the tail measures 9–10 in) and weighs about 3 lb.

PRIMATES

Largest living The average adult male eastern lowland gorilla (*Gorilla g. graueri*) of the lowland forests of eastern Zaïre and southwestern Uganda stands 5 ft 9 in tall and weighs 360 lb.

The mountain gorilla (*Gorilla g. beringei*) of the volcanic mountain ranges of western Rwanda, southwestern Uganda and eastern Zaïre is of comparable size, i.e., 5 ft 8 in tall and 343 lb, and most of the exceptionally large gorillas taken in the field have been of this race.

The greatest height (top of crest to heel) recorded for a gorilla in the wild is 6 ft 2 in for a male of the mountain race shot in the eastern Congo (Zaïre) c. 1920. The tallest gorilla ever kept in captivity is reportedly an eastern lowland male named Colossus (b. 1966), who is currently on display at a zoo in Gulf Breeze, FL. He reportedly stands 6 ft 2 in tall and weighs 575 lb, but these figures have not yet been confirmed.

A western lowland gorilla called Baltimore Jack, who was received at Baltimore Zoo in Maryland in 1956 and later sold to Phoenix Zoo in Arizona, had exceptionally long legs for a gorilla. He reportedly stood 6 ft 3 in tall, but his actual height was somewhere between 5 ft 7 in and 5 ft 9 in (weight 300 lb). He died in 1972.

The heaviest gorilla ever kept in captivity was a male of the mountain race named N'gagi, who died in San Diego Zoo in California on 12 Jan 1944 at the age of 18. He weighed 683 lb at his heaviest in 1943, and 635 lb at the time of his death. He was 5 ft 7¾ in tall and boasted a record chest measurement of 78 in.

Smallest Adult specimens of the rare pen-tailed shrew (*Ptilocercus lowii*) of Malaysia have a total length of 9–13 in (head and body 3.93–5.51 in; tail 5.1–7.5 in) and weigh 1.23–1.76 oz.

The pygmy marmoset (*Cebuella pygmaea*) of the upper Amazon basin and the lesser mouse-lemur (*Microcebus murinus*) of Madagascar are of comparable length to the shrew but heavier, with adults weighing 1.76–2.64 oz and 1.58–2.82 oz respectively.

Rarest The greater bamboo broad-nosed gentle lemur (*Hapalemur simus*) of Madagascar reportedly became extinct in the early 1970s, but in 1986 a group consisting of 60–80 individuals was discovered living in a remote rainforest near Ranomafana in the southeastern part of the island by an expedition from Duke University, Durham, NC.

The golden-rumped tamarin (*Leontopithecus chrysopygus*), which is now restricted to two areas of forest in the state of São Paulo, Brazil, is also on the verge of extinction, with only 75–100 surviving in 1986.

Oldest The greatest irrefutable age reported for a nonhuman primate is about 59 years for a male orangutan (*Pongo pygmaeus*) named Guas, who died in Philadelphia Zoological Garden in Pennsylvania on 9 Feb 1977. He was at least 13 years old on his arrival at the zoo on 1 May 1931.

The famous western lowland gorilla Massa (b. July 1931) died on 30 Dec 1984 at the age of 53 years 5 months. The oldest female gorilla on record was Carolyn (b. 1939) of the New York Zoological Society (Bronx Zoo), New York City who died 27 Sep 1986 at the age of 47.

The oldest chimpanzee (*Pan troglodytes*) on record was a male named Jimmy at Seneca Zoo, Rochester, NY, who died on 17 Sep 1985 at the age of 55 years 6 months.

Strongest In 1924 Boma, a 165-lb male chimpanzee at the New York Zoological Society (Bronx Zoo), New York City recorded a right-handed pull (feet braced) of 847 lb on a dynamometer (compare with 210 lb for a man of equal weight).

On another occasion an adult female chimpanzee named Suzette (estimated weight 135 lb) at the same zoo registered a right-handed pull of 1,260 lb while in a rage. An American record of a 100-lb chimpanzee achieving a two-handed dead lift of 600 lb with ease suggests that a male gorilla could with training raise 2,000 lb.

MONKEYS

Largest The only species of monkey reliably credited with weights of more than 100 lb is the mandrill (*Mandrillus sphinx*) of equatorial West Africa. The greatest reliable weight recorded is 119 lb for a captive male, but an unconfirmed weight of 130 lb has been reported. (Adult females are about half the size of males.)

Smallest The smallest-known monkey is the pygmy marmoset (*Cebuella pygmaea*) of the upper Amazon basin. (See Smallest primates.)

Oldest The world's oldest monkey, a male white-throated capuchin (*Cebus capucinus*) called Bobo, died on 10 Jul 1988 at the age of 53 following complications related to a stroke. He was originally imported from South America and donated to the Mesker Park Zoo in Evansville, IN on 1 Jan 1935. When the zoo disbanded its monkey colony he was given to Dr Raymond T. Bartus, founder of the Geriatric Research Program at Lederle Laboratories, American Cyanamid Company, Pearl River, NY, and lived in the geriatric monkey colony from 31 Oct 1981 until his death.

PINNIPEDS Seals, Sea Lions, Walruses

Largest The largest of the 34 known species of pinniped is the southern elephant seal (*Mirounga leonina*) of the sub-Antarctic islands. Adult bulls average 16½ ft in length from the tip of the inflated snout to the tips of the outstretched tail flippers, have a maximum girth of 12 ft and weigh about 5,000 lb, compared with 10 ft and about 1,500 lb for average adult cows. The largest accurately measured specimen was a bull killed in the South Atlantic at Possession Bay, South Georgia on 28 Feb 1913 which probably weighed at least 4.4 tons and measured 21 ft 4 in after flensing (stripping of the blubber or skin). Its original length was about 22½ ft. The largest recorded live specimen is a bull nicknamed "Stalin" from South Georgia. It was tranquilized by members of the British Antarctic Survey on 14 Oct 1989 when it weighed 5,869 lb and measured 16 ½ ft.

Smallest The smallest pinnipeds are the ringed seal (*Phoca hispida*) of the Arctic and the closely related Baikal seal (*P. sibirica*) of Lake Baikal and the Caspian seal (*P. caspica*) of the Caspian Sea, USSR. Adult males measure up to 5½ ft in length and can weigh up to 280 lb. Females are about two-thirds this size.

Most abundant The total population of the crabeater seal (*Lobodon carci-*

■ **Largest feline**
The largest member of the cat family (Felidae) is the endangered Siberian tiger (Panthera tigris altaica), an inhabitant of grassy or swampy regions. The average adult male is 10 ft 4 in long, stands 39–42 in at the shoulder and weighs 585 lb. Despite its relaxed air, the tiger can leap about 16½ ft from a stationary crouched position. (Photo: Bruce Coleman)

nophagus) of Antarctica was estimated in 1977 to be nearly 15 million.

Rarest The last reliable sighting of the Caribbean or West Indian monk seal (*Monachus tropicalis*) was on Serranilla Bank off the coast of Mexico's Yucatan peninsula in 1952. In 1974 two seals were seen near Cay Verde and Cay Burro, Bahamas, but a search in 1979 found nothing. It has been suggested that these sightings (and others) may have been of California sea-lions (*Zalophus californianus*) which had escaped from captivity; these have been sighted in the Gulf of Mexico on several occasions.

Fastest The highest swimming speed recorded for a pinniped is a short spurt of 25 mph by a California sea lion. The fastest-moving pinniped on land is the crabeater seal, which has been timed at speeds up to 11.8 mph.

Deepest dive In May 1988 a team of scientists from the University of California at Santa Cruz tested the diving abilities of the northern elephant seal (*Mirounga anguistirostris*) off Ano Nuevo Point, CA. One female reached a record depth of 4,135 ft, and another remained submerged for 48 minutes. Similar experiments carried out by Australian scientists on southern elephant seals (*M. leonina*) in the Southern Ocean recorded a dive of 3,720 ft, with other dives lasting nearly two hours also observed. It was discovered that the seals regularly swam down to about 2,500 ft and when they resurfaced apparently had no "oxygen debt."

Oldest A female gray seal (*Halichoerus grypus*) shot at Shunni Wick, Shetland, Great Britain on 23 Apr 1969 was believed to be "at least 46 years old" based on a count of dentine rings. The captive record is an estimated 41 years (1901–42) for a bull gray seal named "Jacob" held in Skansen Zoo, Stockholm, Sweden.

BATS

Largest The only flying mammals are bats (order Chiroptera), of which there are about 950 living species. The bat with the greatest wingspan is the Bismarck flying fox (*Pteropus neohibernicus*) of the Bismarck Archipelago and New Guinea. One specimen preserved in the American Museum of Natural History in New York City has a wing spread of 5 ft 5 in, but some unmeasured bats probably reach 6 ft.

United States Mature specimens of the large mastiff bat (*Eumops perotis*), found in southern Texas, California, Arizona and New Mexico, have a wingspan of 22.04 in.

Smallest The smallest bat in the world is Kitti's hog-nosed bat. (See page 29.)

United States The smallest native bat is the Western pipistrelle (*Pipistrellus hesperus*), found in the western United States. Mature specimens have a wingspan of 0.79 in.

Rarest At least three species of bat are known only from the type specimen. They are: the small-toothed fruit bat (*Neopteryx frosti*) from Tamalanti, Sulawesi (Celebes; 1938–39); *Paracoelops megalotis* from Vinh, Vietnam (1945); and *Latidens salimalii* from the High Wavy Mountains, India (1948).

Fastest Because of the great practical difficulties, little data on bat speeds have been published. The greatest velocity attributed to a bat is 32 mph in the case of a Mexican free-tailed bat (*Tadarida brasiliensis*), but this may have been wind-assisted. In one American experiment using an artificial mine tunnel and 17 different kinds of bat, only four of them managed to exceed 13 mph in level flight.

Oldest The greatest age reliably reported for a bat is 32 years for a banded female little brown bat (*Myotis lucifugus*) in the United States in 1987.

Highest detectable pitch Because of their ultrasonic echolocation, bats have the most acute hearing of any terrestrial animal. Vampire bats (family Desmodontidae) and fruit bats (Pteropodidae) can hear frequencies as high as 120–210 kHz, compared with 20 kHz for the adult human limit and 280 kHz for the common dolphin (*Delphinus delphis*).

Largest colonies The largest concentration of bats found living anywhere in the world today is that of the Mexican free-tailed bat (*Tadarida brasiliensis*) in Bracken Cave, San Antonio, TX, where up to 20 million animals assemble after migration.

Deepest The little brown bat (*Myotis lucifugus*) has been recorded at a depth of 3,805 ft in a zinc mine in New York State. The mine serves as winter quarters for 1,000 members of this species, which normally roost at a depth of 656 ft.

RODENTS

Largest The capybara (*Hydrochoerus hydrochaeris*), also called the carpincho or water hog, of tropical South America, has a head and body length of 3¼–4½ ft and can weigh up to 250 lb (cage-fat specimen).

Smallest The northern pygmy mouse (*Baiomys taylori*) of central Mexico and southern Arizona and Texas measures up to 4.3 in in total length and weighs 0.24–0.28 oz.

Rarest The rarest rodents in the world are Garrido's hutia (*Capromys garridoi*) of the Canarreos Archipelago, Cuba, and the little earth hutia (*C. sanfelipensis*) of Juan Garcia Cay, an islet off southern Cuba. The latter species has not been recorded since its discovery in 1970.

Oldest The greatest reliable age reported for a rodent is 27 years 3 months for a Sumatran crested porcupine (*Hystrix brachyura*) that died in the National Zoological Park, Washington, D.C. on 12 Jan 1965.

Fastest breeder The female meadow vole (*Microtus agrestis*), found in Great Britain, can reproduce from the age of 25 days and can have up to 17 litters of 6–8 young in a year.

INSECTIVORES

Largest The moon rat (*Echinosorex gymnurus*), also known as Raffles' gymnure, which is found in Myanmar (formerly Burma), Thailand, Malaysia, Sumatra and Borneo, has a head and body length of 10.43–17.52 in, a tail measuring 7.87–8.26 in and weighs up to 3.08 lb.

Although the much larger anteaters (families Tachyglossidae and Myrmecophagidae) feed on termites and other soft-bodied insects, they are not insectivores, but belong to the orders Monotremata and Edentata ("without teeth").

Smallest The smallest insectivore is Savi's white-toothed pygmy shrew (*Suncus etruscus*). (See Smallest mammals.)

Oldest The greatest reliable age recorded for an insectivore is over 16 years for a lesser hedgehog-tenrec (*Echinops telfairi*), which was born in Amsterdam Zoo, Netherlands in 1966 and was later sent to Jersey Zoo, Channel Islands, Great Britain. It died on 27 Nov 1982.

ANTELOPES

Largest The rare giant eland (*Taurotragus derbianus*) of western and central Africa may surpass 2,000 lb. The common eland (*Taurotragus oryx*) of eastern and southern Africa has the same shoulder height of up to 5 ft 10 in but is not quite so massive, although there is one record of a 5 ft 5 in bull shot in Malawi *c.* 1937 that weighed 2,078 lb.

Smallest Mature specimens of the royal antelope (*Neotragus pygmaeus*) of western Africa measure 10–12 in at the shoulder and weigh only 7–8 lb, which is the size of a large brown hare (*Lepus europaeus*).

Salt's dik-dik (*Madoqua saltina*) of northeastern Ethiopia and Somalia weighs only 5–6 lb when adult, but this species stands about 14 in at the withers (highest part of the back of an animal).

Rarest Until recently, the Arabian oryx (*Oryx leucoryx*) had not been reported in the wild since 1972 when three were killed and four others captured on the Jiddat-al-Harasis plateau, south Oman. Between March 1980 and August 1983, 17 antelopes from the World Herd at San Diego Zoo in California were released into the desert in south Oman under the protection of a nomadic tribe. Since then there have been at least 43 live births, and at the beginning of 1989 the wild herd totaled 60. The Arabian oryx has also been successfully reintroduced into the Shaumari Reserve in Jordan, where there are now 90 of these animals.

Oldest The greatest reliable age recorded for an antelope is 25 years 4 months for an addax (*Addax nasomaculatus*) that died in Brookfield Zoo, Chicago, IL on 15 Oct 1960.

DEER

Largest The largest deer is the Alaskan moose (*Alces alces gigas*). Adult bulls average 6 ft at the shoulder and weigh *c.* 1,100 lb. A bull standing 7 ft 8 in between pegs and weighing an estimated 1,800 lb was shot on the Yukon River in the Yukon Territory, Canada in September 1897. Unconfirmed measurements of up to 8 ft 6 in at the shoulder and estimated weights of up to 2,600 lb have been claimed.

The record antler spread or "rack" is 78½ in (skull and antlers 91 lb) for a set taken from a moose killed near the headwaters of the Stewart River in the Yukon Territory, Canada in October 1897. The antlers are now on display in the Field Museum, Chicago, IL.

Smallest The smallest true deer (family Cervidae) is the northern pudu (*Pudu mephistopheles*) of Ecuador and Colombia. Mature specimens measure 13–14 in at the shoulder and weigh 16–18 lb.

The smallest ruminant is the lesser Malay chevrotain (*Tragulus javanicus*) of southeast Asia, Sumatra and Borneo. Adults measure 8–10 in at the shoulder and weigh 6–7 lb.

Rarest Until recently, Fea's muntjac (*Muntiacus feae*) was known only from two specimens collected on the borders of southern Myanmar (formerly Burma) and western Thailand. In December 1977 a female was received at Dusit Zoo, in Bangkok, followed by two females in 1981 and three males and three females from Xizang, Tibet between February 1982 and April 1983.

Oldest The world's oldest recorded deer is a red deer (*Cervus elaphus scoticus*) named Bambi (b. 8 Jun 1963), owned by the Fraser family of Kiltarlity, Great Britain.

United States The greatest reliable age recorded for a deer is 26 years 8 months for a red deer (*Cervus elaphus scoticus*) that died in Milwaukee Zoo, WI on 28 Jun 1954.

MARSUPIALS

Largest The adult male red kangaroo (*Megaleia rufa* or *Macropus rufus*) of central, southern and eastern Australia stands up to 7 ft tall, measures up to 8 ft ½ in in total length and weighs up to 187 lb.

Smallest The smallest-known marsupial is the rare long-tailed planigale (*Planigale ingrami*), a flat-skulled mouse of northeastern and northwestern Australia. Adult males have a head and body length of 2.16–2.48 in, a tail length of 2.24–2.36 in and weigh 0.13–0.19 oz.

Oldest The greatest reliable age recorded for a marsupial is 26 years 22 days for a common wombat (*Vombatus ursinus*) that died in London Zoo, Great Britain on 20 Apr 1906.

Fastest speed The fastest speed recorded for a marsupial is 40 mph for a mature female eastern gray kangaroo (*Macropus giganteus* or *M. canguru*). One large male red kangaroo died from his exertions after being paced for one mile at 35 mph.

Highest jump A captive eastern gray kangaroo once cleared an 8-ft fence when an automobile backfired, and there is also a record of a hunted red kangaroo clearing a stack of timber 10 ft high.

Longest jump During the course of a chase in New South Wales, Australia in January 1951, a female red kangaroo made a series of bounds that included one of 42 ft. There is also an unconfirmed report of an eastern gray kangaroo jumping nearly 44 ft 8½ in on level ground.

TUSKS

Longest The longest recorded elephant tusks (excluding prehistoric examples) are a pair from Zaïre preserved in the National Collection of Heads and Horns kept by the New York Zoological Society (Bronx Zoo), New York City. The right tusk measures 11 ft 5½ in along the outside curve and the left tusk measures 11 ft. Their combined weight is 293 lb. A single tusk of 11 ft 6 in has been reported.

Heaviest A pair of tusks in the British Museum (Natural History), London collected from an aged bull shot at the foot of Mt Kilimanjaro, Kenya in 1897 originally weighed 240 lb (length 10 ft 2½ in) and 225 lb (length 10 ft 5½ in) respectively, giving a total weight of 465 lb, but their combined weight today is 440½ lb. A

■ **Rarest antelope**
Saved from the brink of extinction by a captive breeding program at San Diego Zoo, CA and strict protective measures in the wild, the Arabian oryx (Oryx leucoryx) has been successfully reintroduced into the deserts of Oman and Jordan, where its population has now reached at least 150.

(Photo: Bruce Coleman)

MAMMALS

Longest trail

On 8 Feb 1988 Rev. Donald Ewen McEwen, owner-musher of Nekanesu Kennels, Eldorado, Ontario, Canada drove a 76-dog sled for 2 miles single-handedly on the ice and around the shore of Lingham Lake. The team, consisting of 25 Siberian huskies and 51 Alaskan huskies, was assembled for the filming of a British TV commercial.

single elephant tusk collected in Benin, Africa and exhibited at the Paris Exposition, France in 1900 weighed 258 lb.

HORNS

Longest The longest horns grown by any living animal are those of the water buffalo (*Bubalus arnee = B. bubalis*) of India. One huge bull shot in 1955 had horns measuring 13 ft 11 in from tip to tip along the outside curve across the forehead. The longest single horn on record measured 81¼ in along the outside curve and was found on a specimen of domestic ankole cattle (*Bos taurus*) near Lake Ngami, Botswana.

The largest spread recorded for a Texas longhorn steer is 10 ft 6 in. The horns are currently on exhibition at the Heritage Museum, Big Springs, TX.

HORSES AND PONIES

The world's equine population is estimated to be 75 million. For record horse prices see Agriculture, Chapter 8.

Earliest domestication The first domestication of the horse reportedly occurred in what is now the Ukraine, USSR *c.* 6,500 years ago when paleolithic hunters tamed some horses for their flesh and milk.

Largest A 19.2-hand (6½ ft) purebred red roan Belgian (Brabant) stallion named Brooklyn Supreme (1928–48) owned by C. G. Good of Ogden, IA weighed 3,200 lb at its heaviest in 1938 and had a chest girth of 102 in. Each of his 7½-lb shoes measured 14 in across and required 30 in of iron (compare with 22 in for Wandle Goliath—see below).

In April 1973 a weight of 3,218 lb was reported for an 18.2-hand (6 ft 2 in) Belgian (Brabant) mare named Wilma du Bos (foaled 15 Jul 1966) shortly before her journey from Antwerp to her new owner, Virgie Arden of Reno, NV. However, she was heavily in foal at the time (maximum girth 12 ft.) On arrival in New York she weighed 3,086 lb, but returned to her normal weight of 2,400–2,500 lb after foaling.

Tallest The tallest documented horse was the shire gelding Sampson (later renamed Mammoth), bred by Thomas Cleaver of Toddington Mills, Bedfordshire, Great Britain. This horse (foaled 1846) measured 21.2½ hands (7 ft 2½ in) in 1850 and was later said to have weighed 3,360 lb.

Boringdon Black King (foaled 1984), a shire gelding born and bred at the National Shire Horse Center in Plymouth, Great Britain, stands 19.2 hands (6½ ft), making him the world's tallest living horse.

The tallest recorded non-draft horse was a Canadian thoroughbred gelding named Tritonis, owned by Christopher Ewing of Southfield, MI. This show jumper, which died in September 1990 at the age of 7, stood 19.2 hands (6½ ft) and weighed 2,100 lb.

Smallest The Falabela of Argentina was developed over a period of 70 years by inbreeding and crossing a small group of undersized horses originally discovered in the southern part of the country. Most adult specimens stand less than 30 in and average 80–100 lb in weight. The smallest mature horse bred by Julio Falabela of Recco de Roca before he died in 1981 was a mare that stood 15 in and weighed 26 ¼ lb.

The stallion Little Pumpkin (foaled 15 Apr 1973), owned by J.C. Williams Jr. of Della Terra Mini Horse Farm, Inman, SC, stood 14 in and weighed 20 lb on 30 Nov 1975.

Oldest The greatest age reliably recorded for a horse is 62 years in the case of Old Billy (foaled 1760), believed to be a cross between a Cleveland and eastern blood, bred by Edward Robinson of Wild Grave Farm, Woolston, Great Britain. In 1762 or 1763 the horse was sold to the Mersey and Irwell Navigation Company and remained with them in a working capacity (i.e., marshaling and towing barges) until 1819 when he was retired to a farm at Latchford, Great Britain, where he died on 27 Nov 1822. The skull of this horse is preserved in the Manchester Museum, Great Britain, and his stuffed head (fitted with false teeth) is now on display in the Bedford Museum, Great Britain.

The greatest reliable age recorded for a pony is 54 years for a stallion owned by a farmer in central France (foaled 1919). The greatest age recorded for a thoroughbred racehorse is 42 years, in the case of the chestnut gelding Tango Duke (foaled 1935), owned by Mrs Carmen J. Koper of Barongarook, Victoria, Australia. The horse died on 25 Jan 1978.

Strongest The greatest load ever hauled by a pair of draft horses reportedly weighed 144 tons, which two shires with a combined weight of 3,500 lb pulled on a sled litter for a distance of 1,320 ft along a frozen road at the Nester Estate near Ewen, MI on 26 Feb 1893, but this tonnage was exaggerated. The load, which comprised 50 logs of white pine measuring 36,055 board feet, actually weighed about 47 tons.

On 23 Apr 1924 a shire gelding named Vulcan, owned by the Liverpool Corporation, registered a pull equal to a starting load of 32.5 tons on a dynamometer at the British Empire Exhibition at Wembley, Great Britain, and a pair of shires *easily* pulled a starting load of 56 tons, the maximum registered on the dynamometer.

Largest mules Apollo (foaled 1977) and Anak (foaled 1976), owned by Herbert L. Mueller of Chicago, IL, are the largest mules on record. Apollo measures 19.1 hands (6 ft 5 in) and weighs 2,200 lb, with Anak 18.3 hands (6 ft 3 in) and 2,100 lb, giving a combined weight of 4,300 lb. Both are the hybrid offspring of Belgian mares and mammoth jacks.

DOGS

The canine population of the United States for 1990 is estimated by the Pet Food Institute at 54.5 million dogs in 35.0 million households, or 37.3 percent of the households in the United States.

Heaviest The heaviest breeds of domestic dogs (*Canis familiaris*) are the Old English mastiff and the St Bernard, with adult males of both species regularly weighing 170–200 lb. The heaviest (and longest) dog ever recorded is Aicama Zorba of La-Susa (whelped 26 Sep 1981), an Old English mastiff owned by Chris Eraclides of London, Great Britain. Zorba stands 37 in at the shoulder and weighed 343 lb in November 1989. Other statistics include a chest girth of 58¾ in, a length of 8 ft 3½ in and a neck measurement of 37½ in.

The heaviest St Bernard on record is Benedictine Jr. Schwarzwald Hof (whelped 1982), owned by breeders Thomas and Anne Irwin of Grand Rapids, MI. His last recorded weight was 310 lb, with a shoulder height of 39 in.

Tallest The Great Dane and the Irish wolfhound can exceed 39 in at the shoulder. In the case of the Great Dane the extreme recorded example was Shamgret Danzas (whelped 1975), owned by Mr and Mrs Comley of Milton Keynes, Great Britain. He stood 41½ in, or 42 in when his hackles were raised, and weighed up to 238 lb. He died on 16 Oct 1984.

The Irish wolfhound Broadbridge Michael (1920–29), owned by Mary Beynon of Sutton-at-Hone, Great Britain, stood 39½ in at the age of two.

Smallest *Miniature* versions of the Yorkshire terrier, the chihuahua and the toy poodle have been known to weigh less than 16 oz as adults.

The smallest mature dog on record was a matchbox-sized Yorkshire terrier owned by Arthur Marples of Blackburn, Great Britain, a former editor of *Our Dogs*. This tiny atom, which died in 1945 at the age of nearly two years, stood 2½ in at the shoulder and measured 3¾ in from the tip of its nose to the root of its tail. Its weight was an incredible 4 oz.

The smallest living adult dog is a miniature chihuahua named Peanuts (whelped 23 Sep 1986), owned by Grace Parker of Wilson's Mills, NC. She measures 9.84 in from head to tail, 5.5 in at the shoulder and weighed 18 oz on 25 Oct 1988.

Oldest Most dogs live between 8 and 15 years, and authentic records of dogs living over 20 years are rare. They are generally the smaller breeds. The greatest reliable age recorded for a dog is 29 years 5 months for an Australian cattle-dog named Bluey, owned by Les Hall of Rochester, Victoria, Australia. The dog was obtained as a puppy in 1910 and worked among cattle and sheep for nearly 20 years. He was put to sleep on 14 Nov 1939.

Rarest At the last count (18 Mar 1988), there were only 70 living examples of the American hairless terrier, 68 of them owned by Willie and Edwin Scott of Trout, LA.

Largest litter Lena, an American foxhound bitch owned by Cdr W. N. Ely of Ambler, PA produced a litter of 23 on 19 Jun 1944. All the puppies survived.

On 6–7 Feb 1975 Careless Ann, a St Bernard owned by Robert and Alice Rodden of Lebanon, MO, also produced a litter of 23, 14 of which survived. The same number (16 survived) was produced by Shalimar Bootsie, a Great Dane owned by Marjorie Harris of Little Hall, Essex, Great Britain in June 1987.

Most prolific The greatest sire ever was the champion greyhound Low Pressure, nicknamed Timmy (whelped Sep 1957), owned by Bruna Amhurst of London, Great Britain. From Dec 1961 until his death on 27 Nov 1969 he fathered 2,414 registered puppies, with at least 600 others unregistered.

Most valuable In 1907 Mrs Clarice Ashton Cross of Ascot, Great Britain turned down an offer of £32,000 (equivalent to $1,380,000 in 1985!) from the American financier and industrialist J. Pierpont Morgan for her famous pekingese Ch. Ch'érh of Alderbourne (1904–14). Mr Morgan then came back with an "open" check, but again she turned him down. The largest legacy devoted to a dog was by Miss Ella Wendel of New York, who bequeathed her standard poodle Toby $75 million in 1931.

Highest jump The canine "high jump" record for a leap and a scramble over a smooth wooden wall (without ribs or other aids) is held by a German shepherd dog named Volse, who scaled 11 ft 9 in at a demonstration in Avignon, France in November 1989. The dog is owned by Phillipe Clement of Aix-en-Provence, France.

Duke, a three-year-old German shepherd dog, handled by Cpl Graham Urry of the Royal Air Force base at Newton, Great Britain, scaled a ribbed wall with regulation shallow slats to a height of 11 ft 9 in on the British Broadcasting Corporation *Record Breakers* TV program on 11 Nov 1986.

Longest jump A greyhound named Bang jumped 30 ft while chasing a hare at Brecon Lodge, Gloucestershire, Great Britain in 1849. He cleared a 4-ft-6-in gate and landed on a hard road, but despite a damaged pastern bone he still managed to kill the hare.

Tracking In 1925 a Doberman pinscher named Sauer, trained by Detective-Sergeant Herbert Kruger, tracked a stock thief 100 miles across the Great Karroo, South Africa by scent alone.

In 1923 a collie named Bobbie, lost by his owners while they were on vacation in Wolcott, IN, turned up at the family home in Silverton, OR six months later, after covering a distance of some 2,000 miles. The dog, later identified by families who had looked after him along the route, had apparently traveled back through Illinois, Indiana, Nevada and Colorado before crossing the Rocky Mountains in the depths of winter.

Top show dogs The greatest number of Challenge Certificates won by a dog is the 78 compiled by the famous chow chow Ch. U'Kwong King Solomon

(whelped 21 Jun 1968). Owned and bred by Mrs Joan Egerton of Bramhall, Great Britain, Solly won his first CC at the Cheshire Agricultural Society Championship Show on 4 Jun 1969, and his 78th CC was awarded at the City of Birmingham Championship Show on 4 Sep 1976. He died on 3 Apr 1978.

The greatest number of Best-in-Show awards won by any dog in all-breed shows is 203, compiled by the Scottish terrier bitch Ch. Braeburn's Close Encounter (whelped 22 Oct 1978) by 10 Mar 1985. She is owned by Sonnie Novick of Plantation Acres, FL.

Ch. Clayfield's Mon Ami, a German shepherd bitch whelped in 1973, won a unique ten dog show championships on four continents from 1975 to 1987. She is owned by Neal, Sharon, Buffy and Holly Leas of West Des Moines, IA.

Largest show The centennial of the annual Crufts show, held at the National Exhibition Center, Birmingham, Great Britain on 9–12 Jan 1991, attracted a record 22,993 entries.

TOP FIVE BREEDS
(1990)

Breed	Registrations
Cocker spaniels	105,642
Labrador retrievers	95,768
Poodles	71,757
Golden retrievers	64,848
Rottweiler	60,471
Per American Kennel Club	

Top trainer Will Markham of the Corley Dog Training Center in Coventry, Great Britain trained 140 dogs in five basic obedience commands in 6 hours 55 mins on 3 Dec 1989.

United States The fastest trainer is Armand Rabuttinio of Aston, PA. His highest total for a single day (9 A.M.–6 P.M.) is 132 dogs at a training marathon held at Upland, PA on 12 Jun 1982.

Drug sniffing The greatest sniffer-dogs on record are a pair of malinoises called Rocky and Barco. These Belgian sheepdogs (whelped 1984) are members of an American stop-and-search team that patrols the Rio Grande Valley ("Cocaine Alley") along the southern Texas border. In 1988 alone they were involved in 969 seizures of drugs worth $182 million, and they are so proficient at their job that Mexican drug smugglers have put a $30,000 price on their heads. Rocky and Barco were recently awarded honorary titles of sergeant major and always wear their stripes when on duty.

The only sniffer-dog with a 100 percent arrest record was a German shepherd of the US Army called General. From April 1974 to March 1976 this canine detective and his handler, SP4 Michael R. Harris of the 591st Military Police Company in Fort Bliss, TX, carried out 220 searches for narcotics, arrested 220 people for possession and uncovered 330 caches of drugs.

The German shepherd Blue of the Los

Angeles Police Department was reported in January 1986 to have assisted in apprehending 253 suspected felons.

CATS

The feline population of the United States for 1990 was estimated by the Pet Food Institute to be 63.2 million. Of the 93.8 million households in the United States, 29.1 million have at least one cat as a pet.

Largest The largest of the 330 breeds of cat is the ragdoll, with males weighing 15–20 lb. In the majority of domestic cats (*Felis catus*) the average weight of the adult male (tom) is 8.6 lb, compared with 7.2 lb for female or queen. Neuters and spays are generally heavier.

The heaviest domestic cat on record was a neutered male tabby named Himmy, owned by Thomas Vyse of Redlynch, Queensland, Australia. At the time of his death (from respiratory failure) on 12 Mar 1986 at the age of 10 years 4 months he weighed 46 lb 15¼ oz (neck 15 in, waist 33 in, length 38 in).

In February 1988 an unconfirmed weight of 48 lb was reported for a cat named Edward Bear, owned by Jackie Fleming of Sydney, New South Wales, Australia.

Smallest The smallest breed of domestic cat is the Singapura or drain cat of Singapore. Adult males average 6 lb in weight and adult females 4 lb.

A male Siamese cross named Ebony-Eb-Honey Cat, owned by Angelina Johnston of Boise, ID, weighed only 1 lb 12 oz in February 1984 at the age of 23 months.

Oldest Cats generally live longer than dogs. The average life expectancy of intact (unaltered) fed males raised under household conditions and receiving good medical attention is 13–15 years (15–17 years for intact females), but neutered males and females live on the average one to two years longer.

The oldest cat ever recorded was probably the tabby Puss, owned by Mrs T. Holway of Clayhidon, Great Britain, who celebrated his 36th birthday on 28 Nov 1939 and died the next day.

A more recent and better-documented case was that of the female tabby Ma, owned by Alice St George Moore of Drewsteignton, Great Britain. This cat was put to sleep on 5 Nov 1957 at the age of 34.

Oldest twins The oldest twin cats on record were Beau and Bubbles (b. 17 Oct 1963), owned by Diane Phelps of Dearborn, MI. Bubbles died on 29 Apr 1985 at the age of 21 years 6 months and Beau was put to sleep on 28 Dec 1985 at the age of 22 years 2 months. They were longhair and part Persian.

Largest litter A litter of 19 kittens (four stillborn) was delivered by cesarean section from Tarawood Antigone, a four-year-old brown Burmese, on 7 Aug 1970. Her owner, Valerie Gane of Church Westcote, Great Britain, said it was the result of a mismating with a half-Siamese. Of the 15 survivors, 14 were males and one female.

The largest live litter (all of which survived) was one of 14 born in December 1974 to a Persian cat named Bluebell,

LARGEST PET LITTERS

Animal/Breed	No.	Owner	Date	
CAT *Burmese/Siamese*	19[1]	Mrs Valerie Gane, Church Westcote, Great Britain	August	1970
DOG *American foxhound*	23	Cdr W. N. Ely, Ambler, PA	June	1944
DOG *St. Bernard*	23[2]	R. and A. Rodden, Lebanon, MO	February	1975
DOG *Great Dane*	23[3]	Mrs Marjorie Harris, Little Hall, Essex, Great Britain	June	1987
RABBIT *New Zealand white*	24	Joseph Filek, Sydney, Cape Breton, Nova Scotia, Canada		1978
GUINEA PIG (CAVY)	12	Laboratory specimen		1972
HAMSTER *Golden*	26[4]	L. and S. Miller, Baton Rouge, LA	February	1974
MOUSE *House*	34[5]	Marion Ogilvie, Blackpool, Great Britain	February	1982
GERBIL *Mongolian*	14[6]	Sharon Kirkman, Bulwell, Nottingham, Great Britain	May	1983
DOMESTIC FERRET	15	John Cliff, Denstone, Uttoxeter, Great Britain		1981

[1] 4 stillborn [2] 14 survived [3] 16 survived [4] 18 killed by mother [5] 33 survived [6] Litter of 15 recorded 1960s by George Meares, geneticist-owner of gerbil-breeding farm, St. Petersburg, FL. Used special food formula.

Most talkative bird

A number of birds are renowned for their talking ability (i.e., the reproduction of words) but the African gray parrot (*Psittacus erythacus*) excels in this ability.

owned by Elenore Dawson of Wellington, Cape Province, South Africa.

Most prolific A tabby named Dusty (b. 1935) of Bonham, TX produced 420 kittens during her breeding life. She gave birth to her last litter (a single kitten) on 12 Jun 1952.

In May 1987 Kitty, owned by George Johnstone of Croxton, Great Britain, produced two kittens at the age of 30 years, making her the oldest feline mother on record. She died in June 1989, just short of her 32nd birthday, having given birth to a known total of 218 kittens.

Most valuable In 1988 Carl Mayes, a breeder in Atlanta, GA, turned down an offer of $10,000 for his male Singapura Bull, the best-known example of its breed in the United States.

When Mrs Grace Alma Patterson of Joplin, MO died in January 1978, she left her entire estate, worth $250,000, to her 18-lb white alley cat Charlie Chan. When the cat dies, the estate, which includes a three-bedroom house, a 7-acre pet cemetery and a collection of valuable antiques, will be auctioned off and the proceeds donated to humane societies.

RABBITS AND HARES

Largest The largest breed of domestic rabbit (*Oryctolagus cuniculus*) is the Flemish giant. Adults weigh 15.4–18.7 lb (average toe-to-toe length when fully stretched is 36 in), but weights of up to 25 lb have been reliably reported for this breed.

TOP FIVE BREEDS
(1990)

Breed	Registrations
Persian (Traditional)	23,700
Persian (Pointed pattern)	23,123
Persian (Colorpoint pattern)	13,838
Siamese	3,860
Maine Coon cat	2,727

Per Cat Fanciers' Association, Inc.

In April 1980 a five-month-old French lop doe weighing 26.45 lb was exhibited at the Reus Fair in northeast Spain.

The heaviest recorded wild rabbit (av. weight 3½ lb) was one of 8 lb 4 oz, killed by Norman Wilkie of Markinch, Great Britain while ferreting on 20 Nov 1982.

Smallest The Netherland dwarf and the Polish both have a weight range of 2–2½ lb when fully grown. In 1975 Jacques Bouloc of Coulommière, France announced a new cross of the above breeds that weighed 14 oz.

Most prolific The most prolific domestic breeds are the New Zealand white and the Californian. Does produce 5–6 litters a year, each containing 8–12 kittens during their breeding life (compare with five litters and 3–7 young for the wild rabbit).

Longest ears The longest ears are found in the Lop family (four strains), and in particular the English Lop. The ears of a typical example measure about

CAGED PET LONGEVITY

Animal/Species	Name (Owner), etc.	Years	Months
RABBIT	*Flopsy* caught 6 Aug 1964 d. 29 Jun 1983 (L.B. Walker) Longford, Tasmania, Australia	18	10¾
GUINEA PIG	*Snowball* d. 14 Feb 1979 (M. A. Wall) Bingham, Great Britain	14	10½
GERBIL *Mongolian*	*Sahara* May 1973–4 Oct 1981 (Aaron Milstone) Lathrup Village, MI	8	4½
MOUSE *House*	*Fritzy* 11 Sep 1977–24 Apr 1985 (Bridget Beard) West House School, Birmingham, Great Britain	7	7
RAT *Common*	*Rodney* b. Jan 1983 (Rodney Mitchell) Tulsa, OK	7	1

24 in from tip to tip (taken across the skull), and 5.51 in in width. In 1901 a specimen was exhibited in England that had 30.5-in ears; it is not known, however, if this was a natural attainment or if weights had been used to stretch the ears and left the veins inside badly varicosed.

Largest hare In Nov 1956 a Brown hare weighing 15 lb 1 oz was shot near Welford, Great Britain. The average adult weight is 8 lb.

Birds Aves

Largest ratite The largest living bird is the North African ostrich (*Struthio c. camelus*), which is found in reduced numbers south of the Atlas Mountains from Upper Senegal and Niger across to the Sudan and central Ethiopia. Male examples (adult hens are smaller) of this flightless (ratite) subspecies have been recorded up to 9 ft in height and 345 lb in weight. The heaviest subspecies is *S. c. australis*, which can weigh 330 lb, although there is an unsubstantiated record of 353 lb.

Largest carinate The world's heaviest flying birds are the Kori bustard or paauw (*Ardeotis kori*) of northeast and southern Africa and the great bustard (*Otis tarda*) of Europe and Asia. Weights of 42 lb have been reported for the former, and there is an unconfirmed record of 46.3 lb for a male great bustard shot in Manchuria which was too heavy to fly. The heaviest reliably recorded great bustard weighed 39.7 lb.

The mute swan (*Cygnus olor*), which is resident in Britain, can reach 40 lb on very rare occasions, and there is a record from Poland of a male weighing 49.6 lb that had temporarily lost the power of flight.

Bird of prey The heaviest bird of prey is the Andean condor (*Vultur gryphus*), adult males averaging 20–25 lb. A weight of 31 lb has been claimed for an outsized male California condor (*Gymnogyps californianus*) now preserved in the California Academy of Sciences at Los Angeles. This species is appreciably smaller than the Andean condor and rarely exceeds 23 lb.

Largest wingspan The wandering albatross (*Diomedea exulans*) of the southern oceans has the largest wingspan of any living bird, adult males averaging 10 ft 4 in with wings at full stretch. The largest recorded specimen was a very old male with a wingspan of 11 ft 11 in, caught by members of the Antarctic research ship USGS *Eltanin* in the Tasman Sea on 18 Sep 1965. Unconfirmed measurements up to 13 ft 10 in have been claimed for this species.

The only other bird reliably credited with a wingspan exceeding 11 ft is the vulturelike marabou stork (*Leptoptilus crumeniferus*) of tropical Africa. In 1934 an extreme measurement of 13 ft 4 in was

reported for a male shot in central Africa, but this can be discredited.

Smallest The smallest bird in the world is the bee hummingbird (*Mellisuga helenae*) of Cuba and the Isle of Pines. Adult males (females are slightly larger) measure 2.24 in in total length, half of which is taken up by the bill and tail. It weighs 0.056 oz; that means it is lighter than a privet hawkmoth (*Sphinx ligustri*: 0.084 oz). (See Smallest nest.)

The smallest bird of prey is the 1.23-oz white-fronted falconet (*Microhierax latifrons*) of northwestern Borneo, which is sparrow-sized.

The smallest seabird is the least storm petrel (*Halocyptena microsoma*), which breeds on many of the small islands in the Gulf of California, northwestern Mexico. Adult specimens average 5½ in in total length and weigh *c.* 1 oz.

The world's smallest species of duck is the Indian cotton teal, or Indian pygmy goose (*Nettapus coromandelianus*), found in freshwater habitats of tropical Asia and northeastern Australia. The adult bird is 12–14 in long and the drake weighs on average 13.4 oz. In September 1989 the first-ever captive breeding of this duck was achieved at the Pensthorpe Waterfowl Trust in Fakenham, Great Britain when two eggs, removed to the safety of an incubator after being laid in the same tree hole as the eggs of the related African pygmy goose, were successfully hatched.

United States The smallest American bird is the calliope hummingbird (*Stellula calliope*). Adult specimens measure 2¾–3½ in from bill to tail with a wingspan of 4½ in and an approximate weight of ¹⁄₁₀ oz. The calliope is found in the western United States.

Most abundant *Wild bird* The red-billed quelea (*Quelea quelea*), a seed-eating weaver of the drier parts of Africa south of the Sahara, has an estimated adult breeding population of 1.5 billion, and at least 1 billion of these "feathered locusts" are slaughtered annually without having any impact on the population. One huge roost in the Sudan contained 32 million birds.

Sea bird The most abundant is probably the very small Wilson's storm petrel (*Oceanites oceanicus*), which breeds on the Antarctic continent and adjacent sub-Antarctic islands. No population estimates have been published, but the numbers must run into hundreds of millions.

Domesticated bird The most abundant species is the chicken, the tame version of the wild red jungle fowl (*Gallus gallus*) of southeast Asia. According to the FAO (Food and Agriculture Organization of the United Nations), the world's chicken population stood at 8,295,760,000 in 1985; that means there are 1.6 chickens for every member of the human race.

United States The red-winged blackbird (*Agelaius phoeniceus*) had a population of 25.6 million birds as of January 1983. The USFish and Wildlife Service estimates the current total is at least 30 million. The blackbird is found throughout the country, except for desert and mountainous regions.

Rarest The number of threatened bird species worldwide has risen in the past 10 years from 290 to 1,029 as a result of human activity, according to a survey published in October 1988. Because of the practical difficulties in assessing bird populations in the wild, it is virtually impossible to establish the identity of the world's rarest living bird.

The strongest contender until very recently was the dusky seaside sparrow (*Ammospiza nigrescens*), formerly of Titusville Marshes, FL, but the last known example (a male) died at Discovery Island, Disney World, Orlando, FL on 16 May 1987. Some of its tissue has been frozen in the hope that future technology might allow a pure strain of dusky seaside sparrow to be resurrected through genetic cloning.

The Guam flycatcher (*Myiagra freycineti*) and the rufous fantail (*Rhipidura rufifrons*), also of Guam, were last seen in 1984 and may now also be extinct.

The Guam rail (*Rallus owstons*) has only been sighted three times since 1985.

The oa (*Moho braccatus*) of Kauai in the Hawaiian Islands, reportedly extinct, was rediscovered in 1960 in the mountain rain forests of the Alahari swamp. Its nest was found in 1979 and it was seen again in 1981. It is now protected and there may be one or two pairs left.

The crested shellduck (*Tadorna cristata*) is known from only three specimens. The last sighting was in 1971, but it may still survive in the remoter Japanese coastal regions or in adjacent waters.

The imperial woodpecker (*Campephilus imperiali*) of Mexico has not been sighted since 1958 on the Sonora–Chihuahua border, but there were unconfirmed reports from southwest Chihuahua in 1977.

The Socorro dove (*Zenaida graysoni*) of Socorro Island off the west coast of Mexico is now extinct in the wild and survives only in captivity.

The Itombwe owl is known only from the type specimen collected in 1951 while sleeping in long grass high in the Itombwe Mountains, eastern Zaïre, and the Kibale groundthrush (*Turdus kibalensis*) of western Uganda is known only from two males collected in 1966.

The sea-cliff swallow (*Hirunda perdita*) is known only from a dead specimen found

■ **Slowest-flying bird**
Seen here enjoying a well-earned rest, the American woodcock (Scolopax minor) has been timed at 5 mph without sinking during courtship flights. (Photo: Bruce Coleman)

on an islet off Port Sudan in 1984 and has not been recorded since.

In 1979 the Chatham Island black robin (*Petroica traversi*) was another bird on the verge of extinction, with only five surviving. By a pioneering method of cross-breeding the chicks of this wild songbird with local tom tits, however, members of the New Zealand Wildlife Service managed to increase the population to 38 by 1984. There are now over 100 of these robins spread throughout several islands. Another remarkable fact is that every living example of this species is descended from the female known as Old Blue. She lived for *c.* 14 years (over twice the normal lifespan) and remained fertile right to the end. The death of this amazing little bird was officially announced in the New Zealand Parliament and her body has been preserved in a museum.

Spix's macaw (*Cyanopsitta spixii*) of Brazil, the world's most endangered parrot, was reduced to a single specimen in the wild in July 1990. There are only 15 left in captivity around the world.

The Aldabra brush warbler (*Nesillas aldabrabus*) was not discovered until 1967, and five individuals (three males and two females) were ringed between July 1974 and February 1977. One of the males was re-sighted in 1978 and again in September 1983, but this was the last confirmed record. This species is restricted to a coastal strip 1.24 miles long and 162 ft wide on the northern tip of Aldabra Atoll in the Indian Ocean.

United States Under the California Condor Recovery Program administered by the US Fish and Wildlife Service, all condors were captured and placed in captivity. Seven birds were captured between 25 Jun 1985 and 19 Apr 1987, with the last wild California condor (*Gymnogyps californianus*) captured in Kern Co., CA, to join 26 others held for captive breeding in the San Diego Wildlife Park and the Los Angeles Zoo. On 29 Apr 1988 the first California condor ever born in captivity was successfully hatched at the San Diego Wildlife Park and the chick was fed successfully for six months with condor hand puppets. As of April 1991 there were 45 specimens in captivity. It is

hoped that one to three birds can be released back into the wild during the 1991–92 winter.

The ivory-billed woodpecker and the Bachman's warbler have not been seen in at least three decades but are not yet considered extinct.

The Eskimo curlew has not had a verifiable sighting in several decades, but there have been unverified reports at regular intervals in recent years.

After more than three decades, federal officials may remove the bald eagle from the endangered species list, as the official symbol of the nation is no longer in immediate danger of extinction. In 1974 there were fewer than 791 nesting pairs in the lower 48 states; as of March 1990 there were more than 2,660 pairs. A 1989 survey by the National Wildlife Federation lists the bald eagle population, including immature birds, at 11,610. The US government has spent about $25 million helping the bald eagle recover. The five states which would move the bald eagle to the threatened list, one step down from endangered, are Washington, Oregon, Minnesota, Wisconsin, and Michigan.

Fastest-flying The fastest creature on the wing is the peregrine falcon (*Falco peregrinus*) when swooping from great heights during territorial displays. In one series of German experiments, a velocity of 168 mph was recorded at a 30° angle of descent, rising to a maximum of 217 mph at an angle of 45°.

The white-throated spinetail swift (*Hirundapus caudacutus*) of Asia and the alpine swift (*Apus melba*) are also extremely fast during courtship display flights, with the former timed at speeds up to 105.6 mph in tests carried out in the USSR.

The fastest fliers in level flight are found among the ducks and geese (Anatidae); some powerful species such as the red-breasted merganser (*Mergus serrator*), the eider (*Somateria mollissima*), the canvasback (*Aythya valisineria*) and the spur-winged goose (*Plectropterus gambiensis*) can probably exceed an airspeed of 65 mph.

Air speeds up to 70 mph have been claimed for the golden plover (*Pluvialis apricaria*) when flushed, but it is very doubtful whether this rapid-flying bird can exceed 50–55 mph—even in an emergency.

United States America's fastest bird is the white-throated swift (*Aeronautes saxatilis*), which has been estimated to fly at speeds of 200 mph. The peregrine falcon (*Falco peregrinus*) has been credited with a speed of 175 mph while in a dive. The dunlin (*Calidris alpina*) has been clocked from a plane at 110 mph.

Slowest-flying Probably at least 50 percent of the world's flying birds cannot exceed an air speed of 40 mph in level flight. The slowest-flying bird is the American woodcock (*Scolopax minor*), which, during courtship flights, has been timed at 5 mph without stalling.

Fastest-running It is claimed that the wild turkey (*Meleagris gallopavo*) can reach speeds of 30 mph.

Fastest wing-beat The wing-beat of the horned sungem (*Heliactin cornuta*) of tropical South America is 90 beats/sec.

Longest-lived The greatest irrefutable age reported for any bird is over 80 years for a male sulfur-crested cockatoo (*Cacatua galerita*) named Cocky, who died at London Zoo, Great Britain in 1982. He was presented to the zoo in 1925, and had been with his previous owner since 1902 when he was already fully mature.

In 1987 an unconfirmed age of *c.* 82 years was reported for a male Siberian white crane (*Crus leucogeranus*) named Wolfe at the International Crane Foundation, Baraboo, WI. The bird was said to have hatched in a zoo in Switzerland *c.* 1905. He died in late 1988 after breaking his bill while repelling a visitor near his pen.

In 1964 the death was reported of a male Andean condor called Kuzya at Moscow Zoo, USSR. As this bird was already fully grown when it was received in 1892, it must have been at least 77.

The oldest ringed seabird on record is a female royal albatross (*Diomedea epomophora*) named Grandma ("Blue White"), who laid an egg at Taiaroa Head, near Dunedin, South Island, New Zealand in November 1988, when she was 60 years old. She was banded for the first time in 1937 when she was a breeding adult, and such birds do not start breeding until they are 9 years old. Since then she has raised 10 chicks of her own and fostered 3 others. Her mate, Green White Green, is 47.

Longest flights The greatest distance covered by a ringed bird is 14,000 miles by an arctic tern (*Sterna paradisea*), which was banded as a nestling on 5 Jul 1955 in the Kandalaksha Sanctuary on the White Sea coast, USSR, and was captured alive by a fisherman 8 miles south of Fremantle, Western Australia on 16 May 1956. The bird had flown south via the Atlantic Ocean and then circled Africa before crossing the Indian Ocean. It did not survive to make the return journey. There is also a report of an arctic tern flying from Greenland to Australasia, but further details are lacking.

In 1990 six foraging wandering albatrosses (*Diomedea exulans*) were tracked across the Indian Ocean by satellite via radio transmitters fitted by Pierre Jouventin and Henri Weimerskirch of the National Center for Scientific Research at Beauvoir, France. Results showed that the birds covered anywhere between 2,237 and 9,321 miles in a single feeding trip and that they easily maintained a speed of 35 mph over a distance of more than 498 miles with the males going to sea for up to 33 days while their partners remained ashore to incubate the eggs.

Highest-flying Most migrating birds fly at relatively low altitudes (i.e., below 300 ft) and only a few dozen species fly higher than 3,000 ft.

The highest acceptable altitude recorded for a bird is 37,000 ft for a Ruppell's vulture (*Gyps rueppellii*), which collided with a commercial aircraft over Abidjan, Ivory Coast on 29 Nov 1973. The impact damaged one of the aircraft's engines, causing it to shut down, but the plane landed safely without further incident. Sufficient feather remains of the bird were recovered to allow the US Museum of Natural History to make a positive identification of this high-flier, which is rarely seen above 20,000 ft.

United States The highest verified altitude record for a bird in America is 21,000 ft for a mallard (*Meleagris gallopavo*) that collided with a commericial jet on 9 Jul 1963 over Nevada. The jet crashed, killing all aboard.

Most airborne The most aerial of all birds is the sooty tern (*Sterna fuscata*), which, after leaving the nesting grounds, remains continuously aloft from 3–10 years as a sub-adult before returning to land to breed.

The most aerial land bird is the common swift (*Apus apus*), which remains airborne for 2–3 years, during which time it sleeps, drinks, eats and even mates on the wing.

Fastest swimmer The gentoo penguin (*Pygoscelis papua*) has a maximum burst of speed of *c.* 17 mph.

Deepest dive In 1969 a depth of 870 ft was recorded for a small group of 10 emperor penguins (*Aptenodytes forsteri*) at Cape Crozier, Antarctica by a team of US scientists. One bird remained submerged for 18 minutes.

Vision Birds of prey (Falconiformes) have the keenest eyesight in the avian world, and large species with eyes similar in size to those of humans have visual acuity at least twice that of human vision. It has also been calculated that a large eagle can detect a target object at a distance 3–8 times greater than that achieved by humans. Thus the golden eagle (*Aquila chrysaetos*) can detect an 18-in-long hare at a range of 2 miles in good light and against a contrasting background, and a peregrine falcon (*Falco peregrinus*) can spot a pigeon at a range of over 5 miles.

In experiments carried out on the tawny owl (*Strix aluco*) at the University of Birmingham, Great Britain in 1977, it was revealed that the bird's eye on average was only 2½ times more sensitive than the human eye. It was also discovered that the tawny owl sees perfectly adequately in daylight and that its visual acuity is only slightly inferior to that of humans.

g force American experiments have revealed that the beak of the red-headed woodpecker (*Melanerpes erythrocephalus*) hits the bark of a tree with an impact velocity of 13 mph. This means that when the head snaps back the brain is subject to a deceleration of about 10 *g*.

Longest feathers The longest feathers grown by any bird are those of the phoenix fowl or onagadori (a strain of red jungle fowl *Gallus gallus*), which has been bred in southwestern Japan since the mid-17th century. In 1972 a tail covert measuring 34 ft 9½ in was reported for a rooster owned by Masasha Kubota of Kochi, Shikoku, Japan.

Among flying birds the tail feathers of the male crested pheasant (*Rheinhartia ocellata*) of southeast Asia regularly reach 5 ft 8 in in length and 5 in in width, and the central tail feathers of the Reeves' pheasant (*Syrmaticus reevesi*) of central and northern China have reached 8 ft in exceptional cases.

Most and least feathers In a series of feather counts on various species of bird, a whistling swan (*Cygnus columbianus*) was found to have 25,216 feathers, 20,177 of which were on the head and neck. The ruby-throated hummingbird (*Archilochus colubris*) has only 940.

Largest egg The average ostrich (*Struthio camelus*) egg measures 6–8 in in length, 4–6 in in diameter and weighs 3.63–3.88 lb (around two dozen hens' eggs in volume). The egg requires about 40 min for boiling, and the shell, though only 0.059 in thick, can support the weight of a 279.9 lb man. On 28 Jun 1988 a 2-year-old cross between a northern and a southern ostrich (*Struthio c. camelus* and *Struthio c. australis*) laid an egg weighing a record 5.07 lb at the Kibbutz Ha'on collective farm, Israel.

United States The largest egg laid on the list of American birds is that of the trumpeter swan; it measures 4.3 in in length, 2.8 in in diameter. The average California condor egg measures 4.3 in in length and 2.6 in in diameter and weighs 9.5 oz.

Smallest egg Eggs emitted from the oviduct before maturity, known as "sports," are not considered to be of significance. The smallest egg laid by any bird is that of the vervain hummingbird (*Mellisuga minima*) of Jamaica. Two specimens measuring less than 0.39 in in length weighed 0.0128 oz and 0.0132 oz.

United States The smallest egg laid by a bird on the American list is that of the Costa hummingbird (*Calypte costae*); it measures 0.48 in in length and 0.33 in in diameter with a weight of 0.017 oz.

Longest incubation The longest normal incubation period is that of the wandering albatross (*Diomedea exulans*), with a normal range of 75–82 days.

There is an isolated case of an egg of the mallee fowl (*Leipoa ocellata*) of Australia taking 90 days to hatch, against its normal incubation of 62 days.

Shortest incubation The shortest incubation period is 10 days in the case of the great spotted woodpecker (*Dendrocopus major*) and the black-billed cuckoo (*Coccyzus erythropthalmus*).

The idlest of cock birds include hummingbirds (family Trochilidae), the eider duck (*Somateria mollissima*) and the golden pheasant (*Chrysolophus pictus*), among which the hen bird does 100 percent of the incubation, while the female common kiwi (*Apteryx australis*) leaves this to the male for 75–80 days.

Longest bills The bill of the Australian pelican (*Pelicanus conspicillatus*) is

13.3–18.5 in long. The longest bill in relation to overall body length is that of the sword-billed hummingbird (*Ensifera ensifera*) of the Andes from Venezuela to Bolivia. It measures 4 in in length and is longer than the bird's actual body if the tail is excluded.

Shortest bills The shortest bills in relation to body length are found among the smaller swifts (Apodidae) and in particular that of the glossy swiftlet (*Collocalia esculenta*), which is almost nonexistent.

Bird-watcher The world's leading bird-watcher or "twitcher" is Harvey Gilston (b. 12 Oct 1922) of Lausanne, Switzerland, who had logged 6,891 of the 9,016 known species by April 1991.

The greatest number of species spotted in a 24-hour period is 342, by Kenyans Terry Stevenson, John Fanshawe and Andy Roberts on day two of the Birdwatch Kenya '86 event held on 29–30 November. The 48-hour record is held by Don Turner and David Pearson of Kenya, who spotted 494 species at the same event.

Peter Kaestner of Washington, D.C. was the first person to see at least one species of each of the world's 159 bird families. He saw his final family on 1 Oct 1986.

■ **Smallest nest**
The smallest nests in the avian world are built, not surprisingly, by hummingbirds (family Trochilidae). Sizes range from the equivalent of about half a walnut to the deeper thimble-type residence. Pictured here is the broadbill hummingbird (Cynanthus latirostris) (Photo: Bruce Coleman)

Since then Dr Ira Abramson of Miami, FL, Dr Martin Edwards of Kingston, Ontario, Canada and Harvey Gilston (last family seen in December 1988) have also succeeded in this achievement.

Largest nest A nest measuring 9½ ft wide and 20 ft deep was built by a pair of bald eagles (*Haliaeetus leucocephalus*), and possibly their successors, near St Petersburg, FL. It was examined in 1963 and was estimated to weigh more than 2.2 tons. The golden eagle (*Aquila chrysaetos*) also constructs huge nests, and one 15 ft deep was reported from Scotland in 1954. It had been used for 45 years.

The incubation mounds built by the mallee fowl (*Leipoa ocellata*) of Australia are much larger, measuring up to 15 ft in height and 35 ft across, and it has been calculated that the nest site may involve the mounding of 900 ft³ of material weighing 330 tons.

Smallest nest The smallest nests are built by hummingbirds (*Trochilidae*). That of the vervain hummingbird (*Mellisuga minima*) is about half the size of a walnut, while the deeper one of the bee hummingbird (*M. helenea*) is thimble-sized.

DOMESTICATED BIRDS

Earliest The earliest domesticated bird was the graylag goose (*Anser*) of the Neolithic period (20,000 years ago) of southeastern Europe and Asia Minor.

Oldest The longest-lived domesticated bird (excluding the ostrich, which has been known to live up to 68 years) is the domestic goose (*Anser anser domesticus*), which may live about 25 years. On 16 Dec 1976 a gander named George, owned by Florence Hull of Thornton, Great Britain, died at the age of 49 years 8 months. He was hatched in April 1927.

The oldest budgerigar (*Melopsittacus undulatus*) was a hen bird named Charlie, owned by Miss J. Dinsey of London, Great Britain, that died on 20 Jun 1977 at the age of 29 years 2 months.

Most talkative A female specimen named Prudle, formerly owned by Lyn Logue (d. January 1988) and now in the care of Iris Frost of Seaford, Great Britain, won the Best Talking Parrot-like Bird title at the National Cage and Aviary Bird Show in London, Great Britain each December for 12 consecutive years (1965–76). Prudle, who has a vocabulary of nearly 800 words, was taken from a nest at Jinja, Uganda in 1958. She retired undefeated.

Reptiles Reptilia

(Crocodiles, lizards, turtles, tortoises, snakes)

CROCODILIANS

Largest The largest reptile in the world is the estuarine or saltwater crocodile (*Crocodylus porosus*) of southeast Asia, the Malay Archipelago, Indonesia, northern Australia, Papua New Guinea, Vietnam and the Philippines. Adult males average 14–16 ft in length and weigh about 900–1,150 lb. There are four protected estuarine crocodiles at the Bhitarkanika Wildlife Sanctuary, Orissa State, eastern India that measure more than 19 ft 8 in in length. The largest individual is over 23 ft long.

Captive The largest crocodile ever held in captivity is an estuarine/Siamese hybrid named Yai (b. 10 Jun 1972) at the Samutprakarn Crocodile Farm and Zoo, Thailand. He measures 19 ft 8 in in length and weighs 2,465 lb.

Smallest Osborn's dwarf crocodile (*Osteolaemus osborni*), found in the upper region of the Congo River, West Africa, rarely exceeds 3 ft 11 in in length.

Oldest The greatest age authenticated for a crocodile is 66 years for a female American alligator (*Alligator mississipiensis*) which arrived at Adelaide Zoo, South Australia on 5 Jun 1914 as a two-year-old, and died there on 26 Sep 1978.

Another female of this species named Smiley at the Maritime Museum Aquarium, Gothenburg, Sweden, died on 10 Feb 1987 at the age of 65 years after the pool electrical heating was accidentally turned down.

Rarest The total wild population of the protected Chinese alligator (*Alligator sinensis*) of the lower Yangtze River in the Anhui, Zhejiang and Jiangsu provinces of China is currently estimated at no more than a few hundred.

LIZARDS

Largest The largest of all lizards is the komodo monitor or ora (*Varanus komodoensis*), a dragonlike reptile found on the Indonesian islands of Komodo, Rintja, Padar and Flores. Adult males average 7 ft 5 in in length and weigh about 130 lb. Lengths up to 30 ft have been claimed for this species, but the largest specimen to be accurately measured was a male presented to an American zoologist in 1928 by the Sultan of Bima which was taped at 10 ft 0.8 in. In 1937 this animal was put on display in St Louis Zoological Gardens, MO for a short period. It then measured 10 ft 2 in in length and weighed 365 lb.

The longest lizard in the world is the slender Salvadori monitor (*Varanus salvadori*) of Papua New Guinea, which has been reliably measured up to 15 ft 7 in. Nearly 70 percent of the total length, however, is taken up by the tail.

Smallest *Sphaerodactylus parthenopion*, a tiny gecko indigenous to the island of Virgin Gorda, one of the British Virgin Islands, is believed to be the world's smallest lizard. It is known only from 15 specimens, including some pregnant females found between 10 and 16 Aug 1964. The three largest females measured 0.67 in from snout to vent, with a tail of approximately the same length.

It is possible that another gecko, *Sphaerodactylus elasmorhynchus*, may be even smaller. The only known specimen was an apparently mature female with a snout-to-vent measurement of 0.67 in and a tail of the same length. This specimen was found on 15 Mar 1966 among the roots of a tree in the western part of the Massif de la Hotte in Haiti.

Oldest The greatest age recorded for a lizard is over 54 years for a male slow worm (*Anguis fragilis*) kept in the Zoological Museum in Copenhagen, Denmark from 1892 until 1946.

Fastest The fastest speed measured for any reptile on land is 18 mph for a six-lined race runner (*Cnemidophorus sexlineatus*) near McCormick, SC in 1941.

CHELONIANS

Largest The largest living chelonian is the leatherback turtle (*Dermochelys coriacea*), which is circumglobal in distribution. The average adult measures 6–7 ft from the tip of the beak to the end of the tail (carapace 5–5½ ft), about 7 ft across the front flippers and weighs up to 1,000 lb.

The largest leatherback turtle ever recorded is a male found dead on the beach at Harlech, Great Britain on 23 Sep 1988. It measured 9 ft 5½ in in total length over the carapace (nose to tail), 9 ft across the front flippers and weighed an astonishing 2,120 lb. It is now in the possession of the National Museum of Wales, Great Britain and was put on public display on 16 Feb 1990. Most museums refuse to exhibit large turtles because they can drip oil for up to 50 years.

United States The greatest weight reliably recorded is 1,908 lb recorded for a male captured off Monterey, CA on 29 Aug 1961, which measured 8 ft 4 in.

Tortoise The largest living tortoise is the Aldabra giant tortoise (*Geochelone gigantea*) of the Indian Ocean islands of Aldabra, Mauritius and the Seychelles (introduced 1874). A male tortoise named Esmerelda, a longtime resident on Bird Island in the Seychelles, recorded a weight of 657 lb on 26 Feb 1989.

Smallest The smallest marine turtle in the world is the Atlantic ridley (*Lepidochelys kempii*), which has a shell length of 19.7–27.6 in and does not exceed 80 lb. It is also the rarest and most endangered sea turtle, with the total population in 1989 estimated at no more than 900 adult females and an unknown number of males and sub-adults.

Longest-lived The greatest authentic age recorded for a tortoise is over 152 years for a male Marion's tortoise (*Testudo sumeirii*), brought from the Seychelles to Mauritius in 1766 by the Chevalier de Fresne, who presented it to the Port Louis army garrison. This specimen, which went blind in 1908, was accidentally killed in 1918. The greatest proven age of a continuously observed tortoise is more than 116 years for a Mediterranean spur-thighed tortoise (*Testudo graeca*).

The oldest turtle on record was an alligator snapping turtle (*Macrochelys temminckii*) at the Philadelphia Zoo, PA. When it was accidentally killed on 7 Feb 1949 it was 58 years 9 months 1 day old.

Fastest The fastest speed claimed for any reptile in water is 22 mph by a frightened Pacific leatherback turtle.

Slowest In a "speed" test carried out in the Seychelles a male giant tortoise (*Geochelone gigantea*) could cover only 15 ft in 43.5 sec (0.23 mph) despite the enticement of a female.

Deepest dive In May 1987 it was reported by Dr Scott Eckert that a leatherback turtle (*Dermochelys coriacea*) fitted with a pressure-sensitive recording device had dived to a depth of 3,973 ft off the Virgin Islands in the West Indies.

Rarest The world's rarest chelonian is the protected short-necked swamp tortoise (*Pseudemydura umbrina*), which is confined to Ellen Brook and Twin reserves near Perth, Western Australia. The total wild population is now only 20–25, with another 22 held at Perth Zoo.

SNAKES

Longest The reticulated python (*Python reticulatus*) of southeast Asia, Indonesia and the Philippines regularly exceeds 20 ft 6 in. In 1912 a specimen measuring 32 ft 9½ in was shot near a mining camp on the north coast of Celebes in the Malay Archipelago.

Captive The longest (and heaviest) snake ever held in captivity was a female reticulated python named Colossus who died in Highland Park Zoo, PA on 15 Apr 1963. She measured 28 ft 6 in in length, and weighed 320 lb at her heaviest.

United States Three species, in the southeastern United States, have average measurements of 8 ft 6 in. These include the indigo snake (*Drymarchon corais*), the eastern coachwhip (*Masticophis flagellum*) and the black ratsnake (*Elaphe obsoleta*). The indigo snake has been measured at 8 ft 7 ½ in.

Shortest The shortest snake in the world is the rare thread snake (*Leptotyphlops bilineata*), which is known only from the islands of Martinique, Barbados and St Lucia in the West Indies. In one series of eight specimens the two longest both measured 4.25 in.

Heaviest The anaconda (*Eunectes murinus*) of tropical South America and Trinidad is nearly twice as heavy as a reticulated python (*Python reticulatus*) of the same length. A female shot in Brazil *c.* 1960 was not weighed, but as it measured 27 ft 9 in in length with a girth of 44 in, it must have weighed nearly 500 lb. The average adult length is 18–20 ft.

The heaviest venomous snake is probably the eastern diamondback rattle-

snake (*Crotalus adamanteus*) of the southeastern United States. One specimen, measuring 7 ft 9 in in length, weighed 34 lb. Adult examples average 5–6 ft in length and weigh 12–15 lb.

The West African gaboon viper (*Bitis gabonica*) of the tropical rain forests is probably bulkier than this rattlesnake, but its average length is only 4–5 ft. A female 6 ft long was found to weigh 25 lb and another female measuring 5 ft 8½ in weighed 18 lb with an empty stomach.

In February 1973 a posthumous weight of 28 lb was reported for a 14-ft-5-in-long king cobra (*Ophiophagus hannah*) at the New York Zoological Society

(Bronx Zoo) in New York City. It had been ill for some time.

Oldest The greatest reliable age recorded for a snake is 40 years 3 months 14 days for a male common boa (*Boa constrictor constrictor*) named Popeye, who died at the Philadelphia Zoo, PA on 15 Apr 1977.

Fastest The fastest-moving land snake is probably the slender black mamba (*Dendroaspis polylepis*) of the eastern part of tropical Africa. It is possible that this snake can achieve speeds of 10–12 mph in short bursts over level ground.

Most venomous The sea snake (*Hydrophis belcheri*) has a myotoxic

■ **Largest reptile**
The Estuarine of Saltwater crocodile of southeast Asia can average up to 16 ft in length and weigh up to 1,150 lb. At 17 ft 5 ½ in, Gomek, an attraction at the St Augustine Alligator Farm in Florida, is one of the largest examples in captivity. (Photo: St Augustine Alligator Farm)

venom a hundred times as toxic as that of the Australian taipan (*Oxyuranus scutellatus*). The snake abounds at the Ashmore Reef in the Timor Sea, off the coast of northwest Australia.

The most venomous land snake is the 6-ft-6¾-in-long smooth-scaled snake (*Parademansia microlepidotus*) of the Diamantina River and Cooper's Creek drainage basins in Channel County, Queensland and western New South Wales, Australia, which has a venom nine times as toxic as that of the tiger snake (*Notechis scutatus*) of South Australia and Tasmania. One specimen yielded 0.00385 oz of venom after milking, enough to kill 125,000 mice, but so far no human fatalities have been reported.

More people die of snakebites in Sri Lanka than in any comparable area in the world. An average of 800 people are killed annually on the island by snakes, and more than 95 percent of the fatalities are caused by the common krait (*Bungarus caeruleus*), the Sri Lankan cobra (*Naja n. naja*), and Russell's viper (*Vipera russelli pulchella*).

The saw-scaled or carpet viper (*Echis carinatus*) bites and kills more people in the world than any other species. Its geographical range extends from West Africa to India.

■ **Most venomous snake**
Although all sea snakes are venomous, the Hydrophis belcheri, *found among the coral reefs off northwest Australia, has a myotoxin which is 100 times more powerful than that of the Australian taipan* (Oxyuranus scutellatus), *whose bite can kill a man within minutes.* (Photo: Bruce Coleman)

United States The most venomous snake in the United States is the coral snake (*Micrurus fulvius*). In a standard LD99–100 test, which kills 99–100 percent of all mice injected with the venom, it takes 0.55 grain of venom per 2.2 lbs of mouse weight injected intravenously. In this test, the smaller the dosage, the more toxic the venom. However, the teeth of the coral snake point back into its mouth, and therefore it cannot inject the venom until it has a firm hold on the victim.

Longest venomous The longest venomous snake in the world is the king cobra (*Ophiophagus hannah*), also called the hamadryad, of southeast Asia and the Philippines; it has an average adult length of 12–15 ft. A 18-ft-2-in specimen, captured alive near Fort Dickson in the state of Negri Sembilan, Malaya in April 1937, later grew to 18 ft 9 in in London Zoo, Great Britain. It was destroyed at the outbreak of war in 1939.

Shortest venomous The namaqua dwarf adder (*Bitis schneider*) of Namibia has an average adult length of 7.87 in.

Longest fangs The longest fangs of any snake are those of the highly venomous gaboon viper (*Bitis gabonica*) of tropical Africa. In a specimen of 6 ft length they measured 1.96 in. On 12 Feb 1963 a gaboon viper under severe stress sank its fangs into its own back at the Philadelphia Zoo, PA and died from traumatic injury to a vital organ. It did not, as has been widely reported, succumb to its own venom.

Rarest Following a successful conservation campaign and captive breeding of the keel-scaled boa of Round Island, its place as the world's rarest snake has been taken by the St Lucia racer or couresse (*Liophis ornatus*), which inhabits only Maria Island, off St Lucia, West Indies. Estimates by Dr David Corke of the Polytechnic of East London, Great Britain put its population at under 100 in 1989, with no specimens held in captivity.

United States The only snake in the United States on the endangered species list is the San Francisco garter snake (*Thamnophis sirtalis tetrataenia*).

Amphibians Amphibia

Largest The largest species of amphibian is the Chinese giant salamander (*Andrias davidianus*), which lives in northeastern, central and southern China. The average adult measures 3 ft 9 in in length and weighs 55–66 lb. One specimen collected in Hunan province weighed 143 lb and measured 5 ft 11 in in length.

Smallest The smallest-known amphibian is the tiny Cuban frog (*Sminthillus limbatus*), which is less than ½ in long.

Oldest The greatest authentic age recorded for an amphibian is 55 years for a Japanese giant salamander that died in Amsterdam Zoo in the Netherlands in 1881.

Longest gestation The viviparous alpine black salamander (*Salamandra atra*) has a gestation period of up to 38 months at altitudes above 4,600 ft in the Swiss Alps, but this drops to 24–26 months at lower altitudes.

Rarest Only five specimens of the painted frog (*Discoglossus nigriventer*) of Lake Huleh, Israel have been reported since 1940.

Highest and lowest The greatest altitude at which an amphibian has been found is 26,246 ft for a common toad (*Bufo bufo*) collected in the Himalayas. This species has also been found at a depth of 1,115 ft in a coal mine.

Most poisonous The most active known poison is the batrachotoxin derived from the skin secretions of the golden poison-dart frog (*Phyllobates terribilis*) of western Colombia, which was not discovered until 1973. Its skin secretions are at least 20 times more toxic than those of any other known poison-dart frog (human handlers have to wear thick gloves), and an average adult specimen contains enough poison (0.000067 oz) to kill nearly 1,500 people. This species is preyed upon by the frog-eating snake (*Leimadophis epinephelus*), which is thought to be immune to its poison.

Largest frog The largest-known frog is the rare African giant frog or goliath frog (*Conrana goliath*) of Cameroon and Equatorial Guinea. A specimen captured in April 1989 on the Sanaga River, Cameroon by Andy Koffman of Seattle, WA had a snout-to-vent length of 14.5 in (34.5 in overall with legs extended) and weighed 8 lb 1 oz on 30 Oct 1989.

Smallest frog The smallest frog in the world is *Sminthillus limbatus* of Cuba. (See Smallest amphibian.)

Longest jump (*Competition frog jumps are the aggregate of three consecutive leaps.*)

The greatest distance covered by a frog in a triple jump is 33 ft 5½ in by a South African sharp-nosed frog (*Ptychadena oxyrhynchus*) named Santjie at a frog derby held at Lurula Natal Spa, Paulpietersburg, Natal, South Africa on 21 May 1977.

At the annual Calaveras Jumping Jubilee held at Angels Camp, CA on 18 May 1986 an American bullfrog (*Rana catesbeiana*) called Rosie the Ribeter, owned and trained by Lee Giudicci of Santa Clara, CA, leapt 21 ft 5¾ in. Santjie would have been ineligible for this contest because entrants must measure at least 4 in "stem to stern."

Largest toad The largest-known toad is the marine toad (*Bufo marinus*) of tropical South America and Queensland, Australia. An average adult specimen weighs 1 lb.

The largest toad ever recorded was a

female marine toad (*Bufo marinus*) nicknamed "Totally Awesome" (Toad A), owned by Blank Park Zoo, Des Moines, IA. She was purchased from an animal dealer in Miami, FL on 11 May 1983, when she weighed about 2 lb, and attained a peak 5 lb 1½ oz (snout-to-vent length 9½ in) on 19 Nov 1987. She died on 8 Apr 1988, probably from old age.

Smallest toad The smallest toad in the world is the subspecies *Bufo taitanus beiranus*, originally of Mozambique, the largest specimen of which was 0.95 in long

Fishes Gnathostomata, Agnatha

Largest marine The largest fish in the world is the rare plankton-feeding whale shark (*Rhincodon typus*), which is found in the warmer areas of the Atlantic, Pacific, and Indian Oceans. The longest scientifically measured one on record was a 41½-ft specimen captured off Baba Island near Karachi, Pakistan on 11 Nov 1949. It measured 23 ft around the thickest part of the body and weighed an estimated 16.53 tons.

Carnivorous The largest carnivorous fish (excluding plankton-eaters) is the comparatively rare great white shark (*Carcharodon carcharias*), also called the "man-eater." Adult specimens (females are larger than males) average 14–15 ft in length and generally weigh between 1,150–1,700 lb, but larger individuals have been recorded. The length and weight record is held by a 21-ft female caught off Castillo de Cojimar, Cuba in May 1945. It weighed 7,302 lb and yielded a 1,005-lb liver.

On 17 Apr 1987 a female great white shark with a "linear" measurement of 23 ft 5 in and an estimated weight of 6,613 lb was caught off Malta by Alfred Cutajar. Unfortunately the preserved jaws do not confirm this extreme measurement. A formula based on the size of the shark's teeth and the perimeter measurement of its upper jaw indicates a more acceptable measurement of 17½–18 ft.

Bony The longest of the bony or "true" fishes (Pisces) is the oarfish (*Regalecus glesne*), also called the "King of the Herrings," which has a worldwide distribution. In *c.* 1885 a specimen 25 ft long, weighing 600 lb, was caught by fishermen off Pemaquid Point, ME. Another oarfish, seen swimming off Asbury Park, NJ by a team of scientists from the Sandy Hook Marine Laboratory on 18 Jul 1963, was estimated to measure 50 ft in length.

The heaviest bony fish in the world is the ocean sunfish (*Mola mola*), which is found in all tropical, subtropical and temperate waters. On 18 Sep 1908 a specimen was accidentally struck by the SS *Fiona* off Bird Island about 40 miles

from Sydney, New South Wales, Australia and towed to Port Jackson. It measured 14 ft between the anal and dorsal fins and weighed 4,927 lb.

Largest freshwater The largest fish that spends its whole life in fresh or brackish water is the rare pla beuk (*Pangasianodon gigas*). It is confined to the Mekong River and its major tributaries in China, Laos, Cambodia and Thailand. The largest specimen, captured in the River Ban Mee Noi, Thailand, was reportedly 9 ft 10¼ in long and weighed 533.5 lb. This was exceeded by the European catfish or wels (*Silurus glanis*) in earlier times (in the 19th century lengths up to 15 ft and weights up to 720 lb were reported for Russian specimens), but today anything over 6 ft and 200 lb is considered large.

The arapaima (*arapaima glanis*), also called the pirarucu, found in the Amazon and other South American rivers and often claimed to be the largest freshwater fish, averages 6½ ft and 150 lb. The largest authentically recorded measured 8 ft 1½ in in length and weighed 325 lb. It was caught in the Rio Negro, Brazil in 1836.

In September 1978, a Nile perch (*Lates niloticus*) weighing 416 lb was netted in the eastern part of Lake Victoria, Kenya.

Smallest marine The shortest recorded marine fish—and the shortest known vertebrate—is the dwarf goby (*Trimmatom nanus*) of the Chagos Archipelago, central Indian Ocean. In one series of 92 specimens collected by the 1978–79 Joint Services Chagos Research Expedition of the British Armed Forces, the adult males averaged 0.338 in in length and the adult females 0.35 in.

The lightest of all vertebrates and the smallest catch possible for any fisherman is the dwarf goby *Schindleria praematurus* from Samoa, which measures 0.47–0.74 in. Mature specimens have been known to weigh only 0.03 grain, of which there are 14.175 to the oz.

Shark The spined pygmy shark (*Squaliolus laticaudus*) of the western Pacific matures at 5.9 in in length.

Smallest freshwater The shortest and lightest freshwater fish is the dwarf pygmy goby (*Pandaka pygmaea*), a colorless and nearly transparent species found in the streams and lakes of Luzon in the Philippines. Adult males measure only 0.28–0.38 in in length and weigh 0.00014–0.00018 oz.

The world's smallest commercial fish is the now-endangered sinarapan (*Mistichthys luzonensis*), a goby found only in Lake Buhi, Luzon, Philippines. Adult males measure 0.39–0.51 in in length, and a dried 1-lb fish cake contains about 70,000 of them!

Fastest The maximum swimming speed of a fish is dependent on the shape of its body and tail and its internal temperature. The cosmopolitan sailfish (*Istiophorus platypterus*) is considered to be the fastest species of fish over short distances, although the practical difficulties of measuring make data extremely difficult to secure. In a series of speed trials carried out at the Long Key Fishing Camp, FL, one sailfish took out 300 ft of line in 3 sec, which is equivalent to a velocity of 68 mph (compare with 60 mph for the cheetah).

Some American fishermen believe that the bluefin tuna (*Thunnus thynnus*) is the fastest fish in the sea, and bursts of speed up to 56 knots have been claimed for this species, but the fastest speed

■ **Largest fish**
The harmless, plankton-feeding whale shark (Rhincodon typus), found in the warmer waters of the Atlantic, Pacific and Indian Oceans, often reaches 29 ½ ft in length. The longest recorded specimen, captured off Karachi, Pakistan in 1949, measured 41 ½ ft. (Photo: Bruce Coleman)

recorded so far is 43.4 mph in a 20-sec dash. The yellowfin tuna (*Thunnus albacares*) and the wahoo (*Acanthocybium solandri*) are also extremely fast, having been timed at 46.35 mph and 47.88 mph respectively during 10–20 sec sprints.

Oldest Aquaria are of too-recent origin to be able to establish with certainty which species of fish can be regarded as being the longest-lived. Early indications are, however, that it may be the lake sturgeon (*Acipenser fulvescens*) of North America. In one study of the growth rings (annuli) of 966 specimens caught in the Lake Winnebago region in Wisconsin between 1951 and 1954 the oldest sturgeon was found to be a male (length 6 ft 7 in), which gave a reading of 82 years and was still growing.

The perch-like marine fish *Notothenia neglecta* of the Antarctic Ocean, whose blood contains a natural antifreeze, is reported to live up to 150 years, but this claim has not yet been verified.

In July 1974 a growth ring count of 228 years was reported for a female koi fish (a form of fancy carp) named Hanako living in a pond in Higashi Shirakawa, Gifu Prefecture, Japan, but the greatest authoritatively accepted age for this species is "more than 50 years."

In 1948 the death was reported of an 88-year-old female European eel (*Anguilla anguilla*) named Putte in the aquarium at Hälsingborg Museum, southern Sweden. She was allegedly born in the Sargasso Sea, in the North Atlantic, in 1860, and was caught in a river as a 3-year-old elver.

Oldest goldfish Goldfish (*Carassius auratus*) have been reported to live for over 50 years in China.

Shortest-lived The shortest-lived fish are probably certain species of the suborder Cyprinodontei (killifish), found in Africa and South America, which normally live about eight months.

Most abundant The most abundant species is probably the 3-in-long deepsea bristlemouth (*Cyclothone elongata*), which has a worldwide distribution. It would take about 500 of them to weigh 1 lb.

Deepest The greatest depth from which a fish has been recovered is 27,230 ft in the Puerto Rico Trench (27,488 ft) in the Atlantic by Dr Gilbert L. Voss of the US research vessel *John Elliott*, who took a 6½-in-long *Bassogigas profundissimus* in April 1970. It was only the fifth such brotulid ever caught.

Dr Jacques Piccard and Lt Don Walsh of the US Navy reported seeing a sole-like fish about 1 ft long (tentatively identified as *Chascanopsetta lugubris*) from the bathyscaphe *Trieste* at a depth of 35,820 ft in the Challenger Deep (Mariana Trench) in the western Pacific on 24 Jan 1960. This sighting, however, has been questioned by some authorities, who still regard the brotulids of the genus *Bassogigas* as the deepest-living vertebrates.

Most eggs The ocean sunfish (*Mola mola*) produces up to 30 million eggs, each of them measuring about 0.05 in in diameter, at a single spawning.

Fewest eggs The mouth-brooding cichlid *Tropheus moorii* of Lake Tanganyika, East Africa, produces seven eggs or less during normal reproduction.

Most valuable The world's most valuable fish is the Russian sturgeon (*Huso huso*). One 2,706-lb female caught in the Tikhaya Sosna River in 1924 yielded 541 lb of best-quality caviar, which would be worth $326,629 on today's market.

The 30-in-long Ginrin Showa koi, which won the supreme championship in nationwide Japanese koi shows in 1976, 1977, 1979 and 1980, was sold two years later for 17 million yen. In March 1986 this ornamental carp was acquired by Derry Evans, owner of the Kent Koi Centre near Sevenoaks, Great Britain, for an undisclosed sum, but the 15-year-old fish died five months later. It has since been stuffed and mounted to preserve its beauty.

Most venomous The most venomous fish in the world are the stonefish (Synanceidae) of the tropical waters of the Indo-Pacific, and in particular *Synanceja horrida*, which has the largest venom glands of any known fish. Direct contact with the spines of its fins, which contain a strong neurotoxic poison, often proves fatal.

Most ferocious The razor-toothed piranhas of the genera *Serrasalmus*, *Pygocentrus* and *Pygopristis* are the most ferocious freshwater fish in the world. They live in the sluggish waters of the large rivers of South America, and will attack any creature, regardless of size, if it is injured or making a commotion in the water. On 19 Sep 1981 more than 300 people were reportedly killed and eaten when an overloaded passenger-cargo boat capsized and sank as it was docking at the Brazilian port of Obidos. According to one official, only 178 of the boat's passengers survived.

Most electric The most powerful electric fish is the electric eel (*Electrophorus electricus*), which is found in the rivers of Brazil, Colombia, Venezuela and Peru. An average-sized specimen can discharge 400 v at 1 amp, but measurements up to 650 v have been recorded.

Starfishes Asteroidea

Largest The largest of the 1,600 known species of starfish in terms of total arm-span is the very fragile brisingid *Midgardia xandaros*. A specimen collected by the Texas A & M University research vessel *Alaminos* in the southern part of the Gulf of Mexico in the late summer of 1968 measured 54.33 in tip to tip, but the diameter of its disc was only 1.02 in. Its dry weight was 2.46 oz.

The heaviest species of starfish is the five-armed *Thromidia catalai* of the western Pacific. One specimen collected off Ilot Amédée, New Caledonia on 14 Sep 1969 and later deposited in Nouméa Aquarium weighed an estimated 13.2 lb (total arm span 24.8 in).

Smallest The smallest-known starfish is the asterinid sea star *Patiriella parvivipara*, discovered by Wolfgang Zeidler on the west coast of the Eyre peninsula, South Australia in 1975. It has a maximum radius of only 0.18 in and a diameter of less than 0.35 in.

Most destructive The crown of thorns (*Acanthaster planci*) of the Indo-Pacific region and the Red Sea has 12–19 arms and can measure up to 24 in in diameter. It feeds on coral polyps and can destroy $46\frac{1}{2}$–62 in^2 of coral in one day.

Deepest The greatest depth from which a starfish has been recovered is 24,881 ft for a specimen of *Porcellanaster ivanovi* collected by the USSR research ship *Vityaz* in the Mariana Trench, in the western Pacific, c. 1962.

Crustaceans Crustacea

(*Crabs, lobsters, shrimps, prawns, crawfish, barnacles, water fleas, fish lice, woodlice, sandhoppers, krill, etc.*)

Largest marine The largest of all crustaceans (although not the heaviest) is the takashigani or giant spider crab (*Macrocheira kaempferi*), also called the stilt crab, which is found in deep waters off the southeastern coast of Japan. Mature specimens usually have a body measuring 10 × 12 in and a claw-span of 8–9 ft, but unconfirmed measurements up to 19 ft have been reported. A specimen with a claw-span of 12 ft 1½ in weighed 41 lb.

The largest species of lobster, and the heaviest of all crustaceans, is the American or North Atlantic lobster (*Homarus americanus*). On 11 Feb 1977 a specimen weighing 44 lb 6 oz and measuring 3 ft 6 in from the end of the tail fan to the tip of the largest claw was caught off Nova Scotia, Canada and later sold to a New York restaurant owner.

Largest freshwater The largest freshwater crustacean is the crayfish, or crawfish (*Astacopsis gouldi*), found in the streams of Tasmania, Australia. It has been measured up to 2 ft in length and may weigh as much as 9 lb. In 1934 an unconfirmed weight of 14 lb (total length 29 in) was reported for an outsized specimen caught at Bridport.

Smallest Water fleas of the genus *Alonella* may measure less than 0.0098 in in length. They are found in British waters.

The smallest-known lobster is the Cape lobster (*Homarus capensis*) of South Africa, which measures 3.9–4.7 in in total length.

The smallest crabs in the world are the aptly named pea crabs (family Pinnotheridae). Some species have a shell diameter of only 0.25 in, including *Pinnotheres pisum*, which is found in British waters.

Oldest Very large specimens of the American lobster (*Homarus americanus*) may be as much as 50 years old.

Deepest The greatest depth from which a crustacean has been recovered is 34,450 ft for *live* amphipods from the Challenger Deep (Mariana Trench), western Pacific by the US research vessel *Thomas Washington* in November 1980. Amphipods and isopods have also been collected in the Ecuadorean Andes at a height of 13,300 ft.

Largest concentration The largest single concentration of crustaceans ever recorded was an enormous swarm of krill (*Euphausia superba*) estimated to weigh 11 million tons and tracked by US scientists off Antarctica in March 1981.

Arachnids Arachnida

SPIDERS (Araneae)

Largest The world's largest-known spider is the goliath bird-eating spider (*Theraphosa leblondi*) of the coastal rain forests of Suriname, Guyana and French Guiana, northeastern South America; isolated specimens have also been reported from Venezuela and Brazil. In February 1985, Charles J. Seiderman of New York City captured a huge female just north of Paramarido, Suriname. This spider had a maximum leg span of 10½ in (total body length 4 in), 1-in-long fangs, and weighed a peak 4.3 oz before its death from moulting problems in Jan 1986.

An outsized male example collected by members of the Pablo San Martin Expedition at Rio Cavro, Venezuela in April 1965 had a leg span of 11.02 in; the female is built on much heavier lines.

United States The *Rhecosticta californica*, a type of tarantula found in the Southwest, is the heaviest spider and has the longest body. However, the orb web spider (*Nephila clavipes*) of the family *Araneidae*, found in the southern Gulf states, and the wolf spider (*Lycosa carolinensis*) of the family *Lycosidae*, found in the Southeast, equal its leg span.

Smallest The smallest-known spider is *Patu marplesi* (family Symphytognathidae) of Western Samoa in the Pacific. The type specimen (male), found in moss at c. 2,000 ft in Madolelei, Western Samoa in January 1965, measured 0.017 in overall, which means that it was about the size of a period on this page.

United States The *Troglonata paradoxum* of the family *Mysmmenidae* is the smallest spider in the United States.

Most common The crab spiders (family Thomisidae) have a worldwide distribution.

United States The house spider (*Archaearanea tepidariorum*), of the

family *Theridiidae*, has been sighted all over the United States.

Rarest The most elusive of all spiders are the rare trapdoor spiders of the genus *Liphistius*, which are found in southeast Asia.

United States The most elusive spiders in the United States are the *Nesticus Dilutus*, one specimen found by T. S. Barr at Grassy Creek Cave, TN, and the *Nesticus Valentines*, one specimen found by J. M. Valentine at Mt Eagle Saltpeter Cave, TN.

Oldest The longest-lived of all spiders are the primitive *Mygalomorphae* (tarantulas and allied species). One female therasophid collected in Mexico in 1935 lived for an estimated 26–28 years.

United States The longest-lived species of American spider is the *Rhecosticta californica* of the family *Theraphosidae*, which has an average life span of 25 years.

Fastest The fastest-moving arachnids are the long-legged sun spiders of the genus *Solpuga*, which live in the arid semidesert regions of Africa and the Middle East. They feed on geckos and other lizards and can reach speeds of over 10 mph.

Largest webs Aerial webs spun by the tropical orb weavers of the genus *Nephila* have been measured up to 18 ft 9¾ in in circumference.

Smallest webs The smallest webs are spun by spiders such as *Glyphesis cottonae* which cover about 0.75 in². (See Smallest spiders.)

Most venomous The world's most venomous spiders are the Brazilian wandering spiders of the genus *Phoneutria*, and particularly *P. fera*, which has the most active neurotoxic venom of any living spider. These large and highly aggressive creatures frequently enter human dwellings and hide in clothing or shoes. When disturbed they bite furiously several times, and hundreds of accidents involving these species are reported annually. When deaths do occur, they are usually in children under the age of 7. Fortunately, an effective antivenin is available.

SCORPIONS (Scorpiones)

Largest The largest of the 800 or so species of scorpion is the tropical "emperor" *Pandinus imperator* of Guinea, adult males of which can attain a body length of 7 in or more. Its black coloring is indicative of species found in moist or higher mountain habitats.

Smallest The smallest scorpion in the world is *Microbothus pusillus* from the Red Sea coast, which measures about 0.5 in in total length.

Most venomous The most venomous scorpion in the world is the Palestine yellow scorpion (*Leiurus quinquestriatus*), which ranges from the eastern part of North Africa through the Middle East to the shores of the Red Sea. For-

tunately, the amount of venom it delivers is very small (0.000009 oz) and adult lives are seldom endangered; however, it has been responsible for a number of fatalities among children under the age of 5.

Insects Insecta

Earliest The most primitive known insect is an unidentified species of springtail (order Collembola), which dates from at least 300 million years ago. Widely distributed throughout the world, this wingless insect measures 0.04–0.4 in in length.

Heaviest The heaviest living insects are the Goliath beetles (family Scarabaeidae) of Equatorial Africa. The largest members of the group are *Goliathus regius*, *G. goliathus* (=*G. giganteus*) and *G. druryi*, and in one series of fully-grown males (females are smaller) the lengths from the tips of the small frontal horns to the end of the abdomen measured up to 4.33 in and the weights ranged from 2.5–3.5 oz. A single rhinoceros beetle of this family can support 850 times its own weight on its back. (See General records.)

The elephant beetles (*Megasoma*) of Central America and the West Indies attain the greatest dimensions in terms of volume, but they lack the massive build-up of heavy chiton forming the thorax and anterior sternum of the goliaths, and this makes them lighter.

Largest cockroach The world's largest cockroach is *Megaloblatta longipennis* of Colombia. A preserved female in the collection of Akira Yokokura of Yamagata, Japan measures 3.81 in in length and 1.77 in across.

Longest The longest insect in the world is the giant stick-insect (*Pharnacia serratipes*) of Indonesia, females of which have been measured up to 13 in.

The longest-known beetle (excluding antennae) is the Hercules beetle (*Dynastes hercules*) of Central and South America, which has been measured up to

7.48 in. More than half the length, however, is taken up by the prothoracic horn.

Smallest The smallest insects recorded so far are the "feather-winged" beetles of the family Ptiliidae (=trichopterygidae) and the "battledore-wing fairy flies" (parasitic wasps) of the family Mymaridae; they are smaller than some species of protozoa (single-celled animals).

The male bloodsucking banded louse (*Enderleinellus zonatus*) and the parasitic wasp (*Caraphractus cinctus*) may each weigh as little as 5,670,000 to an oz. Eggs of the latter each weigh 141,750,000 to an oz.

Rarest It is estimated that there may be as many as 30 million species of insect—more than all other phyla and classes put together—but thousands are known only from a single or type specimen.

Fastest-flying Experiments have proved that the widely publicized claim by an American scientist in 1926 that the deer botfly (*Cephenemyia pratti*) could attain a speed of 818 mph at an altitude of 12,000 ft was wildly exaggerated. If true, the fly would have had to develop the equivalent of 1.5 hp and consume 1½ times its own weight in food per second to acquire the energy that would be needed and, even if this were possible, it would still be crushed by the air pressure and incinerated by the friction. Acceptable modern experiments have now established that the highest maintainable air speed of any insect, including the deer botfly, hawkmoths (Sphingidae), horseflies (*Tabanus bovinus*) and some tropical butterflies (Hesperiidae) is 24 mph, rising to a maximum of 36 mph for the Australian dragonfly *Austrophlebia costalis* for short bursts.

Fastest-moving The fastest-moving insects are large tropical cockroaches (Dictyoptera), and specimens measuring about 1.18 in in length have been timed at 47–51 in/sec, 2.68–2.90 mph or 40–43 body lengths per second.

Highest g force The click beetle (*Athous haemorrhoidalis*) averages 400 *g* when "jack-knifing" into the air to escape predators. One example measuring 0.47 in in length and weighing 0.00014 oz that jumped to a height of 11¾ in was calculated to have "endured" a peak brain deceleration of 2,300 *g* by the end of the movement.

Oldest The longest-lived insects are the splendor beetles (Buprestidae). On 27 May 1983 a *Buprestis aurulenta* appeared from the staircase timber in the the home of Mr W. Euston of Prittlewell, Great Britain, after 47 years as a larva.

Loudest The loudest of all insects is the male cicada (family Cicadidae). At 7,400 pulses/min its tymbal organs produce a noise (officially described by the US Department of Agriculture as "Tsh-ee-EEEE-e-ou") detectable more than a quarter of a mile distant.

Fastest wing-beat The fastest wing-beat of any insect under natural conditions is 62,760 per min by a tiny midge of the genus *Forcipomyia*. In experiments with truncated wings at a temperature of 98.6° F the rate increased to 133,080 beats/min. The muscular contraction-expansion cycle in 0.00045 or 1/2218th of a sec represents the fastest muscle movement ever measured.

Slowest wing-beat The slowest wing beat of any insect is 300 per min by the swallowtail butterfly (*Papilio machaon*). The average is 460–636 per min.

Largest termite mound In 1968 W. Page photographed a specimen south of Horgesia, Somalia estimated to be 28.5 ft tall.

DRAGONFLIES (Odonata)

Largest *Megaloprepus caeruleata* of Central and South America has been measured up to 4.72 in across the wings and 7.52 in in body length.

United States The giant green darner (*Anax walsinghami*), found in the West, has a body length of up to 4 ½ in.

Smallest The smallest dragonfly in the world is *Agriocnemis naia* of Myanmar (formerly Burma). A specimen in the British Museum (Natural History), London, Great Britain had a wing expanse of 0.69 in and a body length of 0.71 in.

United States The smallest dragonfly in the United States is the elfin skimmer (*Nannothaemis Bella*), which has a body length of ⁴/₅ in.

FLEAS (Siphonaptera)

Largest Siphonapterologists recognize 1830 varieties, of which the largest-known is *Hystrichopsylla schefferi*, which was described from a single specimen taken from the nest of a mountain beaver (*Aplodontia rufa*) at Puyallup, WA in 1913. Females measure up to 0.31 in in length, which is the diameter of a pencil.

Longest jump The champion jumper among fleas is the common flea (*Pulex irritans*). In one American experiment carried out in 1910 a specimen allowed to leap at will performed a long jump of 13 in and a high jump of 7¾ in. In jumping 130 times its own height a flea subjects itself to a force of 200 *g*.

BUTTERFLIES AND MOTHS (Lepidoptera)

Largest The largest-known butterfly is the protected Queen Alexandra's birdwing (*Ornithoptera alexandrae*), which is restricted to the Popondetta Plain in Papua New Guinea. Females may have a wingspan exceeding 11.02 in and weigh over 0.88 oz.

The largest moth in the world (although not the heaviest) is the Hercules moth (*Cosdinoscera hercules*) of tropical Australia and New Guinea. A wing area of up to 40.8 in² and a wingspan of 11 in have been recorded. In 1948 an unconfirmed measurement of 14.17 in was reported for a female captured near the post office at the coastal town of Innisfail, Queensland, Australia, now in the Oberthur collection.

The rare owlet moth (*Thysania agrippina*) of Brazil has been measured up to 12.16 in wingspan in the case of a female taken in 1934 and now in the collection of John G. Powers in Ontario, Canada.

United States The largest *native* butterfly in the United States is the giant swallowtail (*Papilio cresphontes*), found in the eastern states.

Smallest The smallest of the 140,000 known species of Lepidoptera is *Stigmella ridiculosa*, which has a wingspan of 0.079 in with a similar body length and is found in the Canary Islands.

United States The smallest butterfly in the United States is the pygmy blue (*Brephidium exilis*), found in the Southeast.

Rarest The rarest butterfly is considered to be Queen Alexandra's birdwing (*Ornithoptera alexandrae*), which is found with its only source of nutrition, the vine *Aristolochia dielsiana*, in Papua New Guinea. Its population is extremely difficult to estimate as it flies very high and is seldom seen. The caterpillars are also somewhat elusive in their habitat 131 ft above the ground in the vine leaves. However, only three individuals were sighted in 1990 during surveys of an area covering 222.4–321.2 acres. (See also Largest butterfly.) Although another birdwing *Ornithoptera* (= *Troides*) *allottei* of Bougainville, Solomon Islands is known from less than a dozen specimens, this is not a true species, but a natural hybrid of *Ornithoptera victoriae* and *O. urvillianus*. A male from the collection of C. Rousseau Decelle was auctioned for $2,436 in Paris, France on 24 Oct 1966.

United States The rarest butterfly in the United States (30 species) is the Schaus swallowtail (*Papilio aritodemus*).

Most acute sense of smell The most acute sense of smell exhibited in nature is that of the male emperor moth (*Eudia pavonia*), which, according to German experiments in 1961, can detect the sex attractant of the virgin female at the almost unbelievable range of 6.8 miles upwind. This scent has been identified as one of the higher alcohols ($C_{16}H_{29}OH$), of which the female carries less than 0.0000015 grain.

Largest butterfly farm The Stratford-upon-Avon Butterfly Farm, Warwickshire, Great Britain can accommodate 2,000 exotic butterflies in authentic rain forest conditions. The total capacity of all flight areas at the farm, which opened on 15 Jul 1985, is over 141,258 ft³. The complex also comprises insect and plant houses and educational facilities.

United States Butterfly World, in Coconut Creek, FL, accommodates between 2,000 and 3,000 butterflies in authentic rain forest or North American conditions. About 80 species of butterfly can be seen at any one time, and in the course of a year up to 300 species are shown in the 37 screened enclosures. The museum, founded by Mr Boender, Clive Farrell, and John Chalk, cost $1.5 million and was built in five months to open in March 1988.

Centipedes Chilopoda

Longest The longest-known species of centipede is a large variant of the widely distributed *Scolopendra morsitans*, found on the Andaman Islands in the Bay of Bengal. Specimens have been measured up to 13 in in length and 1.5 in in breadth.

United States Tomotaemia parviceps, found in California and Washington, has been measured up to 5.9 in in length and 0.1 in in diameter.

Shortest The shortest recorded centipede is an unidentified species that measures only 0.19 in.

United States Nampabius georgianus, found in Georgia, measures up to 0.19 in in length and 0.03 in in diameter. *Poaaphilus keywinus*, found in Iowa, is smaller in diameter at 0.007 in, but has a length of 0.25 in.

Most legs *Himantarum gabrielis*, found in southern Europe, has 171–177 pairs of legs when adult.

Fastest The fastest centipede is probably *Scrutigera coleoptrata* of southern Europe, which can travel at 1.1 mph.

Millipedes Diplopoda

Longest Both *Graphidostreptus gigas* of Africa and *Scaphistostreptus seychellarum* of the Seychelles in the Indian Ocean have been measured up to 11.02 in in length and 0.78 in in diameter.

United States Orthoporus ornatus, found in Texas and Arizona, measures up to 7.28 in in length and 0.55 in in diameter.

Shortest The shortest millipede in the world is the British species *Polyxenus lagurus*, which measures 0.082–0.15 in.

United States Polyxenus fasciculatus, found in the Southeast, measures only 0.07 in in length and 0.03 in in diameter. The next-shortest millipede is *Buotus carolinus*, found in North Carolina and Virginia, which has been measured at 0.11 in in length and only 0.01 in in diameter.

Most legs The greatest number of legs reported for a millipede is 375 pairs (750 legs) for *Illacme plenipes* of California.

Segmented Worms

Annelida

Longest The longest-known species of

earthworm is *Microchaetus rappi* (= *M. microchaetus*) of South Africa. In *c.* 1937 a giant earthworm measuring 22 ft in length when naturally extended and 0.78 in in diameter was collected in the Transvaal.

Shortest *Chaetogaster annandalei* measures less than 0.019 in in length.

Mollusks Mollusca

(Squids, octopuses, shellfish, snails, etc.)

Largest invertebrate The Atlantic giant squid, *Architeuthis dux*, is the world's largest-known invertebrate. The heaviest ever recorded was a 2.2-ton monster that ran aground in Thimble Tickle Bay, Newfoundland, Canada on 2 Nov 1878. There are numerous types of squids, ranging in size from 0.75 in to the longest ever recorded—a 57-ft giant *Architeuthis longimanus* which was washed up on Lyall Bay, Cook Strait, New Zealand in October 1887. Its two long slender tentacles each measured 49 ft 3 in.

Largest octopus The largest-known octopus is the Pacific giant (*Octopus dofleini*), which ranges from California to Alaska and off eastern Asia south to Japan. It is not known exactly how large these creatures can grow but the average mature male weighs about 51 lb and has an arm span of about 8 ft. The largest recorded specimen, found off western Canada in 1957, had an estimated arm span of 31½ ft and weighed about 600 lb.

One huge specimen of *Octopus apollyon* caught single-handedly by skin diver Donald E. Hagen in Lower Hoods Canal, Puget Sound, WA on 18 Feb 1973 weighed 118 lb 10 oz and had a relaxed radial spread of 23 ft.

Largest eye The Atlantic giant squid has the largest eye of any animal, living or extinct. It has been estimated that the one recorded at Thimble Tickle Bay had eyes 15.75 in in diameter—almost the width of this open book!

Oldest mollusk The longest-lived mollusk is the ocean quahog (*Arctica islandica*), a thick-shelled clam found in the mid-Atlantic. A specimen with 220 annual growth rings was collected in 1982.

SHELLS

Largest The largest of all existing bivalve shells is that of the marine giant clam *Tridacna gigas*, found on the Indo-Pacific coral reefs. An outsized specimen measuring 45.2 in in length and weighing 734 lb was collected off Ishigaki Island, Okinawa, Japan in 1956 but was not scientifically examined until August 1984. It probably weighed just over 750 lb when alive (the soft parts weigh up to 20 lb). Another giant clam collected at Tapanoeli (Tapanula) on the northwest coast of Sumatra before 1817 and now

preserved at Arno's Vale measures 54 in in length and weighs 507 lb.

Smallest The smallest-known shell-bearing species is the gastropod *Ammonicera rota*, which is found in British waters. It measures 0.02 in in diameter.

The smallest bivalve shell is the coinshell *Neolepton sykesi*, which is known only from a few examples collected off Guernsey, Channel Islands, Great Britain and western Ireland. It has an average diameter of 0.047 in.

Most venomous There are some 400–500 species of cone shell (*Conus*), all of which can deliver a poisonous neurotoxin. The geographer cone (*Conus geographus*) and the court cone (*C. aulicus*), marine mollusks found from Polynesia to East Africa, are considered to be the most deadly. The venom is injected by a unique, fleshy harpoon-like proboscis, and symptoms include impaired vision, dizziness, nausea, paralysis and death. Of the twenty-five people known to have been stung by these creatures, five have died, giving a mortality rate exceeding that for common cobras and rattlesnakes.

Most expensive The value of a seashell does not necessarily depend on its rarity or its prevalence. Some rare shells are inexpensive because there is no demand for them, while certain common shells command high prices because they are not readily accessible. In theory the most valuable shells in the world should be some of the unique examples collected in deepsea trawls, but these shells are always dull and unattractive and hold very little interest for the collector. The most sought-after shell at present is probably *Cypraea fultoni*. In 1987 two live specimens were taken by a Russian trawler off Mozambique in the Indian Ocean. The larger of the two was later sold in New York to collector Dr Massilia Raybaudi of Italy for $24,000. The other was put up for sale at $17,000. A third *C. fultoni* went for $6,600 in June 1987 to a Carmel, CA collector. This collector also purchased a *C. teramachii* for $6,500 in a one-week buying spree. Another *C. fultoni*, in the American Museum of Natural History, New York City, was valued at $14,000 a few years ago.

GASTROPODS

Fastest The fastest-moving species of land snail is probably the common garden snail (*Helix aspersa*). It is probable, however, that the carnivorous (and cannibalistic) snail *Euglandina rosea* could outrun other snails in its hunt for prey. The snail-racing equivalent of a four-minute mile is 24 in in 3 min, or a 5½-day mile.

On 20 Feb 1990 a garden snail named Verne completed a 12.2 in course at West Middle School in Plymouth, MI in a record 2 min 13 sec at 0.233 cm/sec. On 9 Jul 1988 another garden snail called Hercules dragged a 8.5-oz stone for 18½ in across a table in 10 min in the Basque town of Val de Trapagua, Spain.

Worm-charming
At the first World Worm Charming Championship held at Willaston, Great Britain on 5 Jul 1980, Tom Shufflebotham (b. 1960) charmed a record 511 worms out of the ground (a 9.84 ft² plot) in the allotted time of 30 min. Garden forks or other implements are vibrated in the soil by competitors to coax up the worms, but water is banned.

Species on the Brink

SPIX'S MACAW (*Cyanopsitta spixii*). Also known as the little blue macaw, the wild population of this 2 ft long parrot has declined to a solitary male driven to mate with an equally endangered blue-winged macaw (*Ara maracana*). Between 1977 and 1987 at least 23 birds were handled illegally by two traders, all taken from the last known population. Only 15 birds are held in legitimate zoological collections and, unless the main contributors to its plight can be persuaded to relinquish their private collections or cooperate in the breeding programs, this species is heading for certain extinction in the wild.

Brazil

A small selection of the world's rarest and most endangered flora and fauna compiled from information supplied by the World Conservation Monitoring Centre, Cambridge, Great Britain. Artwork by Matthew Hillier for Guinness Publishing.

Iriomote, east of Taiwan

IRIOMOTE CAT (*Felis iriomotensis*). Confined to the small (113 miles²) Japanese-owned island from which it takes its name, this average domestic cat-sized feline is not only protected by law, it has also been declared a Japanese national monument. A nocturnal and strictly territorial animal, the Iriomote was only discovered in 1967. Its population has fallen to about 80 because of agricultural development, tourism and indigenous hostility toward conservation, which is considered detrimental to the island's economic development.

BAIJI (or YANGTZE RIVER) DOLPHIN (*Lipotes vexillifer*). The Baiji, which can reach lengths of 8 ft, is probably the most endangered of the cetaceans (whales, dolphins and porpoises). Its population is estimated at about 300 and falling due to competition for fish supplies with China's human population (dolphins are often caught up in fishing gear) and the reduction of overall food because of environmental degradation. Its survival is a high priority of the Chinese government, which has implemented an information program especially aimed at local fishermen, and a captive breeding project is also envisaged.

Lower Yangtze river, China

CHINESE ALLIGATOR (*Alligator sinesis*). This 5 ft long reptile is protected by Chinese law and was thought to be close to extinction in the early 1980s, although a few hundred probably exist in the wild. The population has been severely affected by hunters, traders and the pollution of its diet of fish, snails and crustaceans as a result of heavy use of pesticides. Although captive breeding programs are proving successful, the alligators cannot be reintroduced into the wild because of the lack of suitable remaining habitat, and their extinction outside captivity is expected before the end of the century, if not sooner.

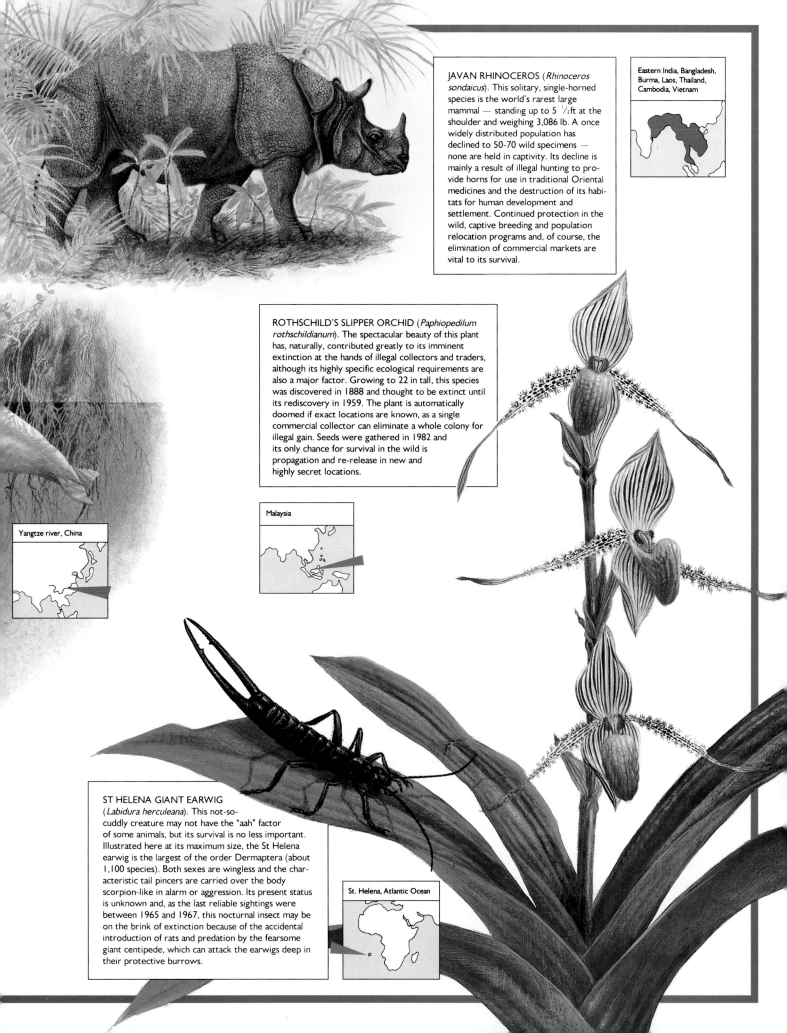

JAVAN RHINOCEROS (*Rhinoceros sondaicus*). This solitary, single-horned species is the world's rarest large mammal — standing up to 5 ¹/₂ft at the shoulder and weighing 3,086 lb. A once widely distributed population has declined to 50-70 wild specimens — none are held in captivity. Its decline is mainly a result of illegal hunting to provide horns for use in traditional Oriental medicines and the destruction of its habitats for human development and settlement. Continued protection in the wild, captive breeding and population relocation programs and, of course, the elimination of commercial markets are vital to its survival.

Eastern India, Bangladesh, Burma, Laos, Thailand, Cambodia, Vietnam

ROTHSCHILD'S SLIPPER ORCHID (*Paphiopedilum rothschildianum*). The spectacular beauty of this plant has, naturally, contributed greatly to its imminent extinction at the hands of illegal collectors and traders, although its highly specific ecological requirements are also a major factor. Growing to 22 in tall, this species was discovered in 1888 and thought to be extinct until its rediscovery in 1959. The plant is automatically doomed if exact locations are known, as a single commercial collector can eliminate a whole colony for illegal gain. Seeds were gathered in 1982 and its only chance for survival in the wild is propagation and re-release in new and highly secret locations.

Malaysia

Yangtze river, China

ST HELENA GIANT EARWIG (*Labidura herculeana*). This not-so-cuddly creature may not have the "aah" factor of some animals, but its survival is no less important. Illustrated here at its maximum size, the St Helena earwig is the largest of the order Dermaptera (about 1,100 species). Both sexes are wingless and the characteristic tail pincers are carried over the body scorpion-like in alarm or aggression. Its present status is unknown and, as the last reliable sightings were between 1965 and 1967, this nocturnal insect may be on the brink of extinction because of the accidental introduction of rats and predation by the fearsome giant centipede, which can attack the earwigs deep in their protective burrows.

St. Helena, Atlantic Ocean

Largest The largest-known gastropod is the trumpet or baler conch (*Syrinx aruanus*) of Australia. One outsized specimen collected off Western Australia in 1979 and now owned by Don Pisor (who bought it from a fisherman in Kaohsiung, Taiwan in November 1979) of San Diego, CA measures 30.39 in in length and has a maximum girth of 39.76 in. It weighed nearly 40 lb when alive.

The largest-known land gastropod is the African giant snail (*Achatina sp.*). A specimen named Gee Geronimo owned by Christopher Hudson (1955–79) of Hove, Great Britain, measured 15½ in from snout to tail when fully extended (shell length 10¾ in) in December 1978 and weighed exactly 2 lb. The snail was collected in Sierra Leone in June 1976.

Ribbon Worms

Nemertina

Longest The longest of the 550 recorded species of ribbon worm, also called nemertines (or nemerteans), is the "boot-lace" worm (*Lineus longissimus*), which is found in the shallow waters of the North Sea, Great Britain. A specimen that washed ashore at St Andrews, Fife, Great Britain in 1864 after a severe storm measured more than 180 ft in length.

Immolation Some ribbon worms absorb themselves when food is scarce. One specimen under observation digested 95 percent of its own body in a few months without apparently suffering any ill effects. As soon as food became available the lost tissue was restored.

Jellyfishes and Corals

Cnidaria

Largest jellyfish The largest jellyfish is the Arctic giant jellyfish (*Cyanea capillata arctica*) of the northwestern Atlantic. One washed up in Massachusetts Bay had a bell diameter of 7 ft 6 in and tentacles stretching 120 ft.

Most venomous The beautiful but deadly Australian sea wasp (*Chironex fleckeri*) is the most venomous jellyfish in the world. Its cardiotoxic venom has caused the deaths of 66 people off the coast of Queensland since 1880, with victims dying within 1–3 minutes if medical aid is not available. One effective defense is women's pantyhose, outsize versions of which are now worn by Queensland lifesavers at surfing tournaments.

Coral The world's greatest stony coral structure is the Great Barrier Reef off Queensland, northeast Australia. It stretches 1,260 miles and covers 80,000 miles^2.

The world's largest reported example of discrete coral is a stony colony of *Galaxea fascicularis* found in Sakiyama Bay off Irimote Island, Okinawa on 7 Aug 1982 by Dr Shohei Shirai of the Institute for Development of Pacific Natural Resources. It has a long axis measurement of 23 ft 9 in, a height of 13 ft 1½ in and a maximum circumference of 59 ft 5 in.

Sponges Porifera

Largest The largest-known sponge is the barrel-shaped loggerhead sponge (*Spheciospongia vesparium*) of the West Indies and the waters off Florida. Individuals measure up to 3 ft 6 in in height and 3 ft in diameter. Neptune's cup or goblet (*Poterion patera*) of Indonesia grows to 4 ft in height, but it is a less bulky animal.

In 1909 a wool sponge (*Hippospongia canaliculatta*) measuring 6 ft in circumference was collected off the Bahamas. When taken from the water it weighed between 80–90 lb but after it had been dried and relieved of all excrescences it weighed 12 lb. (This sponge is now preserved in the National Museum of Natural History, Washington, D.C.)

Smallest The widely distributed *Leucosolenia blanca* measures 0.11 in in height when fully grown.

Deepest Sponges have been recovered from depths of up to 18,500 ft.

Extinct Animals

The first dinosaur to be scientifically described was *Megalosaurus bucklandi* ("great fossil lizard") in 1824. The remains of this bipedal flesh-eater were found by workmen before 1818 in a slate quarry near Woodstock, Great Britain and later placed in the University Museum, in Oxford, Great Britain. The first fossil bone of *Megalosaurus* was actually illustrated in 1677, but its true nature was not realized until much later. It was not until 1841 that the name Dinosauria ("terrible lizards") was given to these newly discovered giants.

Disappearance No wholly satisfactory theory has been offered for the dinosaurs' sudden extinction 65 million years ago. Evidence from the Hell Creek Formation of Montana suggests that dinosaurs dwindled in importance over a period of 5–10 million years and were replaced progressively by mammals. The gradual decline is linked to long-term changes in climates, which became cooler and more seasonal, and in the plants, which changed from lush tropical forms to temperate-zone conifers. The other view which has attracted a great deal of attention is that the dinosaurs, together with many other land and sea groups, were eliminated suddenly and catastrophically by the impact of a giant asteroid, or possibly a shower of comets, on the Earth. The impact(s) supposedly produced a vast cloud of dust which encircled the Earth, blocking out the sun. This caused icy conditions in the northern hemisphere at least, and a cessation of photosynthesis. Plants, and consequently the animals that fed on them, died off. The evidence for this impact theory now seems very strong—the element iridium, a good indicator of extraterrestrial impact, has been found at over 100 locations worldwide. In addition, likely large craters have been identified in Iowa (21.75 miles in diameter), on the Yucatan peninsula, Central America (37.28 miles in diameter) in 1990 and in Siberia, USSR (65.25 miles in diameter) in 1991. However, a clear link between the physical results of a major impact and the selective extinctions that took place 65 million years ago has not yet been established.

Earliest-known The earliest dinosaur is believed to be the *Herrerasaurus*, which is now known from an almost complete skeleton discovered in 1989 in the foothills of the Andes in Argentina by an expedition led by Paul Sereno of the University of Chicago, IL. This specimen is thought to date from

■ **The barrel-shaped loggerhead sponge** (Spheciospongia vesparia) *of the Caribbean can reach 3½ ft in height and 3 ft in diameter. Neptune's cup or goblet* (Poterion patera) *of Indonesia grows to 4 ft, but is less bulky. (Photo: Bruce Coleman)*

230 million years ago and is named after Victorino Herrera, a fossil hunter who discovered fragments of bone years earlier. *Herrerasaurus* was a carnivore that stood about 6 ½–8 ft and weighed over 220 lb, and its importance in the evolutionary process is suggested by its dual-hinged jaw, a feature that did not appear in other dinosaurs for another 50 million years. Other dinosaurs of a similar age from the Late Triassic are known from incomplete remains found in Brazil, Argentina, Morocco, India and Scotland.

Largest The largest-ever land animals were the sauropod dinosaurs, a group of long-necked, long-tailed, four-legged plant-eaters that lumbered around most of the world during the Jurassic and Cretaceous periods 208–65 million years ago. However, it is difficult to determine precisely which of these sauropod dinosaurs was the largest (longest, tallest or heaviest). This is because many of the supposed giants are based only on incomplete fossil remains, and also because many discoverers have tended to exaggerate the sizes of their dinosaur finds. Estimating dinosaur lengths and heights is relatively straightforward when there is a complete skeleton. However, weights are an entirely different matter, and several investigators have simply made estimates by scaling up large modern animals, such as elephants, to dinosaur size.

A more scientific approach has been to make detailed scale models of particular species of dinosaur from clay or plastic. Their volume is estimated by precise measurements of the amount of water they displace from a jar of fixed capacity. The weight can then be calculated by multiplying the volume by the assumed density of a dinosaur. Although the method is simple, results obtained by different scientists studying the same species of dinosaur can vary dramatically. For example, estimates of the body weight of *Brachiosaurus* range from 31.5 to 78.3 tons. Errors arise first because of differences in the assumed corpulence of the animals in the models, and second because of differences in the estimates of dinosaur density. Some scientists regard dinosaurs as having been bulky, slow-moving animals, while others see them as slender and fleet-footed. This can lead to a great range of constructions. Estimates of density used by different investigators range from 49.9 lb/ft^3 to 62.4 lb/ft^3 and these also greatly affect the final weight estimates. Paleontologists now lean toward the lower estimates of weight.

The sauropods are divided into five main groups: cetiosaurids; brachiosaurids; diplodocids; camarasaurids; and titanosaurids. The world's biggest dinosaur has been identified at different times as a brachiosaurid, a diplodocid or a titanosaurid.

Brachiosaurids The largest (and tallest) species for which the whole skeleton is known is the gracile *Brachiosaurus (Giraffatitan) brancai* from the famous Tendaguru site in Tanzania, which was excavated by a German expedition in 1909–11. The bones were later shipped to the Humboldt Museum in Berlin for preparation and assembly, and the specimen (a composite of several partial skeletons of different sizes) was finally put on display in 1937. As it stands today, the world's largest mounted dinosaur measures 72 ft 9½ in in overall length (height at shoulder 19 ft 8 in) and has a raised head height of 46 ft. It weighed an estimated 34.7 tons.

The isolated fibula of another *Brachiosaurus* in the same museum is 13 percent larger than its equivalent in the mounted skeleton and it has been calculated that the bone must have come from a sauropod measuring 82 ft in total length (shoulder height 22 ft 3½ in), which had an estimated height of 52½ ft to the top of its raised head and weighed 49.6 tons.

Brachiosaurus altithorax from the Late Jurassic of western Colorado was similar in size to its African cousin, and weight estimates based on different specimens range from 38.6 to 60.6 tons.

An even larger brachiosaurid was announced from the Uncompahgre Plateau of western Colorado and named *Ultrasaurus macintoshi* ("extreme lizard") in 1986. Estimates of its body length ranged up to 115 ft, and of its weight up to 209.4 tons. However, more detailed study of the incomplete skeleton shows that *Ultrasaurus* is just a large specimen of *Brachiosaurus altithorax*, measuring about 82 ft long and weighing 49.6–60.6 tons.

Fossilized footprints made by sauropod dinosaurs can also give estimates of size for animals that are not known from skeletons. Footprints of a dinosaur called *Breviparopus taghbaloutensis* from Morocco are over 3 ft 3 in long and may have been made by an animal weighing 55.1 tons. A similar body weight is estimated for tracks made by the brachiosaurid *Pleurocoelus* in Texas.

Diplodocids The longest dinosaur known from a complete skeleton is *Diplodocus carnegii* ("double beam"). The remains were found in Wyoming in 1899 and pieced together at the Carnegie Museum, Pittsburgh, PA. The skeleton was so spectacular that casts were requested by other museums, and copies may be seen in London, Great Britain, La Plata, Argentina, Washington, D.C., Frankfurt, Germany and Paris, France. *Diplodocus* was 87½ ft long and weighed 6.4–20.4 tons, the higher estimates being the most likely. Hence, *Diplodocus* was relatively light for its body length, but much of that length was made up of an extremely long whip-like tail.

An even longer diplodocid has been named *Supersaurus vivianae* ("super lizard") in 1986. It was found in the same area of Colorado as *Ultrasaurus*. The length has been estimated as up to 138 ft and the weight as about 55.12 tons, but the skeleton is very incomplete.

In 1985 the remains of another huge diplodocid were excavated from a site near Albuquerque, NM. According to Dr David Gillette at the Division of State History, UT, this giant sauropod, informally named *Seismosaurus* ("earthquake lizard"), measured an estimated 128–154 ft in total length and weighed at least 50 tons. These estimates were given by Gillette in 1989, based on the assumption that *Seismosaurus* was 50–80 percent longer than *Diplodocus*, based on comparisons of individual bones.

Titanosaurids Several titanosaurids ("giant lizards") have also been described as super-sized, and *Antarctosaurus giganteus* ("Antarctic lizard") from Argentina and India probably rivaled the brachiosaurids in terms of weight. Estimates range from 44.1–88.2 tons, with the lower figures being most likely. The skeletons of titanosaurs are generally very incomplete, but there are several thigh bones from Argentina that measure 7½–7¾ ft in length.

Size limits The largest-known sauropods appear to have weighed 55–110 tons, but this does not necessarily represent the ultimate weight limit for a land vertebrate. Theoretical calculations suggest that some dinosaurs approached the maximum body weight possible for a terrestrial animal, namely 132 tons. At weights greater than this, the legs would have to be so massive to support the bulk that the dinosaur could not have moved!

Longest Until very recently the longest dinosaurs on record were believed to be certain attenuated diplodocids. A complete reconstruction of a *Diplodocus carnegii* in the Carnegie Museum of Natural History, Pittsburgh, PA measures 87 ft 6 in in total length—head and body 22 ft, body 15 ft, tail 50 ft 6 in—and has a mounted height of 11 ft 9 in at at the pelvis, the highest point of the body. But, relatively speaking, this giant was a lightweight, weighing an estimated 6.4–20.4 tons.

By comparison, *Supersaurus vivianae* (see Diplodocids) measured an estimated 138 ft in total length, while *Breviparopus* (See Brachiosaurids) attained the astonishing length of 157 ft—making it the longest vertebrate on record. Note, however, that this estimate is based on footprints only.

Largest land predator The largest flesh-eating dinosaur recorded so far is *Tyrannosaurus rex* ("king tyrant lizard"). Seventy million years ago it reigned over what are now the states of Montana, Wyoming and Texas and the provinces of Alberta and Saskatchewan, Canada. A composite skeleton of this nightmarish beast in the American Museum of Natural History, New York City has a bipedal height of 18 ft 6 in (total length 34 ft 9 in), and this animal is estimated to have weighed 6.3 tons, or close to 7.7 tons with large fat reserves. This individual may not, however, have been fully mature, as suggested by the upper jawbone (maxilla) of another *Tyrannosaurus* in the Museum of Paleontology at the University of California,

Most brainless
Stegosaurus ("plated lizard"), which roamed across Colorado, Oklahoma, Utah and Wyoming about 150 million years ago, measured up to 30 ft in total length but had a walnut-sized brain weighing only 2½ oz. This represented 0.004 of 1 percent of its computed body weight of 1.9 tons (compare with 0.074 of 1 percent for an elephant and 1.88 percent for a human).

EXTINCT ANIMALS

Earliest mammals The first true mammals appeared about 220 million years ago during the Late Triassic and by the end of the Cretaceous period, 65 million years ago, the first primate, *Purgatorius*, had emerged. This creature was similar in appearance to modern tree shrews of the order Scandentia.

Berkeley which is 29 percent longer (35.4 in) than the example in the American Museum of Natural History and indicates a 44-ft theropod weighing up to 13.2 tons.

Its Mongolian relative *Tarbosaurus bataar* ("alarming lizard"), known from 13 skeletons, had a longer skull than *Tyrannosaurus* but was less heavily built. It measured 33–46 ft in total length. *Dynamosaurus imperiosus* ("dynamic lizard") of Shandong Province, China was similar in size, measuring up to 46 ft overall (bipedal length 20 ft), but these tyrannosaurids were not as heavily built as their North American relative.

Allosaurs Some of the allosaurs ("other lizards") of North America, Africa, Australia and China also reached exceptional sizes, and one individual excavated near Kenton, OK in 1934 measured 42 ft in total length and had a bipedal height of 16 ft. This specimen was more massively built than the tyrannosaurids and was named *Saurophagus maximus* ("lizard eater"). Later, however, the bones were reexamined and found to be those of another large allosaur, *Acrocanthosaurus* ("very spiky reptile"), which measured about 39 ft overall. Seven skeletons of this terrifying carnivore have been found in Oklahoma since 1950.

Recent collections of the allosaur *Epanterias amplexus* from Masonville, CO have suggested to Dr Robert Bakker of the University of Colorado that this theropod reached a length of 50 ft and a weight of 4.4 tons, but remains are incomplete.

Another allosaur from China, *Yangchuanosaurus magnus*, has been described as the largest non-tyrannosaurid carnosaur so far recorded. Its skull was more massive than that of *Tyrannosaurus rex* and this species is thought to have measured over 34 ft in length overall.

Spinosaurus aegyptiacus ("thorn lizard") of Niger and Egypt was even longer than the largest-known tyrannosaurid, with a total length of *c.* 49 ft, and it combined its tremendous length with 5-ft-3-in-long bladelike spines running down its back, but it was a much more lightly built theropod than the tyrannosaurids and probably did not exceed 4.4 tons.

Ornithomimosaurs Most of the ornithomimosaurs ("ostrich mimic lizards") were of modest size, but one giant from Mongolia, *Deinocheirus mirificus* ("terrible hand"), is represented by a pair of arms each 8 ft long. These suggest a total body size of 24 ft or more.

The megalosaurids ("great lizards") also produced some enormous examples, including *Megalosaurus ingens* from the Tendaguru site in Tanzania, and *Bahariasaurus* from Egypt and Algeria, both of which were nearly as large as *Tyrannosaurus rex*.

Smallest The chicken-sized *Compsognathus* ("pretty jaw") of southern Germany and southeast France, and an undescribed plant-eating fabrosaurid from Colorado, measured 29.5 in from the snout to the tip of the tail and weighed about 15 lb.

Juvenile dinosaurs are even smaller: a *Psittacosaurus* from the Late Cretaceous of Mongolia was smaller than a pigeon (9–10 in long); a *Mussaurus* from the Late Triassic of Argentina was the size of a kitten (8 in long); and an embryo of *Orodromeus*, reported in 1988 from the Late Cretaceous of Montana, still in its egg, was only 4 in long.

Longest neck The sauropod *Mamenchisaurus* ("mamenchi lizard") of the Late Jurassic of Sichuan, China had the longest neck of any animal that has ever lived. It measured 36 ft—half the total length of the dinosaur.

Longest tracks In 1983 a series of four *Apatosaurus* (= *Brontosaurus*) tracks that ran parallel for a distance of over 705 ft were recorded from 145-million-year-old Morrison strata in southeast Colorado.

Fastest Tracks can be used to estimate dinosaur speeds, and one from the Late Morrison of Texas discovered in 1981 indicated that a carnivorous dinosaur had been moving at 25 mph. Some ornithomimids (see above) were even faster, and the large-brained, 220-lb *Dromiceiomimus* ("emu mimic lizard") of the Late Cretaceous of Alberta, Canada could probably outsprint an ostrich, which has a top speed of 40 mph.

Largest footprints In 1932 the gigantic footprints of a large bipedal hadrosaurid ("duckbill") measuring 53½ in in length and 31.8 in wide were discovered in Salt Lake City, UT, and other reports from Colorado and Utah refer to footprints 37.4–39.4 in wide. Footprints attributed to the largest brachiosaurids also range up to 39.3 in wide for the hind feet.

Largest eggs The largest-known dinosaur eggs are those of *Hypselosaurus priscus* ("high ridge lizard"), a 40-ft-long titanosaurid that lived about 80 million years ago. Examples found in the Durance valley near Aix-en-Provence, France in October 1961 would have had, uncrushed, a length of 12 in and a diameter of 10 in (capacity 5.8 pt).

Largest claws The therizinosaurids ("scythe lizards") from the Late Cretaceous of the Nemegt Basin, southern Mongolia, had the largest claws of any known animal, and in the case of *Therizinosaurus cheloniformis* measured up to 36 in around the outer curve (compare with 8 in for *T. rex*). It has been suggested that these sickle claws were designed for grasping and tearing apart large victims, but this creature had a feeble skull partially or entirely lacking teeth and probably lived on termites.

Largest skull The skulls of the long-frilled ceratopsids were the largest of all known land animals and culminated in the long-frilled *Torosaurus sp.* ("piercing lizard"). This herbivore, which measured *c.* 25 ft in total length and weighed up to 8.8 tons, had a skull measuring up to 9 ft 10 in in length (including fringe) and weighing up to 2.2 tons. It ranged from Montana to Texas.

Earliest bird The earliest known fossil bird was the toothed, reptilelike *Archeopteryx lithographica*, which appeared *c.* 175 million years ago. Remains have been found in Upper Jurassic deposits in Bavaria, Germany.

Despite its birdlike skull, this crow-sized animal shared many anatomical features with some of the many smaller bidepal dinosaurs. Its skeletal structure suggests that it glided rather than flew, but the presence of feathers also indicates that, like modern birds, *Archeopteryx* may have been warm-blooded.

Largest bird The largest prehistoric bird was the flightless *Dromornis stirtoni*, a huge emulike creature that lived in central Australia 11 million years ago. Fossil leg bones found near Alice Springs in 1974 indicate that the bird must have stood *c.* 10 ft tall and weighed about 1,100 lb.

The giant moa *Dinornis maximus* of New Zealand was even taller, attaining a maximum height of 12 ft, but it weighed only about 500 lb.

Flying bird The largest-known flying bird was the giant teratorn (*Argentavis magnificens*), which lived in Argentina about 6 million years ago. Fossil remains discovered at a site 100 miles west of Buenos Aires, Argentina in 1979 indicate that this gigantic vulture had a wingspan of 23–25 ft and weighed about 265 lb.

Seabird In 1987 an expedition from the Charleston Museum of South Carolina discovered the fossil remains of a 30-million-year-old giant seabird, *Pseudodontornis sp.*, a relative of pelicans and cormorants. It had a wingspan of about 19 ft and weighed *c.* 90 lb.

Largest flying creature The largest-ever flying creature was the pterosaur *Quetzalcoatlus northropi* ("feathered serpent"). About 70 million years ago it soared over what is now Texas, Wyoming and New Jersey; Alberta, Canada; and Senegal and Jordan. Partial remains discovered in Big Bend National Park, TX in 1971 indicate that this reptile must have had a wingspan of 36–39 ft and weighed about 250 lb.

Largest marine reptile *Kronosaurus queenslandicus*, a short-necked pliosaur from the Early Cretaceous (135 million years ago) of Australia, measured up to 50 ft in length and had a 10-ft-long skull containing 80 massive teeth.

Largest crocodile The largest-known crocodile was the euschian *Deinosuchus riograndensis* ("terrible crocodile"), which lived in the lakes and swamps of what is now Texas about 75 million years ago. Fragmentary remains discovered in Big Bend National Park, TX indicate a hypothetical length of 52 ft 6 in, compared with the 50 ft of the huge gharial *Rhamphosuchus* of northern India (2 million years ago) and the 46 ft of *Sarcosuchus imperator* of Niger.

Largest chelonian The largest prehistoric chelonian was *Stupendemys geographicus*, a pelomedusid turtle that lived about 5 million years ago. Fossil remains discovered by Harvard University paleontologists in northern Venezuela in 1972 indicate that this turtle had a carapace (shell) measuring 7 ft 2 in–7 ft 6½ in in mid-line length, measured 9 ft 10 in in overall length, and had a computed weight of 4,500 lb when alive.

Largest tortoise The largest prehistoric tortoise was probably *Geochelone* (= *Colossochelys*) *atlas*, which lived in what is now northern India, Myanmar (formerly Burma), Java, the Celebes and Timor, about 2 million years ago. In 1923 the fossil remains of a specimen with a carapace 5 ft 11 in long (7 ft 4 in over the curve) and 2 ft 11 in high were discovered near Chandigarh in the Siwalik Hills, India. This animal had a total length of 8 ft and is computed to have weighed 2,100 lb when it was alive.

Longest snake The longest prehistoric snake was the python-like *Gigantophis garstini*, which inhabited what is now Egypt about 38 million years ago. Parts of a spinal column and a small piece of jaw discovered at Fayum in the Western Desert indicate a length of about 37 ft. Another huge fossil snake from the Middle Eocene in Mali was originally credited with a length of 75 ft 6 in, but this measurement was overestimated. It was actually 30 ft.

Largest amphibian The largest amphibian ever recorded was the gharial-like *Prionosuchus plummeri*, which lived 270 million years ago. Fragmented remains were discovered in northern Brazil in 1972. These were reported in 1991 and the total body length was estimated at 30 ft based on a 5-ft-3-in-long skull.

Largest fish No prehistoric fish larger than living species has yet been discovered. The claim, based on ratios from fossil teeth, that the great shark *Carcharodon megalodon*, which abounded in Miocene seas some 15 million years ago, measured 80 ft in length, has now been shown to be in error. Modern estimates suggest that this shark did not exceed 43 ft.

Largest insect The largest prehistoric insect was the dragonfly *Meganeura monyi*, which lived about 300 million years ago. Fossil remains (impressions of wings) discovered at Commentry, France indicate a wing extending up to 27½ in.

Largest land mammal The largest land mammal ever recorded was *Paraceratherium* (= *Baluchitherium*), a long-necked, hornless rhinocerotid which roamed across western Asia and Europe (Yugoslavia) about 35 million years ago. A restoration in the American Museum of Natural History, New York City measures 17 ft 9 in to the top of the shoulder hump and 37 ft in total length, and this particular specimen must have weighed about 22 tons. The bones of this gigantic browser were first discovered in the Bugti Hills of Baluchistan, Pakistan in 1907–1908.

Largest marine mammal The serpentine *Basilosaurus* (*Zeuglodon*) *cetoides*, which swam in the seas which covered modern-day Arkansas and Alabama 50 million years ago, measured up to 70 ft in length.

Largest mammoth The largest prehistoric elephant was the steppe mammoth (*Mammuthus* [*Parelephas*] *trogontherii*), which, one million years ago, roamed what is now central Europe. A fragmentary skeleton found in Mosbach, Germany indicates a shoulder height of 14 ft 9 in.

Largest primate The largest-known primate was *Gigantopithecus* of the Middle Pleistocene in what is now northern Vietnam and southern China. Males would have stood an estimated 9 ft tall and weighed about 600 lb. It is risky, however, to correlate tooth size and jaw depth of primates with their height and body weight, and *Gigantopithecus* may have had a disproportionately large head, jaws and teeth in relation to body size. The only remains discovered so far are three partial lower jaws and more than 1,000 teeth.

Antlers The prehistoric giant deer (*Megaloceros giganteus*), which lived in northern Europe and northern Asia as recently as 8000 B.C., had the longest horns of any known animal. One specimen recovered from an Irish bog had greatly palmated antlers measuring 14 ft across, which corresponds to a shoulder height of 6 ft and a weight of 1,100 lb.

Tusks The longest tusks of any prehistoric animal were those of the straight-tusked elephant (*Paleoloxodon antiquus germanicus*), which lived in northern Germany *c.* 300,000 years ago. The average length for tusks of adult bulls was 16 ft 5 in.

A single tusk of a woolly mammoth (*Mammuthus primigenius*) preserved in the Franzens Museum at Brno, Czechoslovakia measures 16 ft 5½ in along the outside curve.

In about August 1933 a single tusk of an imperial mammoth (*Mammuthus imperator*) measuring at least 16 ft (anterior end missing) was unearthed near Post, TX. In 1934 this tusk was presented to the American Museum of Natural History, New York City.

The heaviest single fossil tusk on record weighed 330 lb with a maximum circumference of 35 in and is now preserved in the Museo Civico di Storia Naturale, Milan, Italy. The specimen, which is in two pieces, measures 11 ft 9 in in length.

The heaviest recorded fossil tusks are a pair belonging to a 13-ft-4-in-tall Columbian mammoth (*Mammuthus columbi*) in the State Museum, Lincoln, NE. The specimens, which have a combined weight of 498 lb and measure 13 ft 9 in and 13 ft 7 in respectively, were found near Campbell, NE in April 1915.

Plant Kingdom Plantea

GENERAL RECORDS

Oldest "King Clone," the oldest-known clone of the creosote plant (*Larrea tridentata*), found in southwest California, was estimated in February 1980 by Prof. Frank C. Vasek to be 11,700 years old. It is possible that crustose lichens in excess of 19.6 in in diameter may be as old. In 1981 it was estimated that Antarctic lichens of more than 3.9 in in diameter are at least 10,000 years old.

Rarest Plants thought to be extinct are rediscovered each year, and there are thus many plants of which specimens are known in only a single locality. The last surviving specimen (a female) of the cycad *Encephalartos woodii*, a palmlike tropical plant of a group known to have existed for 65–225 million years, is held at the Royal Botanic Gardens, Kew, Great Britain. It is possible that this plant is a hybrid of the specimen *Encephalartos altensteinii*, also at Kew. (See Oldest pot plant.)

Pennantia baylisiana, a tree found in 1945 on Three Kings Island off New Zealand, also only exists as a female and cannot bear fruit.

In May 1983 it was reported that there was a sole surviving specimen of the lady's slipper orchid (*Cypripedium calceolus*) in Britain.

Northernmost The yellow poppy (*Papaver radicatum*) and the Arctic

Most valuable flower

In 1954 the Burpee Co. $10,000 prize for the first all-white marigold was won on 12 Aug 1975 by Alice Vonk of Sully, IA.

Longest daisy chain

The longest daisy chain measured 6,980 ft 7 in and was made in 7 hr by villagers of Good Easter, Great Britain on 27 May 1985. The team is limited to 16.

■ **Largest chrysanthemum**

Grown by François Santini of Indre-et-Loire, France, this giant stands 8 ft 2 1/2 in tall and has 4,041 blooms. (Photo: Michael Vohmann)

willow (*Salix arctica*) survive, the latter in an extremely stunted form, on the northernmost land 83° N at Lat.

Southernmost Lichens resembling *Rhinodina frigida* have been found in Moraine Canyon at Lat. 86°09′S, Long. 157°30′W in 1971 and in the Horlick Mountain area, Antarctica at 86°09′S 131°14′W in 1965.

The southernmost recorded flowering plant is the Antarctic hair grass (*Deschampsia antarctica*), which was found at Lat. 68° 21′ S on Refuge Island, Antarctica on 11 Mar 1981.

Highest The greatest certain altitude at which any flowering plants have been found is 21,000 ft on Kamet (25,447 ft) by N.D. Jayal in 1955. They were *Ermania himalayensis* and *Ranunculus lobatus*.

Roots The greatest reported depth to which roots have penetrated is an estimated 400 ft for a wild fig tree at Echo Caves, near Ohrigstad, Transvaal, South Africa. An elm tree root of at least 360 ft was reported from Auchencraig, Great Britain c. 1950. A single winter rye plant (*Secale cereale*) has been shown to produce 387 miles of roots in 1.83 ft³ of earth.

Worst weeds The most intransigent weed is the mat-forming water weed *Salvinia auriculata*, found in Africa. It was detected when Lake Kariba, which straddles the border of Zimbabwe and Zambia, was filled in May 1959, and within 11 months it had choked an area of 77 miles², rising to 387 miles² by 1963.

The world's worst land weeds are purple nut sedge, Bermuda grass, barnyard grass, jungle rice, goose grass

Johnson grass, Guinea grass, Cogon grass and lantana.

United States The most damaging and widespread weed in America is the purple nutsedge (*Cyperus rotundas*), primarily found in the southern states. Its seeds can germinate at 95°F and will withstand temperatures of −68°F for two hours and remain viable. The purple nutsedge will grow to 39 in in height and speeds underground through its system of rhyzones and tubers. It remains dormant underground in extreme weather conditions.

Tallest weeds The tallest weed in the United States is the Melaleuca tree (*Melaleuca quinquenervia*), introduced to Australia in 1900. Growing to an average of 39 ft, the weed has infested 3.7 million acres of the 4.7 million acres of Florida wetlands. Very dense and resistant to fire, the crowns are destroyed but the stem survives. It is a fire hazard in that it contains "essential" petroleums that spread fire quickly.

Most spreading The greatest area covered by a single clonal growth is that of the wild box huckleberry (*Gaylussacia brachyera*), a mat-forming evergreen shrub first reported in 1796. A colony covering about 100 acres was found on 18 Jul 1920 near the Juniata River, PA. It has been estimated that this colony began 13,000 years ago.

Smallest flowering and fruiting The floating, flowering aquatic duckweed (*Wolffia angusta*) of Australia, described in 1980, is only 0.0236 in long and 0.0129 in wide. It weighs about 1/100,000 oz and its fruit, which resembles a minuscule fig, weighs 400,000 to the oz.

United States The smallest plant regularly flowering in the United States is *Wolffia globosa*, which is found in the San Joaquin Valley, central California, and rivers draining the Sierra Nevada mountains. The plant weighs about 150 micrograms, and is listed as 0.015 in to 0.027 in length and 0.011 in width.

Fastest-growing The case of a *Hesperoyucca whipplei* of the family Liliaceae growing 12 ft in 14 days was reported from Tresco Abbey, Isles of Scilly, Great Britain in July 1978.

Slowest-flowering The slowest-flowering of all plants is the rare *Puya raimondii*, the largest of all herbs, discovered at 13,000 ft in Bolivia in 1870. The panicle emerges after about 80–150 years of the plant's life. It then dies. One planted near sea level at the University of California's Botanical Garden, Berkeley in 1958 grew to 25 ft and bloomed as early as August 1986 after only 28 years. (See also Largest flowers.)

Oldest pot plant The world's oldest, and probably rarest, pot plant is the single cycad *Encephalartos altensteinii* brought from South Africa in 1775 and now housed at the Royal Botanic Gardens Kew, Great Britain. (See Rarest plant.)

Biggest collection By October 1988 Dr Julian A. Steyermark (d. 15 Oct 1988) of the Missouri Botanical Garden, St Louis, MO had made an unrivalled total of 138,000 collections, 132,500 of which belonged to his individual continuous numbered series, as opposed to specimens collected jointly with other botanists.

Biggest aspidistra The biggest aspidistra in the world measures 56 in and belongs to Cliff Evans of Kiora, Moruya, New South Wales, Australia.

Earliest flower A flower believed to be 120 million years old was identified in 1989 by Dr Leo Hickey and Dr David Taylor of Yale University, CT from a fossil discovered near Melbourne, Victoria, Australia. The flowering angiosperm, which resembles a modern black pepper plant, had two leaves and one flower and is known as the Koonwarra plant.

United States The oldest fossil of a flowering plant with palmlike imprints in America was found in Colorado in 1953 and dated about 65 million years old.

Largest cactus The largest of all cacti is the saguaro (*Cereus giganteus* or *Carnegiea gigantea*), found in Arizona, southeastern California and Sonora, Mexico. The green fluted column is surmounted by candelabra-like branches rising to a height of 57 ft 11 ¾ in in the case of a specimen discovered in the Maricopa Mountains, 11 miles east of Gila Bend, AZ on 17 Jan 1988 by J.D. and R.M. Fairfield and R.N. and D.J. Wells. The plants have waxy white blooms that are followed by edible crimson fruit.

An armless cactus 78 ft in height was measured in April 1978 by Hube Yates in Cave Creek, AZ. It was toppled in a windstorm in July 1986 at an estimated age of 150 years.

Mosses The tallest variety of moss is the Australian species *Dawsonia Superba*, which can reach a height of 12 in. The smallest variety of moss is the microscopic

pygmy moss (*Ephemerum*) and the longest is the brook moss (*Fontinalis*), which forms streamers up to 3 ft long in flowing water.

SEAWEED

Longest The longest species of seaweed is the Pacific giant kelp (*Macrocystis pyrifera*), which, although it does not exceed 215 ft in length, can grow 18 in in a day.

Deepest The greatest depth at which plant life has been found is 884 ft by Mark and Diane Littler off San Salvadore Island, Bahamas in October 1984. These maroon-colored algae survived although 99.9995 percent of sunlight was filtered out.

VINES AND VINEYARDS

Largest vine This was planted in 1842 at Carpinteria, CA. By 1900 it was yielding more than 9.9 tons of grapes in some years, and averaged 7.7 tons per year until it died in 1920. A single bunch of grapes (Red Thompson seedless) of 20 lb 11½ oz was weighed in Santiago, Chile in May 1984.

Largest vineyard The world's largest vineyard extends over the Mediterranean slopes between the Pyrenees and the Rhône in the *départements* Gard, Hérault, Aude and Pyrénées-Orientales. It covers an area of 2,075,685 acres, 52.3 percent of which is *monoculture viticole*.

United States The largest continuous vineyard in the United States is Minor Thornton Ranch in Fresno, CA. Owned by the Golden State Vintners Corp., the vineyard covers 5,200 acres and produces 6,500 tons of grapes each year.

Most northerly vineyard There is a vineyard at Sabile, Latvia, USSR is just north of Lat. 57° N.

Most southerly vineyard The most southerly commercial vineyards are to be found in central Otago, South Island, New Zealand, south of Lat. 45° S. Renton Burgess Vineyard, south of Alexandra, South Island, is at Lat. 44° 36′ S.

BLOOMS AND FLOWERS

Largest The largest of all blooms are those of the parasitic stinking corpse lily (*Rafflesia arnoldii*), which measure up to 3 ft across and ¾ in thick, and attain a weight of 15 lb. The plants attach themselves to the cissus vines in the jungle of southeast Asia. True to its name, the plant has an extremely offensive scent.

Inflorescence The largest-known inflorescence (as distinct from the largest of all blooms) is that of *Puya raimondii*, a rare Bolivian monocarpic member of the Bromeliaceae family. Its erect panicle (diameter 8 ft) emerges to a height of 35 ft and each of these bears up to 8,000 white blooms. (See also Slowest-flowering plant.) The flower-spike of an agave measured in Berkeley, CA in 1974 was found to be 52 ft long.

Blossoming plant The giant Chinese wisteria (*Wisteria sinensis*) at Sierra Madre, CA was planted in 1892 and now has branches 500 ft long. It covers nearly 1 acre, weighs 248 tons and has an estimated 1.5 million blossoms during its blos-

FRUIT, VEGETABLES, FLOWERS
WORLD RECORDS

In the interest of fairness and to minimize the risk of mistakes being made, all plants should, where possible, be entered in official international, national or local garden contests. Only produce grown primarily for human consumption will be considered for publication. The assistance of *Garden News* and the World Pumpkin Confederation is gratefully acknowledged.

TYPE	SIZE	GROWER	LOCATION	YEAR
APPLE	3 lb 1 oz	V. Loveridge	Ross-on-Wye, Great Britain	1965
BROAD BEAN	23 ⅜ in	T. Currie	Jedburgh, Great Britain	1963
	23 ⅜ in	M. Adrian	Irvine, Great Britain	1982
CABBAGE	124 lb	B. Lavery	Llanharry, Great Britain	1989
CABBAGE, RED[1]	42 lb	R. Straw	Staveley, Great Britain	1925
CANTALOUPE	55 lb	G. Daughtridge	Rocky Mount, NC	1982
CARROT	15 lb 7 oz	I. Scott	Nelson, New Zealand	1978
CELERY	46 lb 1 oz	B. Lavery	Llanharry, Great Britain	1990
CHRYSANTHEMUM	8 ft 2 ½ in	F. Santini	Indre-et-Loire, France	1988
CUCUMBER[2]	17 lb 13 ½oz	P. Vowles	Llanharry, Great Britain	1990
DAHLIA	25 ft 7 in	R. Blythe	Nannup, Western Australia	1990
GARLIC[3]	2 lb 10 oz	R. Kirkpatrick	Eureka, CA	1985
GRAPEFRUIT	6 lb 8 ½oz	J. and A. Sosnow	Tucson, AZ	1984
LEEK (pot)	12 lb 2 oz	P. Harrigan	Linton, Great Britain	1987
LEMON	8 lb 8 oz	C. and D. Knutzen	Whittier, CA	1983
MARROW	108 lb 2 oz	B. Lavery	Llanharry, Great Britain	1990
MELON	59 lb 8 oz	B. Rogerson	Robersonville, NC	1990
ONION	10 lb 14 oz	V. Throup	Silsden, Great Britain	1990
PARSNIP	171 ¾ in	B. Lavery	Llanharry, Great Britain	1990
PETUNIA	13 ft 8 in	B. Lawrence	Windham, NY	1985
PHILODENDRON	1,114 ft	F. Francis	University of Massachusetts	1984
PINEAPPLE[4]	17 lb 8 oz	Dole Philippines Inc.	South Cotabato, Philippines	1984
POTATO	7 lb 1 oz	J. East	Spalding, Great Britain	1963
	7 lb 1 oz	J. Busby	Atherstone, Great Britain	1982
PUMPKIN	816 lb 8 oz	E. and R. Gancarz	Wrightstown, NJ	1990
RADISH	28 lb 1 oz	B. Lavery	Llanharry, Great Britain	1990
RHUBARB	5 lb 14 oz	E. Stone	East Woodyates, Great Britain	1985
RUNNER BEAN	39 ½ in	J. Taylor	Shifnal, Great Britain	1986
RUTABAGA	48 lb 12 oz	A. Foster	Alnwick, Great Britain	1980
SQUASH	821 lb	L. Stellpflug	Rush, NY	1990
STRAWBERRY	8.17 oz	G. Anderson	Folkestone, Great Britain	1983
SUNFLOWER[5]	25 ft 5 ½ in	M. Heijms	Oirschot, Netherlands	1986
TOMATO	7 lb 12 oz	G. Graham	Edmond, OK	1986
TOMATO PLANT[6]	53 ft 6 in	G. Graham	Edmond, OK	1985
WATERMELON[7]	262 lb	B. Carson	Arrington, TN	1990
ZUCCHINI	64 lb 8 oz	B. Lavery	Llanharry, Great Britain	1990

US NATIONAL RECORDS

APPLE	17 ½ in	Mr & Mrs H. Spider	Arcanum, OH	1985
BEET	45 ½lb	R. Meyer	Brawley, CA	1984
COLLARD	35 ft tall	B. Rackley	Rocky Mount, NC	1980
CORN	31 ft high	D. Radda	Washington, IA	1946
DAHLIA	16 ft 5 in	S. & P Barnes	Chattahoochee, FL	1982
EGGPLANT	5 lb 5.4 oz	J. & J Charles	Summerville, SC	1984
GOURD	93 ½ in long	B.W. Saylor	Licking, MT	1986
GOURD (weight)[8]	78 lb	L. Childers	Stinesville, IN	1986
KOHLRABI	36 lb	E. Krejci	Mt Clemens, MI	1979
LIMA BEAN	14 in	N. McCoy	Hubert, NC	1979
OKRA STALK[9]	17 ft 6 ¼ in	C. H. Wilber	Crane Hill, AL	1983
ONION	7 ½ lb	N. W. Hope	Tempe, AZ	1984
PEANUT	3 ¹¹/₁₆ in	B. Senkbeil	Sylvester, GA	1987
PEPPER	13 ½ in	J. Rutherford	Hatch, NM	1975
PEPPER PLANT	8 ft 1 in	R. Allen	Gillespie, IL	1987
RUTABAGA[10]	39 lb	R. & J. Towns	Gresgham, OR	1979
SWEET POTATO	40 ¾ b	O. Harrison	Kite, GA	1982
TOMATO (CHERRY)	28 ft 7 in	C. H. Wilber	Crane Hill, AL	1985
ZUCCHINI[11]	19.92 lb	W. C. Nicholas	Hatley, WI	1984

[1] The Swalwell, County Durham red cabbage of 1865, grown by William Collingwood (d. 8 Oct 1867), reputedly weighed 123 lb and had a circumference of 259 in. [2] A Vietnamese variety 6 ft long was reported by L. Szabo of Debrecen, Hungary in September 1976. The giant cucumbers grown by Eileen Chappel, which were featured for several years, have subsequently been identified as gourds. [3] Elephant garlic variety. The garlic had a circumference of 18 ½ in. [4] Pineapples weighing up to 28 lb 11 oz were reported from Tarauaca, Brazil in 1978. [5] A sunflower with a head measuring 32 ¼ in in diameter was grown by Emily Martin of Maple Ridge, British Columbia, Canada in September 1983. A fully mature sunflower measuring just 2 ⅕ in was grown by Michael Lenke of Lake Oswego, OR in 1985 using a patented bonsai technique. [6] It was reported at the Tsukuba Science Expo Center, Japan on 28 Feb 1988 that a single plant produced 16,897 tomatoes. [7] Bill Rogerson of Robersonville, NC grew a watermelon which weighed 279 lb on 3 Oct 1988, but this was not measured under competition conditions.. [8] A gourd weighing 196 lb was grown in Herringfleet, Great Britain by J. Leather in 1846. [9] This record was tied in 1986 by Buddy and Evelyn Crosby of Brooksville, FL. [10] A rutabaga weighing 51 lb was reported from Alaska in 1981, but this has not been substantiated. [11] A specimen weighing 36 lb 3 oz was grown by M. M. Ricci of Montreal, Canada in 1982.

Apple peeling
The longest single unbroken apple peel on record is one of 172 ft 4 in, peeled by Kathy Wafler of Wolcott, NY in 11 hr 30 min at Long Ridge Mall, Rochester, NY on 16 Oct 1976. The apple weighed 20 oz.

Apple picking
The greatest recorded performance is 15,830 lb picked in 8 hr by George Adrian of Indianapolis, IN on 23 Sep 1980.

Cucumber slicing
Norman Johnson of Blackpool College, Lancashire, Great Britain set a record of 13.4 sec for slicing a 12-in cucumber, 1½ in in diameter, at 22 slices to the inch (total 264 slices) at West Deutscher Rundfunk in Cologne, Germany on 3 Apr 1983.

Potato peeling
The greatest quantity of potatoes peeled by five people to an institutional cookery standard with standard kitchen knives in 45 min is 830 lb 11 oz (net) by Lia Sombroek, Marlene Guiamo, Ria Grol, Yvonne Renting and Nguyet Nguyen at Emmeloord, Netherlands on 15 Sep 1990.

■ **Longest seaweed**
The Pacific giant kelp (Macrocystis pyrifera) can grow to a length of 215 ft. Its distribution is limited because it only reproduces at temperatures below 64–68°F, although it can grow 18 in in one day. (Photo: Bruce Coleman)

soming period of five weeks, when up to 30,000 people pay admission to visit it.

Largest arrangement The largest arrangement of a single variety of flower was made by Johan Weisz, floral designer of Amsterdam, and 15 assistants at the City Hall, Aalsmeer, the Netherlands from 23–25 Sep 1986. It consisted of 35,000 "Zurella" roses and measured 71 ft 6 in in length, 25 ft 2 in in width, and 24 ft 11 in high.

Largest bouquet Thirty-six people took 335 hr to make a bouquet 36 ft 10 in high, consisting of 9,299 flowers, at Annecy, France on 19 Sep 1986.

Largest wreath A wreath made by the Clemsonville Christmas Tree Farm of Union Bridge, MD in December 1989 measured 116 ft in diameter and weighed 8,165 lb.

Largest rhododendron Examples of the scarlet *Rhododendron arboreum* reach a height of 65 ft on Mt Japfu, Nagaland, India. The cross-section of the trunk of a *Rhododendron giganteum*, reputedly 90 ft high, from Yunnan, China, is preserved at Inverewe Gardens, Highland, Great Britain.

Largest rose tree A Lady Banks rose tree at Tombstone, AZ has a trunk 40 in thick, stands 9 ft high and covers an area of 5,380 ft². It is supported by 68 posts and several thousand feet of piping, which enables 150 people to be seated under the arbor. The cutting came from Scotland in 1884.

ORCHIDS

Tallest The largest of all orchids is *Grammatophyllum speciosum*, a native of Malaysia. Specimens have been recorded up to 25 ft in height.

United States The tallest of all American orchids is the *Eulophia ecristata*, with a recorded height of 5.6 ft. There are five species of vanilla orchids that are vines and can spread to almost any length depending on the environment. These include *Phaeantha, Planifolia, Inodora, Dilliana,* and *Barbellata.* These orchids root in the ground and will grow in any direction over their surroundings.

Largest flower The largest orchid flower is that of *Phragmipedium caudatum*, found in tropical areas of America. Its petals grow up to 18 in long, giving it a maximum diameter of 3 ft. The flower is, however, much less bulky than that of the stinking corpse lily. (See Largest bloom.)

A height of 49 ft has been recorded for *Galeola foliata*, a saprophyte of the vanilla family. It grows in the decaying rain forests of Queensland, Australia, but is not freestanding.

United States The largest flowering orchid in America is the yellow ladyslipper (*Cypripedium calceolus*) of the Pubsecens variety. Its petals grow up to 7 in long.

Smallest The smallest orchid is *Platystele jungermannoides*, found in Central America. Its flowers are just 0.04 in in diameter.

United States The smallest orchid is *Lepanthopsis melanantha*, with a petal spread of 0.02 in and a maximum height of 1.6 in.

Most expensive The highest price ever paid for an orchid is 1,150 guineas ($5,868), paid by Baron Schröder to Sanders of St Albans, Great Britain for an *Odontoglossum crispum* (variety *pittianum*) at an auction by Protheroe & Morris of Bow Lane, London, Great Britain on 22 Mar 1906. A cymbidium orchid called Rosanna Pinkiewas sold in the United States for $4,500 in 1952.

FRUITS AND VEGETABLES

Most nutritive An analysis of the 38 commonly eaten raw (as opposed to dried) fruits shows that the one with the highest caloric value is the avocado (*Persea americana*), with 741 calories per edible pound; it also contains vitamins A, C and E and 2.2 percent protein. Avocados probably originated in Central and South America.

Least nutritive That with the lowest caloric value is the cucumber (*Cucumis sativus*), with 73 cal/lb.

HERBS

Herbs are not botanically defined but

consist of plants whose leaves or roots are of culinary or medicinal value.

Most heavily consumed The most heavily consumed is coriander (*Coriandrum sativum*), which is used in curry powder, confections, bread and gin.

FERNS

Largest The largest of the more than 6,000 species of fern is the tree fern (*Alsophila excelsa*) of Norfolk Island in the South Pacific, which attains a height of up to 60 ft.

United States The highest in America is the giant fern (*Acrostichum danaeaefolium*) of the Gulf coast, which measures up to 16.4 ft. However, the bracken fern (*Pteridium aquilinum*) is the largest fern plant. It grows to a height of 4.9 ft above ground, but grows giant clones or stem systems underground that can reach up to a quarter of a mile. This fern is found throughout the United States.

Smallest The world's smallest ferns are *Hecistopteris pumila*, found in Central America, and *Azolla caroliniana*, which is native to the United States and has fronds as small as ½ in.

GRASSES

Commonest The world's commonest grass is Bermuda grass (*Cynodon dactylon*). The Callie hybrid, selected in 1966, grows as much as 6 in a day and stolons reach 18 ft in length.

United States The most common grasses in America include Kentucky Bluegrass (*Poapratensis*), Canada Bluegrass (*Poacompressa*), and annual brome grass (*Bromus tectorum*).

Fastest-growing Some species of the 45 genera of bamboo have been found to grow up to 36 in per day (0.00002 mph).

Tallest A thorny bamboo culm (*Bambusa arundinacea*) felled at Pattazhi, Travancore, India in November 1904 measured 121½ ft.

United States The tallest grass native to America is the giant cane (*Arundinaria gigantea*), which reaches a height of 30 ft.

Shortest In the United States, the shortest grass is false buffalo grass (*Munroa squarrosa*), which has a maximum growing height of 0.8 in, but on average the grass, which is found throughout the states, grows only to a height of 0.4 in.

LEAVES

Largest The largest leaves of any plant belong to the raffia palm (*Raphia raffia*) of the Mascarene Islands in the Indian Ocean, and the Amazonian bamboo palm (*R. toedigera*) of South America, whose leaf blades may measure up to 65 ft in length with petioles up to 13 ft.

The largest undivided leaf is that of *Alocasia macrorrhiza*, found in Sabah, Malaysia. A specimen found in 1966 was 9 ft 11 in long and 6 ft 3½ in wide, with a surface area of 34.12 ft². A specimen of the water lily *Victoria amazonica* (Longwood hybrid) on the grounds of the Stratford-upon-Avon Butterfly Farm, Warwickshire, Great Britain measured 8 ft in diameter on 2 Oct 1989.

United States The largest leaves to be found in outdoor plants in America are those of the climbing fern (*Lygodium japonicum*) of the Gulf coast with leaves of 23 ft.

Fourteen-leafed clover A fourteen-leafed white clover (*Trifolium repens*) was found by Randy Farland near Sioux Falls, SD on 16 Jun 1975. A fourteen-leafed red clover (*Trifolium pratense*) was reported by 12-year-old Paul Haizlip at Bellevue, WA on 22 Jun 1987.

SEEDS

Largest The largest seed in the world is that of the double coconut or coco de mer (*Lodoicea seychellarum*), the single-seeded fruit of which may weigh 40 lb. This grows only in the Seychelles in the Indian Ocean.

Smallest The smallest are those of epiphytic (nonparasitic plants growing on others) orchids, at 35 million/oz (compare with grass pollens at up to 6 billion grains/oz). A single plant of the American ragweed can generate 8 billion pollen grains in five hours.

Most viable The most conclusive claim for the viability of seeds is that made for the Arctic lupine (*Lupinus arcticus*) found in frozen silt at Miller Creek in the Yukon, Canada in July 1954 by Harold Schmidt. The seeds were germinated in 1966 and were radiocarbon dated to at least 8000 B.C., and more probably to 13,000 B.C.

TREES AND WOOD

Earliest The earliest species of tree still surviving is the Maiden-hair tree (*Ginkgo biloba*), of Zhexiang, China, which first appeared about 160 million years ago, during the Jurassic era. It has been grown since *c.* 1100 in Japan, where it was known as *ginkyō* ("silver apricot") and is now known as *icho*.

United States The oldest species is the bristlecone pine, which grows in the desert regions of South California and Nevada. The exact date of the oldest tree is not known; however, some living species are believed to be at least 4,000 years old.

Oldest The oldest recorded tree was a bristlecone pine (*Pinus longaeva*) designated WPN-114, which grew at 10,750 ft above sea level on the northeast face of Mt Wheeler, NV. It was found to be 5,100 years old.

The oldest known *living* tree is the bristlecone pine named Methuselah, growing at 10,000 ft on the California side of the White Mountains, confirmed as 4,700 years old. In March 1974 it was reported that this tree had produced 48 live seedlings. Dendrochronologists estimate the *potential* life span of a bristlecone pine at nearly 5,500 years, and that of a giant sequoia (*Sequoiaden-*

dron giganteum) at perhaps 6,000 years. No single cell lives more than 30 years.

Most massive The most massive living thing on Earth is the biggest-known giant sequoia (*Sequoiadendron giganteum*), a tree named the General Sherman, standing 274.9 ft tall, in the Sequoia National Park, CA. In 1989 it had a girth of 82.3 ft, measured 4.5 ft above the ground. The General Sherman has been estimated to contain the equivalent of 600,120 board feet of timber, sufficient to make 5 billion matches. The foliage is blue-green, and the red-brown bark may be up to 24 in thick in parts. Estimates place its weight, including its root system, at 2,756 tons, but the timber is light (18 lb/ft³).

The seed of a "big tree" weighs only $\frac{1}{6,000}$ of an oz. Its growth at maturity may therefore represent an increase in weight of 13×10^{11}.

The tree canopy covering the greatest area is that of the great banyan (*Ficus benghalensis*) in the Indian Botanical Garden, Calcutta, with 1,775 prop or supporting roots and a circumference of 1,350 ft. It covers some 3 acres and dates from before 1787. However, it is reported that a 550-year-old banyan tree known as "Thimmamma Marrimanu" in Gutibayalu village near Kadiri Taluk, Andrha Pradesh, India spreads over 5.2 acres.

Greatest girth "El Arbol del Tule" in the state of Oaxaca, Mexico is a 135-ft-tall Montezuma cypress (*Taxodium mucronatum*) with a girth in 1982 of 117.6 ft, measured 5 ft above the ground.

A circumference of 190 ft was recorded for the pollarded (trimmed to encourage a more bushy growth) European chestnut (*Castanea sativa*) known as the "Tree of the Hundred Horses" (*Castagno di Cento Cavalli*) on Mt Etna, Sicily, Italy in 1770 and 1780. It is now in three parts, widely separated. Measurements up to 180 ft in circumference have been attributed to baobab trees (*Adansonia digitata*).

United States A Coast Douglas fir at Olympic National Park, WA has a girth of 44.5 ft at a height of 4 ½ ft.

Fastest-growing Discounting bamboo, which is not botanically classified as a tree but as a woody grass, the fastest rate of growth recorded is 35 ft 3 in in 13 months by an *Albizzia falcata* planted on 17 Jun 1974 in Sabah, Malaysia. The youngest recorded age for a tree to reach 100 ft is 64 months for another of the species *A. falcata* planted on 24 Feb 1975, also in Sabah.

The world's most productive forest is a plantation of eucalypts (*Eucalyptus grandis*) at Aracruz, Brazil, where the average growth rate is 2,472 ft³ per 2.5 acres.

Slowest-growing The speed of growth of trees depends largely upon conditions, although some species, such as box and yew, are always slowgrowing. The extreme is represented by the *Dioon edule* (Cycadaceae), measured

in Mexico between 1981 and 1986 by Dr Charles M. Peters, who found the average annual growth rate to be 0.03 in; a specimen 120 years old measured 3.9 in in height.

The growing of miniature trees or *bonsai* is an Oriental cult mentioned as early as *c.* 1320.

Tallest According to the researches of Dr A.C. Carder, the tallest tree ever measured was an Australian eucalyptus (*Eucalyptus regnans*) at Watts River, Victoria, Australia, reported in 1872 by forester William Ferguson. It was 435 ft tall and almost certainly measured over 500 ft originally. Another *Eucalyptus regnans* at Mt Baw Baw, Victoria, Australia is believed to have measured 470 ft in 1885. The closest measured rivals to these champions have been:

415 ft Douglas fir *Pseudotsuga menziesii*, Lynn Valley, British Columbia, 1902.

393 ft Mineral Douglas fir *Pseudotsuga menziesii*, WA, 1905.

380 ft "Nisqually" Douglas fir (*Pseudotsuga menziesii*), Nisqually River, WA, 1899.

375 ft "Cornthwaite" Australian mountain ash, or giant gum (*Eucalyptus regnans*), Thorpdale, Victoria, Australia, 1880.

367.6 ft Coast redwood (*Sequoia sempervirens*), Guerneville, CA, 1873. This tree was felled for timber in 1875.

The tallest tree currently standing is the "National Geographic Society" coast redwood (*Sequoia sempervirens*) in Redwood National Park, Humboldt County, CA. It stood at 373 ft in October 1990, according to Ron Hildebrant of California. The 365 ft "Dyerville" giant redwood in the same park was reported felled in a storm on 27 Mar 1991.

The tallest standing broadleaf tree is an Australian mountain ash, or giant gum (*Eucalyptus regnans*) in the Styx Valley, Tasmania, Australia, at 312 ft.

Most leaves Little work has been done on the laborious task of establishing which species has the most leaves. A large oak has perhaps 250,000 but a cypress may have some 45–50 million leaf scales.

Remotest The tree believed to be the remotest from any other is a sole Nor-

Tree climbing
The fastest time up a 100-ft fir spar pole and back down to the ground is 24.82 sec, by Guy German of Sitka, AK on 3 Jul 1988 at the World Championship Timber Carnival in Albany, OR.

The fastest time up a 29.5-ft coconut tree barefoot is 4.88 sec, by Fuatai Solo, 17, in Sukuna Park, Fiji on 22 Aug 1980.

Tree topping
Guy German climbed a 100-ft spar and sawed off the top in a record time of 53.35 sec at Albany, OR on 3 Jul 1989.

Christmas
The world's tallest cut Christmas tree was a 221 ft Douglas fir (*Pseudotsuga menziesii*) erected at Northgate Shopping Center, Seattle, WA in December 1950.

*T*he National Register of Big Trees, a program of the American Forestry Association (AFA), sponsored by The Davey Tree Expert Company, officially recognizes the largest "champion" tree of each species in the United States. Trees are measured in three sections: circumference (of the tree in inches at 4½ ft from the ground); total vertical height; average diameter of the crown to the nearest foot (calculated by measuring the widest spread and the narrowest, adding them together and dividing by two). To calculate the champion tree the AFA uses a point system based on the following calculation: circumference + height + ¼ of the crown spread.

*G*iant
of the United

	Tree	Circ. (inches)	Height (feet)	Spread (feet)	Points (AFA system)	Location
1	Ash (White) (Fraximus americana)	304	95	82	420	Palisades, NY
2	Ash (Black) (Fraximus nigra)	99	155	108	281	Adrian, MI
3	Beech (American) (Fagus grandifolia)	333	130	75	371	Ashtabula County OH
4	Birch (Yellow) (Betula papyrifera)	252	76	91	351	Deer Isle, ME
5	Birch (Paper) (Betula papytrifera)	217	93	65	326	Hartford, ME
6	Buckeye (Yellow) (Aesculus octandra)	214	145	42	370	Great Smoky Mtn. Natl Park, TN
7	Cedar (Port-Orford) (Chamaecyparis lawsoniana)	451	219	39	680	Siskiyou Natl Forest, OR
8	Cedar (Incense) (Libocedrus decurrens)	462	152	49	626	Marble Mtns Wilderness, CA
9	Cherry (Black)* (Prunus serotina)	181	138	128	351	Washtenaw Co., MI
10	Cherry (Black)* (Prunus serotina)	222	93	122	346	Allegan Co., MI
11	Chestnut (American) (Castanea dentata)	193	69	88	284	Sherwood, OR
12	Cypress (monterey) (Cupressus macrocarpa)	333	97	106	457	Brookings, OR
13	Dogwood (Pacific) (Cornus nuttalli)	169	60	58	244	Clatskanie, OR
14	Douglas-Fir (Coast)* (Pseudotsuga menziesii)	448	298	64	762	Olympic Natl Park, WA
15	Douglas-Fir (Coast)* (Pseudotsuga menziesii)	534	212	48	758	Olympic Natl Park, WA
16	Elm (American) (Ulmus americana)	310	95	116	434	Louisville, KS
17	Eucalyptus (Bluegum) (Eucalyptus globulus)	425	165	126	622	Fort Ross State Park, Sonoma Co., CA
18	Fig (Florida Strangler) (Ficus aurea)	288	80	76	387	Old Cutler Hammock, FL
19	Fir (Noble)* (Abies procera)	340	238	41	588	Gifford Pinchot Natl Forest, WA
20	Fir (Noble)* (Abies procera)	300	272	49	584	Mt St. Helens Natl Monument, WA
21	Hemlock (Western)* (Tsuga heterophylla)	316	202	47	530	Olympia Natl Park, WA
22	Hemlock (Western)* (Tsuga heterophylla)	270	241	67	528	Olympic Natl Park, WA
23	Hemlock (Eastern) (Tsuga canadensis)	224	123	68	364	Aurora, WV

	Tree	Circ. (inches)	Height (feet)	Spread (feet)	Points (AFA system)	Location
24	Hickory (Pignut) (Carya glabra)	157	190	78	367	Robbinsville, NC
25	Juniper (Western) (Juniperus occidentalis)	480	86	58	581	Stanislaus Natl Forest, CA
26	Magnolia (Cucumbertree) (Magnolia acuminata)	293	75	83	389	Waukon, IA
27	Maple (Norway) (Acer platanoides)	288	65	74	372	Lebanon Co., PA
28	Maple (Red) (Acer rubrum)	222	179	120	431	St Clair Co., MI
29	Maple (Sugar) (Acer saccharum)	269	91	80	380	Norwich, CT
30	Oak (White) (Quercus alba)	414	107	145	557	Wye Mills State Park, MD
31	Oak (Shumard) (Quercus shumardii)	765	97	105	384	Lake Providence, LA
32	Oak (Swamp Chestnut) (Quercus michauxii)	197	200	148	434	Fayette Co., AL
33	Pecan (Carya illinoensis)	231	143	115	403	Cocke Co., TN
34	Pine (Western White) (Pinus monticola)	414	157	55	585	El Dorado Natl Forest, CA

Trees

States

	Tree	Circ. (inches)	Height (feet)	Spread (feet)	Points (AFA system)	Location
35	Pine (Ponderosa) (Pinus ponderosa)	287	223	68	527	Plumas, CA
36	Poplar (White) (Populus aalba)	251	96	79	367	Fond du Lac, WI
37	Redcedar (Western) (Juniperus virginiana)	732	178	54	924	Forks, WA
38	Redcedar (Eastern) (Juniperus virginiana)	211	55	68	283	Coffee Co., GA
39	Redwood (Coast) (Sequoia sempervirens)	629	362	74	1010	Humboldt Redwoods State Park, CA
40	Sequoia (Giant) (Sequoiadendron giganteum)	998	275	107	1300	Sequoia Natl Park, CA
41	Spruce (Sitka)* (Picea sitchensis)	707	191	96	922	Seaside, OR
42	Spruce (Sitka)* (Picea sitchensis)	673	206	93	902	Olympic Natl Forest, WA
43	Spruce (Blue) (Picea pungens)	191	126	36	326	Gunnison Natl Forest, CO
44	Spruce (Norway) (Picea abies)	170	94	44	275	Susquehanna Co., PA
45	Sycamore (Platanus occidentalis)	582	129	105	737	Jeromesville, OH
46	Walnut (Black) (Juglans nigra)	271	122	134	427	Humboldt Co., CA
47	Willow (Black) (Salix nigra)	377	109	132	519	Grand Traverse Co., MI
48	Yew (Pacific) (Taxus brevifolia)	180	54	30	242	Lewis Co., WA

* = Two trees listed as largest

Source:
National Register of Big Trees

(Artwork: Maltings Partnership for Guinness Publishing)

■ **Largest leaves**
Specimens of the Amazon, or royal, water lily (Victoria amazonica). The largest recorded example of this species reached a diameter of 8 ft at the Stratford-upon-Avon Butterfly Farm, Great Britain in 1989.

(Photo: Gamma)

wegian spruce on Campbell Island, Antarctica. Its nearest companion would be over 120 miles away on the Auckland Islands.

Most expensive The highest price ever paid for a tree is $51,000 for a single starkspur "Golden Delicious" apple tree from near Yakima, WA, bought by a nursery in Missouri in 1959.

Largest forest The largest forested areas in the world are the vast coniferous forests of the northern USSR, lying between Lat. 55°N and the Arctic Circle. The total wooded area amounts to 2.7 billion acres (25 percent of the world's forests), of which 38 percent is Siberian larch. The USSR is 34 percent forested.

The largest area of forest in the tropics remains the Amazon Basin, amounting to some 815 million acres.

United States The largest forest in the United States is the Tongass National Forest (16.7 million acres), in Alaska. The United States is 32.25 percent forested.

Longest avenue The world's longest avenue of trees comprises three parts converging on Imaichi City in the Tochigi Prefecture of Japan. Known as the Nikko Cryptomeria Avenue, its total length is 22 miles, made up of the Nikko Kaido (10.27 miles), the Reiheishi Kaido (8.18 miles) and the Aizu-nishi Kaido (5.72 miles). The avenue was planted in the period 1628–48 and over 13,500 of its original 200,000 Japanese cedar (*Cryptomeria japonica*) trees survive, at an average height of 88.58 ft.

Heaviest wood Black ironwood (*Olea laurifolia*), also called South African ironwood, has a specific gravity of up to 1.49, and weighs up to 93 lb/ft^3.

United States The heaviest American wood is the lead wood tree (*Krugiodendron ferreum*), with a specific gravity of 1.34:1.42.

Lightest wood The lightest wood is *Aeschynomene hispida*, found in Cuba, which has a specific gravity of 0.044 and a weight of only 2¾ lb/ft^3. The wood of the balsa tree (*Ochroma pyramidale*) is of very variable density—between 2½–24 lb/ft^3. The density of cork is 15 lb/ft^3.

United States The lightest American wood is pithe wood (*Moscheutos*) with a specific gravity of 0.5 or less.

Wood cutting The first recorded lumberjack sports competition was held in 1572 in the Basque region of Spain. The records set at the Lumberjack World Championships at Hayward, WI (founded 1960) are:

Power Saw		**8.71 sec**
Ron Johnson (USA)		1986
One-Man Bucking		**18.96 sec**
Rolin Eslinger (USA)		1987
Standing Block Chop		**22.05 sec**
Melvin Lentz (USA)		1988
Underhand Block Chop		**17.84 sec**
Laurence O'Toole (Australia)		1985
Two-man Bucking		**7.27 sec**
Jim Colbert (USA)		1988
Mike Sullivan (USA)		1988
Springboard Choppping.	**1 min 18.45 sec**	
Bill Youd (Australia)		1985

Kingdom Protista

Protista were first discovered in 1676 by Antonie van Leeuwenhoek of Delft (1632–1723), a Dutch microscopist. Among Protista are characteristics common to both plants and animals. The more plant-like are termed Protophyta (protophytes), including unicellular algae, and the more animal-like are placed in the phylum Protozoa (protozoans), including amoeba and flagellates.

Largest The largest protozoans in terms of volume that are known to have existed were calcareous foraminifera (Foraminiferida) belonging to the genus *Nummulites*, a species of which, in the Middle Eocene rocks of Turkey, attained 8.6 in in diameter.

The largest existing protozoan, a species of the fan-shaped *Stannophyllum* (Xenophyophorida), can exceed this in length (9.8 in has been recorded) but not in volume.

Smallest protophytes The marine microflagellate alga *Micromonas pusilla* has a diameter of less than 2 microns or micrometers (0.00008 in).

Fastest The protozoan *Monas stigmatica* has been found to move a distance equivalent to 40 times its own length in a second. No human can cover even seven times his own length in a second.

Fastest reproduction The protozoan *Glaucoma*, which reproduces by binary fission, divides as frequently as every three hours. Thus in the course of a day it could become a great-great-great-great-great-great-grandparent and the progenitor of 510 descendants!

Kingdom Fungi

Largest Marcia Wallgren of Yellow

Springs, OH found a puffball (*Calvatia gigantea*) 77 in in circumference in 1988. An example of the edible mushroom (*Polyporus frondosus*) weighing 72-lb was reported by Joseph Opple near Solon, OH in September 1976.

Most poisonous The yellowish-olive death cap (*Amanita phalloides*), which can be found in England, is regarded as the world's most poisonous fungus. From 6–15 hours after eating, the victim experiences vomiting, delirium, collapse and death. Among its victims was Cardinal Giulio di' Medici, Pope Clement VII (b. 1478) on 25 Sep 1534.

■ **Below: Most poisonous fungus**
Of the 70–80 species of mushroom or toadstool harmful to humans, the most dangerous is the death cap (Amanita phalloides). After suffering violent symptoms 6–15 hours after eating it, its victim lapses into a coma, resulting in death in over 50 percent of cases. (Photo: Bruce Coleman)

■ **Above: Longest avenue**
Composed of three parts converging on Imaichi City, Japan, the Cryptomeria Avenue stretches for a total of 22 miles.

Aeroflora Fungi were once classified in the subkingdom Protophyta of the kingdom Protista. The highest total fungal spore count was $5,686,860.6/ft^3$ near Cardiff, Great Britain on 21 Jul 1971. A plane tree pollen count of $76,278.24/ft^3$ was recorded near London, Great Britain on 9 May 1971. The lowest counts of airborne allergens are zero.

Kingdom Procaryota

BACTERIA

Antonie van Leeuwenhoek (1632–1723) was the first to observe bacteria, in 1675. The largest of the bacteria is the sulfur bacterium *Beggiatoa mirabilis*, which is 16–45 micrometers in width and may form filaments several millimeters long.

The bacteria *Thermoactinomyces vulgaris* have been found alive in cores of mud taken from the bottom of Windermere, Great Britain and have been dated to 1,500 years before the present.

Smallest free-living entity The smallest of all free-living organisms are the pleuro-pneumonia-like organisms (PPLO) of the *Mycoplasma*. One of these, *Mycoplasma laidlawii*, first discovered in sewage in 1936, has a diameter during its early existence of only 10^{-7} m. Examples of the strain known as H.39 have a maximum diameter of 3×10^{-7} m and weigh an estimated 10^{-16} g. Thus a 209.4-ton blue whale would weigh 1.9×10^{24} times as much.

Highest In April 1967 the National Aeronautics and Space Administration (NASA) reported that bacteria had been discovered at an altitude of 135,000 ft (25.56 miles).

Oldest The oldest deposits from which living bacteria are claimed to have been extracted are salt layers near Irkutsk, USSR, dating from about 600 million years ago, but the discovery was not accepted internationally. The US Dry Valley Drilling Project in Antarctica claimed resuscitated rod-shaped bacteria from caves up to a million years old.

Fastest The rod-shaped bacillus *Bdellovibrio bacteriovorus*, by means of a polar flagellum rotating 100 times/sec, can move 50 times its own length of 2 micrometers per sec. This would be the equivalent of a human sprinter reaching 200 mph or a swimmer crossing the English Channel between England and France in 6 min.

Toughest The bacterium *Micrococcus radiodurans* can withstand atomic radiation of 6.5 million roentgens or 10,000 times the dose that would be fatal to the average person. In March 1983 John Barras (University of Oregon) reported bacteria from sulfurous seabed vents thriving at 583°F in the East Pacific Rise at Lat. 21°N.

VIRUSES

Largest Dmitriy Ivanovsky (1864–1920) first reported filterable objects in 1892, but Martinus Willem Beijerink (1851–1931) first confirmed the nature of viruses in 1898. These are now defined as aggregates of two or more types of chemical (including either DNA or RNA) that are infectious and potentially pathogenic. The longest-known virus is the rod-shaped *Citrus tristeza* virus with particles measuring 2×10^{-5} m.

Smallest The smallest-known viruses are the nucleoprotein plant viruses, such as the satellite of tobacco *Necrosis virus* with spherical particles 17 nm in diameter.

A putative new infectious submicroscopic organism but without nucleic acid, named a "prion," was announced from the University of California in February 1982.

Viroids (RNA cores without protein coating) are much smaller than viruses. They were discovered by Theodor O. Diener (USA) in February 1972. Dr Rohwer of Bethesda, MD stated in September 1984 that scrapie-specific protein was smaller than the concept of a "yet to be identified prion."

Parks, Zoos, Oceanaria, Aquaria

PARKS

Largest The Wood Buffalo National Park in Alberta, Canada (established 1922), has an area of 11,172,000 acres ($17,560$ miles^2).

United States The largest public park in the United States is Wrangell-St Elias National Park and Preserve (13.2 million acres) in Alaska.

ZOOS

It has been estimated that throughout the world there are some 757 zoos with an estimated annual attendance of 350 million.

Largest game reserve The world's largest zoological reserve is the Etosha National Park, Namibia. Established in 1907, its area has grown to 38,427 miles^2.

Oldest zoo The earliest-known collection of animals was the one set up by Shulgi, a third-dynasty ruler of Ur from 2097–2094 B.C., at Puzurish in southeast Iraq.

The oldest-known zoo is the one at Schönbrunn, Vienna, Austria, built in 1752 by the Holy Roman emperor Franz I for his wife Maria Theresa.

The oldest existing public zoological collection in the world is that of the Zoological Society of London, Great Britain, founded in 1826. Its collection, housed partly in Regent's Park, London, Great Britain (36 acres) and partly at Whipsnade Park, Bedfordshire, Great Britain (541 acres; opened 23 May 1931), is the most comprehensive in the United Kingdom. The inventory on 1 Jan 1989 indicated a total of 11,108 specimens. These comprised 2,628 mammals, 1,916 birds, 489 reptiles, 175 amphibians, an estimated total of 2,300 fish and an estimated total of 3,600 invertebrates, excluding some common species. The record annual attendances are 3,031,571 in 1950 for Regent's Park and 756,758 in 1961 for Whipsnade.

United States The Philadelphia Zoo received its charter from the state of Pennsylvania in 1859, but did not open to the public until 1874. Lincoln Park Zoo, a 60-acre public park owned by the city of Chicago, received a gift of two swans from Central Park, New York City in 1868. By 1870 a "small barn and paddocks" had been built to house additional animals that had been donated by the public. The current facility covers 35 acres.

According to the American Association of Zoological Parks and Aquariums, the top zoo for attendance is Lincoln Park Zoo with 4.5 million visitors each year. The next largest total is the San Diego Zoo, CA, which hosts 3.8 million visitors per year.

Earliest without bars The earliest zoo without bars was that at Stellingen, near Hamburg, Germany. It was founded in 1907 by Carl Hagenbeck (1844–1913), who made use of deep pits and large pens instead of cages to separate the exhibits from visitors.

OCEANARIA

Earliest The world's first oceanarium is Marineland of Florida, opened in 1938 at a site 18 miles south of St Augustine, FL. Up to 5.8 million gal of seawater are pumped daily through two major tanks, one rectangular (100 ft long by 40 ft wide by 18 ft deep) containing 375,000 gal, and one circular (233 ft in circumference and 12 ft deep) containing 330,000 gal. The tanks are seascaped, including coral reefs and even a shipwreck.

AQUARIA

Largest In terms of the volume of water held, the Living Seas Aquarium opened in 1986 at the EPCOT Center, FL is the world's largest, with a total capacity of 6.25 million gal. It contains over 3,000 fish representing 90 species.

The Monterey Bay Aquarium in California has the most tanks, specimens and species. The aquarium was opened on 20 Oct 1984 at a cost of $55 million. There are now 95 tanks with a capacity of 750,000 gallons on 2.2 acres of land. It contains over 6,500 specimens of 525 species of fauna and flora. The two largest tanks hold 335,000 and 326,000 gallons.

The Human Being

■ **Earliest hominid footprints**
This trail of hominid footprints was found fossilized in volcanic ash in 1978 at Laetoli, Tanzania. It dates from 3.5 million years ago. (Photo: *Science Photo Library*)

■ **Earliest skeletal remains**
The most complete of the earliest hominid skeletons is that of "Lucy" (40 percent complete), found by Dr Donald C. Johanson and T. Gray near the Awash River, Hadar, Ethiopia in November 1974. (Photo: *Science Photo Library*)

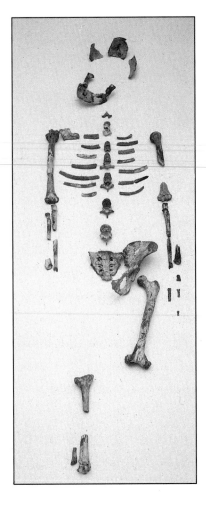

Origins

EARLIEST HUMANS

SCALE OF TIME *If the age of the Earth–Moon system (latest estimate 4.45 billion years) is likened to a single year, hominids appeared on the scene at about 4:15 P.M. on 31 Dec, the Christian era began about 14 seconds before midnight, and the life span of a 120-year-old person (pp 69 & 70) would be about three-quarters of a second. Present calculations indicate that the Sun's increased heat as it becomes a "red giant" will make life on Earth untenable in about 5.5 billion years. Meanwhile there may well be colder epicycles. The period of 1 billion years is sometimes referred to as an eon.*

Human beings (homo sapiens) *are a species in the subfamily Homininae of the family Hominidae of the superfamily Hominoidea of the suborder Simiae (or Anthropoidea) of the order Primates of the infraclass Eutheria of the subclass Theria of the class Mammalia of the subphylum Vertebrata (Craniata) of the phylum Chordata of the subkingdom Metazoa of the animal kingdom.*

Earliest primate Primates appeared in the Paleocene epoch about 69 million years ago. The earliest members of the suborder Anthropoidea are known from both Africa and South America in the early Oligocene, 34–30 million years ago, when the two infra-orders, Platyrrhini and Catarrhini, from the New and Old Worlds respectively, were already distinct. New finds from the Fayum, in Egypt, are being studied and may represent primates from the Eocene period, as old as 38 million years.

Earliest hominoid Recent hominoid remains from Salonika in Greece are claimed to be 25 million years old and are thought to provide a link between humans and their ape ancestors. These finds, however, require more intensive research.

Earliest hominid Characteristics typical of the Hominidae such as the large brain and bipedal locomotion (walking on two legs) do not appear until much later. The earliest hominid relic found is an Australopithecine jawbone with two molars, each 2 in long, found by Kiptalam Chepboi near Lake Baringo, Kenya in February 1984 and dated to 4 million years ago by associated fossils and to 5.6–5.4 million years ago through rock correlation by potassium-argon dating.

The most complete of the early hominid skeletons is that of "Lucy" (40 percent complete), found by Dr Donald C. Johanson and T. Gray at Locality 162 near the Awash River, Hadar, in the Afar region of Ethiopia on 30 Nov 1974. She was estimated to be *c.* 40 years old when she died 3 million years ago, and she was 3 ft 6 in tall.

Parallel tracks of hominid footprints extending over 80 ft were first discovered at Laetoli, Tanzania in 1978, by Paul Abell and Dr Mary Leakey, in volcanic ash dating to 3.5 million years ago. The height of the smallest of the seemingly three individuals was was estimated to be 3 ft 11 in.

Earliest of the genus Homo The earliest species of this genus is *Homo habilis*, or "Handy Man," from Olduvai Gorge, Kenya, named by Louis Leakey, Philip Tobias and John Napier in 1964 after a suggestion from Prof. Raymond Arthur Dart (1893–1988).

The greatest age attributed to fossils of this genus is 1.9 million years for the skull KNM-ER (Kenya National Museum-East Rudolf) 1470 discovered in 1972 by Bernard Ngeneo at Koobi Fora at Lake Turkana, northern Kenya. It was reconstructed by Dr Meave Leakey (nee Epps).

The earliest stone tools are abraded core-choppers dating from *c.* 2.5 million years ago. They were found at Hadar, Ethiopia in November–December 1976 by Hélène Roche (France). Finger-held (as opposed to fist-held) quartz slicers found by Roche and Dr John Wall (New Zealand) close to the Hadar site by the Gona River are also dated to *c.* 2.5 million years ago.

Earliest Homo erectus The oldest example of this species (upright man), the direct ancestor of *Homo sapiens*, was discovered by Kamoya Kimeu on the surface at the site of Nariokotome III to the west of Lake Turkana, Kenya in August 1985. The skeleton of this 5 ft 5 in 12-year-old-boy is the most complete of this species yet found; only a few small pieces are missing. It is dated to 1.6 million years ago.

Earliest Homo sapiens Through the Pleistocene epoch (1.6 million to 10,000 years ago) the trend towards large brains continued. *Homo sapiens* ("wise man") appeared about 300,000 years ago as the successor to *Homo erectus*.

United States Over 500 artifacts 11,000 to 16,000 years old were found in Washington Co., PA in April 1973 after being brought to the attention of the University of Pittsburgh by Albert Miller, whose family owned the land. The dig, led by Dr James Adovasio, started in June 1973 and lasted until June 1983. The artifacts consist mainly of unfluted lanceolate projectile points (either spearheads or darts), an assortment of bifacial and unifacial tools (knives and scrapers), polyhedral blade cores (long thin flakes from which blades are made), and blades struck from this core. These items are all made from chert, a flintlike rock.

The site dates to the Pre-Clovis Paleo-Indian culture and it is believed that the *Homo sapiens* Paleo-Indians were the initial inhabitants of the site. The tools, dated by the mass accelerator spectrometer (MAS) technique, which measures the carbon content present in the amino acids at the time of death, resembled tools found in Manchuria. This supports theories that North America was first inhabited by peoples coming

GIANTS

The only people for whom heights of 8 ft or more have been reliably reported are the eleven listed below. In seven cases, gigantism was followed by acromegaly, a disorder which causes an enlargement of the nose, lips, tongue, lower jaw, hands and feet, due to renewed activity and increase in growth hormone by an already swollen pituitary gland, which is located at the base of the brain.

Robert Wadlow (1918–40), of Alton, IL [1]	8 ft 11 1/10 in
John William Rogan (1871–1905), of Gallatin, TN [2]	8 ft 8 in
John F. Carroll (1932–69) of Buffalo, NY [3]	8 ft 7 3/4 in
Väinö Myllyrinne (1909–63) of Helsinki, Finland [4]	8 ft 3 in
Don Koehler (1925–81) of Denton, MO, later of Chicago [5]	8 ft 2 in
Bernard Coyne (1897–1921) of Anthon, IA [6]	8 ft 2 in
Zeng Jinlain (1964–82) of Yujiang, China [7]	8 ft 1 3/4 in
Patrick Cotter (O'Brien) (1760–1806) of Kinsale, Ireland [8]	8 ft 1 in
"Constantine" (1872–1902) of Reutlingen, Germany [9]	8 ft 0.8 in
Gabriel Estavao Monjane (1944–90) of Monjacaze, Mozambique [10]	c. 8 ft 3/4 in
Sulaimān 'Ali Nashnush (b. 1943–fl.* 1968) of Tripoli, Libya [11]	8 ft 0.4 in

[1] See chart on Wadlow.

[2] Measured in a sitting position. Unable to stand owing to ankylosis (stiffening of the joints through the formation of adhesions) of the knees and hips. Weighed only 175 lb.

[3] Severe kyphoscoliosis (two-dimensional spinal curvature). The figure represents his height with assumed normal spinal curvature, calculated from a standing height of 8 ft measured on 14 Oct 1959. His standing height was 7 ft 8 1/4 in shortly before his death.

[4] Stood 7 ft 3 1/2 in at the age of 21 years. Experienced a second phase of growth in his late thirties and measured 8 ft 1.2 in at the time of his death. In 1931 he reportedly weighed 434 lb.

[5] Abnormal growth started at the age of 10. He had a twin sister who is 5 ft 9 in tall. His

father was 6 ft 2 in and his mother 5 ft 10 in.

[6] Eunuchoidal giant (Daddy long-legs syndrome). Rejected by Army in 1918 when 7 ft 9 in. Still growing at time of death.

[7] Measurement based on assumed normal spinal curvature because she suffered from severe scoliosis and could not stand up straight.

[8] Revised height based on skeletal remeasurement after bones exhumed on 19 Dec 1972.

[9] Eunuchoidal. Height estimated, as both legs were amputated after they turned gangrenous. He claimed a height of 8 ft 6 in.

[10] Died in January 1990 after a fall at his home.

[11] Operation to correct abnormal growth successfully carried out in Rome in 1960.

* Note: fl is the abbreviation for floruit, Latin for "living at the relevant date."

across a natural land bridge between Siberia and Alaska that is now deep beneath the Bering Sea.

In 1968 a burial site containing bones of two individuals believed to be an infant and an adolescent were uncovered by construction workers in Wilsall, MT. The Anzick burial site also contained 120 artifacts with a red ocher covering believed to be grave offerings. These were mainly flint and stone bifacial (flaked by percussion along both sides of the chopping edge) tools and the remains of spear shafts.

The bones were dated by the MAS technique to not less than 10,600 years ago. The remains are believed to be of members of the Paleo-Indian culture, with the artifacts in the style of the Clovis Age.

Oldest mummy Mummification (from the Persian word mūm, wax) dates from 2600 B.C. or the 4th dynasty of the Egyptian pharaohs. The oldest-known mummy is that of a high-ranking young woman who was buried c. 2600 B.C. on a plateau near the Great Pyramid of Cheops

at Giza, or Al-Gizeh, Egypt. Her remains, which appear to represent the first attempts at mummification, were discovered in a 6-ft-deep excavation on 17 Mar 1989, but only her skull was intact. She is believed to have lived in the lost kingdom of Ankh Ptah.

The oldest complete mummy is of Wati, a court musician of c. 2400 B.C. from the tomb of Nefer in Saqqâra, Egypt, found in 1944.

Dimensions

GIANTS

Growth of the body is determined by growth hormone. This is produced by the pituitary gland, set deep in the brain. Overproduction in childhood produces abnormal growth, and true gigantism is the result. The true height of human giants is frequently obscured by exaggeration and commercial dishonesty. The only admissible evidence on the actual height of giants is that collected

since 1870 under impartial medical supervision. Unfortunately, even medical authors are not always blameless and can include fanciful, as opposed to measured, heights.

The Bible states that Goliath of Gath (c. 1060 B.C.) stood 6 cubits (approximately 9 ft) with an arm span of 9 ft 6 1/2 in.

The Jewish historian Flavius Josephus (b. A.D. 37–38, d. c. A.D. 100) and some of the manuscripts of the Septuagint (the earliest Greek translation of the Old Testament) attribute to Goliath the wholly credible height of 4 Greek cubits (approximately 6 ft) and an arm span of 6 ft 10 in.

Giants exhibited in circuses and exhibitions are routinely under contract not to be measured and are, almost traditionally, billed by their promoters at heights up to 18 in in excess of their true heights. The most recent example is Haji Mohammad Alam Channa (b. 1956) of Sehwan Sharif, Pakistan, who allegedly measured 8 ft 2 3/4 in. On 21 Aug 1987 he was measured in New York City and found to be 7 ft 8 in.

TALLEST MEN

Earliest opinion is that the tallest man in medical history of whom there is irrefutable evidence was Robert Pershing Wadlow, born at 6:30 A.M. on 22 Feb 1918 in Alton, IL. Weighing 8 1/2 lb at birth, his abnormal growth started at the age of two following a double hernia operation. On his 13th birthday he stood 7 ft 1 3/4 in tall and by 17 he had reached 8 ft 1/2 in.

On 27 Jun 1940 Dr C.M. Charles, associate professor of anatomy at Washington University's School of Medicine in St Louis, MO, and Dr Cyril MacBryde measured Robert Wadlow at 8 ft 11.1 in (arm span 9 ft 5 3/4 in) in St Louis. Wadlow died 18 days later at 1:30 A.M. on 15 Jul 1940 weighing 439 lb in a hotel in Manistee, MI as a result of a septic blister on his right ankle caused by a poorly fitting brace. He was buried in Oakwood Cemetery, Alton, IL in a coffin measuring 10 ft 9 in.

His greatest recorded weight was 491 lb on his 21st birthday. His shoes were size 37AA (18 1/2 in) and his hands measured 12 3/4 in from the wrist to the tip of the middle finger (compare with the depth of this page at 11 5/8 in).

Living The tallest person in the world is eunochoidal giant Chandra Barman (b. 1962) of Dacca, Bangladesh, who stands 8 ft 3 in and is still growing after starting to grow abnormally at the age of 11.

TALLEST WOMEN

The tallest woman in medical history was the giantess Zeng Jinlian (b. 26 Jun 1964) of Yujiang village in the Bright Moon Commune, Hunan Province, central China, who was 8 ft 1 3/4 in when she died on 13 Feb 1982. This figure, however, represented her height with assumed normal spinal curvature, because she suffered from severe scoliosis (curvature of the spine) and could not stand up straight. She began to grow abnormally from the age of four months and stood 5 ft 1 1/2 in before her fourth birthday and 7 ft 1 1/2 in when she was 13. Her hands measured 10 in and her feet 14 in in length. Both her parents and her brother were of normal size.

Robert Wadlow

Weighing 8 1/2 lb at birth, Robert Wadlow started his abnormal growth at the age of 2 following a double hernia operation. His height progressed as follows:

Age	Height ft in
5	5 4
8	6 0
9	6 2 1/4
10	6 5
11	6 7
12	6 10 1/2
13	7 1 3/4
14	7 5
15	7 8
16	7 10 1/4
17 [1]	8 0 1/2
18	8 3 1/2
19	8 5 1/2
20	8 6 3/4
21	8 8 1/4
22 [2]	8 11 1/10

[1] Following severe influenza and infection of the foot.

[2] Still growing during his terminal illness.

The giantess Ella Ewing (1875–1913) of Gorin, MO was billed at 8 ft 2 in, but this height was exaggerated. She measured 7 ft 4½ in at the age of 23, and may have attained 7 ft 6 in at the time of her death.

Living The world's tallest woman is Sandy Allen, born 18 Jun 1955 in Chicago, IL and now working as a secretary in Indianapolis, IN. A 6½-lb baby, her abnormal growth began soon after birth. At 10 years of age she stood 6 ft 3 in, and she measured 7 ft 1 in when she was 16. On 14 Jul 1977 this giantess underwent a pituitary gland operation, which inhibited further growth at 7 ft 7¼ in. She now weighs 462 lb and takes a size 16 EEE shoe.

Married couple Anna Hanen Swan (1846–88) of Nova Scotia, Canada was said to be 8 ft 1 in but actually measured 7 ft 5½ in. At the church of St Martin-in-the-Fields, London, Great Britain on 17 Jun 1871 she married Martin van Buren Bates (1845–1919) of Whitesburg, KY, who stood 7 ft 2½ in, making them the tallest married couple on record.

TALLEST TWINS

World The world's tallest identical twins are Michael and James Lanier (b. 27 Nov 1969) from Troy, MI. They measured 7 ft 1 in at the age of 14 years and both now stand 7 ft 4 in. Their sister Jennifer is 5 ft 2 in tall.

■ **Smallest living man**
Gul Mohammed (below) of India, 22.5 in tall, standing alongside Mr V.K. Sharma (Photo: Harish Vats)

The world's tallest female identical twins are Heather and Hedi Burge (b. 11 Nov 1971) from Palos Verdes, CA. They are both 6 ft 4¾ in tall.

DWARFS

The strictures that apply to giants apply equally to dwarfs, except that exaggeration gives way to understatement. In the same way as 9 ft may be regarded as the limit towards which the tallest giants tend, so 23 in must be regarded as the limit towards which the shortest adult dwarfs or midgets tend (compare with the average length of newborn babies, which is 18–20 in). In the case of child dwarfs, their *ages* are often exaggerated by their agents or managers.

There are many causes of short stature in humans. They include genetic abnormalities, lack of appropriate hormones and starvation. Dwarfs of the past, whatever the cause of their condition, tended to be smaller because of lower nutritional standards.

Shortest female Adult The shortest mature human of whom there is independent evidence was Pauline Musters, a Dutch dwarf. She was born at Ossendrecht, Netherlands, on 26 Feb 1876 and measured 11.8 in at birth. At nine years of age she was 21.65 in tall and weighed only 3 lb 5 oz. She died on 1 Mar 1895 in New York City at the age of 19. Although she was billed at 19 in, a postmortem examination showed her to be exactly 24 in (there was some elongation after death). Her mature weight varied from 7½–9 lb and her measurements were 18½–19–17 in, which suggests she was overweight.

Child In 1979 a height of 19.68 in and a weight of 4 lb 6 oz were reported for Stamatoula, a nine-year-old Greek girl (1969–85). When she died on 22 Aug 1985 at the Lyrion Convent, Athens, Greece she measured 26.4 in and weighed 11 lb. The child, believed to be the survivor of twins, suffered from Seckel's syndrome, also known as "bird-headed dwarfism."

Shortest male Adult The shortest recorded adult male dwarf is Gul Mohammed (b. 15 Feb 1957) of Delhi, India. On 19 Jul 1990 he was examined at Ram Manohar Hospital, New Delhi, and found to measure 22.5 in in height and weighed 37.47 lb. The other members of his immediate family are of normal height.

Child William E. Jackson, alias "Major Mite" (b. 2 Oct 1864 in Dunedin, New Zealand), measured 9 in long and weighed 12 oz at birth. In November 1880 he stood 21 in and weighed 9 lb. He died in New York City on 9 Dec 1900, when he measured 27 in.

Most famous The most famous midget in history was Charles Sherwood Stratton, alias "General Tom Thumb," born on 4 Jan 1838. When he joined up with Phineas T. Barnum his birth date was changed to 4 Jan 1832, so that when billed at 30½ in at the age of 18 he was in fact 12.

Tom died of apoplexy on 15 Jul 1885 at his birthplace, Bridgewater, CT, age 45 (not 51) and was 3 ft 4 in (70 lb).

Immobile Madge Bester (b. 26 Apr 1963) of Johannesburg, South Africa, is only 25.5 in tall, but she suffers from *Osteogenesis imperfecta* and is confined to a wheelchair. In this disease there is an inherited abnormality of collagen, which, with calcium salts, provides the rigid structure of bones. The disease is characterized by brittle bones and other deformities of the skeleton. Her mother, Winnie, is not much taller, measuring 27.5 in, and she too is confined to a wheelchair.

Twins The shortest twins ever recorded were the primordial dwarfs Matjus and Bela Matina (b. 1903–d. c.1935) of Budapest, Hungary, who later became American citizens. They both measured 30 in.

Living The world's shortest living twins are John and Greg Rice (b. 3 Dec 1951) of West Palm Beach, FL who both measure 34 in.

The shortest identical twin sisters are Dorene Williams of Oakdale and Darlene McGregor of Almeda, CA (b. 1949), who each stand 4 ft 1 in.

Oldest There are only two centenarian dwarfs on record. The oldest was Hungarian-born Susanna Bokoyni ("Princess Susanna") of Newton, NJ, who died at the age of 105 years on 24 Aug 1984. She was 3 ft 4 in tall and weighed 37 lb.

The other was Miss Anne Clowes of Matlock, Derbyshire, Great Britain, who died on 5 Aug 1784 at the age of 103 years. She was 3 ft 9 in tall and weighed 48 lb.

Most variable stature Adam Rainer, born in Graz, Austria in 1899, measured 3 ft 10.45 in at the age of 21. He then suddenly started growing at a rapid rate, and by 1931 he had reached 7 ft 1¾ in. He became so weak as a result that he was bedridden for the rest of his life. At the time of his death on 4 Mar 1950, age 51, he measured 7 ft 8 in and was the only person in medical history to have been both a dwarf and a giant.

Most dissimilar couple Nigel Wilks (b. 1963), 6-ft-6-in tall, of Kingston-upon-Hull, Great Britain on 30 Jun 1984 married Beverley Russell (b. 1963), 4-ft tall, who suffers from a skeletal disorder.

TRIBES

Tallest The tallest major tribes in the world are the slender Tutsi (also known as the Watusi) of Rwanda and Burundi, Central Africa, and the Dinka of the Sudan. In the case of the Tutsi, average adult males and females stand 6 ft 5 in and 5 ft 10 in respectively.

Shortest The smallest pygmies are the Mbuti of the Ituri forest, Zaïre, Central Africa, with an average height of 4 ft 6 in for men and 4 ft 5 in for women.

WEIGHT

Heaviest Male The heaviest human in medical history was Jon Brower Minnoch (b. 29 Sep 1941) of Bainbridge Island, WA, who had suffered from obesity since childhood. The 6-ft-1-in-tall former taxi driver was 392 lb in 1963, 700 lb in 1966, and 975 lb in September 1976.

In March 1978, Minnoch was rushed to University Hospital, Seattle, saturated with fluid and suffering from heart and respiratory failure. It took a dozen firemen and an improvised stretcher to move him from his home to a ferryboat. When he arrived at the hospital he was put in two beds lashed together. It took 13 people just to roll him over. By extrapolating his intake and elimination rates, consultant endocrinologist Dr Robert Schwartz calculated that Minnoch must have weighed more than 1,387 lb when he was admitted. A great deal of this was water accumulation due to his congestive heart failure. After nearly two years on a 1,200-calorie-a-day diet, the choking fluid had gone, and he was discharged at 476 lb. In October 1981 he had to be readmitted, after putting on 197 lb. When he died on 10 Sep 1983 he weighed more than 798 lb.

Female When Mrs Percy Pearl Washington, who suffered from polydipsia (excessive thirst), died in a Milwaukee hospital on 9 Oct 1972 the scales registered only up to 800 lb, but she was credited with a weight of 880 lb. She was 6 ft tall and wore a size 62 dress.

Living Male The heaviest living man is T.J. Albert Jackson (b. 1941 Kent Nicholson), also known as "Fat Albert," of Canton, MS. He recently tipped the scales at 891 lb. He has a 120-in chest, a 116-in waist, 70-in thighs and a 29 ½-in neck.
Female The heaviest woman ever recorded was probably Rosie Carnemolla (b. 1944) of Poughkeepsie, NY, who registered a peak weight of 850 lb on 13 Mar 1988. A week later she was put on a carefully controlled diet that reduced her weight by 250 lb in six months, and then she underwent an operation to reduce the size of her stomach. By September 1988 she was down to 350 lb, during which time her waistline had declined from 98 in to 46 in and her dress size from 70 to 46. Her target weight is 150 lb.

Heaviest twins Billy Leon (1946–79) and Benny Loyd (b. 7 Dec 1946) McCrary, alias McGuire, of Hendersonville, NC were normal in size until the age of six when they both contracted German measles. In November 1978 they weighed 743 lb (Billy) and 723 lb Benny and had 84-in waists. As professional tag-team wrestling performers they were billed at weights up to 770 lb. Billy died at Niagara Falls, Ontario, Canada on 13 Jul 1979.

Weight loss Male Jon Brower Min-

noch (1941–83) had reduced to 476 lb by July 1979, thus achieving a weight loss of at least 924 lb in two years.

Michael Hebranko (b. 14 May 1953) of Brooklyn, NY weighed 905 lb in July 1987. Within 15 months he had lost over 500 lb, and by June 1989 he weighed 217 lb, having shed a total of 688 lb within a period of less than 24 months. His waist measurement was 115 in but is now 36–38 in, a reduction of 79 in.

Richard Stephens of Birmingham, AL, slimmed from 467 lb to 305 ¾ lb in 157 days from 12 April to September 1985.

On 14 Mar 1982 surgeons at a hospital in New York City removed 140 lb of adipose tissue from the abdominal wall of a 798-lb man. They had to use a hoist to lift the layers of fat as they were removed.

Ron Allen (b. 1947) sweated off 21 ½ lb of his 239 lb in Nashville, TN in 24 hours in August 1984.

Female The circus fat lady Mrs. Celesta Geyer (b. 1901), alias Dolly Dimples, went from 552 lb to 152 lb in 1950–51, a loss of 400 lb in 14 months. Her "vital statistics" diminished from 79–84–84 in to a svelte 34–28–36 in. Her book *How I Lost 400 lbs* was not a best-seller, perhaps because of the difficulty of would-be readers in relating to the dressmaking and other problems of losing more than 400 lb when one is 4 ft 11 in tall. In December 1967 she was reportedly down to 110 lb.

Weight gaining The reported record for weight gain is held by Jon Brower Minnoch (see Heaviest male) at 196 lb in 7 days in October 1981 after readmittance to University Hospital, Seattle, WA.

Arthur Knorr (USA; 1916–60), gained 294 lb in the last six months of his life.

Miss Doris James of San Francisco, CA is alleged to have gained 325 lb in the 12 months before her death in August 1965, age 38, at a weight of 675 lb. She was only 5 ft 2 in tall.

Greatest differential The greatest weight difference recorded for a married couple is *c.* 1,300 lb in the case of Jon Brower Minnoch (see Heaviest male) and his 110-lb wife Jeannette in March 1978.

Lightest The thinnest recorded adults of normal height are those suffering from anorexia nervosa. Losses up to 65 percent of original body weight have been recorded in females, with a low of 45 lb in the case of Emma Shaller (1868–90) of St Louis, MO, who stood 5 ft 2 in.

Edward C. Hagner (1892–1962), alias Eddie Masher (USA), is alleged to have weighed only 48 lb at a height of 5 ft 7 in.

Female The lightest adult was Lucia Zarate (San Carlos, Mexico, 1863–89), an emaciated Mexican dwarf of 26 ½ in, who weighed 4.7 lb at the age of 17. She "fattened up" to 13 lb by her 20th birthday. At birth she had weighed 2 ½ lb.

In August 1825 an unsubstantiated claim was made for Claude-Ambroise

Seurat (1797–1826) of Troyes, France giving his biceps measurement as 4 in and the distance between his back and his chest as less than 3 in. According to one report he stood 5 ft 7 ½ in and weighed 78 lb, but in another account he was described as being 15 ft 4 in and only 36 lb.

Reproductivity

MOTHERHOOD

Most children The greatest officially recorded number of children born to one mother is 69, by the first of the two wives of Feodor Vassilyev (b. 1707–*fl.*1782), a peasant from Shuya, 150 miles east of Moscow, USSR. In 27 confinements she gave birth to 16 pairs of twins, seven sets of triplets and four sets of quadruplets. The case was reported to Moscow by the Monastery of Nikolskiy on 27 Feb 1782. At least 67 who were born in the period *c.* 1725–65 survived infancy.

It was reported on 31 Jan 1989 that Mrs Maria Olivera (b. 1939) of San Juan, Argentina had given birth to her 32nd child. All are believed to be still alive.

Oldest mother The oldest recorded mother for whom the evidence satisfied medical verification was Mrs Ruth

REPRODUCTIVITY

Coincident birthdates

It should be mentioned that births are not completely random. There are some days of the year on which more births are recorded than others. It is also true that within families there are tendencies toward births occurring at approximately the same (general) time, if not specific day.

Single family

The only verified example of a family producing five single children with coincident birthdays is that of Catherine (1952), Carol (1953), Charles (1956), Claudia (1961) and Cecilia (1966), born to Carolyn and Ralph Cummins of Clintwood, VA, all on 20 Feb. The odds against five single siblings sharing a birthdate would be one in 17,797,577,730—more than 3 ½ times the world's population.

Coincident generations

Ralph Bertram Williams was born on 4 Jul 1982 in Wilmington, NC. His father, grandfather and, in 1876, his great-grandfather, were also born on 4 July.

Rosemary and Leo Dignan of Palos Heights, IL became grandparents of two girls and one boy within two hours between 11:15 A.M. and 1:04 P.M. on 25 Aug 1989. The three babies were born to two sons and one daughter of the Dignans. The mothers did not know that they were having their babies at the same time.

Alice Kistler (nee Taylor), formerly Mrs Shepard (1899–1982), of Portland, OR. A birth certificate indicated that she gave birth to a daughter, Suzan, at Glendale, near Los Angeles, CA on 18 Oct 1956, when her age was 57 years 129 days.

In the *Gazette Médicale de Liége* (1 Oct 1891) Dr E. Derasse reported the case of one of his patients who gave birth to a healthy baby at the age of 59 years 5 months. The woman already had a married daughter age 40.

Longest pregnancy Claims of up to 413 days have been widely reported, but accurate data are bedeviled by the increasing use of oral contraceptive pills, which is a cause of amenorrhea (abnormal absence of menstruation). *The US Medical Investigator* of 27 Dec 1884 reported a case of 15 months 20 days, and the *Histoire de l'Académie* of 1751 the most extreme case of 36 months.

BABIES

Heaviest Big babies (i.e., over 10 lb) are usually born to mothers who are large, overweight or have some medical problem such as diabetes. The heaviest babies born to healthy mothers were each boys of 22 lb 8 oz, the first born to Signora Carmelina Fedele of Aversa, Italy in September 1955, and the second by cesarean section to Mrs Christina Samane at Sipetu Hospital, Transkei, South Africa on 24 May 1982. The latter boy, named Sithandawe, who suffers from Weaver's syndrome (excessive growth in children because of abnormalities in the parents' genes), weighed 154 lb and stood 5 ft 5 in on his sixth birthday.

Mrs Anna Bates (nee Swan; 1846–88), the 7-ft-5 ½-in Canadian giantess, gave birth to a boy weighing 23 lb 12 oz (length 30 in) at her home in Seville, OH on 19 Jan 1879, but the baby died 11 hours later.

Lightest single births The lowest birth weight recorded for a surviving infant, of which there is definite evidence, is 10 oz in the case of Mrs Marian Taggart (nee Chapman; 1938–83). This baby was born six weeks premature in South Shields, Great Britain. She was born unattended (length 12 in) and was nursed by Dr D.A. Shearer, who fed her hourly for the first 30 hours with brandy, glucose and water through a fountain-pen filler. At three weeks she weighed 1 lb 13 oz and by her first birthday 13 lb 14 oz. Her weight on her 21st birthday was 106 lb.

Lightest twins Mary, 16 oz, and Margaret, 19 oz, were born on 16 Aug 1931 to Mrs Florence Stimson of Old Fletton, Great Britain.

Test-tube babies There are various methods by which babies can be conceived outside of the mother's body. These children are usually known as "test-tube" babies and the technique as IVF (in-vitro fertilization).

Louise Brown (5 lb 12 oz) was delivered by cesarean section from Lesley Brown, age 31, in Oldham General Hospital,

Great Britain at 11:47 P.M. on 25 Jul 1978. Louise was externally conceived on 10 Nov 1977.

United States Elizabeth Carr (5 lb 12 oz) was delivered by cesarean section from Judy Carr, age 28, in Norfolk General Hospital, VA on 28 Dec 1981. Elizabeth was externally conceived on 15 Apr 1981. Dr Howard Jones of Eastern Virginia Medical School performed the in-vitro procedure.

First test-tube quintuplets Alan, Brett, Connor, Douglas and Edward were born to Linda and Bruce Jacobssen at University College Hospital, London, Great Britain on 26 Apr 1985.

Oldest mother to have delivered following IVF A woman 49 years 54 days (b. Cyprus) gave birth by cesarean section to a girl weighing 96 oz in October 1990. The fertilized egg had been implanted in the patient's womb under the supervision of Dr Krinos Trokoudes, Director of the Pedieos IVF Center in Nicosia, Cyprus.

First birth from frozen embryo Zoe (last name withheld) was delivered by cesarean section weighing 5 lb 13 oz on 28 Mar 1984 in Melbourne, Australia. Scientists from Monash University announced the birth.

United States A boy (9 lb 8 oz) was delivered by cesarean section on 4 Jun 1986 from Monique (last name withheld), age 36, in Cottage Hospital, Santa Barbara, CA. A second child (name withheld) was born on 23 Oct 1989 by the same procedure and it is believed that this is the only case of siblings from frozen embryos. Dr Richard Marrs was in charge of the procedure.

Premature—living James Elgin Gill was born to Brenda and James Gill, on 20 May 1987 in Ottawa, Ontario, Canada 128 days premature and weighing 1 lb 6 oz.

United States Ernestine Hudgins was born on 8 Feb 1983 in San Diego, CA about 18 weeks premature and weighing 17 oz.

Twins Joanne and Mark Holding (non-identical twins) were born on 28 Feb 1988 in Portsmouth, Great Britain 105 days premature. Joanne weighed 1 lb 15 oz and Mark 1 lb 8 oz.

Quadruplets Tina Piper of St Leonards-on-Sea, Great Britain, had quadruplets on 10 Apr 1988, at exactly 26 weeks term. Oliver, 2 lb 9 oz (d. Feb 1989), Francesca, 2 lb 2 oz, Charlotte, 2 lb 4 ½ oz, and Georgina, 2 lb 5 oz, were all born at The Royal Sussex County Hospital, Brighton, Great Britain.

MULTIPLE BIRTHS

"Siamese" twins Conjoined twins derive the name "Siamese" from the celebrated Chang and Eng Bunker ("Left" and "Right" in Thai), born at Meklong, Thailand on 11 May 1811 of Chinese parents. They were joined by a cartilaginous band at the chest. They

MULTIPLE BIRTHS

HIGHEST NUMBER REPORTED AT SINGLE BIRTH

10 (decaplets; 2 male, 8 female) in Bacacay, Brazil, 22 Apr 1946 (also report from Spain, 1924 and China, 12 May 1936).

HIGHEST NUMBER MEDICALLY RECORDED

9 (nonuplets; 5 male, 4 female) to Mrs Geraldine Brodrick at Royal Hospital, Sydney, Australia on 13 Jun 1971. 2 males stillborn. Richard (12 oz) survived 6 days.

9 (all died) to patient at University of Pennsylvania, Philadelphia, PA on 29 May 1972.

9 (all died) reported from Bagerhat, Bangladesh, c. 11 May 1977 to 30-year-old mother.

7 (septuplets) to Patti Jorgenson (Mrs Frustaci) on 21 May 1985. The three babies who survived ranged in weight from 1 lb upwards.

HIGHEST NUMBER SURVIVING

6 out of 6 (3 males, 3 females) to Mrs Susan Jane Rosenkowitz (nee Scoones) (b. Colombo, Sri Lanka, 28 Oct 1947) at Mowbray, Cape Town, South Africa on 11 Jan 1974. In order of birth they were: David, Nicolette, Jason, Emma, Grant and Elizabeth They totaled 24 lb 1 oz.

6 out of 6 (4 males, 2 females) to Mrs Rosanna Giannini (b. 1952) at Careggi Hospital, Florence, Italy on 11 Jan 1980. They are Francesco, Fabrizio, Giorgio, Roberto, Letizia and Linda.

QUINTUPLETS[1]

Heaviest
25 lb to Mrs Lui Saulien, Chekiang, China, on 7 Jun 1953.
25 lb to Mrs Kamalammal, Pondicherry, India, on 30 Dec 1956.

QUADRUPLETS

Heaviest
22 lb 13 oz to Mrs Ayako Takeda, Tsuchihashi Maternity Hospital, Kagoshima, Japan, on 4 Oct 1978 (4 girls).

Most Sets
4 to Mme Feodor Vassilyev, Shuya, Russia (d. *ante* 1770).

TRIPLETS[2]

Heaviest
26 lb 6 oz (unconfirmed) Iranian case (2 male, 1 female) on 18 Mar 1968.

Most Sets
15 to Maddalena Granata, Italy (b. 1839–*fl.* 1886).

TWINS

Heaviest
27 lb 12 oz (surviving) to Mrs J. P. Haskin, Fort Smith, AR, on 20 Feb 1924.

Most Sets
16 to Mme Vassilyev (see above). Note also that Mrs Barbara Zulu of

Barbeton, South Africa bore 3 sets of girls and 3 mixed sets in 7 years (1967–73).

[1] The South African press were unable to verify the birth of 5 babies to Mrs Charmaine Craig (nee Peterson) in Cape Town on 16 Oct 1980 and a sixth on 8 November. The reported names were Frank, Salome, John, Andrew, William and, belatedly, Deborah.

[2] Mrs Anna Steynvaait of Johannesburg, South Africa produced 2 sets within 10 months in 1960.

married (in 1843) the Misses Sarah and Adalaide Yates of Wilkes County, NC, and fathered 10 and 12 children respectively. They died within three hours of each other on 17 Jan 1874, age 62.

Rarest The rarest form of conjoined twins is dicephales tetrabrachius dipus (two heads, four arms and two legs). The only known examples are Masha and Dasha Krivoshlyapovy, born in the USSR on 4 Jan 1950.

Earliest successful separation The earliest successful separation of Siamese twins was performed on xiphopagus (joined at the sternum) girls at Mount Sinai Hospital, Cleveland, OH by Dr Jac S. Geller on 14 Dec 1952.

United States Fonda Michelle and Shannon Elaine Beaver of Forest City, NC were born on 9 Feb 1980 and successfully separated in February 1981.

Oldest surviving The oldest surviving unseparated twins are the craniopagus (heads are fused at the crown) pair, Yvonne and Yvette McCarther (b. 1949) of Los Angeles, CA. They have rejected an operation to separate them.

Most twins In Chungchon, South Korea it was reported in September 1981 that there were unaccountably 38 pairs in only 275 families—the highest ratio ever recorded.

Longest-separated twins Through the help of New Zealand's television program *Missing* on 27 Apr 1989, Iris (nee Haughie) Johns and Aro (nee Haughie) Campbell (b. 13 Jan 1914) were reunited after 75 years' separation.

United States Fraternal twins Lloyd Earl and Floyd Ellsworth Clark were born on 15 Feb 1917 in Nebraska. They were separated when only four months old and lived under their adopted names Dewayne William Gramly (Lloyd) and Paul Edward Forbes (Floyd). Both men knew that they had been born twins but it wasn't until 16 Jun 1986 that they were reunited, after having been separated for over 69 years.

Longest interval between twins Mrs Danny Berg (b. 1953) of Rome, Italy, who had been on hormone treatment after suffering two miscarriages, gave birth normally to a girl, Diana, on 23 Dec 1987, but the other twin, Monica, was delivered by cesarean on 30 Jan 1988.

Fastest triplet birth Bradley, Christopher and Carmon were born naturally to Mrs James E. Duck of Memphis, TN in two minutes on 21 Mar 1977.

Septuplets Septuplets were born on 21 May 1985 to Patti Jorgenson Frustaci of Orange, CA, a 30-year-old English teacher who had been taking a fertility drug. One baby was stillborn and the living infants weighed as little as 1 lb. In the weeks that followed, 3 more babies died, but 3 have survived.

Quindecaplets It was announced by Dr Gennaro Montanino of Rome that he had removed by hysterotomy after four months of the pregnancy the fetuses of ten girls and five boys from the womb of a 35-year-old housewife on 22 Jul 1971. A fertility drug was responsible for this unique instance of quindecaplets.

DESCENDANTS

In polygamous countries (countries which allow a man to have more than one wife at a time), the number of a person's descendants can become incalculable. The last Sharifian emperor of Morocco, Moulay Ismail (1672–1727), known as "The Bloodthirsty," was reputed to have fathered a total of 525 sons and 342 daughters by 1703 and achieved a 700th son in 1721.

At his death in April 1984 Adam Borntrager, age 96, of Medford, WI, had 707 direct descendants of whom all but 32 were living. The total extant comprised 11 children, 115 grandchildren, 529 great-grandchildren and 20 great-great-grandchildren.

Mrs Peter L. Schwartz (1902–88) had 14 children, 13 of whom are still living, 175 grandchildren, 477 great-grandchildren and 20 great-great-grandchildren.

Seven-generation family Augusta Bunge (nee Pagel; b. 13 Oct 1879) of Wisconsin learned that she was a great-great-great-great-grandmother when she received news of her great-great-great-great-grandson, Christopher John Bollig (b. 21 Jan 1989).

Great-great-great-grandmother Harriet Holmes of Newfoundland, Canada (b. 17 Jan 1899) became the youngest living great-great-great-grandmother on 8 Mar 1987 at the age of 88 years 50 days.

Most living ascendants Megan Sue Austin (b. 16 May 1982) of Bar Harbor, ME had a full set of grandparents and great-grandparents and five great-great-grandparents, making 19 direct ascendants.

Family tree The lineage of K'ung Ch'iu or Confucius (551–479 B.C.) can be traced back further than that of any other family. His great-great-great-great-grandfather K'ung Chia is known from the 8th century B.C. This man's 85th lineal descendants, Wei-yi (b. 1939) and Wei-ning (b. 1947), live today in Taiwan.

Longevity

No single subject is more obscured by vanity, deceit, falsehood and deliberate fraud than human longevity. Apart from the traces left by accidental markers (e.g. the residual effects of established dated events such as the Chernobyl incident),

there is no known scientific method of checking the age of any part of the living body.

Centenarians surviving beyond their 113th year are in fact extremely rare, and the present absolute proven limit of human longevity does not yet admit of anyone living to celebrate his or her 121st birthday.

From data on documented centenarians, actuaries have shown that only one 115-year life can be expected in 2.1 billion lives (note that the world population was estimated to be *c.* 5.3 billion by mid-1990).

The limits of credulity were reached on 5 May 1933, when a news agency filed a story from China with a Beijing source announcing that Li Chung-yun, the "oldest man on Earth," born in 1680, had just died after 256 years (*sic*).

The latest census in China revealed 3,800 centenarians, of whom two-thirds were women. According to a 1985 census carried out in the Chinese province of Xinjiang Urgur, there were 850 centenarians in the area, four between the ages of 103 and 125. In the United States as of 1 Jul 1989 the figure was 61,000.

In 1989 the United States population of people 65 and over was 31 million, representing 12.5% of the population. Since 1900 the American population 65 and over has increased tenfold from 3.1 million. It is projected that a child born in 1988 has a life expectancy of 74.9 years. In 1900 this figure was 46.9 years.

Oldest authentic centenarian The greatest *authenticated* age to which any human has ever lived is 120 years 237 days in the case of Shigechiyo Izumi of Asan on Tokunoshima, an island 820 miles southwest of Tokyo, Japan. He was born in Asan on 29 Jun 1865 and was recorded as a 6-year-old in Japan's first census of 1871. He died in his ranch house at 12:15 GMT on 21 Feb 1986 after developing pneumonia.

Oldest living The oldest living person in the world whose date of birth can be reliably authenticated is Jeanne Louise Calment, who was born in France on 21

■ Longest-separated twins
Iris Johns (nee Haughie) and Aro Campbell (ne Haughie) were reunited after 75 years of separation. (See above.)

65 +
POPULATION

State	Total (1,000's)
California	3,071
New York	2,341
Florida	2,277
Pennsylvania	1,819
Texas	1,714

Data: AARP/AOA

AUTHENTIC NATIONAL LONGEVITY RECORDS

	Years	Days		Born			Died	
Japan	120	237	Shigechiyo Izumi	29 Jun	1865	21 Feb		1986
United States[1]	115		Carrie White (Mrs; nee Joyner)	18 Nov	1874	14 Feb		1991
France	115		Jeanne Louise Calment	21 Feb	1875	fl.*August		1990
Great Britain[2]	114	208	Anna Eliza Williams (Mrs; nee Davies)	2 Jun	1873	27 Dec		1987
Canada[3]	113	124	Pierre Joubert	15 Jul	1701	16 Nov		1814
Australia	112	330	Caroline Maud Mockridge	11 Dec	1874	6 Nov		1987
Spain[4]	112	228	Josefa Salas Mateo	14 Jul	1860	27 Feb		1973
Norway	112	61	Maren Bolette Torp	21 Dec	1876	20 Feb		1989
Morocco	>112		El Hadj Mohammed el Mokri (Grand Vizier)		1844	16 Sep		1957
Poland	112	+	Roswlia Mielczarak (Mrs)		1868	7 Jan		1981
Ireland	111	327	The Hon. Katherine Plunket	22 Nov	1820	14 Oct		1932
Netherlands[5]	111	241	Jean Michael Reskens	11 May	1878	7 Jan		1990
Scotland[6]	111	238	Kate Begbie (Mrs)	9 Jan	1877	5 Sep		1988
South Africa[7]	111	151	Johanna Booyson	17 Jan	1857	16 Jun		1968
Sweden[8]	111	90	Wilhelmine Sande (Mrs)	24 Oct	1874	21 Jan		1986
Czechoslovakia	111	+	Marie Bernatkova	22 Oct	1857	fl. October		1968
Germany[9]	111		Maria Corba	15 Aug	1878	fl. March		1990
Finland	111	+	Fanny Matilda Nystrom	30 Sep	1878			1989
Channel Islands	110	321	Margaret Ann Neve (nee Harvey)	18 May	1792	4 Apr		1903
Northern Ireland	110	234	Elizabeth Watkins (Mrs)	10 Mar	1863	31 Oct		1973
Yugoslavia	110	150+	Demitrius Philipovitch	9 Mar	1818	fl. August		1928
Greece[10]	110	+	Lambrini Tsiatoura (Mrs)		1870	19 Feb		1981
USSR[11]	110	+	Khasako Dzugayev	7 Aug	1860	fl. August		1970
Italy	110	+	Damiana Sette (Sig)		1874	25 Feb		1985
Denmark	109	265	Maria Louise Augusta Bramsen	4 May	1878	23 Jan		1988
Tasmania (State of)	109	179	Mary Ann Crow (Mrs)	2 Feb	1836	31 Jul		1945
Belgium	108	327	Mathilda Vertommen-Hellemans	12 Aug	1868	4 Jul		1977
Iceland	108	45	Halldóra Bjarndóttir	14 Oct	1873	28 Nov		1981
Portugal[12]	108	+	Maria Luisa Jorge	7 Jun	1859	fl. July		1967
Malaysia	106	+	Hassan Bin Yusoff	14 Aug	1865	fl. January		1972
Luxembourg	105	228	Nicolas Wiscourt	31 Dec	1872	17 Aug		1978

[1] Ex-slave Mrs Martha Graham died at Fayetteville, NC on 25 Jun 1959 apparently aged 117 or 118. Census research shows that she was seemingly born in December 1844 and hence aged 114 years 6 months. Mrs Rena Glover Brailsford died in Summerton, SC on 6 Dec 1977 reputedly aged 118 years. Mrs Rosario Reina Vasquez, who died in California on 2 Sep 1980, was reputedly born in Sonora, Mexico on 3 Jun 1866, which would have made her 114 years 93 days. The 1900 US Federal Census for Crawfish Springs Militia District of Walker County, GA, records an age of 77 for a Mark Thrash. If the Mark Thrash (reputedly born in Georgia in December 1822) who died near Chattanooga, TN on 17 Dec 1943 was he, and the age attributed was accurate, then he would have survived for 121 years. According to Jackson Pollard's Social Security payments, he was born on 15 Dec 1869 in Georgia, but no birth certificate or family bible are available.

[2] British-born Miss Isabella Shepheard was allegedly 115 years old when she died at St Asaph, Clwyd, Great Britain, on 20 Nov 1948, but her actual age was believed to have been 109 years 90 days.

[3] Mrs Ellen Carroll died in North River, Newfoundland, Canada on 8 Dec 1943, reputedly aged 115 years 49 days.

[4] Señor Benita Medrana of Avila died on 28 Jan 1979, allegedly aged 114 years 335 days.

[5] Thomas Peters' birth was recorded on 6 Apr 1745 in Leeuwarden, Netherlands and he died aged 111 years 354 days on 26 Mar 1857 in Arnhem, Netherlands.

[6] Lachlen McDonald, who died on 7 Jun 1858 in Harris, Great Britain, was recorded as being "110 years" on his death certificate.

[7] Mrs Susan Johanna Deporter of Port Elizabeth, South Africa was reputedly 114 years old when she died on 4 Aug 1954. Mrs Sarah Lawrence of Cape Town, South Africa was reputedly 112 on 3 Jun 1968.

[8] Mrs W Sande was born in present-day Norway.

[9] Germany: an unnamed female died in 1979 aged 112 years, and an unnamed male, aged also 112 years, died in 1969. The Austrian record is 108 years (female d. 1975) and the Swiss record is also 108 years (female d. 1967).

[10] The claim that Liakon Efdokia died on 17 Jan 1982 aged 118 years 13 days is not substantiated by the censuses of 1971 or 1981. Birth registration before 1920 was fragmentary.

[11] There are allegedly 21,700 centenarians in the USSR (compared with 54,000 in the United States). Of these, 21,000 are ascribed to the Georgian SSR, i.e., one in every 232. In July 1962 it was reported that 128, mostly male, were in the one village of Medini.

[12] Senhora Jesuina da Conceicao of Lisbon was reputedly 113 years old when she died on 10 Jun 1965.

* Note: fl. is the abbreviation for the Latin *floruit*, meaning he or she was living at the relevant date.

Feb 1875. She now lives in a nursing home in Arles, Southern France.

United States The oldest living person in the United States is Ettie Mae Greene (nee Thomas), who was born in Indian Creek, WV on 8 Sep 1877. She now lives in a nursing home in Lindside, WV.

Oldest twins Eli Shadrack and John Meshak Phipps were born on 14 Feb 1803 at Affinghton, VA. Eli died in Hennessey, OK on 23 Feb 1911 at the age of 108 years 9 days, on which day John was still living in Shenandoah, IA.

Female On 17 Jun 1984, identical twin sisters Mildred Widman Philippi and Mary Widman Franzini of St Louis, MO celebrated their 104th birthday. Mildred died on 4 May 1985, 44 days short of the twins' 105th birthday. The probability of identical twins both reaching 100 is now about one in 50 million.

Oldest living triplets Faith, Hope and Charity Hardwell were born in Sweetwater, TX on 18 May 1899, and live together in a Sweetwater retirement home.

Oldest quadruplets The Ottman quads of Munich, Germany, Adolf, Anne-Marie, Emma and Elisabeth, celebrated their 78th birthday on 5 May 1991.

Anatomy and Physiology

Hydrogen (63 percent) and oxygen (25.5 percent) constitute the most common of the 24 elements regarded as normally being in the human body. Carbon, sodium, potassium, calcium, sulfur, chlorine (as chlorides), phosphorus, iron and zinc are all present in significant quantities. Present in "trace" quantities, but generally regarded as normal in a healthy body (even if their "necessity" is a matter of controversy) are iodine, fluorine, copper, cobalt, chromium, manganese, selenium, molybdenum, vanadium (probably), nickel (probably), silicon (probably), tin (probably) and arsenic.

HANDS, FEET AND HAIR

Touch The extreme sensitivity of the fingers is such that a vibration with a movement of 0.02 microns can be detected.

Longest fingernails Fingernails grow about 0.02 in in a week—four times faster than toenails. The aggregate measurement of those of Shridhar Chillal (b. 1937) of Pune, India, on 19 Mar 1991 was 181 in for the five nails on his left hand (thumb 41 in, index finger 31 in, third and fourth fingers 36 in in each, and the pinkie 37 in). He last cut his nails in 1952.

Least toes The two-toed syndrome exhibited by some members of the Wadomo tribe of the Zambezi Valley, Zimbabwe and the Kalanga tribe of the eastern Kalahari Desert, Botswana is hereditary via a single mutated gene.

They are not handicapped by their deformity, and can walk great distances without discomfort.

Largest feet If cases of elephantiasis are excluded, then the biggest feet known are those of Haji Mohammad Alam Channa of Pakistan, who wears size 22 sandals.

Longest hair Human hair grows at a rate of about 0.5 in in a month. If left uncut it will usually grow to a maximum of 2–3 ft.

In 1780 a head of hair measuring 12 ft in length and dressed in a style known as the Plica Polonica (hair closely matted together) was sent to Dresden after adorning the head of a Polish peasant woman for 52 years. The braid of hair had a circumference of 11.9 in.

In March 1989 a length of 21 ft was claimed for the hair of 74-year-old Mata Jagdamba, a Yogin living in Ujjain, North India.

The hair of Diane Witt of Worcester, MA measured over 11 ft in May 1990. She last cut her hair 9 years ago.

Most valuable hair On 18 Feb 1988 a bookseller from Cirencester, Great Britain, paid £5,575 ($10,035) for a lock of hair that had belonged to British naval hero Lord Horatio Nelson (1758–1805) at an auction held at Crewkerne, Great Britain.

Longest beard The beard of Hans N. Langseth (b. 1846 near Eidsvoll, Norway) measured 17 ½ ft at the time of his burial in Kensett, IA in 1927 after 15 years' residence in the United States. It was presented to the Smithsonian Institution, Washington, D.C., in 1967.

The beard of Janice Deveree, "the bearded lady" (b. Bracken Co., KY, 1842), was measured in 1884 at 14 in.

Longest mustache The mustache of Birger Pellas (b. 21 Sep 1934) of Malmö, Sweden, grown since 1973, reached 10 ft in March 1991.

Karna Ram Bheel (1928–87) was granted permission by a New Delhi prison governor in February 1979 to keep the 7-ft-10-in mustache which he had grown since 1949 during his life sentence. He used mustard, oil, butter and cream to keep it trim.

DENTITION

Earliest Tooth enamel is the only part of the human body which remains basically unchanged throughout life. It is also the hardest substance in the body. The first deciduous or milk teeth normally appear in infants at 5–8 months, these being the upper and lower jaw first incisors. There are many records of children born with teeth, the most distinguished example being Prince Louis Dieudonné, later Louis XIV of France, who was born with two teeth on 5 Sep 1638. Molars usually appear at 24 months, but in a case published in Denmark in 1970, a six-week premature baby was documented with erupted teeth at birth, of which four were in the molar region.

Most teeth at birth Shaun Keaney of Newbury, Great Britain was born on 10 Apr 1990 with 12 teeth, but they were extracted a few days after his birth.

Earliest false teeth From discoveries made in Etruscan tombs, partial dentures of bridgework type were being worn in what is now the Tuscany region of Italy as early as 700 B.C. Some were permanently attached to existing teeth and others were removable.

Most Cases of the growth in late life of a third set of teeth have been recorded several times. A reference to a case in France of a fourth dentition, known as Lison's case, was published in 1896.

Most dedicated dentist Brother Giovanni Battista Orsenigo of the Ospedale Fatebenefratelli, Rome, Italy, a dentist, conserved all the teeth he extracted during the time he exercised his profession from 1868 to 1904. In 1903 the number was counted and found to be 2,000,744 teeth, indicating an average of 185 teeth, or nearly six total extractions, a day.

Most valuable tooth In 1816 a tooth belonging to British scientist Sir Isaac Newton (1643–1727) was sold in London, Great Britain for £730 ($3,650). It was purchased by a nobleman who had it set in a ring, which he wore constantly.

OPTICS

Highest visual acuity The human eye is capable of judging relative position with remarkable accuracy, reaching limits of between 3–5 sec of arc.

In April 1984 Dr Dennis M. Levi of the College of Optometry, University of Houston, TX, repeatedly identified the position of a thin white line within 0.85 sec of arc. This is equivalent to a displacement of some ¼ in at a distance of 1 mile.

Color sensitivity The unaided human eye, under the best possible viewing conditions, comparing large areas of color, in good illumination, using both eyes, can distinguish 10,000,000 different color surfaces. The most accurate photoelectric spectrophotometers possess a precision probably only 40 percent as good as this. About 7.5 percent of men and 0.1 percent of women are colorblind. The most extreme form, monochromatic vision, is very rare. The highest rate of red–green color-blindness is in Czechoslovakia, and the lowest rate among Fijians and Brazilian Indians.

BONES

Longest Excluding a variable number of sesamoids (small rounded bones), there are 206 bones in the adult human body, compared with 300 in children (as they grow, some bones fuse together). The thigh bone or femur is the longest. It constitutes usually 27.5 percent of a person's stature, and may be expected to be 19 ¾ in long in a 6-ft-tall man. The longest recorded bone was the femur of the German giant Constantine, who died in Mons, Belgium, on 30 Mar 1902, age

30. It measured 29.9 in. The femur of Robert Wadlow, the tallest man ever recorded, measured an estimated 29 ½ in. (See Tallest men.)

Smallest The stapes or stirrup bone, one of the three auditory ossicles in the middle ear, measures 0.10–0.17 in in length and weighs from 0.03–0.065 grains.

MUSCLES

Smallest The stapedius, which controls the stapes (see above), an auditory ossicle in the middle ear, is less than 0.05 in long.

Most active It has been estimated that the eye muscles move an incredible 100,000 times a day or more. Many of these eye movements take place during the dreaming phrase of sleep. (See Longest and shortest dreams.)

Largest chest measurements The largest are among endomorphs (those with a tendency towards globularity). In the extreme case of Robert Earl Hughes (USA; 1926–58) this was 124 in, and T. J. Albert Jackson, currently the heaviest living man, has a chest measurement of 120 in. (See Weight, Heaviest living.)

Jamie Reeves (b. 1962) of Sheffield, Great Britain, the "World's Strongest Man," has a chest measurement of 60 in.

■ Longest fingernails
The five nails on the left hand of Shridhar Chillal (above) of Pune, India measure 181 in in total.
(Photo: Gamma Presse)

Lifting with teeth
Walter Arfeuille of Ieper-Vlamertinge, Belgium lifted weights totaling 621 lb a distance of 6¾ in off the ground with his teeth in Paris, France, on 31 Mar 1990.

Hercules John Massis (b. Wilfried Oscar Morbée, 1940–88) of Oostakker, Belgium prevented a helicopter from taking off using only a tooth bit harness in Los Angeles, CA on 7 Apr 1979 for a *Guinness Spectacular* TV show.

■ **Longest hair**
Mata Jagdamba (right), a Yogini living in Ujjain, North India, has hair measuring 21 ft long.

Hair splitting

The greatest reported achievement in hair splitting was that of the former champion cyclist and craftsman Alfred West (1901–85), who succeeded in splitting a human hair 17 times into 18 parts on eight occasions.

Shaving

The fastest barbers on record are Denny Rowe, who shaved 1,994 men in 60 min with a retractor safety razor in Herne Bay, Great Britain on 19 Jun 1988, taking on average 1.8 sec per volunteer, and drawing blood four times; and Gerry Harley, of Gillingham, Great Britain, who on 13 Aug 1984 shaved 235 even-braver volunteers with a cut-throat razor, averaging 15.3 sec per face. He drew blood only once.

With a height of 6 ft 4 in, he weighs 322 lb.

The largest muscular chest measurement recorded so far is that of American power-lifter Isaac "Dr Size" Nesser (b. 21 Apr 1962) of Greensburg, PA, whose chest measures 68.06 in. He is 5 ft 10 in tall and weighs 351 lb.

"Gentleman Dan" Bernhardt of Salt Lake City, UT, had a 70 in expanded chest in 1977.

Largest biceps Isaac "Dr Size" Nesser has biceps of 26 ⅛ in "cold" (not pumped).

WAISTS

Largest The largest waist ever recorded was that of Walter Hudson (b. 1944) of New York, which measured 119 in at his peak weight of 1,197 lb.

Queen Catherine de Medici (1519–89) decreed a waist measurement of 13.77 in for ladies of the French court, but this was at a time when females were more diminutive.

Smallest The smallest waist in someone of normal stature was that of Mrs Ethel Granger (1905–82) of Peterborough, Great Britain, reduced from a natural 22 in to 13 in over the period 1929–39.

A measurement of 13 in was also cliamed for the French actress Mlle Polaire (real name Emile Marie Bouchand; 1881–1939).

NECKS

Longest The maximum measured extension of the neck by the successive fitting of copper coils, as practiced by the women of the Padaung or Kareni tribe of Myanmar (formerly Burma), is 15 ¾ in. When the rings are removed, the muscles developed to support the head and neck shrink to their normal length.

BRAINS

Heaviest In normal brains there is no correlation between intelligence and size.

The heaviest brain ever recorded was that of a 50-year-old male, which weighed 4 lb 8.29 oz and was reported by Dr Thomas F. Hegert, chief medical examiner for District 9, State of Florida, on 23 Oct 1975.

Lightest The lightest "normal" or non-atrophied brain on record was one weighing 2 lb 6.7 oz reported by Dr P. Davis and Professor E. Wright of King's College Hospital, London, Great Britain in 1977. It belonged to a 31-year-old woman.

Most expensive skull The skull of Emanuel Swedenborg (1688–1772), the Swedish philosopher and theologian, was bought in London, Great Britain by the Royal Swedish Academy of Sciences for £5,500 ($10,505) on 6 Mar 1978.

Human computer The fastest extraction of a 13th root from a 100-digit number was achieved by Jaime Garcia Serrano of Bogotá, Colombia in a time of 0.15 sec on 24 May 1989 at the Hilton Hotel, Colombia.

Mrs Shakuntala Devi of India multiplied two 13-digit numbers (7,686,369,774,870 × 2,465,099,745,779) randomly selected by the Computer Department of Imperial College, London, Great Britain on 18 Jun 1980, in 28 seconds. Her answer was 18,947,668,177,995,426,462,773,730 and was correct. Some experts on calculating prodigies refuse to give credence to Mrs Devi on the grounds that her achievements are so vastly superior to the calculating feats of any other investigated prodigy that the authentication must have been defective.

Memory Bhandanta Vicitsara recited 16,000 pages of Buddhist canonical texts in Yangon, Myanmar (formerly Rangoon, Burma) in May 1974.

Gon Yang-ling, 26, has memorized more than 15,000 telephone numbers in Harbin, China, according to the Xinhua News Agency. Rare instances of eidetic memory—the ability to re-project and hence "visually" recall material—are known to science.

Dominic O'Brien of Guildford, Great Britain memorized on a single sighting a random sequence of 35 separate decks of cards (1,820 in all) that had been shuffled together with two corrections, at the Star Inn Furneux Pelham, Great Britain on 22 Jul 1990.

United States George Uhrin of Houston, TX memorized on a single sighting a random sequence of 30 separate decks of cards (1,560) that had been all shuffled together with two errors, at the Texas Commerce Tower, Houston, TX on 16 Jul 1989.

The greatest number of places of π Hideaki Tomoyori (b. 30 Sep 1932) of Yokohama, Japan recited pi from memory to 40,000 places in 17 hr 21 min including 4-hr-15-min breaks on 9–10 Mar 1987 at the Tsukuba University Club House.

Note: It is only the *approximation* of π at $^{22}/_7$ which recurs after its sixth decimal place and can, of course, be recited *ad nauseam*. The true value is a string of random numbers fiendishly difficult to memorize. The average ability for memorizing random numbers is barely more than 8, as proved by the common inability to memorize 9- or-10 digit telephone numbers.

VOICE

Greatest range The normal intelligible outdoor range of the male human voice in still air is 600 ft. The *silbo*, the whistled language of the Spanish-speaking Canary Island of La Gomera, is intelligible across the valleys, under ideal conditions, at 5 miles. There is a recorded case, under freak acoustic conditions, of the human voice being detectable at a distance of 10 ½ miles across still water at night.

Screaming The highest scientifically measured emission has been one of 128 decibels produced by the screaming of Simon Robinson of McLaren Vale, South Australia at The Guinness Challenge at Adelaide, Australia on 11 Nov 1988.

Whistling Roy Lomas achieved 122.5 decibels at 8.20 ft in the Deadroom at the British Broadcasting Corporation studios in Manchester, Great Britain on 19 Dec 1983.

Shouting Donald H. Burns of St George's, Bermuda achieved 119 decibels in shouting when he appeared on the Fuji TV film of *Narvhodo the World* at Liberty State Park, NJ on 18 Jan 1989.

Yodeling Yodeling has been defined as "repeated rapid changes from the chest-voice to falsetto and back again." The most rapid recorded is ten tones (six falsetto) in 0.88 sec, by Jim Whitman of Washington, Tyne & Wear, Great Britain at Bethesda, on 16 Nov 1990.

Lowest detectable sound The intensity of noise or sound is measured in terms of pressure. The pressure of the quietest sound that can be detected by a person of normal hearing at the most sensitive frequency of c. 2,750 Hz is 2×10^{-5} pascal. One-tenth of the logarithm to this standard provides a unit termed a decibel (dB). A noise of 30 dB is zero.

Highest noise levels Prolonged noise above 150 dB will cause permanent deafness, while above 192 dB a lethal over-pressure shock-wave can be formed. Equivalent continuous sound levels (LEQ) above 90 dB are impermissible in factories in many countries, but this compares with 125 emitted by racing cars and 130 by amplified music.

Highest detectable pitch The upper limit is calculated to be 20,000 Hz (cycles per sec), although it has been alleged that children with asthma can detect sounds of 30,000 Hz. Bats emit pulses at up to 90,000 Hz. It was announced in February 1964 that experiments in the USSR had conclusively proved that oscillations as high as 200,000 Hz can be detected if the oscillator is pressed against the skull.

Fastest talker Few people are able to speak *articulately* at a sustained speed above 300 words per minute. The fastest broadcaster has been regarded as Gerry Wilmot (b. Victoria, British Colombia,

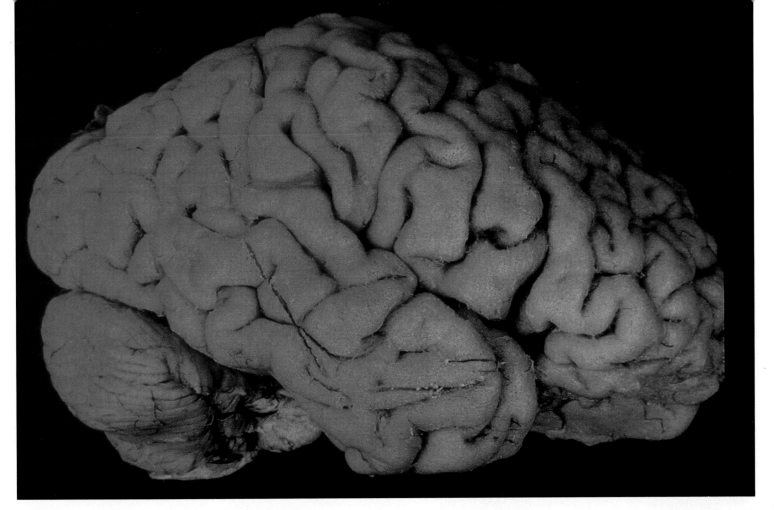

Canada, 6 Oct 1914), the ice hockey commentator of the late forties.

In public life the fastest speed recorded was a burst in excess of 300 words per min in a speech made in December 1961 by President John Fitzgerald Kennedy (1917–63).

Steve Woodmore of Orpington, Great Britain spoke 595 words in a time of 56.01 sec or 637.38 words per minute on ITV Program *Motor Mouth* on 22 Sep 1990.

United States John Moschitta (USA) recited 545 words in 55.8 sec, or 586 words per minute, on 24 May 1988 in Los Angeles, CA.

Backwards talking Steve Briers of Kilgetty, Great Britain recited the entire lyrics of Queen's album *A Night at the Opera* at British Broadcasting Corporation North-West Radio 4's *Cat's Whiskers* on 6 Feb 1990 in a time of 9 min 58.44 sec.

United States David Fuhrer of California recited the entire lyrics of Queen's album *A Night at the Opera* at Trax Recording Studio, CA on 28 Jul 1989 in a time of 10 min 19 sec.

BLOOD

Groups The preponderance of one blood group varies greatly from one locality to another. On a world basis Group O is the most common (46 percent), but in some areas, for example Norway, Group A predominates.

The rarest type in the world is a type of Bombay blood (subtype h-h) found so far only in a Czechoslovak nurse in 1961, and in a brother (Rh positive) and sister (Rh negative) named Jalbert in Massachusetts, reported in February 1968.

The most common subgroup in the United States is O+, which is found in 39 percent of the population. The rarest generic blood group is AB−, which occurs in only 0.6 percent of persons in the United States.

Richest natural resources Joe Thomas of Detroit, MI was reported in August 1970 to have the highest known level of Anti-Lewis B, the rare blood antibody. An American biological supply firm pays him $1,500 per quart. The Internal Revenue Service regards this income as a taxable liquid asset.

Donor and recipient From September 1966 to February 1989, Allen Doster, a self-employed beautician, has made a total of 1,037 platelet donations by both manual and machine plasmapheresis at Roswell Park Memorial Institute, NY. The current limit in America on machine plateletpheresis donations is 24 per year.

A 50-year-old hemophiliac, Warren C. Jyrich, required 2,400 donor units of blood, equivalent to 1,900 pints of blood, when undergoing open-heart surgery at the Michael Reese Hospital, Chicago, IL in December 1970.

Largest vein The largest is the inferior vena cava, which returns the blood from the lower half of the body to the heart.

Largest artery The largest is the *aorta*, which is 1.18 in in diameter where it leaves the heart. By the time it ends at the level of the fourth lumbar vertebra it is about 0.68 in in diameter.

Most alcoholic subject University of California Medical School, Los Angeles reported in December 1982 the case of a confused but conscious 24-year-old female, who was shown to have a blood alcohol level of 1.8 grains per 0.18 pt. After two days she discharged herself.

Tommy Johns of Brisbane, Queensland, Australia died in April 1988 from a brain tumor at the age of 66 years, after having been arrested nearly 3,000 times for being drunk and disorderly in a public place.

Human Body Superlatives

THE SKULL

SMALLEST BONE The stapes or stirrup bone, one of the three auditory ossicles in the middle ear, measures from 1.02 to 1.34 in in length and weighs from 0.00071 to 0.0015 oz.

5 LONGEST MUSCLE NAME The *levator labii superioris alaeque nasi* runs inward and downward on the face, with one branch running to the upper lip and the other to the nostril. It is the muscle which curls the upper lip and its action was particularly well demonstrated in the performances of the late Elvis Presley (1939 –77). In the late 50's he was renowned for his superlative upper lip muscle movement when singing and acting in *Love Me Tender*, one of his many early films.(See above.)

6 MOST INJURED JOINT It is estimated that most sports career-ending injuries are a result of twists, tears or snaps to vital tendons, ligaments and cartilages of the knee joint. One of the few athletes to recover fully from a career-threatening knee injury is Bernard King of the Washington Bullets. Injured in a game in March 1985, King's anterior cruciate ligament had to be replaced with a band of ligaments from his upper leg. King did not play again until March 1987, and his remarkable comeback was highlighted by his selection to the Eastern Conference team in the 1990-91 NBA All-Star Game.

7 STRONGEST JOINT The strongest joint of the body is arguably the hip. The ball on the end of the femur (thigh bone) fits almost perfectly into the socket on the pelvis. It is only put out of joint by enormous force such as a car crash or parachute failure.

8 LONGEST MUSCLE The longest muscle in the human body is the sartorius, which is a narrow, ribbon-like muscle running from the pelvis across the front of the thigh to the top of the tibia below the knee. Its purpose is to draw the lower limb into the cross-legged sitting position, proverbially associated with tailors. As other, stronger muscles in the body can perform this action, the sartorius could be regarded as an "extra" of doubtful merit, since it is extremely painful if torn.

2 STRONGEST MUSCLE The masseter, of which there are two, one on each side of the mouth, is responsible for biting. In August 1986, Richard Hofmann (b. 1949) of Lake City, FL achieved a bite strength of 975 lb for approximately 2 secs. This figure is more than six times the normal biting strength.

3 TEETH Tooth enamel is the hardest substance in the body, with a Knoop number of over 300. It is also the only part of the body which remains basically unchanged throughout life. Thus a person in his 70's with a full set of teeth has enamel in his mouth that was originally formed in his mother's womb.

4 The biggest tooth is the first upper molar, which usually has three roots.

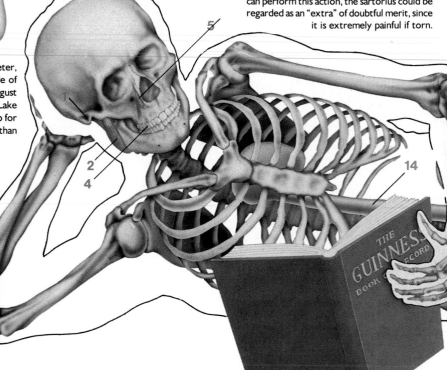

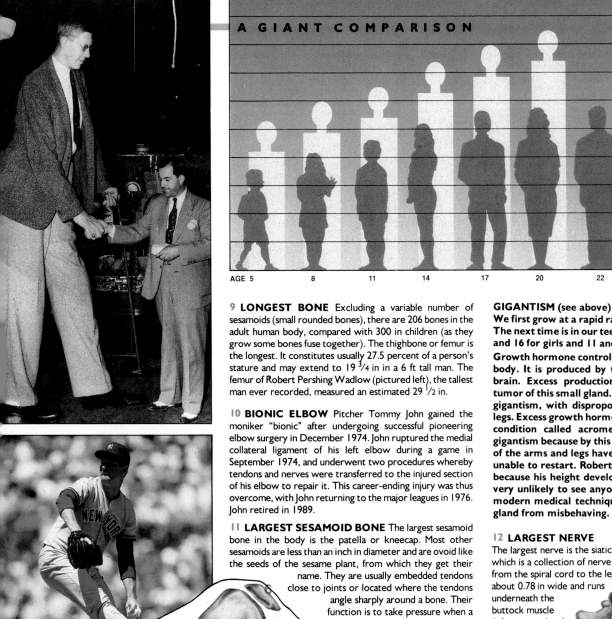

A GIANT COMPARISON

AGE 5   8   11   14   17   20   22   ROBERT WADLOW AT 22 YEARS

9 LONGEST BONE Excluding a variable number of sesamoids (small rounded bones), there are 206 bones in the adult human body, compared with 300 in children (as they grow some bones fuse together). The thighbone or femur is the longest. It constitutes usually 27.5 percent of a person's stature and may extend to 19 ¾ in in a 6 ft tall man. The femur of Robert Pershing Wadlow (pictured left), the tallest man ever recorded, measured an estimated 29 ½ in.

10 BIONIC ELBOW Pitcher Tommy John gained the moniker "bionic" after undergoing successful pioneering elbow surgery in December 1974. John ruptured the medial collateral ligament of his left elbow during a game in September 1974, and underwent two procedures whereby tendons and nerves were transferred to the injured section of his elbow to repair it. This career-ending injury was thus overcome, with John returning to the major leagues in 1976. John retired in 1989.

11 LARGEST SESAMOID BONE The largest sesamoid bone in the body is the patella or kneecap. Most other sesamoids are less than an inch in diameter and are ovoid like the seeds of the sesame plant, from which they get their name. They are usually embedded tendons close to joints or located where the tendons angle sharply around a bone. Their function is to take pressure when a tendon is going around a joint, as when kneeling.

GIGANTISM (see above)

We first grow at a rapid rate in our mothers' womb. The next time is in our teens, between the ages of 11 and 16 for girls and 11 and 18 for boys.

Growth hormone controls the growth of the human body. It is produced by the pituitary gland in the brain. Excess production is usually caused by a tumor of this small gland. In childhood this results in gigantism, with disproportionately long arms and legs. Excess growth hormone in adult life produces a condition called acromegaly. It does not cause gigantism because by this stage of life the long bones of the arms and legs have stopped growing and are unable to restart. Robert Wadlow was a true giant because his height developed in childhood. We are very unlikely to see anyone like him again because modern medical techniques can stop the pituitary gland from misbehaving.

12 LARGEST NERVE
The largest nerve is the siatic nerve. This broad flat nerve, which is a collection of nerve fibers from the spiral cord to the leg, is about 0.78 in wide and runs underneath the buttock muscle (*gluteus maximus*).

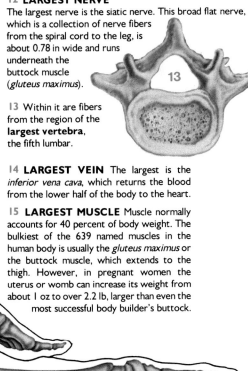

13 Within it are fibers from the region of the **largest vertebra**, the fifth lumbar.

14 LARGEST VEIN The largest is the *inferior vena cava*, which returns the blood from the lower half of the body to the heart.

15 LARGEST MUSCLE Muscle normally accounts for 40 percent of body weight. The bulkiest of the 639 named muscles in the human body is usually the *gluteus maximus* or the buttock muscle, which extends to the thigh. However, in pregnant women the uterus or womb can increase its weight from about 1 oz to over 2.2 lb, larger than even the most successful body builder's buttock.

Artwork: Pat Gibbon. Photos: All-Sport, Alton Telegraph and RCA Records.

Cardiopulmonary resuscitation

Three teams of two, consisting of David Bailey and Les Williams, Angie Drinkard and Rich Martel, and Michelle Tyler and Sherri Johnson, all completed CPR marathons (cardiopulmonary resuscitation—15 compressions alternating with two breaths) of 120 hr 6 min from 1–6 Sep 1988 at Melbourne, FL.

Lung power

The inflation of a standardized meteorological balloon to a diameter of 8 ft against time was achieved by Nicholas Berkeley Mason in 45 min 8 sec at the British Broadcasting Corporation TV Center, London, Great Britain on 25 Sep 1989, later shown on the *Record Breakers* television program.

AIDS STATISTICS

State	Cases
New York	36,459
California	32,547
Florida	15,277
Texas	12,947
New Jersey	10,955

City	Cases
New York	31,635
Los Angeles	11,409
San Francisco	9,943
Houston	5,086
Washington, D.C.	4,886

Data: Centers for Disease Control (31 Mar 1991)

William Pitt the Younger (1759–1806), the British prime minister, once allegedly drank 574 bottles of claret, 854 bottles of Madeira and 2,410 bottles of port in a single year!

CELLS

Biggest The biggest cell body is the ovum (egg cell) which comes from the female ovary. It is about the size of the period at the end of this paragraph.

Smallest Some of the smallest cells are brain cells in the cerebellum that measure about 0.005 mm.

Longest The longest cells are neurons of the nervous system. Motor neurons 4.26 ft long have cell bodies (gray matter) in the lower spinal cord with axons (white matter) which carry nerve impulses 4.26 ft from the spinal cord down to the big toe. Even longer are the cell systems which carry certain sensations (vibration and positional sense) back from the big toe to the brain. Their uninterrupted length, from the toe and up the posterior part of the spinal cord to the medulla of the brain, is about equal to the height of the body.

Fastest turnover of body cells The fastest turnover of body cells, i.e., the shortest life, is in the lining of the alimentary tract (guts), where the cells are shed every three days.

Longest life Those with the longest life are brain cells, which last for life. They may be three times as old as bone cells, which may live 25–30 years.

Longest memory The lymphocyte has probably the longest memory of any cell. As successive generations of lymphocytes are produced during life the cells never forget an enemy. So, for example, once a measles virus has introduced itself to the lymphocytes in the first years of life, these stalwarts of the immune system will still be ready to recognize and destroy the measles virus 70 years later. In other words, you cannot get measles twice.

Largest blood cell The largest blood cell is the megakaryocyte. It spends its life in the bone marrow, rarely venturing out into the main stream of the blood itself. In the marrow it produces perhaps the "stickiest" particles in the body—the platelets. There are about 250,000 platelets in each pin-prick (cu. mm) of blood. They have an important role in stopping bleeding. Once a hole is formed in a blood vessel the platelets quickly gather at the site and stick to it, thus sealing the breach.

BODY TEMPERATURE

Highest Willie Jones, 52, was admitted to Grady Memorial Hospital, Atlanta, GA on 10 Jul 1980 with heatstroke on a day when the temperature reached 90° F with 44 percent humidity. His temperature was found to be 115.7° F. After 24 days he was discharged "at prior baseline status."

Lowest People may die of hypothermia with body temperatures of 95° F. There are three recorded cases of individuals surviving body temperatures as low as 60.8° F: Dorothy Mae Stevens (1929–1974), who was found in an alley in Chicago, IL on 1 Feb 1951 with a pulse that had dropped to 12 beats per min; Vickie Mary Davis, age 2 years 1 month, discovered in an unheated house in Marshalltown, IA on 21 Jan 1956; and 2-year old Michael Troke, found in the snow near his home in Milwaukee, WI on 19 Jan 1985.

ILLNESS AND DISEASE

Commonest The commonest non contagious disease is periodontal disease, such as gingivitis (inflammation of the gums). In their lifetime few people completely escape the effects of tooth decay.

The commonest contagious disease in the world is coryza (acute nasopharyngitis), or the common cold.

Infestation with pinworm (*Enterobius vermicularis*) approaches 100 percent in some tropical areas of the world.

United States The greatest reported loss of working time in the United States, as reported by the Bureau of Labor Statistics, is from sprains and strains. In 1987 63.3 days per 100 employees were lost to illness or injury in the private sector. In 1988 76.1 days were lost.

Rarest The last case of endemic smallpox was recorded in Ali Maow Maalin in Merka, Somalia on 26 Oct 1977. This disease is now extinct.

Kuru (literally, "the shakes") is now believed to be extinct and was only found among the Fore tribe of Papua New Guinea. It is believed that the virus was transmitted during ritual mourning, when the brain of the deceased was eaten by women and children.

Most infectious and most fatal The pneumonic form of plague, as evidenced by the Black Death of 1347–51, had a mortality rate of 100 percent. A quarter of the population of Europe perished during the outbreak.

Highest mortality Rabies in humans has been regarded as uniformly fatal when associated with the hydrophobia symptom (a pathological fear of drinking fluids because of painful spasms while swallowing). A 25-year-old woman, Candida de Sousa Barbosa of Rio de Janeiro, Brazil, following surgery by Dr Max Karpin, was believed to be the first-ever survivor of the disease in November 1968.

Some sources prefer the case of an unnamed seven-year-old boy living near Tampa, FL who, on 23 Jun 1953, was bitten on the chest by a rabid common vampire bat (*Desmodus rotundus*). The boy was put on a course of prophylactic immunization and eventually made a full recovery.

While the *disease* rabies is regarded as being almost universally fatal, this is not to be confused with being bitten by a rabid animal. With immediate treatment the virus can be prevented from invading the nervous system and chances of survival can be as high as 95 percent.

The virus AIDS (Acquired Immune Deficiency Syndrome) was first reported in 1981. The Human Immunodeficiency Virus (HIV), which causes AIDS, was jointly discovered in January 1983 by Luc Montagnier, Françoise Barré Sinoussi and Jean-Claude Chermann at the Institute Pasteur, Paris, France, and Robert Gallo and co-workers at the National Institutes of Health, Bethesda, MD as the Human T-lymphotrophic Type III (HTLV III) virus. The World Health Organization (WHO) reported 345,553 HIV positive cases worldwide by 1 Apr 1991. WHO estimates that there are 8–10 million HIV-infected people worldwide. Out of 180 countries that report to WHO, 162 show at least one or more reported cases. There have not yet been any cases of recovery from AIDS.

By April 1991 the total number of HIV positive cases in the United States was 171,876. This total included 168,913 adults and 2,963 children under 13. The total number of deaths was 108,731, with 107,210 adults and 1,521 children.

Leading cause of death In industrialized countries, arteriosclerosis (thickening of the arterial wall) underlies much coronary and cerebrovascular disease. In 1988, the top five causes of death in the United States were: heart disease, 765,156; cancer, 485,048; brain disease, 150,517; accidents, including automobile, 97,100; and lung disease and related conditions, 82,853.

Most notorious carrier The most publicized of all typhoid carriers was Mary Mallon (real name Maria Anna Caduff), known as Typhoid Mary, who was born in Graubunden, Switzerland in 1855 and arrived as an immigrant in New York City, on 11 Jan 1868. In her job as a cook she was the source of 53 outbreaks, including the 1903 epidemic of 1,400 cases in Ithaca, NY, and three deaths. She was placed under permanent detention at Riverside Hospital on North Brother Island in the East River, New York City from 1915 until her death from bronchopneumonia on 11 Nov 1938.

MEDICAL EXTREMES

Postmortem birth The longest gestation interval in a postmortem birth was one of 84 days in the case of a girl born on 5 Jul 1983 to a brain-dead woman in Roanoke, VA who had been kept on a life support machine since April.

Heart arrest The longest is four hours in the case of a Norwegian fisherman, Jan Egil Refsdahl (b. 1936), who fell overboard in the icy waters off Bergen on 7 Dec 1987. He was rushed to nearby Haukeland Hospital after his body temperature fell to 77° F and his heart stopped beating, but he made a full recovery after he was connected to a heart–lung machine normally used for heart surgery.

United States On 9 Oct 1986, Allen Smith, age 2, fell into the swollen waters of the Stanislaus River in Oakdale, CA. He was spotted 90 minutes later and rushed to Modesto Memorial Hospital, where 2 hours later his heart began beating again spontaneously.

Pulse rates A normal adult rate is 70–78 beats per min at rest for males and 75–85 for females. (The abnormal heart may beat as fast as 300 times per min, or the beat may be so slow as to be virtually undetectable). The heart rate may increase to 200 or more during violent exercise in the unfit. Super-fit athletes do not have to increase their heart rates nearly as much as this. The reason is that with training the fit heart can put out much more blood with each contraction. Thus it is able to produce the necessary increase of blood during exercise by raising its rate to perhaps only 140 beats per minute.

Longest coma Elaine Esposito (b. 3 Dec 1934) of Tarpon Springs, FL, never stirred after an appendectomy on 6 Aug 1941, when she was 6 years old. She died on 25 Nov 1978 at the age of 43 years 357 days, having been in a coma for 37 years 111 days.

Longest and shortest dreams Dreaming sleep is characterized by rapid eye movements known as REM, first described in 1953 by William Dement of the University of Chicago. The longest recorded period of REM is one of 2 hr 23 min on 15 Feb 1967 at the Department of Psychology, University of Illinois, Chicago on Bill Carskadon, who had had his previous sleep interrupted. In July 1984 the Sleep Research Center, Haifa, Israel recorded no REM in a 33-year-old male who had a shrapnel brain injury. (See Most active muscle.)

Longest in "iron lung" Mrs. Laurel Nisbet (1912–85) of La Crescenta, CA was in an "iron lung" for 37 years 58 days continuously until her death.

Fastest nerve impulses The results of experiments published in 1966 have shown that the fastest messages transmitted by the human nervous system can travel at 180 mph. With advancing age, impulses are carried 15 percent more slowly.

Heaviest organ The skin is medically considered to be an organ. It weighs around 5.9 lb in an average adult. The heaviest internal organ is the liver at 3.3 lb. This is four times heavier than the heart.

Hiccupping The longest recorded attack of hiccupping is that which afflicted Charles Osborne (1894–1990) of Anthon, IA for 69 years, since 1922. He contracted it when slaughtering a hog and was unable to find a cure, but led a reasonably normal life in which he had two wives and fathered eight children. He admitted, however, that he could not keep his false teeth in. In July 1986 he was reported to be hiccupping at a rate of 20–25 per minute, down from his earlier high of 40.

Sneezing The longest-lasting sneezing fit ever recorded is that of Donna Griffiths (b. 1969) of Pershore, Great Britain. She started sneezing on 13 Jan 1981 and surpassed the previous duration record of 194 days on 27 Jul 1981. She sneezed an estimated million times in the first 365 days.

She achieved her first sneeze-free day on 16 Sep 1983—the 978th day.

The fastest speed at which particles expelled by sneezing have ever been measured to travel is 103.6 mph.

Snoring The highest sound level recorded by any chronic snorer peaked at 90 decibels, measured at the Department of Medicine, University of British Columbia, Vancouver, Canada during the evening of 3 Nov 1987. The meter was placed 2 ft above the head of Mark Thompson Hebbard (b. 28 Feb 1947) of Richmond, British Columbia, Canada, who maintained an overall level of 85 decibels. As a Vancouver city traffic bylaw for acceptable noise stipulates a maximum of 80 decibels, he wonders if he is legally entitled to sleep there.

Sleeplessness Victims of the very rare condition known as chronic colestites (total insomnia) have been known to go without definable sleep for many years.

Motionlessness The longest that anyone has continuously remained motionless is 24 hours, by William Fuqua at Glendale, CA, on 17–18 May 1985 while sitting on a motorcycle.

Antonio Gomes dos Santos of Zare, Portugal continuously stood motionless for 15 hr 2 min 55 sec on 30 Jul 1988 at the Amoreiras Shopping Center, Lisbon.

Fire-breathers Reg Morris blew a flame from his mouth to a distance of 31 ft at the Miner's Rest, Chasetown, Great Britain on 29 Oct 1986.

Fire extinguishers Inge Widar Svingen, alias "Benifax" of Norway, on 10 Aug 1990 extinguished 25,270 torches of flame in his mouth in 2 hrs at Kolvereid in Nord-Trøndelag, Norway.

On 26 Jul 1986 at Port Lonsdale, Victoria, Australia, Sipra Ellen Lloyd set a female record by extinguishing 8,357 torches. *Note: Fire-eating is potentially a highly dangerous activity.*

Human salamanders The highest dry-air temperature endured by naked men in US Air Force experiments in 1960 was 400° F, and for heavily clothed men 500° F. (Steaks require only 325° F to cook.) Temperatures of 284° F have been found quite bearable in saunas.

Swallowing The worst reported case of compulsive swallowing of objects involved an insane female, Mrs H., who at the age of 42 complained of a "slight abdominal pain." She proved to have 2,533 objects, including 947 bent pins, in her stomach. These were removed by Drs Chalk and Foucar in June 1927 at the Ontario Hospital, Canada. In a more recent case, 212 objects were removed from the stomach of a man admitted to Groote Schuur Hospital, Cape Town, South Africa in May 1985. They included 53 toothbrushes, two telescopic aerials, two razors and 150 handles of disposable razors.

Another compulsive swallower in the United States, a 24-year-old psychoneurotic woman, gulped down a 5-in-long iron hinge bolt from a hospital door, which amazingly passed through the curve of the duodenum and the intestinal tract and broke the bedpan when the patient successfully passed the object.

Hunger strike Doctors estimate that a well-nourished individual can survive without medical consequences on a diet of sugar and water for 30 days or more. The longest period for which anyone has gone without solid food is 382 days in the case of Angus Barbieri (b. 1940) of Tayport, Great Britain, who lived on tea, coffee, water, soda water and vitamins in Maryfield Hospital, Dundee, Great Britain, from June 1965 to July 1966. His weight declined from 472 lb to 178 lb. *Note: Records claimed without continuous medical surveillance are inadmissible.*

The longest recorded case of survival without food *and* water is 18 days by Andreas Mihavecz, then 18, of Bregenz, Austria, who was put in a holding cell on 1 Apr 1979 in a local government building in Höchst, and then was totally forgotten by the police. On 18 Apr 1979 he was discovered close to death, having had neither food nor water. He had been a passenger in a car that crashed.

Under water In 1986 two-year-old Michelle Funk of Salt Lake City, UT, made a full recovery after spending 66 minutes under water. The toddler fell into a swollen creek near her home while playing. When she was eventually discovered, rescue workers found she had no pulse or heartbeat. Her life was saved by the first successful bypass machine; it warmed her blood, which had dropped to 66° F. Doctors at the hospital described the time she had spent underwater as the "longest documented submergence with an intact neurological outcome."

g forces The highest g value endured on a water-braked rocket sled is 2.9 oz for 0.04 sec by Eli L. Beeding, Jr. at Holloman Air Force Base, NM on 16 May 1958. He was subsequently hospitalized for three days.

A land diver of Pentecost Island, Vanuatu (formerly the New Hebrides) dove from a platform 81 ft 3 in high with liana vines attached to his ankles on 15 May 1982. His body speed was 50 ft per sec, or 34 mph. The jolt transmitted a momentary g force in excess of 110.

Longest stay in a hospital Miss Martha Nelson was admitted to the Columbus State Institute for the Feeble-Minded in Ohio in 1875. She died in January 1975 at the age of 103 years 6 months in the Orient State Institution, OH after spending more than 99 years in hospitals.

Pill-taking The highest recorded total of pills swallowed by a patient is 565,939 between 9 Jun 1967 and 19 Jun 1988 by C.H.A. Kilner (1926–88) of Bindura, Zimbabwe.

Most injections A diabetic, Mrs Evelyn Ruth Winder (b. 1921) of Invercargill, New Zealand gave an estimated 62,948 insulin injections to herself over 60 years to March 1991.

Most tattoos The ultimate in being tattooed is represented by Tom Leppard of the Isle of Skye, Scotland. He has chosen a leopard-skin design, with all the

Standing The longest period on record that anyone has continuously stood is more than 17 years in the case of Swami Maujgiri Maharaj when performing the *Tapasya* or penance from 1955 to November 1973 in Shahjahanpur, Uttar Pradesh, India. When sleeping he would lean against a plank. He died at the age of 85 in September 1980.

Balancing on one foot The longest recorded duration for balancing on one foot is 34 hr by N. Ravi in Sathyamangalam City, Tamil Nadu, India on 17–18 Apr 1982. The disengaged foot may not be rested on the standing foot nor may any object be used for support or balance.

Eating Michel Lotito (b. 15 Jun 1950) of Grenoble, France, known as Monsieur Mangetout, has been eating metal and glass since 1959. Gastroenterologists have X-rayed his stomach and described his ability to consume 2 lb of metal per day as unique. His diet since 1966 has included 10 bicycles, a supermarket cart (in 4½ days), 7 TV sets, 6 chandeliers and a low-calorie Cessna light aircraft, which he ate in Caracas, Venezuela. He is said to have provided the only example in history of a coffin (handles and all) ending up inside a man.

Stretcher bearing

The record for carrying a stretcher case with a 140-lb "body" is 142.3 miles in 38 hr 39 min by two four-man teams from 1 Field Ambulance, Canadian Forces Base, Calgary, Canada on 5–7 Apr 1989.

The record limited to youth organizations (under 20 years of age) and 8-hr carrying is 42.02 miles by 8 members of the Henry Meoles School, Moreton, Great Britain on 13 Jul 1980.

skin between the dark spots tattooed saffron yellow. The area of his body covered is approximately 3,002 in^2, 99.2 percent of totality. Bernard Moeller of Pennsylvania claimed to have 8,960 individual tattoos on 4 Dec 1989, and Walter Stiglitz of New Jersey claims 5,488 separate tattoos by six different artists.

The world's most decorated woman is strip artiste "Krystyne Kolorful" (b. 5 Dec 1952, Alberta, Canada). Her 95 percent bodysuit took 10 years to complete.

OPERATIONS

Longest The most protracted reported operation was one of 96 hr performed from 4–8 Feb 1951 in Chicago, IL on Mrs Gertrude Levandowski for the removal of an ovarian cyst. During the operation her weight fell from 616 lb to 308 lb. The patient suffered from a weak heart and surgeons had to exercise the utmost caution during the operation.

Most Dr M.C. Modi, a pioneer of mass eye surgery in India since 1943, together with assistants, has performed as many as 833 cataract operations in one day, visited 45,416 villages and 10,094,632 patients, making a total of 595,019 operations to February 1990.

Dr Robert B. McClure (b. 1901) of Toronto, Ontario, Canada performed a career total of 20,423 major operations from 1924 to 1978.

On 2 Mar 1977 Mr Jens Kjaer Jension (b. 1914) of Hoven, Denmark was discharged from a local hospital after having had 32,131 thorns removed from his body during 248 visits over a period of six years. In 1967 he had tripped and fallen into a pile of spiky barberry cuttings in his garden and was rushed unconscious to the hospital. Even today he is still troubled by thorns working their way out through the skin of his legs.

Oldest patient The greatest recorded age at which anyone has undergone an operation is 111 years 105 days in the case of James Henry Brett, Jr. (1849–1961) of Houston, TX. He underwent a hip operation on 7 Nov 1960.

Earliest appendectomy The earliest recorded successful appendix operation was performed in 1736 by Claudius Amyand (1680–1740). He was Serjeant Surgeon to King George II (r. 1727–1760).

Earliest general anesthesia The earliest recorded operation under general anesthesia was for the removal of a cyst from the neck of James Venable by Dr Crawford Williamson Long (1815–78), using diethyl ether ($C_2H_5)_2O$, in Jefferson, GA on 30 Mar 1842.

Fastest amputation The shortest time recorded for a leg amputation in the pre-anesthetic era was 13–15 sec by Napoleon's chief surgeon, Dominique Larrey. There could have been no ligation of blood vessels.

Largest tumor The largest tumor ever recorded was Spohn's case of an ovarian cyst weighing 328 lb taken from a woman in Texas in 1905. She made a full recovery.

Largest gallbladder On 15 Mar 1989 at the National Naval Medical Center in Bethesda, MD, Prof. Bimal C. Ghosh removed a gallbladder that weighed 23 lb from a 69-year-old woman. The patient had been complaining of increasing swelling around the abdomen, and after removal of this enlarged gallbladder, which weighed more than three times as much as the average newborn baby, the patient felt perfectly well and left the hospital 10 days after the operation.

Surgical instruments The largest instruments are robot retractors used in abdominal surgery, introduced by Abbey Surgical Instruments of Chingford, Great Britain in 1968 and weighing 11 lb. Some bronchoscopic forceps measure 23½ in in length.

The smallest is the microcystotome, a super microknife for cutting the lens capsule in eye microsurgery. The working part is 0.011 in long and 2.03 in wide. The instrument is licensed by the Research and Technology Complex of the Russian Ministry of Health, Moscow.

TRANSPLANTS

Heart The first heart transplant operation was performed on Louis Washkansky, age 55, at the Groote Schuur Hospital, Cape Town, South Africa between 1 A.M. and 6 A.M., on 3 Dec 1967, by a team of 30 headed by Professor Christiaan Neethling Barnard. The donor was Miss Denise Ann Darvall, age 25. Washkansky lived for 18 days.

United States The first operation was performed on a 2½-week-old baby boy at Maimonides Hospital, Brooklyn, NY on 6 Dec 1967 by a team of 22 headed by Dr Adrian Kantrowitz. The donor was a newborn infant. The baby boy lived 6½ hours. The first adult transplant took place at the Stanford Medical Center in Palo Alto, CA on 6 Jan 1968 by Dr Norman E. Shumway and was performed on 54-year-old Mike Kasperak. Mr Kasperak, a retired steelworker, lived 14 days. From December 1967 until February 1990 there have been 7,831 heart transplants. In 1989 there was a total of 1,621 transplants.

Double heart transplant The first double heart transplant operation in the United States was performed on Darrell Hammarley, age 56, at the Stanford Medical Center in Palo Alto, CA on 20 Nov 1968 by Dr Norman E. Shumway. The first heart implanted failed to beat steadily and was replaced by a second transplant two hours later.

Longest surviving William George van Buuren of California (b. 24 May 1929) received an unnamed person's heart at the Stanford Medical Center, Palo Alto, CA on 3 Jan 1970 and is still alive today. The surgeon who performed the operation was Dr Edward Stinson.

Youngest Paul Holt of Vancouver, British Columbia, Canada underwent a heart transplant at Loma Linda Hospital in California on 16 Oct 1987 at the age of 2 hr 34 min. He was born six weeks premature weighing 6 lb 6 oz.

First transplantee to give birth Betsy Sneith, 23, gave birth to a girl, Sierra (7 lb 10 oz), at the Stanford Medical Center, Palo Alto, CA on 17 Sep 1984. She had received a donor heart in Feb 1980.

Animal-to-human transplant The first operation in the United States was carried out on 23 Jan 1964 at the University of Mississippi Medical Center in Jackson, MS by a team of 12 headed by Dr James D. Hardy. The patient, age 64, received the heart of a chimpanzee, which beat for 90 minutes.

Five-organ Tabatha Foster (1984–1988) of Madisonville, KY, at 3 years 143 days of age, received a transplanted liver, pancreas, small intestine, portions of stomach and large intestine in a 15-hour operation at the Children's Hospital, Pittsburgh, PA on 31 Oct 1987. Before the operation, she had never eaten solid food.

Heart–lung–liver The first triple transplant took place on 17 Dec 1986 at Papworth Hospital, Cambridge, Great Britain when Mrs Davina Thompson (b. 28 Feb 1951) of Rawmarsh, Great Britain, underwent surgery for seven hours by a team of 15 headed by chest surgeon Dr. John Wallwork and Professor Sir Roy Calne.

Artificial heart On 1–2 Dec 1982 at the Utah Medical Center, Salt Lake City, UT, Dr Barney B. Clark, 61, of Des Moines, IA was the first recipient of an artificial heart. The surgeon was Dr William C. DeVries. The heart was a Jarvik-7 designed by Dr Robert K. Jarvik. Dr Clark died on 23 Mar 1983, 112 days later. William J. Schroeder survived 620 days with an artificial heart in Louisville, KY from 25 Nov 1984 to 7 Aug 1986. The Food and Drug Administration (FDA) recalled the Jarvik-7 on 11 Jan 1990. At the time of the recall it was the only artificial heart approved by the FDA and thus the only one allowed in the United States.

First synthetic heart implant Haskell Karp, age 47, of Skokie, IL received the first synthetic heart implant on 4 Apr 1969, at St Luke's Episcopal Hospital, Houston, TX. Dr Denton A. Cooley led the team of doctors, which included the developer of the heart, Dr Domingo Liotta. The artifical heart was replaced by a human transplant on 7 April.

Kidney Dr Richard H. Lawler (USA; b. 1895) performed the first transplant of a kidney in a human at Little Company of Mary Hospital, Chicago, IL, on 17 Jun 1950. The first successful kidney transplant operation was performed at Peter Bent Brigham Hospital (now Brigham and Women's Hospital) in Boston, MA on 23 Dec 1954 by a team of surgeons headed by Dr John P. Merrill. The patient, Richard Herrick, age 23, received a kidney from his identical twin, Ronald. The longest surviving kidney transplant patient is Kathleen Severson (b. 25 Jul 1943) of Minnesota, whose operation was performed with her brother as donor on 8 Jul 1964, at the University of Minnesota Hospital.

Lung The first lung transplant operation in the United States took place on 11 Jun 1963 at the University of Mississippi Medical Center in Jackson, MS. The surgery, which was headed by Dr James D. Hardy, lasted three hours and involved the replacement of the patient's left lung. The patient, John Richard Russell, survived 18 days.

The Human World

■ **Previous page**
Lhasa, Tibet (Photo: Horizon)

Political and Social

Largest political division The Commonwealth, a free association of 50 independent states and their dependencies that are, or have been at some time, ruled by Great Britain, covers an area of 11,339,513 miles² with a population estimated in 1988 to be 1,384,631,000. The British Empire began to expand when Henry VII patented trade monopolies to John Cabot in Mar 1496 and when the East India Co. was incorporated on 31 Dec 1600.

COUNTRIES

The world comprises 171 sovereign countries and 60 separately administered nonsovereign or other territories, making a total of 231.

The United Nations still lists the *de jure* territories of East Timor (now incorporated into Indonesia), Western Sahara (now in Morocco), the former mandated territory of Palestine and the uninhabited Canton and Enderbury Islands (now disputed between the United States and Kiribati) but does not list the three Baltic states of Estonia, Latvia and Lithuania, though their forcible incorporation into the USSR in 1940 has never been internationally recognized. Neither does it list the *de facto* territories of Taiwan, Mayotte or Spanish North Africa, the territories claimed by various countries in Antarctica, or the Australian Territory of Coral Sea Islands and Heard and McDonald Islands.

Largest The country with the greatest area is the Union of Soviet Socialist Republics (USSR), comprising 15 union (constituent) republics with a total area of 8,649,500 miles² or 15 percent of the world's total land area, and a total coastline (including islands) of 66,090 miles. The country measures 5,580 miles from east to west and 2,790 miles from north to south and is 2.4 times the size of the United States. Its population in mid-1990 was an estimated 291 million.

The United States covers 3,618,770 miles², a land area of 3,539,289 miles² and a water area of 79,481 miles². It ranks fifth in the world in area behind the USSR, Canada, China and Brazil.

■ **Sovereign countries**
There are currently 171 sovereign countries. The most recent independence ceremony was in March 1990, when Namibia celebrated its sovereignty. (Photos: United Nations, New York)

WORLD POPULATION			
Date	**Millions**	**Date**	**Millions**
8000 B.C.	c. 6	1970	3,698
A.D. 1	c. 255	1975	4,080
1000	c. 254	1980	4,450
1250	416	1981	4,528
1500	460	1982	4,607
1600	579	1983	4,684
1700	679	1984	4,760
1750	770	1985	4,854
1800	954	1986	4,917
1900	1,633	1987 *	4,998
1920	1,862	1988	5,096
1930	2,070	1989	5,194
1940	2,295	1990	5,292
1950	2,515	1991†	5,390
1960	3,019	2000†	6,251
		2025†	8,467

* *The Population Institute of Washington, D.C. declared that the landmark of 5 billion was reached on 7 Jul 1987, whereas the United Nations nominated 11 Jul 1987 "Baby Five Billion Day."*

† *These projections are from the latest UN publication* World Population Prospects 1988. *This gives no projection beyond 2025. An earlier publication in 1984 forecast that the world population will not stabilize until 2095 at about 10.5 billion, but revised estimates in May 1988 said that it might be as high as 14 billion in 2050. Note: The all-time peak annual increase of 2.06 percent in the period 1965–70 had declined to 1.73 percent by 1985–90. By 2025 this should decline to 0.98 percent. In spite of the reduced percentage increase, world population is currently growing by 98 million people every year.*

Using estimates made by the French demographer J.N. Biraben and others, A.R. Thatcher, former Director of the Office of Population Censuses and Surveys, has calculated that the number of people who died between 40,000 B.C. and A.D. 1990 was nearly 60 billion. This estimate implies that the current world population is about one eleventh of all those who have ever lived.

Smallest The smallest independent country in the world is the State of Vatican City or Holy See (Stato della Città del Vaticano), which was made an enclave within the city of Rome, Italy on 11 Feb 1929. The enclave has an area of 108.7 acres. The maritime sovereign country with the shortest coastline is Monaco, with 3.49 miles, excluding piers and breakwaters. The world's smallest republic is Nauru, less than 1 degree south of the equator in the western Pacific, which became independent on 31 Jan 1968. It has an area of 5,263 acres and a population of 9,000 (latest estimate 1989).

The smallest colony in the world is Gibraltar (since 1969, the City of Gibraltar), with an area of 2½ miles². However, Pitcairn Island, the only inhabited island (49 people in Mar 1990) of a group of four (total area 18½ miles²), has an area of 960 acres/1½ miles². It was named after Midshipman Robert Pitcairn of HMS *Swallow* in July 1767.

The official residence, since 1834, of the Grand Master of the Order of the Knights of Malta, totaling 3 acres and comprising the Villa del Priorato di Malta on the lowest of Rome's seven hills, the 151-ft Aventine, retains certain diplomatic privileges, as does 68 via Condotti, also in Rome. The Order has accredited representatives to foreign governments and is hence sometimes cited as the world's smallest "state."

Flattest and most elevated The country with the lowest "high point" is Maldives; it attains 8 ft. The country with the highest "low point" is Lesotho. The egress of the Senqu (Orange) riverbed is 4,530 ft above sea level.

Longest and shortest frontier The longest *continuous* frontier in the world is that between Canada and the United States, which (including the Great Lakes boundaries) extends for 3,987 miles (excluding the frontier of 1,538 miles with Alaska).

The frontier which is crossed most frequently is that between the United States and Mexico. It extends for 1,933 miles and there are more than 120 million crossings every year. The Sino-Soviet frontier, broken by the Sino-Mongolian border, extends for 4,500 miles, with no reported figure for crossings. The "frontier" of the Holy See in Rome measures 2.53 miles. The land frontier between Gibraltar and Spain at La Linea, closed between June 1969 and February 1985, measures 1 mile. Zambia, Zimbabwe, Botswana and Namibia, in Africa, almost meet at a single point.

Most frontiers China has the most land frontiers, with 13—Mongolia, USSR, North Korea, Hong Kong, Macao, Vietnam, Laos, Myanmar (formerly Burma), India, Bhutan, Nepal, Pakistan and Afghanistan. These extend for 14,900 miles. France, if all her overseas territories are included, may, on extended territorial waters, have 20.

POPULATIONS

World The average daily increase in the world's population is about 270,000 or an average of just under 200 per minute. There are, however, seasonal variations in the numbers of births and deaths throughout the year. For past, present and future estimates, see table.

Matej Gaspar, born 11 Jul 1987 in Yugoslavia, was symbolically named the world's 5-billionth inhabitant by the United Nations Secretary-General.

United States On 6 Mar 1990 the population of the United States reached the 250 million mark, according to the Census Bureau, which also predicts that the country's population will reach 267 million by the year 2000.

Most populous country The most populated country is China, which in *pinyin* is written Zhongguo (meaning "central land"). The census of July 1990 revealed a population of 1,133,682,501, and involved 7 million census-takers. The rate of natural increase in the People's Republic of China is now estimated to be 35,068 a day or 12.8 million per year. India is expected to overtake China in size of population by A.D. 2050, with 1.591 billion against 1.555 billion for China.

Least populous country The independent state with the smallest population is Vatican City or the Holy See (see Smallest country, above), with 750 inhabitants in 1989 and no births.

Most densely populated The most densely populated territory in the world is the Portuguese province of Macao, on the southern coast of China. It has an estimated population of 479,000 (1988) in an area of 6.5 miles², giving a density of 73,692/mile². The principality of Monaco, on the south coast of France, has a population of 29,000 (1989) in an area of just 473 acres, a density equal to 39,242/mile².

Of territories with an area of more than 386 miles², Hong Kong (400.5 miles²) contains an estimated 5.8 million (1990), giving the territory a density of 14,482/mile². Hong Kong is now the most populous of all colonies. The transcrip-

1990 US CENSUS

State	Population 1990
California	29,760,021
New York	17,990,455
Texas	16,986,510
Florida	12,937,926
Pennsylvania	11,881,643
Illinois	11,430,602
Ohio	10,847,115
Michigan	9,295,297
New Jersey	7,730,188
North Carolina	6,628,637
Georgia	6,478,216
Virginia	6,187,358
Massachusetts	6,016,425
Indiana	5,544,159
Missouri	5,117,073
Wisconsin	4,891,769
Tennessee	4,877,185
Washington	4,866,692
Maryland	4,781,468
Minnesota	4,375,099
Louisiana	4,219,973
Alabama	4,040,587
Kentucky	3,685,296
Arizona	3,665,228
South Carolina	3,486,703
Colorado	3,294,394
Connecticut	3,287,116
Oklahoma	3,145,585
Oregon	2,842,321
Iowa	2,776,755
Mississippi	2,573,216
Kansas	2,477,574
Arkansas	2,350,725
West Virginia	1,793,477
Utah	1,722,850
Nebraska	1,578,385
New Mexico	1,515,069
Maine	1,227,928
Nevada	1,201,833
New Hampshire	1,109,252
Hawaii	1,108,229
Idaho	1,006,749
Rhode Island	1,003,464
Montana	799,065
South Dakota	696,004
Delaware	666,168
North Dakota	638,800
District of Columbia	606,900
Vermont	562,758
Alaska	550,043
Wyoming	453,588

Census Bureau

WORST DISASTERS IN THE WORLD
(By Category)

TYPE OF DISASTER	NUMBER KILLED	LOCATION	DATE
Pandemic	75,000,000	Eurasia: The Black Death (bubonic, pneumonic and septicaemic plague)	1347–51
Genocide	c. 35,000,000	Mongol extermination of Chinese peasantry	1311–40
Famine[1]	c. 30,000,000	Northern China	1959–61
Influenza	21,640,000	Worldwide	1918–19
Earthquake	1,100,000	Near East and E. Mediterranean	c. July 1201
Circular Storm[2]	1,000,000	Ganges Delta Islands, Bangladesh	12–13 Nov 1970
Flood	900,000	Hwang-ho River, China	Oct 1887
Landslides (triggered off by single earthquake)	180,000	Kansu Province, China	16 Dec 1920
Atomic Bomb	155,200	Hiroshima, Japan (including radiation deaths within year)	6 Aug 1945
Conventional Bombing[3]	c. 140,000	Tokyo, Japan	10 Mar 1945
Volcanic Eruption	92,000	Tambora, Sumbawa, Indonesia	5–7 Apr 1815
Avalanches[4]	c. 18,000	Yungay, Huascarán, Peru	31 May 1970
Marine (Single Ship)	c. 7,700	Wilhelm Gustloff (28,542.1 tons) German liner torpedoed off Danzig by USSR submarine S-13 (only 903 survivors)	30 Jan 1945
Dam Burst[5]	c. 5,000	Machhu River Dam, Morvi, Gujarat, India	11 Aug 1979
Panic	c. 4,000	Chungking (Zhong qing) China, air raid shelter	6 Jun 1941
Industrial (Chemical)	3,350	Union Carbide methylisocyanate plant, Bhopal, India	2–3 Dec 1984
Smog	2,850	London fog, Great Britain (excess deaths)	5–13 Dec 1952
Tunneling (Silicosis)	c. 2,500	Hawk's Nest hydroelectric tunnel, West Virginia	1931–35
Fire[6] (Single building)	c. 1,670	The Theatre, Canton, China	May 1845
Explosion[7]	1,635	Halifax, Nova Scotia, Canada	6 Dec 1917
Mining[8]	c. 1,572	Honkeiko Colliery, China (coal dust explosion)	26 Apr 1942
Tornado	c. 1,300	Shaturia, Bangladesh	26 Apr 1989
Riot	c. 1,200	New York anticonscription riots	13–16 Jul 1863
Mass Suicide[9]	960	Jewish Zealots, Masada, Israel	73
Railway	>800	Bagmati River, Bihar, India	6 Jun 1981
Fireworks	>800	Dauphin's wedding, Seine, Paris, France	16 May 1770
Aircraft (Civil)[10]	583	KLM-Pan Am Boeing 747 ground crash, Tenerife, Canary Islands, Spain	27 Mar 1977
Man-eating Animal	436	Champawat district, India, tigress shot by Col. Jim Corbet (died 1955)	1907
Terrorism	329	Bomb aboard Air-India Boeing 747, crashed into Atlantic southwest of Ireland. Sikh extremists suspected	23 Jun 1985
Hail	246	Moradabad, Uttar Pradesh, India	20 Apr 1888
Road[11]	176	Petrol tanker explosion inside Salang Tunnel, Afghanistan	3 Nov 1982
Offshore Oil Platform	167	Piper Alpha oil production platform, North Sea	6 Jul 1988
Submarine	130	Le Surcouf rammed by US merchantman Thomas Lykes in Caribbean	18 Feb 1942
Helicopter	54	Israel, military Sea Stallion, West Bank	10 May 1977
Ski Lift (Cable car)	42	Cavalese resort, northern Italy	9 Mar 1976
Nuclear Reactor[12]	31	Chernobyl No. 4, Ukraine, USSR	26 Apr 1986
Mountaineering[13]	23	Mount Fuji, Japan	20 Mar 1972
Elevator (Lift)	23	Vaal Reefs gold mine lift fell 1.2 miles	27 Mar 1980
Lightning	21	Hut in Chinamasa Krael, near Mutari, Zimbabwe (single bolt)	23 Dec 1975
Yacht Racing	19	28th Fastnet Race—23 boats sank or abandoned in Force 11 gale	13–15 Aug 1979
Space Exploration	7	US Challenger 51L Shuttle, Cape Canaveral, FL	28 Jan 1986
Nuclear Waste Accident[14]	high but undisclosed	Venting of plutonium extraction wastes, Kyshtym, USSR	c. Dec 1957

FOOTNOTES

[1] It has been estimated that more than 5 million died in the post-World War I famine of 1920–21 in the USSR. The USSR government in July 1923 informed Mr (later President) Herbert Hoover that the ARA (American Relief Administration) had since August 1921 saved 20 million lives from famine and famine-related diseases.

[2] This figure published in 1972 for the Bangladeshi disaster was from Dr Afzal, Principal Scientific Officer of the Atomic Energy Authority Centre, Dacca. One report asserted that less than half of the population of the four islands of Bhola, Charjabbar, Hatia and Ramagati (1961 census 1.4 million) survived. The most damaging hurricane recorded was Hurricane Hugo from 17-22 Sep 1989, which was estimated to have done $7 billion worth of damage.

[3] The number of civilians killed by the bombing of Germany has been put variously at 593,000 and "over 635,000," including some 35,000 deaths in the raids on Dresden, Germany from 13–15 Feb 1945. Total Japanese fatalities were 600,000 (conventional) and 220,000 (nuclear).

[4] A total of 18,000 Austrian and Italian troops were reported to have been lost in the Dolomite valleys of northern Italy on 13 Dec 1916 in more than 100 snow avalanches. Some of the avalanches were triggered by gunfire.

[5] The dynamiting of a Yangtze Kiang dam at Huayuan Kow by the Kuomintang during the Sino-Japanese war in 1938 is reputed to have resulted in 900,000 deaths.

[6] >200,000 killed in the sack of Moscow, as a result of fires started by the invading Tartars in May 1571. Worst-ever hotel fire, 162 killed, Hotel Daeyungak, Seoul, South Korea 25 Dec 1971. Worst circus fire killed 168 in Hartford, CT 6 Jul 1944.

[7] Some sources maintain that the final death toll was over 3,000 on 6–7 December. Published estimates of the 11,000 killed at the BASF chemical plant explosion at Oppau, Germany on 21 Sep 1921 were exaggerated. The most reliable estimate is 561 killed.

[8] The worst gold-mining disaster in South Africa was when 182 were killed in Kinross gold mine on 16 Sep 1986.

[9] As reported by the historian Flavius Josephus (c. 37–100). In modern times, the greatest mass suicide was on 18 Nov 1978 when 913 members of the People's Temple cult died of mass cyanide poisoning near Port Kaituma, Guyana. 22,000 Japanese civilians jumped off a cliff to their deaths in June 1943 during the US Marines' assault of the island of Tarawa (now in Kiribati).

[10] The crash of JAL's Boeing 747, flight 123, near Tokyo on 12 Aug 1985, in which 520 passengers and crew perished, was the worst single plane crash in aviation history.

[11] Western estimates gave the number of deaths at c. 1,100. The global aggregate death toll in road accidents was put at 25 million by September 1975. The worst year for road deaths in the United States was 1972 (56,278).

[12] Explosion at 0123 hrs Soviet European time 26 Apr 1986. Thirty-one was the official Soviet total of immediate deaths. On 29 Apr 1991 Vladimir Shovkoshitny stated in the Ukranian Parliament that 7,000 "clean-up" workers had already died from radiation. The estimate for the eventual death toll has been put as high as 75,000 by Dr Robert Gale, a US bone transplant specialist.

[13] Some people have claimed that 40 mountaineers were killed in a Soviet expedition on Mount Everest in December 1952, but this is discounted by many authorities on the matter.

[14] More than 30 small communities in a 460 mile² area have been eliminated from USSR maps since 1958, with 17,000 people evacuated. Possibly an ammonium nitrate-hexone explosion was the cause.

tion of the name is from a local pronunciation of the Beijing dialect version of Xiang gang (meaning "a port for incense"). The 1976 census showed that the West Area of the urban district of Mong Kok on the Kowloon Peninsula had a density of 652,910/mile^2. In 1959, at the peak of the housing crisis, it was reported that in one house designed for 12 people the number of occupants was 459, including 104 in one room and four living on the roof.

Of countries over 1,000 miles^2 the most densely populated is Bangladesh, with a population of 114,800,000 (1990) living in 55,598 miles^2 at a density of 2,065/mile^2. The Indonesian island of Java (with an area of 48,763 miles^2) has a population of 100.3 million (1987), giving a density of 2,056/mile^2.

Most sparsely populated Antarctica became permanently occupied by relays of scientists from 1943 on. The population varies seasonally and reaches 2,000 at times.

The least populated territory, apart from Antarctica, is Kalaallit Nunaat (formerly Greenland), with a population of 55,400 (1989) in an area of 840,000 miles^2, giving a density of one person to every 15.16 miles^2. Some 84.3 percent of the island comprises an ice cap.

Emigration More people emigrate from Mexico than from any other country. An estimated 800,000 illegally entered the United States in 1980 alone. The Soviet invasion of Afghanistan in December 1979 caused an influx of 2.9 million refugees into Pakistan and a further 2.2 million into Iran. By 1989 the number of Afghan refugees in Pakistan had increased to 3,622,000.

Immigration The country that regularly receives the most legal immigrants is the United States. During fiscal year 1990 (October 1989–September 1990) 1,536,483 people legally entered the United States. Of these, 679,068 were

from Mexico, by far the largest intake from a single country.

In fiscal year 1990 a total of 1,169,939 people were apprehended for immigration violations. The largest group by nationality were 1,092,258 from Mexico. The most common violation is people entering without inspection (EWI), and of these, 1,116,254 were apprehended crossing the Mexican border, 4,901 the Canadian border and 10,299 at other parts of the United States border.

Biggest demonstration A figure of 2.7 million was reported from China for the demonstration against the USSR in Shanghai on 3–4 Apr 1969 following the border clashes.

Most patient "refusenik" The USSR citizen who waited longest for an exit visa was Benyamin Bogomolny, who first applied in 1966. He arrived in Vienna on 14 Oct 1986. The USSR citizen who has currently been waiting the longest is Vladimir Raiz, who first applied to emigrate in February 1973.

Tourism The most popular tourist destination is France, which in 1989 received 49,544,000 foreign tourists. The country with the greatest receipts from tourism is the United States, with $15.4 billion in 1987. The biggest spenders are Germans, who in 1987 spent $23.6 billion on foreign tourism.

Birthrate *Highest and lowest* The crude birthrate—the number of births per 1,000 population—for the whole world was estimated to be 27.1 per 1,000 in 1985–90. The highest rate estimated by the United Nations for 1985–90 is 53.9 per 1,000 for Kenya. Excluding Vatican City, where the rate is zero, the lowest recorded rate is 9.3 per 1,000 (1985) for San Marino.

United States The National Center for Health Statistics (NCHS) estimates that 4.2 million babies were born in 1990. The estimated United States birthrate (the

number of babies for every 1,000 people) is 16.7 percent. The most recent official statistics issued by the NCHS show that in 1988, 3,909,510 live births took place in the United States (2,002,424 boys, 1,907,086 girls), which works out to an official birthrate of 15.9 percent. For statistical purposes the NCHS divides the States into nine geographic areas. The Pacific division (WA, OR, CA, AK and HA), had the most live births registered in 1988, with 675,980; New England (ME, NH, VT, MA, RI and CT) had the fewest, 193,142. The most live births registered in the United States were 4,300,000 in 1957. The highest birthrate recorded after 1909, the first year official records were recognized, was 30.1 percent in 1910.

Death rate The crude death rate—the number of deaths per 1,000 population of all ages—for the whole world was an estimated 9.9 per 1,000 in 1985–90. The estimated death rate in Cambodia (or Kampuchea) of 40.0 per 1,000 from 1975–80 subsided to 16.6 in 1985–90. The estimated figure for Ethiopia from 1985–90 was 23.6.

United States The crude death rate for the USA in 1988 was 8.8 per 1,000 persons or 2,123,323 people.

Natural increase The rate of natural increase (crude birthrate minus crude death rate) for the whole world is estimated to be 17.2 (27.1 minus 9.9) per 1,000 in 1985–90 compared with a peak 22 per 1,000 in 1965. The highest of the latest available recorded rates is 42.9 (53.9 minus 11) from Kenya in 1985–90.

Marriage and divorce The marriage rate for the Northern Mariana Islands, in the Pacific Ocean, is 31.2 per 1,000 population.

In the United States the median age at first marriage in 1989 was 26.2 years (bridegrooms) and 23.8 years (brides). In 1990 2.5 million couples were married. The marriage rate was 9.8 per 1,000 people.

The country with the most divorces is the United States, with a total of 1.2 million in 1990—a rate of 4.7 per thousand population. The all-time high rate was 5.4 per thousand population in 1979. In 1986 some 2 percent of all *existing* marriages in the United States broke up.

Sex ratio There were estimated to be 1,012 males in the world for every 1,000 females in 1988. The country with the largest recorded shortage of males is the USSR, with an estimated 1,112 females to every 1,000 males in 1988. The country with the largest recorded shortage of women is the United Arab Emirates, with an estimated 484 females to every 1,000 males in 1988.

Infant mortality The world infant mortality rate—the number of deaths at ages under one year per 1,000 live births—in 1987 was 80.0 per 1,000 live births. Based on deaths before one year of age, the lowest of the latest recorded rates is 5.0 in Japan in 1987.

In Ethiopia the infant mortality rate was unofficially estimated to be nearly 550 per 1,000 live births in 1969. The highest rate recently estimated is 172.1 per 1,000 in Afghanistan (1985–90).

The infant mortality rate for the United States in 1989 was 10.1 per 100,000 live births, or 34,408.

Expectation of life at birth World expectation of life is rising from 47.4 years (1950–55) towards 64.5 years (1995–2000). In the decade 1890–1900 the expectation of life among the population of India was 23.7 years.

The highest average expectation of life is in Japan, with 81.9 years for women and 75.8 years for men in 1988. The lowest expectation of life at birth recently estimated is 39.4 years for males in Ethiopia and Sierra Leone, and 42.0 years for females in Afghanistan.

Housing For comparison purposes, a dwelling unit is defined as a structurally separated room or rooms occupied by a private household of one or more people and having separate access or a common passageway to the street.

The country with the greatest number of housing units is China, with 249,270,175 in 1986.

United States In March 1988 there were 91,066,000 households in the United States. Of these, 58,214,000 were owner-occupied (63.9 percent) and 32,853,000 were rentals.

Physicians The country with the most physicians is the USSR, with 1,232,300, or one for every 235 persons. China had an estimated 1.4 million paramedical personnel, known as "barefoot doctors," by 1981.

Dentists The country with the most dentists is the United States, where 150,000 were registered members of the American Dental Association in 1990.

Psychiatrists/Psychologists The country with the most psychiatrists is the United States. The registered membership of the American Psychiatric Association (instituted in 1844) was 36,335 in 1990, and the membership of the American Psychological Association (instituted in 1892) was 96,000. The No. 1 city in the 1987 couch rankings is Boston, MA with one psychiatrist for 328 heads.

Largest hospital World The largest psychiatric hospital in the world is the Pilgrim State Hospital, West Brentwood, NY, with 3,816 beds. It formerly contained 14,200 beds. The largest psychiatric institute is at the University of California, Los Angeles (UCLA).

The busiest maternity hospital in the world has been the Mama Yemo Hospital, Kinshasa, Zaïre, with 42,987 deliveries in 1972. The record "birthquake" occurred on a day in May 1976, with 175 babies born. The hospital had 599 beds.

STATES

Most populous The most populous state in the United States in 1990 was California, with 29.76 million people.

Least populous The least populous state was Wyoming with 453,588 people in 1990.

Thirteen original states The thirteen original states were Connecticut, Delaware, Georgia, Maryland, Massachusetts, New Hampshire, New Jersey, New York, North Carolina, Pennsylvania, Rhode Island, South Carolina and Virginia.

Confederate states Eleven states seceded from the union between December 1860 and June 1861. They were (in order of secession): South Carolina, Mississippi, Florida, Alabama, Georgia, Louisiana, Texas, Virginia, Arkansas, North Carolina and Tennessee.

COUNTIES

As of April 1991 there were 3,141 counties in the United States (in Alaska counties are known as divisions and in Louisiana they are called parishes). The largest is San Bernardino County, CA, with an area of 20,119 miles². The state with the most counties is Texas with 254 and the state with the fewest is Delaware with three (Kent, New Castle and Sussex).

TOWNS AND CITIES

Oldest The oldest known walled town in the world is Arihā (Jericho). Radiocarbon dating on specimens from the lowest levels reached by archaeologists indicates habitation there by perhaps 2,700 people as early as 7800 B.C. The settlement of Dolní Věstonice, Czechoslovakia has been dated to the Gravettian culture c. 27,000 B.C. The oldest capital city in the world is Dimashq (Damascus), Syria. It has been continuously inhabited since c. 2500 B.C.

United States The oldest town of European origin in the United States is St Augustine, St. John's County, FL (present population 12,000), founded on 8 Sep 1565, on the site of Seloy by Pedro Menendez de Aviles.

The oldest incorporated city is York, ME (present population 14,000), which received an English charter in March 1642, and was incorporated under the name Georgiana.

Most populous The most populous urban agglomeration in the world is the Tokyo-Yokohama Metropolitan Area or "Keihin Metropolitan Area" in Japan, which was listed in the United Nations *Prospects of World Urbanization, 1988* as having a population of 19,040,000 in 1985. The population of the Mexico City urban agglomeration in 1985 was given in the same publication as 16,650,000, but by 2000 it is expected to have a population of 24,440,000, against 21,320,000 for Tokyo-Yokohama.

The 1990 United States census shows that 76 percent of all Americans live in metropolitan areas—central cities and their surrounding suburbs—up from 56 percent in 1950. The largest metropolitan area is that of New York City with 18,087,251 residents.

Largest in area The world's largest town (densely populated settlement), in area, is Mount Isa, Queensland, Australia. The area administered by the City Council is 15,822 miles².

Highest The highest capital in the world, before the domination of Tibet by China, was Lhasa, at an elevation of 12,087 ft above sea level. La Paz, administrative and *de facto* capital of Bolivia, stands at an altitude of 11,916 ft. Its airport, El Alto, is at 13,385 ft. The city was founded in 1548 by

TEN MOST POPULOUS METROPOLITAN AREAS

Area	Population in 1990
New York City	18,087,251
Los Angeles, CA	14,531,529
Chicago, IL	8,065,633
San Francisco, CA	6,253,311
Philadelphia, PA	5,899,345
Detroit, MI	4,665,236
Boston, MA	4,171,463
Washington, D.C.	3,923,574
Dallas, TX	3,885,415
Houston, TX	3,711,043

Census Bureau

■ Highest capital
La Paz, administrative and de facto capital of Bolivia, stands at an altitude of 11,916 ft above sea level. Its airport, El Alto, is at 13,385 ft. (Photo: Images)

Capt. Alonso de Mendoza on the site of an Indian village named Chuquiapu. It was originally called Ciudad de Nuestra Señora de La Paz (City of Our Lady of Peace), but in 1825 was renamed La Paz de Ayacucho, its present official name. Sucre, the legal capital of Bolivia, stands at 9,301 ft above sea level. The new town of Wenzhuan, founded in 1955 on the Qinghai–Tibet road north of the Tangla range, is the highest in the world at 16,732 ft above sea level.

United States The highest incorporated city in the United States in Leadville, CO, at an elevation of 10,152 ft. Founded in 1878, Leadville's current population is 2,629.

Lowest The settlement of Ein Bokek, which has a synagogue, on the shores of the Dead Sea is the lowest in the world, at 1,291 ft below sea level.

United States The lowest incorporated city in the United States is Calipatria, CA, at 184 ft below sea level. Founded on 28 Feb 1919, it has a current population of 2,696. The flagpole outside city hall is 184 ft tall, allowing "Old Glory" to fly at sea-level.

Northernmost The northernmost village is Ny Ålesund (78° 55′ N), a coal-mining settlement on King's Bay, Vest Spitsbergen, in the Norwegian territory of Svalbard, inhabited only during the winter season. The northernmost capital is Reykjavik, Iceland (64° 08′ N). Its population was estimated to be 95,800 in 1988.

United States The northernmost city in the United States is Barrow, AK (71° 17′ N).

Southernmost The world's southernmost village is Puerto Williams (population about 350) on the north coast of Isla Navarino, Tierra del Fuego,

Chile, 680 miles north of Antarctica. Wellington, North Island, New Zealand, with a 1989 population of 324,600, is the southernmost capital city (41° 17′ S). The world's southernmost administrative center is Port Stanley, Falkland (Malvinas) Islands (51° 43′ S), with a population of 1,200.

United States The southernmost city in the United States is Hilo, HI (19° 43′ N).

Most remote from sea The large town most remote from the sea is Wu-lu-mu-ch'i (formerly Ürümqi) in Xinjiang, the capital of China's Xinjiang Uighur Autonomous Region, at a distance of about 1,500 miles from the nearest coastline. Its population was estimated to be 1,060,000 in late 1987.

Heads of State and Royalty

Forty-six of the world's 171 sovereign states are not republics. They are headed by 1 emperor, 13 kings, 3 queens, 2 sultans, 1 grand duke, 2 princes, 3 emirs, an elected monarch, the pope, a president chosen from and by 7 hereditary sheiks, a head of state currently similar to a constitutional monarch, and 2 nominal nonhereditary "princes" in one country. Queen Elizabeth II is head of state of Great Britain and 16 other Commonwealth countries.

Reigns Longest all-time The longest recorded reign of any monarch is that of Phiops II (also known as Pepi II), or Neferkare, a Sixth Dynasty pharaoh of ancient Egypt. His reign began *c.* 2281 B.C., when he was 6 years of age, and is believed to have lasted *c.* 94 years. Musoma Kanijo, chief of the Nzega

district of western Tanganyika (now part of Tanzania), reputedly reigned for more than 98 years from 1864, when he was 8 years old, until his death on 2 Feb 1963. Minhti, King of Arakan (now part of Myanmar, formerly Burma), is reputed to have reigned for 95 years between 1279 and 1374. The longest reign of any European monarch was that of Afonso I Henriques of Portugal, who ascended the throne on 30 Apr 1112 and died on 6 Dec 1185 after a reign of 73 years 220 days, first as a count and then as king.

Shortest Crown Prince Luis Filipe of Portugal was mortally wounded at the same time that his father was killed by a bullet that severed his carotid artery (one of the two great arteries carrying blood to the head), in the streets of Lisbon on 1 Feb 1908. He was thus technically King of Portugal (Dom Luis III) for about 20 minutes.

Highest post-nominal numbers The highest post-nominal number ever used to designate a member of a royal house was 75, briefly enjoyed by Count Heinrich LXXV Reuss zu Schleiz (1800–1801). All male members of this branch of the German family are called Heinrich and are successively numbered from I upwards in three sequences—the first began in 1695 (and ended with Heinrich LXXV), the second began in 1803 (and ended with Heinrich XLVII) and the third began in 1910. These are purely *personal* numbers and should not be confused with *regnal* numbers (years of a royal reign).

Longest-lived royal The longest-lived royal on record was Zita, Empress of Austria and Queen of Hungary, whose husband reigned as Emperor Charles I of Austria and King Charles IV of Hungary from 1916–18; she died on 14 Mar 1989 at the age of 96 years 309 days, after living in exile from 23 Mar 1919 (see Most prolific, below).

Youngest king and queen The country with the youngest king is Swaziland, where King Mswati III was crowned on 25 Apr 1986 at the age of 18 years 6 days. He was born Makhosetive, the 67th son of King Subhusa II. The country with the youngest queen is Denmark, with Queen Margrethe II (b. 16 Apr 1940).

Heaviest monarch The world's heaviest monarch is the 6-ft-3-in-tall King Taufa'ahau of Tonga, who in September 1976 was weighed on the only adequate scales in the country at the airport, recording 462 lb. By 1985 he was reported to have slimmed down to 308 lb. His embassy car in London, Great Britain has the license plate "1 TON."

Most prolific The most prolific monogamous "royals" were Prince Hartmann of Liechtenstein (1613–86), who had 24 children, of whom 21 were born live, by Countess Elisabeth zu Salm-Reifferscheidt (1623–88). HRH Duke Roberto I of Parma (1848–1907) also had 24 children, but by two wives.

One of his daughters, Zita, Empress of Austria and Queen of Hungary (1892–

1989), was exiled on 23 Mar 1919, but visited Vienna, her titles intact, on 17 Nov 1982, reminding republicans that her father succeeded to the throne of Parma in 1854. (See Longest-lived, above.)

Heads of state *Oldest and youngest* The oldest head of state in the world is Félix Houphouët-Boigny, president of Ivory Coast (b. 18 Oct 1905). The youngest is King Mswati III of Swaziland (b. 19 Apr 1968). (See Youngest King and Queen, above.)

First female presidents Isabel Perón (b. 1931) of Argentina became the world's first female president when she succeeded her husband on his death on 1 Jul 1974. She held office until she was deposed in a bloodless coup on 24 Mar 1976. President Vigdis Finnbogadottir (b. 1930) of Iceland became the world's first democratically elected female head of state on 30 Jun 1980.

Meeting The largest meeting of heads of

state and heads of government took place on the occasion of the World Summit for Children, held on 29–30 Sep 1990. The conference at the headquarters of the United Nations in New York

City was attended by 71 world leaders and dealt with the plight of children worldwide.

Legislatures— United States

PRESIDENTS

Oldest The oldest president was Ronald Wilson Reagan, who was 69 years 349 days old when he took the oath of office. He was reelected at age 73.

Youngest The youngest president to assume office was Theodore Roosevelt. Vice-President Roosevelt became President at the age of 42 years, 10 months when President William McKinley was assassinated in 1901. The youngest president ever elected was John Fitzgerald Kennedy, who took the oath of office at age 43 years 236 days in 1961.

Term of office Franklin Delano Roosevelt served the longest term—12 years 39 days (1933–45) as President of the United States. The shortest term in office was 32 days (4 Mar–4 Apr 1841) by William Henry Harrison.

Most ex-presidents living Between 4 Mar 1861 (the inauguration of Abraham Lincoln) and the death of ex-president Tyler on 18 Jan 1862, there were five ex-presidents living: Martin

PRESIDENTS OF THE UNITED STATES

PRESIDENT	TERM IN OFFICE	PARTY	BIRTH	DEATH
George Washington *	1789–1797	Federalist	22 Feb 1732	14 Dec 1799
John Adams	1797–1801	Federalist	30 Oct 1735	4 Jul 1826
Thomas Jefferson	1801–1809	Dem-Rep	13 Apr 1743	4 Jul 1826
James Madison	1809–1817	Dem-Rep	16 Mar 1751	28 Jun 1836
James Monroe	1817–1825	Dem-Rep	28 Apr 1758	4 Jul 1831
John Quincy Adams	1825–1829	Dem-Rep	11 Jul 1767	23 Feb 1848
Andrew Jackson	1829–1837	Democratic	15 Mar 1767	8 Jun 1845
Martin Van Buren	1837–1841	Democratic	5 Dec 1782	24 Jul 1862
William H. Harrison †	1841	Whig	9 Feb 1773	4 Apr 1841
John Tyler	1841–1845	Whig	29 Mar 1790	18 Jan 1862
James K. Polk	1845–1849	Democratic	2 Nov 1795	15 Jun 1849
Zachary Taylor †	1849–1850	Whig	24 Nov 1784	9 Jul 1850
Millard Fillmore	1850–1853	Whig	7 Jan 1800	8 Mar 1874
Franklin Pierce	1853–1857	Democratic	23 Nov 1804	8 Oct 1869
James Buchanan	1857–1861	Democratic	23 Apr 1791	1 Jun 1868
Abraham Lincoln ±	1861–1865	Republican	12 Feb 1809	15 Apr 1865
Andrew Johnson **	1865–1869	Union	29 Dec 1808	31 Jul 1875
Ulysses S. Grant	1869–1877	Republican	27 Apr 1822	23 Jul 1885
Rutherford B. Hayes	1877–1881	Republican	4 Oct 1822	17 Jan 1893
James A. Garfield ±	1881	Republican	19 Nov 1831	19 Sep 1881
Chester A. Arthur	1881–1885	Republican	5 Oct 1829	18 Nov 1886
S. Grover Cleveland	1885–1889	Democratic	18 Mar 1837	24 Jun 1908
Benjamin Harrison	1889–1893	Republican	20 Aug 1833	13 Mar 1901
S. Grover Cleveland	1893–1897	Democratic	18 Mar 1837	24 Jun 1908
William McKinley ±	1897–1901	Republican	29 Jan 1843	14 Sep 1901
Theodore Roosevelt	1901–1909	Republican	27 Oct 1858	6 Jan 1919
William H. Taft	1909–1913	Republican	15 Sep 1857	8 Mar 1930
T. Woodrow Wilson	1913–1921	Democratic	28 Dec 1856	3 Feb 1924
Warren G. Harding †	1921–1923	Republican	2 Nov 1865	2 Aug 1923
J. Calvin Coolidge	1923–1929	Republican	4 Jul 1872	5 Jan 1933
Herbert C. Hoover	1929–1933	Republican	10 Aug 1874	20 Oct 1964
Franklin D. Roosevelt †	1933–1945	Democratic	30 Jan 1882	12 Apr 1945
Harry S. Truman	1945–1953	Democratic	8 May 1884	26 Dec 1972
Dwight D. Eisenhower	1953–1961	Republican	14 Oct 1890	28 Mar 1969
John F. Kennedy ±	1961–1963	Democratic	29 May 1917	22 Nov 1963
Lyndon B. Johnson	1963–1969	Democratic	27 Aug 1908	22 Jan 1973
Richard M. Nixon ‡	1969–1974	Republican	9 Jan 1913	
Gerald R. Ford	1974–1977	Republican	14 Jul 1913	
James E. Carter, Jr	1977–1981	Democratic	1 Oct 1924	
Ronald W. Reagan	1981–1989	Republican	6 Feb 1911	
George H. W. Bush	1989–	Republican	12 Jun 1924	

* There was no party system in place at the creation of the presidency; the system appeared during Washington's first term. † Died in office. ± Assassinated. ** Impeached. ‡ Resigned.

Handshaking

The record number of hands shaken by a public figure at an official function was 8,513 by President Theodore Roosevelt (1858–1919) at a New Year's Day White House presentation in Washington, D.C. in 1907.

Rainer Vikström of Turku, Finland shook 19,592 different hands in 8 hours on 15 May 1988 during Turku's Fourth Annual Spring Market "Manun Markkinat."

PRESIDENTIAL RECORDS

Article II of the Constitution provides for the office of the presidency. The President is head of all executive agencies, and has full responsibility for the execution of the laws, is commander in chief of the armed forces, conducts foreign affairs, and with the advice and consent of Congress appoints cabinet members and any other executive officials. The Constitution sets the term of office at four years and requires that the position should be filled by election through the electoral college. The Twenty-second Amendment (1951) limits a President to two consecutive four-year terms. To be eligible for the presidency one must be a native-born citizen, over 35 years old, and at least 14 years resident in the United States.

LONGEST TERM IN OFFICE	12 years 39 days	Franklin Delano Roosevelt	1933–45
SHORTEST TERM IN OFFICE	32 days	William Henry Harrison	4 Mar–4 Apr 1841
YOUNGEST TO ASSUME OFFICE	42 years 10 months	Theodore Roosevelt	1901–09
YOUNGEST ELECTED	43 years 236 days	John Fitzgerald Kennedy	1961–63
OLDEST ELECTED	69 years 349 days	Ronald Wilson Reagan	1981–89
TALLEST	6 ft 4 in	Abraham Lincoln	1861–65
SHORTEST	5 ft 4 in	James Madison	1809–17
LONGEST LIVED	90 years 258 days	John Adams	1797–1801
SHORTEST LIVED	46 years 6 months	John Fitzgerald Kennedy	1961–63
LONGEST LIFE AFTER PRESIDENCY	31 years 7 months	Herbert Clark Hoover	1929–33
SHORTEST LIFE AFTER PRESIDENCY	105 days	James K. Polk	1845–49
HEAVIEST	354 lb	William Howard Taft	1909–13
MOST CHILDREN	15	John Tyler	1841–45
MOST CHILDREN (one spouse)	10	William Henry Harrison	1841
BACHELOR		James Buchanan	1857–61
IMPEACHED		Andrew Johnson	1865–69
RESIGNED		Richard M. Nixon	1969–74
ASSASSINATED	14 Apr 1865	Abraham Lincoln	1861–65
	2 Jul 1881	James A. Garfield	1881
	6 Sep 1901	William H. McKinley	1897–1901
	22 Nov 1963	John Fitzgerald Kennedy	1961–63

FIRST LADIES

Barbara Bush is the 37th first lady. The term itself dates only from the time of Lucy Ware Webb Hayes, who was the 16th first lady in 1887–81.

FIRST AND EARLIEST BORN	21 Jun 1731	Martha Dandridge Custis (1731–1802)	m George Washington
LONGEST TENURE	12 years 39 days 1933–45	(Anna) Eleanor Roosevelt (1884–1962)	m Franklin D Roosevelt
SHORTEST TENURE	31 days in 1841	Anna Tuthill Symmes (1775–1864)	m William H Harrison
MOST CHILDREN	6 sons, 4 daughters	Anna Tuthill Symmes	m William H. Harrison
LEAST CHILDREN	None	Five first ladies were childless: Martha Dandridge Custis Washington (1731–1802), Dorothea "Dolley" Payne Madison (1768–1849), Sarah Childress Polk (1803–91), Edith Bolling Galt Wilson (1872–1961) and Florence (Kling) De Wolfe Harding (1860–1924)	
LARGEST GATHERING	8	At inauguration of John F. Kennedy (1917–63) in Washington, D.C. on 20 Jan 1961, his wife, 4 past and 3 future first ladies	
COMMONEST HOME STATE	New York (8)	17 other states represented. Only foreign-born First Lady has been Louisa Catherine Johnson (1775–1852), in London, England on 12 Feb 1775 and there married John Quincy Adams on 26 Jul 1797.	
COMMONEST ANCESTRY		All 37 have British ancestry; 25 have purely English ancestry	
RAREST ANCESTRY		Only 1 has Native American blood—Edith Bolling Galt Wilson (see above) was a ninth-generation descendant of Princess Pocahontas (c. 1595–1617)	

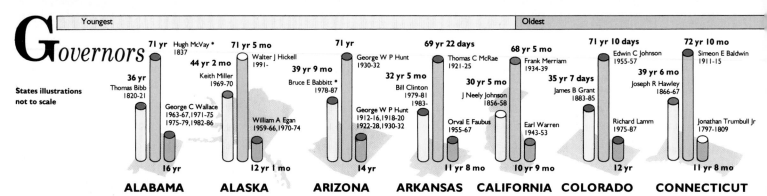

Governors

Youngest | Oldest

States illustrations not to scale

ALABAMA
71 yr — Hugh McVay * 1837
36 yr — Thomas Bibb 1820-21
44 yr 2 mo — George C Wallace 1963-67,1971-75 1975-79,1982-86
16 yr

ALASKA
71 yr 5 mo — Walter J Hickell 1991-
44 yr 2 mo — Keith Miller 1969-70
William A Egan 1959-66,1970-74
12 yr 1 mo

ARIZONA
71 yr
39 yr 9 mo — Bruce E Babbitt * 1978-87
George W P Hunt 1912-16,1918-20 1922-28,1930-32
14 yr

ARKANSAS
69 yr 22 days — George W P Hunt 1930-32
32 yr 5 mo — Bill Clinton 1979-81 1983-
Thomas C McRae 1921-25
11 yr 8 mo

CALIFORNIA
68 yr 5 mo — Frank Merriam 1934-39
30 yr 5 mo — J Neely Johnson 1856-58
Orval E Faubus 1955-67
Earl Warren 1943-53
10 yr 9 mo

COLORADO
71 yr 10 days — Edwin C Johnson 1955-57
35 yr 7 days — James B Grant 1883-85
Richard Lamm 1975-87
12 yr

CONNECTICUT
72 yr 10 mo — Simeon E Baldwin 1911-15
39 yr 6 mo — Joseph R Hawley 1866-67
Jonathan Trumbull Jr 1797-1809
11 yr 8 mo

Notes: Thomas Bibb was appointed governor following the death of Gov. Wyatt Bibb, his brother. Hugh McVay was appointed following the resignation of Gov. Comer.

Notes: Babbitt was appointed governor following the death of Gov. Wesley H. Bolin. He won the November 1978 election.

Key: ● Democrat ● Republican ● Dem-Rep ○ Other

Van Buren, Millard Fillmore, Franklin Pierce, James Buchanan and John Tyler.

Largest gathering The largest gathering of men who had been or would become President of the United States was eight, on 30 Dec 1834 in the old House Chamber of the Capitol: ex-president John Quincy Adams; ex-president Andrew Jackson; Vice-president Martin Van Buren; Senator John Tyler; Senator James Buchanan and Representatives James K. Polk, Millard Fillmore and Franklin Pierce.

VICE-PRESIDENTS

Fourteen men have held the offices of both President and Vice-President of the United States. Eight became President following the death of the incumbent: John Tyler (1841–45); Millard Fillmore (1850–53); Andrew Johnson (1865–69); Chester Arthur (1881–85); Theodore Roosevelt (1901–09); Calvin Coolidge (1923–29); Harry Truman (1945–53); Lyndon Johnson (1963–69). Five gained the presidency via election: John Adams (1797–1801); Thomas Jefferson (1801–1809); Martin Van Buren (1837–41); Richard Nixon (1969–74); George Bush (1989–present). Gerald Ford (1974–77) became President following the resignation of the incumbent Richard Nixon.

Longest term of office Only five Vice-Presidents have served two full four-year terms in office: John Adams (1789–97), Thomas R. Marshall (1913–1921), John Nance Garner (1933–41), Richard Nixon (1953–61) and George Bush (1981–89).

Youngest to hold office The youngest man to become Vice-President was John Cabell Breckinridge (Democrat; b. 21 Jan 1821), who took office on 4 Mar 1857 at the age of 36 years 1 month.

Oldest to hold office Alben William Barkley (Democrat; b. 24 Nov 1877) took office on 20 Jan 1949 at the age of 71 years 40 days. He served a full four-year term.

Longest-lived The longest-lived Vice-President was John Nance Garner, who served under Franklin D. Roosevelt from 1933 to 1941. He was born in 1868 and died on 7 Nov 1967 at the age of 98.

CONGRESS

Speaker of the House of Representatives In 1947 Congress enacted a law placing the Speaker of the House first in line to the presidency should both the President and Vice-President die, become incapacitated or be disqualified from office. James K. Polk is the only person to hold the offices of Speaker (1835–89) and President (1845–49).

Longest term The longest term served by any speaker was 17 yrs by Samuel Taliaferro Rayburn (1882–1961; D-Texas). Rayburn served three terms: 1940–47, 1949–53, 1955–61.

Shortest term The shortest term of any speaker is one day, 3 Mar 1869, served by Theodore Medad Pomeroy (1824–1905; R-New York).

Oldest speaker The oldest speaker was Sam Rayburn (D-Texas), who was reelected speaker for the 87th Congress on 3 Jan 1961 at age 78 years 11 months.

Youngest speaker The youngest speaker was Robert Mercer Taliaferro Hunter (1809–87; D-Virginia), who was chosen Speaker for the 26th Congress on 2 Dec 1839 at age 30 years 7 months.

Highest-paid legislators The most highly paid of all the world's legislators are members of the US Congress. The annual salary for members of the House of Representatives is $125,100. The basic annual salary for members of the Senate is $101,900, with an honoraria limit of $23,068. The President of the United States has an annual salary of $200,000, and a lifetime pension of $138,900 per year.

Most roll calls Senator William Proxmire (D-Wisconsin) did not miss a single one of the 9,695 roll calls from Apr 1966 to 27 Aug 1987. Rep. William H. Natcher (D-Kentucky) has cast 12,627 consecutive roll call votes and responded in person to 4,175 recorded quorum calls, for a total of 16,443 votes to the end of 1990. He has not missed a roll call or quorum call since being sworn in as a House member on 6 Jan 1954, a total of 37 years.

Filibusters The longest continuous speech in the history of the US Senate was that of Senator Wayne Morse (1900–74) of Oregon on 24–25 Apr 1953, when he spoke on the Tidelands Oil Bill for 22 hr 26 min without resuming his

seat. Interrupted only briefly by the swearing-in of a new senator, Senator Strom Thurmond (b. 1902) (R-South Carolina) spoke against a civil rights bill for 24 hr 19 min on 28–29 Aug 1957. The US national duration record on a state level is 43 hr by Texas State Senator Bill Meier, who spoke against nondisclosure of industrial accidents, in May 1977.

Fastest amendment The constitutional amendment that took the shortest time to ratify after congressional approval was the 26th Amendment in 1971, which gave 18-year-olds the right to vote.

POLITICAL OFFICE HOLDERS

Congressional service Carl Hayden (d. 25 Jan 1972; D-Arizona) holds the record for the longest congressional service, a total of 56 consecutive years (1927–69), of which 42 years were spent as a senator and the remainder as a representative.

House of Representatives The longest any representative has ever served is 50 years 2 months. Rep. Carl Vinson (D-Georgia) first entered the House on 3 Nov 1914 and retired on 3 Jan 1965.

The current longest-serving member of the House of Representatives is Jamie L. Whitten (D-Mississippi). Whitten began his career as a representative on 4 Nov 1941 and has served 25 consecutive two-year terms as of 1990.

■ **Filibusters**
Interrupted only briefly by the swearing-in of a new senator, South Carolina senator Strom Thurmond (b. 1902) spoke against a civil rights bill for 24 hr 19 min on 28–29 Aug 1957. Now a Republican but formerly both a Democrat and an independent, he is currently the oldest member of Congress.

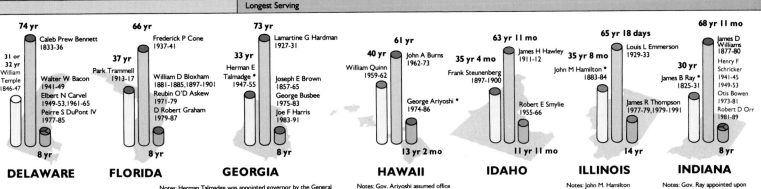

Longest Serving

	DELAWARE	FLORIDA	GEORGIA	HAWAII	IDAHO	ILLINOIS	INDIANA
Longest	74 yr — Caleb Prew Bennett 1833-36	66 yr — Frederick P Cone 1937-41	73 yr — Lamartine G Hardman 1927-31	61 yr — John A Burns 1962-73	63 yr 11 mo — James H Hawley 1911-12	65 yr 18 days — Louis L Emmerson 1929-33	68 yr 11 mo — James D Williams 1877-80

DELAWARE
31 or 32 yr — William Temple 1846-47
Walter W Bacon 1941-49
Elbert N Carvel 1949-53, 1961-65
Peirre S DuPont IV 1977-85
8 yr

FLORIDA
37 yr — Park Trammell 1913-17
William D Bloxham 1881-1885, 1897-1901
Reubin O'D Askew 1971-79
D Robert Graham 1979-87
8 yr

GEORGIA
33 yr — Herman E Talmadge * 1947-55
Joseph E Brown 1857-65
George Busbee 1975-83
Joe F Harris 1983-91
8 yr

HAWAII
40 yr — William Quinn 1959-62
George Ariyoshi * 1974-86
13 yr 2 mo

IDAHO
35 yr 4 mo — Frank Steunenberg 1897-1900
Robert E Smylie 1955-66
11 yr 11 mo

ILLINOIS
35 yr 8 mo — John M Hamilton * 1883-84
James R Thompson 1977-79, 1979-1991
14 yr

INDIANA
30 yr — James B Ray * 1825-31
Henry F Schricker 1941-45, 1949-53
Otis Bowen 1973-81
Robert D Orr 1981-89
8 yr

Notes: Herman Talmadge was appointed governor by the General Assembly following the death of Gov.-elect Eugene Talmadge, Herman's father. In February 1947 the appointment was upheld in court. Gov. Talmadge won the subsequent 1948 election.

Notes: Gov. Ariyoshi assumed office 10/1973 upon resignation of Gov. Burns.

Notes: John M. Hamilton appointed to complete term of governor who resigned.

Notes: Gov. Ray appointed upon resignation of Gov. William Hendricks—Gov. Ray later elected.

LEGISLATURES

■ **Smallest quorum**
Expressed as a percentage of eligible voters, the House of Lords, the upper chamber of the British Parliament, has the smallest quorum of any legislative body in the world—less than one-third of 1 percent. To transact business, there must be three peers present, including the lord chancellor or his deputy. The picture at right shows HM Queen Elizabeth II in the House of Lords for the State Opening of Parliament in 1964. (Photo: Hulton Picture Company)

■ **Oldest national constitution**
(far right) The world's oldest national constitution still in force is that of the United States of America, ratified by the necessary ninth state (New Hampshire) on 21 Jun 1788 and declared to be in effect on 4 Mar 1789. (Photo: Zefa)

Youngest elected The youngest man ever to serve in the House was William Charles Cole Claiborne (1775–1817; Jeffersonian Democrat-Tennessee), who, in contravention of the 25-year age requirement of the Constitution, was elected in August 1787 at the age of 22.

Oldest elected The oldest man ever elected representative was Claude Denson Pepper (1900–89; D-Florida), who was reelected on 8 Nov 1988 at age 88 years 2 months.

Senate The longest any senator has ever served is 37 years. Senator Francis E. Warren (1844–1929; R-Wyoming), first elected in November 1890, served through 1893, won reelection in 1895, and served continuously until his death on 24 Nov 1929.

The current longest-serving member of the Senate is Strom Thurmond (R-South Carolina). Thurmond began his career in the Senate on 24 Dec 1954 and has served six consecutive six-year terms as of 1990. He was originally a Democrat but changed to the Republican Party in 1964.

Oldest elected The greatest age at which anyone has been returned as a senator is 87 years 1 month, the age at which Theodore Francis Green (1867–1966; D-Rhode Island) was reelected in November 1956.

Youngest elected The youngest person ever elected senator was Brig. Gen. Armistead Thomson Mason (1787–1819; D-Virginia), who was elected on 3 Jan 1816 and was sworn in on 22 January at the age of 28 years 5 months 18 days.

The youngest-ever senator was John Henry Eaton (1790–1856; D-Tennessee), who was appointed on 5 Sep 1818 and sworn in on 16 November at age 28 years 4 months 29 days.

ELECTIONS

Largest popular majority Since the introduction of the popular vote in presidential elections in 1872, the greatest majority won was 17,994,460 votes in 1972 when President Richard M. Nixon (Republican) defeated George S. Mc-

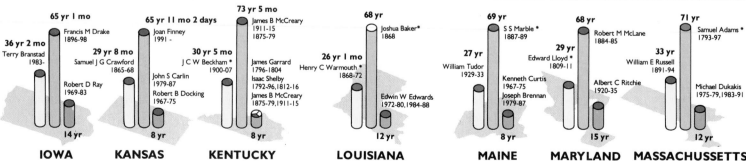

Youngest | Oldest

IOWA
- 36 yr 2 mo — Terry Branstad 1983-
- 65 yr 1 mo — Francis M Drake 1896-98
- 29 yr 8 mo — Samuel J G Crawford 1865-68
- Robert D Ray 1969-83
- 14 yr

KANSAS
- 65 yr 11 mo 2 days — Joan Finney 1991 -
- John S Carlin 1979-87
- Robert B Docking 1967-75
- 8 yr

KENTUCKY
- 73 yr 5 mo — James B McCreary 1911-15
- 30 yr 5 mo — J C W Beckham * 1900-07
- James Garrard 1796-1804
- Isaac Shelby 1792-96,1812-16
- James B McCreary 1875-79,1911-15
- 8 yr

Notes: Gov. Beckham appointed to complete term of Gov. William Goebel who died in 1900.

LOUISIANA
- 68 yr — Joshua Baker* 1868
- 26 yr 1 mo — Henry C Warmouth * 1868-72
- Edwin W Edwards 1972-80, 1984-88
- 12 yr

Notes: Both Warmouth and Baker were appointed governor by military commanders during Reconstruction. Warmouth was elected by popular vote in August 1868. Baker only served 6 months. The oldest governor, excluding Reconstruction appointments, was Joseph M. Walker (Dem), who took office in January 1850 at 63 years 6 months.

MAINE
- 69 yr — S S Marble * 1887-89
- 27 yr — William Tudor 1929-33
- Kenneth Curtis 1967-75
- Joseph Brennan 1979-87
- 8 yr

Notes: S. S. Marble, 1887-1889, appointed governor upon death of J. Bodwell.

MARYLAND
- 68 yr — Robert M McLane 1884-85
- 29 yr — Edward Lloyd * 1809-11
- Albert C Ritchie 1920-35
- 15 yr

Notes: Gov. Lloyd was elected by the General Assembly. The youngest governor elected by popular vote was Gov. Enoch L. Lowe (Rep); he served 1851-1854.

MASSACHUSSETTS
- 71 yr — Samuel Adams * 1793-97
- 33 yr — William E Russell 1891-94
- Michael Dukakis 1975-79, 1983-91
- 12 yr

Notes: Samuel Adams took office upon the death of Gov. Hancock. He won reelection in May 1794.

Key: ● Democrat ● Republican ● Dem-Rep ○ Other

Govern (Democrat) with 47,165,234 votes to 29,170,774.

Smallest popular majority The smallest popular majority was 7,023 votes in 1880 when President James A. Garfield (Republican) defeated Winfield Scott Hancock (Democrat) with 4,449,053 votes to 4,442,030.

Largest electoral college majority Since 1872, the greatest electoral college majority was 515 votes in 1936 when President Franklin D. Roosevelt (Democrat) defeated Alfred M. Landon (Republican) with 523 votes to 8.

Legislatures—World

PARLIAMENTS

Earliest and oldest The earliest-known legislative assembly or *ukkim* was a bicameral one in Erech, Iraq, *c.* 2800 BC. The oldest legislative body is the Althing of Iceland, founded in A.D. 930. This body, which originally comprised 39 local chieftains at Thingvellir, was abolished in 1800, but restored by Denmark to a consultative status in 1843 and a legislative status in 1874. The legislative assembly with the oldest continuous history is the Court of Tynwald in the Isle of Man, Great Britain, which celebrated its millennium in 1979.

Largest The largest legislative assembly in the world is the National People's Congress of the People's Republic of China, which has 2,978 members who are indirectly elected for a five-year term. The seventh congress convened in March 1988.

Smallest quorum The House of Lords has the smallest quorum, expressed as a percentage of eligible voters, of any legislative body in the world—less than one-third of 1 percent. To transact business, there must be three peers present, including the lord chancellor or his deputy. The House of Commons' quorum of 40 MPs, including the Speaker or his deputy, is 13 times as exacting.

Longest membership The longest span as a legislator was 83 years, by József Madarász (1814–1915). He first attended the Hungarian Parliament from 1832–36 as *oblegatus absentium* (i.e., on behalf of an absent deputy). He was a full member from 1848–50 and from 1861 until his death on 31 Jan 1915.

Longest UN speech The longest speech made in the United Nations was one of 4 hr 29 min on 26 Sep 1960 by President Fidel Castro Ruz (b. 13 Aug 1927) of Cuba.

Oldest treaty The oldest treaty still in force is the Anglo-Portuguese Treaty of Alliance, which was signed in London, Great Britain over 618 years ago on 16 Jun 1373. The text was confirmed "with my usual flourish" by John de Banketre, Clerk.

Constitutions The world's oldest national constitution still in force is that of the United States of America, ratified by the necessary ninth state (New Hampshire) on 21 Jun 1788 and declared to be in effect on 4 Mar 1789.

Woman's suffrage The earliest legislature with female voters was that of the Territory of Wyoming in 1869, followed by that of the Isle of Man, Great Britain in 1881. The earliest country to have universal woman's suffrage was New Zealand in 1893.

United States In 1920 the 19th Amendment to the Constitution granted nationwide suffrage to women.

PRIME MINISTERS AND STATESMEN

Oldest The longest-lived prime minister of any country was Naruhiko Higashikuni (Japan), who was born on 3 Dec 1887 and died on 20 Jan 1990, at age 102 years 48 days. He was his country's first prime minister after World War II, but held office for less than two months, resigning in October 1945.

El Hadji Muhammad el Mokri, Grand Vizier of Morocco, died on 16 Sep 1957 at a reputed age of 116 Muslim (*Hijri*) years, equivalent to 112½ Gregorian years.

The oldest age at first appointment was 81, by Morarji Ranchhodji Desai of India (b. 29 Feb 1896) in March 1977.

Youngest Currently the youngest head of government is HM Druk Gyalpo ("Dragon King") Jigme Singye Wangchuk of Bhutan (b. 11 Nov 1955), who

has been head of government since March 1972.

Longest term of office The longest-serving current prime minister is HRH Prince Fatafehi Tu'ipelehake (b. 7 Jan 1922) of Tonga, who has held office since 16 Dec 1965.

Marshall Kim Il Sung (ne Kim Sung Chu; b. 15 Apr 1912) has been head of government or head of state of the Democratic People's Republic of Korea since 25 Aug 1948.

Andrei Andreievich Gromyko (1909–89) had been Minister of Foreign Affairs of the USSR since 15 Feb 1957 (having been

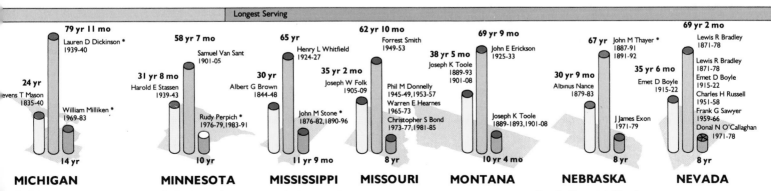

Longest Serving

MICHIGAN
- 79 yr 11 mo — Lauren D Dickinson * 1939-40
- 24 yr — Stevens T Mason 1835-40
- 14 yr — William Milliken * 1969-83

Notes: Gov. Dickinson became governor upon the death of Gov. Frank D. Fitzgerald. Gov. Milliken took office in 1969 when Gov. Romney resigned to take a cabinet post.

MINNESOTA
- 58 yr 7 mo — Samuel Van Sant 1901-05
- 31 yr 8 mo — Harold E Stassen 1939-43
- 10 yr — Rudy Perpich * 1976-79, 1983-91

Notes: Gov. Perpich appointed to complete term of Gov. Wendell R. Anderson, who resigned to take a seat in the US Senate.

MISSISSIPPI
- 65 yr — Henry L Whitfield 1924-27
- 30 yr — Albert G Brown 1844-48
- 11 yr 9 mo — John M Stone * 1876-82, 1890-96

Notes: Gov. Stone appointed to complete term of Gov. Adelbert Ames, who had resigned.

MISSOURI
- 62 yr 10 mo — Forrest Smith 1949-53
- 35 yr 2 mo — Joseph W Folk 1905-09
- Phil M Donnelly 1945-49, 1953-57
- Warren E Hearnes 1965-73
- Christopher S Bond 1973-77, 1981-85
- 8 yr

MONTANA
- 69 yr 9 mo — John E Erickson 1925-33
- 38 yr 5 mo — Joseph K Toole 1889-93, 1901-08
- Joseph K Toole 1889-1893, 1901-08
- 10 yr 4 mo

NEBRASKA
- 67 yr — John M Thayer * 1887-91, 1891-92
- 30 yr 9 mo — Albinus Nance 1879-83
- J James Exon 1971-79
- 8 yr

Notes: Gov. Thayer contested November 1890 election results. Gov. Thayer was reinstated 5/5/1891-2/8/1892; Gov. James E. Boyd, who had won the election, was not finally seated until 2/8/1892.

NEVADA
- 69 yr 2 mo — Lewis R Bradley 1871-78
- 35 yr 6 mo — Emet D Boyle 1915-22
- Lewis R Bradley 1871-78
- Emet D Boyle 1915-22
- Charles H Russell 1951-58
- Frank G Sawyer 1959-66
- Donal N O'Callaghan 1971-78
- 8 yr

Deputy Foreign Minister since 1946), when he was elected President of the USSR on 2 Jul 1985, a position he held until 30 Sep 1988. Piotr Lomako (1904–90) served in the government of the USSR as Minister for Non-Ferrous Metallurgy from 1940–86. He was relieved of his post on 1 Nov 1986 after 46 years at age 82, having served on the Central Committee of the Communist Party of the Soviet Union (CPSU) since 1952.

Woman Sirimavo Bandaranaike (b. 1916) of Ceylon (now Sri Lanka) became the first woman prime minister of any country when her party, the Sri Lanka ("Blessed Ceylon") Freedom Party, won the general election in July 1960.

ELECTIONS

Largest The largest elections in the world were those beginning on 22 Nov 1989 for the Indian Lok Sabha (Lower House), which has 543 elective seats. Out of an electorate of 498,647,786, a total of 304,126,600 people cast their votes; 291 parties contested the elections; and there were more than 593,000 polling stations manned by a staff of 3.5 million. As a result of the election a new government was formed under the leadership of Viswanath Pratap Singh of Janata Dal (People's Party), which has now disbanded.

Closest The ultimate in close general elections occurred in Zanzibar (now part of Tanzania) on 18 Jan 1961, when the Afro-Shirazi Party won by a single seat, after the seat of Chake-Chake on Pemba Island had been gained by a single vote.

The narrowest recorded percentage win in an election would seem to be for the office of Southern District Highway Commissioner in Mississippi on 7 Aug 1979. Robert E. Joiner was declared the winner over W. H. Pyron, with 133,587 votes to 133,582. The loser thus obtained more than 49.999 percent of the votes.

Most decisive North Korea recorded a 100 percent turnout of electors and a 100 percent vote for the Workers' Party of Korea in the general election of 8 Oct 1962. The closest to a unanimous vote was in Albania on 14 Nov 1982, when a single voter spoiled national unanimity for the official (and only) Communist

candidates, who consequently obtained 99.99993 percent of the vote in a 100 percent turnout of 1,627,968.

Most crooked In the Liberian presidential election of 1927, President Charles D.B. King (1875–1961) was returned with an officially announced majority of 234,000 over his opponent, Thomas J.R. Faulkner of the People's Party. President King thus claimed a "majority" more than 15½ times greater than the entire electorate.

Highest personal majority The highest-ever personal majority for any politician was 4,726,112 by Boris Yeltsin, the unofficial Moscow candidate, in the parliamentary elections held in the Soviet Union on 26 Mar 1989. Yeltsin received 5,118,745 votes out of the 5,722,937 that were cast in the Moscow constituency, his closest rival obtaining 392,633 votes. In 1956 W.R.D. Bandaranaike achieved 91.82 percent of the vote, with 45,016 votes, in the Attanagalla constituency of Sri Lanka (then Ceylon).

Communist parties *Largest* The party membership in mainland China was estimated to be 48 million in 1989.

Largest field of candidates There were 301 candidates running to represent Belgaum City in the State Assembly (Vidhan Sabha) elections in Karnataka, India held on 5 Mar 1985.

Most coups Statisticians contend that Bolivia, since it became a sovereign country in 1825, has had 191 coups, the latest on 30 Jun 1984, when President Hernan Siles Zuazo, age 70, was kidnapped from his official residence by more than 60 armed men.

Judicial

LEGISLATION AND LITIGATION

Statutes *Oldest* The earliest surviving judicial code was that of King Ur-Hammu during the third dynasty of Ur, Iraq, *c.* 2110 B.C.

Most inexplicable Certain pieces of legislation have always defied interpre-

tation, and the most inexplicable must be a matter of opinion. A judge of the Court of Session of Scotland once sent the Editor his candidate, which reads: *"In the Nuts (unground), (other than ground nuts) Order, the expression nuts shall have reference to such nuts, other than ground nuts, as would but for this amending Order not qualify as nuts (unground) (other than ground nuts) by reason of their being nuts (unground)."*

Most protracted litigation The longest-contested lawsuit ever recorded ended in Poona, India on 28 Apr 1966, when Balasaheb Patloji Thorat received a favorable judgment on a suit filed by his ancestor Maloji Thorat 761 years earlier in 1205. The points at issue were rights of presiding over public functions and precedences at religious festivals.

Longest hearing The longest civil case heard before a jury is *Kemner v. Monsanto Co.*, which concerned an alleged toxic chemical spill in Sturgeon, MO in 1979. The trial started on 6 Feb 1984, at St Clair County Court House, Belleville, IL before Circuit Judge Richard P. Goldenhersh, and ended on 22 Oct 1987. The testimony lasted 657 days, following which the jury deliberated for two months. The verdict was returned on 22 October when the plaintiffs secured sums of $1 nominal compensatory damage and $16,250,000 punitive damage.

Litigants in person Dr Mark Feldman, a chiropodist, of Lauderhill, FL became the first litigant in person to secure seven figures ($1 million) before a jury in compensatory and punitive damages in September 1980. The case concerned conspiracy and fraud alleged against six other doctors.

Highest bail The world record for bail was set at $100 billion on Jeffrey Marsh, Juan Mercado, Yolanda Kravitz and Alvin Kravitz at the Dade County Courthouse, Miami, FL on 16 Oct 1989. The four defense attorneys in the case, which concerned an armed robbery, stipulated the bail, and although a reduction was subsequently requested, this was denied. The presiding judge was David L. Tobin.

Best-attended trial The greatest attendance at any trial was at that of Major Jesús Sosa Blanco, age 51, for an

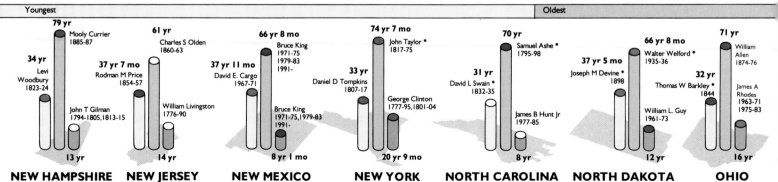

alleged 108 murders. At one point in the 12½-hr trial (5:30 P.M. to 6 A.M., 22–23 Jan 1959), 17,000 people were present in the Havana Sports Palace, Cuba. He was executed on 18 Feb 1959.

Greatest damages *Personal injury* The greatest personal injury damages ever awarded were $78 million to the model Marla Hanson, 26, on 29 Sep 1987. Her face was slashed with razors in Manhattan, New York City in June 1987. The three men convicted and now serving 5–15 years have no assets and Miss Hanson is entitled to 10 percent of their post-prison earnings.

On 18 Jul 1986 a Bronx Supreme Court jury awarded $65,086,000 to Mrs Agnes Mae Whitaker against the New York City Health and Hospitals Corporation for medical malpractice.

The compensation for the disaster in 1984 at the Union Carbide Corporation plant in Bhopal, India was set at $470 million. The Supreme Court of India passed the order for payment on 14 Feb 1989 after the settlement between the corporation and the Indian government, which represented the interests of more than 500,000 claimants.

Civil damages The largest damages awarded in legal history were $11.12 billion to Pennzoil Company against Texaco Inc. concerning the latter's allegedly unethical tactics in January 1984 in attempting to break up a merger between Pennzoil and Getty Oil Company, by Judge Solomon Casseb, Jr. in Houston, TX on 10 Dec 1985. An out-of-court settlement of $5.5 billion was reached after a 48-hour negotiation on 19 Dec 1987.

Defamation Richard A. Sprague, a prominent lawyer from Philadelphia, PA, was awarded a record $34 million against the *Philadelphia Inquirer* on 3 May 1990 for a series of articles which the newspaper had published about him in 1973.

The $39.6 million awarded in Columbus, OH on 1 Mar 1980 to Robert Guccione, publisher of *Penthouse*, against Larry Flynt, publisher of *Hustler*, for defamation, was reduced by Judge Craig Wright to $4 million on 17 Apr 1980.

Media (television) The U.S. Supreme Court on 4 Apr 1988 let stand a $3,050,000

libel award against CBS Inc., its Chicago station WBBM and anchorman Walter Jacobsen. The damages awarded to Brown & Williamson Tobacco Corp. were the largest against a news media defendant in the United States.

Media (newspaper) The record libel award actually paid was $2,771,000 by the *Pittsburgh Post-Gazette* to former judge Richard Disalle. Damages had been set by a Washington, PA jury in 1985, the Supreme Court declined to hear an appeal on 3 Jul 1988 and the award was paid on 11 Jul 1988.

Greatest compensation for imprisonment Robert McLaughlin, 29, was awarded $1,935,000 in October 1989 for wrongful imprisonment as a result of a murder in New York City in 1979 which he did not commit. He had been sentenced to 15 years in prison and had actually served six years, from 1980 to 1986, when he was released after his foster father succeeded in showing the authorities that he had had nothing to do with the crime.

Largest alimony suit Belgian-born Sheika Dena Al-Fassi, 23, filed the highest-ever alimony claim of $3 billion against her former husband, Sheik Mohammed Al-Fassi, 28, of the Saudi Arabian royal family, in Los Angeles, CA in February 1982. Attorney Marvin Mitchelson, explaining the size of the settlement claim, alluded to the Sheik's wealth, which included 14 homes in Florida alone and numerous private aircraft. On 14 Jun 1983 the claimant was awarded $81 million and declared she would be "very very happy" if she was able to collect.

Largest divorce settlement The reported settlement achieved in 1982 by the lawyers of Soraya Khashóggi was £500 million ($950 million) plus property from her husband Adnan. Mrs Anne Bass, former wife of Sid Bass of Texas, was reported to have rejected $535 million as inadequate to live in the style to which she had been made accustomed.

Patent case Polaroid Corporation was awarded $909.5 million in Boston, MA on 12 Oct 1990 in a suit involving Eastman Kodak Company for infringing patents for instant photography cameras and films. Polaroid had filed

suit in 1976, claiming that Kodak had infringed patents used in Polaroid's 1972 SX-70 system.

Largest suit The highest amount of damages ever sought to date is $675 trillion (then equivalent to 10 times the US national wealth) in a suit by Mr I. Walton Bader brought in the US District Court, New York City on 14 Apr 1971 against General Motors and others for polluting all 50 states.

Highest costs The Guinness case, involving the takeover bid by the Company of Distillers in 1986, is estimated to have cost approximately £10 million ($17 million). The trial at Southwark Crown Court, London, Great Britain, which lasted 107 days, ended on 27 Aug 1990 and resulted in jail sentences for three of the four defendants—Ernest Saunders, Gerald Ronson and Anthony Parnes. The fourth defendant, Sir (later

■ **Patent case**
Polaroid Corporation was awarded a record $909.5 million in Boston, MA on 12 Oct 1990 in a suit involving Eastman Kodak Co. for infringing patents for instant photography cameras and films. The picture above shows Edwin Hand, the founder of Polaroid, in his laboratory in Cambridge, MA in 1947. (Photo: Gamma/Liaison)

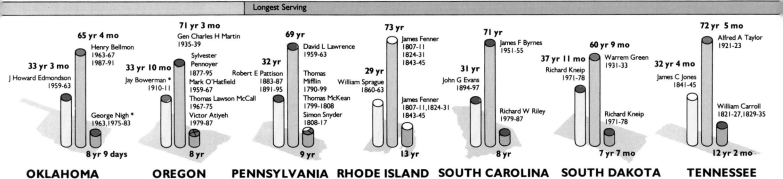

Longest Serving

OKLAHOMA
33 yr 3 mo — J Howard Edmondson 1959-63
65 yr 4 mo — Henry Bellmon 1963-67 1987-91
George Nigh * 1963,1975-83
8 yr 9 days

Notes: Gov. Nigh served January 6-14 1963 to complete term of Gov. Edmondson, who resigned to assume US Senate seat.

OREGON
71 yr 3 mo — Gen Charles H Martin 1935-39
Sylvester Pennoyer 1877-95
Mark O'Hatfield 1959-67
Thomas Lawson McCall 1967-75
Victor Atiyeh 1979-87
33 yr 10 mo — Jay Bowerman * 1910-11
8 yr

Notes: Gov. Bowerman appointed governor following the incapacity of Gov. Frank W. Benson.

PENNSYLVANIA
69 yr — David L Lawrence 1959-63
32 yr — Robert E Pattison 1883-87 1891-95
Thomas Mifflin 1790-99
Thomas McKean 1799-1808
Simon Snyder 1808-17
9 yr

RHODE ISLAND
73 yr — James Fenner 1807-11 1824-31 1843-45
29 yr — William Sprague 1860-63
James Fenner 1807-11,1824-31 1843-45
13 yr

Notes: Gov. Fenner changed party to Jacksonian Dem. in election of 1830; Whig (election of 1843); Law and Order Party (1844-45).

SOUTH CAROLINA
71 yr — James F Byrnes 1951-55
31 yr — John G Evans 1894-97
Richard W Riley 1979-87
8 yr

SOUTH DAKOTA
60 yr 9 mo — Warrem Green 1931-33
37 yr 11 mo — Richard Kneip 1971-78
Richard Kneip 1971-78
7 yr 7 mo

TENNESSEE
72 yr 5 mo — Alfred A Taylor 1921-23
32 yr 4 mo — James C Jones 1841-45
William Carroll 1821-27,1829-35
12 yr 2 mo

Mr) Jack Lyons, was fined £3 million ($5.1 million).

United States The McMartin Preschool case in Los Angeles, CA is estimated to have cost $15 million. The trial, concerning the alleged abuse of children at the school in Manhattan Beach, CA, had begun with jury selection on 20 Apr 1987 and resulted in the acquittal on 18 Jan 1990 of the two defendants on 52 counts of child molestation and conspiracy. Peggy McMartin Buckey, the former director of the school, and her son Raymond, who had been a teacher's aide, had spent nearly two and five years in jail respectively since their arrest in 1984. A second trial, of Raymond Buckey, began on 7 May but he was acquitted on 27 July. Afterwards Deputy Los Angeles District Attorney Joseph Martinez declared, "The McMartin case is over."

Longest lease There is a lease concerning a plot for a sewage tank adjoining Columb Barracks, Mullingar, Ireland, which was signed on 3 Dec 1868 for 10 million years. It is to be assumed that a future civil servant will bring up the matter for review early in A.D. 10,001,868. Leases in Ireland lasting "forever" are quite common.

Wills *Shortest* The shortest valid will in the world consists of the words "Vše zene," the Czech for "All to wife," written and dated 19 Jan 1967 by Herr Karl Tausch of Langen, Germany.

Most durable judge The oldest recorded active judge was Judge Albert R. Alexander (1859–1966) of Plattsburg, MO. He was the magistrate and probate judge of Clinton County until his retirement at the age of 105 years 8 months on 9 Jul 1965.

Youngest judge No collated records on the ages of judicial appointments exist. However, David Elmer Ward had to await the legal age of 21 before taking office after nomination in 1932 as judge of the County Court in Fort Myers, FL.

Muhammad Ilyas passed the examination enabling him to become a civil judge in July 1952 at the age of 20 years 9 months, although formalities such as medicals meant that it was not until eight months later that he started work as a civil judge in Lahore, Pakistan.

Most judges In *R. v. Canning* at the Old Bailey, London, Great Britain in 1754 Elizabeth Canning was deported to Connecticut for willful perjury, by 19 judges voting 10 to 9.

CRIME

Mass killings *China* The greatest massacre ever imputed by the government of one sovereign nation against the government of another is that of 26.3 million Chinese during the regime of Mao Zedong between 1949 and May 1965. This accusation was made by an agency of the USSR government in a radio broadcast on 7 Apr 1969. The broadcast broke down the figure into four periods: 2.8 million (1949–52); 3.5 million (1953–57); 6.7 million (1958–60); and 13.3 million (1961–May 1965).

The Walker Report published by the US Senate Committee of the Judiciary in Jul 1971 placed the parameters of the total death toll within China since 1949 between 32.25 and 61.7 million. An estimate of 63.7 million was published by the *Figaro* magazine of 19–25 Nov 1978.

In Chinese history of the 13th–17th centuries there were three periods of wholesale massacre. The numbers of victims attributed to these events are assertions rather than reliable estimates. The figures given for the Mongolian invasions of northern China from 1210–19 and from 1311–40 are both on the order of 35 million, while the number of victims of the bandit leader Chang Hsien-chung (c. 1605–47), known as the "Yellow Tiger," from 1643–47 in the Siechuan province has been put at 40 million.

USSR The total death toll in the Great Purge, or *Yezhovshchina*, in the USSR from 1936–38 has never been published. Evidence of its magnitude may be found in population statistics, which show a decline in population from *before* the outbreak of the 1941–45 war. Nobel laureate Alexander Solzhenitsyn estimated the loss of life from state repression and terrorism from October 1917 to December 1959 under Lenin, Stalin and Khrushchev at 66.7 million.

Nazi Germany The most reliable estimate of the number of Jewish victims of the Holocaust or the genocidal "Final Solution" (*Endlösung*) ordered by Adolf Hitler (1889–1945) in April 1941 and continuing into May 1945 is 5.8 million. At the SS (*Schutzstaffel*) extermination camp (*Vernichtungslager*) known as Auschwitz-Birkenau (Oświecim-Brzezinka), near Oświecim (Auschwitz) in southern Poland, a minimum of 920,000 people (Soviet estimate is 4 million) were killed from 14 Jun 1940 to 18 Jan 1945. The greatest number killed in a day was 6,000.

Cambodia As a percentage of a nation's total population the worst genocide appears to have been that in Cambodia (or Kampuchea). According to the Khmer Rouge Foreign Minister, Teng Sary, more than a third of the 8 million Khmers were killed between 17 Apr 1975 and January 1979. The philosophy of class conflict induced indifference to individual suffering to the point of serving as a warrant for massacre. Under the rule of Saloth Sar, alias Pol Pot, a founding member of the CPK (Communist Party of Kampuchea, formed in September 1960), towns, money and property were abolished and economical execution by bayonet and club was introduced for such offenses as falling asleep during the day, asking too many questions, playing noncommunist music, being old and feeble, being the offspring of an "undesirable" or being too well educated. Deaths at the Tuol Sleng interrogation center reached 582 in a day.

Saving of life The greatest number of people saved from extinction by one person is an estimated 90,000 Jews in Budapest, Hungary from July 1944 to January 1945 by the Swedish diplomat Raoul Wallenberg (b. 4 Aug 1912). After escaping an assassination attempt by the Nazis, he was imprisoned without trial in the Soviet Union. On 6 Feb 1957 Mr Gromyko said prisoner Wallenberg had died in a cell in Lubyanka Jail, Moscow on 16 Jul 1947. Sighting reports within the Gulag system persisted for years after his disappearance. He was made an Honorary Citizen of the United States on 5 Oct 1981, and on 7 May 1987 a statue to him was unveiled in Budapest to replace an earlier one that had been removed.

Largest criminal organization The largest syndicate of organized crime is the Mafia or La Cosa Nostra. The

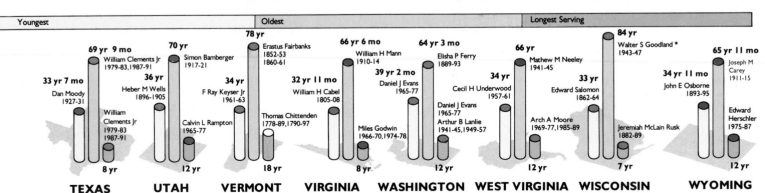

TEXAS
33 yr 7 mo — Dan Moody 1927-31
69 yr 9 mo — William Clements Jr 1979-83, 1987-91
8 yr — William Clements Jr 1979-83 1987-91

UTAH
70 yr — Simon Bamberger 1917-21
36 yr — Heber M Wells 1896-1905
12 yr — Calvin L Rampton 1965-77

VERMONT
78 yr — Erastus Fairbanks 1852-53 1860-61
34 yr — F Ray Keyser Jr 1961-63
18 yr — Thomas Chittenden 1778-89, 1790-97

VIRGINIA
66 yr 6 mo — William H Mann 1910-14
32 yr 11 mo — William H Cabel 1805-08
8 yr — Miles Godwin 1966-70, 1974-78

WASHINGTON
64 yr 3 mo — Elisha P Ferry 1889-93
39 yr 2 mo — Daniel J Evans 1965-77
12 yr — Daniel J Evans 1965-77

WEST VIRGINIA
66 yr — Mathew M Neeley 1941-45
34 yr — Cecil H Underwood 1957-61
12 yr — Arch A Moore 1969-77, 1985-89

WISCONSIN
84 yr — Walter S Goodland * 1943-47
33 yr — Edward Salomon 1862-64
7 yr — Jeremiah McLain Rusk 1882-89

WYOMING
65 yr 11 mo — Joseph M Carey 1911-15
34 yr 11 mo — John E Osborne 1893-95
12 yr — Edward Herschler 1975-87

Arthur B Lanlie 1941-45, 1949-57

Youngest | Oldest | Longest Serving

Notes: Gov. Goodland appointed following death of Gov.-elect Orland S. Loomis. Goodland died in office in March 1947.

Key: ● Democrat ● Republican ● Dem-Rep ○ Other

name "Mafia" is thought to be derived from the first letters of each word of the slogan *"Morte alla Francia Italia anela"*—"Death to the French is Italy's cry." It consists of some 3,000 to 5,000 individuals in 25 "families" federated under "The Commission," with an annual turnover in vice, gambling, protection rackets, tobacco, bootlegging, hijacking, narcotics, loan-sharking and prostitution that was estimated by *US News & World Report* in Dec 1982 at $200 billion, and a profit estimated in Mar 1986 by US District Attorney Rudolph Giuliani at $75 billion. Its origin in the United States dates from 1869 in New Orleans, LA.

Murder rate   Highest and lowest The country with the highest recorded murder rate is Brazil, with 104 homicides for each 100,000 of the population in 1983, or 370 per day.

The highest homicide rates recorded in New York City were 58 in a week in July 1972 and 15 in a day in June 1989.

In the Indian state of Sikkim, in the Himalayas, murder is practically unknown, while in the Hunza area of Kashmir, in the Karakoram, only one definite case of murder by a Hunzarwal has been recorded since 1900.

Most prolific murderers It was established at the trial of Behram, the Indian Thug, that he had strangled at least 931 victims with his yellow and white cloth strip or *ruhmal* in the Oudh district between 1790 and 1840. It has been estimated that at least 2 million Indians were strangled by Thugs (*burtotes*) during the reign of the Thugee (pronounced tugee) cult from 1550 until its final suppression by the British raj in 1853.

The greatest number of victims ascribed to a murderess was 650, in the case of Countess Erzsebet Bathory (1560–1614) of Hungary. At her trial, which began on 2 Jan 1611, a witness testified to seeing a list of her victims in her own handwriting totaling this number. All were alleged to be young girls from near her castle at Csejthe, where she died on 21 Aug 1614. She had been walled up in her room for 3½ years after being found guilty.

20th century A total of 592 deaths was attributed to one Colombian bandit leader, Teófilo ("Sparks") Rojas, 27, between 1948 and his death in an ambush near Armenia, Colombia on 22 Jan 1963. Some sources attribute 3,500 slayings to him during *La Violencia* of 1945–62.

In a drunken rampage lasting 8 hours on 26–27 Apr 1982, policeman Wou Bom-Kon, 27, killed 57 people and wounded 35 with 176 rounds of rifle ammunition and hand grenades in the Kyong Sang-Namdo province of South Korea. He then blew himself up with a grenade.

Suicide The estimated daily rate of suicide throughout the world surpassed 1,000 in 1965. The country with the highest suicide rate is Hungary, with a rate of 40 per 100,000 in 1989. The country with the lowest recorded rate is Jordan, with just a single case in 1970 and hence a rate of 0.04 per 100,000. The number in China rose to 382 per day, or 16 per hour, in 1987–88.

Mass poisoning On 1 May 1981 the first of more than 600 victims of the Spanish cooking oil scandal died. On 12 June it was discovered that this 8-year-old boy's cause of death was the use of "denatured" industrial oil from rape seed. The trial of 38 defendants, including the manufacturers Ramón and Elias Ferrero, lasted from 30 Mar 1987 to 28 Jun 1988. The 586 counts on which the prosecution demanded jail sentences totaled 60,000 years.

Robbery The greatest robbery on record was that of the Reichsbank following Germany's collapse in April–May 1945. The Pentagon in Washington described the event, first published in *The Guinness Book of Records* in 1957, as "an unverified allegation." *Nazi Gold* by Ian Sayer and Douglas Botting, published in 1984, however, finally revealed full details and estimated the total haul at what were then current values as £2.5 billion ($3.75 billion).

Treasury bills and certificates of deposit worth £292 million ($484.72 million) were stolen when a mugger attacked a money-broker's messenger in the financial sector of London, Great Britain on 2 May 1990. Because details of the documents stolen were quickly flashed on market dealing screens and given to central banks worldwide, the chances of anyone being able to benefit from the theft were considered to be very remote.

Art On 18 Mar 1990, 11 paintings by Rembrandt, Vermeer, Degas, Manet and Vlaminck, plus a Chinese bronze beaker of about 1200 B.C., in total worth an estimated $200 million, were stolen from the Isabella Stewart Gardner Museum in Boston, MA. Although the paintings were insured against damage, none of them was insured against theft.

On 24 Dec 1985, 140 priceless gold, jade and obsidian artifacts were stolen from the National Museum of Anthropology, Mexico City. The majority of the stolen objects were recovered in June 1989 from the Mexico City home of a man described by officials as the mastermind of the theft.

Bank During the extreme civil disorder prior to 22 Jan 1976 in Beirut, Lebanon, a guerrilla force blasted the vaults of the British Bank of the Middle East in Bab Idriss and cleared out safe deposit boxes with contents valued by former Finance Minister Lucien Dahadah at $50 million and by another source at an "absolute minimum" of $20 million.

Train The greatest recorded train robbery occurred between 3:03 A.M. and 3:27 A.M. on 8 Aug 1963, when a General Post Office mail train from Glasgow, Great Britain was ambushed at Sears Crossing and robbed at Bridego Bridge near Mentmore, Great Britain. The gang escaped with about 120 mailbags containing £2,631,784 ($7.41 million) worth of banknotes being taken to London for destruction. Only £343,448 ($961,654) was recovered.

Jewels The greatest recorded theft of jewels was from the bedroom of the "well-guarded" villa of Prince Abdel Aziz bin Ahmed Al-Thani near Cannes, France on 24 Jul 1980. The jewels were valued at $16 million.

Greatest kidnapping ransom Historically the greatest ransom paid was that for Atahualpa by the Incas to Francisco Pizarro in 1532–33 at Cajamarca, Peru, which constituted a hall full of gold and silver, worth some $170 million on today's market.

The greatest ransom ever reported in modern times was 1,500 million pesos ($60 million) for the release of the brothers Jorge Born, 40, and Juan Born, 39, of Bunge and Born, paid to the left-wing urban guerrilla group Montoneros in Buenos Aires, Argentina on 20 Jun 1975.

Greatest hijack ransom The highest amount ever paid to aircraft hijackers was $6 million, by the Japanese government in the case of a JAL DC-8 at Dacca Airport, Bangladesh on 2 Oct 1977, with 38 hostages. Six convicted criminals were also exchanged. The Bangladesh government had refused to sanction any retaliatory action.

Largest narcotics haul The greatest drug haul ever achieved was on 28 Sep 1989, when cocaine with an estimated street value of $6–7 billion was seized in a raid on a warehouse in Los Angeles, CA. The haul of 22 tons was prompted by a tip-off from a local resident who had complained about heavy truck traffic and people leaving the warehouse "at odd hours and in a suspicious manner."

The bulkiest haul was 3,200 tons of Colombian marijuana in the 14-month-long "Operation Tiburon," carried out by the Drug Enforcement Administration. The arrest of 495 people and the seizure of 95 vessels was announced on 5 Feb 1982.

Greatest bank note forgery The greatest forgery was the German Third Reich's forging operation, code name "Bernhard," engineered by SS Sturmbannführer Alfred Naujocks of the Technical Dept of the German Secret Service Amt VI F in Berlin in 1940–41. It involved £150 million worth ($604.5 million) of £5 notes (worth $20.15).

Biggest bank fraud The Banca Nazionale del Lavoro, Italy's leading bank, admitted on 6 Sep 1989 that it had been defrauded of an estimated $3 billion, with the disclosure that its branch in Atlanta, GA had made unauthorized loan commitments to Iraq. Both the bank's chairman, Nerio Nesi, and its director general, Giacomo Pedde, resigned following the revelation.

Computer fraud Between 1964 and 1973, 64,000 fake insurance policies were created on the computer of the Equity Funding Corporation in the United States, involving $2 billion.

Art robbery
It is arguable that the *Mona Lisa*, though never valued, is the most valuable object ever stolen. It disappeared from the Louvre, Paris, France on 21 Aug 1911. It was recovered in Italy in 1913, when Vincenzo Perruggia was charged with its theft.

Kidnapping
The youngest person ever kidnapped was Carolyn Wharton, born at 12:46 P.M. on 19 Mar 1955 in the Baptist Hospital, TX and kidnapped, by a woman disguised as a nurse, at 1:15 P.M. at the age of 29 minutes.

JUDICIAL

Largest object stolen by a single man

On a moonless night at dead calm high water on 5 Jun 1966, at Wolfe's Cove, St Lawrence Seaway, Canada, N. William Kennedy, armed with only a sharp ax, slashed free the mooring lines of the 10,639-ton SS *Orient Trader* owned by Steel Factors Ltd of Ontario. The vessel drifted to a waiting blacked-out tug, thus escaping a ban on any shipping movements during a violent wildcat waterfront strike. She then sailed for Spain.

Stanley Mark Rifkin (b. 1946) was arrested in Carlsbad, CA by the FBI on 6 Nov 1978 and charged with defrauding a Los Angeles bank of $10.2 million by manipulation of a computer system. He was sentenced to 8 years' imprisonment in June 1980.

Theft It was estimated in November 1983 that the greatest theft in the world is running at $160 billion per year. This is the value of "bosses' time" paid for but not worked in the United States in 1983/84.

The government of the Philippines announced on 23 Apr 1986 that it had succeeded in identifying $860.8 million salted away by former President Ferdinand Edralin Marcos (1917–89) and his wife Imelda. The total since November 1965 was believed to be $5–$10 billion.

Maritime fraud A cargo of 198,414 tons of Kuwaiti crude oil on the supertanker *Salem* at Durban was sold without title to the South African government in December 1979. The ship mysteriously sank off Senegal on 17 Jan 1980, leaving the government to pay £148 million ($318.2 million) to Shell International, which owned the shipment.

CAPITAL PUNISHMENT

Capital punishment is known to date at least from the Iron Age, as evidenced by the finding of Tollund man in Denmark. The countries in which capital punishment is still *prevalent* include China (hundreds of shootings per year), South Africa (about 100 hangings for rape, robbery and murder), Turkey, Iran, Saudi Arabia, Malaysia, United States (reintroduced in 38 states since January 1983 for the most heinous murders) and the USSR (23 capital offenses, including profiteering, speculation and currency offenses, for which 253 persons were shot in 1989). Capital punishment was first abolished *de facto* in 1798 in Liechtenstein.

Through April 1991, 144 people have been put to death in the United States since the Supreme Court permitted states to restore the death penalty. Executions have been permitted in 16 states; Texas has executed 38 men, the most of any state.

Earliest The earliest recorded execution among white settlers in the United States was that of John Billington for murder at Plymouth, MA on 30 Sep 1630. The earliest judicial electrocution was of William Kemmler at Auburn Prison, NY, on 6 Aug 1890, for the murder of Matilda Zeigler 495 days before.

Largest hanging The most people hanged from one gallows were 38 Sioux Indians by William J. Duly outside Mankato, MN for the murder of unarmed citizens on 26 Dec 1862. The Nazi Feldkom-mandant simultaneously hanged 50 Greek resistance fighters as a reprisal measure in Athens on 22 Jul 1944.

Last public hanging The last public hanging in the United States occurred at Owensboro, KY in 1936.

Last from yardarm The last naval execution at the yardarm was the hanging of Private John Dalliger, Royal Marines, aboard HMS *Leven* in Victoria Bay near Lu-da, China, on 13 Jul 1860. Dalliger had been found guilty of two attempted murders.

Last guillotinings The last person to be publicly guillotined in France was the murderer Eugene Weidmann, before a large crowd at Versailles, near Paris, France at 4:50 A.M. on 17 Jun 1939. The executioner was Henri Desfourneaux, who was succeeded by his nephew André Obrecht (1897–1983) in 1951, who was in turn succeeded by his niece's husband, Marcel Chevalier, in January 1978. Dr Joseph Ignace Guillotin (1738–1812) died a natural death. He had advocated the use of the machine designed by Dr Antoine Louis in 1789 in the French constituent assembly.

The last use before abolition on 9 Sep 1981 was on 10 Sep 1977 at Baumettes Prison, Marseille, for torturer and murderer Hamida Djandoubi, age 28.

Death row The longest sojourn on death row was the 39 years of Sadamichi Hirasawa (1893–1987) in Sendai Jail, Japan. He was convicted in 1948 of poisoning 12 bank employees with potassium cyanide to effect a theft of $403, and died in prison at the age of 94. Willie Jasper Darden, 54, survived a record six death warrants in 14 years on death row for the murder of a storekeeper in 1973. His final TV interview was interrupted by a power failure caused by a test of the Florida electric chair in which he died on 15 Mar 1988.

On 31 Oct 1987 Liong Wie Tong, 52, and Tan Tian Tjoen, 62, were executed for robbery and murder by firing squad in Jakarta, Indonesia after 25 years on death row.

Lynching The worst year in the twentieth century for lynchings in the United States was 1901, with 130 lynchings, while the first year with no reported cases was 1952.

PRISON SENTENCES

Longest sentences Chamoy Thipyaso, a Thai woman known as the queen of underground investing, and seven of her associates were each jailed for 141,078 years by the Bangkok Criminal Court, Thailand on 27 Jul 1989 for swindling the public through a multi-million dollar deposit-taking business.

For failing to deliver 42,768 letters, a sentence of 384,912, years or 9 years per letter, was demanded at the prosecution of mailman Gabriel Mar Grandos, 22, at Palma de Mallorca, Spain on 11 Mar 1972.

The longest sentence imposed on a mass murderer was 21 consecutive life sentences and 12 consecutive death sentences in the case of John Wayne Gacy Jr., who killed 33 boys and young men between 1972 and 1978 in Illinois. He was sentenced by a jury in Chicago, IL on 13 Mar 1980.

Longest time served Paul Geidel (1894–1987) was convicted of second-degree murder on 5 Sep 1911 when he was a 17-year-old porter in a hotel in New York. He was released from the Fishkill Correctional Facility, Beacon, NY at the age of 85 on 7 May 1980, having served 68 years, 8 months and 2 days—the longest recorded term in US history. He first refused parole in 1974.

Oldest Bill Wallace (1881–1989) was the oldest prisoner on record, spending the last 63 years of his life in Aradale Psychiatric Hospital, at Ararat, Victoria, Australia. He had shot and killed a man at a restaurant in Melbourne, Victoria in December 1925, and having been found unfit to plead, was transferred to the responsibility of the Mental Health Department in February 1926. He remained at Aradale until his death on 17 Jul 1989, shortly before his 108th birthday.

Most arrests A record for arrests was set by Tommy Johns (1922–88) in Brisbane, Queensland, Australia on 9 Sep 1982 when he faced his 2,000th conviction for drunkenness since 1957. His total at the time of his last drink on 30 Apr 1988 was "nearly 3,000."

Greatest mass arrest The greatest mass arrest reported in a democratic country was of 15,617 demonstrators on 11 Jul 1988, rounded up by South Korean police to ensure security in advance of the 1988 Olympic Games in Seoul.

FINES

Heaviest The largest fine ever was one of $650 million, which was imposed on the US securities firm of Drexel Burnham Lambert in December 1988 for insider trading. This figure represented $300 million in direct fines, with the balance to be put into an account to satisfy claims of parties who could prove they were defrauded by Drexel's actions.

The record for an individual is $200 million, which Michael Milken (see also The Business World, Highest salary) agreed to pay on 24 Apr 1990. In addition, he agreed to settle civil charges filed by the Securities and Exchange Commission and is now serving a 10-year prison sentence. The payments were in settlement of a criminal racketeering and securities fraud suit brought by the US government.

PRISONS

Most secure prison After it became a maximum security federal prison in 1934, no convict was known to have lived to tell of a successful escape from the prison on Alcatraz Island in San Francisco Bay, CA. A total of 23 men attempted it, but 12 were recaptured, five were shot dead, one drowned and five were presumed drowned. On 16 Dec 1962, just before the prison was closed on 21 Mar 1963, one man reached the mainland alive, only to be recaptured on the spot. John Chase held the record for the longest time spent in Alcatraz, 26 years.

Most expensive prison Spandau Prison, Berlin, originally built in 1887 for 600 prisoners, was used solely for the Nazi war criminal Rudolf Hess (26 Apr 1894–17 Aug 1987) for the last twenty years of his life. The cost of maintenance of the staff of 105 was estimated in 1976 to be $415,000 per year. On 19 Aug 1987 it was announced that Hess had strangled himself with a piece of electric cord and that he had left a note in old German script. He had remained in lone confinement at Spandau for a total of forty years. Two months after his death, the prison was demolished.

Longest escape The longest recorded escape by a recaptured prisoner was that of Leonard T. Fristoe, 77, who escaped from Nevada State Prison on 15 Dec 1923 and was turned in by his son on 15 Nov 1969 at Compton, CA. He had had 46 years of freedom under the name of Claude R. Willis. He had killed two sheriff's deputies in 1920.

Greatest jail break In February 1979 a retired US Army colonel, Arthur Bull Simons, led a band of 14 to break into Gasre Prison, Tehran, Iran to rescue two fellow Americans. Some 11,000 other prisoners took advantage of this and the Islamic revolution in what became history's largest-ever jail break.

In July 1971, Raoul Sendic and 105 other Tupamaro guerrillas escaped from a Uruguayan prison through a tunnel 298 ft long.

Honors, Decorations and Awards

Oldest order The earliest honor known was the "Gold of Honor" for extraordinary valor awarded in the 18th Dynasty c. 1440–1400 B.C. A statuette was found at Qan-el-Kebri, Egypt. The oldest true order was the Order of St John of Jerusalem (the direct descendant of which is the Sovereign Military Order of Malta), legitimized in 1113.

Most titles The most titled person in the world is the 18th Duchess of Alba (Alba de Tormes), Doña Maria del Rosario Cayetana Fitz-James Stuart y Silva. She is 8 times a duchess, 15 times a marchioness, 21 times a countess and 19 times a Spanish grandee.

Top jet ace The greatest number of kills in jet-to-jet battles is 16, a record shared by Lt-Col. Heinz Bär (Germany) in 1945 and Capt. Joseph Christopher McConnell, Jr., USAF, in the Korean war (1950–53). Capt. McConnell was killed on 25 Aug 1954. It is possible that an Israeli ace may have surpassed this total in the period 1967–70, but the identity of pilots is subject to strict security.

Top woman ace The record score for any woman fighter pilot is 12, by Jnr-Lt Lydia Litvak (USSR; b. 1921) on the Eastern Front between 1941 and 1943. She was killed in action on 1 Aug 1943.

Youngest awardee The youngest age at which an official gallantry award has ever been won is eight years in the case of Anthony Farrer, who was given the Albert Medal on 23 Sep 1916 for fighting

NOBEL PRIZES

Earliest 1901 for Physics, Chemistry, Physiology or Medicine, Literature and Peace.

Most Prizes The United States has won outright or shared 206 prizes, including most for Physiology or Medicine (69); Physics (55); Chemistry (36), Peace (18); Economics (18). France has most for Literature (12).

Oldest Laureate Professor Francis Peyton Rous (USA; 1879–1970) in 1966 shared in Physiology or Medicine prize at the age of 87.

Youngest Laureates *At time of award:* Professor Sir Lawrence Bragg (Great Britain; 1890–1971) 1915 Physics prize at 25. *At time of work:* Bragg, and Theodore W. Richards (USA; 1868–1928) 1914 Chemistry prize at 23. *Literature:* Rudyard Kipling (Great Britain; 1865–1936) 1907 prize at 41. *Peace:* Mrs Mairead Corrigan-Maguire (Republic of Ireland; b. 27 Jan 1944) 1976 prize (shared) at 32.

Most 3 Awards: International Committee of the Red Cross, Geneva (founded 1863) Peace 1917, 1944 and 1963 (shared); 2 Awards: Dr Linus Carl Pauling (USA; b. 28 Feb 1901) Chemistry 1954 and Peace 1962; Mme Marja Sklodowska Curie (Polish-French; 1867–1934) Physics 1903 (shared) and Chemistry 1911; Professor John Bardeen (USA; 1908–91) Physics 1956 (shared) and 1972 (shared); Professor Frederick Sanger (b. 13 Aug 1918) Chemistry 1958 and 1980 (shared); Office of the United Nations' High Commissioner for Refugees, Geneva (founded 1951) Peace 1954 and 1981.

Highest Prize Sw Kr 6,000,000 (for 1991), equivalent to $969,000.

Lowest Prize Sw Kr 115,000 (1923).

off a cougar at Cowichan Lake, Vancouver Island, Canada to save Doreen Ashburnham. She was also awarded the Albert Medal, which, in 1971, was exchanged for the George Cross.

Highest military award

United States The highest US military decoration is the Congressional Medal of Honor. Five Marines received both the Army and Navy Medals of Honor for the same deeds in 1918, and 14 officers and men received the medal on two occasions between 1864 and 1915 for two distinct acts. The Defense Department refuses to recognize any military hero as having the most awards, but various heroes have been nominated by unofficial groups. Since medals and decorations cannot be compared as to value, the title of most decorated can only be a matter of subjective evaluation. General Douglas MacArthur (1880–1964), because of his high rank and his years of military service spanning three wars, would seem to hold the best claim to "Most Decorated American Soldier." In addition to the Congressional Medal of Honor, he also received 58 separate awards and decorations with 16 Oak Leaf Clusters, plus 18 campaign stars.

Germany The Knight's Cross of the Iron Cross with swords, diamonds and golden oak-leaves was uniquely awarded to Col. Hans Ulrich Rudel

(1916–82) for 2,530 operational flying missions on the Eastern Front in the period 1941–45. He destroyed 519 Soviet armored vehicles.

USSR The USSR's highest award for valor is the Gold Star of a Hero of the Soviet Union, of which 12,709 have been awarded, 11,040 of them during World War II. The only wartime triple awards were to Marshal Georgi Konstantinovich Zhukov (1896–1974; subsequently awarded a fourth Gold Star), and to the leading air aces Guards Colonel (later Marshal of Aviation) Aleksandr Ivanovich Pokryshkin (1913–85) and Aviation Maj Gen Ivan Nikitovich Kozhedub (b. 8 Jun 1920) (Order of the Red Banner, seven times) (Zhukov also uniquely had the Order of Victory (twice), the Order of Lenin (six times) and the Order of the Red Banner (three times). The highest award of civil honor is the Gold Star of Socialist Labor, 20,424 of which have been awarded since it was established in 1938. There have been 15 awards of a third Gold Star of Socialist Labor. Leonid Ilyich Brezhnev (1906–82) was four times Hero of the Soviet Union and Hero of Socialist Labor, Order of Victory (withdrawn in 1990), Order of Lenin (eight times) and Order of the Red Banner (twice).

Anti-submarine successes The highest number of U-boat kills attributed to one ship in World War II was 15, to HMS *Starling* (Capt Frederic John Walker , RN). Captain Walker was in command at the sinking of a total of 25 U-boats between 1941 and the time of his death on 9 Jul 1944. The US Destroyer Escort *England* sank six Japanese submarines in the Pacific between 18 and 30 May 1944.

Most successful submarine captains The most successful of all World War II submarine commanders was Lieutenant Otto Kretschmer, captain of the U.23 and U.99, who up to March 1941 sank one destroyer and 44 Allied merchantmen totaling 266,629 gross registered tons.

In World War I Lieutenant (later Vice Admiral) Lothar von Arnauld de la Périère, in the U.35 and U.139, sank 195 Allied ships totaling 458,856 gross registered tons. The most successful boats were the U.35, which in World War I sank 54 ships of 90,350 gross registered tons in a single voyage and 224 ships of 539,711 gross registered tons all told, and the U.48, which sank 51 ships of 310,007 gross registered tons in World War II. The largest target ever sunk by a submarine was the Japanese aircraft carrier *Shinano* (66,131 tons) by USS *Archerfish* (Cdr Joseph F. Enright, USN) on 29 Nov 1944.

Most valuable annual prize The value of each of the 1991 Nobel Prizes (see left, Nobel Prizes) was Sw Kr 6 million, which at the time of printing was equivalent to approximately $969,000. The ceremonial presentations for the annual prizes in physics, chemistry, physiology or medicine, litera-

MILITARY AND DEFENSE

Shortest war

The shortest war on record was that between Great Britain and Zanzibar (now part of Tanzania), which lasted from 9:02 to 9:40 A.M. on 27 Aug 1896. The British battle fleet under Rear-Admiral Harry Rawson (1843–1910) delivered an ultimatum to the self-appointed Sultan Sa'īd Khalid to evacuate his palace and surrender. This was not forthcoming until after 38 minutes of bombardment. Admiral Rawson received the Brilliant Star of Zanzibar (first class) from Hamud ibn Muhammad, the new sultan. It was proposed at one time that elements of the local populace should be compelled to defray the cost of the broadsides fired.

Youngest conscripts

President Francisco Macias Nguema of Equatorial Guinea (deposed in August 1979) in March 1976 decreed compulsory military service for all boys between the ages of 7 and 14. The edict stated that any parent refusing to hand over his or her son "will be imprisoned or shot."

ture, and economics take place in Stockholm, Sweden, and the presentations for peace take place in Oslo, Norway.

Most statues The world record for raising statues to oneself was set by Generalissimo Dr Rafael Leónidas Trujillo y Molina (1891–1961), former president of the Dominican Republic. In March 1960 a count showed that there were "over 2,000." The country's highest mountain was named Pico Trujillo (later Pico Duarte). One province was called Trujillo and another Trujillo Valdez. The capital was named Ciudad Trujillo (Trujillo City) in 1936, but reverted to its old name of Santo Domingo de Guzmán on 23 Nov 1961. Trujillo was assassinated in an automobile ambush on 30 May 1961, and 30 May is now celebrated as a public holiday.

The man to whom the most statues have been raised is Buddha. The 20th-century champion is Vladimir Ilyich Ulyanov, alias Lenin (1870–1924), busts of whom have been mass-produced. This also has been the case with Mao Zedong (1893–1976); and with Ho Chi Minh (1890–1969).

Military and Defense

WAR

Earliest conflict The oldest known offensive weapon is a broken wooden spear found in April 1911 at Clacton-on-Sea, Great Britain by S. Hazzledine Warren. It is much beyond the limit of radiocarbon dating but is estimated to have been fashioned before 200,000 B.C.

Longest The longest war was the Hundred Years War between England and France, which lasted from 1338 to 1453 (115 years), although it could be said that the nine Crusades, from the First (1096–1104) to the Ninth (1270–91), extending over 195 years, comprised a single holy war.

Bloodiest By far the most costly war in terms of human life was World War II (1939–45), in which the total number of fatalities, including battle deaths and civilians of all countries, is estimated to have been 54.8 million, assuming 25 million USSR fatalities and 7.8 million Chinese civilians killed. The country that suffered most was Poland, with 6,028,000 or 17.2 percent of its population of 35.1 million killed.

The total combatant death toll from World War I was 9.7 million, compared with the 15.6 million from World War II. In the Paraguayan war of 1864–70 against Brazil, Argentina and Uruguay, Paraguay's population was reduced from 1.4 million to 220,000 survivors, of whom only 30,000 were adult males.

Dr William Brydon (1811–73) and two natives were the sole survivors of the seven-day retreat of 13,000 soldiers and camp-followers from Kabul, Afghanistan. Dr Brydon's horse died 2 days after

his arrival at Jellalabad, some 70 miles to the east on the route to the Khyber Pass, on 13 Jan 1842.

Bloodiest civil The bloodiest civil war in history was the *Taiping* ("Great Peace") rebellion, which was a revolt against the Chinese Ch'ing Dynasty between 1851 and 1864. The rebellion was led by the deranged Hung Hsiu-ch'üan (later executed), who imagined himself to be a younger brother of Jesus Christ. His force was named *Taiping Tienguo* ("Heavenly Kingdom of Great Peace"). According to the best estimates the loss of life was some 20 million, including more than 100,000 killed by government forces in the sack of Nanjing on 19–21 Jul 1864.

Most costly The material cost of World War II far transcended that of all the rest of history's wars put together and has been estimated at $1.5 trillion. The total cost to the Soviet Union was estimated in May 1959 at 2.5 trillion rubles, while a figure of $530 billion has been estimated for the United States.

Bloodiest battle *Modern* The battle with the greatest recorded number of *military* casualties was the first Battle of the Somme, France, from 1 July–19 Nov 1916, with 1,043,896; of these 623,907 were Allied and the rest German. The published German figure of *c.* 670,000 is no longer accepted. Gunfire was heard in London, Great Britain.

The greatest death toll in a single battle (military and civilian) has been estimated at *c.* 2.1 million in the Battle of Stalingrad, USSR ending with the German surrender on 31 Jan 1943 by Field Marshal Friedrich von Paulus (1890–1957). The Soviet garrison commander was Gen Vasiliy Chuikov. Only 1,515 civilians out of a prewar population of more than 500,000 were found alive after the battle.

The final drive on Berlin, Germany by the Soviet Army and the battle for the city which followed, from 16 April–2 May 1945, involved 3.5 million men, 52,000 guns and mortars, 7,750 tanks and 11,000 aircraft on both sides.

Ancient Modern historians give no credence, on logistic grounds, to the casualty figures attached to ancient battles, such as the 250,000 reputedly killed at Plataea (Greeks *v.* Persians) in 479 B.C. or the 200,000 allegedly killed in a single day at Châlons-sur-Marne, France (Huns *v* Romans) in A.D. 451.

United States The American Civil War (1861–65) is the bloodiest war fought on American soil. The bloodiest battles between the Northern (Union) and the Southern (Confederate) forces were at Shiloh Church, near Pittsburg Landing in Hardin Co., TN on 6–7 Apr 1862 when each side reported casualties of over 10,000; at Fredericksburg, VA on 13 Dec 1862 when Union losses were over 12,000, more than double those of the Confederacy; and at Gettysburg, PA on 1–3 Jul 1863 when the Union reported losses of 23,000 and the Confederacy

25,000 (a disputed figure). The Civil War officially ended when Confederate General Robert E. Lee surrendered to Union General Ulysses S. Grant at Appomattox Courthouse, VA on 9 Apr 1865.

Greatest naval battle The greatest number of ships and aircraft ever involved in a sea–air action was 231 ships and 1,996 aircraft in the Battle of Leyte Gulf, in the Philippines. It raged from 22–27 Oct 1944, with 166 Allied and 65 Japanese warships engaged, of which 26 Japanese and six US ships were sunk. In addition, 1,280 US and 716 Japanese aircraft were engaged. The greatest purely naval battle of modern times was the Battle of Jutland on 31 May 1916, in which 151 British Royal Navy warships were involved against 101 German warships. The Royal Navy lost 14 ships and 6,097 men and the German fleet 11 ships and 2,545 men.

The greatest of ancient naval battles was the Battle of Salamis, Greece in Sep 480 B.C. There were an estimated 800 vessels in the defeated Persian fleet and 380 in the victorious fleet of the Athenians and their allies, with a possible involvement of 200,000 men. The death toll at the Battle of Lepanto on 7 Oct 1571 has been estimated at 33,000.

Greatest invasion *Seaborne* The greatest invasion in military history was the Allied land, air and sea operation against the Normandy coast of France on D-day, 6 Jun 1944. Thirty-eight convoys of 745 ships moved in on the first three days, supported by 4,066 landing craft, carrying 185,000 men, 20,000 vehicles and 347 minesweepers. The air assault comprised 18,000 paratroopers from 1,087 aircraft. The 42 available divisions had air support from 13,175 aircraft. Within a month 1.1 million troops, 200,000 vehicles and 840,000 tons of stores were landed. The Allied invasion of Sicily from 10–12 Jul 1943 involved the landing of 181,000 men in three days.

Airborne The largest airborne invasion was the Anglo-American assault of three divisions (34,000 men), with 2,800 aircraft and 1,600 gliders, near Arnhem, in the Netherlands, on 17 Sep 1944.

Greatest evacuation The greatest evacuation in military history was that carried out by 1,200 Allied naval and civilian craft from the beachhead at Dunkerque (Dunkirk), France between 27 May and 4 Jun 1940. A total of 338,226 British and French troops were evacuated.

Worst sieges The worst siege in history was the 880-day siege of Leningrad, USSR by the German Army from 30 Aug 1941 until 27 Jan 1944. The best estimate is that between 1.3 and 1.5 million defenders and citizens died. This included 641,000 people who died of hunger in the city and 17,000 civilians killed by shelling. More than 150,000 shells and 100,000 bombs were dropped on the city.

The longest recorded siege was that of Azotus (now Ashdod), Israel, which according to Herodotus was besieged by

Psamtik I of Egypt for 29 years, during the period 664–610 B.C.

Chemical warfare The greatest number of people killed through chemical warfare were the estimated 4,000 Kurds who died at Halabja, Iraq in March 1988 when President Saddam Hussein used chemical weapons against Iraq's Kurdish minority in revenge for the support it had given to Iran in the Iran–Iraq war.

DEFENSE SPENDING

In 1989 it was estimated that the world's spending on armaments was running at an annual rate of some $1,100 billion, or 5.4 percent of the world's gross national product. In 1987 there were 28,123,000 full-time armed forces regulars or conscripts plus 40,289,400 reservists totaling 68,412,400. The budgeted expenditure on defense by the US government for the fiscal year 1990 was $291.4 billion. The defense expenditure of the USSR is given as 70.97 billion rubles in 1990, or $117.48 billion, but Western intelligence agencies still maintain that by NATO definition standards, spending is about twice as large as claimed.

ARMED FORCES

Largest Numerically the largest regular armed force in the world is that of the USSR, with 3,988,000 members (1990). China's People's Liberation Army's strength in 1990 was estimated to be 3.0 million (comprising land, sea and air forces), with reductions continuing. Her reserves number around 1.2 million and her paramilitary forces of armed and unarmed militias are estimated by the International Institute for Strategic Studies, London, Great Britain at "some 12 million." The military forces of the United States for 1990 totaled 2,117,900.

Navies *Largest* The largest navy in the world in terms of personnel is the United States Navy, with a total of 590,500 plus 195,300 Marines in mid-1990. The active strength in 1990 included six nuclear-powered aircraft carriers, with nine conventionally powered aircraft carriers, four battleships, 34 ballistic missile submarines, 90 nuclear attack submarines and one diesel attack submarine, 43 cruisers, 59 destroyers, 100 frigates and 65 amphibious warfare ships.

The navy of the USSR has a larger submarine fleet, comprising 323 vessels (including 63 nuclear attack). It also has five aircraft carriers, 43 cruisers, 31 destroyers, 148 frigates and 77 amphibious warfare ships.

Armies *Oldest* The oldest army in the world is the 80–90 strong Pontifical Swiss Guard in Vatican City, with a regular foundation dating back to 21 Jan 1506. Its origins, however, predate 1400.

Largest Numerically, the world's largest army is that of the People's Republic of China, with a total strength of some 2.3 million in mid-1990. The total size of the USSR's army in mid-1990 was estimated by the International Institute for Strategic Studies, London, Great Britain at 1.5 million (including 27,000–30,000 Spetsnaz), believed to be organized into 197 divisions.

Oldest soldier The oldest "old soldier" of all time was probably John B. Salling of the Army of the Confederate States of America and the last accepted survivor of the US Civil War (1861–65). He died in Kingsport, TN on 16 Mar 1959, aged 113 years 1 day.

Youngest soldier Marshall Duke of Caxias (25 Aug 1803–7 May 1880), Brazilian military hero and statesman, entered his infantry regiment at the age of five in 1808.

Tallest soldier The tallest soldier of all time was Väinö Myllyrinne (1909–63), who was conscripted into the Finnish Army when he was 7 ft 3 in and later grew to 8 ft 3 in. (See Giants.)

Greatest mutiny In World War I, 56 French divisions, comprising some 650,000 men and their officers, refused orders on the Western front sector of General Robert Nivelle in April 1917 after the failure of his offensive.

Longest march The longest march in military history was the famous Long March by the Chinese Communists in 1934–35. In 368 days, of which 268 were days of movement, from October to October, their force of some 100,000 covered 6,000 miles from Juichin, in Jiangxi, to Yanan, in Sheanxi. They crossed 18 mountain ranges and 24 rivers, and eventually reached Yanan with only about 8,000 survivors, following continual rearguard actions against nationalist Kuomintang (KMT) forces.

Air forces *Oldest* The earliest autonomous air force is the Royal Air Force, which can be traced back to 1878, when the War Office commissioned the building of a military balloon. The Royal Engineers Balloon Section and Depot was formed in 1890 and the Air Battalion of the Royal Engineers followed on 1 Apr 1911. On 13 May 1912 the Royal Flying Corps (RFC) was formed, with both Military and Naval Wings, the latter being renamed the Royal Naval Air Service (RNAS). The Royal Air Force was formed on 1 Apr 1918 from the RFC and the RNAS, and took its place alongside the Royal Navy and the Army as a separate service with its own Ministry. The Prussian Army used a balloon near Strasbourg, France as early as 24 Sep 1870.

Largest The largest air force of all time was the United States Army Air Corps (now the US Air Force), which had 79,908 aircraft in July 1944 and 2,411,294 personnel in March 1944. The US Air Force, including strategic missile forces, had 571,000 personnel and 7,642 aircraft in early 1990. The USSR Air Force 420,000 personnel in mid-1990. It had 10,723 aircraft. In addition, the USSR's Offensive Strategic Rocket Forces had about 260,000 operational personnel in mid-1990.

BOMBS

Heaviest The heaviest conventional bomb ever used operationally was the Royal Air Force's *Grand Slam*, weighing 22,000 lb and measuring 25 ft 5 in long, dropped on Bielefeld railroad viaduct, Germany on 14 Mar 1945.

In 1949 the United States Air Force tested a bomb weighing 42,000 lb at Muroc Dry Lake, CA. The heaviest-known nuclear bomb was the MK 17 carried by US B-36 bombers in the mid-1950s. It weighed 42,000 lb and was 24 ft 6 in long.

Atomic The first atom bomb dropped on Hiroshima, Japan by the United States at 8:16 A.M. on 6 Aug 1945 had an explosive power equivalent to that of 12.5 kilotons of trinitrotoluene ($C_7H_5O_6N_3$), called TNT. Code-named *Little Boy*, it was 10 ft long and weighed 9,000 lb. It burst c. 1,900 ft above the city center.

The most powerful thermonuclear device so far tested is one with a power equivalent to that of 57 megatons of TNT, detonated by the USSR in the Novaya Zemlya area at 8:33 A.M. GMT on 30 Oct 1961. The shock-wave circled the world three times, taking 36 hr 27 min for the first circuit. Some estimates put the power of this device at between 62 and 90 megatons. The largest US H-bomb tested was the 18–22 megaton *Bravo* at Bikini Atoll, Marshall Islands on 1 Mar 1954.

On 9 Aug 1961, Nikita Khrushchev, then the Chairman of the Council of Ministers of the USSR, declared that the Soviet Union was capable of constructing a 100-megaton bomb, and announced the possession of one during a visit to what was then East Berlin, East Germany on 16 Jan 1963. Such a device could make a crater in rock 355 ft deep and 1.8 miles wide, with a fireball 8.6 miles in diameter.

Largest nuclear weapons The most

Gun running
The record for the Royal Tournament Naval Field Gun Competition (instituted 1907, with present rules since 1913) is 2 min 40.6 sec, by the Portsmouth Command Field Gun crew at Earl's Court, London, Great Britain on 19 Jul 1984. The barrel alone weighs 800 lb. The wall is 5 ft high and the chasm 28 ft across.

Field gun pull
Three teams of eight members from 55 Ordnance Company (Volunteers) Royal Army Ordnance Corps pulled a 25-pounder field gun over a distance of 85.7 miles in 24 hr in Hounslow, Great Britain on 15–16 Apr 1988.

■ Largest mortar
The largest mortars ever constructed were the Little David of World War II, made in the United States, and Mallet's mortar, built in London, Great Britain in 1857. Each had a caliber of 36 in, but neither was ever used in action. Little David is now located at Aberdeen Proving Ground, MD, and Mallet's mortar is at the Woolwich Arsenal, London.

powerful ICBM (intercontinental ballistic missile) is the USSR's SS-18 (Model 5), believed to be armed with ten 750-kiloton MIRVs (multiple independently targetable reentry vehicles). Earlier models had a single 20-megaton warhead. The US Titan II carrying a W-53 warhead was rated at 5–9 megatons but has now been withdrawn, leaving the 1–2 megaton W-56 as the most powerful US weapon.

Largest "conventional" explosion
The largest use of conventional explosives was for the demolition of the fortifications and U-boat pens at Helgoland, Germany on 18 Apr 1947. A net charge of 7,122 tons gross was detonated by Commissioned Gunner E.C. Jellis of the naval team headed by Lt F.T. Woosnam RN aboard HMS *Lasso* lying 9 miles out to sea.

TANKS

Earliest
The first tank was *No. 1 Lincoln*, modified to become *Little Willie*, built by William Foster & Co. Ltd of Lincoln, Great Britain. It first ran on 6 Sep 1915. Tanks were first taken into action by the Heavy Section, Machine Gun Corps, which later became the Royal Tank Corps, at the Battle of Flers-Courcelette in France on 15 Sep 1916. The Mark I Male tank, armed with a pair of 6-pounder guns and four machine guns, weighed 31.3 ton and was driven by a motor developing 105 hp, which gave it a maximum road speed of 3–4 mph.

Heaviest and fastest
The heaviest tank ever constructed was the German Panzer Kampfwagen Maus II, which weighed 211.6 tons. By 1945 it had reached only the experimental stage and was not developed further.

The heaviest operational tank used by any army was the 83-ton 13-man French Char de Rupture 2C bis of 1922. It carried a 155-mm howitzer and had two 250 hp engines giving a maximum speed of 8 mph. The world's most heavily armed tank since 1972 has been the Soviet T-72, with a 4⅞ in high velocity gun. The world's fastest tank is the British Scorpion AFV, which can reach a speed of 50 mph with a 75 percent payload.

GUNS

Earliest
Although it cannot be accepted as proven, it is believed that the earliest guns were constructed in both China and North Africa in c. 1250. The earliest antiaircraft gun was an artillery piece on a high-angle mounting used in the Franco-Prussian War of 1870 by the Prussians against French balloons.

Largest
The largest gun ever constructed was used by the Germans in the siege of Sevastopol, USSR in Jul 1942. It was of a caliber of 31½ in with a barrel 94 ft 8½ in long. Internally it was named Schwerer Gustav, and was one of three guns which were given the general name of Dora, although the other two were not finished and so were not used in action. It was built by Krupp, and its remains were discovered near Metzenhof, Bavaria in August 1945. The whole assembly of the gun was 141 ft long and weighed 1,481.5 ton, with a crew of 1,500. The range for an 8.9-ton projectile was 29 miles.

Greatest range
The greatest range ever attained by a gun was achieved by the HARP (High Altitude Research Project) gun, consisting of two 16½ in caliber barrels in tandem 119.4 ft long and weighing 165 tons, at Yuma, AZ. On 19 Nov 1966 an 185-lb projectile was fired to an altitude of 111.8 miles or 590,550 ft. The static V3 underground firing tubes built in 50° shafts near Mimoyècques, near Calais, France by Germany during World War II, to bombard London, Great Britain were never operative. The famous long-range gun that shelled Paris, France in World War I was the *Kaiser Wilhelm Geschütz*, with a caliber of 8¼ in, a designed range of 79½ miles and an achieved range of 76 miles from the Forest of Crépy in March 1918. The *Big Berthas* were mortars of 16.53 in caliber and with a range of less than 9 miles.

Mortars
The largest mortars ever constructed were Mallet's mortar (Woolwich Arsenal, London, Great Britain, 1857); and the *Little David* of World War II, made in the United States. Each had a caliber of 36 in, but neither was ever used in action.

The heaviest mortar ever employed was the tracked German 23.6 in siege piece *Karl*; there were seven such mortars built. Only six of these were actually used in action, although never all at the same time—at Sevastopol, USSR in 1942; at Warsaw, Poland in 1944; and at Budapest, Hungary, also in 1944.

Largest cannon
The highest-caliber cannon ever constructed is the *Tsar Pushka* (*King of Cannons*), now housed in the Kremlin, Moscow, USSR. It was built in the 16th century with a bore of 36.2 in and a barrel 10 ft 5 in long. It weighs 44.1 tons.

The Turks fired up to seven shots per day from a bombard 26 ft long, with an internal caliber of 42 in, against the walls of Constantinople (now Istanbul) from 12 April–29 May 1453. It was dragged by 60 oxen and 200 men and fired a 1,200-lb stone cannonball.

Military engines
The largest military catapults, or onagers, could throw a missile weighing 60 lb a distance of 500 yd.

Education

Compulsory education was first introduced in 1819 in Prussia.

University Oldest
The Sumerians had scribal schools or *É-Dub-ba* soon after 3500 B.C. The oldest existing educational institution in the world is the University of Karueein, founded in A.D. 859 in Fez, Morocco. The University of Bologna, the oldest in Europe, was founded in 1088.

The oldest college in the United States is Harvard College, founded in 1636 as Newtowne College and renamed in 1638 after its first benefactor, John Harvard. It was incorporated in 1650. The second oldest college in the US is the College of William and Mary, at Williamsburg, VA. It was chartered in 1693, opened in 1694, and acquired university status in 1779. However, its antecedents were in the planned university at Henrico, VA (1619–22) which was postponed because of the Indian massacre of 1622.

Largest
The largest existing university building in the world is the M.V. Lomonosov State University on the Lenin Hills, south of Moscow, USSR. It stands 787 ft 5 in tall, and has 32 stories and 40,000 rooms. It was constructed from 1949–53.

Most graduates in family
Mr and Mrs Harold Erickson of Naples, FL saw all of their 14 children—11 sons and three daughters—obtain university or college degrees between 1962 and 1978.

Youngest undergraduate and graduate
The most extreme recorded case of undergraduate juvenility was that of William Thomson (1824–1907), later Lord Kelvin, who entered Glasgow University at the age of 10 years 4 months in Oct 1834 and matriculated on 14 Nov the same year.

Adragon Eastwood De Mello (b. 5 Oct 1976) of Santa Cruz, CA obtained his BA in Mathematics from the University of California in Santa Cruz on 11 Jun 1988 at the age of 11 years 8 months.

Youngest doctorate
On 13 Apr 1814 the mathematician Carl Witte of Lochau was made a Doctor of Philosophy of the University of Giessen, Germany at the age of 12.

School Most expensive
The annual cost of keeping a pupil at the Gstaad International School, Gstaad, Switzerland (founded 1974) in 1988/89 was SFr200,000 ($37,800). The school is run by Alain Souperbiet, its founder.

The annual cost of keeping a pupil at the most expensive school in the United States for the academic year 1990/91 is $26,250 at the Oxford Academy (founded 1906), in Westbrook, CT.

Youngest college president The youngest president of a major college was Ellen Futter, who was appointed to head Barnard College in May 1981 at the age of 31.

Most schools The greatest documented number of schools attended by a pupil is 265, by Wilma Williams, now Mrs R. J. Horton, from 1933–43 when her parents were in show business in the United States.

Highest endowment The greatest single gift in the history of higher education was $125 million, to Louisiana State University by C.B. Pennington in 1983.

Religions

Oldest Human burial, which has religious connotations, is known from *c.* 60,000 B.C. among *Homo sapiens neanderthalensis* in the Shanidar cave, northern Iraq.

Largest Religious statistics are necessarily only approximate. The test of adherence to a religion varies widely in rigor, while many individuals, particularly in the East, belong to two or more religions. Christianity is the world's most widely practiced religion, with some 1,711,897,000 adherents in 1989, or 33.0 percent of the world's population. In 1989 there were 890,907,000 Roman Catholics, or 17.5 percent of the world's population in the same year. The largest non-Christian religion is Islam (Muslim) with some 880,555,000 followers in 1988.

The total of world Jewry is estimated to be 18.2 million. The highest concentration is in the United States, with 5,944,000. The total in Israel is 3,537,000. The total in Tokyo, Japan is only 750.

Largest clergies The world's largest religious organization is the Roman Catholic Church, with 144 cardinals, 738 archbishops, 3,224 bishops, 401,930 priests and 893,418 nuns in 1989.

PLACES OF WORSHIP

Earliest Many archaeologists are of the opinion that the decorated Upper Paleolithic caves of Europe (*c.* 30,000–10,000 B.C.) were used as places of worship or religious ritual. Claims have been made that the El Juyo cave in northern Spain contains an actual shrine, dated to *c.* 12,000 B.C.

The oldest surviving Christian church in the world is a converted house in Qal'at es Salihiye (formerly Douro-Europos) in eastern Syria, dating from A.D. 232.

Oldest Church The oldest standing Protestant edifice in the United States and the only remaining example of Colonial Gothic Church is the Newport Parish Church, commonly known as St Luke's, in Isle Wright County, VA, four miles south of Smithfield, VA. The church was built *c.* 1632 and was originally called Warris-

■ Largest temple
The largest religious structure ever built is Angkor Wat ("City Temple"), enclosing 402 acres in Cambodia. The whole complex of 72 major monuments, begun c. A.D. 900, extends over 15 × 5 miles. (Photo: Bettmann Archive, NY)

quioke Parish Church. In 1637 it was renamed the Isle of Wight Parish Church and its present name was instituted in 1957.

Synagogue The oldest synagogue in the United States is Touro Synagogue, Newport, RI. Construction was started in 1759 and completed in 1763. The synagogue was dedicated during the Channukah celebration of 1763. Originally called the Jewish Synagogue of Newport, the synagogue was closed in 1820, but reopened in 1883, renamed Touro Synagogue.

Largest temple The largest religious structure ever built is Angkor Wat ("City Temple"), enclosing 402 acres in Cambodia (or Kampuchea), Southeast Asia. It was built to the Hindu god Vishnu by the Khmer King Suryavarman II in the period A.D. 1113–50. Its curtain wall measures 4,199 × 4,199 ft and its population, before it was abandoned in 1432, was 80,000. The whole complex of 72 major monuments, begun c. A.D. 900, extends over 15 × 5 miles.

The largest Buddhist temple in the world is Borobudur, near Jogjakarta, Indonesia, built in the eighth century. It is 103 ft tall and 403 ft square.

The largest Mormon temple is the Salt Lake Temple, UT, dedicated on 6 Apr 1893, with a floor area of 253,015 ft^2 or 5.8 acres.

Largest cathedral The world's largest cathedral is the cathedral church of the Diocese of New York, St John the Divine, with a floor area of 121,000 ft^2 and a volume of 16,822,000 ft^3. The cornerstone was laid on 27 Dec 1892, and work on the Gothic building was stopped in 1941. Work was restarted in earnest in July 1979, but is still not finished. The nave is the longest in the world at 601 ft, with a vaulting 124 ft in height.

The cathedral covering the largest area is that of Santa Mariá de la Sede in Sevilla (Seville), Spain. It was built in Spanish Gothic style between 1402 and 1519, and is 414 ft long, 271 ft wide and 100 ft high to the vault of the nave.

Smallest The smallest church in the world designated as a cathedral is that of the Christ Catholic Church, Highlandville, MO. It was consecrated in July 1983. It measures 14 × 17 ft and has seating for 18 people.

Largest church The largest church in the world is the Basilica of St Peter, built

between 1506 and 1614 in Vatican City, Rome, Italy. Its length, including the walls of the apse and façade, is 717 ft 6 in. The area is 247,572 ft². The inner diameter of the famous dome is 139 ft 8 in and its center is 393 ft 4 in high. The external height is 448 ft 1 in. Taller, although not as tall as the cathedral in Ulm, Germany (see Tallest spire), is the Basilica of Our Lady of Peace (Notre Dame de la Paix) at Yamoussoukro, Ivory Coast, completed in 1989. Including its golden cross, it is 519 ft high.

The elliptical Basilica of St Pius X at Lourdes, France, completed in 1957 at a

cost of $5.6 million, has a capacity of 20,000 under its giant span arches and a length of 656 ft.

Longest The crypt of the underground Civil War Memorial Church in the Guadarrama Mountains, 28 miles from Madrid, Spain, is 853 ft in length. It took 21 years (1937–58) to build, at a reported cost of $392 million, and is surmounted by a cross 492 ft tall.

Smallest church The world's smallest church is the chapel of Santa Isabel de Hungría, in Colomares, a monument to Christopher Columbus at

■ **Largest church**
The largest church in the world is the Basilica of St Peter, built between 1506 and 1614 in Vatican City, Rome, Italy. Its length, including the walls of the apse and façade, is 717 ft 6 in. Its area is 247,572 ft². (Photo: Spectrum)

Singing
Acharya Prem Bhikshuji (d. 18 Apr 1970) started chanting the Akhand Rama-Dhoon at Jamnagar, Gujarat, India on 31 Jul 1964 and devotees were still continuing the chant in May 1990.

Benalmádena, Málaga, Spain. It is of irregular shape and has a total floor area of 21⅛ ft².

United States The smallest church is the United States is Cross Island Chapel, at Oneida, NY, with a floor area of 29.1 ft² (6 ft 9 ½ in × 4 ft 3 ½ in).

Largest synagogue The largest synagogue in the world is the Temple Emanu-El on Fifth Avenue at 65th Street, New York City. The temple, completed in Sep 1929, has a frontage of 150 ft on Fifth Avenue and 253 ft on 65th Street. The sanctuary proper can accommodate 2,500 people, and the adjoining Beth-El Chapel seats 350. When all the facilities are in use, more than 6,000 people can be accommodated.

Largest mosque The largest mosque is Shah Faisal Mosque, near Islamabad, Pakistan. The total area of the complex is 48.87 acres, with the covered area of the prayer hall being 1.19 acreas. It can accommodate 100,000 worshippers in the prayer hall and the courtyard, and a further 200,000 people in the adjacent grounds.

Tallest minaret The tallest minaret in the world is that of the Great Hassan II Mosque, Casablanca, Morocco, measuring 576 ft. The cost of construction of the mosque was $381.5 million. The Qutb Minar, south of New Delhi, India, built in 1194, is 238 ft tall.

Tallest and oldest pagoda The world's tallest pagoda is the Phra Pathom Chedi at Nakhon Pathom, Thailand, which was built for King Mongkut between 1853 and 1870. It rises to 377 ft. The oldest pagoda in China is Sung-Yo Ssu in Henan, built with 15 12-sided stories in A.D. 523. The 326-ft-tall Shwedagon Pagoda, Yangon (formerly Rangoon), Myanmar (formerly Burma) is built on the site of a 27-ft-tall pagoda of 585 B.C.

Sacred object The sacred object with the highest intrinsic value is the 15th-century gold Buddha in Wat Trimitr Temple in Bangkok, Thailand. It is 10 ft tall and weighs an estimated 6.06 tons. At the March 1991 price of $360.93 per fine ounce, its intrinsic worth was $35.92 million. The gold under the plaster exterior was found only in 1954.

Tallest spire The tallest cathedral spire in the world is that of the Protestant Cathedral of Ulm in Germany. The building is early Gothic and was begun in 1377. The tower, in the center of the west facade, was not finally completed until 1890 and is 528 ft high.

The world's tallest church spire is that of the Chicago Temple of the First Methodist Church on Clark Street, Chicago, IL. The building consists of a 22-story skyscraper (erected in 1924) surmounted by a parsonage at 330 ft, a "Sky Chapel" at 400 ft and a steeple cross at 568 ft above street level.

Stained glass *Oldest* Pieces of stained glass dated before A.D. 850, some possibly even to the seventh century, excavated by Prof. Rosemary Cramp, were set into a window of that date in the nearby St Paul's Church, Jarrow, Great Britain. The oldest complete stained glass in the world represents the Prophets in a window of the Cathedral of Augsburg, Germany, dating from the second half of the 11th century.

The oldest figured stained-glass window in the United States is in Christ Church, Pelham Manor, NY and was designed by William Jay Bolton and John Bolton in 1843.

Largest The largest stained-glass window is that of the Resurrection Mausoleum in Justice, IL, measuring 22,381 ft² in 2,448 panels, completed in 1971.

Although not one continuous window, the Basilica of Our Lady of Peace (Notre Dame de la Paix) at Yamoussoukro, Ivory Coast contains a number of stained-glass windows covering a total area of 80,000 ft².

The tallest stained glass is the 135-ft-high back-lit glass mural installed in 1979 in the atrium of the Ramada Hotel, Dubai.

Brasses The world's oldest monumental brass is that commemorating Bishop Yso von Wölpe in the Andreaskirche, Verden, near Hanover, Germany, dating from 1231.

An engraved coffin plate of St Ulrich (died 973), laid in 1187, was found buried in the Church of SS Ulrich and Afra, Augsburg, Germany in 1979.

CHURCH PERSONNEL

There are more than 2,000 "registered" saints, of whom around two-thirds are either Italian or French.

The first native-born American Roman Catholic saint was Mother Elizabeth Ann Bayley Seton (1774–1821), canonized 14 Sep 1975.

Most rapidly canonized The shortest interval that has elapsed between the death of a saint and his or her canonization was in the case of St Peter of Verona, Italy, who died on 6 Apr 1252 and was canonized 337 days later on 9 Mar 1253.

For the other extreme of 857 years, see table of Popes and Cardinals.

Bishop The oldest Roman Catholic bishop in recent years was Bishop Angelo Teutonico, formerly Bishop of Aversa, Italy (b. 28 Aug 1874), who died at the age of 103 years 276 days on 31 May 1978. He had celebrated mass about 24,800 times.

Youngest The youngest bishop of all time was HRH the Duke of York and Albany, the second son of George III, who was elected Bishop of Osnabrück, through his father's influence as Elector of Hanover, at the age of 196 days on 27 Feb 1764. He resigned after 39 years' enjoyment.

United States The first consecrated Roman Catholic Bishop of the United States was John Carroll (1735–1815) of Baltimore, MD. In 1808, Carroll, a Jesuit, became the first Catholic archbishop of the United States, with suffragan sees at Boston, New York City, Philadelphia and Baidstown, KY. Carroll also founded Georgetown University in 1789.

Oldest parish priest Father Alvaro Fernandez (8 Dec 1880–6 Jan 1988) served as a parish priest at Santiago de Abres, Spain from 1919 until he was 107 years old.

The oldest Anglican clergyman, Rev. Clement Williams (b. 30 Oct 1879), died at the age of 106 years 3 months on 3 Feb 1986. He stood on the route at Queen Victoria's funeral and was ordained in 1904.

Longest service Rev. K.M. Jacob (b. 10 Jul 1880) was made a deacon in the Marthoma Syrian Church of Malabar in Kerala, southern India in 1897. He served his church until his death on 28 Mar 1984, 87 years later.

Longest-serving chorister John Love Vokins (1890–1989) was a chorister for 92 years. He joined the choir of Christ Church, Heeley, Great Britain in 1895 and that of St Michael's, Hathersage, Great Britain 35 years later, and was still singing in 1987.

Sunday school Sunday schools were established by Congregationalists in Neath and Tirdwyncyn, Great Britain in 1697. F. Otto Brechel (1890–1990) of Mars, PA completed 88 years (4,576 Sundays) of perfect attendance at Church School at three different churches in Pennsylvania—the first from 1902 to 1931, the second from 1931 to 1954, and the third from 1954 onwards.

United States Bill Tom Adams (b. 30 Aug 1898) of Monroe, LA is currently the record-holder, having not missed Sunday school since Jun 1905, although there have been occasions when ill-health has meant that someone from his class has come to his bedside and taught the lesson.

Largest crowds The greatest recorded number of human beings assembled with a common purpose was an estimated 15 million at the Hindu festival of Kumbh mela, which was held at the confluence of the Yamuna (formerly the Jumna), the Ganges and the invisible "Saraswathi" at Allahabad, Uttar Pradesh, India on 6 Feb 1989. (See also Largest funerals.)

Largest funerals The funeral of the charismatic C.N. Annadurai (died 3 Feb 1969), Madras Chief Minister, was attended by 15 million people, according to a police estimate.

The line at the grave of the Russian singer and guitarist Vladimir Visotsky (died 28 Jul 1980) stretched for 6.2 miles.

■ **Previous page**
Particle accelerator (Photo: ACE After Image)

Elements

All known matter in, on and beyond the Earth is made up of chemical elements. It is estimated that there are 10^{87} electrons in the known universe. The total of naturally occurring elements is 94, comprising, at ordinary temperatures, 2 liquids, 11 gases and 81 solids (including 72 metals). The so-called fourth state of matter is plasma, when negatively charged electrons and positively charged ions are in flux; 99 percent of all visible matter is in this form.

SUBNUCLEAR PARTICLES

As of April 1990, physicists accepted the existence of three gauge bosons, six leptons and 136 hadron multiplets (77 meson multiplets and 59 baryon multiplets), representing the eventual discovery of 256 particles and an equal number of anti-particles.

Heaviest The heaviest particle accepted is the neutral gauge boson, the $Z°$, of mass 91.18 GeV and lifetime 2.64×10^{-25} sec, which was discovered in May 1983 by the UA1 Collaboration, CERN, Geneva, Switzerland. Precise determination of these values indicates that there are only three "families" of quarks and leptons. The theoretical masses of the graviton (the as-yet unobserved gravitational gauge boson), the photon, and the three neutrino leptons should all be zero. Current experimental limits are less than 7.6×10^{-67} g for the graviton, less than 5.3×10^{-60} g for the photon, and less than 10 eV (less than 1.8×10^{-32} g) for the electron neutrino.

The heaviest hadron accepted is the upsilon (11020) meson of mass 11.02 GeV and lifetime 8.3×10^{-24} sec, which consists of a bottom/anti-bottom quark combination and which was discovered in October 1984 by two groups using the Electron Storage Ring facilities at Cornell University, Ithaca, NY.

Lightest The lightest hadron is the neutral pion meson of mass 134.974 MeV

and lifetime 8.4×10^{-17} sec, which was discovered in September 1949 at the University of California Radiation Laboratory, Berkeley, CA. It consists of a "linear combination" of up/anti-up and down/anti-down quarks.

Quarks The lightest quark is the "up" with a short-range or current mass of 6 MeV and a long-range mass of 350 MeV, while the heaviest is the as-yet unobserved "top" quark with a predicted mass of 140 GeV.

Most and least stable The "Grand Unified Theory" of the weak, electromagnetic, and strong forces predicts that the proton will not be stable, but experiments indicate that the lifetime of the most likely decay mode (to a positron and a neutral pion) has a lower limit of 3.1×10^{32} years, which is over 40 times longer than the maximum lifetime predicted by the theory.

The shortest-lived hadrons are the two baryons N(2220) and N(2600), both with lifetimes 1.6×10^{-24} sec (but see $Z°$ lifetime above).

Newest Of the seven new particles accepted in April 1990, the most recently discovered is the neutral charmed meson D_3 (2,460)° of mass 2,459 MeV and lifetime 3.5×10^{-23} sec, discovered in September 1988 by the Tagged Photon Spectrometer Collaboration at Fermilab, Fermi National Accelerator Laboratory, Batavia, IL, and the neutral charmed strange xi baryon Ξ°_{c}, of mass 2,473 MeV and lifetime 1.1×10^{-22} sec, discovered in November 1988 at the CLEO detector of the Electron Storage Ring facilities, Cornell University, Ithaca, NY.

CHEMICAL EXTREMES

Smelliest substance The most evil of the 17,000 smells so far classified must be a matter of opinion, but ethyl mercaptan (C_2H_5SH) and butyl seleno-mercaptan (C_4H_9SeH) are pungent claimants, each with a smell reminiscent of a combination of rotting cabbage, garlic, onions, burned toast and sewer gas.

Most expensive perfume Retail prices tend to be fixed with an eye to public relations rather than dictated soley by the market cost of ingredients and packaging. The Chicago-based firm Jōvan marketed in March 1984 a cologne called Andron, which contains a trace of the attractant pheromone androstenol, costing $2,750 per oz.

Most potent poison The rickettsial disease Q-fever can be instituted by a *single* organism, though it is fatal in only 1 in 1,000 cases. About 10 organisms of *Francisella tularenesis* (formerly *Pasteurella tularenesis*) can institute tularemia, variously called alkali disease, Francis disease or deerfly fever. This is fatal in upwards of 10 cases in 1,000.

Most powerful nerve gas VX, 300 times more toxic than phosgene ($COCl_2$), used in World War I, was developed at the Chemical Defense Experimental Establishment, Porton Down, Great Britain, in 1952. Patents

were applied for in 1962 and published in Feb 1974 showing it to be ethyl S-2-diisopropylaminoethylmethylphosphonothiolate. The lethal dosage is 10 mg-minute/m³ airborne or 0.3 mg orally.

Most absorbent substance The US Department of Agriculture Research Service announced on 18 Aug 1974 that "H-span" or Super Slurper, composed of one-half starch derivative and one-fourth each of acrylamide and acrylic acid, can, when treated with iron, retain water 1,300 times its own weight.

Finest powder The ultimate is solid helium, which was first postulated to be a monatomic powder as early as 1964.

Most lethal man-made chemical TCDD (2, 3, 7, 8-tetrachlorodibenzo-p-dioxin), the most deadly of the 75 known dioxins, is admitted to be 150,000 times more deadly than cyanide, at 3.1 trillion moles/kg.

Most refractory substance The most refractory substance is tantalum carbide ($TaC_{0.88}$), which melts at 7,214°F.

Least dense substance These are the silica aerogels in which tiny spheres of bonded silicon and oxygen atoms are joined into long strands separated by pockets of air. In February 1990 the lightest of these aerogels, with a density of only 5 oz/ft³, was produced at the Lawrence Livermore Laboratory, CA. The main use will be in space to collect micrometeoroids and the debris present in comets' tails.

Highest superconducting temperature In March 1988, bulk superconductivity with a transition to zero resistance at $-234°$ F was obtained at the IBM Almaden Research Center, San Jose, CA for a mixed oxide of thallium, calcium, barium and copper ($Tl_2Ca_2Ba_2Cu_3O_x$).

Strongest acid and alkaline solutions Normal solutions of strong acids such as perchloric acid ($HClO_4$) and strong alkalis such as sodium hydroxide ($HaOH$), or potassium hydroxide ($N[CH_3]_4OH$), tend towards pH values of 0 and 14 respectively. However, this scale is inadequate for describing the "superacids," the strongest of which is estimated to be an 80 percent solution of antimony pentafluoride in hydrofluoric acid (fluoroantimonic acid $HF : SbF_5$). The acidity function, H_0 of this solution has not been measured but even a 50 percent solution has an acidity function of -30, so that this acid mixture is a quintillion (10^{18}) times stronger than concentrated sulfuric acid.

Sweetest substance Talin from arils of katemfe (*Thaumatococcus Daniellii*), discovered in West Africa, is 6,150 times as sweet as a one percent sucrose solution.

Most magnetic substance The most magnetic substance is neodymium iron boride ($Nd_2Fe_{14}B$) with a maximum energy product (the highest energy that a magnet can supply when operating at a

■ **Hardest substance and highest melting point**
A mixture of natural and synthetic diamonds. Diamond is a naturally occurring form of carbon that crystallizes under great pressure. The crystals may be colorless and transparent or yellow, brown or black. Diamond is the hardest known mineral and poor qualities are used in industry for cutting and grinding tools.

(Photo: Science Photo Library)

particular operating point) of up to 280 kJ/m³.

The 109 Elements

There are 94 naturally occurring elements, while to date a further 15 transuranic elements (elements 95 to 109) have been claimed, of which 10 are undisputed. By 1984 6,845,000 chemical compounds had been produced from these elements, of which some 65,000 were in common use.

Commonest Extraterrestrial Hydrogen (H) accounts for 90 percent of all known matter in the universe and 70.68 percent by mass in the solar system.

Earth's lithosphere The commonest is oxygen (O) at 46.40 percent by weight.

Atmosphere The commonest is nitrogen (N) at 78.08 percent by volume (75.52 percent by mass).

Rarest of the 94 natural elements
Earth's lithosphere Only 0.0056 oz of astatine (At) is present in the Earth's crust, of which the isotope astatine 215 (At 215; discovered by B. Karlik and T. Bernert [Austria] in 1943) accounts for only 1.6×10^{-10} oz.

Atmosphere The rarest is radon (Rn) at 6×10^{-20} parts per million by volume. This is only 5.3 lb overall, but concentration of this radioactive gas in certain granitic areas has been blamed for a number of cancer deaths. The total amount of radon in the Earth's crust available to replenish the atmosphere is estimated to be 157 tons.

Density *Solid* The least dense element at room temperature is the metal lithium (Li) at 0.01927 lb/in³, although the density of solid hydrogen at its melting point of $-434.546\,°F$ is only 0.00315 lb/in³. The densest solid at room temperature is osmium (Os) at 0.8161 lb/in³.

Gas At NTP (Normal Temperature and Pressure, 0 °C and one atmosphere) the lightest gas is hydrogen (H) at 0.005612 lb/ft³. The heaviest gas is radon (Rn) at 0.6274 lb/ft³.

Melting/boiling point *Highest* Metallic tungsten (W) melts at 6,188°F and boils at 10,580°F. On the assumption that graphite transforms to carbyne forms above 4,172°F, the nonmetal with the highest melting and boiling points would be carbon (C) at 6,386°F and 6,998°F respectively. However, this is disputed; an alternative suggestion is that graphite remains stable at high temperatures, sublimes directly to vapor at 6,728°F and cannot be obtained in a liquid form unless the temperature exceeds 8,006°F and the pressure 10 MPa.

Lowest Helium (He) cannot be obtained at a solid atmospheric pressure, the minimum pressure being 24.985 atm (2.532 MPa), which occurs at a temperature of $-458.275\,°F$. The boiling point of helium is $-452.070\,°F$. Monatomic hydrogen (H) is expected to be a non-liquefiable superfluid gas. The metal with the lowest melting and boiling points is mercury (Hg) at $-37.892\,°F$ and 673.92°F respectively.

Thermal expansion At room temperature the metal with the highest expansion is cesium (Cs), at 94×10^{-6} per deg C, while the diamond allotrope of carbon (C) has the lowest expansion at 1.0×10^{-6} per deg C.

Hardest substance The carbon (C) allotrope diamond has a Knoop value of 8,400.

Most ductile 1 oz of gold (Au) can be drawn to a length of 43 miles.

Highest tensile strength The element with the highest tensile strength is boron (B) at 5.7 GPa 8.3×10^5 lb/in² (redetermined at the Technical Research Center of Finland).

Purest In April 1978 P.V.E. McClintock of the University of Lancaster, Great Britain, reported success in obtaining the isotope helium 4 (He4) with impurity levels at less than two parts in 10^{15}.

Most expensive For commercially available elements, californium (Cf) was sold in 1970 for $10 per microgram.

Newest The discovery of element 108 or unniloctium (Uno) (provisional IUPAC name) was announced in April 1984 by G. Münzenberg et al. and was based on the observation of only three atoms at the Gesellschaft für Schwerionenforschung (GSI), Darmstadt, Germany. A less-substantiated claim was made in June of the same year by Yu.Ts. Oganessian et al. of the Joint Institute for Nuclear Research, Dubna, USSR. The single atom of unnilennium (Une) produced at GSI on 29 Aug 1982 counts as the highest atomic number (109) and the heaviest atomic mass (266) obtained; a tentative Soviet claim to have detected element 110 or ununnillium (Uun) with a probable mass of 272 has not been substantiated.

Isotopes *Most* The elements with the most isotypes (36 each) are xenon (Xe) (9 stable isotopes identified by F.W. Aston [Great Britain] 1920–22 and 27 radioactive identified 1939–81) and cesium (Cs; 1 stable identified by Aston in 1921 and 35 radioactive identified 1935–83).

Least There are three confirmed isotopes for hydrogen (H) including two stable (identified by Aston in 1920 [protium] and by H.C. Urey, F.G. Brickwedde and G.M. Murphy in 1931 [deuterium]) and one radioactive (tritium) first identified by M.L.E Oliphant, P. Harteck and Lord Rutherford (Great Britain) in 1934 but characterized as a radioactive isotope by L.W. Alvarez and R. Cornog (USA) in 1939.

Most stable The most stable radioactive isotope is the double-beta decaying tellurium 128 (Te128), with a half-life of 1.5×10^{24} years. It was first identified as being naturally occurring by F.W. Aston (Great Britain) in 1924 and confirmed as being the longest-living by E.C.

Alexander Jr., B. Srinivasan and O.K. Manuel (USA) in 1968. The alpha-decay record is 8×10^{15} years for samarium 148 (Sm148) and the beta-decay record is 9×10^{15} years for cadmium 113 (Cd113). Both isotopes were identified as being naturally occurring by Aston in 1933 and 1924 respectively, while proof of their radioactivity was first obtained by T.R. Wilkins and A.J. Dempster (USA) in 1938 for Sm148 and by D.E. Watt and R.N. Glover (Great Britain) in 1961 for Cd113.

Least stable Lithium 5 (Li5), with a lifetime of 4.4×10^{-22} sec, was first characterized by E.W. Titterton and T.A. Brinkley (Australia/Great Britain) in 1950.

Liquid range Based on the differences between melting and boiling points, the element with the shortest liquid range is the inert gas neon (Ne) at only 4.575 degrees (from $-415.469\,°$ F to $-410.894\,°$ F) while that with the longest liquid range is the radioactive transuranium element neptunium (Np) at 6,215 degrees (from 1,179° F to 7,394° F). However, based on the true range of liquids from their melting points to their critical points, the shortest range is for helium (He) at 9.351 degrees (from absolute zero, $-459.67\,°$ F, to $-450.319\,°$ F), and the largest range is for tungsten (W) at 18,360 degrees (from 6,188°F to 24,548°F).

Toxic The most stringent restriction placed on a nonradioactive element is for beryllium (Be), with a threshold limit value in air of only 2 micrograms/m³. For radioactive isotopes, which occur naturally or are produced in nuclear installations and have ecologically significant half-lives (i.e., in excess of six months), the severest restriction in air is placed on thorium 228 (Th228) or radiothorium—first observed by O. Hahn (Germany) in 1905 at 2.4×10^{-16} grams/m³ (equivalent radiation itensity 0.0074 becquerel/m³). The severest restriction in water is placed on radium 228 (Ra228 or mesothorium 1, discovered by Hahn in 1907) at 1.1×10^{-13} grams/liter (equivalent radiation intensity 1.1 becquerel/liter).

Physical Extremes

Smallest optical prism Researchers at the National Institute of Standards and Technology laboratories in Boulder, CO have created a glass prism with sides 0.001 in—barely visible to the naked eye. This should find application in fiber optics research and instrumentation.

Highest temperature Temperatures produced in the center of a thermonuclear fusion bomb are of the order of 540,0320,000–720,032,000° F. Of controllable temperatures, the highest effective laboratory figure reported is 392 million° F achieved in the Tokamak Fusion Test Reactor at the Princeton Plasma Physics Laboratory, Princeton, NJ in June 1986.

Lowest temperature The absolute zero of temperature, 0 K on the Kelvin scale, corresponds to −459.67° F. The lowest temperature ever reached is 2×10^{-9} Kelvin, i.e., two billionths of a degree above absolute zero. This was achieved at the Low Temperature Laboratory, Helsinki University of Technology, Finland in a nuclear demagnetization device by a team led by Prof. Olli V. Lounasmaa, including Dr Pertii Hakonen of Helsinki University and Dr Shi Yin of Michigan State University, and was announced in October 1989.

Smallest thermometer Dr Frederich Sachs, a biophysicist at the State University of New York at Buffalo, has developed an ultra-microthermometer for measuring the temperature of single living cells. The tip is one micron in diameter, about one-fiftieth the diameter of a human hair.

Largest barometer A water barometer 39 ft in height was constructed in 1987 by Bert Bolle, curator of the Barometer Museum, Maartensdijk, Netherlands, where the instrument is situated.

Highest pressures A sustained laboratory pressure of 1.70 megabars (11,000 tons force/in²) was achieved in the giant hydraulic diamond-faced press at the Carnegie Institution's Geophysical Laboratory, Washington, D.C. and reported in June 1978. This laboratory announced solid hydrogen achieved at 57 kilobars pressure on 2 Mar 1979. If created, metallic hydrogen is expected to be silvery-white but soft, with a

density of 0.040 lb/in³. The pressure required for the transition is estimated by H.K. Mao and P.M. Bell to be 1 megabar at 77° F. Using dynamic methods and impact speeds of up to 18,000 mph, momentary pressures of 75 million atmospheres (490,000 tons/in²) were reported from the United States in 1958.

Highest velocity The highest velocity at which any solid visible object has been projected is 93 miles/sec in the case of a plastic disc at the Naval Research Laboratory, Washington, D.C., reported in August 1980.

Finest balance The Sartorius Model 4108 manufactured in Göttingen, Germany can weigh objects of up to 0.018 oz to an accuracy of 3.5×10^{-10} oz, equivalent to little more than one sixtieth of the weight of the ink on this period.

Largest bubble chamber The $7 million installation, completed in Oct 1973 at Weston, IL, is 15 ft in diameter. It contains 7,259 gallons of liquid hydrogen at a temperature of −413° F and has a superconducting magnet of 3 tesla (a unit of magnetic induction).

Fastest centrifuge Ultra-centrifuges were invented by Theodor Svedberg (b. 30 Aug 1884; Sweden) in 1923.

The highest man-made rotary speed ever achieved and the fastest speed of any earthbound object is 4,500 mph by a swirling tapered 6-in carbon fiber rod in a vacuum at Birmingham University, Great Britain reported on 24 Jan 1975.

Finest cut The $13 million large optics diamond turning machine at the Lawrence Livermore National Laboratory, CA was reported in June 1983 to be able to sever a human hair 3,000 times lengthwise.

Longest echo The longest echo in any building is one of 15 sec following the closing of the door of the Chapel of the Mausoleum, Hamilton, Great Britain, built 1840–55.

Most powerful electric current If fired simultaneously, the 4,032 capacitors comprising the Zeus capacitor at the Los Alamos Scientific Laboratory, NM would produce, for a few microseconds, twice as much current as that generated anywhere else on Earth.

Hottest flame The hottest is carbon subnitride (C_4N_2), which at one atm (atmosphere) can produce a flame calculated to reach 9,010° F.

Highest measured frequency The highest *directly* measured frequency is a visible yellow-green light at 520.2068085 terahertz (a terahertz being a million million hertz or cycles per second) for the o-component of the 17–1 P (62) transition line of iodine 127.

The highest measured frequency determined by precision metrology is a green light at 582.491703 terahertz for the b 21 component of the R+ (15) 43–0 transition line of iodine 127. However, with the decision on 20 Oct 1983 by the *Conférence Générale des Poids et Mesures* (CGPM)

to define the meter (m) exactly in terms of the velocity of light (c) such that "the meter is the length of the path traveled by light in vacuum during a time interval of 1/299792458 of a second" then frequency (f) and wavelength (λ) are exactly interchangeable through the relationship $f\lambda = c$.

Lowest friction The lowest coefficient of static and dynamic friction of any solid is 0.04, in the case of polytetrafluoroethylene ($[C_2F_4]n$), called PTFE—equivalent to wet ice on wet ice. It was first manufactured in quantity by E.I. Pont de Nemours & Co. Inc. in 1943, and is marketed in the United States as Teflon.

In the centrifuge at the University of Virginia a 30-lb rotor magnetically supported has been spun at 1,000 rev/sec in a vacuum of 10^{-6} mm of mercury pressure. It loses only one revolution per second per day, thus spinning for years.

Smallest hole A hole of 40 Å was shown visually using a JEM 100C electron microscope and Quantel Electronics devices at the Department of Metallurgy, Oxford University, Great Britain on 28 Oct 1979. To find such a hole is equivalent to finding a needle in a haystack—a haystack with sides of 1.2 miles.

An electron microscope beam on a sample of sodium beta-alumina at the University of Illinois in May 1983 accidentally bored a hole 2×10^{-9} m in diameter.

Most powerful laser beams The first illumination of another celestial body was achieved on 9 May 1962, when a beam of light was successfully reflected from the moon by the use of a laser attached to a 48 in telescope at the Massachusetts Institute of Technology, Cambridge, MA. The spot was estimated to be 4 miles in diameter on the moon. The device was propounded in 1958 by the American Dr Charles Hard Townes (b. 1915). Such a flash for $1/5,000$th of a second can bore a hole through a diamond by vaporization at 18,032° F, produced by 2×10^{23} photons. The "Shiva" laser was reported at the Lawrence Livermore Laboratory, CA to be concentrating 2.6×10^{13} watts into a pinhead-sized target for 9.5×10^{-11} sec in a test on 18 May 1978.

Brightest light The brightest artificial sources are "laser" pulses generated at the Los Alamos National Laboratory, NM, announced in March 1987 by Dr Robert Graham. An ultraviolet flash lasting 1 picosecond (1 trillionth sec) is intensified to an energy of 5×10^{15} watts.

The most powerful searchlight ever developed was one produced during World War II by the General Electric Company Ltd at the Hirst Research Center in London, Great Britain. It had a consumption of 600 kW and gave an arc luminance of 300,000 candles/in² and a maximum beam intensity of 2.7 billion candles from its parabolic mirror (diameter 10 ft).

Heaviest magnet
The heaviest magnet is in the Joint Institute for Nuclear Research at Dubna, near Moscow, USSR, for the 10 GeV synchrophasotron measuring 196 ft in diameter and weighing 42,518 tons.

Smallest microphone
Prof. Ibrahim Kavrak of Bogazici University, Istanbul, Turkey developed a microphone for a new technique of pressure measurement in fluid flow in 1967. It has a frequency response of 10 Hz–10 kHz and measures 0.06 × 0.03 in.

Of continuously burning sources, the most powerful is a 313 kW high-pressure argon arc lamp of 1.2 million candle-power, completed by Vortek Industries Ltd of Vancouver, British Columbia, Canada in March 1984.

Shortest light pulse Charles Z. Shank and colleagues of the AT&T Laboratories in New Jersey achieved a light pulse of 8 femtoseconds (8×10^{-15} sec), announced in April 1985. The pulse comprised only four or five wavelengths of visible light.

Largest electromagnet The world's largest electromagnet is part of the L3 detector, another experiment on LEP (large electron–positron collider). The octagonal-shaped magnet consists of 6,400 tons of low carbon steel yoke and 1,100 tons of aluminum coil. The yoke elements, welded pieces of up to 30 tons each, were manufactured in the Soviet Union. The coil was manufactured in a modular technique in Switzerland and consists of 168 turns welded together to form an eight-sided frame. Thirty thousand amperes of current flow through the aluminum coil to creat a uniform magnetic field of 5 kilogauss. The magnet is higher than a four-story building, with a volume of approximately $39 \times 39 \times 39$ ft. The total weight of the magnet, including the frame, coil and inner support tube, is 7,810 tons. The L3 magnet is composed of more metal than the Eiffel Tower.

Magnetic fields The strongest continuous field strength achieved was a total of 35.3 ± 0.3 teslas at the Francis Bitter National Magnet Laboratory, Massachusetts Institute of Technology in Cambridge, MA, on 26 May 1988, employing a hybrid magnet with holmium pole pieces. This had the effect of enhancing the central magnetic field generated in the heart and brain.

The weakest magnetic field measured is one of 8×10^{-15} tesla in the heavily shielded room at the same laboratory. It is used by Dr David Cohen for research into the very weak magnetic field generated in the heart and brain.

Most powerful microscope The scanning tunneling microscope (STM) invented at the IBM Zürich research laboratory, Switzerland, in 1981 has a magnifying ability of 100 million and is capable of resolving down to one-hundredth the diameter of an atom (3×10^{-10} m). The fourth generation of the STM now being developed is said to be "about the size of a fingertip."

By using field ion microscopy, the tips of probes of scanning tunneling microscopes have been shaped to end in a single atom—the last three layers constituting the world's smallest man-made pyramid, consisting of 7, 3 and 1 atoms. It was announced in January 1990 that D.M. Eigler and E.K. Schweizer of the IBM Almaden Research Center, San Jose, CA had used an STM to move and reposition single atoms of xenon on a nickel surface in order to spell out the initials "IBM." (See also Language.)

Loudest noise The loudest in a laboratory has been 210 dB, or 400,000 acoustic watts, reported by NASA from a 48 ft steel and concrete test bed for the Saturn V rocket static with 60 ft deep foundations, at Marshall Space Flight Center, Huntsville, AL in October 1965. Holes could be bored in solid material by this means, and the audible range was in excess of 100 miles.

Highest note A laser beam striking a sapphire crystal at the Massachusetts Institute of Technology, Cambridge, MA in September 1964 generated a note of 60 gigahertz.

Most powerful particle accelerator The 1.25-mile diameter proton synchrotron at the Fermi National Accelerator Laboratory near Batavia, IL is the highest energy "atomsmasher" in the world. On 14 May 1976 an energy of 500 giga electron volts (5×10^{11}) was achieved for the first time. On 13 Oct 1985 a center of mass energy of 1.6 TeV (1.6×10^{11} electron volts) was achieved by colliding beams of protons and antiprotons. This involves 1,000 superconducting magnets maintained at a temperature of $-452°$ F by means of the world's largest (1,188 gallons per hour) helium liquefying plant, which began operating on 18 Apr 1980.

On 16 Aug 1983 the US Department of Energy set up a study for the $6 billion super superconductivity collider (SSC) 1995 with two 20 TeV proton and anti-proton colliding beams with a diameter of 52 miles at Waxahachie, TX. White House approval was announced on 30 Jan 1987. On 6 Aug 1990 the cost estimated was put at $11.7 billion compared with a cost of $9 billion estimated in November 1988.

Largest scientific instrument The largest scientific instrument so far is the 16.57 mile circumference electron-positron storage ring "LEP" at CERN, which began operations on 13 Aug 1989. The tunnel, 12.46 ft in diameter, runs between 164 and 492 ft under the Earth's surface, and is accessible through 18 vertical shafts. Over 60,000 tons of technical equipment have been installed in the tunnel and its eight underground work zones. It is intended to be a "Z° factory" producing up to 10,000 of these neutral weak gauge bosons every day in order to obtain a deeper understanding of the subatomic nature of matter. The aim is that by 1992 the electron and positron beams should have energies of 96 GeV each.

Quietest place The "dead room," measuring 35×28 ft in the Bell Telephone System laboratory at Murray Hill, NJ, is the most anechoic room in the world, eliminating 99.98 percent of reflected sound.

Sharpest objects and smallest tubes The sharpest objects yet made are glass micropipette tubes used in intracellular work on living cells. Techniques developed and applied by Prof. Kenneth T. Brown and Dale G. Flaming of the Department of Physiology, University of California, San Francisco achieved by

1977 beveled tips with an outer diameter of 0.02 μm and an 0.01 μm inner diameter. The latter is smaller than the smallest known nickel tubing by a factor of 340 and is 6,500 times thinner than a human hair.

Highest vacuum The highest vacuum was obtained at the IBM Thomas J. Watson Research Center, Yorktown Heights, NY in Oct 1976 in a cryogenic system with temperatures down to $-452°$ F.

Lowest viscosity The California Institute of Technology first announced on 1 Dec 1957 that there was no measurable viscosity, i.e., perfect flow, in liquid helium II, which exists at temperatures close to absolute zero ($-459.67°$ F).

Highest voltage The highest-ever potential difference obtained in a labor-

■ **Largest scientific instrument**
At top is an aerial view of CERN laboratory. The ring around it indicates the position of the LEP and SPS tunnels. The picture below is the interior section of the electron-positron storage ring.
(Photo: CERN and Gamma/Norvan)

atory was 32 ± 1.5 million volts by the National Electrostatics Corporation at Oak Ridge, TN on 17 May 1979.

Numbers

In dealing with large numbers, scientists use the notation of 10 raised to various powers to eliminate a profusion of zeros. For example, 19.16 trillion miles would be written 1.916×10^{13} miles. Similarly, a very small number, for example 0.0000154324 of a gram, would be written $1.543\,24 \times 10^{-5}$. Of the prefixes used before numbers the smallest is "yocto," symbol y, of power 10^{-24}, and the largest is "yotta," symbol Y, of power 10^{24}. Both are based on the Greek *octo*, eight (for the eighth power of 10^3).

Highest numbers The highest lexicographically accepted named number in the system of successive powers of ten is the centillion, first recorded in 1852. It is the hundredth power of a million, or 1 followed by 600 zeros.

The number 10^{100} is designated a googol. The term was suggested by the nine-year-old nephew of Dr Edward Kasner (USA). Ten raised to the power of a googol is described as a googolplex. Some conception of the magnitude of such numbers can be gained when it is considered that the number of electrons in some models of the observable universe does not exceed 10^{87}. The highest named number outside the decimal notation is the Buddhist *asankhyeya*, which is equal to 10^{140} and mentioned in Jain works of *c.* 100 B.C.

The highest number ever used in a mathematical proof is a bounding value published in 1977 and known as Graham's number. It concerns bichromatic hypercubes and is inexpressible without the special "arrow" notation, devised by Knuth in 1976, extended to 64 layers.

Prime numbers A prime number is any positive integer (excluding unity 1) having no integral factors other than itself and unity, e.g., 2, 3, 5, 7 or 11. The lowest prime number is thus 2. The highest *known* prime number is $391,581 \times 2^{216,193} - 1$, discovered on 6 Aug 1989 by a team known as the "Amdahl Six." The number contains 65,087 digits and was found on an Amdahl 1200 supercomputer in Santa Clara, CA. The "team" also discovered the largest-known twin primes, $1,706,595 \times 2^{11,235} - 1$ and $1,706\,595 \times 2^{11,235} + 1$. The lowest nonprime or composite number (excluding 1) is 4.

Perfect numbers A number is said to be perfect if it is equal to the sum of its divisors other than itself, e.g., $1 + 2 + 4 + 7 + 14 = 28$. The lowest perfect number is 6 ($= 1 + 2 + 3$). The highest known, and the 31st so far discovered, is $(2^{216,091} - 1) \times 2^{216,090}$. It is a consequence of the largest Mersenne prime (also the second largest prime known) being $2^{216,091} - 1$.

Newest mathematical constant The study of turbulent water, the weather and other chaotic phenomena has revealed the existence of a new universal constant, the Feigenbaum number. Named after its discoverer, Mitchell Feigenbaum (USA), it equals approximately 4.669201609102990.

Most-proved theorem A book published in 1940 contained 370 different proofs of Pythagoras' theorem, including one by President James Garfield.

Longest proof The proof of the classification of all finite simple groups is spread over more than 14,000 pages in nearly 500 papers in mathematical journals, contributed by more than 100 mathematicians over a period of more than 35 years.

Oldest mathematical puzzle The oldest mathematical puzzle dates from 1650 B.C. This is an English version:

As I was going to St Ives, I met a man with seven wives. Every wife had seven sacks, every sack had seven cats. Every cat has seven kits. Kits, cats, sacks and wives, how many were going to St Ives?

Largest claimed accurate number in physics Sir Arthur Eddington announced in 1938 that there are exactly
15,747,724,136,275,002,577,605,653,961,
181,555,468,044,717,914,527,116,
709,366,231,425,076,185,631,031,296
protons in the universe, and the same number of electrons. Unfortunately for Eddington, no one else accepted his over-precise calculation, which is now discredited.

Most prolific mathematician Leonard Euler (Switzerland; 1707–83) was so prolific that his papers were still being published for the first time more than 50 years after his death. His collected works have been printed bit by bit since 1910 and will eventually occupy more than 75 large quarto volumes.

Greatest mathematical prodigy Blaise Pascal (1623–62), the French philosopher and mathematician, discovered the theorem now known as Pascal's theorem at the age of 16.

Largest mathematical prize ever offered Dr Paul Wolfskell left prize money in his will for the first person to solve the last theorem of Pierre Fermat (1601–65). This prize was worth 100,000 deutsch marks in 1908. As a result of inflation, the prize is now just over 10,000 deutsch marks.

Longest computer computation for a yes–no answer The twentieth Fermat number, $2^{2^{20}} + 1$, was tested on a CRAY-2 supercomputer in 1986 to see if it was a prime number. After 10 days of calculation the answer was no.

Most accurate and most inaccurate value of pi In 1989 the greatest number of decimal places to which $pi\ (\pi)$ had been calculated was 1,011,196,691 by David and Gregory Chudnovsky at Columbia University, New York City. The calculation was performed twice on an IBM 3090 mainframe and on a CRAY-2 supercomputer, and the results matched. Places 762–767 comprise six consecutive 9's.

In 1853 William Shanks published his calculation of π to 707 decimal places, all calculated by hand. Ninety-two years later, in 1945, it was discovered that the last 180 digits were in fact all incorrect. In 1897 the General Assembly of Indiana enacted Bill No. 246 stating that *pi* was *de jure* 4.

Earliest measures The earliest known measure of weight is the *beqa* of the Amratian period of Egyptian civilization *c.* 3800 B.C., found at Naqada, Egypt. The weights are cylindrical, with rounded ends, and weigh 6.65–7.45 oz.

The unit of length used by the megalithic tomb-builders in northwestern Europe *c.* 3500 B.C. appears to have been 2.72 ± 0.003 ft. This was deduced by Prof. Alexander Thom (1894–1985) in 1966.

Time measure Because of variations in the length of a day, which is estimated to be increasing irregularly at an average rate of about a millisecond per century due to the moon's tidal drag, the second has been redefined. Instead of being 1/86,400th part of a mean solar day, it has, since 1960, been reckoned as 1/315,569,259,747th part of the solar (or tropical) year at A.D. 1900, January 0.12 hr, Ephemeris time. In 1958 the second of Ephemeris time was computed to be equivalent to $9,192,631,770 \pm 20$ cycles of the radiation corresponding to the transition of cesium 133 atoms when unperturbed by exterior fields. The greatest diurnal change recorded was 10 milliseconds on 8 Aug 1972, due to the most violent solar storm recorded in 370 years of observations.

The accuracy of the cesium beam frequency standard approaches eight parts in 10^{14}, compared to two parts in 10^{13} for the methane-stabilized helium-neon laser and six parts in 10^{13} for the hydrogen maser.

The longest measure of time is the *kalpa* in Hindu chronology. It is equivalent to 4,320 million years. In astronomy a cosmic year is the period of rotation of the sun around the center of the Milky Way galaxy, i.e., 225 million years. In the Late Cretaceous Period of *c.* 85 million years ago the Earth rotated faster, resulting in 370.3 days per year, while in Cambrian times, *c.* 600 million years ago, there is evidence that the year extended over 425 days.

Borings and Mines

Deepest The deepest penetration into the Earth's crust is a geological exploratory drilling near Zapolarny, Kola peninsula, USSR, begun on 24 May 1970. By April 1991 a depth of 39,776 ft had been surpassed. The eventual target of 49,212 ft is expected in 1995. The drill bit is mounted on a turbine driven by a mud pump. The temperature at 7.45 miles was already 229° F. The Germans announced the test drilling of the Erbendorf hole, Upper Bavaria on 9 Oct 1986. The planned depth of the $263 million project is 8.6 miles or 45,900 ft.

MINE RECORDS

EARLIEST ● 41,250 B.C. ± 1,600 Lion Cavern, Haematite (red iron ore) at Ngwenya, Hhohho, Swaziland.

DEEPEST [1] ● 11,749 ft, Gold, Western Deep Levels (temp 131°F) at Carletonville, South Africa.

FASTEST DRILLING
The most footage drilled in one month is 34,574 ft of a hole drilled during June 1988 by Harkins & Company Rig Number 13 while drilling four wells in McMullen County, TX.

COPPER *Deepest open pit* ● 2,625 ft Bingham Canyon (begun 1906), location near Salt Lake City, UT.
Largest underground ● 356 miles of tunnels, San Manuel Mine, Magma Copper Co in AZ.

LEAD *Largest* ● >10 percent of world output, Viburnum Trend in southeast Missouri.

GOLD MINING *Area* ● >51 percent of world output, 38 mines of the Witwatersrand Discovery, South Africa, in 1886.

GOLD *Largest* [2] ● 12,100 acres, East Rand Proprietary Mines Ltd at Boksburg, Transvaal, South Africa.
Richest ● 49.4 million fine oz, Crown Mines (all-time yield) in Transvaal, South Africa.

IRON *Largest* ● 22.4 billion tons rich ore, Lebedinsky (45–65% ore), Kursk region, USSR.

PLATINUM *Largest* ● 30.8 tons per annum, Rustenburg Platinum Mines Group, Rustenburg Platinum, mine location Western Transvaal, South Africa.

TUNGSTEN *Largest* ● 2,205 tons per day, Union Carbide Mount Morgan mine, near Bishop, CA.

URANIUM *Largest* ● 5,600 tons of uranium oxide, Rio Tinto Zinc open cast pit at Rössing, Namibia.

SPOIL DUMP *Largest* ● 275 million yd[3], New Cornelia Tailings at Ten Mile Wash, AZ.

QUARRY *Largest* ● 2.81 miles², 3,698 million tons extracted, Bingham Canyon, UT.

COAL, OPEN CAST MINE ● 1,103 ft deep 8 mile² area, Fortuna-Garsdorf (lignite) (begun 1955), near Bergheim, Germany.

COAL MINE *Oldest, US* [3] ● c. 1750 at James River coalfield near Richmond, VA. This site is now abandoned.

[1] *Sinking began in July 1957. Scheduled to reach 12,370 ft by 1992, with 14,000 ft or 2.65 miles regarded as the limit. No. 3 vertical ventilation shaft is the world's deepest shaft at 9,675 ft. This mine requires 141,150 tons of air per day and refrigeration, which uses the energy it would take to make 41,440 short tons of ice. An underground shift comprises 11,150 men. The deepest exploratory coal-mining shaft is one reaching 6,700 ft near Thorez in the Ukrainian Donbas field, USSR in August 1983.*

[2] *The world's most productive gold mine may be Muruntau, Kyzyl Kum, Uzbekistan, USSR. According to one Western estimate it produces 88 tons of gold in a year. It has been estimated that South Africa has produced in 96 years (1886–1982) 40,768 tons or more than 31 percent of all gold mined since 3900 B.C.*
[3] *The first recorded discovery of coal in the United States was in 1679 by French explorers, who reported a "coal mine" on the Illinois River.*

Ocean drilling The deepest recorded drilling into the seabed by the *Glomar Challenger* of the US Deep Sea Drilling Project is one of 5,709 ft off northwest Spain in 1976.

The deepest site is now 23,077 ft below the surface on the western wall of the Mariana Trench, Pacific Ocean. The deepest drilling in the North Sea, Great Britain was in 2,611 ft of water on 11–12 Jun 1986 by the British-built *Sovereign Explorer*, a propulsion-assisted semisubmersible drilling unit operated by Scotdrill Offshore Co., Great Britain and contracted to Chevron Petroleum.

Oil fields In 1989 the world's largest oil producer was the USSR, with 121.5 million barrels per day, followed by the United States with 7.5 million.

The world's largest oil field is the Ghawar field, Saudi Arabia, developed by ARAMCO, which measures 150 × 22 miles.

United States The largest oil field in the United States is Permian Basin, which covers approximately 100,000 miles² in southeast New Mexico and western and northwestern Texas.

In 1989, the United States imported 7,979,000 barrels of oil per day.

Oil refineries The world's largest refinery is the Petroleos de Venezuela S.A. refinery in Judibana, Falcón, Venezuela. It is operated by the Lagoven subsidiary of Petroleos and produces 571,000 barrels of crude oil per day.

United States The largest refinery in the United States is Exxon Co. USA's Baytown, TX refinery, which has a capacity of 426,000 barrels per calender day and 448,700 barrels per stream day.

Gas deposits The largest gas deposit in the world is at Urengoi, USSR, with an eventual production of 261.6 billion yd³ per year through six pipelines from proved reserves of 9.156 trillion yd³. The trillionth (10^{12}) cubic meter was produced on 23 Apr 1986.

Oil platforms *Heaviest* The world's heaviest oil platform is the *Gullfaks C* in the North Sea, Great Britain, built and operated by the Norwegian oil company

WORST US OIL SPILLS

SPILL	LOCATION	BARRELS LOST	DATE
Ranger TX (Drilling Rig)	Gulf of Mexico, off Texas coast	326,000	6 Nov 1985
Exxon Valdez (Tanker)	Prince William Sound, AK	258,000	24 Mar 1989
Burmah Agate (Tanker)	Gulf of Mexico, 5 miles south of Galveston, TX	255,000	1 Nov 1979
Texaco Oklahoma (Tanker)	Atlantic Ocean, 120 miles northeast of Cape Hatteras, NC	220,000	March 1971

US Coast Guard, 1990

Statoil. The platform is of the Condeep type, with a steel deck and modules on top of a concrete gravity base. Total dry weight of the £1.3 billion ($2.3 billion) structure is 932.5 tons. Total height is 115.82 ft. The gravity base was built by Norwegian Contractors, Stavanger, and the deck by Aker, Stord.

Tallest The world's tallest production platform stands in water 1,760 ft deep about 100 miles off the Louisiana coast. It is operated by Conoco and co-owned by Conoco, Texas and Occidental Petroleum.

Gushers The greatest wildcat ever recorded blew at Alborz No. 5 well, near Qum, Iran on 26 Aug 1956. The uncontrolled oil gushed to a height of 170 ft at 120,000 barrels per day at a pressure of 9,000 lb/in². It was closed after 90 days' work by B. Mostofi and Myron Kinley of Texas.

The Lake View No. 1 gusher in California on 15 Mar 1910 may have yielded 125,000 barrels in its first 24 hours.

Oil spills The slick from the Mexican marine blow-out beneath the drilling rig *Ixtoc I* in the Gulf of Campeche, Gulf of Mexico, on 3 Jun 1979 reached 400 miles by 5 Aug 1979. It was eventually capped on 24 Mar 1980 after a loss of 3,000,000 barrels (599,200 tons).

The *Exxon Valdez* in Prince William Sound, AK struck a reef on 24 Mar 1989, spilling 10 million gallons of crude slick spread over 2,600 miles².

The worst oil spill in history was of 260,140 tons of oil from two supertankers, *Atlantic Empress* and *Aegean Captain*, when they collided off Tobago on 19 Jul 1979.

Flare The greatest gas fire was the one that burned at Gassi Touil in the Algerian Sahara from noon on 13 Nov 1961 to 9:30 A.M. on 28 Apr 1962. The pillar of flame rose 450 ft and the smoke 600 ft. It was eventually extinguished by Paul Neal ("Red") Adair (b. 1916) of Houston, TX, using 550 lb of dynamite. His fee was understood to be about $1 million plus expenses.

Water well The world's deepest water bore is the Stensvad Water Well 11-W1 of 7,320 ft, drilled by the Great Northern Drilling Co. Inc. in Rosebud County, MT

UNITED STATES CRUDE OIL IMPORTS*
(January–November 1990)

Country	Barrels
Saudi Arabia	391,683
Nigeria	270,922
Mexico	232,959
Venezuela	223,069
Canada	212,153
Iraq	185,859
Angola	79,153
Great Britain	53,984
Colombia	46,905
Indonesia	35,665
Norway	34,362
Kuwait	28,942
China	26,710
Trinidad & Tobago	25,896
Gabon	22,418
Algeria	20,139
Australia	15,216
Ecuador	13,502
Malaysia	13,348
Oman	13,037
Congo	8,457
Egypt	8,301
Zaire	7,650
Yemen	6,993
Cameroon	4,604
Thailand	4,120
United Arab Emirates	3,300
Argentina	3,033
Brunei	2,463
Benin	1,387
Guatemala	1,295
Qatar	1,293
Syria	813
Italy	669
Turkey	499
Tunisia	331
USSR	297
India	210
Total:	**2,001,637**

* Includes crude oil imported for storage in the Strategic Petroleum Reserve. American Petroleum Institute

in October–November 1961. The Thermal Power Co. geothermal steam well, begun in Sonoma County, CA in 1955, is down to 9,029 ft.

Power

Largest power plant Currently, the most powerful installed power station is the Grand Coulee, WA, with 7.4 million kW/hr (ultimately 10,830 MW), which began operating in 1942.

The $11-billion Itaipu power station on the Paraná River near the Brazil–Paraguay border began generating power formally on 25 Oct 1984 and will attain 13,320 kW from 18 turbines. Construction began in 1975 with a work force approaching 28,000. A 20,000 MW power station project on the Tunguska River, USSR was announced in February 1982.

Largest boiler The largest boilers ever designed were those ordered in the United States from Babcock & Wilcox (USA), with a capacity of 1,330 MW, involving the evaporation of 9.33 million lb of steam per hour.

Largest generator Dynamos in the 2,000,000 kW (or 2,000 MW) range are

■ **Smallest gas turbine**
The minature gas turbine poised at the intake of the DeHavilland Ghost jet engine. (Photo: Geoff Knights)

now in the planning stages both in Great Britain and the United States.

The largest operational is a turbo generator of 1,450 MW (net) being installed at the Ignalina atomic power station in Lithuania, USSR.

Turbines The largest hydraulic turbines are those rated at 815,000 kW (equivalent to 1.1 million hp), 32 ft in diameter with a runner and a shaft installed by Allis-Chalmers at the Grand Coulee Third Powerplant, WA.

Pump The world's largest reversible pump-turbine is that made by Allis-Chalmers for the Bath County project, VA. It has a maximum rating of 457 MW as a turbine and maximum operating head of 1,289 ft. The impeller/runner diameter is 20 ft 9 in, with a synchronous speed of 257.1 rpm.

Gas The largest gas turbine is type GT 13 E from BBC Brown Boveri AG, with a maximum output of 140 MW. The first machine is being installed in Holland in order to increase the general output of a 500 MW steam-powered plant (Hemweg 7) by more than 46 percent.

The smallest self-sustaining gas turbine is one with 2 in compressor and turbine wheels built by Geoff Knights of London, Great Britain. It has an operating speed of 50,000 RPM.

Battery *Largest* The 10 MW lead-acid battery at Chino, CA has a design capacity of 40 MW/h. It will be used at an electrical substation for leveling peak demand loads. This $13 million project is a cooperative effort by Southern California Edison Company Electric Power Research Institute and International Lead Zinc Research Organization Inc.

Longest-lasting The zinc foil and sulfur dry-pile batteries made by Watlin and Hill of London, Great Britain in 1840 have powered ceaseless tintinnabulation inside a bell jar at the Clarendon Laboratory, Oxford, Great Britain since that year.

Earliest atomic pile The world's first atomic pile was built in a disused doubles squash court at Stagg Field, University of Chicago, IL. It went "critical" at 3:25 P.M. on 2 Dec 1942.

Nuclear power station The first nuclear power station producing electricity was the EBR-1 in the United States on 20 Dec 1951.

The world's largest nuclear power station, with 10 reactors and an output of 9,096 MW, is the station in Fukushima, Japan.

Nuclear reactor The largest single nuclear reactor in the world is the 1,450 MW (net) reactor at the Ignalina station, Lithuania, USSR, put on full power in January 1984.

The largest under construction is the CHOOZ-B1 reactor in France. Work began on site in July 1982 and the first reactor is scheduled for operation in 1991 with a net capacity of 1,457 MW.

Fusion power Tokamak-7, the experimental thermonuclear apparatus, was declared in January 1982 by USSR academician Velikhov to be operating "reliably for months on end." An economically viable thermonuclear reactor is not anticipated until "about 2030."

The recent temperature attained in the Joint European Torus (JET) at Culham, Great Britain was 180 million° F on 10 Oct 1988.

Solar power plant The largest solar electric-generating system in the world is the LUZ plant, located in the Mojave Desert, 140 miles northeast of Los Angeles, CA. It is currently operating the world's nine largest solar electric generating systems (SEGS), which account for more than 92 percent of the the world's solar electricity. LUZ is now producing 354 MW. SEGS IX is the second phase in a six-plant, $1.5 billion solar development program due for completion in 1994 which will bring the total to 675 MW.

The $30 million thermal solar energy system at the Packerland Packing Co. Bellevue Plant, Green Bay, WI, completed in January 1984, comprises 9,750 4 × 8 ft collectors covering 7.16 acres. It will yield up to 8,000 million BTUs a month.

Tidal power station The world's first major station is the *Usine marémotrice de la Rance*, officially opened on 26 Nov 1966 on the Rance estuary in the Golfe de St-Malo, Brittany, France. It was built in five years at a cost of 420 million francs, and has a net annual output of 544 million kW. The 2,640 ft barrage contains 24 turbo alternators.

The $1 billion Passamaquoddy project for the Bay of Fundy in Maine and New Brunswick, Canada remains a project. The $46 million pilot Annapolis River project for the Bay of Fundy was begun in 1981.

Biggest blackout The greatest power failure in history struck seven northeastern US states and Ontario, Canada on 9–10 Nov 1965. About 30 million people in 80,000 miles[2] were plunged into darkness. Only two people died as a result of the blackout. In New York City the power failed at 5:27 P.M. and was not fully restored for 13½ hr.

The total losses in the 52-min New York City power failure of 13 Jul 1977, including looting, were put at $1 billion.

Windmill The earliest recorded windmills were those used for grinding corn in Persia (now Iran) in the 7th century A.D.

Tallest The De Noord windmill in Schiedam, Netherlands at 109 ft 4 in is the tallest in Europe.

Largest The world's first 3,000 kW wind generator was the 492 ft tall turbine built by Grosse Windenergie–Anlage, which was set up in 1982 on the Friesian coast of Germany.

The $14.2 million GEC MOD-5A installation on the north shore of Oahu, HI will produce 7,300 kW when the wind reaches 32 mph with 400 ft rotors. Installation was started in March 1984.

Tidal mill On 12 Nov 1989 the Eling Tide Mill, Great Britain attained 16 hr 7 min rotation of the waterwheel in one day. It is the only surviving mill in the world harnessing the power of the tide for regular production of wholemeal flour.

Engineering

Oldest machinery The earliest mechanism still in use is the *dâlu*—a water-raising instrument known to have been in use in the Sumerian civilization, which originated *c.* 3500 B.C. in what is now lower Iraq. The *dâlu* is thus even earlier than the *saqiyas* on the Nile.

Blast furnace The world's largest blast furnace has an inner volume of 185,224 ft³ and a 49 ft diameter hearth at ZBF at the Oita Works, Kyūshū, Japan, completed in October 1976 with 4,314,300 tons annual capacity.

Catalytic cracker The world's largest catalytic cracker is Exxon's Bayway Refinery plant at Linden, NJ, with a fresh feed rate of 5.04 million gals per day.

Concrete pumping The world record distance for pumping ready-mixed concrete without a relay pump is 4,986 ft, set on the Lake Chiemsee, Bavaria sewage tunnels project in the summer of 1989.

Conveyor belt The world's longest single-flight conveyor belt is one of 18 miles in Western Australia installed by Cable Belt Ltd of Camberley, Great Britain.

The world's longest multiflight conveyor was one of 62 miles between the phosphate mine near Bucraa and the port of El Aiún, Morocco, built by Krupps and completed in 1972. It had 11 flights of 5.6–6.8 miles and was driven at 10.06 mph. It has since been closed down.

Most powerful crane The most powerful cranes are the two aboard the semisubmersible vessel *Micoperi 7000* (623.35 ft in length and 292 ft in breadth) operated by Officine Meccaniche Reggiane, designed by American Hoist & Derrick Company, built by Monfalcone, Gorizia, Italy and launched 15 Dec 1986. Each has a capacity of 7,716 tons. In tandem they can lift 16,534.7 tons. In their first six months of operation they achieved a record lift of 6,283 tons.

Gantry crane The 92.3 ft wide Rahco (R.A. Hanson Disc Ltd) gantry crane at the Grand Coulee Dam Third Powerplant was tested to lift a load of 2,570.5 tons in 1975. It lowered a 1,972 ton generator rotor with an accuracy of 1.32 in.

Tallest mobile crane The 893 ton Rosenkranz K10001, with a lifting capacity of 1,102 tons, and a combined boom and jib height of 663 ft, is carried on 10 trucks, each limited to a length of 75 ft 8 in and an axle weight of 130 tons. It can lift 33 tons to a height of 525 ft.

Most powerful diesel engines Five 12RTA84 type diesel engines have been constructed by Sulzer Brothers of Winterthur, Switzerland, for container ships built for the American President Lines. Each 12-cylinder power unit gives a maximum continuous output of 57,000 bhp at 95 rev/min. The first of these ships, the *President Truman*, was handed over in April 1988 and the most recent in September of that year.

Most powerful rocket engine The most powerful rocket engine was built in the USSR by Scientific Industrial Corporation of Energetic Engineering in 1980. The engine has a thrust of 2,645.5 tons in open space and a thrust of 4,409.5 tons at the Earth's surface. The RD-170 has a turbopump of 190 MW and burns liquid oxygen and kerosene.

Dragline The Ural Engineering Works (named after Ordzhonikidze) in Sverdlovsk, USSR, completed in March 1962, has a dragline known as the ES-25(100), with a boom of 328 ft, and a bucket with a capacity of 848 ft³.

The world's largest walking dragline is "Big Muskie," the Bucyrus-Erie 4250W with an all-up weight of 13,227 tons and a bucket capacity of 5,933 ft³ on a 310 ft boom. This is the largest mobile land machine and is now operating on the Central Ohio Coal Co. Muskingum site in Ohio.

Earthmover The giant wheeled loader developed for open-air coal mining in Australia by SMEC, a consortium of 11 manufacturers in Tokyo, Japan, is 55.1 ft in length, weighs 198 tons, and has rubber tires 11.5 ft in diameter. The bucket has a capacity of 671 ft³.

Escalator The term "escalator" was registered in the United States on 28 May 1900, but the earliest "Inclined Escalator" was installed by Jesse W. Reno on the pier at Coney Island, NY in 1896. The escalators on the Leningrad underground, USSR at Lenin Square have 729 steps and a vertical rise of 195 ft 9½ in.

The world's longest *ride* is on the four-section outdoor escalator at Ocean Park, Hong Kong, which has an overall length of 745 ft and a total vertical rise of 377 ft. The world's longest "moving sidewalks" are those installed in 1970 in the Neue Messe Center, Dusseldorf, Germany, which measure 738 ft between comb plates.

The ultimate in absurdity for weary shoppers is the escalator at the shopping mall at Kawasaki-shi, Japan. It has a vertical height of 32.83 in and was installed by Hitachi Ltd.

Excavator The world's largest excavator is the bucket wheel excavator being assembled at the open-cast lignite mine at Hambach, Germany, with a rating of 2.15 million ft² per 20 hr working day. It is 690 ft in length and 269 ft tall. The wheel is 222 ft in circumference with 16 ft buckets.

Forging The largest forging on record is one of a 225 ton, 55 ft long generator shaft

■ **Largest solar electric-generating system**
The LUZ plant has nine solar plants in operation in the Mojave Desert in California. By 1994 the plants will produce 675 MW of electricity, providing enough energy for one million people.
(Photo: LUZ International Ltd)

■ **Most powerful diesel engine**
The President Polk *is one of five 12RTA84 type container ships with the most powerful diesel engines, constructed by Sulzer Brothers of Switzerland. Each 12-cylinder power unit gives a maximum continuous output of 57,000 bhp.*
(Photo: Sulzer)

ENGINEERING

Escalator riding
The record distance traveled on a pair of "up" and "down" escalators is 133.18 miles, by David Beattie and Adrian Simons at Top Shop in London, Great Britain, from 17 to 21 Jul 1989. They each completed 7,032 circuits.

for Japan, forged by the Bethlehem Steel Corporation of Pennsylvania in October 1973.

Fork lift truck Kalmar LMV of Sweden manufactured in 1985 ten counterbalanced forklift trucks capable of lifting loads up to 88 tons at a load center of 90.5 in. They were built to handle the large-diameter pipeline in the Libyan Great Man-made River Project.

Lathe The largest is the 126 ft long 460 ton giant lathe built by Waldrich Siegen of Germany in 1973 for the South African Electricity Supply Commission at Rosherville. It has a capacity for 330-ton workpieces and a swing-over bed of 16 ft 5 in in diameter.

Greatest lift The heaviest lifting operation in engineering history was the raising of the entire 0.745 mile long offshore Ekofisk complex in the North Sea, Great Britain, owing to subsidence of the seabed. The complex consists of eight platforms weighing some 44,092 tons. During 17–18 Aug 1987 it was raised 21 ft 4 in by 122 hydraulic jacks requiring a computer-controlled hydraulic system developed and supplied by Hydraudyne Systems & Engineering bv of Boxtel, Netherlands.

Slowest machine A nuclear environmental machine for testing stress corrosion has been developed by Nene

Instruments of Wellingborough, Great Britain that can be controlled at a speed as slow as one million millionth of a millimeter per minute, or one meter (3.28 ft) in about 2 billion years.

Oil tank The largest oil tanks ever constructed are the five ARAMCO 1½-million-barrel storage tanks at Ju'aymah, Saudi Arabia. They are 72 ft tall with a diameter of 386 ft and were completed in March 1980.

Passenger elevator The fastest domestic passenger elevators in the world are the express elevators to the 60th floor of the 787.4 ft tall "Sunshine 60" building, Ikebukuro, in Tokyo, Japan, completed 5 Apr 1978. They were built by Mitsubishi Corporation and operate at a speed of 2,000 ft/min or 22.72 mph.

Much higher speeds are achieved in the winding cages of mine shafts. A hoisting shaft 6,800 ft deep, owned by Western Deep Levels Ltd in South Africa, winds at speeds of up to 40.9 mph (3,595 ft/min). Otitis media (popping of the ears) presents problems above even 10 mph.

Pipelines *Earliest* The world's earliest pipeline, of 2 in diameter cast iron, laid at Oil Creek, PA in 1863, was torn up by Luddites (persons engaged in seeking to obstruct progress).

Longest The longest crude oil pipeline

in the world is the Interprovincial Pipe Line Company installation from Edmonton, Alberta, Canada to Buffalo, NY, a distance of 1,775 miles. Along the length of the pipe, 13 pumping stations maintain a flow of 8.3 million gals of oil per day.

The eventual length of the Trans-Siberian pipeline will be 2,319 miles, running from Tuimazy through Omsk and Novosibirsk to Irkutsk. The first 30 mile section was opened in July 1957.

Gas The world's longest submarine pipeline is that of 264 miles for natural gas from the Union Oil platform to Rayong, Thailand, opened on 12 Sep 1981. The longest natural gas pipeline in the world is the Trans-Canada pipeline, which by 1974 had 5,654 miles of pipe up to 42 in in diameter.

There is a 2,690-mile-long gas pipeline which travels from Tyumen to Brandenburg through Chelyabinsk and Moscow. The large-caliber Urengoi-Nzhgorod line to Western Europe, begun in November 1982, covers 2,765 miles and was completed on 25 Jul 1983. It has a capacity of 1.13 trillion ft^3 per year.

Water The world's longest water pipeline runs a distance of 350 miles to the Kalgoorlie goldfields from near Perth in Western Australia. Engineered in 1903, the system has since been extended fivefold by branches.

Most expensive The world's most expensive pipeline is the Alaska pipeline running 800.3 miles from Prudhoe Bay to Valdez. On completion of the first phase in 1977, it had cost $8 billion. The pipe is 48 in in diameter and it capacity is now 2.1 million barrels per day. In 1990 the capacity averaged 1.8 million per day.

Press The world's two most powerful production machines are forging presses in the United States. The Loewy closed-die forging press, in a plant leased from the US Air Force by the Wyman-Gordon Company at North Grafton, MA, weighs 9,462 tons and stands 114 ft 2 in high, of which 66 ft is sunk below the operating floor. It has a rated capacity of 43,896 tons and became operational in October 1955. A similar press is at the plant of the Aluminum Company of America in Cleveland, OH.

In January 1986 ASEA Metallurgy's QUINTUS department delivered a sheet metal forming press to BMW AG, Munich, Germany. This press, which is the largest in the world in terms of forming pressure and press force, is a QUINTUS fluid cell press with a press force of 116,844 tons. The Bêché & Grohs counter-blow forging hammer, manufactured in Germany, is rated at 66,138 tons.

Printer The world's fastest printer is the Radiation Inc. electro-sensitive system at the Lawrence Radiation Laboratory, Livermore, CA. High-speed recording of up to 30,000 lines, each containing 120 alphanumeric characters per minute, is attained by controlling electronic pulses through chemically impregnated recording paper that is moving rapidly under closely spaced fixed styli. It can thus print the entire wordage of the Bible (773,692 words) in 65 seconds—3,306 times as fast as the world's fastest typist.

Radar installation The largest of the three installations in the US Ballistic Missile Early Warning System (BMEWS) is that near Thule, in Kalaallit Nunaat (Greenland), 931 miles from the North Pole. It was completed in 1960 at a cost of $500 million.

Its sister stations are one at Cape Clear, AK, which was completed in 1961, and the $115 million radar installation at Fylingdales Moor, Great Britain which was completed in Jun 1963.

The largest scientific radar installation is the 21-acre ground array at Jicamarca, Peru.

Ropes The largest rope ever made was a coir fiber launching rope with a circumference of 47 in made in 1858 for the British liner *Great Eastern* by John and Edwin Wright of Birmingham, Great Britain. It consisted of four strands, each of 3,780 yarns. The longest fiber rope ever made without a splice was one of 11.36 miles of 6½ in circumference manila by Frost Brothers (now British Ropes Ltd) in London, Great Britain in 1874.

The strongest cable-laid wire rope strop made is one 15½ in diameter with a breaking strain of 8,300 tons and manufactured by ScanRope Ltd of Norway. The sling was used to lift the steel jacket for the Veslefrikk Offshore Field in the Norwegian sector of the North Sea in 1989.

Ropeway or téléphérique The longest ropeway in the world is the *Compagnie Minière de l'Ogooué*, or COMILOG, installation built in 1959–62 for the Moanda manganese mine in Gabon, which extends 47.2 miles. It has 858 towers and 2,800 buckets, with 96.3 miles of wire rope running over 6,000 idler pulleys.

The highest and longest passenger-carrying aerial ropeway in the world is the *Teleférico Mérida* in Venezuela, from Mérida City (5,379 ft) to the summit of Pico Espejo (15,629 ft), a rise of 10,250 ft. The ropeway is in four sections, involving three car changes in the 8 mile ascent in one hour. The fourth span is 10,070 ft in length. The two cars work on the pendulum system—the carrier rope is locked and the cars are hauled by means of three pull ropes powered by a 233 hp motor. They have a maximum capacity of 45 persons and travel at 32 ft/sec (21.8 mph).

The longest single-span ropeway is the 13,500 ft span from the Coachella Valley to Mt San Jacinto (10,821 ft), CA, inaugurated on 12 Sep 1963.

Shovel The Marion 6360 has a reach of 236.75 ft, a dumping height of 153 ft and a bucket capacity of 4,860 ft³. Manufactured in 1964 by the Marion Power Shovel Co., Marion, OH, it weighs 24.3 million lb and uses 20 electric motors that generate 45,000 hp to operate its 220.5-ft-long boom arm. It is operated for open-cast coal mining near Percy, IL by the Arch Mineral Corporation.

Snow-plow blade A blade measuring 32 ft 3 in in length was designed and constructed by the Thomas Sedgwick Construction Co., Inc. of Syracuse, NY for use at Hancock International Airport. With a 6 in snowfall the plow can push away 229,506 ft³ of snow in one hour.

Transformers The world's largest single-phase transformers are rated at 1,500,000 kVA, of which eight are in service with the American Electric Power Service Corporation. Of these, five step down from 765 to 345 kV.

Transmission lines The longest span between pylons of any power line in the world is that across the Sogne Fjord, Norway, between Rabnaberg and Fatlaberg. Supplied in 1955 by Whitecross of Warrington, Great Britain, and projected and erected by A.S. Betonmast of Oslo as part of the high-tension power cable from Refsdal power station at Vik, it has a span of 16,040 ft and a weight of 13.3 tons. In 1967 two further high-tensile steel/aluminum lines 16,006 ft long, and weighing 36.4 tons, manufactured by Whitecross and BICC, were erected here.

Highest The world's highest transmission lines are those across the Straits of Messina, Italy, with towers of 675 ft (Sicily side) and 735 ft (Calabria side) and 11,900 ft apart.

Highest voltages The highest voltages now carried are 1,330,000 volts for 1,224 miles on the D.C. Pacific Inter-tie in the United States. The Ekibastuz D.C. transmission lines in Kazakhstan, USSR are planned to be 1,490 miles long with 1,500,000 volt capacity.

Valve The world's largest valve is the 32 ft diameter, 187 ton butterfly valve designed by Boving & Co. Ltd of London, Great Britain for use at the Arnold Air Force Base engine test facility in Tennessee.

Wire ropes The longest wire ropes in the world are the four made at British Ropes Ltd, Wallsend, Great Britain, each measuring 14.9 miles. The ropes are 1.3 in in diameter, weigh 120 tons each and were ordered by the CEGB for use in the construction of the 2,000 MW cross-Channel power cable.

The thickest ever manufactured are spliced crane strops from wire ropes 11¼ in thick with 2,392 individual wires made in Mar 1979 by British Ropes Ltd of Doncaster at Willington Quay, Great Britain, and designed to lift loads of up to 3,307 tons. The suspension cables on the Seto Grand Bridge, Japan, completed in 1988, are 41 in in diameter.

The heaviest-ever wire ropes (four in number) are each of 143 tons, made for the twin shaft system of Western Deep Levels gold mine, South Africa by Haggie Rand Ltd of Johannesburg.

Wind tunnel The world's largest wind tunnel is that of the NASA Ames Research Center in Mountain View, Palo Alto, CA. The new tunnel, 40 × 80 ft, was opened on 11 Dec 1989 and powered by six 22,500 hp motors enabling a best speed of 345 mph.

Timepieces

Largest sundial The world's largest sundial is the Samrat Yantra, with a gnomon height (rod of sundial that shows time by its shadow on marked surface) of 88.5 ft and a vertical height of 118 ft. It was built in 1724 at Jaipur, India.

On 1 Mar 1991, Walt Disney World in Orlando, FL unveiled the largest cylindrical sundial, measuring 120 ft high, 122 ft in diameter at the base. The sundial was designed by Arata Isozaki of Tokyo, Japan.

Most accurate time measurer The most accurate timekeeping devices are the twin atomic hydrogen masers installed in 1964 in the US Naval Research Laboratory, Washington, D.C. They are based on the frequency of the hydrogen atom's transition period of 1,420,450,751,694 cycles/sec. This permits an accuracy to within 1 sec in 1,700,000 years.

Clock *Oldest* The earliest mechanical clock—that is, one with an escapement—was completed in China in A.D. 725 by I Xing and Liang Lingzan.

The oldest surviving working clock in the world is the faceless clock dating from 1386, or possibly earlier, at Salisbury Cathedral, in Great Britain, which was restored in 1956, having struck the hours for 498 years and ticked more than 500 million times. Earlier dates, ranging back to c. 1335, have been attributed to the weight-driven clock in Wells Cathedral, Somerset, Great Britain, but only the iron frame is original.

Largest The world's most massive clock is the astronomical clock in the Cathedral of St-Pierre, Beauvais, France, constructed between 1865 and 1868. It contains 90,000 parts and is 40 ft high, 20 ft wide and 9 ft deep.

The Su Sung clock, built in China at Kaifeng in 1088–92, had a 23 ton bronze armillary sphere for 1.7 tons of water. It was removed to Beijing (formerly Peking) in 1126 and was last known to be working in its 40 ft high tower in 1136.

"Timepiece," a clock that measures 51 × 51 × 51 ft, is suspended over five stories in the atrium of the International Square building in Washington, D.C. Computer-driven and accurate to within 1/100th of a second, it weighs 2.3 tons. It is lit by 400 ft of neon tube lighting and requires 1,500 ft of cable and wiring. Twelve tubes at its base light up to tell the hour and the minute. The clock, designed by the sculptor John Safer, also indicates when the sun is at its zenith in 12 international cities.

Top-spinning
The duration record for spinning a clock-balance wheel by unaided hand is 5 min 26.8 sec by Philip Ashley, 16, of Leigh, Great Britain on 20 May 1968.

The record using 36 in of string with a 7¼-oz top is 58 min 20 sec, by Peter Hodgson at Southend-on-Sea, Great Britain on 4 Feb 1985.

A team of 25 from the Mizushima Plant of Kawasaki Steel Works in Okayama, Japan spun a giant top 6 ft 6¾ in tall and 8 ft 6¼ in in diameter, weighing 793.6 lb, for 1 hr 21 min 35 sec on 3 Nov 1986.

Pendulum

The longest pendulum in the world is 73 ft 9 ¾ in on the water-mill clock installed by the Hattori Tokeiten Co. in the Shinjuku NS building in Tokyo, Japan in 1983.

Clock faces The world's largest is that of the floral clock 68 ft 10 ¾ in in diameter, manufactured by Seiko for the Koryu Fujisho Co. and installed in June 1988 inside the Rose Building in the city of Hokkaido, Japan. The large hand of the clock is 27 ft 10 ½ in long.

The digital, electronic, two-sided clock that revolves on top of the Texas Building in Fort Worth, TX has dimensions of 44 × 44 × 28 ft.

The largest vertical outdoor clock face is the octagonal Colgate clock in Jersey City, NJ, with a diameter of 50 ft and a minute hand 27 ft 3 in in length. In 1989 it was dismantled from the position it had occupied since 1908 at the top of the company's factory, which is being redeveloped. There are plans to relocate it at another site.

Four-faced Tallest The tallest four-faced clock in the world is that of the Williamsburgh Savings Bank in Brooklyn, New York City. It is 430 ft above street level.

Largest The largest four-faced clock in the world is that on the building of the Allen Bradley Co. of Milwaukee, WI. Each face has a diameter of 40 ft 3 ½ in with a minute hand 20 ft in overall length.

Most accurate mechanical The Olsen clock, completed for the Copenhagen Town Hall, Denmark in Dec 1955, has more than 14,000 units, and took 10 years to make; the mechanism functions in 570,000 different ways. The celestial pole motion will take 25,753 years to complete a full circle and is the slowest-moving designed mechanism in the world. The clock is accurate to 0.5 sec in 300 years—50 times more accurate than the previous record.

Most expensive The highest price paid for any clock is £880,000 ($1,540,000) for a Thomas Tompion (1639–1713) unrecorded miniature long-case, known as a "night clock," at Christie's, London, Great Britain on 6 Jul 1989.

Watch

Oldest The oldest portable clockwork timekeeper is one made of iron by Peter Henlein in Nürnberg (Nüremberg), Germany, c. 1504.

The earliest wristwatches were those of Jacquet-Droz and Leschot of Geneva, Switzerland, dating from 1790.

Largest The largest watch was a "Swatch" 531 ft 6 in long and 65 ft 7 ½ in in diameter, made by D. Tomas Feliu, which was set up on the Bank of Bilbao building, Madrid, Spain from 7–12 Dec 1985.

The Eta "watch" on the Swiss pavilion at Expo 86 in Vancouver, British Columbia, Canada from May–October weighed 38.5 tons and stood 80 ft high.

Smallest The smallest watches are those produced by Jaeger le Coultre of Switzerland. Equipped with a 15-jeweled movement, they measure just over ½ in long and ³⁄₁₆ in in width. Movement and case weigh under 0.25 oz.

Astronomical The entirely mechanical Planetarium Copernicus, made by Ulysse Nardin of Switzerland, is the only wristwatch that indicates the time of day, the date, the phases of the moon, and the astronomical position of the sun, Earth, moon and the planets known in Copernicus' day. It also represents the Ptolemaic universe showing the astrological "aspects" at any given time.

Most expensive The record price paid for a watch is $28,007,686 at Habsbury Feldman, Geneva, Switzerland on 9 Apr 1989 for a Patek Philippe "Calibre '89" with 1,728 separate parts.

Excluding watches with jeweled cases, the most expensive standard man's pocket watch is Heaven at Hand, known to the connoisseurs as the Packard and made in 1922 by Patek Philippe for the American automobile magnate James Packard. The timepiece is the most outstanding example of a "complicated" pocket watch in the world and was bought back by Patek Philippe in September 1988 for $1,200,000. To satisfy Packard's eccentric demands, Patek Philippe created a perfect celestial chart in enamel on the watch in gold casing to show the heavens as they moved over Packard's hometown of Warren, OH—in fact, exactly as he could see them from his bedroom window.

Computers

Earliest The earliest programmable electronic computer was the 1,500-valve Colossus formulated by Prof. Max H.A. Newman (1897–1985) and built by T.H. Flowers. It was run in December 1943 at Bletchley Park, Great Britain to break the German coding machine Enigma. It arose from a concept published in 1936 by Dr Alan Mathison Turing (1912–54) in his paper *On Computable Numbers with an Application to the Entscheidungsproblem*. Colossus was declassified on 25 Oct 1975.

The world's first stored-program computer was the Manchester University (Great Britain) Mark I, which incorporated the Williams storage cathode ray tube (patented 11 Dec 1946). It ran its first program, by Prof. Tom Kilburn (b. 1921), for 52 min on 21 Jun 1948.

The concept of the integrated circuit, which has made micro-miniaturization possible, was first published on 7 May 1952 by Geoffrey W.A. Dummer (b. 1909) in Washington, D.C.

The invention of the microcomputer was attributed to a team led by M.E. Hoff, Jr. of Intel Corporation with the production of the microprocessor chip "4004" in 1969–71. However, on 17 Jul 1990 print-

■ **Smallest modem**
The SRM-3A ultra-miniature asynchronous short-range modem is used for local data distribution connecting terminals to computers.

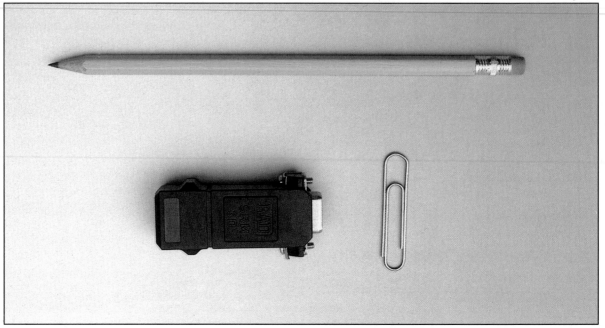

ing was accorded to Gilbert Hyatt (b. 1938), who devised a single chip microcomputer at Micro Computer Inc. of Van Nuys, Los Angeles in 1968–71 with the award of US Patent No. 4942516.

Most powerful and fastest The world's most powerful and fastest computer is the liquid-cooled CRAY-2, named after Seymour R. Cray of Cray Research Inc., Minneapolis, MN. Its memory has a capacity of 256 million 64-bit words, resulting in a capacity of 32 million bytes of main memory. (A "byte" is a unit of storage comprising eight "bits" that are collectively equivalent to one alphabetic symbol or two numericals.) It attains speeds of 250 million floating point operations per second.

Sandia National Laboratory, NM on 18 Mar 1988 announced a "massively parallel" hypercube computer with 1,024 parallel processors, which, by breaking down problems into parts for simultaneous solution, proved 1,019 times faster than a conventional mainframe computer.

In May 1988 NEC (Nippon Electric Co.) announced a $2.8 billion research program to attain a fifth generation computer able to read handwriting and understand speech in many languages, and incorporating superconduction and Josephson functions (See also Numbers—Longest computer computation and Most accurate and inaccurate value of *pi*.)

Computer company The world's largest computer firm is International Business Machines (IBM) Corporation of Armonk, NY. In December 1990, its assets were $87.6 billion and gross income was $69 billion. The company has 373,816 employees worldwide and 789,046 stockholders.

Smallest modem Modems are devices that allow electron signals to be transmitted over large distances by MOdulating the signal at one end, and DEModulating the signal back to its original form at the destination. The smallest is the SRM-3A, which is 2.4 in long, 1.2 in wide, and 0.8 in high, and weighs 1.1 oz. It is currently manufactured by RAD Data Communications Ltd of Tel Aviv, Israel.

Smallest word processor The Easi-Text 1350 was introduced by Minimicro of Huntington, Great Britain in April 1986. It is based on the Sharp PC-1350 computer, which measures 7.2 × 2.8 × 0.6 in, and the entire system, including a letter-size Epson P-80 printer, fits into an executive briefcase.

Megabits The megabit barrier was broken in February 1984, with the manufacture of a 1,024K-bit integrated circuit the size of a thumbtack head and as thin as a human hair, by four Japanese companies: Hitachi, NEC, NTT Atsugi Electrical Communications and Toshiba. Toshiba announced that manufacture of an 80-picosecond LSI (large scale integration) chip of gallium arsenide had started in 1985–86.

Fastest transistor A transistor capable of switching 230 billion times per second was announced by Illinois State University on 5 Oct 1986.

Telecommunications

Telephones There were approximately 423,618,819 telephones in the world on 1 Jan 1989. The country with the greatest number was the United States, with 118,400,662. The territory reported to have the fewest reported telephone lines is Pitcairn Island, with 24.

The city with the most telephones in the world is Tokyo, Japan with 5,511,000. The greatest number of calls made in any country is in the United States with 421,022 million per year.

Longest telephone cable The world's longest submarine telephone cable is ANZCAN, which runs for 9,415 miles (8,181 nautical miles) from Port Alberni, Canada to Auckland, New Zealand and Sydney, Australia via Fiji and Norfolk Island. It cost some $379 million and was inaugurated by Her Majesty Queen Elizabeth II in Nov 1984.

Longest terrestrial call A telephone call around the world, over an estimated 98,700 miles, was made on 28 Dec 1985 from, and back to, the Royal Institute, London, Great Britian, during one of the Christmas lectures given by David Pye, Prof. of Zoology, University of London. The international telecommunications "rule," that only one communication satellite be used at a time, was suspended for the demonstration so that both geostationary Intelsats, one over the Indian Ocean and one over the Pacific, could be employed. The two "telephonists," Anieka Russell and Alison Risk, experienced a delay in their conversation of 530 milliseconds.

Largest and smallest telephones
Largest The world's largest operational telephone was exhibited at a festival on 16 Sep 1988 to celebrate the 80th birthday of Centraal Beheer, an insurance company based in Apeldoorn, the Netherlands. It was 8 ft 1 in high and 19 ft 11 in long, and weighed 3.8 tons. The handset, being 23 ft 5 in long, had to be lifted by crane in order to make a call.

Smallest The smallest operational telephone was created by Jeff Smith of GTE Northwest, Everett, WA in 1988 and measured 4 1/8 × 3/4 × 1 1/2 in.

Busiest telephone exchange GPT (GEC Plessey Telecommunications Ltd) demonstrated the ability of the "System X" telephone exchange to handle 1,558,000 calls in an hour through one exchange at Beeston, Great Britain on 27 Jun 1989.

Largest switchboard The world's biggest switchboard is the one in the Pentagon, Washington, D.C., with 25,000 lines handling over 200,000 calls per day through 100,000 miles of telephone cable.

Facsimile machine *Largest* The largest facsimile machine is manufactured by WideCom Group Inc of Ontario, Canada. "Wide Fax" has scanning and printing facilities to 24 in.

Smallest The world's smallest facsimile machine is capable of sending and receiving A4-size documents, together with an error correction mode. The RICOH PF-1 portable measures 11 × 7 × 2 in and weighs 5.5 lb.

Telescopes

Earliest It is not known when the first telescopes were made. The refractive properties of lenses were certainly known in ancient times, and spectacles were in use in the 13th century. Roger Bacon (*c.* 1214–92) in England wrote extensively about lenses, and claims have been made on behalf of various others, notably the Elizabethan scientists Diggs and Dee. Leonardo da Vinci (1452–1519) is said to have used some sort of reflecting device to "make the moon seem larger," though this is not fully authenticated. It is very probable that the

■ **Widest facsimile**
With a scanning and printing width of up to 24 in, this facsimile machine is manufactured by WideCom Group Inc., Ontario, Canada. (Photo: Mel Loynd)

Message in a bottle
The longest recorded interval between drop and pickup is 73 years in the case of a message thrown from the SS *Arawatta* out of Cairns, Queensland, Australia on 9 Jun 1910 in a lotion bottle and reported as found on Moreton Island on 6 Jun 1983.

Morse code
The highest recorded speed at which anyone has received Morse code is 75.2 words per minute—over 17 symbols per second. This was achieved by Ted R. McElroy of the United States in a tournament at Asheville, NC on 2 Jul 1939.

The fastest speed recorded for hand-key transmitting is 175 symbols a minute by Harry A. Turner of the US Army Signal Corps at Camp Crowder, MO on 9 Nov 1942.

TELESCOPES

Planetaria The ancestor of the modern planetarium is the rotatable Gottorp Globe, built by Andreas Busch in Denmark about 1660. It was 34.6 ft in circumference, weighed nearly 3.9 tons and is now preserved in Leningrad, USSR. The stars were painted on the inside. The first modern planetarium was opened in 1923 in Jena, Germany; it was designed by Walther Bauersfelt of the Carl Zeiss company.

United States The Rueben H. Fleet Space Theater & Science Center in San Diego, CA and The Ethyl Universe Planetarium & Space Theater in Richmond, VA both have dome diameters of 75.5 ft.

The American Museum–Hayden Planetarium, New York City has a dome diameter of 75.1 ft, but has the largest seating capacity of any planetarium in the United States with 650 seats.

The Adler Planetarium in Chicago, IL, which opened on 12 May 1930, is the oldest planetarium in the United States. Its dome is 68 ft in diameter and it seats 450 people.

first telescope actually constructed was a refractor made by H. Lippershey in Holland in 1608. The first astronomical observations with telescopes were made shortly afterwards, notably in 1609 by Thomas Harriot, who even drew a telescopic map of the moon—though the first really systematic telescopic observations were made by Galileo from January 1610.

The first reflecting telescope was made by Isaac Newton, and was presented to the Royal Society in 1671 and thought to have been constructed in 1668 or 1669.

Largest reflector The largest single-mirror telescope now in use is the 19 ft 8 in reflector sited on Mount Semirodriki, near Zelenchukskaya in the Caucasus Mountains, USSR, at an altitude of 6,830 ft and completed in 1976. It has never come up to expectations, partly because it is not set up on a really good observing site. The largest satisfactory single-mirror telescope is the 200 in Hale reflector at Mount Palomar, CA. Though the Hale was completed in 1948, it is now much more efficient than it was, as it is used with electronic devices that are more sensitive than photographic plates. The CCD (Charged-Coupled Device) increases the sensitivity by a factor of around 100.

Metal-mirror This 72 in reflector was made by the third Earl of Rosse, and set up at Birr Castle, Ireland in 1845. The mirror was of speculum metal (an alloy of copper and tin). With it, Lord Rosse discovered the spiral forms of the galaxies. It was last used in 1909.

Largest partially completed telescope The Keck telescope on Mauna Kea, HI now being constructed will have a 393.70 in mirror, made up of 36 segments fitted together to produce the correct curve. Each segment is 72 in in aperture. An active support system holds each segment in place, and ensures that the images produced are brought to the same focus. The first image of the spiral galaxy 1232 was obtained on 24 Nov 1990, when nine of the segments were in place. It has been estimated that all the segments will be in place by the end of 1991, and that the first regular observational programs will begin in 1992.

Multiple-mirror The MMT (Multiple-Mirror Telescope) at the Whipple Observatory at Mount Hopkins, AZ uses six 600.3 in mirrors together, giving a light-grasp equal to a single 176 in mirror. There are, however, considerable operational problems.

Largest planned The largest telescope of the century should be the VLT (Very Large Telescope) being planned by the European Southern Observatory. It will consist of four 26.24 ft telescopes working together, providing a light-grasp equal to a single 52.49 ft mirror. The chosen site is Paranal in northern Chile, well to the north of the La Silla Observatory in the Atacama Desert of northern Chile. It is hoped to have the

first units working by 1995, and the complete telescope by 2000.

Infrared The largest infrared reflector in Great Britain is the UKIRT (United Kingdom Infrared Telescope) on Mauna Kea, HI with a 147 in mirror. It is so good that it can be used for visual work as well as infrared.

Solar The McMath solar telescope at Kitt Peak, AZ has a 6.88 ft primary mirror; the light is sent to it via a 32° inclined tunnel from a coelostat (rotatable mirror) at the top end. Extensive modifications to it are now being planned.

Southern The largest southern telescope is the 157.87 in reflector at Cerro Tololo in the Atacama Desert, northern Chile. The Anglo-Australian Telescope (AAT) at Siding Spring in New South Wales has a 153.14 in mirror.

Submillimeter The James Clark Maxwell telescope on Mauna Kea, HI has a 49.21 ft paraboloid primary, and is used for studies of the submillimeter part of the electromagnetic spectrum (0.01–0.03 in). It does not produce a visual image.

Largest refractor A 62 ft long 40 in refractor completed in 1897 is situated at the Yerkes Observatory, Williams Bay, WI and belongs to the University of Chicago, IL. Although nearly 100 years old, it is still in full use on clear nights. A larger refractor measuring 59.05 in was built in France and shown at the Paris Exhibition in 1900. However, it was a failure and was never used for scientific work.

Largest radio dish Radio waves from the Milky Way galaxy were first detected by Karl Jansky of Bell Telephone Laboratories, Holmdel, NJ in 1931 when he was investigating static with an improvised 100 ft aerial. The only radio telescope built for that purpose before the outbreak of the war in 1939 was made by an amateur, Grote Reber, who detected radio emissions from the sun. The diameter of the dish was 31.16 ft.

The first really large "dish" was the 250 ft telescope at Jodrell Bank, Cheshire, Great Britain, now known as the Lovell Telescope, completed in 1957. It is part of the MERLIN network, which includes other dishes in various parts of Britain.

The world's largest fully steerable dish is the 328 ft diameter, 3,360 ton assembly at the Max Planck Institute for Radio Astronomy of Bonn in the Effelsberger Valley, Germany; it was completed in 1971.

Largest radio installation The largest radio installation is the Australian Telescope, which includes dishes at Parkes (210 ft), Siding Spring (72 ft) and Culgoora (72 ft). There are also links with tracking stations at Usuada and Kashima, Japan, and with the TDRS (Tracking and Data Relay Satellite), which is in a geosynchronous orbit. This is equivalent to a radio telescope with an

effective diameter of 2.16 Earth diameters (17,102 miles).

The VLA (Very Large Array) of the US National Science Foundation is Y-shaped, with each arm 13 miles long and with 27 mobile antennae (each of 82 ft diameter) on rails. It is 50 miles west of Socorro in the Plains of San Augustin, NM. It was completed on 10 Oct 1980.

First telescope to use active optics Active optics involves automatic correction of the mirror curve as the telescope is moved around. It gives a great increase in resolution. The first major telescope to use active optics was the New Technology Telescope (NTT) at La Silla in the Atacama Desert of northern Chile, the observing site of the ESO (European Southern Observatory). The NTT, like all modern telescopes, has an altazimuth mount, and is probably the most effective ground-based telescope in use in the world today. It will shortly incorporate adaptive optics, which involves compensating the shape of the mirror for minor short-term variations in the atmosphere.

Observatory Oldest The oldest observatory building extant is the "Tower of the Winds" used by Andronichus of Cyrrhus in Athens, Greece *c.* 100 B.C., and equipped with sundials and clepsydra (water clock).

Highest The high-altitude observatory at Denver, CO is at 14,100 ft and was opened in 1973. The main instrument is a 24 in reflector. It is slightly higher than the observatory at the summit of Mauna Kea in Hawaii at 13,760 ft.

Lowest The lowest "observatory" is at Homestake Mine, SD, where the "telescope" is a tank of cleaning fluid (perchioroethylene), which contains chlorine, and can trap neutrinos from the sun. The installation is 1.56 miles below ground level, in the shaft of a gold mine; the detector has to be at this depth, as otherwise the experiments would be confused by cosmic rays. The Homestake Observatory has been operating since 1964 and has provided results of tremendous value, as the solar neutrinos are far less numerous than had been predicted by theory—a result amply confirmed by other neutrino detectors in Japan and the USSR.

Largest Schmidt telescope A Schmidt telescope is invaluable in astronomy, as it uses a spherical mirror with a correcting plate and can cover a very wide field with a single exposure. The largest is the 6.56 ft instrument at the Karl Schwarzschild Observatory at Tautenberg, Germany. It has a clear aperture of 53 in with a 78.7 in mirror, focal length 13.12 ft. It was brought into use in 1960. Next in size is the Palomar Schmidt at the Palomar Observatory, CA with a clear aperture of 49.5 in and a 72 in mirror, operational in 1948.

Space telescope Largest The largest is the $1.55 billion NASA Edwin P. Hubble Space Telescope of 12 tons and 43 ft in overall length with a 94.5 in reflector. It was placed in orbit at

381 miles altitude aboard a US space shuttle on 24 Apr 1990. When it had been launched, it was found to have a defective mirror, because of a mistake in the original construction, giving serious problems of spherical aberration. It is hoped it can be repaired in the future. Nevertheless, it is doing excellent work in some areas of research in which it can out-perform any ground-based telescope.

Rocketry and Missiles

Earliest uses War rockets, propelled by gunpowder (charcoal-saltpeter-sulfur), were described by Zeng Kung Liang of China in 1042. This early form of rocket became known in Europe by 1258.

The first launching of a liquid-fueled rocket (patented 14 Jul 1914) was by Dr Robert Hutchings Goddard (1882–1945; USA), at Auburn, MA, on 16 Mar 1926, when his rocket reached an altitude of 41 ft and traveled a distance of 184 ft.

The USSR's earliest rocket was the semiliquid-fueled GIRD-IX (Gruppa Izucheniya Reaktivnogo Dvizheniya), begun in 1931 and tested on 17 Aug 1933.

Highest velocity The first space vehicle to achieve the Third Cosmic velocity—sufficient to break out of the solar system—was *Pioneer 10*. The Atlas SLV-3C launcher with a modified Centaur D second stage and a Thiokol Te-364-4 third stage left the Earth at an unprecedented 32,114 mph on 2 Mar 1972.

However, the fastest escape velocity from Earth was 34,134 mph, achieved by the ESA *Ulysses* spacecraft, powered by an IUS-Pam upper stage after deployment from the Space Shuttle Discovery on 18 Oc 1989, en route to a solar polar orbit via Jupiter.

Mariner 10 reached a recorded solar system speed of 131,954 mph as it passed Mercury in September 1974, but the fastest speed of approximately 158,000 mph is recorded by the NASA-German *Helios B* solar probe each time it reaches the perihelion of its solar orbit. Sister spaceship *Helios A* will also exceed *Mariner 10*'s velocity. (See Closest approach to the sun.)

Most powerful rocket The USSR's NI booster, first launched from Baikonur on 21 Feb 1969, had a thrust of 5,092.7 tons. It exploded at takeoff + 70 secs. The USSR's current booster *Energia*, first launched on 15 May 1987 from the Baikonur Cosmodrome, when fully loaded weighs 2,645.6 tons and has a thrust of over 4,724 tons. It is capable of placing 165 tons into low Earth orbit and measures 193.56 ft tall with a maximum diameter of 52.5 ft. It comprises a core stage powered by four liquid oxygen and hydrogen engines—the first cryogenic units flown by the Russians. There are also four strap-on boosters powered by single RD 170 engines burning liquid oxygen and kerosene.

Closest approach to the sun by a rocket The research spacecraft *Helios B* approached within 27 million miles of the sun, carrying both US and German instrumentation, on 16 Apr 1976. (See Highest velocity.)

Remotest man-made object *Pioneer 10*, launched from Cape Canaveral, FL, crossed the mean orbit of Pluto on 17 Oct 1986, being then at a distance of 3.670 billion miles from Earth. In A.D. 34,593 it will make its nearest approach to the star *Ross 248*, 10.3 light-years distant. *Voyager 1*, traveling faster, will surpass *Pioneer 10* in remoteness from the Earth. *Pioneer 11* and *Voyager 2* are also leaving the solar system.

Space Flight

The physical laws controlling the flight of artificial satellites were first propounded by Sir Isaac Newton (1642–1727) in his *Philosophiae Naturalis Principia Mathematica* ("Mathematical Principles of Natural Philosophy"), begun in March 1686 and first published in July 1687.

The first artificial satellite was successfully put into orbit at an altitude of 142.588 miles and a velocity of more than 17,750 mph from the Baikonur Cosmodrome at Tyuratam, 170 miles east of the Aral Sea and 155.34 miles south of the town of Baikonur on the night of 4 Oct 1957. This spherical satellite, called *Sputnik 1* ("Fellow Traveler"), was officially designated "Satellite 1957 Alpha 2." It weighed 184.3 lb, with a diameter of 22.8 in, and its lifetime is believed to have been 92 days, ending on 4 Jan 1958. The 96 ft 8 in SL-4 launcher was designed under the direction of former Gulag prisoner Dr Sergei Pavlovich Korolyov (1907–66).

Earliest manned satellite The earliest manned spaceflight ratified by the world governing body, the *Fédération Aéronautique Internationale* (FAI, founded 1905), was by Cosmonaut Flight Major (later Col.) Yuri Alekseyevich Gagarin (1934–68) in *Vostok 1* on 12 Apr 1961.

Details filed showed takeoff to be from the Baikonur Cosmodrome at 6:07 A.M. GMT and the landing near Smelovka, near Engels, in the Saratov region, USSR, 108 minutes later. Col. Gagarin landed separately from his spacecraft, by parachute, after ejecting as planned, as did all the Vostok pilots. The flight time of the capsule is not recorded.

The maximum altitude during *Vostok 1*'s 25,394.5 mile flight was listed at 203.2 miles, with a maximum speed of 17,560 mph.

Col. Gagarin, invested a Hero of the Soviet Union and awarded the Order of Lenin and the Gold Star Medal, was killed in a jet plane crash near Moscow on 27 Mar 1968.

United States On 5 May 1961, aboard *Mercury 3*, Alan B. Shepard, Jr. became the first American to man a spaceflight. The suborbital flight, which lasted 15½ minutes, covered 302 miles and reached an altitude of 116.5 miles.

John H. Glenn was the first American to orbit the Earth. His flight aboard *Mercury 6* (*Friendship 7*) was launched at 9:47 A.M. EST on 20 Feb 1962 and splashed down into the Atlantic Ocean at 2:43 P.M. EST that same day. Glenn completed three orbits of the Earth and traveled approximately 81,000 miles.

First woman in space The first woman to orbit the Earth was Junior Lt (now Lt.-Col. Eng) Valentina Vladimirovna Tereshkova (b. 6 Mar 1937), who was launched in *Vostok 6* from Tyuratam, USSR, at 9:30 A.M. GMT on 16 Jun 1963, and landed at 8:16 A.M. on 19 June, after a flight of 2 days 22 hr 50 min, during which she completed over 48 orbits (1.23 million miles) and passed momentarily within three miles of *Vostok 5*.

United States The first American woman in space was Sally Ride, who was launched in the US space shuttle *Challenger STS-7* on 18 Jun 1983, and returned to Earth 24 Jun.

Space fatalities The greatest published number to perish in any of the 140 attempted spaceflights to December 1990 is seven (five men and two women) aboard the *Challenger 51L* on 28 Jan 1986, when an explosion occurred 73 sec after liftoff, at a height of 47,000 ft. Four people, all Soviet, have been killed during actual spaceflight—Vladimir Komarov on 24 Apr 1967 on *Soyuz 1*, which crashed on landing; and the unspacesuited Georgi Dobrovolsky, Viktor Patsayev and Vladislav Volkov, who died when their *Soyuz 11* spacecraft depressurized during reentry on 29 Jun 1971.

Astronaut *Oldest* The oldest astronaut of the 242 people in space was Vance DeVoe Brand (b. 9 May 1931; USA), age 59, while on the space shuttle mission aboard the *Columbia STS 35* on 2 Dec 1990. The oldest woman was Shannon Lucid (USA) at the age of 46 on space shuttle mission *Atlantis STS 34* on 18 Oct 1989.

Youngest The youngest was Major (later Lt-Gen) Gherman Stepanovich Titov (b. 11 Sep 1935), who was 25 years 329 days when launched in *Vostok 2* on 6 Aug 1961. The youngest woman in space was Valentina Tereshkova, 26. (See First woman in space.)

The youngest American astronaut was Sally Ride (b. 26 May 1951), who on 18 Jun 1983, at the age of 32 years 169 days, was launched in the space shuttle *Challenger*.

Longest and shortest manned spaceflight The longest manned flight was by Col. Vladimir Georgeyevich Titov (b. 1 Jan 1947) and Flight Engineer Musa Khiramanovich Manarov (b. 22 Mar 1951), who were launched to the Mir space station aboard *Soyuz TM4* on 21 Dec 1987, and landed, in *Soyuz TM6* (with French spationaut Jean-Loup

Lt-Col. (now Maj Gen) Aleksey Arkhipovich Leonov (b. 20 May 1934) from *Voskhod 2* was the first person to engage in EVA ("extra-vehicular activity") on 18 Mar 1965. Capt. Bruce McCandless II (b. 8 Jun 1937; USN), from the space shuttle *Challenger*, was the first to engage in untethered EVA, at an altitude of 164 miles above Hawaii, on 7 Feb 1984. His MMU (Manned Maneuvering Unit) back-pack cost $15 million to develop. The first woman to perform an EVA was Svetlana Savitskaya from *Soyuz T12/Salyut 7* on 25 Jul 1985.

The first American to "walk" in space was Edward H. White II (1930–67) from the spacecraft *Gemini 4* on 3 Jun 1965. Between 3–7 Jun, White and James McDivitt completed 62 circuits in orbit around the Earth, and it was during the third orbit that White left the capsule and, using a 25-ft lifeline, maneuvered for 20 minutes in space.

The first American woman to "walk" in space was Kathryn D. Sullivan, on 11 Oct 1984, as part of the space shuttle *Challenger* mission 5–13 Oct 1984.

Duration record on the moon

The crew of *Apollo 17* collected a record 253 lb of rock and soil during their longest EVA of 22 hr 5 min. They were Capt. Eugene A. Cernan, USN (b. 14 Mar 1934) and Dr Harrison H. (Jack) Schmitt (b. 3 Jul 1935), who became the 12th man on the moon. The crew were on the lunar surface for 74 hr 59 min during this longest of lunar missions, which took 12 days 13 hr 51 min on 7–19 Dec 1972.

Longest spacewalk

The longest spacewalk was the second lunar EVA by Eugene Cernan and Jack Schmitt on *Apollo 17*. It lasted 7 hr 37 min. The longest recorded spacewalk in Earth orbit was made outside space shuttle *Discovery STS 511* in September 1985, lasting 7 hr 20 min, by James van Hoften and Bill Fisher, although this may have been exceeded by *Soyuz TM9's* Anatoli Solovyov and Alexander Balandin during an EVA outside the Mir space station on 1 Jul 1990.

■ **Largest crew**
On 30 Oct 1985, Challenger 9 STS 6A *lifted off with eight crew members aboard.* (Photo: NASA)

Chretien), at a secondary recovery site near Dzhezkazgan, Kazakhstan, USSR, on 21 Dec 1988, after a spaceflight lasting 365 days 22 hr 39 min 47 sec. The shortest manned flight was made by Cdr Alan B. Shepard, Jr. (USN) aboard *Mercury Redstone 3* on 5 May 1961. His suborbital mission lasted 15 min 28 sec.

The most experienced space traveler is Musa Manarov, who clocked up 500 days on two spaceflights in 1977–78 and 1990–91 on 14 Apr 1991. At the end of his *Soyuz TM11* mission on 20 May 1991 he had clocked 534 days in space.

United States Gerald P. Carr, Edward G. Gibson and William R. Pogue manned the longest American flight aboard *Skylab SL–4*, which was launched 16 Nov 1974 and splashed down 8 Feb 1975, after 2,017 hrs 15 min 32 sec in space.

Most journeys Capt. John Watts Young (USN ret.) (b. 24 Sep 1930) completed his sixth spaceflight on 8 Dec 1983, when he relinquished command of *Columbia STS 9/Spacelab* after a space career of 34 days 19 hr 41 min 53 sec.

Largest crew The largest crew on a single space mission was eight. This included one female and was launched on space shuttle *Challenger 9 STS 61A*, the 22nd shuttle mission, on 30 Oct 1985, carrying the German Spacelab D1 laboratory. The mission, commanded by Hank Warren Hartsfield, lasted 7 days 44 min 51 sec.

Most in space The greatest number of people in space at any one time has been 12, seven Americans aboard the space

shuttle *Columbia STS 35* and two Soviet spationauts aboard the Mir space station and two spationauts and one Japanese journalist aboard *Soyuz TM11* on 2–10 Dec 1990.

Lunar conquest Neil Alden Armstrong (b. 5 Aug 1930), command pilot of the *Apollo 11* mission, became the first man to set foot on the moon, on the Sea of Tranquility, at 02:56 and 15 sec GMT on 21 Jul 1969. He was followed out of the lunar module *Eagle* by Col. Edwin Eugene Aldrin, Jr., USAF (b. 20 Jan 1930) while the command module *Columbia*, piloted by Lt. Col. Michael Collins, USAF (b. 31 Oct 1930), orbited above.

Eagle landed at 20:17 and 42 sec GMT on 20 July and lifted off at 17:54 GMT on 21 July, after a stay of 21 hr 36 min. *Apollo 11* had blasted off from Cape Canaveral, FL at 13:32 GMT on 16 July and was a culmination of the US space program, which, at its peak, employed 376,600 people and attained in 1966–67 a record budget of $5.9 billion.

Altitude The greatest altitude attained by humans was when the crew of the *Apollo 13* were at apocynthion (i.e., their furthest point 158 miles above the lunar surface, and 248,655 miles above the Earth's surface) at 1:21 A.M. BST on 15 Apr 1970. The crew were Capt. James Arthur Lovell, Jr., USN (b. 25 Mar 1928), Fred Wallace Haise, Jr. (b. 14 Nov 1933) and John L. Swigert (1931–82).

The greatest altitude attained by an American woman is 381 miles by astronaut Kathryn D. Sullivan during her

flight in space shuttle *Discovery* on 24 Apr 1990.

Speed The fastest speed at which humans have traveled is 24,791 mph when the command module of *Apollo 10* carrying Col. (now Brig. Gen) Thomas Patten Stafford, USAF (b. 17 Sep 1930), and Cdr Eugene Andrew Cernan, USN (b. 14 Mar 1934) and Cdr (now Capt.) John Watts Young, USN (b. 24 Sep 1930), reached this maximum value at the 400,000 ft altitude interface on its trans-Earth round-trip flight on 26 May 1969.

The fastest speed recorded by a woman is 17,864 mph by Kathryn Sullivan at the start of reentry at the end of the *Discovery STS 31* shuttle mission on 29 Apr 1990. The highest recorded by a Soviet space traveler is 17,470 mph by Junior Lt (now Lt-Col.) Valentina Vladimirovna Tereshkova of the USSR in *Vostok 6* on 16 Jun 1983, although because orbital injection of Soyuz spacecraft occurs at marginally lower altitude, it is probable that Tereshkova's speed was exceeded twice by Svetlana Savistkaya aboard *Soyuz TM7* and *TM12* on 19 Aug 1982 and 17 Jul 1984.

First extraterrestrial vehicle The first wheeled vehicle landed on the moon was the unmanned *Lunokhod I*, which began its Earth-controlled travels on 17 Nov 1970. It moved a total of 6.54 miles on gradients up to 30° in the Mare Imbrium and did not break down until 4 Oct 1971. The lunar speed and distance record was set by the unmanned *Apollo 16* Rover, with 11.2 mph downhill and 22.4 miles.

Heaviest and largest space objects The heaviest object orbited is the *Saturn V* third stage of the *Apollo 15* spacecraft, which, prior to translunar injection into parking orbit, weighed 309,690 lb. The 442 lb US RAE (Radio Astronomy Explorer) B, or *Explorer 49*, launched on 10 Jun 1973, had, however, antennae 1,500 ft from tip to tip.

Most expensive project The total cost of the US manned space program up to and including the 28 Apr 1991 *Discovery* space shuttle mission has been estimated to be $76,982,400,000. The first 15 years of the USSR space program, from 1958 to September 1973, have been estimated to have cost $45 billion. The cost of the NASA shuttle program was $42.8 billion, including the launch of *Discovery*.

First reusable spacecraft The US space shuttle *Columbia STS 1*, the world's first reusable spacecraft, lifted off from its launch pad at Cape Canaveral, FL, on 12 Apr 1981 at 7 A.M. EST. After 36 orbits and 54 hours in space, the craft glided to a perfect landing on a dry lake bed at Edwards Air Force Base in the Mojave Desert, CA on 14 Apr at 1:21 P.M. EST. The craft was manned by John W. Young, USN and Robert L. Crippen. Through 28 Apr 1991 there were 40 space shuttle flights using four shuttle craft: *Columbia*, *Challenger*, *Discovery* and *Atlantis*. *Discovery* has flown the most times with 12 missions.

Building and Structures

Brick carrying

The greatest distance achieved for carrying a 9-lb brick in a nominated ungloved hand in an uncradled downward pincer grip is 61¾ miles, by Reg Morris of Walsall, Great Britain on 16 Jul 1985.

The women's record for a 9-lb-12-oz brick is 22½ miles, by Wendy Morris of Walsall, Great Britain on 28 Apr 1986.

Hod carrying

Russell Bradley of Worcester, Great Britain carried bricks totaling 456 lb 6 oz up a ladder of the minimum specified length of 12 ft on 28 Jan 1991 at Worcester City Football Club.

He also carried bricks with a total weight of 574.1 lb in a 105.8 lb hod a distance of 16 ft 5 in on level ground before ascending a runged ramp to a height of 7 ft at Worcester Rugby Club on 17 Mar 1991.

Buildings for Working

EARLIEST STRUCTURES

World The earliest-known human structure may be a windbreak. It is a rough circle of loosely piled lava blocks found on the lowest cultural level at the Lower Paleolithic site at Olduvai Gorge in Tanzania, revealed by Dr Mary Leakey in January 1960. The ring of several hundred stones was associated with artifacts and bones on a workfloor, dating from c. 1,750,000 B.C.

The earliest evidence of *buildings* yet discovered is that of 21 huts with hearths or pebble-lined pits and delimited by stake-holes found in October 1965 at the Terra Amata site in Nice, France, thought to belong to the Acheulian culture of c. 400,000 years ago. Excavation carried out between 28 Jun and 5 Jul 1966 revealed one hut with palisaded walls with axes of 49 ft and 20 ft.

The remains of a stone tower 20 ft high originally built into the walls of Jericho have been excavated and are dated to 5000 B.C. The foundations of the walls themselves have been dated to as early as 8350 B.C.

The oldest freestanding structures in the world are now believed to be the megalithic temples at Mgarr and Skorba in Malta. With those at Ggantija in Gozo, they date from c. 3250 B.C., some 3 ½ centuries earlier than the earliest Egyptian pyramid.

LARGEST

Construction project The Madinat Al-Jubail Al-Sinaiyah project in Saudi Arabia is believed to be the largest public works project in modern times. Construction started in 1976 for an industrial city covering 250,705 acres. At the peak of construction nearly 52,000 workers were employed, representing 62 nationalities. The total earth dredging and moving volume has reached 953.5 billion ft³, enough to construct a belt around the Earth at the equator 23 ft × 3.3 ft high. The seawater cooling system is believed to be the world's largest canal system, bringing 353 million ft³ of seawater per day to cool the industrial establishment.

Industrial The largest multilevel industrial building is the 15-level building developed for warehouse and container freight at Terminal 3, Port of Kwaichung, Hong Kong by Asia Terminals Ltd. The building measures 905.5 × 958 ft and 359.25 ft high. It has a total floor area of 9321851.4 ft² and a cubic capacity of 206,589,680 ft³. The entire area in each floor of the building is directly accessible by 45.92 ft container trucks, and the complex comprises 16.6 miles of roadway and 2,610 container truck parking bays.

Commercial The greatest ground area covered by any commercial building in the world under one roof is the flower auction building of the Co-operative VBA (Verenigde Bloemenveilingen Aalsmeer), Aalsmeer, Netherlands, with dimensions of 2,546 × 2,070 ft. The original floor surface of 84.82 acres was extended in 1986 to 91.05 acres.

The assembly plant with the largest cubic capacity in the world is the Boeing Company's main assembly plant at Everett, WA, completed in 1968, with a capacity of 200 million ft³.

Scientific The most capacious scientific building is the Vehicle Assembly Building (VAB) at Complex 39, the selected site for the final assembly and launching of the *Apollo* spacecraft on the Saturn V rocket, at the John F. Kennedy Space Center on Merritt Island, Cape Canaveral, FL. Construction was begun in April 1963 by the Ursum Consortium. It is a steel-framed building measuring 716 ft in length, 518 ft in width and 525 ft high. The building contains four bays, each with its own door 460 ft high. Its floor area is 343,500 ft² and its capacity is 129.5 million ft³. The building was "topped out" on 14 Apr 1965, the cost then amounting to $108,700,000.

Administrative The largest ground area covered by any office building is that of the Pentagon, in Arlington, VA. Built to house the US Defense Department's offices, it was completed on 15 Jan 1943 and cost an estimated $83 million. Each of the outermost sides is 921 ft long and the perimeter of the building is about 4,609.58 ft. Its five stories enclose a floor area of 6.5 million ft². The corridors total 17 miles in length and there are 7,748 windows to be cleaned. Twenty-nine thousand people work in the building, which has over 44,000 telephones connected by 160,000 miles of cable. Two hundred and twenty employees handle 280,000 calls a day. Two restaurants, six cafeterias, ten snack bars and a staff of 675 form the catering department.

Office The complex with the largest rentable space is the World Trade Center in New York City with a total of 4.37 million ft² in each of the twin towers, the taller of which, Tower Two (formerly B), is 1,368 ft high. The tip of the TV antenna on Tower One is 1,710 ft above street level and is thus 3 ft taller than the antennae on top of the Sears Tower. (See Tallest, below.)

Rentals The highest rentals in the world for prime offices, according to *World Rental Levels* by Richard Ellis of London, Great Britain, are in Tokyo, Japan at $187 per ft² per year (January 1990). With added service charges and rates Tokyo is also top at $204 per ft².

A typical apartment in the commercial and residential Kioicho building in Akasaka, Japan costs over $17,000 per month—payable ten months in advance!

TALLEST

The tallest office building in the world is the Sears Tower, national headquarters of Sears, Roebuck & Co. on Wacker Drive, Chicago, IL, with 110 stories rising to 1,454 ft. Its gross area is 4.4 million ft². Construction was started in August 1970 and it was "topped out" on 4 May 1973, having surpassed the World Trade Center in New York City in height at 2:35 P.M. on 6 Mar 1973 with the first steel column reaching to the 104th story. The addition of two TV antennae brought the total height to 1,707 ft. The building's population is 16,700, served by 103 elevators and 18 escalators. It has 16,000 windows.

SHALLOWEST

The shallowest commercial building is the 6-ft-wide, 100-ft-long Sam Kee Building at 8 West Pender, Vancouver, Canada. It was erected in 1912.

HABITATIONS

Greatest altitude The highest inhabited buildings in the world are those in the Indo-Tibetan border fort of Bāsisi by the Māna Pass (Lat. 31° 04′N, Long. 79° 24′E) at c. 19,700 ft.

In April 1961, however, a three-room dwelling was discovered at 21,650 ft on Cerro Llullaillaco (22,057 ft), on the Argentina–Chile border, believed to date from the late pre-Columbian period c.1480. A settlement on the T'e-li-mo trail in southern Tibet is sited at an altitude of 19,800 ft.

Northernmost The Danish scientific station set up in 1952 in Pearyland, northern Kalaallit Nunaat (Greenland) is over 900 miles north of the Arctic Circle. Inuit hearths dated to before 1000 B.C. were discovered in Pearyland in 1969. Polar Inuits were discovered in Inglefield Land, northwest Greenland in 1818.

The USSR's drifting research station "North Pole 15" passed within 1 ¼ miles of the North Pole in December 1967.

The most northerly continuously inhabited place is the Canadian Department of National Defense outpost at Alert on Ellesmere Island, Northwest Territories at Lat. 82° 30′ N, Long. 62° W, set up in 1950.

Southernmost The most southerly permanent human habitation is the United States' Amundsen–Scott South Polar Station, completed in 1957 and replaced in 1975.

EMBASSIES AND CIVIC BUILDINGS

Largest The USSR embassy on Bei Xiao Jie, Beijing, China, in the northeastern corner of the northern walled city, occupies the whole 45 acre area of the old Orthodox Church Mission (established 1728), now known as the *Beiguan*. It was handed over to the USSR in 1949.

United States The largest American embassy is in Bonn, Germany. It is 285,416 ft² in area.

EXHIBITION CENTERS

Largest The International Exposition Center in Cleveland, OH, the world's largest, is situated on a 175 acre site adjacent to Cleveland Hopkins International Airport in a building that measures 2.5 million ft². An indoor terminal provides direct rail access and parking for 10,000 cars.

SHOPPING CENTERS

The world's first shopping center was built in 1896 at Roland Park, Baltimore, MD.

The world's largest center is the $1.1 billion West Edmonton Mall in Alberta, Canada, which was opened on 15 Sep 1981 and completed four years later. It covers 5.2 million ft² on a 121 acre site and encompasses 828 stores and services as well as 11 major department stores. Parking is provided for 20,000 vehicles for more than 500,000 shoppers per week.

The world's largest wholesale merchandise mart is the Dallas Market Center on Stemmons Freeway, Dallas, TX, with nearly 9.3 million ft² in eight buildings. The complex covers 150 acres and houses some 3,400 permanent showrooms displaying merchandise of more than 26,000 manufacturers. The center attracts 600,000 buyers each year to its 38 annual markets and trade shows.

The longest mall in the world is part of the £40 million ($68 million) shopping center at Milton Keynes, Great Britain. It measures 2,133 ft².

INDUSTRIAL STRUCTURES

Tallest chimneys The Ekibastuz, USSR coal power plant No. 2 stack is 1,377 ft tall and was built at a cost of 7.89 million rubles. It was started on 15 Nov 1983 and completed on 15 Oct 1987 by the Soviet Building Division of the Ministry of Energy. The diameter tapers from 144.35 ft at the base to 46.58 ft at the top. It weighs 42,996 tons and became operational in 1991.

The $5.95 million International Nickel Company's stack at Copper Cliff, Sudbury, Ontario, Canada, completed in 1970 is 1,245 ft 8 in tall. It was built by Canadian Kellogg Ltd in 60 days, and the diameter tapers from 116.4 ft at the base to 51.8 ft at the top. It weighs 42,996 tons and became operational in 1971.

The world's most massive chimney is one of 1,148 ft at Puentes de Garcia Rodriguez, northwest Spain, built by M.W. Kellog Co. It contains 549,840 ft³ of concrete and 2.9 million lb of steel and has an internal volume of 6.7 million ft³.

Cooling towers The largest is that adjacent to the nuclear power plant at Uentrop, Germany, which is 590 ft tall, completed in 1976.

HANGARS

Largest Hangar 375 ("Big Texas") at Kelly Air Force Base, San Antonio, TX, completed on 15 Feb 1956, has four doors each 250 ft wide, 60 ft high and weighing 598 tons. The high bay area measures 2,000 × 300 × 90 ft and is surrounded by a 44 acre concrete apron.

Delta Airlines' jet base on a 140 acre site at Hartsfield International Airport, Atlanta, GA has a 36 acre roof area.

GRAIN ELEVATOR

Largest The single-unit elevator operated by the C-G-F Grain Co. at Wichita, KS consists of a triple row of storage tanks, 123 on each side of the central loading tower or "head house." The unit is 2,717 ft long and 100 ft wide. Each tank is 120 ft high, with an inside diameter of 30 ft, giving a total storage capacity of 20 million bushels of wheat.

The world's largest collection of grain elevators are the 23 at Thunder Bay, Ontario, Canada, on Lake Superior, with a total capacity of 103.9 million bushels.

SEWAGE WORKS

Largest The West-Southwest Treatment Plant, opened in 1940 on a site of 501 acres in Chicago, IL, serves an area containing 2,940,000 people. It treated an average of 835 million gal of waste per day in 1973 and the capacity of its sedimentation and aeration tanks is 45.2 trillion ft³.

WOODEN BUILDING

Largest The two US Navy airship hangars built in 1942–43 at Tillamook, OR are now used by the Louisiana-Pacific Corporation as a sawmill. They measure 1,000 ft long, 170 ft high at the crown and 296 ft wide at the base.

AIR-SUPPORTED BUILDING

Largest The 80,600-capacity octagonal Pontiac Silverdome Stadium, Pontiac, MI is 522 ft wide and 722 ft long. The air pressure is 5 lb/in² supporting the 10 acre translucent Fiberglas roofing. The structural engineers were Geiger-Berger Associates of New York City.

The largest standard size air hall (air-supported structure) is one 860 ft long, 140 ft wide and 65 ft high. One was first sited at Lima, OH, made by Irvin Industries of Stamford, CT.

Buildings for Living

WOODEN BUILDINGS

Oldest The oldest extant wooden buildings in the world are those comprising the Pagoda, Chumanar Gate and Temple of Horyu (Horyu-ji) at Nara, Japan, dating from c. A.D. 670 and completed in 715. The wood used was from 1,000-year-old Hinoki trees. The nearby Daibutsuden, built in 1704–11, once measured 285.4 ft long, 167.3 ft wide and 153.3 ft tall. Presently the dimensions are 188 × 165.3 × 159.4 ft.

CASTLES

Earliest The castle at Gomdan in Yemen originally had 20 stories and dates from before A.D. 100.

Largest The largest inhabited castle in the world is the royal residence of Windsor Castle at Windsor, Great Britain. It is primarily of 12th-century construc-

tion and is in the form of a waisted parallelogram measuring 1,890 × 540 ft.

Forts The largest ancient castle in the world is Hradčany Castle, Prague, Czechoslovakia, originating in the 9th century. It is an oblong irregular polygon with an axis of 1,870 ft and an average transverse diameter of 420 ft; it has a surface area of 18 acres.

Thickest walls Urnammu's city walls at Ur (now Muqayyar, Iraq), destroyed by the Elamites in 2006 B.C., were 88 ft thick and made of mud brick.

PALACES

Largest The Imperial Palace (Gu gong) in the center of Beijing, China, covers a rectangle 3,150 × 2,460 ft, an area of 177.9 acres. The outline survives from the construction of the third Ming emperor, Yung Lo (1402–24), but due to constant rearrangements most of the intramural buildings are 18th century. These consist of five halls and 17 palaces, of which the one occupied by the last empress until 1924 was the Palace of Accumulated Elegance (Chu xia gong).

The Palace of Versailles, 14 miles south-

■ **Highest rentals**
High-rise rents at the commercial and residential Kioicho building in Akasaka, Japan (above) are over $17,000 per month—payable ten months in advance! (Photo: Gamma/Wada)

Los Angeles was sold for a record $1.2 million per room, for a total cost of $110 million, to the Sekitei Kaihatsu Co. of Tokyo, Japan.

Most mobile The three-story brick Hotel Fairmount (built 1906) in San Antonio, TX, which weighed 1,714 tons, was moved on 36 dollies with pneumatic tires over city streets approximately five blocks and over a bridge, which had to be reinforced. The move by Emmert International of Portland, OR took four days, 30 Mar–2 Apr 1985, and cost $650,000.

Spas Spas are named after the town of Spa, a watering place in the Liège province of Belgium, where hydropathy was developed from 1626.

The largest spa, measured by number of available hotel rooms, is Vichy, Allier, France, with 14,000 rooms.

The highest French spa is Barèges, Hautes-Pyrénées, at 4,068 ft above sea level.

HOUSING

According to the National Association of Realtors, the median price of existing homes sold in the 83 largest metropolitan areas in the United States during the first quarter of 1990 was $91,700. The metropolitan with the highest median price was Honolulu, HI, at $367,500.

Largest house The 250-room Biltmore House in Asheville, NC is owned by George and William Cecil, grandsons of George Washington Vanderbilt II (1862–1914). The house was built between 1890 and 1895 in an estate of 119,000 acres, at a cost of $4.4 million; it is now valued at $5.5 million with 12,000 acres.

Most expensive The most expensive private house ever built is the Hearst Ranch at San Simeon, CA. It was built from 1922–39 for William Randolph Hearst (1863–1951), at a total cost of more than $30 million. It has more than 100 rooms, a 104-ft-long heated swimming pool, a 83-ft-long assembly hall and a garage for 25 limousines. The house required 60 servants to maintain it.

Highest price paid for residential property It was reported in June 1990 that entertainment mogul David Geffen had paid $47.5 million for the nine-acre Jack Warner estate in Beverly Hills, CA. The estate features "a French-style chateau, three-hole golf course, waterfall, a bevy of fountains, gardens and a tree-lined driveway."

Largest non-palatial residence St Emmeram Castle, Regensburg, Germany, valued at more than $177 million, contains 517 rooms with a floor space of 231,000 ft^2. Only 95 rooms are personally used by the family of the late Prince Johannes von Thurn und Taxis.

Longest continuous home construction Winchester House in San Jose, CA has been under construction for 38 years. The original house was an eight-room farmhouse with separate barn on the 161-acre estate of Oliver Winchester, who did not invent the Winchester rifle, but owned its patent. Sarah Winchester, widowed in 1886, consulted a psychic in Boston, who told her that she alone could

west of Paris, France, has a façade 1,902 ft in length, with 375 windows. The building, completed in 1682 for Louis XIV, occupied over 30,000 workmen under Jules Hardouin-Mansert (1646–1708).

Residential The palace (Istana Nurul Iman) of HM the Sultan of Brunei in the capital Bandar Seri Begawan, completed in January 1984 at a reported cost of $350 million, is the largest in the world, with 1,788 rooms and 257 lavatories. The underground garage accommodates the sultan's 110 cars.

Largest moat From plans drawn by French sources it appears that those which surround the Imperial Palace in Beijing (see above) measure 162 ft wide and have a total length of 10,800 ft. In all, the city's moats total 23 ½ miles.

HOTELS

Largest The $290-million Excalibur Hotel/Casino, NV, built on a 17 acre site, was opened in April 1990. It has 4,032 deluxe rooms and employs a staff of 4,000. Its facilites include seven theme restaurants and a total of 11 food outlets throughout the hotel and casino.

The Las Vegas Hilton, Reno, NV, built on a 63 acre site in 1974–81, has 3,174 rooms, 13 international restaurants and a staff of 3,600. It has a 10 acre rooftop recreation deck, a 48,000 ft^2 pillar-free ballroom and 125,000 ft^2 of convention space.

The Hotel Rossiya in Moscow opened in 1967 with 3,200 rooms, but because of its high proportion of dormitory accommodations, it is not now internationally listed among the largest hotels.

The Izmailovo Hotel complex, opened in July 1980 for the 22nd Olympic Games in Moscow, was designed to accommodate 9,500 people.

Hoteliers Following its acquisition of Holiday Inns North America in February 1990, Bass plc, Great Britain's largest brewing company, became the world's largest hotel operator. The company now owns, manages and franchises 1,697 hotels totaling 326,388 rooms in 50 countries. (See Business World—Brewers.)

Largest lobby The lobby at the Hyatt Regency, San Francisco, is 350 ft long, and 160 ft wide, and at 170 ft is the height of a 17-story building.

Tallest Measured from the street level of its main entrance to the top, the 741.9-ft-tall 73-story Westin Stamford in Raffles City, Singapore was "topped out" in March 1985. The $235 million hotel is operated by Westin Hotel Co. and owned by Raffles City Pte Ltd. However, the Westin at the Renaissance Center in Detroit, MI, is 748 ft tall when measured from the rear entrance.

Smallest Punta Grande Hotel, Las Puntas, Hierro Island, Tenerife in the Canary Islands has a total area of 6,459. ft^2. There are four double bedrooms looking on to a small terrace, a lounge, a bar-restaurant and a solarium. Reconstructed in 1987, the building is more than 150 years old.

Most expensive The Penthouse Suite in the Fairmont Hotel, San Francisco, CA can be rented for $6,000 per night, plus tax. The price includes an around-the-clock butler and maid, and airport limousine service. The suite was built in 1927 atop the Fairmont's main building. It has an immense drawing room with grand piano, a dining room accommodating up to 50, a two-story circular library with the celestial constellations in gold on a domed ceiling, a game room, three bedrooms and four bathrooms with 24-carat gold-plated fittings.

In May 1989 the 92-room Hotel Bel-Air in

balance the ledger for those killed by Winchester firearms by never stopping construction of the estate.

Mrs. Winchester moved to California, where she transformed the farmhouse into a mansion, which now has 13 bathrooms, 52 skylights, 47 fireplaces, 10,000 windows, 40 staircases, 2,000 doorways and closets opening into blank walls, secret passageways, trap doors, three $10,000 elevators and more. The house remodeling is intended to confuse the resident ghosts.

APARTMENTS

Tallest The 716-ft Metropolitan Tower on West 57 Street, New York City is 78 stories; the upper 48 are residential.

The tallest purely residential apartment house is Lake Point Tower, Chicago, IL, which has 879 units consisting of 70 stories and stands 639.4 ft high.

Buildings for Entertainment

STADIUMS

Largest The open Strahov Stadium in Prague, Czechoslovakia was completed in 1934 and can accommodate 240,000 spectators for mass displays of up to 40,000 Sokol gymnasts.

Football The Maracaña Municipal Stadium in Rio de Janeiro, Brazil, has a normal capacity of 205,000, of whom 155,00 can be seated. A crowd of 199,854 was accommodated for the World Cup final between Brazil and Uruguay on 16 Jul 1950. A dry moat, 7 ft wide and more than 5 ft deep, protects players from spectators and vice versa.

The largest stadium in the United States is the Rose Bowl, Pasadena, CA, which has a current seating capacity of 102,083. The largest crowd ever to attend an event there was 106,869 for the Rose Bowl game on New Year's Day, 1973. USC defeated Ohio State 42–27.

Covered The Azteca Stadium, Mexico City, opened in 1968, has a capacity of 107,000. Nearly all seats are under cover.

Retractable roof The world's largest covers the 54,000-seating-capacity Sky-Dome, Toronto, Ontario, Canada, completed in June 1989. The diameter is 679 ft.

Indoor The $173 million 273 ft tall Louisiana Superdome in New Orleans, LA, covering 13 acre, 273 ft high, was completed in May 1975. Its maximum seating capacity for conventions is 97,365, or 76,791 for football. Boxes rent for $35,000, excluding the price of admission. A gondola with six 25.98 ft TV screens produces instant replay.

Largest roof The transparent acrylic glass "marquee" roof over the Munich Olympic Stadium, Germany measures 914,940 ft² in area, resting on a steel net supported by masts.

The longest roof span in the world is the 680 ft diameter of the Louisiana Superdome in New Orleans, LA. The major axis of the elliptical Texas Stadium, completed in 1971 at Irving, TX, is, however, 787 ft 4 in.

Amusement resort *Largest* Disney World is set in 28,000 acres of Orange and Osceola counties, 20 miles southwest of Orlando in central Florida. It was opened on 1 Oct 1971 after a $400 million investment.

Most attended Disneyland, Anaheim, CA (opened 1955) received its 250-millionth visitor on 24 Aug 1985 at 9:52 A.M. Disneyland welcomed its 300-millionth visitor in 1989.

Largest pleasure beach Virginia Beach, VA has 28 miles of beachfront on the Atlantic and 10 miles of estuary frontage. The area embraces 255 miles² with 134 hotels and motels.

Piers *Origins* The origin of piers goes back to the origin of man-made harbors. The one at Caesarea reputedly had the first freestanding breakwaters in 13 B.C. However, it is possible that the structures associated with the "great harbors" of the ancient world in Crete, Alexandria and Carthage predate this.

Longest The longest pleasure pier in the world is Southend Pier at Southend-on-Sea, Great Britain. It is 1.34 miles in length and was first opened in August 1889, with final extensions made in 1929. In 1949–50 the pier had a peak 5.75 million visitors. The pier railroad closed in October 1978, and reopened on 2 May 1986.

Most piers The resort with the most piers was Atlantic City, NJ with seven, though currently only five remain: the Garden Pier (1912), Million Dollar (1906; now called Shops on Ocean One), Auditorium (1900; now the Steeplechase), Steel (1898) and Applegates (1883), now known as Central.

FAIRS

Earliest The earliest major international fair was the Great Exhibition of 1851 in the Crystal Palace, London, Great Britain, which in 141 days attracted 6,039,195 admissions.

Largest The site of the Louisiana Purchase Exposition at St Louis, MO covered 1,271.76 acres and there was an attendance of 19,694,855. The 1904 Olympic Games were also staged there.

Big wheel The original Ferris Wheel, named after its constructor, George W. Ferris (1859–96), was erected in 1893 at the Midway at the Chicago World's Fair for $385,000. It was 250 ft in diameter, 790 ft in circumference, weighed 1,283.8 tons and carried 36 cars each seating 60 people, making a total of 2,160 passengers. The structure was removed in 1904 to St Louis, MO for the Louisiana Purchase Exposition (see above) and was eventually sold as scrap for $1,800.

The largest-diameter wheel now operating is the Cosmoclock 21 at Yokohama City, Japan. It is 344.48 ft high and 328 ft in diameter, with 60 gondolas each with eight seats. With such features as illumination by laser beams and acoustic effects by sound synthesizers, the 60 arms holding the gondolas each serve as a second hand for the 42.65-ft-long electric clock mounted at the hub.

Roller coaster The maximum speeds claimed for switchbacks, scenic railroads or roller coasters have long been exaggerated for commercial reasons.

Longest The longest roller coaster in the world is *The Beast* at Kings Island near Cincinnati, OH. The run of 1.40 miles incorporates 800 ft of tunnels and a 540-degree banked helix.

Highest vertical drop The $8 million *Magnum XL-200*, opened in May 1989 at Cedar Point Park, Sandusky, OH, has a vertical drop of 194.8 ft on which a speed of 72 mph is reached. Cedar Point has nine coasters, making its total more than that of any other park.

Tallest The tallest is the *Moonsault Scramble* at the Fujikyu Highland Park, near Kawaguchi Lake, Japan, opened on 24 Jun 1983. It is 230 ft tall.

Wooden The latest design of Curtis D. Summers, who has already designed over 30 wooden coasters, is the *Texas Giant* at Six Flags over Texas, Arlington, TX. At its highest point it is 143 ft, with a top speed of up to 62 mph. It carries 28 passengers.

Tallest looping At its highest point 188 ft above the ground the *Viper* at Six Flags Magic Mountain, Valencia, CA

■ **Most expensive hotel suite**
The Penthouse suite at the Fairmont Hotel, San Francisco, CA costs $6,000 a night, plus tax. The suite was added to the hotel in 1927, 20 years after its construction, to the design of John Drum. The two-story circular library (left) has a domed ceiling with handpainted constellations of the heavens in gold leaf. Rich oak adorns the walls, and the doors are of the finest mahogany. (Photos: Fairmont Hotel)

Largest harem

The Winter Harem of the Grand Seraglio at Topkapi, Istanbul, Turkey was completed in 1589 and has 400 rooms. By the time Abdul Hamid II was deposed in 1909 the number of *carge* ("those who serve") had dwindled from 1,200 to 370 odalisques, with 127 eunuchs.

■ **Largest diameter Ferris wheel**
Cosmoclock 21 is 328 ft in diameter and 344.88 ft high. The 60 arms holding the gondalas serve as a second hand for the clock and light up one per second.

sends riders upside-down seven times over a 3,830 ft track.

Longest slide The Bromley Alpine Slide on Route 11 in Peru, VT, has a length of 4,600 ft and a vertical drop of 820 ft.

Night clubs The earliest night club (*boîte de nuit*) was "Le Bal des Anglais" at 6 rue des Anglais, Paris, France. Established in 1843, it closed *c.* 1960.

Largest Gilley's Club (formerly Shelly's), built in 1955, was extended in 1971 on Spencer Highway, Houston, TX, with a seating capacity of 6,000 under one roof covering 4 acres.

The largest night club in the world in the more classic sense of the term is The Mikado in the Akasaka district of Tokyo, Japan, with a seating capacity of 2,000. Binoculars are essential to an appreciation of the floor show.

Lowest The Minus 206 in Tiberias, Israel, on the shores of the Sea of Galilee, is 676 ft below sea level. An alternative candidate is the oft-raided "Outer Limits," opposite the Cow Palace, San Francisco, CA. It has been called "The Most Busted Joint" and "The Slowest to Get the Message."

Restaurants *Earliest* The Casa Botin was opened in 1725 in Calle de Cuchilleros 17, Madrid, Spain.

Largest The Tump Nak restaurant in Bangkok, Thailand consists of 65 adjoining houses built on 10 acres. A thousand waiters are available to serve the 3,000 potential customers.

Highest The highest restaurant in the world is in the Chacaltaya ski resort, Bolivia, at 17,519 ft.

Restaurateurs The world's largest restaurant chain is operated by McDon-

ald's Corporation of Oak Brook, IL, founded in 1955 by Ray A. Kroc (1902–84) after buying out the brothers Dick and "Mac" McDonald, pioneers of the fast-food drive-in. By April 1991 McDonald's licensed and owned 12,000 restaurants in 53 countries. Its largest outlet, and the first in the USSR, opened in Moscow on 31 Jan 1990, when 630 specially-trained local staff were faced with 20,000 Muscovites lining up for their first taste of *Big Mak* at the 700-seater restaurant. Worldwide sales in 1990 were $18.7 billion.

Fish and chip restaurant The world's largest fish and chip eatery is Harry Ramsden's at White Cross, Guiseley, Great Britain, with 140 employees serving 1 million customers per year, who consume 235 tons of fish and 392 tons of potatoes. On 30 Oct 1988, between 11:30 A.M. and 10:00 P.M., Harry Ramsden's celebrated its Diamond Jubilee by serving 10,182 servings of fish and chips at 1928 prices.

BARS

Largest The largest beer-selling establishment in the world is the "Mathäser," Bayerstrasse 5, Munich, Germany, where daily sales reach 84,470 pts. It was established in 1829, demolished in World War II and rebuilt by 1955. It now seats 5,500 people.

The beer consumption at the Dube beer halls in the Bantu township of Soweto, Johannesburg, South Africa may, however, be higher on some Saturdays when the average daily consumption of 48,000 pts is far exceeded.

Tallest bar Humperdink's Seafood and Steakhouse Bar in Dallas, TX is 25 ft 3 in high with two levels of shelving containing over 1,000 bottles. The lower level has four rows of shelves approximately 40 ft across and can be reached from floor level. If an order has to be met from the upper level, which has five rows of shelves, it is reached by climbing a ladder.

Longest bars The world's longest permanent bar is the 340-ft-long bar in "Lulu's Roadhouse," Kitchener, Ontario, Canada, opened on 3 Apr 1984. The "Bar at Erickson's," on Burnside Street, Portland, OR, in its heyday (1883–1920) possessed a bar measuring 684 ft that ran continuously around and across the main saloon. The chief bouncer, Edward "Spider" Johnson, had an assistant named "Jumbo" Reilly, who weighed 322 lb and was said to resemble "an ill-natured orangutan." Beer was five cents for 16 fluid ounces. Temporary bars of greater length have been erected.

Towers and Masts

TALLEST STRUCTURES

World The tallest structure in the world, the guyed Warszawa Radio mast at Konstantynow, 60 miles northwest of the capital of Poland, is 2,120 ⅔ ft tall

or more than four-tenths of a mile. It was completed on 18 Jul 1974 and put into operation on 22 Jul 1974. It was designed by Jan Polak and weighs 606 tons. The mast is so high that anyone falling off the top would reach terminal velocity and hence cease to be accelerating before hitting the ground. Work was begun in July 1970 on this tubular steel construction, with its 15 steel guy ropes. It recaptured for Europe, after 45 years, a record held in the United States since the Chrysler Building surpassed the Eiffel Tower in 1929.

TALLEST TOWERS

The tallest self-supporting tower (as opposed to a guyed mast) in the world is the $44 million CN Tower in Metro Center, Toronto, Ontario, Canada, which rises to 1,815 ft 5 in. Excavation began on 12 Feb 1973 for the erection of the 143,300 ton reinforced, post-tensioned concrete structure, which was "topped out" on 2 Apr 1975. The 416-seat restaurant revolves in the Sky Pod at 1,140 ft, from which the visibility extends to hills 74 ½ miles distant. Lightning strikes the top about 200 times (30 storms) per year.

The tallest tower built before the era of television masts is the Eiffel Tower in Paris, France, designed by Alexandre Gustav Eiffel (1832–1923) for the Paris Exhibition and completed on 31 Mar 1889. It was 985 ft 11 in tall, now extended by a TV antenna to 1,052 ⅓ ft, and weighs 8,090 tons. The maximum sway in high winds is 5 in. The whole iron edifice, which has 1,792 steps, took 2 years, 2 months and 2 days to build and cost 7,799,401 francs 31 centimes.

Bridges

Oldest Arch construction was understood by the Sumerians as early as 3200 B.C., and a reference exists to a Nile bridge in 2650 B.C.

The oldest surviving datable bridge in the world is the slab stone single-arch bridge over the River Meles in Izmir (formerly Smyrna) Turkey, which dates from *c.* 850 B.C.

LONGEST

Cable suspension The world's longest bridge span is the main span of the Humber Estuary Bridge, Humberside, Great Britain, at 4,626 ft. Work began on 27 Jul 1972, after a decision announced on 22 Jan 1966. The towers are 533 ft 1 ⅝ in tall and are 1 ⅜ in out of parallel to allow for the curvature of the Earth. Including the Hessle and the Barton side spans, the bridge stretches 1.37 miles. It was structurally completed on 18 Jul 1980 at a cost of £96 million ($192 million) and was opened by HM Queen Elizabeth II on 17 Jul 1981. Tolls range between 70 pence ($1.25) for motorcycles and £10.90 ($19.10) for heavy vehicles; pedestrians and pedal cyclists cross for free.

HIGHEST STRUCTURES IN THE UNITED STATES

Feet	Stories	Tower	Year
1,454	110	Sears Tower, Chicago, IL	1974
1,368	110	World Trade Center (North), New York City	1972
1,362	110	World Trade Center (South), New York City	1973
1,250	102	Empire State Building, New York City	1931
1,136	80	Amoco Building, Chicago, IL	1973
1,127	100	John Hancock Center, Chicago, IL	1968
1,046	77	Chrysler Building, New York City	1930
1,012	75	Library Square Tower, Los Angeles, CA	1989
1,000	79	Texas Commerce Plaza, Houston, TX	1982
970	71	Allied Bank Plaza, Houston, TX	1983

Council of Tall Buildings and Urban Habitat; Lehigh University, Bethlehem, PA

The Akashi-Kaikyo road bridge linking Honshū and Shikoku, Japan was started in 1988 and completion is planned for 1998. The main span will be 6,528 ft in length with an overall suspended length, with side spans, totaling 12,828 ft. Two towers will rise 974.40 ft above water level, and the two main supporting cables will be 1,100 mm in diameter, making both dimensions a world record.

The Seto-Ohashi double-deck road and rail bridge linking Kojima, Honshū with Sakaide, Shikoku, Japan opened on 10 Apr 1988 at a cost of $8.33 billion and 17 lives. The tolls for cars are $42 each way for the 12 ft spans and viaducts. The Minami Bisan-seto Bridge on this link has the world's longest suspension bridge span—3,609 ft for combined road-railroad traffic.

The longest cable-stayed bridge span in the world is the 1,608 ft Ikuchi Bridge in Japan between Honshu and Shikoku on the Onomichi-Imabari Route, completed in 1991.

The Tatara Bridge on the Onomichi-Imabari Route, Japan, is due for completion in 1999, and will be the leading long-span cable-stayed bridge in the world, with a main span of 2,920 ft.

The Mackinac Straits Bridge between Mackinac City and St Ignace, MI is the longest suspension bridge between anchorages (1.58 miles), and has an overall length, including approaches, of 5 miles.

United States The longest suspension bridge in the USA is the Verrazano–Narrows Bridge, which measures 4,260 ft. The bridge spans Lower New York Bay and connects Staten Island to Brooklyn. Construction was completed in 1964.

Cantilever The Quebec Bridge (Pont de Québec) over the St Lawrence River in Canada has the longest cantilever truss span of any in the world— 1,800 ft between the piers and 3,239 ft overall. It carries a railroad track and two carriageways. Begun in 1899, it was finally opened to traffic on 3 Dec 1917 at cost of 87 lives and Cdn$22.5 million.

United States The longest cantilever bridge in the USA is the John Barry

Bridge, in Chester, PA. It spans the Delaware River and measures 1,644 ft. Work was completed in 1974.

Steel arch The longest is the New River Gorge bridge, near Fayetteville, WV, completed in 1977, with a span of 1,700 ft.

Floating The longest is the Second Lake Washington Bridge, Evergreen, Seattle, WA. Its total length is 12,596 ft and its floating section measures 7,518 ft. It was built at a total cost of $15 million and completed in August 1963.

Covered The longest is that at Hartland, New Brunswick, Canada, measuring 1,282 ft overall, completed in 1899.

Bridge sale

The largest antique ever sold was London Bridge in Great Britain in March 1968. The sale was made by Ivan F. Luckin of the Court of Common Council of the Corporation of London to the McCulloch Oil Corporation of Los Angeles, CA for £1,029,000 ($2,469,600). The 11,810.5 tons of façade stonework were re-assembled, at a cost of $7.2 million at Lake Havasu City, AZ and rededicated on 10 Oct 1971.

Bridge building

British soldiers from the 35th Engineer Regiment based at Hameln, Germany constructed a bridge across a 26 ft gap using a five-bay single-story MGB (medium girder bridge) in 8 min 31 sec at Quebec Barracks, Osnabruck, Germany on 17 Oct 1989.

■ **Largest concrete dam**

The Grand Coulee Dam on the Columbia River, WA became operational on 22 Mar 1941. It weighs approximately 21.5 million tons, has a crest length of 4,173 ft, and is 550 ft high. (Photo: Telegraph Colour Library)

Railway The longest is the Huey P. Long Bridge, Metairie, LA, with a railroad section 23,235 ft long (4.4 miles), including approach roads. It has a 3-span tress: 529 ft, 790 ft and 531 ft, folllowed by a single span of 531.5 ft. It was completed on 16 Dec 1935.

Longest bridging The Second Lake Pontchartrain Causeway was completed on 23 Mar 1969, joining Lewisburg and Mandeville, LA. It has a length of 126,055 ft. It cost $29.9 million and is 228 ft longer than the adjoining First Causeway, completed in 1956.

Stone arch The longest stone arch bridge is the 3,810 ft-long Rockville Bridge north of Harrisburg, PA, with 48 spans containing 216,051 tons of stone. It was completed in 1901.

The longest stone arch span is the Planen Bridge in Germany at 295 ft.

Concrete arch The longest concrete arch is the Jesse H. Jones Memorial Bridge, which spans the Houston Ship Canal in Texas. Completed in 1982, the bridge measures 1,500 ft.

Widest The widest long-span bridge is the 1,650 ft Sydney Harbor Bridge, Australia (160 ft wide). It carries two electric overhead railroad tracks, eight lanes of roadway and bicycle and pedestrian lanes. It was officially opened on 19 Mar 1932.

The Crawford Street Bridge in Providence, RI has a width of 1,148 ft.

Bicycle bridge The longest bicycle bridge is over the 17 railroad tracks of Cambridge Station, Great Britain. It has a tower 114.82 ft high and two 164-ft-long approach ramps, and is 779.52 ft in length.

HIGHEST

The highest bridge in the world is over the Royal Gorge of the Arkansas River in Colorado, and is 1,053 ft above the water level. It is a suspension bridge with a main span of 880 ft and was constructed in six months, ending on 6 Dec 1929.

Railway The highest railroad bridge in the world is the Mala Rijeka viaduct of Yugoslav Railways at Kolasin on the Belgrade–Bar line. It is 650 ft high and was opened on 1 Jun 1976. It consists of steel spans mounted on concrete piers.

Road The road bridge at the highest altitude in the world, 18,380 ft, is the 98.4-ft-long Bailey Bridge, designed and constructed by Lt Col. S.G. Vombatkere and an Indian Army team in August 1982 near Khardung-La, in Ladakh, India.

TALLEST

The tallest bridge in the world is the Golden Gate Bridge, which connects San Francisco and Marin Co., CA. The towers of this suspension bridge extend 745 ft above the water. Completed in 1937, the bridge has an overall length of 9,266 ft.

AQUEDUCTS

Longest ancient The greatest of ancient aqueducts was the aqueduct of Carthage in Tunisia, which ran 87.6 miles from the springs of Zaghouan to Djebel Djougar. It was built by the Romans during the reign of Publius Aelius Hadrianus (A.D. 117–138). In 1895, 344 arches still survived. Its original capacity has been calculated at 7 million gal per day.

The tallest of the 14 arches of the Aguas Livres aqueduct, built in Lisbon, Portugal, in 1784 is 213 ¼ ft .

Longest modern The world's longest aqueduct, in the nonclassical sense of water conduit, excluding irrigation canals, is the California State Water Project aqueduct, completed in 1974, with a length of 826 miles, of which 385 miles is canalized.

Canals

Earliest Relics of the oldest canals in the world, dated by archaeologists c. 4000 B.C., were discovered near Mandali, Iraq early in 1968.

Longest The longest canal of the ancient world was the Grand Canal of China from Beijing to Hangzhou. It was begun in 540 B.C. and not completed until A.D. 1327, by which time it extended (including canalized river sections) for 1,107 miles. The estimated work force c. A.D. 600 reached 5 million on the Bian section. By 1950 it had been allowed to silt up to the point that it was nowhere more than 6 ft deep; however, it is now plied by vessels of up to 2,205 tons.

The Beloye More (White Sea) Baltic Canal from Belomorsk to Povenets, in the USSR, is 141 miles long and has 19 locks. It was completed with the use of forced labor in 1933. It cannot accommodate ships of more than 16 ft in draft.

The world's longest big-ship canal is the Suez Canal linking the Red and Mediterranean Seas, opened on 16 Nov 1869 but inoperative from June 1967 to June 1975. The canal was planned by the French diplomat Comte Ferdinand de Lesseps (1805–94) and work began on 25 Apr 1859. The work force consisted of 8,213 men and 368 camels. It is 100.6 miles in length from Port Said lighthouse to Suez Roads, and 197 ft wide.

The largest vessel to transit the Suez Canal has been SS *Settebello*, of 355,432 tons (length 1,110.3 ft; beam 188.1 ft at a maximum draft of 73.3 ft). This was southbound in ballast on 6 Aug 1986. USS *Shreveport* transited southbound on 15–16 Aug 1984 in a record 7 hr 45 min.

United States The longest canal in the USA is the Erie Barge Canal, connecting the Hudson River at Troy, NY, with Lake Erie at Buffalo, NY. It is 365 miles long, 150 ft wide and 12 ft in depth. The Erie Barge is part of the main waterway of the New York State Barge Canal System, which covers a distance of 525 miles.

Busiest The busiest ship canal is the Kiel Canal linking the North Sea, Great Britain with the Baltic Sea in Germany. Over 45,000 transits were recorded in 1987. Next comes the Suez Canal, with over 20,000 transits, and third the Panama Canal, with over 10,000.

Busiest in terms of tonnage of shipping using it is the Suez Canal, with nearly 440 million grt.

Longest artificial seaway The St Lawrence Seaway is 189 miles in length along the New York State–Ontario border from Montreal to Lake Ontario. It enables ships up to 728 ft long and 26.2 ft draft (some of which weigh 29,100 tons) to sail 2,342 miles from the North Atlantic up the St Lawrence estuary and across the Great Lakes to Duluth, MN. The project, begun in 1954, cost $470 million and the seaway was opened on 25 Apr 1959.

Longest irrigation The Karakumsky Kanal stretches 745.66 miles from Haun-Khan to Ashkhabad, Turkmenistan, USSR. The "navigable" length in 1991 will be 497 miles.

LOCKS

Largest The Berendrecht lock, which links the river Scheldt with docks at the port of Antwerp, Belgium, is the largest sea lock in the world. First used in April 1989, it has a length of 1,640.41 ft, a width of 223 ft and a sill level of 44.29 ft. Each of its four sliding lock gates weighs 1,771.5 tons. The total cost of construction was approximately BFr 12,000 million.

Deepest The Zaporojie on the Dnieperbug Canal, USSR can raise or lower barges at 128 ft.

United States The John Day dam lock

on the River Columbia, in Oregon and Washington State, was completed in 1963. It can raise or lower barges 113 ft and is served by a 1,100-ton gate.

Highest rise and longest flight The world's highest lock elevator overcomes a head of 225 ft at Ronquières on the Charleroi–Brussels Canal, Belgium. The two 236-wheeled caissons, each able to carry 1,510 tons, take 22 minutes to cover the 4,698-ft-long inclined plane.

Largest cut The Corinth Canal, Greece, opened in 1893, is 3.940 miles long, 26.24 ft deep, with an average depth of cutting of 1,003 ft over some 2.6 miles, and an extreme depth of 1,505 ft.

The Gaillard Cut (known as "the Ditch") on the Panama Canal is 270 ft deep between Gold Hill and Contractor's Hill with a bottom width of 500 ft. In one day in 1911 as many as 333 trains, each carrying 400 tons of earth, left this site.

Dams

Earliest The earliest-known dams were those uncovered by the British School of Archaeology in 1974 and at Jawa in Jordan in 1975. These stone-faced earthen dams are dated to *c.* 3200 B.C.

Most massive Measured by volume, the earth- and rock-filled Pati Dam on the Paraná River, Argentina has a volume of 8.4 billion ft^3. It is 108.6 miles in length and 118 ft high. This volume will be surpassed by the Syncrude Tailings dam in Canada with 19 billion ft^3.

Largest concrete The Grand Coulee Dam on the Columbia River, WA was begun in 1933 and became operational on 22 Mar 1941. It was finally completed in 1942 at a cost of $56 million. It has a crest length of 4,173 ft and is 550 ft high; 285 million ft^3 of concrete were used in its construction. It weighs approximately 21.5 million tons.

Highest The highest will be the 1,098-ft-high Rogunskaya earth-filled dam across the river Vakhsh, Tadzhikistan, USSR, with a crest length of only 1,975 ft and a volume of 3.002 billion ft^3. Preparations for building started in 1976, and construction began in March 1981. The completion date is set for early 1992. Meanwhile the tallest dam completed is the 984-ft-high Nurek dam, USSR, of 2.05 billion ft^3 volume.

United States The embankment-earthfill Oroville Dam is the United States' highest dam, reaching 754 ft and spanning the Feather River of California. It was completed in 1968.

Longest The 134 ½-ft-high Yacyreta–Apipe Dam across the Paraná on the Paraguay–Argentina border will extend for 43.24 miles. It is due for completion in 1992.

The Kiev Dam across the Dnieper,

Ukraine, USSR, completed in 1964, has a crest length of 256 miles. The Chapeton Dam under construction on the Paraná River, Argentina will have a crest length of 139 miles and is due to be completed in 1996.

In the early 17th century an impounding dam of moderate height was built in Lake Hungtze, Jiangsu, China, of a reputed length of 62 miles.

The longest sea dam in the world is the Afsluitdijk, stretching 20.195 miles across the mouth of the Zuider Zee in two sections of 1.553 miles (mainland of North Holland to the Isle of Wieringen) and 18.641 miles from Wieringen to Friesland. It has a sea-level width of 293 ft and a height of 24 ft 7 in.

Strongest On completion, the strongest will be the 803.8-ft-high Sayano-Shushenskaya Dam on the River Yenisey, USSR, which is designed to bear a load of 19.8 million tons from a fully filled reservoir of 1.1 trillion ft^3 capacity.

Largest reservoir The most voluminous man-made reservoir is the Bratskoe reservoir, on the Angara River in Siberia, USSR with a volume of 5978.74 ft^3 and an area of 2,111.98 $miles^2$. It extends for 372 miles with a width of 21 miles. It was filled in 1961–67.

The world's largest artificial lake measured by surface area is Lake Volta, Ghana, formed by the Akosombo Dam, completed in 1965. By 1969 the lake had filled to an area of 3,275 $miles^2$, with a shoreline 4,500 miles in length.

The completion in 1954 of the Owen Falls Dam near Jinja, Uganda, across the northern exit of the White Nile from the Victoria Nyanza, marginally raised the level of that natural lake by adding 218.9 million acre-feet, and technically turned it into a reservoir with a surface area of 17.2 million acres.

The $4-billion Tucurui Dam in Brazil of 2.27 billion ft^2 had, by 1984, converted the Tocantins River into a 1,180-mile-long chain of lakes.

United States The largest wholly artificial resevoir in the USA is Lake Mead in Nevada. It was formed by the Hoover Dam, which was completed in 1936. The lake has a capacity of 1,241,445 million ft^3 and a surface area of 28,255,000 acre–ft.

Largest polder (land reclaimed from the sea) Of the five great polders in the old Zuider Zee, Netherlands, the largest will be the Markerwaard, of 149,000 acres (232.8 $miles^2$). Work on the 66-mile-long surrounding dike was begun in 1957. The water area remaining after the erection of the 1927–32 dam (20 miles in length) is called IJsselmeer, and will have a final area of 487 ½ $miles^2$.

Largest levees The most massive ever built are the Mississippi levees, begun in 1717 but vastly augmented by the federal government after the disastrous floods of 1927. They extend for 1,732 miles

along the main river from Cape Girardeau, MO to the Gulf of Mexico and comprise more than 27 billion ft^3 of earthworks. Levees on the tributaries comprise an additional 2,000 miles.

Tunnels

LONGEST

Water-supply tunnel The longest tunnel of any kind is the New York City West Delaware water-supply tunnel, begun in 1937 and completed in 1944. It has a diameter of 13 ½ ft and runs for 105 miles from the Rondout Reservoir into the Hillview Reservoir, on the border of Yonkers, NY and New York City.

Rail The 33.46-mile-long Seikan Rail Tunnel was bored 787 ft beneath sea level and 328 ft below the seabed of the Tsugaru Strait between Tappi Saki, Honshū, and Fukushima, Hokkaidō, Japan. Tests started on the subaqueous section (14 ½ miles) in 1964 and construction began in June 1972. It was holed through on 27 Jan 1983 after a loss of 34 lives. The cost by the completion of tunneling after 20 years 10 months in March 1985 and subsequent maintenance to February 1987 was $8.3 billion. The first test run took place on 13 Mar 1988.

Proposals for a Brenner Base Tunnel between Innsbruck, Austria and Italy envisage a rail tunnel 36–39 miles long.

The Channel Tunnel, an electric railroad under the English Channel, is being constructed as a joint Anglo-French project at an estimated cost of £7.7 billion ($13.5 billion). Nonstop through trains, operated by the national railroads, will carry passengers and freight. The system will consist of three bored tunnels—two main tunnels each carrying a single railroad track and a central tunnel containing essential services such as electricity, ventilation and drainage. Some 23 miles will be under the sea and the journey will take about 35 minutes. The project is due for completion in 1993.

United States The longest main-line tunnel railroad in the USA is the Moffat Tunnel, which cuts through a 6.2 mile section of the Rocky Mountains in Colorado. Tunnel construction was completed in 1928.

Continuous subway The Moscow Metro underground railroad line from Medvedkovo to Bittsevsky is *c.* 23.55 miles long and was completed in early 1990.

Road tunnel The 10.14-mile-long two-lane St Gotthard road tunnel from Göschenen, Switzerland to Airolo, Italy opened to traffic on 5 Sep 1980. Nineteen lives were lost during its construction, begun in fall 1969, at a cost of SFr 686 million ($414 million).

United States The longest road tunnel in the USA is the 2.5 mile Lincoln Tunnel, linking New York City and New

Jersey. The tunnel was dug beneath the Hudson River and was completed in 1937.

Largest The largest-diameter road tunnel in the world is that blasted through Yerba Buena Island, San Francisco, CA. It is 76 ft wide, 56 ft high and 540 ft long. More than 90 million vehicles pass through on its two decks every year.

Hydroelectric irrigation The 51½-mile-long Orange–Fish Rivers tunnel, South Africa, was begun in 1967 at an estimated cost of £60 million ($144 million). It was completed in April 1973. The lining to a minimum thickness of 9 in will give a completed diameter of 17½ ft.

The Majes dam project in Peru involves 60.9 miles of tunnels for hydroelectric and water-supply purposes. The dam is at 13,780 ft altitude.

Sewerage The Chicago TARP (Tunnels and Reservoir Plan) in Illinois involves 120 miles of sewerage tunneling.

The Viikinmäki Central Treatment Plant in Helsinki, Finland is the world's first major waste-water plant to be built underground. It will involve the excavation of nearly 35,314 ft³ of rock before its completion in 1993.

Bridge-tunnel The Chesapeake Bay Bridge-Tunnel extends 17.65 miles from the Eastern Shore peninsula to Virginia Beach, VA. It cost $200 million and was completed in 42 months. It opened to traffic on 15 Apr 1964. The longest bridged section is Trestle C (4.56 miles long) and the longest tunnel section is the Thimble Shoal Channel Tunnel (1.09 miles).

Longest and largest canal-tunnel The Rove Tunnel on the Canal de Marseille au Rhône in the south of France was completed in 1927 and is 23,359 ft

Largest fumigation
Carried out during the restoration of the Mission Inn complex in Riverside, CA on 28 Jun–1 Jul 1987 to rid the buildings of termites, the fumigation was performed by Fume Masters Inc. of Riverside. Over 350 tarpaulins were used, each weighing up to 350 lb, and the operation involved completely covering the 70,000 ft² site and buildings—domes, minarets, chimneys and balconies, some of which exceeded 100 ft in height.

■ **Largest conspicuous sign**
Although dismantled in 1936, the world's most conspicuous sign was on the Eiffel Tower in Paris, France. The sign read Citroën and could be seen from a distance of 24 miles away. (Photo: Archiv Für Kunst)

long, 72 ft wide and 37 ft high. Built to be navigated by seagoing ships, it was closed in 1963 following a collapse of the structure and has not been reopened.

Oldest navigable The Malpas tunnel on the Canal du Midi in southwest France was completed in 1681 and is 528 ft long. Its completion enabled vessels to navigate from the Atlantic Ocean to the Mediterranean Sea via the river Garonne to Toulouse and the Canal du Midi to Sète.

Tunneling The longest unsupported example of a machine-bored tunnel is the Three Rivers water tunnel, 30,769 ft long with a 10.5 ft diameter, constructed for the city of Atlanta, GA from April 1980 to February 1982.

Specialized Structures

Largest Lego statue The sculpture of the Indian chief Sitting Bull, at the Legoland Park, Billund, Denmark, measures 25 ft to the top of the feather. The largest statue ever constructed from Lego, it required 1.5 million bricks, individually glued together to withstand the weather.

Advertising signs *Highest* The highest are the four Bank of Montreal logos at the top of the 72-story 935-ft-tall First Canadian Place, Toronto, Ontario, Canada. Each sign, built by Claude Neon Industries Ltd, measures 20 × 22 ft. The signs were lifted into place by helicopter.

The most conspicuous sign ever erected was the electric Citroën sign on the Eiffel Tower, Paris, France. It was switched on on 4 Jul 1925, and could be seen 24 miles away. It was in six colors with 250,000 lamps and 56 miles of electric cables. The letter "N" that terminated the name "Citroën" between the second and third levels measured 68 ft 5 in in height. The sign was dismantled in 1936.

Neon The longest is the letter "M" installed on the Great Mississippi River Bridge, Old Man River at Memphis, TN. It is 1,800 ft long and comprises 200 high-intensity lamps.

The largest neon sign measures 210 × 55 ft and was built for Marlboro cigarettes at Hung Hom, Kowloon, Hong Kong in May 1986. It contains 35,000 ft of neon tubing and weighs approximately 126 tons.

An interior-lit fascia advertising sign in Clearwater, FL completed by the Adco Sign Corp in April 1983 measured 1,168 ft 6½ in in length.

Billboards The world's largest billboard is Bassat Ogilvy Promotional Campaigns for Ford España, measuring 475 ft 9 in in length and 78 ft 9 in in width. It is sited at Plaza de Toros Monumental de Barcelona, Barcelona, Spain.

Illuminated The world's longest illumi-

nated sign measures 196 ft 7½ in × 65.6 ft. It is illuminated by 62,400 W metal-halide projectors and was erected by Abudi Signs Industry Ltd of Israel.

Animated The world's most massive is the one outside the Circus Circus Hotel, Reno, NV, and is named Topsy the Clown. It is 127 ft tall and weighs over 45 tons, with 1.4 miles of neon tubing. Topsy's smile measures 14 ft across.

Longest airborne Reebok International Ltd of Massachusetts flew a banner from a single-seater plane which read "Reebok Totally Beachin'." The banner measured 50 ft in height and 100 ft in length, and was flown from 13–16 and 20–23 Mar 1990 for four hours each day at Daytona Beach, FL.

Bonfire The largest was constructed in Espel, in the Noordoost Polder, Netherlands. It stood 91 ft 5 in high with a base circumference of 276 ft 11 in and was lit on 19 Apr 1987.

Breakwater The world's longest breakwater is the one that protects the Port of Galveston, TX. The granite South Breakwater is 6.74 miles in length.

Buildings demolished by explosives The largest was the 21-story Traymore Hotel, Atlantic City, NJ on 26 May 1972 by Controlled Demolition Inc. of Towson, MD. This 600-room hotel had a cubic capacity of 6.5 million ft³.

The tallest chimney ever demolished by explosives was the Matla Power Station chimney, Kriel, South Africa, on 19 Jul 1981. It stood 902 ft and was brought down by the Santon (Steeplejack) Co. Ltd of Greater Manchester, Great Britain.

Cemetery *Largest* Rookwood Necropolis, New South Wales, Australia is the largest cemetery, covering an area of 728 acres, with over 575,536 interments. It has been in continuous use since 1867.

The United States' largest cemetery is Arlington National Cemetery, which is situated on the Potomac River in Virginia, directly opposite from Washington, D.C. It is 612 acres in extent and more than 200,000 members of the armed forces are buried there. Presidents William Howard Taft and John Fitzgerald Kennedy are also buried there.

Tallest The permanently illuminated Memorial Cemitério Ecumencio, São Paulo, Brazil is 10 stories high, occupying an area of 4.448 acres. When full, the final capacity will be 20,000.

Tallest columns The tallest are the thirty-six 90-ft-tall fluted pillars of Vermont marble in the colonnade of the Education Building, Albany, NY. Their base diameter is 6½ ft.

The tallest load-bearing stone columns in the world are those measuring 69 ft in the Hall of Columns of the Temple of Amun at Karnak, opposite Thebes on the Nile, the ancient capital of Upper Egypt. They were built in the 19th dynasty in the reign of Rameses II c. 1270 B.C.

Crematorium The largest crematorium in the world is at the Nikolo-Arkhangelskoye Cemetery, east Moscow, USSR with seven twin cremators of British design, completed in March 1972. It has several Halls of Farewell for atheists.

Dome The largest is the Louisiana Superdome, New Orleans, which has a diameter of 680 ft.

The largest dome of ancient architecture is that of the Pantheon, built in Rome in A.D. 112, with a diameter of 142 ½ ft.

Doors *Largest* The four doors in the Vehicle Assembly Building near Cape Canaveral, FL have a height of 460 ft.

Heaviest The heaviest is that of the laser target room at Lawrence Livermore National Laboratory, CA. It weighs 360 tons, is up to 8 ft thick and was installed by Overly.

Largest dry dock With a maximum shipbuilding capacity of 1.34 million tons dwt, the Daewoo Okpo No. 1 Dry Dock, Koje Island in South Korea measures 1,738.84 ft long × 430 ft wide and was completed in 1979. The dock gates, 46 ft high and 32.8 ft thick at the base, are the world's most massive.

Largest earthworks The largest prior to the mechanical era were the Linear Earth Boundaries of the Benin Empire in the Bendel state of Nigeria. Their existance was first reported in 1900 and partially surveyed in 1967. In April 1973 it was estimated by Patrick Darling that the total length of the earthworks was probably between 4,000 and 8,000 miles, with the amount of earth moved estimated at 13.4–16 billion ft^3.

Fence *Longest* The dingo-proof wire fence enclosing the main sheep areas of Australia is 6 ft high, 1 ft underground and stretches for 3,437 miles. The Queensland state government discontinued full maintenance in 1982.

Tallest The world's tallest fences are security screens 65.6 ft high erected by Harrop-Allin of Pretoria, South Africa in November 1981 to protect fuel depots and refineries at Sasolburg from terrorist rockets.

Tallest flagpole Erected outside the Oregon Building at the 1915 Panama-Pacific International Exposition in San Francisco, CA, and trimmed from a Douglas fir, the flagpole stood 299 ft 7 in in height and weighed 51.8 tons.

The tallest unsupported flagpole in the world is the 282-ft-tall steel pole weighing 120,000 lb, which was erected on 22 Aug 1985 at the Canadian Expo 86 exhibition in Vancouver, British Columbia and supports a gigantic ice hockey stick 205 ft in length. Sherrold Haddad of Flag Chevrolet Oldsmobile Ltd was instrumental in moving and reconstructing the flagpole at its present location at the company's premises on 104th Avenue, Surrey, British Columbia.

Tallest fountain The tallest is the fountain at Fountain Hills, AZ, built at a cost of $1.5 million for McCulloch Properties Inc. At full pressure of 375 lb/in^2 and at a rate of 5,828 gal/min, the 560-ft-tall column of water weighs more than 8.8 tons. The nozzle speed achieved by the three 600 hp pumps is 146.7 mph.

Largest gas tank The largest gas tanks are at Fontaine L'Eveque, Belgium, where disused mines have been adapted to store up to 17.6 billion ft^3 of gas at ordinary pressure.

Probably the largest conventional gas tank is that at Wien-Simmering, Vienna, Austria, completed in 1968, with a height of 275 ft and a capacity of 10.59 million ft^3.

Longest deep-water jetty The Quai Hermann du Pasquier at Le Havre, France, with a length of 5,000 ft, is part of an enclosed basin and has a constant depth of water of 32 ft on both sides.

Lamppost The tallest lighting columns are the four made by Petitjean & Cie of Troyes, France and installed by Taylor Woodrow at Sultan Qaboos Sports Complex, Muscat, Oman. They stand 208 ft 4 in high.

Lighthouse *Tallest* The 348 ft steel tower near Yamashita Park in Yokohama, Japan has a power of 600,000 candelas and a visibility range of 20 miles.

Greatest range The lights with the greatest range are those 1,089 ft above the ground on the Empire State Building, New York City. Each of the four-arc mercury bulbs has a rated candlepower of 450 million, visible 80 miles away on the ground and 300 miles away from aircraft.

Marquee *Largest* A marquee covering an area of 188,368 ft^2 (4.32 acres) was erected by the firm of Deuter of Augsburg, Germany for the 1958 "Welcome Expo" in Brussels, Belgium.

Maze The oldest datable representation of a labyrinth is that on a clay tablet from Pylos, Greece c.1200 B.C.

The world's largest hedge maze is the one at Longleat, near Warminster, Wiltshire, Great Britain, designed for Lord Weymouth by Greg Bright, which has 1.69 miles of paths flanked by 16,180 yew trees. It was opened on 6 Jun 1978 and measures 381 × 187 ft.

"Il Labirinto" at Villa Pisani, Stra, Italy, in which Napoleon was "lost" in 1807, had 4 miles of pathways.

Menhir *(prehistoric upright monolith)* The tallest found is the 418.8 ton Grand Menhir Brisé, now in four pieces, which originally stood 72 ft high at Locmariaquer, Brittany, France. Recent research suggests a possible 75-ft-high menhir, in three pieces, weighing 280 tons, also at Locmariaquer.

Monuments *Tallest* The stainless-steel Gateway to the West arch in St Louis, MO, completed on 28 Oct 1965 to commemorate the westward expansion after the Louisiana Purchase of 1803, is a sweeping arch spanning 630 ft and rising to the same height of 630 ft. It cost $29 million. It was designed in 1947 by the Finnish-American architect Eero Saarinen (1910–61).

Tallest column Constructed from 1936–39, at a cost of $1.5 million, the tapering column that commemorates the Battle of San Jacinto (21 Apr 1836), on the bank of the San Jacinto River near Houston, TX, is 570 ft tall, 47 ft square at the base, and 30 ft square at the observation tower, which is surmounted by a star weighing 220 tons. It is built of concrete with buff limestone, and weighs 35,150 tons.

The largest trilithons exist at Stonehenge, to the south of Salisbury Plain, Wiltshire, Great Britain, with single sarsen blocks weighing over 49.6 tons and requiring over 550 men to drag them up a 9 degree gradient. The earliest stage of the construction of the ditch has been dated to 2800 B.C. Whether Stonehenge, which required some 30 million man-years, was

Demolition work
Fifteen members of the Black Leopard Karate Club demolished a seven-room wooden farmhouse west of Elnora, Alberta, Canada in 3 hr 18 min by foot and unaided hand on 13 Jun 1982.

Grave digging
It is recorded that Johann Heinrich Karl Thieme, sexton of Aldenburg, Germany, dug 23,311 graves during a 50-year career. In 1826 his understudy dug *his* grave.

Garbage dump
Reclamation Plant No. 1, Fresh Kills, Staten Island, NY, opened in March 1974, is the world's largest sanitary landfill. In its first four months of operation 503,751 tons of refuse from New York City carried by 700 barges was dumped on the site.

SPECIALIZED STRUCTURES

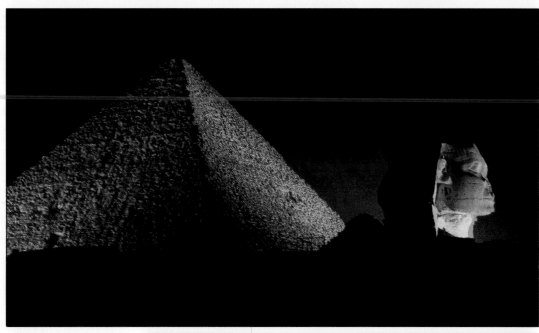

Largest revolving globe
The 33-ton 32.81-ft diameter sphere called "Globe of Peace" was built in five years, from 1982 to 1987, by Orfeo Bartolucci from Apecchio, Pesaro, Italy.

built as a place of worship, as a lunar calendar, as an eclipse predictor, or as a navigation school is still debated.

Largest artificial mound The gravel mound built as a memorial to the Seleucid King Antiochus I (r. 69–34 B.C.) stands on the summit of Nemrud Dagi (8,182 ft), southeast of Malatya, eastern Turkey. It measures 197 ft tall and covers 7.5 acres.

Naturist resort *Oldest* The oldest resort is Der Freilichtpark, Klingberg, Germany, established in 1903.

The center Helio-Marin at Cap d'Agde, southern France, which covers 222 acres, is visited by 100,000 people each year.

Largest standing obelisk (monolithic) The "skewer" or "spit" (from the Greek *obeliskos*) of Tuthmosis III brought from Aswan, Egypt by Emperor Constantius in the spring of A.D. 357 was repositioned in the Piazza San Giovanni in Laterane, Rome on 3 Aug 1588. Once 118.1 ft tall, it now stands 107.6 ft and weighs 501.5 tons.

The unfinished obelisk, probably commissioned by Queen Hatshepsut c. 1490 B.C., at

Aswan, Egypt is 136.8 ft in length and weighs 1,287 tons.

The obelisk that has remained *in situ* for the longest time is the one still standing at Heliopolis, near Cairo, erected by Senwosret I c.1750 B.C.

Tallest The world's tallest obelisk is the Washington Monument in Washington, D.C. Situated in a 106 acre site and standing 555 ft 5 1/8 in high, it was built to honor George Washington (1732–99), the first President.

Longest piers The Dammam Pier, Saudi Arabia, on the Persian Gulf, with an overall length of 6.79 miles, was begun in July 1948 and completed on 15 Mar 1950. The area was subsequently developed by 1980 into the King Abdul Aziz Port, with 39 deep-water berths. The original causeway, greatly widened, and the port extend for 7.95 miles.

Longest covered promenade The Long Corridor in the Summer Palace in Beijing is a covered promenade running for 2,388.45 ft. It is built entirely of wood and divided by crossbeams into 273 sections. These crossbeams, as well as the ceiling

and side pillars, have over 10,000 paintings of famous Chinese landscapes, episodes from folk tales, and flowers and birds.

Pyramid *Largest* The largest pyramid, and the largest monument ever constructed, is the Quetzalcóatl at Cholula de Rivadabia, 63 miles southeast of Mexico City. It is 177 ft tall and its base covers an area of nearly 45 acres. Its total volume has been estimated at 116.5 million ft^3 compared with 88.2 million ft^3 for the Pyramid of Khufu or Cheops (a fourth dynasty Eyptian pharoah).

The largest-known single block comes from the Third Pyramid (Pyramid of Mycerinus) and weighs 320 tons.

Oldest The Djoser step pyramid at Saqqâra, Egypt, constructed by Imhotep to a height of 204 ft, and originally with a Tura limestone casing, dates from c. 2680 B.C.

The oldest New World pyramid is that on the island of La Venta in southeastern Mexico, built by the Olmec people c. 800 B.C. It stands 100 ft tall with a base dimension of 420 ft.

Scaffolding The largest freestanding scaffolding is believed to be the one erected for the restoration of the Goldstone antenna in California. It was 170 ft high, 70 ft deep and went 180 ft around the circumference of the structure.

Scarecrow The tallest scarecrow ever built was "Stretch II," constructed by the Speers family of Paris, Ontario, Canada and a crew of 15 at the Paris, Ontario Fall Fair on 2 Sep 1989. It measured 103 ft 6 3/4 in in height.

Snow and ice constructions A snow palace 87 ft high, one of four structures which together spanned 702.7 ft, was unveiled on 7 Feb 1987 at Asahikawa City, Hokkaidō, Japan.

The world's largest ice construction was the ice palace built in January 1986, using 9,000 blocks of ice, at St Paul, MN during the Winter Carnival. Designed by Ellerbe Associates Inc., it stood 128 ft 9 in high—the equivalent of a 13-story building.

Snowman The tallest was Fubukikun, the Blizzard Man, built by villagers of Sumon and Niigata, Japan between March and April 1990, which stood 66.92 ft tall.

United States "Super Frosty," built by a team in Anchorage, AK led by Myron L. Ace between 20 Feb and 5 Mar 1988, stood 63.56 ft.

Longest stairway The service staircase for the Niesenbahn funicular near Spiez, Switzerland rises to 7,759 ft. It has 11,674 steps and a bannister.

The stone-cut Taichan temple stairs of 6,600 steps in the Shandong Mountains, China ascend 4700 ft.

The tallest spiral staircase is on the outside of the chimney Bobila Almirall located in Angel Sallent in Tarrasa, Barcelona, Spain. Built by Mariano

Masana i Ribas in 1956, it is 207.34 ft high and has 217 steps.

The longest spiral staircase is one 1,103 ft deep with 1,520 steps installed in the Mapco-White County Coal Mine, Carmi, IL by Systems Control Inc. in May 1981.

Statue Longest Near Bamiyan, Afghanistan there are the remains of the recumbent Sakya Buddha, built of plastered rubble, which was "about 1,000 ft" long and is believed to date from the 3rd or 4th century A.D.

Tallest A full-figure statue, that of "Motherland," an enormous prestressed concrete female figure on Mamayev Hill, outside Volgograd, USSR, was designed in 1967 by Yevgeny Vuchetich, to commemorate victory in the Battle of Stalingrad (1942–43). The statue from its base to the tip of the sword clenched in the right hand measures 270 ft.

The statue of Maitreya is carved out of a single piece of wood from a white sandalwood tree and it stands 85.30 ft high. It is located northwest of Beijing at the Lama Temple (Yonghegong), built in 1649. The Imperial Court took two years to carve the statue in the Pavilion House of Ten Thousand Fortunes and finished the project in 1750.

United States The Statue of Liberty, originally named Liberty Enlightening the World, is the tallest statue in the United States. Designed and built in France to commemorate the friendship of the two countries, the 152 ft statue was shipped to New York City, where its copper sheets were assembled. President Grover Cleveland accepted the statue for the USA on 28 Oct 1886.

The statue, which became a national monument in 1924, stands on Liberty Island in Upper New York Bay. The base of the statue is an eleven-pointed star; a 150 ft pedestal is made of concrete faced with granite. The statue was closed to the public on 23 Jun 1985 in order to complete restoration work, at a cost of $698 million. The statue was officially reopened by President Ronald Reagan on 4 Jul 1986 during a weekend-long celebration of the statue's 100th birthday.

Tallest swing A glider swing 30 ft high was constructed by Kenneth R. Mack, Langenburg, Saskatchewan, Canada for Uncle Herb's Amusements. The swing is capable of taking its four sides 25 ft off the ground.

Largest tomb The Mount Li tomb, belonging to Zeng, the first emperor of China, dates to 221 B.C. and is situated 25 miles east of Xianyang. The two walls surrounding the grave measure 7,129 × 3,195 ft and 2,247 × 1,896 ft. Several pits in the tomb contained a vast army of an estimated 8,000 life-sized terracotta soldiers.

A tomb housing 180,000 World War II dead on Okinawa, Japan was enlarged in 1985 to accommodate another 9,000 bodies thought to be buried on the island.

Totem pole A 173-ft-tall pole was raised on 6 Jun 1973 at Alert Bay, British Columbia, Canada. It tells the story of the Kwakiutl tribe and took 36 man-weeks to carve.

Vats Largest The largest wooden wine cask in the world is the Heidelberg Tun, completed in 1751, in the cellar of the Friedrichsbau, Heidelberg, Germany. Its capacity is 40,790 gal.

"Strongbow," used by H. P. Bulmer Ltd, the English cider-makers of Hereford,

SPECIALIZED STRUCTURES

operated by the Elizabethtown Water Co.

Largest waterwheel The Mohammadieh Noria wheel at Hamah, Syria has a diameter of 131 ft and dates from Roman times.

Largest window The largest sheet of glass ever manufactured was one of 538.2 ft², or 65 ft 7 in by 8 ft 2 ¼ in, exhibited by the Saint Gobin Co. in France at the *Journées Internationales de Miroiterie* in March 1958.

The largest single windows in the world are those in the Palace of Industry and Technology at *Rondpoint de la Défense*, Paris, France, with an extreme width of 715.2 ft and a maximum height of 164 ft.

The largest sheet of tempered (safety) glass ever processed was one made by P.T. Sinar Rasa Kencana of Jakarta, Indonesia. It measures 22.96 ft long by 7.02 ft wide and is 0.05 in thick.

Largest wine cellar The cellars at Paarl, those of the Ko-operative Wijnbouwers Vereeniging, known as KWV, near Cape Town, in the center of the wine-growing district of South Africa, cover an area of 25 acres and have a capacity of 30 million gal.

The Cienega Winery of the Almaden Vineyards in Hollister, CA covers 4 acres and can house 37,300 oak barrels containing 1.83 million gallons of wine.

Ziggurat The largest ziggurat (from the Assyrian *ziqqurati*, meaning summit, height) ever built was that of the Elamite King Untas, *c.* 1250 B.C., known as the Ziggurat of Choga Zanbil, 18.6 miles from Haft Tepe, Iran. The outer base was 344 × 344 ft and the fifth "box" 91.8 × 91.8 ft, nearly 164 ft above.

The largest partially surviving ziggurat is the Ziggurat of Ur (now Muquyyar, Israel) with a base 200 × 150 ft, built to three stories and surmounted by a summit temple. The first and part of the second stories now survive to a height of 60 ft. It was built in the reign of Ur-nammu (*c.* 2113–2096 B.C.).

■ **Tallest wooden statue**
Above: This magnificent statue of Maitreya is carved out of a single white sandalwood tree standing 85.30 ft high. It is situated in the Pavilion House of Ten Thousand Fortunes of the Lama Temple northwest of Beijing, China. (Photo: Beijing Tourist Office).

■ **Largest waterwheel**
Right: The Mohammadieh Noria wheel at Hamah, Syria has a wheel diameter of 131 ft. (Photo: Explorer)

Window cleaning
Keith Witt of Amarillo, TX cleaned three standard 42½ × 47 in office windows with an 11.8-in-long squeegee and 1.98 gal of water in 10.50 sec on 21 Jan 1990 in Orlando, FL.

Great Britain, measures 64 ½ ft in height and 75 ½ ft in diameter, with a capacity of 1.6 million gal.

Oldest The world's oldest is that in use ut-Rhin, Germany by 12 generations of the family.

Longest wall The Great Wall of China has a main-line length of 2,150 miles. Completed during the reign of Qin Shi Huangdi (221–210 B.C.), it has a further 1,780 miles of branches and spurs. Its height varies from 15–39 ft and it is up to 32 ft thick. It runs from Shanhaikuan, on the Gulf of Bohai, to Yumenkuan and Yang-guan, and was kept in repair up to the 16th century. Some 32 miles of the wall have been destroyed since 1966 and part of the wall was blown up to make way for a dam in July 1979. On 6 Mar 1985 a report from China stated that a five-year survey proved that the total length had been 6,200 miles. In October 1990 it was reported that after two years of struggle Lin Yu-tian became the first person to walk its entire length, and the average pedometer reading indicated a length of 3,415 miles.

Indoor waterfall The tallest indoor waterfall measures 114 ft in height and consists of 2,525 ft² of marble. It is situated in the lobby of Greektown's International Center Building, Detroit, MI.

Water tower The Union water tower in New Jersey, built in 1965, rises to a height of 210 ft, with a capacity of 250,000 gal. The tower is owned and

Transport

■ **Previous page**
Balloons in flight (Photo: All Sport/Vandystadt)

■ **Marine circumnavigations**
David Scott Cowper holds a record for the first circumnavigation via the Northwest Passage (see table on page 136). This picture shows him off Cape Town, South Africa. (Photo: Gamma)

Ships

EARLIEST SEAGOING BOATS –

Aborigines are thought to have been able to cross the Torres Strait from New Guinea to Australia, then at least 43 ½ miles across, as early as 60,000 B.C. They are believed to have used double canoes.

The earliest surviving "vessel" is a pinewood dugout found in Pesse, Netherlands and dated to *c.* 6315 B.C. ± 275, now in the Provincial Museum, Assen.

The earliest representation of a boat is a matter for dispute; there are possible rock-art outlines of Mesolithic skin-boats in Høgnipen, Norway (*c.* 8000–7000 B.C.); in Minateda, Spain (7000–3000 B.C.); and in Kobystan, USSR (8000–6000 B.C.).

An 18-in-long paddle was found at the Star Carr site in Great Britain, discovered in 1948. It has been dated to *c.* 7600 B.C. and is now in the Cambridge Museum of Archaeology, Great Britain.

The oldest surviving boat is a 27-ft-long 2 ½-ft-wide wooden eel-catching canoe discovered at Tybrind Vig on the Baltic island of Fünen, which is dated to *c.* 4490 B.C.

The oldest shipwreck ever found is one of a Cycladic trading vessel located off the islet of Dhókós, near the Greek island of Hydra, reported in May 1975 and dated to 2450 B.C. ± 250.

A wreck about 2,400 years old is currently being excavated in the crater of a live volcano off the northern coast of Sicily. The cargo includes large quantities of classical Greek pottery.

Earliest power Marine propulsion by steam engine was first achieved when in 1783 the Marquis Claude-François-Dorothée Jouffroy d'Abbans (1751–1832) ascended a reach of the river Saône near Lyons, France, in the 198-ton paddle wheeler *Pyroscaphe.*

The tug *Charlotte Dundas* was the first successful power-driven vessel. She was a stern paddle wheel steamer built for the Forth and Clyde Canal, Great Britain in 1801–02 by William Symington (1763–1831), using a double-acting condensing engine constructed by James Watt (1736–1819).

The world's oldest active paddle wheeler continuously operated as such is *Skibladner*, which has plied Lake Mjøsa, Norway since 1856. She was built in Motala, Sweden and has had two major refits.

Oldest active The world's oldest active oceangoing ship is the *MV Doulos* (Greek for "servant"), built in 1914 in the USA and first named *Medina*. She is currently operating as an international educational and Christian service vessel with approximately 300 crew members, personnel and passengers on board from 30 different nations.

WARSHIPS

Largest battleships The largest battleships in active service are the USS *Missouri* and USS *Wisconsin*, 887 ft long with a full-load displacement of 63,934 tons. Both were first commissioned in 1944, and following major refits were recommissioned in 1986 and 1988 respectively. Each has nine 16-inch guns which were used for shore bombardment during the Gulf War in early 1991. The 16-inch projectiles of 2,700 lb can be fired a distance of 23 miles.

Two other ships of the same class, USS *New Jersey* and USS *Iowa*, last saw action off Lebanon in 1983–84.

The Japanese battleships *Yamato* (completed on 16 Dec 1941 and sunk southwest of Kyūshū, Japan by US planes on 7 Apr 1945) and *Musashi* (sunk in the Philippine Sea by 11 bombs and 16 torpedoes on 24 Oct 1944) were the largest battleships ever commissioned, each with a full-load displacement of 81,545 tons. With an overall length of 863 ft, a beam of 127 ft and a full-load draft of 35 ½ ft, they mounted nine 18.1 in guns in three triple turrets. Each gun weighed 181.5 tons and was 75 ft in length, firing a 3,200 lb projectile.

Fastest warship A hovercraft, the 78-ft-long 110-ton US Navy test vehicle SES-100B, achieved a speed of 91.9 knots (105.8 mph). (See Hovercraft, fastest.)

Fastest destroyer The fastest speed attained by a destroyer was 45.25 knots (51.83 mph) by the 3,120 ton French destroyer *Le Terrible* in 1935. She was built in Blainville, France and was powered by four Yarrow small-tube boilers and two Rateau geared turbines, giving 100,000 shp. She was removed from the active list at the end of 1957.

AIRCRAFT CARRIERS

Largest The warships with the largest full-load displacement in the world are the Nimitz class US Navy aircraft carriers USS *Nimitz, Dwight D. Eisenhower, Carl Vinson, Theodore Roosevelt* and *Abraham Lincoln* at 100,846 tons. They are 1,092 ft in length overall, with 4 ½ acres of flight deck, and have a speed well in excess of 30 knots from their four nuclear-powered 260,000 shp geared steam turbines. They have to be refueled after about 900,000 miles of steaming. Their full complement of personnel is 5,986.

SUBMARINES

Largest The world's largest submarines are of the USSR Typhoon class. The launch of the first at the covered shipyard at Severodvinsk in the White Sea, USSR was announced by NATO on 23 Sep 1980. They are believed to have a dive displacement of 27,557 tons, to measure 557.6 ft overall and to be armed with 20 SS NX 20 missiles with a 4,800-nautical-mile range, each with seven warheads. By late 1987 two others built in Leningrad were operational, each deploying 140 warheads.

The longest submarine patrol that ever dove unsupported is 111 days by HM Submarine *Warspite* in the South Atlantic from 25 Nov 1982 to 15 Mar 1983. She sailed 30,804 nautical miles.

Fastest The Russian Alfa class nuclear-powered submarines have a reported maximum speed of 45 knots plus (51.8 mph). With the use of titanium alloy in the hull, they are believed to be able to dive to 2,500 ft. A US spy satellite over Leningrad's naval yard on 8 Jun 1983 showed they were being lengthened and are now 260.1 ft long.

TRANSATLANTIC AND TRANSPACIFIC MARINE RECORDS

(Compiled by Nobby Clarke and Richard Boehmer)

CATEGORY	VESSEL	SKIPPER	START	FINISH	DURATION
FIRST CRUISE	*Lively* 140-ton brig	Shuttleworth (Great Britain) guests and 25 crew	Great Britain 1783 Hudson Bay, Canada	Florida Great Britain 1784	420 days
FIRST SOLO SAILING E–W	15-ton gaff sloop	Josiah Shackford (USA)	Bordeaux, France, 1786	Surinam (Guiana)	35 days
FIRST ROWING	Ship's boat 20 ft	John Brown and 5 British deserters from garrison	St Helena 10 Jun 1799	Belmonte, Brazil (fastest-ever row)	28 days (83 mpd)
FIRST MULTIHULL (raft)	*Non Pareil* 25 ft	John Mikes and 2 crew (USA)	New York, 1868	Southampton, Great Britain	51 days
FIRST SOLO SAILING W–E	*Centennial* 20 ft	Alfred Johnson (USA)	Shag Harbor, ME, 1876	Wales	46 days
FIRST MOTORBOAT	*Abiel Abbott Low* 38 ft (engine: 10hp kerosene)	William C. Newman (USA) Edward (son)	New York, 1902	Falmouth, Great Britain	36 days (83.3 mpd)
FIRST WOMAN SOLO	Lugger 18 ft	Gladys Gradeley (USA)	Nova Scotia, 1903	Devon, Great Britain	60 days
FIRST SOLO ROWING E–W	*Britannia* 22 ft	John Fairfax (Great Britain)	Las Palmas, Canary Islands 20 Jan 1969	Ft Lauderdale, FL 19 Jul 1969	180 days
FIRST SOLO ROWING W–E	*Super Silver* 20 ft	Tom McClean (Ireland)	St John's, Newfoundland 1969	Black Sod Bay, Ireland 27 Jul 1969	70.7 days
FIRST OUTBOARD	*Trans-Atlantic* 26 ft (2.65 hp Evinrudes)	Al Grover (USA) Dante (son)	St Pierre, Newfoundland 1985 (via Azores)	Lisbon	34 days (88 mpd approx.)
YOUNGEST SOLO SAILING	*Sea Raider* 35 ft	David Sandeman (Great Britain) (17 years 176 days)	Jersey, Channel Islands 1976	Newport, RI	43 days
OLDEST SOLO SAILING	*Tawny Pipit* 25 ft	Stefan Szwarnowski (Great Britain) (76 years 165 days)	New Jersey 2 Jun 1989	Bude 13 Aug 1989	72 days
YOUNGEST SOLO ROWING	*Finn Again* 20 ft 6 in	Sean Crowley (Great Britain; 25 years 306 days)	Halifax, Nova Scotia, 17 Jun 1988	Co. Galway, Ireland, 21 Sep 1988	95 days 22 hr
OLDEST SOLO ROWING	*Khaggavisana* 19 ³/₄ ft	Sidney Genders (Great Britain; 51 years)	Penzance, Great Britain, 1970	Miami, FL via Antigua	160 days 8 hr
FASTEST POWER W–E	*Gentry Eagle* 110 ft	Tom Gentry (USA)	Ambrose Light Tower, NJ 13:49 BST 24 Jul 1989	Bishop Rock Light 03:56 BST 27 Jul 1989	2 days 14 hr 7 min 47 sec (45.7 knots smg)
FASTEST SAIL W–E Non-solo in multihull	*Jet Services 5* 75 ft catamaran sloop	Serge Madec (France)	Ambrose Light Tower, NJ 2 Jun 1990	Lizard Lighthouse, Great Britain 9 Jun 1990	6 days 13 hr 3 min 32 sec (18.4 knots smg)
FASTEST SAIL W–E Non-solo in monohull	*Phocea* 243 ft ULDB schooner	Philippe Morinay (France)	Ambrose Light Tower, NJ 26 Jun 1988	Lizard Lighthouse, Great Britain 3 Jul 1988	8 days 3 hr 29 min (14.8 knots smg)
FASTEST SAIL W–E Solo in multihull	*Pierre 1er* 60 ft trimaran sloop	Florence Arthaud (France)	Ambrose Light Tower, NJ 24 Jul 1990	Lizard Lighthouse, Great Britain 3 Aug 1990	9 days 21 hr 42 min (12.2 knots smg)
FASTEST SAIL W–E Clipper ship	*Red Jacket* 251 ft 3-masted ship	Asa Eldridge (USA)	Sandy Hook, NJ 11 Jan 1854	Liverpool Bar, Great Britain 23 Jan 1854	12 days (approx. 260 mpd av.)
FASTEST SAIL E–W Non-solo in multihull	*Elf Aquitaine III* 60 ft trimaran sloop	Jean Maurel (France)	Plymouth, Great Britain 10 Jun 1990	Newport, RI 21 Jun 1990	10 days 23 hr 15 min (11.0 knots smg)
FASTEST SAIL E–W Non-solo in monohull	*Allied Bank* 60 ft ULDB sloop	John Martin (South Africa)	Plymouth, Great Britain 10 Jun 1990	Newport, RI 26 Jun 1990	15 days 13 hr 40 min (7.8 knots smg)
FASTEST SAIL E–W Solo in multihull	*Fleury Michon (IX)* 60 ft trimaran	Philippe Poupon (France)	Plymouth, Great Britain (STAR) 5 Jun 1988	Newport, RI 15 Jun 1988	10 days 9 hr 15 min 9 sec (11.6 knots smg)
FASTEST SAIL E–W Solo in monohull	*Thursday's Child* 60 ft ULDB cutter	Warren Luhrs (USA)	Plymouth, Great Britain (STAR) 2 Jun 1984	Newport, RI 19 Jun 1984	16 days 22 hr 27 min (7.1 knots smg)
FASTEST SAIL E–W Clipper ship	*Andrew Jackson* 220 ft 3-masted ship	W.S. Johnson (USA)	Liverpool, Great Britain 3 Nov 1860	New York 18 Nov 1860	15 days (approx. 210 mpd av.)
FIRST RAFT Shore to shore	*La Balsa* 42 ft (balsa logs)	Vital Alsar (Spain) and 3 crew	Guayaquil, Ecuador 1970	Mooloolaba, Australia	160 days
FIRST ROWING	*Britannia II* 35 ft	John Fairfax (Great Britain) Sylvia Cook (Great Britain)	San Francisco 26 Apr 1971	Hayman I., Australia 22 Apr 1972	362 days
FASTEST SAIL CALIFORNIA–HAWAII Non-solo in multihull	*Aikane X-5* 63 ft catamaran	Rudy Choy (USA)	Los Angeles 17 Aug 1989	Honolulu 24 Aug 1989	6 days 22 hr 41 min 12 sec (13.3 knots smg)
FASTEST SAIL CALIFORNIA–HAWAII Non-solo in monohull	*Merlin* 67 ft ULDB sloop	Bill Lee (USA)	Los Angeles (TransPac) 2 Jul 1977	Honolulu 10 Jul 1977	8 days 11 hr 1 min 45 sec (11.0 knots smg)
FASTEST SAIL CALIFORNIA–HAWAII Solo in multihull	*Bullfrog Sunblock* 40 ft trimaran	Ian Johnston (Australia)	San Francisco (SoloTP) 14 Jun 1986	Kauai 24 Jun 1986	10 days 10 hr 3 min 43 sec (8.5 knots smg)
FASTEST SAIL CALIFORNIA–HAWAII Solo in monohull	*Intense* 30 ft ULDB sloop	Bill Strange (USA)	San Francisco (SoloTP) 25 Jun 1988	Kauai 7 Jul 1988	11 days 15 hr 21 min (7.6 knots smg)
FASTEST SAIL CALIFORNIA–JAPAN	*Pen Duick V* 35 ft sloop	Eric Tabarly (France)	San Francisco 15 Mar 1969	Tokyo, Japan 24 Apr 1969	39 days 15 hr 44 min (4.66 knots smg)

Notes:— The earliest single-handed Pacific crossings were achieved East–West by Bernard Gilboy (USA) in 1882 in the 18 ft double-ender *Pacific* to Australia, and West–East by Fred Rebel (Latvia) in the 18 ft *Elaine*, (from Australia) and Edward Miles (USA) in the 36 ³/₄ ft *Sturdy II* (from Japan) both in 1932, the latter via Hawaii. ULDB = Ultra-light displacement boat. All mileages are nautical miles. STAR is a transatlantic race. smg = speed made good.

MARINE CIRCUMNAVIGATION AND OTHER MARINE RECORDS

(Compiled by Nobby Clarke and Richard Boehmer)

Strictly speaking, a circumnavigation involves someone passing through a pair of antipodal points. Of the records listed below, only those with an asterisk are actually known to have met this requirement. A nonstop circumnavigation is entirely self-maintained; no water supplies, provisions, equipment or replacements of any sort may be taken aboard en route. Vessel may anchor, but no physical help may be accepted apart from passing mail or messages.

CATEGORY	VESSEL	SKIPPER	START	FINISH
* FIRST	*Victoria* Expedition of Fernão de Magalhães (Ferdinand Magellan)	Juan Sebastián de Elcano or del Cano (d. 1526) and 17 crew	Seville 20 Sep 1519	San Lucar 6 Sep 1522 30,700 nm
FIRST FORE-AND-AFT RIGGED VESSEL	*Union* 98 tons (sloop)	John Boit Junior, aged 19–21 (USA) and 22 crew	Newport, RI 1794 (via Cape Horn westabout)	Newport, RI 1796
FIRST YACHT	*Nancy Dawson* (schooner)	Robert Shedden (Great Britain) and crew (died in Mexico, 1849)	Thames, Great Britain 1847	Thames, Great Britain 1850
* FIRST SOLO	*Spray* 36 ft 9 in gaff yawl	Capt Joshua Slocum, 51 (USA) (a nonswimmer)	Newport, RI, via Magellan Straits 24 Apr 1895	3 Jul 1898 46,000 nm
FIRST MOTORBOAT	*Speejacks* 98 ft	Albert Y. Gowen (USA) plus wife and crew	New York City 1921	New York City 1922
* FIRST SUBMERGED	*Triton* Nuclear submarine	Capt Edward L. Beach USN plus 182 crew	New London, CT 16 Feb 1960	10 May 1960 84 days 19 hr, 36,300 nm
* FIRST MULTIHULL	*Rehu Moana* 40 ft catamaran cutter	David Lewis (New Zealand)	Plymouth, Great Britain 23 May 1964	27 Jul 1967 660 days + 500 days in port, 41,609 nm
* FIRST NONSTOP SOLO W–E	*Suhaili* 32.4 ft Bermudan ketch	Robin Knox-Johnston (Great Britain)	Falmouth, Great Britain 14 Jun 1968	22 Apr 1969 (312 days)
* FIRST SOLO MULTIHULL	*Victress* 40 ft Bermudan ketch	Nigel Tetley (Great Britain) (b. South Africa)	Plymouth, Great Britain 16 Sep 1968 (W–E via Cape Horn)	21 May 1969 (trimaran sank after circumnavigation was completed)
* FIRST NONSTOP SOLO E–W	*British Steel* 59 ft ketch	Chay Blyth (Great Britain)	Hamble River, Great Britain 18 Oct 1970	6 Aug 1971 (292 days)
* FIRST WOMAN SOLO	*Express Crusader* 53 ft cutter	Dame Naomi James (New Zealand)	Dartmouth, Great Britain 9 Sep 1977	Dartmouth, Great Britain 8 Jun 1978 265 sailing days + 7 days in port
* FIRST BY NORTHWEST PASSAGE	*Mabel E. Holland* 42 ft motor lifeboat	David Scott Cowper (Great Britain)	Newcastle-upon-Tyne, Great Britain 14 Jul 1986	Newcastle-upon-Tyne, Great Britain, 24 Sep 1990 (approx. 260 days motoring)
FASTEST SAIL NONSTOP W–E Solo in monohull	*Ecureuil d'Aquitaine II* 60 ft ULDB cutter	Titouan Lamazou (France)	Les Sables, France (VGC) 26 Nov 1989	Les Sables, France (via 5 capes) 16 Mar 1990 109 days 8 hr 48 min 50 sec (205.7 mpd)
* FASTEST SAIL WITH STOPS W–E Solo in multihull	*Un Autre Regard* 75 ft trimaran	Olivier de Kersauson (France)	Brest, France 28 Dec 1988	Brest, France (via 5 capes and 2 stops) 5 May 1989 125 d 19 h 32 m 33 s + 2 days in port
FASTEST SAIL WITH STOPS W–E Solo in monohull	*Groupe Sceta* 60 ft ULDB sloop	Christophe Auguin (France)	Newport, RI (BOC) 15 Sep 1990	Newport, RI (via 3 capes and 3 stops) 23 Apr 1991 120 d 22 h 36 m 35 s + 98 d 14 h 34 m 47 s in port
* FASTEST SAIL WITH STOPS W–E Non-solo in monohull	*UBS Switzerland* 80 ft IOR sloop	Pierre Fehlmann (Switzerland)	Portsmouth, Great Britain (WRWR) 28 Sep 1985	Portsmouth, Great Britain (via 4 capes and 3 stops) 9 May 1986, 117 d 14 h 31 m 42 s + 105 d 5 h 49 m 58 s in port
FASTEST SAIL WITH STOP W–E Clipper ship	*James Baines* 266 ft 3-masted ship	Charles McDonnell (Great Britain)	Liverpool, Great Britain 10 Dec 1854	Liverpool, Great Britain (via Melbourne) 20 May 1855 133 days + 28 days in port

CATEGORY	VESSEL	SKIPPER	START	FINISH	DURATION
LONGEST TIME AND DISTANCE NONSTOP BY SAIL	*Parry Endeavour* 44 ft Bermudan sloop	Jon Sanders (Australia)	Fremantle, Australia 25 May 1986	Fremantle, Australia 13 Mar 1988	(71,000 nm in 658 days) (4.5 knots)
GOLD RUSH ROUTE Fastest multihull	*Great American* 60 ft trimaran	Georgs Kolesnikovs (Canada)	New York 10 Mar 1989	San Francisco 26 May 1989	76 days 23 hr 20 min (7.36 knots smg)
GOLD RUSH ROUTE Fastest monohull	*Thursday's Child* 60 ft ULDB cutter	Warren Luhrs (USA)	New York 24 Nov 1988	San Francisco 12 Feb 1989	80 days 18 hr 39 min (includes 3-day stop)
BEST DAY'S RUN Non-solo in multihull	*Jet Services 5* 60 ft catamaran sloop	Serge Madec (France)	42.638° N 62.626° W 22:22 GMT 3 Jun 1990	45.750° N 51.480° W 21:58 GMT 4 Jun 1990	514.01 nm (GCD)/23 hr 36 min (21.8 knots smg)
BEST DAY'S RUN Non-solo in monohull	*Phocea* 243 ft ULDB schooner	Philippe Morinay (France)	During transatlantic record run in 1988		490 nm/24 hr (20.4 knots smg)
BEST DAY'S RUN Solo in multihull	*Laiterie Mont St Michel* 60 ft trimaran	Olivier Moussy (France)	50° 13' N 11° 30' W 18:18 GMT 6 Jun 1988	48° 18' N 23° 30' W 21:17 GMT 7 Jun 1988	430.8 nm (GCD)/24 hr (18.0 knots smg)
BEST DAY'S RUN Solo in monohull	*Generali Concorde* 60 ft sloop	Alain Gautier (France)	50.300° S 42.550° E 15:39 GMT 2 Dec 1990	51.800° S 50.617° E 15:16 GMT 3 Dec 1990	317.1 nm (GCD)/23 hr 37 min (13.43 knots smg)
BEST DAY'S RUN Sailboard	*Fanatic board* Gaastra sail	Françoise Canetos (France)	Sète, France 13 Jul 1988	14 Jul 1988	227 nm/24 hr (9.46 knots smg)
ONE NAUTICAL MILE Fastest sail	*Crédit Agricole (II)* 74 ft catamaran	Philippe Jeantot (France)	Martinique January 1985		2 min 13 sec (27.1 knots smg)
500 METERS Fastest	Naish sailboard with ART sail	Pascal Maka (France)	Saintes Maries de-la-Mer, France 27 Feb 1990		22.65 sec (42.91 knots)
500 METERS Fastest sailboat	*Longshot* 20 ft 9 in trifoiler	Russell Long (USA)	Lethbridge, Canada 12 Oct 1990		26.17 sec (37.14 knots)

Eduard Roditi, author of *Magellan of the Pacific*, advances the view that Magellan's slave, Enrique, was the first circumnavigator. He had been purchased in Malacca and it was shown that he already understood the Filipino dialect Vizayan when he reached the Philippines from the east. He "tied the knot" off Limasawa on 28 Mar 1521. ULDB = Ultra-light displacement boat. VGC = Vendée Globe Challenge Race. BOC = British Oxygen Corp. Challenge Around Alone Race. IOR = International Offshore Rule. WRWR = Whitbread Round World Race. All mileages are nautical miles. GCD = Great circle distance. smg = speed made good. All mileages are nautical miles.

Deepest The US Navy deep submergence vessel *Sea Cliff* (DSV 4), 30 tons, commissioned in 1973, reached in March 1985 a depth of 20,000 ft.

PASSENGER LINERS

Largest The largest and longest is the *Norway*, 1,035 ft 7 ½ in in overall length, with a capacity of 2,400 passengers. She was built as the *France* in 1961 and renamed after purchase in June 1979 by Knut Kloster of Norway. She is normally employed in cruises in the Caribbean and is based at Miami, FL. Work undertaken during an extensive refit, including two new decks, during the fall of 1990 increased the *Norway*'s tonnage to 76,000 grt.

The RMS *Queen Elizabeth* (finally 82,998 but formerly 83,673 grt), of the Cunard fleet, was the largest passenger vessel ever built and had the largest displacement of any liner in the world. She had an overall length of 1,031 ft, was 118 ft 7 in in breadth and was powered by steam turbines that developed 168,000 hp. Her last passenger voyage ended on 15 Nov 1968. In 1970 she was removed to Hong Kong to serve as a floating marine university and renamed *Seawise University*. She was burned out on 9 Jan 1972 when three *simultaneous* outbreaks of fire strongly pointed to arson. The gutted hull had been cut up and removed by 1978. *Seawise* was a pun on the owner's initials—C.Y. Tung (1911–82).

TANKERS

Largest The *Happy Giant*, formerly the *Seawise Giant*, is 622,511.7 tons dwt. She is 1,504 ft long overall, with a beam of 225 ft 11 in, and has a draft of 80 ft 9 in. She was lengthened by Nippon Kokan in 1980 by adding a 265 ft 8 in midship section. She was attacked by Iraqi Mirage jets off Larak Island in the Persian Gulf on 22 Dec 1987 and was severely damaged in another attack on 14 May 1988. Despite this damage, she was bought by a Norwegian, and is to be returned to service after refitting in South Korea. A new diesel engine in place of her steam turbines will result in her deadweight tonnage being reduced to approximately 420,000.

The largest tanker and ship of any kind in service is the 611,832.7 ton dwt *Hellas Fos*, a steam turbine tanker built in 1979. Of 254,583 grt and 227,801 nrt, she is owned by the Bilinder Marine Corporation of Athens, Greece.

CARGO VESSELS

Largest The largest ship carrying dry cargo is the Norwegian ore carrier *Berge Stahl*, 402,082.6 tons dwt, built in South Korea for the Norwegian owner Signora Bergesen. She has a length of 1,125 ft, a beam measuring 208 ft and was launched on 5 Nov 1986.

Largest whale factory The USSR's *Sovietskaya Ukraina* (35,878 tons), with a summer dwt of 51,519 tons, was completed in October 1959. She is 714½ ft in length and 84 ft 7 in abeam.

Barges The world's largest RoRo (roll-on, roll-off) ships are four *El Rey* class barges, weighing 18,408 tons and measuring 580 ft in length. They were built by the FMC Corp of Portland, OR and are operated by Crowley Maritime Corp of San Francisco between Florida and Puerto Rico with tri-level lodging for up to 376 truck-trailers.

Containership Earliest Shipborne containerization began in 1955 when the tanker *Ideal X* was converted by Malcolm McLean (USA). She carried containers only on deck.

Largest The 12 built for United States Lines in Korea in 1984–85 are capable of carrying 4,482 TEU containers with a gross tonnage of 57,075. They were named *American Alabama, California, Illinois, Kentucky*, etc. Following the financial collapse of United States Lines, the fleet was sold and the 12 ships now have such names as *Sea-Land Atlantic, Achiever, Commitment, Integrity*, etc., while others have the prefix "Nedlloyd" (*Nedlloyd Holland*) or the suffix "Bay" (*Galveston Bay*). Their new owners have decided to limit their capacity to 3,456 TEU in normal operation. American President Lines has built five ships in Germany: *President Adams, President Jackson, President Kennedy, President Polk* and *President Truman*, that are termed post-Panamax, being the first container vessels too large for transit of the Panama Canal. They are 902.69 ft in length and 129.29 ft abeam; the maximum beam for the Panama transit is 105.97 ft. These vessels have a quoted capacity of 4,300 TEU; they have in fact carried in excess of this in normal service.

Most powerful tugs The *Nikolay Chiker* and *SB–134*, commissioned in April–May 1989, and built by Hollming Ltd of Sweden for V/O Sudoiport, USSR,

have 24,480 hp and are capable of 250 tons bollard pull at full power. They are 324.80 ft long and 63.81 ft wide.

Largest car ferry The world's largest car and passenger ferry is the 58,376 grt *Silja Serenade*, which entered service between Stockholm and Helsinki in 1990 and is operated by the Silja Line. She is 666 ft long and 103.34 ft wide, and can carry 2,500 passengers and 450 cars.

Fastest The fastest is the 24,065 grt gas-turbine powered *Finnjet*, built in 1977, which operates in the Baltic between Helsinki, Finland and Travemunde, Germany and is capable of exceeding 30 knots (34.47 mph).

Largest rail ferry The operating area of the biggest international rail ferries, *Klaipeda, Vilnius, Mukran* and *Greifswald*, is in the Baltic sea, between the ports of Klaipeda, Lithuania, USSR and Mukran, Germany. Consisting of two decks 625 ft in length, 301.4 ft in breadth and 13,104 tons dwt, they were built in Wismar, Germany. Each of them can lift 103 railcars of standard 48.65 ft length and weighing up to 84 tons. The ferries can cover a distance of 273 nautical miles (314.2 miles) in 17 hours.

Largest propeller The largest propeller ever made is the triple-bladed screw of 36 ft 1 in diameter made by Kawasaki Heavy Industries, Japan, and delivered on 17 Mar 1982 for the 233,787 ton bulk carrier *Hoei Maru* (now renamed *New Harvest*).

Largest hydrofoil The 212-ft-long *Plainview* (347 tons full-load) naval hydrofoil was launched by the Lockheed Shipbuilding and Construction Co. at Seattle, WA on 28 Jun 1965. She has a service speed of 57.2 mph.

Three 185-ton Supramar PTS 150 Mk III hydrofoils carry 250 passengers at 40 knots across the Öre Sound between

■ **Aircraft carrier**
The USS Dwight D. Eisenhower *is one of four of the world's largest full-load displacement warships at 100,846 metric tons. The flight deck covers 4 ½ acres. This view was taken at Monaco. (Photo: US Navy)*

Most landings
The greatest number of landings on an aircraft carrier in one day was 602, achieved by Marine Air Group 6 of the United States Pacific Fleet Air Force aboard the USS *Matanikau* on 25 May 1945 between 8 A.M. and 5 P.M.

Riveting
The world record for riveting is 11,209 rivets in 9 hr, by John Moir at the Workman Clark Ltd shipyard, Belfast, Northern Ireland in June 1918. His peak hour was his 7th, with 1,409 rivets, an average nearly 23½ per min.

Fastest building

The fastest times in which complete ships of more than 10,000 tons were ever built were achieved at Kaiser's Yard, Portland, OR during the wartime program for building 2,742 liberty ships in 18 shipyards from 27 Sep 1941. In 1942 No. 440, named *Robert E. Peary*, had her keel laid on 8 November, was launched on 12 November and was operational after 4 days 15½ hr on 15 November. She was broken up in 1963.

Message in a bottle

The longest recorded interval between drop and pickup is 73 years in the case of a message thrown from the SS *Arawatta* out of Cairns, Queensland, Australia on 9 Jun 1910 in a lotion bottle and reported found on Moreton Island on 6 Jun 1983.

Stowaway

The most rugged stowaway was Socarras Ramirez, who escaped from Cuba on 4 Jun 1969 by stowing away in an unpressurized wheel well in the starboard wing of a Douglas DC 8 from Havana, Cuba to Madrid, Spain in a 5,600-mile Iberian Airlines flight.

Malmö, Sweden and Copenhagen, Denmark. They were built by Westermoen Hydrofoil Ltd of Mandal, Norway.

Riverboat The world's largest inland boat is the 382-ft *Mississippi Queen*, designed by James Gardner of London, Great Britain. The vessel was commissioned on 25 Jul 1976 in Cincinatti, OH and is now in service on the Mississippi River.

Most powerful icebreakers The most powerful icebreaker built for that purpose is the 28,000 ton 460-ft-long *Rossiya*, powered by 75,000 hp nuclear engines, built in Leningrad, USSR and completed in 1985.

A 100,000 hp 636-ft-long polar icebreaker of the Class 8 type was ordered by the Canadian government in October 1985. Its cost was $Can 500 million.

The largest *converted* icebreaker was the 1,007-ft-long SS *Manhattan* (43,000 shp), which was converted by the Humble Oil Co. into a 168,000 ton icebreaker. She made a double voyage through the Northwest Passage in Arctic Canada from 24 Aug to 12 Nov 1969.

The Northwest Passage was first navigated by Roald Engebereth Gravning Amundsen (Norway; 1872–1928) in the sealing sloop *Gjöa* in 1906.

Yacht *Most expensive* The fitting-out of the 470 ft Saudi Arabian royal yacht *Abdul Aziz*, built in Denmark, was completed on 22 Jun 1984 at Vospers Yard, Southampton, Great Britain. It was estimated in September 1987 to be worth more than $100 million.

Longest The private (nonroyal) yacht *Nabila*, originally costing some $29 million, was the longest at 282 ft. She was sold in September 1987 by the Sultan of Brunei to New York property dealer Donald Trump (b. 1946) for close to that price and was renamed *Trump Princess*. Her original owner was Adnan Kashoggi, who installed a helicopter pad and an operating theater.

Most powerful dredger The 468.4-ft-long *Prins der Nederlanden* of 10,586 grt can dredge up 19,700 tons of sand from a depth of 115 ft via two suction tubes in less than an hour.

Wooden ship *Heaviest* The *Richelieu*, 333⅔ ft long and weighing 8,534 tons, was launched in Toulon, France on 3 Dec 1873.

HM battleship *Lord Warden*, completed in 1869, displaced 7,940 tons.

Longest The longest ever built was the New York–built *Rochambeau* (1867–72), formerly the *Dunderberg*, which measured 377 ft 4 in overall.

It should be noted that the biblical length of Noah's ark was 300 cubits, or, at 18 in to a cubit, 450 ft.

Largest human-powered The giant ship *Tessarakonteres*, a three-banked catamaran galley with 4,000 rowers, built for Ptolemy IV c. 210 B.C. in Alexandria, Egypt, measured 420 ft with up to

eight men to an oar of 38 cubits (57 ft) in length.

Longest canoe The 117-ft-long Kauri wood Maori war canoe *Nga Toki Matawhaorua* was shaped with adzes at Kerikeri Inlet, New Zealand in 1940. The crew numbered 70 or more.

The "Snake Boat" *Nadubhagóm*, 135 ft long, from Kerala, southern India, has a crew of 109 rowers and nine "encouragers."

SAILING SHIPS

Largest The largest vessel ever built in the era of sail was the *France II* (5,806 gross tons), launched at Bordeaux, France in 1911. The *France II* was a steel-hulled, five-masted barque (square-rigged on four masts and fore-and-aft rigged on the aftermost mast). Her hull measured 418 ft overall. Although principally designed as a sailing vessel with a stump topgallant rig, she was also fitted with two auxiliary engines; however, these were removed in 1919 and she became a pure sailing vessel. She was wrecked off New Caledonia on 13 Jul 1922.

The only seven-masted sailing schooner ever built was the 375.6-ft-long *Thomas W. Lawson* (5,218 gross tons), built at Quincy, MA in 1902 and wrecked off the Isles of Scilly, Great Britain on 15 Dec 1907. (See Largest junks, below.)

Largest in service The largest now in service is the 385½ ft *Sedov*, built in 1921 in Kiel, Germany and used for training in the USSR. She is 48 ft wide, with a displacement of 6,300 grt (4,267.2 tons) and a sail area of 45,123 ft ^{2}.

The world's only surviving first rate ship-of-the-line is the Royal Navy's 104-gun battleship HMS *Victory*, laid down at Chatham, Great Britain on 23 Jul 1759 and constructed from the wood of some 2,200 oak trees. She bore the body of Admiral Nelson from Gibraltar to Portsmouth, Great Britain, arriving 44 days after serving as his victorious flagship at the Battle of Trafalgar on 21 Oct 1805. In 1922 she was moved to No. 2 dock, Portsmouth—site of the world's oldest graving dock. The length of her cordage (both standing and running rigging) is 19.12 miles.

Oldest active The oldest active square-rigged sailing vessel in the world is the restored SV *Maria Asumpta* (formerly the *Ciudad de Inca*), built near Barcelona, Spain in 1858. She is 125 ft overall and weighs 142.3 tons. She was restored in 1981–82 and is used for film work, promotional appearances at regattas and sail training. She is operated by The Friends of *Maria Asumpta* of Lenham, Great Britain.

Longest The longest is the 613-ft-long French-built *Club Med 1* with five aluminum masts. The 2,500 ft ^{2} polyester sails are computer-controlled. She is operated as a Caribbean cruise vessel for 425 passengers bound for Club Med. With her small sail area and powerful engines she is really a motor-sailer.

Largest junks The largest on record was the seagoing *Cheng Ho*, flagship of Admiral Cheng Ho's 62 treasure ships, c. 1420, with a displacement of 3,472 tons and a length variously estimated up to 538 ft. She is believed to have had nine masts.

A river junk 361 ft long, with treadmill-operated paddle wheels, was recorded in 1161.

In c. A.D. 280 a floating fortress 600 ft square, built by Wang Chün on the Yangtze River, took part in the Qin-Wu river war. Present-day junks do not, even in the case of the Jiangsu traders, exceed 170 ft in length.

Longest day's run under sail Calculated for any commercial vessel under sail, the longest day's run was one of 462 nautical miles by the clipper *Champion of the Seas* (3,048.7 tons) of the Liverpool Black Ball Line, running before a northwesterly gale in the south Indian Ocean under the command of Capt. Alex Newlands in 1854. The elapsed time between the fixes was 23 hr 17 min, giving an average of 19.97 knots (23 mph).

Largest sails Sails are known to have been used for marine propulsion since 3500 B.C. The largest spars ever carried were those in HM Battleship *Temeraire*, completed at Chatham, Kent, Great Britain, on 31 Aug 1877. She was broken up in 1921. The fore and main yards measured 115 ft in length. The foresail contained 5,100 ft of canvas weighing 2.23 tons, and the total sail area was 25,000 ft ^{2}.

HM Battleship *Sultan* was ship-rigged when completed at Chatham, Kent, Great Britain on 10 Oct 1871 and carried 34,100 ft ^{2} of sails plus 15,300 ft ^{2} of stunsails. She was broken up in 1946.

Tallest mast The *Velsheda*, a J-class sailing vessel, is the tallest known single-masted yacht in the world. Measured from heel fitting to the mast truck, she is 169 ¼ ft in height. Built in 1933, the second of the four British J-class yachts, she is unusual in that she was the only one ever built that was not intended to race for the America's Cup. With a displacement of 160 tons, she supports a sail area of 7,500 ft ^{2}.

Largest wreck The 312,186 dwt very large crude carrier (VLCC) *Energy Determination* blew up and broke in two in the Straits of Hormuz on 12 Dec 1979. Her full value was $58 million.

The largest wreck removal was carried out in 1979 by Smit Tak International, which removed the remains of the French tanker *Betelgeuse*, 120,000 tons, from Bantry Bay, Republic of Ireland, within 20 months.

Most massive collision The closest an irresistible force has come to striking an immovable object occurred on 16 Dec 1977, 22 miles off the coast of southern Africa, when the tanker *Venoil* (330,954 dwt) struck her sister ship *Venpet* (330,869 dwt).

OCEAN CROSSINGS

Earliest Atlantic The earliest crossing of the Atlantic by a power vessel, as opposed to an auxiliary-engined sailing ship, was a 22-day voyage begun in April 1827, from Rotterdam, Netherlands, to the West Indies, by the *Curaçao*. She was a 127-ft wooden paddle boat of 490.5 tons, built as the *Calpe* in Dover, Great Britain in 1826 and purchased by the Dutch government for the West Indian mail service.

The earliest Atlantic crossing entirely under steam (with intervals for desalting the boilers) was by HMS *Rhadamanthus*, from Plymouth, Great Britain to Barbados in 1832.

The earliest crossing under continuous steam power was by the condenser-fitted packet ship *Sirius* (787 tons) from Queenstown (now Cóbh), Ireland to Sandy Hook, NJ, in 18 days 10 hr, from 4–22 Apr 1838.

Fastest Atlantic Under the rules of the Hales Trophy or "Blue Riband," which recognize the highest average speed rather than the shortest duration, the record is held by *Hoverspeed Great Britain* with an average speed of 36.966 knots (46.02 mph) between the Nantucket Light Buoy and Bishop Rock Lighthouse on 20–23 Jun 1990. However, although she is a passenger vessel, *Hoverspeed Great Britain* is not intended for the North Atlantic, and traditionalists still feel that the Blue Riband should be held by the vessel making the best passage in regular liner service.

That distinction goes to the *United States* (then 51,988, now 38,216 grt),

former flagship of the United States Lines. On her maiden voyage between 3–7 Jul 1952 from New York to Le Havre, France and Southampton, Great Britain, she averaged 35.39 knots (40.75 mph) for three days 10 hr 40 min (6:36 P.M. GMT, 3 July to 5:16 A.M., 7 July) on a route of 2,949 nautical miles from the Ambrose Light Vessel to the Bishop Rock Lighthouse, Isles of Scilly, Great Britain. During this run, on 6–7 July, she steamed the greatest distance ever covered by any ship in a day's run (24 hr)—868 nautical miles (998.9 miles), thus averaging 36.17 knots (41.65 mph). The maximum speed attained from her 240,000 shp engines was 44.13 mph in trials on 9–10 Jun 1952.

Fastest Pacific The fastest crossing from Yokohama to Long Beach, CA (4,840 nautical miles [5,567.64 miles]) took 6 days 1 hr 27 min (30 Jun–6 Jul 1973) by the container ship *Sea-Land Commerce* (56,353 tons), at an average speed of 33.27 knots (38.31 mph).

Water speed The fastest speed ever achieved on water is an estimated 300 knots (345.48 mph) by Kenneth Peter Warby (b. 9 May 1939) on the Blowering Dam Lake, New South Wales, Australia on 20 Nov 1977 in his unlimited hydroplane *Spirit of Australia*.

The official world water speed record is 277.57 knots (319.63 mph) set on 8 Oct 1978 by Warby on Blowering Dam Lake.

Fiona, Countess of Arran (b. 1918) drove her 15-ft three-point hydroplane *Stradag* (Gaelic "The Spark") to the first world water speed record for electrically propelled powerboats at a speed of 45.13 knots (51.973 mph), at the National Water Sports Center, Nottingham, Great Britain, on 22 Nov 1989.

Carriage driving
The only man to drive 48 horses in a single hitch is Dick Sparrow of Zearing, IA, between 1972 and 1977. The lead horses were on reins 135 ft long.

Longest
A 100-ft-long 26-wheeled limo was designed by Jay Ohrberg of Burbank, CA. It has many features, including a swimming pool, a diving board and a king-sized water bed. It is designed to be driven as one piece or it can be changed to bend in the middle. Its main purpose is for use in films and exhibitions.

Lowest car
Perry Wakins and Danny Curtis of Aylesbury, Great Britain built a Hillman Imp, the *Impressed*, which stands 26 ½ in from the highest point on its open top roof to the road.

MERCHANT SHIPPING

Total The world total of merchant shipping, excluding vessels of less than 100 gross tonnage, sailing vessels and barges, was 423,627,198 gross tonnage on 1 Jul 1990.

As of 1 Nov 1990, there were 406 privately owned deep draft merchant ships with a gross tonnage of 1,000 or more in the United States. These ships are either oceangoing or Great Lakes motor carriers. Their carrying capacity is 30.539 million deadweight tons.

Shipbuilding Worldwide production completed in 1990 was 15.9 million gross tonnage of ships, excluding sailing ships, nonpropelled vessels and vessels of less than 100 gross tonnage. The figures for the USSR, Romania and the People's Republic of China are incomplete. Japan completed 6.8 million gross tonnage (43 percent of the world total) in 1990.

The world's leading shipbuilder in 1990 was Hyundai of South Korea, which completed 35 ships of 1.8 million gross tonnage.

Biggest owner The largest ship owners are the Japanese NYK Group, whose fleet of owned vessels totals 12,821,406 deadweight tons.

United States The largest shipping owner and operator in the United States is Exxon Corporation, whose fleets of owned/managed and chartered tankers in 1987 totaled a daily average of 10.42 million deadweight tons.

Largest fleet The largest merchant fleet in the world in mid-1990 was that under the flag of Liberia with a fleet totaling 54,699,564 gross tonnage.

PORTS

Largest The largest port in the world is the Port of New York and New Jersey. The port has a navigable waterfront of 755 miles (295 miles in New Jersey), stretching over 92 miles ^{2}. A total of 261 general cargo berths and 130 other piers gives a total berthing capacity of 391 ships at any one time. The total warehousing floor space is 422.4 acres.

Busiest The world's busiest port and largest artificial harbor is Rotterdam-Europoort in the Netherlands, which covers 38 miles ^{2}, with 76 miles of wharfs. In 1990 it handled 317.1 million tons of seagoing cargo, 99.2 million tons more than the port of Singapore, the world's second busiest.

Although the port of Singapore handled less tonnage, in terms of numbers of ships it was busier, with 36,000 ships calling there during 1988.

United States The busiest port in the USA is New Orleans, LA, which handled 1.775 million tons of cargo in 1989.

HOVERCRAFT (skirted air-cushion vehicles)

Fastest The world's fastest warship-hovercraft is the 78-ft-long 110.2 ton US Navy test vehicle SES-100B. She attained a world record 91.9 knots (105.8 mph) on 25 Jan 1980 on the Chesapeake Bay Test Range, MD. As a result of the success of this test craft, a 3,307 ton US Navy Large Surface Effect Ship (LSES) was built by Bell Aerospace under contract from the Department of Defense in 1977–81.

Longest journey The longest hovercraft journey was one of 5,000 miles, by the British Trans-African Hovercraft Expedition, under the leadership of David Smithers, through eight West African countries in a Winchester class SRN6, between 15 Oct 1969 and 3 Jan 1970.

Highest The highest altitude reached by a Hovercraft was on 11 Jun 1990 when *Neste Enterprise* and her crew of ten reached the navigable source of the Yangtze River, China at 16,050 ft.

The greatest altitude at which a hovercraft is operating is on Lake Titicaca, Peru, where since 1975 an HM2 Hoverferry has been hovering 12,506 ft above sea level.

Road Vehicles

COACHING

The longest horse-drawn procession was a cavalcade of 68 carriages that measured 3,018 ft "nose to tail," organized by the Spies Travelling Company of Denmark on 7 May 1986. It carried 810 people through the woods around Copenhagen to celebrate the coming of spring.

AUTOMOBILES

The total number of vehicles constructed worldwide in 1989 was 485,607,800, of which 35,057,630 were automobiles.

In 1990 the number of automobiles constructed in the United States was 6,077,449. The leading manufacturer was General Motors Corporation, which produced 2,755,284. The number of trucks manufactured in 1990 was 3,702,787; General Motors was the leading manufacturer with 1,467,249.

The world's largest manufacturer of motor vehicles and parts (and the largest manufacturing company) is General Motors Corporation of Detroit, MI. The company has on average 761,400 employees, and revenues for 1990 were $126 billion producing 5,571,905 vehicles.

Largest plant The largest single automobile plant in the world is the Volkswagenwerk at Wolfsburg, Germany, with 61,000 employees and a capacity for producing 4,100 vehicles daily. The factory buildings cover an area of 371 acres and the whole plant covers 1,878 acres, with 43.5 miles of rail sidings.

The largest automobile plant in the United States as calculated by its "straight-time capacity" (the number of cars or trucks built using two eight-hour shifts, five days per week), is Honda of America Manufacturing Inc.'s Marysville, OH plant with a capacity of 3,600,000 cars per year. It is estimated that Nissan Motor Manufacturing Corp's Smyrna, TN plant will have a capacity of 450,000 cars and compact pickup trucks when its expansion is completed in 1992.

Earliest automobiles *Model* The earliest "automobile" of which there is a record was a two-foot-long steam-powered model constructed by Ferdinand Verbiest (d. 1687), a Belgian Jesuit priest, and described in his *Astronomia Europaea*. His model of 1668 was possibly inspired either by Giovanni Branca's description of a steam turbine, published in his *La Macchina* in 1629, or by *Nan Huai-Jen* (writings on "fire carts") in the Chu dynasty (*c.* 800 B.C.).

The earliest full-scale automobile was the first of two military steam tractors completed at the Paris Arsenal in 1769 by Nicolas-Joseph Cugnot (1725–1804). This reached 2 ¼ mph. Cugnot's second, larger tractor, completed in May 1771, today survives in the *Conservatoire Nationale des Arts et Métiers* in Paris, France.

Passenger-carrying The world's first passenger-carrying automobile was a steam-powered road vehicle carrying eight passengers and built by Richard Trevithick (1771–1833). It first ran on 24 Dec 1801 in Camborne, Great Britain.

Internal combustion The Swiss Isaac de Rivaz (d. 1828) built a carriage powered by his "explosion engine" in 1805. The first practical internal combustion engined vehicle was that built by the Londoner Samuel Brown (British Patent Number. 5350, 25 Apr 1826), whose 4 hp two-cylinder atmospheric gas 88 liter engined carriage climbed Shooters Hill, Kent, Great Britain in May 1826.

The first successful gasoline-driven car, the Motorwagen, built by Karl-Friedrich Benz (1844–1929) of Karlsruhe, Germany, ran at Mannheim, Germany in late 1885. It was a 3 cwt three-wheeler reaching 8–10 mph. Its single-cylinder engine (bore 3.6 in, stroke 6.3 in) delivered 0.85 hp at 400 rpm. It was patented on 29 Jan 1886. Its first 1.62 mile road test was reported in the local newspaper, the *Neue Badische Landeszeitung*, of 4 Jun 1886, under the heading "Miscellaneous."

FASTEST CARS

Land speed The *official* one-mile land-speed record is 633.468 mph, set by Richard Noble (b. 1946) on 4 Oct 1983 over the Black Rock Desert, NV in his 17,000 lb thrust Rolls-Royce Avon 302 jet-powered *Thrust 2*, designed by John Ackroyd. (See also table, Fastest Cars.)

The fastest reputed land speed record in one direction is 739.666 mph or Mach 1.0106 by Stan Barrett (USA) in the *Budweiser Rocket*, a rocket-engined three-wheeled car, at Edwards Air Force Base, CA on 17 Dec 1979 (see also table).

The fastest land speed recorded by a woman is 524.016 mph by Mrs Kitty Hambleton (nee O'Neil; USA) in the 48,000 hp rocket-powered three-wheeled SM1 *Motivator* over the Alvard Desert, OR on 6 Dec 1976. Her official two-way

FASTEST CARS

CATEGORY	MPH	CAR	DRIVER	PLACE	DATE
JET ENGINED *official*	633.468	Thrust 2	Richard Noble (GB)	Black Rock Desert, NV	4 Oct 1983
ROCKET ENGINED *official*	622.287	Blue Flame	Gary Gabelich (USA)	Bonneville, UT	23 Oct 1970
*unofficial**	739.666	Budweiser Rocket	Stan Barrett (USA)	Edwards Air Force Base,CA	17 Dec 1979
WHEEL DRIVEN *turbine*	429.311	Bluebird	Donald Campbell (GB)	Lake Eyre, Australia	17 Jul 1964
multipiston engine	418.504	Goldenrod	Robert Summers (USA)	Bonneville, UT	12 Nov 1965
single piston engine	397.996	Speed O Motive	Al Teague (USA)	Bonneville, UT	9 Nov 1989

* This published speed of Mach 1.0106 is *not* officially sanctioned by the USAF, whose Digital Instrumented Radar was not calibrated or certified. The radar information was *not* generated by the vehicle directly but by an operator aiming the dish by means of a TV screen. To claim a speed to six significant figures appears quite unsustainable.

record was 512.710 mph and she probably touched 600 mph momentarily.

Diesel engined The prototype 3 liter Mercedes C 111/3 attained 203.3 mph in tests on the Nardo Circuit, southern Italy on 5–15 Oct 1978, and in April 1978 averaged 195.398 mph for 12 hours, thus covering a world record 2,399.76 miles.

Rocket-powered sleds The fastest speed recorded on ice is 247.93 mph by *Oxygen*, driven by Sammy Miller (b. 15 Apr 1945) on Lake George, NY on 15 Feb 1981.

Electric car The land speed record for an electric car over a distance of 1 km (0.621 mile) flying start was achieved by Christopher Sleath of Market Harborough, Great Britain with a speed of 62.18 mph, at Bruntingthorpe Training Ground, Great Britain on 25 Jun 1990.

Steam car On 19 Aug 1985 Robert E. Barber broke the 79-year-old record for a steam car driving No. 744, *Steamin' Demon*, built by the Barber-Nichols Engineering Co, which reached 145.607 mph at Bonneville Salt Flats, UT.

Road cars Various revved up track cars have been licensed for road use but are not normal production models.

Lamborghini asserted a speed of 202 mph for their Diablo at the Nardo Test Track, Italy, reported in March 1990.

LARGEST CARS

Of cars produced for private use, the largest was the Bugatti Royale type 41, of which only six were assembled (although it is believed that seven were built) at Molsheim, France by the Italian Ettore Bugatti. First built in 1927, this machine has an eight-cylinder engine of 12.7 liters capacity, and measures over 22 ft in length. The hood is over 7 ft long.

Largest engines The largest car ever used was the White Triplex, sponsored by J.H. White of Philadelphia, PA. Completed early in 1928, after two years' work, the car weighed about 4.5 tons and was powered by three Liberty V12 aircraft engines with a total capacity of 81,188 cc, developing 1,500 brake horsepower (bhp) at 2,000 rpm. It was used to break the world speed record but crashed at Daytona, FL on 13 Mar 1929.

Most powerful *Production car* The highest engine capacity of a production car was 2.5 gallon, for the US Pierce-Arrow 6–66 Raceabout of 1912–18, the US Peerless 6–60 of 1912–14 and the Fageol of 1918.

The most powerful current production car is the Cizeta V16T, which develops 520 bhp.

Heaviest The heaviest car in production today (up to twenty-five made annually) appears to be the Soviet-built Zil–41047 limousine with a 12.72 ft wheelbase. It weighs 7,352 lb (3.3 tons). The "stretched" Zil (four to five made annually) used by President Mikhail Gorbachev weighs 6.6 tons and is made of three-inch armor-plated steel. The eight-cylinder, 7-liter engine guzzles fuel at a rate of 6 miles to the gallon.

MISCELLANEOUS CARS

Highest mileage The highest recorded mileage for a car was 1.2 million authenticated miles by August 1978 for a 1957 Mercedes 180 D owned by Robert O'Reilly of Olympia, WA. Its subsequent fate is unknown.

Longest in production Among mass-production models, the Volkswagen "Beetle" dates from 1938.

United States The luxury model Cadillac Fleetwood has been in continuous production since 1936. The oldest mass-production model still in production is the Chrysler Imperial, which was in production from 1926–84 and 1990–present.

Registrations
Earliest The world's first license plates were introduced by the Paris police in France in 1893.

License plate No. 8 was sold at a Hong Kong government auction for HK\$5 million (approximately \$602,250) on 13 Feb 1988 to Law Tingpong, a textile manufacturer. The number 8 is considered a lucky number.

United States In 1989 there were 143,081,443 automobiles registered in the United States. As of 1 May 1991, it was estimated that there were 145,000,000 cars and 45,218,000 trucks in the United States.

■ **Heaviest car**
The heaviest car in production today is the Soviet-built ZIL-41047. It weighs 7,352 lb, can carry seven passengers comfortably and uses 5.8 gallons of gasoline per 62 miles. (Photo: Gamma/Brissaud)

Car collection
The unrivaled collector of Rolls-Royces was Bhagwan Shree Rajneesh (Osho; ne Chandra Mohan Jain [1931–90]), the Indian mystic of Rajneeshpuram, OR. His disciples bestowed 93 of these upon him before his deportation from the USA in November 1985.

Car wrecking
The greatest number of cars wrecked in a stunting career is 1,997 through 1 Jun 1990 by Dick Sheppard of Glouchester, Great Britain.

ROAD VEHICLES

Lightest Louis Borsi of London, Great Britain has built and driven a 21 lb car with a 2.5-cc engine. It is capable of 15 mph.

PRICE EXTREMES

Most expensive The most expensive car ever built was the US Presidential 1969 Lincoln Continental Executive delivered to the US Secret Service on 14 Oct 1968. It has an overall length of 21 ft 6.3 in with a 13 ft 4 in wheelbase, and with the addition of 2.2 tons of armor plate, weighs 6 tons (12,000 lb). The estimated cost of research, development and manufacture was $500,000, but it is rented at $5,000 per year. Even if all four tires were shot out it can travel at 50 mph on inner rubber-edged steel discs.

In March 1979 Carriage House Motor Cars of New York completed four years' work on converting a 1973 Rolls-Royce, including lengthening it by 30 in. The price tag was $500,000.

Used Although higher prices have been reported for sales by private treaty, the greatest price paid at a public auction was £6.4 million ($10.83 million), including commission, for a 1962 Ferrari 250 GTO sold by Sotheby's on 22 May 1990 at Monte Carlo, Monaco. It was bought by Hans Thulin.

Most inexpensive The cheapest car of all time was the 1922 Red Bug Buckboard, built by the Briggs & Stratton Co. of Milwaukee, WI, listed at $125–$150. It had a 62 in wheel-base and weighed 245 lb. Early models of the King Midget cars were sold in kit form for self-assembly for as little as $100 in 1948.

DRIVING

Around the world The fastest circumnavigation embracing more than an equator's length of driving (26,078 road miles) is one of 39 days 23 hr 35 min. Driving two Rover 827Si Saloon cars, six members (three male and three female) of the Transworld Venture organized by the Royal Army Ordnance Corps left the Tower of London, Great Britain on 13 May 1990 and returned to the same place on 22 June. On their epic journey they traveled through six continents and covered 25 countries. The distance covered was 25,187.8 miles.

Amphibious circumnavigation The only circumnavigation by an amphibious vehicle was by Ben Carlin (Australia; d. 7 Mar 1981) in the amphibious jeep *Half-Safe*. He completed the last leg of the Atlantic crossing (the English Channel) on 24 Aug 1951. He arrived back in Montreal, Canada on 8 May 1958, having completed a circumnavigation of 39,000 miles over land and 9,600 miles by sea and river. He was accompanied on the transatlantic stage by his ex-wife Elinore (USA) and on the long transpacific stage (Tokyo, Japan to Anchorage, AK) by Broye Lafayette De-Mente).

One-year duration record The greatest distance ever covered in one year is 354,257 miles by two Opel Rekord 2 liter passenger sedans, both of which covered this distance between 18 May 1988 and the same date in 1989 without any major mechanical breakdowns. The vehicles were manufactured by the Delta Motor Corporation, Port Elizabeth, South Africa, and were driven on tar and gravel roads in the Northern Cape by a team of company drivers from Delta. The entire undertaking was monitored by the Automobile Association of South Africa.

Trans-Americas Garry Sowerby (Canada), with Tim Cahill (USA) as co-driver and navigator, drove a 1988 GMC Sierra K3500 four-wheel-drive pickup truck powered by a 6.2 liter V8 Detroit diesel engine from Ushuaia, Tierra del Fuego, Argentina to Prudhoe Bay, AK, a distance of 14,739 miles, in a total elapsed time of 23 days 22 hr 43 min from 29 Sep to 22 Oct 1987. The vehicle and team were surface-freighted from Cartagena, Colombia to Balboa, Panama so as to bypass the Darien Gap.

The Darien Gap was first traversed by the Land Rover *La Cucaracha Carinosa* (The Affectionate Cockroach) of the Trans-Darién Expedition 1959–60, crewed by Richard E. Bevir (Great Britain) and engineer Terence John Whitfield (Australia). They left Chepo, Panama on 3 Feb 1960 and reached Quibdó, Colombia on 17 June, averaging 660 ft per hour of indescribable difficulty.

Trans-America Jeremiah L. Burr (driver/leader), Kurt E. Detlefsen (driver) and Thaddeus E. Burr (navigator) of Connecticut completed the first documented traverse of all the contiguous 48 states of the United States from 13 May to 19 May 1991, in a total elapsed time of 5 days, 7 hours and 15 minutes and a total distance of 7,217.8 miles. The team drove a 1990 Chevrolet Astro Van and stopped only for fuel. Dehydrated foods and 9 gallons of water made the team self-sufficient.

Gasoline consumption An experimental Japanese vehicle achieved the equivalent of 6,409 mpg in the Shell Mileage Marathon at Silverstone, Great Britain on 30 Jun 1988.

Longest fuel range The greatest distance driven without refueling on a single fuel fill in a standard vehicle (40.7 gal carried in factory-optional twin fuel tanks) is 1,438.2 miles by a 1990 Toyota LandCruiser diesel pickup. Driven by Ewan Kennedy and Ray Barker with Ian Lee (observer) from Perth, Western Australia to Port Augusta, South Australia in 31 hr 51 min in September 1990, the average speed was 45.2 mph, giving 35.3 mpg.

Driving in reverse Charles Creighton (1908–70) and James Hargis of Maplewood, MO drove their Model A Ford 1929 roadster in reverse from New York 3,340 miles to Los Angeles, CA, from 26 Jul–13 Aug 1930 without once stopping the engine. They arrived back in New York in reverse on 5 September, having completed 7,180 miles in 42 days.

The highest average speed attained in any nonstop reverse drive exceeding 500 miles was achieved by Gerald Hoagland, who drove a 1969 Chevrolet Impala 501 miles in 17 hr 38 min at Chemung Speed Drome, NY on 9–10 Jul 1976, to average 28.41 mph.

Brian "Cub" Keene and James "Wilbur" Wright drove their Chevrolet Blazer 9,031 miles in 37 days (1 Aug–6 Sep 1984) through 15 American states and Canada. Though it was prominently named "Stuck in Reverse," law-enforcement officers in Oklahoma refused to

believe it and insisted they drive in *reverse* reverse—i.e., forward—out of the state.

Two-side-wheel driving *Car* Bengt Norberg (b. 23 Oct 1951) of Äppelbo, Sweden drove a Mitsubishi Colt GTi-16V on two side wheels nonstop for a distance of 192.873 miles in a time of 7 hr 15 min 50 sec. He also achieved a distance of 30.328 miles in 1 hr at Rattvik Horse Track, Sweden on 24 May 1989.

Sven-Erik Söderman (b. 26 Sep 1960) achieved a speed of 102.14 mph over a 100 m (328.1 ft) flying start on the two wheels of an Opel Kadette at Mora Siljan airport, Dalecarlia, Sweden on 2 Aug 1990. Söderman also broke the 1,000 m (3,280.84 ft) flying kilometer at 95.04 mph at the same venue on 24 Aug 1990.

Truck Sven-Erik Söderman of Sweden drove a Daf 2800 7.5 ton truck on two wheels for a distance of 5.9 miles for 31 minutes at Mora Siljan airport, Delecarlia, Sweden on 10 Nov 1990.

Wheelie Steve Murty drove a Multi-Part Skytrain truck on its rear wheels for 1,353 ⅓ ft at Mondello Park, Co. Kildare, Republic of Ireland on 23 Aug 1987. The 66-ton truck was powered by a 500 bhp Cummins turbocharged 14 liter engine and had a ZF-Ecomat 600 hp five-speed automatic gearbox.

Most durable driver The Goodyear Tire and Rubber Co. test driver Weldon C. Kocich drove 3,141,946 miles from 5 Feb 1953 to 28 Feb 1986, thus averaging 95,210 miles per year.

Oldest driver Roy M. Rawlins (b. 10 Jul 1870) of Stockton, CA was given a warning for driving at 95 mph in a 55 mph zone in June 1974. On 25 Aug 1974 he was awarded a California State license valid until 1978, but he died on 9 Jul 1975, one day short of his 105th birthday.

Mrs Maude Tull of Inglewood, CA, who took to driving at the age of 91 after her husband died, was issued a renewal on 5 Feb 1976 when she was 104.

Drivers' licenses Regular drivers' licenses are issued to 15-year-olds without a driver-education course only in Hawaii and Mississippi. Thirteen states issue restricted juvenile licenses at 14.

SERVICES

Parking lots The world's largest is the one in the West Edmonton Mall, Edmonton, Alberta, Canada, which can hold 20,000 vehicles. There are overflow facilities on an adjoining lot for 10,000 more cars.

Garage The largest private garage is one of two stories built outside Bombay, India for the private collection of 176 cars owned by Pranlal Bhogilal (b. 1939).

The KMB Overhaul Center, operated by the Kowloon Motor Bus Co. (1933) Ltd, Hong Kong, is the world's largest multistory service center. Built expressly for double-decker buses, it has four floors occupying more than 11.6 acres.

Filling stations The largest concentration of pumps is 204—96 of them Tokheim Unistar (electronic) and 108 Tokheim Explorer (mechanical)—in Jeddah, Saudi Arabia.

The highest filling station in the world is at Leh, Ladakh, India, at 12,001 ft, operated by the Indian Oil Corporation.

Unleaded gasoline Under the provisions of the Clean Air Act (1970), the Environmental Protection Agency (EPA) was given a mandate to set a timetable for the introduction of unleaded gasoline to service stations throughout the United States. On 22 Feb 1972 the EPA announced proposed regulations that required all large service stations to carry low-octane nonleaded gas (with a minimum lead content of 0.05 grams per gallon). On 27 Dec 1972 the EPA set a deadline of 1 Jul 1974 for stations to carry nonleaded gas.

Tires *Largest* The largest ever manufactured were by the Goodyear Tire & Rubber Co. for giant dump trucks. They measure 12 ft in diameter, weigh 12,500 lb and cost $74,000. A tire 17 ft in diameter is believed to be the limit of what is practical.

Fattest The widest tire in normal production is the Pirelli P Zero, with 335/35Z5R17 dimensions.

Tow The longest on record was one of 4,759 miles from Halifax, Nova Scotia to Canada's Pacific coast, when Frank J. Elliott and George A. Scott of Amherst, Nova Scotia, Canada persuaded 168 passing motorists in 89 days to tow their Model T Ford (in fact engineless) to win a $1,000 bet on 15 Oct 1927.

After his 1969 MGB broke down in the vicinity of Moscow, USSR, the late Eddie McGowan of Chipping Warden, Great Britain was towed a distance of 1,456 miles from Moscow to Berlin, Germany on a 7-ft single nylon tow rope from 12–17 Jul 1987.

Skid marks The skid marks made by the jet-powered *Spirit of America*, driven by Norman Craig Breedlove, after the car went out of control at Bonneville Salt Flats, UT, on 15 Oct 1964, were nearly 6 miles long.

MISCELLANEOUS VEHICLES

Land *Largest* The most massive automotive land vehicle is "Big Muskie," the 12,004 ton mechanical shovel built by Bucyrus Erie for the Musk mine. It is 487 ft long, 151 ft wide and 222 ft high, with a grab capacity of 364 tons.

Longest The Arctic Snow Train owned by the world-famous tightrope-walker Steve McPeak (USA) has 54 wheels and is 572 ft long. It was built by R. G. Le Tourneau Inc. of Longview, TX for the US Army. Its gross train weight is 441 tons, with a top speed of 20 mph, and it was driven by a crew of six when used as an "overland train" for the military. McPeak undertook all repairs, including every punctured wheel, single-

handedly in often sub-zero temperatures in Alaska. It generates 4,680 shp and has a fuel capacity of 7,832 gal.

Largest ambulance The world's largest are the 59 ft ½-in-long articulated Alligator Jumbulances Marks VI, VII, VIII and IX, operated by the ACROSS Trust to convey the sick and handicapped on vacations and pilgrimages across Europe. They are built by Van Hool of Belgium with Fiat engines, cost $350,000 and carry 44 patients and staff.

Crawler The most massive vehicle ever constructed is the Marion eight-caterpillar crawler used for conveying Saturn V rockets to their launch pads at Cape Canaveral, FL. It measures 131 ft 4 in × 114 ft and the two built cost $12.3 million. The loaded train weight is 9,000 tons. The windshield wiper blades are 42 in long and are the world's largest.

Buses *Earliest* The first municipal bus service in the world was inaugurated on 12 Apr 1903 and ran between Eastbourne railroad station and Meads, Great Britain.

Longest The longest are the articulated buses, with 121 passenger seats and room also for 66 "strap-hangers," built by the Wayne Corporation of Richmond, IN for use in the Middle East. They are 76 ft long and weigh 23,957 lb.

The longest rigid single bus is 49 ft long and carries 69 passengers. It was built by Van Hool of Belgium.

The longest regularly scheduled bus route in the United States is by Greyhound, which runs a service from Miami, FL to Los Angeles, CA. The route is 2,642 miles, taking 61 hours 45 min.

Largest fleet The 6,580 single-decker buses in Rio de Janeiro, Brazil make up the world's largest bus fleet.

Longest route The longest regularly scheduled bus route is operated by "Across Australia Coach Lines," which inaugurated a regular scheduled service between Perth and Brisbane on 9 Apr 1980. The route is 3,389 miles long, taking 75 hr 55 min.

■ **Two-side-wheel truck drive**
Sven-Erik Söderman of Sweden drove this truck a distance of 5.9 miles for 31 minutes.

Ramp jumping
The longest ramp jump in an automobile, with the car landing on its wheels and being driven on, is 232 ft, by Jacqueline De Creed (nee Creedy) in a 1967 Ford Mustang at Santa Pod Raceway, Bedfordshire, Great Britain on 3 Apr 1983.

Tire supporting
The greatest number of tires supported in a free-standing lift is 96, by Gary Windebank of Romsey, Great Britain in February 1984. The total weight was 1,440 lb. The tires used were Michelin XZX 155 × 13.

Worst exit to miss

The longest distance between controlled access exits in the United States is 51.1 miles from Florida Turnpike exit 193 (Yeehaw Junction, FL) to exit 244 (Kissimee, FL). The worst exit to miss on any interstate highway is 37.7 miles from I-80 exit 41 (Knolls, UT) to exit 4 (Bonneville Speedway, UT).

Fire pump handling

The longest unaided tow of a fire appliance in excess of 1,120 lb in 24 hr on a closed circuit is 223 miles, by a 32-man team of the Dublin Fire Brigade with a 1,144-lb fire pump on 20–21 Jun 1987.

Fire pumping

The greatest gallonage stirrup-pumped by a team of eight in an 80 hr charity pump is 27,414 gal by fire-fighters representing Grampian Fire Brigade, from 17–20 Aug 1989 at Aberdeen, Great Britain.

Lawn mowers

The widest gang mower in the world is the 5.6 ton 60 ft wide 27-unit "Big Green Machine" used by the turf farmer Jay Edgar Frick of Monroe, OH. It mows an acre in 60 sec.

Longest distance

The longest drive on a power lawn mower was 3,034 miles, when Ian Ireland of Harlow, Great Britain drove an Iseki SG15 between Harlow and Southend Pier, Great Britain from 13 Aug to 7 Sep 1989. He was assisted by members of 158 Round Table, Luton, Great Britain and raised over £15,000 ($26,250) in aid of the Leukemia Research Fund.

Greatest passenger volume The city with the greatest passenger volume in the United States in 1990 was New York City, with 724.094 million unlinked passenger trips. In 1989 the city with the highest aggregate for passenger miles traveled was Los Angeles, CA, where bus riders logged 1.6 billion miles.

Campers Largest The largest two-wheeled two-story camper was built in 1990 by H.E Sheik Hamad Bin Hamdan Al Nahyan of Abu Dhabi, United Arab Emirates. It is 66 ft long, 39.37 ft wide and stands 39.37 ft. Weighing 120 tons, it comprises eight bedrooms, eight bathrooms, four garages and water storage for 6,340 gal.

Longest journey The continuous motor camper journey of 143,716 miles by Harry B. Coleman and Peggy Larson in a Volkswagen Camper from 20 Aug 1976 to 20 Apr 1978 took them through 113 countries.

Fastest The world speed record for a camper is 124.91 mph by an Alpha 14 towed by a Le Mans Aston Martin V8 saloon driven by Robin Hamilton, at RAF Elvington, North Yorkshire, Great Britain on 14 Oct 1980.

Dump truck The world's largest is the Terex Titan 33–19 manufactured by General Motors Corporation and now in operation at Westar Mine, British Columbia, Canada. It has a loaded weight of 604.7 tons and a capacity of 350 tons. When tipped its height is 56 ft. The 16 cylinder engine delivers 3,300 hp. The fuel tank holds 1,300 gal.

Fire engines The world's most powerful fire appliance is the 860 hp eight-wheel Oshkosh firetruck used for aircraft fires. It can discharge 41,600 gal of foam through two turrets in just 150 sec. It weighs 66 tons.

Fastest The fastest on record is the Jaguar XJ12 "Chubb Firefighter," which on 2 Nov 1982 atttained a speed of 130.57 mph in tests when servicing the *Thrust 2* land-speed record trials. (See Fastest cars—Land speed.)

Go karts The highest mileage recorded in 24 hours on a closed indoor circuit by a four-man team is 3,833 laps of a 238.5 yd track at Silvia Park, Auckland, New Zealand on 1–2 Sep 1990. The 5 hp 144-cc Honda-engined kart was driven by Andrew Hill, Harry and Matt Redward and Rhodri Griffiths.

The greatest distance recorded in a 48-hour marathon is 1,696.3 miles by Denis Wedes, Stephen Mantle, Len Nicholson and Janice Bennett, driving a Yamaha RC100SE kart powered by a KT100J 100 cc engine at Mount Sugarloaf Circuit, Newcastle, New South Wales, Australia on 25–27 Mar 1983.

The highest mileage of the 100 cc non-gearbox six-hour record is 194.81 miles by Emily Newman at Rye House Raceway, Hoddesdon, Great Britain on 25 Jun 1986.

Solar-powered The fastest speed attained by a solely solar-powered land vehicle is 48.71 mph by Molly Brennan driving the General Motors *Sunraycer* at Mesa, AZ on 24 Jun 1988. The fastest speed of 83.88 mph using solar/battery power was achieved by Star Micronics solar car *Solar Star* driven by Manfred Hermann on 5 Jan 1991 at Richmond RAAF Base, Richmond, New South Wales, Australia.

Taxis The largest taxi fleet is that in Mexico City, with 60,000 "normal" taxis, *pesaros* (communal fixed-route taxis) and *settas* (airport taxis).

Carmen Fasanella (b. 19 Feb 1903) was continuously licensed as a taxi-cab owner and driver in the Borough of Princeton, NJ for 68 years 243 days from 1 Feb 1921 to 2 Nov 1989.

The city with the largest taxi fleet in the USA is New York City, which on 1 May 1991 had 11,787 registered yellow medallion cabs and 40,000 drivers. In addition, there are approximately 40,000 rental service vehicles in New York City.

The longest taxicab ride on record is one of 13,670 miles with the meter running at a cost of £31,446 ($55,030.50). Ned Kelly and Dr John Morgan, accompanied by taxi drivers Guy Smith and Kanelli Tsiros, left London, Great Britain on 19 Aug 1988 and arrived in Sydney, Australia on 27 Oct 1988 as part of the Australian Bicentenary celebrations.

Tractor The world's largest tractor is a $459,000 US Department of Agriculture Wide Tractive Frame Vehicle completed by Ag West of Sacramento, CA in June 1982. It measures 33 ft between its wheels, which are designed to run on permanent paths, and weighs 24.5 tons.

The sport of tractor-pulling was put on a national US championship basis in 1967 at Bowling Green, OH, where the winner was "The Purple Monster" built and driven by Roger E. Varns. Today there are 12 classes ranging up to "12,200 lb unlimited."

Trams Longest journey The longest tram journey now possible is from Krefeld St Tönis to Witten Annen Nord, Germany. With luck at the eight interconnections, the 65.5 mile trip can be achieved in 5 ½ hours.

By early 1991 Leningrad, USSR had the most extensive tramway system, with 2,402 cars on 64 routes and 429.13 miles of track.

Most powerful truck A 1987 Ford LTL 9000 truck, owned and driven by Ken Warby of Cincinnati, OH, is outfitted with a General Electric J 79 tuned to produce 20,000 lbf of thrust. Weighing 4.8 tons, it has achieved 210.2 mph in 7.7 sec over a quarter-mile course from a standing start.

Wrecker The world's most powerful wrecker is the Twin City Garage and Body Shop's 22.7-ton, 36-ft-long International M6-23 "Hulk" 1969 stationed at Scott City, MO. It can lift in excess of 325 tons on its short boom.

LOADS

Heaviest load On 14–15 Jul 1984 John Brown Engineers & Contractors BV moved the Conoco Kotter Field production deck with a roll-out weight of 325 tons for the Continental Netherlands Oil Co. of Leidsenhage, Netherlands.

MODEL CARS

Nonstop duration A Scalextric Jaguar XJ8 ran nonstop for 866 hr 44 min 54 sec and covered a distance of 1,771.2 miles from 2 May to 7 Jun 1989. The event was organized by the Rev. Bryan G. Apps and church members of Southbourne, Great Britain.

24 hour slot car racing Under the rules of the BSCRA (British Slot Car Racing Association) a 24-hour world-record was set for 1/32 scale cars. On 5–6 Jul 1986 the North London Society of Model Engineers team at the ARRA club in Southport, Great Britain achieved a distance of 305.949 miles, 11,815 laps of the track driving a Rondeau M482C Group C Sports car, built by Ian Fisher.

MOTORCYCLES

In 1989, there were 4,433,915 motorcycles registered in the United States. As of 1 May 1991 it was estimated that there were 4,274,000 motorcycles in the United States.

Earliest The earliest internal combustion-engined motorized bicycle was a wooden-framed machine built at Bad Cannstatt, Germany in October–November 1885 by Gottlieb Daimler (1834–1900) of Germany and first ridden by Wilhelm Maybach (1846–1929). It had a top speed of 12 mph and developed one-half of one horsepower from its single-cylinder 264 cc four-cycle engine at 700 rpm. Known as the "Einspur," it was lost in a fire in 1903.

The earliest factory which made motorcycles in quantity was opened in 1894 by Heinrich and Wilhelm Hildebrand and Alois Wolfmüller in Munich, Germany. In its first two years this factory produced over 1,000 machines, each having a water-cooled 1488 cc twin-cylinder four-cycle engine developing about 2.5 bhp at 600 rpm—the highest-capacity motorcycle engine ever put into production.

Fastest production road machine The 151 hp 1-litre Kawasaki Tu Atara YB6 EI has a road-tested top speed of 186 mph.

Fastest racing machine There is no satisfactory answer to the identity of the fastest track machine other than to say that the current Honda, Suzuki and Yamaha machines have all been geared to attain speeds marginally in excess of 186.4 mph under race conditions.

Fastest speeds Official world speed records must be set with two runs over a measured distance made in opposite directions within a time limit—1 hr for FIM records and 2 hr for AMA records.

Donald A. Vesco (USA; b. 8 Apr 1939), riding his 6.4 m long *Lightning Bolt* streamliner, powered by two 1016 cc Kawasaki engines on Bonneville Salt

Flats, UT on 28 Aug 1978 set AMA and FIM absolute records with an overall average of 318.598 mph and had a fastest run at an average of 318.865 mph.

The world record for 0.62 miles from a standing start is 16.68 sec by Henk Vink (Netherlands; b. 24 Jul 1939) on his supercharged 984 cc four-cylinder Kawasaki, at Elvington Airfield, North Yorkshire, Great Britain on 24 Jul 1977. The faster run was made in 16.09 sec.

The world record for 1,320 ft from a standing start is 8.805 sec by Henk Vink on his supercharged 1132 cc four-cylinder Kawasaki at Elvington Airfield, Great Britain on 23 Jul 1977. The faster run was made in 8.55 sec.

The fastest time for a single run over 440 yd from a standing start is 7.08 sec by Bo O'Brechta (USA) riding a supercharged 1200 cc Kawasaki-based machine in Ontario, CA in 1980.

The highest terminal velocity recorded at the end of a 440 yd run from a standing start is 199.55 mph by Russ Collins (USA) in Ontario, CA on 7 Oct 1978.

Smallest Magnor Mydland of Norway constructed a motorcycle with a wheelbase of 4.72 in, a seat height of 5.82 in and wheel diameters of 1.49 in for the front and 3.39 in for the back. He rode a distance of 1,870 ft, reaching a speed of 7.2 mph.

Simon Timperley and Clive Williams of Progressive Engineering Ltd, Ashton-under-Lyne, Lancashire, Great Britain designed and constructed a motorcycle with a wheelbase of 4.25 in, a seat height of 3¾ in and a wheel diameter of 0.75 in for the front and 0.95 in for the back. Simon rode the bike a distance of 3.2 ft, reaching a speed of 2 mph.

Duration The longest time a motor scooter, a Kinetic Honda DX 100 cc, has been kept in nonstop motion is 1,001 hrs. It was ridden by Har Parkash Rishi, Amarjeet Singh and Navjot Chadha, covering a distance of 49,831 miles at Traffic Park, Pune, Maharashtra, India between 22 Apr–3 Jun 1990.

Biggest pyramid The White Helmets, of the Royal Signals Motorcycle Display team, successfully achieved an eight-bike 36-man pyramid for 984 ft on 2 Sep 1986. They also achieved a 13-man pyramid, held together by muscle and determination only, on straps, harnesses or any other aids, mounted on three motorcycles which traveled a distance of 0.8 mile in 2 min 6.6 sec at Catterick Airfield, Great Britain, on 30 Sep 1988.

Wheelie *Distance* Yasuyuki Kudoh at the Japan Automobile research Institute, Tsukuba City, Ibaragi-pref, Japan covered 205.7 miles nonstop on the rear wheel of his Honda TLM 220 R 216 cc motorcycle on 5 May 1991.

United States Doug Domokos on the Alabama International Speedway, Talladega on 27 Jun 1984 covered 145 miles nonstop on the rear wheel of his Honda XR 500. He stopped only when the gasoline ran out.

Two-wheel sidecar riding Graham John Martin drove a distance of 198.9 miles on a Yamaha XS 1100 cc bike in a time of 3 hr 5 min at Gerotek Test Track, Pretoria, South Africa on 21 Aug 1988.

Most on one machine The record for the most people on a single machine is all 46 members of the Illawarra Mini Bike Training Club, New South Wales, Australia. They rode on a 1000 cc motorcycle and traveled a distance of 1 mile on 11 Oct 1987.

BICYCLES

Earliest The first design for a machine propelled by cranks and pedals with connecting rods has been attributed to Leonardo da Vinci (1452–1519) or one of his pupils, c. 1493.

The earliest such design actually built was in 1839–40 by Kirkpatrick Macmillan (1810–78) of Dumfries. The machine is now in the Science Museum, London, Great Britain.

The first practical bicycle was the *vélocipède* built in March 1861 by Pierre Michaux and his son Ernest of Rue de Verneuil, Paris, France.

In 1870, James Starley of Coventry, Great Britain, constructed the first "penny-farthing" or ordinary bicycle. It had wire-spoked wheels for lightness and was available with an optional-speed gear.

Bicycle parade The greatest participation was one involving 30,000 cyclists (2.75 percent of the population of Puerto Rico) at San Juan on 17 Apr 1988. It was organized by TV personality "Pacheco" Joaquín Monserrat.

Trishaw The longest trishaw parade on record was when 177 trishaw peddlers rode in single file in Penang, Malaysia on 23 Nov 1986.

Longest The longest true tandem bicycle ever built (i.e., without a third stabilizing wheel) is one of 66 ft 11 in for 35 riders built by Pedaalstompers Westmalle of Belgium. The riders covered c. 195 ft in practice on 20 Apr 1979. The machine weighs 2,425 lb.

Terry Thessman of Pahiatua, New Zealand designed and built a bike measuring 72.96 ft long and weighing 340 lb. It was ridden by four riders a distance of 807 ft on 27 Feb 1988.

Smallest Jacques Puyoou of Pau, Pyrénées-Atlantiques, France has built a tandem of 14.1 in wheel diameter, which has been ridden by him and Madame Puyoou.

Largest The largest bicycle as measured by the front-wheel diameter is "Frankencycle," built by Dave Moore of Rosemead, CA and first ridden by Steve Gordon of Moorpark, CA, on 4 Jun 1989. The wheel diameter is 10 ft and it is 11 ft 2 in high.

HPVs *Fastest land* The world speed records for human-powered vehicles (HPVs), 200 m (656.2 ft) flying start (single rider), are 65.484 mph by Fred

Markham at Mono Lake, CA on 11 May 1986 and 62.92 mph (multiple riders) by Dave Grylls and Leigh Barczewski at the Ontario Speedway, CA, on 4 May 1980. The one-hour standing start (single rider) record is held by Pat Kinch, riding *Kingcycle Bean*, averaging a speed of 46.96 mph on 8 Sep 1990 at Millbrook Proving Ground, Great Britain.

Water cycle The men's 6,562 ft (single rider) record is 12.84 mph by Steve Hegg in *Flying Fish* at Long Beach, CA on 20 Jul 1987.

Wheelie A duration record of 5 hr 12 min 33 sec was set by David Robilliard at the Beau Sejour Leisure Center, St Peter Port, Guernsey, Channel Islands on 28 May 1990.

Unicycles *Tallest* The tallest unicycle ever mastered is one 101 ft 9 in tall ridden by Steve McPeak (with a safety wire suspended by an overhead crane) for a distance of 376 ft in Las Vegas, NV in October 1980.

Smallest Peter Rosendahl of Las Vegas, NV rode a unicycle with a wheel diameter of 2.988 in in a radius of 4 ft for 30 sec at Circus Circus Hotel, Las Vegas, NV on 4 Aug 1990.

Endurance Deepak Lele of Maharashtra, India unicycled 3,963 miles from New York to Los Angeles from 6 Jun–25 Sep 1984.

Takayuki Koike of Kanagawa, Japan set a unicycle record for 100 miles in 6 hr 44 min 21.84 sec on 9 Aug 1987.

John Foss of Westbury, NY rode 100 m (328.1 ft) in 13.71 sec in Tokyo, Japan on 1 Aug 1987.

Backwards Peter Rosendahl of Las

■ **Unicycle records**
Peter Rosendahl of Nevada currently holds four unicycle records; smallest rideable, backwards distance, fastest sprint from standing, and flying starts.

Snowmobile
Tony Lenzini of Duluth, MN drove his 1986 Arctic Cat Cougar snowmobile a total of 7,211 miles in 60 riding days between 28 Dec 1985 and 20 Mar 1986.

Pedal car
The record from Marble Arch, London, Great Britain to the Arc de Triomphe, Paris, France, including a channel crossing by ferry, is 23 hr 21 min 27 sec, for a distance of 249 miles, by six members of Lea Manor High School and Community College, Luton, Great Britain on 27–28 May 1989.

Ramp jumping
The longest distance ever achieved for motorcycle long jumping is 246 ft, by Todd Seeley at a World of Wheels show in Tampa, FL on 28 Feb 1988.

Wall of death
The greatest endurance feat on a wall of death was 6 hr 7 min 38 sec, by Hugo Dabbert (b. Hildesheim, Germany on 24 Sep 1938) at Rüsselsheim on 14 Aug 1980. He rode 6,841 laps on the 32.8 ft diameter wall on a Honda CM 400T, averaging 21.8 mph for the 133.4 miles.

Underwater tricycling
A team of 32 divers pedaled a distance of 116.66 miles in 75 hr 20 min on a standard tricycle at Diver's Den, Santa Barbara, CA on 16–19 Jun 1988 to raise money for the Muscular Dystrophy Association.

Vegas, NV rode his 24 in wheel unicycle backwards for a distance of 46.7 miles in 9 hr 25 min on 19 May 1990.

Sprint Peter Rosendahl at the Wet 'N Wild Show, Las Vegas on 1 Jul 1990 set a sprint record from a standing start over 100 m (328.1 ft) of 12.74 secs and from a flying start for the same distance of 12.43 secs.

Roads

Road mileages The country with the greatest length of road is the United States (all 50 states), with 3,876,501 miles of graded road. The state with the most miles of road is Texas (305,692), while Hawaii has the least, with 4,082 miles.

Longest driveable road The Pan-American Highway, from northwest Alaska to Santiago, Chile, then eastward to Buenos Aires, Argentina and terminating in Brasilia, Brazil is over 15,000 miles in length. There remains a gap known as the Tapon del Darién in Panama and another at the Atrato Swamp, Colombia.

The longest highway solely in the United States is US-20, which runs 3,365 miles from Boston, MA to Newport, OR. The longest highway in the interstate system is I-90, 3,107 miles from Boston, MA to Seattle, WA.

Highest roads The highest trail in the world is an 8 mile stretch of the Kang-ti-suu between Khaleb and Xingi-fu, Tibet, which in two places exceeds 20,000 ft.

The highest traversable road in the world is one 733.2 miles long between Tibet and southwestern Xinjiang, China, completed in October 1957, which takes in passes at altitudes up to 18,480 ft above sea level.

Lowest roads The lowest road is along the Israeli shores of the Dead Sea at 1,290 ft below sea level.

The world's lowest "pass" is Rock Reef Pass, Everglades National Park, FL, which is 3 ft above sea level.

Widest roads The widest road in the world is the Monumental Axis, running for 1½ miles from the Municipal Plaza to the Plaza of the Three Powers in Brasilia, the capital of Brazil. The six-lane boulevard was opened in April 1960 and is 820.2 ft wide.

The San Francisco–Oakland Bay Bridge Toll Plaza has 23 lanes (17 westbound) serving the bridge in Oakland, CA.

Greatest traffic volume The most heavily traveled stretch of road is Route 10, Junction Route 13.80, Normandie Avenue Interchange, Los Angeles, CA with a rush-hour traffic volume 18,000 vehicles.

The territory with the highest traffic density in the world is Hong Kong. By 1 Jan 1987 there were 300,000 motor vehicles on 867 miles of serviceable roads, giving a density of 4.53 yd per vehicle.

Bridge The world's busiest bridge is the Howrah Bridge across the river Hooghly in Calcutta, India. In addition to 57,000 vehicles per day it carries an incalculable number of pedestrians across its 1,500-ft-long 72-ft-wide span.

Longest traffic jams The longest ever reported was that of 16 Feb 1980, which stretched northwards from Lyons 109.3 miles towards Paris, France.

A record traffic jam was reported for 1½ million cars crawling bumper-to-bumper over the East-West German border on 12 Apr 1990.

Streets *Longest* The longest designated street in the world is Yonge Street, running north and west from Toronto, Ontario, Canada. The first stretch, completed on 16 Feb 1796, ran 34 miles. Its official length, now extended to Rainy River on the Ontario–Minnesota border, is 1,178.3 miles.

Narrowest The world's narrowest street is in the village of Ripatransone in the Marche region of Italy. It is called *Vicolo della Virilita* ("Virility Alley") and is 16.9 in wide.

Shortest The title of "The Shortest Street in the World" is claimed by Bacup, Great Britain, where Elgin Street, situated by the old market ground, measures just 17 ft.

Steepest The steepest street in the world is Baldwin Street, Dunedin, New Zealand, which has a maximum gradient of 1 in 1.266.

United States The crookedest and steepest street in the US is Lombard Street, San Francisco, CA. It has eight consecutive 90-degree turns of 20-ft radius.

Squares *Largest* Tiananmen ("Gate of

Heavenly Peace") Square in Beijing, described as the navel of China, covers 98 acres.

The Maiden e Shah Square in Isfahan, Iran extends over 20.1 acres.

Railroading

TRAINS

Earliest The first practical electric railroad was Werner von Siemens' oval meter gauge demonstration track, about 984 ft long, at the Berlin Trades Exhibition in Germany on 31 May 1879.

Fastest The world's fastest speed with passengers in a non-railed vehicle is 249 mph by the Maglev (magnetic levitation) MLU-001 test train over the 4.3-mile-long JNR experimental track at Miyazaki, Japan on 4 Feb 1987.

The fastest speed recorded on any national rail system is 320 mph by the French SNCF high-speed train TGV (*Train à Grande Vitesse*) between Courtalain and Tours on 18 May 1990. It was brought into service on 27 Sep 1981. By September 1983 it had reduced its scheduled time for the Paris–Lyons run in France of 264 miles to exactly 2 hours, thus averaging 132 mph.

The highest speed ever ratified for a steam locomotive was 125 mph over 1,320 ft, by the LNER 4-6-2 No. 4468 *Mallard* (later numbered 60022), which hauled seven coaches weighing 267.9 tons down Stoke Bank, near Essendine, Great Britain on 3 Jul 1938. Driver Joseph Duddington was at the controls with Fireman Thomas Bray. The engine suffered some damage.

Longest nonstop Steam Locomotive No. 4472, *Flying Scotsman*, completed a nonstop run, hauling 590 tons between Parkes and Broken Hill in New South Wales, Australia on 6 Aug 1989. The total distance covered was 422 miles in a time of 9 hr 25 min 15 sec.

Most powerful The world's most powerful steam locomotive, measured by tractive effort, was No. 700, a triple-articulated or triplex 2-8-8-8-4 wheels and a six-cylinder engine built by the Baldwin Locomotive Works in 1916 for the Virginian Railway. It had a tractive force of 166,300 lb when working compound and 199,560 lb when working simple.

Probably the heaviest train ever hauled by a single engine was one of 17,135 tons made up of 250 freight cars stretching 1.6 miles by the *Matt H. Shay* (No. 5014), a 2-8-8-8-2 engine, which ran on the Erie Railroad from May 1914 until 1929.

Greatest load The world's strongest rail carrier, with a capacity of 838 tons, is the 36-axle "Schnabel," 301 ft 10 in long, built for a US railroad by Krupp, Germany in March 1981.

The heaviest load ever moved on rails is the 11,971 ton Church of the Virgin

Mary (built in 1548 in the village of Most, Czechoslovakia), in October–November 1975, moved because it was in the way of coal operations. It was moved 2,400 ft at 0.0013 mph over four weeks, at a cost of $17 million.

Freight trains The world's longest and heaviest freight train on record, with the largest number of cars recorded, made a run on the 3 ft 6 in gauge Sishen–Saldanha railroad in South Africa on 26–27 Aug 1989. The train consisted of 660 cars each loaded to 105 tons gross, a tank car and a caboose, moved by nine 50 kV electric and seven diesel-electric locomotives distributed along the train. The train was 4 ½ miles long and weighed 77,720 tons excluding locomotives. It traveled a distance of 535 miles in 22 hr 40 min.

United States The longest and heaviest freight train on record was about 4 miles in length. It comprised 500 coal motor cars with three 3600 hp diesels pulling and three more in the middle, on the Iaeger, WV, to Portsmouth, OH stretch of 157 miles on the Norfolk and Western Railway on 15 Nov 1967. The total weight was nearly 47,040 tons.

TRACKS

Longest The world's longest run is one of 5,864½ miles on the Trans-Siberian line from Moscow to Nakhodka, USSR, in the Soviet Far East. There are 97 stops on the journey, which takes 8 days 4 hr 25 min.

The 1,954 mile Baikal–Amur (BAM) main line (USSR), begun with forced labor in 1938, was restarted in 1974 and put into service on 27 Oct 1984. A total of 13.5 billion ft³ of earth had to be moved and 3,901 bridges built in this $12 billion project.

Longest straight The Commonwealth Railways Trans-Australian line over the Nullarbor Plain, from Mile 496 between Nurina and Loongana, Western Australia to Mile 793 between Ooldea and Watson, South Australia, is 297 miles dead straight, although not level.

United States The longest straight track in the United States is 78.86 miles on CSX Railroad, between Wilmington and Hamlet, NC.

Widest and narrowest gauge The widest in standard use is 5 ft 6 in. This width is used in Spain, Portugal, India, Pakistan, Bangladesh, Sri Lanka, Argentina and Chile.

The narrowest gauge on which public services are operated is 10¼ in on the Wells Harbor (0.7 mile) and the Wells-Walsingham Railways (4 miles) in Norfolk, Great Britain.

Highest line At 15,806 ft above sea level, the standard gauge (4 ft 8½ in) track on the Morococha branch of the Peruvian State Railways at La Cima is the highest in the world.

Lowest line The world's lowest is in the Seikan Tunnel between Honshu and Hokkaido, Japan. The rails are 786 ft

below the Tsugaro Straits. The tunnel was opened on 13 Mar 1988 and is 33.4 miles long.

Steepest gradient The world's steepest standard-gauge gradient by adhesion is 1:11, between Chedde and Servoz on the meter-gauge SNCF Chamonix line, France.

Busiest system The railroad carrying the largest number of passengers is the East Japan Railway Co., which in 1989 carried 14,660,000 passengers daily. Among articles lost in 1989 were 377,712 umbrellas, 141,200 clothing items, 143,761 books and stationery items, 4,359 accessories and 89,799 purses.

Greatest length of railroad The country with the greatest length of railroad is the United States, with 184,235 miles of track.

RAIL TRAVEL

Most countries in 24 hours The greatest number of countries traveled through entirely by train in 24 hours is 10, by Aaron Kitchen on 16–17 Feb 1987. His route started in Yugoslavia and continued through Austria, Italy, Liechtenstein, Switzerland, France, Luxembourg, Belgium and the Netherlands, arriving in Germany 22 hr 42 min later.

Handpumped railcars A speed of 20.51 mph for a 984 ft course was achieved by Gold's Gym, Surrey, British Columbia, Canada at the Annual World Championship Handcar Races, Port Moodby, British Columbia with their five-man team (one pusher, four pumpers) in a time of 32.71 sec on 2 Jul 1986.

STATIONS

Largest The world's largest is Grand Central Terminal, Park Avenue and 42nd Street, New York City, built from 1903–13. It covers 48 acres on two levels with 41 tracks on the upper level and 26 on the lower. On average more than 550 trains and 180,000 people per day use it.

Busiest The busiest railroad junction in the world is Clapham Junction, London, Great Britain, in the Southern Region of British Rail, with an average of 2,200 trains passing through each 24 hours.

Highest The Condor station in Bolivia at 15,705 ft on the meter gauge Rio Mulato to Potosi line is the highest in the world.

Waiting rooms The world's largest waiting rooms are the four in Beijing Station, Chang'an Boulevard, Beijing, China, opened in September 1959, with a total standing capacity of 14,000.

Platforms The longest railroad platform in the world is the Kharagpur platform, West Bengal, India, which measures 2,733 ft in length.

The State Street Center subway platform on "The Loop" in Chicago, IL measures 3,500 ft in length.

The two platforms comprising the New Misato railroad station on the Musa-

Suggestion boxes
The most prolific
example on record of
the use of a suggestion
box is that of John
Drayton (1907–87) of
Newport, Great
Britain, who plied the
British rail system with
a total of 31,400 sug-
gestions from 1924 to
August 1987. More than
one in seven were
adopted and 100 were
accepted by London
Transport. In 1983 he
was presented with a
chiming clock by
British Rail to mark
almost 60 years of sug-
gestions.

shino line, Saitama, Japan are 984 ft
apart and are connected by a bridge.

SUBWAY SYSTEMS

Most extensive The subway with most
stations in the world is the New York
City Metropolitan Transportation Authority subway (first section opened on
27 Oct 1904). The network covers 231.73
route miles and 469 subway stations, and
served an estimated 5 million riders per
day in 1990.

Traveling *New York subway* The
record for traveling the whole system is
26 hr 21 min 08 sec set by Kevin Foster
(USA) on 25–26 Oct 1989.

Moscow Metro The record transit on 9
Dec 1988 (all 123 named stations) was
9 hr 39 min 50 sec by Peter Altman and
Miss Jackie Smith (both Great Britain).

Busiest The world's busiest metro
system is that in Greater Moscow,
USSR, with as many as 3.3 billion passengers per year. There are 141 stations
(18 of which have more than one name,
being transfer stations) and 140 miles of
track. The 5 kopek fare has just been
increased to 15 kopeks for the first time
since the Metro went into operation in
1935.

Aircraft

*The use of the Mach scale for aircraft
speeds was introduced by Prof. Ackeret of
Zürich, Switzerland. The Mach number
is the ratio of the velocity of a moving body
to the local velocity of sound. This ratio
was first employed by Dr Ernst Mach
(1838–1916) of Vienna, Austria in 1887.
Thus Mach 1.0 equals 760.98 mph at sea
level at 59°F, and is assumed, for conven-
ience, to fall to a constant 659.78 mph in
the stratosphere, i.e., above 36,089 ft.*

EARLIEST FLIGHTS

The first controlled and sustained
power-driven flight occurred near Kill
Devil Hill, Kitty Hawk, NC, at 10:35 A.M.
on 17 Dec 1903, when Orville Wright
(1871–1948) flew the 12 hp chain-driven
Flyer I for a distance of 120 ft at an
airspeed of 30 mph, a ground speed of
6.8 mph and an altitude of 8–12 ft for
about 12 seconds, watched by his brother
Wilbur (1867– 1912), four men and a boy.
Both brothers, from Dayton, OH, were
bachelors because, as Orville put it, they
had not the means to "support a wife as
well as an airplane." The *Flyer* is now in
the National Air and Space Museum at
the Smithsonian Institution, Washington,
D.C.

The first hop by a passenger-carrying
airplane entirely under its own power was
made when Clément Ader (1841–1925) of
France flew in his *Eole* for about 164 ft at
Armainvilliers, France on 9 Oct 1890. It
was powered by a lightweight steam
engine of his own design, which developed
about 20 hp.

The earliest "rational design" for a flying
machine, according to the Royal Aeronau-
tical Society, London, Great Britain was
that published by Emanuel Swedenborg
(1688–1772) in Sweden in 1717.

Jet-engined Proposals for jet propulsion date back to Capt. Marconnet
(1909) of France, and Henri Coanda
(1886–1972) of Romania, and to the
turbojet proposals of Maxime Guillaume
in 1921.

The first flight by an airplane powered
by a turbojet engine was made by the
Heinkel He 178, piloted by Flug Kapitän
Erich Warsitz, at Marienehe, Germany
on 27 Aug 1939. It was powered by a
Heinkel He S3b engine weighing 834 lb
(as installed with long tailpipe) designed by Dr Hans "Pabst" von Ohain
and first tested in August 1937.

Transatlantic The first crossing of
the North Atlantic by air was made by
Lt-Cdr Albert Cushion Read (1887
–1967) and his crew (Stone, Hinton,
Rodd, Rhoads and Breese) in the 84 knot
US Navy/Curtiss flying boat NC-4 from
Trepassey Harbor, Newfoundland,
Canada, via the Azores, to Lisbon, Portugal from 16–27 May 1919. The whole
flight of 4,717 miles, originating from
Rockaway Air Station, Long Island, NY
on 8 May, required 53 hr 58 min, terminating at Plymouth, Great Britain on 31
May. The Newfoundland–Azores flight
of 1,200 miles took 15 hr 18 min at
81.7 knots (94.1 mph).

Nonstop The first nonstop transatlantic
flight was achieved 18 days later. The
pilot, Capt John Williams Alcock (1892–
1919), and navigator, Lt Arthur Whitton
Brown (1886–1948) left Lester's Field,
St John's, Newfoundland, Canada at
4:13 P.M. GMT on 14 Jun 1919, and landed
at Derrygimla Bog near Clifden, Republic
of Ireland, at 8:40 A.M. GMT, 15 June,
having covered a distance of 1,960 miles in
their Vickers Vimy, powered by two 360 hp
Rolls-Royce Eagle VIII engines.

Solo The first solo transatlantic flight
was achieved by Capt. Charles Augustus
Lindbergh (1902–74), who took off in his
220 hp Ryan monoplane *Spirit of St Louis*
at 12:52 P.M. GMT on 20 May 1927 from
Roosevelt Field, Long Island, NY. He
landed at 10:21 P.M. GMT on 21 May 1927
at Le Bourget Airfield, Paris, France. His
flight of 3,610 miles lasted 33 hr 29½ min
and he won a prize of $25,000. The *Spirit of
St Louis* is now in the National Air and
Space Museum at the Smithsonian Institution, Washington, D.C.

Most flights Between March 1948 and
his retirement on 1 Sep 1984, Flight
Service Manager Charles M. Schimpf
logged a total of 2,880 Atlantic
crossings—a rate of 6.4 per month.

Transpacific The first nonstop flight
was by Maj. Clyde Pangborn and Hugh
Herndon in the Bellanca cabin monoplane *Miss Veedol*. They took off from
Sabishiro Beach, Japan and covered the
distance of 4,558 miles to Wenatchee,
WA in 41 hr 13 min from 3–5 Oct 1931.
(For earliest crossing, see Circumnavigational flights, below.)

Circumnavigational flights Strict
*circumnavigation of the globe requires
the plane to pass through two antipodal
points, thus covering a minimum distance
of 24,859.75 miles.*

Earliest The earliest such flight, of
26,345 miles, was by two US Army Douglas DWC amphibians in 57 "hops"
between 6 April and 28 Sep 1924, beginning and ending in Seattle, WA. The
Chicago was piloted by Lt Lowell H.
Smith and Lt Leslie P. Arnold, and the
New Orleans by Lt Erik H. Nelson and Lt
John Harding.

Fastest The fastest flight under the FAI
(*Fédération Aéronautique Internationale*)
rules, which permit flights that exceed
the length of the Tropic of Cancer or
Capricorn (22,858.754 miles), was that of
the 23,125 mile eastbound flight of 36 hr

54 min 15 sec by the Boeing 747SP *Friendship One* (Capt. Clay Lacy) from Seattle, WA with 141 passengers from 28–30 Jan 1988. The plane reached 803 mph over the Atlantic and refueled only in Athens, Greece and Taipei, Taiwan.

First without refueling Dick Rutan and Jeana Yeager, in their specially constructed aircraft *Voyager*, designed by Dick's brother Burt Rutan, flew from Edwards Air Force Base, CA from 14–23 Dec 1986. Their flight took 9 days 3 min 44 sec and they covered a distance of 25,012.665 miles, averaging 115.8 mph. The plane, with a wingspan of 110.8 ft, was capable of carrying 1,240 gal of fuel weighing 8,934 lb. It took over two years and 22,000 man-hours to construct. The pilot flew from a cockpit measuring 5.6 × 1.8 ft and the off-duty crew member occupied a cabin 7 ½ × 2 ft. *Voyager* is now in the National Air and Space Museum at the Smithsonian Institution, Washington, D.C.

First circumpolar Capt. Elgen M. Long, 44, achieved the first circumpolar flight in a Piper Navajo from 5 Nov–3 Dec 1971. He covered 38,896 miles in 215 flying hours. The cabin temperature sank to −40°F over Antarctica.

First single-engined circumpolar Richard Norton, an American airline captain, and Calin Rosetti, head of satellite navigation systems at the European Space Agency, made the first single-engined circumpolar flight in a Piper PA-46-310P Malibu. This began and finished at Le Bourget Airport, Paris, France, from 21 Jan–15 Jun 1987. They traveled 34,342 miles in a flying time of 185 hr 41 min.

Largest wingspan The aircraft with the largest wingspan ever constructed is the $40-million Hughes H.4 Hercules flying boat (*Spruce Goose*). She was raised 70 ft into the air in a test run of 3,000 ft, piloted by Howard Hughes (1905–76), off Long Beach Harbor, CA, on 2 Nov 1947, but after this she never flew again. The eight-engined 212 ton aircraft had a wingspan of 319 ft 11 in and a length of 218 ft 8 in. In a delicate engineering feat she was moved bodily by the Goldcoast Corporation, aided by the US Navy barge crane YD-171, on 22 Feb 1982, to her final resting place 6 miles across the harbor under a 415-ft-diameter, clear-span aluminum dome, the world's largest.

Among current aircraft, the Soviet Antonov An-124 has a span of 240 ft 5 ¾ in, and the Boeing 747-400 one of 213 ft.

A modified six-engine version of the An-124, known as An-225 and built to carry the Soviet space shuttle *Buran*, has a wingspan of 290 ft (see Heaviest, below).

The $34-million Piasecki Heli-Stat, comprising a framework of light alloy and composite materials, to mount four Sikorsky SH-34J helicopters and the envelope of a Goodyear ZPG-2 patrol airship, was exhibited on 26 Jan 1984 at Lakehurst, NJ. Designed for use by the US Forest Service and designated Model 94-37J Logger, it had an overall length of 343 ft and was intended to carry a payload of 24 tons. It crashed on 1 Jul 1986.

Heaviest The aircraft with the highest standard maximum takeoff weight is the Antonov An-225 *Myira* ("Dream") at 560 tons. (See also Most capacious, below.) The aircraft lifted a payload of 344,579 lb to a height of 40,715 ft on 22 Mar 1989. This flight was achieved by Capt. Alexander Galunenko and his crew of seven pilots. The flight was made along the route Kiev–Leningrad–Kiev without landing at a range of 1,305 miles and lasted 3 hr 47 min.

Electric plane The MB-E1 is the first electrically propelled aircraft. A Bosch 10.7 hp motor is powered by Varta FP25 nickel-cadmium 25 Ah batteries. The aircraft, with a wingspan of 39.4 ft, is 23 ft long and weighs 882 lb. It was designed by the model aircraft constructor Fred Militky (USA) and made its maiden flight on 21 Oct 1973.

Ultralight On 3 Aug 1985 Anthony A. Cafaro (b. 30 Nov 1951) flew an ultralight aircraft (ULA; maximum weight 245 lb, maximum speed 65 mph, fuel capacity 5 gal) single-seater Gypsy Sky-cycle for 7 hr 31 min at Dart Field, Mayville, NY. Nine fuel "pickups" were completed during the flight.

Smallest The smallest plane ever flown is the *Bumble Bee Two*, designed and built by Robert H. Starr of Arizona. It was 8 ft 10 in long, with a wingspan of 5 ft 6 in, and weighed 396 lb empty. The fastest speed attained was 190 mph. On 8 May 1988 it flew to a height of approximately 400 ft, crashed, and was totally destroyed.

The smallest jet is the 280 mph Silver Bullet, weighing 432 lb, with a 17 ft wingspan, built by Bob Bishop (USA).

Bombers *Heaviest* The eight-jet swept-wing Boeing B-52H Stratofortress has a maximum takeoff weight of 242.5 tons. It is 157 ft 6 ¾ in in length. It has a speed of over 650 mph. The B-52 can carry 12 SRAM thermonuclear short-range attack missiles or 24 750-lb bombs under its wings and eight more SRAMs, or 84 500-lb bombs, in the fuselage.

The ten-engined Convair B-36J, weighing 204 tons, had a greater wingspan at 230 ft, but it is no longer in service. Its top speed was 435 mph.

Fastest The world's fastest operational bombers include the French Dassault Mirage IV, which can fly at Mach 2.2 (1,450 mph) at 36,000 ft.

The American variable-geometry or "swing-wing" General Dynamics FB-111A has a maximum speed of Mach 2.5, and the Soviet swing-wing Tupolev Tu-22M, known to NATO as "Backfire," has an estimated over-target speed of Mach 2.0 but could be as fast as Mach 2.5.

Largest airliner The highest-capacity jet airliner is the Boeing 747 "Jumbo Jet," first flown on 9 Feb 1969, which has a capacity of from 385 to more than 500 passengers and a maximum speed of 602 mph. Its wingspan is 231.8 ft and its length 195.7 ft. It entered service on 22 Jan 1970. The first 747-400 entered service with Northwest Airlines on 26 Jan 1988 with a wingspan of 213 ft, a range exceeding 8,000 miles and a capacity for 422 passengers. Theoretical accommodation is available for 516 passengers seated 10 abreast in the main cabin plus up to 69 in the stretched upper deck in the 747-300.

A stretched version of the McDonnell Douglas MD-11 airliner was being contemplated, with accommodation for 515 passengers in the main cabin and up to 96 in a lower "panorama deck" forward

■ Largest wing span *The $40 million Hughes H.4 Hercules flying boat Spruce Goose (left), once piloted by Howard Hughes (1905–76), had a wingspan of 319 ft 11 in. She is now at her permanent site at Long Beach Harbor, CA. (Photo: Spectrum)*

AIRCRAFT

Solar-powered

The *Solar Challenger*, designed by a team led by Dr Paul MacCready, was flown for the first time entirely under solar power on 20 Nov 1980. On 7 Jul 1981, piloted by Steve Ptacek (USA), the *Solar Challenger* became the first aircraft of this category to cross the English Channel. After takeoff from Pontoise-Cormeilles, Paris, France, the 163 mile journey to Manston, Great Britain was completed in 5 hr 23 min at a maximum altitude of 11,000 ft. The aircraft has a wingspan of 47 ft.

Wing walking

Roy Castle, the host of the British Broadcasting Corporation *Record Breakers* television program, flew on the wing of a Boeing Stearman airplane for 3 hr 23 min on 2 Aug 1990, taking off from Gatwick, Great Britain and landing at Le Bourget, near Paris, France.

Around the world

The fastest time for a circumnavigation on scheduled flights is 44 hr 6 min by David J. Springbett (b. 2 May 1938) of Taplow, Great Britain. His route took him from Los Angeles, CA eastwards via London, Bahrain, Singapore, Bangkok, Manila, Tokyo and Honolulu from 8–10 Jan 1980 over a 23,068 mile course.

London–New York

The record from central London, Great Britain to downtown New York City by helicopter and Concorde is 3 hr 59 min 44 sec, and the return 3 hr 40 min 40 sec, both by David J. Springbett and David Boyce on 8–9 Feb 1982.

of the wing. This has given way to the MD-12, proposed in early 1990.

The greatest passenger load recorded was one of 306 adults, 328 children and 40 babies (total 674) from cyclone-devastated Darwin to Sydney, New South Wales, Australia on 29 Dec 1974.

Fastest airliner

The supersonic BAC/Aérospatiale Concorde, first flown on 2 Mar 1969, with a designed capacity of 128 passengers, cruises at up to Mach 2.2 (1,450 mph). It has a maximum takeoff weight of 408,000 lb. It flew at Mach 1.05 on 10 Oct 1969, exceeded Mach 2 for the first time on 4 Nov 1970, and became the first supersonic airliner used in passenger service on 21 Jan 1976. In service with Air France and British Airways, Concorde is designed to carry 100 passengers. The New York–London, Great Britain record is 2 hr 55 min 15 sec, set on 14 Apr 1990.

Most capacious

The Aero Spacelines Super Guppy has a cargo hold with a usable volume of 49,790 ft^3 and a maximum takeoff weight of 87.5 tons. Its wingspan is 156 ft 3 in and its length 141 ft 3 in. Its cargo compartment is 108 ft 10 in long with a cylindrical section 25 ft in diameter.

The Soviet Antonov An-124 *Ruslan* has a cargo hold with a usable volume of 35,800 ft^3 and a maximum takeoff weight of 446 tons. It is powered by four Lotarev D-18T turbofans giving a cruising speed of up to 528 mph at 39,370 ft and a range of 2,796 miles. A special-purpose heavy-lift version of the An-124, known as An-225 *Myira* ("Dream"), has been developed with a stretched fuselage providing as much as 42,000 ft^3 usable volume. A new wing center section carries an additional two engines, providing an estimated total 310,000 lb thrust. Having flown first on 21 Dec 1988, the aircraft was used to carry the Soviet space shuttle *Buran* for the first time on 13 May 1989, when it was airborne for 13 hr 13 min. (See Heaviest, above.)

Soviet manufacturer Antonov and British charter company Air Foyle claim a record for the heaviest commercial air cargo movement after carrying three transformers weighing 47.4 tons each and other equipment weighing 147.14 tons, from Barcelona, Spain to Noumea, New Caledonia, between 10–14 Jan 1991. Antonov and Soviet state air-line Aeroflot carried a one-piece newsprint press weighing 60.6 tons from Helsinki Finland to Melbourne, Australia in November 1989 on behalf of forwarding agent Röhlig Australia. Total pay-load was 134.5 tons.

Largest propeller

The largest ever used was the 22 ft 7½ in diameter Garuda propeller, fitted to the Linke-Hofmann R II built in Breslau, Germany (now Wrocław, Poland), which flew in 1919. It was driven by four 260 hp Mercedes engines and turned at only 545 rpm.

Most flights by propeller-driven airliner

A Convair CV-580 turboprop

airliner was reported by the manufacturer in April 1991 to have achieved 139 368 flights. Exact age was not announced but even if it were the first such airliner the figure equates to more than nine flights a day since 1952.

Most flights by jet airliner

A survey of aging airliners or so-called "geriatric jets" in *Flight International* Magazine for April 1990 reported a McDonnell Douglas DC 9 which had logged 90,914 flights in less than 21 years. This comes to ten flights a day and 11 daily flights on weekends, but after allowing for "downtime" for maintenance the real daily average is higher.

Scheduled flights

Longest The nonstop flights of United Airlines and Qantas from Los Angeles, CA to Sydney, Australia last 14 hr 50 min in a Boeing 747SP, a journey of over 7,487 miles.

The longest delivery flight by a commercial jet is 11,250 miles from London, Great Britain to Sydney, Australia by a Qantas Boeing 747-400 *Longreach*, using 176.6 tons of specially formulated Shell Jet A-1 high-density fuel, in 20 hr 9 min on 16–17 Aug 1989. It is the first time this route has been completed nonstop by an airliner.

A Boeing 767-200ER flight from Seattle, WA to Nairobi, Kenya on 8–9 Jun 1990 was the subject of claims for speed and endurance records and is likely to be the longest delivery flight by a twin-engined commercial jet. The Royal Brunei Airlines Boeing 767 flew 8,040 nautical miles (great-circle distance) in 18 hr 29 min, consuming 74.2 tons of fuel.

Shortest The shortest scheduled flight is by Loganair between the Orkney Islands of Westray and Papa Westray which has been flown with Britten-Norman Islander twin-engined 10-seat transports since September 1967. Though scheduled for 2 minutes, in favorable wind conditions it has been accomplished in 58 sec by Capt. Andrew D. Alsop. The check-in time for the 2 min flight is 20 min.

United Airlines provides the shortest scheduled flight by jet, by Boeing 727 between San Francisco and Oakland, CA. There are three daily return flights; the time averages 5 minutes for the 12 mile journey.

Gary W. Rovetto of Island Air on 21 Mar 1980 flew on a scheduled flight from Center Island to Decatur Island, WA in 41 sec.

FASTEST SPEED

Official record

The airspeed record is 2,193.167 mph, by Capt. Eldon W. Joersz and Maj. George T. Morgan, Jr., in a Lockheed SR-71A near Beale Air Force Base, CA over a 15½ mile course on 28 Jul 1976.

Air-launched record

The fastest fixed-wing aircraft in the world was the US North American Aviation X-15A-2, which flew for the first time (after modification from the X-15A) on 25 Jun 1964, powered by a liquid oxygen and ammonia rocket-propulsion system.

Ablative materials on the airframe enabled it to withstand a temperature of 3,000°F. The landing speed was momentarily 242 mph. The fastest speed attained was 4,520 mph (Mach 6.7) when piloted by Maj. William J. Knight, USAF (b. 1930), on 3 Oct 1967.

An earlier version piloted by Joseph A. Walker (USAF; 1920–66) reached 354,200 ft also over Edwards Air Force Base, CA on 22 Aug 1963. The program was suspended after the final flight of 24 Oct 1968.

US NASA Rockwell International space shuttle orbiter *Columbia*, commanded by Cdr John W. Young, USN and piloted by Robert L. Crippen, was launched from the Kennedy Space Center, Cape Canaveral, FL on 12 Apr 1981 after expenditure of $9.9 billion since 1972. *Columbia* broke all records in space by a fixed-wing craft, with 16,600 mph at main engine cutoff. After reentry from 75.8 miles, experiencing temperatures of 3,920° F, she glided home weighing 107 tons, and with a landing speed of 216 mph, on Rogers Dry Lake, CA on 14 Apr 1981.

Under a new FAI (Fédération Aéronautique Internationàle) Category P for aerospacecraft, the *Columbia* is holder of the current absolute world record for duration—10 days 7 hr 47 min 23 sec to main touchdown—when on its sixth mission, STS 9 Spacelab 1, with six crewmen, launched on 28 Nov 1983.

Orbiter *Atlantis* holds the shuttle altitude record of 320 miles, achieved on 3 Oct 1985 on its maiden flight.

The greatest mass lifted by the shuttle and placed in orbit was 261,679 lb by orbiter *Discovery* STS 51A, launched on 8 Nov 1984.

Fastest jet

The USAF Lockheed SR-71, a reconnaissance aircraft, is the world's fastest jet (see official record, above). First flown on 22 Dec 1964, it was reportedly capable of attaining an altitude ceiling of close to 100,000 ft. It has a wingspan of 55.6 ft and a length of 107.4 ft and weighs 85 tons at takeoff. Its reported range at Mach 3 was 2,982 miles at 78,750 ft. At least 30 are believed to have been built before the plane was retired by the US Air Force.

It was reported on 15 Jan 1988 that the US Air Force was developing secretly a Mach 5 3,800 mph high-altitude (above 100,000 ft) stealth aircraft.

Fastest combat jet

The fastest combat jet is the USSR Mikoyan MiG-25 fighter (NATO code name "Foxbat"). The reconnaissance "Foxbat-B" has been tracked by radar at about Mach 3.2 (2,110 mph). When armed with four large underwing air-to-air missiles known to NATO as "Acrid," the fighter "Foxbat-A" is limited to Mach 2.8 (1,845 mph). The single-seat "Foxbat-A" has a wingspan of 45 ft 9 in, is 278 ft 2 in long and has an estimated maximum takeoff weight of 82,500 lb.

Fastest biplane

The fastest is the

Italian Fiat CR42B, with a 1,010 hp Daimler-Benz DB601A engine, which attained 323 mph in 1941. Only one was built.

Fastest piston-engined aircraft
The fastest speed is for a cut-down privately-owned Hawker Sea Fury which attained 520 mph in level flight over Texas in August 1966. It was piloted by Mike Carroll (killed 1969) of Los Angeles, CA.

The FAI-accredited record for a piston-engined aircraft is 517.055 mph over Mojave, CA by Frank Taylor (USA) in a modified North American P-51D Mustang powered by a 2,237 kW Packard Merlin, over a 15 ½ mile course, on 30 Jul 1983.

Fastest propeller-driven aircraft
The Soviet Tu-114 turboprop transport achieved a record speed of 545.076 mph carrying heavy payloads over measured circuits. It was developed from the Tupolev Tu-95 bomber, known to NATO as the "Bear," and has four 11,033 kW engines.

The turboprop-powered Republic XF-84H prototype US Navy fighter which flew on 22 Jul 1955 had a top *design* speed of 670 mph, but was abandoned.

McDonnell Douglas expected its projected MD-91X, powered by counter-rotating multi-bladed fans, to cruise at about Mach 0.78 (514 mph). In tests during 1987–88 with an MD-80 experimentally fitted with a General Electric GE36 engine driving two fans (in place of one of the two standard Pratt & Whitney JT8D turbofans) a maximum speed of Mach 0.865 was attained.

Fastest transatlantic flight
The flight record is 1 hr 54 min 56.4 sec by Maj. James V. Sullivan, 37, and Maj. Noel F. Widdifield, 33, flying a Lockheed SR-71A eastwards on 1 Sep 1974. The average speed, slowed by refueling by a KC-135 tanker aircraft, for the New York–London stage of 3,461.53 miles was 1,806.963 mph.

The solo record (Gander to Gatwick) is 8 hr 47 min 32 sec by Capt. John J.A. Smith in a Rockwell 685 on 12 Mar 1978.

Fastest climb
Heinz Frick of British Aerospace took a Harrier GR5 powered by a Rolls-Royce 11-61 Pegasus engine from a standing start to 39,370 ft in 126.63 sec at the Rolls-Royce flight test center, Bristol, Great Britain on 15 Aug 1989.

Aleksandr Fedotov (USSR) in a Mikoyan E 266M (MiG-25) aircraft established the fastest time-to-height record on 17 May 1975, reaching 98,425 ft in 4 min 11.7 sec after takeoff.

Duration
The longest flight on record is 64 days 22 hr 19 min 5 sec, set by Robert Timm and John Cook in the Cessna 172 *Hacienda*. They took off from McCarran Airfield, Las Vegas, NV just before 3:53 P.M. local time on 4 Dec 1958 and landed at the same airfield just before 2:12 P.M. on 7 Feb 1959. They covered a distance equivalent to six times around the world, refueling without landing.

AIRPORTS

Largest The largest is the $3.6 billion King Khalid International Airport outside Riyadh, Saudi Arabia, which covers an area of 86 miles². It also has the world's largest control tower, 243 ft in height. It was opened on 14 Nov 1983.

The Hajj Terminal at the $4.76 billion King Abdul-Aziz Airport near Jeddah, Saudia Arabia is the world's largest roofed structure, covering 370 acres.

The present six runways and four terminal buildings of Dallas/Fort Worth Airport, TX are planned to be extended to eight runways, 13 terminals, and 260 gates, with an ultimate capacity for 150 million passengers.

The world's largest airport terminal is at Hartsfield Atlanta International Airport, GA, opened on 21 Sep 1980, with floor space covering 2.4 million ft² and still expanding. It has 146 gates handling 48,024,566 passengers in 1990, but has capacity for 75 million.

The planned Denver International Airport is scheduled to open in October 1993. It will occupy 53 miles², have 4 operating runways (12 runways are planned for the final development), 3 terminal modules with 72–85 gates and capacity for 28 million passengers.

Busiest The busiest airport is Chicago International Airport, O'Hare Field, IL, with a total of 59,130,007 passengers and 780,658 operation movements in the year 1989. This represents a takeoff or landing every 40.4 sec around the clock.

In terms of freight operations, New York City's Kennedy International Airport handled 1.18 tons in 1988, while Tokyo International Airport at Narita handled 1.12 tons of international freight.

Non-airline airport Among airports served by very few airlines, Van Nuys in Southern California is the busiest. In 1989, the airport saw 492,936 movements, of which less than one percent were by scheduled airlines, which averages more than 55 non-airline takeoffs or landings per hour throughout the year.

The busiest landing area ever was Bien Hoa Air Base, South Vietnam, which handled approximately 1,000,000 takeoffs and landings in 1970.

Helipad The world's largest helipad is at An Khe, South Vietnam. The heliport at Morgan City, LA, one of a string used by helicopters flying energy-related

■ **Largest airport**
The King Khalid International Airport (top) outside Riyadh, Saudi Arabia covers an area of 86 miles². It also has the world's tallest control tower (bottom) at 243 ft.
(Photos: Gamma/Guenet).

Los Angeles–Washington
The record time from Los Angeles to Washington, D.C. is 68 min 17 sec by Lieut. Col. Ed Yeilding, pilot, and Lt. Col. J. T. Vida, reconnaissance systems officer, aboard the SR-71 Blackbird spy plane during its retirement flight on 7 Mar 1990. The Blackbird was refueled over the Pacific Ocean at 60,000 ft before heading east from the California coastline and crossing the finish line near Salisbury, MD. The plane flew at 2,153.24 mph between Los Angeles and Washington.

Longest runways
The longest runway in the world at 7 miles in length (of which 15,000 ft is concrete) is at Edwards Air Force Base on the bed of Rogers Dry Lake at Muroc, CA. The whole test center airfield extends over 65 miles². In an emergency, an auxiliary 12 mile strip is available along the bed of the Dry Lake. The *Voyager* aircraft, taking off on its around-the-world unrefueled flight (see Circumnavigational flights) used 14,200 ft of concrete runway at Edwards Air Force Base.

Longest runways

The world's longest civil airport runway is one of 3.04 miles at Pierre van Ryneveld Airport, Upington, South Africa, constructed in five months from August 1975 to January 1976. A paved runway 3.88 miles long appears on maps of Jordan at Abu Husayn.

The most southerly major runway (1.6 miles) in the world is at Mount Pleasant, East Falkland (Lat 51° 50′ S), built in 16 months and completed in May 1985.

Longest air ticket

A ticket 39 ft 4 ½ in long was issued for $4,500 to M. Bruno Leunen of Brussels, Belgium in December 1984 for a 53,203 mile trip on 80 airlines with 109 layovers.

■ Helicopter hover

Doug Daigle, one of four pilots mastering his skills during a hover record in December 1989 at Anaheim, CA. Four fresh eggs were taped to the helicopter's wheels to verify that it did not touch the ground for 50 hrs 50 secs.

offshore operations into the Gulf of Mexico, has pads for 46 helicopters.

Landing fields *Highest* The highest is La Sa (Lhasa) Airport, People's Republic of China, at 14,315 ft.

Lowest The lowest landing field is El Lisan on the east shore of the Dead Sea, 1,180 ft below sea level, but during World War II BOAC Short C-class flying boats operated from the surface of the Dead Sea at 1,292 ft below sea level.

The lowest international airport is Schiphol, Amsterdam, Netherlands, at 15 ft below sea level.

Furthest and nearest to city or capital The airport furthest from the city center it allegedly serves is Viracopos, Brazil, which is 60 miles from São Paulo. Gibraltar Airport is a mere 2,625 ft from the city center.

AIRLINES

Busiest The country with the busiest airlines system is the United States, where the total number of passengers for air carriers in domestic operations in 1990 was 964,114,000.

Largest The USSR state airline Aeroflot, so named since 1932, was instituted on 9 Feb 1923. It operates 1,650 aircraft over 620,000 miles of routes, employs 500,000 people and carried 132 million passengers and 3.3 million tons of freight in 1989. Seventy percent of its routes are international; it serves 160 passenger and five cargo routes outside the country, making regular flights to 99 countries. Its domestic network covers 3,600 towns.

Oldest The oldest airline, Koninklijke-Luchtvaart-Maatschappij NV (KLM), the national airline of the Netherlands, was established on 7 Oct 1919. It opened its first scheduled service (Amsterdam–London, Great Britain) on 17 May 1920, seven months after its establishment.

Delag (Deutsche Luftschiffahrt AG) was founded at Frankfurt am Main,

Germany on 16 Nov 1909 and started a scheduled airship service in June 1910.

Chalk's International Airline has been flying amphibious planes from Miami, FL to the Bahamas since July 1919. Albert "Pappy" Chalk flew from 1911–75.

Aerospace company The world's largest aerospace company is Boeing of Seattle, WA, with 1990 sales of $27.6 billion and a workforce of 160,000 worldwide. Cessna Aircraft Company of Wichita, KS had total sales of $600.9 million in 1989. The company has produced more than 177,000 aircraft since Clyde Cessna's first was built in 1911.

HELICOPTERS

Earliest Leonardo da Vinci (1452–1519) proposed the idea of a helicopter-type craft, although it is known that the French had built helicopter toys before this time.

Igor Sikorsky built a helicopter in Russia in 1909, but the first practical machine was the Focke-Achgellis, first flown in 1936.

Fastest Under FAI rules, the world's speed record for helicopters was set by Trevor Eggington, who averaged 249.09 mph over Somerset, Great Britain on 11 Aug 1986 in a Westland Lynx company demonstrator helicopter.

Largest The Soviet Mil Mi-12 (NATO code-name "Homer"), also known as the V-12, is powered by four 6,500 hp turboshaft engines and has a span of 219 ft 10 in over its rotor tips, with a length of 121 ft 4 ½ in. It weighs 114 tons.

Highest altitude The record for helicopters is 40,820 ft by an Aérospatiale SA315B Lama, over France on 21 Jun 1972.

The highest recorded landing was at 23,000 ft, below the southeast face of Mt Everest in a rescue sortie in May 1971.

Longest hover Doug Daigle, Brian Watts and Dave Meyer of Tridair Helicopters, together with Rod Anderson of Helistream, Inc. of California maintained a continuous hovering flight in a 1947 Bell B model for 50 hr 50 sec between 13 and 15 Dec 1989.

Circumnavigation H. Ross Perot and Jay Coburn, both of Dallas, TX, made the first helicopter circumnavigation in *Spirit of Texas* on 1–30 Sep 1982.

The first solo around-the-world flight in a helicopter was completed by Dick Smith (Australia) on 22 Jul 1983. Taking off from and returning to the Bell Helicopter facility at Fort Worth, TX, in a Bell Model 206L, *Long Ranger III*, his unhurried flight began on 5 Aug 1982 and covered a distance of 35,258 miles.

AUTOGYROS

Earliest The autogyro, or gyroplane, a rotorcraft with an unpowered rotor turned by the airflow in flight, preceded the practical helicopter with an engine-driven rotor.

Juan de la Cierva (Spain) designed the first successful gyroplane with his model C.4 (commercially named Autogiro), which flew at Getafe, Spain on 9 Jan 1923.

Speed, altitude and distance records Wing-Cdr Kenneth H. Wallis (Great Britain) holds the straight-line distance record of 543.27 miles set in his WA-116F autogyro on 28 Sep 1975 with a nonstop flight from Lydd to Wick, Great Britain. On 20 Jul 1982, flying from Boscombe Down, Great Britain, he established a new autogyro altitude record of 18,516 ft in his WA-121/Mc. Wing-Cdr Wallis also flew his WA-116, with a 72-hp McCulloch engine, to a record speed of 120 ½ mph over a 1.86 mile straight course on 18 Sep 1986.

It was reported that on 8 Apr 1931, Amelia Earhart (USA) reached a height in excess of 19,000 ft in an autogyro at Pitcairn Aviation Field, PA.

FLYING BOATS

Fastest The fastest flying boat ever built was the Martin XP6M-1 Seamaster, the US Navy four-jet-engined minelayer flown in 1955–59, with a top speed of 646 mph. In September 1946 the Martin JRM-2 Mars flying boat set a payload record of 68,327 lb.

The official flying boat speed record is 566.69 mph, set by Nikolay Andreievski and crew of two in a Soviet Beriev M-10, powered by two AL-7 turbojets, over a 9.3–15 ½ mile course on 7 Aug 1961.

The M-10 holds all 12 records listed for jet-powered flying boats, including an altitude record of 49,088 ft set by Georgiy Buryanov and crew over the Sea of Azov, USSR on 9 Sep 1961.

AIRSHIPS

Earliest flight The earliest flight in an airship was by Henri Giffard from Paris, France in his steam-powered coal-gas airship 88,300 ft³ in volume and 144 ft long, on 24 Sep 1852.

Largest *Rigid* The largest was the 235 ton German *Graf Zeppelin II* (LZ 130), with a length of 803.8 ft and a capacity of 7.06 million ft³. She flew her maiden flight on 14 Sep 1938 and in May and August 1939 made radar spying missions in British air space. She was dismantled in April 1940. Her sister ship, *Hindenburg*, was 5.6 ft longer.

Non-rigid The largest ever constructed was the US Navy ZPG 3-W, which had a capacity of 1.5 million ft³, a length of 403 ft, a diameter of 85.1 ft and a crew of 21. She first flew on 21 Jul 1958 but crashed into the sea in June 1960.

Hot-air The world altitude record of 10,365 ft is held by the Cameron D-38 hot-air airship flown at Cunderin, Western Australia, on 27 Aug 1982. It was flown by R.W. Taaffe (Australia).

Oscar Lindstrom in a Colt AS 63 hot-air airship achieved a distance and duration record of 57.8 miles in a time of 3 hr 41 min 55 sec, from Stockholm to Tobo, Sweden on 20 Mar 1988.

Greatest passenger load The most people ever carried in an airship was 207, in the US Navy *Akron* in 1931. The transatlantic record is 117, by the German *Hindenburg* in 1937.

The largest airship currently certifed for the public transport of passengers (13) is the 193.6 ft-long non-rigid Skyship 600 series of 235,400 ft³ capacity, built by Airship Industries.

Distance records The FAI accredited straight-line distance record for airships is 3,967.1 miles, set by the German *Graf Zeppelin*, captained by Dr Hugo Eckener, between 29 Oct and 1 Nov 1928.

From 21–25 Nov 1917 the German *Zeppelin L59* flew from Yambol, Bulgaria to a point south of Khartoum, Sudan and returned, covering a minimum of 4,500 miles.

Duration record The longest recorded flight by a non-rigid airship (without refueling) is 264 hr 12 min by a US Navy Goodyear-built ZPG-2 class ship (Cdr J.R. Hunt, USN) that flew 9,448 miles from South Weymouth Naval Air Station, MA to Key West, FL, on 4–15 Mar 1957.

BALLOONING

Earliest The earliest recorded ascent was by a model hot-air balloon invented by Father Bartolomeu de Gusmão (ne Lourenço; 1685–1724), which was flown indoors at the Casa da India, Terreiro do Paço, Portugal on 8 Aug 1709.

Distance record The record distance traveled by a balloon is 5,208.68 miles, by the Raven experimental helium-filled balloon *Double Eagle V* (capacity 399.053 ft³) from 9–12 Nov 1981. The journey started at Nagashima, Japan and ended at Covello, CA. The crew for this first manned balloon crossing of the Pacific Ocean was Ben L. Abruzzo, 51, Rocky Aoki (Japan), 43, Ron Clark, 41, and Larry M. Newman, 34.

Ex-USAF Col. Joe Kittinger (see also Parachuting) became the first man to complete a solo transatlantic crossing by balloon. Accomplished in the 105,944 ft³ helium-filled balloon *Rosie O'Grady* between 14 and 18 Sep 1984, Kittinger lifted off from Caribou, ME and completed a distance of approximately 3,543 miles before landing at Montenotte, Italy 86 hours later.

The first balloon crossing of the North Atlantic was made from 12–17 Aug 1978 (137 hr 6 min) in the gas balloon *Double Eagle II*, crewed by Ben L. Abruzzo, Maxie L. Anderson and Larry M. Newman.

The first crossing of the United States was by the helium-filled balloon *Super Chicken III* (pilots Fred Gorell and John Shoecraft), flying 2,515 miles from Costa Mesa, CA to Blackbeard's Island, GA from 9–12 Oct 1981.

Highest   Unmanned The highest altitude attained by an unmanned balloon was 170,000 ft by a Winzen balloon, with a 47.8 million ft³ capacity, launched at Chico, CA in October 1972.

PARACHUTING RECORDS

It is estimated that the human body reaches 99 percent of its low-level terminal velocity after falling 1,880 ft, which takes 13–14 sec. This is 117–125 mph at normal atmospheric pressure in a random posture, but up to 185 mph in a head-down position.

FIRST ● Tower[1] **●** Louis-Sébastien Lenormand (1757–1839), quasi-parachute, Montpellier, France, 1783.

Balloon ● André-Jacques Garnerin (1769–1823), 2,230 ft, Monceau Park, Paris, France, 22 Oct 1797.

Aircraft ● *Man:* "Captain" Albert Berry, an aerial exhibitionist, St Louis, MI, 1 Mar 1912. *Woman:* Mrs Georgina "Tiny" Broadwick (b. 1893), Griffith Park, Los Angeles, CA, 21 Jun 1913.

LONGEST-DURATION FALL ● Lt Col Wm H. Rankin, USMC, 40 min due to thermals, North Carolina, 26 Jul 1956.

LONGEST-DELAYED DROP ● World ● *Man:* Capt Joseph W. Kittinger,[2] 84,700 ft (16.04 miles), from balloon at 102,800 ft, Tularosa, NM, 16 Aug 1960. *Woman:* E. Fomitcheva (USSR), 48,556 ft over Odessa, USSR, 26 Oct 1977.

MID-AIR RESCUE ● Earliest ● Miss Dolly Shepherd (1886-1983) brought down Miss Louie May on her single 'chute from balloon at 11,000 ft, Longton, Great Britain, 9 Jun 1908.

Lowest ● Gregory Robertson saved Debbie Williams (unconscious) collision at 9,000 ft, pulled her ripcord at 3,500 ft—10 secs from impact, Coolidge, AZ, 18 Apr 1987.

HIGHEST ESCAPE ● Flt Lt J. de Salis, RAF and Fg Off P. Lowe, RAF, 56,000 ft, Moynash, Derby, Great Britain, 9 Apr 1958.

Lowest ● S/Ldr Terence Spencer DFC, RAF, 30–40 ft, Wismar Bay, Baltic, 19 Apr 1945.

HIGHEST LANDING ● Ten USSR parachutists,[3] 23,405 ft, Lenina Peak, USSR, May 1969.

LOWEST INDOOR JUMP ● Andy Smith and Phil Smith, 192 ft, Houston Astrodome, TX, 16–17 Jan 1982.

MOST SOUTHERLY ● T/Sgt Richard J. Patton (USA; d. 1973), Operation Deep Freeze, South Pole, 25 Nov 1956.

MOST NORTHERLY ● Dr Jack Wheeler (USA); pilot Capt. Rocky Parsons, −25° F, in Lat. 90° 00′ N, 15 Apr 1981.

CROSS-CHANNEL (LATERAL FALL) ● Sgt Bob Walters with three soldiers and two Royal Marines, 22 miles from 25,000 ft, Dover, Kent, Great Britain to Sangatte, France, 31 Aug 1980.

TOTAL SPORT PARACHUTING DESCENTS ● *Man:* Roch Charmet (France; d. 20 Feb 1989), 14,650 ft, various locations. *Woman:* Valentina Zakoretskaya (USSR), 8,000 ft, over USSR, 1964–Sep 1980.

24-HOUR TOTAL ● Dale Nelson (USA), 301 (in accordance with United States Parachute Association rules), PA, 26–27 May 1988.

MOST TRAVELED ● Kevin Seaman from a Cessna Skylane (pilot Charles E. Merritt), 12,186 miles, jumps in all 50 US states, 26 Jul–15 Oct 1972.

HEAVIEST LOAD ● US Space Shuttle *Columbia*, external rocket retrieval, 80 ton capacity, triple array, each 120 ft diameter, Atlantic, off Cape Canaveral, FL, 12 Apr 1981.

HIGHEST COLUMN ● 24 Royal Marine Team, Dunkeswell, Great Britain, 20 Aug 1986.

LARGEST FREE-FALL FORMATION ● 144, held for 8.8 sec, from 16,000 ft, Quincy, IL, 11 Jul 1988.

OLDEST ● *Man:* Edwin C. Townsend (d. 7 Nov 1987), 89 years, Vermillion Bay, LA, 5 Feb 1986. *Woman:* Mrs Sylvia Brett (GB), 80 years 166 days, Cranfield, Great Britain, 23 Aug 1986.

LONGEST FALL WITHOUT PARACHUTE ● World ● Vesna Vulovic (Yugoslavia), air hostess in DC–9 which blew up at 33,330 ft over Serbska Kamenice, Czechoslovakia, 26 Jan 1972.

[1] *The king of Ayutthaya, Siam in 1687 was reported to have been diverted by an ingenious athlete parachuting with two large umbrellas. Faustus Verancsis is reputed to have descended in Hungary with a framed canopy in 1617.*
[2] *Maximum speed in rarefied air was 625.2 mph at 90,000 ft—marginally supersonic.*
[3] *Four were killed.*

Manned The highest altitude reached in a manned balloon is an unofficial 123,800 ft by Nicholas Piantanida (1933–66) of Bricktown, NJ, from Sioux Falls, SD on 1 Feb 1966. He landed in a cornfield in Iowa but did not survive.

The official record (closed gondola) is 113,740 ft by Cdr Malcolm D. Ross, USNR and the late Lt Cdr Victor A. Prother, USN, in an ascent from the deck of the USS *Antietam* over the Gulf of Mexico on 4 May 1961 in a balloon of 12 million ft³ capacity.

Because of an oversight, Keith Lang and Harold Froelich, scientists from Minneapolis, MN, ascended in an open gondola and without the protection of pressure suits to an altitude of 42,150 ft, just under 8 miles, on 26 Sep 1956. During their 6½-hour flight, at maximum altitude and without goggles, they observed the Earth and measured a temperature of −72°F.

Largest The largest balloons ever built have an inflatable volume of 70 million ft³ and stand 1,000 ft tall. They are unmanned. The manufacturers are Winzen Research Inc. of Minnesota.

Hot-air The modern revival of this form of ballooning began in the USA in 1961, and the first world championships were held in Albuqerque, NM on 10–17 Feb 1973.

Mass ascent The greatest mass ascent of hot-air balloons from a single site took place within one hour on 15 Aug 1987 when 128 participants at the Ninth Bristol International Balloon Festival in Bristol, Great Britain took off.

Atlantic crossing Richard Branson (Great Britain) and his pilot, Per Lindstrand (Great Britain), were the first to cross the Atlantic in a hot-air balloon, on 2–3 Jul 1987. They ascended from Sugarloaf, ME and covered the distance

Greatest load On 3 Feb 1982 at Podmoscovnoe in the USSR, a Mil Mi-26 heavy-lift helicopter, crewed by G. V. Alfeurov (pilot) and L. A. Indeyev (co-pilot), lifted a total mass of 62.5 tons to 6,560 ft.

Smallest helicopter The Aerospace General Co. one-person rocket-assisted minicopter weighs about 160 lb and can cruise for 250 miles at 185 mph.

Largest number to jump from a balloon

On 5 Apr 1990 12 members of the Red Devils Free Fall Parachute Team together made a jump from a Cameron A210, hot-air balloon over Bath, Great Britain, at a height of 6,000 ft.

Plane pulling

Dave Gauder single-handedly pulled a Concorde 40 ft across the tarmac at Heathrow Airport, London, Great Britain on 11 Jun 1987.

---

of 3,075 miles to Limavady, Great Britain in 31 hours 41 minutes.

Pacific crossing Richard Branson and Per Lindstrand crossed the Pacific in the *Virgin Otsuka Pacific Flyer* from the southern tip of Japan to Lac la Matre, Yukon, northwestern Canada on 15–17 Jan 1991 in a 2.6 million ft^3 capacity hot-air balloon (the largest ever flown) to set FAI records for duration (46 hr 15 min) and distance (great circle 4,768 miles). Unofficial world best performances were also set for the fastest speed from takeoff to landing of 147 mph. A speed of 239 mph was sustained over one hour.

Altitude Per Lindstrand (Great Britain) achieved the altitude record of 64,996 ft in a Colt 600 hot-air balloon over Laredo, TX on 6 Jun 1988.

The FAI endurance and distance record for a gas and hot-air balloon is 96 hr 24 min and 2,074.817 miles by *Zanussi*, crewed by Donald Allan Cameron (Great Britain) and Maj. Christopher Davey (Great Britain). The balloon failed by only 103 miles to achieve the first balloon crossing of the Atlantic on 30 Jul 1978.

Highest, most passengers The balloon *Miss Champagne*, of 2.6 million ft^3 capacity, was built by Tom Handcock of Portland, ME. Tethered, it rose to a height of 50 ft with 61 passengers on board on 19 Feb 1988.

The Dutch balloonist Henk Brink made an unthethered flight of 656 ft in the 850,000 ft^3 capacity Nashua Number One, carrying a total of 50 passengers and crew. The flight, on 17 Aug 1988, began from Lelystad Airport, Netherlands, lasted 25 minutes, and reached an altitude of 328 ft.

PERSONAL AVIATION RECORDS

Oldest and youngest passengers

Airborne births are reported every year. The oldest person to fly was Mrs. Jessica S. Swift (b. Anna Stewart, 17 Sep 1871), age 110 years 3 months. She flew from Vermont to Florida in December 1981.

Pilots Youngest The youngest age at which anyone has ever qualified as a military pilot is 15 years 5 months, by Sgt Thomas Dobney (b. 6 May 1926) of the Royal Air Force (RAF). He had overstated his age (14 years) on entry.

Wholly untutored, James A. Stoodley, age 14 years 5 months, took his 13-year-old brother, John, on a 29-minute joy ride in an unattended US Piper Cub trainer aircraft near Ludgershall, Great Britain in December 1942.

Oldest The world's oldest pilot is Ed McCarty (b. 18 Sep 1885) of Kimberley, ID, who in 1979 was flying his rebuilt 30-year-old Ercoupe at the age of 94.

Longest interval between transatlantic flights

Wing Cdr A.G. Evenden first flew the Atlantic as a crew member of the British R34, the first airship to cross the Atlantic, between 2–6 Jul 1919. Sixty years later, on 2 Jul 1979, he made the crossing on the Concorde.

Most flying hours Pilot John

Edward Long (USA; b. 10 Nov 1915) between 1 May 1933 and 7 Sep 1989 logged 53,290 hr 5 min of flight time as a pilot—more than six years airborne.

Passenger The record for a supersonic passenger is held by Fred Finn, who made his 687th Concorde crossing in February 1991. He commutes regularly from New Jersey to London, Great Britain. In April 1991 he became the first passenger to achieve 10 million miles.

Most takeoffs and landings

Al Yates and Bob Phoenix of Texas made 193 takeoffs and daylight landings at unduplicated airfields in 14 hr 57 min in a Piper Seminole, on 15 Jun 1979.

Most planes flown

James B. Taylor, Jr. (1897–1942) flew 461 different types of powered aircraft during his 25 years as an active experimental test and demonstration pilot for the US Navy and a number of American aircraft manufacturing companies. The planes flown included the most advanced military fighter and attack aircraft of their day. He was one of the few pilots of the 1920s and 1930s qualified to perform terminal velocity dives. During one dive in 1939, he may have become the first pilot in history to fly faster than 500 mph and live.

Most flying records

Brendan O'Brien of Croydon, Great Britain holds 201 point-to-point speed records as verified by the FAI (*Fédération Aéronautique Internationàle*), flying a Fournier RF4 single-seater single-engine plane on 2 Jul 1985.

Human-powered flight

The Daedalus Project, centered at the Massachusetts Institute of Technology, Cambridge, MA, achieved its goal of human-powered flight from Crete to the island of Santorini, Greece, a distance of 74 miles, on 23 Apr 1988, when Kanellos Kanellopoulos (b. 25 Apr 1957) averaged 18.5 mph in his 112 ft wingspan machine.

MODEL AIRCRAFT

Altitude, speed and duration

Maynard L. Hill (USA), flying radio-controlled models, established the world record for altitude of 26,929 ft on 6 Sep 1970, and on 4 Jul 1983 he set a closed-circuit distance record of 1,231 miles.

The free-flight speed record is 213.70 mph, achieved by V. Goukoune and V. Myakinin (both USSR), with a radio-controlled model at Klementyevo, USSR on 21 Sep 1971.

The record duration flight is one of 32 hr 7 min 40 sec by Eduard Svoboda (Czechoslovakia), flying a radio-controlled glider on 23–24 Aug 1980.

An indoor model with a rubber motor designed by J. Richmond (USA) set a duration record of 52 min 14 sec on 31 Aug 1979.

Largest glider

In January 1990 *Eagle III*, a radio-controlled glider weighing 14.5 lb with a wingspan of 32 ft 6 in, was designed and constructed by Carlos Reńe Tschen and Carlos Reńe Tschen Jr. of Colonia San Lázaro, Guatemala.

Cross-Channel

The first model helicopter flight was achieved by an 11 lb

model Bell 212, radio controlled by Dieter Zeigler for 32 miles between Ashford, Great Britain and Ambleteuse, France on 17 Jul 1974.

Smallest

The smallest to fly is one weighing 0.004 oz, powered by attaching a horsefly and designed by insectonaut Don Emmick of Seattle, WA. On 24 Jul 1979 one flew for 5 minutes at Kirkland, WA.

Paper aircraft

The flight duration record for a paper aircraft is 16.89 sec, by Ken Blackburn in the Reynolds Coliseum, North Carolina State University, on 29 Nov 1983.

The indoor record with a 12 ft ceiling is 1 min 33 sec set in the Fuji TV studios, Tokyo, Japan on 21 Sep 1980.

A paper plane was reported by "Chick" C.O. Reinhart to have flown 1 ¼ miles from a tenth-story office window at 60 Beaver Street, New York City across the East River to Brooklyn in August 1933, helped by a thermal from a coffee-roasting plant.

An indoor distance of 193 ft was recorded by Tony Felch at the La Crosse Center, WI on 21 May 1985.

Largest The largest flying paper airplane, with a wingspan of 16 ft 4 in, was constructed by pupils of Pendleton Heights High School, IN and flown on 24 May 1990. It was launched from a 10-ft high platform and flown for a distance of 85 ft 3 in.

KITE FLYING

The following records are all recognized by *Kite Lines* Magazine.

Longest

The longest kite flown was 3,394 ft in length. It was made and flown by Michel Trouillet and a team of helpers at Nîmes, France on 18 Nov 1990.

Largest

The largest kite flown was one of 5,952 ft^2. It was first flown by a Dutch team on the beach at Scheveningen, Netherlands on 8 Aug 1981.

Highest

The record height of 31,955 ft was reached by a train of eight kites over Lindenberg, Germany on 1 Aug 1919.

The altitude record for a single kite is 12,471 ft, in the case of a kite flown by Henry Helm Clayton and A.E. Sweetland at the Blue Hill Weather Station, Milton, MA on 28 Feb 1898.

Fastest

The fastest speed attained by a kite was 120 mph for a kite flown by Pete DiGiacomo at Ocean City, MD on 22 Sep 1989.

Greatest lift

The greatest lift by a single kite was one of 728 lb, achieved by a kite flown by G. William Tyrrell, Jr., also at Ocean City, MD on 23 Sep 1984.

Most on a single line

The greatest number of kites flown on a single line is 11,284, by Sadao Harada and a team of helpers at Sakurajima, Kagoshima, Japan on 18 Oct 1990.

Longest duration

The longest recorded flight is one of 180 hr 17 min by the Edmonds Community College team at Long Beach, WA from 21–29 Aug 1982. Managing the flight of the J-25 parafoil was Harry N. Osborne.

■ **Previous page**
Bank vault (Photo: ACE
Photo Library)

Greatest auction

The greatest auction was of the Hughes Aircraft Co. for $5 billion by General Motors of Detroit, MI on 5 Jun 1985.

Greatest barter deal

The biggest barter in trading history was 30 million barrels of oil, valued at $1,710 million, exchanged for ten Boeing 747s for the Royal Saudi Airline in July 1984.

Rummage sale

The Cleveland Convention Center, OH White Elephant Sale (instituted 1933) on 18–19 Oct 1983 raised $427,935.21. The greatest amount of money raised at a one-day sale was $170,139.76 at the 56th one-day rummage sale organized by the Winnetka Congregational Church, IL on 12 May 1988.

Brickworks

The largest brickworks in the world is the London Brick Co. Ltd plant at Stewartby, Great Britain. Established in 1898, the plant now covers 221 acres and has a weekly production capacity of 10.5 million bricks and brick equivalent.

Bank note collection

Colin Dealey of Berkhamsted, Great Britain has accumulated banknotes from 178 different countries in three years since he started collecting in 1988.

Commerce

Oldest industry The oldest-known industry is flint knapping, involving the production of chopping tools and hand axes, dating from 2.5 million years ago in Ethiopia. The earliest evidence of trading in exotic stone and amber dates from *c.* 28,000 B.C. in Europe. Agriculture is often described as "the oldest industry in the world," but in fact there is no firm evidence yet that it was practiced before *c.* 11,000 B.C.

Oldest company The Faversham Oyster Fishery Co. is referred to in the Faversham Oyster Fishing Act of 1930 as having existed "from time immemorial," i.e., in English law, from before 1189.

Stora Kopparbergs Bergslags of Falun, Sweden's oldest industrial enterprise, has been in continuous operation since the 11th century. It is first mentioned in historical records in the year 1288, when a Swedish bishop bartered an eighth share in the enterprise. Originally concerned with the mining and processing of copper, it is today the largest privately owned power producer in Sweden.

Largest company The largest manufacturing company in the world is General Motors Corporation of Detroit, MI, with operations throughout the world. Apart from its core business of motor vehicles and components, it produces defense and aerospace materials and provides computer and communication services. Its total revenue in 1990 was $126.017 billion, a drop of 8 percent from its 1989 figures. It is estimated that GM took a $1.9 billion loss in 1990; however, its assets are valued at $180.2365 billion, the greatest of any corporation. The company's total 1990 payroll was $28.8 billion for 761,400 staff. Dividends paid in 1990 were $1.9 billion.

Largest employer The world's largest employer is Indian Railways, with 1,646,704 employees on 31 Mar 1990.

Greatest sales The first company to surpass the $1 billion mark in annual sales was the United States Steel (now USX) Corporation of Pittsburgh, PA in 1917.

The *Fortune* 500 list of leading industrial corporations in April 1991 is headed by the General Motors Corporation of Detroit, MI, with sales of $126 billion for 1990.

Greatest profit The greatest net profit ever made by a corporation in 12 months is $7.6 billion by American Telephone and Telegraph Co. (AT&T) from 1 Oct 1981 to 30 Sep 1982.

Greatest loss The Argentine-government-owned oil company Yacimientos Petrolíferos (YPF) was reported to have had a trading loss of $4.6 billion in 1983.

Takeover The highest bid in a corporate takeover was $21 billion for RJR Nabisco Inc., the tobacco, food and beverage company, by the Wall Street leveraged buyout firm Kohlberg Kravis Roberts (KKR), which offered $90 a share on 24 Oct 1988. By 1 Dec 1988 the bid, led by Henry Kravis, had reached $109 per share to total $25 billion.

Bankruptcies Rajendra Sethia (b. 1950) was arrested in New Delhi, India on 2 Mar 1985 on charges including criminal conspiracy and forgery. He had been declared bankrupt by the High Court in London, Great Britain on 18 Jan 1985, when Esal Commodities was said to be in debt for a record £170 million ($177 million). His personal debts were estimated at £140 million ($146 million).

William G. Stern (b. 1936) of London, Great Britain, a US citizen since 1957, who set up the Wilstar Group Holding Co. in the London property market in 1971, was declared bankrupt for £104 million ($235 million) in February 1979. This figure rose to £143 million ($272 million) by February 1983.

Accountants The world's largest firm of accountants and management consultants is KPMG Peat Marwick McLintock, whose worldwide fee income totaled $5.36 billion on 30 Sep 1990. The company had 77,300 employees in 802 offices on 31 Mar 1991.

Banks The International Bank for Reconstruction and Development (founded on 27 Dec 1945 and known as the World Bank) is the world's largest multilateral development bank. Based in Washington, D.C., the bank had an authorized share capital of $171.4 billion on 31 Dec 1988. There were 151 members with a subscribed capital of $102 billion on 31 Dec 1988, at which time the World Bank also had unallocated reserves and accumulated net income of $9.2 billion.

The International Monetary Fund (IMF), also in Washington, D.C., had 155 members with total quotas of $131 billion as of February 1991.

The world's biggest commercial bank is the Dai-Ichi Kangyo Bank Ltd of Japan, with assets on 31 Mar 1989 of $414.1 billion.

The bank with most branches is the State Bank of India, which had 12,462 outlets on 1 Jan 1991 and assets of $37.4 billion.

The largest commercial bank in the

LARGEST AMERICAN CORPORATIONS	
Corporation	**Sales (1990) $ Millions**
General Motors, MI	126,017
Exxon, TX	105,885
Ford Motor, MI	98,275
Int'l Business Machines, NY	69,018
Mobil, VA	58,770

Fortune 500 Directory, 1991

United States is Citibank, N.A., located in New York City, with total assets of $216.99 billion and deposits of $142.45 billion as of 1 May 1991.

The oldest bank in the United States in continuous operation is The Bank of New York, founded in 1834 by Alexander Hamilton.

CEOs, highest paid The highest paid CEOs in the United States in 1990 in terms of salary, bonus and long-term compensation were Donald Pels of LIN Broadcasting ($186,200,000), Stephen J. Ross of Time Warner ($78,113,000) and Stephen Wolf of UAL ($18,301,000). The majority of Donald Pels' income for 1990 was from a windfall in LIN stock-options after the LIN/McCaw Cellular Communications merger in 1990. Stephen Ross' salary for 1990 was $3,200,000; his total pay of over $78 million included a bonus triggered by Time's merger with Warner. Stephen Wolf's pay for 1990 was $1,150,000; he also earned $12 million in stock owned, $2,376,000 compensation and stock gains of $14,774,000

Chemicals The largest manufacturer of chemicals in the United States is E. I. Du Pont de Nemours & Co. Inc. of Wilmington, DE. *Fortune* Magazine lists 1990 sales at $39.8 billion, with 143,961 employees.

Confectioners The largest chocolate and confectionary factory is that built by Hershey Chocolate United States in Hershey, PA in 1903–05. It has 2 million ft^2 of floor space.

Department stores Woolworth Corporation now operates more than 8,700 general stores worldwide. Frank Winfield Woolworth opened his first store, "The Great Five Cent Store," in Utica, NY on 22 Feb 1879. The net income for 1990 was $317 million.

The world's largest department store is R.H. Macy & Co. Inc. at Herald Square, New York City. It covers 50.5 acres and has 14,000 employees handling 400,000 items. Total sales for the company's 150 stores in 1990 were $7.3 billion. Rowland Hussey Macy's sales on his first day in his fancy goods store on Sixth Avenue, on 27 Oct 1858, were recorded as $11.06.

Employment agency Blue Arrow became the world's largest employment agency when, on 5 Sep 1987, it bid successfully for the US company Manpower, at £825 million ($1.331 billion).

Grocery stores The largest grocery chain in the United States is American Stores, of Salt Lake City, UT, with 1990 sales of $22.001 billion. Kroger Co. of Cincinnati, OH has the most stores in the United States with 2,245.

Sales per unit area Stew Leonard's Supermarket in Norwalk, CT has the greatest sales per unit area in the United States, with sales of $3,470 per ft^2 for the calendar year 1990 (total sales $114,968,000).

Insurance The company with the highest volume of insurance in force in the world is the Metropolitan Life Insurance Co. of New York City, with $908.6

billion at year end 1990. The Prudential Insurance Company of America of Newark, NJ has the greatest volume of consolidated assets, totaling $169 billion on 31 Dec 1990. The largest single association in the world is the Blue Cross and Blue Shield Association, the American-based hospital insurance organization. It had a membership of 71 million on 31 Dec 1990, and benefits paid out in 1990 totaled $55.9 billion.

The largest life insurance policy ever issued was for $100 million, bought by a major American entertainment corporation on the life of a leading American entertainment industry figure. The policy was sold in July 1990 by Peter Rosengard of London, Great Britain and was placed by Shel Bachrach of Albert G. Ruben & Co. Inc. of Beverly Hills, CA and Richard Feldman of the Feldman Agency, East Liverpool, OH with nine insurance companies to spread the risk. The second-largest life insurance policy ever written was one for $44 million for a Calgary land developer, Victor T. Uy, in February 1982 by Transamerica Occidental Life Assurance Co. The salesman was local manager Lorenzo F. Reyes.

The highest payout on a single life was reported on 14 Nov 1970 to be some $18 million to Linda Mullendore, widow of an Oklahoma rancher. Her murdered husband had paid $300,000 in premiums in 1969.

The largest-ever marine insurance loss was approximately $836 million for the Piper Alpha Oil Field in the North Sea, Great Britain. On 6 Jul 1988 a leak from a gas compression chamber underneath the living quarters ignited and triggered a series of explosions which which blew Piper Alpha apart. Of the 232 people on board, only 65 survived. The largest sum claimed for consequential losses was approximately 1,700 billion against owning, operating and building corporations and Claude Phillips, resulting from the 55 million gallon oil spill from MT *Amoco Cadiz* on the Brittany coast, France on 16 Mar 1978.

Law firm The world's largest law firm is Baker & McKenzie, employing 1,579 lawyers, 491 of whom are partners, in 51 offices in 30 countries on 1 May 1991. Billings for fiscal year 1990 were $404 million. The firm was founded in Chicago, IL in 1949.

Paper company The world's largest producer of paper, fiber and wood products is International Paper of Purchase, NY, with sales in 1990 of $12.9 billion. The company employs 69,000 workers.

Pharmaceuticals The world's largest pharmaceutical company is Bristol-Meyers Squibb Co. in New York City, with 1990 global sales of $10.3 billion, $7.017 billion in the United States, and 52,900 employees worldwide.

The world's largest health care products company is Johnson & Johnson of New Brunswick, NJ. The company employed a work force of 82,200, generating sales

of $11.2 billion in 1990. Total assets for the year were $9.5 billion.

The largest chain of drug stores in the world is Rite Aid Corporation of Shiremanstown, PA, which in 1989 had 2,353 branches throughout the United States. The Walgreen Co. of Deerfield, IL has fewer shops, but a larger volume of sales, totaling $5.3 billion in 1989.

Public relations The world's largest public relations firm is Burson Marsteller. Based in New York, the company had a net fee income of $210.372 million in 1990. Burson Marsteller operates 62 offices worldwide with a staff of 2,299.

Hill and Knowlton Inc. has most offices worldwide, with 68, in 25 countries. The company generated a net fee income solely within the United States of $119.66 million for 1990.

Retailer The largest retailer in the United States, based on 1990 sales, was Wal-Mart, Inc. of Bentonville, AR with revenues of $32.6 billion. Wal-Mart was founded by Sam Moore Walton in Rogers, AR in 1962, and as of April 1991 Wal-mart had 1,591 retail locations employing 325,000 workers.

The largest retailing firm in the United States based on current assets is Sears, Roebuck and Co. (founded by Richard Warren Sears in North Redwood, MN in 1886) of Chicago, IL, with $25.539 billion. Sears Merchandise Group had 847 retail stores, 1,731 sales offices and 1,769 independent catalog merchants in the United States in 1989.

Savings and Loan association The world's biggest lender is the Japanese government-controlled House Loan Corporation.

The largest Savings and Loan Association (S&L) in the United States is Home Savings of America, FA in Irwindale, CA, with total assets of $43.975 billion and total deposits of $32.266 billion as of year-end 1990. Home Savings also has the most branch offices of any S&L, with 333. Great Western Bank Association in Beverly Hills, CA has the most deposit accounts, with 2.631 million.

Steel companies From data available, the world's largest producer of steel is believed to be the Nippon Steel Corporation of Japan, which produced 31.7 million tons of crude steel in 1990. It employs 54,062 workers.

The Pohang works of the Pohang Iron & Steel Co. Ltd (POSCO) of South Korea produced 32 million tons of crude steel in 1988, the highest amount produced by a single integrated works.

United States The largest producer of steel in the United States in 1990 was USX Corporation, of Pittsburgh, PA, which produced 13.6 million tons of raw steel.

Undertakers The world's largest undertaking business is SCI (Service Corporation International) of Houston, TX, with 551 funeral homes and 126 cemeteries. Its annual revenue in this

most recession-proof of industries in the year ending 31 Dec 1989 was $519 million.

Economics

MONETARY AND FINANCIAL —

Largest budget The greatest governmental expenditure ever made by any country was $1,251.7 billion by the United States government for the fiscal year 1990. The highest-ever revenue figure was $1,031.3 billion in the same fiscal year.

The greatest fiscal surplus ever was $8,419,469,844 in the United States in 1947/48. The worst deficit was $221.1 billion in the US fiscal year 1986.

Foreign aid The greatest donor of foreign aid has been the United States—the total net foreign aid given by its government between 1 Jul 1945 and 1 Jan 1990 was $300.8 billion.

The country receiving most US aid in 1990 was Israel with $3 billion. Egypt was second with $2.3 billion. These totals are for both economic and military aid. US foreign aid began with $50,000 to Venezuela for earthquake relief in 1812.

Least taxed The sovereign countries with the lowest income tax in the world are Bahrain, Brunei, Kuwait and Qatar, where the rate, regardless of income, is zero. No tax is levied on the Sarkese (inhabitants of Sark), in the Channel Islands, Great Britain, or on the inhabitants of Tristan da Cunha.

United States The lowest income rate in United States history was 1 percent between 1913 and 1915.

Highest taxation rates The country with the most confiscatory taxation is Norway, where in January 1974 the Labor Party and Socialist Alliance abolished the 80 percent limit. Some 2,000 citizens were then listed in the *Lignings Boka* as paying more than 100 percent of their taxable income. The shipping magnate Hilmar Reksten (1897–1980) was assessed at 491 percent.

United States The highest income tax rate in United States history was implemented in 1944 by the Individual Tax Act with a 91 percent bracket. The current highest income tax bracket is 33 percent.

Balance of payments The record balance of payments deficit for any country for a fiscal year is $143.7 billion in 1987 by the United States. The preliminary figure for the United States balance of payments deficit for the fourth quarter of 1990 is $99.3 billion. The record balance of payments surplus is $87.0 billion in 1987 by Japan.

Highest tax levy The highest recorded personal tax levy is one for $336 million on 70 percent of the estate of Howard Hughes.

National debt The largest national debt of any country in the world is that

Store coupons

A record 306.8 billion store coupons were issued in 1990, up from the 263 billion in 1989. It is estimated that only 4 percent of coupons are redeemed annually.

Toy store

The world's biggest toy store is Hamleys, founded in 1760 in London. Its selling space covers 45,000 ft^2 on six floors, and it employs 400 staff during the Christmas season.

Faux pas

If measured by financial consequence, the greatest *faux pas* on record was that of the young multimillionaire James Gordon Bennett (1841–1918), committed on 1 Jan 1877 at the family mansion of his demure fiancée, one Caroline May, on Fifth Avenue in New York City. Bennett arrived in a two-horse carriage, late and obviously drunk. By dint of intricate footwork, he entered the drawing room, where he was the center of attention. He mistook the fireplace for a plumbing fixture more usually reserved for another purpose. The May family broke the engagement and Bennett was obliged to spend the rest of his footloose and fancy-free life based in Paris, France, with the resultant noncollection of millions of dollars in tax by the US Treasury.

of the United States, where the gross federal public debt of the federal government surpassed the trillion (10^{12}) dollar mark on 30 Sep 1981. By the end of 1989 it had reached $2.9 trillion, with net interest payments on the debt of $169.1 billion.

The total federal debt in the United States for the fiscal year ending 1990 was $3.233 trillion, with net interest payments of $264.8 billion, which is the highest national debt in US history. The lowest national debt figure was $33,533 in 1835.

Most foreign debt The country most heavily in overseas debt in early 1990 was the United States, with $675 billion, although the size of its debt is small relative to its economic strength. Among developing countries, Brazil has the highest foreign debt, with $123 billion at the end of 1990.

Gross national product The country with the largest gross national product is the United States, which, having reached $3 trillion (3 × 10^{12}) in 1981, was running at $5.5 trillion at the end of the fiscal year 1990.

National wealth The richest country as listed in the 1990 *World Bank Atlas* ranking is Switzerland, which in 1988 had an average gross national product (GNP) per capita of $27,370. The United States, which had held the lead from 1910 to 1973, was sixth. It has been estimated that the value of all physical assets in the United States on 1 Jan 1983 was $12.5 trillion.

According to figures released by the Commerce Department's Bureau of Economic Analysis, in 1990 Connecticut enjoyed the highest per capita income level of any state, at 135.7 percent of the national average ($25,358), while Mississippi continued to be the lowest at 68 percent of the national average ($12,735).

The median household income in the United States in 1990 was $28,906. Connecticut enjoyed the highest level at $42,000 and Mississippi was the lowest at $19,774.

Poorest country Mozambique had the lowest GNP per capita in 1988, with $100, although there are several sovereign countries for which the *World Bank Atlas* is not able to include data.

Gold reserves The country with the greatest monetary gold reserves is the United States, whose Treasury held 262.02 million fine oz as of 30 Sep 1990. Valued at $355 per fine oz, these amounts would translate to $93.02 billion.

The United States Bullion Depository at Fort Knox, 30 miles southwest of Louisville, KY, has been the principal federal depository of US gold since December 1936. Gold is stored in 446,000 standard mint bars of 400 troy ounces measuring 7 × 3⅝ × 1⅝ in. Gold's peak price was $875 per fine oz on 21 Jan 1980.

Inflation The United States Department of Labor measures changes in the Consumer Price Index (CPI) in twelve-month periods ending in December. The Bureau of Labor Statistics first began keeping the CPI in 1913. Since that time the change of the greatest magnitude was a 20.4 percent increase for the twelve-month period ending December 1918, and the largest decline was −10.8 percent in December 1921. The largest peacetime increase recorded in December 1979 was 13.3 percent. Figures are based on the United States city average CPI for all urban consumers.

Worst The world's worst inflation occurred in Hungary in June 1946, when the 1931 gold pengö was valued at 130 million trillion (1.3 × 10^{20}) paper pengös. Notes were issued for "Egymillard billion" (one sextillion or 1,000,000,000,000,000,000,000) pengös on 3 June and withdrawn on 11 Jul 1946. Vouchers for 1 billion trillion (10^{27}) pengös were issued for taxation payment only. On 6 Nov 1923 Germany's Reichsbank marks circulation reached 400,338,326,350,700,000,000 and inflation was 755,700 millionfold at 1913 levels.

The country with the worst inflation in 1990 was Nicaragua, where the rate was 13,500 percent.

Least The country with the least inflation over a year in recent times was Equatorial Guinea, which had a rate of −17.8 percent in 1986.

WEALTH AND POVERTY

Comparisons and estimates of extreme personal wealth are beset with intractable difficulties. Quite apart from reticence and the element of approximation in the valuation of assets, as Jean Paul Getty (1892–1976) once said: "If you can count your millions you are not a billionaire." The term millionaire was invented *c.* 1740 and billionaire in 1861. The earliest dollar centimillionaire was Cornelius Vanderbilt (1794–1877), who left $100 million in 1877. The earliest billionaires were John Davison Rockefeller (1839–1937); Henry Ford (1863–1947) and Andrew William Mellon (1855–1937).

Richest men Much of the wealth of the world's monarchs represents national rather than personal assets. The least fettered and most monarchical is HM Sir Muda Hassanal Bolkiah Mu'izzaddin Waddaulah (b. 15 Jul 1946) of Brunei. He appointed himself Prime Minister, Finance Minister and Home Affairs Minister on 1 Jan 1984. *Fortune* Magazine reported in September 1990 that his fortune was $25 billion.

Forbes Magazine estimated in its issue of 23 Jul 1990 that Yoshiaki Tsutsumi (b. 1934) of Japan was the world's richest man, with assets of $16 billion. He heads Japan's Seibu Railway Group, and his empire includes golf courses, hotels and ski resorts.

Forbes Magazine reported in its issue of 22 Oct 1990 that the richest man in the United States is John Kluge of Charlottesville, VA, with a personal fortune of $5.6 billion. At the age of 76, Kluge is chairman of Metromedia.

Richest women The title of the world's wealthiest woman has been wrongly conferred upon the recluse Hideko Osano (b. 1930), widow since October 1986 of the Japanese tycoon Kenji Osano. The US press first estimated her wealth at $25 billion. In fact much of her husband's wealth was diverted from her.

Her Majesty Queen Elizabeth II is asserted by some to be the wealthiest woman, and *The Sunday Times* of London, Great Britain estimated in April 1991 that she had assets worth £7 billion ($11.9 billion). However, few of her assets under the perpetual succession of the Crown are either personal or disposable.

The cosmetician Madame C. J. Walker (nee Sarah Breedlove; 1867–1919) is reputed to have been the first self-made millionairess. She was an uneducated black orphan whose fortune was founded on a hair relaxer.

Richest families It has been tentatively estimated that the combined value of the assets nominally controlled by the Du Pont family of some 1,600 members may be on the order of $150 billion. The family arrived in the United States from France on 1 Jan 1800. Capital from Pierre Du Pont (1730–1817) enabled his son Eleuthère Irénée Du Pont to start his explosives company in the United States.

Youngest millionaires The youngest person ever to accumulate a million dollars was the American child film actor Jackie Coogan (1914–84), co-star with Charlie Chaplin (1889–1977) in *The Kid*, made in 1920.

The youngest millionairess was Shirley Temple (b. on 23 Apr 1928), now Mrs Charles Black, who accumulated wealth exceeding $1 million before she was 10. Her childhood acting career spanned the years 1934 to 1939.

Highest incomes The largest incomes derive from the collection of royalties per barrel by rulers of oil-rich sheikhdoms who have not formally revoked personal entitlement. Shaikh Zayid ibn Sultan an-Nuhayan (b. 1918), head of state of the United Arab Emirates, arguably has title to some $9 billion of the country's annual gross national product.

Largest dowry The largest recorded dowry was that of Elena Patiño, daughter of Don Simón Iturbi Patiño (1861–1947), the Bolivian tin millionaire, who in 1929 bestowed $39 million from a fortune at one time estimated to be worth $607.5 million.

Greatest miser If meanness is measurable as a ratio between expendable assets and expenditure then Henrietta (Hetty) Howland Green (nee Robinson; 1835–1916), who kept a balance of over $31.4 million in one bank alone, was the all-time world champion. Her son had to have his leg amputated because of her delays in finding a *free* medical clinic. She herself ate cold cereal because she

was too thrifty to heat it. Her estate proved to be worth $95 million.

Return of cash The largest amount of cash ever found and returned to its owners was $500,000, discovered by Lowell Elliott, 61, on his farm at Peru, IN. It had been dropped in June 1972 by a parachuting hijacker.

Jim Priceman, 44, assistant cashier at Doft & Co. Inc., returned an envelope containing $37.1 million in *negotiable* bearer certificates found outside 110 Wall Street to A.G. Becker Inc. of New York on 6 Apr 1982. In announcing a reward of $250, Becker was acclaimed as being "all heart."

Greatest bequests The greatest bequest in the lifetime of a billionaire was that of Ryoichi Sasakawa, chairman of the Japanese Shipbuilding Industry Foundation, who made total donations of 644,699,912,000 yen ($5.16 billion) in the years 1962–88.

The largest single bequest in the history of philanthropy was the art collection belonging to the American publisher Walter Annenberg, which was worth $1 billion. He announced on 12 Mar 1991 that he would be leaving the collection to the Metropolitan Museum of Art in New York City.

The largest single cash bequest was the $500 million gift, announced on 12 Dec 1955, to 4,157 educational and other institutions by the Ford Foundation (established 1936) of New York.

Highest salary It was reported by the US government that Michael Milken, the "junk bond king" at Drexel Burnham Lambert Inc., was paid $550 million in salary and bonuses in 1987. (See also Fines.)

Highest fees The highest-paid investment consultant in the world is Harry D. Schultz, who operates from Monte Carlo and Zurich, Switzerland. His standard consultation fee for 60 minutes is $2,400 on weekdays and $3,400 on weekends. Most popular are the five-minute phone consultations at $200 (i.e., $40 a minute). His "International Harry Schultz Letter," instituted in 1964, sells

for $50 per copy. A life subscription costs $2,400.

Golden handshake *Business Week* Magazine reported in May 1989 that the largest "golden handshake" ever given was one of $53.8 million, to F. Ross Johnson, who left RJR Nabisco as chairman in February 1989.

PAPER MONEY

The Department of the Treasury reported that in fiscal year 1990, 3. billion $1 bills were printed, the most of any denomination. Other bills were printed as follows: $5 (0.9 billion), $10 (0.8 billion), $20 (1.8 billion), $50 (0.1 billion) and $100 (0.2 billion).

Earliest Paper money was an invention of the Chinese, first tried in A.D. 812 and prevalent by A.D. 970. The world's earliest banknotes (*banco-sedler*) were issued in Stockholm, Sweden in July 1661, the oldest survivor being one of five dalers dated 6 Dec 1662.

Largest and smallest The largest paper money ever issued was the one-kwan note of the Chinese Ming Dynasty issue of 1368–99, which measured 9 × 13 in.

The smallest national note ever issued was the 10-bani note of the Ministry of Finance of Romania, in 1917. It measured (printed area) 1.09 × 1.49 in. Of German *Notgeld*, the smallest were the 1–3 pfg notes of Passau (1920–21), measuring 0.70 × 0.72 in.

Highest values The highest-value notes in circulation are US Federal Reserve $10,000 banknotes, bearing the head of Salmon P. Chase (1808–73). It was announced in 1969 that no further notes higher than $100 would be issued, and only 345 $10,000 bills remain in circulation or unretired. The highest value ever issued by the US Federal Reserve System is a note for $100,000, bearing the head of Woodrow Wilson (1856–1924), which is only used for transactions between the Federal Reserve and the Treasury Department.

Lowest values The lowest value (and the lowest denomination) legal tender

bank note is the 1-sen (or $^1/_{100}$th of a rupiah) Indonesian note. Its exchange value in early 1991 was more than 194,000 to the dollar.

Most expensive The record price paid for a single lot of banknotes was £240,350 (including buyer's premium [$478,897.37]) by Richard Lobel, on behalf of a consortium, at Phillips, London, Great Britain on 14 Feb 1991. The lot consisted of a cache of British military notes which were found in a vault in Berlin, Germany, and contained more than 17 million notes.

CHECKS AND COINS

Largest The greatest amount paid by a single check in the history of banking was £1.425 trillion ($2.494 trillion). Issued on 11 Jul 1989 and signed by 3 treasurers, the check represented a payment from the expiring Abbey National Building Society in favor of the newly created Abbey National plc.

A larger one, for $4,176,969,623.57, was drawn on 30 Jun 1954, although this was an internal US Treasury check.

Collection—record price The highest price ever paid for a coin collection was $25,235,360 for the Garrett family collection of US and colonial coins, which had been donated to Johns Hopkins University, Baltimore, MD. The sales were made at a series of four auctions held on 28–29 Nov 1979 and 25–26 Mar 1981 at the Bowers & Ruddy Galleries in Wolfeboro, NH. The collection was put together by members of the Garrett family between 1860 and 1942.

Hoards The most valuable hoard of coins was one of about 80,000 aurei found in Brescello near Modena, Italy in 1714, and believed to have been deposited *c.* 37 B.C. The largest deliberately buried hoard ever found was the Brussels hoard of 1908 containing *c.* 150,000 coins.

The largest accidental hoard on record was the 1715 Spanish Plate Fleet, which sank off the coast of Florida. A reasonable estimate of its contents would be some 60 million coins, of which about half were recovered by Spanish authorities shortly after the event. Of the remaining 30 mil-

■ **Most expensive coin**
The record price paid for an individual coin is $1,500,000, for this US 1907 Double Eagle Ultra High Relief $20 gold coin. It was sold by MTB Banking Corporation of New York to a private investor on 9 Jul 1990.
(Photos: MTB Banking)

Coin balancing
Hiem Shda of Kiriat Mozkien, Israel stacked a pyramid of 847 coins on the edge of a coin freestanding vertically on the base of a coin, which was on a table, on 30 Jul 1989.

lion pieces, perhaps 500,000 have been recovered by modern salvagers. The other 29½ million coins are, presumably, still on the bottom of the sea, awaiting recovery.

The record in terms of weight is 47.4 tons of gold, from the White Star Liner HMS *Laurentic*, which was mined in 132 ft of water off Fanad Head, Donegal, Ireland in 1917. The Royal Navy, Cossum Diving Syndicate and Consortium Recovery Ltd. have since recovered 3,191 of the 3,211 gold ingots.

Largest mint The largest mint in the world is that of the US Treasury. It was built from 1965–69 on Independence Mall, Philadelphia and covers 11½ acres, with an annual production capacity on a three-shift seven-day week of 15 billion coins. One new high-speed stamping machine can produce coins at a rate of 40,000 per hour.

Most popular coin More than 250 billion pennies with Lincoln's head have been minted in the 80 years since its première issue in 1909 for the 100th anniversary of Lincoln's birth. If lined up, the 250 billion coins would stretch 2,808,586 miles and if piled up (17 to an inch) they would tower 220,851 miles into space.

Charity fund-raising The "Sport Aid" event, conceived by Chris Long and organized by Bob Geldof, took place in 277 cities in 78 countries on 25 May 1986 and raised a worldwide figure of over $100 million.

The greatest recorded amount raised by a charity walk or run is Cdn$24.7 million by Terry Fox (1958–81) of Canada who, with an artificial leg, ran from St John's, Newfoundland to Thunder Bay, Ontario in 143 days from 12 Apr–2 Sep 1980. He covered 3,339 miles.

Column of coins The most valuable column of coins was worth £15,606

COINS

OLDEST

c. 630 B.C. electrum staters of King Gyges of Lydia, Turkey. [1]

EARLIEST DATED

Samian silver tetradrachm struck in Zankle (now Messina), Sicily, dated year 1, *viz*. 494 B.C.—shown as "A". *Christian Era:* MCCXXXIIII (1234) Bishop of Roskilde coins, Denmark (6 known).

HEAVIEST

43 lb 7¼ oz Swedish 10-daler copper plate 1644. [2]

LIGHTEST

14,000 to the oz Nepalese silver ¼ jawa c. 1740.

MOST EXPENSIVE

Set: $3,190,000 for the King of Siam Proof Set, a set of 1804 and 1834 US coins which had once been given to the King of Siam, purchased by Iraj Sayah and Terry Brand at Superior Galleries, Beverly Hills, CA on 28 May 1990. Included in the set of nine coins was the 1804 silver dollar, which had an estimated value of about $2,000,000.

Individual: $1,500,000 for the US 1907 Double Eagle Ultra High Relief $20 gold coin, sold by MTB Banking Corporation of New York to a private investor on 9 Jul 1990.

RAREST

Many "singletons" known; e.g., the Axumite gold coin of Wazeba in the Bibliothèque Nationale, Paris and the Axumite ½ tremissis of Aphilas of c. A.D. 250 owned by Dr Bent Juel-Jensen of Oxford.

---

[1] Chinese uninscribed "spade" money of the Zhou dynasty has been dated to c. 550 B.C.
[2] The largest coinlike medallion was completed on 21 Mar 1986 for the World Exposition in Vancouver, British Columbia, Canada, Expo 86—a $1,000,000 gold piece. Its dimensions were 37.5 in diameter and ¾ in thick and it weighed 365 lb 15 oz or 5,337 oz (troy) of gold.

($30,338) and was 6 ft 1½ in high. It was built by pupils of Middlecroft School, Staveley, Great Britain at Ringwood Hall Hotel, Brimington, Great Britain on 26 Aug 1990.

Line of coins The most valuable line of coins was made up of 662,353 quarters to a value of $165,588. It was 10 miles 5 ft 7 in long, and was laid at Central City Park, Atlanta, GA on 16 Mar 1985.

A carpet of 1,945,223 Belgian one-franc coins, 0.83 in diameter and thus with a total length of 25.38 miles, was laid in Geel, Belgium by members of Mepp-Stegeta on 25 Jun 1988.

Pile of coins The Copper Mountain, devised by Terry Pitts Fenby for the National Society for the Prevention of Cruelty to Children, at Selfridges, Oxford Street, in London, Great Britain, consisted of over 3 million coins accumulated

---

in 350 days (24 May 1984– –7 May 1985), with a total value of £57,051.34 ($69,032).

LABOR

First labor union The first officially recognized labor organization in the United States was formed by the Shoemakers and Coopers of Boston, MA. They were granted a three-year charter by King Charles II in 1648. The charter was not renewed.

Largest labor union The world's largest union is Professionalniy Soyuz Rabotnikov Agro-Promyshlennogo Kompleksa (Agro-Industrial Complex Workers' Union) in the Soviet Union, with 36,634,613 members on 1 Jan 1990.

United States As of 31 Dec 1990 the largest union in the United States was the National Education Association (NEA), which has 2 million members.

Smallest labor union The ultimate in small unions was the Jewelcase and Jewelry Display Makers Union (JJDMU), founded in 1894. It was dissolved on 31 Dec 1986 by its general secretary, Charles Evans. The motion was seconded by Fergus McCormack, its only other surviving member.

Longest name The union with the longest name is the International Association of Marble, Slate and Stone Polishers, Rubbers and Sawyers, Tile and Marble Setters' Helpers and Marble, Mosaic and Terrazzo Workers' Helpers, or the IAMSSPRSTM-SHMMTWH, of Washington, D.C.

Earliest labor dispute A labor dispute concerning monotony of diet and working conditions was recorded in 1153 B.C. in Thebes, Egypt. The earliest recorded strike was one by an orchestra leader named Aristos from Greece, in Rome c. 309 BC. The dispute concerned meal breaks.

Longest strike The world's longest recorded strike ended on 4 Jan 1961, after 33 years. It concerned the employment of barbers' assistants in Copenhagen, Denmark.

United States The longest recorded major strike was that at the plumbing fixtures factory of the Kohler Co. in Sheboygan, WI, between April 1954 and October 1962. The strike is alleged to have cost the United Automobile Workers' Union about $12 million to sustain.

Unemployment Lowest In December 1973 in Switzerland (population 6.6 million), the total number of unemployed was reported to be 81.

United States The highest annual unemployment average in United States history was 24.9 percent, or 12,830,000 people in 1933 during the Great Depression, and the lowest average was 1.2 percent, or 670,000 people, in 1944 during World War II. These figures are based on a labor force age of fourteen and older. Since 1948 the United States Department of Labor has kept statistics based on households members aged sixteen and older. According to these figures, the highest annual unemployment average since 1948 was 9.7 percent, or 10,717,000 people, in 1982, and the lowest was 2.9 percent, or 1,834,000 people, in 1953.

Working career The longest working life was one of 98 years by Mr Izumi, who began work goading draft animals at a sugar mill at Isen, Tokunoshima, Japan in 1872. He retired as a sugar cane farmer in 1970 at the age of 105.

Working week A case of a working week of 142 hours (with an average each day of 3 hr 42 min 51 sec for sleep) was recorded in June 1980 by Dr Paul Ashton, 32, the anesthetics registrar at Birkenhead General Hospital, Merseyside, Great Britain. He described the week in question as "particularly bad but not untypical."

ENERGY CONSUMPTION

To express the various forms of available energy (coal, liquid fuels, water power, etc., but omitting vegetable fuels and peat), it is the practice to convert them all into terms of coal.

The highest consumption in the world is in the US Virgin Islands, with an average of 597.4 cwt per person per year. The highest in a sovereign country is 430.7 cwt in Qatar.

The lowest average is 28.6 lb per person, most recently recorded in Bhutan in 1987.

United States The Energy Information Administration reports that in 1990, total consumption of energy in the United States was 81.497 quadrillion Btu (British thermal units—the amount of energy needed to raise the temperature of 1 lb of water one degree at 39.2° F). Total consumption of coal was 19.094 quadrillion Btu; natural gas, 19.424 quadrillion Btu; petroleum, 33.644 quadrillion Btu; hydroelectric power, 2.492 quadrillion Btu, and nuclear electric power, 6.186 quadrillion Btu.

STOCK EXCHANGES

The oldest stock exchange of the 138 listed throughout the world is that of Amsterdam, Netherlands, founded in 1602 with dealings in printed shares of the United East India Company of the Netherlands in the Oude Zijds Kapel. The largest in trading volume in 1990 was Tokyo, with 1.45 trillion yen, ahead of New York City with $957 billion and London, Great Britain with $608.5 billion.

New York Stock Exchange The highest index figure on the Dow Jones Industrial agerage (instituted 8 Oct 1896) of selected stocks at the close of a day's trading was 3,035.33 on 3 Jun 1991, a rise of 7.83 points on the day. The index closed above 3,000 points for the first time on 17 Apr 1991, at 3,004.46, although it had edged past the 3,000 barrier on Friday 13 Jul 1990 after a strong run.

The record day's trading was 608,148,710 shares on 20 Oct 1987. The old record trading volume in a day on the New York Stock Exchange of 16,410,030 shares on 29 Oct 1929, the "Black Tuesday" of the famous "crash," was unsurpassed until April 1968.

The Dow Jones Industrial average, which reached 381.71 on 3 Sep 1929, plunged 30.57 points on 29 Oct 1929, on its way to the Depression's lowest point of 41.22 on 2 Jul 1932. The largest decline in a day, 508 points (22.6 percent), occurred on 19 Oct 1987.

The total lost in security values from 1 Sep 1929 to 30 Jun 1932 was $74 billion. The greatest paper loss in a year was $210 billion in 1974.

The record daily increase of 69.89 on 3 Apr 1986 was most recently bettered on 21 Oct 1987 with a rise of 186.84 points to 2,027.85.

The largest stock trade in the history of the New York Stock Exchange was a 48,788,800-share block of Navistar International Corporation stock at $10 in a $487,888,000 transaction on 10 Apr 1986.

The highest price paid for a seat on the New York Stock Exchange was $1.15 million in 1987. The lowest 20th-century price was $17,000 in 1942.

The market value of stocks listed on the New York Stock Exchange reached an all-time high of $3.2 trillion at the end of March 1991.

Most valued companies The market capitalization of Nippon Telegraph and Telephone (NTT) was quoted as $87.4 billion in September 1990, falling from $112.2 billion in the preceding three-month period.

The market value of the American Telephone and Telegraph Co. (AT&T), formerly the company with the greatest assets, on 31 Dec 1983 was $59.4 billion, held among 3 million ordinary stockholders. A total of 20,109 stockholders attended the annual general meeting in April 1961, setting a world record.

The largest recorded rights issue was one of £921 million ($1.57 billion) by Barclays Bank, Great Britain, announced on 7 Apr 1988.

Gold prices The highest closing spot price for gold on the Commodities Exchange (COMEX) in New York City was $875.00 per fine oz on 21 Jan 1980.

Silver prices The highest closing spot price for silver on the Commodities Exchange (COMEX) in New York City was $50.35 per fine oz on 18 Jan 1980.

Largest and smallest equity The greatest aggregate market value of any corporation at year end was $127.48 billion for International Business Machines (IBM) Corporation on 31 Dec 1990. The smallest aggregate market value of any corporation was $35 million for International Technology of Torrance, CA on 31 Dec 1990.

Highest par value The highest denomination of any share quoted in the world is a single share in Moeara Enim Petroleum Corporation, worth 164,000 Dutch florins ($74,980) on 17 Aug 1989.

Largest flotation The largest-ever flotation in stock market history was the £5.2 billion ($9.9 billion) sale of the 12 Great Britain regional electricity companies to 5.7 million stockholders at the end of 1990.

The earlier flotation of British Gas plc in 1986 had an equity offer which produced the higher sum of £7.75 billion ($10.85 billion), but to only 4.5 million stockholders.

Largest investment house The largest securities company in the United States, and formerly the world's largest partnership, with 124 partners before becoming a corporation in 1959, is Merrill Lynch, Pierce, Fenner & Smith Inc. (founded 6 Jan 1914) of New York. At the end of 1990 its parent, Merrill Lynch and Co. Inc., had $110 billion worth of assets under management, held $356 billion in client assets, had 39,000 employees and operated 510 offices worldwide.

POSTAL SERVICES

The practice of numbering houses began on the Pont Notre Dame, in Paris, France in 1463.

Largest mail The country with the largest mail service in the world is the United States, whose population mailed 161.6 billion letters and packages in the year ending 30 Sep 1989, when the US Postal Service employed 763,743 people,

■ **Stock Exchange**
The New York Stock Exchange in 1987, a year in which records were set for a day's trading (over 608 million shares), the greatest decline in a day (508 points), and the highest price paid for a seat ($1.15 million). (Photo: Gamma/Liaison)

■ **Most expensive stamps**
Relative to their total face value, the most expensive stamps ever produced were the 1847 1-penny and 2-penny Mauritius "Post Office" stamps. J. Barnard was paid ten guineas (£10.50 [$52.50]) for engraving the die and printing 500 of each. Thus the production costs far outweighed the revenue from sales, as the total face value of the 1,000 stamps was only £6.25 ($31.25). (Photo: Gamma)

Combine harvesting

Philip Baker of West End Farm, Merton, Great Britain harvested 182.5 tons of wheat in eight hours using a Massey Ferguson MF 38 combine on 8 Aug 1989. On 9 Aug 1990 an international team from CWS Agriculture, led by estate manager Ian Hanglin, harvested 394.73 tons of wheat in eight hours from 108.72 acres at Cockayne Hatley Estate, Sandy, Great Britain. The equipment consisted of a Claas Commandor 228 combine fitted with a Shelbourne Reynolds SR 6000 stripper head.

with the world's largest civilian vehicle fleet of 182,533 cars and trucks.

Switzerland takes first place in the average number of letters and packages which each person mails during one year. The figure was 655 in 1988.

In the United States, the average number of letters and packages which each person mails during one year was 645 in 1988.

Oldest mailboxes The first orthodox system of roadside mailboxes was established in 1653 in Paris, France, to facilitate the interchange of correspondence in the city. The mailboxes were erected at the intersections of main thoroughfares and were emptied three times a day.

Post offices The country with the greatest number of post offices is India, with 144,829 in 1988.

Agriculture

Origins It has been estimated that about 21 percent of the world's land surface is cultivable and that only 7.6 percent is actually under cultivation.

Evidence adduced in 1971 from Nok Nok Tha and Spirit Cave, Thailand tends to confirm that plant cultivation was part of the Hoabinhian culture c. 11,000 B.C., but it is still likely that hominids (humans and their human-like ancestors) probably survived for 99.93 percent of their known history without cultivating plants or domesticating animals.

A village site found near Nineveh, Iraq, dated provisionally to 9,000 B.C., shows evidence of agricultural practices. The earliest evidence for maize cultivation comes from samples taken of sediments in Lake Ayauchi, near the Rio Santiago tributary of the Amazon, which was dated to at least 5,300 years ago. Rice was grown in China by c. 5,000 B.C. at Hemudu, near Shanghai.

It has been suggested that reindeer (*Rangifer tarandus*) may have been domesticated as early as 18,000 B.C., but definite proof is still lacking. The earliest-known animals domesticated for food were probably descendants of the wild goats of Bezoar (*Capra aegagrus = hircus*), which were herded at Asiah, Iran c. 7,700 B.C. Sheep (*Ovis aries*) have been dated to c. 7,200 B.C. at Argissa Magula in Thessaly,

Greece, and pigs (*Sus domestica*) and cattle (*Bos primigenius = taurus*) to c. 7,000 B.C. at the same site.

The earliest definite date for the horse (*Equus caballus*) is c. 4350 B.C. from Dereiska, Ukraine, USSR, but evidence from southern France indicates that horses may have been tethered earlier

than 30,000 B.C. The oldest evidence for the possible domestic use of camels (*Camelus*) came from the site at Sihi, Saudi Arabia, where a jawbone has been carbon-dated to c. 7,200–7,100 B.C.

Chickens were domesticated before 6000 B.C. in Indochina and by 5900–5400 B.C. had spread to North China, as shown by radiocarbon dating from a Neolithic site at Peiligan, near Zhengzou, and also at Cishan and Beixin.

FISHERIES

United Nations Food and Agricultural Organization figures for 1988 showed the world's leading fishing nation to be Japan, with a total catch of 13.1 million tons, followed by the USSR (12.5 million tons), China (11.4 million tons), perhaps surprisingly Peru (7.3 million tons) and the United States (6.5 million tons). The total worldwide was 107.9 million tons.

The record for a single trawler is $473,957 from a 41,776 ton catch by the Icelandic vessel *Videy* at Hull, Great Britain on 11 Aug 1987. The greatest catch ever recorded from a single throw is 2,724 tons by the purse seine-net boat M/S *Flømann* from Hareide, Norway in the Barents Sea on 28 Aug 1986. It was estimated that more than 120 million fish were caught in this shoal.

REAL ESTATE

Landowners The world's largest landowner is the United States government, with a holding of 728 million acres, which is bigger than the world's eighth largest country, Argentina, and 12 times larger than Indiana. It has been suggested that the Soviet government constitutionally owns all the land in the USSR, with the exception, perhaps, of that on which foreign embassies stands—a total of 8,649,500 miles^2.

The world's largest private landowner is reputed to be International Paper Co. of Purchase, NY, with 9 million acres at its disposal.

Price, most expensive The most expensive piece of property ever recorded, the land around the central Tokyo retail food store Mediya Building in the Ginza district, was quoted in October 1988 by the Japanese National Land Agency at 358.5 million yen per ft^2 (then equivalent to $248,000).

FARMS

Largest The largest farms in the world are *kolkhozy*—collective farms in the USSR. These have been reduced in number from 235,500 in 1940 to 26,900 in 1988 and represent a total cultivated area of 417.6 million acres. Units of over 60,000 acres are not uncommon.

The pioneer farm owned by Laucidio Coelho near Campo Grande, Mato Grosso, Brazil c. 1901 covered 3,358 miles^2 and supported 250,000 head of cattle at the time of the owner's death in 1975.

Cattle ranch The world's largest cattle ranch is the 11,600 miles^2 Anna Creek ranch in South Australia owned by the Kidman family. The biggest component is Strangway at 5,500 miles^2.

Until 1915 the Victoria River Downs Station in Northern Territory, Australia had an area of 35,000 miles^2.

Chicken farm The Croton Egg Farm in Ohio has 4.8 million hens laying some 3.7 million eggs daily.

Community garden The largest such project is the one operated by the City Beautiful Council and the Benjamin Wegerzyn Garden Center in Dayton, OH. It comprises 1,173 plots, each measuring 812 ft^2.

Hop farm The world's leading hop growers are John I. Haas Inc., with farms in Idaho, Oregon and Washington; Tasmania, Australia; and Kent, Great Britain, covering a total net area of 5,163 acres. The largest field covers 1,715 acres near Toppenish, WA.

Mushroom farm The world's largest mushroom farm is owned by Moonlight Mushrooms Inc. and was founded in 1937 in a disused limestone mine near Worthington, PA. The farm employs over 1,000 people who work in a maze of underground galleries 110 miles long, producing over 22,500 tons of mushrooms per year. The French annual consumption is unrivaled at 7 lb per capita.

Pig farm The world's largest pig farm is the Sljeme pig unit in Yugoslavia, which is able to process 300,000 pigs in a year.

Rice farm The largest wild rice (*Zizania aquatica*) farm in the world is that of Clearwater Rice Inc. in Clearbrook, MN, covering 2,000 acres. In 1986 it yielded 577,000 lb, the largest amount to date.

Sheep ranch The largest sheep ranch in the world is Commonwealth Hill, in the northwest of South Australia. It grazes between 60,000 and 70,000 sheep, along with 24,000 uninvited kangaroos, in an area of 4,080 miles^2 enclosed by 119 miles of dog-proof fencing. The head count on Sir William Stevenson's 40,970 acre Lochinver station in New Zealand was 110,460 on 1 Jan 1991.

The largest sheep move on record occurred when 27 horsemen moved a flock of 43,000 sheep 40 miles from Barcaldine to Beaconsfield station, Queensland, Australia in 1886.

Turkey farm The world's largest turkey farm is that of Bernard Matthews plc in Norfolk, Great Britain, where 2,600 employees tend 9 million turkeys.

CROP PRODUCTION

Barley The total amount of land farmed for barley production in the 1990/91 season was estimated to be 18 million acres, with total production of 200.1 million tons and an average yield of 6.75 tons per acre. The world's leading grower of barley is the USSR, which is estimated to produce 62.83 million tons from about 64.2 million acres.

United States In 1990 7.4 million acres

of barley were farmed in the United States, with an average yield of 8.2 tons per acre and a total production of 10.03 million tons.

Cotton The total area of land used for cotton production in 1990/91 was estimated to be 83.02 million acres, giving a total production of 87 million bales, each weighing 480 lb. The leading cotton producer is China, with figures esti-

mated at 20.5 million such bales from 13.6 million acres.

United States It is estimated that 11.6 million acres will be planted for cotton production in the United States during the 1990/91 growing season. The average yield per acre will be 38.7 lb, with a total production of 15.5 480-lb bales.

Corn The total amount of land used for growing corn in 1990/91 was 316.8 mil-

Bale rolling
Michael Priestley and Marcus Stanley of Heckington Young Farmers Club rolled a 3-ft-11-in-wide cylindrical bale over a 164-ft course in 18.06 sec at the Lincolnshire Federation of Young Farmers' Clubs annual sports day at Sleaford, Great Britain on 25 Jun 1989.

Ploughing
The world championship (instituted 1953) has been staged in 18 countries and won by competitors from 12 nations. Great Britain has been most successful, winning ten championships. The only person to take the title three times is Hugh B. Barr of Northern Ireland, in 1954–56.

The fastest recorded time for plowing an acre by the Society of Ploughmen (Great Britain) rules is 9 min 49.88 sec by Joe Langcake at Hornby Hall Farm, Brougham, Great Britain on 21 Oct 1989. He used a case IH 7140 Magnum tractor and Kverneland four-furrow plow.

The greatest area plowed with a six-furrow plow to a depth of 9 in in 24 hours is 173 acres. This was achieved by Richard Gaisford and Peter Gooding of Wiltshire Young Farmers, using a Case IH tractor and Lemken plow, at Manor Farm, Pewsey, Great Britain on 25–26 Sep 1990.

Knitting

The Exeter Spinners—
Audrey Felton,
Christine Heap, Eileen
Lancaster, Marjorie
Mellis, Ann Sander-
cock and Maria Scott—
produced a sweater by
hand from raw fleece in
1hr 55min 50.2 sec on 25
Sep 1983 at British
Broadcasting Corpor-
ation Television
Center, London, Great
Britain.

Crochet

Barbara Jean Sonntag
(b. 1938) of Craig, CO
crocheted 330 shells
plus five stitches
(equivalent to 4,412
stitches) in 30 min at a
rate of 147 stitches per
min on 13 Jan 1981.

Ria van der Honing of
Wormerveer, Nether-
lands completed a cro-
chet chain 38.83 miles
long on 14 Jul 1986.

lion acres, producing an estimated 520.3
tons, of which 97 million tons was produced by China from an estimated 51.9
million acres.

Oats The worldwide production of oats
in 1990/91 was an estimated 47.18 million
tons harvested from about 53.4 million
acres, most of which, 19.3 million tons, is
produced by the USSR from some 26
million acres.

United States In 1990 5.9 million acres
of oats were farmed in the United States,
with an average yield of 2.38 tons and a
total production of 5.62 million tons.

Rice About half of the world's
population, including virtually the
whole of East Asia, is totally dependent
on rice as the staple food. The total
amount of land used for rice production
is 362.7 million acres, with India leading
in the area farmed, at 104.3 million
acres. The world's leading producer,
however, is China with estimated yields
of 203.93 million tons from 80.8 million
acres.

United States In 1990 2.7 million acres
of rice were planted in the United States,
with an average yield of 7.4 tons and a
total production of 7.74 million tons.

Sugar beets The highest recorded
yield for sugar beets is 62.4 tons per acre
by Andy Christensen and Jon Giannini
in the Salinas Valley, CA.

Wheat An estimated 569 million acres
of land is used for wheat production
worldwide, giving a yield of 650.5 million
tons. The leading grower is the USSR,

UNITED STATES CROP SUMMARY—1990		
Crop	Yield Per Acre	Production
Barley	3.32	10,052,538
Coffee	1.39	1,323
Corn (for grain)	8.20	222,125,850
Corn (for silage)	35.04	86,843,989
Hay	5.89	146,984,980
Hops	1.98	28,429
Lentils	1.04	43,751
Oats	2.38	5,714,381
Potatoes	35.80	19,693,362
Rice	2.72	17,493,371
Rye	2.06	282,743
Sorghum (for grain)	4.35	16,001,524
Sorghum (for silage)	25.22	5,479,997
Sugarcane	84.60	27,089,992
Sweet potatoes	17.79	651,003
Tobacco	2.72	803,431
Wheat	2.93	82,157,800

*Source: Agricultural Statistics Board
(NASS, USDA)*

which produces 119.05 million tons from
about 117.4 million acres farmed.

The largest single fenced field sown with
wheat measured 35,000 acres and was
sown in 1951 southwest of Lethbridge,
Alberta, Canada.

United States In 1990 69.4 million acres
of wheat were farmed in the United
States, with an average yield of 2.93 tons
and a total production of 82.12 million
tons.

Baling A rick of 40,400 bales of straw
was built between 22 Jul and 3 Sep 1982
by Nick and Tom Parsons with a gang of

eight at Cuckoo Pen Barn Farm, Birdlip,
Great Britain. It measured 150
× 30 × 60 ft high and weighed some
784 tons. The team baled, hauled and
ricked 24,200 bales in seven consecutive
days from 22–29 July.

Svend Erik Klemmensen of Trustrup,
Djursland, Denmark baled 220 tons of
straw in 9 hr 54 min using a Hesston 4800
baling machine on 30 Aug 1989.

LIVESTOCK PRICES

*Note: Some exceptionally high livestock
auction prices are believed to result from
collusion between buyer and seller to
raise the ostensible price levels of the
breed concerned. Others are marketing
and publicity exercises with little relation
to true market prices.*

Cattle The highest price ever paid was
$2.5 million for the beefalo (a ⅜ bison, ⅜
Charolais, ¼ Hereford) Joe's Pride, sold
by D. C. Basalo of Burlingame, CA to the
Beefalo Cattle Co. of Calgary, Canada
on 9 Sep 1974.

Cow The highest price paid for a cow is
$1.3 million for a Holstein at auction in
East Montpelier, VT in 1985.

Goat On 25 Jan 1985 an Angora buck
bred by Waitangi Angoras of Waitangi,
New Zealand was sold to Elliott Brown
Ltd of Waipu, New Zealand for NZ
$140,000.

Horse The highest price paid for a draft
horse is $47,000 by C.G. Good of Ogden,
IA for the seven-year-old Belgian stallion Farceur at Cedar Falls, IA on 16 Oct
1917.

■ **From field to loaf**
*The fastest time for pro-
ducing 13 loaves (a
baker's dozen) from
growing wheat is 23 min
49 sec, by Tendring Hun-
dred Farmers' Club
(right) and bakers (far
right) from Read
Woodrow Ltd at St
Osyth, Great Britain on
16 Aug 1990.*

Pig The highest price ever paid for a pig is $56,000 for a cross-bred barrow named Bud, owned by Jeffrey Roemisch of Hermleigh, TX and bought by E.A. Bud Olson and Phil Bonzio on 5 Mar 1983.

Sheep The highest price ever paid for a sheep is $A450,000 ($358,750) by Willogoleche Pty Ltd for the Collinsville stud "JC&S 43" at the 1989 Adelaide Ram Sales, South Australia.

Wool The highest price ever paid for wool is $A3,008.5 per kg greasy wool for a bale of Tasmania superfine at the wool auction in Tasmania, Australia on 23 Feb 1989 by Fujii Keori Ltd of Osaka, Japan—top bidders since 1973.

CATTLE

As of 1989 the world's leading producer of cattle was India, with 269.2 million head. However, the leading producer of milk in 1989 was the USSR, with a total of 119.6 million tons.

In 1990 there were 99,436,000 head of cattle farmed in the United States. The leading cattle producer was Texas with 13,400,000 head.

Largest The heaviest breed of cattle is the Chianini, which was brought to the Chiana Valley in Italy from the Middle East in pre-Roman times. Four types of the breed exist, the largest of which is the Val di Chianini, found on the plains and low hills of Arezzo and Sienna. Mature bulls average 5 ft 8 in at the forequarters and weigh 2,865 lb (cf. 1,873 lb for cows), but Chianini oxen have been known to attain heights of 6 ft 2¾ in. The sheer expense of feeding such huge cattle has put the breed under threat of extinction in Italy, but farmers in North America, Mexico and Brazil are still enthusiastic buyers of the breed.

The heaviest on record was a Holstein–Durham cross named Mount Katahdin, exhibited by A.S. Rand of Maine from 1906–10, which frequently weighed in at an even 5,000 lb. He was 6 ft 2 in at the shoulder with a 13 ft girth, and died in a barn fire c. 1923.

Smallest The smallest breed of domestic cattle is the Ovambo of Namibia. Mature bulls and cows average 496 lb and 353 lb respectively.

Oldest Big Bertha, a Dremon owned by Jerome O'Leary of Blackwatersbridge,

County Kerry, Republic of Ireland, was born on 17 Mar 1944. (See also Reproductivity.)

Reproductivity On 25 Apr 1964 it was reported that a cow named Lyubik had given birth to seven calves in Mogilev, USSR. Five short-lived and one stillborn calf were recorded from a Friesian at Te Puke, North Island, New Zealand on 27 Jul 1980. A case of five live calves at one birth was reported in 1928 by T.G. Yarwood of Manchester, Great Britain.

The lifetime breeding record is 39 in the case of Big Bertha (b. 17 Mar 1944), a Dremon owned by Jerome O'Leary of Blackwatersbridge, Republic of Ireland. (See also Oldest.)

Soender Jylland's Jens, a Danish black-and-white bull, left 220,000 surviving progeny by artificial insemination when he was put away at the age of 11 in Copenhagen in September 1978. Bendalls Adema, a Friesian bull, died at the age of 14 in Clondalkin, Dublin, Republic of Ireland on 8 Nov 1978, having sired an estimated 212,000 progeny by artificial insemination.

Birth weights The heaviest recorded live birth weight for a calf is 225 lb for a British Friesian cow at Rockhouse Farm, Bishopston, Great Britain in 1961. On 28 May 1986 a Holstein cow owned by Sherlene O'Brien of Simitar Farms, Henryetta, OK gave birth to a perfectly formed stillborn calf weighing 270 lb. The sire was an Aberdeen-Angus bull which had "jumped the fence."

Lightest The lowest live birth weight recorded for a calf is 17 lb 10 oz for a bull (breed not identified) born on Jan van Rensberg's farm at Kankus, Orange Free State, South Africa in August 1972. It stood 15 ¾ in at the hindquarters and measured 21½ in overall.

Milk yields As of 1989, the world's leading producer of cow's milk was the Soviet Union with 119.6 million tons. The United States produced 72.09 million tons in 1989. The highest recorded world lifetime yield of milk is 465,224 lb by the unglamorously named cow No. 289 owned by M.G. Maciel & Son of Hanford, CA, to 1 May 1984.

The greatest recorded yield for one lactation (maximum 365 days) is 55,661 lb in 1975 by the Holstein Beecher Arlinda Ellen, owned by Mr and Mrs Harold L. Beecher of Rochester, IN. The highest reported milk yield in a day is 241 lb by a cow named Urbe Blanca in Cuba on or about 23 Jun 1982.

Butterfat yields The world record lifetime yield is 16,370 lb by the US Holstein Breezewood Patsy Bar Pontiac in 3,979 days.

The world record for 365 days is 3,126 lb by Roybrook High Ellen, a Holstein owned by Yashuhiro Tanaka of Tottori, Japan.

Cheese The oldest and most primitive cheeses are the Arabian *kishk*, made of the dried curd of goats' milk. Today there are 450 named cheeses in 18 major varieties, but many are merely named after different towns and differ only in shape or the method of packing. France has 240 varieties. The world's biggest producer of cheese is the United States, with a factory production of 2.43 million tons in 1980.

The most active cheese-eaters are the people of France, with an annual average in 1983 of 43.6 lb per person.

GOATS

Largest The largest goat ever recorded was a British Saanen named Mostyn Moorcock, owned by Pat Robinson of Ewyas Harold, Great Britain, which reached a weight of 400 lb (shoulder height 44 in and overall length of 66 in). He died in 1977 at the age of four.

Smallest Some pygmy goats weigh only 33–44 lb.

Oldest The oldest goat on record is a Toggenburg feral cross named Hongi (b. August 1971), belonging to April Koch of Glenorchy, near Otago, New Zealand, which was still alive in mid-March 1989 at the age of 17 years 8 months.

Reproductivity According to the British Goat Society, at least one or two cases of quintuplets are recorded annually out of the 10,000 goats registered, but some breeders only record the females born.

On 14 Jan 1980 a nanny goat named Julie, owned by Galen Cowper of Nampah, ID, gave birth to septuplets, but they all died, including the mother.

Milk yields The highest recorded milk yield for any goat is 7,714 lb in 365 days by Osory Snow-Goose, owned by Mr and Mrs G. Jameson of Leppington, New South Wales, Australia, in 1977.

Snowball, the goat owned by Don Papin of Tipton, CA, lactated continuously for 12 years 10 months between 1977 and 1989.

PIGS

The world's leading producer of hogs in 1989 was China, with 342,220,000 head. As of 1 Dec 1990 there were 54,562,000 head of hogs farmed in the United States. The leading producer was Iowa with 14 million head.

Largest The heaviest pig ever recorded was a Poland–China hog named Big Bill, who was so obese that his belly dragged along the ground. Bill weighed an astonishing 2,552 lb just before he was put away after suffering a broken leg in an accident en route to the Chicago World's Fair for exhibition in 1933. Other statistics included a shoulder height of 5 ft and a length of 9 ft. At the request of his owner, W.J. Chappall, this prized possession was mounted and put on display in Weekly County, TN until 1946, when he was acquired by a traveling carnival. On the death of the carnival's proprietor his family reportedly donated Big Bill to a museum, but no trace has been found of him since.

Smallest The smallest breed of pig is the Mini Maialino, developed by Stefano Morini of St Golo d'Enza, Italy, after 10 years of experimentation with Viet-

Lowest price
The lowest price ever realized for livestock was at a sale at Kuruman, Cape Province, South Africa in 1934, where donkeys were sold for less than 2 p (less than 5 cents) each.

Hand-milking of cows
Andy Faust at Collinsville, OK in 1937 achieved a yield of 99.92 gal in 12 hours.

Egg shelling
Two kitchen hands, Harold Witcomb and Gerald Harding, shelled 1,050 dozen eggs in a 7¼-hr shift at Bowyers, Great Britain on 23 Apr 1971. Both men were blind.

Egg dropping
The greatest height from which fresh eggs have been dropped (to the ground) and remained intact is 650 ft, by David S. Donoghue from a helicopter on 2 Oct 1979 on a golf course in Tokyo, Japan.

Chicken and turkey plucking
Ernest Hausen (1877–1955) of Fort Atkinson, WI died undefeated after 33 years as champion chicken plucker. On 19 Jan 1939 he was timed at 4.4 sec.

Vincent Pilkington of Cootehill, Co. Cavan, Republic of Ireland killed and plucked 100 turkeys in 7 hr 32 min on 15 Dec 1978. His record for a single turkey is 1 min 30 sec in Dublin on 17 Nov 1980.

Fine spinning

The longest thread of wool, hand-spun and plied to weigh 0.35 oz, was one with a length of 1,815 ft 3 in, achieved by Julitha Barber of Bull Creek, Western Australia, at the International Highland, Great Britain Spin-In, Bothwell, Tasmania, Australia on 1 Mar 1989.

Sheep to shoulder

At the International Wool Secretariat Development Center, Ilkley, West Yorkshire, Great Britain, a team of eight using commercial machinery produced a sweater—from shearing sheep to the finished article—in 2 hr 28 min 32 sec on 3 Sep 1986.

Sheep's survival

On 24 Mar 1978 Alex Maclennan found one ewe still alive after he had dug out 16 sheep buried in a snowdrift for 50 days near the river Skinsdale on Mrs Tyser's Gordonbush Estate in Sutherland, Great Britain after the great January blizzard. The sheep's hot breath creates airholes in the snow, and the animals gnaw their own wool for protein, enabling them to survive in a snowdrift for a considerable length of time.

namese pot-bellied pigs. The piglets weigh 14 oz at birth and 20 lb at maturity.

Reproductivity A breeding sow will live 12 years or more before it is slaughtered, but the maximum potential lifespan is 20 years.

The highest recorded number of piglets in one litter is 34, farrowed on 25–26 Jun 1961 by a sow owned by Aksel Egedee of Denmark.

In February 1955 a Wessex sow belonging to E.C. Goodwin of Paul's Farm, Leigh, Great Britain also had a litter of 34, of which 30 were stillborn. A litter of 32 piglets (eight stillborn) was farrowed in February 1971 by a British Saddleback owned by Mr R. Spence of Toddington, Great Britain

A Large White owned by H.S. Pedlingham farrowed 385 pigs in 22 litters from December 1923 to September 1934. A Newsham Large White × Landrace sow of Meeting House Farm, Staintondale, Great Britain had farrowed 189 piglets (seven stillborn) in nine litters up to 22 Mar 1988. Between 6 May 1987 and 9 Feb 1988 she gave birth to 70 piglets.

Birth weights The average birth weight for a piglet is 3 lb. A Hampshire × Yorkshire sow belonging to Rev. John Schroeder of Mountain Grove, MO farrowed a litter of 18 on 26 Aug 1979. Five were stillborn, including one male that weighed 5 lb 4 oz.

The highest recorded weight for a piglet at weaning (eight weeks) is 81 lb for a boar, one of a litter of nine farrowed on 6 Jul 1962 by the Landrace gilt Manorport Ballerina 53rd, alias "Mary," and sired by a Large White named Johnny at Kettle Lane Farm, West Ashton, Great Britain.

In Nov 1957 a total weight of 1,134 lb was reported at weaning for a litter of 18 piglets farrowed by an Essex sow owned by Mrs B. Ravel of Seaton House, Thorugumbald, Great Britain.

POULTRY

Figures for 1989 showed the United States to be the largest producer of chicken meat, with a total of 11.9 million tons. The leading egg producer, however, is China, where 143 billion were laid in 1990, compared with 67.9 billion in the United States.

Chicken Largest The heaviest breed of chicken is the White Sully developed by Grant Sullens of West Point, CA by crossing and recrossing large Rhode Island Reds with other varieties. One monstrous rooster named Weirdo reportedly weighed 22 lb in January 1973 and was so aggressive that he killed two cats and crippled a dog that ventured too close. The heaviest chicken is currently a White Ross 1 rooster named Bruno, owned by John Steele of Kirkhills Farms, Boyndie, Great Britain. On 4 Jul 1989 this outsized bird recorded a weight of 22 lb 1 oz.

Reproductivity The highest authenticated rate of egg-laying is by a White Leghorn, No. 2988, which laid 371 eggs in 364 days in an official test conducted by

Prof. Harold V. Biellier ending on 29 Aug 1979 at the College of Agriculture, University of Missouri.

The highest recorded annual average per bird for a flock is 313 eggs in 52 weeks from 1,000 Warren-Stadler SSL layers (from 21 weeks of age), owned by Eric Savage of White Lane Farm, Albury, Great Britain in 1974–75.

Largest egg The heaviest egg reported was one of 16 oz, with double yolk and double shell, laid by a White Leghorn at Vineland, NJ on 25 Feb 1956. The largest egg recorded was one of nearly 12 oz for a five-yolked egg measuring 12¼ in around the long axis and 9 in around the short, laid by a Black Minorca at Mr Stafford's Damsteads Farm, Mellor, Great Britain in 1896.

Smallest egg An egg measuring 0.8 × 0.6 in was laid on 15 Jan 1991 by a hen owned by David Kay of Chippenham, Great Britain.

Most yolks The highest claim for the number of yolks in a hen's egg is nine, reported by Diane Hainsworth of Hainsworth Poultry Farms, Mount Morris, NY in July 1971, and also from a hen in Kirgizya, USSR in August 1977.

Flying Sheena, a barnyard bantam owned by Bill and Bob Knox, flew 630 ft 2 in at Parkesburg, PA on 31 May 1985.

Duck Reproductivity An Aylesbury duck belonging to Annette and Angela Butler of Princes Risborough, Great Britain laid 457 eggs in 463 days, including an unbroken run of 375 in as many days. The duck died on 7 Feb 1986.

Another duck of the same breed owned by Edmond Walsh of Gormanstown, Republic of Ireland laid eggs every year right up to her 25th birthday. She died on 3 Dec 1978 at the age of 28 yr 6 months.

Goose The heaviest goose egg on record was one of 24 oz that measured 13½ in around the long axis and had a maximum circumference of 9½ in around the short axis. It was laid on 3 May 1977 by a white goose named Speckle, owned by Donny Brandenberg of Goshen, OH. The average weight is 10–12 oz.

Turkey The greatest dressed weight recorded for a turkey is 86 lb for a stag named Tyson reared by Philip Cook of Leacroft Turkeys Ltd, Peterborough, Great Britain. It won the annual "heaviest turkey" competition held in London, Great Britain on 12 Dec 1989 and was auctioned for charity for a record £4,400 ($7,480). Stags of this size have been so overdeveloped for meat production that they are unable to mate because of their shape and the hens have to be artificially inseminated.

SHEEP

Not surprisingly, the world's leading producer of sheep is Australia, with a total of 174 million head in 1989. As of 1 Jan 1991 there were 11,200,000 head of sheep farmed in the United States. The leading producer was Texas with 2 million head.

Largest The largest sheep ever

recorded was a Suffolk ram named Stratford Whisper 23H, which weighed 545 lb and stood 43 in tall in March 1991. It is owned by Joseph and Susan Schallberger of Boring, OR.

Smallest The smallest breed of sheep is the Soay, which is now confined to the island of Hirta in the St Kilda group, Outer Hebrides, Great Britain. Adults weigh 55–60 lb.

Reproductivity A case of eight lambs at a birth was reported by D.T. Jones of Priory Farm, Gwent, Great Britain in June 1956 and also by Ken Towse of Buckton, Great Britain in March 1981, but none lived. A Border Leicester × Merino sheep owned by Roger Saunders gave birth to 4 ram and 3 ewe live lambs at Strathdownie, Victoria, Australia on 19 Jun 1984. Seven live lambs (4 rams and 3 ewes) were also reported for a Finn × Targhoe ewe owned by Elsward Meine of Crookston, MN on 24 Mar 1980. Pedigree Cambridge ewe No. 8125AP, owned by Peter Adorian, gave birth to seven live lambs weighing 42 lb at Gibbons Mill Farm, Billingshurst, Great Britain on 19 Mar 1990, and a Welsh mule owned by Dennis and Martin Swain of Holt Farm, Sherborne, Great Britain gave birth to seven live lambs on 2 Jan 1991.

Birth weights The highest recorded birth weight for a lamb is 38 lb at Clearwater, Sedgwick County, KS in 1975, but neither lamb nor ewe survived. Another lamb of the same weight was born on 7 Apr 1975 on the Gerald Neises Farm, Howard, SD but died soon afterwards.

A four-year-old Suffolk ewe owned by Gerry H. Watson of Augusta, KS gave birth to two live sets of triplets on 30–31 Jan 1982. The total weight of the lambs was 49½ lb.

The lowest live birth weight recorded for a lamb is 2 lb 4 oz for a ram named Tiny, born in April 1980 and owned by Jeanette Fox of Daisy Bank Farm, Barthomley, Great Britain. It was nursed to full health.

Oldest A crossbred sheep owned by Griffiths & Davies of Dolclettwr Hall, Taliesin, Great Britain gave birth to a healthy lamb in the spring of 1988 at the grand old age of 28, after lambing successfully more than 40 times. She died on 24 Jan 1989 just one week before her 29th birthday.

Shearing The fastest speed for sheep shearing in a working day was that recorded by Alan McDonald, who machine-sheared 805 lambs in nine hours (an average of 89.4) at Waitnaguru, New Zealand on 20 Dec 1990.

Peter Casserly of Christchurch, New Zealand achieved a solo blade (i.e., hand-shearing) record of 353 lambs in nine hours on 13 Feb 1976.

In a 24-hour shearing marathon, Alan MacDonald and Keith Wilson machine-sheared 2,220 sheep at Warkworth, Auckland Province, New Zealand on 26 Jun 1988. Lavor Taylor (1896–1989) of Ephraim, UT claimed to have sheared 515,000 sheep to May 1984.

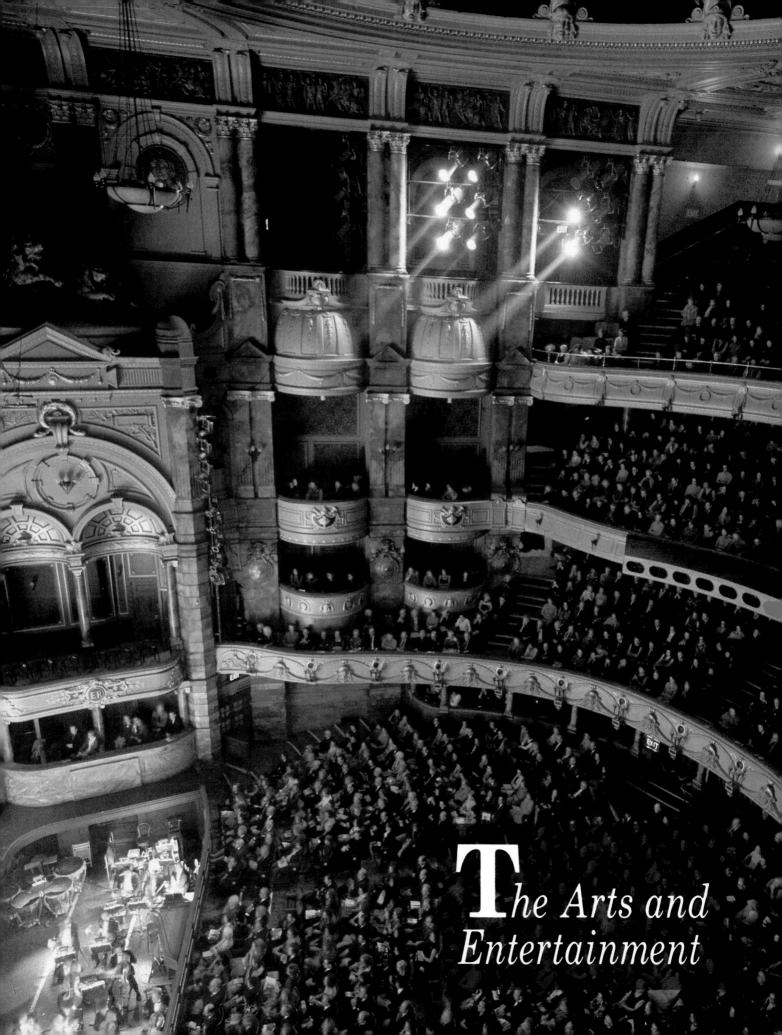

The Arts and Entertainment

PAINTING

■ **Previous page**
London Coliseum, Great Britain
(Photo: ACE Photo Library)

Finest standard brush

The finest standard brush sold is the 000 in Series 7 by Winsor and Newton, known as a "triple goose." It is made of 150–200 Kolinsky sable hairs weighing 0.000529 oz.

Poster

A poster measuring 134,550 ft² was painted by 30,000 inhabitants of Miyazaki, Japan and unveiled on 17 Mar 1990 on the banks of the Oyodo River to celebrate the annual Himuka-no-Saiten Festival.

Sand sculpture

The longest sand sculpture ever made—with the sculpture meticulously carved—was the 55,154-ft-6-in-long sculpture named "The GTE Directories Ultimate Sand Castle" built by more than 8,000 volunteers at Myrtle Beach, SC on 4 Jul 1990.

The tallest was the "Invitation to Fairyland," which was 56 ft 2 in high, and was built by 2,000 local volunteers at Kaseda, Japan on 26 Jul 1989 under the supervision of Gerry Kirk of Sand Sculptors International of San Diego and Shogo Tashiro of Sand Sculptors International of Japan.

Painting

Origins Evidence of Paleolithic art was first found in 1833 at Veyrier, three miles southwest of Geneva, Switzerland, when François Mayor (1779–1854) found two harpoonlike objects corated with geometric figures. Recently discovered pieces of bone bearing geometric engraved marks from an Old Stone Age site at Bilzingsleben, near Erfurt, Germany, could possibly be the world's oldest examples of art. They are dated to *c.* 350,000 years ago.

The oldest-known dated examples of representational art come from La Ferrassie, near Les Eyzies in the Périgord, France, in layers dated to *c.* 25,000 B.C. Blocks of stone were found with engraved animals and female symbols; some of the blocks also had symbols painted in red ocher.

Pieces of ocher with ground facets have been found at Lake Mungo, New South Wales, Australia in a context *ante* 30,000 B.C., but there is no evidence to show whether these were used for body-painting or for pictorial art.

Largest The largest-ever painting measures 72,437 ft² after allowing for shrinkage of the canvas. It is made up of brightly colored squares with a Smiley face superimposed, and was painted by students of Robb College at Armidale, New South Wales, Australia, aided by local schoolchildren and students from neighboring colleges. The canvas was completed by its designer, Australian artist Ken Done, and unveiled at the University of New England at Armidale on 10 May 1990.

Panorama of the Mississippi, completed by John Banvard (1815–91) in 1846, showing the river for 1,200 miles in a strip probably 5,000 ft long and 12 ft wide, was the largest painting in the world, with an area of more than 60,000 ft². The painting is believed to have been destroyed when the rolls of canvas, stored in a barn at Cold Spring Harbor, Long Island, NY, caught fire shortly before Banvard's death on 16 May 1891. *The Battle of Gettysburg*, completed in 1883, after 2½ years of work, by Paul Philippoteaux (France) and 16 assistants, was 410 ft long, 70 ft high and weighed 6 tons. It depicts the climax of the battle, in southern Pennsylvania, on 3 Jul 1863. In 1964 it was bought by Joe King of Winston-Salem, NC after being stored by E.W. McConnell in a Chicago warehouse since 1933, but, because of deterioration, the sky was trimmed, thus decreasing the area of the painting.

Jackson Bailey's *Life of Christ*, exhibited by Religious Art Institute of America Inc. of Atlanta, GA, comprises 50 panels 11 × 20 ft each, and was complete by 1971 with an area of 11,000 ft².

"Old Master" The largest "Old Master" is *Il Paradiso*, by Jacopo Robusti, alias Tintoretto (1518–94), and his son Domenico (1565–1637) on the east wall of the Sala del Maggior Consiglio in the Palazzo Ducale (Doge's Palace) in Venice, Italy between 1587 and 1590. The work is 72 ft 2 in long, 22 ft 11½ in high and contains some 350 human figures.

Auction The largest painting ever auctioned was Carl Larsson's *Midvinterblot*, painted in Stockholm, Sweden from 1911 to 1915 and sold at Sotheby's, London, on 25 Mar 1988 for £880,000 ($1,496,000) to the Umeda Gallery of Japan. The painting measured 44 × 9 ft.

Most valuable The "Mona Lisa" (*La Gioconda*) by Leonardo da Vinci (1452–1519) in the Louvre, Paris, France, was assessed for insurance purposes at $100 million for its move to Washington, D.C. and New York City for exhibition from 14 Dec 1962 to 12 Mar 1963. However, insurance was not purchased because the cost of the closest security precautions was less than that of the premiums. It was painted *c.* 1503–07 and measures 30.5 × 20.9 in. It is believed to portray either Mona (short for Madonna) Lisa Gherardini, the wife of Francesco del Giocondo of Florence, or Constanza d'Avalos, coincidentally nicknamed La Gioconda, mistress of Giuliano de Medici. King Francis I of France bought the painting for his bathroom in 1517 for 4,000 gold florins, or 92 oz of gold.

Most prolific painter Pablo Diego José Francisco de Paula Juan Nepomuceno Crispin Crispiano de la Santisima Trinidad Ruiz y Picasso (1881–1973) of Spain was the most prolific of all painters in a career that lasted 78 years. It has been estimated that Picasso produced about 13,500 paintings or designs, 100,000 prints or engravings, 34,000 book illustrations and 300 sculptures or ceramics. His lifetime *oeuvre* has been valued at over $800 million.

Largest galleries The world's largest art gallery is the Winter Palace and the neighboring Hermitage in Leningrad, USSR. One has to walk 15 miles to visit each of the 322 galleries, which house nearly 3 million works of art and objects of archaeological interest.

The Georges Pompidou National Center for Art and Culture, Beauborg, opened in Paris, France, in 1977, has 183,000 ft² of floor space.

Most heavily endowed The J. Paul Getty Museum at Malibu, CA, was established with an initial $1.4 billion budget in January 1974 and now has an annual budget of $180 million for acquisitions to stock its 38 galleries.

MOSAICS

Largest mosaic The world's largest mosaic is on the walls of the central library of the Universidad Nacional Autónoma de Mexico in Mexico City. Of the four walls, the two largest measure 12,949 ft², and the scenes on each represent the pre-Hispanic past.

MURALS

Earliest The earliest-known murals on man-made walls are the clay relief leopards at Catal Hüyük in southern Anatolia, Turkey, discovered by James Malaart at level VII in 1961 and dating from *c.* 6200 B.C.

Largest A mural on the 23-story Vegas World Hotel, Las Vegas, NV covers an area of 95,442 ft². A mural covering an area of 17,963 ft² is painted on the walls of the Royal Liverpool Children's Hospital, Liverpool, Great Britain.

HIGHEST PRICE

Painting Following the collapse of Australian tycoon Alan Bond's business empire in 1989, he was forced to part with Vincent Van Gogh's *Irises*, which he had bought in 1987 for a then-record price of $53.9 million. The sale followed reports that Sotheby's had loaned Mr Bond $27 million towards the purchase, a practice which the auction house has subsequently reviewed. *Irises* was resold to the Getty Museum for an undisclosed sum in April 1990. On 15 May 1990 this record was shattered again when another Van Gogh, *Portrait of Dr Gachet*, was sold within three minutes for $82.5 million at Christie's, New York. The painting depicts Van Gogh's physician and was completed only weeks before the artist's suicide in 1890. The new owner was subsequently identified as Ryoei Saito, Japan's second-largest paper manufacturer.

Art collection The most valuable art collection of a single owner sold at auction realized $131,297,870 at Sotheby's, New York in October 1990. The collection was formed by John T. Dorrance, Jr., and included *Femme a l'Ombrelle Rouge Assise de Profil* (1921), by Henri Matisse, which raised $12.375 million.

Miniature The record price is the £352,000 ($621,632) paid by the Alexander Gallery of New York at Christie's, London on 7 Nov 1988 for a 2⅛-in-high miniature of George Washington. It was painted by the Irish-American miniaturist John Ramage (*c.* 1748–1802) in 1789.

20th-century painting The record bid at auction for a 20th-century painting is $47.8 million for a self-portrait by Picasso (1881–1973), *Yo Picasso* (1901), at Sotheby's, New York on 9 May 1989.

Living artist The highest price paid at auction for a work by a living artist is $20.68 million for *Interchange*, an abstract by the American painter Willem de Kooning (b. Rotterdam, Netherlands, 1904) at Sotheby's, New York on 8 Nov 1989. Painted in 1955, it was bought by Japanese dealer-cum-collector "Mountain Turtle."

Print The record price for a print at auction was £561,600 ($786,000) for a 1655 etching of *Christ Presented to the People* by Rembrandt (1606–69) at Christie's, London on 5 Dec 1985. It was sold by the Chatsworth Settlement Trustees.

Drawing The highest price ever paid for a drawing is $8.36 million for the pen-and-ink scene *Jardin de Fleurs*, drawn by Vincent Van Gogh in Arles, France in 1888 and sold at Christie's, New York on 14 Nov 1990 to an anonymous buyer.

Poster The record price for a poster is £62,000 ($74,400) for an advertisement for the 1902 Vienna Exhibition by Koloman Moser (1868–1918), sold at Christie's, London on 1 Apr 1985.

Sculpture

Earliest A piece of ox rib found in 1973 at Pech de l'Aze, Dordogne, France in an early Middle Paleolithic layer of the Riss glaciation of *c.* 105,000 B.C. has several engraved lines on one side, thought to be possibly intentional. A churingo or curved ivory plaque rubbed with red ocher from the Middle Paleolithic Mousterian site at Tata, Hungary has been dated to 100,000 B.C. by the thorium/uranium method.

The earliest-known examples of sculpture date from the Aurignacian culture of *c.* 28,000–22,000 B.C. and include the so-called "Venus" figurines from Austria and numerous figurines from northern Italy and central France. A carving in mammoth ivory from the Magdalenian culture (*c.* 11–17,000 years ago) of a horse measuring 2½ in was found in the Vogelherd cave in southwest Germany.

Most expensive The record price for a sculpture at auction is £6.82 million ($12 million) at Sotheby's, London on 7 Dec 1989 for a bronze garden ornament, *The Dancing Faun*, made by the Dutch-born sculptor Adrien de Vries (1545/6–1626). London dealer Cyril Humpris bought the figure from an unnamed couple who had paid £100 ($240) in the 1950s and in whose garden it had stood undiscovered for 40 years.

The highest price paid for the work of a sculptor during his lifetime is the $1,265,000 given at Sotheby's, New York on 21 May 1982 for the 75-in-long elmwood *Reclining Figure* by Henry Moore (1898–1986).

United States The highest price paid at auction for a sculpture by an American sculptor is $4.4 million for *Coming Through the Rye*, by Frederic Remington (1861–1909), at Christie's, New York on 25 May 1989.

Largest The mounted figures of Jefferson Davis (1808–89), Gen Robert Edward Lee (1807–70) and Gen Thomas Jonathan (Stonewall) Jackson (1824–63) cover 1.33 acres on the face of Stone Mountain, near Atlanta, GA. They are 90 ft high. Roy Faulkner was on the mountain face for 8 years 174 days with a thermo-jet torch, working with the sculptor Walker Kirtland Hancock and other helpers, from 12 Sep 1963 to 3 Mar 1972.

If completed, the world's largest sculpture will be that of the Indian chief Tashunca-Uitco (*c.* 1849–77), known as Crazy Horse, of the Oglala tribe of the Dakota or Nadowessioux (Sioux) group, on horseback. The sculpture was begun on 3 Jun 1948 near Mount Rushmore, SD. A projected 563 ft high and 641 ft long, it was the uncompleted life work of one man, Korczak Ziólkowski (1908–82). The horse's nostril is 50 ft deep and 35 ft in diameter. In 1985–86 another 44,800 tons of granite blasted off the mountain face brought the total to 9.2 million tons.

The largest scrap-metal sculpture was built by Sudhir Deshpande of Nashik, India and unveiled in February 1990. Named *Powerful*, the colossus weighs 29.8 tons and stands 55 ¾ ft tall.

Ground figures In the Nazca Desert, 185 miles south of Lima, Peru, there are straight lines (one more than 7 miles long), geometric shapes, and outlines of plants and animals drawn on the ground some time between 100 B.C. and A.D. 600 for an uncertain but probably religious, astronomical or even economic purpose by an imprecisely identified civilization. They were first detected from the air *c.* 1928 and have been described as the world's longest works of art.

Hill figures A 330-ft-tall figure was found on a hill above Tarapacá, Chile in August 1968.

Antiques

All prices quoted are inclusive of the buyer's premium. The largest and oldest firm of art auctioneers in the world is the Sotheby Group of London, Great Britain and New York City, founded in 1744, which until 1778 traded primarily in books. Christie's held its first art auction in 1766. Sotheby's turnover in 1989 was a record $4.93 billion. A single-session record of $286 million was set at Sotheby's, New York on 17 May 1990.

Art nouveau The highest auction price for any piece of art nouveau is $1.78 million for a standard lamp in the form of three lotus blossoms by the Daum Brothers and Louis Majorelle of France, sold at Sotheby's, New York on 2 Dec 1989.

Blanket The most expensive blanket was a Navajo Churro hand-spun serape of *c.* 1852 sold for $115,500 at Sotheby's, New York on 22 Oct 1983.

Bottle A cobalt-blue bottle made by the Isabella Glassworks of New Jersey *c.* 1855–65 was sold for $26,400 at the Robert W. Skinner Galleries in Bolton, MA on 7 Oct 1989.

Carpet In 1946 the Metropolitan Museum in New York City privately paid $1 million for the 26.5 × 13.6 ft Anhalt Medallion carpet, made in Tabriz or Kashan, Persia (now Iran) *c.* 1590.

The highest price paid at auction for a carpet is $672,400 for a Louis XV Savonnerie at Christie's, Monaco in June 1989.

Ceramics The highest auction price for any ceramic is £3.74 million ($6.4 million) for a Chinese Tang dynasty (A.D. 681–907) horse sold by the British Rail Pension Fund and bought by a Japanese dealer at Sotheby's, London, on 12 Dec 1989. The horse was stolen from a warehouse in Hong Kong on 14 November, but was recovered on 2 December in time for the sale.

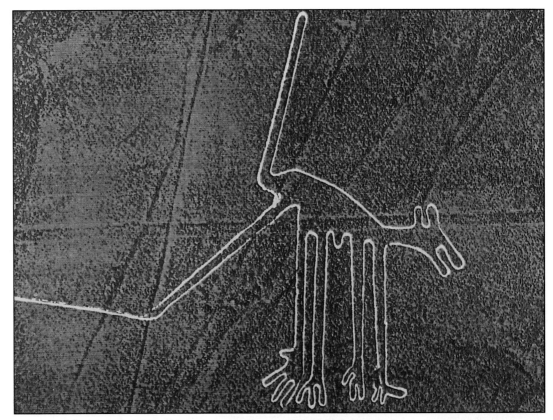

■ Ground figures
This computer-enhanced picture of an unidentified animal shows just one of the unexplained geometric shapes drawn in the Nazca Desert of Peru between 100 B.C. and A.D. 600. (Photo: Images)

Auctioneering
The longest one-man auction on record was of 60 hr, conducted by Reg Coates at Gosport, Great Britain from 9–11 Sep 1988.

Chamber pot A 33 oz silver pot, made by David Willaume and engraved for the 2nd Earl of Warrington, Great Britain, sold for £9,500 ($13,300) at Sotheby's, London on 14 Jun 1984.

Cigarette card The most valuable card is one of the six known baseball series cards of Honus Wagner (who was a nonsmoker), which was sold at Sotheby's, New York for $451,000 on 22 Mar 1991. The buyers were Bruce McNall, owner of the Los Angeles Kings hockey club, and team member Wayne Gretzky, the game's most successful player.

Doll The highest price paid at auction for a doll is £90,200 ($153,340) for a 1909 bisque Kämmer and Reinhardt doll at Sotheby's, London, on 16 Feb 1989. It was bought by Mme Dina Vierny, who planned to open a Museum of Childhood in France.

Furniture The highest price ever paid for a single piece of furniture is £8.58 million ($15.2 million) at Christie's, London on 5 Jul 1990 for the 18th-century Italian "Badminton Cabinet" owned by the Duke of Beaufort. It was bought by Barbara Piasecka Johnson of Princeton, NJ.

United States The highest price ever paid for a single piece of American furniture is $12.1 million at Christie's, New York on 3 Jun 1989 for a mahogany desk-cum-bookcase, made in the 1760s by master craftsman John Goddard of Newport, RI for the eminent statesman Nicholas Brown. It was bought by Israel Sack, one of New York's leading dealers in American furniture.

Glass The auction record is £520,000 ($1,175,200) for a Roman glass cage-cup of *c.* A.D. 300, measuring 7 in in diameter and 4 in in height, sold at Sotheby's, London, on 4 Jun 1979 to Robin Symes.

Gold plate The record for any gold artifact is £950,400 ($1,140,000) for the 22-carat font made by Paul Storr to the design of Humphrey Repton in 1797. It was sold at Christie's, London by Lady Anne Cavendish-Bentinck and bought by Armitage of London, Great Britain on 11 Jul 1985.

Guns The highest price ever paid for a single gun is £125,000 ($318,750) paid by the London dealers F. Partridge for a French flintlock fowling piece made for Louis XIII *c.* 1615 and attributed to Pierre le Bourgeoys of Lisieux, France (d. 1627). This piece was included in the collection of the late William Goodwin Renwick (USA), sold by Sotheby's, London on 21 Nov 1972. It is now in the Metropolitan Museum of Art, New York City.

A set of rare, 24-carat gold-inlaid Colt 1851 model Navy presentation revolvers was sold for $352,000 at Christie's, New York on 26 Jan 1991.

Helmet The highest price ever paid for an item of headwear is $66,000 by the Alaska State Museum at an auction in New York City in November 1981 for a native North American Tlingit Kiksadi ceremonial frog helmet dating from *c.* 1600.

Jade The highest price ever paid for an item in jade is $2,042,857 at Christie's, Geneva, Switzerland on 12 May 1988 for a jade, ruby and diamond necklace.

Jewelry The world's largest jewelry auction, which included a Van Cleef and Arpels 1939 ruby and diamond necklace, realized over $50 million when the collection belonging to the Duchess of Windsor (1896–1986) was sold at Sotheby's, Geneva, Switzerland on 3 Apr 1987.

The highest auction price for individual items of jewelry is $6.2 million for two pear-shaped diamond drop earrings of 58.6 and 61 carats bought and sold anonymously at Sotheby's, Geneva on 14 Nov 1980.

Music box The highest price paid for a music box is £20,900 ($22,990) for a Swiss example made for a Persian prince in 1901 and sold at Sotheby's, London on 23 Jan 1985.

Playing cards The highest price for a deck of playing cards is $143,352 paid by the Metropolitan Museum of Art, New York City at Sotheby's, London on 6 Dec 1983.

Scientific instrument The highest auction price paid for a scientific instrument is £385,000 ($654,500) for a 13½ in Dutch gilt-brass astrolabe of 1559 by Walter Arsenius, sold at Christie's, London on 29 Sep 1988.

Sculpture An 8-in-high, 6,000-year-old neolithic sculpture of a seated goddess from the estate of James Johnson Sweeney was sold for $1.32 million at Sotheby's, New York on 24 Nov 1986 to Mrs Shelby White Levy of New York.

Silver A Sicilian table fountain, after Giovanni Angelo Montorsoli's *Fountain of Orion* in Messina, was sold for $1.98 million at Christie's, New York on 19 Apr 1990.

The record for a single piece of English silver is £1,485,000 ($2,578,700) for the "Maynard" sideboard dish made by the Huguenot silversmith Paul de Lamerie in 1736, which was sold at Christie's, London on 22 May 1991.

The 100-piece Paul de Lamerie dinner service made for the 7th Earl of Thanet *c.* 1745 was sold by Lord Hothfield at Sotheby's, London on 22 Nov 1984 for £825,000 ($1.155 million).

Snuffbox The highest price paid for a snuffbox is $1,070,750 at Christie's, Geneva, Switzerland on 11 Nov 1986 for a pale-green chrysoprase and diamond gold box once owned by Frederick the Great of Prussia.

Spoons A set of 13 Henry VIII Apostle spoons owned by Lord Astor of Hever was sold for £120,000 ($238,800) on 24 Jun 1981 at Christie's, London. A Wiener Werkstätte spoon made by Josef Hoffmann of Austria *c.* 1905 was sold at Sotheby's, London, Great Britain for £17,600 ($29,900) on 28 Apr 1983.

Sword The highest price paid for a sword is $1,316,800 for the Duke of Windsor's Royal Navy officer's sword (presented to him by King George V in 1913) at Sotheby's, Geneva, Switzerland on 3 Apr 1987.

Tapestry The highest auction price for a tapestry is £638,000 ($1,124,794), paid by Swiss dealer Peter Kleiner at Christie's, London on 3 Jul 1990 for a fragment of a rare Swiss example woven near Basle in the 1430s. The tapestry was in the Benedictine Abbey at Muri until 1840 before descending through the Vischer family.

Teddy bear The highest price paid for a teddy bear at auction is £55,100 ($86,350). The dual-plush brown bear, made by Steiff of Germany *c.* 1920, was bought at Sotheby's, London on 19 Sep 1989 by dealer James Fox.

Thimble The record auction price for a thimble is £8,000 ($17,600) paid by London dealer Winifred Williams at Christie's, London on 3 Dec 1979 for a Meissen dentil-shaped porcelain piece dated *c.* 1740.

Toys The most expensive antique toy, and the first to bring $1 million, was sold privately by London dealers Mint & Boxed to an unnamed European in mid-1990. The work is a hand-painted tin-plate replica of the "Charles" hose reel, a piece of fire-fighting equipment pulled by two firemen, measuring 15 × 23 in and built *c.* 1870 by George Brown & Co. of Forestville, CT.

The highest price paid for a single toy soldier is £3,375 ($5,714) for a uniformed scale figure of Hitler's deputy, Rudolf Hess, made by the Lineol company of Brandenburg, Germany. The figure was among several sold by the Danish auction house Boyes in London, Great Britain on 23 Apr 1991.

Typewriter The highest price paid for an antique typewriter is £9,900 ($17,325) for an 1890 black enamel Guhl & Harbeck at Christie's, London on 10 Aug 1989.

Walking stick The highest auction price for a walking stick is $24,200 at Sotheby's, New York in 1983 for an octagonal whale-ivory knobbed stick decorated by scrimshaw carvers in 1845.

Language

Earliest The ability to speak is believed to be dependent upon physiological changes in the height of the larynx between *Homo erectus* and *Homo sapiens sapiens* as developed *ante* 45,000 B.C. The discovery of a hyoid bone (from the base of the tongue) from a cave site on Mt Carmel, Israel shows that a Neanderthal man was capable of speech 60,000 years ago.

Oldest English words It was first suggested in 1979 that languages ancestral to English and to Latvian (both Indo-European) split *c.* 3500 B.C. According to researches completed in 1989, about 40 words of a pre-Indo-European substratum survive in English, among them apple (apal), bad (bad), gold (gol) and tin (tin).

Commonest language Today's world total of languages and dialects still spoken is about 4,000–5,000, some 845 of which are spoken in India.

The language used by more people than any other is Mandarin, spoken by an estimated 68 percent of China's population, and hence by about 770 million people in 1990. The so-called national language (*Guóyǔ*) is a standardized form of northern Chinese (*Běifānghuà*) as spoken in the Beijing area. This was alphabetized into *zhùyīn fùhào* of 37 letters in 1913 by Wa Chih-hui (1865–1953). On 11 Feb 1938 the *Hanyu-Pinyin-Fang'an* system, which is a phonetic pronunciation guide, was introduced.

The next most commonly spoken language, and the most widespread, is English, with an estimated 330 million native speakers and nearly twice as many using it as a second or third language.

Most languages The former Australian territory of Papua New Guinea has, because of its many isolated valleys, the greatest concentration of separate languages in the world, with more than 10 percent of the world's total of 4,000–5,000.

Most complex The following extremes of complexity have been noted: Chippewa, the North American Indian language of Minnesota, has the most verb forms, with up to 6,000; Haida, the North American Indian language, has the most prefixes, with 70; Tabassaran, a language of Daghestan, USSR, uses the most noun cases, 48; and Inuit uses 63 forms of the present tense, and simple nouns have as many as 252 inflections.

The 40-volume *Chung-wén Tà Tz'u-tiĕn* Chinese dictionary lists 49,905 characters. The fourth tone of "i" (i⁴) has 84 meanings, varying as widely as "dress," "hiccup" and "licentious." The written language provides 92 different characters of "i⁴." The most complex written character in Chinese is that representing *xiè*, consisting of 64 strokes and meaning "talkative." The most complex in current use is *nang*, with 36 strokes, meaning "a blocked-up nose."

Least irregular verbs Esperanto, with no irregular verbs, was first published by its inventor, Dr Ludwig Zamenhof (1859–1917) of Warsaw, in 1887. It is now estimated (by textbook sales) to have a million speakers. The even earlier interlanguage Volapük, invented by Johann Martin Schleyer (1831–1912), also has absolutely regular configuration.

The Turkish language has a single irregular verb — *olmak*, meaning "to be."

Most irregular verbs According to *The Morphology and Syntax of Present-day English* by Prof. Olu Tomori, English has 283 irregular verbs, 30 of which are formed merely by adding prefixes.

Rarest sounds The rarest speech sound is probably the one written "ř" in Czech, which occurs in very few languages and is the last sound mastered by Czech children. In the southern Bushman language !xo, there is a click articulated with both lips, which is written ☉. In some contexts the "l" sound in the Arabic word *Allah* is pronounced uniquely in that language.

Commonest sound No language is known to be without the vowel "a" (as in the English "father."

Vocabulary The English language contains about 490,000 words plus another 300,000 technical terms, the most in any language, but it is doubtful if any individual speaker uses more than 60,000. The members of the International Society for Philosophical Enquiry (no admission for IQs below 148) have an average vocabulary of 36,250 words. Shakespeare employed a vocabulary of *c.* 33,000 words.

Greatest linguist If the yardstick of

Icon
The record price for an icon is $150,000, paid at Christie's, New York on 17 Apr 1980 for the *Last Judgment* (from the George R. Hann collection, Pittsburgh, PA), made in Novgorod, USSR in the 16th century.

Most succinct word

The most challenging word for any lexicographer to define briefly is the Fuegian (southernmost Argentina and Chile) word *mamihlapinatapai*, meaning "looking at each other hoping that either will offer to do something which both parties desire but are unwilling to do."

Most synonyms

The condition of being inebriated has more synonyms than any other condition or object. Delacorte Press of New York City has published a selection of 1,224 from a list of 2,241 compiled by Paul Dickson of Garrett Park, MD.

Most contrived name

In the United States the determination to derive commercial or other benefit from being the last listing in the local telephone book has resulted in self-given names starting with up to nine "Z's" — an extreme example being Zachary Zzzzzzzzzra in the San Francisco book.

ability to speak with fluency and reasonable accuracy is maintained, it is doubtful whether any human being could maintain fluency in more than 20 to 25 languages concurrently or achieve fluency in more than 40 in a lifetime.

The world's greatest linguist is believed to be George Campbell (b. 9 Aug 1912), who is retired from the British Broadcasting Corporation Overseas Service, where he worked with 54 languages. Powell Alexander Janulus (b. 1939) has worked with 41 languages in the Provincial Court of British Columbia, Vancouver, Canada.

In terms of oral fluency, the most multilingual living person is Derick Herning of Lerwick, Great Britain, whose command of 22 languages earned him victory in the inaugural "Polyglot of Europe" contest held in Brussels, Belgium in May 1990.

The 1975 edition of *Who's Who in the United Nations* listed "only" 19 languages for Georges Schmidt (1914–90), Chief of the UN Terminology Section in 1965–71, because he was then unable to find time to "revive" his former fluency in 12 others. Louis Jay Herman of New York City *worked* with 25 languages as a translator for the United Nations between 1958 and 1980.

Historically, the greatest linguists have been proclaimed to be Prof. Rask (1787–1832) of Denmark, Sir John Bowring (1792–1872) and Dr Harold Williams of New Zealand (1876–1928), who were all fluent in 28 languages, and Cardinal Mezzofanti (1774–1849) of Italy (fluent in 26 or 27 languages).

ALPHABET

Earliest The earliest-known example of alphabetic writing was found at Ugarit (now Ras Sharma), Syria, dated to c. 1450 B.C. It comprised a tablet of 32 cuneiform letters.

Oldest letter The letter "O" is unchanged in shape since its adoption in the Phoenician alphabet c. 1300 B.C.

Newest letters The newest letters to be added to the English alphabet are "j" and "v," which are of post-Shakespearean use (c. 1630). Formerly they were used only as variants of "i" and "u." There are 65 alphabets in use worldwide.

Longest The language with the most letters in its alphabet is Cambodian, with 72 (some have no current use).

Shortest Rotokas of central Bougainville Island, Papua New Guinea has the fewest letters, with 11 (a, b, e, g, i, k, o, p, ř, t and u).

Most and least consonants The language with the greatest number of distinct consonantal sounds is Ubykhs in the Caucasus, with 80–85. Rotokas has the least, with six consonants. The English word "latchstring" contains six consecutive consonants, while the Georgian *gyprtskvins* ("he is feeling us") has eight separately pronounced consonants.

LONGEST WORDS

JAPANESE[1]
Chi-n-chi-ku-ri-n (12 letters)
a very short person (slang)

SPANISH
Superextraordinarisimo (22 letters)
extraordinary

FRENCH
Anticonstitutionnellement (25 letters)
anticonstitutionally

CROATIAN
Prijestolonasljednikovica (25 letters)
wife of an heir apparent

ITALIAN
Precipitevolissimevolmente (26 letters)
as fast as possible

PORTUGUESE
Inconstitucionalissimamente (27 letters)
with the highest degree of unconstitutionality

ICELANDIC
Haecstaréttarmálaflutningsmaður (29 letters)
supreme court barrister

RUSSIAN
Ryentgyenoelyektrokardiografichyeskogo
(33 Cyrillic letters, transliterating as 38)
of the X-ray electrocardiographic

HUNGARIAN
Megszentségtelenithetetlenségeskedéseitekért
(44 letters)
for your unprofanable actions

DUTCH[2]
Kindercarnavalsoptochtvoorbereidingswerkzaamheden (49 letters)
preparation activities for a children's carnival procession

MOHAWK[3]
Tkanuhstasrihsranuhwe'tsraaksahsrakaratattsrayeri
(50 letters)
the praising of the evil of the liking of the finding of the house is right

TURKISH[2]
Cekoslovakyalılaştırabilemediklerimizlerdenmisiniz
(50 letters)
"are you not of that group of persons that we were said to be unable to Czechoslovakianize?"

GERMAN[2,4]
Donaudampfschiffahrtselectrizitaetenhauptbetriebswerkbauunterbeamtengesellschaft (80 letters)
The club for subordinate officials of the head-office management of the Danube steamboat electrical services (name of a pre-war club in Vienna)

SWEDISH[2]
Nordöstersjökustartilleriflygspaningssimulatoranläggningsmaterielunderhållsuppföljningssystemdiskussionsinläggsförberedelsearbeten
(130 letters)
Preparatory work on the contribution to the discussion on the maintaining system of support of the material of the aviation survey simulator device within the northeast part of the coast artillery of the Baltic

[1] Patent applications sometimes harbor long compound "words." An extreme example is one of 13 kana (Japanese syllabary) that transliterates to the 40-letter Kyūkitsūrohekimenfuchakunenryōsekisanryō meaning "the accumulated amount of fuel condensed on the wall face of the air intake passage."

[2] Agglutinative words are limited only by imagination and are not found in standard dictionaries. The first 100-letter such word was published in 1975 by the late Eric Rosenthal in Afrikaans.

[3] Lengthy concatenations are a feature of Mohawk.

[4] The longest dictionary word in everyday usage is Rechtsschutzversicherungsgesellschaften (39 letters) meaning "insurance companies which provide legal protection."

Most and least vowels The language with the most vowels is Sedang, a Vietnamese language with 55 distinguishable vowel sounds, and the one with the fewest is the Caucasian language Abkhazian, with two. *Cauaiauaia* in Angola has nine consecutive vowels. The name of a language in Pará State, Brazil consists of seven vowels—*uoiauai*, and the Estonian *jääärne* ("the edge of the ice"), has the same four vowels consecutively.

Smallest letters In April 1990 the letters IBM were etched into a nickel crystal by an instrument called a scanning tunneling microscope to form a corporate logo measuring 1.27 nm (10^{-9}) long. It took physicists Donald Eigler and Erhard Schweizer at IBM's Almaden Research Center in San Jose, CA 22 hr to drag the 35 xenon atoms across the bumpy nickel surface, which had been chilled to near absolute zero. Their creation flew apart when the temperature rose above $-380°$F. In February 1991 it was announced that scientists at the Hitachi Central Research Laboratory in Tokyo, Japan had used the same technique at room temperature to etch sulfur atoms on molybdenum-disulfide into the message "PEACE '91 HCRL."

WORDS

Longest Lengthy concatenations and some compound or nonce words are or have been written in the closed-up style of a single word, e.g., the 182-letter fricassee of 17 sweet and sour ingredients in Aristophanes' comedy *The Ecclesiazusae* in the 4th century B.C. A compound "word" of 195 Sanskrit characters (which transliterates into 428 letters in the Roman alphabet) describing the region near Kanci, Tamil Nadu, India appears in a 16th-century work by Tirumalāmbā, Queen of Vijayanagara.

English The longest real word in the *Oxford English Dictionary* is *floccipaucinihilipilification* (alternatively hyphenated with an "n" in place of the "p" as the seventh letter), with 29 letters, meaning "the action of estimating as worthless," which was first used in 1741, and later by Sir Walter Scott (1771–1832).

The longest made-up word in the *Oxford English Dictionary* is *pneumonoultramicroscopicsilicovolcanoconiosis* (-koniosis), which has 45 letters and allegedly means "a lung disease caused by the inhalation of very fine silica dust." *Webster's Third International Dictionary* lists *pneumonoultramicroscopicsilicovolcanoconiosises* (47 letters), the plural of this term. The medical term *hepaticocholangiocholecystenterostomies* (39 letters) refers to the surgical creation of new communications between gallbladders and hepatic ducts and between intestines and gallbladders.

The longest regularly formed English word is *praetertranssubstantiationalistically* (37 letters), used by Mark McShane in his 1963 novel *Untimely*

Ripped. *Interdenominationalism* (22 letters) is found in *Webster's Ninth New Collegiate Dictionary*, and hence *interdenominationalistically* (28 letters) is perhaps permissible. The longest words in common use are *disproportionableness* and *incomprehensibilities* (21 letters).

Longest palindromes The longest known palindromic word is *saippuakivikauppias* (19 letters), which is Finnish for "a dealer in lye" (caustic soda). The longest in English is *tattarrattat*, with 12 letters, which appears in the *Oxford English Dictionary*. Some baptismal fonts in Greece and Turkey bear the circular 25-letter inscription ΝΙΨΟΝ ΑΝΟΜΗΜΑΤΑ ΜΗ.Μ.ΟΝΑΝ ΟΨΙΝ, meaning "wash (my) sins not only (my) face."

Longest scientific name The systematic name for *deoxyribonucleic acid* (DNA) of the human mitochondria contains 16,569 nucleotide residues and is thus *c.* 207,000 letters long. It was published in key form in *Nature* on 9 Apr 1981.

Longest anagrams The longest nonscientific English words that can form anagrams are the 19-letter transpositions *representationalism* and *misrepresentational*. The longest scientific transposals are *hydroxydesoxycorticosterone* and *hydroxydeoxycorticosterones*, with 27 letters.

Longest abbreviation The initials S.K.O.M.K.H.P.K.J.C.D.P.W.B., which stand for the Syarikat Kerjasama Orang-orang Melayu Kerajaan Hilir Perak Kerana Jimat Cermat Dan Pinjam-meminjam Wang Berhad. This is the Malay name for The Cooperative Company of the Lower State of Perak Government's Malay People for Money Savings and Loans Ltd, in Teluk Anson, Perak, West Malaysia (formerly Malaya). The abbreviation for this abbreviation is Skomk.

The 55-letter full name of Los Angeles (El Pueblo de Nuestra Señora la Reina de los Angeles de Porciuncula) is abbreviated to L.A., or 3.63 percent of its length.

Longest acronym The longest acronym is NIIOMTPLABOPARMBETZHELBETRABSBOMONIMONKONOTDTEKHSTROMONT with 56 letters (54 in Cyrillic) in the *Concise Dictionary of Soviet Terminology*, meaning: the Laboratory for Shuttering, Reinforcement, Concrete and Ferroconcrete Operations for Composite-monolithic and Monolithic Constructions of the Department of the Technology of Building-Assembly Operations of the Scientific Research Institute of the Organization for Building Mechanization and Technical Aid of the Academy of Building and Architecture of the USSR.

Commonest words and letters The most frequently used words in written English are, in descending order of frequency: *the, of, and, to, a, in, that, is, I, it, for* and *as*. The most commonly used in conversation is "*I.*" The commonest letter is "e." More words begin with the letter "s" than with any other, but the most commonly *used* initial letter is "t" as in "the," "to," "that" or "there."

Most meanings The most overworked word in English is "set," to which Dr Charles Onions of Oxford University Press gave 58 uses as a noun, 126 uses as a verb and ten as a participle adjective.

PERSONAL NAMES

Earliest The earliest personal name that has survived seems to be that of a predynastic king of Upper Egypt *ante* 3050 B.C., who is indicated by the hieroglyphic sign for a scorpion. It has been suggested that the name should be read as Sekhen.

Longest personal name The longest name appearing on a birth certificate is that of Rhoshandiatellyneshiaunneveshenk Koyaanfsquatsiuty Williams, born to Mr and Mrs James Williams in Beaumont, TX on 12 Sep 1984. On 5 Oct 1984 the father filed an amendment that expanded his daughter's first name to 1,019 letters and her middle name to 36 letters.

Most first names Laurence Watkins (b. 9 Jun 1965) of Auckland, New Zealand claims a total of 2,310 first names, added by deed poll in 1991 after official opposition by the registrar and a prolonged court battle. The great-great-grandson of Carlos III of Spain, Don Alfonso de Borbón y Borbón (1866–1934), had 94 first names, several of which were lengthened by hyphenation.

Shortest The commonest single-letter surname is "O," prevalent in Korea but with 52 examples in US telephone books (1973–81) and 12 in Belgium. This name causes great distress to those concerned with the prevention of cruelty to computers. Every other letter, except "Q," has been traced as a surname in US telephone books by A. Ross Eckler.

Commonest family name The Chinese name Chang is borne, according to estimates, by between 9.7 and 12.1 percent of the Chinese population. Even at the lower estimate this means that there are at least some 104 million Changs—more than the entire population of all but seven of the other 170 sovereign countries of the world.

The commonest surname in the English-speaking world is Smith. There are an estimated 2,382,509 Smiths in the United States.

Most versions Edward A. Nedelcov of Regina, Saskatchewan, Canada has collected 1,201 versions of the spelling of his surname since January 1960. Mzilikazi of Zululand (b. *c.* 1795) had his name chronicled in 325 spellings, according to researches by Dr R. Kent Rasmussen.

PLACE-NAMES

Earliest The world's earliest-known place-names are pre-Sumerian, e.g., Kish, Ur and the now-lost Attara, and therefore earlier than *c.* 3600 B.C.

Longest The official name for Bangkok, the capital city of Thailand, is Krungthep Mahanakhon. However, the full name is Krungthep Mahanakhon Bovorn Ratanakosin Mahintharayutthaya Mahadilokpop Noparatratchathani Burirom Udomratchanivet mahasathan Amornpiman Avatarnsathit Sakkathattiyavisnukarmprasit (167 letters), which in its most scholarly transliteration emerges with 175 letters.

The longest place-name now in use in the world is Taumatawhakatangihangakoauauotamateaturipukakapikimaungahoronukupokaiwhenuakitanatahu, the unofficial 85-letter version of the name of a hill (1,002 ft above sea level) in the Southern Hawke's Bay district of North Island, New Zealand. The Maori translation means "The place where Tamatea, the man with the big knees, who slid climbed and swallowed mountains, known as landeater, played his flute to his loved one."

Shortest The shortest place-names in the world are the French village of Y (population 143), so named since 1241, the Danish village Å on the island Fyn, the Norwegian village of Å (pronounced "Aw"), the Swedish place Å in Vikholandet, U in the Caroline Islands, Pacific Ocean, and the Japanese town of Sosei, which is alternatively called Aioi or O.

There was once a town called "6" in West Virginia.

Most spellings The spelling of the Dutch town of Leeuwarden has been recorded in 225 versions since A.D. 1046. Bromesberrow, Great Britain is recorded in 161 spellings since the 10th century as reported by local historian Lester Steynor.

Literature

Earliest The earliest written language discovered is on Yangshao culture pottery from Paa-t'o, near Xi'an (Sian) in the Shaanxi (Sheanxi) province of China, found in 1962. This bears protocharacters for the numbers 5, 7 and 8 and has been dated to 5000–4000 B.C. The earliest dated pictographs are on clay tablets from Nippur, southern Iraq, from one of the lowest excavation levels, equivalent to Uruk V/VI and dated in 1979 to *c.* 3400 B.C. Tokens or tallies from Tepe Asiab and Ganji-I-Dareh Tepe in Iran have, however, been dated to 8500 B.C.

The oldest surviving printed work is the Dharani scroll or *sutra* from wooden printing blocks found in the foundations of the Pulguk Sa pagoda, Kyŏngju, South Korea on 14 Oct 1966. It has been dated to no later than A.D. 704.

Paper dated to between 71 B.C. and A.D. 21, i.e., 100 years earlier than the previous presumed date for paper's invention, has been found in northwest China.

The oldest medical literature, a small clay tablet in the Sumerian script from Nippur (now in Iraq), is dated to *c.* 2100 B.C. It is

LITERATURE

Christmas cards

The earliest-known Christmas card was sent out by Sir Henry Cole (1808–82) in 1843, but this practice did not become an annual ritual until 1862.

The greatest number of personal Christmas cards sent by an individual is believed to be 62,824 by Werner Erhard of San Francisco, CA in December 1975. Many must have been to unilateral acquaintances.

Christmas card exchange

Frank Rose of Burnaby, British Columbia, Canada and Gordon Loutet of Lake Cowichan, British Columbia have exchanged the same Christmas card every year since 1929.

Warren Nord of Mesa, AZ and Thor (Tut) Andersen (d. 11 Sep 1988) of Ashtabula, OH exchanged the same Christmas card every year from 1930–87.

now in the University Museum of Philadelphia, PA and gives details of various ointments and plasters made of crushed turtle shell, nagasi plant, salt and mustard. Beer formed an ingredient of some of the ointments.

Oldest mechanically printed It was claimed in November 1973 that a 28-page book of Tang dynasty poems at Yonsei University, Korea was printed from metal type c. 1160. It is widely accepted that the earliest mechanically printed full-length book was the 42-line-per-page Gutenberg Bible, printed in Mainz, Germany c. 1454 by Johann Henne zum Gensfleisch zur Laden, called "zu Gutenberg" (c. 1398–1468).

Work on watermarks published in 1967 indicates that a copy of a surviving printed "Donatus" Latin grammar was made from paper c. 1450. The earliest exactly dated printed work is the Psalter completed on 14 Aug 1457 by Johann Fust (c. 1400–66) and Peter Schöffer (1425–1502), who had been Gutenberg's chief assistant. The earliest printing by William Caxton (c. 1422–91), though undated, would appear to be *The Recuyel of the Historyes of Troye* in Cologne in late 1473 to spring 1474.

Largest book The "thickest" printed book on record was produced by Peter Troendle of Basle, Switzerland. It has a cover size of 2 × 1⅘ in and is 9 ft thick.

Smallest book The smallest marketed bound printed book is one printed on 22 gsm paper measuring ¹⁄₂₅ × ¹⁄₂₅ in, comprising the children's story *Old King Cole!* and published in 85 copies in March 1985 by The Gleniffer Press of Paisley, Great Britain. The pages can be turned (with care) only by the use of a needle.

Largest publication The 1,112-volume set of *British Parliamentary Papers* was published by the Irish University Press in 1968–72. A complete set weighs 3.6 tons and would take six years to read at ten hours per day. The production involved the death of 34,000 Indian goats and the use of $30,000 worth of gold ingots. The total printing is 500 sets and the price per set in 1987 was $79,200.

In 1990 The British Library published its *General Catalogue of Printed Books to 1975* on a set of three CD-ROMs, priced at £9,000 ($15,750). Alternatively, readers can spend six months scanning 178,000 catalog pages in 360 volumes.

The entire Buddhist scriptures are inscribed on 729 marble slabs measuring 5 × 3½ ft housed in 729 stupas in the Kuthodaw Pagoda, south of Mandalay, Myanmar (formerly Burma). They were incised in 1860–68.

Largest dictionary *Deutsches Wörterbuch*, started by Jacob and Wilhelm Grimm in 1854, was completed in 1971 and consists of 34,519 pages and 33 volumes.

The Dictionary of Chinese Characters (Sichuan and Huber) in eight volumes will contain 20 million characters when completed in 1989.

English-speaking The largest English-language dictionary is the 20-volume *Oxford English Dictionary*, with 21,728 pages. The first edition was published between 1884 and 1928. A first Supplement of 964 pages appeared in 1932, and a second one in four volumes, between 1972 and 1986. Work on the second edition began in 1984, and the work involved represented 500 person-years. Published in March 1989, it defines a total of 616,500 word-forms, with 2,412,400 illustrative quotations and approximately 350 million letters and figures. Now computerized, the dictionary required 625 million bytes to store in machine-readable form. The longest entry in the second edition is that for the verb *set*, with over 75,000 words of text.

Specialized The *New Grove Dictionary of Music and Musicians*, edited by Stanley Sadie (b. 30 Oct 1930) and published in 20 volumes by Macmillan in February 1981, contains over 22 million words and 4,500 illustrations and is the largest specialized dictionary.

United States The largest English-language dictionary published in the United States is *Webster's Third New International Dictionary Unabridged*, published in 1986 by Merriam-Webster Inc. It defines 470,000 word-forms, with 99,943 illustrative quotations and approximately 60 million letters and numerics. The longest entry is for the verb *turn*, with over 5,500 words of text.

The best-selling dictionary in the United States is *Webster's Ninth New Collegiate Dictionary*, published in 1983 and 1990 by Merriam-Webster Inc. The 1983 edition has reportedly sold over one million copies each year.

Longest novel The longest novel of note ever published is *Les hommes de bonne volonté* by Louis-Henri-Jean Farigoule (1885–1972), alias Jules Romains, of France, published in 27 volumes in 1932–46. The English version, *Men of Good Will*, was published in 14 volumes in 1933–46 as a "novel-cycle." The 4,959-page edition published by Peter Davies Ltd has an estimated 2,070,000 words, excluding the 100-page index.

The novel *Tokuga-Wa Ieyasu* by Sohachi Yamaoka has been serialized in Japanese daily newspapers since 1951. Now completed, it will require nearly 40 volumes.

Earliest encyclopedias The earliest-known encyclopedia was compiled by Speusippus (*post* 408–c. 338 B.C.), a nephew of Plato, in Athens c. 370 B.C.

Largest encyclopedia The largest encyclopedia ever compiled was the *Yung-lo ta tien* (the great thesaurus of the Yung-lo reign) of 22,937 manuscript chapters (370 of which still survive) in 11,095 volumes. It was written by 2,000 Chinese scholars in 1403–08. Currently, the largest encyclopedia is *La Enciclopedia Universal Ilustrada Europeo-Americana* (J. Espasa & Sons, Madrid and Barcelona) totaling 105,000 pages

with an annual supplement since 1935. The encyclopedia comprises 165.2 million words. The number of volumes in the set in August 1983 was 104, and the price $2,325.

The most comprehensive English-language encyclopedia is *The New Encyclopaedia Britannica*, first published in Edinburgh, Great Britain in December 1768. A group of booksellers in the United States acquired reprint rights in 1898 and completed ownership in 1899. The current 32-volume 15th edition contains 32,330 pages and 44 million words from more than 4,000 contributors. It is now edited in Chicago, IL.

Longest index The tenth collective index of *Chemical Abstracts*, completed in June 1983, contains 23,948,253 entries in 131,445 pages and 75 volumes and weighs 380 lb.

Who's Who The longest of the 79,400 entries in *Who's Who in America* (46th edition) is that of Mr Thomas Capper Eakin (b. 16 Dec 1933), with an all-time record of 128 lines.

MAPS

Oldest A clay tablet depicting the river Euphrates flowing through northern Mesopotamia (Iraq) dates to c. 2250 B.C. The earliest printed map in the world is one of western China dated to 1115.

Largest A giant relief map of California, *Paradise in Panorama* by Reuben Hall, measuring 45 × 18 ft and weighing 43 tons, was displayed in the Ferry Building, San Francisco from 1924–60. It required 29 person-years and $147,000 to build and is now stored at the Hamilton Air Force Base in Novato, CA.

HIGHEST PRICES

Book The highest price paid for any book is £8.14 million ($12 million) for the 226-leaf manuscript *The Gospel Book of Henry the Lion, Duke of Saxony* at Sotheby's, London on 6 Dec 1983. The book, which measures 13½ × 10 in, was illuminated c. 1170 by the monk Herimann at Helmershansen Abbey, Germany with 41 full-page illustrations. The book was bought by Hans Kraus for the Hermann Abs consortium.

The highest price ever paid for a *printed* book is $5.39 million for an Old Testament (Genesis to the Psalms) Gutenberg Bible printed in 1455 in Mainz, Germany. It was bought by Tokyo booksellers Maruzen Co. Ltd at Christie's New York on 22 Oct 1987. The most expensive new book is the reproduction of the full set of ornithological prints *The Birds of America* by John James Audubon (1785–1851), published by Abbeville Press at $15,000.

Broadsheet The highest price ever paid for a broadsheet was $2,420,000 for one of the 24 known copies of *The Declaration of Independence*, printed by Samuel T. Freeman & Co. in Philadelphia, PA in 1776, and sold to Donald J. Scheer of Atlanta, GA on 13 Jun 1991.

Manuscript The highest price ever paid for a complete manuscript is £2.97 million ($11.4 million) by London dealers Quaritch at Sotheby's, London on 29 Nov 1990 for the 13th-century *Northumberland Bestiary*, a colourful and highly illustrated encyclopedia of real and imaginary animals.

Musical The auction record for a musical manuscript is $4,394,500 at Sotheby's, London on 22 May 1987 for a 510-page, 8½ × 6½ in bound volume of nine complete symphonies in Mozart's hand. The manuscript is owned by Robert Owen Lehman and is on deposit at The Pierpont Morgan Library in New York City.

The record price paid for a single musical manuscript is £880,000 ($1,540,000) for the autograph copy of Schumann's first (and only complete) piano concerto at Sotheby's, London on 22 Nov 1989.

Mozart's 14-page autograph manuscript of the *Fantasia in C minor* and *Sonata in C minor* (K475 and K457) for solo piano also sold for £880,000 ($1,734,000) at Sotheby's, London on 21 Nov 1990.

Scientific The highest price paid for a scientific manuscript was $1.16 million for a 72-page document by Albert Einstein, which explained his theory of relativity, on 2 Dec 1987 at Sotheby's, New York.

Atlas The highest price paid for an atlas is $1,925,000 for a copy of Ptolemy *Cosmographia*, which sold at Sotheby's Sotheby's, New York City on 31 Jan 1990.

BIBLE

Oldest The earliest biblical texts are from two silver amulets found under the Scottish Church, Jerusalem in 1979 bearing Numbers Chapter 6 verse 22–27 and dated to *c.* 587 B.C. In 1945 various papyrus texts were discovered at Nag Hammodi, Egypt, including gnostic gospels or secret books (apocrypha) ascribed to Thomas, James, John, Peter and Paul. They were buried *c.* A.D. 350 but the originals are thought to have been written *c.* A.D. 120–150.

The oldest-known Bible is the *Codex Vaticanus* written in Greek *ante* A.D. 350 and preserved in the Vatican Museum, Rome. The earliest complete Bible *printed* in English was edited by Miles Coverdale, Bishop of Exeter (*c.* 1488–1569), while living in Antwerp, Belgium, and printed in 1535. William Tyndale's New Testament in English was, however, printed in Cologne and Worms, Germany in 1525, and John Wycliffe's first manuscript translation dates from 1382.

Longest and shortest book The longest book in the Authorized Version of the Bible is the Book of Psalms, and the longest book including prose is the Book of the Prophet Isaiah, with 66 chapters. The shortest is the Third Epistle of John, which has only 294 words in 14 verses. The Second Epistle of John has only 13 verses but 298 words.

Longest and shortest psalm Of the 150 psalms, the longest is the 119th, with 176 verses, and the shortest is the 117th, with two verses.

Longest and shortest verse The shortest verse in the Authorized Version (King James) of the Bible is verse 35 of Chapter XI of the Gospel according to St John, consisting of the two words "Jesus wept." The longest is verse 9 of Chapter VIII of the Book of Esther, which extends to a 90-word description of the Persian empire.

Total letters and words The total number of letters in the Bible is 3,566,480. The total number of words depends on the method of counting hyphenated words, but is usually given as between 773,692 and 773,746. According to Colin McKay Wilson of the Salvation Army, the word *"and"* appears 46,227 times. According to the Interpreters Dictionary of the Bible, there are 212,916 references to "God" (in all forms) in the Bible.

Longest name The longest actual name in English language bibles is the 18-letter Maher-shalal-hash-baz, the symbolic name of the second son of Isaiah (Isaiah, Chapter VIII, verses 1 and 3).

The caption of Psalm 22, however, contains a Hebrew title sometimes rendered as Al-Ayyeleth Hash-Shahar (20 letters).

DIARIES AND LETTERS

Longest-kept diary Col. Ernest Loftus of Harare, Zimbabwe began his daily diary on 4 May 1896 at the age of 12 and continued it until his death on 7 Jul 1987 at the age of 103 years 178 days. George C. Edler (1889–1987) of Bethesda, MD kept a handwritten diary continuously from 20 Sep 1909, a total of 78 years. Alisa Morris of New York City has a diary which comprised an estimated 15 million words in 238 volumes to date.

Longest and most letters Uichi Noda, former vice minister of treasury and minister of construction in Japan, from July 1961 until his bedridden wife Mitsu's death in March 1985, wrote her 1,307 letters amounting to 5 million characters during his overseas trips. These letters have been published in 25 volumes totaling 12,404 pages. Rev. Canon Bill Cook and his fiancée/wife Helen of Diss, Norfolk, Great Britain exchanged 6,000 love letters during their 4¼ year separation from March 1942–May 1946.

Longest letter to an editor The *Upper Dauphin Sentinel* of Pennsylvania published a letter of 25,513 words spread over eight issues from August to November 1979, written by John Sultzbaugh of Lykens, PA.

Most letters to an editor David Green, author and solicitor, of Castle Morris, Dyfed, Great Britain, had his 128th letter published in the main correspondence columns of *The Times*

(London) on 10 Apr 1991. His record year was 1972 with 12.

Shortest correspondence The shortest correspondence on record was that between Victor Marie Hugo (1802–85) and his publisher, Hurst and Blackett, in 1862. The author was on vacation and was anxious to know how his new novel *Les Misérables* was selling. He wrote "?" and received the reply "!"

Most personal mail The highest confirmed amount of mail received by any private citizen in a year is 900,000 letters by the baseball star Henry Louis "Hank" Aaron (b. 1934), reported by the US Postal Department in June 1974. About a third were letters of hate engendered by his bettering of George Herman "Babe" Ruth's career record for home runs set in 1927. (See also Baseball.)

Pen pals The longest sustained correspondence on record is one of 75 years between Mrs Ida McDougall of Tasmania, Australia and Miss R. Norton of Sevenoaks, Kent, Great Britain from 11 Nov 1904 until Mrs McDougall's death on 24 Dec 1979.

AUTOGRAPHS AND SIGNATURES

Earliest The earliest surviving examples of autographs are those made by scribes on cuneiform clay tablets from Tell Abu Salābīkh, Iraq dated to the early Dynastic III A *c.* 2600 B.C. A scribe named "a-du" has added "dub-sar" after his name, thus translating to "Adu, scribe." The earliest surviving signature on a papyrus is that of the scribe Amen-'aa, held in the Leningrad Museum, USSR and dated to the Egyptian Middle Kingdom, which began *c.* 2130 B.C.

A signum (Latin = "a sign") exists for William I (the Conqueror) from *c.* 1070. The earliest full signature extant is that of Richard II, dated 26 Jul 1386. The Magna Carta does not bear even the mark of King John (r. 1199–1216), but carries only his seal affixed on 19 Jun 1215.

Most expensive The highest price ever paid on the open market for a single signed autograph letter was $360,000 on 29 Oct 1986 at Sotheby's, New York for a letter written by Thomas Jefferson in 1818 condemning prejudice against Jews. It was sold by Charles Rosenbloom of Pittsburgh, PA. The highest price paid for an autograph letter signed by a living person is $12,500 at the Hamilton Galleries on 22 Jan 1981 for a letter from President Ronald Reagan praising Frank Sinatra.

Rarest and most valuable Only one example of the signature of Christopher Marlowe (1564–93) is known. It is in the County Archives in Kent, Great Britain on a will of 1583. It is estimated that a seventh Shakespearean signature, should it ever come to light, would realize more than $1.5 million at auction.

The only known document that bears ten US presidential signatures is a letter sent by President Franklin Delano

Longest literary gestation

The standard German dictionary *Deutsches Wörterbuch* was begun by the brothers Grimm (Jacob and Wilhelm, 1785–1863 and 1786–1859 respectively) in 1854 and finished in 1971. *Acta Sanctorum*, begun by Jean Bolland in 1643, arranged according to saints' days, reached the month of November in 1925 and an introduction for December was published in 1940.

Oxford University Press received back its proofs of *Constable's Presentments* from the Dugdale Society in December 1984. They had been sent out for correction 35 years earlier, in December 1949.

Slowest seller

The accolade for the world's slowest-selling book (a category known in publishing as slooow sellers) probably belongs to David Wilkins' translation of the New Testament from Coptic into Latin, published by Oxford University Press (OUP) in 1716 in a printing of 500 copies. Selling an average of one each 20 weeks, it remained in print for 191 years.

Roosevelt to Richard C. Corbyn, then of Dallas now of Amarillo), TX, dated 26 Oct 1932. It was subsequently signed by Herbert Hoover, Harry S. Truman, Dwight D. Eisenhower, Gerald Ford, Lyndon Johnson, Jimmy Carter, Ronald Reagan and George Bush. Richard Nixon's first signature was signed with an auto-pen but he later re-signed it.

AUTHORS

Most prolific The champion of the goose quill era was Józef Ignacy Kraszewski (1812–87) of Poland, who produced more than 600 volumes of novels and historical works.

A lifetime output of 72–75 million words has been calculated for Charles Harold St John Hamilton, alias Frank Richards (1876–1961), the creator of Billy Bunter. In his peak years (1915–26) he wrote up to 80,000 words a week for the boys' school weeklies *Gem* (1907–39), *Magnet* (1908–40) and *Boys' Friend*.

Soho Tokutomi (1863–1957) wrote the history *Kinsei Nippon Kokuminshi* in 100 volumes of 42,468 pages and wrote 19,452,952 letters in 35 years.

Most novels The greatest number of novels published is 904 by Kathleen Lindsay (Mrs Mary Faulkner; 1903–73) of Somerset West, Cape Province, South Africa. She wrote under two other married names and eight pen names.

Baboorao Arnalkar (b. 9 Jun 1907) of Maharashtra State, India published 1,092 short mystery stories in book form and several nonfiction books between 1936 and 1984.

After receiving a probable record 743 rejection slips, British novelist John Creasey (1908–73), under his own name and 25 *noms de plume*, had 564 books totaling more than 40 million words published from 1932 to his death.

Enid Mary Blyton (1898–1968; Mrs Darrell Waters) completed 700 children's stories, many of them brief, with 59 in 1955. Her books have been translated into about 40 languages.

Greatest advance The greatest advance paid for any book is $5 million for *Whirlwind*, to James Clavell at auction in New York City on 11 Jan 1986 by William Morrow & Co. and Avon Books. On 11 Jul 1990 it was reported that Jeffrey Archer had signed a deal worth between $20 and $30 million with HarperCollins for two unwritten novels and a collection of short stories. Stephen King received $30 million from Penguin for a four-book deal in 1990. Danielle Steel received $60 million from Delacorte for five books in 1990.

Top-selling It was announced on 13 Mar 1953 that 672,058,000 copies of the works of Generalissimo Stalin (b. Yózef Vissarionovich Dzhugashvili, 1879–1953) had been sold or distributed in 101 languages.

The top-selling authoress is currently Dame Barbara Cartland, with global sales of over 600 million for 540 titles published in 25 languages. She has

averaged 23 titles per year for the last 16 years and, in 1988, received *La Medaille de Vermeil de la Ville de Paris* for sales in France, which have now reached over 30 million. She was made a Dame of the Order of the British Empire by Her Majesty Queen Elizabeth II in the 1991 New Year's Honours List for services to literature and the community.

The all-time estimate of book sales for US writer Erle Stanley Gardner (1889–1970) to date is 323,062,565 copies in 37 languages.

The world's top-selling writer of fiction is Dame Agatha Christie (nee Miller, later Lady Mallowan, 1890–1976), whose 78 crime novels have sold an estimated 2 billion copies in 44 languages. Her famous Belgian detective, Hercule Poirot, is featured in 33 books and 56 stories, while his English counterpart, Miss Marple, has appeared in 12 books and 20 stories. Agatha Christie also wrote 19 plays and six romantic novels under the pseudonym Mary Westmacott. All 78 novels were reissued to commemorate the centenary of her birth in 1990, and in 1989 Harper & Row paid $9.6 million for the rights to 33 titles. Royalty earnings are estimated to be worth $4.25 million per year.

An estimated 600 million copies of Belgian novelist Georges Simenon's (1903–89) works have been sold in 47 languages.

Biography Georges Simenon (1903–89) wrote 22 autobiographical books from 1972 to 1989. The longest biography in publishing history is that of Sir Winston Churchill by his son Randolph (4,832 pages) and Martin Gilbert (17,811 pages), to date comprising some 9,694,000 words.

Most rejections The greatest recorded number of publishers' rejections for a manuscript is 242 to date for the 150,000-word *World Government Crusade*, written in 1966 by Gilbert Young (b. 1906) of Bath, Great Britain.

The record for rejections before publication is 176 (and non-acknowledgement from many other publishers) in the case of Bill Gordon's *How Many Books Do You Sell in Ohio?* from October 1983 to November 1985. The record was then spoiled by Mr Gordon's rejection of a written offer from Aames-Allen.

Oldest The oldest author in the world was Alice Pollock (nee Wykeham-Martin, 1868–1971) of Haslemere, Great Britain, whose first book, *Portrait of My Victorian Youth* (Johnson Publications), was published in March 1971 when she was aged 102 years 8 months. The oldest living author is Griffith R. Williams of Llithfaen, Great Britain, whose autobiography, *Cofio Canrif*, was published on his 102nd birthday on 5 Jun 1990.

Longest poem The longest poem ever published was the Kirghiz folk epic *Manas*, which appeared in printed form in 1958 but has never been translated into English. According to the *Dictionary of Oriental Literatures*, this

three-part epic runs to about 500,000 lines. Short translated passages appear in *The Elek Book of Oriental Verse*. Roger Brien's (b. Montreal, 1910) *Prométhée — dialog des vivants et des morts* runs to 456,047 lines, written from 1964–81. Brien has written another 497,000 lines of French poetry in over 90 published works.

The longest poem ever written in the English language is one on the life of King Alfred by John Fitchett (1766–1838) of Liverpool, Great Britain, which ran to 129,807 lines and took 40 years to write. His editor, Robert Riscoe, added the concluding 2,585 lines.

In contrast, the 24-line Kamassian poem *Lament* is the only known literary work in this Samoyed language (distantly related to Hungarian), spoken in the Sayan Mountains near Lake Baikal, Siberia, USSR but on the verge of extinction. This little poem is chronicled in the Hungarian publication *Ancient Cultures of the Uralian Peoples* and is printed in International Phonetics because Kamassian has no written form of its own.

Most successful poem *If* by Rudyard Kipling (1865–1936), first pub-lished in 1910, has been translated into 27 languages and, according to Kipling, "anthologized to weariness."

HIGHEST PRINTINGS

The world's most widely distributed book is the Bible, which has been translated into 318 languages, and portions of it into a further 1,628 languages. This compares with 222 languages for Lenin. It has been estimated that between 1815 and 1975 some 2.5 billion copies of the Bible were printed, of which 1.5 billion were handled by bible societies. Since 1976, combined global sales of Today's English Version (*Good News*) New Testament and Bible (which is copyrighted by the bible societies) have exceeded 111.3 million copies. Apart from the King James version (averaging some 13 million copies printed annually), there are at least 14 other copyrights on other versions of the Bible. The oldest publisher of bibles is the Cambridge University Press, which began with the Geneva version in 1591.

It has been reported that 800 million copies of the red-covered booklet *Quotations from the Works of Mao Zedong* were sold or distributed between June 1966, when possession became virtually mandatory in China, and September 1971, when its promoter Marshal Lin Biao died in an air crash.

It is believed that in the United States, Van Antwerp Bragg and Co. printed some 60 million copies of the 1879 edition of *The McGuffey Reader*, compiled by Henry Vail in the pre-copyright era for distribution to public schools.

The total dispersal through noncommercial channels by Jehovah's Witnesses of *The Truth that Leads to Eternal Life*, published by the Watchtower Bible and Tract Society of New York City on 8 May

1968, reached 107,073,279 in 117 languages by April 1991.

BEST-SELLING BOOKS

Excluding versions of the Bible, the world's all-time best-selling book is *The Guinness Book of Records*, first published in October 1955 by the Guinness Brewery and edited by Norris Dewar McWhirter (b. 12 Aug 1925) and his twin brother Alan Ross McWhirter (killed 27 Nov 1975). Global sales in 39 languages surpassed 65 million in October 1990.

Best-seller lists The longest duration on the *New York Times* best-seller list (founded 1935) has been for *The Road Less Traveled* by M. Scott Peck, which on 2 Oct 1988 had its 258th week on the lists.

Fiction The novel with the highest sales has been *Valley of the Dolls* (first published March 1966) by Jacqueline Susann (Mrs Irving Mansfield; 1921–74) with a worldwide total of 28,712,000 to 30 Mar 1987. In the first six months Bantam sold 6.8 million copies. Alistair Stuart MacLean (1922–87) wrote 30 books that have been translated into 28 languages, and 13 have been filmed. It has been estimated that a MacLean novel is purchased every 18 seconds. *The Cruel Sea* by Nicholas Monsarrat (1910–79), published in 1951 by Cassell, reached sales of 1.2 million in its original edition.

PUBLISHERS AND PRINTERS

Oldest publisher Cambridge University Press has a continuous history of printing and publishing since 1584. The University received a Royal Letters Patent to print and sell all manner of books on 20 Jul 1534. In 1978 the Oxford University Press (OUP) celebrated the 500th anniversary of the printing of the first book in the City of Oxford, Great Britain in 1478. This was before OUP itself was in existence.

United States The firm of Lea Febiger of Malvern, PA (founded as Matthew Carey) has a continuous history of publishing since 1785.

Most prolific publisher At its peak in 1989, Progress Publishers (founded in 1931 as the Publishing Association of Foreign Workers in the USSR) of Moscow, USSR printed over 750 titles in 50 languages annually.

Largest publisher The world's largest publishing company is Time Warner of New York. It has 41,000 employees and sales in 1990 totaled $2.926 billion.

Fastest publisher A thousand bound copies of Sir Frederick Mason's village history *Ropley—Past and Present* were produced in 12 hr 26 min from raw disk by publishers Scriptmate Editions in conjunction with printers Scan Laser Ltd.

Largest printer The largest printers in the world are believed to be R.R. Donnelley & Sons Co. of Chicago, IL. The company, founded in 1864, has nearly 100 manufacturing facilities, offices, service centers and subsidiaries worldwide, turning out $3.5 billion worth of work per year.

The largest printer under one roof is the United States Government Printing Office (founded 1861) in Washington, D.C. Encompassing 34.4 acres of floor space, the central office processes an average of 1,954 print orders daily, and uses 98 million lb of paper annually. The Superintendent of Documents sells approximately $75.7 million worth of US government publications every year and maintains an inventory of over 16,500 titles in print, receiving 5,600 mail orders each day.

Largest print order The initial print order for the 1990/91 Automobile Association (Great Britain) *Members' Handbook* was 6,153,000 copies. Stacked on top of each other, this would be seven times the height of Mt Everest. The total print since 1908 is 97,673,000, and it is currently printed by web offset by Petty & Sons Ltd of Leeds, Great Britain and Jarrolds Printing Ltd of Norwich, Great Britain.

Bookstore The bookstore with the most titles and the longest shelving (30 miles) in the world is W. & G. Foyle Ltd of London, Great Britain. First established in 1904 in a small store, the company now has a site of 75,825 ft². The most capacious individual bookstore in the world measured by square footage is the Barnes & Noble Bookstore at 105 Fifth Ave at 18th Street, New York City. It covers 154,250 ft² and has 12.87 miles of shelving.

LIBRARIES

Earliest One of the earliest-known collections of archival material was that of King Ashurbanipal at Nineveh (668–627 B.C.). He had clay tablets referring to events and personages as far back as the Dynasty of Agode c. 23rd century B.C.

United States The first library in America was established at Harvard University in 1638. The first subscription library in the country was the Philadelphia Library Company in 1731. The first library in America that meets the definition of a modern public library was in Peterboro, NH, established on 9 Apr 1833. The Peterboro Town Library was the first free public library in the country and was tax-supported with $750 from the New Hampshire State Literary Fund. The original collection contained 700 books, mainly religious, historical, biographical and educational works. The current collection of Peterboro Library numbers 49,000 books, and circulation is automated.

Largest The United States Library of Congress (founded on 24 Apr 1800) in Washington, D.C. contains 97,264,237 items, including 15,095,645 books in the classified collections and 82,168,592 items in the nonclassified collections. The library occupies approximately 3,857,000 net usable ft² of space in the three Capitol Hill buildings. Additionally, the library has some 350,000 ft² of space in six different remote locations. As of May 1991 there were 585 miles of shelving.

The largest nonstatutory library in the world is the New York Public Library (founded 1895) on Fifth Avenue, New York City with a floor space of 525,276 ft² and 88 miles of shelving, plus an underground extension with the capacity for an additional 92 miles. Its collection, including 82 branch libraries, embraces 13,887,774 volumes, 18,349,585 manuscripts and 381,645 maps.

Oldest museum The world's oldest extant museum is the Ashmolean in Oxford, Great Britain, built between 1679 and 1683 and named after the collector Elias Ashmole (1617–92). Since 1924 it has housed an exhibition of historic scientific instruments.

Largest museum The Smithsonian Institution comprises 15 museums containing over 139 million items and has 6,400 employees.

The American Museum of Natural History in New York City was founded in 1869 and comprises 22 interconnected buildings. The buildings of the museum and the planetarium contain 1.5 million ft² of floor space, accommodating more than 30 million artifacts and specimens. Its exhibits are viewed by more than 3 million visitors each year.

Most popular The highest attendance for any museum is that at the Smithsonian's National Air and Space Museum, Washington, D.C., opened in July 1976. The record-setting day on 14 Apr 1984, with an attendance of over 118,437, required the doors to be temporarily closed.

NEWSPAPERS

Oldest A copy has survived of a news pamphlet published in Cologne, Germany in 1470. The oldest existing newspaper in the world is the Swedish official journal *Post och Inrikes Tidningar*, founded in 1645 and published by the Royal Swedish Academy of Letters. The oldest existing commercial newspaper is the *Haarlems Dagblad/Oprechte Haarlemsche Courant*, published in Haarlem, Netherlands, first issued as the *Weecke- lycke Courante van Europa* on 8 Jan 1656. A copy of issue No. 1 survives.

United States The oldest continuously published newspaper in the United States is the *Hartford Courant*, established by Thomas Greene on 29 Oct 1764. Originally a weekly four-page newspaper, it had an estimated circulation of 8,000 during the American Revolution, when it printed the Declaration of Independence and the Constitution. In

US FICTION BEST-SELLERS (1990)		
TITLE	**AUTHOR**	**SALES**
The Plains of Passage (Crown)	Jean M. Auel	1,686,589
Four Past Midnight (Viking)	Stephen King	1,277,268
The Burden of Proof (Farrar, Straus & Giroux)	Scott Turow	1,044,513
Memories of Midnight (Morrow)	Sidney Sheldon	1,040,217
Message from Nam (Delacorte)	Danielle Steel	1,037,006
Publishers Weekly, 8 Mar 1991		

Overdue books

The record for an unreturned and overdue library book was set when a book in German on the Archbishop of Bremen, published in 1609, was borrowed from Sidney Sussex College, Cambridge, Great Britain by Colonel Robert Walpole in 1667–68. It was found by Prof. Sir John Plumb in the library of the then-Marquess of Cholmondeley at Houghton Hall, Norfolk, Great Britain and returned 288 years later. No fine was exacted.

United States The most overdue book in the United States was a book on febrile diseases (London, 1805, by Dr J. Currie) checked out in 1823 from the University of Cincinnati Medical Library and returned 7 Dec 1968 by the borrower's great-grandson Richard Dodd. The calculated fine of $2,264 was waived.

Most syndicated cartoon strip

"Peanuts" by Charles Schulz of Santa Rosa, CA, first published in October 1950, currently appears in 2,300 newspapers in 68 countries and 26 languages. In 1990 Schulz's income was estimated at $5 million per month.

Most durable cartoon strip

The longest-lived newspaper comic strip is "The Katzenjammer Kids" (Hans and Fritz), created by Rudolph Dirks and first published in the *New York Journal* on 12 Dec 1897.

Newspaper correction

On 20 Jan 1991, 199 years and 27 days after its initial report, the *Observer*, a British newspaper, published a correction for its inaccurate account of the death of Wolfgang Amadeus Mozart. The original article, published on 25 Dec 1791, described Mozart as German and reported that he died on 15 Dec 1791. The correction stated "We are now able to confirm that the composer died on 5 Dec and was, in fact, Austrian. As today is his birthday, we should like to take this opportunity to apologize to the composer's family for any distress . . ."

Slowest solution

In May 1966 *The Times* of London received an announcement from a Fijian woman that she had just succeeded in completing their crossword No. 673, published in the issue 4 Apr 1932.

1836 the *Courant* became a daily newspaper and in 1913 started a Sunday edition. It was acquired by the Times Mirror organization in 1979 and has outlasted 40 other newspapers published at one time or another out of Hartford. Its current circulation figures are 229,060 daily and 312,244 Sunday papers, as of March 1991.

The oldest continuously published daily newspaper in the United States is the *New York Post*, established as the *New York Evening Post* by Alexander Hamilton on 16 Nov 1801. Originally four pages, the newspaper had an estimated circulation of 600 in 1801. Its current circulation is 644,738, as of April 1991.

Largest The most massive single issue of a newspaper has been of the *Sunday New York Times*, which weighed 12 lb and contained 1,612 pages, on 14 Sep 1987. The largest page size ever used was 51×35 in for *The Constellation*, printed in 1859 by George Roberts as part of the July 4th celebrations in New York City.

Smallest The smallest original page size was the $3 \times 3\frac{3}{4}$ in of the *Daily Banner* (25 cents per month) of Roseberg, OR, issues of which, dated 1 and 2 Feb 1876, survive. The British Library Newspaper Library contains the *Watford News and Advertiser* of 1 Apr 1899, which measures 2.9×3.9 in.

Longest editorship Sir Etienne Dupuch (b. 16 Feb 1899) of Nassau, Bahamas was editor-in-chief of *The Tribune* from 1 Apr 1919 to 1972, and is a contributing editor to the present time, entering his 73rd year as an editor on 1 Apr 1991.

Most Pulitzer prizes The New York Times has won 63 Pulitzer prizes, more than any other news organization. The Pulitzer is the highest award given annually for American journalism and arts.

Most durable feature Eric Hardy of Liverpool, Great Britain is in his 64th year as a regular natural history contributor to the *Daily Post* of Liverpool, Great Britain, with a weekly "Countryside" feature.

Most syndicated columnist In 1987 Ann Landers (nee Eppie Lederer, b. 4 Jul 1918) appeared in over 1,200 newspapers with an estimated readership of 90 million. Her only serious rival was "Dear Abby" (Mrs Pauline Phillips), her identical twin sister based in Beverly Hills, CA.

Earliest cartoon strip "The Yellow Kid" first appeared in the *New York Journal* on 18 Oct 1896.

CIRCULATION

In 1990 the total number of morning and evening newspapers published in the United States was 1,611 with a total circulation of 62,324,156. There were 865 Sunday newspapers with a circulation of 62,409,541. The peak year for US newspapers was 1910, when there were 2,202.

The country with the leading number of newspaper readers in the world is Sweden, where 580 newspapers are sold for every 1,000 people.

Earliest million The first newspaper to achieve a circulation of one million copies was *Le Petit Journal*, published in Paris, France, which reached this figure in 1886, when selling at 5 centimes.

Highest The highest circulation for any newspaper in the world is that for *Komsomolskaya Pravda* (founded 1925), the Soviet youth paper, which had a peak daily circulation of 21,975,000 copies in May 1990. The eight-page weekly newspaper *Argumenty i Fakty* (founded 1978) of Moscow, USSR attained a figure of 33,431,100 copies in May 1990. It has an estimated readership of over 100 million.

United States The highest circulation daily newspaper in the United States is The *Wall Street Journal* (founded 1889), published by Dow Jones & Co. As of March 1991, circulation was 1.97 million copies.

Most read The national newspaper that achieves the closest to a saturation circulation is the *Sunday Post*, established in Glasgow, Great Britain in 1914. In 1989 its estimated readership in Scotland of 2,213,000 represented 54 percent of the entire population aged 15 and over. The *Arran Banner* (founded March 1974) has a readership of 97+ percent on Britain's seventh largest offshore island.

PERIODICALS

Oldest The oldest continuing periodical in the world is *Philosophical Transactions of the Royal Society*, published in London, Great Britain, which first appeared on 6 Mar 1665. Curtis's *Botanical Magazine* has been in continuous publication since 1 Feb 1787 as several "parts" a year forming a series of continuously numbered volumes.

Largest circulations The peak circulation of any weekly periodical has been that of *TV Guide*, which in 1974 became the first magazine to sell a billion copies in a year. The world's highest-circulation magazine is currently *Modern Maturity*, with a figure in January–July 1988 of 17,924,783.

In its 39 basic international editions, *Reader's Digest* (established February 1922) circulates 28 million copies monthly in 17 languages, including a US edition of more than 16.25 million copies and a Great Britain edition (established 1939) of 1,533,700 copies (ABC July–December 1989). *Parade*, the syndicated color magazine, is distributed with 338 US newspapers every Sunday. The circulation in July 1991 was 35.4 million.

Weightiest The heaviest magazine ever published was the February/March 1990 issue of the Conde Nast publication *Bride's*, which ran to 1,034 back-breaking pages.

Annual *Old Moore's Almanack* has been published annually since 1697, when it first appeared as a broadsheet produced by Dr Francis Moore (1657–1715) of London, Great Britain to advertise his "physiks." The annual sale certi-

fied by its publishers, W. Foulsham & Co. Ltd of Slough, Great Britain, is one million copies, and its aggregate sale is estimated to be in excess of 108 million.

CROSSWORDS

First The earliest-known crossword was a 9×9 Double Diamond published in *St Nicholas* for September 1875 in New York City. This was discovered by Dr Kenneth Miller (Great Britain), inventor of the color crossword in 1983. However, a 25-letter acrostic of Roman provenance was discovered on a wall in Cirencester, Great Britain in 1868.

Largest published crossword In July 1982 Robert Turcot of Québec, Canada compiled a crossword comprising 82,951 squares. It contained 12,489 clues across, 13,125 down and covered 38.28 ft^2.

Most durable compilers Adrian Bell (1901–1980) of Barsham, Suffolk, Great Britain contributed a record 4,520 crosswords to *The Times* (London) from 2 Jan 1930 until his death.

The most prolific compiler is Roger F. Squires of Ironbridge, Great Britain, who compiles 42 published puzzles single-handedly each week. His total output to September 1991 was over 37,500 crosswords, and his millionth clue was published in the *Daily Telegraph* (London) on 6 Sep 1989.

ADVERTISING

Highest rates *Newspapers* The world's highest newspaper advertising rate is 41.55 million yen ($299,179.65) for a full page in the morning edition and 32.37 million yen ($233,179.65) for a full page in the evening edition of the *Yomiuri Shimbun* of Tokyo (April 1989).

Magazines The highest-ever price for a single page was $527,400, for a four-color back cover in *Parade* (circulation 35.4 million per week) in July 1991. The record for a four-color inside page is $451,000 in *Parade*, with a black-and-white page costing $365,000.

Advertising revenue The advertising revenue from the November 1982 US edition of *Reader's Digest* was a peak $14,716,551.

Avertising expenditure The highest expenditure ever incurred for a single advertisement in a periodical is 3,851,684 by Walt Disney Productions, celebrating

TOP TEN ADVERTISERS, 1990	
Corporation	**Spending ($ millions)**
Phillip Morris	2,072
Proctor & Gamble	1,779
Sears, Roebuck	1,432
General Motors	1,363
Grand Met. (UK)	823
PepsiCo	786
McDonald's	774
Eastman-Kodak	718
RJR Nabisco	703
Kellogg	611
Advertising Age	

Mickey Mouse's 60th birthday, on 7 Nov 1988 in *Time* Magazine.

Largest group The largest advertising group in the world is WPP Group plc of London, Great Britain. *Advertising Age* lists the group's billings for 1990 at $18.1 billion.

Largest agency The largest advertising *agency* is Dentsu Inc. of Tokyo, Japan, with billings for 1990 quoted as $9.7 billion by *Advertising Age*.

Biggest advertiser The biggest advertiser in the world is Phillip Morris, which spent $2.072 billion in 1990. (See also Advertising table.)

Most durable advertiser The Jos Neel Co., a clothing store in Macon, GA (founded 1880) has run an ad in the *Macon Telegraph* every day in the upper-left corner of page 2 since 22 Feb 1889.

Music

Whistles and flutes made from perforated phalange bones have been found at Upper Paleolithic sites of the Aurignacian period (*c.* 25,000–22,000 B.C.) at Istallóskö, Hungary and in Moldova, USSR. A heptatonic scale deciphered from a clay tablet by Dr Duchesne-Guillemin in 1966–67 was found at a site in Nippur, Sumer, now Iraq. The world's earliest surviving musical notation dates from *c.* 1800 B.C. An Assyrian love song, also *c.* 1800 B.C., to an Ugaritic god from a tablet of notation and lyric was reconstructed for an 11-string lyre at the University of California, Berkeley on 6 Mar 1974. Musical history can, however, be traced back to the third millennium B.C., when the yellow bell (*huang chung*) had a recognized standard musical tone in Chinese temple music.

The human voice Before this century the extremes were a staccato E in *alt altissimo* (e[iv]) by Ellen Beach Yaw (1869–1947) in Carnegie Hall, New York City on 19 Jan 1896, and an A₁ (55 Hz [cycles per sec]) by Kasper Foster (1617–73).

Madeleine Marie Robin (1918–60), the French operatic coloratura, could produce and sustain the B above high C in the Lucia mad scene in Donizetti's *Lucia di Lammermoor*. Since 1950 singers have achieved high and low notes far beyond the hitherto accepted extremes. However, notes at the bass and treble extremities of the register tend to lack harmonics and are of little musical value. Ivan Rebroff, the German singer, has a voice which extends easily over four octaves from a low F to a high F, one and a quarter octaves above C.

The highest note put into song is G[iv], occurring in Mozart's *Popoli di Tessaglia*. The lowest vocal note in the classical repertoire is in Mozart's *Die Entführung aus dem Serail* in Osmin's aria, which calls for a low D (73.4 Hz).

INSTRUMENTS

Earliest piano The earliest piano-forte in existence is one built in Florence, Italy in 1720 by Bartolommeo Cristofori (1655–1731) of Padua, and now preserved in the Metropolitan Museum of Art, New York City.

Grandest piano The grandest grand piano was one of 1.4 tons and 11 ft 8 in in length made by Chas H. Challen & Son Ltd of London, Great Britain in 1935. The longest bass string measured 9 ft 11 in, with a tensile strength of 33 tons.

Most expensive piano The highest price ever paid for a piano was $390,000 at Sotheby Parke Bernet, New York City on 26 Mar 1980 for a Steinway grand of *c.* 1888 sold by the Martin Beck Theater. It was bought by a non-pianist.

Smallest piano The smallest playable piano is a one-eighth scale model of a 1910 Knabe. It measures 7½ × 3⅜ × 6½ in and was built by Emil J. Cost.

Largest organ The largest and loudest musical instrument ever constructed is the now only partially functional Auditorium Organ in Atlantic City, NJ. Completed in 1930, this heroic instrument had two consoles (one with seven manuals and another movable one with five), 1,477 stop controls and 33,112 pipes, ranging in tone from ⅕ in to the 64 ft tone. It had the volume of 25 brass bands, with a range of seven octaves. The world's largest fully functional organ is the six manual 30,067 pipe Grand Court Organ installed in the Wanamaker Store, Philadelphia, PA in 1911 and enlarged between then and 1930. It has a 64 ft tone gravissima pipe.

The world's largest church organ is that in Passau Cathedral, Germany. It was completed in 1928 by D. F. Steinmeyer & Co. and has 16,000 pipes and five manuals. The chapel organ at the United States Military Academy at West Point, NY has, since 1911, been expanded from 2,406 to 18,200 pipes. The world's most powerful electronic organ is Robert A. Nye's 7000-watt "Golden Spirit" organ, designed by Henry N. Hunsicker. It has 700 speakers and made its public concert debut in Trump Castle, Atlantic City, NJ on 9 Dec 1988.

Loudest organ stop The Ophicleide stop of the Grand Great in the Solo Organ in the Atlantic City Auditorium (see above) is operated by a pressure of water 3½ lb/in² and has a pure trumpet note of ear-splitting volume, more than six times the volume of the loudest locomotive whistles.

Largest pan pipes The world's largest pan pipes, created by Simon Desorgher and Lawrence Casserley, consist of five contrabass pipes, each 4 in in diameter, with lengths of 19 in, 16 in, 14 in, 12 in and 10 in respectively, and five bass pipes of 2 in diameter with lengths of 9.5 in, 8 in, 7 in, 6 in and 5 in. Their first public appearance was at Jubilee Gardens, London, Great Britain on 9 Jul 1988.

Most durable musicians Elsie Maude Stanley Hall (1877–1976) gave piano recitals for 90 years, giving her final concert in Rustenburg, Transvaal, South Africa at the age of 97. The longest international career in the history of Western music was crowned by Mieczyslaw Horszowski (b. Poland, July 1892) with a recital given at the Wigmore Hall, London, Great Britain on 4 Jun 1991, three weeks before his 99th birthday. He played for Emperor Franz-Joseph in Vienna, Austria in 1899.

James Herbert "Eubie" Blake (1883–1983) was a pianist and composer of ragtime music and show tunes from the 1890s until his death, aged 97, in 1983. Norwegian pianist Reidar Thommesen (1889–1986) played over 30 hours a week in theater cafés when a nonagenarian. Charles Bridgeman (1779–1873) of All Saints Parish Church, Hertford, Great Britain, who was appointed organist in 1792, was still playing 81 years later in 1873.

The world's oldest active musician is Violet Loader (b. 9 Nov 1889) of Lymington, Hampshire, Great Britain, who has been the regular organist at the church of Our Lady of Mercy and St Joseph in Lymington since 1924. Mrs Loader's record is very nearly matched by Yiannis Pipis (b. 25 Nov 1889) of Nicosia, Cyprus, who has been a professional folkloric violinist since 1912. Rolland S. Tapley retired as a violinist from the Boston Symphony Orchestra after reputedly playing for an unrivaled 58 years from February 1920 to 27 Aug 1978.

Largest brass instrument The largest recorded brass instrument is a tuba standing 7½ ft tall, with 39 ft of tubing and a bell 3 ft 4 in across. This contrabass tuba was constructed for a world tour by the band of American composer John Philip Sousa (1854–1932), *c.* 1896–98. It is now owned by a circus promoter in South Africa.

Largest stringed instrument The largest movable stringed instrument ever constructed was a pantaleon with 270 strings stretched over 50 ft² used by George Noel in 1767. The greatest number of musicians required to operate a single instrument was the six required to play the gigantic orchestrion, known as the Apollonican, built in 1816 and played until 1840.

Most expensive standard-sized guitar A Fender Stratocaster belonging to legendary rock guitarist Jimi Hendrix (1942–70) was sold by his former drummer Mitch Mitchell to an anonymous buyer for £198,000 ($338,580) at Sotheby's, London on 25 Apr 1990.

Largest double bass A double bass measuring 14 ft tall was built in 1924 in Ironia, NJ by Arthur K. Ferris, allegedly on orders from the Archangel Gabriel. It weighed 11.6 cwt with a sound box 8 ft across, and had leather strings totaling 104 ft. Its low notes could be felt rather than heard.

Most valuable cello The highest auction price for a violoncello is £143,000

■ **Most expensive
guitar**
The left-handed Jimi Hendrix (1942–70) demonstrating his unusual "upside-down" playing style on the Fender Stratocaster, which was sold for £198,000 ($338,580) at Sotheby's, London on 25 Apr 1990 by his former drummer "Mitch" Mitchell. (Photo: London Features International)

Drumming

Four hundred separate drums were played in 31.78 sec by Rory Blackwell at Finlake Country Park, Chudleigh, Great Britain on 30 May 1988.

Longest rendering of a national anthem

"God Save the King" was played nonstop 16 or 17 times by a German military band on the platform of Rathenau railroad station, Brandenburg, Germany on the morning of 9 Feb 1909. The reason was that King Edward VII was struggling inside the train to put on the uniform of a German field-marshal before he could emerge.

Bottle orchestra

In an extraordinary display of oral campanology (bell ringing), the Brighton Bottle Orchestra—Terry Garoghan and Peter Miller—performed a musical medley on 444 Gordon's gin bottles at the Brighton International Festival, Great Britain on 21 May 1991. It took 18 hours to tune the bottles, and about 10 times the the normal rate of puff (90 breaths/min) to play them.

($242,242) at Christie's, London on 26 Apr 1991 for a favorite of the late Pablo Casals, made in the 18th century by Carlo Tonini.

Most valuable violin The highest price paid at auction for a violin is £902,000 ($1.76 million) for the 1720 "Mendelssohn" Stradivarius, named after the German banking family who were descendants of the composer. It was sold to a mystery buyer at Christie's, London on 21 Nov 1990.

Stradivarius' (1644–1737) Alard violin was confirmed by Jacques Français to have been sold by private treaty by W. E. Hill for $1.2 million to a Singaporean in 1982.

Largest drum A drum with a 13 ft diameter was built by the Supreme Drum Co., London, Great Britain and played at the Royal Festival Hall, London on 31 May 1987.

Largest drum kit A drum kit consisting of 81 pieces — 45 drums, including six bass drums, 15 cymbals, five temple blocks, two triangles, two gongs, two sets of wind chimes, one solid bar chime, six assorted cowbells, a drum set tambourine, a vibra slap and an icebell—is owned by Darreld MacKenzie of Calgary, Alberta, Canada.

Longest alphorn A 154 ft 8 in (excluding mouthpiece) long alphorn weighing 227 lb was completed by Swissborn Peter Wutherich, of Boise, ID in December 1989. The diameter at the bell is 24½ in and the sound takes 105.7 milliseconds to emerge from the bowl after entry into the mouthpiece.

Highest and lowest notes The extremes of orchestral instruments (excluding the organ) range from a handbell tuned to g^v (6,272 cycles/sec) to the sub-contrabass clarinet, which can reach C_{11} or 16.4 cycles/sec. The highest note on a standard pianoforte is c^v (4,186 cycles/sec), which is also the violinist's limit.

In 1873 a sub-double bassoon able to reach $B_{111}\pm$ or 14.6 cycles/sec was constructed, but no surviving specimen is known. The extremes for the organ are g^{vi} (the sixth G above middle C) (12.544 cycles/sec) and C_{111} (8.12 cycles/sec) obtainable from ¾ in and 64 ft pipes respectively.

SONGS

Oldest The *shaduf* chant has been sung since time immemorial by irrigation workers on the human-powered, pivoted-rod bucket raisers of the Nile water mills (or *saqiyas*) in Egypt.

The oldest-known harmonized music performed today is the English song *Sumer is icumen in*, which dates from c. 1240.

National anthems The oldest national anthem is the *Kimigayo* of Japan, the words of which date from the 9th century, although the music was written in 1881. The oldest music belongs to the anthem of the Netherlands, *Vilhelmus*, which was written c. 1570.

The anthem of Greece constitutes the first two verses of the Solomos poem, which has 158 stanzas. The shortest anthems are those of Japan, Jordan and San Marino, each with only four lines. Of the 11 wordless national anthems, the oldest is that of Spain, dating from 1770.

Top songs The most frequently sung songs in English are *Happy Birthday to You* (based on the original *Good Morning to All*), by Kentucky Sunday School teachers Mildred Hill and Patty Smith Hill of New York (written in 1893 and under copyright from 1935 to 2010); *For He's a Jolly Good Fellow* (originally the French *Malbrouk*), known at least as early as 1781; and *Auld Lang Syne* (originally the Strathspey *I Fee'd a Lad at Michaelmass*), some words of which were written by Robert Burns (1759–1796). *Happy Birthday* was sung in space by the *Apollo IX* astronauts on 8 Mar 1969.

Top-selling sheet music Sales of three uncopyrighted pieces are known to have exceeded 20 million—namely *The Old Folks at Home* by Stephen Foster (1855), *Listen to the Mocking Bird* (1855) and *The Blue Danube* (1867).

Of copyrighted material, the two top sellers are *Let Me Call You Sweetheart* (1910, by Whitson and Friedman) and *Till We Meet Again* (1918, by Egan and Whiting), each with some six million copies sold by 1967. Other huge sellers have been *St Louis Blues, Stardust* and *Tea for Two*.

Songwriters The songwriters responsible for the most number-one singles are John Lennon (1940–80) and Paul McCartney (b. 18 Jun 1942). McCartney is credited as writer on 32 number-one hits in the United States to Lennon's 26 (with 23 co-written), whereas Lennon authored 29 Great Britain number-ones to McCartney's 28 (25 co-written).

In the United States Barry Gibb of the Bee Gees has written or co-written 16 number-ones. The most successful female songwriter in the United States is Carole King (nee Carole Klein, 9 Feb 1942) with eight number-ones, and in Great Britain it is Madonna with seven.

HYMNS

Earliest There are more than 950,000 Christian hymns in existence. The music and parts of the text of a hymn in the *Oxyrhynchus Papyri* from the 2nd century are the earliest known hymnody. The earliest exactly datable hymn is the *Heyr Himna Smióur* (Hear, the Maker of Heaven) from 1208 by the Icelandic bard and chieftain Kolbeinn Tumason (1173–1208).

Longest The *Hora novissima tempora pessima sunt; vigilemus* by Bernard of Cluny (mid-12th century) runs to 2,966 lines. The longest in English is *The Sands of Time Are Sinking* by Anne Ross Cousin (nee Cundell, 1824–1906), which runs to 152 lines in full, though only 32 lines appear in the Methodist Hymn Book.

Most prolific hymnists Mrs Frances (Fanny) Jane van Alstyne (nee Crosby, 1820–1915) of the United States wrote

8,500 hymns and is reputed to have knocked off one hymn in 15 minutes.

Oldest choral society The oldest active choral society in the United States is the Handel and Haydn Society of Boston, which gave its first concert performance on Christmas Day 1815 at Stone Chapel (now King's Chapel). The Handel and Haydn Society also gave the first complete performance of The Messiah in the United States on 25 Dec 1818 at Boylston Hall, Boston. It celebrated its 175th anniversary in 1990.

BELLS

Oldest The tintinnabulum found in the Babylonian Palace of Nimrod in 1849 by Mr (later Sir) Austen Henry Layard (1817–94) dates from *c.* 1100 B.C. The oldest-known tower bell is one in Pisa, Italy dated MCVI (1106).

United States The oldest bell in the United States is located at St Stephens Episcopal Church in East Haddam, CT. The bell was cast in Spain in 815 A.D. and shipped to the US in 1834.

Heaviest The Tsar Kolokol, cast by Russian brothers I.F. and M.I. Motorin on 25 Nov 1735 in Moscow, weighs 222.6 tons, measures 22 ft in diameter and 20 ft high, and its greatest thickness is 24 in. The bell was cracked in a fire in 1737 and a fragment, weighing about 12.91 tons, was broken from it. The bell has stood, unrung, on a platform in the Kremlin in Moscow since 1836 with the broken section alongside.

The heaviest bell still in use is the Mingun bell, weighing 101 tons with a diameter of 16 ft 8½ in at the lip, in Mandalay, Myanmar (formerly Burma). The bell is struck by a teak boom from the outside. It was cast at Mingun late in the reign of King Bodawpaya (1782–1819). The heaviest swinging bell in the world is the Petersglocke in the southwest tower of Cologne Cathedral, Germany, cast in 1923, with a diameter of 11 ft 1¾ in, weighing 28 tons.

Peals A ringing peal is defined as a diatonic "ring" of five or more bells hung for full-circle change ringing. Of 5,500 rings so hung, only 70 are outside the British Isles. The heaviest ring in the world is that of 13 bells cast in 1938–39 for the Anglican Cathedral in Liverpool, Great Britain. The total bell weight is 18.5 tons, of which Emmanuel, the tenor bell note A, weighs 82 cwt 11 lb.

Largest carillon The largest carillon (minimum of 23 bells) in the world is the Laura Spelman Rockefeller Memorial Carillon in Riverside Church, New York City with 74 bells weighing 114.2 tons. The bourdon, giving the note lower C, weighs 20 tons. Cast in England with a diameter of 10 ft 2 in, this is the largest *tuned* bell in the world.

ORCHESTRAS

Oldest The first modern symphony orchestra—basically four sections consisting of woodwind, brass, percussion and bowed string instruments—was founded at the court of Duke Karl Theodor at Mannheim, Germany in 1743. The oldest existing symphony orchestra, the Gewandhaus Orchestra of Leipzig, Germany, was also established in 1743. Originally known as the Grosses Concert and later as the Liebhaber-Concerte, its current name dates from 1781.

United States The oldest orchestra in the United States is the Philharmonic-Symphony Society of New York, which was founded by Ureli Corelli Hill in 1842. It was established in the same year as the Vienna Symphony Orchestra and both will celebrate their sesquicentennial in 1992/93.

Largest On 17 Jun 1872, Johann Strauss the younger (1825–99) conducted an orchestra of 987 pieces supported by a choir of 20,000, at the World Peace Jubilee in Boston, MA. The number of first violinists was 400.

On 4 Nov 1990 a 1,500-piece orchestra consisting of 13 youth orchestras from Mexico and Venezuela gave a full concert, including works by Handel, Tchaikovsky, Beethoven and Dvorak, under the baton of Mexican conductor Fernando Lozano at the Magdalena Mixhiuca Sports Center, Mexico City.

Largest band The most massive band ever assembled was one of 20,100 players at the Ullevaal Stadium, Oslo, Norway from Norges Musikkorps Forbund bands on 28 Jun 1964.

On 17 Apr 1982, 6,179 "musicians" congregated at Bay Shore Mall, Milwaukee, WI for a rendering of Sousa's "Stars and Stripes Forever." According to one music critic, the "instruments" included "kazoos, 7-Up bottles, one-man-band contraptions, coffee cans, bongo drums and anything-you-can-thump-on." "At times," the report concludes, "you could almost tell what they were playing."

One-man band Rory Blackwell, of Starcross, Great Britain, aided by his double left-footed perpendicular percussion-pounder, plus his three-tier right-footed horizontal 22-pronged differential beater, and his 12-outlet bellow-powered horn-blower, played 108 different instruments (19 melody and 89 percussion) simultaneously in Dawlish, Great Britain on 29 May 1989. He also played 314 instruments in a single rendition in 1 min 23.07 sec, again at Dawlish, on 27 May 1985.

Largest marching band The largest marching band was one of 4,524, including 1,342 majorettes, under the direction of entertainer Danny Kaye (1913–87) at Dodger Stadium, Los Angeles, CA on 15 Apr 1985.

Musical march The longest recorded musical march was one of 42.5 miles at Wheeling, WV by the Wheeling Park High School Marching Band on 21 Oct 1989. Of the 69 members who started, 31 managed to complete the march, in 14 hr 53 min.

Most successful bands The most successful pipe band is the Shotts & Dykehead Caledonian Pipe Band, with their 10th world title in August 1980.

Conductors Austrian conductor Herbert von Karajan (1908–89), principal conductor of the Berlin Philharmonic Orchestra for 35 years before his retirement from the position shortly before his death, was the most prolific conductor ever, having made over 800 recordings of all the major works. Despite a reputation for being temperamental, Karajan had also led the Philharmonia of London, the Vienna State Opera and La Scala Opera of Milan.

The 1991–92 season was the Cork Symphony Orchestra's 58th under the baton of Dr Aloys Fleischmann.

Sir Georg Solti (b. 22 Oct 1912), the Hungarian-born principal conductor of the Chicago Symphony Orchestra, has won a record 29 Grammy awards for his recordings. (See also Grammy awards.)

United States The Chicago Symphony Orchestra was directed by Frederic Stock from 1905 until his death in 1942, a total of 37 seasons.

Largest choir Excluding "sing alongs" by stadium crowds, the greatest choir is one of 60,000, which sang in

Bell ringing

Eight bells have been rung to their full "extent" (40,320 unrepeated changes) only once without relays. This took place in a bell foundry at Loughborough, Great Britain, beginning at 6:52 A.M. on 27 Jul 1963 and ending at 12:50 A.M. on 28 July, after 17 hr 58 min. The peal was composed by Kenneth Lewis of Altrincham, Great Britain and the eight ringers were conducted by Robert B. Smith of Marple, Great Britain. Theoretically it would take 37 years 355 days to ring 12 bells (maximus) to their full extent of 479,001,600 changes.

The greatest number of peals (minimum of 5,000 changes, all in tower bells) rung in a year is 303, by Colin Turner of Abingdon, Great Britain in 1989.

The late George E. Fearn rang 2,666 peals from 1928 to May 1974. Matthew Lakin (1801–1899) was a regular bell-ringer at Tetney Church near Grimsby, Great Britain for 84 years.

■ **One-man band** *Rory Blackwell of Starcross, Great Britain succeeded in playing 108 different instruments (19 melody and 89 percussion) simultaneously on 29 May 1989.*

Baton twirling

The greatest number of complete spins done between tossing a baton into the air and catching it is 10 by Donald Garcia, on the British Broadcasting Corporation *Record Breakers* TV program on 9 Dec 1986.

The record for women is seven, shared by Lisa Fedick on the same program; Joanne Holloway, at Great Britain National Baton Twirling Association Championships in Paignton, Great Britain on 29 Oct 1987, and Rachel Hayes on 18 Sep 1988, also later shown on the British Broadcasting Corporation *Record Breakers* TV program.

Singing

The longest recorded choir-singing marathon is one of 80 hr 32 min, by the Danville High School Contemporaires Swing Choir, Danville, IL from 8–12 Feb 1991.

Musical chairs

The largest game on record was one starting with 8,238 participants, ending with Xu Chong Wei on the last chair, which was held at the Anglo-Chinese School, Singapore on 5 Aug 1989.

Longest silence

The longest interval between the known composition of a piece by a major composer and its performance in the manner intended is from 3 Mar 1791 until 9 Oct 1982 (over 191 years), in the case of Mozart's *Organ Piece for a Clock*, a fugue fantasy in F minor (K 608), arranged by the organ builders Wm Hill & Son and Norman & Beard Ltd at Glyndebourne, Great Britain.

unison as a finale of a choral contest among 160,000 participants in Breslau, Germany on 2 Aug 1937.

ATTENDANCES

Classical An estimated 800,000 attended a free open-air concert by the New York Philharmonic conducted by Zubin Mehta, on the Great Lawn of Central Park, New York City on 5 Jul 1986, as part of the Statue of Liberty Weekend.

Rock/pop festival Estimating the size of audiences at open-air events where no admission is paid is often left to the police, media reporters, promoters and publicity agents. Estimates therefore vary widely and there is no way to check the accuracy of claims. The best claim is believed to be 725,000 for Steve Wozniak's 1983 US Festival in San Bernardino, CA. The Woodstock Music and Art Fair held on 15–17 Aug 1969 at Bethel, NY is thought to have attracted an audience of 300,000–500,000.

Solo performer The largest *paying* audience ever attracted by a solo performer was an estimated 180,000–184,000 in the Maracaña Stadium, Rio de Janeiro, Brazil to hear Paul McCartney (b. 1942) on 2 Apr 1990. Jean-Michel Jarre, the *son et lumière* specialist, entertained an estimated audience of two million in Paris, France at a free Bastille Day concert in 1990.

Most successful concert tour The Rolling Stones' 1989 "Steel Wheels" North American tour earned an estimated $310 million and was attended by 3.2 million people in 30 cities.

Most successful concert series Michael Jackson sold out for seven nights at Wembley, London, Great Britain in the summer of 1988. The stadium has a capacity of 72,000, so a total of 504,000 people saw Jackson perform 14–16, 22–23 Jul and 26–27 Aug 1988.

Largest concert On 21 Jul 1990, Potsdamer Platz, straddling East and West Berlin, was the site of the largest single rock concert in terms of participants and organization ever staged. Roger Waters' production of Pink Floyd's "The Wall" involved 600 people performing on a stage measuring 551 × 82 ft at its highest point. An estimated 200,000 people gathered for the symbolic building and demolition of a wall made of 2,500 styrofoam blocks.

COMPOSERS

Most prolific The most prolific composer of all time was probably Georg Philipp Telemann (1681–1767) of Germany. He composed 12 complete sets of services (one cantata every Sunday) for a year, 78 services for special occasions, 40 operas, 600 to 700 orchestral suites, 44 passions, plus concertos and chamber music. The most prolific symphonist was Johann Melchior Molter (c. 1695–1765) of Germany, who wrote 169 symphonies. Franz Joseph Haydn (1732–1809) of Austria wrote 108 numbered symphonies, many of which are regularly played today.

Most rapid Among composers of the classical period, the most prolific was Wolfgang Amadeus Mozart (1756–91) of Austria, who wrote c. 1,000 operas, operettas, symphonies, violin sonatas, divertimenti, serenades, motets, concertos for piano and many other instruments, string quartets, other chamber music, masses and litanies, of which only 70 were published before he died at the age of 35. His opera *La Clemenza di Tito* (1791) was written in 18 days, and three symphonic masterpieces, Symphony No. 39 in E flat major, Symphony No. 40 in G minor and Symphony No. 41 in C major (the *Jupiter*), were reputedly written in the space of 42 days in 1788. His overture *Don Giovanni* was written in full score at one sitting in Prague in 1787 and finished on the day of its opening performance.

Longest symphony The longest of all single classical symphonies is the orchestral Symphony No. 3 in D minor by Gustav Mahler (1860–1911) of Austria. This work, composed in 1896, requires a contralto, a women's and a boys' choir in addition to a full orchestra. A full performance requires 1 hr 40 min, of which the first movement alone takes between 30 and 36 min.

The Symphony No. 2 (the Gothic), composed from 1919–22 by British-born William Havergal Brian (1876–1972), was played by over 800 performers (four brass bands) in the Victoria Hall, Hanley, Staffordshire, Great Britain on 21 May 1978 (conductor Trevor Stokes). A recent broadcast required 1 hr 45½ min. Brian wrote an even vaster work based on Shelley's "Prometheus Unbound" lasting 4 hr 11 min, but the full score has been missing since 1961.

The symphony *Victory at Sea*, written by US composer Richard Rodgers (1902–1979) and arranged by Robert Russell Bennett for NBC TV in 1952, lasted 13 hours.

Longest piano composition The longest continuous nonrepetitious piano piece ever published is *The Well-Tuned Piano* by La Monte Young, first presented by the Dia Art Foundation at the Concert Hall, Harrison St, New York City on 28 Feb 1980. The piece lasted 4 hr 12 min 10 sec.

Symphonic Variations, composed in the 1930s for piano and orchestra by the British-born Kaikhosru Shapurji Sorabji (1892–1988) on 500 pages of close manuscript in three volumes, would last for six hours at the prescribed tempo.

PERFORMERS

Highest-paid pianist Wladziu Valentino Liberace (1917–87) earned more than $2 million each 26-week season, with a peak of $138,000 for a single night's performance at Madison Square Garden, New York City in 1954. The highest-paid classical concert pianist was Ignace Jan Paderewski (1860–1941), Prime Minister of Poland (1919–20), who accumulated a fortune estimated at $5 million, of which

$500,000 was earned in a single season in 1922/23. The *nouveau riche* wife of a US industrialist once required him to play in her house behind a curtain. The pianist Artur Rubinstein (1887–1982) between 1937 and 1976 commanded 70 percent of the gross from his concerts.

Most successful singer Of great fortunes earned by singers, the highest on record are those of Enrico Caruso (1873–1921), the Italian tenor, whose estate was worth about $9 million, and the Italian-Spanish coloratura soprano Amelita Galli-Curci (1889–1963), who received about $3 million. The Irish tenor Count John Francis McCormack (1884–1945) gave up to ten concerts to capacity audiences in a single season in New York City.

David Bowie drew a fee of $1.5 million for a single show at the US Festival in Glen Helen Regional Park, San Bernardino County, CA on 26 May 1983. The four-man Van Halen rock band attracted a matching fee. The total attendance at Michael Jackson's world tour, September 1987–December 1988, brought in a tour gross revenue of over $124 million.

Largest contract It was reported on 21 Mar 1991 that Michael Jackson (b. 29 Aug 1958) had signed a 15-year contract worth $890 million with the Sony Corporation of Japan for a series of music, television and film projects. Not wanting to be left out, in the same month Michael's sister Janet signed a deal with Virgin Records reportedly worth $32 million for as few as two albums.

Singer's pulling power In 1850, up to $653 was paid for a single seat at the US concerts of Johanna ("Jenny") Maria Lind (1820–87), the "Swedish nightingale." She had a range from g to e[111], of which the middle register is still regarded as unrivaled.

Fastest rapper Daddy Freddy rapped 528 syllables in 60 sec at the Guinness World of Records Exhibition in the Empire State Building, New York City on 24 May 1991.

OPERA

Longest The longest of commonly performed operas is *Die Meistersinger von Nürnberg* by Wilhelm Richard Wagner (1813–83) of Germany. A normal uncut performance of this opera as performed by the Sadler's Wells company between 24 Aug and 19 Sep 1968 entailed 5 hr 15 min of music. *The Heretics* by Gabriel von Wayditch (1888–1969), a Hungarian-American, is orchestrated for 110 pieces and lasts 8½ hr.

Shortest The shortest opera published was *The Deliverance of Theseus* by Darius Milhaud (1892–1972), first performed in 1928, which lasted 7 min 27 sec.

Longest aria The longest single aria, in the sense of an operatic solo, is Brünnhilde's immolation scene in Wagner's *Götterdämmerung*. A well-known recording of this has been precisely timed at 14 min 46 sec.

Largest opera houses The Metropolitan Opera House, Lincoln Center, New York City, completed in September 1966 at a cost of $45.7 million, has a capacity of 3,800 seats in an auditorium 451 ft deep. The stage is 234 ft wide and 146 ft deep. The tallest opera house is in a 42-story building on Wacker Drive in Chicago, IL, which houses the Chicago Lyric Opera Company. The Teatro della Scala (La Scala) in Milan, Italy shares with the Bolshoi Theatre in Moscow, USSR the distinction of having the greatest number of tiers. Each has six, with the topmost being nicknamed the *Galiorka* by Russians.

First opera company The first opera company in the United States was The American Company, founded in 1752 by Lewis Hallam. The oldest continuously performing opera company in the United States is the Metropolitan Opera Company of New York City; its first season was in 1883.

Youngest opera singers Ginetta Gloria La Bianca, born in Buffalo, NY on 12 May 1934, sang Rosina in *The Barber of Seville* at the Teatro dell' Opera, Rome, Italy on 8 May 1950 at the age of 15 years 361 days, having appeared as Gilda in *Rigoletto* at Velletri 45 days earlier. Ginetta La Bianca was taught by Lucia Carlino and managed by Angelo Carlino.

■ **Largest concert**
In the biggest single rock concert ever staged, 200,000 people gathered in Potsdamer Platz, straddling the former East and West Berlin, Germany, on 21 Jul 1990 for a production of Pink Floyd's The Wall. *It involved 600 performers and included the symbolic building and demolition of a styrofoam wall to celebrate German reunification. (Photo: Gamma)*

■ **Highest-paid pianist**
Left: Ignace Jan Paderewski (1860–1941), concert pianist and former Prime Minister of Poland, earned $500,000 in a single season in 1922/23. (Photo: Hulton Picture Library)

183

MUSIC

Worst singer
While no agreement exists as to the identity of history's greatest singer, there is unanimity on the worst. The excursions of the soprano Florence Foster Jenkins (1868–1944) into lieder and even high coloratura culminated on 25 Oct 1944 in her sellout concert at Carnegie Hall, New York City. The diva's high F, was said to have been made still higher in 1943 by a crash in a taxi. It is one of the tragedies of musicology that Madame Jenkins' *Clavelitos*, accompanied by Cosme McMoon, was never recorded for posterity.

Most curtain calls
On 24 Feb 1988 Luciano Pavarotti received 165 curtain calls and was applauded for 1 hr 7 min after singing the part of Nemorino in Gaetano Donizetti's *L'elisir d'Amore* at the Deutsche Oper in Berlin, Germany.

Clapping
The duration record for continuous clapping (sustaining an average of 160 claps per min, audible at 120 yd) is 58 hr 9 min by V. Jeyaraman of Tamil Nadu, India from 12–15 Feb 1988.

Longest encore
The longest operatic encore listed in the *Concise Oxford Dictionary of Opera* was of the entire opera *Il Matrimonio Segreto* by Cimarosa at its premiere in 1792. This was at the command of the Austro-Hungarian emperor Leopold II (r. 1790–92).

Oldest opera singer The tenor Giovanni Martinelli sang Emperor Altoum in *Turandot* in Seattle, WA on 4 Feb 1967 when he was 81. Danshi Toyotake (b. 1 Aug 1891) has been singing *Musume Gidayu* for 91 years.

BALLET

Fastest "entrechat douze" In the *entrechat* (a vertical spring from the fifth position with the legs extended crisscrossing at the lower calf), the starting and finishing position each count as one, so that in an *entrechat douze* there are five crossings and uncrossings. This feat was performed by Wayne Sleep for the British Broadcasting Corporation *Record Breakers* TV program on 7 Jan 1973. He was in the air for 0.71 sec.

Grands jetés On 28 Nov 1988, Wayne Sleep completed 158 grands jetés along the length of Dunston Staiths, Great Britain in 2 min.

Most turns The greatest number of spins called for in classical ballet choreography is 32 *fouettés rond de jambe en tournant* in *Swan Lake* by Piotr Ilyich Tchaikovsky (1840–93). Miss Rowena Jackson (later Chatfield; b. Invercargill, New Zealand, 1925) achieved 121 such turns at her class in Melbourne, Victoria, Australia in 1940.

Most curtain calls The greatest recorded number of curtain calls ever received is 89 by Dame Margot Fonteyn de Arias (nee Margaret Evelyn Hookham; 1919-91) and Rudolf Hametovich Nureyev (born on a train near Irkutsk, USSR, 17 Mar 1938) after a performance of *Swan Lake* at the Vienna Staatsoper, Austria in October 1964.

Dancing

Marathon dancing must be distinguished from choreomania (dancing mania), or tarantism, which is a pathological condition. The worst outbreak of the latter was at Aachen, Germany in July 1374, when hordes of men and women broke into a frenzied and compulsive choreomania in the streets. It lasted for many hours until injury or complete exhaustion ensued.

Largest and longest dances An estimated 25,000 people attended a "Moonlight Serenade" outdoor evening of dancing to the music of the Glenn Miller Orchestra in Buffalo, NY on 20 Jul 1984. An estimated total of 20,000 dancers took part in a single dance with one caller at the National Square Dance Convention at Louisville, KY on 26 Jun 1983.

The most taxing marathon dance staged as a public spectacle was one by Mike Ritof and Edith Boudreaux, who logged 5,148 hr 28½ min to win $2,000 at Chicago's Merry Garden Ballroom, Belmont and Sheffield, IL from 29 Aug 1930 to 1 Apr 1931. Rest periods were progressively cut from 20 to 10 to 5 to zero minutes per hour, with 10-inch steps and

a maximum of 15 seconds for closure of eyes.

"Rosie Radiator" (Rose Marie Ostler) led an ensemble of 14 dancers through the streets of San Francisco, CA on 18 Jul 1987, covering a distance of 7¾ miles.

Ballroom The world's most successful professional ballroom dancing champions have been Bill and Bobbie Irvine, who won 13 world titles between 1960 and 1968. The oldest competitive ballroom dancer was Albert J. Sylvester (1889–1989) of Corsham, Great Britain, who retired at the age of 94.

Conga The longest recorded conga was the Miami Super Conga, held in conjunction with Calle Ocho—a party to which Cuban-Americans invite the rest of Miami for a celebration of life together. Held on 13 Mar 1988, the conga line consisted of 119,986 people.

Country dancing The most complex Scottish country dance ever held was a 256-person reel, choreographed by Ian Price, which took place on 24 Apr 1988 in Vancouver, British Columbia, Canada.

Flamenco The fastest flamenco dancer ever measured is Solero de Jerez, age 17, who in Brisbane, Australia in September 1967 attained 16 heel taps per second, in an electrifying routine.

Limbo The lowest height for a bar (flaming) under which a limbo dancer has passed is 6 in off the floor, by Dennis Walston, alias King Limbo, at Kent, WA on 2 Mar 1991. Junior J. Renaud (b. 7 Jun 1954) became the first Official World Limbo Champion at the inaugural International Limbo Competition on 19 Feb 1974 at Port of Spain, Trinidad.

The record for a performer on roller skates is 5¼ in, first achieved by Denise Culp of Rock Hill, SC on 22 Jan 1984. This has since been equaled by Tracey O'Callaghan on 2 Jun 1984 and Sandra Siviour on 30 Mar 1985, both at Bexley North, New South Wales, Australia; Jessie Ball on 27 Jun 1985 at Beverley Hills, New South Wales; and Kelly Foley on 22 May 1987, Magdalena Petrik and Meegan Anderson, both on 13 Apr 1988, and Michelle Boyle, Donna Bray and Jessica McLeish on 21 May 1988, all at Parramatta, New South Wales. On 28 Jun 1988 Erika Howell of Brunswick, GA equaled this height, as did Kellie Boyle at Burwood, New South Wales on 9 Aug 1989, Bahar (Jenny) Sonmez at Gosford, New South Wales on 26 Nov 1989, and Lindee Watmough, also at Gosford, on 30 Sep 1990.

Tap The fastest *rate* ever measured for tap dancing is 32 taps per second by Stephen Gare of Sutton Coldfield, Great Britain, at the Grand Hotel, Birmingham, Great Britain on 28 Mar 1990. Roy Castle, host of the British Broadcasting Corporation *Record Breakers* TV program, achieved one million taps in 23 hr 44 min at the Guinness World of Records exhibition, London, Great Britain on 31 Oct–1 Nov 1985. The greatest-ever

assemblage of tap dancers in a single routine numbered 5,271 outside Macy's department store in New York City on 12 Aug 1990.

Recorded sound

Origins The phonograph was first conceived by Charles Cros (1842–88), a French poet and scientist, who described his idea in sealed papers deposited with the French Academy of Sciences on 30 Apr 1877. However, the realization of a practical device was first achieved by Thomas Alva Edison (1847–1931) of the United States.

The first successful wax cylinder machine was constructed by his mechanic, John Kruesi, on 4–6 Dec 1877, demonstrated on 7 Dec and patented on 19 Feb 1878. The horizontal disc was introduced by Emile Berliner (1851–1929) and first demonstrated in Philadelphia on 18 May 1888.

Earliest recordings The earliest voice recording is believed to be a speech made by Lord Stanley of Preston, governor-general of Canada, during the opening of the Toronto Industrial Exhibition on 11 Sep 1888. Copies of this speech are held in the National Sound Archive, London, Great Britain. The earliest commercial disc recording was manufactured in 1895.

Tape recording Magnetic recording was invented by Valdemar Poulsen (1869–1942) of Denmark with his steel wire Telegraphone in 1898 (US Pat. No. 661619). Fritz Pfleumer (German Patent 500900) introduced tape in 1928. Tapes were first used at the Blattner Studios, Elstree, Great Britain in 1929. Plastic tapes were devised by BASF of Germany in 1932–35, but were first marketed in 1950 by Recording Associates of New York.

Largest record collection The British Broadcasting Corporation record library contains over one million recordings, including 5,250 with no known matrix. The oldest records in the library are white wax cylinders dating from 1888. The world's largest private collection is believed to be that of Stan Kilarr (b. 1915) of Klamath Falls, OR, with some 500,000.

Smallest functional record Six titles of 1 5/16 in diameter were recorded by HMV's studio at Hayes, Great Britain on 26 Jan 1923 for Queen Mary's Doll House. Some 92,000 of these miniature records were pressed, including 35,000 of *God Save The King*.

Earliest jazz records *Indiana* and *The Dark Town Strutters Ball* were recorded for the Columbia label in New York City on or about 30 Jan 1917, by the Original Dixieland Jazz Band, led by Dominick (Nick) James La Rocca (1889–1961). The record was released on 31 May 1917. The first jazz record to be released was the Original Dixieland Jazz Band's *Livery Stable Blues* (recorded 26 Feb), backed by *The Dixie Jass Band One-Step* (recorded 26 Feb), released by Victor on 7 Mar 1917.

Most successful singer The most successful singer on records is Madonna (Madonna Louise Veronica Ciccone, b. 16 Aug 1959). Her album *True Blue*, with sales of over 17 million, was number one in 28 countries (See also Biggest sellers [albums].)

Most successful solo recording artist No independently audited figures have ever been published for Elvis Aron Presley (1935–77). In view of Presley's worldwide tally of over 170 major hits on singles and over 80 top-selling albums from 1956 continuing after his death, it may be assumed he must have succeeded Bing Crosby as the top-selling solo artist of all time.

On 9 Jun 1960 the Hollywood Chamber of Commerce presented Harry Lillis (alias Bing) Crosby Jr. (1904–77) with a platinum disc to commemorate the alleged sale of 200 million records from the 2,600 singles and 125 albums he had recorded. On 15 Sep 1970 he received a second platinum disc when Decca claimed a sale of 300.6 million discs. No independently audited figures of his global lifetime sales have ever been published, and the figures are believed to be exaggerated.

Most successful group The singers with the greatest sales of any group have been the Beatles. This group from Liverpool, Great Britain was made up of George Harrison (b. 25 Feb 1943), John Ono (formerly John Winston) Lennon (b. 9 Oct 1940–k. 8 Dec 1980), James Paul McCartney (b. 18 Jun 1942) and Richard Starkey, alias Ringo Starr (b. 7 Jul 1940). The all-time Beatles sales up to May 1985 have been estimated by EMI at over one billion discs and tapes. All four ex-Beatles sold many million more records as solo artists.

Since the Beatles' breakup in 1970, it is estimated that the most successful group in the world in terms of record sales is the Swedish foursome ABBA (Agnetha Faltskog, Anni-Frid Lyngstad, Bjorn Ulvaeus and Benny Andersson), with total sales of 215 million discs and tapes up to May 1985.

Earliest golden discs The first actual golden disc was one sprayed by RCA Victor for the US trombonist and bandleader Alton "Glenn" Miller (1904–44) for his *Chattanooga Choo Choo* on 10 Feb 1942. The first record eventually to aggregate a total sale of a million copies was of performances by Enrico Caruso (b. Naples, Italy, 1873, d. 2 Aug 1921) of the aria "Vesti la giubba" ("On with the Motley") from the opera *I Pagliacci* by Ruggiero Leoncavallo (1858–1919), the earliest version of which was recorded with piano on 12 Nov 1902. The first single recording to surpass the million mark was *Carry Me Back to Old Virginny*, sung by Alma Gluck, on the Red Seal Victor label on the twelve-inch single-faced (later backed) record No. 74420.

Most golden discs The only *audited*

measure of gold, platinum and multiplatinum singles and albums within the United States is certification by the Recording Industry Association of America (RIAA), introduced on 14 Mar 1958.

Out of the 5,943 RIAA awards (1,206 gold singles, 3,433 gold albums, 98 platinum singles and 1,206 platinum albums) made to 31 Dec 1990, the Beatles, with 47 (20 gold singles, 25 gold albums and 2 platinum albums) have the most for any group. The Beatles also received a gold disc for work performed with Billy Preston, giving them 48 in total.

The individual artist to receive the most gold and platinum discs is Paul McCartney, with 75 (48 as a member of the Beatles, and 27 as a member of the Wings, as a solo artist and from duets with Stevie Wonder and Michael Jackson). The solo artist to receive the most awards is Elvis Presley (1935–77), with 56 (16 gold singles, 32 gold albums and 8 platinum albums). It is estimated that Presley's total of million-selling singles is 80 worldwide. The female solo artist to receive the most awards is Barbra Streisand, with 55 (7 gold singles, 29 gold albums and 19 platinum albums). The group with the most gold albums is the Rolling Stones, with 34.

The first platinum album was awarded to the Eagles for *Greatest Hits, 1971–75* in 1976. The Rolling Stones and Chicago share the record for most platinum albums, with 15. Barbra Streisand holds the record for a solo artist, with 19, while Billy Joel holds the record for a male solo artist, with 11.

Most recordings In what is believed to be the largest-ever recording project devoted to a single composer, 180 compact discs containing the complete set of authenticated works by Mozart were produced by Philips Classics for release in 1990/91 to commemorate the bicentennial of the composer's death. The complete set comprises over 200 hours of music and would occupy 6½ ft of shelving.

In the period between February 1987 and August 1989, Genesis P. Orridge and his band Psychic TV released 14 live albums on the Temple Records label. The albums are part of a series of 23.

Biggest sellers (singles) The greatest seller of any phonograph record to date is *White Christmas* by Irving Berlin (b. Israel Bailin, 1888–1989), recorded by Bing Crosby on 29 May 1942. It was announced on Christmas Eve 1987 that North American sales alone reached 170,884,207 copies by 30 Jun 1987.

The highest claim for any "pop" record is an unaudited 25 million for *Rock*

■ **Best-selling albums** Opera stars Placido Domingo, José Carreras and Luciano Pavarotti, whose In Concert, recorded at the 1990 Soccer World Cup in Rome, Italy, became the best-selling classical album, with sales of over 5 million copies worldwide. (Photo: Gamma)

Square dance calling
Alan Covacic called for 26 hr 2 min for the Wheelers and Dealers Square Dance Club at RAF Halton, Aylesbury, Great Britain from 18–19 Nov 1988.

Dancing dragon
The longest dancing dragon, created by schoolchildren and volunteers from St Helens, Merseyside, Great Britain in June and July 1989, was 985 ft long. It was made from foil, paper, bamboo and cane and decorated with scales. Five hundred people then brought it to life in dance as part of the Mayor's Carnival in St Helens on 30 Jul 1989.

Phonographic identification
Dr Arthur B. Lintgen (b. 1932) of Rydal, PA, has an as-yet unique and proven ability to identify the music on phonograph records purely by visual inspection without hearing a note.

Largest record store

HMV opened the world's largest record store at 150 Oxford Street, London, Great Britain on 24 Oct 1986. Its trading area measures 36,684 ft².

Most Grammy awards

An all-time record 29 awards (including a special Trustees' award presented in 1967) have been won since 1958 by the British conductor Sir Georg Solti (Hungary; 21 Oct 1912). The greatest number won in a year is eight by Michael Jackson in 1984.

Gladiatorial combat

Emperor Trajan of Rome (A.D. 98–117) staged a display involving 4,941 pairs of gladiators over 117 days. Publius Ostorius, a freedman, survived 51 combats in Pompeii.

Around the Clock, copyrighted in 1953 by James E. Myers under the name Jimmy DeKnight and the late Max C. Freedmann and recorded on 12 Apr 1954 by Bill Haley (1927–1981) and the Comets.

Biggest sellers (albums)

The best-selling album of all time is *Thriller* by Michael Jackson (b. Gary, IN 29 Aug 1958), with global sales of over 40 million copies by May 1990.

The best-selling album by a group is Fleetwood Mac's *Rumours* with over 21 million sales by May 1990. *In Concert* is the best-selling classical album, with sales of 5 million to date. It was recorded by those operatic heavyweights José Carreras, Placido Domingo and Luciano Pavarotti at the 1990 Soccer World Cup Finals in Rome, Italy.

The best-selling album by a woman is *True Blue* by Madonna, which had sold almost 17 million copies by October 1990. *Whitney Houston* by Whitney Houston, released in 1985, is the best-selling debut album of all time. It had sold over 14 million copies by May 1987, including over nine million in the United States, one million in Great Britain, and a further million in Canada. Whitney Houston also shares the record for most No. 1 singles for a female artist—9 in all—with Madonna (see also Most successful singer).

The best-selling movie soundtrack is *Saturday Night Fever*, with sales of over 26.5 million by May 1987.

The charts (US singles)

Singles record charts were first published by *Billboard* on 20 Jul 1940, when the No. 1 was *I'll Never Smile Again* by Tommy Dorsey (1905–56). *Near You* by Francis Craig stayed at the No. 1 spot for 17 weeks in 1947.

The Beatles have had the most No. 1's (20), Conway Twitty the most Country No. 1's (35) and Aretha Franklin the most Rhythm and Blues No. 1's (20). Aretha Franklin is also the female solo artist with the most million-selling singles, with 14 between 1967 and 1973. Elvis Presley has had the most hit singles on *Billboard*'s Hot 100—149 from 1956 to May 1990. Bing Crosby's *White Christmas* spent a total of 72 weeks on the chart between 1942 and 1962, while *Tainted Love* by Soft Cell stayed on the chart for 43 *consecutive* weeks from January 1982.

The charts (US albums)

Billboard first published an album chart on 15 Mar 1945 when the No. 1 was *King Cole Trio* featuring Nat "King" Cole (1919–65). *South Pacific* was No. 1 for 69 weeks (non-consecutive) from May 1949. *Dark Side of the Moon* by Pink Floyd enjoyed 730 weeks on the *Billboard* charts to April 1989.

The Beatles had the most No. 1's (15), Elvis Presley was the most successful male soloist (nine), and Simon and Garfunkel the top duo with three. Elvis Presley has had the most hit albums (94 from 1956 to April 1989).

The woman with the most No. 1 albums (six), and most hit albums in total (40 between 1963 and April 1989), is Barbra Streisand, 29 of whose albums have been certified gold (500,000 sales) and 19 platinum (one million sales) by the RIAA, making Streisand the best-selling female singer of all time.

Fastest-selling

The fastest-selling non-pop record of all time is *John Fitzgerald Kennedy—A Memorial Album* (Premium Albums), recorded on 22 Nov 1963, the day of President Kennedy's assassination, which sold 2.1 million copies at 99 cents in six days (7–12 Dec 1963), thus ironically beating the previous speed record set by the satirical LP *The First Family* in 1962/63.

Advance sales

The greatest advance sale for a single worldwide is 2.1 million for *Can't Buy Me Love* by the Beatles. Released on 21 Mar 1964, it also holds the British record of one million jointly with another Beatles single, *I Want to Hold Your Hand*, released on 29 Nov 1963.

Fastest live recording to stores

A limited edition of Midge Ure's *Dear God* single, including two live tracks *All Fall Down* and *Strange Brew* on the B-side, was delivered to stores 81 hrs 15 min after the live performance at The Venue, Edinburgh, Great Britain where the tracks were recorded on 21 Nov 1988.

Compact discs

Announced by Philips in 1978 and introduced by the same company in 1982, the compact disc (CD) increasingly challenges the LP and cassette as a recording medium. The first CD to sell a million copies worldwide was Dire Straits' *Brothers in Arms* in 1986. It subsequently topped a million sales in Europe alone.

Theater

Oldest

Theater in Europe has its origins in Greek drama performed in honor of a god, usually Dionysus. The earliest amphitheaters date from the 5th century B.C. The first stone-built theater in Rome, erected in 55 B.C., could accommodate 40,000 spectators.

Oldest indoor theater

The oldest indoor theater in the world is the Teatro Olimpico in Vicenza, Italy. Designed in the Roman style by Andrea di Pietro, alias Palladio (1508–80), it was begun three months before his death and finished by his pupil Vicenzo Scamozzi (1552–1616) in 1583. It is preserved today in its original form.

Largest

The world's largest building used for theater is the National People's Congress Building (*Ren min da hui tang*) on the west side of Tiananmen Square, Beijing, China. It was completed in 1959 and covers an area of 12.9 acres. The theater seats 10,000 and is occasionally used as such, as in 1964 for the play *The East Is Red*.

The theater with the largest capacity is the Perth Entertainment Center, Western Australia, completed in November 1976, with 8,003 seats. The stage area is 12,000 ft².

United States

The highest capacity theater currently in use on Broadway is the Gershwin Theater (formerly the Uris Theater), with 1,933 seats. Designed by Ralph Alswang, the theater opened on 28 Nov 1972. Its name was changed on 5 Jun 1983 to honor the famed composer George Gershwin.

Smallest

The smallest regularly operated professional theater in the world is the Piccolo in Juliusstrasse, Hamburg, Germany. It was founded in 1970 and has a maximum capacity of 30 seats.

Largest amphitheater

The Flavian amphitheater or Colosseum of Rome, Italy, completed in A.D. 80, covers 5 acres and has a capacity of 87,000. It has a maximum length of 612 ft and a maximum width of 515 ft.

Largest stage

The largest stage in the world is in the Ziegfeld Room, Reno, NV, with 176 ft passerelle, three main elevators each capable of raising 1,200 show girls (72 tons), two 62½-ft-circumference turntables and 800 spotlights.

Longest runs

The longest continuous run of any show in the world is *The Mousetrap* by Dame Agatha Christie (nee Miller; 1890–1976). This thriller opened on 25 Nov 1952 at the Ambassadors Theatre, London, Great Britain (capacity 453) and moved after 8,862 performances to the St Martin's Theatre next door on 25 Mar 1974. The 16,000th performance was on 6 May 1991, and the box office total was £19 million ($32.3 million) from more than nine million attenders.

The Vicksburg Theater Guild, MS has been playing the melodrama *Gold in the Hills* by J. Frank Davis discontinuously but every season since 1936.

Revue

The greatest number of performances of any theatrical presentation is 47,250 (to April 1986) in the case of *The Golden Horseshoe Revue*, a show staged at Disneyland, Anaheim, CA. It started on 16 Jul 1955, and closed on 12 Oct 1986 after being seen by 16 million people. The main performers were Fulton Burley, Dick Hardwick (who replaced Wally Boag, who had appeared from the opening day until his retirement in 1983) and Betty Taylor, who played to as many as five houses a day in a routine that lasted 45 minutes.

Broadway

A Chorus Line opened on 25 Jul 1975 and closed on 28 Apr 1990 after a record run of almost 15 years and 6,137 performances. It was created by Michael Bennett (1943–87).

Musical shows

The off-Broadway musical show *The Fantasticks* by Tom Jones and Harvey Schmidt opened on 3 May 1960, and the total number of performances to 6 Jun 1991 is 12,897 at the Sullivan Street Playhouse, Greenwich Village, New York City.

Shortest runs

The shortest run on record was that of *The Intimate Revue* at the Duchess Theatre, London, Great Britain, on 11 Mar 1930. Anything that could go wrong did. With scene changes taking up to 20 min apiece, the management scrapped seven scenes to get the finale on before midnight. The run was described as "half a performance."

The greatest loss sustained by a theatrical show was by the Royal Shakespeare Company's musical *Carrie*, which closed after five performances on Broadway on 17 May 1988 at a cost of $7 million. *King*, the musical about Martin Luther King, incurred a loss of £3 million ($5.04 million) in a six-week run ending on 2 Jun 1990, thus matching the London, Great Britain record losses of *Ziegfeld* in 1988.

Tony awards Harold (Hal) S. Prince (b. 1928) has won 16 "Tonys"—the awards of the American Theater Wing, instituted on 6 Apr 1947—the most of any individual. Prince has won eight awards as a producer, seven as a director and one special award. Three plays share the record for most Tonys, with five: *A Man for All Seasons* (1962), *Who's Afraid of Virginia Woolf?* (1963) and *Amadeus* (1981).

The only person to win five Tonys in a starring role is Julie Harris, in *I am a Camera* (1952), *The Lark* (1956), *Forty Carats* (1969), *The Last of Mrs Lincoln* (1973) and *The Belle of Amherst* (1977).

The record number of awards for a starring role in a musical is four, by Angela Lansbury: *Mame* (1966), *Dear World* (1969), *Gypsy* (1975) and *Sweeney Todd* (1979). Gwen Verdon has also won four Tonys; three in leading roles: *Damn Yankees* (1956), *New Girl in Town* (1958), *Redhead* (1959), and one in a supporting role, *Can-Can* (1954). The musical that has won the most awards is *Hello Dolly!* (1964), with 10.

Youngest Broadway producer Margo Feiden (nee Margo Eden; b. New York, 2 Dec 1944) produced the musical *Peter Pan*, which opened on 3 Apr 1961, when she was 16 years 5 months old. She wrote *Out Brief Candle*, which opened on 18 Aug 1962. She is now a leading art dealer.

One-man shows The longest run of one-man shows is 849, by Victor Borge (b. Copenhagen, 3 Jan 1909) in his *Comedy in Music* from 2 Oct 1953 to 21 Jan 1956 at the Golden Theater, Broadway, New York City.

The world aggregate record for one-man shows is 1,700 performances of *Brief Lives* by Roy Dotrice (b. Guernsey, 26 May 1923), including 400 straight at the Mayfair Theatre, London, Great Britain ending on 20 Jul 1974. He was on stage for more than 2½ hr per performance of this 17th-century monologue and required 3 hr for makeup and 1 hr for removal of makeup, thus aggregating 40 weeks in the chair.

Most durable actors and actresses Kanmi Fujiyama (b. 1929) played the lead role in 10,288 performances by the comedy company Sochiku Shikigeki

from November 1966 to June 1983. Lore Noto co-starred in 6,438 performances of *The Fantasticks*, the world's longest-running musical, between December 1970 and June 1986. (See Musical shows.) David Raven played Major Metcalfe in *The Mousetrap* on 4,575 occasions between 22 Jul 1957 and 23 Nov 1968.

Dame Anna Neagle (1904–86) played the lead role in *Charlie Girl* at the Adelphi Theatre, London, Great Britain for 2,062 of 2,202 performances between 15 Dec 1965 and 27 Mar 1971. She played the role a further 327 times in Australasia. Jack Howarth (1896–1984) was an actor on the stage and in television for 76 years from 1907 until his last appearance after 23 years as Albert Tatlock in *Coronation Street* on 25 Jan 1984. Frances Etheridge has played Lizzie, the housekeeper, in *Gold in the Hills* more than 660 times over a span of 47 years since 1936. (See Longest runs.)

Advance sales The musical *Miss Saigon*, produced by Cameron Mackintosh and starring Jonathan Pryce and Lea Salonga, opened on Broadway in April 1991 after generating record advance sales of $36 million. Its move from London, Great Britain had been under threat because of a controversy over casting.

Most roles The greatest recorded number of theatrical, film and television roles portrayed is 3,385, from 1951 to March 1989, by Jan Leighton (USA).

Most theatrical roles Kanzaburo Nakamura (b. July 1909) has performed in 806 Kabuki titles from November 1926 to January 1987. Since each title in this classical Japanese theatrical form lasts 25 days, he has therefore played 20,150 performances.

Shakespeare The first all-amateur company to have staged all 37 plays was The Southsea Shakespeare Actors, Hampshire, Great Britain (founded 1947) in October 1966 when, under K. Edmonds Gateley, they presented *Cymbeline*. The longest Shakespeare play is *Hamlet* with 4,042 lines and 29,551 words. Of Shakespeare's 1,277 speaking parts, the longest is Hamlet with 11,610 words.

Longest chorus line The longest chorus line in performing history numbered up to 120 in some of the early *Ziegfeld Follies*. In the finale of *A Chorus Line* on the night of 29 Sep 1983, when it broke the record as the longest-running Broadway show ever, 332 top-hatted "strutters" performed on stage. An even tighter squeeze was achieved by 369 dancers—including the original Tiller Girls and a number of British TV personalities—in a specially choreographed routine performed on the British Broadcasting Corporation *Record Breakers* TV program broadcast on 14 Dec 1990.

Highest cabaret fee Dolly Parton received up to $400,000 per live concert. Johnny Carson's fee for the non-televised Sears Roebuck Centennial Gala in October 1984 was set at $1 million.

Ice shows Holiday On Ice Productions Inc., founded by Morris Chalfen in 1945, stages the world's most costly live entertainment, with up to seven productions playing simultaneously in several of 75 countries. By 8 Mar 1988 the show had been seen by 250 million spectators. The total skating and other staff exceeds 900.

The most prolific producer of ice shows was Gerald Palmer (1908–83) with 137 since 1945, including 34 consecutive

Lowest theater attendance The ultimate in low attendance was in December 1983, when the comedy *Bag* in Grantham, Great Britain opened to a zero attendance.

Most ardent theatergoer Dr H. Howard Hughes (b. 1902), Prof. Emeritus of Texas Wesleyan College, Fort Worth, TX has attended 6,136 shows in the period 1956–87.

■ **Longest chorus line** *A record 369 dancers fill the studio for the finale of the BBC* Record Breakers *TV program, broadcast on 14 Dec 1990. (Photo: BBC Record Breakers)*

Joke-telling

Felipe Carbonell of Lima told jokes for 100 hr at the Lima Sheraton Hotel, Peru from 30 Aug–3 Sep 1990.

Magician, fastest

Eldon D. Wigton, alias Dr Eldoonie, performed 225 different tricks in 2 min at Kilbourne, OH on 21 Apr 1991.

shows at the Empire Pool, Wembley, London, Great Britain with attendances up to 850,000.

Arts festival The world's largest arts festival is the annual Edinburgh Fringe Festival (instituted in 1947). In 1990, 537 groups gave 9,504 performances of 1,103 shows between 12 Aug and 1 Sep. Prof. Gerald Berkowitz of Northern Illinois University attended a record 145 separate performances at the 1979 Festival from 15 Aug–8 Sep.

Fashion shows The most prolific producer of fashion shows is Adalene Ross Riley of San Francisco, CA with totals of over 4,721 to April 1989.

The greatest distance covered by female models on a catwalk is 71.1 miles, by Roberta Brown and Lorraine McCourt at Parke's Hotel, Dublin, Republic of Ireland from 19–21 Sep 1983. Male model Eddie Warke covered a further 11.9 miles on the catwalk.

Beauty contests The first international beauty contest was staged by P.T. Barnum (with the public to be the judges) in the United States in June 1855. The world's largest annual beauty pageants are the Miss World and Miss Universe contests (inaugurated in 1951 and 1952 respectively). The most successful country in the latter contest has been the USA, with winners in 1954, 1956, 1960, 1967, 1980 and 1982.

The greatest number of countries represented in the Miss Universe contest was 81 in 1983. The country that has produced the most winners in the Miss World contest is Great Britain, with five. They were Rosemarie Frankland (1961); Ann Sidney (1964); Lesley Langley (1965); Helen Morgan (1974), who resigned; and Sarah-Jane Hutt (1983). The maximum number of contestants was 84 in November 1988. The shortest reign as Miss World was 18 hr, by Miss Germany (Gabriella Brum) in 1980.

Circus

The world's largest permanent circus is Circus Circus, Las Vegas, NV, opened on 18 Oct 1968 at a cost of $15 million. It covers an area of 129,000 ft^2, covered by a marquee-shaped plexiglass roof 90 ft high. The largest traveling circus is the Gold Unit of Ringling Bros. and Barnum & Bailey Circus. It seats 7,000 people and is 394 × 197 × 66 ft. It was first used for a show at Sapporo, Japan on 1 Jul 1988.

The largest circus crowd comprised 52,385 people who attended a performance of "The Greatest Show on Earth" at the Superdome in New Orleans, LA on 14 Sep 1975.

Flying trapeze Downward circles or "muscle grinding"—1,350 by Sarah Denu (USA) at the age of 14, in Madison, WI, on 21 May 1983. Single-heel hang on swinging bar, by Angela Revelle (Angelique), in Australia, in 1977.

Highest aerial act Ian Ashpole (b. 15 Jan 1956) of Ross-on-Wye, Great Britain performed a trapeze act suspended from a hot-air balloon between St Neots, Great Britain and Newmarket, Great Britain at 16,420 ft on 16 May 1986.

Triple-twisting double somersault Tom Robin Edelston performed a triple-twisting double somersault to catcher John Zimmerman, at Circus World, FL on 20 Jan 1981.

Full twisting triple and the quadruple Vazquez Troupe. Miguel Vazquez performed a full twisting triple and the quadruple to catcher Juan Vazquez at Ringling Bros, Amphitheater, Chicago, IL in November 1981. On 20 Sep 1984 he performed a triple somersault in a layout position (no turn) to catcher Juan Vazquez at the Sports Arena, Los Angeles, CA.

Triple back somersault with 1½ twists Terry Cavaretta Lemus (now Mrs St Jules) performed a triple back somersault with 1½ twists at Circus Circus, Las Vegas, NV in 1969.

Teeter board A seven-person-high perch pyramid was established by the Bulgarian "Kehaiovi Troupe" at the Tower Circus, Blackpool, Great Britain on 16 Jul 1986. It was finished off with a leap from the top by 13-year-old member Magdelena.

Trampoline Septuple twisting back somersault to bed and quintuple twisting back somersault to shoulders was performed by Marco Canestrelli to Belmonte Canestrelli at Madison Square Garden, NY on 5 Jan and 28 Mar 1979. Richard Tison (France) performed a triple-twisting triple back somersault for television near Berchtesgaden, Germany on 30 Jun 1981.

Flexible pole Double full-twisting somersault to a 2-in-diameter pole was performed by Roberto Tabak (at the age of 11) in Sarasota, FL in 1977. A triple full-twisting somersault was performed by Corina Colonelu Mosoianu (at the age of 13) at Madison Square Garden, New York City on 17 Apr 1984.

Human pyramid (or tuckle) Twelve people, 3 high and a combined total weight of 1,700 lb, were supported by a single under-stander, Tahor Douis of the Hassani Troupe, at British Broadcasting Corporation's TV Pebble Mill Studio, Birmingham, Great Britain on 17 Dec 1979. A nine-high human pyramid was created by top-mounter Josep-Joan Martínez Lozano, age 10, of the Colla Vella dels Xiquets, 39 ft tall on 25 Oct 1981 in Valls, Spain.

Oldest clown Charlie Rivel (b. José Andreu, Spain, 1896) performed for 82 years, making his first public appearance when he was three years old in 1899. He died in 1983 at the age of 87.

Human cannonball The first human cannonball was Emilio Onra (ne Maîtrejean) at The Cirque d'Hiver, Paris, France on 21 Nov 1875.

The record distance a human has been fired from a cannon is 175 ft, in the case of Emanuel Zacchini, son of the pioneer Hugo Zacchini, in the Ringling Bros. and Barnum & Bailey Circus, Madison Square Garden, New York City in 1940. His muzzle velocity has been estimated at 54 mph. On his retirement the management was fortunate in finding that his daughter Florinda was of the same caliber.

Lion taming The greatest number of lions mastered and fed in a cage by an unaided lion tamer was 40, by "Captain" Alfred Schneider in 1925. Clyde Raymond Beatty handled more than 40 "cats" (lions and tigers) simultaneously. Beatty (1903–65) was the featured attraction at every show he appeared in for more than 40 years. He insisted upon being called a lion *trainer*. More than 20 lion tamers have died of injuries since 1900.

Plate spinning The greatest number of plates spun simultaneously is 84, by Dave Spathaky on British Broadcasting Corporation's *Record Breakers* TV program on 21 Oct 1986.

Stilt-walking The fastest stilt-walker on record is Masaharu Tatsushiro, who covered 328 ft on 1-ft-high stilts in 14.15 sec in Tokyo, Japan on 30 Mar 1980. Over a long distance, the fastest is M. Garisoain of Bayonne, France, who in 1892 walked the 4.97 miles from Bayonne to Biarritz on stilts in 42 min, an average speed of 7.10 mph.

The greatest distance ever walked on stilts is 3,008 miles, from Los Angeles, CA to Bowen, KY by Joe Bowen from 20 Feb–26 Jul 1980. In 1891 Sylvain Dornon stilt-walked from Paris, France to Moscow, USSR via Vilna in 50 stages, covering 1,830 miles. Another source gives his time as 58 days. Either way, although Bowen's distance was greater, Dornon walked at a much higher speed.

Even with a safety or Kirby wire, very high stilts are *extremely* dangerous—25 steps are deemed to constitute "mastery." The tallest stilts ever mastered measured 40 ft 6½ in from ground to ankle; they were used by Eddy Wolf ("Steady Eddy") of Loyal, WI to walk a distance of 27 steps without touching his safety handrail wires at Yokohama Dreamland Park, Yokohama, Japan on 9 Mar 1986. The stilts were of aluminum and weighed 55 lb each.

The heaviest stilts mastered weighed 56 lb each and were used by Joe Long (b. Kenneth Caesar), who has suffered five fractures, at the British Broadcasting Corporation Television Center, London, Great Britain on 8 Dec 1978. They were 24 ft high.

Photography

CAMERAS

Earliest The earliest veiled reference to a photograph on glass taken in a camera was in a letter dated 19 Jul 1822 from Joseph Nicéphore Niépce (1765–

1833), a French scientist. It was a photograph of a copper engraving of Pope Pius VII taken at Gras, near Chalon-sur-Saône, France, and it was rediscovered in London, Great Britain in February 1952 by the photohistorian Helmut Gernsheim after six years' research. The world's earliest aerial photograph was taken in 1858 by Gaspard Félix Tournachon (1820–1910), alias Nadar, from a balloon near Villacoublay, on the outskirts of Paris, France.

Largest The largest and most expensive industrial camera ever built is the 30 ton Rolls-Royce camera now owned by BPCC Graphics Ltd of Derby, commissioned in 1956. It measures 8 ft 10 in high, 8¼ ft wide and 46 ft in length. The lens is a 63 in f 16 Cooke Apochromatic and the bellows were made by Camera Bellows Ltd of Birmingham, Great Britain.

A pinhole camera was created from a Portakabin unit measuring 34 × 9½ × 9 ft by photographers John Kippen and Chris Wainwright at the National Museum of Photography, Film and Television at Bradford, Great Britain on 25 Mar 1990. The unit produced a direct positive measuring 33 × 6 ft.

Largest lens The National Museum of Photography, Film and Television, Bradford, Great Britain has the largest lens on display, made by Pilkington Special Glass Ltd, St Asaph, Clwyd, Great Britain. Its dimensions are: focal length 333 in, diameter 54 in, weight 474 lb. Its focal length allows writing on the museum's walls to be read from a distance of 40 ft.

Smallest Apart from cameras built for intracardiac surgery and espionage, the smallest that has been marketed is the circular Japanese "Petal" camera, with a diameter of 1.14 in and a thickness of 0.65 in. It has a focal length of 0.47 in.

The smallest functional bellows camera is a model Edwardian field camera designed and built by William Pocklington of Ascot, Great Britain in 1989, although the bellows were made by Camera Bellows Ltd. Constructed from matchsticks with brass fittings, when mounted for use on its collapsible tripod this replica stands 5.9 in high and has a body measuring 1.3 in × 1.3 in × 1.9 in with bellows extended. When closed it measures just 1.3 in × 1.3 in × 0.75 in. Fitted with a reversing back for landscape and portrait format, the camera produces pictures measuring 0.78 in × 0.67 in.

Fastest A camera built for research into high-power lasers by The Blackett Laboratory of Imperial College of Science and Technology, London, Great Britain registers images at a rate of 33 billion per sec. The fastest production camera is currently the Imacon 675, made by Hadland Photonics Ltd of Bovingdon, Great Britain, at up to 600 million frames per sec.

Most expensive The most expensive complete range of camera equipment in the world is that of Nikon Corporation

of Tokyo, Japan, which in May 1991 marketed its complete range of 26 cameras with 84 lenses and 617 accessories at a total cost of $225,174.49 excluding tax.

The highest auction price for a camera is £26,400 ($44,880) for a Leica R6 sold at Christie's, London on 9 Nov 1989 to De Liugi Garibaldi.

Longest negative On 1 Jul 1988 Christopher Creighton of Port Hope, Ontario, Canada, using a 24 in focal length Turner-Reich lens, fitted to a Kodak 8 Cirkut camera, made a portrait of an estimated 1,500 inhabitants of Port Hope, achieving a 355 degree view in a single shot. The resulting negative measured 11 ft 10½ in × 7¾ in.

Most expensive photograph The platinum print *Roses, Mexico* taken by Tina Modotti in 1925 was sold at Sotheby's, New York on 17 Apr 1991 for a record $165,000.

Cinema

FILMS

The earliest motion pictures ever taken were by Louis Aimé Augustin Le Prince (1842–90). He was attested to have achieved dim moving outlines on a whitewashed wall at the Institute for the Deaf, Washington Heights, New York City as early as 1885–87. The earliest surviving film (sensitized 2⅛ in wide paper roll) is from his camera, patented in Britain on 16 Nov 1888, taken in early October 1888, of the garden of his father-in-law, Joseph Whitley, in Roundhay, Great Britain at 10 to 12 frames per second.

The first commercial presentation of motion pictures was at Holland Bros' Kinetoscope Parlor at 1155 Broadway, New York City on 14 Apr 1894. Viewers could see five films for 25 cents or ten for 50 cents from a double row of Kinetoscopes developed by William Kennedy Laurie Dickson (1860–1935), assistant to Thomas Alva Edison (1847–1931), in 1889–91. The earliest publicly presented film on a *screen* was *La Sortie des Ouvriers de l'Usine Lumière*, probably shot in August or September 1894 in Lyons, France. It was exhibited at 44 rue de Rennes, Paris, France on 22 Mar 1895 by the Lumière brothers, Auguste-Marie-Louis-Nicholas (1862–1954) and Louis-Jean (1864–1948).

Earliest "talkie" The earliest sound-on-film motion picture was achieved by Eugene-Augustin Lauste (1857–1935), who patented his process on 11 Aug 1906 and produced a workable system using a string galvanometer in 1910 at Benedict Road, London, Great Britain. The earliest public presentation of sound on film was by the Tri-ergon process at the Alhambra Theater, Berlin, Germany on 17 Sep 1922.

United States The earliest screening of a sound-on-picture motion picture in the

United States before a paying audience was at the Rivoli Theater in New York City on 15 Apr 1923. The first all-talking motion picture was Warner Brothers' *Lights of New York*, shown at the Strand Theater, New York City on 6 Jul 1928.

Country with largest output India's production of feature-length films was a record 948 in 1990 and its annual output has exceeded 700 every year since 1979.

Most expensive film At the time of its release in July 1991, *Terminator 2: Judgment Day*, was reported to have cost Carolco Pictures a blockbusting $104 million, plus print and advertising costs of about $20 million. Its star, Arnold Schwarzenegger, was believed to have received a fee of $15 million for this sequel.

Least expensive full-length feature film The total cost of production for the 1927 film *The Shattered Illusion*, by Victorian Film Productions, was £300 ($1,458). It took 12 months to complete and included spectacular scenes of a ship being overwhelmed by a storm.

Most expensive film rights The highest price ever paid for film rights was $9.5 million announced on 20 Jan 1978 by Columbia for *Annie*, the Broadway musical by Charles Strouse starring Andrea McCardle, Dorothy Loudon and Reid Shelton.

Longest film The longest commercially released film was Rainer Werner Fassbinder's 15 hr 21 min epic *Berlin Alexanderplatz*, which was shown in full at the Vista Theater, Hollywood, CA on 6–7 Aug 1983 with a two-hour break for dinner. At 15 hr 40 min, the slightly longer *Heimat* (1984) was shown throughout Germany and in London, Great Britain, but over two days at weekend screenings.

Highest box office gross The box office gross champion is Steven Spielberg's *ET: The Extra-Terrestrial*, released on 11 Jun 1982, which had grossed over $700 million (including videos) by December 1989.

On 24 Jun 1989, *Batman* (Warner Brothers) grossed $14,600,000, for a single-day record. The highest opening-day gross was also scored by *Batman*, on 23 Jun 1989, with a take of $13.1 million.

Largest loss Michael Cimino's 1980 production *Heaven's Gate* earned $1.5 million in North American rentals against an estimated negative cost of $44 million and a total cost, including distribution and overheads, of $57 million.

Highest earnings Jack Nicholson stood to receive up to $60 million for playing "The Joker" in Warner Brothers' $50 million *Batman*, through a percentage of the film's receipts in lieu of salary.

The highest-paid actresses are Meryl Streep (b. Summit, NJ, 1949), with $4 million for *Out of Africa* and the same for *Heartburn*, and Barbra Streisand, with $6 million for *Prince of Tides*.

Stuntman Dar Robinson was paid $100,000 for the 1,100 ft leap from the CN Tower, Toronto, Ontario, Canada in November 1979 for *High Point*. His parachute opened just 300 ft above the ground. He died on 21 Nov 1986 at the age of 39.

Longest series still continuing Japan's *Tora-San* films have now stretched from *Tora-San I* in August 1969 to *Tora-San XL* in 1988, with Kiyoshi Atsumi (b. 1929) starring in each for Shochiku Co.

Most portrayed character The character most frequently recurring on the screen is Sherlock Holmes, created by Sir Arthur Conan Doyle (1859–1930). The Baker Street sleuth has been portrayed by some 72 actors in over 204 films since 1900, his most recent incarnation being Christopher Lee (with Patrick Macnee as Dr Watson) in a series of TV films which began production in August 1990.

In horror films the character most often portrayed is Count Dracula, created by the Irish writer Bram Stoker (1847–1912). Representations of the Count or his immediate descendants outnumber those of his closest rival, Frankenstein's monster, by 160 to 112.

Largest number of extras It is believed that over 300,000 extras appeared in the funeral scene of Sir Richard Attenborough's *Gandhi* (1982).

Largest studios The largest complex of film studios in the world is the one at Universal City, Los Angeles, CA. The back lot contains 573 buildings and there are 34 sound stages on the 420-acre site.

Largest studio stage The world's largest studio stage is the 007 stage at Pinewood Studios, Buckinghamshire, Great Britain. It was designed by Ken Adam and Michael Brown and built in 1976 for the James Bond film *The Spy Who Loved Me*. It measures 336 × 139 × 41 ft, and accommodates 1.2 million gal-

lons of water, a full-scale 672,000 ton oil tanker and three nuclear submarines.

Largest film set The largest film set ever built was the 1,312 × 754 ft Roman Forum designed by Veniero Colosanti and John Moore for Samuel Bronston's production of *The Fall of the Roman Empire* (1964). It was built on a 55 acre site outside Madrid, Spain, where 1,100 workmen spent seven months laying the surface of the Forum with 170,000 cement blocks, erecting 22,000 ft of concrete stairways, 601 columns and 350 statues, and constructing 27 full-size buildings.

Longest directorial career The directorial career of Wallis Vidor (1894–1982) lasted for 66 years, beginning with the two-reel comedy *The Tow* and culminating in another short, a documentary called *The Metaphor* (1980).

Oldest director Joris Ivens (b. Netherlands 1898) directed the Franco-Italian co-production *Le Vent* in 1988 at the age of 89. He made his directorial debut with the Dutch film *De Brug* in 1928.

Most durable performers The

record for the longest screen career is held by German actor Curt Bois (b. 1900), who made his debut in *Mutterliebe* at the age of nine and whose recent films include *Der Himmel über Berlin* (1987). American actress Helen Hayes (b. 10 Oct 1900) first appeared on screen at the age of 10 in *Jean and the Calico Doll*, but much of her later work has been on the stage. The most enduring stars of the big screen are French actor Charles Vanel (b. 1892), who marked his 75th anniversary as a film actor in *Les Saisons du Plaisir* (1988), and Lillian Gish (b. 14 Oct 1893) — although her birthdate is usually given as 1896. She made her debut in *An Unseen Enemy* (1912) and most recently appeared in *The Whales of August* (1987).

Most generations of screen actors in a family There are four generations of screen actors in the Redgrave family. Roy Redgrave (1872–1922) made his screen debut in 1911 and continued to appear in Australian films until 1920. His son, Sir Michael Redgrave, married actress Rachel Kempson, and their two daughters Vanessa and Lynn and son Corin all went into films. Vanessa's two daughters, Joely and Natasha, and

Corin's daughter Jemma, are already successful actresses with films such as *Wetherby*, *A Month in the Country* and *The Dream Demon* to their respective credit.

Costumes The largest number of costumes used for any one film was 32,000 for the 1951 film *Quo Vadis*. Elizabeth Taylor changed costume 65 times in *Cleopatra* (1963). The costumes were designed by Irene Sharaff and cost $130,000.

Most expensive Constance Bennett's sable coat in *Madam X* was valued at $50,000. The most expensive costume designed and made specially for a film was Edith Head's mink and sequins dance costume worn by Ginger Rogers in *Lady in the Dark*. It cost Paramount $35,000. The ruby slippers, a personal prop worn by Judy Garland in the 1939 film *The Wizard of Oz*, were sold on 2 Jun 1988 to a mystery buyer at Christie's, New York for $165,000.

Longest screen kiss The most prolonged osculatory marathon in movie history was one of 185 sec by Regis Toomey and Jane Wyman (b. Sarah Jane Faulks, 4 Jan 1914, later Mrs Ronald

Reagan) in *You're in the Army Now*, released in 1940.

Oscar winners Walter (Walt) Elias Disney (1901–66) won more "Oscars"— the awards of the United States Academy of Motion Picture Arts and Sciences, instituted on 16 May 1929 and named after Mr Oscar Pierce of Texas— than any other person. The physical count comprises 20 statuettes and 12 other plaques and certificates, including posthumous awards.

The only person to win four Oscars in a starring role is Katharine Hepburn (b. Hartford, CT, 8 Nov 1909) for *Morning Glory* (1932/33), *Guess Who's Coming to Dinner* (1967), *The Lion in Winter* (1968) and *On Golden Pond* (1981). She has been nominated 12 times.

Eight actors have won two Oscars in starring roles (the year the award was presented is given in each case): Ingrid Bergman (1945 and 1956), Marlon Brando (1955 and 1973), Gary Cooper (1942 and 1953), Jane Fonda (1972 and 1979), Dustin Hoffman (1979 and 1988), Vivien Leigh (1940 and 1952), Frederic March (1933 and 1947) and Spencer Tracy (1938 and 1939). Edith Head

■ **Largest multiplex**
An audience at the Kinepolis multiplex in Brussels, Belgium. Opened in 1988, the building houses 24 screens and has seating for 7,000. (Photo: Gamma/ Photonews)

Biggest screen

The largest permanently installed theater screen, with an area of 96 × 70½ ft, is located at the Keong Emas Imax Theatre, Taman Mini Park, Jakarta, Indonesia, opened on 20 Apr 1984. The Six Flags Great America Pictorium, Gurnee, ID, opened in 1979, has a screen of equal size, but it is 3D. A temporary screen measuring 297 × 33 ft was used at the 1937 Paris Exposition in France.

Most films seen

Gwilym Hughes of Dolgellau, Great Britain had seen 20,064 films by March 1991. He saw his first film in 1953 while in the hospital.

United States

Albert E. van Schmus (b. 1921) saw 16,945 films in 32 years (1949–1982) as a rater for the Motion Picture Association of America Inc.

Longest continuous broadcast

Radio Telefís Éireann transmitted an unedited reading of *Ulysses* by James Joyce (1882–1941) for 29 hr 38 min 47 sec on 16–17 Jul 1982.

Most assiduous radio ham

The late Richard C. Spenceley of KV4AA at St Thomas, VI built his contacts (QSOs) to a record level of 48,100 in 365 days in 1978.

(1907–81) won eight individual awards for costume design.

The youngest-ever winner was Shirley Temple (b. 23 Apr 1928), who was given an honorary Oscar at the age of 5. The oldest recipients, George Burns (b. 20 Jan 1896) for *The Sunshine Boys* in 1976 and Jessica Tandy (b. 7 Jun 1909) for *Driving Miss Daisy* in 1990, were both 80 at the time of the presentation.

The film with the most awards is *Ben Hur* (1959) with 11. The film with the most nominations was *All About Eve* (1950) with 14. It won six (Best Supporting Actor: George Sanders; Best Picture; Best Costume Design: Edith Head, Charles Le Maire; Best Director: Joseph L. Mankiewicz; Best Sound Recording; Best Screenplay: Joseph L. Mankiewicz).

Most honored entertainer

The most honored entertainer in history is Bob Hope (ne Leslie Townes Hope; London, Great Britain, 29 May 1903). He has been uniquely awarded the USA's highest civilian honors—the Medal of Freedom (1969); Congressional Gold Medal (1963); Medal of Merit (1966); Distinguished Public Service Medal (1973); Distinguished Service Gold Medal (1971)—and is also an Hon CBE (1976) and was appointed Hon. Brigadier of the US Marine Corps. He also has 44 honorary degrees.

MOVIE THEATERS

Earliest

The earliest structure designed and used exclusively for exhibiting projected films is believed to be one erected at the Atlanta Show, GA in October 1895 to exhibit C. F. Jenkins' phantoscope.

Largest

The largest theater in the world is the Radio City Music Hall, New York City, opened on 27 Dec 1932, with 5,945 (now 5,874) seats. Kinepolis, the first eight screens of which opened in Brussels, Belgium in 1988, is the world's largest theater complex. It has 24 screens and a total seating capacity of 7,000.

Most and fewest theaters

The country with the largest number of theaters in relation to population is San Marino, with one theater for every 3,190 inhabitants (a total of seven). In comparison, the United States has one theater for every 11,000 inhabitants. As of 31 Dec 1990 there were 23,814 commercial movie theaters in the United States. California leads the nation with 2,530, with Delaware last with only 49. Saudi Arabia (population 8 million) has no theaters, the public presentation of films being illegal as contrary to strict Islamic belief.

Highest movie theater attendance

The Chinese Ministry of Culture reported in September 1987 that there were 21 billion movie theater attendances in 1986—or nearly 21 per person per year.

Highest box office gross

In 1990, domestic gross box office receipts (USA and Canada) were $5.021 billion.

Radio

In the United States, the most popular formats for listeners (12 years and older) as of 1 Apr 1991, per a survey conducted by Arbitron Co. and Billboard *magazine, were adult contemporary (18.3 percent), news talk (14.6 percent), contemporary hit radio–top 40 (11.9 percent), country (11.0 percent) and album-orientated rock (9.1 percent). The survey did note that listener ratings were affected by coverage of the Persian Gulf War.*

Earliest patent

The earliest patent for telegraphy without wires (wireless) was received by Dr Mahlon Loomis (USA; 1826–86). It was entitled "Improvement in Telegraphy" and was dated 20 Jul 1872 (US Pat. No. 129 971). He in fact demonstrated only potential differences on a galvanometer between two kites 14 miles apart in Loudoun County, VA in October 1866.

The authentic first patent for a system of communication by means of electromagnetic waves, numbered No. 12039, was granted on 2 Jun 1896 to the Italian-Irish Marchese Guglielmo Marconi (1874–1937). A public demonstration of wireless transmission of speech was, however, given in the town square of Murray, KY in 1892 by Nathan B. Stubblefield. He died destitute on 28 Mar 1928. The first permanent wireless installation was at The Needles on the Isle of Wight, Great Britain, by Marconi's Wireless Telegraph Co. Ltd, in November 1897.

Earliest broadcast

The world's first advertised broadcast was made on 24 Dec 1906 by the Canadian-born Prof. Reginald Aubrey Fessenden (1868–1932) from the 420 ft mast of the National Electric Signalling Company at Brant Rock, MA. The transmission included Handel's *Largo*. Fessenden had achieved the broadcast of speech as early as November 1900 but it was highly distorted.

Transatlantic transmissions

The earliest claim to have received wireless signals (the letter S in Morse Code) across the Atlantic was made by Marconi, George Stephen Kemp and Percy Paget from a 10 kW station at Poldhu, Cornwall, Great Britain, to Signal Hill, St John's, Newfoundland, Canada, at 12:30 P.M. on 12 Dec 1901.

Human speech was first heard across the Atlantic in November 1915 when a transmission from the US Navy station at Arlington, VA was received by US radio-telephone engineers on the Eiffel Tower.

Earliest radio-microphones

The radio-microphone, which was in essence also the first " bug," was devised by Reg Moores (Great Britain) in 1947 and first used on 76 MHz in the ice show *Aladdin* at Brighton Sports Stadium, Great Britain in September 1949.

Biggest prize

Mary Buchanan, 15, on WKRQ, Cincinnati, won a prize of $25,000 for 40 years (or $1 million) on 21 Nov 1980.

Most durable programs

Rambling with Gambling, the early morning program on WOR, New York City, was first broadcast in March 1925 and celebrated its 20,000th show in March 1989. The show has been hosted by three generations of the Gambling family: John B. Gambling (1925–59), John A. Gambling (1959–present) and John R. Gambling (1985–present). The show currently airs six days per week, year round. The weekly sports report "The Tenpin Tattler" first broadcast on WCFL, Chicago, IL on 24 Aug, 1935. Fifty-three years and 2,756 broadcasts later, it still continues on WGN, Chicago.

Most hours broadcast per week

Larry King's radio and television programs are broadcast a combined 46 hours per week, the most of any broadcaster heard nationwide. He has been broadcast ten hours per week on CNN since 1985. He has broadcast 36 hours per week on Mutual Broadcasting since 1978.

Most stations

The country with the greatest number of radio broadcasting stations is the United States, where there were 10,889 authorized broadcast stations as of 30 Apr 1991, made up of 4,987 AM (amplitude modulation) stations and 5,902 FM (frequency modulation) stations.

Highest listening

The peak recorded listenership on British Broadcasting Corporation Radio was 30 million on 6 Jun 1950 for the boxing match between Lee Savold (USA) and Bruce Woodcock (Great Britain; b. 1921). Surveys carried out in 90 countries showed that, in 1990, the global estimated audience for the British Broadcasting Corporation World Service, broadcast in 38 languages, was 120 million regular listeners—greater than the combined listenership of Voice of America, Radio Moscow and *Deutsche Welle*. This is, however, a conservative estimate because figures are unavailable for several countries, including China, Cuba, Myanmar (formerly Burma), Iran, Afghanistan and Vietnam.

Highest response

The highest recorded response from a radio show occurred on 27 Nov 1974 when, on a 5-hr talk show on WCAU, Philadelphia, PA, astrologer Howard Sheldon registered a call count of 388,299 on the *Bill Corsair Show*.

Television

As of 30 Apr 1991 there were 1,477 commercial and educational licensed television stations in the United States.

Invention

The invention of television, the instantaneous viewing of distant objects by electrical transmission, was not an act but a process of successive and interdependent discoveries.

The first commercial cathode ray tube

was introduced in 1897 by Karl Ferdinand Braun (1850–1918), but was not linked to "electric vision" until 1907 by Prof. Boris Rosing (disappeared 1918) of Russia in St Petersburg (Leningrad). A.A. Campbell Swinton (1863–1930) published the fundamentals of television transmission on 18 Jun 1908 in a brief letter to the publication *Nature* entitled "Distant Electric Vision."

The earliest public demonstration of television was given on 27 Jan 1926 by John Logie Baird (1888–1946) of Scotland, using a development of the mechanical scanning system patented by Paul Gottlieb Nipkow (1860–1940) on 6 Jan 1884. He had achieved the transmission of a Maltese Cross over 10 ft at 8 Queen's Arcade, Hastings, Great Britain, by February 1924 and the first facial image (of William Taynton, 15) at 22 Frith Street, London, Great Britain on 30 Oct 1925. Baird launched his first television "service" via a British Broadcasting Corporation transmitter on 30 Sep 1929 and marketed the first sets, Baird Televisors, in May 1930.

A patent application for the Iconoscope had been filed on 29 Dec 1923 by Dr Vladimir Kosma Zworykin (1889–1982) but was not issued until 20 Dec 1938. Kenjiro Takayanagi (b. 20 Jan 1899) succeeded in transmitting a 40-line electronic picture on 25 Dec 1926 with a Braun cathode ray tube and a Nipkow disc at Hamamatsu Technical College, Japan.

Earliest service The world's first high-definition (i.e., 405 lines) television broadcasting service was opened from Alexandra Palace, London, Great Britain on 2 Nov 1936, when there were about 100 sets in all of Great Britain. The chief engineer was Mr Douglas Birkinshaw. A television station in Berlin, Germany made a low-definition (180-line) transmission starting on 22 Mar 1935, but the transmitter burned out in August of that year.

Transatlantic transmission On 9 Feb 1928 the image of J. L. Baird and of a Mrs Howe was transmitted from Station 2 KZ at Coulsdon, Great Britain to Station 2 CVJ, Hartsdale, NY.

The earliest transatlantic transmission by satellite was achieved at 1 A.M. on 11 Jul 1962, via the active satellite *Telstar 1* from Andover, ME to Pleumeur Bodou, France. The picture was of Frederick R. Kappell, chairman of the American Telephone and Telegraph Company, which owned the satellite. The first "live" broadcast was made on 23 Jul 1962 and the first woman to appear was the *haute couturière* Ginette Spanier, director of Balmain, the next day.

Longest telecast The longest pre-scheduled telecast on record was a continuous transmission for 163 hr 18 min by GTV 9 of Melbourne, Australia, covering the *Apollo XI* moon mission from 19–26 Jul 1969.

The longest continuous TV transmission under a single director was a student production on WOCC TV3 at Otterbein College, Westerville, OH transmitted over 48 hr 3 min on 17–19 Feb 1990 under the direction of Ben Kehoe.

Earliest videotape recording Alexander M. Poniatoff first demonstrated videotape recording, known as Ampex (his initials plus "ex" for excellence), in 1956.

The earliest demonstration of a home video recorder was on 24 Jun 1963 at the British Broadcasting Corporation News Studio at Alexandra Palace, London, Great Britain, of the Telcan, developed by Norman Rutherford and Michael Turner of the Nottingham Electronic Valve Co.

Most durable shows The world's most durable TV show is NBC's *Meet the Press*, first transmitted on 6 Nov 1947 and broadcast weekly since 12 Sep 1948. As of 26 May 1991, 2,190 shows had been broadcast. The show was originated by Lawrence E. Spivak, who served as host and chief analyst through 1975.

On 1 Jun 1986 Joe Franklin presented the 21,700th version of his show, started in 1951. Since 1949 over 150,000 individual episodes of the TV show *Bozo the Clown*, by Larry Harmon Pictures, have been aired daily on 150 stations in the United States and abroad.

ALL-TIME TOP VIDEO RENTALS

Movie	Rentals*
Top Gun (Paramount)	105.5
Crocodile Dundee (Paramount)	66.2
Dirty Dancing (Vestron)	62.6
Three Men and a Baby (Disney)	52.8
Platoon (HBO)	50.2
Based on times rented, in millions (Alexander & Associates)	

The greatest number of hours on camera on US national television is 10,190 hr 30 min by the TV personality Hugh Downs in over 46 years up to 7 Jun 1991.

Most sets The United States had, by March 1991, 92.8 million TV households, with 54.96 million receiving cable. A total 71,072,100 homes owned a videocassette recorder as of April 1991. The global total of homes with television surpassed 500 million in 1987, led by the USA with 89.13 million. The number of US homes with color sets was 8.3 million (97 percent) by January 1989. More than 60 percent of homes in the United States have two or more TV sets.

On 15 Feb 1988 the New China News Agency announced that China's number of TV viewers had risen to 600 million from 100 million sets.

TV watching In June 1988 it was reported that the average US child sees at least 26,000 murders on TV by his or her 18th birthday. Between the ages of 2 and 11 the average viewing time is 31 hours 52 minutes per week. There are 8,250 TV transmitting stations worldwide, of which 1,241 are in the United States. There are 364 TV sets per 1,000 people in the USA, compared with 348 in Sweden and 330 in Britain.

Greatest audience An estimated 2.5 billion viewers tuned in to the live and recorded transmissions of the XXIIIrd Olympic Games in Los Angeles, CA from 27 Jul to 13 Aug 1984. The American Broadcasting Co. airing schedule comprised 187 ½ hours of coverage on 56 cameras.

The estimated viewership for the Live Aid concerts organized by Bob Geldof and Bill Graham, via a record 12 satellites, was 1.6 billion, or nearly one-third of the world's population.

■ **Highest listening**
The newsroom of the British Broadcasting Corporation World Service. Surveys of 90 countries show that at least 120 million listeners tuned in regularly in 1990—more than the combined audience of Voice of America, Radio Moscow and Deutsche Welle. (Photo: BBC)

Fastest video production
Tapes of the Royal Wedding of HRH Prince Andrew and Miss Sarah Ferguson on 23 Jul 1986 were produced by Thames Video Collection. Live filming ended with the departure of the honeymoon couple from Chelsea Hospital by helicopter at 4:42 P.M. The first fully edited and packaged VHS tapes were purchased 5 hr 41 min later by Fenella Lee and Lucinda Burland of London at the Virgin Megastore in Oxford Street, London, Great Britain at 10:23 P.M.

Most takes
The highest number of takes for a TV commercial is 28 in 1973 by Pat Coombs, the comedienne. Her explanation was "every time we came to the punch line I just could not remember the name of the product."

■ Largest TV screen
The main feature at the Tsukuba International Exposition '85, near Tokyo, Japan, was the Sony JumboTRON, measuring 131 × 82 ft. A remote control is recommended, as the screen is best viewed from a distance of about 165–1,650 ft, although it can be seen from over ½ mile away. (Photo: Spectrum)

The program that attracted the highest-ever viewership was the "Goodbye, Farewell and Amen" final episode of M*A*S*H (the acronym for Mobile Army Surgical Hospital 4077), transmitted by CBS on 28 Feb 1983 to 60.3 percent of all households in the United States. It was estimated that some 125 million people tuned in, taking a 77 percent share of all viewing.

The estimated global audience for the 1990 Soccer World Cup finals played in Italy from 8 June to 8 July was 26.5 billion.

The *Muppet Show* is the most widely viewed program in the world, with an estimated audience of 235 million in 106 countries as of August 1989.

Emmy awards *Instituted on 25 Jan 1949 by the Academy of Television Arts & Sciences, the Emmy is awarded for achievement in national nighttime television programming.*

Most The most Emmys won by any individual is 15, by television producer Dwight Arlington Hemion (b. 14 Mar 1926). He also holds the record for most nominations, with 35. *The Mary Taylor Moore Show* (CBS) has won the most awards for a series, with 29. M*A*S*H (CBS) has received the most nominations, with 99. The most Emmys awarded to a miniseries was 9, to *Roots* (ABC) in 1977. In 1977 *Eleanor and Franklin: The White House Years* (ABC) received the most Emmys, 11, for a television movie. Columbia Broadcasting System (CBS) holds the record for most Emmys won by a network in a single season, with 44 in 1973–74.

Most expensive production The *Winds of War*, a seven-part Paramount World War II saga aired by ABC, was the most-expensive-ever TV production, costing $42 million over 14 months' shooting. The final episode on 13 Feb 1983 attracted a rating of 41 percent of the total number of viewers, and a 56 percent share of total sets that were turned on.

Largest contracts John William (Johnny) Carson (b. 23 Oct 1925), the host of *The Tonight Show*, has a contract with NBC reportedly calling for annual payment of $5 million for his one-hour evening shows aired four times weekly. The highest-paid current affairs or news performer is Dan Rather of CBS, who reportedly signed an $8 million contract for five years starting in 1982. Marie Osmond signed a contract worth $7 million for seven hours of transmission, paid by NBC on 9 Mar 1981. The figure includes talent and production costs.

Highest-paid entertainer The highest-paid television performer is currently Bill Cosby, who was reported by *Forbes* Magazine in October 1990 to have earned an estimated $115 million in 1989 and 1990. A survey in the *National Enquirer* published in February 1988 contended that the royalty income of Paul McCartney was running at $41 million per year and that his estimated personal fortune was $560 million.

Most successful telethon The world record for a telethon is $78,438,573 in pledges in 21½ hours by the 1989 Jerry Lewis Labor Day Telethon on 4 September. *The Comic Relief '89 Appeal*, the second "Red Nose Day" in Great Britain, was hosted by comedians Lenny Henry and Griff Rhys-Jones raised £26,660,145 ($46,655,253).

Biggest sale The greatest number of episodes of any TV program ever sold was 1,144 episodes of *Coronation Street* by Granada Television to CBKST Saskatoon, Saskatchewan, Canada, on 31 May 1971. This constituted 20 days 10 hr 44 min of continuous viewing. A further 728 episodes (January 1974–January 1981) were sold to CBC in August 1982.

Most prolific scriptwriter The most prolific television writer in the world is the Rt Hon Lord Willis (b. 13 Jan 1918). Since 1949 he has created 41 series, including the first seven years and 2.25 million words of *Dixon of Dock Green*, which ran on British Broadcasting Corporation television from 1955 to 1976; 36 stage plays; and 39 feature films. He has had 26 plays produced and his total output since 1942 is estimated to be 19.8 million words.

TV producer The most prolific producer in television history is game show producer Mark Goodson (b. 1915). Since 1948, Goodson has produced 38,000 episodes totaling more than 20,800 hours of air-time. Since February 1950, a Mark Goodson-produced show has appeared on national television at least once every week.

Aaron Spelling (b. 1928) has produced more than 1,770 TV episodes totaling 2,583 hours of air time, including 117 hours of TV movies. The total 2,583 broadcast hours is equal to 14.2 million ft of film and, projected 24 hours a day, it would take 108 days to screen it all. The average American TV is turned on six hours per day. At this rate, Spelling has produced enough film to last 678 days.

Highest TV advertising rates The highest TV advertising rate was $800,000 per 30 sec for ABC network prime time during the transmission of Super Bowl XXV on 27 Jan 1991.

Commercial records It was reported in March 1988 that Pepsi Cola had paid Michael Jackson $12 million to do four TV commercials for them.

Largest and smallest sets The Sony Jumbo Tron color TV screen at the Tsukuba International Exposition '85 near Tokyo, Japan in March 1985 measured 80 ft × 150 ft. The largest cathode ray tubes for color sets are 37 in models manufactured by Mitsubishi Electric of Japan.

The Seiko TV-Wrist Watch, launched on 23 Dec 1982 in Japan, has a 1.2 in screen and weighs only 2.8 oz. Together with the receiver unit and headphones, the entire black and white system, costing 108,000 yen, weighs only 11.3 oz. The smallest single-piece set is the Casio-Keisanki TV-10, weighing 11.9 oz with a 2.7 in screen, launched in Tokyo in July 1983. The smallest color set is the liquid crystal display (LCD) Japanese Epson, launched in 1985, with dimensions of 3 × 6¾ × 1⅛ in, weighing, with batteries and its 52,800 crystals, only 16 oz.

Human
Achievements

■ Previous page
Tightrope walking in France. (Photo: Gamma)

■ Most traveled man
The world's most traveled men are Giorgio Ricatto, from Turin, Italy, and Parke G. Thompson, from Akron, OH (see entry, right). Ricatto's travels have taken him to remote Antarctica and to markets in Cameroon. Not surprisingly, he has a large collection of passports which are full as a result (Photos: Giorgio Ricatto)

Endurance and Endeavor

Most traveled The world's most traveled men are Parke G. Thompson, from Akron, OH, and Giorgio Ricatto, from Turin, Italy, both of whom have visited all of the 171 sovereign countries and 59 of the 60 nonsovereign or other territories (see Countries, Chapter 4). Both men have yet to go to the Heard and McDonald Islands, an island group in the southern Indian Ocean.

The most traveled couple is Robert and Carmen Becker of East Northport, NY, both of whom have visited 169 of the 171 sovereign countries (the exceptions being Afghanistan and Iraq) and 53 of the 60 nonsovereign or other territories.

The most traveled man in the era before motor vehicles was believed to be the Methodist preacher Bishop Francis Asbury (b. Handsworth, Great Britain, 1745), who traveled 264,000 miles in North America between 1771 and 1815. During this time he preached some 16,000 sermons and ordained nearly 3,000 ministers.

John W. Black is the first person to visit all of the 3,104 counties and county equivalents in the United States, from 1925 to 1991. He has generally traveled by car, but has used most other forms of transport as well to achieve his record.

Most isolated The farthest any human has been removed from his nearest living fellow human is 2,233.2 miles in the case of the Command Service Module pilot Alfred M. Worden on the US *Apollo 15* lunar mission of 30 Jul–1 Aug 1971.

Longest walks The first person reputed to have "walked around the world" is George Matthew Schilling (USA) from 3 Aug 1897 to 1904. But the first *verified* achievement in this category was by David Kunst (b. 1939) from 20 Jun 1970 to 5 Oct 1974.

Tomas Carlos Pereira (b. Argentina, 16 Nov 1942) spent ten years, from 6 Apr 1968 to 8 Apr 1978, walking 29,825 miles around five continents. Steven Newman of Bethel, OH spent four years, from 1 Apr 1983 to 1 Apr 1987, walking 22,500 miles around the world, covering 20 countries and five continents.

Rick Hansen (b. Canada, 1957), who was paralyzed from the waist down in 1973 as a result of an auto accident, wheeled his wheelchair over 24,901.55 miles through four continents and 34 countries. He started his journey from Vancouver, British Columbia on 21 Mar 1985 and arrived back there on 22 May 1987.

George Meegan (b. 2 Oct 1952) from Rainham, Great Britain walked 19,019 miles from Usuaia, in the southern tip of South America, to Prudhoe Bay in northern Alaska, taking 2,426 days from 26 Jan 1977 to 18 Sep 1983. He thus completed the first north–south traverse of the western hemisphere on foot.

Sean Eugene Maguire (b. 15 Sep 1956; USA) walked 7,327 miles from the Yukon River, north of Livengood, AK to Key West, FL in 307 days, from 6 Jun 1978 to 9 Apr 1979. The trans-Canada (Halifax to Vancouver) record walk of 3,764 miles is 96 days by Clyde McRae, age 23, from 1 May to 4 Aug 1973. John Lees (b. 23 Feb 1945) of Brighton, Great Britain walked 2,876 miles across the United States from City Hall, Los Angeles to City Hall, New York City in 53 days 12 hr 15 min (averaging 53.75 miles a day) between 11 April and 3 Jun 1972.

North Pole conquest The claims of the two Arctic explorers Dr Frederick Albert Cook (1865–1940) and Cdr (later Rear-Ad.) Robert Edwin Peary (1856–1920), of the US Naval Civil Engineering branch, to have reached the North Pole are not subject to positive proof, and several recent surveys have produced conflicting conclusions. On excellent pack ice and modern sleds, Wally Herbert's 1968–69 expedition (see Arctic crossing, below) attained a best day's route mileage of 23 miles in 15 hr. Cook (see above) claimed 26 miles twice, while Peary claimed a surely unsustain-

able average of 38 miles over eight consecutive days.

The first people definitely to have reached the North Pole at ground level—the exact point at Lat. 90° 00′ 00″ N (± 300 meters)—were Pavel Afanasyevich Geordiyenko, Pavel Kononovich Sen'ko, Mikhail Mikhaylovich Somov and Mikhail Yemel'yenovich Ostrekin (all USSR), on 23 Apr 1948. They arrived and departed by air.

The earliest indisputable attainment of the North Pole by surface travel over the sea-ice took place at 3 P.M. Central Standard Time on 19 Apr 1968, when expedition leader Ralph Plaisted (USA), accompanied by Walter Pederson, Gerald Pitzel and Jean Luc Bombardier, reached the pole after a 42-day trek in four skidoos (snowmobiles). Their arrival was independently verified 18 hr later by a US Air Force weather aircraft. The party returned by aircraft.

Naomi Uemura (1941–84), the Japanese explorer and mountaineer, became the first person to reach the North Pole in a solo trek across the Arctic ice cap at 4:45 A.M. GMT on 1 May 1978. He had traveled 450 miles, setting out on 7 March from Cape Edward, Ellesmere Island in northern Canada. He averaged nearly eight miles per day with his sled *Aurora* drawn by 17 huskies. He also left by aircraft.

Dr Jean-Louis Etienne, age 39, was the first to reach the pole solo and without dogs, on 11 May 1986 after 63 days. On 20 Apr 1987 Fukashi Kazami, age 36, of Tokyo, Japan reached the North Pole from Ward Hunt Island, northern Canada in 44 days, having started on his 250-cc motorcycle on 8 March. Both left by aircraft.

The first woman to set foot on the North Pole was Mrs Fran Phipps (Canada) on 5 Apr 1971. She traveled there with her husband, a bush pilot. Galina Aleksandrovna Lastovskaya (b. 1941) and Lilia Vladislavovna Minina (b. 1959) were crew members of the USSR atomic icebreaker *Arktika*, which reached the pole on 17 Aug 1977.

South Pole conquest The first men to cross the Antarctic Circle (Lat. 66° 33′ S) were the 193 crew members and Capt. James Cook, Royal Navy (1728–79) of the *Resolution* (509 tons) and the *Adventure* (370 tons), captained by Lt Tobias Furneaux, on 17 Jan 1773 at 39° E.

The first person known to have sighted the Antarctic ice shelf was Capt. Thaddeus Thaddevich Bellingshausen (Russia; 1778–1852) on 27 Jan 1820 from the vessel *Vostock* accompanied by the *Mirnyy*. The first people known to have sighted the mainland of the continent were Capt. William Smith (1790–1847) and Master Edward Bransfield, Royal Navy, in the brig *Williams*. They saw the peaks of Trinity Land three days later, on 30 Jan 1820.

The South Pole (alt. 9,186 ft on ice and 336 ft bedrock) was first reached at 11 A.M. on 14 Dec 1911 by a Norwegian party of five men led by Capt. Roald Engebereth Gravning Amundsen (1872 –1928), after a 53-day march with dog sleds from the Bay of Whales, to which he had penetrated in the vessel *Fram*. Subsequent calculations showed that Olav Olavson Bjaaland and Helmer Hanssen probably passed within 1,310–1,970 ft of the exact location of the South Pole. The other two members were Sverre H. Hassell (died 1928) and Oskar Wisting (died 1936).

The first woman to set foot on Antarctica was Mrs Karoline Mikkelsen, a whaling captain's wife, on 20 Feb 1935. It was not until 11 Nov 1969 that a woman stood at the South Pole. On that day Lois Jones, Eileen McSaveney, Jean Pearson, Terry Lee Tickhill (all USA), Kay Lindsay (Australia) and Pam Young (New Zealand) arrived by air at Amundsen-Scott station and walked to the exact point from there.

First to see both poles The first people to see both poles were Amundsen and Oskar Wisting (see above) when they flew aboard the airship *Norge* over the North Pole on 12 May 1926, having previously been to the South Pole on 14 Dec 1911.

First to visit both poles Dr Albert Paddock Crary (USA; 1911–87) reached the North Pole in a Dakota aircraft on 3 May 1952. On 12 Feb 1961 he arrived at the South Pole by Sno Cat on a scientific traverse party from the McMurdo Station.

First to walk to both poles The first man to walk to both the North and the South Pole was Robert Swan (b. 1956). He led the three-man Footsteps of Scott expedition, which reached the South Pole on 11 Jan 1986, and three years later headed the eight-man Icewalk expedition, which arrived at the North Pole on 14 May 1989.

Arctic crossing The first crossing of the Arctic sea-ice was achieved by the British Trans-Arctic Expedition, which left Point Barrow, AK on 21 Feb 1968 and arrived at the Seven Island archipelago northeast of Spitzbergen, Svalbard, Norway 464 days later, on 29 May 1969. This involved a haul of 2,920 statute miles with a drift of 700 miles, compared with the straight-line distance of 1,662 miles. The team was made up of Wally Herbert (leader), 34, Major Ken Hedges, RAMC, 34, Allan Gill, 38, Dr Roy Koerner (glaciologist), 36, and 40 huskies. The only crossing achieved in a single season was that by Fiennes and Burton (see Polar circumnavigation, below) from Alert via the North Pole to the Greenland Sea in open snowmobiles. Both reached the North Pole and returned by land.

Antarctic crossing The first surface crossing of the Antarctic continent was completed at 1:47 P.M. on 2 Mar 1958, after a trek of 2,158 miles lasting 99 days from 24 Nov 1957, from Shackleton Base to Scott Base via the pole. The crossing party of 12 was led by Dr (now Sir) Vivian Ernest Fuchs (Great Britain; b. 11 Feb 1908). The 2,600 mile trans-Antarctic leg from Sanae to Scott Base of the 1980–82 British Trans-Globe Expedition was achieved in 67 days, from 28 Oct 1980 to 11 Jan 1981, having reached the South Pole on 15 Dec 1980. The three-man party on snowmobiles comprised Sir Ranulph Fiennes (b. 1944), Oliver Shepard and Charles Burton.

Polar circumnavigation The first polar circumnavigation was achieved by Sir Ranulph Fiennes and Charles Burton of the British Trans-Globe Expedition, who traveled south from Greenwich, Great Britain (2 Sep 1979), via the South Pole (15 Dec 1980) and the North Pole (10 Apr 1982), and back to Greenwich, arriving on 29 Aug 1982 after a 35,000 mile trek.

Longest sled journeys The longest totally self-supporting polar sled journey ever made was one of 1,080 miles from west to east across Greenland (now Kalaallit Nunaat) from 18 Jun to 5 Sep 1934 by Capt. M. Lindsay (later Sir Martin Lindsay of Dowhill, Great Britain; 1905–81), Lt Arthur S. T. Godfrey (later Lt-Col., killed 1942), Andrew N. C. Croft (later Col.), and 49 dogs.

The Ross Sea Party of ten (three died) sledded over 2,000 miles in 300 days from 6 May 1915.

The International Trans-Antarctic Expedition (six members) sledded a distance of some 2,300 miles in 117 days from 7 Nov 1989 (Patriot Hills) to 3 Mar 1990 (Mirnyy). The journey had started at Seal Nunataks on 27 Jul 1989, but the dogs accompanying the expedition were flown out from Patriot Hills to South America for a period of rest before returning to the Antarctic. The expedition was supported by aircraft throughout its duration.

Greatest ocean descent The record ocean descent was achieved in the Challenger Deep of the Mariana Trench, 250 miles southwest of Guam in the Pacific Ocean, when the Swiss-built US Navy bathyscaphe *Trieste*, manned by Dr Jacques Piccard (Switzerland; b. 1914) and Lt Donald Walsh, USN, reached a depth of 35,813 ft at 1:10 P.M. on 23 Jan 1960. The pressure of the water was 16,883 lbf/in^2 and the temperature 37.4° F. The descent took 4 hr 48 min and the ascent 3 hr 17 min.

Deep-diving records The record depth for the extremely dangerous activity of breath-held diving is 351 ft by Angela Bandini (Italy) off Elba, Italy on 3 Oct 1989. She was underwater for 2 min 46 sec.

The record dive with scuba (self-contained underwater breathing apparatus) is 437 ft by John J. Gruener and R. Neal Watson (USA) off Freeport, Grand Bahama on 14 Oct 1968. For women it is 345 ft by Marty Dunwoody (USA) off Bimini, Bahama Islands on 20 Dec 1987.

The record dive utilizing gas mixtures (nitrogen, oxygen and helium) was a simulated dive of 2,250 ft in a dry chamber by Stephen Porter, Len Whitlock

Submergence
The *continuous* duration record (i.e., no rest breaks) for scuba (i.e., self-contained and without surface air hoses) is 212 hr 30 min, by Michael Stevens of Birmingham, Great Britain in a Royal Navy tank at the National Exhibition Center, Birmingham from 14–23 Feb 1986.

High-altitude diving
The record for high-altitude diving is 16,200 ft in Lake Donag-Tsho in the Himalayas, Nepal, by Frank B. Mee, Dr John Leach and Dr Andy McLean on 4 Mar 1989. They dove to a depth of 92 ft, having first cut through 5 ft of ice in temperatures of −18° F.

Longest on a raft
The longest recorded survival alone on a raft is 133 days (4½ months) by Second Steward Poon Lim (b. Hong Kong) of Great Britain Merchant Navy, whose ship, the SS *Ben Lomond*, was torpedoed in the Atlantic 565 miles west of St Paul's Rocks at Lat. 00° 30′ N, Long. 38° 45′ W at 11:45 A.M. on 23 Nov 1942. He was picked up by a Brazilian fishing boat off Salinópolis, Brazil on 5 Apr 1943 and was able to walk ashore.

Maruice and Maralyn Bailey of Derby survived 118⅓ days (4 Mar–30 Jun 1973) in an inflatable dingy 4½ ft in diameter in the Pacific

ENDURANCE AND ENDEAVOR

Best man
The world champion "best man" is Ting Ming Siong, from Sibu, Sarawak, in Malaysia, who officiated for the 658th time since 1976 in April 1991.

Longest engagement
The longest engagement on record was between Octavio Guillen and Adriana Martinez. They finally took the plunge after 67 years in June 1969 in Mexico City. Both were then 82 years old.

Most married
Ralph and Patsy Martin of Quartzsite, AZ have married each other a total of 51 times, their first wedding having been in 1960. Richard and Carole Roble of South Hempstead, NY have also married each other 51 times, with their first wedding being in 1969. Both couples have chosen different locations each time.

Youngest married
It was reported in 1986 that an 11-month-old boy was married to a 3-month-old girl in Bangladesh to end a 20-year feud between two families over a disputed farm.

and Erik Kramer at Duke University Medical Center in Durham, NC on 3 Feb 1981, in a 43-day trial in a sphere of 8 ft diameter.

A team of six divers (four Comex and two French Navy) descended and worked efficiently during a period of six days to a depth of 1,706 ft off Marseilles, France, as part of the Hydra VIII operation in the spring of 1988. This involved the use of "hydreliox," a synthetic breathing mixture containing a high percentage of hydrogen. Arnaud de Nechaud de Feral performed a saturation dive of 73 days from 9 Oct–21 Dec 1989 in a hyperbaric chamber simulating a depth of 985 ft, as part of the Hydra IX operation carried out by Comex at Marseilles, France. He was breathing "hydrox," a mixture of hydrogen and oxygen.

Deepest underwater escapes The deepest underwater rescue ever achieved was of the *Pisces III*, in which Roger R. Chapman (28) and Roger Mallinson (35) were trapped for 76 hours when their vessel sank to 1,575 ft, 150 miles southeast of Cork, Republic of Ireland on 29 Aug 1973. It was hauled to the surface on 1 September by the cable ship *John Cabot* after work by *Pisces V*, *Pisces II* and the remote-control recovery vessel US CURV.

The greatest depth from which an actual escape without any equipment has been made is 225 ft, by Richard A. Slater from the rammed submersible *Nekton Beta* off Catalina Island, CA on 28 Sep 1970. The record for an escape with equipment was by Norman Cooke and Hamish Jones on 22 Jul 1987. During a naval exercise they escaped from a depth of 601 ft from the submarine HMS *Otus* in Bjornefjorden, off Bergen, Norway. They were wearing standard suits with a built-in life jacket, from which air expanding during the ascent passes into a hood over the escaper's head.

Deepest salvage The greatest depth at which salvage has been successfully carried out is 16,500 ft. The bathyscaphe *Trieste II* (Lt-Cdr Mel Bartels, USN) was used to attach cables to an "electronic package" on the seabed 400 miles north of Hawaii on 20 May 1972.

The deepest salvage operation ever achieved with divers was on the wreck of HM cruiser *Edinburgh*, sunk on 2 May 1942 in the Barents Sea off northern Norway, inside the Arctic Circle, in 803 ft of water. Over 32 days (from 7 Sep–7 Oct 1981), 12 divers dove on the wreck in pairs, using a bell from the *Stephaniturm* (1,594 tons), under the direction of former Royal Navy officer Michael Stewart. A total of 460 gold ingots (the only 100 percent salvage to date) was recovered, John Rossier being the first person to touch the gold.

Greatest penetration into the Earth The deepest penetration made into the ground by human beings is in the Western Deep Levels Mine at Carletonville, Transvaal, South Africa, where a record depth of 11,749 ft was attained

on 12 Jul 1977. The virgin rock temperature at this depth is 131° F.

Shaft-sinking record The one-month (31 days) world record is 1,251 ft for a standard shaft 26 ft in diameter at Buffelsfontein Mine, Transvaal, South Africa, in March 1962.

Most marriages The greatest number of marriages contracted by one person in the monogamous world is 27 by former Baptist minister Glynn "Scotty" Wolfe (b. 25 Jul 1908) of Blythe, CA, who first married in 1927. His latest wife is Daisy Delgado (b. 29 Dec 1970), a Filipino from Liloan, Cebu. His total number of children is, he believes, 41.

The greatest number of monogamous marriages by a woman is 21 by Linda Lou Essex of Anderson, IN. She has been married to 15 different men since 1957, having divorced the last one in 1988.

The record for bigamous marriages is 104 by Giovanni Vigliotto—one of many aliases used by either Fred Jipp (b. New York, 3 Apr 1936) or Nikolai Peruskov (b. Siracusa, Sicily, 3 Apr 1929) during 1949–81 in 27 states and 14 foreign countries. Four victims were aboard one ship in 1968 and two were in London, Great Britain. On 28 Mar 1983 in Phoenix, AZ he received a sentence of 28 years for fraud and six for bigamy, and was fined $336,000.

Oldest bride and bridegroom The oldest recorded bridegroom was Harry Stevens, age 103, who married Thelma Lucas, 84, at the Caravilla Retirement Home, WI on 3 Dec 1984.

The oldest recorded bride is Minnie Munro, age 102, who married Dudley Reid, 83, at Point Clare, New South Wales, Australia on 31 May 1991.

Longest marriage The longest recorded marriages were both of 86 years. Sir Temulji Bhicaji Nariman and Lady Nariman, who were married from 1853 to 1940, were cousins, and the marriage took place when both were age five. Sir Temulji (b. 3 Sep 1848) died, at the age of 91 years 11 months, in August 1940 in Bombay, India.

Lazarus Rowe (b. Greenland, NH in 1725) and Molly Webber were recorded as marrying in 1743. He died first in 1829, also after 86 years of marriage.

Golden weddings The greatest number of golden weddings in a family is ten, the six sons and four daughters of Joseph and Sophia Gresl of Manitowoc, WI all celebrating golden weddings between April 1962 and September 1988, and the six sons and four daughters of George and Eleonora Hopkins of Patrick County, VA all celebrating their golden weddings between November 1961 and October 1988.

Mass ceremony The largest mass wedding ceremony was one of 6,516 couples officiated over by Sun Myung Moon (b. 1920) of the Holy Spirit Association for the Unification of World Christianity at a factory near Seoul, South Korea on 30 Oct 1988.

Most expensive wedding The wedding of Mohammed, son of Shaik Rashid Bin Saeed Al Maktoum, to Princess Salama in Dubai in May 1981 lasted seven days and cost an estimated $44 million. It was held in a stadium built especially for the occasion, accommodating 20,000 wedding guests.

Oldest divorced On 2 Feb 1984 a divorce was granted in Milwaukee, WI to Ida Stern, age 91, and her husband Simon, 97.

Banquets It was estimated that some 30,000 guests attended a military feast given at Radewitz, Poland on 25 Jun 1730 by King August II (1709–33).

The greatest number of people served indoors at a single sitting was 18,000 municipal leaders at the Palais de l'Industrie, Paris, France on 18 Aug 1889.

At the wedding of cousins Menachem Teitelbaum and Brucha Sima Melsels in Uniondale, NY on 5 Dec 1984, the attendance of the Satmar sect of Hasidic Jews was estimated to be 17,000–20,000.

The most expensive menu ever served was for the main banquet at the Imperial Iranian 2,500th Anniversary gathering at Persepolis in October 1971. The feast, which lasted 5½ hr, comprised quails' eggs stuffed with Iranian caviar, a mousse of crawfish tails in Nantua sauce, stuffed rack of roast lamb, a main course of roast peacock stuffed with *foie gras*, fig rings and raspberry sweet champagne sherbet. The wines included *Château Lafite-Rothschild* 1945 at $160 (now $400) per bottle from Maxime's, Paris, France.

Dining out The world champion for eating out is Fred E. Magel of Chicago, IL, who since 1928 has dined out 46,000 times in 60 countries as a restaurant grader. He claims that the restaurant which served the largest helpings was Zehnder's Hotel, Frankenmuth, MI. Mr Magel's favorite dishes are South African rock lobster and mousse of fresh English strawberries.

The greatest altitude at which a formal meal has been held is 22,205 ft, at the top of Mt Huascaran, Peru, when nine members of the Ansett Social Climbers from Sydney, Australia scaled the mountain on 28 Jun 1989 with a dining table, chairs, wine and a three-course meal. At the summit they put on top hats and thermal evening attire for their dinner party, which was marred only by the fact that the wine turned to ice.

Party-giving The International Year of the Child children's party in Hyde Park, London, Great Britain on 30–31 May 1979 was attended by the British royal family and 160,000 children.

The world's biggest birthday party was attended by 54,972 people at The Plaza, Robinson Town Centre, in Pittsburgh, PA from 20–22 Jul 1990 to mark the first anniversary of the shopping center.

The largest Christmas party ever staged was the one thrown by the Boeing Co. in the 65,000-seat Kingdome, Seattle, WA. The party was held in two parts on 15 Dec 1979, and a total of 103,152 people attended.

During St Patrick's week of 11–17 Mar 1985, Houlihan's Old Place hosted St Pat's Parties at the 48 Kansas City, MO based Gilbert/Robinson restaurants, for a total of 206,854 documented guests.

Lecture fees Dr Ronald Dante was paid $3,080,000 for lecturing students on hypnotherapy at a two-day course held in Chicago on 1–2 Jun 1986. He taught for 8 hr each day, and thus earned $192,500 per hr.

Longest pension Miss Millicent Barclay was born on 10 Jul 1872, three months after the death of her father, Col. William Barclay, and became eligible for a Madras Military Fund pension to continue until her marriage. She died unmarried on 26 Oct 1969, having drawn the pension for every day of her life of 97 years 3 months.

Medical families The four sons and five daughters of Dr Antonio B. Vicencio of Los Angeles, CA, all earned medical degrees during the period 1964–82.

Miscellaneous Endeavors

It is intended to continue the process of phasing out the record categories in the "Human Achievements" chapter where the duration of the event is the only criterion for inclusion. If you are planning an attempt on an endurance marathon you should contact us at a very early stage to check whether that category is likely to be retained in future editions of the book.

Accordion playing Ted Larkin, alias "The Great Garaibaldi," played an accordian for 90 hr from 4–8 Jun 1991 at the Elephant and Castle Shopping Centre, London, Great Britain.

Bag carrying In the greatest nonstop bag carrying feat, 100 lb of household coal in an open bag was carried 34 miles by Neil Sullivan, 37, of Small Heath, Great Britain, in 12 hr 45 min on 24 May 1986.

Barrel rolling The record for rolling a full 36-gallon metal beer barrel over a measured mile is 8 min 7.2 sec, by Phillip Randle, Steve Hewitt, John Round, Trevor Bradley, Colin Barnes and Ray Glover of Haunchwood Collieries Institute and Social Club, Nuneaton, Great Britain on 15 Aug 1982.

A team of ten rolled a 140 lb barrel 150 miles in 30 hr 31 min in Chlumčany, Czechoslovakia on 27–28 Oct 1982.

Barrow pushing The heaviest loaded one-wheeled barrow pushed for a minimum 200 level feet was one loaded with bricks weighing a gross 8,275 lb. It was pushed a distance of 243 ft by John Sarich at London, Ontario, Canada on 19 Feb 1987.

Barrow racing The fastest time attained in a 1 mile wheelbarrow race is 4 min 48.51 sec, by Piet Pitzer and Jaco Erasmus at the Transvalia High School, Vanderbijlpark, South Africa on 3 Oct 1987.

Bathtub racing The record for a 36 mile bathtub race is 1 hr 22 min 27 sec, by Greg Mutton at the Grafton Jacaranda Festival, New South Wales, Australia on 8 Nov 1987. Tubs are limited to 75 in and 6 hp motors. The greatest distance for paddling a hand-propelled bathtub in 24 hr is 90½ miles, by 13 members of Aldington Prison Officers Social Club, near Ashford, Great Britain on 28–29 May 1983.

Bed making The pair record for making a bed with one blanket, two sheets, an undersheet, an uncased pillow, one bedspread and "hospital" corners is 17.3 sec, by Sister Sharon Stringer and Nurse Michelle Benkel of the Royal Masonic Hospital, London, Great Britain on 19 Sep 1990, shown on the British Broadcasting Corporation's *Record Breakers* TV program.

The record time for one person to make a bed is 28.2 sec, by Wendy Wall, 34, of Hebersham, Sydney, Australia on 30 Nov 1978.

Bed pushing The longest recorded push of a normally stationary object is of 3,233 miles, in the case of a wheeled hospital bed by a team of nine employees of Bruntsfield Bedding Center, Edinburgh, Great Britain from 21 Jun–26 Jul 1979.

Bed race The course record for the 10 mile Chew Valley Lake race (established 1977) in Avon, Great Britain is 50 min, by the Westbury Harriers' three-man bed team.

Beer coaster flipping Dean Gould of Felixstowe, Great Britain flipped and caught a pile of 102 coasters (490 gsm wood pulp board) through 180 degrees in Hamburg, Germany on 18 Mar 1988.

Beer keg lifting Tommy Gaskin raised a keg of beer weighing 137.79 lb above his head 656 times in the space of 6 hr at Newry, Northern Ireland on 28 Oct 1989.

Beer stein carrying Barmaid Rosie Schedelbauer covered a distance of 49 ft 2½ in in 4 sec with five full steins in each hand in a televised contest at Königssee, Germany on 29 Jun 1981.

Brick lifting Russell Bradley of Worcester, Great Britain lifted 30 bricks laid side by side off a table, raising them to chest height and holding them there for two seconds on 17 Nov 1990. The greatest weight of bricks lifted was also by Russell Bradley on the same day, when he succeeded in lifting 26 far-heavier bricks weighing a total of 189 lb 9 oz, again holding them for two seconds.

Bubble David Stein of New York City created a 50 ft long bubble on 6 Jun 1988.

He made the bubble using a bubble wand, dishwashing liquid and water.

Bubble-gum blowing The greatest reported diameter for a bubble-gum bubble under the strict rules of this highly competitive activity is 22 in, by Susan Montgomery Williams of Fresno, CA in June 1985.

Catapulting The greatest recorded distance for a catapult shot is 1,362 ft by James M. Pfotenhauer, using a patented 17 ft 1½ in Monarch IV Supershot and a 53-caliber lead musket ball on Ski Hill Road, Escanaba, MI on 10 Sep 1977.

Cigar box balancing Bruce Block balanced 213 cigar boxes (without modification) on his chin for 9.2 sec at the Guinness World of Records exhibition, London, Great Britain on 5 Nov 1990, later shown on the British Broadcasting Corporation's *Record Breakers* TV program.

Crawling The longest continuous voluntary crawl (progression with one or other knee in unbroken contact with the ground) on record is 28½ miles, by Reg Morris of Walsall, Great Britain on 29 Jul 1988. The crawl took place on a measured course 1½ miles long. It took 9 ½ hr and 19 laps of the track to attain the record. Over a space of 15 months ending on 9 Mar 1985, Jagdish Chander, 32, crawled 870 miles from Aligarh to Jamma, India to propitiate his favorite Hindu goddess, Mata.

Ducks and drakes (stone skipping) The record is 29 skips (14 plinkers

■ **Bubble**
David Stein of New York City created a 50 ft long bubble on 6 Jun 1988. He made the bubble using a bubble wand, dishwashing liquid and water. (Photo: Gelman & Gray/Lowry)

■ **Cigar box balancing**
Bruce Block managed to balance 213 cigar boxes (without modification) on his chin for 9.2 sec at the Guinness World of Records exhibition, London, Great Britain on 5 Nov 1990. (Photo: Rex Features)

and 15 pitty-pats), by Arthur Ring, 69, at Midway Beach, CA on 4 Aug 1984; and Jerdone "Jerry" McGhee, 42, at Wimberley, TX on 18 Nov 1986.

Egg and spoon racing Dale Lyons of Meriden, Great Britain ran 29.9 miles while carrying a dessert spoon with a fresh egg on it in 4 hr 18 min on 23 Apr 1990.

United States Chris Riggio of San Francisco, CA completed a 28.5 mile fresh egg and dessert spoon marathon in 4 hr 34 min on 7 Oct 1979.

Egg hunt The greatest egg hunt on record in the United States involved 120,000 plastic and candy eggs at a community Easter egg hunt at Coquina Beach in Manatee, FL on 23 Mar 1991. The event, hosted by Meals on Wheels PLUS of Manatee, Inc., involved more than 40,000 children.

Footbag This sport originated in Oregon in 1972 and was invented by John Stalberger (USA).

The world record for keeping a footbag airborne is 48,825 consecutive kicks or hacks by Ted Martin (USA) in Memphis, TN on 4 Jun 1988. The women's record is held by Francine Beaudry (Canada), with 15,458 on 28 Jul 1987 at Golden, CO.

The greatest number of kicks in five minutes is 850 by Gary Lautt (USA) at Berkeley, CA on 27 May 1990, and for women the record is 665 by Jody Welch (USA) on 31 Jul 1990, again at Golden, CO.

Garbage collection The greatest number of volunteers involved in collecting garbage in one location on one day is 18,143, along the coastline of Florida on 22 Sep 1990 as part of the Center for Marine Conservation's National Beach Cleanup program.

Gold panning The fastest time for "panning" eight planted gold nuggets in a 10 in diameter pan is 7.55 sec by Don Roberts of Diamond Bar, CA in the 27th World Gold Panning Championship on 16 Apr 1989 at Dahlonega, GA.

The female record is 10.03 sec, by Susan Bryeans of Fullerton, CA at the 23rd World Gold Panning Championship on 6 Mar 1983 at Knott's Berry Farm, Buena Park, CA.

Grape catching The greatest distance at which a grape thrown from level ground has been caught in the mouth is

327 ft 6 in by Paul J. Tavilla at East Boston, MA on 27 May 1991.

Gum wrapper chain The longest gum wrapper chain on record was 5,967 ft in length, and was made by Cathy Ushler of Redmond, WA between 1969 and 1987.

Hopscotch The greatest number of games of hopscotch successfully completed in 24 hr is 307 by Ashrita Furman of Jamaica, NY in Zürich, Switzerland on 5–6 Apr 1991.

Hula-hooping The longest marathon for a single hoop is 90 hr, by Roxann Rose of Pullman, WA from 2–6 Apr 1987, but she used her arm to keep the hoop whirling when tired. Tonya Lynn Mistal of Cottonwood, CA completed 88 hr of hula-hooping without the use of her arm, at Ted's Burgers in Idaho from 9–14 Jul 1986.

Simultaneous hula-hooping The record for simultaneous hula-hooping is 2,010 participants, at the St John Labatt's Lite 24 Hour Relay in St John, New Brunswick, Canada on 21 Sep 1990.

Human centipede The largest "human centipede" to move 98 ft 5 in (with ankles firmly tied together) consisted of 1,148 students and staff of University College Dublin (UCD), Republic of Ireland as part of UCD Science Day on 20 Feb 1991. Not one single person fell over in the course of the walk.

Kissing Alfred A.E. Wolfram of New Brighton, MN kissed 8,001 women in 8 hr at the Minnesota Rennaissance Festival on 15 Sep 1990.

Knitting The world's most prolific hand-knitter has been Mrs Gwen Matthewman of Featherstone, Great Britain. She attained a speed of 111 stitches per min in a test at Phildar's Wool Shop, Leeds, Great Britain on 29 Sep 1980.

Knot-tying The fastest recorded time for tying the six Boy Scout Handbook Knots (square knot, sheet bend, sheep shank, clove hitch, round turn and two half hitches, and bowline) on individual ropes is 8.1 sec by Clinton R. Bailey, Sr., 52, of Pacific City, OR on 13 Apr 1977.

Land rowing The greatest distance covered by someone on a land rowing machine is 3,280 miles by Rob Bryant of Fort Worth, TX, who "rowed" across the United States. He left Los Angeles, CA on 2 Apr 1990, reaching Washington, D.C. on 30 July.

Leapfrogging The greatest distance covered was 888.1 miles by 14 members of the class of 1988 of Hanover High School, in Hanover, NH, who started leapfrogging on 10 Jun 1988 and stopped 189 hr 49 min later, on 18 Jun 1988.

Log rolling The record number of International Championships won is 10, by Jubiel Wickheim of Shawnigan Lake, British Columbia, Canada, between 1956 and 1969. At Albany, OR on 4 Jul 1956 Wickheim rolled on a 14 in log against Chuck Harris of Kelso, WA for 2 hr 40 min before losing.

The youngest international log-rolling champion is Cari Ann Hayer (b. 23 Jun 1977), who won her first championship on 15 Jul 1984 at Hayward, WI.

Merry-go-round The greatest distance traveled on a merry-go-round is 2,462 miles by 14 people at the Mississippi–Alabama State Fair, Meridian, MS from 21 Sep–7 Oct 1990.

Milk bottle balancing The greatest distance walked by a person continuously balancing a full pint milk bottle on the head is 43.7 miles around a track at a park in New York City by Ashrita Furman on 12 Aug 1990.

Milk crate balancing Frank Charles balanced 24 milk crates, with a total weight of 74 lb, on his chin for 19 sec at Leyton Youth Center, London, Great Britain on 30 Jul 1988.

Needle threading The record number of times that a strand of cotton has been threaded through a number 13 needle (eye $\frac{1}{2}$ in × $\frac{1}{16}$ in) in 2 hr is 7,238, set by Brajesh Shrivastava at Gautam Nagar, Bhopal, India on 12 Dec 1990.

United States The record number of times that a strand of cotton has been threaded through a number 13 needle (eye $\frac{1}{2}$ in × $\frac{1}{16}$ in) in 2 hr is 5,370, set by Diane Sharp on 1 Aug 1987 at the Charitable Union's centennial event, Battle Creek, MI.

Oyster opening The record for opening oysters is 100 in 2 min 20.07 sec, by Mike Racz in Invercargill, New Zealand on 16 Jul 1990.

Pogo stick jumping The greatest number of jumps achieved is 130,077, by Gary Stewart in Reading, OH on 8–9 Mar 1985. Ashrita Furman of Jamaica, NY set a distance record of 13.06 miles in 5 hr 23 min on 15 Sep 1989 in New York City.

Rope slide The greatest distance recorded in a rope slide is from the top of Blackpool Tower, Lancashire, Great

Britain—a height of 454 ft 11 in—to a fixed point 1,120 ft from the base of the tower. Set up by the Royal Marines, the rope was descended on 8 Sep 1989 by Sgt Alan Heward and Cpl Mick Heap of the Royal Marines, John Herbert of Blackpool Tower, and Cheryl Baker and Roy Castle of the British Broadcasting Corporation's *Record Breakers* TV program. The total length descended was 1,202 ft.

Shorthand The highest recorded speeds ever attained under championship conditions are 300 words per min (99.64 percent accuracy) for five minutes and 350 wpm (99.72 percent accuracy—that is, two insignificant errors) for two minutes by Nathan Behrin (USA) in tests in New York in December 1922. Behrin (b. 1887) used the Pitman system, invented in 1837.

Morris I. Kligman, official court reporter of the US Court House, New York City, has taken 50,000 words in 5 hr (a sustained rate of 166.6 wpm). Rates are much dependent upon the nature, complexity and syllabic density of the material. Mr G.W. Bunbury of Dublin, Ireland held the unique distinction of writing at 250 wpm for 10 minutes on 23 Jan 1894. Mr Arnold Bradley achieved a speed of 309 wpm without error using the Sloan-Duployan system, with 1,545 words in 5 minutes in a test in Walsall, West Midlands, Great Britain on 9 Nov 1920.

Spitting Randy Ober of Bentonville, AR spat a tobacco wad 47 ft 7 in at the Calico 5th Annual Tobacco Chewing and Spitting Championships, held north of Barstow, CA on 4 Apr 1982. The record for projecting a watermelon seed is 68 ft 9⅛ in by Lee Wheelis at Luling, TX on 24

Jun 1989. The greatest recorded distance for a cherry stone is 72 ft 7½ in, by Rick Krause at Eau Claire, MI on 2 Jul 1988.

String ball, largest The largest ball of string on record is one of 12 ft 9 in in diameter, 40 ft in circumference and weighing 11 tons, amassed by Francis A. Johnson of Darwin, MN between 1950 and 1978.

Stroller pushing The greatest distance covered in pushing a stroller in 24 hr is 350.23 miles by 60 members of the Oost-Vlanderen branch of Amnesty International at Lede, Belgium on 15 Oct 1988. A ten-man team from the Royal Marines School of Music, Deal, Great Britain, with an adult "baby," covered a distance of 271.7 miles in 24 hr from 22–23 Nov 1990.

Tightrope walking The oldest tightrope walker was "Professor" William Ivy Baldwin (1866–1953), who crossed the South Boulder Canyon, CO on a 320 ft wire with a 125 ft drop on his 82nd birthday on 31 Jul 1948.

The world tightrope endurance record is 185 days, by Henri Rochatain (b. 1926) of France, on a wire 394 ft long, 82 ft above a supermarket in Saint Etienne, France from 28 Mar–29 Sep 1973. His ability to sleep on the wire has left doctors puzzled.

Ashley Brophy of Neilborough, Victoria, Australia walked 7.18 miles on a wire 147.64 ft long and 32.81 ft above the ground at the Adelaide Grand Prix, Australia on 1 Nov 1985 in 3½ hr.

The greatest drop over which anyone has walked on a tightrope is 10,335 ft, above the French countryside, by Michel Menin of Lons-le-Saunier, France, on 4 Aug 1989.

■ **Merry-go-round**
The greatest distance traveled on a merry-go-round is 2,462 miles by 14 people at the Mississippi–Alabama State Fair, Meridian, MS from 21 Sep–7 Oct 1990. Most of the record holders are in this picture, at the scene of their successful attempt.

Largest garbage can
The largest garbage can ever constructed was made by Glasdon UK Ltd of Blackpool, Great Britain for "Spring Clean Day" on 29 Mar 1990. The 18 ft 6 in tall replica of their standard bin has a capacity of 5,719 gal.

Typewriting The world duration record for typewriting on an electric machine is 264 hr, set by Violet Gibson Burns at the Royal Easter Show, Sydney, Australia from 29 Mar–9 Apr 1985. The longest duration in a typing marathon on a manual machine is 142 hr 50 min, by M. Kanagasundaram of Dindigul, India, from 25–31 Jul 1990. His marathon consisted of nearly 916,000 strokes.

The highest recorded speeds attained with a ten-word penalty per error on a manual machine are:

Five minutes: 176 wpm by Mrs Carole Forristall Waldschlager Bechen at Dixon, IL on 2 Apr 1959. *One hour:* 147 wpm by Albert Tangora (USA) on an Underwood Standard, 22 Oct 1923.

The official hour record on an electric typewriter is 9,316 words (40 errors) on an IBM machine, giving a net rate of 149 words per min, by Margaret Hamma, now Mrs Dilmore (USA), in Brooklyn, NY on 20 Jun 1941. In an official test in 1946, Stella Pajunas, now Mrs Garnand, attained a rate of 216 words in a minute on an IBM machine.

Mary Ann Morel (South Africa) set a numerical record at the CABEX '85 Exhibition in Johannesburg, South Africa on 6 Feb 1985 by typing spaced numbers from 1 to 781 in 5 min.

Unsupported circle The highest recorded number of people who have demonstrated the physical paradox of all being seated without a chair is an unsupported circle of 10,323 employees of the Nissan Motor Co. at Komazawa Stadium, Tokyo, Japan on 23 Oct 1982.

Whip cracking The longest stock whip ever "cracked" is one of 140 ft (excluding the handle), wielded by Gary Brophy at Adelaide, Australia on 1 Nov 1985.

Yo-yo A yo-yo was a toy in Grecian times and is depicted on a bowl dated 450 B.C. It was also a Filipino jungle fighting weapon recorded in the 16th century, weighing 4 lb with a 20 ft thong. The word means "come-come." Though illustrated in a book in 1891 as a bandalore, the craze did not begin until Donald F. Duncan of Chicago, IL initiated it in 1926. The most difficult modern yo-yo trick is the "whirlwind," incorporating both inside and outside horizontal loop-the-loops. The individual continuous endurance record is 130 hr 13 min, by Jason Stremble and Scott Fletcher at Variety Village, Scarborough, Ontario, Canada from 17–22 Jul 1989.

"Fast" Eddy McDonald of Toronto, Ontario, Canada completed 21,663 loops in 3 hr on 14 Oct 1990 in Boston, MA, having previously set a 1 hr speed record of 8,437 loops in Cavendish, Prince Edward Island, Canada on 14 Jul 1990. Dr Allen Bussey in Waco, TX on 23 Apr 1977 completed 20,302 loops in 3 hr.

Juggling

8 clubs (flashed) Anthony Gatto (USA), 1989.

7 clubs (juggled) Albert Petrovski (USSR), 1963; Sorin Munteanu (Romania), 1975; Jack Bremlov (Czechoslovakia), 1985; Albert Lucas (USA), 1985; Anthony Gatto (USA), 1988.

8 plates Enrico Rastelli (Italy), 1896–1931; Albert Lucas (USA), 1984.

10 balls Enrico Rastelli (Italy), 1896–1931; Albert Lucas (USA), 1984.

12 rings (flashed) Albert Lucas (USA), 1985.

11 rings (juggled) Albert Petrovski (USSR), 1963–66; Eugene Belaur (USSR), 1968; Sergei Ignatov (USSR), 1973.

7 flaming torches Anthony Gatto (USA), 1989.

Bounce juggling Tim Nolan (USA), 10 balls, 1988.

Basketball spinning Bruce Crevier (US), 15 basketballs (whole body), 1991.

Ball spinning (on one hand) François Chotard (France), 9 balls, 1990.

Duration: 5 clubs without a drop 45 min 2 sec, Anthony Gatto (USA), 1989.

Duration: 3 objects without a drop Jas Angelo (Great Britain), 8 hr 57 min 31 sec, 1989.

7 ping-pong balls with mouth Tony Ferko (Czechoslovakia), 1987.

Pirouettes with 3 cigar boxes Kris Kremo (Switzerland) (quadruple turn with 3 boxes in mid-air), 1977.

5 balls inverted Bobby May (USA), 1953.

Most objects aloft 821 jugglers kept 2,463 objects in the air simultaneously, each person juggling at least three objects, 1990. (See also Track and Field.)

Food

Apple pie The largest apple pie ever baked was made by chef Glynn Christian in a 40 × 23 ft dish at Hewitts Farm, Chelsfield, Great Britain from 25–27 Aug 1982. Over 600 bushels of apples were included in the pie, which weighed 30,115 lb. It was cut by Rear-Admiral Sir John Woodward.

Banana split The longest banana split ever created measured 4.55 miles in length, and was made by residents of Selinsgrove, PA on 30 Apr 1988.

Barbecue The record attendance at a one-day barbecue was 35,072, at the Iowa State Fairgrounds, Des Moines, IA on 21 Jun 1988. The greatest meat consumption ever recorded at a one-day barbecue was at the same event—20,130 lb of pork consumed in 5 hr. The greatest quantity of meat consumed at any barbecue was 21,112 lb of beef at the Sertoma Club Barbecue, New Port Richey, FL, from 7–9 Mar 1986.

Cakes The largest cake ever created weighed 128,238 lb 8 oz, including 16,209 lb of icing. It was made to celebrate the 100th birthday of Fort Payne, AL, and was in the shape of Alabama. The cake was prepared by a local bakery, Earth-Grains, and the first cut was made by 100-year old resident Ed Henderson on 18 Oct 1989. The tallest cake was 101 ft 2½ in high, created by Beth Cornell and her team of helpers at the Shiwassee County Fairgrounds, MI. It consisted of 100 tiers and work was completed on 5 Aug 1990. The Alimentarium, a museum of food in Vevey, Switzerland, has on display the world's oldest cake, which was sealed and "vacuum-packed" in the grave of Pepionkh, who lived in ancient Egypt around 2200 B.C. The 4.3-in-wide cake has sesame on it and honey inside, and was possibly made with milk.

Candy The largest candy was a marzipan chocolate weighing 4,078.5 lb, made at the Ven International Fresh Market, Diemen, Netherlands on 11–13 May 1990.

Cheese The largest cheese ever created was a cheddar of 40,060 lb, made on 13–14 Mar 1988 at Simon's Specialty Cheese, Little Chute, WI. It was subsequently taken on tour in a specially designed, refrigerated "Cheesemobile."

Cherry pie The largest cherry pie on record weighed 37,740.65 lb and contained 36,800 lb of cherry filling. It measured 20 ft in diameter, and was baked by members of the Oliver Rotary Club in Oliver, British Columbia, Canada on 14 Jul 1990.

Chocolate model The largest chocolate model was one weighing 3,968.3 lb, of the 1992 Olympic Center, Barcelona, Spain. It was made by Gremi Provincial de Pastisseria, Confitería i Bolleria school, Barcelona in November 1985 and measured 32 ft 9½ in × 16 ft 4 ¾ in × 2 ft 4¾ in.

Cocktail The largest cocktail on record was a "Cabanas Surprise" of 462.9 gal, made by Sun City Cabanas at Sun City, Bophuthatswana, South Africa on 2 Mar 1991.

United States The largest cocktail on record in the USA was one of 300 gal created by Bacardi Imports in Miami, FL on 9 Mar 1989, and named "Cuba Libre."

Doughnut The largest doughnut ever made was lemon-filled and weighed 2,099 lb, with a diameter of 22 ft. It was baked by Ed Sanderson at Crystal River, FL on 10 Dec 1988.

Easter eggs The heaviest chocolate Easter egg ever made was one weighing 7,561 lb 13½ oz, 10 ft high, by Siegfried Berndt at Macopa Patisserie, Leicester, Great Britain, and completed on 7 Apr 1982. A chocolate egg 18 ft 11½ in tall was constructed by Tobler Suchard of Bedford, Great Britain on 10 Apr 1987.

Food, most expensive The most expensive food (as opposed to spice) is First Choice Black Périgord truffle

■ **Lasagne**
The largest lasagne was one weighing 3,609.6 lb and measuring 50 × 5 ft. It was made by Andreano Rossi of Dolmio, second from the left, and a team of helpers at the Royal Dublin Society Spring Show in Dublin, Republic of Ireland on 11 May 1990. (Photo: Masterfoods Ltd)

Condiment, rarest
The world's most prized condiment is Cà Cuong, a secretion recovered in minute amounts from beetles in North Vietnam. Because of war conditions, the price had risen to $100 per oz before supplies virtually ceased in 1975.

Dish
The largest item on any menu in the world is roasted camel, prepared occasionally for Bedouin wedding feasts. Cooked eggs are stuffed into fish, the fish stuffed into cooked chickens, the chickens stuffed into a roasted sheep's carcass and the sheep stuffed into a whole camel.

Omelet making
The greatest number of two-egg omelettes made in 30 min is 427, by Howard Helmer at the International Poultry Trade Show held at Atlanta, GA on 2 Feb 1990.

Pancake tossing
The greatest number of times a pancake has been tossed in 2 min is 281, by Judith Aldridge in the Merry Hill shopping center at Dudley, Great Britain on 27 Feb 1990.

(*Tuber melanosporum*), which is sold at Harrods in London, Great Britain for £17.50 ($30) per 0.44 oz jar. However, in January 1985 in the Hafr El-Baten market, Riyadh, Saudi Arabia, local truffles sold for SR 5,000 for 6.6 lb, equivalent to $85 for 0.44 oz.

Hamburger The largest hamburger on record was one of 5,520 lb, made at the Outgamie County Fairgrounds, Seymour, WI on 5 Aug 1989.

Ice-cream sundae The largest ice cream sundae was one weighing 54,914.8 lb, made by Palm Dairies Ltd under the supervision of Mike Rogiani in Edmonton, Alberta, Canada on 24 Jul 1988. It consisted of 44,689.5 lb of ice cream, 9,688.1 lb of syrup and 537.2 lb of topping.

Jello The world's largest Jello, a 7,700 gal watermelon-flavored pink Jello made by Paul Squires and Geoff Ross, worth $14,000, was set at Roma Street Forum, Brisbane, Queensland, Australia on 5 Feb 1981 in a tank supplied by Pool Fab.

Kebab The longest kebab ever was one 1,065 ft 11 in long, made by George Psarias of the Olive Tree Greek Restaurant, Rodley, Great Britain on 26 Aug 1990.

Lasagne The largest lasagne was one weighing 3,609.6 lb and measuring 50 × 5 ft. It was made by Andreano Rossi of Dolmio and a team of helpers at the Royal Dublin Society Spring Show in Dublin, Republic of Ireland on 11 May 1990.

Loaf The longest loaf on record was a Rosca de Reyes 3,491 ft 9 in long, baked at the Hyatt Regency Hotel in Guadalajara, Mexico on 6 Jan 1991. If a consumer of the "Rosca," or twisted loaf, finds the embedded doll, that person has to host the Rosca party (held annually at Epiphany) the following year.

The largest pan loaf ever baked weighed 3,163 lb 10 oz and measured 9 ft 10 in × 4 ft 1 in × 3 ft 7 in, by the staff of Sasko in Johannesburg, South Africa on 18 Mar 1988.

United States The longest loaf on record in the United States was one 2,357 ft 10 in long, baked by the Northlands Job Corps, Vergennes, VT on 3 Nov 1987. Some 35,840 lb of dough were required in the preparation of the loaf, and over 4,480 lb of charcoal and 4,700 ft of aluminum foil were used to bake it.

Lollipop The world's largest ice lollipop was one of 7,080 lb, constructed by students and staff at Lawrence University, Appleton, WI on 17 Feb 1990. The largest "regular" lollipop weighed 2,220.5 lb and was made by Lolly Pops/Johnson's Confectionary in Sydney, Australia on 18–19 Aug 1990.

Meat pie The largest meat pie on record weighed 19,908 lb and was the 9th in the series of pies baked in Denby Dale, Great Britain. It was baked on 3 Sep 1988 to mark the bicentennial of Denby Dale pie-making, the first one having been made in 1788 to celebrate King George III's return to sanity. The fourth (Queen Victoria's Jubilee, 1887) went a bit "off" and had to be buried in quicklime.

Milk shake The largest milk shake was a chocolate one of 1,891.69 gal, made by the Smith Dairy Products Co. at Orrville, OH on 20 Oct 1989.

Omelet The largest omelet in the world had an area of 1,324 ft² and was made in a skillet 41 ft 1 in in diameter. It was cooked by staff and pupils of the Municipal School for Special Education at Opwijk, Belgium on 10 Jun 1990.

United States The largest omelet in the USA was one with an area of 706 ft 8 in², made with 54,763 eggs and 531 lb cheese in a skillet 30 ft in diameter. It was cooked by Michael McGowan, assisted by his staff and the Sunrise Jaycees of Las Vegas, NV on 25 Oct 1986.

Paella The largest paella measured 52 ft 6 in in diameter and was made by Josep Gruges ("Pepitu") on 25 Aug 1987 in the Playa de Aro, Gerona, Spain. The ingredients included 8,140 lb of rice, 6,600 lb of meat, 3,300 lb of mussels, 1,540 lb each of beans and peppers, 440 lb of garlic and 88 gal of oil. The paella was eaten by 40,000 people, who washed it all

Yard of ale

Peter Dowdeswell of Earls Barton, Great Britain drank a yard of ale (2½ pints) in 5.0 sec at RAF Upper Heyford, Great Britain on 4 May 1975.

Wine tasting

The largest wine tasting ever reported was the one staged by the Wine Institute at the St Francis Hotel, San Francisco, CA on 17 Jul 1980, with 125 pourers, 90 openers and a consumption of 3,000 bottles.

Champagne cork flight

The longest flight of a cork from an untreated and unheated bottle 4 ft from level ground is 177 ft 9 in, reached by Prof. Emeritus Heinrich Medicus, RPI, at the Woodbury Vineyards Winery, NY on 5 Jun 1988.

■ **Champagne fountain**
The greatest number of stories achieved in a champagne fountain, successfully filled from the top and using 10,404 traditional long-stemmed glasses, is 44 (height 24 ft 8 in). This was achieved by Pascal Leclerc at the Biltmore Hotel, Los Angeles, CA on 18 Jun 1984. (Photo: Rex Features)

down with 8,000 bottles of Catalan champagne.

Pancake The largest pancake was 32 ft 11 in in diameter and 1 in deep, and weighed 2,866 lb. It was made and flipped at Dijkerhoek, Holten, Netherlands on 13 May 1990.

Pastry The longest pastry in the world was an apple strudel 2,018 ft 2 in in length, made by Port Macquarie College of Technical and Further Education at Port Macquarie, New South Wales, Australia on 30 Sep 1990.

United States The longest pastry in the USA was the "record" pastry 1,683 ft 2½ in in length made by chefs at the Hyatt Regency Ravinia, Atlanta, GA on 26 Jul 1986.

Pizza The largest pizza ever baked was one measuring 122 ft 8 in in diameter, made at Norwood Hypermarket, Norwood, South Africa on 8 Dec 1990.

United States The largest pizza in the United States was one measuring 100 ft 1 in in diameter, organized by L. Amato and L. Piancone and completed at Highway 27, Havana, FL on 11 Oct 1987.

Popcorn The largest container of popcorn contained 3,791.8 ft³ of popped corn. It measured 32 × 32 ft and was filled by the 1990 marketing block class at Fresno State University, CA from 25–28 Apr 1990. The average depth was 3 ft 8½ in.

Potato chips The Pringles plant in Jackson, TN produced a Pringle potato chip 23 in x 14½ in on 19 Apr 1990. Pringles potato chips are made from potato flour.

Salami The longest salami on record was one 61 ft 3½ in long with a circumference of 24 in, weighing 1,202.5 lb, made by the Kutztown Bologna Co., PA and displayed at the Lebanon Bologna Fest in Kutztown on 11–13 Aug 1989.

Sausage The longest continuous sausage on record was one of 13.125 miles, made at the premises of Keith Boxley at Wombourne, Great Britain in 15 hr

33 min on 18–19 Jun 1988.

Soda float The largest soda float ever made was one produced in a 2,000 gallon container and consisted of 1,200 lbs skim milk and 936 gallons Coca Cola. It was made by Coleman Quality Chekd Dairy, Inc., Cool 95 FM, and Coca Cola of Arkansas at the Arkansas State Fairgrounds, Little Rock, AR on 14 Oct 1990.

Spice, most expensive Prices for wild ginseng (root of *Panax quinquefolium*) from the Chan Pak Mountain area of China, thought to have aphrodisiac qualities, were reported in November 1979 to be as high as $23,000 per ounce in Hong Kong. Total annual shipments from Jilin Province do not exceed 140 oz a year.

Spice, "hottest" The hottest of all spices is claimed to be siling labuyo from the Philippines. The chili pepper or capsicum known as tepin, of the southwestern United States, comes in pods ⅜ in in diameter. A single dried gram will produce detectable "heat" in 68.3 lb of bland sauce.

Strawberry bowl The largest bowl of strawberries ever picked had a net weight of 4,832 lb. The strawberries were picked at Walt Furlong's farm at New Ross, Republic of Ireland during the Enniscorthy Strawberry Fair on 9 Jul 1989.

Drink

Since 1 Jan 1981 the strength of spirits has been expressed only in terms of percentage volume of alcohol at 68° F. Absolute or "100 percent volume" alcohol was formerly expressed as 75.35° over proof, or 75.35° OP. In the USA proof is double the actual percentage of alcohol by volume at 60° F, so that absolute alcohol is 200 percent proof spirit. "Hangovers" are said to be aggravated by the presence of such toxic congenerics as amyl alcohol ($C_5H_{11}OH$).

Beer Strongest Roger & Out, brewed at the Frog & Parrot in Sheffield, Great Britain, from a recipe devised by W.R. Nowill and G.B. Spencer, has an alcohol volume of 16.9 percent. It was first brewed in July 1985 and has been selling ever since.

The strongest lager is Samichlaus Dark 1987, brewed by Brauerei Hürlimann of Zürich, Switzerland. It is 14.93 percent alcohol by volume at 68°F.

Bottles Largest A bottle 6 ft 11 in tall and 5 ft 4½ in in circumference was displayed at the Laidley Tourist Festival, Laidley, Queensland, Australia on 2 Sep 1989. The bottle was filled with 92 gal of Laidley Gold, a wheat beer only available in Laidley.

The largest bottles normally used in the wine and spirit trade are the Jeroboam (equal to 4 bottles of champagne or, rarely, of brandy, and from 5–6½ bottles of claret according to whether blown or molded) and the double magnum (equal, since c. 1934, to 4 bottles of claret or, more rarely, red Burgundy). A complete set of champagne bottles would consist of a quarter bottle, through a half bottle, bottle, magnum, Jeroboam, Rehoboam, Methuselah, Salmanazar and Balthazar, to the Nebuchadnezzar, which has a capacity of 28.14 pt, and is equivalent to 20 bottles.

A bottle containing 33.7 liters of Château Lalande Sourbet 1985, equal in volume to almost 45 standard wine bottles, was auctioned on 10 Oct 1989 in Copenhagen, Denmark.

Martell Cognac is available in a range of 21 bottle sizes from 0.05 pt to 6.65 pt.

Smallest The smallest bottles of liquor now sold are of White Horse Scotch Whisky; they stand just over 2 in high and contain 22 minims. A mini case of 12 bottles costs about £7 ($12), and measures 2 1/16 × 1 7/8 × 1 5/16 in. The distributor is Cumbrae Supply Co., Linwood, Scotland.

Brewers The oldest brewery in the world is the Weihenstephan Brewery, Freising, near Munich, Germany, founded in A.D. 1040. Old Bushmills Distillery, County Antrim, Ireland, licensed in 1608, claims to have been in production in 1276.

The largest single brewing organization in the world is Anheuser-Busch Inc. of St Louis, MO, with 12 breweries in the United States. In 1990 the company sold 86.5 million barrels, the greatest annual volume ever produced by a brewing company. The company's St Louis plant covers 100 acres, and after the completion of current modernization projects in 1993, the plant will have an annual capacity of 416.6 million gallons.

The largest brewery on a single site is Coors Brewing Co. of Golden, CO, where 597.99 million gallons were produced in 1990.

Distillers The world's largest distilling company is the Seagram Co. Ltd, of

Canada, with sales in the year ending 31 Jan 1990 totaling $5.6 billion. The company employs about 17,600 people.

The largest blender and bottler of Scotch whiskey is United Distillers, the spirits company of Guinness plc, at their Shieldhall plant in Glasgow, Great Britain, which has the capacity to fill an estimated 144 million bottles of Scotch a year. This is equivalent to approximately 20 million gal, most of which is exported. The world's best-selling brands of Scotch and gin, Johnnie Walker Red Label and Gordon's, are both products of United Distillers.

Most alcoholic drinks During independence (1918–40) the Estonian Liquor Monopoly marketed 98 percent potato alcohol (196 proof US). In 31 states, Everclear, 190 proof or 95 percent volume alcohol, is marketed by the American Distilling Co. "primarily as a base for home-made cordials." The Royal New Zealand Navy still issues Navy rum at 4.5 Under Proof and is the only navy in the world that does so.

Spirits Most expensive The most expensive spirit is Springbank 1919 Malt Whisky, which is sold at Harrods in London, Great Britain for £6,500 ($11,050; including tax) per bottle.

Vintners The world's oldest champagne firm is Ruinart Père et Fils, founded in 1729. The oldest cognac firm is Augier Frères & Cie, established in 1643.

Wine Oldest Evidence of wine dating from c. 3,500 B.C. was detected at Godin Tepe, Iran in early 1991. Excavations there revealed the remains of a Sumerian jar containing a large red stain. This was analyzed, and the results showed the presence of tartaric acid, a chemical naturally abundant in grapes.

The oldest bottle of wine to have been sold at auction was a bottle of 1648 Johannisberger, which was bought by Scharlachberg brandy distillery for 19,720 DM (including buyer's premium) through Weichmann auctioneers at Wiesbaden, Germany in December 1981. At the time the sum paid was equivalent to $7,000.

Most expensive £105,000 ($131,250) was paid for a bottle of 1787 Château Lafite claret, sold to Christopher Forbes (USA) at Christie's, London, Great Britain on 5 Dec 1985. The bottle was engraved with the initials of Thomas Jefferson (1743–1826), "Th J"—a factor that greatly affected the bidding. In November 1986 its cork, dried out by exhibition lights, slipped. Although the wine has not been tasted, it is assumed to be undrinkable as a result.

The record price for a half bottle of wine is Fr180,000 ($30,600), for a 1784 Château Margaux, also bearing the initials of Thomas Jefferson, which was sold by Christie's at Vinexpo in Bordeaux, France on 26 Jun 1987.

The record price for a glass of wine is Fr4,000 ($800), for the first glass of Beaujolais Nouveau 1990 released in

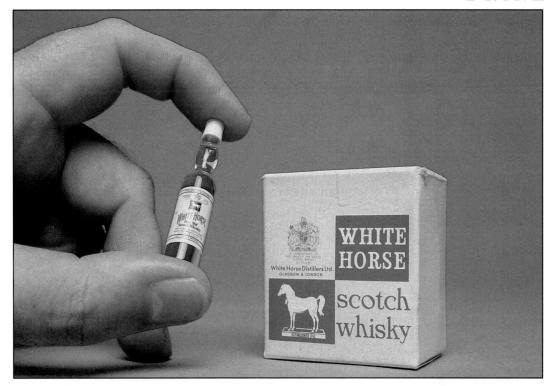

Beaune, in the wine region of Burgundy, France. It was bought by Bernard Repolt at Pickwick's, a British pub in Beaune, on 15 Nov 1990.

Auction The largest single sale of wine was conducted by Christie's of London, Great Britain on 10–11 Jul 1974 at Quaglino's Ballroom, London, when 2,325 lots comprising 432,000 bottles realized $2,400,000.

Soft drinks Pepsico of Purchase, NY topped the Fortune 500 list for beverage companies in April 1991, with total sales for 1990 of $17.8 billion, compared with $10.4 billion for the Coca-Cola Company of Atlanta, GA. Coca-Cola is, however, the world's most popular soft drink, with sales in 1990 of over 471 million drinks per day, representing an estimated 45 percent of the world market.

Mineral water The world's largest mineral water firm is Source Perrier, near Nîmes, France, with an annual production of more than 2.5 billion bottles, of which 1.1 billion now come from Perrier. The French drink about 152 pints of mineral water per person per year.

Manufactured Articles

So many articles are submitted to us as being of record interest for their size (either large or small) that we can rarely monitor and identify records individually.

Because of the infinite number of objects it is possible to collect, we can include only a small number of claims which reflect proven widespread interest. We are more likely to consider claims for items accumulated on a personal basis over a significant period of time, made

through appropriate organizations, established and recognized, as these are often better placed to comment authoritatively in record terms.

Amplifier The largest working guitar amplifier is 9.04 ft high, weighs 718 lb, and houses 32 10 in speakers driven by 600 watts of all tube power. However, it can handle 1,400 watts output. This Ampeg Mega SVT Bass Amp System was unveiled at the NAMM EXPO in Chicago, IL by St Louis Music of St Louis, MO.

Armor The highest auction price paid for a suit of armor was £1,925,000 ($3,657,000), by B.H. Trupin (USA) on 5 May 1983 at Sotheby's, London, Great Britain for a suit made in Milan by Giovanni Negroli in 1545 for Henri II of France. It came from the Hever Castle Collection in Kent, Great Britain.

■ **Smallest bottles**
The smallest bottles of liquor now sold are of White Horse Scotch Whisky; they stand just over 2 in high and contain 22 minims. A mini case of 12 bottles costs about £7 ($12), and measures $2^1/_{16} \times 1^7/_8 \times 1^5/_{16}$ in. (Photo: Guinness Publishing/Cumbrae Supply Company).

■ **Most expensive wine**
A bottle of 1787 Château Lafite claret was sold for £105,000 ($131,250) to Christopher Forbes (USA) at Christie's, London on 5 Dec 1985. The bottle was engraved with the initials of Thomas Jefferson (1743–1826)—"Th J"— a factor which greatly affected the bidding. (Photo: Christie's)

Wool blanket

The world's largest wool blanket was made by the people of Perth, Western Australia in a joint venture between the Living Stone Foundation Inc. and Radio 6PR. Comprising hand-knitted, machine-knitted and crocheted sections, it measured 27,976 ft² and was unveiled on 6 Aug 1989.

Bottle cap pyramid

A pyramid consisting of 263,810 bottle caps was constructed by 12 students of Nanyang Technological Institute, Singapore from 10–17 Jun 1990. Between 2 April and 10 May 1990, 16 members of the Belgian army based in Lüdenscheid, Germany constructed a hexagonal-based pyramid consisting of 276,681 crown caps.

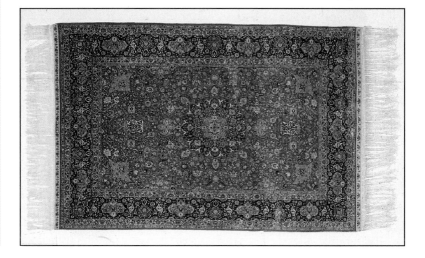

■ **Most finely woven carpet**
The "Hereke Treasure" carpet, made for Ozipek Halicilik A.S. of Hereke, Turkey and now owned by Gandhara Carpet Japan Co. Ltd of Tokyo, contains 3,716 strands per in² and was woven by five women over a period of five years. (Photo: Gandhara Carpet Japan Co. Ltd)

Basket The world's biggest basket is a hand-woven maple example made by the Longaberger Company of Dresden, OH in 1990, measuring 48 × 23 × 19 ft.

Beds In Bruges, Belgium, Philip, Duke of Burgundy had a bed 12½ ft × 19 ft erected for the perfunctory *coucher officiel* ceremony with Princess Isabella of Portugal in 1430.

A promotional 1½ ton 19 ft 8 in × 14 ft 5 in pinewood bed accommodating 39 people was exhibited by a French company in August 1986.

Beer cans Beer cans date from a test marketing by Krueger Beer of Newark, NJ, in Richmond, VA in 1935. The largest collection has been made by John F. Ahrens of Mount Laurel, NJ, with nearly 15,000 different cans. A Rosalie Pilsner can sold for $6,000 in the United States in April 1981. A collection of 2,502 unopened bottles and cans of beer from 103 countries was bought for A$25,000 by the Downer Club ACT of Australia at the Australian Associated Press Financial Markets Annual Charity Golf Tournament on 23 Mar 1990.

Beer labels (labology) Jan Solberg of Oslo, Norway has amassed 348,000 different labels from around the world to date.

Beer tankard The largest tankard was made by the Selangor Pewter Co. of Kuala Lumpur, Malaysia and unveiled on 30 Nov 1985. It measures 6½ ft in height and has a capacity of 615 gal.

Bottle caps Since 1950 Helge Friholm (b. 1909) of Søborg, Denmark has amassed 67,330 different bottle caps from 170 countries.

Bottle collections David L. Maund of Upham, Hampshire, Great Britain, has a collection of unduplicated miniature Scotch whiskey bottles amounting to 8,732 as of July 1990.

George E. Terren of Southboro, MA had a collection of 29,508 miniature and distilled spirit and liquor bottles on 1 Mar 1988. Ted Shuler of Germantown, TN has a collection of 2,401 different bottled beers, including specimens from 99 countries.

The world's biggest collection of whiskey bottles is one of 4,800 unduplicated, assembled by Signor Edward Giaccone at his *whiskeyteca*, Salo, Lake Garda, Italy. The largest reported collection of spirits and liqueurs is 2,890 unduplicated bottles collected by Ian Boasman at Bistro French, Preston, Lancashire, Great Britain by February 1990.

Bowl, wooden The largest one-piece wooden bowl was made by Dan Cunningham, David Tarleton and Scott Hare in Kamuela, HI in September 1990. The bowl, which took 2,978 man-hours to complete, was constructed of monkey-pod wood, stands 6 ft 7 in tall, and its widest diameter is 5 ft 9 ⅝ in with a circumference of 18 ft 1 in.

Candles A candle 80 ft high and 8½ ft in diameter was exhibited at the 1897 Stockholm Exhibition by the firm of Lindahls. Including the candlestick, the overall height was 127 ft.

A candle constructed by Enham Industries at the Charlton Leisure Center, Andover, Great Britain on 2 Jul 1989 measured 101.7 ft high.

Cards The world's largest greeting card was produced by seven members of Oceanway PTA, Jacksonville, FL. It measured 37 ft 3 in × 54 ft 9 in. It was delivered by the United States Postal Service to Oceanway Seventh Grade Center on 21 Apr 1989.

Carpets and rugs The earliest carpet known is a Seythian woolen pile-knotted carpet measuring 6 ft² and dating from the 4th–3rd centuries B.C. It was discovered by the Russian archaeologist Sergei Ivanovich Rudenko in 1947 in the Pazyryk Valley in southern Siberia and is now preserved in the Hermitage, Leningrad, USSR.

Of ancient carpets, the largest was a gold-enriched silk carpet of Hashim (dated A.D. 743) of the Abbasid caliphate in Baghdad, Iraq. It is reputed to have measured 180 × 300 ft. A 52,225 ft², 31.4 ton red carpet was laid on 13 Feb 1982, by the Allied Corporation, from Radio City Music Hall to the New York Hilton along the Avenue of the Americas, in New York City.

The most finely woven carpet known is one having 3,716 strands per in², selected from 3,000 weaving specialists, for Ozipek Halicilik A.S. of Hereke, Turkey. The project took five years to complete and the finished product, named *Hereke Treasure*, was sold to Gandhara Carpet Japan Co. Ltd, Tokyo in March 1988. The most magnificent carpet ever made was the Spring carpet of Khusraw made for the audience hall of the Sassanian palace at Ctesiphon, Iraq. It was about 7,000 ft² of silk and gold thread, and was encrusted with emeralds. It was cut up as booty by looters in A.D. 635 and from the known realization value of the pieces must have had an original value of some $170 million.

Chair An enlarged version, 53 ft 4 in tall, of the chair George Washington sat in while presiding at the Constitutional Convention was made by the NSA and brought to Washington, D.C. for the 1989 inauguration.

Chandeliers The world's largest set of chandeliers was created by the Kookje Lighting Co. Ltd of Seoul, Korea. It is 39 ft high, weighs 11.8 tons and has 700 bulbs. Completed in November 1988, it occupies three floors of the Lotte Chamshil Department Store in Seoul.

Check The world's largest check was made by the Christmas Cracker project and measured 52½ × 26 ft. The £50 ($85) check, representing "One million hours of time and energy," was presented in London, Great Britain on 28 Sep 1990.

Cigarettes World production in 1985 was 9.8 trillion cigarettes. The people of China were estimated to have consumed 1576 billion cigarettes in 1989. In Senegal 80 percent of urban males smoke.

The longest cigarettes ever marketed were *Head Plays*, each 11 in long and sold in packets of five in the United States in about 1930, to save tax. The shortest were *Lilliput* cigarettes, each 1¼ in long and ⅛ in in diameter, made in Great Britain in 1956.

The world's largest collection of cigarettes is that of Robert E. Kaufman, of New York. To date he has 8,390 different cigarettes made in 173 countries and territories. The oldest brand represented is *Lone Jack*, made in the USA c. 1885. Both the longest and shortest (see above) are represented. In the Philippines there is a brand with 1.1 grain nicotine per cigarette.

Cigarette cards The earliest known tobacco card is "Vanity Fair" dated 1876, issued by Wm S. Kimball & Co., Rochester, NY. The earliest British example appeared c. 1883 in the form of a calendar issued by Allen & Ginter, of Richmond, VA, trading from Holborn Viaduct, City of London, Great Britain. The largest-known collection is that of Mr Edward Wharton-Tigar (b. 1913) of London, Great Britain with more than 1 million cigarette and trade cards in about 45,000 sets. This collection has been accepted as a bequest by the British Museum, where it will eventually be available for public study.

Cigars The largest cigar ever made measures 16 ft 8½ in in length and weighs 577 lb 9 oz. It took 243 hours to make and used 3,330 full tobacco leaves. It was made by Tinus Vinke and Jan Weijmer in February 1983 and is in the Tobacco Museum in Kampen, Netherlands.

The largest marketed cigar in the world is the 14 in Valdez Emperador manufactured by Fábrica de Puros Santa Clara of San Andrés Tuxtla, Veracruz, Mexico and exclusively distributed by Tabacos San Andrés.

Coasters (Tegestology) The world's largest collection of coasters is owned by Leo Pisker of Vienna, Austria, who has collected 135,480 different coasters from 154 countries to date.

Credit cards The largest collection of valid credit cards to date is one of 1,265 (all different) by Walter Cavanagh (b. 1943) of Santa Clara, CA. The cost of acquisition to "Mr Plastic Fantastic" was zero, and he keeps them in the world's longest wallet—250 ft long, weighing 35 lb and worth more than $1.6 million in credit.

Doll, rag The largest rag doll in the United States is one 41 ft 11 in in total length, created by Apryl Scott at Autoworld in Flint, MI on 20 Nov 1990.

Dress A wedding outfit created by Helene Gainville with jewels by Alexander Reza is believed to be worth $7,301,587.20 precisely. The dress is embroidered with diamonds mounted on platinum and was unveiled in Paris, France on 23 Mar 1989. A robe for Emperor Field Marshal Jean-Bédel Bokassa with a 39 ft long train and encrusted with 785,000 pearls and 1,220,000 crystal beads was made by Guiselin of Paris, France for $135,000. It was for his coronation at Bangui, Central African Empire (now Republic) on 4 Dec 1977 (see also Shoes).

The world's longest wedding dress train measured 171 ft 3 in and was made by Agnès Remaud of La Roche-sur-Yon, France in 1990.

Egg The largest and most elaborate jeweled egg stands 2 ft tall and was fashioned from 37 lb of gold studded with 20,000 pink diamonds. Designed by British jeweler Paul Kutchinsky, the Argyle Library Egg took six British craftsmen 7,000 hours to create and has a price tag of £7 million ($12 million). It was unveiled on 30 Apr 1990 before going on display at the Victoria and Albert Museum, London, Great Britain.

Fabrics The oldest surviving fabric discovered from Level VI A at Çatal Hüyük, Turkey has been radiocarbon dated to 5900 B.C. The most expensive fabric is Vicuña cloth manufactured by Fujii Keori Ltd of Osaka, Japan, retailing at 1 million yen ($7,600) per meter in January 1988.

The finest denier nylon yarn ever produced is the 5 denier produced by Nilit Ltd of Tel Aviv, Israel and used by Pretty Polly for women's hosiery in Great Britain. The sheerest stockings normally available are 9 denier. A hair from the average human head is about 50 denier.

Fan An intricately carved wooden fan measuring 10.9 ft when unfolded and 6 ft high was completed by Wang Xianbao of Shanghai, China in January 1987.

Fireworks The largest firework ever produced was Universe I Part II, exploded for the Lake Toya Festival, Hokkaidō, Japan on 15 Jul 1988. The 1,543 lb shell was 1354.7 in in diameter and burst to a diameter of 3,937 ft.

The longest firecracker display was produced by the Johor Tourism Department, the United Malaysian Youth Movement and Mr Yap Seng Hock, and took place on 20 Feb 1988 at Pelangi Garden, Johor Bahru, Johor, Malaysia. The total length of the display was 18,777 ft and consisted of 3,338,777 firecrackers and 1,468 lb of gunpowder. It burned for 9 hr 27 min.

Flags The oldest known flag is one dated to c. 3000 B.C. found in 1972 at Khabis, Iran. It is of metal and measures 9 × 9 in and depicts an eagle, two lions and a goddess, three women and a bull.

The largest flag in the world, one of the Republic of China presented to the city of Kaohsiung, Taiwan by Unichamps Inpe'l Corp. on 9 Apr 1989, measured 413 × 275½ ft and weighed 1,807.7 lb. The largest flag *flown* from a flagpole is a Brazilian national flag measuring 229 ft 8 in × 328 ft 1 in in Brasilia.

Float The largest float was the 155 ft long, 24 ft wide "Merry Christmas America" float bearing three double arches, a 17-ft Christmas tree, two 15-ft peppermint candy sticks and 5,380 ft² of wrapping paper, used at the 40th Annual Christmas Parade, Baton Rouge, LA on 5 Dec 1986.

Glass The most priceless example of the art of glassmaking is usually regarded as the glass Portland Vase, which dates from late in the first century B.C. or first century A.D. It was made in Italy, and was in the possession of the Barberini family in Rome from at least 1642. It was eventually bought by the Duchess of Portland in 1792 but was smashed while in the British Museum by William Lloyd on 7 Feb 1845.

The thinnest glass, type D263, has a minimum thickness of 0.00137 in and a maximum thickness of 0.0021 in. It is made by Deutsche Spezialglas AG, Grünenplan, Germany for use in electronic and medical equipment.

Gold The gold coffin of the 14th-century B.C. Pharaoh Tutankhamun, discovered by Howard Carter on 16 Feb 1923 in the Valley of the Kings, western Thebes, Egypt, weighed 243 lb.

Hammock A 145½ ft long hammock was woven by members of the Åboland Crafts Guild, Pargas, Finland in July 1988. The completed hammock was suspended between large oak trees and accommodated 21 people.

Jigsaw puzzles The earliest jigsaws were made as "dissected maps" by John Spilsbury (1739–69) in Russell Court off Drury Lane, London, Great Britain c. 1762.

The world's largest jigsaw puzzle measures 9,905.5 ft² and consists of 187,220 pieces. It was made by Robert Longstaff Workshops of Longworth, Oxfordshire, Great Britain for the Family Heart Association and was assembled on 22–26 Oct 1990 at Harrow Leisure Center, London, Great Britain.

Most expensive Custom-made Stave puzzles made by Steve Richardson of Norwich, VT of 2,640 pieces cost $8,680 in March 1991.

Kettle The largest antique copper kettle was one standing 3 ft high with a 6 ft girth and a 20 gal capacity, built in Taunton, Somerset, Great Britain, for the hardware merchants Fisher and Son c. 1800.

■ Longest wedding dress train
This train, measuring 171 ft 3 in, was created by Agnès Remaud of La Roche-sur-Yon, France in 1990. (Photo: Gamma/Charneau)

Scarf
The longest scarf ever knitted measured an amazing 20 miles 13 ft long. It was knitted by residents of Abbeyfield Houses for the Abbeyfield Society in Great Britain and was completed on 29 May 1988.

Can construction
A stadium-shaped structure consisting of 2 million empty beverage cans was built in Verona, Italy by 150 members of AVIS–AIDO with the cooperation of Rail (producers of aluminum cans). It was completed on 1 Dec 1989 after 18,000 hours of work.

Greeting cards
Craig Shergold of Carshalton, Great Britain was reported to have collected a record 33 million get-well cards by May 1991. Jarrod Booth of Salt Spring Island, British Columbia, Canada had a collection of 205,120 Christmas cards in February 1990.

■ Largest jeweled egg
Revealed here (left) are some of the inner chambers and the gear mechanism of the magnificent Paul Kutchinsky Argyle Library Egg, which took 7,000 hours to create and is valued at $11.9 million. (Photo: The Rowland Company/Gamma/Wada).

MANUFACTURED ARTICLES

Matchbox labels
The oldest matchbox label of accepted provenance is that of Samuel Jones c. 1830. The finest collection of trademark matchbox labels (excluding any pub/bar or other advertising labels) is some 280,000 pieces collected by the phillumenist Robert Jones of Indianapolis, IN. Teiichi Yoshizawa (b. 1904) of Chiba-Ken, Japan has amassed 712,118 matchbox labels (including advertising labels) from 150 countries since 1925.

Paper clip
An iron paper clip measuring 23 ft and weighing 1,328 lb was made by O. Mustad & Son of Norway and unveiled at the Norwegian School of Management in Sandvika in honor of Johan Valer, pioneer of the paper clip, in 1989.

Quilt
The world's largest quilt was made by 7,000 citizens of North Dakota for the 1989 centennial of North Dakota. It measured 85 × 134 ft.

Stuffed toy, longest
A snake measuring 274 ft and weighing 154.3 lb was made in a total of 60 hours by members of Brettell Lane Day Center, Amblecote, West Midlands, Great Britain in February 1990.

Knife
The penknife with the greatest number of blades is the Year Knife made by cutlers Joseph Rodgers & Sons, of Sheffield, Great Britain, whose trademark was granted in 1682. The knife was made in 1822 with 1,822 blades, and a blade was added every year until 1973 when there was no further space. It was acquired by Britain's largest hand tool manufacturers, Stanley Works (Great Britain) Ltd of Sheffield, Great Britain, in 1970.

Lantern
A 12 ft 1¾ in high lantern with a 39 ft 4 in circumference was made on 29 Apr 1989 by members of the Lotus Lantern International Buddhist Center and staff of the Seoul Hilton International Hotel, South Korea.

Lego tower
The tallest Lego tower, 59½ ft, was built in Tel Aviv, Israel in May 1990 and consisted of 221,560 bricks.

Matchstick
The longest matchstick, made by Stichting "De Langste Daag" at Tegelen, Netherlands on 25 Jun 1988, measured 61 ft 8 in, weighed 2,204 lb and burned for 6 hr 45 min 1 sec.

Needles
Needles made of bone have been found in sites of the Upper Paleolithic Aurignacian period in France dated c. 28,000–24,000 B.C. The longest is one 6 ft 1 in long made by George Davies of Thomas Somerfield, Bloxwich, Great Britain for stitching on mattress buttons lengthwise. One is preserved in the National Needle Museum at Forge Mill, Great Britain.

Pens
The most expensive writing pen is the 5003.002 Caran D'Ache 18-carat solid gold Madison slimline ballpoint pen incorporating white diamonds of 6.35 carats, exclusively distributed by Jakar International Ltd of London, Great Britain. Its recommended retail price, including tax, in 1992 is £23,950 ($40,545).

A Japanese collector paid 1.3 million French francs in Feb 1988 for the "Anémone" fountain pen made by Réden, France. It was encrusted with 600 precious stones, including emeralds, amethysts, rubies, sapphires and onyx, and took skilled craftsmen over a year to complete.

Photographs with stars
Barbara Ann Thomas of Fredericksburg, VA has photos of herself taken with 206 Hollywood stars. Husband John acts as photographer while they vacation at film locations in Hollywood, CA.

Pistols
In Dec 1983 it was reported that Ray Bily (USA) owned an initialed gold pistol made for Adolf Hitler that was valued for insurance at $375,000. The pistol with the largest magazine capacity is the .22LR M.100P with 103 rounds of continuous firepower, manufactured by Calico, Bakersfield, CA.

Postcards
Deltiology—postcard collecting—is claimed to be the third largest collecting hobby, after stamps and coins. Austria issued the first postcards in 1869, followed by Britain in 1872. The highest price paid for a postcard was $4,400 for one of the five known Mucha Waverly Cycle postcards. It was sold by Susan Brown Nicholson of Lisle, IL in September 1984.

Pottery
The largest vase on record is one 11 ft high, weighing 3,968 lb, thrown by Aksel Krog and Jorgen Hansen of Denmark on 10–13 Feb 1989. The Chinese ceramic authority Ching-wah Lee of San Francisco, CA was reported in August 1978 to have appraised a unique 39 in Kang Hxi four-sided vase then in a bank vault in Phoenix, AZ at $60 million.

Shoes
James Smith, founder of James Southall & Co. of Norwich, Great Britain, introduced sized shoes in 1792. The firm began making "Startrite" children's shoes in 1923.

Emperor Bokassa of the Central African Empire (now Republic) commissioned pearl-studded shoes from the House of Berluti, Paris, France for his self-coronation on 4 Dec 1977 at a cost of $85,000.

The most expensive shoes are mink-lined golf shoes with 18-carat gold embellishments and ruby-tipped spikes made by Stylo Matchmakers International of Northampton, Great Britain, which retail for $18,500 per pair.

A pair of women's cream kid and braid high-heeled slap-soled shoes c. 1660 was sold by Lord Hereford at Sotheby's, London, Great Britain in September 1987 to Mrs Sonia Bata for £21,000 ($33,600). An export license was reportedly refused on 20 Jun 1988.

Excluding cases of elephantiasis, the largest shoes ever sold are a pair size 42 built for the giant Harley Davidson of Avon Park, FL. The normal limit is size 14. For advertising and display purposes, facsimiles of shoes weighing up to 1.6 tons have been constructed.

Silver
The largest single pieces of silver are a pair of water jugs of 10,408 troy oz (4.77 cwt) made in 1902 for the Maharaja of Jaipur (1861–1922). They are 5 ft 3 in tall, with a circumference of 8 ft 1½ in, and have a capacity of 1,800 gallons. They are now in the City Palace, Jaipur, India. The silversmith was Gorind Narain.

Sofa
The longest standard sofa manufactured is the Augustus Rex Sofa, 12¼ ft in length, made by Dodge & Son of Sherborne, Great Britain.

In April 1990 a 21 ft 9 in long jacquard fabric sofa was specially manufactured by Mountain View Interiors of Collingwood, Ontario, Canada with an estimated value of $8,000.

Suit
EVA suits for extravehicular activity worn by space shuttle crews since 1982 have a unit cost of $3.4 million.

Table
The longest table was set up in Pesaro, Italy on 20 Jun 1988 by the US Libertas Scavolini Basketball team. It was 10,072 ft in length and was used to seat 12,000 people.

Tablecloth
The world's largest tablecloth is 1,502 ft long, 4½ ft wide and was made by the Sportex division of Artex International in Highland, IL on 17 Oct 1990.

Tapestry
The earliest-known examples of tapestry woven linen are three pieces from the tomb of the Egyptian pharaoh Thutmose IV dated to 1483–1411 B.C.

The largest tapestry ever woven is the *History of Irak*, with an area of 13,370.7 ft². It was designed by the Yugoslavian artist Frane Delale and produced by the Zivtex Regeneracija Workshop in Zabok, Yugoslavia. The tapestry was completed in 1986 and it now adorns the wall of an amphitheater in Baghdad, Iraq.

The famous Bayeux *Telle du Conquest, dite tapisserie de la reine Mathilde*, a hanging tapestry 19½ in × 23 ft, depicts events of 1064–66 in 72 scenes and was probably worked in Canterbury, Great Britain, c. 1086. It was "lost" for 2½ centuries from 1476 until 1724.

The Overlord Embroidery of 34 panels each 8 × 3 ft, commissioned by Lord Dulverton (b. 1915) from the Royal School of Needlework in London, Great Britain, was completed in 1979 after 100 person-years of work and is 41 ft longer than the Bayeux. It has the largest area of any embroidery, 816 ft².

Tartan
The earliest evidence of tartans is the so-called Falkirk tartan, found stuffed in a jar of coins in Bells Meadow, Scotland. It is of a dark and light brown pattern and dates from c. A.D. 245. The earliest reference to a specific named tartan is to a Murray tartan in 1618, although Mackay tartan was probably worn earlier. There are 2,179 tartans known to The Tartans Museum at the headquarters of the Scottish Tartans Society in Comrie, Perth, Tayside, Great Britain. HRH Prince of Wales is eligible to wear 11, including the Balmoral, which has been exclusive to the British royal family since 1852.

Time capsule
The world's largest time capsule is the Tropico Time Tunnel of 10,000 ft³ in a cave in Rosamond, CA, sealed by the Kern Antelope Historical Society on 20 Nov 1966 and intended for opening in A.D. 2866.

Wallet
The most expensive wallet ever made is a platinum-cornered, diamond-studded crocodile creation made by Louis Quatorze of Paris, France and Mikimoto of Tokyo, selling in September 1984 for $84,000.

Wreath
The most expensive wreath on record was that presented to Sri Chinmoy in New York on 11 Jul 1983 by Ashrita Furman and Pahar Meltzer. It was handled by the Garland of Divinity's Love Florist, contained 10,000 flowers, and cost $3,500.

Zipper
The world's longest zipper was laid around the center of Sneek, Netherlands on 5 Sep 1989. The brass zipper, made by Yoshida (Netherlands) Ltd, is 9,353.56 ft long and consists of 2,565,900 teeth.

Sports
and Games

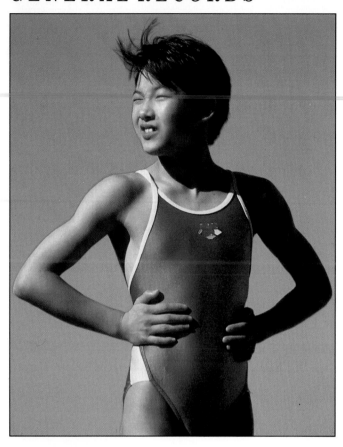

General Records

Origins Sport stems from the time when self-preservation ceased to be the all-consuming human preoccupation. Archery, although a hunting skill in Mesolithic times (by c. 8000 B.C.), did not become an organized sport until later—possibly as early as c. 1150 B.C., since an archery competition is described in Homer's *Iliad*, and certainly by c. A.D. 300, among the Genoese. The earliest dated evidence for any sport is c. 2750–2600 B.C. for wrestling. Ball games played by girls, depicted on Middle Kingdom murals at Beni Hasan, Egypt, have been dated to c. 2050 B.C.

Fastest The fastest speed reached in a nonmechanical sport is in skydiving, in which a speed of 185 mph is attained in a head-down free-falling position, even in the lower atmosphere. In delayed drops, speeds of 625 mph have been recorded at high, rarefied altitudes.

The fastest projectile speed in any moving ball game is c. 188 mph, in jai alai. This compares with 170 mph (electonically timed) for a golf ball driven off a tee.

Largest playing field The largest playing field for any ball game is 12.4 acres for polo, or a maximum length of 900 ft and a width, without sideboards, of 600 ft. With boards the width is 480 ft.

Twice a year in the Parish of St Columb Major, Cornwall, Great Britain, a game called hurling (not to be confused with the Irish game) is played on a "pitch," which consists of the entire parish—approximately 25 square miles.

World record breakers *Youngest* The youngest age at which anybody has broken a nonmechanical world record is 12 yr 298 days for Gertrude Caroline Ederle (USA; b. 23 Oct 1906), with 13 min 19.0 sec for women's 880 yd freestyle swimming, at Indianapolis, IN on 17 Aug 1919.

Oldest Gerhard Weidner (Germany; b. 15 Mar 1933) set a 20-mile walk record on 25 May 1974, at age 41 yr 71 days, the oldest to set an official world record recognized by an international governing body. Lee Chin-yong (South Korea; b. 15 Aug 1925) was 62 yr

273 days when he broke the consecutive chins record on 14 May 1988.

Most prolific Between 24 Jan 1970 and 1 Nov 1977, Vasiliy Alekseiev (USSR; b. 7 Jan 1942) broke 80 official world records in weightlifting.

Champion *Youngest* The youngest successful competitor in a world title event was a French boy, whose name is not recorded, who coxed the Netherlands' Olympic pair at Paris, France on 26 Aug 1900. He was not more than ten and may have been as young as seven.

Fu Mingxia (China) won the women's world title for platform diving at Perth, Australia on 4 Jan 1991, at the age of 12.

The youngest individual Olympic winner was Marjorie Gestring (USA; b. 18 Nov 1922), who took the springboard diving title at the age of 13 yr 268 days at the Olympic Games in Berlin, Germany on 12 Aug 1936.

Oldest Fred Davis (b. 14 Feb 1913) won (and retained) the world professional billiards title in 1980, at age 67.

Youngest international The youngest age at which any person has won international honors is eight in the case of Joy Foster, the Jamaican singles and mixed doubles table tennis champion, in 1958.

Oldest competitor at major games William Edward Pattimore (b. 1 Mar 1892) competed for Wales at bowls (lawn bowling) at the 1970 Commonwealth Games in Edinburgh, Great Britain at the age of 78, the oldest competitor at such an international event open to competitors of all ages.

Most versatile Charlotte "Lottie" Dod (1871–1960) won the Wimbledon singles tennis title five times between 1887 and 1893, the British Ladies' Golf Championship in 1904, an Olympic silver medal for archery in 1908, and represented England at field hockey in 1899.

Mildred "Babe" Zaharias (nee Didrikson; 1914–56) won two gold medals (80 meter hurdles and javelin) and a silver (high jump) at the 1932 Olympic Games. She set world records in those three events in 1930–32. She was an All-American basketball player for three years and set the world record for throwing a baseball—296 ft. Switching to golf, she won the US Women's Amateur title in 1946 and the US Women's Open in 1948, 1950 and 1954.

Charles Burgess Fry (Great Britain; 1872–1956) was perhaps the most versatile male sportsman at the highest level. On 4 Mar 1893 he equaled the world long jump record of 23 ft 6½ in. He represented England v. Ireland at soccer (1901) and played first class rugby for the Barbarians. His greatest achievements, however, were at cricket, where he headed the English batting averages in six seasons and captained England in 1912.

All-Star game selection Bo Jackson is believed to be the only athlete selected to the All-Star games in two professional sports. He was the MVP of the All-Star game (baseball), on 11 Jul 1989 at Anaheim, CA. Jackson played for the American League and hit a home run and had 2 RBI's. He was selected for the 1990 NFL Pro Bowl as a running-back for the AFC team. However, due to injury, he was unable to participate in the game played 3 Feb 1991 in Hawaii.

Longest reign Jacques Edmond Barre (France; 1802–73) was a world champion for 33 years (1829–62) at court tennis.

Largest contract In March 1990, the National Football League concluded a deal worth $3.64 billion for four years' coverage by the five major TV and cable networks—ABC, CBS, NBC, ESPN and TBS. This represented $26.1 million for each league team in the first year, escalating to $39.1 million in the fourth.

Largest crowd The greatest number of live spectators for any one-day sporting spectacle is the estimated 2.5 million who have lined the route of the New York City Marathon. However, spread over three weeks, it is estimated that more than 10 million see the annual Tour de France cycling race.

Olympic The total attendance at the 1984 Summer Games held at Los Angeles, CA, was given as 5,797,923 for all sports, including 1,421,627 for soccer and 1,129,465 for track and field events.

Single sporting venue More than 400,000 travel to the annual Grand Prix d'Endurance (Le Mans 24 hours) auto race on the Sarthe circuit near Le Mans, France.

Stadium A crowd of 199,854 attended the Brazil v Uruguay soccer match, in the Maracaña Municipal Stadium, Rio de Janeiro, Brazil on 16 Jul 1950.

Most participants On 15 May 1988 an estimated 110,000 (including unregistered athletes) ran in the *Examiner* Bay to Breakers 7.6-mile race in San Francisco, CA.

The 1988 Women's International Bowling Congress (WIBC) Championship tournament attracted 77,735 bowlers for the 96-day event held 31 March–4 July at Reno/Carson City, NV.

Worst disasters The stands at the Hong Kong Jockey Club racetrack collapsed and caught fire on 26 Feb 1918, killing an estimated 604 people.

During the reign of Antoninus Pius (A.D. 138–161), 1,112 spectators were killed when the upper wooden tiers in the Circus Maximus, Rome collapsed during a gladiatorial combat.

Aerobatics

Origins The first aerobatic "maneuver" is generally considered to be the sustained inverted flight in a Bleriot

flown by Célestin-Adolphe Pégoud (1889–1915), at Buc, France on 21 Sep 1913, but Lt Capt. Petr Nikolayevich Nesterov (1887–1914), of the Imperial Russian Air Service, performed a loop in a Nieuport Type IV monoplane at Kiev, USSR on 27 Aug 1913.

World Championships In this competition, held biennially since 1960 (except 1974), scoring is based on a system originally devised by Col. José Aresti of Spain. The competition consists of two compulsory and a free program.

The USSR has won the men's team competition a record six times.

Petr Jirmus (Czechoslovakia) is the only man to become world champion twice, in 1984 and 1986.

Betty Stewart (USA) won the women's competition in 1980 and 1982.

Lyubov Nemkova (USSR) won a record five medals: first in 1986, second in 1982 and 1984, and third in 1976 and 1978. The oldest-ever world champion has been Henry Haigh (USA; b. 12 Dec 1924), age 63 in 1988.

Inverted flight The duration record is 4 hr 9 min 5 sec by John "Hal" McClain in a Swick Taylorcraft on 23 Aug 1980 over Houston International Raceways, TX.

Loops On 21 Jun 1980, R. Steven Powell performed 2,315⅝ inside loops in a Bellanca Decathlon over Almont, MI. Joann Osterud achieved 208 outside loops in a "Supernova" Hyperbipe over North Bend, OR on 13 Jul 1989.

Archery

Origins Though the earliest pictorial evidence of the existence of bows is seen in Mesolithic cave paintings in Spain, archery as an organized sport appears to have developed in the third century A.D. Competitive archery may, however, date back to the 12th century B.C. The National Archery Association of America was established in 1879. The inaugural National Outdoor Target Championship was held in 1884. The world governing body is the *Fédération Internationàle de Tir à l'Arc* (FITA), founded in 1931.

Highest championship scores The highest scores achieved in either a world or Olympic championship for Double FITA rounds are: men, 2,617 points (possible 2,880) by Darrell Owen Pace (USA; b. 23 Oct 1956) and Richard Lee McKinney (USA; b. 20 Oct 1963) at Long Beach, CA on 21–22 Oct 1983; and for women, 2,683 points by Kim Soo-nyung (South Korea; b. 5 Apr 1971) at Seoul, South Korea on 27–30 Sep 1988.

World Championships The most titles won by a man is four by Hans Deutgen (Sweden; 1917–89) in 1947–50 and by a woman is seven by Janina Spychajowa-Kurkowska (Poland; b. 8

World Archery Records			Single FITA rounds	
Event	Points	Name and Country	Possible Score	Year
MEN				
FITA	1,352	Vladimir Yesheyev (USSR)	1,440	1990
90 m	330	Vladimir Yesheyev (USSR)	360	1990
70 m	344	Hiroshi Yamamoto (Japan)	360	1990
50 m	345	Richard McKinney (USA)	360	1982
30 m	357	Takayoshi Matsushita (Japan)	360	1986
Final	345	Vladimir Esheev (USSR)	360	1989
Team	3,963	USSR (Stanislav Zabrodskiy, Vadim Shikarev, Vladimir Yesheyev)	4,320	1989
Final	1,005	South Korea (Sun-Bin Kin, Chang-Hoon Yang, Jae-Pyo Park)	1,080	1990
WOMEN				
FITA	1,370	Lee Eun-Kyung (South Korea)	1,440	1990
70 m	341*	Kim Soo-nyung (South Korea)	360	1989
60 m	347	Kim Soo-nyung (South Korea)	360	1989
50 m	337	Lee Eun-Kyung (South Korea)	360	1990
30 m	357	Joanne Edens (Great Britain)	360	1990
Final	346	Kim Soo-nyung (South Korea)	360	1990
Team	4,025	South Korea (Kim Soo-nyung, Wang Hee-nyung, Kim Kyung-wook)	4,320	1989
Final	1,010	South Korea (Kim Soo-nyung, Wang Hee-nyung, Kim Kyung-wook)	4,320	1989

* unofficial

Indoor Double FITA rounds at 25 meters

MEN	591	Erwin Verstegen (Netherlands)	600	1989
WOMEN	592	Petra Ericsson (Sweden)	600	1990

Indoor FITA rounds at 18 meters

MEN	591	Vladimir Yesheyev (USSR)	600	1989
WOMEN	587	Denise Parker (USA)	600	1989

FLIGHT SHOOTING

CROSSBOW: 2,047 yd 2 in, Harry Drake (USA; b. 7 May 1915), "Smith Creek" Flight Range near Austin, NV, 30 Jul 1988.
UNLIMITED FOOTBOW: 1 mile 268 yd, Harry Drake, Ivanpah Dry Lake, CA, 24 Oct 1971.
RECURVE BOW: Men: 1,336 yd 1 ft 3 in, Don Brown (USA), "Smith Creek" Flight Range, 2 Aug 1987. Women: 1,039 yd 1 ft 1 in, April Moon (USA), Wendover, UT, 13 Sep 1981.
CONVENTIONAL FOOTBOW: Men: 1,542 yd 2 ft 10 in, Harry Drake, Ivanpah Dry Lake, 6 Oct 1979. Women: 1,113 yd 2 ft 6 in, Arlyne Rhode (USA; b. 4 May 1936), Wendover, UT, 10 Sep 1978.
COMPOUND BOW: Men: 1,159 yd 2 ft 6 in, Bert McCune, Jr. (USA), "Smith Creek" Flight Range, 2 Aug 1987. Women: (25 kg) 904 yd 4 in, April Moon, "Smith Creek" Flight Range, 5 Oct 1989.
BROADHEAD FLIGHT BOWS: Unlimited Compound Bow: Men: 742 yd 2 in, Jesse Morehead (USA), Wendover, UT, 24 Jun 1990. Women: 481 yd 4 in, April Moon, Salt Lake City, 29 Jun 1989.

Feb 1901) in 1931–34, 1936, 1939 and 1947. The USA has a record 14 men's and eight women's team titles.

Oscar Kessels (Belgium; 1904–68) participated in 21 world championships.

The most individual world titles by a US archer is three, by Richard McKinney: 1977, 1983 and 1985. Jean Lee, 1950 and 1952, is the only US woman to have won two individual world titles. Luann Ryon (b. 13 Jan 1953) was Olympic women's

Slowest
In wrestling, before the rules were modified to favor "brighter wrestling," contestants could be locked in holds for so long that a single bout once lasted for 11 hr 40 min.

In the extreme case of the 2 hr 41 min pull in the regimental tug o' war in Jubbulpore, India, on 12 Aug 1889, the winning team moved a net distance of 12 ft at an average speed of 0.00084 mph.

Heaviest sportsman
Professional wrestler William J. Cobb of Macon, GA, who in 1962 was billed as "Happy Humphrey," weighed 802 lb.

The heaviest player of any ball game was Bob Pointer, the 487-lb football tackle formerly on the 1967 Santa Barbara High School team, CA.

**■ Highest
championship score at
archery**
*The highest score
achieved in either a
World or Olympic cham-
pionship for men's
Double FITA rounds is
2,617 points (out of a
possible 2,880) by Darrell
Owen Pace (USA; b. 23
Oct 1956) at Long Beach,
CA on 21–22 Oct 1983.*

Greatest draw
on a longbow
Gary Sentmam, of Rose-
berg, OR drew a long-
bow weighing a record
176 lb to the maximum
draw on the arrow of
28¼ in at Forksville,
PA on 20 Sep 1975.

---

champion in 1976 and also world champion in 1977.

Olympic Games Hubert van Innis
(Belgium; 1866–1961) won six gold and
three silver medals at the 1900 and 1920
Olympic Games.

The most successful US archer at the
Olympic Games has been Darrell Pace,
gold medalist in 1976 and 1984. He was
also world champion in 1975 and 1979.

US championships The most US
archery titles won is 17, by Lida Howell
(nee Scott; 1859–1939), from 20 contested between 1883 and 1907. She won
three Olympic gold medals in 1904, for
Double National and Double Columbia
rounds and for the US team.

The most men's titles is nine (three
individual, six pairs), by Richard McKinney, 1977, 1979–83, 1985–87. The greatest
span of title winning is 29 years, by
William Henry Thompson (1848–1918),
who was the first US champion in 1879,

and won his fifth and last men's title in
1908.

*Twenty-four   hours—target
archery* The highest recorded score
over 24 hours by a pair of archers is
76,158 during 70 Portsmouth Rounds (60
arrows per round at 20 yd at 2 ft FITA
targets) by Simon Tarplee and David
Hathaway at Evesham, Great Britain on
1 Apr 1991. During this attempt Simon
Tarplee set an individual record
of 38,500.

Auto racing

Origins There are various conflicting
claims, but the first automobile race was
the 201-mile Green Bay to Madison, WI
run in 1878, won by an Oshkosh steamer.
In 1887 Count Jules Félix Philippe
Albert   de   Dion   de   Malfiancé
(1856–1946) won the *La Vélocipéde* 19.3

INDY 500 Career Miles

Driver	Races	Miles
A.J. Foyt, Jr.	34	11,785.5
Al Unser	25	9,892.5
Gordon Johncock	23	7,745.0
Johnny Rutherford	24	6,980.0
Mario Andretti	26	6,872.5

LAP LEADERS

Driver	Laps
Al Unser	625
Ralph DePalma	613
A. J. Foyt, Jr.	555
Wilbur Shaw	508
Parnelli Jones	492

TOP MONEY EARNERS

Driver	Victories	Earnings
Rick Mears	4—1979, 1984 1988, 1991	$4,162,989
Al Unser	4—1970–71 1978, 1987	$2,814,615
E. Fittipaldi	1—1989	$2,450,597
A. J. Foyt, Jr.	4—1961, 1964 1967, 1977	$2,448,080
Mario Andretti	1—1969	$2,157,833

mile race in Paris, France in a De Dion
steam quadricycle in which he is reputed
to have exceeded 37 mph. The first
"real" race was in France, from Paris
to Bordeaux and back (732 miles) on 11–
13 Jun 1895. The first to finish was Emile
Levassor (1844–97) of France, in a
Panhard-Levassor two-seater, with a 1.2-
liter Daimler engine producing 3½ hp.
His time was 48 hr 47 min (average speed
15.01 mph). The first closed circuit race
was held over five laps of a mile-long
dirt track at Narragansett Park, Crans-
ton, RI on 7 Sep 1896. It was won by
A.H. Whiting, driving a Riker electric.

The oldest race in the world still regu-
larly run is the Royal Automobile Club
(RAC) Tourist Trophy, first staged on 14
Sep 1905, in the Isle of Man, Great
Britain. The French Grand Prix was
first held on 26–27 Jun 1906. The Coppa
Florio, in Sicily, has been irregularly
held since 1906.

Fastest circuits The highest average
lap speed attained on any closed circuit
is 250.958 mph in a trial by Dr Hans
Liebold (Germany; b. 12 Oct 1926), who
lapped the 7.85 mile high-speed track at
Nardo, Italy in 1 min 52.67 sec in a
Mercedes-Benz C111-IV experimental
coupé on 5 May 1979. It was powered by a
V8 engine with two KKK turbochargers,
with an output of 500 hp at 6,200 rpm.

The fastest road circuit was the Francorchamps circuit near Spa, Belgium,
then 8.76 miles in length, which was
lapped in 3 min 13.4 sec (average speed
163.086 mph) on 6 May 1973, by Henri
Pescarolo (France; b. 25 Sep 1942) driving a 2,993-cc V12 Matra-Simca MS670

Group 5 sports car.

Fastest pit stop Robert William "Bobby" Unser (USA; b. 20 Feb 1934) took 4 seconds to take on fuel on lap 10 of the Indianapolis 500 on 30 May 1976.

Fastest race The fastest race is the Busch Clash at Daytona, FL over 50 miles on a 2½-mile 31-degree banked track. In 1987 Bill Elliott (USA; b. 8 Oct 1955) averaged 197.802 mph in a Ford Thunderbird. Al Unser, Jr. (USA; b. 19 Apr 1962) set the world record for a 500 mile race when he won the Michigan 500 on 9 Aug 1990 at an average speed of 189.727 mph.

INDIANAPOLIS 500

The Indianapolis 500 mile race (200 laps) was inaugurated in the USA on 30 May 1911. Three drivers have four wins: Anthony Joseph "A.J." Foyt, Jr. (USA; b. 16 Jan 1935) in 1961, 1964, 1967 and 1977; Al Unser (USA; b. 29 May

Most Le Mans wins

The race has been won
by Porsche cars twelve
times, in 1970–71,
1976–77, 1979, 1981–87.
The most wins by one
man is six by Jacques
Bernard "Jacky" Ickx
(Belgium; b. 1 Jan
1945), 1969, 1975–77
and 1981–82.

1939) in 1970–71, 1978 and 1987; and Rick Mears (USA; b. 3 Dec 1951) in 1979, 1984, 1988 and 1991. The record time is 2 hr 41 min (185.981 mph) by Arie Luyendyk (Netherlands) driving a Lola-Chevrolet on 27 May 1990. The record average speed for four laps qualifying is 225.301 mph by Emerson Fittipaldi (Brazil; b. 12 Dec 1946) in a Penske-Chevrolet on 13 May 1990. On the same day he set the one-lap record of 225.575 mph. The track record is 228.502 mph by Al Unser, Jr. on 11 May 1990. A.J. Foyt, Jr. has started a record 34 races, 1959–90, and Rick Mears has started from pole position a record six times, 1979, 1982, 1986, 1988–89, and 1991. The record prize fund is $7,009,150 and the individual prize record is $1,219,704 by Rick Mears, both in 1991.

First woman driver The first and only woman to compete in the Indianapolis 500 is Janet Guthrie (USA; b. 7 Mar 1938). She passed her rookie test in May 1976, and earned the right to compete in the qualifying rounds, but was unable to win a place on the starting line when the Vollstedt-Offenhauser she drove was withdrawn from the race after repeated mechanical failures. In the 61st running of the Indianapolis 500, in 1977, Guthrie became the first woman to compete, although her car developed mechanical problems which forced her to retire after 27 laps. In 1978, she completed the race, finishing in 9th place after 190 laps.

Indy Car Championships (CART)

The first Indy Car Championship was held in 1909 under the auspices of the American Automobile Association (AAA). In 1959 the United States Automobile Club (USAC) took over the running of the Indy series. Since 1979 Championship Auto Racing Teams Inc. (CART) has organized the Indy Championship, which since 1979 has been called the PPG Indy Car World Series Championship.

Most wins National Championships The most successful driver in Indy car history is A. J. Foyt, Jr., who has won 67 races and seven championships (1960–61, 1963–64, 1967, 1975 and 1979). The record for the most victories in a season is ten, shared by two drivers: A.J. Foyt, Jr. (1964) and Al Unser (1970). Mario Andretti (USA; 28 Feb 1940) has the most laps (7,392) in Indy championships as of 9 Jun 1991; he also holds the record for most pole positions at 64.

As of 6 Jun 1991, Rick Mears holds the career earnings mark for Indy drivers with $9,701,701. The single season earnings record was set at $2,166,078 in 1989 by Emerson Fittipaldi.

NASCAR (National Association for Stock Car Auto Racing)

The first NASCAR championship was held in 1949. Since 1971 the championship series has been called the Winston Cup Championship. The championship has been won a record seven times by Richard Lee Petty (USA; b. 2 Jul 1937)—1964, 1967, 1971–72, 1974–75 and 1979.

Petty won 200 NASCAR Winston Cup races in 1,137 starts from 1958 to 26 May 1991, and his best season was 1967, with 27 wins. Petty, on 1 Aug 1971, was the first driver to pass $1 million in career earnings.

The NASCAR career money record is $13,339,694 to 26 May 1991, by Dale Earnhardt (USA; b. 29 Apr 1952). Earnhardt won a season record $3,083,056 in 1990. Geoff Bodine (USA; b. 18 Apr 1949) won 55 races in NASCAR Modified racing in 1978.

Shawna Robinson (USA; b. 30 Nov 1954) became the first woman to win a NASCAR race when she won an event in the NASCAR Dash Series at Asheville, NC on 10 Jun 1978.

Daytona 500 The Daytona 500 has been held at the 2½ mile oval Daytona International Speedway in Daytona, FL since 1959. The race is the major event of the NASCAR season. Richard Petty has a record seven wins—1964, 1966, 1971, 1973–74, 1979 and 1981. The record average speed for the race is 177.602 mph by Buddy Baker in an Oldsmobile in 1980. The qualifying speed record is 210.364, by Bill Elliott in a Ford Thunderbird in 1987.

FORMULA ONE GRAND PRIX MOTOR RACING

Most successful drivers The World Drivers' Championship, inaugurated in 1950, has been won a record five times by Juan-Manuel Fangio (Argentina; b. 24 Jun 1911) in 1951 and 1954–57. He retired in 1958, after having won 24 Grand Prix races (two shared) from 51 starts.

Alain Prost (France; b. 24 Feb 1955) holds the records for both the most Grand Prix points in a career, 676.5, and the most Grand Prix victories, 44 from 175 races, 1980–91. The most Grand Prix victories in a year is eight by Ayrton Senna (Brazil; b. 21 Mar 1960) in 1988. The most Grand Prix starts is 214 to 1 Jul 1991 by Ricardo Patrese (Italy; b. 17 Apr 1954) from 1977. The greatest number of pole positions is 56 by Ayrton Senna from 116 races (30 wins), 1985–91.

Two Americans have won the World Drivers' Championship—Phil Hill in 1961, and Mario Andretti in 1978. Andretti has the most Grand Prix wins by a US driver: 12 in 128 races, 1968–82.

Oldest and youngest The youngest world champion was Emerson Fittipaldi, who won his first World Championship on 10 Sep 1972 at the age of 25 yr 273 days.

The oldest world champion was Juan-Manuel Fangio, who won his last World Championship on 4 Aug 1957 at the age of 46 yr 41 days.

The youngest Grand Prix winner was Bruce Leslie McLaren (1937–70) of New Zealand, who won the United States Grand Prix at Sebring, FL on 12 Dec 1959, age 22 yr 104 days. Troy Ruttman (USA) was 22 yr 80 days when he won

the Indianapolis 500 on 30 May 1952, which was part of the World Championships at the time. The oldest Grand Prix winner (in pre-World Championship days) was Tazio Giorgio Nuvolari (Italy; 1892–1953), who won the Albi Grand Prix at Albi, France on 14 Jul 1946, age 53 yr 240 days. The oldest Grand Prix driver was Louis Alexandre Chiron (Monaco; 1899–1979), who finished sixth in the Monaco Grand Prix on 22 May 1955, age 55 yr 292 days. The youngest driver to qualify for a Grand Prix was Michael Christopher Thackwell (New Zealand; b. 30 Mar 1961) at the Canadian Grand Prix on 28 Sep 1980, age 19 yr 182 days.

Manufacturers Ferrari has won a record eight manufacturers' World Championships, 1961, 1964, 1975–77, 1979, 1982–83. Ferrari has 103 race wins in 476 Grands Prix, 1950–91.

The greatest dominance by one team since the Constructor's Championship was instituted in 1958 was by McLaren in 1988 when the team won 15 of the 16 Grands Prix. Ayrton Senna had eight wins and three seconds, Alain Prost had seven wins and seven seconds. The McLarens, powered by Honda engines, amassed over three times the points of their nearest rivals, Ferrari. Excluding the Indianapolis 500 race, then included in the World Drivers' Championship, Ferrari won all seven races in 1952 and the first eight (of nine) in 1953.

Fastest race The fastest overall average speed for a Grand Prix race on a circuit in current use is 146.284 mph by Nigel Mansell (Great Britain) in a Williams-Honda at Zeltweg in the Austrian Grand Prix on 16 Aug 1987. The qualifying lap record was set by Keke Rosberg (Finland) at 1 min 05.59 sec, an average speed of 160.817 mph, in a Williams-Honda at Silverstone in the British Grand Prix on 20 Jul 1985.

Closest finish The closest finish to a World Championship race was when Ayrton Senna (Brazil) in a Lotus beat Nigel Mansell (Great Britain) in a Williams by 0.014 sec in the Spanish Grand Prix at Jerez de la Frontera on 13 Apr 1986. In the Italian Grand Prix at Monza on 5 Sep 1971, 0.61 sec separated winner Peter Gethin (Great Britain) from the fifth-placed driver.

LE MANS

The greatest distance ever covered in the 24-hour *Grand Prix d'Endurance* (first held on 26–27 May 1923) on the old Sarthe circuit at Le Mans, France is 3,314.222 miles by Dr Helmut Marko (Austria; b. 27 Apr 1943) and Gijs van Lennep (Netherlands; b. 16 Mar 1942) in a 4907-cc flat-12 Porsche 917K Group 5 sports car, on 12–13 Jun 1971. The record for the greatest distance ever covered for the current circuit is 3,313.241 miles (av speed 137.718 mph) by Jan Lammers (Netherlands), Johnny Dumfries and Andy Wallace (both from Great Britain) in a Jaguar XJR9 on 11–12 Jun 1988.

The race lap record (now 8.410 mile lap) is 3 min 21.27 sec (average speed 150.429 mph) by Alain Ferté (France) in a Jaguar XRJ-9 on 10 Jun 1989. Hans Stück (West Germany) set the practice lap record of 3 min 14.8 sec (av. speed 156.62 mph) on 14 Jun 1985.

RALLYING

The earliest long rally, from Beijing, China to Paris, France, over about 7,500 miles from 10 Jun 1907, was promoted by the Parisian daily *Le Matin*. The winner, Prince Scipione Borghese (1872–1927) of Italy, arrived in Paris on 10 Aug 1907 in his 40-hp Itala accompanied by his chauffeur, Ettore, and Luigi Barzini.

Longest The longest-ever rally was the *Singapore Airlines* London–Sydney Rally over 19,329 miles from Covent Garden, London, Great Britain on 14 Aug 1977 to Sydney Opera House, Australia, won on 28 Sep 1977 by Andrew Cowan, Colin Malkin and Michael Broad in a Mercedes 280E. The longest held annually is the Safari Rally (first run in 1953 as the Coronation Rally, through Kenya, Tanzania and Uganda, but now restricted to Kenya). The race has covered up to 3,874 miles, as in the 17th Safari held from 8–12 Apr 1971. It has been won a record five times by Shekhar Mehta (Kenya; b. 20 Jun 1945) in 1973, 1979–82.

The Paris–Dakar '92 rally between 25 Dec 1991 and 22 Jan 1992 is scheduled to be raced over about 7,890 miles from Paris, France to Cape Town, South Africa. It will no longer go near the Senegalese capital.

Monte Carlo The Monte Carlo Rally (first run in 1911) has been won a record four times by: Sandro Munari (Italy; b. 27 Mar 1940) in 1972, 1975, 1976 and 1977; and Walter Röhrl (West Germany; b. 7 Mar 1947) (with co-driver Christian Geistdorfer) in 1980, 1982–84, each time in a different car. The smallest car to win was an 851-cc Saab driven by Erik Carlsson (Sweden; b. 5 Mar 1929) and Gunnar Häggbom (Sweden; b. 7 Dec 1935) on 25 Jan 1962, and by Carlsson and Gunnar Palm on 24 Jan 1963.

World Championship Two World Drivers' Championships (instituted 1979) have been won by Walter Röhrl, 1980 and 1982, Juha Kankkunen (Finland; b. 2 Apr 1959), 1986–87; and Mikki Biasion (Italy) 1988–89. The most wins in World Championship races is 19 by Hannu Mikkola and Markku Alen (Finland) to the end of 1990. Lancia have won a record eight manufacturers' World Championships. The first winner of the women's World Championships, inaugurated in 1990, was Louise Aitken-Walker (Great Britain).

DRAG RACING

Piston-engined The lowest official elapsed time recorded by a piston-engined dragster from a standing start for 440 yd is 4.897 sec by Joe Amato (USA; b. 1944) at Gainesville, FL on 24

Mar 1991. A lower time of 4.881 sec by Gary Ormsby (USA; b. 11 Nov 1941) with the highest terminal velocity reached at the end of a 440 yd run of 296.05 mph in qualifying for the NHRA Heartlands Nationals at Topeka, KS on 29 Sep 1990 was not officially recognized. The lowest elapsed time for a woman is 4.962 sec by Shirley Muldowney (USA; b. 1940) at Topeka on 29 Sep 1989. For a gasoline-driven piston-engined car the lowest elapsed time is 7.184 sec by Darrell Alderman (USA; b. 1949), driving a Dodge Daytona, on 13 Oct 1990 in Dallas, TX, and the highest terminal velocity is 192.18 mph by Warren Johnson (b. 1943) in an Oldsmobile Cutlass Supreme in Dallas, TX on 13 Oct 1990. The lowest elapsed time for a gasoline-driven piston-engined motorcycle is 7.697 sec by John Myers (USA; b. 1958) at Gainesville, FL on 8 Mar 1990, and the highest terminal velocity is 176.47 mph by John Mafaro (USA; b. 1949) at Indianapolis on 4 Sep 1989.

Most wins The greatest number of wins in National Hot Rod Association national events is 80 by Bob Glidden in Pro Stock, 1973–91.

Rocket or jet engined The highest terminal velocity recorded by any dragster is 392.54 mph by Kitty O'Neil (USA) at El Mirage Dry Lake, CA on 7 Jul 1977. The lowest elapsed time is 3.58 sec by Sammy Miller in a Pontiac "Funny Car" in 1986.

Fastest speeds The most successful land speed record breaker was Sir Malcolm Campbell (Great Britain; 1885

–1948). He broke the official record nine times between 25 Sep 1924, with 146.157 mph in a Sunbeam, and 3 Sep 1935, when he achieved 301.129 mph in the Rolls-Royce–engined Bluebird.

Badminton

Origins Badminton is a descendant of the children's game of battledore and shuttlecock. It is believed that a similar game was played in China more than 2,000 years ago. Badminton takes its name from Badminton House in England, where the Duke of Beaufort's family and guests popularized the game in the 19th century. British army officers took the game to India in the 1870s, and the first modern rules were codified there in 1876. The world governing body is the International Badminton Federation, formed in 1934.

A battledore shuttlecock is described in the 1864 *American Boy's Book of Sports and Games.* The first badminton club formed in the United States was the Badminton Club of New York founded in 1878. The game was not organized at the national level until 1935, when the American Badminton Association (ABA) was founded in Boston, MA. In 1978 the ABA was renamed the United States Badminton Association.

World Championships (instituted 1977) A record five titles have been won by Park Joo-bong (South Korea), men's doubles 1985 and 1991 and

mixed doubles 1985, 1989 and 1991. Three Chinese players have won two individual world titles: men's singles: Yang Yang, 1987 and 1989; women's singles: Li Lingwei in 1983 and 1989; Han Aiping in 1985 and 1987.

The most wins at the men's International Championship for the Thomas Cup (instituted 1948) is eight, by Indonesia (1958, 1961, 1964, 1970, 1973, 1976, 1979 and 1984).

The most wins at the women's International Championship for the Uber Cup (instituted 1956) is five by Japan (1966, 1969, 1972, 1978 and 1981).

United States The USA has never won the Thomas Cup, but won the Uber Cup on the first three occasions that it was contested, 1957, 1960 and 1963. Judy Hashman (nee Devlin; b. 22 Oct 1935) was the only player on all three teams.

All-England Championships This competition was instituted in 1899. Rudy Hartono Kurniawan (Indonesia; b. 18 Aug 1948) has won a record eight men's singles in 1968–74 and 1976. The greatest number of titles won (including doubles) is 21, by George Alan Thomas (1881–1972), between 1903 and 1928. The women's singles was won ten times by Judy Hashman, in 1954, 1957–58, 1960–64, 1966–67. She also equaled the greatest number of titles won, 17, by Meriel Lucas (later Mrs King Adams) from 1899 to 1910.

United States Championships Judy Hashman won a record 31 US titles: 12 women's singles, 1954, 1956–63, 1965–67; 12 women's doubles, 1953–55,

1957–63, 1966–67 (11 with her sister Susan); and 7 mixed doubles, 1956–59, 1961–62, 1967. David Freeman won 7 single titles: 1939–42, 1947–48, 1953.

Baseball

Origins In 1908, the Spalding Commission, sponsored by Albert G. Spalding, a sporting goods tycoon, concluded that the game of baseball was invented by Abner Doubleday in 1839 at Cooperstown, NY, and the legend of Doubleday's efforts has since become deeply embedded in American folklore. Despite this tradition, Spalding's official version of baseball history is disputed by sports historians. They argue that baseball in North America evolved from such English games as cricket, paddleball, trap ball and rounders. Printed references to "base ball" in England date to 1700 and in the USA to the mid-eighteenth century. It is uncontested that Alexander Cartwright, Jr. formulated the rules of the modern game in 1845, and that the first match under these rules was played on 19 Jun 1846 when the New York Nine defeated the New York Knickerbockers, 23–1, in four innings. On 17 Mar 1871 the National Association of Professional Base Ball Players was formed—the first professional league in the United States. Today there are two main professional baseball associations, the National League (organized in 1876) and the American League (organized in 1901, recognized in 1903), which together form the major leagues, along with approximately 20 associations that make up the minor leagues. The champions of the two leagues first played for the World Series in 1903 and have played continuously since 1905. (For further details on World Series history, see below.)

The first night game was played on 2 Jun 1883 (M.E. College *v* professionals from Quincy, IL). The major leagues were slow to adopt this innovation, then considered radical. The Cincinnati Reds were the first big-league team to play under lights when they hosted the Philadelphia Phillies on 24 May 1935. President Franklin D. Roosevelt pressed a button at the White House to flick the switch at Crosley Field.

MAJOR LEAGUE

Most games played Peter Edward "Pete" Rose (b. 14 Apr 1941) played in a record 3,562 games with a record 14,053 at bats for the Cincinnati Reds (NL) 1963–78 and 1984–86, the Philadelphia Phillies (NL) 1979–83, and the Montreal Expos (NL) 1984. Henry Louis "Lou" Gehrig (1903–41) played in 2,130 successive games for the New York Yankees (AL) from 1 Jun 1925 to 30 Apr 1939.

Most home runs Career Henry Louis "Hank" Aaron (b. 5 Feb 1934) holds the major league career record with 755 home runs—733 for the Milwaukee

(1965–65) and Atlanta (1966–74) Braves in the National League and 22 for the Milwaukee Brewers (AL) 1975–76. On 8 Apr 1974 he bettered the previous record of 714 by George Herman "Babe" Ruth (1895–1948). Ruth hit his home runs from 8,399 times at bat, the highest home run percentage of 8.5 percent. Joshua Gibson (1911–47) of the Homestead Grays and Pittsburgh Crawfords, Negro League clubs, hit an estimated 900 home runs in his career, including an unofficial season record of 84 in 1931. These totals are believed to include exhibition games.

Season The major league record for home runs in a season is 61 by Roger Eugene Maris (1934–85) for the New York Yankees in 162 games in 1961. The most official home runs in a minor league season is 72 by Joe Bauman of the Roswell Rockets of the Longhorn League in 1954. Bauman hit his record "dingers" in 138 games, while batting .400 and driving in 224 runs.

Game The most home runs in a major league game is four, first achieved by Robert Lincoln "Bobby" Lowe (1868 –1951) for Boston *v.* Cincinnati on 30 May 1894. The feat has been achieved a further ten times since then.

Consecutive games The most home runs hit in consecutive games is eight, set by Richard Dale Long (b. 6 Feb 1926) for the Pittsburgh Pirates (NL), 19–28 May 1956, and tied by Donald Arthur

"Don" Mattingly (b. 21 Apr 1961) for the New York Yankees (AL), on 18 Jul 1987.

Grand slams Seven players have hit two grand slams in a single game. They are: Anthony Michael "Tony" Lazzeri (1903–46) for the New York Yankees (AL) on 24 May 1936, James Reubin "Jim" Tabor (1916–53) for the Boston Red Sox (AL) on 4 Jul 1946, James Edward "Diamond Jim" Gentile (b. 3 Jun 1934) for the Baltimore Orioles (AL) on 9 May 1961, Tony Lee Cloninger (b. 13 Aug 1940) for the Atlanta Braves (NL) on 3 Jul 1966, James "Jim" Thomas Northrup (b. 24 Nov 1939) for the Detroit Tigers (AL) on 24 Jun 1968 and Frank Robinson (b. 31 Aug 1935) for the Baltimore Orioles (AL) on 26 Jun 1970.

Don Mattingly of the New York Yankees (AL) hit 6 grand slams in 1987. Lou Gehrig hit 23 grand slams during his 16 seasons with the New York Yankees (AL), 1923–39.

Most career hits The career record for most hits is 4,256, by Pete Rose. Rose's record hits total came from a record 14,053 at-bats, which gave him a career batting average of .303.

Most consecutive hits Michael Franklin "Pinky" Higgins (1909–69) had 12 consecutive hits for the Boston Red Sox (AL) in a four-game span, 19–21 Jun 1938. This was equaled by Walter "Moose" Dropo (b. 30 Jan 1923) for the Detroit Tigers (AL), 14–15 Jul 1952.

Longest rallies In the men's singles final of the 1987 All-England Championships between Morten Frost (Denmark) and Icuk Sugiarto (Indonesia), there were two successive rallies of over 90 strokes.

Most shuttles In the final of the Indian National Badminton Championships in 1986, when Syed Modi beat Vimal Kumar 15–12, 15–12, 182 shuttles were used in the 66-minute period.

Shortest game In the 1969 Uber Cup in Tokyo, Japan, Noriko Takagi (later Mrs Nakayama) (Japan) beat Poppy Tumengkol (Indonesia) in 9 min.

MAJOR LEAGUE RECORDS
American League (AL)
National League (NL)

Career batting records

Batting average	**.367**	Tyrus Raymond "Ty" Cobb (Detroit–AL, Philadelphia–AL)	1905–28
Runs scored	**2,245**	Ty Cobb	1905–28
Runs batted in (RBI's)	**2,297**	Henry Louis "Hank" Aaron (Milwaukee, Atlanta–NL, Milwaukee–AL)	1954–76
Base hits	**4,256**	Peter Edward "Pete" Rose (Cincinnati–NL, Philadelphia–NL, Montreal–NL)	1963–86
Total bases	**6,856**	Hank Aaron (Milwaukee, Atlanta–NL, Milwaukee–AL)	1954–76

Season batting records

Batting average	**.438**	Hugh Duffy (Boston–NL; 236 hits in 539 at-bats)	1894
modern record (1900–present)	**.424**	Rogers Hornsby (St Louis–NL; 227 in 536 at-bats)	1924
Runs scored	**196**	William Robert Hamilton (Philadelphia–NL; in 131 games)	1894
modern record (1900–present)	**177**	George Herman "Babe" Ruth (New York–AL; in 152 games)	1921
Runs batted in (RBI's)	**190**	Lewis Robert "Hack" Wilson (Chicago–NL; in 155 games)	1930
Base hits	**257**	George Harold Sisler (St Louis–AL; 631 times at bat, 143 games)	1920
Singles	**202**	William H. "Wee Willie" Keeler (Baltimore–NL; in 128 games)	1898
modern record (1900–present)	**198**	Lloyd James Waner (Pittsburgh–NL; in 150 games)	1927
Doubles	**67**	William Earl Webb (Boston–AL; in 151 games)	1931
Triples	**36**	John Owen Wilson (Pittsburgh–NL; in 152 games)	1912
Total bases	**457**	Babe Ruth (New York–AL); 85 singles, 44 doubles, 16 triples, 59 home runs	1921

Single game batting records

Runs batted in (RBI's)	**12**	James LeRoy Bottomley (St Louis–NL) v Brooklyn	16 Sep 1924
Base hits	**9**	John Henderson Burnett (Cleveland–AL; in 18 innings)	10 Jul 1932
Total bases	**18**	Joseph Wilbur "Joe" Adcock (Milwaukee–AL; 1 double, 4 home runs	31 Jul 1954

Career pitching records

Games won	**511**	Denton T. "Cy(clone)" Young (in 906 games; Cleveland, St Louis, Boston–NL and Cleveland, Boston–AL)	1890–1911
Shutouts	**110**	Walter Perry Johnson (Washington–AL; in 802 games)	1907–27
Strikeouts	***5,394**	Lynn Nolan Ryan (New York–NL, California–AL, Houston–NL, Texas–AL)	1968–91

*Through 10 Jun 1991

Season pitching records

Games won	**60**	Charles Gardner "Old Hoss" Radbourn (Providence–NL; and 12 losses)	1884
modern record(1900–present)	**41**	John Dwight "Jack" Chesbro (New York–AL)	1904
Shutouts	**16**	George Washington Bradley (St Louis–NL; in 64 games)	1876
modern record (1900–present)	**16**	Grover Cleveland "Pete" Alexander (Philadelphia–NL; 48 games)	1916
Strikeouts	**513**	Matthew Aloysius Kilroy (Baltimore–AL)	1886
modern record (1900–present)	**383**	Lynn Nolan Ryan (California–AL)	1973

Single game pitching records

Strikeouts (9 innings)	**20**	William Roger Clemens (Boston–AL) v Seattle	29 Apr 1986
Strikeouts in extra innings	**21**	Thomas Edgar Cheney (Washington–AL) v Baltimore (16 innings)	12 Sep 1962

■ **Most games won by a pitcher**
"Cy" Young (1867–1955), had a record 511 wins and a record 750 complete games from a total of 906 games and 815 starts in his career. In his honor, the Cy Young Award is awarded annually (since 1956) to the outstanding pitcher in the major leagues. (Photo: National Baseball Library, Cooperstown, NY)

Joseph Paul "Joe" DiMaggio (b. 25 Nov 1914) hit in a record 56 consecutive games for the New York Yankees (AL) in 1941; he went to bat 223 times, with 91 hits, totaling 56 singles, 16 doubles, 4 triples and 15 home runs.

Home runs and stolen bases The only player to hit 40 or more home runs and have 40 stolen bases in a season was José Canseco (b. 2 Jul 1964) for the Oakland Athletics (AL) in 1988. His totals were 42 and 40 respectively.

Stolen bases On 1 May 1991 Rickey Henley Henderson (b. 25 Dec 1958) of the Oakland Athletics (AL) broke baseball's all-time record for stolen bases when he stole his 939th base, surpassing Lou Brock's mark. As of 17 Jun 1991, Henderson had extended his record to 961 stolen bases. Henderson also holds the mark for most stolen bases in a season, which he set in 1982 when he stole 130 bases.

Walks Babe Ruth holds the record for career walks, 2,056, and the single season record, 170 in 1923.

Two players share a record six walks for a single game: James E. "Jimmy" Foxx (1907–67) of the Boston Red Sox (AL) set the mark on 16 Jun 1938, and Andre Thornton (b. 13 Aug 1949) of the Cleveland Indians (AL) tied the record on 2 May 1984 in a game that went 18 innings.

Strikeouts The batter with the career strikeout record is Reginald Martinez "Reggie" Jackson (b. 18 May 1946), with 2,597 in 21 seasons with four teams. The season's record is 189, by Bobby Lee Bonds (b. 15 Mar 1946), right fielder for the San Francisco Giants in 1970. The longest run of games without striking out is 115, by Joseph Wheeler "Joe" Sewell (b. 9 Oct 1898) while playing third base of the Cleveland Indians (AL) in 1929. He had a record seven seasons batting at least 500 times with less than ten strikeouts, and struck out only 114 times in his 14-year career.

Most games won by a pitcher Denton True "Cy" Young (1867–1955) had a record 511 wins and a record 750 complete games from a total of 906 games and 815 starts in his career for the Cleveland Spiders (NL) 1890–98, the St Louis Cardinals (NL) 1899–1900, the Boston Red Sox (AL) 1901–08, the Cleveland Indians (AL) 1909–11 and the Boston Braves (NL) 1911. He pitched a career total of 7,356 innings. The career record of most pitching appearances is 1,070 by James Hoyt Wilhelm (b. 26 Jul 1923) for a total of nine teams between 1952 and 1969; he set the career record with 143 wins by a relief pitcher. The season's record is 106 appearances by Michael Grant Marshall (b. 15 Jan 1943) for the Los Angeles Dodgers (NL) in 1974.

Most consecutive games won by a pitcher Carl Owen Hubell (1903–88) pitched for the New York Giants (NL) to win 24 consecutive games, 16 in 1936 and

8 in 1937.

Shutouts The record for the most shutouts in a career is 110, pitched by Walter Perry Johnson (1887–1946) in his 21-season career with the Washington Senators (AL), 1907–27. Donald Scott "Don" Drysdale (b. 23 Jul 1936) pitched 6 consecutive shutouts for the Los Angeles Dodgers (NL) between 14 May and 4 Jun 1968. Orel Leonard Hershiser IV (b. 16 Sep 1958) pitched a record 59 consecutive shutout innings for the Los Angeles Dodgers (NL) from 30 Aug to 28 Sep 1988.

No-hitters Nolan Ryan, playing for the Texas Rangers (AL) against the Toronto Blue Jays (AL), pitched his record seventh no-hitter on 1 May 1991. John Samuel "Johnny" Vander Meer (b. 2 Nov 1914) of the Cincinnati Reds (NL) is the only player in baseball history to have pitched consecutive no-hitters, 11–15 Jun 1938.

Perfect game A perfect nine-inning game, in which the pitcher allowed the opposition no hits, no runs and did not allow a man to reach first base, was first achieved by John Lee Richmond (1857–1929) for Worcester, MA against Cleveland in the NL on 12 Jun 1880. There have been 14 subsequent perfect games over nine innings, but no pitcher has achieved this feat more than once. On 26 May 1959 Harvey Haddix Jr. (b. 18 Sep 1925) for Pittsburgh pitched a perfect game for 12 innings against Milwaukee in the National League, but lost in the 13th.

Saves Robert Thomas "Bobby" Thigpen (b. 17 Jul 1963) saved a record 57 games for the Chicago White Sox (AL) in 1990. The career record for saves is 341, by Roland Glen "Rollie" Fingers in his 18 seasons playing for the Oakland Athletics (AL), the San Diego Padres (NL) and the Milwaukee Brewers (AL), 1968–85. Fingers completed his record save total in 907 relief appearances.

Youngest player Frederick Joseph Chapman (1872–1957) pitched for Philadelphia in the American Association at 14 yr 239 days on 22 Jul 1887, but did not play again.

The youngest major league player of all time was the Cincinnati Reds (AL) pitcher Joseph Henry "Joe" Nuxhall (b. 30 Jul 1928), who played one game in Jun 1944, age 15 yr 314 days. He did not play again in the National League until 1952. The youngest player to play in a minor league game was Joe Louis Reliford (b. 29 Nov 1939), who played for the Fitzgerald Pioneers against the Statesboro Pilots in the Georgia State League, age 12 yr 234 days on 19 Jul 1952.

Oldest player Leroy Robert "Satchel" Paige (1906–82) pitched for the Kansas City A's (AL) at 59 years 80 days on 25 Sep 1965.

Shortest and tallest players The shortest major lea ie player was Eddie Gaedel, a 3 ft 7 ı, 65 lb midget, who pinch-hit for the St Louis Browns (AL) v

the Detroit Tigers (AL) on 19 Aug 1951. Wearing number ⅛, the batter with the smallest-ever major league strike zone walked on four pitches. Following the game, major league rules were hastily rewritten to prevent the recurrence of such an affair. The tallest major leaguer of all time is Randy Johnson (b. 10 Sep 1963) of the Seattle Mariners (AL), a 6 ft 10 in pitcher, who played in his first game for the Montreal Expos on 15 Sep 1988.

Most Valuable Player Award The most selections in the annual vote (instituted in 1931) of the Baseball Writers' Association for Most Valuable Player of the Year (MVP) in the major leagues is three, won by: National League: Stanley Frank "Stan" Musial (b. 21 Nov 1920; St Louis), 1943, 1946, 1948; Roy Campanella (b. 19 Nov 1921; Brooklyn), 1951, 1953, 1955; Mike Schmidt (b. 27 Sep 1949; Philadelphia), 1980–81, 1986. American League: James Emory "Jimmie" Foxx (1907–67; Philadelphia), 1932–33, 1938; Joe Di Maggio (New York), 1939, 1941, 1947; Yogi Berra (New York), 1951, 1954–55; Mickey Mantle (b. 20 Oct 1931; New York), 1956–57, 1962.

Cy Young Award Awarded annually from 1956 on to the outstanding pitcher in the major leagues, the most wins is three: National League: George Thomas "Tom" Seaver (b. 17 Nov 1944; New York), 1969, 1973, 1975; Stephen Norman "Steve" Carlton (b. 22 Dec 1944; Philadelphia), 1977, 1980, 1982. American League: Sanford "Sandy" Koufax (b. 30 Dec 1935; Los Angeles), 1963, 1965–66; James Alvin "Jim" Palmer (b. 15 Oct 1945; Baltimore), 1973, 1975–76.

Dwight Eugene Gooden (b. 16 Nov 1964) of the New York Mets became the youngest pitcher to win the Cy Young Award in 1985 by unanimous vote of the 24 sportswriters who make the selection.

Father and son On 31 Aug, 1990, Ken Griffey, Sr. and Ken Griffey, Jr., of the Seattle Mariners (AL), had been the first father and son to play for the same league team at the same time. Griffey Sr., an 18-year veteran, was signed by

Seattle on 29 Aug. In 1989 the Griffeys became the first father/son combination to play in the major leagues at the same time—Griffey Sr. played for the Cincinnati Reds (NL) during that season, while Griffey, Jr. was in his first season with the Mariners.

Longest and shortest games The Brooklyn Dodgers (NL) and the Boston Braves (NL) played to a 1–1 tie after 26

WORLD SERIES RECORDS
American League (AL), National League (NL)

Most wins	22 New York Yankees–AL	1923–78
Most series played	14 Lawrence Peter "Yogi" Berra (New York Yankees–AL)	1947–63
Most series played by pitcher	11 Edward Charles "Whitey" Ford (New York Yankees–AL)	1950–64

World Series career records

Batting average (min. 75 at bats)	.391 Louis Clark "Lou" Brock (St Louis Cardinals–NL; 34 hits in 87 at bats, 3 series)	1964–68
Runs scored	42 Mickey Charles Mantle (New York Yankees–AL)	1951–64
Runs batted in (RBI's)	40 Mickey Mantle (New York Yankees–AL)	1951–64
Base hits	71 Yogi Berra (New York Yankees–AL)	1947–63
Home runs	18 Mickey Mantle (New York Yankees–AL)	1951–64
Victories pitching	10 Whitey Ford (New York Yankees–AL)	1950–64
Strikeouts	94 Whitey Ford (New York Yankees–AL)	1950–64

World Series single series records

Batting average (4 or more games)	.750 William Augustus "Billy" Hatcher (Cincinnati Reds–NL; 9 hits in 12 at bats in four-game series)	1990
Runs scored	10 Reginald Martinez "Reggie" Jackson (New York Yankees–AL)	1977
Runs batted in (RBI's)	12 Robert Clinton "Bobby" Richardson (New York Yankees–AL)	1960
Base hits (7-game series)	13 Bobby Richardson (New York Yankees–AL)	1960
	13 Lou Brock (St Louis Cardinals–NL)	1968
	13 Martin "Marty" Barrett (Boston Red Sox–AL)	1986
Home runs	5 Reggie Jackson (New York Yankees–AL; in 20 at bats)	1977
Victories pitching	3 Christopher "Christy" Matthewson (New York Yankees–AL; in five-game series)	1905
	3 John Wesley "Jack" Coombs (Philadelphia A's–AL; in five-game series	1910
	Ten other pitchers have won three games in more than five games.	
Strikeouts	35 Robert "Bob" Gibson (St Louis Cardinals–NL; in 7 games)	1968
	23 Sanford "Sandy" Koufax (Los Angeles Dodgers–NL; in 4 games)	1963

World Series single game records

Home runs	3 Babe Ruth (New York Yankees–AL) v St Louis Cardinals	6 Oct 1926
	3 Babe Ruth (New York Yankees–AL) v St Louis Cardinals	9 Oct 1928
	3 Reggie Jackson (New York Yankees–AL) v Los Angeles Dodgers	18 Oct 1977
Runs batted in (RBI's) in a game	6 Bobby Richardson (New York Yankees–AL) v Pittsburgh Pirates	8 Oct 1960
Strikeouts by pitcher in a game	17 Bob Gibson (St Louis Cardinals–NL) v Detroit Tigers	2 Oct 1968
Perfect game (9 innings)	Donald James "Don" Larson (New York Yankees–AL) v Brooklyn Dodgers	8 Oct 1956

Fastest base runner

The fastest time for circling bases is 13.3 sec by Ernest Evar Swanson (1902–73) at Columbus, OH in 1932, at an average speed of 18.45 mph.

Longest throw

Glen Edward Gorbous (Canada; b. 8 Jul 1930) threw 445 ft 10 in on 1 Aug 1957. Mildred Ella "Babe" Didrikson (USA [later Mrs Zaharias]; 1914–56) threw 296 ft at Jersey City, NJ on 25 Jul 1931.

innings on 1 May 1920. The New York Giants (NL) beat the Philadelphia Phillies (NL), 6–1, in 9 innings in 51 min on 28 Sep 1919. (A minor league game, Atlanta v Mobile in the Southern Association on 19 Sep 1910, took 33 min [see below].) The Chicago White Sox (AL) played the longest ballgame in elapsed time—8 hours 6 min—beating the Milwaukee Brewers, 7–6, in the 25th inning on 9 May 1984 in Chicago. The game started on Tuesday night and was still tied at 3–3 when the 1 A.M. curfew caused suspension until Wednesday night.

Longest baseball game The actual longest game was a minor league game in 1981 which lasted 33 innings. At the end of 9 innings the score was tied, 1–1, with the Rochester (NY) Red Wings battling the home team Pawtucket (RI) Red Sox. At the end of 21 innings it was tied 2–2, and at the end of 32 innings, the score was still 2–2, when the game was suspended. Two months later, play was resumed, and 18 minutes later, Pawtucket scored one run and won. The winning pitcher was the Red Sox's Bob Ojeda.

Record attendances The all-time season record for attendance for both leagues is 55,173,597 in 1989. The record for an individual league is 30,331,417 for the American League in 1990, and this included an individual team record of 3,885,284 for the home games of the Toronto Blue Jays.

Managers Connie Mack (b. Cornelius Alexander McGillicuddy; 1862–1956) managed in the major leagues for a record 53 seasons and achieved a record 3,731 regular season victories (and a record 3,948 losses)—139 wins and 134 losses for the Pittsburgh Pirates (NL) 1894–96 and 3,592 wins and 3,814 losses for the Philadelphia Athletics (AL), a team he later owned, 1901–50. The most successful in the World Series was Charles Dillon "Casey" Stengel (1890–1975), who managed the New York Yankees (AL) to seven wins in ten World Series, winning in 1949–53, 1956 and 1958, and losing in 1955, 1957 and 1960. Joseph Vincent "Joe" McCarthy (1887–1978) also coached the New York Yankees to seven wins, 1932, 1936–39, 1941, 1943, and his teams lost in 1929 (Chicago) and 1942 (New York). He had the highest win percentage of managers who achieved at least 1,500 regular season wins, with .614, 2,126 wins and 1,335 losses in his 24-year career, with the Chicago Cubs (NL) 1926–30, the New York Yankees (AL) 1931–46, and the Boston Red Sox (AL) 1948–50, in which he never had an overall losing season.

Origins Played annually between the winners of the National League and the American League, the World Series was first staged unofficially in 1903, and officially from 1905. The most wins is 22 by the New York Yankees between 1923 and 1978, during a record 33 Series appearances after winning the American League titles between 1921 and 1981. The most National League wins is 19 by the Dodgers—Brooklyn 1890–1957, Los Angeles 1958–88.

Most Valuable Player The only players to have won the award twice are: Sandy Koufax (b. 30 Dec 1935) (Los Angeles, NL 1963, 1965), Bob Gibson (b. 9 Nov 1935) (St Louis, NL, 1964, 1967) and Reggie Jackson (b. 18 May 1946) (Oakland AL, 1973, New York, AL, 1977).

Attendance The record attendance for a Series is 420,784 for the six games when the Los Angeles Dodgers beat the Chicago White Sox 4–2 between 1 and 8 Oct 1959. The single game record is 92,706 for the fifth game of this series at the Memorial Coliseum, Los Angeles on 6 Oct 1959.

COLLEGE BASEBALL

Various forms of college baseball have been played throughout the twentieth century; however, the National Collegiate Athletic Association (NCAA) did not organize a championship until 1947 and did not begin to keep statistical records until 1957.

NCAA Division I regular season Hitting records The most career home runs was 100, by Pete Incaviglia for Oklahoma State in three seasons, 1983–85. The most career hits was 118, by Phil Stephenson for Wichita State in four seasons, 1979–82.

Pitching records Don Heinkel won 51 games for Wichita State in four seasons, 1979–82. Derek Patsumo struck out 541 batters for the University of Hawaii in three seasons, 1977–79.

College World Series The first College World Series was played in 1947 in Kalamazoo, MI. The University of California at Berkeley defeated Yale University 8–7. Since 1950 the College World Series has been played continuously at Rosenblatt Stadium, Omaha, NE.

Most championships The most wins in Division I is 11 by the University of Southern California (USC) in 1948, 1958, 1961, 1963, 1968, 1970–74 and 1978.

Hitting records The record for most home runs in a College World Series is four, shared by four players: Bud Hollowell (University of Southern California), 1963; Pete Incaviglia (Oklahoma State), 1983–85; Ed Sprague (Stanford University), 1987–88; and Gary Hymel (Louisiana State University), 1991.

Longest home run
The longest measured home run in a regular-season major league game was 573 ft by Dave Nicholson (b. 29 Aug 1939) for the Chicago White Sox *v* Kansas City Athletes on 6 May 1964 at Comisky Park in Chicago.

In a minor league game at Emeryville Ball Park, CA on 4 Jul 1929, Roy Edward "Dizzy" Carlyle (1900–56) hit a home run measured at 618 ft. In 1919 Babe Ruth hit a 587 ft homer in a Boston Red Sox *v* New York Giants exhibition game in Tampa, FL.

Keith Moreland of the University of Texas holds the record for the most hits in a College World Series career with 23 hits in three series, 1973–75.

Pitching records The record for most wins in the College World Series is four games, shared by nine players: Bruce Gardner (University of Southern California), 1958, 1960; Steve Arlin (Ohio State), 1965–66; Bert Hooton (University of Texas at Austin), 1969–70; Steve Rogers (University of Tulsa), 1969, 1971; Russ McQueen (University of Southern California), 1972–73; Mark Bull (Unversity of Southern California), 1973–74; Greg Swindell (University of Texas), 1984–85; Kevin Sheary (University of Miami of Florida), 1984, 1985; Greg Brummett (Wichita State), 1988–89.

Carl Thomas of the University of Arizona struck out 64 batters in three College World Series, 1954–56.

World Amateur Championships Instituted in 1938, the most successful nation has been Cuba with 19 wins between 1939 and 1988. Baseball has been a demonstration sport at six Olympic Games, and American teams have won the tournament four times, 1912, 1956, 1964 and 1988.

Basketball

Origins The game of "Pok-ta-Pok" was played in the 10th century B.C. by the Olmecs in Mexico, and closely resembled basketball in its concept. "Ollamalitzli" was a variation of this game played by the Aztecs in Mexico as late as the 16th century. If the solid rubber ball was put through a fixed stone ring the player was entitled to the clothing of all the spectators. Modern basketball (which may have been based on the German game *Korbball*) was devised by the Canadian-born Dr James A. Naismith (1861–1939) at the Training School of the International YMCA College in Springfield, MA in mid-December 1891. The first game played under modified rules was on 20 Jan 1892. The International Amateur Basketball Federation (FIBA) was founded in 1932; it has now dropped the word Amateur from its title.

Highest score In a senior international match, Iraq scored 251 against Yemen (33) at New Delhi, India, in Nov 1982 at the Asian Games.

Individual Mats Wermelin, 13 years old (Sweden), scored all 272 points in a 272–0 win in a regional boys' tournament in Stockholm, Sweden on 5 Feb 1974.

Tallest players Suleiman Ali Nashnush (b. 1943) was reputed to be 8 ft when he played for the Libyan team in 1962. Aleksandr Sizonenko of Kuibyshev Stroitel and USSR is 7 ft 10 in tall. The tallest woman player was Iuliana Larionovna Semenova (USSR; b. 9 Mar 1952) at a reported 7 ft 2 in and weighing 281 lb.

Longest goal Christopher Eddy (b. 13 Jul 1971) scored a field goal measured at 90 ft 2¼ in for Fairview High School *v.* Iroquois High School at Erie, PA on 25 Feb 1989. The shot was made as time expired in overtime and it won the game for Fairview, 51–50.

NATIONAL BASKETBALL ASSOCIATION

Origins The Amateur Athletic Union (AAU) organized the first national tournament in the USA in 1897. The first professional league was the National Basketball League (NBL), founded in 1898, but this league only lasted two seasons. The American Basketball League was formed in 1925, but declined, and the NBL was refounded in 1937. This organization merged with the Basket-

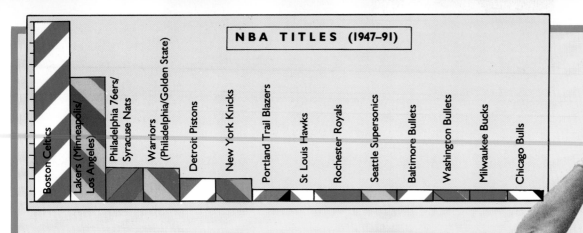

NBA TITLES (1947–91)

Boston Celtics · Lakers (Minneapolis/Los Angeles) · Philadelphia 76ers/Syracuse Nats · Warriors (Philadelphia/Golden State) · Detroit Pistons · New York Knicks · Portland Trail Blazers · St Louis Hawks · Rochester Royals · Seattle Supersonics · Baltimore Bullets · Washington Bullets · Milwaukee Bucks · Chicago Bulls

"WILT" CHAMBERLAIN

1960	† * 2,707	1967	† 1,956
1961	* 3,033	1968	† 1,992
1962	* 4,029	1969	1,664
1963	* 3,586	1970	328
1964	* 2,948	1971	1,696
1965	* 2,534	1972	1,213
1966	† * 2,649	1973	1,084

* = Season's leading scorer
† = NBA Most Valuable Player for the season

This building was the unlikely setting for the first-ever game of basketball in mid-December 1891, in Springfield, MA.

MICHAEL JORDAN

1985	2,313
1986	408
1987	* 3,041
1988	† * 2,868
1989	* 2,633
1990	* 2,752
1991	† * 2,580

* = Season's leading scorer
† = NBA Most Valuable Player for the season

NCAA DIVISION I
MEN'S CHAMPIONSHIP RECORDS

TEAM RECORDS

Most wins **10** UCLA 1964-65, 1967-73, 1975
Most points *(Championship game)* **103** UNLV (v. Duke) 1990
Most points *(Tournament game)* **149** Loyola Marymount (v. Michigan) 1990

Source: NCAA

INDIVIDUAL RECORDS

Most points *(Championship game)* **44**
Bill Walton, UCLA (v. Memphis State) 1973
Most points *(Tournament game)* **61**
Austin Carr, Notre Dame (v. Ohio State) 1970
Most points *(Tournament season)* **184**
Glen Rice, Michigan (6 games) 1989
Most points *(Tournament career)* **358**
Elvin Hayes, Houston (13 games) 1966-68

KAREEM ABDUL-JABBAR

Year	Score
1970	2,361
1971	† * 2,596
1972	† * 2,822
1973	2,292
1974	† 2,191
1975	1,949
1976	† 2,275
1977	† 2,152
1978	1,600
1979	1,903
1980	† 2,034
1981	2,095
1982	1,818
1983	1,722
1984	1,717
1985	1,735
1986	1,846
1987	1,366
1988	1,165
1989	748

* = Season's leading scorer
† = NBA Most Valuable Player
for the season

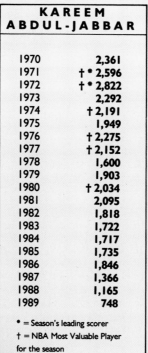

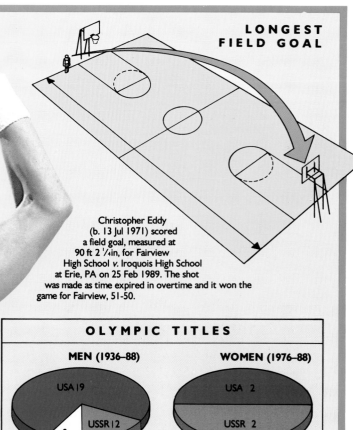

LONGEST FIELD GOAL

Christopher Eddy (b. 13 Jul 1971) scored a field goal, measured at 90 ft 2 ¼ in, for Fairview High School v. Iroquois High School at Erie, PA on 25 Feb 1989. The shot was made as time expired in overtime and it won the game for Fairview, 51-50.

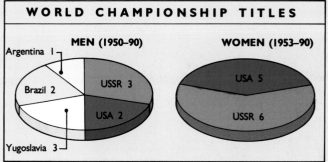

OLYMPIC TITLES

MEN (1936–88)

USA 19
USSR 12
Yugoslavia 1

WOMEN (1976–88)

USA 2
USSR 2

WORLD CHAMPIONSHIP TITLES

MEN (1950–90)

Argentina 1
Brazil 2
Yugoslavia 3
USSR 3
USA 2

WOMEN (1953–90)

USA 5
USSR 6

100 Years of **B**asketball

Dr James A. Naismith
inventor of basketball

First basketball team
including James Naismith
(right in center row)

Dribbling
Peter del Masto (USA) dribbled a basketball without "traveling" from near Lee to Provincetown, MA, a distance of 265.2 miles, from 12–25 Aug 1989.

Bob Nickerson of Gallitzin, PA and Dave Davlin of Garland, TX are the only people to have successfully demonstrated the ability to dribble four basketballs simultaneously.

ball Association of America in 1949 to form the National Basketball Association (NBA).

Most championships The Boston Celtics have won a record 16 NBA titles —1957, 1959–66, 1968–69, 1974, 1976, 1981, 1984, 1986.

Individual scoring Wilton Norman "Wilt" Chamberlain (b. 21 Aug 1936) set an NBA record with 100 points for Philadelphia v New York at Hershey, PA on 2 Mar 1962. This included a record 36 field goals and 28 free throws (from 32 attempts) and a record 59 points in a half (the second). The free throws game record was equaled by Adrian Dantley (b. 28 Feb 1956) for Utah v Houston at Las Vegas on 5 Jan 1984. The most points scored in an NBA game in one quarter is 33 in the second quarter, by George Gervin for San Antonio v New Orleans on 9 Apr 1978.

Most games Kareem Abdul-Jabbar (formerly Ferdinand Lewis Alcindor) (b. 16 Apr 1947) took part in a record 1,560 NBA regular season games over 20 seasons, totaling 57,446 minutes played, for the Milwaukee Bucks, 1969–75, and the Los Angeles Lakers, 1975–89. He also played a record 237 playoff games. The most successive games is 906 by Randy Smith for the Buffalo Braves, the San Diego Clippers, the Cleveland Cavaliers and the New York Knicks from 18 Feb 1972 to 13 Mar 1983. The record for playing complete games in one season is 79, by Wilt Chamberlain for Philadelphia in 1962, when he was on court for a record 3,882 minutes. Chamberlain went through his entire career of 1,045 games without fouling out. On 21 Apr 1991 Moses Malone played his 1,047th consecutive game without fouling out. Malone has fouled out five times during his career.

Most points Kareem Abdul-Jabbar set NBA career records with 38,887 points, including 15,837 field goals, in regular season games, and 5,762 points, including 2,356 field goals, in playoff games. The previous record holder, Wilt Chamberlain, had an average of 30.1 points per game for his total of 31,419 for the Philadelphia Warriors 1959–62, the San Francisco 76ers 1962–65, the Philadelphia Warriors 1964–68 and the Los Angeles Lakers 1968–73. He scored 50 or more points in 118 games, including 45 in 1961/62 and 30 in 1962/63, to the next-best career total of 17. He set season records for points and scoring average with 4,029 at 50.1 per game, and also for field goals, 1,597, for Philadelphia in 1961/62. The highest career average for players exceeding 10,000 points is 32.6, by Michael Jordan (b. 17 Feb 1963), 16,596 points in 509 games for the Chicago Bulls, 1984–91. Jordan also holds the career scoring average record for playoffs at 34.6, 2,425 points in 70 games 1984–91.

Kareem Abdul-Jabbar (Milwaukee, Los Angeles) had a record nine seasons scoring more than 2,000 points: 1970–74, 1976–77, 1980–81; and 19 scoring more than 1,000, 1970–88.

Steals The most steals in an NBA game is 11, by Larry Kenon for San Antonio at Kansas City on 26 Dec 1976. Alvin Robertson (b. 22 Jul 1962) set season records for San Antonio in 1985/86 with 301 at a record average of 3.67 per game.

Blocked shots The record for most blocked shots in an NBA game is 17, by Elmore Smith for Los Angeles v Portland at Los Angeles on 28 Oct 1973.

Most Valuable Player Kareem Abdul-Jabbar was elected the NBA's most valuable player a record six times, 1971–72, 1974, 1976–77 and 1980.

Youngest and oldest player The youngest NBA player has been Bill Willoughby (b. 20 May 1957), who made his debut for the Atlanta Hawks on 23 Oct 1975 at 18 yr 156 days. The oldest NBA regular player was Kareem Abdul-Jabbar, who made his last appearance for the Los Angeles Lakers at age 42 yr 59 days in 1989.

Tallest player Tallest in NBA history has been Manute Bol (Sudan; b. 16 Oct 1962) of the Washington Bullets, Golden State Warriors and Philadelphia 76ers at 7 ft 6 ¾ in. He made his pro debut in 1985.

Highest score The highest aggregate score in an NBA match is 370, when the Detroit Pistons (186) beat the Denver Nuggets (184) at Denver, CO on 13 Dec 1983. Overtime was played after a 145–145 tie in regulation time. The record in regulation time is 318, when the Denver Nuggets beat the San Antonio Spurs 163–155 at Denver on 11 Jan 1984. The most points in a half is 107, by the Phoenix Suns in the first half v Denver Nuggets on 11 Nov 1990. The most points in a quarter is 58 in the fourth quarter, by Buffalo at Boston on 20 Oct 1972.

NBA RECORDS

Career records

Points	38,387	Kareem Abdul-Jabbar: Milwaukee Bucks, Los Angeles Lakers	1970–89
Field goal percentage	.599	Artis Gilmore: Chicago Bulls, San Antonio Spurs, Boston Celtics; min. 2,000 field goals	1977–88
Free throws made	7,694	Oscar Palmer Robertson: Cincinnati Royals, Milwaukee Bucks of 9,185 attempts	1961–74
Free throw percentage	.900	Rick Barry: San Francisco / Golden State Warriors, Houston Rockets; 3,818 from 4,243 attempts (technically .89983)	1965–80
Field goals	15,837	Kareem Abdul-Jabbar	1970–89
Rebounds	23,924	Wilt Chamberlain: Philadelphia / San Francisco Warriors, Philadelphia 76ers, Los Angeles Lakers	1960–73
Assists	9,921	Earvin "Magic" Johnson: Los Angeles Lakers	1980–91
Steals	2,194	Maurice Cheeks: Philadelphia 76ers, San Antonio Spurs, New York Knicks	1979–91

Season records

Points	4,029	Wilt Chamberlain: Philadelphia Warriors	1962
Field goal percentage	.727	Wilt Chamberlain: Los Angeles Lakers; 426 of 586 attempts	1972
Free throws made	840	Jerry West: Los Angeles Lakers; of 977 attempts	1966
Free throw percentage	.958	Calvin Murphy: Houston Rockets; 206 of 215 attempts	1981
Field goals	1,597	Wilt Chamberlain: Philadelphia Warriors	1962
Rebounds	2,149	Wilt Chamberlain: Philadelphia Warriors	1961
Assists	1,164	John Stockton: Utah Jazz	1991
Steals	301	Alvin Robertson: San Antonio Spurs	1986

Single game records

Points	100	Wilt Chamberlain: Philadelphia Warriors v New York Knicks	2 Mar 1962
Field goals	36	Wilt Chamberlain	2 Mar 1962
Free throws made	28	Wilt Chamberlain	2 Mar 1962
	28	Adrian Dantley: Utah Jazz v Houston Rockets	5 Jan 1984
Rebounds	55	Wilt Chamberlain: Philadelphia Warriors v Boston Celtics	24 Nov 1960
Assists	30	Scott Skiles: Orlando Magic v Denver Nuggets	30 Dec 1990
Steals	11	Larry Kenon: San Antonio Spurs v Kansas City Kings	26 Dec 1976

NBA PLAYOFF RECORDS

Most games played	237	Kareem Abdul-Jabbar: Milwaukee Bucks, Los Angeles Lakers	1970–89

Career records

Points	5,762	Kareem Abdul-Jabbar (in 237 playoff games)	1970–89
Field goals	2,356	Kareem Abdul-Jabbar: Milwaukee Bucks, Los Angeles Lakers	1970–89
Free throws made	1,213	Jerry West: Los Angeles Lakers (from 1,507 attempts)	1961–74
Assists	2,142	Magic Johnson: Los Angeles Lakers	1980–91
Rebounds	4,104	Bill Russell: Boston Celtics	1957–69

Series records

Points	284	Elgin Baylor: Los Angeles Lakers (v Boston Celtics); in 7 games	1962
Field goals	113	Wilt Chamberlain: San Francisco (v St Louis); in 6 games	1964
Free throws made	86	Jerry West: Los Angeles Lakers (v Baltimore); in 6 games	1965
Rebounds	220	Wilt Chamberlain: Philadelphia 76ers (v Boston Celtics); in 7 games	1965
Assists	115	John Stockton: Utah Jazz (v Los Angeles Lakers); in 7 games	1988

Single game records

Points	63	Michael Jordan: Chicago Bulls (v Boston Celtics); includes two overtime periods	20 Apr 1986
	61	Elgin Baylor: Los Angeles Lakers (v Boston Celtics)	14 Apr 1962
Field goals	24	Wilt Chamberlain: Philadelphia 76ers v Syracuse Nationals; in 42 attempts	14 Mar 1960
	24	John Havelicek: Boston Celtics (v Atlanta Hawks); in 36 attempts	1 Apr 1973
	24	Michael Jordan: Chicago Bulls (v Cleveland Cavaliers); in 45 attempts	1 May 1988
Free throws made	30	Bob Cousy: Boston Celtics (v Syracuse Nationals); includes four overtime periods and 32 attempts	21 Mar 1953
	23	Michael Jordan: Chicago Bulls (v New York Knicks); in 28 attempts	14 May 1989
Rebounds	41	Wilt Chamberlain: Philadelphia 76ers (v Boston Celtics)	5 Apr 1967
Assists	24	Magic Johnson: Los Angeles Lakers (v Phoenix Suns)	15 May 1984
	24	John Stockton: Utah Jazz (v Los Angeles Lakers)	17 May 1988

Shooting speed

The greatest goal-shooting demonstration was by Ted St Martin of Jacksonville, FL who, on 25 Jun 1977, scored 2,036 consecutive free throws. Also at Jacksonville, he scored 175 out of 185 free throws in 10 min on 27 Jan 1990 and 90 out of 97 attempts in five minutes on 24 Feb 1990. On 14 Dec 1990, Jeff Liles scored 224 out of 237 attempts in ten minutes at Southern Nazarene University, Bethany, OK. These speed records were both achieved with one ball and one rebounder.

In 24 hours Fred Newman scored 20,371 free throws from a total of 22,049 taken (92.39 percent) at Caltech, Pasadena, CA on 29–30 Sep 1990.

Steve Bontrager (USA; b. 1 Mar 1959) of Polycell Kingston scored 21 points in a minute from seven positions in a demonstration for the British Broadcasting Corporation's *Record Breakers* TV program on 29 Oct 1986.

Winning margin The greatest winning margin in an NBA game was the 63 points by which Los Angeles Lakers, 162, beat the Golden State Warriors, 99, on 19 Mar 1972.

Winning streak The Los Angeles Lakers won a record 33 NBA games in succession from 5 Nov 1971 to 7 Jan 1972, as during the 1971/72 season they won a record 69 games with 13 losses.

Coaches The most successful coach in NBA history has been Arnold "Red" Auerbach (b. 1917) with 938 wins (1,037 including playoffs), with the Washington Capitols 1946–49, the Tri-Cities Blackhawks 1949–50, and the Boston Celtics 1950–66. He led the Boston Celtics to a record nine NBA titles, including eight in succession in 1959–66.

In his nine seasons with the Los Angeles Lakers (1981–90), coach Pat Riley won

■ **Most assists**

John Stockton of the Utah Jazz holds the NBA regular season record for assists, with 1,164. He also holds the play-off series record for assists, with 115; and shares the playoffs record for single game assists, with 24. The photo at right show his record-setting style.

(Photo: Utah Jazz)

NCAA DIVISION I RECORDS
Through 1990/91 Season

Career records

Points	**3,667**	Peter "Pistol Pete" Maravich: Louisiana State	1968–70
Field goals	**1,387**	Pistol Pete Maravich: Louisiana State	1968–70
Best percentage	**68.5**	Stephen Sheffler: Purdue	1987–90
Rebounds	**2,243**	Tom Gola: La Salle	1952–55
Assists	**1,038**	Chris Corchiani, North Carolina State	1988–91

Season records

Points	**1,381**	Pistol Pete Maravich: Louisiana State	1970
Field goals	**522**	Pistol Pete Maravich: Lousiana State (from 1,168 attempts)	1970
Best percentage	**74.9**	Steve Johnson: Oregon State	1981
Three-point goals	**158**	Darrin Fitzgerald: Butler (in 362 attempts)	1987
Free throws	**355**	Frank Selvy: Furman (in 444 attempts)	1954
Best percentage	**95.9**	Craig Collins: Penn State	1985
Rebounds	**734**	Walt Dukes: Seton Hall (in 33 games)	1953
Assists	**406**	Mark Wade: Nevada–Las Vegas	1987
Blocked shots	**207**	David Robinson: Navy (in 35 games)	1986

Game records

Points	**100**	Frank Selvy: Furman (v Newberry)	13 Feb 1954
Field goals	**41**	Frank Selvy: Furman	13 Feb 1954
Three-point goals	**14**	Dave Jamerson: Ohio (v Charleston)	21 Dec 1989
Free throws	**30**	Pistol Pete Maravich: Louisiana State (v Oregon State)	22 Dec 1969
Rebounds	**51**	Bill Chambers: William and Mary (v Virginia)	14 Feb 1953
Assists	**22**	Tony Fairly: Baptist (v Armstrong State)	9 Feb 1987
	22	Avery Johnson: Southern–B.R. (v Texas Southern)	25 Jan 1988
	22	Sherman Douglas: Syracuse (v Providence)	28 Jan 1989
Blocked shots	**14**	David Robinson: Navy (v North Carolina–Wilmington)	4 Jan 1986
	14	Shawn Bradley: BYU (v Eastern Kentucky)	7 Dec 1990

NCAA WOMEN'S DIVISION I CHAMPIONSHIP GAME RECORDS

Team records

Most championships	**2**	Louisiana Tech (1982, 1988), USC (1983–84), Tennessee (1987, 1989)	
First championships		Louisiana Tech v Cheyney State; 76–62	1982
Most points	**97**	Texas (v USC)	1986
Most field goals	**40**	Texas (v USC)	1986
Highest field-goal percentage	**58.8**	Texas (v USC; 40–68)	1986
Most 3-point field goals	**11**	Stanford (v Auburn)	1990
Rebounds	**57**	Old Dominion (v Georgia)	1985
Assists (since 1985)	**22**	Texas (v USC)	1986
Blocked shots (since 1988)	**7**	Tennessee (v Auburn)	1989
Steals (since 1988)	**12**	Louisiana Tech (v Auburn)	1988

Individual records

Most points	**27**	Cheryl Miller, USC (v Louisiana Tech)	1983
	27	Cynthia Cooper, USC (v Texas)	1987
	27	Bridgette Gordon, Tennessee (v Auburn)	1989
Most field goals	**12**	Erica Westbrooks, Louisiana Tech (v Auburn)	1988
Highest field-goal percentage	**88.9**	Jennifer White, Louisiana Tech (v USC; 8–9)	1983
Most 3-point field goals (since 1988)	**6**	Katy Steding, Stanford (v Auburn)	1990
Rebounds	**20**	Tracy Claxton, Old Dominion (v Georgia)	1985
Assists (since 1985)	**10**	Kamie Ethridge, Texas (v USC)	1986
	10	Melissa McCray, Tennessee (v Auburn)	1989
Blocked shots (since 1988)	**5**	Sheila Frost, Tennessee (v Auburn)	1989
Steals (since 1988)	**6**	Erica Westbrooks, Louisiana Tech (v Auburn)	1988

■ Most points

Cheryl Miller shares the record for most points in an NCAA championship, with 27, for USC against Louisiana Tech in 1983.

(Photo: All-Sport/ Alvin Chung)

102 playoff games to set the NBA all-time mark. Riley also compiled a league record .733 (533–194) regular season winning percentage.

Record attendance The Minnesota Timberwolves set an NBA record for total attendance of 1,072,572 during the 1989–90 season, the Timberwolves' first in the league. The average crowd was 26,160 fans at the Metrodome in Minneapolis.

NCAA RECORDS

Origins First contested in 1939, the record for most Division I titles is 10, by the University of California at Los Angeles (UCLA), 1964–65, 1967–73, 1975. The only player to have been voted the most valuable player in the NCAA final three times has been Lew Alcindor of UCLA in 1967–69. He subsequently changed his name to Kareem Abdul-Jabbar.

Points The most points by an individual for an NCAA Division I team in a game is 100, by Frank Selvy for Furman v Newberry on 13 Feb 1954, including a record 41 field goals. In Division II, Clarence "Bevo" Francis scored 113

BASKETBALL

Fastest century

Walter Lindrum made an unofficial 100 break in 27.5 sec in Australia on 10 Oct 1952. His official record is 100 in 46.0 sec set in Sydney, Australia in 1941.

Biggest board game

The world's biggest board game was a version of the game "Goose", and was organized by "Jong Nederland." It stretched for 2,090 ft and was played by 1,631 participants at Someren, Netherlands on 16 Sep 1989.

Shortest backgammon game

Alan Malcolm Beckerson (b. 21 Feb 1938) devised a game of just 16 throws in 1982.

points for Rio Grande v Hillsdale on 2 Feb 1954.

Career and season scoring

Peter "Pistol Pete" Maravich (1947–88) set unmatched NCAA scoring records while at Louisiana State University: 1,138 points, an average 43.8 per game, in 1968; 1,148 at 44.2 per game in 1969; and the season record 1,381 at 44.5 per game in 1970—the three highest season averages in NCAA history, for a total 3,667 points in 83 games. Maravich scored a career record 1,387 field goals. The career field goal percentage record (minimum 400 scored) is 67.8 percent by Steve Johnson, 828 of 1,222 attempts for Oregon State, 1976–81. In Division II competition, Travis Grant of Kentucky State scored a record 4,045 points in 121 games, 1969–72, and a season average record was set at 46.5 points by Clarence "Bevo" Francis, with 1,255 points in 27 games for Rio Grande in 1954. In all collegiate competition, Philip Hutcheson of David Lipscomb University scored 4,106 points in his career, 1987–90.

Coaches

The man to have coached most victories in NCAA Division I competition is Adolph Rupp (1901–77) at Kentucky, with 875 wins (and 190 losses), 1931–72. John Wooden (b. 1910) coached UCLA to all its ten NCAA titles.

Record attendances

The highest paid attendance for a college game is 66,144 for Louisiana State's 82–80 victory over Georgetown at the Louisiana Superdome, New Orleans, LA on 28 Jan 1989.

Women's

The record for a women's college game is 24,563 in Knoxville, TN for a game between the University of Tennessee and the University of Texas on 9 Dec 1987.

Women's championships

First contested in 1982, the record for most Division I titles is two by the University of Southern California, 1983–84, Tennessee, 1987 and 1989, and Louisiana Tech University, 1982 and 1988. The regular season match aggregate record is 261, when St Joseph's (Indiana) beat North Kentucky 131–130 on 27 Feb 1988.

Coaches

Jody Conradt of the University of Texas has won the most games in Women's NCAA Division I competition with 577 victories through the 1990/91 season.

OTHER RECORDS

Most points

The women's record for most points scored in a college career is 4,061 by Pearl Moore. She scored 177 points in eight games for Anderson Junior College, Anderson, SC, and 3,884 points for Francis Marion College, Florence, SC, 1975–79. Francis Marion was a member of the Association of Intercollegiate Athletics for Women (AIWA) during Moore's career. The career points leader in NCAA Division I competition is Patricia Hoskins of Mississippi

Valley State with 3,122 points (1985–89).

Vertical dunk height record

Joey Johnson of San Pedro, CA successfully dunked a basketball at a rim height of 11 ft 7 in at the One-on-One Collegiate Challenge on 25 Jun 1990 at Trump Plaza Hotel and Casino in Atlantic City, NJ.

Olympic Games

Three men and two women have won two Olympic gold medals: Robert Albert "Bob" Kurland (b. 23 Dec 1924) in 1948 and 1952; William Marion "Bill" Houghland (b. 20 Jun 1930) in 1952 and 1956; Burdette Eliele Haldorson (b. 12 Jan 1934) in 1956 and 1960; Anne Theresa Donovan (b. 1 Nov 1961) and Theresa Edwards, both in 1984 and 1988.

Most titles

Olympic The USA has won nine men's Olympic titles. From the time the sport was introduced to the Games in 1936 until 1972 the USA won 63 consecutive matches in the Olympic Games, until it lost 51–50 to the USSR in the disputed final match in Munich, Germany. The USA won its 8th and 9th titles in 1976 and 1984.

The women's title was won by the USSR in 1976 and 1980, and by the USA in 1984 and 1988.

World The USSR has won most titles at both the men's World Championships (instituted 1950) with three (1967, 1974 and 1982) and women's (instituted 1953), with six (1959, 1964, 1967, 1971, 1975 and 1983). Yugoslavia has also won three men's world titles: 1970, 1978 and 1990.

Billiards

Origins

The earliest recorded mention of billiards was in France in 1429, and Louis XI, King of France 1461–83, is reported to have had a billiard table.

Most titles

The greatest number of World Championships (instituted 1870) won by one player is eight, by John Roberts Jr. (Great Britain; 1847–1919), in 1870 (twice), 1871, 1875 (twice), 1877 and 1885 (twice). The record for world amateur titles is four, by Robert James Percival Marshall (Australia; b. 10 Apr 1910), in 1936, 1938, 1951 and 1962.

Youngest champion

The youngest winner of the world professional title is Mike Russell (b. 3 Jun 1969), age 20 yr 49 days, when he won at Leura, Australia on 23 Jul 1989.

Highest breaks

Tom Reece (1873–1953) made an unfinished break of 499,135, including 249,152 cradle cannons (two points each) in 85 hr 49 min against Joe Chapman at Burroughes' Hall, Soho Square, London, Great Britain between 3 Jun and 6 Jul 1907. This was not recognized because press and public were not continuously present.

The highest certified break made by the

anchor cannon is 42,746 by William Cook (England) from 29 May to 7 Jun 1907.

The official world record under the then balkline rule is 1,784 by Joe Davis in the United Kingdom Championship on 29 May 1936.

Walter Albert Lindrum (Australia; 1898–1960) made an official break of 4,137 in 2 hr 55 min against Joe Davis at Thurston's on 19–20 Jan 1932, before the balkline rule was in force.

Davis had an unofficial personal best of 2,502 (mostly pendulum cannons) in a match against Tom Newman (England; 1894–1943) in Manchester, Great Britain in 1930.

The highest break recorded in amateur competition is 1,149, by Michael Ferreira (India) at Calcutta, India on 15 Dec 1978.

Under the more stringent "two pot" rule, restored on 1 Jan 1983, the highest break is Ferreira's 962 unfinished, in a tournament at Bombay, India on 29 Apr 1986.

THREE CUSHION

Origins

This pocketless variation dates back to 1878. The world governing body, the *Union Mondiale de Billiard* (UMB), was formed in 1928.

Most titles

William F. "Willie" Hoppe (USA; 1887–1959) won 51 billiards championships in all forms, spanning the pre- and post-international era from 1906 to 1952.

UMB Raymond Ceulemans (Belgium; b. 12 Jul 1935) has won 19 world three-cushion championships (1963–73, 1975–80, 1983, 1985).

Board Games

BACKGAMMON

Origins

Forerunners of the game have been traced back to a dice and board game found in excavations at Ur, dated to 3000 B.C. Later the Romans played a game remarkably similar to the modern one. The name "backgammon" is variously ascribed to Welsh "little battle," or Saxon "back game."

BINGO

Bingo is a lottery game which, as keno, was developed in the 1880s from lotto, whose origin is thought to be the 17th-century Italian game *tumbule*. The winner was the first to complete a random selection of numbers from 1 to 90. The USA version called Bingo differs in that the selection is from 1 to 75.

Largest house

The largest "house" in bingo sessions was 15,756, at the Canadian National Exhibition, Toronto on 19 Aug 1983. Staged by the Variety Club of Ontario Tent Number 28, there was total prize money of $Cdn250,000 with a record one-game payout of $Cdn100,000.

Earliest and latest full house A "full house" call occurred on the 15th number by Norman A. Wilson at Guide Post Working Men's Club, Bedlington, Great Britain on 22 Jun 1978; by Anne Wintle of Brynrethin, Great Britain, on a coach trip to Bath, Great Britain on 17 Aug 1982; and by Shirley Lord at Kahibah Bowling Club, New South Wales, Australia on 24 Oct 1983.

"House" was not called until the 86th number at the Hillsborough Working Men's Club, Sheffield, Great Britain on 11 Jan 1982. There were 32 winners.

CHECKERS

Origins Checkers, known as draughts in Europe, is believed to have originated on the French/Spanish border in the 12th century, when backgammon men were placed on a chessboard and moved as in the well-known game of the time, *alquerque*. The earliest book on the game was by Antonio Torquemada of Valencia, Spain in 1547.

World champions Walter Hellman (USA; 1916–75) won a record eight world titles during his tenure as world champion 1948–75.

Dr Marion Tinsley (USA; b. 3 Feb 1927), the current world champion, has been internationally undefeated in match-play from 1947 to 1990.

Youngest and oldest national champion Asa A. Long (b. 20 Aug 1904) became the youngest US national champion, at age 18 yr 64 days, when he won in Boston, MA on 23 Oct 1922. He became the oldest, age 79 yr 334 days, when he won his sixth title in Tupelo, MS on 21 Jul 1984. He was also world champion from 1934 to 1938.

Most opponents Major H. Roy White played a record 222 games simultaneously, winning 221 and drawing 1, at the Canadian Forces Base, Cornwallis, Nova Scotia, Canada on 27 Oct 1990.

The largest number of opponents played without a defeat or draw is 172 by Nate Cohen of Portland, ME at Portland on 26 Jul 1981. This was not a simultaneous attempt, but consecutive play over a period of four hours.

Newell W. Banks (1887–1977) played 140 games simultaneously, winning 133 and drawing seven, in Chicago, IL in 1933. His total playing time was 145 min, thus averaging about one move per sec. In 1947 he played blindfolded for 4 hr per day for 45 consecutive days, winning 1,331 games, drawing 54 and losing only two, while playing six games at a time.

Longest and shortest games In competition the prescribed rate of play is not less than 30 moves per hour, with the average game lasting about 90 min. In 1958 a game between Dr Marion Tinsley (USA) and Derek Oldbury (Great Britain) lasted 7 hr 30 min (played under the 5-minutes-a-move rule).

The shortest possible game is one of 20 moves composed by Alan Malcolm Beckerson (Great Britain) in 1977.

CHESS

Origins The game is believed to have originated in ancient India under the name *Chaturanga* (literally "four-corps")—the name for the four traditional army divisions. The name *chess* is derived from the Persian word *shah* (a king or ruler). The earliest written reference is from the Middle Persian *Chatrang Namak* (*c.* A.D. 590–628). The oldest pieces identified as chesspieces were found at Nashipur, datable to *c.* A.D. 900. Chess reached Britain *c.* 1255. The *Fédération Internationale des Echecs* (FIDE) was established 1924.

World championships World champions have been officially recognized since 1886. The longest undisputed tenure was 26 yr 337 days, by Dr Emanuel Lasker (1868–1941) of Germany, from 1894 to 1921.

The women's world championship title was held by Vera Francevna Stevenson-Menchik (USSR, later Great Britain; 1906–44) from 1927 until her death, and was successfully defended a record seven times.

The first American to be regarded as world champion was Paul Charles Morphy (1837–89) in 1858.

Team The USSR has won the biennial men's team title (Olympiad) a record 18 times between 1952 and 1990, and the women's title 11 times from its introduction in 1957 to 1986.

The USA has won the men's title five times: 1931, 1933, 1935, 1937 and 1976.

Youngest Gary Kimovich Kasparov (USSR; b. 13 Apr 1963) won the title on 9 Nov 1985 at age 22 yr 210 days.

Maya Grigoryevna Chiburdanidze (USSR; b. 17 Jan 1961) won the women's title in 1978 when only 17.

Oldest Wilhelm Steinitz (Austria, later USA; 1836–1900) was 58 yr 10 days when he lost his title to Lasker on 26 May 1894.

Most active Anatoliy Yevgenyevich Karpov (USSR; b. 23 May 1951) in his tenure as champion, 1975–85, averaged 45.2 competitive games per year, played in 32 tournaments and finished first in 26.

Grand Masters The youngest individual to qualify as an International Grand Master is Robert James "Bobby" Fischer (USA; b. 9 Mar 1943), age 15 yr 185 days on 10 Sep 1958.

Highest rating The highest rating ever attained on the officially adopted Elo System is 2,800, by Gary Kasparov (USSR) at the end of 1989.

The highest-rated woman player is Judit Polgar (Hungary; b. 25 Jul 1976), who is currently at 2,540 but has achieved a peak rating of 2,555.

Least games lost by a world champion José Raúl Capablanca (Cuba; 1888–1942) lost only 34 games (out of 571) in his adult career, 1909–39.

He was unbeaten from 10 Feb 1916 to 21 Mar 1924 (63 games) and was world champion 1921–27.

US Championships The most wins since the US Championships became determined by match play competition in 1888 is eight, by Bobby Fischer, 1958–66. Fischer, world champion 1972–75, reached a rating on the Elo system of 2,785, the highest ever until surpassed by Gary Kasparov in 1989.

Most opponents The record for most consecutive games played is 663, by Vlastimil Hort (Czechoslovakia, later Germany; b. 12 Jan 1944) over 32½ hours at Porz, Germany on 5–6 Oct 1984. He played 60–120 opponents at a time, scoring over 80 percent wins and averaging 30 moves per game. He also holds the record for most games played simultaneously, 201 during 550 consecutive games of which he only lost ten, in Seltjarnes, Iceland on 23–24 Apr 1977.

Eric G. J. Knoppert (Netherlands; b. 20 Sep 1959) played 500 games of ten-minute chess against opponents, averaging 2,002 on the Elo scale on 13–16 Sep 1985. He scored 413 points (1 for win, ½ for draw), a success rate of 82.6 percent.

MONOPOLY

Monopoly, a real-estate trading game, of which Parker Brothers has sold in excess of 100 million copies worldwide in 23 languages (the most recent in Russian), was devised by Charles Darrow (1889–1967) of Germantown, PA, in 1923. While unemployed as a heating engineer during the Depression, he created the game using the street names of Atlantic City, NJ, where he spent his vacations.

World Champions The current holder of the World Monopoly Championship trophy and medal is Ikuo Hiyakuta of Japan. He won the eighth World Monopoly Tournament (held every three years under the auspices of Parker Brothers) at the Park Lane Hotel, London, Great Britain in 1988 after two days of grueling play. His prize was $15,140 and a personal computer.

SCRABBLE Crossword Game

Origins The crossword game was invented by Alfred M. Butts in 1931 and was developed, refined and trademarked as Scrabble Crossword Game by James Brunot in 1948.

Highest scores The highest competitive game score is 1,049 by Phil Appleby (b. 9 Dec 1957) in June 1989. His opponent scored 253, and the margin of victory, 796 points, is also a record. His score included a single turn of 374 for the word "OXIDIZERS."

The highest competitive single turn score recorded, however, is 392, by Dr Saladin Karl Khoshnaw (of Kurdish origin) in Manchester, Great Britain in April 1982. He laid down "CAZIQUES," which means "native chiefs of West Indian aborigines."

Most moves

The Master chess game with most moves on record was one of 269 moves, when Ivan Nikolić drew with Goran Arsović in a Belgrade, Yugoslavia tournament, on 17 Feb 1989. It took a total of 20 hr 15 min.

Domino stacking

David Coburn successfully stacked 291 dominoes on a single supporting domino on 19 Aug 1988 in Miami, FL.

Domino toppling

The greatest number set up single-handedly and toppled is 281,581 out of 320,236 by Klaus Friedrich, 22, at Fürth, Germany on 27 Jan 1984. The dominoes fell within 12 min 57.3 sec, having taken 31 days (10 hr daily) to set up.

Thirty students at Delft, Eindhoven and Twente Technical Universities in the Netherlands set up 1,500,000 dominoes representing all the European Community member countries. Of these, 1,382,101 were toppled by one push on 2 Jan 1988.

Most tournaments Chuck Armstrong, a hospital worker from Saline, MI, has won the most tournaments—65 to the end of 1989.

Bobsled and Luge

BOBSLEDDING

Origins The oldest known sled is dated *c.* 6500 B.C. and came from Heinola, Finland. The first known bobsled race took place at Davos, Switzerland in 1889. The International Federation of Bobsled and Luge was formed in 1923, followed by the International Bobsled Federation in 1957.

Most titles The Olympic four-man bob title (instituted 1924) has been won five times by Switzerland (1924, 1936, 1956, 1972 and 1988).

The USA (1932, 1936), Switzerland (1948, 1980), Italy (1956, 1968), West Germany (1952, 1972) and East Germany (1976, 1984) have won the Olympic two-man bob event twice.

The most gold medals won by an individual is three, by Meinhard Nehmer (East Germany; b. 13 Jun 1941) and Bernhard Germeshausen (East Germany; b. 21 Aug 1951) in the 1976 two-man, 1976 and 1980 four-man events.

The most medals won is six (two gold, two silver, two bronze) by Eugenio Monti (Italy; b. 23 Jan 1928), 1956 to 1968.

World and Olympic The world four-man bob title (instituted 1924) has been won 19 times by Switzerland (1924, 1936, 1939, 1947, 1954–57, 1971–73, 1975, 1982–83, 1986–90), including their five Olympic victories.

Italy won the two-man title 14 times (1954, 1956–63, 1966, 1968–69, 1971 and 1975).

Eugenio Monti was a member of 11 world championship crews, eight two-man and three four-man, in 1957–68.

Most titles Two American bobsledders have won two gold medals: driver William Mead Lindsley "Billy" Fiske III (1911–40) and crewman Clifford Barton Grey (1887–1941) in 1928 and 1932. At age 16 yr 260 days in 1928 Fiske was America's youngest-ever Winter Games gold medalist.

Oldest gold medalist The oldest age at which a gold medal has been won at any sport at the Winter Olympics is 49 yr 7 days, for James Jay O'Brien (USA; 1883–1940) at four-man bob.

LUGEING

In lugeing the rider adopts a supine, as opposed to a sitting position. Official international competition began at Klosters, Switzerland in 1881. The first European championships were at Reichenberg, Germany in 1914 and the first World Championships at Oslo, Norway in 1953. The International Luge Federation was formed in 1957. Lugeing became an Olympic sport in 1964.

Most titles The most successful riders in the World Championships have been Thomas Köhler (East Germany; b. 25 Jun 1940), who won the single-seater title in 1962, 1964 (Olympic), 1965 and 1967 and shared the two-seater title in 1967 and 1968 (Olympic), and Hans Rinn (East Germany; b. 19 Mar 1953), Olympic champion two-seater 1976 and 1980 and world champion at single-seater 1973 and 1977, two-seater 1977 and 1980. Margit Schumann (East Germany; b. 14 Sep 1952) has won five women's titles, 1973–75, 1976 (Olympic) and 1977.

Steffi Walter (nee Martin [East Germany]; b. 17 Sep 1962) became the first rider to win two Olympic single-seater luge titles, with victories at the women's event in 1984 and 1988.

Fastest speed The fastest recorded photo-timed speed is 85.38 mph, by Asle Strand (Norway) at Tandådalens Lin-

bana, Sälen, Sweden on 1 May 1982.

TOBOGGANING

Origins The word *toboggan* comes from the Micmac American Indian word *tobaakan*. The St Moritz Luge Club, Switzerland, founded in 1887, is the oldest toboggan club in the world. It is notable for being the home of the Cresta Run, which dates from 1884, and for the introduction of the one-man skeleton racing toboggan.

Cresta Run The course is 3,977 ft long with a drop of 514 ft, and the record is 50.91 sec (av. 53.26 mph) by Franco Gansser of Switzerland on 22 Feb 1987. On 21 Feb 1986 Nico Baracchi (Switzerland) set a record from Junction (2,920 ft) of 41.58 sec. The greatest number of wins in the Grand National (instituted in 1885) is eight, by the 1948 Olympic champion Nino Bibbia (Italy; b. 15 Mar 1922) in 1960–64, 1966, 1968 and 1973, and by Franco Gansser in 1981, 1983–86, 1988–89 and 1991. The greatest number of wins in the Curzon Cup (instituted 1910) is eight, by Bibbia in 1950, 1957–58, 1960, 1962–64 and 1969. He thus won the double in 1960 and 1962–64.

SLED DOG RACING

Longest trail Racing between har-

Cresta run winners
The only men to have won the four most important races (Curzon Cup, Brabazon Trophy, Morgan Cup and Grand National) in one season are: Bruno Bischofberger (1972), Paul Felder (1974), Nico Baracchi (1982) and Franco Gansser (1988), all of Switzerland.

Highest bowling score—24 hours
A team of six scored 202,015 at Verdes Tropicana at West Palm Beach, FL on 24–25 Aug 1990. This total included an individual 24 hr record of 44,695 by Mike Cernobyl.

nessed dog teams (usually huskies) had been practiced by the Inuits and the northern Indians of North America and in Scandinavia, but the first formal record of a race was in 1908, when the All-Alaskan Sweepstakes were contested on a run of 408 miles from Nome to Candle and back.

Now established as the world's most prestigious sled dog race, the Iditarod trail has existed since 1910 and has been raced annually since 1967 by dog teams, 1,049 miles from Anchorage to Nome, AK. The inaugural winner, Dick Wilmarth, took 20 days 49 min and 41 sec to complete the course, beating 33 other racers.

The fastest time was set by Susan Butcher (winner 1986–88 and 1990) in 1990 with 11 days 1 hr 53 min 23 sec. Rick Swenson has won the race a record five times (1977–79, 1981–82 and 1991).

Bowling

Origins The ancient German game of nine-pins (*Heidenwerfen*—"knock down pagans") was exported to the United States in the early 17th century. In 1841 the Connecticut State Legislature prohibited the game, and other states followed. Eventually a tenth pin was added to evade the ban; but there is some evidence of ten pins being used in Suffolk, Great Britain about 200 years ago.

The first body to standardize rules was the American Bowling Congress (ABC), established in New York City on 9 Sep 1895.

World Championships The World (*Fédération Internationale des Quilleurs*) Championships were instituted for men in 1954 and for women in 1963.

The highest pinfall in the individual men's event is 5,963 (in 28 games) by Ed Luther (USA) at Milwaukee, WI on 28 Aug 1971.

For the current schedule of 24 games the men's record is 5,261 by Richard Clay "Rick" Steelsmith (b. 1 Jun 1964), and the women's record is 4,894 by Sandra Jo Shiery (USA), both at Helsinki, Finland in June 1987.

Highest scores The highest individual score for three sanctioned games (out of a possible 900) is 899, by Thomas Jordan (USA; b. 27 Oct 1966) at Union, NJ on 7 Mar 1989. He followed with a 299, setting a four-game series record of 1,198 pins.

The record by a woman is 864, by Jeanne Maiden (b. 10 Nov 1957) at Tacoma, WA OH on 23 Nov 1986.

The maximum 900 for a three-game series was achieved by Glenn Richard Allison (USA; b. 22 May 1930) at the La Habra Bowl in Los Angeles, CA on 1 Jul 1982, but this was not recognized by the

ABC due to the oiling patterns on the boards.

It has been recorded five times in unsanctioned games—by Leon Bentley at Lorain, OH on 26 Mar 1931; by Joe Sargent at Rochester, NY in 1934; by Jim Murgie in Philadelphia, PA on 4 Feb 1937; by Bob Brown at Roseville Bowl, CA on 12 Apr 1980; and by John Strausbaugh at York, PA on 11 Jul 1987. Such series must have consisted of 36 consecutive strikes (i.e., all pins down with one ball).

The record for consecutive strikes in sanctioned match play is 33, first achieved by John Pezzin (b. 1930) at Toledo, OH on 4 Mar 1976.

Youngest and oldest 300 shooters The youngest bowler to score 300 is said to be Richard Daff, Jr. of Crownsville, MD (b. 28 Aug 1978), who performed this feat at age 11, on 8 Apr 1990. The oldest bowler to score 300 is Leo Sites of Witchita, KS, who performed the feat on 10 Apr 1985 at age 80.

Largest bowling center The Fukuyama Bowl, Osaka, Japan has 144 lanes. The Tokyo World Lanes Center, Japan, now closed, had 252 lanes.

United States The largest bowling center in the USA is Showboat Lanes in Las Vegas, NV, with 106 lanes.

In the United States there were 8,103 bowling establishments with 153,403 lanes in 1988/89 and about 71 million bowlers.

PROFESSIONAL BOWLERS ASSOCIATION (PBA)

Most titles Earl Anthony (b. 27 Apr 1938) of Dublin, CA has won a lifetime total of 41 PBA titles through 1990. The record number of titles won in one PBA season is 8, by Mark Roth (b. 10 Apr 1951) of North Arlington, NJ, in 1978.

Consecutive titles Only three bowlers have ever won three consecutive professional tournaments—Dick Weber (b. 23 Dec 1929) (three times), in 1959, 1960 and 1961, Johnny Petraglia (b. 3 Mar 1947) in 1971, and Mark Roth in 1977.

Perfect games A total of 141 perfect (300-pin) games were bowled in PBA tournaments in 1990, the most ever for one year.

Dick Weber rolled three perfect games in one tournament (Houston, TX) in 1965, as did Billy Hardwick (b. 25 Jul 1941) of Louisville, KY (in the Japan Gold Cup competition) in 1968, John Wilcox (at Detroit, MI), in 1979, Norm Meyers of St Louis (at Peoria, IL) in 1979, Ray Shackelford of Hartwood, VA (at St Louis, MO) in 1982, Shawn Christensen of Denver (at Denver, CO) in 1984, and Amleto Monacelli (b. 27 Aug 1961) of Venezuela (at Tuscon, AZ) in 1989.

Amleto Monacelli rolled seven perfect games on the 1989 tour and Guppy Troup

(b. 18 Jan 1950) of Savannah, GA, rolled six perfect games on the 1979 tour.

Triple crown The United States Open, the PBA National Championship and the Firestone Tournament of Champions comprise the Triple Crown of men's professional bowling. No bowler has won each of the three titles in the same year, and only three have managed to win all three during a career.

The first bowler to accumulate the three legs of the triple crown was Billy Hardwick: National Championship (1963); Firestone Tournament of Champions (1965); US Open (1969). Hardwick's feat was matched by Johnny Petraglia: Firestone (1971); US Open (1977); National (1980); and by Pete Weber: Firestone (1987); US Open (1988); National (1989).

US Open Since its inauguration in 1942, the most wins in this tournament is four by two bowlers: Don Carter in 1953–54 and 1957–58, and Dick Weber in 1962–63 and 1965–66.

PBA National championship Since its inauguration in 1960, the most wins in this tournament is six by Earl Anthony in 1973–75 and 1981–83.

Firestone Tournament of Champions Since its inauguration in 1965, the most wins in this tournament is three by Mike Durbin in 1972, 1982 and 1984.

Highest earners Marshall Holman (b. 29 Sep 1954) won a record $1,925,957 to the end of 1990 in Professional Bowlers Association (PBA) competition. Earl Roderick Anthony (b. 27 Apr 1938) was the first to win $1 million.

Mike Aulby (b. 25 Mar 1960) of Indianapolis, IN set a single-season earnings mark of $298,237 in 1989.

Television bowling Nelson Burton, Jr. (b. 5 Jun 1942) of St Louis rolled the best series, 1,050, for four games (278–279–257–236) at Dick Weber Lanes in Florissant, MO, 11 Feb 1984.

AMERICAN BOWLING CONGRESS (ABC)

Highest score The highest individual score for three games is 899 by Thomas Jordan at Union, NJ on 7 Mar 1989 (see Bowling—Highest scores). Highest three-game team score is 3,858 by Budweisers of St Louis on 12 Mar 1958.

The highest season average attained in sanctioned competition is 245.63 by Doug Vergouven of Harrisonville, MO in the 1989/90 season.

The all-time ABC-sanctioned two-man single-game record is 600, held jointly by the teams of John Cotta (300) and Steve Larson (300) on 1 May 1981, at the Manteca, CA, Bowling Association Tournament; Jeff Mraz and Dave Roney of Canton, OH on 8 Nov 1987 in the Ann Doubles Classic in Canton, OH; William Gruner and Dave Conway of Oceanside,

CA on 27 Feb 1990; and Scott Williams and Willie Hammar of Utica, NY on 7 Jan 1990.

The two-man team series record is 1,655 by Tom Jordon (899) and Ken Yorker, Jr. (856) in Union, NJ on 7 Mar 1989.

Perfect scores The highest number of sanctioned 300 games is 42, by Bob Learn, Jr. of Erie, PA.

Two perfect games were rolled back-to-back *twice* by Al Spotts of West Reading, PA on 14 Mar 1982 and again on 1 Feb 1985.

ABC CHAMPIONSHIPS TOURNAMENT

Highest score Highest three-game series in the ABC Championships tournament in singles is 826 by Ed Deines of Ft. Collins, CO in 1991. Best three-game total in any ABC event is 857 by Norm Duke of Albuquerque, NM in 1989. George Hall of Mundelein, IL holds the record for a nine-game All-Events total with 2,227 (747–747–733) set in Wichita, KS in 1989.

ABC Hall of Famers Fred Bujack of Detroit, MI, Bill Lillard of Houston, TX and Nelson Burton, Jr. of St Louis, MO have won the most championships with eight each. Bujack shared in three team and four team All-Events titles between 1949 and 1955, and also won the individual All-Events title in 1955. Lillard bowled on regular and team All-Events champions in 1955 and 1956, the Classic team champions in 1962 and 1971, and won regular doubles and All-Events titles in 1956. Burton shared in three Classic team titles, two Classic doubles titles and has won Classic singles twice and Classic All-Events.

Highest doubles The ABC national tournament record of 561 was set in 1989 by Rick McCardy and Steve Mesmer of Redford, MI. The record score in a doubles series is 1,505 set in 1991 by Jimmy Johnson (784) of Columbus, OH and Dan Nadeau (721) of Las Vegas, NV.

Perfect scores Les Schissler of Denver scored 300 in the Classic team event in 1967, and Ray Williams of Detroit scored 300 in regular team play in 1974, the first two perfect games bowled in team competition. In all, there have been only 146 perfect games in the regular ABC tournament through 1991.

Best finishes Mike Newman of Buffalo, NY won the doubles, All-Events, and was on two winning teams in 1989 to tie Ed Lubanski of Detroit, MI and Bill Lillard of Houston, TX as the only men to win four ABC crowns in one year.

Youngest and oldest winners The youngest champion was Ronnie Knapp of New London, OH, who was a member of the 1963 Booster team champions when he was 16 years old.

The oldest champion was Joe Detloff of Chicago, IL who, at the age of 72, was a winner in the 1965 Booster team event. The oldest doubles team in ABC compe-

tition totaled 165 years in 1955: Jerry Ameling (83) and Joseph Lehnbeutter (82), both from St Louis.

Strikes and spares in a row In the greatest finish to win an ABC title, Ed Shay set a record of 12 strikes in a row in 1958, when he scored a perfect game for a total of 733 in singles. Most strikes in a row is 20 by Lou Veit of Milwaukee, WI in 1977. The most spares in a row is 23 by Lt Hazen Sweet of Battle Creek, MI in 1950.

Most tournament appearances Bill Doehrman of Fort Wayne, IN competed in 71 consecutive ABC tournaments, beginning in 1908. (No tournaments were held 1943–45.)

WOMEN'S INTERNATIONAL BOWLING CONGRESS (WIBC)

Highest scores Patty Ann of Appleton, WI, had a record five-year composite average of 227 through the 1985/86 season. She also had the best one-season average, 232, in the 1983/84 season.

Jeanne Maiden of Tacoma, WA, has rolled 17 perfect games to set the WIBC career record. She also set a record of 40 consecutive strikes in 1986 and rolled an 864 on games of 300–300–264.

The highest five-woman team score for a three-game series is 3,493, by Lisa's Flowers and Gift Shop, Franklin, WI in the 1989/90 season. The highest game score by a five-woman team is 1,244 by Chamberlain Wholesale of Detroit, MI in the 1987/88 season.

Championship Tournaments The highest score for a three-game series in the annual WIBC Championship Tournament is 773 by Debbie Kuhn of Baltimore, MD in the 1991 singles event. She also holds the record for highest All-Events score (nine games), with 2,036 in 1991.

The record for one game is 300 by Lori Gensch of Milwaukee, WI in the 1979 doubles event, by Rose Walsh of Pomona, CA in the 1986 singles event, and by Linda Kelly of Huber Heights, OH in the 1987 singles event.

Dorothy Miller of Chicago, IL has won ten WIBC Championship Tournament events, the most by an individual. Millie Ignizo is the only one to have won three WIBC Queens Tournaments, in 1967, 1970, and 1971.

The highest WIBC Championship Tournament lifetime average is 199.17 by Dorothy Fothergill of Lincoln, RI, who has bowled for ten years, but is now inactive.

Oldest and youngest players Mary Covell of Chicago, IL participated in her 60th WIBC tournament in 1991. The oldest participant was Ethel Brunnick (b. 30 Aug 1887) of Santa Monica, CA, at age 99 in 1987.

Mary Ann Keiper of St Louis, MO was only 5 years old when she participated in the 1952 tournament.

The youngest champion was Leila

Wagner (b. 12 Jul 1960) of Annapolis, MD, who was 18 when she was a member of the championship five-woman team in 1979.

Perfect games The most 300 games rolled in a career is 17 by Jeanne Maiden of Tacoma, WA. The oldest woman to bowl a perfect game (12 strikes in a row) was Helen Duval of Berkeley, CA, at age 65 in 1982. Of all the women who rolled a perfect game, the one with the lowest average was Diane Ponza of Santa Cruz, CA who had a 112 average in the 1977/78 season.

Consecutive strikes, spares and splits The record for most consecutive strikes is 40 by Jeanne Maiden (see above). Mabel Henry of Winchester, KY had 30 consecutive spares in the 1986/87 season. Shirley Topbigh of Las Vegas, NV, holds the unenviable record of rolling 14 consecutive splits in 1968/69.

Boxing

Origins Boxing with gloves was depicted on a fresco, dated *c.* 1520 B.C. from the Isle of Thera, Greece. The earliest prizering code of rules was formulated in England on 16 Aug 1743 by the champion pugilist Jack Broughton (1704–89), who reigned from 1734 to 1750. Boxing in 1867 came under the Queensberry Rules formulated for John Sholto Douglas, 8th Marquess of Queensberry (1844–1900).

New York was the first state to legalize boxing in the United States, in 1896. Today professional boxing is regulated in each state by athletic or boxing commissions.

Longest fights The longest recorded fight with gloves was between Andy Bowen of New Orleans (1867–94) and Jack Burke at New Orleans, LA on 6–7 Apr 1893. It lasted 110 rounds, 7 hr 19 min (9:15 P.M.–4:34 A.M.), and was declared a no contest (later changed to a draw). Bowen won an 85-round bout on 31 May 1893.

The longest bare-knuckle fight was 6 hr 15 min between James Kelly and Jack Smith at Fiery Creek, Dalesford, Victoria, Australia on 3 Dec 1855.

The greatest number of rounds was 276 in 4 hr 30 min when Jack Jones beat Patsy Tunney in Cheshire, Great Britain in 1825.

Shortest fights There is a distinction between the quickest knockout and the shortest fight. A knockout in 10½ sec (including a 10 sec count) occurred on 23 Sep 1946, when Al Couture struck Ralph Walton while the latter was adjusting a gum shield in his corner at Lewiston, ME. If the time was accurately recorded it is clear that Couture must have been more than halfway across the ring from his own corner at the opening bell.

The shortest fight on record appears to

■ Largest attendance
Muhammad Ali (l) and Leon Spinks (r) square off during their WBA World Heavyweight title fight at the Superdome, New Orleans on 15 Sep 1978. The fight attracted a crowd of 63,350, the largest ever for an indoor fight. Ali won on points and regained the world title for a record second time. (Photo: All-Sport [USA])

have been one in a Golden Gloves tournament at Minneapolis, MN on 4 Nov 1947, when Mike Collins floored Pat Brownson with the first punch and the contest was stopped, without a count, 4 sec after the opening bell.

The shortest world title fight was 45 sec, when Lloyd Honeyghan (Great Britain; b. 22 Apr 1960) beat Gene Hatcher (USA) in an IBF welterweight bout at Marbella, Spain on 30 Aug 1987. Some sources also quote the Al McCoy (1894–1966) first round knockout of George Chip in a middleweight contest on 7 Apr 1914 as being in 45 sec.

The shortest-ever heavyweight world title fight was the James J. Jeffries (1875–1953)–Jack Finnegan bout at Detroit, MI on 6 Apr 1900, won by Jeffries in 55 sec.

Eugene Brown, on his professional debut, knocked out Ian Bockes at Leicester, Great Britain, on 13 Mar 1989. The fight was officially stopped after ten seconds of the first round. Bockes got up after a count of six but the referee stopped the contest.

Tallest The tallest boxer to fight professionally was Gogea Mitu (b. 1914) of Romania, in 1935. He was 7 ft 4 in and weighed 327 lb.

John Rankin, who won a fight in New Orleans, LA in November 1967, was reputedly also 7 ft 4 in.

Jim Culley, "The Tipperary Giant," who fought as a boxer and wrestled in the 1940s, is also reputed to have been 7 ft 4 in.

Most fights without loss Edward Henry "Harry" Greb (USA; 1894–1926) was unbeaten in a sequence of 178 bouts, but these included 117 "no decision," of which five were unofficial losses, in 1916–23.

Of boxers with complete records, Packey McFarland (USA; 1888–1936) had 97 fights (5 draws) in 1905–15 without a defeat.

Pedro Carrasco (Spain; b. 7 Nov 1943) won 83 consecutive fights from 22 April 1964 to 3 Sep 1970, drew once and had a further nine wins before his loss to Armando Ramos in a WBC lightweight contest on 18 Feb 1972.

Most knockouts The greatest number of finishes classed as "knockouts" in a career (1936–63) is 145 (129 in professional bouts), by Archie Moore (USA; b. Archibald Lee Wright, 13 Dec 1913 or 1916).

The record for consecutive KO's is 44 by Lamar Clark (USA; b. 1 Dec 1934) from 1958 to 11 Jan 1960. He knocked out six in one night (five in the first round) at Bingham, UT on 1 Dec 1958.

Largest purse The total purse for the world heavyweight fight between Mike Gerard Tyson (USA; b. 30 Jun 1966) and Michael Spinks (USA; b. 22 Jul 1956) at Convention Hall, Atlantic City, NJ on 27 Jun 1988, was estimated as at least $35.8 million, $22 million for Tyson and $13.8 million for Spinks, who was knocked out after 1 min 31 sec of the first round.

Attendances *Highest* The greatest paid attendance at any boxing match was 120,757 (with a ringside price of $27.50) for the Gene T. Tunney v Jack D. Dempsey world heavyweight title fight at the Sesquicentennial Stadium, Philadelphia, PA on 23 Sep 1926.

The indoor record is 63,350, at the Muhammad Ali v Leon Spinks (b. 11 Jul 1953) fight in the Superdome, New Orleans, LA on 15 Sep 1978.

The highest nonpaying attendance is 135,132, at the Tony Zale v Billy Pryor fight at Juneau Park, Milwaukee, WI on 16 Aug 1941.

Lowest The smallest attendance at a world heavyweight title fight was 2,434, at the Cassius Clay (Muhammad Ali) v Sonny Liston fight at Lewiston, ME on 25 May 1965.

WORLD HEAVYWEIGHT

Earliest title fight Long accepted as the first world heavyweight title fight, with gloves and 3-min rounds, was that between John Lawrence Sullivan (1858–1918) and James John "Gentleman Jim" Corbett (1866–1933) in New Orleans, LA on 7 Sep 1892. Corbett won in 21 rounds. However, the fight between Sullivan, then the world bare-knuckle champion, and Dominick F. McCafferey in Chester Park, Cincinnati, OH on 29 Aug 1885 was staged under Queensberry Rules with the boxers wearing gloves over six rounds. The referee, Billy Tait, left the ring without giving a verdict, but when asked two days later said that Sullivan had won.

Reign *Longest* Joe Louis (USA; b. Joseph Louis Barrow, 1914–81) was champion for 11 years 252 days, from 22 Jun 1937, when he knocked out James Joseph Braddock in the eighth round at Chicago, IL, until announcing his retirement on 1 Mar 1949. During his reign Louis made a record 25 defenses of his title.

Shortest 83 days for WBA champion James "Bonecrusher" Smith (USA; b. 3 Apr 1955), 13 Dec 1986 to 7 Mar 1987, and for Ken Norton (USA; b. 9 Aug 1945), recognized by the WBC as champion from 18 Mar–9 Jun 1978. Tony Tucker (USA; b. 28 Dec 1958) was IBF champion for 64 days, 30 May–2 Aug 1987.

Most recaptures Muhammad Ali is the only man to regain the heavyweight championship twice. Ali first won the title on 25 Feb 1964, defeating Sonny Liston. He defeated George Foreman on 30 Oct 1974, having been stripped of the title by the world boxing authorities on 28 Apr 1967. He won the WBA title from Leon Spinks on 15 Sep 1978, having previously lost to him on 15 Feb 1978.

Undefeated Rocky Marciano (USA; b. Rocco Francis Marchegiano, 1923–69) is the only world champion at any weight to have won every fight of his entire professional career (1947–56); 43 of his 49 fights were by knockouts or stoppages.

Oldest "Jersey Joe" Walcott (USA; b. Arnold Raymond Cream, 31 Jan 1914) was 37 yr 168 days when he knocked out Ezzard Mack Charles (1921–75) on 18 Jul 1951 in Pittsburgh, PA. He was also the oldest holder, at 38 yr 236 days, losing his title to Rocky Marciano on 23 Sep 1952.

Youngest Mike Tyson (USA) was 20 yr 144 days when he beat Trevor Berbick (USA) to win the WBC version at Las Vegas, NV on 22 Nov 1986. He added the WBA title when he beat James "Bonecrusher" Smith on 7 Mar 1987 at 20 yr 249 days. He became universal champion on 2 Aug 1987 when he beat Tony Tucker (USA) for the IBF title.

Tallest There is uncertainty as to the tallest world champion. Ernest Terrell (USA; b. 4 Apr 1939), WBA champion 1965–67, was reported to be 6 ft 6 in. Slightly higher figures had been given for earlier champions, but, according to measurements by the physical education director of the Hemingway Gymnasium, Harvard University, Cambridge, MA, Primo Carnera was 6 ft 5.4 in, although widely reported and believed to be up to 6 ft 8½ in. Jess Willard (1881–1968), who won the title in 1915, often stated to be 6 ft 6¼ in, was in fact 6 ft 5¼ in.

Shortest Tommy Burns, world champion from 23 Feb 1906 to 26 Dec 1908, stood 5 ft 7 in and weighed between 168–180 lb.

WORLD CHAMPIONS
Any weight

Reign *Longest* The Joe Louis heavyweight duration record of 11 yr 252 days stands for all divisions.

Shortest Tony Canzoneri (USA; 1908–59) was world light welterweight champion for 33 days, 21 May to 23 Jun 1933, the shortest period for a boxer to have won and lost the world title in the ring.

Youngest Wilfred Benitez (b. New York, 12 Sep 1958) of Puerto Rico, was 17 yr 176 days when he won the WBA light welterweight title in San Juan, Puerto Rico on 6 Mar 1976.

Oldest Archie Moore, who was recognized as a light heavyweight champion up to 10 Feb 1962 when his title was removed, was then believed to be between 45 and 48 years old.

Longest career Bob Fitzsimmons had a career of over 31

years, from 1883 to 1914. He had his last world title bout on 20 Dec 1905 at the age of 42 yr 208 days. Jack Johnson (USA; 1878–1946) also had a career of over 31 years, from 1897–1928.

Longest fight The longest world title fight (under Queensberry Rules) was that between the lightweights Joe Gans (1874–1910), of the USA, and Oscar Matthew "Battling" Nelson (1882–1954), the "Durable Dane," at Goldfield, NV on 3 Sep 1906. It was terminated in the 42nd round when Gans was declared the winner on a foul.

Most different weights The first to have won world titles at four weight categories was Thomas Hearns (USA; b. 18 Oct 1958), WBA welterweight in 1980, WBC super welterweight in 1982, WBC light heavyweight in 1987 and WBC middleweight in 1987. He added a fifth weight division when he won the super middleweight title recognized by the newly created World Boxing Organization (WBO) on 4 Nov 1988, and he won the WBA light heavyweight title in 1991.

Most titles recognized by the WBA and the WBC Sugar Ray Leonard (USA; b. 17 May 1956) won world titles at his fourth and fifth weight categories, when he beat Donny Lalonde (Canada) on 7 Nov 1988, to annex both WBC light heavyweight and super middleweight titles. He had previously won the WBC welterweight title in 1979 and 1980, WBA junior middleweight title in 1981 and WBC middleweight title in 1987.

The only man to hold world titles at three weights *simultaneously* was Henry "Homicide Hank" Armstrong (USA; 1912–88), at featherweight, lightweight and welterweight from August to December 1938. In recent years there has been a proliferation of weight categories and governing bodies but

Heaviest Primo Carnera (Italy; 1906–67), the "Ambling Alp," who won the title from Jack Sharkey in New York City on 29 Jun 1933, scaled 260½ lb for this fight, but his peak weight was 270 lb. He had an expanded chest measurement of 54 in and the longest reach at 85½ in (fingertip to fingertip).

Lightest heavyweight Robert James "Bob" Fitzsimmons (1863–1917) from Great Britain weighed 167 lb when he won the title by knocking out James J. Corbett at Carson City, NV on 17 Mar 1897.

■ **Longest-lived**
Jack Sharkey (b. Joseph Paul Cukoschay, 26 Oct 1902) is the longest-lived world heavyweight champion, surpassing the previous record of 87 yr 341 days held by Jack Dempsey (1895–1983), on 3 Oct 1990. Sharkey won the title on 21 Jun 1932, defeating Max Schmeling on points, but lost in his first defense to the "Ambling Alp," Primo Carnera, on 29 Jun 1933. (Photo: Hulton Picture Library)

Canoe raft
A raft of 376 kayaks and canoes, organized by the People's Association Youth Movement, was held together by hands only, while free-floating for 30 seconds, on the Johor Strait at Sembawang, Singapore on 26 Jun 1990.

Armstrong was undisputed world champion at widely differing weights, which makes his achievement all the more remarkable.

Most recaptures The only boxer to win a world title five times at one weight is "Sugar Ray" Robinson (USA; b. Walker Smith Jr., 1921–89), who beat Carmen Basilio (USA) in Chicago Stadium, IL on 25 Mar 1958 to regain the world middleweight title for the fourth time.

The record number of title bouts in a career is 37, of which 18 ended in "no decision," by three-time world welterweight champion Jack Britton (USA; 1885–1962) in 1915–22. The record containing no "no decision" contests is 27 (all heavyweight), by Joe Louis between 1937–50.

Greatest weight difference When Primo Carnera (Italy), 270 lb, fought Tommy Loughran (USA), 184 lb, for the world heavyweight title at Miami, FL on 1 Mar 1934, there was a weight difference of 86 lb between the two fighters. Carnera won the fight on points.

Greatest "tonnage" The greatest "tonnage" recorded in any fight is 700 lb when Claude "Humphrey" McBride (Oklahoma), 340 lb, knocked out Jimmy Black (Houston, TX), 360 lb, in the third round at Oklahoma City, OK on 1 Jun 1971.

The greatest "tonnage" in a world title fight was 488 ¾ lb, when Carnera, then 259 ½ lb, fought Paolino Uzcudun (Spain), 229 ¼ lb, in Rome, Italy on 22 Oct 1933.

Most knockdowns in title fight Vic Toweel (South Africa; b. 12 Jan 1929) knocked down Danny O'Sullivan of London, Great Britain 14 times in ten rounds in their world bantamweight fight at Johannesburg, South Africa on 2 Dec 1950, before the latter retired.

Twins When Khaokor Galaxy (Thailand) won the WBA bantamweight title on 8 May 1988, he and his twin brother, Khaosai, were the first twins ever to be world boxing champions. Khaosai Galaxy had been WBA super flyweight champion since 21 Nov 1984.

AMATEUR

Most Olympic titles Only two boxers have won three Olympic gold medals: southpaw László Papp (Hungary; b. 25 Mar 1926), middleweight winner 1948, light-middleweight winner 1952 and 1956; and Teofilo Stevenson (Cuba; b. 23 Mar 1952), heavyweight winner 1972, 1976 and 1980.

The only man to win two titles in one Olympic celebration was Oliver L. Kirk (USA) who won both bantam and featherweight titles in St Louis, MO in 1904, but he needed only one bout in each class.

A record that will stand forever is that of the youngest Olympic boxing champion: Jackie Fields (ne Finkelstein [USA]; b. 9 Feb 1908), who won the 1924 featherweight title at 16 yrs 162 days.

The minimum age for Olympic boxing competitors is now 17.

Oldest gold medalist Richard Kenneth Gunn (Great Britain; 1871–1961) won the Olympic featherweight gold medal on 27 Oct 1908 in London, Great Britain at the age of 37 yr 254 days.

World Championships Two boxers have won three world championships (instituted 1974): Teofilo Stevenson (Cuba), heavyweight winner 1974, 1978 and super-heavyweight winner 1986, and Adolfo Horta (Cuba; b. 3 Oct 1957) bantam winner 1978, feather winner 1982 and lightweight winner 1986.

Most US titles US Amateur Championships were first staged in 1888. The most titles won is five by middleweight W. Rodenbach, 1900–04.

Canoeing

Origins The acknowledged pioneer of canoeing as a modern sport was John Macgregor (1825–92), a British attorney, who founded the Canoe Club in Surrey, Great Britain on 26 Jul 1866.

The oldest club in the United States is the New York Canoe Club, founded at St George, Staten Island, NY in 1871. The American Canoe Association was formed on 3 Aug 1880.

Most titles *Olympics* Gert Fredriksson (Sweden; b. 21 Nov 1919) won a record six Olympic gold medals, 1948–60. He added a silver and a bronze for a record eight medals.

The most by a woman is three by Lyudmila Iosifovna Pinayeva (nee Khvedosyuk [USSR]; b. 14 Jan 1936), 1964–72 and Birgit Schmidt (nee Fischer [East Gremany]; b. 25 Feb 1962), one in 1980 and two in 1988.

The most gold medals at one Games is three by Vladimir Parfenovich (USSR; b. 2 Dec 1958) in 1980 and by Ian Ferguson (New Zealand; b. 20 Jul 1952) in 1984.

United States The only American canoeist to have won two Olympic gold medals is Gregory Mark Barton (b. 2 Dec 1959), who won at K1 and K2 1,000 m events in 1988. He also has a US record three medals, as he took bronze at K1 1,000 m in 1984.

World Including the Olympic Games, a

■ **Canoeing**
Greg Barton (right), gold medalist at K1 and K2 100 meter races in 1988, is the only American to win two Olympic gold medals at canoeing. (Photo: All-Sport [USA]/Mike Powell)

women's record 22 titles have been won by Birgit Schmidt, 1978–88.

The men's record is 13, by Gert Fredriksson, 1948–60, Rüdiger Helm (East Germany; b. 6 Oct 1956), 1976–83, and Ivan Patzaichin (Romania; b. 26 Nov 1949) 1968–84.

Most US titles Marcia Ingram Jones Smoke (b. 18 Jul 1941) won 35 US national titles bewtween 1962 and 1981, as well as 24 North American Championships and three gold medals at the 1967 Pan-American Games. The men's record is 33 US titles by Ernest Riedel (b. 13 Jul 1901) between 1930 and 1948, mostly at kayak events.

Fastest speed The Hungarian four-man kayak Olympic champions in 1988 at Seoul, South Korea covered 1,000 m in 2 min 58.54 sec in a heat. This represents an average speed of 12.53 mph.

In this same race the Norwegian four achieved a 250 m split of 42.08 sec between 500 m and 750 m for a speed of 13.29 mph.

Longest journey Father and son Dana and Donald Starkell paddled from Winnipeg, Manitoba, Canada by ocean and river to Belem, Brazil, a distance of 12,181 miles, from 1 Jun 1980 to 1 May 1982. All portages were human-powered.

Without portages or aid of any kind, the longest is one of 6,102 miles, by Richard H. Grant and Ernest "Moose" Lassy, circumnavigating the eastern USA via Chicago, New Orleans, Miami, New York City and the Great Lakes from 22 Sep 1930 to 15 Aug 1931.

Longest race The Canadian Government Centennial Voyageur Canoe Pageant and Race from Rocky Mountain House, Alberta to the Expo 67 site at Montreal, Quebec was 3,283 miles. Ten canoes represented Canadian provinces and territories. The winner of the race, which took from 24 May to 4 Sep 1967, was the Province of Manitoba canoe *Radisson*.

24 hours *Men* Zdzislaw Szubski paddled 157.1 miles in a Jaguar K1 canoe on the Vistula River, Wlocklawek to Gdansk, Poland, on 11–12 Sep 1987.

Women Lydia Formentin paddled 97.2 miles on the Swan River, Western Australia in 1979.

Flat water Thomas J. Mazuzan paddled, without benefit of current, 123.98 miles on the Barge Canal, New York State on 24–25 Sep 1986.

Open sea Randy Fine (USA) paddled 120.6 miles along the Florida coast on 26–27 Jun 1986.

Greatest lifetime distance Fritz Lindner of Berlin, Germany, totaled 64,278 miles from 1928 to 1987.

Highest altitude In September 1976 Dr Michael Leslie Jones (1951–78) and Michael Hopkinson of the British Everest Canoe Expedition canoed down the River Dudh Kosi, Nepal from an altitude of 17,500 ft.

Eskimo rolls with paddle Ray Hud-spith (b. 18 Apr 1960) achieved 1,000 rolls in 34 min 43 sec at the Elswick Pool, Newcastle-upon-Tyne, Great Britain on 20 Mar 1987. He completed 100 rolls in 3 min 7.25 sec at Killingworth Leisure Center, Great Britain on 3 Mar 1991.

Randy Fine (USA) completed 1,796 continuous rolls at Biscayne Bay, Miami, FL on 8 Jun 1991.

"Hand rolls" Colin Brian Hill (b. 16 Aug 1970) achieved 1,000 rolls in 31 min 55.62 sec at Consett, County Durham, Great Britain on 12 Mar 1987. He also achieved 100 rolls in 2 min 39.2 sec in London, Great Britain on 22 Feb 1987. He completed 3,700 continuous rolls at Durham City Swimming Baths, Great Britain on 1 May 1989.

Card Games

CONTRACT BRIDGE

Origins Bridge (a corruption of *biritch*, a now-obsolete Russian word whose meanings include "declarer") is thought either to be of Levantine origin, similar games having been played there in the early 1870s, or to have come from India.

Auction bridge (highest bidder names trump) was invented *c.* 1902. The contract principle, present in several games (notably the French game *plafond, c.* 1917), was introduced to bridge by Harold Stirling Vanderbilt (USA; 1884–1970) on 1 Nov 1925 during a Caribbean voyage aboard the SS *Finland*. It became a worldwide craze after the USA *v* Great Britain challenge match between Romanian-born Ely Culbertson (USA; 1891–1955) and Lt Col Walter Thomas More Buller (Great Britain; 1887–1938) at Almack's Club, London, Great Britain in September 1930. The USA won the 200-hand match by 4,845 points.

Biggest tournament The Epson World Bridge Championship, held on 7 Jun 1991, was contested by almost 90,000 players playing the same hands at centers in 95 countries.

Most world titles The World Championship (Bermuda Bowl) has been won a record 13 times by Italy's Blue Team (*Squadra Azzura*), 1957–59, 1961–63, 1965–67, 1969, 1973–75, and by the USA, 1950–51, 1953–54, 1970–71, 1976–77, 1979, 1981, 1983, 1985, 1987. Italy also won the team Olympiad in 1964, 1968 and 1972 and the US won in 1988.

Giorgio Belladonna (b. 7 Jun 1923) was on all the Italian winning teams.

The USA has a record five wins in the women's world championship for the Venice Trophy, 1974, 1976, 1978, 1987 and 1989, and three women's wins at the World Team Olympiad, 1976, 1980 and 1984.

Most world championship hands In the 1989 Bermuda Bowl in Perth, Australia, Marcel Branco and Gabriel Chagas, both of Brazil, played a record 752 out of a possible 784 boards.

Most master points In the latest ranking list based on Master Points awarded by the World Bridge Federation during the last ten years, the leading players in the world are (men) Robert Hamman (b. 1938) of Dallas, TX, with 597 and (women) Sandra Landy (Great Britain), with 284.

The all-time leading Master Point winner was Giorgio Belladonna (Italy) with 1,821 1/4 points.

The world's leading woman player is Jacqui Mitchell (USA), with 347 points.

Barry Crane of Los Angeles, CA led the American Contract Bridge League rankings from 1968 to his murder in 1985. He amassed a record total of 35,137.6 Master Points. The current leader is Paul Soloway, with 35,219 to July 1991.

The most master points scored in a year is 3,270, by Grant Baze (USA) in 1984.

The first man to win 10,000 Master Points was Oswald Jacoby (USA; 1902–84), in October 1967. He had been a member of the winning World Championship team in 1935, and on 4 Dec 1983 became the oldest member of a winning team of a major open team championship, in the Curtis Reisinger Trophy.

Rika "Rixi" Markus (Austria, later Great Britain; b. 27 Jun 1910) has won numerous titles during an illustrious career and became the first woman World Grand Master in 1974.

Youngest Life Master Joel Wooldridge (b. 19 Jul 1979) of Synder, NY became the world's youngest-ever Life Master on 2 Dec 1990 at 11 yr 4 months 13 days.

The youngest-ever woman Master is Patricia Thomas (b. 10 Oct 1968), at 14 yr 28 days in 1982.

CRIBBAGE

Origins The invention of the game (once spelled cribbidge) is credited to the English dramatist Sir John Suckling (1609–42).

Rare hands Four maximum 29-point hands have been achieved by William E. Johnson of Waltham, MA, 1974–81, and by Mrs Mary Matheson of Springhill, Nova Scotia, Canada, 1974–85. Paul Nault of Athol, MA had two such hands within eight games in a tournament on 19 Mar 1977.

Most points in 24 hours The most points scored by a team of four, playing singles in two pairs, is 111,201, by Christine and Elizabeth Gill, Jeanette MacGrath and Donald Ward at Grannie's Healin' Hame, Embo, Great Britain on 2–3 May 1987.

Cricket

Origins Cricket originated in England in the Middle Ages. It is impossible to

Card throwing Kevin St Onge threw a standard playing card 185 ft 1 in at the Henry Ford Community College campus, Dearborn, MI on 12 Jun 1979.

Perfect deals The mathematical odds against dealing 13 cards of one suit are 158,753,389,899 to 1, while the odds against a named player receiving a "perfect hand" consisting of all 13 spades are 635,013,559,599 to 1. The odds against each of the four players' receiving a complete suit (a "perfect deal") are 2,235,197,406,895,366-368,301,559,999 to 1.

Possible auctions The number of possible auctions with North as dealer is 128,745,650-347,030,683,120,231,926-111,609,371,363,122,697-557.

Card holding Georgios Stefanidis held 292 standard playing cards in a fan in one hand, so that the value and color of each one was visible, at Reutlingen, Germany on 16 Mar 1991.

CROQUET

Largest cross-country field
The largest recorded field in any cross-country race was 11,763 starters (10,810 finished), in the 18.6 miles Lidingöloppet, near Stockholm, Sweden on 3 Oct 1982.

■ **East African cross-country dominance**
In 1991 Kenya uniquely won all four cross-country running competitions—men and women, senior and junior—in the World Championships in Antwerp, Belgium, and Ethiopia came in second in all of them. The photo on the right shows action in the senior race, in which Africans, including eight Kenyans, took all of the first 13 places. In the junior race the first 16 runners were African.
(Photo: All-Sport)

pinpoint its exact origin; however, historians believe that the modern game developed in the mid-16th century. The earliest surviving scorecard is from a match played between England and Kent, Great Britain on 18 Jun 1744. The Marylebone Cricket Club (MCC) was founded in 1787 and, until 1968, was the world governing body for the sport. The International Cricket Conference (ICC) is responsible for international (Test) cricket, while the MCC remains responsible for the laws of cricket. The first international match was played between Canada and the USA in 1844. Fifteen years later those countries were host to the first English touring team.

First-class records *Career* The most runs scored in a career is 61,237, by Sir John Berry "Jack" Hobbs (1882–1963) for Surrey, Great Britain and England, 1905–34. The most wickets taken by an individual is 4,187, by Wilfred Rhodes (1877–1973) for Yorkshire and England, 1898–1930. The most dismissals by a wicket-keeper is 1,649 by Robert William Taylor (b. 17 Jul 1941) for Derbyshire and England, 1960–88. The most catches by a fielder is 1,018 by Frank Edward Woolley (1887–1978) for Kent, Great Britain and England, 1906–38.

TEST CRICKET

Origins The first match, now considered as a Test, was played at Melbourne, Australia on 15–19 Mar 1877 between Australia and England. Neither side was representative of its country, and indeed such was the case for many matches, now accepted as Tests, played over the next 50 years or so. Eight nations have played Test cricket: Australia, England, India, New Zealand, Pakistan, South Africa, Sri Lanka and West Indies.

Career records The most runs scored by an individual is 10,122, by Sunil Manohar Gavaskar (India; b. 10 Jul 1949) in 125 Tests, 1971–87. The most wickets taken by a bowler is 431, by Sir Richard John Hadlee (New Zealand; b. 3 Jul 1951) in 86 Tests, 1973–90. The most dismissals by a wicket-keeper is 355 by Rodney William Marsh (Australia; b. 11 Nov 1947), in 96 Tests, 1970–84. The most catches by a fielder is 130, by Allan Robert Border (Australia; b. 27 Jul 1955) in 125 Tests, 1978–91.

NATIONAL CRICKET CHAMPIONSHIPS

Australia The premier event in Australia is the Sheffield Shield, an interstate competition contested since 1891–92. New South Wales has won the title a record 40 times.

England The major championship in England is the County Championships, an intercounty competition officially recognized since 1890. Yorkshire has won the title a record 30 times.

India The Ranji Trophy is India's premier cricket competition. Established in 1934 in memory of K. S. Ranjitsinhji, it is contested on a zonal basis, culminating in a playoff competition. Bombay has won the tournament a record 30 times.

New Zealand Since 1975, the major championship in New Zealand has been the Shell Trophy. Otago, Wellington and Auckland have each won the competition four times.

Pakistan Pakistan's national championship is the Quaid-e-Azam Trophy, established in 1953. Karachi has won the trophy a record seven times.

South Africa The Currie Cup, donated by Sir Donald Currie, was first contested in 1889. Transvaal has won the competition a record 28 times.

West Indies The Red Stripe Cup, established in 1966, is the premier prize played for by the association of Caribbean islands (plus Guyana) that form the West Indies Cricket League. Barbados has won the competition a record 13 times.

Croquet

Origins Its exact origins are obscure, but croquet was probably derived from the French game *jeu de mail*, first mentioned in the 12th century. A game resembling croquet, possibly of foreign origin, was played in Ireland in the 1830s, and was introduced to England. Although croquet had been played in the United States for a number of years, a national body was not established until the formation of the United States Croquet Association (USCA) in 1976. The first United States Championship was played in 1977.

International trophy The MacRobertson International Shield (instituted 1925) has been won a record eight times by Great Britain in 1925, 1937, 1956, 1963, 1969, 1974, 1982 and 1990.

A record seven appearances have been made by John G. Prince (New Zealand),

in 1963, 1969, 1975, 1979, 1982, 1986 and 1990; on his debut he was the youngest-ever international, at 17 yr 190 days.

USCA National Championships J. Archie Peck has won the singles title a record four times (1977, 1979–80, 1982). Ted Prentis has won the doubles title four times with three different partners (1978, 1980–81, 1988). The teams of Ted Prentis and Ned Prentis (1980–81) and Dana Dribben and Ray Bell (1985–1986) have each won the doubles title twice. The New York Croquet Club has won a record six National Club Championships (1980–83, 1986, 1988).

Cross-country Running

Origins The earliest recorded international cross-country race took place over 9 miles 18 yd from Ville d'Avray, outside Paris, France on 20 Mar 1898 between England and France (England won by 21 points to 69).

World Championships The inaugural International Cross-Country Championships took place at the Hamilton Park Racecourse, Great Britain on 28 Mar 1903.

The greatest margin of victory is 56 sec or 390 yd by John "Jack" Thomas Holden (England; b. 13 Mar 1907) at Ayr Racecourse, Strathclyde, Great Britain on 24 Mar 1934.

Since 1973 the events have been official world championships under the auspices of the International Amateur Athletic Federation.

The USA has never won the men's team race, but Craig Steven Virgin (b. 2 Aug 1955) won the individual race twice, 1980–81.

Most wins The greatest number of team victories has been by England, with 45 for men, 11 for junior men and seven for women.

The USA and USSR each have a record eight women's team victories.

The greatest team domination was by Kenya at Auckland, New Zealand on 26 Mar 1988. Their senior men's team finished eight men in the first nine, with a low score of 23 (six to score), and their junior men's team set a record low score, 11 (four to score) with six in the first seven.

The greatest number of men's individual victories is four, by: Jack Holden (England) in 1933–35 and 1939; by Alain Mimoun-o-Kacha (France; b. 1 Jan 1921), in 1949, 1952, 1954 and 1956; by Gaston Roelants (Belgium; b. 5 Feb 1937) in 1962, 1967, 1969 and 1972; and by John Ngugi (Kenya; b. 10 May 1962), 1986–89.

The women's race has been won five times by: Doris Brown-Heritage (USA; b. 17 Sep 1942), 1967–71; and Grete Waitz (nee Andersen [Norway]; b. 1 Oct 1953), 1978–81 and 1983.

US championship In this competition, first staged in 1890, the most wins in the men's race is eight, by Patrick Ralph Porter (b. 31 May 1959), 1982–89. The women's championship was first contested in 1972, and the most wins is five, by Lynn A. Jennings (b. 1 Jul 1960), 1985, 1987–90.

Most appearances Marcel van de Wattyne (Belgium; b. 7 Jul 1924) ran in a record 20 races, 1946–65.

The women's record is 16 by Jean Lochhead (Wales; b. 24 Dec 1946), 1967–79, 1981, 1983–84.

Curling

Origins Although a 15th-century bronze figure in the Florence Museum appears to be holding a curling stone, the earliest illustration of the sport was in one of the Flemish painter Pieter Brueghel's winter scenes *c.* 1560. The game was probably introduced into Scotland by Flemings in the 15th century. The earliest documented club is Muthill, Great Britain, formed in 1739. Organized administration began in 1838, with the formation in Edinburgh, Great Britain of the Grand (later Royal) Caledonian Curling Club, the international legislative body until the foundation of the International Curling Federation in 1966, which was renamed the World Curling Federation in 1991.

The USA won the first Gordon International Medal series of matches, between Canada and the United States, at Montreal in 1884. In 1832, Orchard Lake Curling Club, MI, was founded, the first in the United States. The oldest club in continuous existence in the USA is Milwaukee Curling Club, WI, formed circa 1850. Regional curling associations governed the sport in the USA until 1947, when the United States Women's Curling Association was formed, followed in 1958 by the Men's Curling Association. In 1986, the United States Curling Association was formed and is

the current governing body for the sport. In Canada, the Dominion Curling Association was formed in 1935, renamed the Canadian Curling Association in 1968. Curling has been a demonstration sport at the Olympic Games of 1924, 1932, 1964 and 1988.

Most titles Canada has won the men's World Championships (instituted 1959) 20 times, 1959–64, 1966, 1968–72, 1980, 1982–83, 1985–87, 1989–90.

The most Strathcona Cup (instituted 1903) wins is seven by Canada (1903, 1909, 1912, 1923, 1938, 1957, 1965) against Scotland.

The most women's World Championships (instituted 1979) is six, by Canada (1980, 1984–87, 1989).

The US has won the men's world title four times, with Bud Somerville skip on the first two winning teams, 1965 and 1974.

United States National Championship *Men* First held in 1957, two curlers have been skips on five championship teams: Bud Somerville (Superior Curling Club, WI in 1965, 1968–69, 1974, 1981), and Bruce Roberts (Hibbing Curling Club, MN in 1966–67, 1976–77, 1984). Bill Strum of the Superior Curling Club has been a member of five title teams in 1965, 1967, 1969, 1974 and 1978.

Women First held in 1977, Nancy Langley, Seattle, WA has been the skip of a record four championship teams, 1979, 1981, 1983 and 1988.

The Labatt Brier (formerly the Macdonald Brier 1927–79) The Brier is the Canadian Men's Curling championship. The competition was first held at the Granite Club, Toronto in 1927. Sponsored by Macdonald Tobacco Inc., it was known as the Macdonald Brier; since 1980 Labatt Brewery has sponsored the event. The most wins is 22 by Manitoba (1928–32, 1934, 1936, 1938, 1940, 1942, 1947, 1949, 1952–53, 1956, 1965, 1970–72, 1979, 1981, 1984). Ernie Richardson (Saskatchewan) has

■ **Olympic gold**
Curling has been a demonstration sport at the Olympic Games of 1924, 1932, 1936 (when a specialized German version of the game was played), 1964 and 1988. In 1988 Canada won the women's title, defeating Sweden in the final. (Photo: All-Sport [USA]/Leah)

been winning skip a record four times (1959–60, 1962–63). His brothers Arnold and Sam Richardson were also members of each championship team.

"Perfect" game Stu Beagle, of Calgary, Alberta, Canada, played a perfect game (48 points) against Nova Scotia in the Canadian Championships (Brier) at Fort William (now Thunder Bay), Ontario on 8 Mar 1960.

Bernice Fekete, of Edmonton, Alberta, Canada, skipped her rink to two consecutive eight-enders on the same ice at the Derrick Club, Edmonton on 10 Jan and 6 Feb 1973.

Two eight-enders in one bonspiel were

Fastest game in curling

Eight curlers from the Burlington Golf and Country Club curled an eight-end game in 47 min 24 sec, with time penalties of 5 min 30 sec, at Burlington, Ontario, Canada on 4 Apr 1986, following rules agreed on with the Ontario Curling Association. The time is taken from when the first rock crosses the near hogline until the game's last rock comes to a complete stop.

Highest cycling

Canadians Bruce Bell, Philip Whelan and Suzanne MacFadyen cycled at an altitude of 22,834 ft on the peak of Mt Aconcagua, Argentina on 25 Jan 1991.

Greatest distance in one hour

The greatest distance covered in one hour is 76 miles 504 yd by Leon Vanderstuyft (Belgium; 1890–1964) on the Montlhéry Motor Circuit, France, on 30 Sep 1928, achieved from a standing start paced by a motorcycle.

Fastest roller-cycling speed

James Baker (USA) achieved a record speed of 153.2 mph at El Con Mall, Tucson, AZ on 28 Jan 1989.

■ **Cycling**
Rebecca Twigg holds the record for the most world titles by a US cyclist with four, at the pursuit in 1982, 1984–85 and 1987. Here she is in action in the 1984 Olympic road race, where she took the silver medal behind teammate Connie Carpenter-Phinney. (Photo: All-Sport [USA]/Steve or Mike Powell)

scored at the Parry Sound Curling Club, Ontario, Canada from 6–8 Jan 1983.

Andrew McQuiston skipped the Scotland team to a perfect game *v* Switzerland at the Uniroyal Junior Men's World Championship at Kitchener, Ontario, Canada in 1980.

Longest throw The longest throw of a curling stone was a distance of 576 ft 4 in, by Eddie Kulbacki (Canada) at Park Lake, Neepawa, Manitoba, Canada on 29 Jan 1989. The attempt took place on a specially prepared sheet of curling ice on frozen Park Lake, a record 1,200 ft long.

Largest bonspiel The largest bonspiel (curling tournament) in the world is the Manitoba Curling Association Bonspiel, held annually in Winnipeg, Canada. In 1988 there were 1,424 teams of four men, a total of 5,696 curlers, using 187 sheets of curling ice.

Cycling

Origins The earliest recorded bicycle race was a velocipede race over 1.24 miles at the Parc de St Cloud, Paris, France on 31 May 1868, won by Dr James Moore (Great Britain; 1847–1935) (later *Chevalier de la Légion d'Honneur*).

The first recorded cycle race in the United States was in September 1883 when G. M. Hendrie beat W. G. Rowe in a road race.

Fastest speed The fastest speed ever achieved on a bicycle is 152.284 mph, by John Howard (USA) behind a windshield at Bonneville Salt Flats, UT on 20 Jul 1985. It should be noted that considerable help was provided by the slipstreaming effect of the lead vehicle.

The 24 hr record behind pace is 1216.8 miles by Michael Secrest at Phoenix International Raceway, AZ on 26–27 Apr 1990.

Most titles *Olympic* The most gold medals won is three, by Paul Masson (France; 1874–1945) in 1896, Francisco Verri (Italy; 1885–1945) in 1906; and Robert Charpentier (France; 1916–66) in 1936. Daniel Morelon (France) won two in 1968, and a third in 1972; he also won a silver in 1976 and a bronze in 1964. In the "unofficial" 1904 cycling program, Marcus Latimer Hurley (USA; 1885–1941) won four events.

Burton Cecil Down (1885–1929) won a record six medals at the 1904 Games, two gold, three silver and one bronze. The only American woman to win a cycling gold medal is Helen Constance "Connie" Carpenter-Phinney (b. 26 Feb 1957), who won the individual road race in 1984. She became the first woman to compete in the winter and summer Olympics, as she had competed as a speed skater in 1972.

World World Championships are contested annually. They were first staged for amateurs in 1893 and for professionals in 1895.

The most wins at a particular event is ten, by Koichi Nakano (Japan; b. 14 Nov 1955), professional sprint 1977–86.

The most wins at a men's amateur event is seven, by: Daniel Morelon (France; b. 28 Jul 1944), sprint 1966–67, 1969–71, 1973, 1975; and Leon Meredith (Great Britain; 1882–1930), 100 km motor paced 1904–05, 1907–09, 1911, 1913.

The most women's titles is eight, by Jeannie Longo (France; b. 31 Oct 1958), pursuit 1986 and 1988–89; road 1985–87 and 1989 and points 1990.

The most world titles won by a US cyclist is four, at women's 3 kilometers pursuit by Rebecca Twigg (b. 26 Mar 1963), 1982,

1984–85 and 1987. The most successful man has been Greg LeMond (b. 26 Jun 1960), winner of the individual road race in 1983 and 1989.

Tour de France The world's premiere stage race was first contested in 1903. Held over a three-week period, the longest race ever staged was over 3,569 miles in 1926. The greatest number of wins in the *Tour de France* (inaugurated in 1903) is five by Jacques Anquetil (France; 1934–1987), 1957, 1961–64; Eddy Merckx (Belgium; b. 17 Jun 1945), 1969–72 and 1974; and Bernard Hinault (France; b. 14 Nov 1954), 1978–79, 1981–82 and 1985.

Greg LeMond became the first American winner in 1986, and returned from serious injury to win again in 1989 and 1990.

The closest race ever was in 1989 when after 2,030 miles over 23 days (1–23 July) Greg LeMond (USA; b. 26 Jun 1960) who completed the Tour in 87 hr 38 min 35 sec, beat Laurent Fignon (France; b. 12 Aug 1960) in Paris, France by only 8 sec.

The fastest average speed was 24.16 mph by Pedro Delgado (Spain; b. 15 Apr 1960) in 1988.

The longest-ever stage was the 486 km from Les Sables d'Olonne to Bayonne in 1919. The most participants was 210 starters in 1986.

Women The inaugural women's *Tour de France* was staged in 1984. Jeannie Longo (France) has won the event a record four times, 1987–90.

Six-day races The most wins in six-day races is 88 out of 233 events, by Patrick Sercu (Belgium; b. 27 Jun 1944), 1964–83.

Longest one-day race The longest single-day "massed start" road race is the 342–385 mile Bordeaux–Paris, France event. Paced over all or part of the route, the highest average speed was 29.32 mph, by Herman van Springel (Belgium; b. 14 Aug 1943) for 363.1 miles in 13 hr 35 min 18 sec, in 1981.

Cross-America The trans-America solo record recognized by the Ultra-Marathon Cycling Association for men is 8 days 8 hr 45 min, by Paul Selon at age 35 from Costa, CA to New York, in the 1989 Race Across AMerica. Selon won the race while wearing a plastic neck brace. The women's record is 9 days 9 hr 9 min, by Susan Notorangelo at age 35, also in the 1989 Race Across AMerica. She clipped 16 hr 55 min off the previous women's record.

Michael Secrest of Scottsdale, AZ set a transcontinental record of 7 days 23 hr 16 min in Jun 1990 from Huntington Beach, CA to Atlantic City, NJ, a distance of 2,916 miles. It was the fastest-ever crossing on a bicycle.

Cross-Canada The trans-Canada record is 13 days 15 hr 4 min, by Ronald J. Dossenbach of Windsor, Ontario, 3,800 miles from Vancouver, British Columbia to Halifax, Nova Scotia on 30 Jul–13 Aug 1988, a distance of 3,800 miles.

WORLD RECORDS

Records are recognized by the Union Cycliste Internationàle (UCI) for both professionals and amateurs on open air and indoor tracks for a variety of distances at unpaced flying and standing starts and for motor-paced. In this list only the best are shown, with an asterisk * to signify those records set by a professional rather than an amateur.

OPEN-AIR TRACKS

MEN

Distance	hr:min:sec	Name and country	Venue	Date
Unpaced standing start				
1 km	1:02.091	Maic Malchow (East Germany)	Colorado Springs, CO	28 Aug 1986
4 km	4:31.160	Gintautas Umaras (USSR)	Seoul, South Korea	18 Sep 1987
5 km	5:44.700	Gregor Braun (West Germany)*	La Paz, Bolivia	12 Jan 1986
10 km	11:39.720	Francesco Moser (Italy)*	Mexico City, Mexico	19 Jan 1984
20 km	23:21.592	Francesco Moser (Italy)*	Mexico City, Mexico	23 Jan 1984
100 km	2:09:11.312	Kent Bostick (USA)	Colorado Springs, CO	13 Oct 1989
1 hour	51.151 km	Francesco Moser (Italy)*	Mexico City, Mexico	23 Jan 1984
Unpaced flying start				
200 meters	10.118	Michael Hübner (East Germany)	Colorado Springs, CO	27 Aug 1986
500 meters	26.776	Philippe Boyer (France)*	La Paz, Bolivia	June 1989
1 km	58.269	Dominguez Rueda Efrain (Colombia)*	La Paz, Bolivia	13 Dec 1986
Motor-paced				
50 km	35:21.108	Aleksandr Romanov (USSR)	Tbilisi, USSR	6 May 1987
100 km	1:10:29.420	Giovanni Renosto (Italy)	Bassano del Grappa, Italy	16 Sep 1988
1 hour	85.067 km	Giovanni Renosto (Italy)	Bassano del Grappa, Italy	16 Sep 1988

WOMEN

Unpaced standing start				
1 km	1:14.249	Erika Salumyae (USSR)	Tashkent, USSR	17 May 1984
3 km	3:38.190	Jeannie Longo (France)	Mexico City, Mexico	5 Oct 1989
5 km	6:14.135	Jeannie Longo (France)	Mexico City, Mexico	27 Sep 1989
10 km	12:59.435	Jeannie Longo (France)	Mexico City, Mexico	1 Oct 1989
20 km	25:59.883	Jeannie Longo (France)	Mexico City, Mexico	1 Oct 1989
100 km	2:28:26.259	Francesca Galli (Italy)	Milan, Italy	26 Oct 1987
1 hour	46.35270 km	Jeannie Longo (France)	Mexico City, Mexico	1 Oct 1989
Unpaced flying start				
200 meters	11.383	Isabelle Gautheron (France)	Colorado Springs, CO	16 Aug 1986
500 meters	30.59	Isabelle Gautheron (France)	Cali, Colombia	14 Sep 1986
1 km	1:10.463	Erika Salumyae (USSR)	Tashkent, USSR	15 May 1984

Many of the above venues, such as La Paz, Colorado Springs, Cali and Mexico City, are at high altitude. The UCI recognizes separate world records for the classic one-hour event at venues below 600 meters. These are: MEN: 49.80193 km Francesco Moser on 3 Oct 1986. WOMEN: 43.58789 km Jeannie Longo on 30 Sep 1986, both at Milan, Italy.

INDOOR TRACKS

MEN

Unpaced standing start				
1 km	1:02.576	Aleksandr Kirichenko (USSR)	Moscow, USSR	2 Aug 1989
4 km	4:28.900	Vyachselav Yekimov (USSR)	Moscow, USSR	20 Sep 1986
5 km	5:39.316	Vyachselav Yekimov (USSR)	Moscow, USSR	26 Oct 1990
10 km	11:31.968	Vyachselav Yekimov (USSR)	Moscow, USSR	7 Jan 1989
20 km	23:14.553	Vyachselav Yekimov (USSR)	Moscow, USSR	3 Feb 1989
100 km	2:10:08.287	Beat Meister (Switzerland)	Stuttgart, West Germany	22 Sep 1989
4 km team	4:10.877	USSR (Vyacheslav Yekimov, Dmitriy Nelyubin, Mikhail Orlov, Yevgeniy Berzin)	Moscow, USSR	4 Aug 1989
1 hour	50.644 km	Francesco Moser (Italy)	Stuttgart, West Germany	21 May 1988
Unpaced flying start				
200 meters	10.117	Nikolay Kovch (USSR)	Moscow, USSR	5 Feb 1988
500 meters	26.649	Aleksandr Kirichenko (USSR)	Moscow, USSR	29 Oct 1988
1 km	57.260	Aleksandr Kirichenko (USSR)	Moscow, USSR	25 Apr 1989
Motor-paced				
50 km	32:56.746	Aleksandr Romanov (USSR)	Moscow, USSR	21 Feb 1987
100 km	1:05:58.031	Aleksandr Romanov (USSR)	Moscow, USSR	21 Feb 1987
1 hour	91.131 km	Aleksandr Romanov (USSR)	Moscow, USSR	21 Feb 1987

WOMEN

Unpaced standing start				
1 km	1:13.377	Erika Salumyae (USSR)	Moscow, USSR	21 Sep 1983
3 km	3:43.490	Jeannie Longo (France)	Paris, France	14 Nov 1986
5 km	6:22.713	Jeannie Longo (France)	Grenoble, France	2 Nov 1986
10 km	12:54.26	Jeannie Longo (France)	Paris, France	19 Oct 1989
20 km	26:51.222	Jeannie Longo (France)	Moscow, USSR	29 Oct 1989
100 km	2:24:57.618	Tea Vikstedt-Nyman (Finland)	Moscow, USSR	30 Oct 1990
1 hour	45.016 km	Jeannie Longo (France)	Moscow, USSR	29 Oct 1989
Unpaced flying start				
200 meters	11.164	Galina Yenyukhina (USSR)	Moscow, USSR	6 Aug 1990
500 meters	29.655	Erika Salumyae (USSR)	Moscow, USSR	6 Aug 1987
1 km	1:05.232	Erika Salumyae (USSR)	Moscow, USSR	30 May 1987

LONG DISTANCE BESTS (unpaced)

24 hr	830.79 km	Michael L. Secrest (USA)	Montreal, Canada	13–14 Mar 1985
1,000 km	32 hr 4 min	Herman de Munck (Belgium)	Keerbergen, Belgium	23–24 Sep 1983
1,000 miles	51:12:32	Herman de Munck (Belgium)	Keerbergen, Belgium	23–25 Sep 1983

Cycling the length of the Americas

Daniel Buettner, Bret Anderson, Martin Engel and Anne Knabe cycled the length of the Americas, from Prudhoe Bay, AK to the Beagle Channel, Ushuaia, Argentina from 8 Aug 1986 to 13 Jun 1987. They cycled a total distance of 15,266 miles.

Speed records in darts

The fastest time taken to complete three games of 301, finishing on doubles, is 1 min 47 sec, by Keith Deller on British Broadcasting Corporation's *Record Breakers* TV program on 22 Oct 1985.

The record time for going around the board clockwise in "doubles" at arm's length is 9.2 sec by Dennis Gower at the Millers Arms, Hastings, Great Britain on 12 Oct 1975, and 14.5 sec in numerical order by Jim Pike (1903–60) at the Craven Club, Newmarket, Great Britain in Mar 1944.

The record for this feat at the 9-ft throwing distance, retrieving own darts, is 2 min 13 sec by Bill Duddy (b. 29 Sep 1932) at The Plough, London, Great Britain on 29 Oct 1972.

Longest horse ride

Henry G. Perry, a stockman from Mollongghip, Victoria, Australia, rode 14,021 miles around Australia in 157 days, 1 May to 4 Oct 1985, with six horses.

Endurance Thomas Edward Godwin (Great Britain; 1912–75), cycling every day during the 365 days of 1939, covered 75,065 miles, or an average of 205.65 miles per day. He then completed 100,000 miles in 500 days to 14 May 1940.

Jay Aldous and Matt DeWaal cycled 14,290 miles on an around-the-world trip from Place Monument, Salt Lake City, UT in 106 days, from 2 Apr–16 Jul 1984.

Nicholas Mark Sanders (b. 26 Nov 1957) of Glossop, Great Britain circumnavigated the world (13,035 road miles) in 78 days 3 hr 30 min between 5 Jul and 21 Sep 1985.

Cycle touring The greatest mileage amassed in a cycle tour was more than 402,000 miles, by the itinerant lecturer Walter Stolle (b. Sudetenland, 1926) from 24 Jan 1959 to 12 Dec 1976. Starting from Romford, Great Britain, he visited 159 countries.

From 1922 to 25 Dec 1973 Tommy Chambers (1903–84) of Glasgow, Great Britain rode a verified total of 799,405 miles.

Visiting every continent, John W. Hathaway (b. Great Britain, 13 Jan 1925) of Vancouver, British Columbia, Canada covered 50,600 miles from 10 Nov 1974 to 6 Oct 1976. Veronica and Colin Scargill, of Bedford, Great Britain, traveled 18,020 miles around-the-world on a tandem, 25 Feb 1974–27 Aug 1975.

The most participants in a bicycle tour were 31,678 in the 56 mile London to Brighton Bike Ride (Great Britain) on 19 Jun 1988.

The most participants in a tour in an excess of 1,000 km is 2,037 (from 2,157 starters) for the Australian Bicentennial Caltex Bike Ride from Melbourne to Sydney, from 26 Nov–10 Dec 1988.

CYCLO-CROSS

The greatest number of World Championships (instituted 1950) has been won by Eric de Vlaeminck (Belgium; b. 23 Aug 1945) with the Amateur and Open in 1966 and six Professional titles in 1968–73.

Darts

Origins Darts can be dated from the use by archers of heavily weighted ten-inch throwing arrows for self-defense in close-quarters fighting. The "dartes" were used in Ireland in the 16th century, and darts was played on the *Mayflower* by the Plymouth pilgrims in 1620. The modern game dates from 1896, when Brian Gamlin of Bury, Lancashire, Great Britain is credited with inventing the present numbering system on the board. The first recorded highest possible score of 180 was achieved by John Reader at the Highbury Tavern in Sussex, Great Britain in 1902.

Most titles Eric Bristow (Great

Britain; b. 25 Apr 1957) has the most wins in the World Masters Championship (instituted 1974) with five, 1977, 1979, 1981 and 1983–84, the World Professional Championship (instituted 1978) with five, 1980–81 and 1984–86, and the World Cup Singles (instituted 1977), four, 1983, 1985, 1987 and 1989.

Seven men have won the annual *News of the World* Individual Championship twice—most recently Eric Bristow, 1983–84 and Mike Gregory (b. 16 Dec 1956), 1987–88.

John Lowe (Great Britain; b. 21 Jul 1945) is the only other man to have won each of the four major titles: World Masters, 1976 and 1980; World Professional, 1979 and 1987; World Cup Singles, 1981; and *News of the World*, 1981.

Record prize John Lowe won £102,000 for achieving the first 501 scored with the minimum nine darts in a major event on 13 Oct 1984 at Slough, Great Britain in the quarter-finals of the World Match-play Championships. His darts were six successive treble 20s, treble 17, treble 18 and double 18.

Least darts Scores of 201 in four darts, 301 in six darts, 401 in seven darts and 501 in nine darts have been achieved on various occasions.

Roy Edwin Blowes (Canada; b. 8 Oct 1930) was the first person to achieve a 501 in nine darts, "double-on, double-off," at the Widgeons Pub, Calgary, Canada on 9 Mar 1987. His scores were: bull, treble 20, treble 17, five treble 20s and a double 20 to finish.

The lowest number of darts thrown for a score of 1,001 is 19, by Cliff Inglis (b. 27 May 1935) (160, 180, 140, 180, 121, 180, 40) at the Bromfield Men's Club, Devon, Great Britain on 11 Nov 1975; and by Jocky Wilson (Great Britain) (140, 140, 180, 180, 180, 131, Bull) at The London Pride, Bletchley, Great Britain on 23 Mar 1989.

A score of 2,001 in 52 darts was achieved by Alan Evans (Great Britain; b. 14 Jun 1949) at Ferndale, Great Britain on 3 Sep 1976.

A score of 3,001 in 73 darts was thrown by Tony Benson at the Plough Inn, Gorton, Great Britain on 12 Jul 1986.

Linda Batten (b. 26 Nov 1954) set a women's 3,001 record of 117 darts at the Old Wheatsheaf, London, Great Britain on 2 Apr 1986.

A score of 100,001 was achieved in 3,732 darts by Alan Downie of Stornoway, Great Britain on 21 Nov 1986.

Equestrian Sports

Origins Evidence of horse riding dates from a Persian engraving dated *c.* 3000 B.C. Pignatelli's academy of horsemanship at Naples dates from the 16th century. The earliest jumping compe-

tition was at the Agricultural Hall, London, in 1869. Equestrian events have been included in the Olympic Games since 1912. Dressage competition derived from the exercises taught at 16th century Italian and French horsemanship academies, while the three-day event developed from cavalry endurance rides. The world governing body for all three disciplines is the *Fédération Equestre Internationàle* (FEI), founded in Brussels, Belgium in 1921.

SHOW JUMPING

Olympic Games The most Olympic gold medals won by a rider is five, by Hans-Günter Winkler (West Germany; b. 24 Jul 1926), four team wins in 1956, 1960, 1964 and 1972 and the individual Grand Prix in 1956. He also won team silver in 1976 and team bronze in 1968, for a record seven medals overall.

The most team wins in the Prix des Nations is six, by Germany in 1936, 1956, 1960, 1964 and as West Germany in 1972 and 1988.

The lowest score obtained by a winner is no faults, by Frantisek Ventura (Czechoslovakia; 1895–1969) on Eliot, 1928, and Alwin Schockemöhle (West Germany; b. 29 May 1937) on Warwick Rex, 1976.

Pierre Jonquères d'Oriola (France; b. 1 Feb 1920) uniquely won the individual gold medal twice, in 1952 and 1964.

United States Two US riders have won individual gold medals: William "Bill" Clark Steinkraus (b. 12 Oct 1925) won in 1968 and also won two silver and a bronze medal, 1952–68; and Joseph Halpin "Joe" Fargis (b. 4 Feb 1948) won both individual and team gold medals in 1984 as well as team silver in 1988.

World Championships The men's World Championships (instituted 1953) have been won twice by Hans-Günter Winkler (West Germany; 1954–55) and Raimondo d'Inzeo (Italy; b. 8 Feb 1925) (1956 and 1960).

The women's title (1965–74) was won twice by Jane "Janou" Tissot (nee Lefebvre [France]; b. Saigon, 14 May 1945) on Rocket (1970 and 1974).

President's Cup The world team championship (instituted 1965) has been won a record 13 times by Great Britain, 1965, 1967, 1970, 1972–74, 1977–79, 1983, 1985–86, 1989.

World Cup Instituted in 1979, double winners have included Conrad Homfeld (USA; b. 25 Dec 1951), 1980 and 1985, Ian Miller (Canada; b. 6 Jan 1947), 1988 and 1989; and John Whitaker (Great Britain; b. 5 Aug 1955), 1990 and 1991.

Jumping records The official *Fédération Equestre Internationàle* records are: high jump 8 ft 1¼ in, by Huasó, ridden by Capt. Alberto Larraguibel Morales (Chile) at Viña del Mar, Santiago, Chile on 5 Feb 1949; long jump over water, 27 ft 6¾ in, by Something, ridden by André Ferreira (South Africa) at Johannesburg, South Africa on 25 Apr 1975.

THREE-DAY EVENT

Olympic Games and World Championships Charles Ferdinand Pahud de Mortanges (Netherlands; 1896–1971) won a record four Olympic gold medals, team 1924 and 1928, individual (riding Marcroix) 1928 and 1932; he also won a team silver medal in 1932.

Bruce Oram Davidson (USA; b. 13 Dec 1949) is the only rider to have won two world titles (instituted 1966), on Irish Cap in 1974 and Might Tango in 1978.

United States The most medals won for the USA is six, by John Michael Plumb (b. 28 Mar 1940); team gold 1976 and 1984, and four silver medals, team 1964, 1968 and 1972, and individual 1976. Edmund Sloane "Tad" Coffin (b. 9 May 1955) is the one US rider to have won both team and individual gold medals in 1976.

DRESSAGE

Olympic Games and World Championships Germany (West Germany 1968–90) has won a record seven team gold medals, 1928, 1936, 1964, 1968, 1976, 1984 and 1988, and has the most team wins, six, at the World Championships (instituted 1966). Dr Reiner Klimke (West Germany; b. 14 Jan 1936) has won a record six Olympic golds (team 1964–88, individual, 1984). He won individual bronze in 1976, for a record seven medals overall, and is the only rider to have won two world titles, on Mehmed in 1974 and Ahlerich in 1982. Henri St Cyr (Sweden; 1904–79) won a record two individual Olympic gold medals, in 1952 and 1956.

World Cup Instituted in 1986, this competition has had only one double winner: Christine Stückelberger (Switzerland; b. 22 May 1947) on Gauguin de Lully in 1987–88.

CARRIAGE DRIVING

World Championships were first held in 1972. Three team titles have been won by Great Britain, 1972, 1974, and 1980; Hungary 1976, 1978 and 1984; and the Netherlands, 1982, 1986 and 1988.

Two individual titles have been won by György Bárdos (Hungary), 1978 and 1980, and by Tjeerd Velstra (Netherlands), 1982 and 1986.

Fencing

Origins Fencing (fighting with single sticks) was practiced as a sport, or as a part of a religious ceremony, in Egypt as early as c. 1360 B.C. The first governing body for fencing in Great Britain was the Corporation of Masters of Defense founded by Henry VIII before 1540, and fencing has been practiced as a sport, notably in prize fights, since that time. The modern foil was introduced in France as a practice weapon for the short court sword in the mid-17th century. In the late 19th century the épée was developed in France and the light fencing sabre in Italy.

Fencing was included in the first Olympic Games of the modern era at Athens in 1896, and is one of only six sports to be featured in every Olympiad. The *Fédération Internationale d'Escrime* (FIE), the world governing body, was founded in Paris, France, in 1913. The first European Championships were held in 1921 and were expanded into World Championships in 1935.

In the United States the Amateur Fencers League of America (AFLA) was founded on 22 Apr 1891 in New York City. This group assumed supervision of the sport in the United States. In June 1981 the AFLA changed its name to the United States Fencing Association (USFA).

Most titles *World* The greatest number of individual world titles won is five, by Aleksandr Romankov (USSR; b. 7 Nov 1953), at foil 1974, 1977, 1979, 1982 and 1983, but Christian d'Oriola (France) won four world foil titles, 1947, 1949, 1953–54 as well as two individual Olympic titles.

Five women foilists have won three world titles: Hélène Mayer (Germany; 1910–53), 1929, 1931, 1937; Ilona Schacherer-Elek (Hungary; 1907–88), 1934–35, 1951; Ellen Müller-Preis

■ World Cup show jumping
Since it was instituted in 1979, there have been three double winners, and the most recent is John Whitaker (Great Britain; b. 5 Aug 1955) in 1990 and 1991. Here he is seen in action during the 1990 World Championships in Stockholm. (Photo: Pressens Bild Ab/S. Norling)

Longest field hockey game

The longest international field hockey game on record was one of 145 min (into the sixth period of extra time), when the Netherlands beat Spain 1–0 in the Olympic tournament at Mexico City on 25 Oct 1968.

Club matches of 205 min have twice been recorded: the Hong Kong Football Club beat Prison Sports Dept as the first to score in a "sudden death" playoff after 2–2 at full time on 11 Mar 1979, and Gore Court beat Hampstead in the first round of the English Club Championships in 1983.

(Austria; b. 6 May 1912), 1947, 1949–50; Cornelia Hanisch (West Germany; b. 12 Jun 1952), 1979, 1981, 1985; and Anja Fichtel (West Germany; b. 17 Aug 1968), 1986, 1988 and 1990. Of these only Ilona Schacherer-Elek also won two individual Olympic titles (1936 and 1948). The longest span for winning an individual world or Olympic title is 20 years, by Aladár Gerevich (Hungary; b. 16 Mar 1910) at sabre, 1935–55; Gerevich also had a 28-year span for winning Olympic team gold medals.

Olympic The most individual Olympic gold medals won is three, by Ramón Fonst (Cuba; 1883–1959) in 1900 and 1904 (two) and by Nedo Nadi (Italy; 1894–1952) in 1912 and 1920 (two). Nadi also won three team gold medals in 1920, making five gold medals at one celebration, the record for fencing and a record for any sport at that time.

Edoardo Mangiarotti (Italy; b. 7 Apr 1919), with six gold, five silver and two bronze, holds the record of 13 Olympic medals. He won them for foil and épée from 1936 to 1960.

The most gold medals won by a woman is four (one individual, three team) by Yelena Dmitryevna Novikova (nee Byelova [USSR]; b. 28 Jul 1947) from 1968 to 1976, and the record for all medals is seven (two gold, three silver, two bronze) by Ildikó Sági (formerly Ujlaki, nee Retjö [Hungary]; b. 11 May 1937) from 1960 to 1976.

United States The only US Olympic champion was Albertson Van Zo Post (1866–1938), who won the men's single sticks and team foil (with two Cubans) at the 1904 Games.

United States National Championships The most US titles won at one weapon is 12 at sabre, by Peter J. Westbrook, in 1974, 1975, 1979–86, 1988 and 1989. The women's record is 10 at foil, by Janice Lee York Romary in 1950–51, 1956–57, 1960–61, 1964–66 and 1968.

The most men's individual foil championships won is seven, by Michael Marx in 1977, 1979, 1982, 1985–87 and 1990. L. G. Nunes won the most épée championships, with six—1917, 1922, 1924, 1926, 1928 and 1932. Vincent Bradford won a record number of women's épée championships with four in 1982–84 and 1986.

NCAA Championship Division I (Men)

Since this competition was inaugurated in 1941, New York University has won the most titles: 12 (1947, 1954, 1957, 1960–61, 1966–67, 1970–71, 1973–74, 1976). The longest consecutive title streak is four wins by Wayne State (MI), 1982–85.

Michael Lofton, New York University, has won the most titles in a career with four victories in the sabre, 1984–87. Abraham Balk, New York University, is the only man to win two individual titles in one year, 1947 (foil and épée).

(Women)

Since this competition was inaugurated in 1982, Wayne State (MI) has won the most titles: three (1982, 1988–89).

Caitlin Bilodeaux (Columbia-Barnard) and Molly Sullivan (Notre Dame) have both won the individual title twice—Bilodeaux in 1985 and 1987; Sullivan in 1986 and 1988.

In 1990, the NCAA team competition was combined for the first time. Penn State have won both the 1990 and 1991 titles.

Field hockey

Origins A representation of two players with curved snagging sticks apparently in an orthodox "bully" position was found in Tomb No. 17 at Beni Hasan, Egypt, and has been dated to c. 2050 B.C. The modern game evolved in south London, Great Britain in the 1870s.

The *Fédération Internationàle de Hockey* was formed on 7 Jan 1924.

The sport was introduced to the United States in 1921 by a British teacher, Constance M.K. Applebee. The Field Hockey Association of America (FHAA) was founded in 1928 by Henry Greer. The first game was staged between the Germantown Cricket Club and the Westchester Field Hockey Club, also in 1928.

Most Olympic medals India was Olympic champion from the reintroduction of Olympic hockey in 1928 until 1960, when Pakistan beat India 1–0 in Rome. India had its eighth win in 1980. Of the seven Indians who have won three Olympic team gold medals, two have also won a silver medal—Leslie Walter Claudius (b. 25 Mar 1927), in 1948, 1952, 1956 and 1960 (silver), and Udham Singh (b. 4 Aug 1928), in 1952, 1956, 1964 and 1960 (silver).

A women's tournament was added in 1980, when Zimbabwe was the winners. The Netherlands won in 1984 and Australia in 1988.

United States The US men won the bronze medal in 1932, but only three teams played that year, and the US women won the bronze in 1984.

World Cup The World Cup for men was first held in 1971, and for women in 1974. The most wins are: men: three by Pakistan, 1971, 1978 and 1982; women: five by the Netherlands, 1974, 1978, 1983, 1986 and 1990.

Champions' Trophy In this competition, first held in 1978 and contested annually since 1980 by the top six men's teams in the world, the most wins is five, by Australia, 1983–85, 1989–90. The first women's Champions' Trophy was won by the Netherlands in 1987. South Korea won in 1989.

MEN

The first international match was the Wales *v.* Ireland match at Rhyl, Clwyd, Great Britain on 26 Jan 1895. Ireland won 3–0.

Highest international score The highest score was when India defeated the USA 24–1 at Los Angeles, CA in the 1932 Olympic Games.

Most international appearances Heiner Dopp (b. 27 Jun 1956) represented West Germany 286 times between 1975 and 1990, indoors and out.

Greatest scoring feats The greatest number of goals scored in international hockey is 267, by Paul Litjens (Netherlands; b. 9 Nov 1947) in 177 games.

Fastest goal in an international match John French scored 7 sec after the bully-off for England *v.* West Germany at Nottingham, Great Britain on 25 Apr 1971.

Best goalkeeping Richard James Allen (India; b. 4 Jun 1902) did not concede a goal during the 1928 Olympic tournament and gave up a total of only three in 1936.

WOMEN

The first national association was the Irish Ladies' Hockey Union, founded in 1894.

The first international match was an England *v.* Ireland game in Dublin in 1896. Ireland won 2–0.

Most international appearances Valerie Robinson made a record 144 appearances for England, 1963–84.

United States Sheryl Johnson has made a record 137 appearances for the USA from 1978 to 1990.

Highest scores The highest score in an international match was when England beat France 23–0 at Merton, Greater London, Great Britain on 3 Feb 1923.

WORLD RECORDS—FRESHWATER AND SALTWATER

A selection of All-Tackle records ratified by the International Game Fish Association as of January 1991

Species	Weight lb oz	Caught By	Location	Date	
ARAWANA	10 2	Gilberto Fernandes	Puraquequara Lake, Amazon, Brazil	3 Feb	1990
BARRACUDA, BLACKFIN	15 0	Alejandron Caniz	Puerto Quetzal, Guatemala	29 Oct	1988
BARRACUDA, GREAT	83 0	K. J. W. Hackett	Lagos, Nigeria	13 Jan	1952
BARRACUDA, MEXICAN	21 0	E. Greg Kent	Phantom Isle, Costa Rica	27 Mar	1987
BASS, GIANT SEA	536 8	James D. McAdam, Jr.	Anacapa Island, CA	20 Aug	1968
BASS, LARGEMOUTH	22 4	George W. Perry	Montgomery Lake, GA	2 Jun	1932
BASS, SMALLMOUTH	11 15	David L. Hayes	Dale Hollow Lake, KY	9 Jul	1955
BASS, STRIPED	78 8	Albert R. McReynolds	Atlantic City, NJ	21 Sep	1982
BASS, STRIPED (landlocked)	66 0	Theodore Furnish	O'Neill Forebay, Los Ramos, CA	29 Jun	1988
BASS, WHITEROCK	24 3	David N. Lambert	Lessville Lake, VA	12 May	1989
BLUEFISH	31 12	James M. Hussey	Hatteras, NC	30 Jan	1972
BONEFISH	19 0	Brian W. Batchelor	Zululand, South Africa	26 May	1962
CARP	75 1	Leo van der Gugten	Lac de St. Cassien, France	21 May	1987
CATFISH, BLUE	97 0	Edward B. Elliot	Missouri River, SD	16 Sep	1959
COD, ATLANTIC	98 12	Alphonse J. Bielevich	Isle of Shoals, NH	8 Jun	1969
CONGER	102 8	Raymond E. Stewart	Plymouth, Great Britain	18 Jul	1983
FLOUNDER, SUMMER	22 7	Charles Nappi	Montauk, NY	15 Sep	1975
GROUPER, BLACK	112 6	Donald W. Bone	Dry Tortugas, FL	27 Jan	1990
HALIBUT (Pacific)	356 0	Gregory C. Olsen	Juneau, AK	8 Nov	1986
MARLIN, BLACK	1,560 0	Alfred C. Glassell, Jr	Cabo Blanco, Peru	4 Aug	1953
MARLIN, BLUE (Atlantic)	1,282 0	Larry Martin	St Thomas, Virgin Islands	6 Aug	1977
MARLIN, BLUE (Pacific)	1,376 0	Jay Wm de Beaubien	Kaaiwi Point, Kona Coast, HI	31 May	1982
MARLIN, STRIPED	494 0	Bill Boniface	Tutukaka, New Zealand	16 Jan	1986
MARLIN, WHITE	181 14	Evandro Luiz Coser	Vitoria, Brazil	8 Dec	1979
MUSKELLUNGE	69 15	Arthur Lawton	St Lawrence River, NY	22 Sep	1957
PERCH, NILE	152 1	Kurt M. Fenster	Tende Bay, Entebbe, Uganda	4 Jun	1989
PIKE, NORTHERN	55 1	Lothar Louis	Lake of Grefeern, Germany	16 Oct	1986
SAILFISH (Atlantic)	128 1	Harm Steyn	Luanda, Angola	27 Mar	1974
SAILFISH (Pacific)	221 0	C. W. Stewart	Santa Cruz Island, Ecuador	12 Feb	1947
SALMON, CHINOOK	97 4	Les Anderson	Kenia River, AK	17 May	1985
SALMON, COHO	33 4	Jerry Lifton	Pulaski, NY	27 Sep	1989
SHARK, BLUE	437 0	Peter Hyde	Catherine Bay, NSW, Australia	2 Oct	1976
SHARK, HAMMERHEAD	991 0	Allen Ogle	Sarasota, FL	30 May	1982
SHARK, MAKO	1,115 0	Patrick Guillanton	Black River, Mauritius	16 Nov	1988
SHARK, TIGER	1,780 0	Walter Maxwell	Cherry Grove, SC	14 Jun	1964
SHARK, WHITE	2,664 0	Alfred Dean	Ceduna, South Australia	21 Apr	1959
SNAPPER, CUBERA	121 8	Mike Hebert	Cameron, LA	5 Jul	1982
SNAPPER, RED	46 1	E. Lane Nicholls	Destin, FL	1 Oct	1985
STINGRAY	294 0	Iain Foulger	River Gambia, The Gambia	4 Nov	1988
STURGEON	468 0	Joey Pallotta III	Benicia, CA	9 Jul	1983
SWORDFISH	1,182 0	L. Marron	Iquique, Chile	17 May	1953
TARPON	283 0	M. Salazar	Lake Maracaibo, Venezuela	19 Mar	1956
TROUT, BROWN	35 15	Eugenio Cavaglia	Nahuel Huapi, Argentina	16 Dec	1952
TROUT, LAKE	65 0	Larry Daunis	Great Bear Lake, NWT, Canada	8 Aug	1970
TROUT, RAINBOW	42 2	David Robert White	Bell Island, AK	22 Jun	1970
TUNA, BIGEYE (Pacific)	435 0	Dr Russel V. A. Lee	Cabo Blanco, Peru	17 Apr	1957
TUNA, BIGEYE (Atlantic)	375 8	Cecil Browne	Ocean City, MD	26 Apr	1977
TUNA, BLUEFIN	1,496 0	Ken Fraser	Aulds Cove, Nova Scotia, Canada	26 Oct	1979
WAHOO	155 8	William Bourne	San Salvador, Bahamas	3 Apr	1990
WALLEYE	25 0	Mabry Harper	Old Hickory Lake, TN	1 Apr	1960

Highest attendance The highest attendance was 65,165 for the match between England and the USA at Wembley, London, Great Britain on 11 Mar 1978.

NCAA Division I (Women) In this competition, inaugurated in 1981, Old Dominion University, Norfolk, VA has won the most championships with five titles: 1982–84, 1988 and 1991.

Fishing

Oldest existing club The Ellem Fishing Club was formed by a number of Edinburgh and Berwickshire gentlemen in Scotland in 1829. Its first annual general meeting was held on 29 Apr 1830.

Largest single catch The largest officially ratified fish ever caught on a rod was a man-eating great white shark (*Carcharodon carcharias*) weighing 2,664 lb and measuring 16 ft 10 in long, caught on a 130 lb test line by Alf Dean at Denial Bay, near Ceduna, South Australia on 21 Apr 1959. A great white shark weighing 3,388 lb was caught by Clive Green off Albany, Western Australia on 26 Apr 1976 but will remain unratified, as whale meat was used as bait.

In June 1978 a great white shark measuring 20 ft 4 in in length and weighing over 5,000 lb was harpooned and landed by fishermen in the harbor of San Miguel, Azores.

The largest marine animal killed by *hand* harpoon was a blue whale 97 ft in length, by Archer Davidson in Twofold Bay, New South Wales, Australia in

1910. Its tail flukes measured 20 ft across and its jawbone 23 ft 4 in.

The largest fish ever taken underwater was an 804 lb giant black grouper or jewfish by Don Pinder of the Miami Triton Club, FL in 1955.

World Freshwater Championship The *Confédération Internationàle de la Pêche Sportive* (CIPS) championships were inaugurated as European championships in 1953 and recognized as world championships in 1957.

France won the European title in 1956 and 12 world titles between 1959 and 1990. Robert Tesse (France) took the individual title a record three times, 1959–60 and 1965.

Casting The longest freshwater cast ratified under ICF (International Casting Federation) rules is 574 ft 2 in, by

Longest fight The longest recorded individual fight with a fish is 32 hr 5 min by Donal Heatley (New Zealand; b. 1938) with a black marlin (estimated length 20 ft and weight 1,500 lb) off Mayor Island, Tauranga, North Island, New Zealand on 21–22 Jan 1968. It towed the 13.2-ton launch 50 miles before breaking the line.

Walter Kummerow (Germany), for the Bait Distance Double-Handed 30 g event held at Lenzerheide, Switzerland in the 1968 Championships.

At the currently contested weight of 17.7 g, known as 18 g Bait Distance, the longest Double-Handed cast is 457 ft ½ in by Kevin Carriero (USA) at Toronto, Ontario, Canada on 24 Jul 1984.

The longest Fly Distance Double-Handed cast is 319 ft 1 in by Wolfgang Feige (Germany) at Toronto, Ontario, Canada on 23 Jul 1984.

IGFA world records The International Game Fish Association (IGFA) recognizes world records for game fish—both freshwater and saltwater—for a large number of species of fish. Its thousands of categories include all-tackle, various line classes and tippet classes for fly fishing. New records recognized by the IGFA reached an annual peak of 1,074 in 1984.

The heaviest freshwater category recognized by the IGFA is for the sturgeon, record weight 468 lb, caught by Joey Pallotta on 9 Jul 1983 off Benicia, CA.

Football

Origins On 6 Nov 1869, Princeton and Rutgers Universities staged what is generally regarded as the first intercollegiate football game at New Brunswick,

NJ. In Oct 1873 the Intercollegiate Football Association was formed (Columbia, Princeton, Rutgers and Yale), with the purpose of standardizing rules. At this point football was a modified version of soccer. The first significant move towards today's style of play came when Harvard accepted an invitation to play McGill University (Montreal, Canada) in a series of three challenge matches, the first being in May 1874, under modified rugby rules. Walter Camp (1859–1925) is credited with organizing the basic format of the current game. Between 1880 and 1906, Camp sponsored the concepts of scrimmage lines, 11-man teams, reduction in field size, "downs" and yards to gain and a new scoring system. In 1902 the first Rose Bowl game was played in Pasadena, CA, and has been played there continuously since 1916.

The first professional game was played on 31 Aug 1895 at Latrobe, PA, Latrobe YMCA defeating Jeanette Athletic Club 12–0. In 1920 the American Professional Football Association (APFA) was formed in Canton, OH. This organization was reorganized a number of times and in 1922 was renamed the National Football League (NFL). In 1944 the All-America Conference League was established, but eventually merged with the NFL in 1949. In 1959 the American Football League (AFL) was formed and competed with the NFL until a merger was agreed on in 1966, which led to the creation of the Super Bowl game, first played in January 1967. In 1970 the AFL and the NFL merged to form the present NFL.

NATIONAL FOOTBALL LEAGUE (NFL) RECORDS

Most championships The Green Bay Packers have won a record 11 NFL titles, 1929–31, 1936, 1939, 1944, 1961–62, 1965–67.

Most consecutive wins (regular season and playoffs) The Chicago Bears have won 18 consecutive games

■ **Most successful passer**
In a 17-year career with the Minnesota Vikings and the New York Giants, Fran Tarkenton passed for an NFL record total of 47,003 yards. Not surprisingly, he also holds the record for the greatest number of passes completed, 3,686. (Photo: Sports Illustrated)

NFL RECORDS

MOST POINTS

Career 2,002, George Blanda (Chicago Bears, Baltimore Colts, Houston Oilers, Oakland Raiders), 1949–75. **Season** 176, Paul Hornung (Green Bay Packers), 1960. **Game** 40, Ernie Nevers (Chicago Cardinals), 28 Nov 1929.

MOST TOUCHDOWNS

Career 126, Jim Brown (Cleveland Browns), 1957–65. **Season** 24, John Riggins (Washington Redskins), 1983. **Game** 6, Ernie Nevers (Chicago Cardinals), 28 Nov 1929; William "Dub" Jones (Cleveland Browns) 25 Nov 1951; Gale Sayers (Chicago Bears), 12 Dec 1965.

MOST YARDS GAINED RUSHING

Career 16,726, Walter Payton (Chicago Bears), 1975–87. **Season** 2,105, Eric Dickerson (Los Angeles Rams), 1984. **Game** 275, Walter Payton (Chicago Bears), 20 Nov 1977. **Highest career average** 5.22 yds per game (2,359 from 12,312), Jim Brown (Cleveland Browns), 1957–65.

MOST YARDS GAINED RECEIVING

Career 13,089, Steve Largent (Seattle Seahawks), 1976–89. **Season** 1,746, Charley Hennigan (Houston Oilers), 1961. **Game** 336, Willie "Flipper" Anderson (Los Angeles Rams), 26 Nov 1989.

MOST YARDS GAINED PASSING

Career 47,003, Fran Tarkenton (Minnesota Vikings, New York Giants), 1961–78. **Season** 5,084, Dan Marino (Miami Dolphins), 1984. **Game** 554, Norm Van Brocklin (Los Angeles Rams), 28 Sep 1951.

PASSING ATTEMPTS

Career 6,467, Fran Tarkenton (Minnesota Vikings, New York Giants), 1961–78. **Season** 623, Dan Marino (Miami Dolphins), 1986. **Game** 68, George Blanda (Houston Oilers), 1 Nov 1964.

MOST PASSES COMPLETED

Career 3,686, Fran Tarkenton (Minnesota Vikings, New York Giants), 1961–78. **Season** 378, Dan Marino (Miami Dolphins), 1986. **Game** 42 (from 59 attempts), Richard Todd (New York Jets), 21 Sep 1980. **Consecutive** 22, Joe Montana (San Francisco 49ers), 29 Nov 1987 *v* Cleveland Browns (5); 6 Dec 1987 *v* Green Bay Packers (17).

PASS RECEPTIONS

Career 819, Steve Largent (Seattle Seahawks), 1976–89. **Season** 106, Art Monk (Washington Redskins), 1984. **Game** 18, Tom Fears (Los Angeles Rams), 3 Dec 1950.

FIELD GOALS

Career 373, Jan Stenerud (Kansas City Chiefs, Green Bay Packers, Minnesota Vikings), 1967–85. **Season** 35, Ali Haji-Sheikh (New York Giants), 1983. **Game** 7, Jim Bakken (St Louis Cardinals), 24 Sep 1967; Rich Karlis (Minnesota Vikings), 5 Nov 1989. **Longest** 63 yds, Tom Dempsey (New Orleans Saints), 8 Nov 1970.

PUNTING

Career 1,154, Dave Jennings (New York Giants, New York Jets), 1974–87. **Season** 114, Bob Parsons (Chicago Bears), 1981. **Game** 15, John Teltschik (Philadelphia Eagles *v* New York Giants), 6 Dec 1987.

SACKS

Career 114.5, Lawrence Taylor (New York Giants), 1982–90. **Season** 22, Mark Gastineau (New York Jets), 1984. **Game** 7, Derrick Thomas (Kansas City Chiefs *v* Seattle Seahawks), 11 Nov 1990.

MOST INTERCEPTIONS

Career 81, Paul Krause (Washington Redskins; Minnesota Vikings), 1964–79. **Season** 14, Dick "Night Train" Lane (Los Angeles Rams), 1952. **Game** 4, 16 players have achieved this feat.

twice, in 1933–34 and 1941–42. This was matched by the Miami Dolphins in 1972–73 and the San Francisco 49ers in 1989–90. The most consecutive games without defeat is 25 by the Canton Bulldogs (22 wins and 3 ties) in 1921–23.

Most games played George Frederick Blanda (b. 17 Sep 1927) played in a record 340 games in a record 26 seasons in the NFL, for the Chicago Bears (1948–58), the Baltimore Colts (1950), the Houston Oilers (1960–66), and the Oakland Raiders (1967–75).

The most consecutive games played is 282, by Jim Marshall for the Cleveland Browns (1960) and the Minnesota Vikings (1961–79).

Longest run from scrimmage Anthony Drew "Tony" Dorsett (b. 7 Apr 1954) completed a touchdown after a run of 99 yards for the Dallas Cowboys *v* the Minnesota Vikings on 3 Jan 1983.

Longest field goal 63 yards by Thomas John "Tom" Dempsey (b. 12 Jan 1947) for the New Orleans Saints *v* the Detroit Lions, 8 Nov 1970.

Longest pass completion Pass completions for a touchdown of 99 yards were achieved by: Frank Filchok (to Andy Farkas), Washington Redskins *v* Pittsburgh Steelers, 15 Oct 1939; George Izo (to Bobby Mitchell), Washington Redskins *v* Cleveland Browns, 15 Sep 1963; Karl Sweetan (to Pat Studstill), Detroit Lions *v* Baltimore Colts, 16 Oct 1966; Sonny Jurgensen (to Gerry Allen), Washington Redskins *v* Chicago Bears, 15 Sep 1968; Jim Plunkett (to Cliff Branch), Los Angeles Raiders *v* Washington Redskins, 2 Oct 1983; Ron Jaworski (to Mike Quick), Philadelphia Eagles *v* Atlanta Falcons, 10 Nov 1985.

Longest punt 98 yards by Steve O'Neal for New York Jets *v* Denver Broncos, 21 Sep 1969.

Consecutive games *Scoring* 151, by Fred Cox for the Minnesota Vikings from 1963 to 1973.

Scoring touchdowns 18, by Lenny Moore for the Baltimore Colts, 1963–65.

Pass receptions 177, by Steve Largent for the Seattle Seahawks, 1977–89.

Field goals 24, by Kevin Butler for the Chicago Bears, 1988–89.

Greatest comeback in NFL history On 7 Dec, 1980, the San Francisco 49ers, playing at home, trailed the New Orleans Saints 35–7 at halftime. In the 2nd half, the 49ers, led by Joe Montana, scored 31 unanswered points to win the game 38–35. The 49ers had overcome a deficit of 28 points, the largest in NFL history.

Coaches The winningest coach in NFL history was George Stanley Halas (1895–1983), whose Chicago Bears teams won 325 games (and 7 NFL titles) to 151 losses and 31 ties while he was coach in 1920–29, 1933–42, 1946–55 and 1958–67. The highest winning percentage was .740 percent achieved by Vin-

cent Thomas "Vince" Lombardi (1913–70): 105 wins, 35 losses and 6 ties with the Green Bay Packers 1959–67 and the Washington Redskins 1969.

Most seasons 40, George Halas, with the Decatur/Chicago Staleys/Chicago Bears (1920–29, 1933–42, 1946–55, 1958–67).

THE SUPER BOWL

The Super Bowl was first held in 1967 between the winners of the NFL and AFL championships. Since 1970 it has been contested by the winners of the National and American Conferences of the NFL. The most wins is four, by the Pittsburgh Steelers in 1974–75, 1978–79, coached by Chuck Noll on each occasion, and by the San Francisco 49ers in 1981, 1984, 1988 and 1989, coached by Bill Walsh (1981, 1984, 1988) and George Seifert (1989).

Most appearances The most Super Bowl appearances is five, by the Dallas Cowboys (2 wins, 3 losses), 1970, 1971, 1975, 1977–78, and by the Miami Dolphins (2 wins, 3 losses), 1971–73, 1982, 1984.

The most appearances by a player is also five, shared by seven players: Marv Fleming (Green Bay Packers 1966–67, Miami Dolphins 1971–73); Larry Cole Dallas Cowboys 1970–71, 1975, 1977–78); Cliff Harris (Dallas Cowboys

1970–71, 1975, 1977–78); D. D. Lewis (Dallas Cowboys 1970–71, 1975, 1977–1978); Preston Pearson (Baltimore Colts 1968, Pittsburgh Steelers 1974, Dallas Cowboys 1975, 1977–78); Charlie Waters (Dallas Cowboys 1970–71, 1975, 1977–1978); Rayfield Wright (Dallas Cowboys 1970–71, 1975, 1977–78).

Don Shula has coached six Super Bowls to set the all-time mark: Baltimore Colts, 1968; Miami Dolphins, 1971–73, 1982, 1984. He won two games and lost four.

Highest scores The highest aggregate score was 66 points when the Pittsburgh Steelers beat the Dallas Cowboys 35–31 on 21 Jan 1979. The highest team score and record victory margin was when the San Francisco 49ers beat the Denver Broncos 55–10 in New Orleans, LA on 28 Jan 1990. In their 42–10 victory over the Denver Broncos on 31 Jan 1988, the Washington Redskins scored a record 35 points in the second quarter. The narrowest margin of victory was one point, when the New York Giants defeated the Buffalo Bills 20–19 on 27 Jan 1991.

Most valuable player Joseph C. Montana, Jr. (b. 11 Jun 1956), quarterback of the San Francisco 49ers, has been voted the Super Bowl MVP on a record three occasions: Super Bowl XVI, XIX, and XXIV.

For further details on the Super Bowl, see pages 248 and 249.

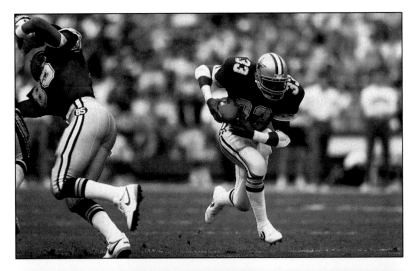

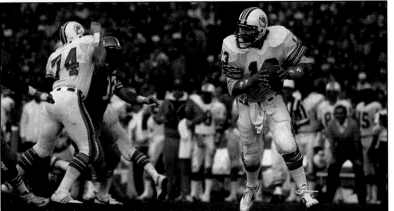

■ **Longest run from scrimmage**
Tony Dorsett (b. 7 Apr 1954) scored on a touchdown run of 99 yd for the Dallas Cowboys v. the Minnesota Vikings on 3 Jan 1983. (Photo: All-Sport [USA]/Stewart)

■ **Most pass completions**
Despite completing a Super Bowl record 29 passes, quarterback Dan Marino of the Miami Dolphins still ended up on the losing side against the San Francisco 49ers in Super Bowl XIX at Stanford, CA on 20 Jan 1985. (Photo: All-Sport [USA]/Duffy)

OFFENSIVE STATISTICS

PITTSBURGH STEELERS

| Game | Net Yardage Gained | | | Intercepted | Touchdowns/ |
	Rushing	Passing	Total		Points Scored
IX	249	84	333	0	2/ 16
X	149	190	339	0	2/ 21
XIII	66	291	357	1	5/ 35
XIV	84	309	393	3	4/ 31
Total:	**548**	**874**	**1,422**	**4**	**13/103**

SAN FRANCISCO 49ers

| Game | Net Yardage Gained | | | Intercepted | Touchdowns/ |
	Rushing	Passing	Total		Points Scored
XVI	127	148	275	0	2/ 26
XIX	211	326	537	0	5/ 38
XXIII	111	343	454	0	2/ 20
XXIV	144	317	461	0	8/ 55
Total:	**593**	**1,134**	**1,727**	**0**	**17/139**

Steelers celebrate the team's first Super Bowl victory at Super Bowl IX. Linebacker Andy Russell (34) holds aloft his game ball, which he later presented to owner Art Rooney, who had waited 42 years for his first NFL title.

DEFENSIVE STATISTICS

PITTSBURGH STEELERS

| Game | Net Yardage Allowed | | | Interceptions | Touchdowns/ |
	Rushing	Passing	Total		Points Allowed
IX	17	102	119	3	1/ 6
X	108	162	270	3	2/17
XIII	154	176	330	1	4/31
XIV	107	194	301	1	2/19
Total:	**386**	**634**	**1,020**	**8**	**9/73**

SAN FRANCISCO 49ers

| Game | Net Yardage Allowed | | | Interceptions | Touchdowns/ |
	Rushing	Passing	Total		Points Allowed
XVI	72	284	356	2	3/21
XIX	25	289	314	2	1/16
XXIII	106	123	229	1	1/16
XXIV	64	103	167	2	1/10
Total:	**267**	**799**	**1,066**	**7**	**6/63**

FRANCO HARRIS Elected to the Pro Football Hall of Fame in 1990, Harris was the main weapon in the Pittsburgh Steelers' running attack during its four championship triumphs. Harris's last Super Bowl was in 1980, yet he still shares or holds outright several Super Bowl records: career touchdowns scored (4), career points scored (24), career rushing attempts (101) and career yards gained rushing (354). Harris was named MVP of Super Bowl IX.

SUPER BOWL RESULTS

Bowl	Date	Winner	Loser	Score	Site	Crowd
I	15 Jan 1967	Green Bay Packers	Kansas City Chiefs	35–10	Los Angeles, CA	61,946
II	14 Jan 1968	Green Bay Packers	Oakland Raiders	33–14	Miami, FL	75,546
III	12 Jan 1969	New York Jets	Baltimore Colts	16–7	Miami, FL	75,389
IV	11 Jan 1970	Kansas City Chiefs	Minnesota Vikings	23–7	New Orleans, LA	80,562
V	17 Jan 1971	Baltimore Colts	Dallas Cowboys	16–13	Miami, FL	79,204
VI	16 Jan 1972	Dallas Cowboys	Miami Dolphins	24–3	New Orleans, LA	81,023
VII	14 Jan 1973	Miami Dolphins	Washington Redskins	14–7	Los Angeles, CA	90,182
VIII	13 Jan 1974	Miami Dolphins	Minnesota Vikings	24–7	Houston, TX	71,882
IX	12 Jan 1975	Pittsburgh Steelers	Minnesota Vikings	16–6	New Orleans, LA	80,997
X	18 Jan 1976	Pittsburgh Steelers	Dallas Cowboys	21–17	Miami, FL	80,187
XI	9 Jan 1977	Oakland Raiders	Minnesota Vikings	32–14	Pasadena, CA	103,438
XII	15 Jan 1978	Dallas Cowboys	Denver Broncos	27–10	New Orleans, LA	75,583
XIII	21 Jan 1979	Pittsburgh Steelers	Dallas Cowboys	35–31	Miami, FL	79,484
XIV	20 Jan 1980	Pittsburgh Steelers	Los Angeles Rams	31–19	Pasadena, CA	103,985
XV	25 Jan 1981	Oakland Raiders	Philadelphia Eagles	27–10	New Orleans, LA	76,135
XVI	24 Jan 1982	San Francisco 49ers	Cincinnati Bengals	26–21	Pontiac, MI	81,270
XVII	30 Jan 1983	Washington Redskins	Miami Dolphins	27–17	Pasadena, CA	103,667
XVIII	22 Jan 1984	Los Angeles Raiders	Washington Redskins	38–9	Tampa, FL	72,920
XIX	20 Jan 1985	San Francisco 49ers	Miami Dolphins	38–16	Stanford, CA	84,059
XX	26 Jan 1986	Chicago Bears	New England Patriots	46–10	New Orleans, LA	73,818
XXI	25 Jan 1987	New York Giants	Denver Broncos	39–20	Pasadena, CA	101,063
XXII	31 Jan 1988	Washington Redskins	Denver Broncos	42–10	San Diego, CA	73,302
XXIII	22 Jan 1989	San Francisco 49ers	Cincinnati Bengals	20–16	Miami, FL	75,129
XXIV	28 Jan 1990	San Francisco 49ers	Denver Broncos	55–10	New Orleans, LA	72,919
XXV	27 Jan 1991	New York Giants	Buffalo Bills	20–19	Tampa, FL	73,813

Since 1971 the Vince Lombardi Trophy has been presented to the winner of the Super Bowl. Awarded at the first AFL-NFL World Championship Game (Super Bowl I), the trophy was renamed in honor of Lombardi, whose Green Bay Packer teams won the first two Super Bowls, following his death in September 1970.

SUPER BOWL GAME AND CAREER RECORDS

POINTS *Game*		18	Roger Craig (San Francisco 49ers)	1985
		18	Jerry Rice (San Francisco 49ers)	1990
	Career	24	Franco Harris (Pittsburgh Steelers)	1975–76, 1979–80
		24	Roger Craig (San Francisco 49ers)	1985, 1989–90
		24	Jerry Rice (San Francisco 49ers)	1989–90
TOUCHDOWNS SCORED *Game*		3	Roger Craig (San Francisco 49ers)	1985
			Jerry Rice (San Francisco 49ers)	1990
	Career	4	Franco Harris (Pittsburgh Steelers)	1975–76, 1979–80
		4	Roger Craig (San Francisco 49ers)	1985, 1989–90
		4	Jerry Rice (San Francisco 49ers)	1989–90
TOUCHDOWN PASSES *Game*		5	Joe Montana (San Francisco 49ers)	1990
	Career	11	Joe Montana (San Francisco 49ers)	1982, 1985, 1989–90
HIGHEST PASSING PERCENTAGE *Game*	.880		Phil Simms (New York Giants)	1987
	Career	.680	Joe Montana (San Francisco 49ers; 40 attempts)	1982, 1985,1989–90)
YARDS GAINED PASSING *Game*		357	Joe Montana (San Francisco 49ers)	1989
	Career	1,142	Joe Montana (San Francisco 49ers)	1982, 1985, 1989–90
YARDS GAINED RECEIVING *Game*		215	Jerry Rice (San Francisco 49ers)	1989
	Career	364	Lynn Swann (Pittsburgh Steelers)	1975–76, 1979–80
PASSES COMPLETED *Game*		29	Dan Marino (Miami Dolphins)	1985
	Career	83	Joe Montana (San Francisco 49ers)	1982, 1985, 1989–90
PASS RECEPTIONS *Game*		11	Dan Ross (Cincinnati Bengals)	1982
		11	Jerry Rice (San Francisco 49ers)	1989
	Career	20	Roger Craig (San Francisco 49ers)	1985, 1989–90
YARDS GAINED RUSHING *Game*		204	Timmy Smith (Washington Redskins)	1988
	Career	354	Franco Harris (Pittsburgh Steelers)	1975–76, 1979–80
FIELD GOALS *Game*		4	Don Chandler (Green Bay Packers)	1968
		4	Ray Wersching (San Francisco 49ers)	1982
	Career	5	Ray Wersching (San Francisco 49ers)	1982, 1985
LONGEST (yds)		48	Jan Stenerud (Kansas City Chiefs)	1970
		48	Rich Karlis (Denver Broncos)	1987
INTERCEPTIONS *Game*		3	Rod Martin (Oakland Raiders)	1981
	Career	3	Rod Martin (Oakland Raiders)	1981, 1984
		3	Chuck Howley (Dallas Cowboys)	1971, 1972
MOST VALUABLE PLAYER		3	Joe Montana (San Francisco 49ers)	1982, 1985, 1990

The Super Bowl

During its twenty-five year history, two teams have dominated the Super Bowl: the Pittsburgh Steelers and the San Francisco 49ers, both having won four titles.
The Steelers, led by quarterback Terry Bradshaw and its famed "steel curtain" defense, won Super Bowl's IX, X, XIII and XIV. The 49ers, led by quarterback Joe Montana and its noted innovative offensive, won Super Bowl's XVI, XIX, XXIII and XXIV. Although the "team of the seventies" can never meet the "team of the eighties" on the field of play, it is interesting to compare their Super Bowl statistics and fun to add fuel to the unanswerable question...Who is the best ever?

RESULTS

RECORDS and CHAMPIONS

In 1966, the National Football League (NFL) and the American Football League (AFL) agreed to merge their competing leagues to form an expanded NFL. Regular-season play would not begin until 1970, but the two leagues agreed to stage an annual AFL–NFL World Championship Game beginning in January 1967. The proposed championship game was dubbed the Super Bowl, and in 1969 the NFL officially recognized the title. Super Bowl I was played on 15 Jan 1967, the Green Bay Packers (NFL) defeating the Kansas City Chiefs (AFL), 35–10. The Packers repeated as champions in 1968. In Super Bowl III, the New York Jets (AFL) pulled off one of the great upsets in sports when they defeated the Baltimore Colts (NFL), 16–7, and thus became the first AFL team to win the Super Bowl. This game established the reputation of the Super Bowl and it has grown into an "American Event" since that time.

JOE MONTANA The greatest quarterback in Super Bowl history, Montana was at the helm at each of the San Francisco 49ers four Super Bowl victories. Montana holds numerous Super Bowl records, among them: the most touchdown passes in a game (5, *v* the Denver Broncos in 1990), the most yards gained passing in a game (357, *v* the Cincinnati Bengals in 1989), career touchdown passes (11), career yards gained passing (1,142) and the most MVP awards (3 – 1982, 1985 and 1990). In his Super Bowl career, Montana has completed 83 of 122 passes for 1,142 yards, with no interceptions and 11 touchdowns.

Photo credits: All-Sport, All-Sport USA and Pittsburgh Steelers

COLLEGE FOOTBALL (NCAA) —

The oldest collegiate series still contested is that between Yale and Princeton, first played in November 1873, three years before the formation of the Intercollegiate Football Association. The first Rose Bowl game was held in Pasadena, CA on 1 Jan 1902, when Michigan beat Stanford 49–0. The National Collegiate Athletic Association began classifying college teams into Divisions I, II and III in 1973. Five years later Division I was subdivided into 1-A and 1-AA.

Career Records (Divisions 1-A, 1-AA, II And III) *Points scored* 474, Joe Dudek, Plymouth State (Div. III), 1982–85.

Rushing (yards) 6,320, Johnny Bailey, Texas A&I (Div. II), 1986–89.

Passing (yards) 13,220, Neil Lomax, Portland State (Div II; 1-AA), 1977; 1978–80.

Receptions (yards) 4,693, Jerry Rice, Mississippi Valley (Div. 1-AA), 1981–84.

Receptions (most) 301, Jerry Rice, Mississippi Valley (Div. 1-AA), 1981–84.

Field goals (game) 8, Goran Lingmerth, Northern Arizona (Div. 1-AA). Booting 8 out of 8 kicks, Lingmerth set the record on 25 Oct 1986 *v* Idaho.

Longest plays *Run from scrimmage* 99 yards by four players: Gale Sayers (Kansas *v* Nebraska), 1963; Max Anderson (Arizona State *v* Wyoming), 1967; Ralph Thompson (West Texas State *v* Wichita State), 1970; Kelsey Finch (Tennessee *v* Florida), 1977.

Field goal 67 yards by three players: Russell Erxleben (Texas *v* Rice), 1977; Steve Little (Arkansas *v* Texas), 1977; Joe Williams (Wichita State *v* Southern Illinois), 1978. Ove Johansson kicked a 69-yard field goal for Abilene Christian University *v* East Texas State on 16 Oct 1976, but this was in an NAIA game.

Pass completion 99 yards by seven players: Fred Owens (to Jack Ford), Portland *v* St. Mary's, CA, 1947; Bo Burris (to Warren McVea), Houston *v* Washington State, 1966; Colin Clapton (to Eddie Jenkins), Holy Cross *v* Boston U, 1970; Terry Peel (to Robert Ford), Houston *v* Syracuse, 1970; Terry Peel (to Robert Ford), Houston *v* San Diego State, 1972; Chris

Collingsworth (to Derrick Gaffney), Florida *v* Rice, 1977; Scott Ankrom (to James Maness), TCU *v* Rice, 1984.

Punt 99 yards by Pat Brady, Nevada-Reno *v* Loyola, CA in 1950.

Highest score The most points ever scored in a college game is 222, by Georgia Tech *v* Cumberland College (0) of Lebanon, TN on 7 Oct 1916. Tech set records for 63 points in a quarter, 32 touchdowns, and 30 points after touchdown in a game.

Longest streak The University of Oklahoma won 47 successive games from 1953 to 1957, when they were beaten 7–0 by Notre Dame. The longest unbeaten streak is 63 (59 won, 4 tied) by Washington from 1907 to 1917, ended by a 27–0 loss to California.

Coaches In Division 1-A competition, Paul "Bear" Bryant (1913–83) won more games than any other coach, with 323 wins over 38 years: Maryland 1945, Kentucky 1946–53, Texas A&M 1954–57 and Alabama 1958–82. He led Alabama to five national titles and 15 bowl wins, including 7 Sugar Bowls. The best win percentage in

Division 1-A was 0.881 by Knute Rockne (1888–1931), with 105 wins, 12 losses and 5 ties, 12,847 points for and 667 against, at Notre Dame 1918–30. In overall NCAA competition, Eddie Robinson, Grambling (Division 1-AA) holds the mark for most victories with 366 through 1990.

Record attendances The highest attendances at college football games were estimated crowds of 120,000 at Soldier Field, Chicago, IL on 26 Nov 1927 when Notre Dame beat Southern California 7–6, and on 13 Oct 1928 when Notre Dame beat Navy 7–0. The highest average attendance for home games is 105,588 for the six games played by Michigan in 1985.

National College Football Champions The most wins in the national journalists' poll, established in 1936, to determine the college team of the year is eight by Notre Dame, 1943, 1946–47, 1949, 1966, 1973, 1977 and 1988. Notre Dame was also declared winner in 1924 and 1929–30.

Bowl games The oldest college bowl game is the Rose Bowl. It was first played on 1 Jan 1902 at Tournament Park, Pasadena, CA, when Michigan beat Stanford 49–0. The second game did not take place until 1916, and the game has been played continuously since. The University of Southern California (USC) has a record 19 wins in the Rose Bowl. The University of Alabama has made a record 43 bowl appearances and 23 wins. Most wins in the other "big four" bowl games: Orange Bowl: 11, Oklahoma; Sugar Bowl: 7, Alabama; Cotton Bowl: 9, Texas.

Heisman Memorial Trophy This award has been given annually since 1935 by the Downtown Athletic Club of New York to the top college football player as determined by a poll of journalists. It was originally called the D.A.C. Trophy but the name was changed in 1936. Its full title is the John W. Heisman Memorial Trophy and it is named after the first athletic director of the Downtown Athletic Club. The only double winner has been Archie Griffin of Ohio State, 1974–75. The University of Notre Dame has had more Heisman Trophy winners than any other school with seven selections.

NCAA DIVISION 1-A INDIVIDUAL RECORDS

POINTS
Game	48	Howard Griffith (Illinois v Southern Illinois; 8 touchdowns)	22 Sep 1990
Season	234	Barry Sanders (Oklahoma State; 39 touchdowns in 11 games)	1988
Career	394	Anthony Thompson (Indiana; 65 touchdowns, 4 point-after-touchdowns)	1986–89

TOTAL YARDAGE
Game	732	David Klinger (Houston v Arizona State; 716 passing, 16 rushing)	1 Dec 1990
Season	5,221	David Klinger (Houston; 5,140 passing, 81 rushing)	1990
Career	11,317	Doug Flutie (Boston College; 10,579 passing, 738 rushing)	1981–84

YARDS GAINED RUSHING
Game	377	Anthony Thompson (Indiana v Wisconsin)	11 Nov 1989
Season	2,628	Barry Sanders (Oklahoma State; 344 rushes in 11 games, record av. 238.9)	1988
Career	6,082	Tony Dorset (Pittsburgh; 1,074 rushes)	1973–76

YARDS GAINED PASSING
Game	716	David Klinger (Houston v Arizona State)	1 Dec 1990
Season	5,188	Ty Detmer (Brigham Young)	1990
Career	11,425	Todd Santos (San Diego State; completed 910 of 1,484)	1984–87

PASS COMPLETIONS
Game	48	David Klinger (Houston v SMU)	20 Oct 1990
Season	374	David Klinger (Houston)	1990
Career	910	Todd Santos (San Diego State; 1,484 attempts)	1984–87

TOUCHDOWN PASSES
Game	11	David Klinger (Houston v Eastern Washington)	17 Nov 1990
Season	54	David Klinger (Houston)	1990
Career	86	Ty Detmer (Brigham Young)	1988–90

PASS RECEPTIONS
Game	22	Jay Miller (Brigham Young v New Mexico; 263 yards)	3 Nov 1973
Season	142	Emmanuel Hazard (Houston)	1969
Career	263	Terance Mathis (New Mexico)	1985–87, 1989

YARDS GAINED RECEIVING
Game	349	Chuck Hughes (UTEP v North Texas; caught 10)	18 Sep 1965
Season	1,779	Howard Twilley (Tulsa; caught 134 in 10 games)	1965
Career	4,254	Terance Mathis (New Mexico)	1985–87, 1989

PASS INTERCEPTIONS
Game	5	Dan Rebsch, (Miami [Ohio] v Western Michigan; 88 yards; three others with less yards)	4 Nov 1972
Season	14	Al Worley (Washington; 130 yards, in 10 games)	1968
Career	29	Al Brosky (Illinois; 356 yards, 27 games)	1950–52

TOUCHDOWNS (Receiving)
Game	6	Tim Delaney (San Diego State v New Mexico State)	15 Nov 1969
Season	22	Emmanuel Hazard (Houston)	1989
Career	38	Clarkston Hines (Duke)	1986–89

FIELD GOALS
Game	7	Mike Prindle (West Michigan v Marshall)	29 Sep 1984
	7	Dale Klein (Nebraska v Missouri)	19 Oct 1985
Season	29	John Lee (UCLA)	1984
Career	80	Jeff Jaeger (Washington)	1983–86
Consecutive	30	Chuck Nelson (Washington)	1981–82

TOUCHDOWNS
Game	8	Howard Griffith (Illinois v Southern Illinois)	22 Sep 1990
Season	39	Barry Sanders (Oklahoma State)	1988
Career	65	Anthony Thompson (Indiana)	1986–89

Gaelic Football

Origins The game developed from inter-parish "free for alls," with no time limit, specific playing area, or rules. The earliest reported match was Meath v Louth, at Slane, Ireland in 1712. Standardization came with the formation of the Gaelic Athletic Association in Thurles, Ireland on 1 Nov 1884.

All-Ireland Championships The greatest number of All-Ireland Championships won by one team is 30, by Ciarraidhe (Kerry) between 1903 and 1986.

The greatest number of successive wins is four, by Wexford (1915–18) and Kerry twice (1929–32, 1978–81).

The most finals contested by an individual is ten, including eight wins by the Kerry players Pat Spillane, Paudie O'Shea and Denis Moran, 1975–76, 1978–82, 1984–86.

The highest team score in a final was when Dublin, 27 (5 goals, 12 points), beat Armagh, Great Britain, 15 (3 goals, 6 points), on 25 Sep 1977. The highest combined score was 45 points, when Cork (26) beat Galway (19) in 1973. A goal equals three points.

The highest individual score in an All-Ireland final has been 2 goals, 6 points by Jimmy Keaveney (Dublin) v Armagh, Great Britain, in 1977, and by Michael Sheehy (Kerry) v Dublin in 1979.

Largest crowd The record crowd was 90,556 for the Down v Offaly final at Croke Park, Dublin in 1961.

Gliding

Origins Research by Isadore William Deiches has shown evidence of the use of gliders in ancient Egypt *c.* 2500–1500 B.C. Emanuel Swedenborg (1688–1772) of Sweden made sketches of gliders *c.* 1714. The earliest human-carrying glider was designed by Sir George Cayley (1773–1857) and carried his coachman possibly John Appleby) about 500 yd across a valley in Brompton Dale, Great Britain in the summer of 1853.

Most titles The most World Individual

GLIDING WORLD RECORDS
(Single-seaters)

DISTANCE	NAME	TYPE OF GLIDER	LOCATION	DATE
STRAIGHT DISTANCE ... 907.7 miles	Hans-Werner Grosse (West Germany)	ASW-12	Lübeck, Germany to Biarritz, France	25 Apr 1972
DECLARED GOAL DISTANCE ... 779.4 miles	Bruce Drake (New Zealand)	Nimbus 2	Te Anau to Te Araroa, New Zealand	14 Jan 1978
	David Speight (New Zealand)	Nimbus 2	Te Anau to Te Araroa, New Zealand	14 Jan 1978
	S. H. "Dick" Georgeson (New Zealand)	Nimbus 2	Te Anau to Te Araroa, New Zealand	14 Jan 1978
GOAL AND RETURN ... 1,023.2 miles	Tom Knauff (USA)	Nimbus 3	Williamsport, PA to Knoxville, TN	25 Apr 1983
ABSOLUTE ALTITUDE ... 49,009 ft	Robert R. Harris (USA)	Grob G102	California	17 Feb 1986
HEIGHT GAIN ... 42,303 ft	Paul Bikle (USA)	Schweitzer SGS1-23E	Mojave, CA	25 Feb 1961

SPEED OVER TRIANGULAR COURSE

DISTANCE	SPEED KM/H	MPH	NAME	TYPE OF GLIDER	PLACE	DATE
100 km	195.3	121.35	Ingo Renner (Australia)	Nimbus 3	Australia	14 Dec 1982
300 km	169.49	105.32	Jean-Paul Castel (France)	Nimbus 3	South Africa	15 Nov 1986
500 km	170.06	105.67	Beat Bunzli (Switzerland)	Nimbus 3	South Africa	18 Dec 1987
750 km	158.40	98.43	Hans-Werner Grosse (West Germany)	ASW-22	Australia	8 Jan 1985
1,000 km	145.32	90.29	Hans-Werner Grosse (West Germany)	ASW-17	Australia	3 Jan 1979
1,250 km	133.24	82.79	Hans-Werner Grosse (West Germany)	ASW-17	Australia	9 Jan 1980

Biggest bunker
The world's biggest bunker is Hell's Half Acre on the 585 yd seventh hole of the Pine Valley course, Clementon, NJ, built in 1912 and generally regarded as the world's most trying course.

championships (instituted 1937) won is four, by Ingo Renner (Australia) in 1976 (Standard class), 1983, 1985 and 1987 (Open).

The most titles won by a US pilot is two, by George Moffat, in the Open category, 1970 and 1974.

Women's altitude records The women's single-seater world record for absolute altitude is 41,449 ft, by Sabrina Jackintell (USA) in an Astir GS on 14 Feb 1979.

The height gain record is 33,506 ft, by Yvonne Loader (New Zealand) at Omarama, New Zealand on 12 Jan 1988.

HANG GLIDING

Origins In the 11th century the monk Eilmer is reported to have flown from the 60-ft tower of Malmesbury Abbey, Wiltshire, Great Britain. The earliest modern pioneer was Otto Lilienthal (Germany; 1848–96) with about 2,500 flights in gliders of his own construction between 1891 and 1896. In the 1950s Professor Francis Rogallo of the National Space Agency developed a flexible "wing" from his space capsule reentry research.

World Championships The World Team Championships (officially instituted in 1976) have been won most often by Great Britain (1981, 1985, 1989 and 1991).

World records The *Fédération Aéronautique Internationàle* recognizes world records for rigid-wing, flex-wing and multiplace flex-wing. The following records are the greatest in each category—all by flex-wing gliders.

MEN Greatest distance in straight line and declared goal distance: *303.36 miles* Larry Tudor (USA), Wills Wing Hobbs Airpark, NM to Elkhart, KS, 3 Jul 1990.

Height gain: *14,250 ft* Larry Tudor (USA), Owens Valley, CA, 4 Aug 1985.

Out and return distance: *192.818 miles* Larry Tudor (USA) and Geoffrey Loyns (Great Britain), Owens Valley, 26 Jun 1988.

Triangular course distance: *104.4 miles* Hans Ulrich Bluimenthal, Markus Hangstangl and Sepp Singhammer (all West Germany), St. André-les-Alps, France, 9 Aug 1990.

WOMEN Greatest distance: *181.02 miles* Kari Castle (USA), Hobbs Airpark, 1 Jul 1990.

Height gain: *10,997 ft* Tover Buas-Hansen (Norway) and Keven Klinefelder (USA), Owens Valley, 6 Jul 1989.

Out and return distance: *181.48 miles* Kari Castle (USA), Hobbs Airpark, 3 Jul 1990. *81.99 miles* Tover Buas-Hansen, Owens Valley, 6 Jul 1989.

Declared goal distance: *132.04 miles* Liavan Mallin (Ireland), Owens Valley, 13 Jul 1989.

Triangular course distance: Jenney Ganderton (Australia), *66.3 miles*, Forbes, Australia, 23 Jan 1990.

Greatest descent John Bird piloted a hang glider from a height of 39,000 ft when he was released from a hot-air balloon to the ground, landing in Edmonton, Alberta, Canada on 29 Aug 1982. He touched down 50 miles from his point of departure.

Golf

Origins The Chinese Nationalist Golf Association claims the game is of Chinese origin (*ch'ui wan*—the ball-hitting game) in the 3rd or 2nd century B.C. There were official ordinances prohibiting a ball game with clubs in Belgium and Holland from 1360. Gutta percha balls succeeded feather balls in 1848, and by 1902 were in turn succeeded by rubber-cored balls, invented in 1899 by Coburn Haskell (USA). Steel shafts were authorized in the United States in 1925.

The first evidence of golf in the USA is that the game was played in Charleston, NC and in Virginia, in the mid-18th century. The first club organized for the playing of golf in North America was in Canada, when the Royal Montreal Golf Club was formed on Nov 4 1873. The United States Golf Association (USGA) was founded in 1894 as the governing body of golf in the United States.

Oldest club The oldest club of which there is written evidence is the Gentlemen Golfers (now the Honourable Company of Edinburgh Golfers) formed in March 1744—ten years prior to the institution of the Royal and Ancient Club of St Andrews, Fife, Scotland. However, the Royal Burgess Golfing Society of Edinburgh, Great Britain claims to have been founded in 1735.

Two golf clubs claim to be the first established in the United States: the Foxberg Golf Club, Clarion Co., PA (1887) and St Andrews Golf Club of Yonkers, NY (1888).

Highest course The Tuctu Golf Club in Morococha, Peru, is 14,335 ft above sea level at its lowest point. Golf has, however, been played in Tibet at an altitude of over 16,000 ft.

Lowest course The Furnace Creek course in Death Valley, CA is 220 ft below sea level.

Longest hole The longest hole in the world is the 7th hole (par-7) of the Sano Course, Satsuki Golf Club, Japan, which measures 909 yd.

Largest green Probably the largest green in the world is that of the par-6 695 yd fifth hole at International Golf Club, Bolton, MA, with an area greater than 28,000 ft^2.

Longest course The world's longest course is the par-77 8,325 yd International Golf Club (see also above) in Bolton, MA from the "Tiger" tees, remodeled in 1969 by Robert Trent Jones.

Floyd Satterlee Rood used the entire United States as a course, when he played from the Pacific surf to the Atlantic surf from 14 Sep 1963 to 3 Oct 1964 in 114,737 strokes. He lost 3,511 balls on the 3,397.7 mile trail.

Longest drives In officially regulated long driving contests over level ground the greatest distance recorded is 437 yd 2 ft 4 in by Jack L. Hamm (USA), at an altitude of 5,280 ft, on 25 Oct 1989 in Denver, CO. The longest recorded drive in a regulated competition at sea level is 411 yd by Cary B. Schuman (USA) at the Navy Marine Golf Course, Oahu, HI on 7 May 1989.

On an airport runway, Kelly Murray (Canada) drove a Wilson Ultra 432 ball 684.8 yd at Fairmont Hot Springs, British Columbia, Canada on 25 Sep 1990.

The women's record is held by Helen Dobson (Great Britain), who drove a Titleist Pinnacle 531 yd at RAF Honnington, Suffolk, Great Britain on 31 Oct 1987.

The longest recorded drive on an ordinary course is one of 515 yd by Michael Hoke Austin (b. 17 Feb 1910) of Los Angeles, CA, in the US National Seniors Open Championship at Las Vegas, NV on 25 Sep 1974. Austin, 6 ft 2 in tall and weighing 210 lb, drove the ball to within a yard of the green on the par-4 450 yd fifth hole of the Winterwood Course and it rolled 65 yd past the flagstick. He was aided by an estimated 35 mph tailwind.

A drive of 2,640 yd (1½ miles) across ice was achieved by an Australian meteorologist named Nils Lied at Mawson Base, Antarctica in 1962.

On the moon the energy expended on a mundane 300 yd drive would achieve, craters permitting, a distance of 1 mile.

Longest putt The longest recorded holed putt in a major tournament was one of 86 ft on the vast 13th green at the Augusta National, GA by Cary Middlecoff (USA; b. 6 Jan 1921) in the 1955 Masters' Tournament.

Robert Tyre "Bobby" Jones Jr. (1902–71) was reputed to have sunk a putt in excess of 100 ft at the fifth green in the first round of the 1927 Open at St Andrews.

Bob Cook (USA) sank a putt measured at 140 ft 2¾ in on the 18th at St Andrews in the International Fourball Pro Am Tournament on 1 Oct 1976.

SCORES

Lowest nine holes Nine holes in 25 (4, 3, 3, 2, 3, 3, 1, 4, 2) was recorded by A. J. "Bill" Burke in a round in 57 (32 + 25) on the 6,389 yd par-71 Normandie course at St Louis, MO on 20 May 1970.

The professional tournament record is 27, by Mike Souchak (USA; b. 10 May 1927) for the second nine (par-35), first round of the 1955 Texas Open (see Lowest 72 holes); Andy North (USA; b. 9 Mar 1950), for the second nine (par-34), first round, 1975 B.C. Open at En-Joie Golf Club, Endicott, NY; José Maria Canizares (Spain; b. 18 Feb 1947), for the first nine, third round, in the 1978 Swiss Open on the 6,811 yd Crans Golf Club, Crans-sur-Seine; and Robert Lee (Great Britain; b. 12 Oct 1961), for the first nine,

first round, in the Monte Carlo Open on the 6,249 yd Mont Agel course on 28 Jun 1985.

Lowest 18 holes *Men* At least four players have played a long course (over 6,561 yd) in a score of 58, most recently Monte Carlo Money (USA; b. 3 Dec 1954), on the par-72, 6,607 yd Las Vegas Municipal Golf Club, NV on 11 Mar 1981.

Alfred Edward Smith (1903–85) scored 55 (15 under par 70) on his 18-hole home course of 4,248 yd on 1 Jan 1936, scoring 4, 2, 3, 4, 2, 4, 3, 4, 3 = 29 out, and 2, 3, 3, 3, 3, 2, 5, 4, 1 = 26 in.

The PGA tournament record for 18 holes is 59 (30 + 29), by Al Geiberger (b. 1 Sep 1937) in the second round of the Danny Thomas Classic, on the 72-par 7,249 yd Colonial Golf Club course, Memphis, TN on 10 Jun 1977.

Other golfers to have recorded 59 over 18 holes in major non-PGA tournaments include: Samuel Jackson "Sam" Snead (USA; b. 27 May 1912), at the Sam Sneed Festival (third round) at White Sulphur Springs, WV on 16 May 1959; Gary Player (South Africa; b. 1 Nov 1935), in the second round of the Brazilian Open in Rio de Janeiro on 29 Nov 1974; David Jagger (Great Britain; b. 9 Jun 1949) in a Pro-Am tournament prior to the 1973 Nigerian Open at Ikoyi Golf Club, Lagos; and Miguel Martin (Spain) in the Argentine Southern Championship at Mar del Plata on 27 Feb 1987.

Women The lowest recorded score on an 18-hole course (over 5,600 yd) for a woman is 62 (30 + 32) by Mary "Mickey" Kathryn Wright (USA; b. 14 Feb 1935) on the Hogan Park Course (par-71, 6,286 yd) at Midland, TX, in November 1964; Vicki Fergon at the 1984 San Jose

Classic, San Jose, CA; and Janice Arnold (New Zealand; 31 + 31) on the Coventry Golf Course (5,815 yd) on 24 Sep 1990.

Wanda Morgan (b. 22 Mar 1910) recorded a score of 60 (31 + 29) on the Westgate and Birchington Golf Club course, Kent, Great Britain, over 18 holes (5,002 yd) on 11 Jul 1929.

Lowest 36 holes The record for 36 holes is 122 (59 + 63), by Sam Snead in the 1959 Sam Snead Festival on 16–17 May 1959.

Horton Smith (1908–63) scored 121 (63 + 58) on a short course on 21 Dec 1928 (see Lowest 72 holes).

Lowest 72 holes The lowest recorded score on a first class course is 255 (29 under par), by Leonard Peter Tupling (Great Britain; b. 6 Apr 1950) in the Nigerian Open at Ikoyi Golf Club, Lagos in February 1981, made up of 63, 66, 62 and 64 (average 63.75 per round).

The lowest 72 holes in a PGA tour event is 257 (60, 68, 64, 65), by Mike Souchak in the 1955 Texas Open at San Antonio.

The 72 holes record on the European tour is 258 (64, 69, 60, 65) by David Llewellyn (Wales; b. 18 Nov 1951) in the Biarritz Open on 1–3 Apr 1988. This was equaled by Ian Woosnam (Wales; b. 2 Mar 1958) (66, 67, 65, 60) in the Monte Carlo Open on 4–7 Jul 1990.

Trish Johnson scored 242 (64, 60, 60, 58; 21 under par) in the Bloor Homes Eastleigh Classic at the Fleming Park Course (4,402 yd) at Eastleigh, Great Britain on 22–25 Jul 1987.

Most shots for one hole In a competition at Peacehaven, East Sussex, Great Britain in 1890, A. J. Lewis had 156 putts

Most shots for one hole
A woman player in the qualifying round of the Shawnee Invitational for Ladies at Shawnee-on-Delaware, PA, c. 1912, took 166 strokes for the short 130 yd 16th hole. Her tee shot went into the Binniekill River and the ball floated. She put out in a boat with her exemplary but statistically minded husband at the oars. She eventually beached the ball 1½ miles downstream but was not yet out of the woods. She had to play through one on the home run.

■ **Highest earnings**
Ian Woosnam (Wales) won a season's record £574,166 ($980,000) in European Order of Merit tournaments in 1990. In 1991 he attained number 1 in the Sony rankings and confirmed his position by immediately winning his first major, the Masters.
(Photo: All-Sport/S. Munday)

PGA Tour All-Time Scoring Records

Lowest score (9 holes)	27	Mike Souchak, Texas Open (back nine)	1955
	27	Andy North, B.C. Open (back nine)	1975
Lowest score (18 holes)	59	Al Geiberger, Danny Thomas Memphis Classic (2nd round)	1977
Lowest score (36 holes)	125	Ron Streck, Texas Open (3rd and 4th rounds)	1988
	125	Blaine McCallister, Hardee's Golf Classic (2nd and 3rd rounds)	1988
Lowest score (54 holes)	189	Chandler Harper, Texas Open (2nd, 3rd and 4th rounds)	1954
Lowest score (72 holes)	257	Mike Souchak, Texas Open	1955
Most shots under par	27	Ben Hogan, Portland Invitational	1945
	27	Mike Souchak, Texas Open	1955
Most birdies in a row	8	Bob Goalby, St Petersburg Open (4th round)	1961
	8	Fuzzy Zoeller, Quad Cities Open (1st round)	1976
	8	Dewey Arnette, Buick Open (1st round)	1987
Fewest putts (18 holes)	18	Sam Trahan, IVB-Philadelphia Golf Classic (4th round)	1979
	18	Mike McGee, Federal Express St Jude Classic (1st round)	1987
	18	Kenny Knox, MCI Heritage Classic (1st round)	1989
	18	Andy North, Anheuser Busch Golf Classic (2nd round)	1990
Fewest putts (72 holes)	93	Kenny Knox, MCI Heritage Classic	1989

Source: PGA Tour

Highest shot on Earth

Timothy J. Ayers played a shot from the summit of Mt McKinley, AK (20,320 ft) on 23 May 1984.

Throwing a golf ball

The lowest recorded score for throwing a golf ball around 18 holes (over 6,000 yd) is 82 by Joe Flynn (USA), 21, at the 6,228 yd Port Royal course, Bermuda on 27 Mar 1975.

on one green without holing out. The highest score for a single hole in the British Open is 21, by a player in the inaugural meeting at Prestwick in 1860. Double figures have been recorded on the card of the winner only once, when Willie Fernie (1851–1924) scored a ten at Musselburgh, Lothian, Scotland in 1883.

Ray Ainsley of Ojai, CA took 19 strokes for the par-4 16th hole during the second round of the US Open at Cherry Hills Country Club, Denver, CO on 10 Jun 1938. Most of the strokes were used in trying to extricate the ball from a brook.

Hans Merell of Mogadore, OH took 19 strokes on the par-3 16th (222 yd) during the third round of the Bing Crosby National Tournament at Cypress Point Club, Del Monte, CA on 17 Jan 1959.

Fastest rounds *Individual* With such variations in lengths of courses, speed records, even for rounds under par, are of little comparative value. The fastest round played when the golf ball comes to rest before each new stroke is 27 min 9 sec, by James Carvill (b. 13 Oct 1965) at Warrenpoint Golf Course, County Down, Northern Ireland (18 holes, 6,154 yd) on 18 Jun 1987.

Team Forty-eight players completed the 18-hole 7,108 yd Kyalami course, near Johannesburg, South Africa in 9 min 51 sec on 23 Feb 1988, using only one ball. They scored 73!

Slowest rounds The slowest stroke-play tournament round was one of 6 hr 45 min, taken by South Africa in the first round of the 1972 World Cup at the Royal Melbourne Golf Club, Australia. This was a four-ball medal round; everything holed out.

Most holes in 24 hours *On foot* Ian Colston, 35, played 22 rounds plus five holes (401 holes in all) at Bendigo Golf Club, Victoria, Australia (par-73, 6,061 yd) on 27–28 Nov 1971.

Using golf carts Charles Stock played

783 holes at Boston Hills Golf Club, Hudson, OH (9 holes, 3,110 yd) on 20 Jul 1987.

Terry Zachary played 391 holes in 12 hours on the 6,706 yd course at Connaught Golf Club, Alberta, Canada on 16 Jun 1986.

Most holes played in a week Steve Hylton played 1,128 holes at the Mason Rudolph Golf Club (6,060 yd), Clarkesville, TN from 25–31 Aug 1980. Using a golf cart for transport, Colin Young completed 1,260 holes at Patshull Park Golf Club (6,412 yd), Pattingham, Shropshire from 2–9 Jul 1988.

MEN'S CHAMPIONSHIP RECORDS

Grand Slam In 1930 Bobby Jones won the United States and British Opens and the United States and British Amateur Championships. These four victories were christened the Grand Slam of golf. In 1960 the professional Grand Slam (the Masters, US Open, British Open and Professional Golfers Association [PGA] Championships) gained recognition when Arnold Palmer won the first two legs, the Masters and the US Open. However, he did not complete the set of victories, and the Grand Slam has still not been attained. Ben Hogan came closest to succeeding in 1951, when he won the first three legs, but he could not return to the United States from Britain in time for the PGA Championship.

The four grand slam events are also known as "the majors." Jack Nicklaus (b. 21 Jan 1940) has won the most major championships with 18 professional titles (6 Masters, 4 US Opens, 3 British Opens and 5 PGA Championships). Additionally, Nicklaus has won two US Amateur titles, which are often included in calculating major championship victories.

The Masters (played on the 6,980 yd Augusta National Golf Course, GA, first in 1934) *Most wins:* Jack Nick-

laus has won six green jackets (1963, 1965–66, 1972, 1975, 1986). Two players have won consecutive Masters: Jack Nicklaus (1965–66) and Nick Faldo (Great Britain; 1989–90).

LOWEST SCORE Any round: 63, by Nicholas Raymond Leige Price (Zimbabwe; b. 28 Jan 1957) in 1986.

Total aggregate: 271, by: Jack Nicklaus (67, 71, 64, 69) in 1965, and Raymond Loran Floyd (65, 66, 70, 70) in 1976.

Oldest winner The oldest winner of the Masters was Jack Nicklaus, age 46 years 81 days in 1986. Severiano Ballesteros (Spain) was the youngest player to win the Masters, at 23 years 2 days in 1980.

US Open (inaugurated 1895) *Most wins:* Four players have won the titles four times: Willie Anderson (1901, 1903–05), Bobby Jones (1923, 1926, 1929–30), Ben Hogan (1948, 1950–51, 1953) and Jack Nicklaus (1962, 1967, 1972, 1980). The only player to gain three successive titles was Willie Anderson, from 1903 to 1905.

LOWEST SCORE Any round: 63, by Johnny Miller (b. 29 Apr 1947) on the 6,921 yd par-71 Oakmont Country Club, PA on 17 Jun 1973; by Jack Nicklaus and Tom Weiskopf (USA; b. 9 Nov 1942), both on 12 Jun 1980 at Baltusrol Country Club, Springfield, NJ.

Total aggregate: 272 (63, 71, 70, 68) by Jack Nicklaus on the lower course (7,015 yd) at Baltusrol Country Club, 12–15 Jun 1980.

Oldest winner The oldest US Open champion was Hale Irwin (b. 3 Jun 1945), at 45 yr 15 days on 18 Jun 1990.

Youngest winner The youngest winner of the Open was John J. McDermott at 19 years 317 days in 1911; this is also the record for the youngest winner of any PGA event in the United States.

British Open (inaugurated 1860, Prestwick, Strathclyde, Scotland) *Most wins:* Harry Vardon won a record six titles in 1896, 1898–99, 1908, 1911 and 1914. Tom Morris, Jr. is the only player to win four successive British Opens, from 1868 to 1872 (the event was not held in 1871).

LOWEST SCORE First nine holes: 28, by Denis Durnian (b. 30 Jun 1950), at Royal Birkdale, Southport, Great Britain in the second round on 15 Jul 1983.

Any round: 63, by Mark Stephen Hayes (USA; b. 12 Jul 1949) at Turnberry, Strathclyde, Scotland, on 7 Jul 1977; Isao Aoki (Japan; b. 31 Aug 1942), at Muirfield, Lothian, Scotland on 19 Jul 1980; Gregory John Norman (Australia; b. 10 Feb 1955), at Turnberry, on 18 Jul 1986; and Paul Broadhurst (Great Britain; b. 14 Aug 1965) at St Andrews, Fife, Scotland on 21 Jul 1990.

Total aggregate: 268 (68, 70, 65, 65) by Thomas Sturges Watson (USA; b. 4 Sep 1949) at Turnberry, in July 1977.

Youngest and oldest champions The youngest winner of the British Open was Tom Morris, Jr. (1851–75) at Preswick, Strathclyde, Scotland, in 1868 at the age of 17 yr 249 days.

The oldest British Open champion was "Old Tom" Morris (1821–1908), age 46 yr 99 days when he won at Prestwick in 1867. The oldest this century has been the 1967 champion, Roberto de Vicenzo (Argentina) at 44 yr 93 days.

Professional Golfers Association (PGA) Championship *Most wins:* Two players have won the title five times: Walter Hagen (1921, 1924–27) and Jack Nicklaus (1963, 1971, 1973, 1975, 1980). Walter Hagen won a record four consecutive titles from 1924 to 1927.

LOWEST SCORE Any round: 63, by Bruce Crampton (Australia; b. 28 Sep 1935) at Firestone Country Club, Akron, OH in 1975; and by Raymond Loran Floyd (b. 4 Sep 1942) at Southern Hills, Tulsa, OK in 1982.

Total aggregate: 271, by Bobby Nicholls (64, 71, 69, 67) at Columbus Country Club, OH in 1964.

The oldest winner of the PGA was Julius Boros (USA; b. 3 Mar 1920) at the age of 48 years 110 days in 1968. Eugene "Gene" Sarazen (USA; b. 27 Feb 1902) was the youngest PGA winner in 1922 at the age of 20 years 170 days.

WOMEN'S CHAMPIONSHIP RECORDS

Grand Slam The Grand Slam of women's golf has consisted of four tournaments since 1955. From 1955–66, the US Open, Ladies Professional Golfers Association (LPGA) Championship, Western Open and Titleholders Championship served as the "majors." From 1967 to 1982 the Grand Slam events changed, as first the Western Open (1967) and then the Titleholders Championship (1972) were discontinued.

Since 1983, the US Open, LPGA Championship, du Maurier Classic and Nabisco Dinah Shore have been the major events. Patty Berg has won 15 professional Grand Slam events: US Open (1), Titleholders (7), Western Open (7); the latter two are now defunct. She also won one US Amateur title.

US Open This competition was first held in 1946 at Spokane, WA at match-play, but at 72 holes of stroke-play annually on different courses from 1947. The most wins is four by Elizabeth Earle "Betsy" Rawls (b. 4 May 1928), 1951, 1953, 1957 and 1960, and by Mickey Wright (b. 14 Feb 1935), in 1958–59, 1961 and 1964. The biggest margin of victory is 14 strokes by Mae Louise Suggs (b. 7 Sep 1923) with an aggregate of 291 in 1949. The oldest winner has been Fay Crocker at 40 yrs 11 months in 1955, and the youngest Catherine Lacoste (France; b. 27 Jun 1945) at 22 yrs 5 days in 1967. The lowest 72 holes aggregate is 279 by Pat Bradley (b. 24 Mar 1951) in 1981. The record for the lowest round is 65 by Sally Little (South Africa; b. 12 Oct

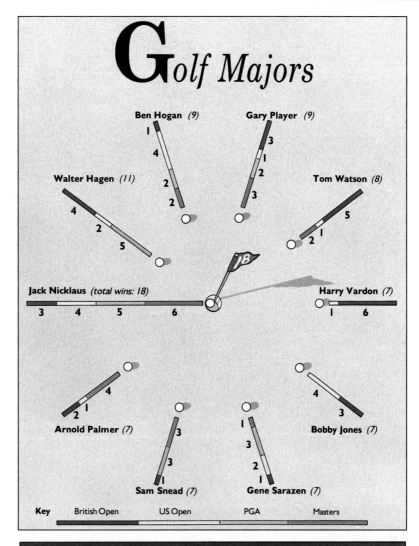

Golf Majors

Ben Hogan (9)

Gary Player (9)

Walter Hagen (11)

Tom Watson (8)

Jack Nicklaus (total wins: 18)

Harry Vardon (7)

Arnold Palmer (7)

Bobby Jones (7)

Sam Snead (7)

Gene Sarazen (7)

Key British Open   US Open   PGA   Masters

World one-club record
Thad Daber (USA), with a 6-iron, played the 6,037 yd Lochmore Golf Club course, Cary, NC in 70 to win the 1987 World One-club Championship.

■ **Most majors**
These ten great golfers have won seven or more "majors"—the Masters, the US Open, the British Open, and the PGA—and, as the feature shows, the greatest of these is Jack Nicklaus. He is the only golfer to have won each of these titles twice, and he holds the record for the lowest four-round total in both the Masters and the US Open. (Photo: All-Sport/Cannon)

Oldest LPGA winner

The oldest LPGA tour event champion was Jo Anne Carter (nee Gunderson: b. 4 Apr 1939) at the 1985 Safeco Classic at the age of 46 yrs 163 days.

Youngest LPGA winner

The youngest LPGA tour event winner was Marlene Hagge (b. 16 Feb 1934), who won the 1952 Sarasota Open at the age of 18 yrs 14 days.

Youngest and oldest national golf champions

Thuashni Selvaratnam (b. 9 Jun 1976) won the 1989 Sri Lankan Ladies Amateur Open Golf Championship, aged 12 yr 324 days, at Nuwara Eliva Golf Course on 29 Apr 1989. Angela Uzelli (b. 1 Feb 1940) won the English Women's Championship, aged 50 yr 114 days, at Rye, Great Britain on 26 May 1990.

1951) in the fourth round in 1978 and by Judy Dickinson (b. 4 Mar 1950) in the third round in 1985.

Consecutive wins Five players have won twice: Mickey Wright (1958–59); Donna Caponi (1969–70); Susie Berning (1972–73); Hollis Stacy (1977–78); Betsy King (1989–90).

Ladies Professional Golfers Association (LPGA) Championship (inaugurated 1955, Orchard Ridge Country Club, Fort Wayne, IN; since 1987 officially called the Mazda LPGA Championship) *Most wins:* four, Mickey Wright in 1958, 1960–61 and 1963. *Consecutive wins:* Two, by two players: Mickey Wright (1960–61); Patty Sheehan (1983–84).

LOWEST CHAMPIONSHIP SCORES 18 holes: 63, by Patty Sheehan at the Jack Nicklaus Sports Center at Kings Island, OH in 1984. *72 holes:* 272 by Patty Sheehan at the Jack Nicklaus Sports Center in 1984.

Du Maurier Classic (inaugurated 1973, Royal Montreal Golf Club, Montreal, Canada; formerly called La Canadienne [1973] and the Peter Jackson Classic [1974–83]): Pat Bradley holds the record for most wins with three titles won in 1980, 1985–86. The lowest score for 18 holes is 64, by JoAnne Carner at the St Georges Country Club, Canada in 1978.

72 holes: Pat Bradley and Ayako Okamoto share the record for the lowest score for 72 holes, 276, at the Board of Trade Country Club, Toronto, Ontario, Canada in 1986. Cathy Johnson matched Bradley and Okamoto in 1990 at Westmount Golf and Country Club, Kitchener, Ontario, Canada.

Nabisco Dinah Shore (inaugurated 1972, Mission Hills Country Club, Rancho Mirage, CA, the permanent site): The most wins is three, by Amy Alcott (1983, 1988 and 1991).

Nancy Lopez holds the record for the lowest score for 18 holes, 64, in 1981. The lowest score for 72 holes is 273, by Amy Alcott in 1991.

LPGA Tour 18 holes: Mickey Wright scored 62 on the Hogan Park course, Midland, TX in the first round of the 1964 Tall City Open, as did Vicki Fergon (b. 29 Sep 1955) at Almaden Golf & Country Club in the second round of the 1984 San Jose Classic.

36 holes: 129 (64 + 65), by Judy Dickinson at Pasadena Yacht & Country Club, St Petersburg, FL in the 1985 S&H Golf Classic.

72 holes: Nancy Lopez (b. 6 Jan 1957) scored 268 (66, 67, 69, 66), at the Willow Creek Golf Club, NC in the 1985 Henredon Classic.

TEAM COMPETITIONS

Ryder Cup The biennial Ryder Cup professional match between the USA and Europe (British Isles or Great Britain prior to 1979) was instituted in 1927. The USA has won 21 to 5 (with 2 draws) to date.

Arnold Palmer has the record of winning most Ryder Cup matches, with 22 out of 32 played, with two halved and 8 lost in six contests from 1963 to 1973. Christy O'Connor, Sr. (Ireland; b. 21 Dec 1924) played in a record ten contests, 1955–73. The most contests and matches for the USA is 8 and 37 (with 20 wins) by Billy Casper (b. 24 Jun 1931).

World Cup (formerly Canada Cup) The World Cup (instituted as the Canada Cup in 1953) has been won most often by the USA, with 17 victories between 1955 and 1988. The only men to have been on six winning teams have been Arnold Palmer (b. 10 Sep 1929; 1960, 1962–64, 1966–67) and Jack Nicklaus (1963–64, 1966–67, 1971 and 1973). Only Nicklaus has taken the individual title three times (1963–64, 1971).

The lowest aggregate score for 144 holes is 544, by Australia, Bruce Devlin (b. 10 Oct 1937) and Anthony David Graham (b. 23 May 1946), at San Isidro, Buenos Aires, Argentina from 12–15 Nov 1970. The lowest individual score was 269, by Roberto de Vicenzo (Argentina; b. 14 Apr 1923), also in 1970.

Walker Cup The series was instituted in 1921 (for the Walker Cup since 1922 and now held biennially). The USA has won 28, Great Britain and Ireland three (in 1938, 1971 and 1989) and the 1965 match was tied.

Jay Sigel (USA; b. 13 Nov 1943) has won a record 14 matches, with five halved and eight lost, 1977–89. Joseph Boynton Carr (Great Britain & Ireland; b. 18 Feb 1922) played in ten contests, 1947–67.

Curtis Cup The biennial ladies' Curtis Cup match between the USA and Great Britain and Ireland was first held in 1932. The USA has won 20, Great Britain and Ireland four (1952, 1956, 1986 and 1988), and two matches have been tied.

Mary McKenna (Great Britain and Ireland; b. 29 Apr 1949) played in a record 9th match in 1986, when for the first time she was on the winning team. Anne Sander (nee Quast, later Decker, Welts; b. 31 Aug 1937) played in a US record eighth match in 1990, when at 52 years 332 days she became the oldest-ever player in the series.

INDIVIDUAL RECORDS

Richest prize The greatest first place prize money ever won is $1 million, awarded annually from 1987 to 1990 to the winners of the Sun City Challenge, Bophuthatswana, South Africa. Ian Woosnam (Wales) was the first winner.

The greatest total prize money is $2.5 million (including $450,000 first prize) for the Nabisco Championship of Golf at Hilton Head Island, SC on 26–29 Oct 1989.

Highest earnings *PGA and LPGA circuits:* The all-time top professional money-winner is Tom Kite (USA; b. 9 Dec 1949) with $6,689,127, to May 1991.

He also holds the earnings record for a year on the US PGA circuit, $1,395,278 in 1989. The record career earnings for a woman is by Pat Bradley (b. 24 Mar 1951), with $3,629,130 to 20 Jun 1991. The season's record is $863,578 by Beth Daniel in 1990.

Most tournament wins John Byron Nelson (USA; b. 4 Feb 1912) won a record 18 tournaments (plus one unofficial) in one year, including a record 11 consecutively from 8 Mar to 4 Aug 1945.

The LPGA record is 13 by Mickey Wright (1963). She also holds the record for most wins in scheduled events, with four between August and September 1962 and between May and June 1963, a record matched by Kathrynne "Kathy" Ann Whitworth (b. 27 Sep 1939) between March and April 1969.

Sam Snead, who turned professional in 1934, won 84 official PGA tour events, 1936–65. The ladies' PGA record is 88 by Kathy Whitworth from 1962 to 1985.

Consecutive wins Four, by two players: Mickey Wright (1962); Kathy Whitworth (1969).

Successive wins Between May and June 1978, Nancy Lopez won all five tournaments that she entered; however, these events did not follow each other and are therefore not considered consecutive tournament victories.

Oldest winner Sam Snead won a PGA tournament at the age of 52 years 312 days at the 1965 Greater Greensboro Open.

Greatest winning margin The greatest margin of victory in a professional tournament is 21 strokes by Jerry Pate (USA; b. 16 Sep 1953), who won the Colombian Open with 262, from 10–13 Dec 1981.

Cecilia Leitch won the Canadian Ladies' Open Championship in 1921 by the biggest margin for a national title, 17 up and 15 to play.

Willie Smith won the US Open in 1899 by 11 strokes, with a score of 315. Jack Nicklaus won the US Masters in 1965 with a nine-stroke margin, scoring 271.

Arthur D'Arcy "Bobby" Locke (South Africa; 1917–87) achieved the greatest winning margin in a PGA tour event by 16 strokes in the Chicago Victory National Championship in 1948. Kathy Whitworth won eight times—1965–68, 1970–73.

NCAA Championships The only golfer to win three NCAA titles is Ben Daniel Crenshaw (b. 11 Jan 1952) of the University of Texas in 1971–73, tying with Tom Kite in 1972.

Most club championships Marjorie Edey (1913–81) was ladies champion at Charleswood Golf Course, Winnipeg, Manitoba, Canada 36 times between 1937 and 1980. Bernard Charles Cusack (b. 24 Jan 1920) was men's champion 34 times, at the Narembeen Golf Course, Western Australia, between 1943 and 1982.

Longest odds

Apollo Prince won at odds of 250–1 at Sandown Greyhound Race Course, Springvale, Victoria, Australia on 14 Nov 1968.

Somersaults

Ashrita Furman performed 8,341 forward rolls in 10 hr 30 min over 12 miles 390 yards from Lexington to Charleston, MA on 30 Apr 1986.

Shigeru Iwasaki (b. 1960) somersaulted backwards 54.68 yd in 10.8 sec at Tokyo, Japan on 30 Mar 1980.

Static wall "sit" (or Samson's Chair)

Paddy Doyle stayed in an unsupported sitting position against a wall for 4 hr 40 min at The Magnet Center, Erdington, Great Britain on 18 Apr 1990.

Gymnastics/aerobics display

The now-discontinued Czechoslovak Spartakiad featured gymnastics displays by about 180,000 participants. Held at the Strahov Stadium, Prague until 1989, the competition drew 200,000 spectators for each of the four days. On the 15-acre infield there were markers for 13,824 gymnasts at a time.

■ **Youngest champion**
Aurelia Dobre (Romania; b. 6 Nov 1972) (right) won the women's overall world gymnastics title at the age of 14 yr 352 days on 23 Oct 1987. Here she is seen in action on the balance beam, for which she also won the individual title in 1987.

(Photo: All-Sport [USA]/Martin)

At different clubs, Peter Toogood (Australia; b. 11 Apr 1930) has won 35 championships in Tasmania. At different clubs in the United States, Frances Miles-Maslon Hirsh (USA) was ladies champion 44 times between 1951–90.

Largest tournament The Volkswagen Grand Prix Open Amateur Championship in the United Kingdom attracted a record 321,778 (206,820 men and 114,958 women) competitors in 1984.

HOLES IN ONE

Longest The longest straight hole ever holed in one shot was, appropriately, the tenth (447 yd) at Miracle Hills Golf Course, Omaha, NE, by Robert Mitera (b. 1944) on 7 Oct 1965. Mitera stood 5 ft 6 in tall and weighed 165 lb. He was a two-handicap player who normally drove 245 yd. A 50 mph gust carried his shot over a 290 yd drop-off.

The longest "dog-leg" hole achieved in one shot is the 480 yd fifth at Hope Country Club, AR by L. Bruce on 15 Nov 1962. The women's record is 393 yd, by Marie Robie on the first hole of the Furnace Brook Golf Club, Wollaston, MA on 4 Sep 1949.

Consecutive There are at least 18 cases of "aces" being achieved in two consecutive holes, of which the greatest was Norman L. Manley's unique "double albatross" on the par-4 330 yd seventh and par-4 290 yd eighth holes on the Del Valle Country Club course, Saugus, CA on 2 Sep 1964.

The first woman to record consecutive "aces" was Sue Prell, on the 13th and 14th holes at Chatswood Golf Club, Sydney, Australia on 29 May 1977.

The closest to achieving three consecutive holes in one were Dr Joseph Boydstone on the third, fourth and ninth at Bakersfield Golf Club, CA, on 10 Oct 1962; and the Rev Harold Snider (b. 4 Jul 1900), who aced the 8th, 13th and 14th holes of the par-3 Ironwood course in Arizona on 9 Jun 1976.

Youngest and oldest The youngest golfer recorded to have shot a hole-in-one is Coby Orr (5 years) of Littleton, CO on the 103 yd fifth at the Riverside Golf Course, San Antonio, TX in 1975.

The youngest American woman to score an ace was Mrs Shirley Kunde (nee Caley) in Aug 1943, at age 13.

The oldest golfers to have performed this feat are: (men) 99 yr 244 days, Otto Bucher (Switzerland; b. 12 May 1885) on the 130 yd 12th at La Manga Golf Club, Spain on 13 Jan 1985; (women) 95 yr 257 days, Erna Ross (b. 9 Sep 1890) on the 112 yd 17th at The Everglades Club, Palm Beach, FL on 23 Apr 1986.

The oldest player to score his age is C. Arthur Thompson (1869–1975) of Victoria, British Columbia, Canada, who scored 103, on the Uplands course of 6,215 yd in 1973.

Greyhound Racing

Origins The first greyhound meeting was staged at Hendon, London, Great Britain, with a railed hare operated by a windlass, in September 1876. Modern greyhound racing originated with the perfecting of the mechanical hare by Owen Patrick Smith at Emeryville, CA, in 1919. St Petersburg Kennel Club, located in St Petersburg, FL, which opened on 3 Jan 1925, is the oldest greyhound track in the world still in operation on its original site.

Derby Two greyhounds have won the American Derby twice, at Taunton, MA: Real Huntsman in 1950–51, and Dutch Bahama in 1984–85.

Fastest greyhound The fastest speed at which any greyhound has been timed is 41.72 mph (410 yd in 20.1 sec) by The Shoe on the then-straightaway track at Richmond, New South Wales, Australia on 25 Apr 1968. It is estimated that he covered the last 100 yd in 4.5 sec or at 45.45 mph.

United States Tiki's Ace ran a distance of $5/16$ mile in 29.61 sec in Naples, Ft Myers, FL in 1988. The fastest $3/8$ mile time was 36.43 sec by P's Rambling in Hollywood, FL in 1987. Old Bill Drozd ran a $7/16$ mile track in 42.83 sec in Tucson, AZ in 1973.

Most wins The most career wins is 143, by the American greyhound JR's Ripper of Multnomah, Fairview, OR and Tuscon, AZ in 1982–86. The most wins in a year is 61 by Indy Ann in Mexico and the United States in 1966.

The most consecutive victories is 32 in Great Britain, by Ballyregan Bob, owned by Cliff Kevern and trained by George Curtis, from 25 Aug 1984 to 9 Dec 1986, including 16 track record times.

His race wins were by an average of more than nine lengths.

Joe Dump of Greenetrack, Eutaw, AL holds the US record, with 31 consecutive wins from 18 Nov 1978 to 1 Jun 1979.

Highest earnings The career earnings record is held by Homespun Rowdy with $297,000 in the United States, 1984–87.

The richest first prize for a greyhound race is $125,000 won by Ben G Speedboat in the Great Greyhound Race of Champions at Seabrook, NH on 23 Aug 1986.

Most stakes victories Real Huntsman achieved ten wins in 1949–51, including the American Derby twice.

Highest syndicated price P's Rambling was syndicated for $500,000 in 1987.

Gymnastics

Origins A primitive form of gymnastics was practiced in ancient Greece and Rome during the period of the ancient Olympic Games (776 B.C. to A.D. 393) but Johann Friedrich Simon was the first teacher of modern gymnastics, at Basedow's School, Dessau, Germany in 1776.

World Championships *Women* The greatest number of titles won in the World Championships (including Olympic Games) is 12 individual wins and five team, by Larisa Semyonovna Latynina (USSR; b. 27 Dec 1934) between 1956 and 1964.

The USSR has won the team title on 19 occasions (ten world and nine Olympic).

Men Boris Anfiyanovich Shakhlin (USSR; b. 27 Jan 1932) won ten individual titles between 1954 and 1964. He also had three team wins. The USSR has won the team title a record 11 times

EXERCISES
SPEED AND STAMINA

Records are accepted for the most repetitions of the following activities within the given time span.

CHINS (CONSECUTIVE) *370* Lee Chin-yong (South Korea; b. 15 Aug 1925) at Backyon Gymnasium, Seoul, South Korea on 14 May 1988.

CHINS (ONE ARM) (FROM A RING)—CONSECUTIVE *22* Robert Chisnall (b. 9 Dec 1952) at Queen's University, Kingston, Ontario, Canada on 3 Dec 1982. (Also 18 two-finger chins, 12 one-finger chins).

PARALLEL BAR DIPS—1 HOUR *3,645* Simon Kent (Great Britain) at Mablethorpe, Great Britain on 29 Aug 1990.

PUSH-UPS—24 HOURS *37,350* Paddy Doyle (Great Britain) at the Holiday Inn, Birmingham, Great Britain on 1–2 May 1989.

PUSH-UPS IN A YEAR Paddy Doyle achieved a documented 1,500,230 push-ups of which the 24-hour record was a part, from October 1988 to October 1989.

PUSH-UPS (ONE ARM)—5 HOURS *7,643* Paddy Doyle at the Albany Hotel, Birmingham, Great Britain on 31 Jul 1990.

PUSH-UPS (FINGERTIP)—5 HOURS *6,011* Vince Manson (Great Britain) at HM Prison Albany, Newport, Isle of Wight on 25 Jul 1990.

PUSH-UPS (ONE FINGER)—CONSECUTIVE *100* Harry Lee Welch Jr at Durham, NC on 31 Mar 1985.

SIT-UPS—24 HOURS *60,690* Louis Scripa, Jr. (USA) at Jack La Lanne's American Health & Fitness Spa, Sacramento, CA on 5–6 Aug 1985.

LEG LIFTS—12 HOURS *41,788* Lou Scripa, Jr. at Jack La Lanne's American Health & Fitness Spa, Sacramento, CA on 2 Dec 1988.

SQUATS—1 HOUR *2,550* Ashrita Furman (USA) at Philadelphia, PA on 3 Nov 1989.

SQUAT THRUSTS—1 HOUR *2,998* Paul Wai Man Chung at the Chung Sze Kung Fu (HK) Association, Kowloon, Hong Kong on 14 Apr 1991.

BURPEES—1 HOUR *1,551* Ashrita Furman at the Natural Physique Centre, New York City on 13 Mar 1990.

PUMMEL HORSE DOUBLE CIRCLES—CONSECUTIVE *75* by Lee Thomas (Great Britain) on British Broadcasting Corporation on 12 Dec 1985.

(seven World Championships, four Olympics) between 1952 and 1989.

The most successful US gymnast has been Kurt Bittereaux Thomas (b. 29 Mar 1952), who won three gold medals: floor exercises 1978 and 1979, horizontal bar 1979.

Youngest champions Aurelia Dobre (Romania; b. 6 Nov 1972) won the women's overall world title at age 14 yr 352 days on 23 Oct 1987. Daniela Silivas (Romania) revealed in 1990 that she was born on 9 May 1971, a year later than previously claimed, so that she was age 14 yr 185 days when she won the gold medal for balance beam on 10 Nov 1985.

The youngest male world champion was Dmitriy Bilozerchev (USSR; b. 17 Dec 1966), at 16 yr 315 days at Budapest, Hungary on 28 Oct 1983.

Olympics Japan has won the men's team title most often (in 1960, 1964, 1968, 1972 and 1976). The USSR has won the women's title nine times (1952–80, 1988). The most men's individual gold medals is six, by: Boris Shakhlin (USSR), one in 1956, four (two shared) in 1960 and one in 1964; and Nikolay Yefimovich Andrianov (USSR; b. 14 Oct 1952), one in 1972, four in 1976 and one in 1980. Vera Caslavska-Odlozil (Czechoslovakia; b. 3 May 1942) has won most individual gold medals, with seven, three in 1964 and four (one shared) in 1968.

Larisa Latynina won six individual gold medals and was on three winning teams from 1956–64, earning nine gold medals. She also won five silver and four bronze, 18 in all—an Olympic record.

The most medals for a male gymnast is 15, by Nikolay Andrianov (USSR), seven gold, five silver and three bronze, from 1972–80.

Aleksandr Nikolaivich Dityatin (USSR; b. 7 Aug 1957) is the only man to win a medal in all eight categories in the same Games, with three gold, four silver and one bronze at Moscow in 1980.

United States The best US performances were in the 1904 Games, when there was only limited foreign participation. Anton Heida (b. 1878) won five gold medals and a silver, and George Eyser (b. 1871), who had a wooden leg, won three gold, two silver and a bronze medal. Mary Lou Retton (b. 24 Jan 1968) won a women's record five medals in 1984, gold at all-around, two silver and two bronze. The most medals won by a US male gymnast since 1904 is four, by Mitchell Jay "Mitch" Gaylord (b. 10 Mar 1961), a team gold and a silver and two bronze in individual events in 1984, when both Bart Conner (b. 28 Mar 1958) and Peter Glen Vidmar (b. 3 Jun 1961) won two gold medals.

Highest score Nadia Comaneci (Romania; b. 12 Nov 1961) was the first to achieve a perfect score (10.00) in the Olympics, and achieved seven in all at Montreal, Canada in July 1976.

Club swinging Albert Rayner set a world record of 17,512 revolutions (4.9 per sec) in 60 min at Wakefield, Great Britain on 27 Jul 1981.

Stair climbing The 100-story record for stair climbing was set by Dennis W. Martz in the Detroit Plaza Hotel, Detroit, MI on 26 Jun 1978 at 11 min 23.8 sec.

Dale Neil, 22, ran a vertical mile on the stairs of the Peachtree Plaza Hotel, Atlanta, GA in continuous action of 2 hr 1 min 25 sec on 9 Mar 1984.

Russell Gill made 50 ascents of the Rhodes State Office Tower, Columbus, OH on 3 Mar 1991 (descending by elevator) in 10 hr 32 min 24 sec. He climbed 41,750 stairs for a vertical height of 25,520 ft.

The record for the 1,760 steps (vertical height 1,122 ft) in the world's tallest freestanding structure, Toronto's CN Tower, Canada, is 7 min 52 sec by Brendan Keenoy on 29 Oct 1989.

The record for the 1,336 stairs of the world's tallest hotel, the Westin Stamford Hotel, Singapore, is 6 min 55 sec by Balvinder Singh, in the third Vertical Marathon on 4 Jun 1989.

Scott Elliott raced up the 1,575 steps of the Empire State Building, New York City on 14 Feb 1990 in 10 min 47 sec.

Youngest international (gymnastics)

Pasakevi "Voula" Kouna (b. 6 Dec 1971) was age 9 yr 299 days at the start of the Balkan Games at Serres, Greece on 1 Oct 1981, when she represented Greece.

Highest prices

The highest prices paid were $19.2 million for Nihilator (a pacer), who was syndicated by Wall Street Stable and Almahurst Stud Farm in 1984; and $6 million, for Mack Lobell (a trotter) by John Erik Magnusson of Vislanda, Sweden in 1988.

Greatest winnings

For any harness horse the amount is $4,408,857, by the trotter Ourasi (France), who won 32 races to the end of 1990.

The single season records are $2,091,860 by the pacer Beach Towel in 1990, and $1,610,608 by the trotter Prakas in 1985.

The largest-ever purse was $2,161,000 for the Woodrow Wilson two-year-old race over one mile at The Meadowlands, East Rutherford, NJ on 16 Aug 1984. Of this sum a record $1,080,500 went to the winner, Nihilator, driven by William O'Donnell (b. 4 May 1948).

World Cup

Gymnasts who have won two World Cup (instituted 1975) overall titles are three men: Nikolay Andrianov (USSR), Aleksandr Dityatin (USSR) and Li Ning (China; b. 8 Sep 1963), and one woman: Maria Yevgenyevna Filatova (USSR; b. 19 Jul 1961).

US Championships

Alfred A. Jochim (1902–81) won a record seven men's all-around US titles, 1925–30 and 1933, and a total of 34 at all exercises between 1923 and 1934. The women's record is six all-around, 1945–46 and 1949–52, and 39 at all exercises, including 11 in succession at balance beam, 1941–51, by Clara Marie Schroth Lomady (b. 5 Oct 1920).

McDonald's American Cup

The American Cup was created by the USGF in 1976. Since 1980 it has been called the McDonald's American Cup.

Most wins Mary Lou Retton has won the title three times (1983–85), more than any other woman gymnast. Kurt Thomas has also won three consecutive times (1978–80), making him champion of the men's division.

Modern rhythmic gymnastics

The most overall individual world titles in modern rhythmic gymnastics is three, by Maria Gigova (Bulgaria) in 1969, 1971 and 1973 (shared).

Bulgaria has a record eight team titles, in 1969, 1971, 1973, 1981, 1983, 1985, 1987 and 1989 (shared). Bianka Panova (b. 27 May 1960) of Bulgaria won all four apparatus gold medals, all with maximum scores, and won a team gold in 1987.

Marina Lobach (USSR; b. 26 Jun 1970) won the 1988 Olympic title with perfect scores for all events. Lilia Ignatova (Bulgaria) has won both the individual World Cup titles that have been held, in 1983 and 1986.

Handball (Team)

Origins

Handball was first played c. 1895 in Germany. It was introduced into the Olympic Games at Berlin in 1936 as an 11-a-side outdoor game, with Germany winning, but when reintroduced in 1972 it was an indoor game with seven-a-side, the standard team size since 1952.

The International Handball Federation was founded in 1946. The first international match was held at Halle/Saale on 3 Sep 1925, when Austria beat Germany 6–3.

Most championships

Olympic The USSR has won four titles—men 1976 and 1988, women 1976 and 1980. Yugoslavia has also won two men's titles, in 1972 and 1984.

World Championships (instituted 1938)

Romania has won four men's and three women's titles (two outdoor, one indoor) from 1956 to 1974. Three women's titles have also been won by East Germany, in 1971, 1975 and 1978, and the USSR, 1982, 1986 and 1990.

East Germany has also won three women's titles, in 1971, 1975 and 1978.

Highest score

The highest score in an international match was recorded when the USSR beat Afghanistan 86–2 in the "Friendly Army Tournament" at Miskolc, Hungary in August 1981.

Harness Racing

Origins

Trotting races were held in Valkenburg, the Netherlands in 1554. In Great Britain the trotting gait (the simultaneous use of the diagonally opposite legs) was known in the 16th century. The sulky first appeared in 1829. Pacers thrust out their fore and hind legs simultaneously on one side.

The sport became very popular in the United States in the 19th century, and the National Trotting Association was founded, originally as the National Association for the Promotion of the Interests of the Trotting Turf, in 1870. It brought needed controls to a sport which had been threatened by gambling corruption.

Most successful driver

The most successful sulky driver in North American harness racing history has been Herve Filion (b. 1 Feb 1940) of Québec, Canada, who had achieved 12,964 wins and prize earnings of $72,670,641 through 19 May 1991, including a record 814 wins in a year, 1989.

John D. Campbell (USA; b. 8 Apr 1955) has the highest career earnings, $93,857,322 through 19 May 1991. This includes a season record of $11,622,778 in 1990, when he won 543 races.

Hambletonian

The most famous trotting race in North America, the Hambletonian Stakes, run annually for three-year-olds, was first staged at Syracuse, NY in 1926. The race is named after the great sire Hambletonian, born in 1849, from whom almost all harness horses trace their pedigree. The race

record time is 1 min 53³⁄₅ sec, by Mack Lobell, driven by John Campbell in 1987.

Little Brown Jug

Pacing's three-year-old classic has been held annually at Delaware, OH from 1946. The name honors a great 19th century pacer. The race record time is 1 min 52¹⁄₅ sec by Nihilator, driven by Bill O'Donnell in 1985.

Hockey

Origins

There is pictorial evidence that a hockey-like game (*kalv*) was played on ice in the early 16th century in The Netherlands. The game was probably first played in North America on 25 Dec 1855 at Kingston, Ontario, Canada, but Halifax also lays claim to priority. The International Ice Hockey Federation was founded in 1908.

NATIONAL HOCKEY LEAGUE (NHL)

Origins

The National Hockey League (NHL) was founded on 22 Nov 1917 in Montreal, Canada following the collapse of the National Hockey Association of Canada (NHA). Four teams formed the original league: the Montreal Canadiens, the Montreal Wanderers, the Ottawa Senators and the Québec Bulldogs. The Toronto Arenas were admitted as a 5th team, but the Bulldogs were unable to operate, and the league began as a four-team competition. The first NHL game was played on 19 Dec 1917. The NHL is now comprised of 21 teams, seven from Canada and 14 from the United States, divided into two divisions within two conferences: Adams and Patrick Divisions in the Wales Conference; Norris and Smythe Division in the Campbell Conference. At the end of the regular season, 16 teams compete in the Stanley Cup playoffs to decide the NHL championship. (For further details of the Stanley Cup see below.)

Team records

The Montreal Canadiens won a record 60 games and 132 points (with 12 ties) in 80 games played in 1976/77; their eight losses were also a record, the least ever in a season of 70 or more games. The highest percentage of wins in a season was .875 achieved by the Boston Bruins, with 30 wins in 44 games in 1929/30.

The longest undefeated run during a season, 35 games (25 wins and ten ties), was established by the Philadelphia Flyers from 14 Oct 1979 to 6 Jan 1980.

The New York Islanders won 15 consecutive games from 21 Jan–20 Feb 1982.

The most goals scored in a season is 446 by the Edmonton Oilers in 1983/84, when they also achieved a record 1,182 points.

The most shutouts in a season is 22 in 1928/29 by the Montreal Canadiens, in just 44 games, all by George Hainsworth, who also achieved a record low for goals against percentage of 0.98 that season.

HARNESS RACING MILE RECORDS

TROTTING	Horse (driver)	Place	Date
World... 1:52 ¹⁄₅	Mack Lobell (John Campbell)	Springfield, IL	21 Aug 1987
PACING			
World... 1:48 ²⁄₅	Matt's Scooter (Michel Lachance)	Lexington, KY	23 Sep 1988
Race...... 1:49 ³⁄₅	Nihilator (William O'Donnell)	East Rutherford, NJ	3 Aug 1985
1:49 ³⁄₅	Call For Rain (Clint Galbraith)	Lexington, KY	1 Oct 1988

Most games played Gordon "Gordie" Howe (Canada; b. 31 Mar 1928) played in a record 1,767 NHL regular season games (and 157 playoff games) over a record 26 seasons, from 1946 to 1971, for the Detroit Red Wings and in 1979/80 for the Hartford Whalers. He also played 419 games (and 78 playoff games) for the Houston Aeros and for the New England Whalers in the World Hockey Association from 1973 to 1979, for a grand total of 2,421 professional hockey games.

Most consecutive games played A record of 962 consecutive games played was achieved by Doug Jarvis for the Montreal Canadiens, the Washington Capitals and the Hartford Whalers from 8 Oct 1975–5 Apr 1987.

Fastest goals The fastest goal was after 4 sec by Joseph Antoine Claude Provost (b. 17 Sep 1933; Montreal Canadiens) *v* Boston Bruins in the second period at Montreal on 9 Nov 1957, and by Denis Joseph Savard (b. 4 Feb 1961; Chicago Black Hawks) *v* Hartford Whalers in the third period at Chicago on 12 Jan 1986. From the opening whistle, the fastest is 5 sec, by Doug Smail (b. 2 Sep 1957; Winnipeg Jets) *v* St Louis Blues at Winnipeg on 20 Dec 1981, and by Bryan John Trottier (b. 17 Jul 1956; New York Islanders) *v* Boston Bruins at Boston on 22 Mar 1984. Bill Mosienko (b. 2 Nov 1921; Chicago Black Hawks) scored three goals in 21 sec *v* New York Rangers on 23 Mar 1952. Toronto scored eight goals in 4 min 52 sec *v* New York Americans on 19 Mar 1938.

Most goals *Team* The NHL record is 21 goals, when the Montreal Canadiens beat Toronto St Patrick's, 14–7, at Montreal on 10 Jan 1920, and the Edmonton Oilers beat the Chicago Black Hawks, 12–9, at Chicago on 11 Dec 1985. The NHL single team record is 16 by the Montreal Canadiens *v* the Québec Bulldogs 3, at Québec City on 3 Nov 1920.

Most goals and points *Career* The North American career record for goals is 1,071 (including a record 801 in the NHL) by Gordie Howe (Detroit Red Wings, Houston Aeros, New England Whalers and Hartford Whalers) from 16 Oct 1946 in 32 seasons ending in 1979/80. He took 2,204 games to achieve the 1,000th goal, but Robert Marvin "Bobby" Hull (Great Britain; b. 3 Jan 1939; Chicago Black Hawks and Winnipeg Jets) scored his 1,000th in 1,600 games on 12 Mar 1978.

Wayne Gretzky (Edmonton Oilers 1979–88, Los Angeles Kings 1988–91) has the NHL record for assists, 1,424, and points, 2,142.

Season The most goals scored in a season in the NHL is 92 in the 1981/82 season by Wayne Gretzky (b. 26 Jan 1961) for the Edmonton Oilers. He scored a record 215 points, including a record 163 assists in 1985/86.

Game The most goals in an NHL game is seven, by Michael Joseph "Joe" Malone

(b. 28 Feb 1890) in Québec's 10–6 win over Toronto St. Patricks at Québec City on 31 Jan 1920.

The most assists in an NHL game is seven, by William "Billy" Taylor (b. 3 May 1919) for Detroit, 10–6 at Chicago on 16 Mar 1947, and three by Wayne Gretzky for Edmonton, 8–2 *v* Washington on 15 Feb 1980, 12–9 at Chicago on 11 Dec 1985, and 8–2 *v* Québec on 14 Feb 1986.

The record number of assists in one period is five, by Dale Hawerchuk, for the Winnipeg Jets *v* the Los Angeles Kings on 6 Mar 1984.

Consecutive games Harry Broadbent scored in 16 consecutive games for Ottawa in the 1921/22 season.

Most hat tricks The most hat tricks (three or more goals in a game) in a career is 48, by Wayne Gretzky through the 1990/91 season for the Edmonton Oilers and the Los Angeles Kings. Wayne Gretzky also holds the record for most hat tricks in a season, ten, in both the 1982 and 1984 seasons for the Oilers.

Most consecutive 50-or-more-goal seasons Mike Bossy (New York Islanders) scored at least 50 goals in nine consecutive seasons from 1977/78 through 1985/86. Wayne Gretzky (Ed-

monton Oilers, Los Angeles Kings) has also scored at least 50 goals in one season nine times, but his longest streak is eight seasons.

Most points in one game The North American major league record for most points scored in one game is ten by Jim Harrison (b. 9 Jul 1947; three goals, seven assists) for Alberta, later Edmonton Oilers in a World Hockey Association match at Edmonton on 30 Jan 1973, and by Darryl Sittler (b. 18 Sep 1950; six goals, four assists) for the Toronto Maple Leafs *v* the Boston Bruins in an NHL game at Toronto on 7 Feb 1976.

Period The most points in one period is six, by Bryan Trottier, three goals and three assists in the second period, for the New York Islanders *v* the New York Rangers (9–4) on 23 Dec 1978. Nine players have a record four goals in one period.

Most consecutive points The most consecutive games scoring points was 51, by Wayne Gretzky from 5 Oct 1983–27 Jan 1984 for the Edmonton Oilers.

Goaltending *Career* Terrance "Terry" Gordon Sawchuk (1929–70) played a record 971 games as a goaltender, for the Detroit Red Wings, the Boston Bruins, the Toronto Maple

Stanley Cup goaltending
Jacques Plante holds the record for most shutouts in a playoff career, with 14, with the Montreal Canadiens (1953–63) and the St. Louis Blues (1969–1970). The record for most victories in a playoff career is 88, by Billy Smith for the New York Islanders (1975–88).

Longest hockey game

The longest game was 2 hr 56 min 30 sec (playing time) when the Detroit Red Wings beat the Montreal Maroons 1–0 in the sixth period of overtime at the Forum, Montreal, at 2:25 A.M. on 25 Mar 1936. Norm Smith, the Red Wings goaltender, turned aside 92 shots for the NHL's longest single shutout.

■ **Most points**

Mario Lemieux (Pittsburgh Penguins) shares the record for most goals scored in a Stanley Cup game, with 5, and most points (8—5 goals and 3 assists). (Photo: All-Sport [USA])

Leafs, the Los Angeles Kings and the New York Rangers from 1949 to 1970. He achieved a record 435 wins (to 337 losses, and 188 ties). Jacques Joseph Ormar Plante (1929–86), with 434 NHL wins, surpassed Sawchuk's figure by adding 15 wins in his one season in the WHA for a total of 449 in 868 games.

Season Bernie Parent (b. 3 Apr 1945) achieved a record 47 wins in a season, with 13 losses and 12 ties, for Philadelphia in 1973/74.

Most successful goaltending The most shutouts played by a goaltender in an NHL career is 103 by Terry Sawchuck of Detroit, Boston, Toronto, Los Angeles and New York Rangers, between 1949 and 1970. Gerry Cheevers (b. 2 Dec 1940; Boston Bruins) went a record 32 successive games without a defeat in 1971/72. George Hainsworth completed 22 shutouts for the Montreal Canadiens in 1928/29. Alex Connell played 461 min 29 sec without conceding a goal for Ottawa in the 1928/29 season. Roy Worters saved 70 shots for the Pittsburgh Pirates *v* New York Americans on 24 Dec 1925.

Defensemen Denis Potvin (New York Islanders 1973–88) set career records for most goals (310), assists (742) and points (1,052) by a defenseman. Paul Coffey (Edmonton Oilers) scored a record 48 goals in 1985/86. Bobby Orr (Boston Bruins) holds the single season marks for assists (102) and points (139), both of which were set in 1970/71.

Player awards The Hart Trophy, awarded annually starting with the 1923/24 season by the Professional Hockey Writers Association as the Most Valuable Player award of the NHL, has been won a record nine times by Wayne Gretzky, 1980–87, 1989. Gretzky has also won the Art Ross Trophy a record eight

times, 1981–87 and 1990; this has been awarded annually since 1947/48 to the NHL season's leading scorer. Bobby Orr of Boston won the James Norris Memorial Trophy, awarded annually starting with the 1953/54 season to the league's leading defenseman, a record eight times, 1968–75.

Coaches Scotty Bowman holds the records for most victories and highest winning percentage by an NHL coach. He won 739 games (110, St Louis Blues 1967–71; 419, Montreal Canadiens 1971–79; 210, Buffalo Sabres 1979–87). His career record is 739 wins, 327 losses, 210 ties for a record .661 winning percentage. Dick Irvine has coached a record 1,437 games with three teams: Chicago Blackhawks (1930–31; 1955–56); Toronto Maple Leafs (1931–40); Montreal Canadiens (1940–55). Irvin's career record was 690 wins, 521 losses, 226 ties.

STANLEY CUP

The top NHL teams compete annually for the Stanley Cup, which was first presented in 1893 (original cost Cdn$48.67) by Lord Stanley of Preston, then Governor-General of Canada. Starting in 1894 it was contested by amateur teams for the Canadian Championship. From 1910 it became the award for the winners of the professional league playoffs. It has been won most often by the Montreal Canadiens with 23 wins in 1916, 1924, 1930-31, 1944, 1946, 1953, 1956-60, 1965-66, 1968-69, 1971, 1973, 1976-79, 1986, out of a record 31 finals. The longest Stanley Cup final game was settled after 115 min 13 sec, in the third period of overtime, when the Edmonton Oilers beat the Boston Bruins 3–2 on 15 May 1990.

Most games played Larry Robinson has played in 225 Stanley Cup playoff games for the Montreal Canadiens

(1973–89) and the Los Angeles Kings (1990–91).

Scoring records Wayne Gretzky (the Edmonton Oilers and the Los Angeles Kings) has scored a record 299 points in Stanley Cup games, a record 93 goals and a record 206 assists. Gretzky scored a playoff record 47 points (16 goals, record 31 assists) in 1985. The most goals in a season is 19 by Reggie Leach for Philadelphia in 1976 and Jari Kurri for Edmonton in 1985.

Five goals in a Stanley Cup game were scored by Maurice Richard (b. 14 Aug 1924) in Montreal's 5–1 win over the Toronto Maple Leafs on 23 Mar 1944; by Darryl Glen Sittler (b. 18 Sep 1950) for Toronto's 8–5 victory over Philadelphia on 22 Apr 1976; by Reggie Leach for Philadelphia's 6–3 victory over the Boston Bruins on 6 May 1976; and by Mario Lemieux (b. 1965) for the Pittsburgh Penguins' 10–7 victory over Philadelphia on 25 Apr 1989. Reggie Leach (Philadelphia) scored at least one goal in nine consecutive playoff games in 1976. The streak started on 17 Apr *v* the Toronto Maple Leafs, and ended on 9 May when he was shut out by the Montreal Canadiens. Overall, Leach scored 14 goals during his record-setting run.

A record six assists in a game were achieved by Mikko Leinonen for the New York Rangers in their 7–3 victory over Philadelphia on 8 Apr 1982 and by Wayne Gretzky for Edmonton's 13–3 victory over Los Angeles on 9 Apr 1987, when his team set a Stanley Cup game record of 13 goals. The most points in a game is eight, by Patrik Sundström, three goals and five assists, for the New Jersey Devils (10) *v* the Washington Capitals (4) on 22 Apr 1988, and by Mario Lemieux, five goals and three assists, for the Pittsburgh Penguins (10) *v* the Philadelphia Flyers (7) on 25 Apr 1989.

Point-scoring streak Bryan Trottier (New York Islanders) scored a point in 27 playoff games over three seasons (1980–82), scoring 16 goals and 26 assists for 42 points.

Defensemen During his career with the Edmonton Oilers, 1980–87, Paul Coffey set marks for the most points in a playoff game (6) and in a season (37)—both set in 1985. Also in 1985, Coffey set the record for most goals by a defenseman in a playoff season with 12 in 18 games. The record for most goals in a game by a defenseman is three shared by five players: Bobby Orr (Boston Bruins *v* Montreal Canadiens, 11 Apr 1971); Dick Redmond (Chicago Blackhawks *v* St. Louis Blues, 4 Apr 1973); Denis Potvin (New York Islanders *v* Edmonton Oilers, 17 Apr 1981); Paul Reinhart twice, (Calgary Flames *v* Edmonton Oilers, 14 Apr 1983; *v* Vancouver Canucks, 8 Apr 1984); Doug Halward (Vancouver Canucks *v* Calgary Flames, 7 Apr 1984).

Most valuable player The Conn Smythe Trophy for the most valuable player in the play-offs has been awarded annually since 1965. The only players to

win it twice have been Bobby Orr 1970 and 1972, Bernie Parent (Philadelphia) 1974 and 1975, and Wayne Gretzky (Edmonton) 1985 and 1988.Henri Richard played on a record 11 winning teams for the Montreal Canadiens between 1956 and 1973.

Coaches "Toe" Blake coached the Montreal Canadiens to eight championships (1956–60, 1965–66, 1968), the most of any coach. Al Arbour and Scotty Bowman share the record for most playoff wins at 114: Arbour (four, St. Louis Blues, 1970–73; 110, New York Islanders, 1973–86, 1988–90); Bowman (26, St Louis Blues, 1967–71; 70, Montreal Canadiens, 1971–79; 18, Buffalo Sabres, 1979–87).

WORLD CHAMPIONSHIPS AND OLYMPIC GAMES

World Championships were first held for amateurs in 1920 in conjunction with the Olympic Games, which were also considered world championships up to 1968. Sicne 1977, World Championships have been open to professionals. The USSR won 22 world titles between 1954 and 1990, including the Olympic titles of 1956, 1964 and 1968. It has a record seven Olympic titles with a further four in 1972, 1976, 1984 and 1988. The longest Olympic career is that of Richard Torriani (Switzerland; 1911–88) from 1928 to 1948. The most gold medals won by any player is three, achieved by USSR players Vitaliy Semyenovich Davydov, Anatoliy Vasilyevich Firssov, Viktor Grigoryevich Kuzkin and Aleksandr Pavlovich Ragulin in 1964, 1968 and 1972, and by Vladislav Aleksandrovich Tretyak in 1972, 1976 and 1984.

Women The first world championships were won by Canada, which beat the USA 5–2, at Ottawa, Canada on 24 Mar 1990.

Most goals The greatest number of goals recorded in a world championship match was when Australia beat New Zealand 58–0 at Perth on 15 Mar 1987.

Fastest goals In minor leagues, Per Olsen scored two seconds after the start of the match for Rungsted against Odense in the Danish First Division at Hørsholm, Denmark on 14 Jan 1990. Three goals in 10 seconds was achieved by Jørgen Palmgren Erichsen for Frisk v. Holmen in a junior league match in Norway on 17 Mar 1991. The Skara Ishockeyclubb, Sweden, scored three goals in 11 seconds against Örebro IK at Skara on 18 Oct 1981. The Vernon Cougars scored five goals in 56 seconds against the Salmon Arm Aces at Vernon, British Columbia, Canada on 6 Aug 1982. The Kamloops Knights of Columbus scored seven goals in 2 min 22 sec v the Prince George Vikings on 25 Jan 1980.

Horse Racing

Origins Horsemanship was an important part of the Hittite culture of Anato-lia, Turkey dating from 1400 B.C. The 33rd ancient Olympic Games of 648 B.C. in Greece featured horse racing. Horse races can be traced in England from the 3rd century. The first sweepstakes race was originated by the 12th Earl of Derby at his estate in Epsom in 1780. The Epsom Derby is still run today, and is the classic race of the English flat racing season.

Horses were introduced to the North American continent from Spain by Cortez in 1519. In colonial America, horse racing was common. Colonel Richard Nicholls, commander of English forces in New York, is believed to have staged the first organized race at Salisbury Plain, Long Island, NY in 1665. Thoroughbred racing was first staged at Saratoga Springs, NY in 1863. The first Jockey Club to be founded was at Charleston, SC in 1734.

Breeders' Cup The highest prize money for a day's racing is $10 million, for the Breeders' Cup series of seven races staged annually since 1984. Included each year is a record $3 million for the Breeders' Cup Classic.The jockey who has won the most Breeders' Cup races is Laffit Pincay, Jr. with six from 1985 to 1990, and the trainer with the most wins is D. Wayne Lukas, with ten.

HORSES

Most successful The horse with the best win–loss record was Kincsem, a Hungarian mare foaled in 1874, who was unbeaten in 54 races (1876–79) throughout Europe, including the Goodwood Cup of 1878.

Longest winning sequence Camarero, foaled in 1951, was undefeated in 56 races in Puerto Rico from 19 Apr 1953 to his first defeat on 17 Aug 1955 (in his career to 1956, he won 73 of 77 races).

Career Galgo Jr. (foaled 1928) won 137 of 159 starts in Puerto Rico between 1930 and 1936; in 1931 he won a record 30 races in one year.

Career—United States The most wins is 89, by Kingston in 138 starts, 1886–94. This included 33 in stakes races, but the horse with the most wins in stakes races in the USA is Exterminator (foaled 1915), with 34 between 1918 and 1923. John Henry (foaled 1975) won a record 25 graded stakes races, including 16 at Grade 1, 1978–84. On his retirement in 1984, his career prize money was $6,597,947, nearly twice as much as the next best. Of 83 races he won 39, was second 15 times and third 9 times.

Same race Doctor Syntax (foaled 1811) won the Preston Gold Cup on seven successive occasions, 1815–21.

Triple Crown winners The Triple Crown (Kentucky Derby, Preakness Stakes, Belmont Stakes) has been achieved 11 times, most recently by Affirmed in 1978. Eddie Arcaro is the only jockey to board two Triple Crown winners, Whirlaway in 1941 and Citation in 1948. Two trainers have schooled double Triple Crown winners: James Fitzsimmons, Gallant Fox in 1930 and Omaha in 1935; Ben A. Jones, Whirlaway in 1941 and Citation in 1948.

Greatest winnings The career earnings record is $6,679,242, by the 1987 Kentucky Derby winner Alysheba (foaled 1984), from 1986–88. The most prize money earned in a year is $4,578,454 by Sunday Silence (foaled 1986) in the USA in 1989. His total included $1,350,000 from the Breeders' Cup Classic and a $1 million bonus for the best record in the Triple Crown races: he won the Kentucky Derby and Preakness Stakes and was second in the Belmont Stakes. The leading money-winning mare is Lady's Secret (foaled 1982), with $3,021,325 in the USA,

Biggest payout Anthony A. Speelman and Nicholas John Cowan (both Great Britain) won $1,627,084.40, after federal income tax of $406,768.00 was withheld, on a $64 nine-horse accumulator at Santa Anita racetrack, CA on 19 Apr 1987. Their first seven selections won and the payout was for a jackpot, accumulated over 24 days.

■ **Triple Crown winner**
Affirmed *at the Kentucky Derby in 1978, when he became the eleventh (and last to date) winner of the Triple Crown. This feat was first achieved by* Sir Barton *in 1919. Affirmed was ridden by* Steve Cauthen. *(Photo: Sports Illustrated)*

MAJOR RACE RECORDS

RACE (instituted)	RECORD TIME	MOST WINS Jockey	Trainer	Owner	LARGEST FIELD
TRIPLE CROWN					
Kentucky Derby (1875) 1¼ miles Churchill Downs, Louisville, KY	1 min 59.4 sec *Secretariat* 1973	5–Eddie Arcaro 1938, 41, 45, 48, 52 5–Bill Hartack 1957, 60, 62, 64, 69	6–Ben Jones 1938, 41, 44, 48, 49, 52	8–Calumet Farm 1941, 44, 48, 49, 52, 57, 58, 68	23 (1974)
Preakness Stakes (1873) 1 mile 1½ f Pimlico, Baltimore, MD	1 min 53.2 sec *Tank's Prospect* 1985	6–Eddie Arcaro 1941, 48, 50, 51, 55, 57	7–Robert Wyndham Walden 1875, 78, 79, 80, 81, 82, 88	5–George Lorillard 1878, 79, 80, 81, 82	18 (1928)
Belmont Stakes (1867) 1½ miles Belmont Park, New York	2 min 24.0 sec *Secretariat* 1973 (By a record 31 lengths)	6–Jimmy McLaughlin 1882, 83, 84, 86, 87, 88 6–Eddie Arcaro 1941, 42, 45, 48, 52, 55	8–James Rowe Sr 1883, 84, 1901, 04, 07, 08, 10, 13	5–Dwyer Bros 1883, 84, 86, 87, 88 5–James R. Keene 1901, 04, 07, 08, 10 5–William Woodward Sr (Belair Stud) 1930, 32, 35, 36, 39	15 (1983)
FAMOUS INTERNATIONAL RACES					
Derby (1780) 1½ miles Epsom Downs, Great Britain	2 min 33.8 sec *Mahmoud* 1936 2 min 33.84 sec *Kahyasi* 1988 (Electronically timed)	9–Lester Piggott 1954, 57, 60, 68, 70, 72, 76, 77, 83	7–Robert Robson 1793, 1802, 09, 10, 15, 17, 23 7–John Porter 1868, 82, 83, 86, 90, 91, 99 7–Fred Darling 1922, 25, 26, 31, 38, 40, 41	5–3rd Earl of Egremont 1782, 1804, 05, 07, 26 5–HH Aga Khan III 1930, 35, 36, 48, 52	34 (1862)
Prix de l'Arc de Triomphe (1920) 1 mile 864 yd Longchamp, France	2 min 26.3 sec *Trempolino* 1987	4–Jacques Doyasbère 1942, 44, 50, 51 4–Frédéric "Freddy" Head 1966, 72, 76, 79 4–Yves Saint-Martin 1970, 74, 82, 84 4–Pat Eddery 1980, 85, 86, 87	4–Charles Semblat 1942, 44, 46, 49 4–Alec Head 1952, 59, 76, 81 4–François Mathet 1950, 51, 70, 82	6–Marcel Boussac 1936, 37, 42, 44, 46, 49	30 (1967)
VRC Melbourne Cup (1861) 1 mile 1739 yd Flemington, Victoria, Australia	3 min 16.3 sec *Kingston Rule* 1990	4–Bobby Lewis 1902, 15, 19, 27 4–Harry White 1974, 75, 78, 79	8–Bart Cummings 1965, 66, 67, 74, 75, 77, 79, 90	4–Etienne de Mestre 1861, 62, 67, 78	39 (1890)
Grand National (1839) 4½ miles Aintree, Liverpool, Great Britain	8 min 47.8 sec *Mr Frisk* 1990	5–George Stevens 1856, 63, 64, 69, 70	4–Fred Rimell 1956, 61, 70, 76	3–James Machell 1873, 74, 76 3–Sir Charles Assheton-Smith 1893, 1912, 13 3–Noel Le Mare 1973, 74, 77	66 (1929)

Biggest weight
The biggest weight ever carried is 420 lb by both Mr Maynard's mare and Mr Baker's horse in a match won by the former over a mile at York, Great Britain on 21 May 1788.

Perfect card
The only recorded instance of a racing correspondent forecasting ten out of ten winners on a race card was at Delaware Park, Wilmington, DE on 28 Jul 1974, by Charles Lamb of the *Baltimore News American*.

1984–87. The one-race record is $2.6 million by Spend A Buck (foaled 1982), for the Jersey Derby, Garden State Park, NJ on 27 May 1985, of which $2 million was a bonus for having previously won the Kentucky Derby and two preparatory races at Garden State Park.

Oldest winners The oldest horses to win on the flat have been the 18-year-olds Revenge, at Shrewsbury, Great Britain on 23 Sep 1790; Marksman at Ashford, Great Britain, on 4 Sep 1826; and Jorrocks, at Bathurst, Australia on 28 Feb 1851. At the same age Wild Aster won three hurdle races in six days in March 1919 and Sonny Somers won two steeplechases in February 1980.

World speed records The fastest race speed recorded is 43.26 mph by Big Racket, 20.8 sec for ¼ mile, at Mexico City, Mexico on 5 Feb 1945. The four-year-old carried 114 lb. The record for 1½ miles is 37.82 mph by 3-year-old Hawkster (carrying 121 lb) at Santa Anita Park, Arcadia, CA on 14 Oct 1989, with a time of 2 min 22.8 sec.

JOCKEYS

Most successful Billie Lee "Willie" Shoemaker (USA; b. weighing 2½ lb, 19 Aug 1931, whose racing weight was 97 lb at 4 ft 11 in), rode a record 8,833 winners out of 40,350 mounts from his first ride on 19 Mar 1949 and first winner on 20 Apr 1949 to his retirement on 3 Feb 1990. Laffit Pincay, Jr. (USA; b. 29 Dec 1946) has earned a career record $154,659,844 from 1964 to the end of 1990.

The most races won by a jockey in a year is 597 in 2,312 rides, by Kent Desormeaux (b. 27 Feb 1970) in 1989. The greatest amount won in a year is 2,356,280,400 yen (c. $16,250,000) by Yutaka Take (b. 1969) in Japan in 1990. The greatest amount won in the United States in a year is $14,877,298, by José Adeon Santos (USA; b. 26 Apr 1961, Chile) in 1988.

Wins The most winners ridden in one day is nine, by Chris Wiley Antley (USA; b. 6 Jan 1966) on 31 Oct 1987. They consisted of four in the afternoon at Aqueduct, NY and five in the evening at The Meadowlands, NJ.

One card The most winners ridden on one card is eight by six riders, most recently (and in fewest rides) by Pat Day, in only nine rides at Arlington, IL on 13 Sep 1989.

Consecutive The longest winning streak is 12, by: Sir Gordon Richards (Great Britain; 1904–86); one race at Nottingham, Great Britain on 3 October, six out of six at Chepstow on 4 October and the first five races next day at Chepstow in 1933; and Pieter Stroebel at Bulawayo, Southern Rhodesia (now Zimbabwe), 7 Jun–7 Jul 1958.

TRAINERS

Jack Charles Van Berg (USA; b. 7 Jun 1936) has the greatest number of wins in a year, 496 in 1976. The career record is 5,540 by Dale Baird (USA; b. 17 Apr 1935) from 1962 to 1990. The greatest amount won in a year is $17,842,358, by Darrell Wayne Lukas (USA; b. 2 Sep 1935) in 1988.

The only trainer to saddle the first five finishers in a championship race is Michael William Dickinson (Great Britain; b. 3 Feb 1950), in the Cheltenham Gold Cup on 17 Mar 1983; he won a record 12 races in one day, 27 Dec 1982.

and 1952–54, while Doyle's were in 1949–51, 1958, 1961–62 and 1964–65. Ring also played in a record 22 interprovincial finals (1942–63), and was on the winning side 18 times.

Highest and lowest scores The highest score in an All-Ireland final (60 min) was in 1989, when Tipperary, 41 (4 goals, 29 points) beat Antrim, Great Britain (3 goals, 9 points). The record aggregate score was when Cork, 39 (6 goals, 21 points), defeated Wexford, 25 (5 goals, 10 points), in the 80-minute final of 1970. A goal equals three points. The highest recorded individual score was by Nick Rackard (Wexford), who scored 7 goals and 7 points against Antrim, Great Britain in the 1954 All-Ireland semifinal. The lowest score in an All-Ireland final was when Tipperary (1 goal, 1 point) beat Galway (zero) in the first championship at Birr in 1887.

Largest crowd The largest crowd was 84,865 for the All-Ireland final between Cork and Wexford at Croke Park, Dublin in 1954.

Ice Skating

Origins The earliest reference to ice skating is in early Scandinavian literature referring to the 2nd century, although its origins are believed, on archaeological evidence, to be ten centuries earlier than that. The earliest English account of ice skating in 1180 refers to skates made of bone. The earliest skating club was the Edinburgh Skating Club, formed in 1742.

The first recorded race was from Wisbech to Whittlesey, Cambridgeshire, Great Britain in 1763. The first artificial rink in the world was opened in London, Great Britain on 7 Dec 1842, although the surface was not of ice. The first artificial ice rink was opened in London, Great Britain on 7 Jan 1876.

The International Skating Union was founded at Scheveningen, Netherlands in 1892.

FIGURE SKATING

In North America, the first national body was the Amateur Association of Canada, founded on 30 Nov 1887. The Skating Club of the USA was founded in Philadelphia in 1887.

Most titles *Olympic* The most Olympic gold medals won by a figure skater is three: by Gillis Grafström (Sweden; 1893–1938) in 1920, 1924 and 1928 (also silver medal in 1932); by Sonja Henie (Norway; 1912–69) in 1928, 1932 and 1936; and by Irina Konstantinovna Rodnina (USSR; b. 12 Sep 1949) with two different partners in the Pairs in 1972, 1976 and 1980.

World The greatest number of men's individual world figure skating titles (instituted 1896) is ten, by Ulrich Salchow (Sweden; 1877–1949) in 1901–05 and 1907–11. The women's record (insti-

OWNERS

The most lifetime wins by an owner is 4,775, by Marion H. Van Berg (1895–1971), in North America in 35 years. The most wins in a year is 494, by Dan R. Lasater (USA) in 1974. The greatest amount won in a year is $5,858,168, by Ogden Phipps (USA) in 1988.

Hurling

Origins A game of very ancient origin, hurling was included in the Tailteann Games (instituted 1829 B.C.). It only

became standardized with the formation of the Gaelic Athletic Association in Thurles, Ireland on 1 Nov 1884. The Irish Hurling Union was formed in 1879.

Most titles *All-Ireland* The greatest number of All-Ireland Championships won by one team is 27, by Cork between 1890 and 1990. The greatest number of successive wins is four by Cork (1941–44).

Most appearances The most appearances in All-Ireland finals is ten, shared by Christy Ring (Cork and Munster) and John Doyle (Tipperary). They also share the record of All-Ireland medals, won with eight each. Ring's appearances on the winning side were in 1941–44, 1946

Distance

Robin John Cousins (Great Britain; b. 17 Aug 1957) achieved 19 ft 1 in in an axel jump and 18 ft with a back flip at Richmond Ice Rink, Surrey, Great Britain on 16 Nov 1983.

Barrel jumping on ice skates

The official distance record is 29 ft 5 in over 18 barrels, by Yvon Jolin at Terrebonne, Quebec, Canada on 25 Jan 1981. The women's record is 20 ft 4¼ in over 11 barrels, by Janet Hainstock in Michigan on 15 Mar 1980.

tuted 1906) is also ten individual titles, by Sonja Henie between 1927 and 1936. Irina Rodnina won ten pairs titles (instituted 1908), four with Aleksey Nikolayevich Ulanov (b. 4 Nov 1947), 1969–72, and six with her husband Aleksandr Gennadyevich Zaitsev (b. 16 Jun 1952), 1973–78. The most ice dance titles (instituted 1952) won is six, by Lyudmila Alekseyevna Pakhomova (1946–86) and her husband Aleksandr Georgiyevich Gorshkov (USSR; b. 8 Oct 1946), 1970–74 and 1976. They also won the first-ever Olympic ice dance title in 1976.

Richard Totten "Dick" Button (b. 18 Jul 1929) set US records with two Olympic gold medals, 1948 and 1952, and five world titles, 1948–52. Five women's world titles were won by Carol Elizabeth Heise (b. 20 Jan 1940), 1956–60, as well as the 1960 Olympic gold.

United States The US Championships were first held in 1914. The most titles won by an individual is nine by Maribel Y. Vinson (1911–61), 1928–33 and 1935–37. She also won six pairs titles, and her aggregate of 15 titles is equaled by Therese Blanchard (nee Weld; 1893–

1978), who won six individual and nine pairs titles between 1914 and 1927. The men's individual record is seven, by Roger Turner, 1928–34, and by Dick Button, 1946–52. At age 16 in 1946, Button was the youngest-ever winner.

Highest marks The highest tally of maximum six marks awarded in an international championship was 29 to Jayne Torvill and Christopher Dean (Great Britain) in the World Ice Dance Championships at Ottawa, Canada on 22–24 Mar 1984. This comprised seven in the compulsory dances, a perfect set of nine for presentation in the set pattern dance and 13 in the free dance, including another perfect set from all nine judges for artistic presentation. They previously gained a perfect set of nine sixes for artistic presentation in the free dance at the 1983 World Championships in Helsinki, Finland and at the 1984 Winter Olympic Games in Sarajevo, Yugoslavia. In their career Torvill and Dean received a record total of 136 sixes.

The most by a soloist is seven: by Donald George Jackson (Canada; b. 2 Apr 1940) in the World Men's Championship at Prague, Czechoslovakia in 1962; and by

Midori Ito (Japan; b. 13 Aug 1969) in the World Women's Championships at Paris, France in 1989.

Most mid-air rotations Kurt Browning (Canada; b. 18 Jun 1966) was the first to achieve a quadruple jump in competition—a toe loop—in the World Championships at Budapest, Hungary on 25 Mar 1988. The first woman to do so was Suruya Bonaly (France; b. 15 Dec 1973) in the Women's World Championships at Munich, Germany on 16 Mar 1991.

Largest rink The world's largest indoor ice rink is in the Moscow Olympic arena, which has an ice area of 86,800 ft². The five rinks at Fujikyu Highland Skating Center in Japan total 285 243 ft².

SPEED SKATING

Most titles *Olympic* The most Olympic gold medals won in speed skating is six by Lidiya Pavlovna Skoblikova (USSR; b. 8 Mar 1939) in 1960 (two) and 1964 (four). The men's record is by Clas Thunberg (Finland; 1893–1973) with five gold (including one tied), and also one silver and one tied bronze, in 1924 and 1928. Eric Arthur Heiden (USA; b. 14 Jun 1958) also won five gold medals, uniquely at one Games at Lake Placid, NY in 1980.

World The greatest number of world overall titles (instituted 1893) won by any skater is five—by Oscar Mathisen (Norway; 1888–1954) in 1908–09 and 1912–14; and by Clas Thunberg in 1923, 1925, 1928–29 and 1931. The most titles won in the women's events (instituted 1936) is five by Karin Kania (nee Enke [East Germany], b. 20 Jun 1961) in 1982, 1984, 1986–88. Kania also won a record six overall titles at the World Sprint Championships 1980–81, 1983–84, 1986–1987. A record four men's sprint overall titles have been won by Eric Heiden, 1977–80, and by Igor Zhelezovskiy (USSR), 1985–86, 1989 and 1991.

The record score achieved for the world overall title is 157.396 points by Johann-Olav Koss (Norway) at Heerenveen, Netherlands on 9–10 Feb 1991. The record low women's score is 171.630 points by Jacqueline Börner (East Germany) at Calgary, Canada on 10–11 Feb 1990.

Eric Heiden won a US record three overall world titles, 1977–79. His sister Elizabeth Lee "Beth" Heiden (b. 27 Sep 1959) became the only US woman's overall champion in 1979. She completed a unique double championship when the following year she became the first American woman to win the cycling road race world title. Later, at the University of Vermont, she took up cross country skiing, and won the NCCA title.

World Short-track Championships The most successful skater in these championships (instituted 1978) has been Sylvia Daigle (Canada; b. 1 Dec 1962), women's overall champion in 1979, 1983 and 1989–90.

Longest race The "Elfstedentocht" ("Tour of the Eleven Towns"), which

SPEED SKATING WORLD RECORDS

MEN

Meters	min sec	Name (Country)	Place	Date
500	36.45	Uwe-Jens Mey (East Germany)	Calgary, Canada	14 Feb 1988
	36.23 *	Nick Thometz (USA)	Medeo, USSR	26 Mar 1987
1,000	1:12.58	Igor Zhelezovskiy (USSR)	Heerenveen, Netherlands	25 Feb 1989
	1:12.58 †	Pavel Pegov (USSR)	Medeo, USSR	25 Nov 1983
	1:12.05 *	Nick Thometz (USA)	Medeo, USSR	27 Mar 1987
1,500	1:52.06	André Hoffmann (East Germany)	Calgary, Canada	20 Feb 1988
3,000	3:57.52	Johann Olav Koss (Norway)	Heerenveen, Netherlands	13 Mar 1990
	3:56.65 *	Sergey Martyuk (USSR)	Medeo, USSR	11 Mar 1977
5,000	6:41.73	Johann-Olav Koss (Norway)	Heerenveen, Netherlands	9 Feb 1991
10,000	13:43.54	Johann-Olav Koss (Norway)	Heerenveen, Netherlands	10 Feb 1991

* *Unofficial.* † *Set at high altitude.*

WOMEN

Meters	min sec	Name (Country)	Place	Date
500	39.10	Bonnie Blair (USA)	Calgary, Canada	22 Feb 1988
1,000	1:17.65	Christa Rothenburger (now Luding; East Germany)	Calgary, Canada	26 Feb 1988
1,500	1:59.30	Karin Kania (East Germany)	Medeo, USSR	22 Mar 1986
3,000	4:10.80	Gunda Kleeman (Germany)	Calgary, Canada	9 Dec 1990
5,000	7:14.13	Yvonne van Gennip (Netherlands)	Calgary, Canada	28 Feb 1988
10,000 *	15:25.25	Yvonne van Gennip (Netherlands)	Heerenveen, Netherlands	19 Mar 1988

* *Record not officially recognized for this distance.*

WORLD SHORT TRACK SPEED SKATING RECORDS

MEN

Meters	min sec	Name (Country)	Place	Date
500	44.46	Orazio Fagone (Italy)	Budapest, Hungary	16 Jan 1988
1,000	1:31.80	Tsutomu Kawasaki (Japan)	Amsterdam, Netherlands	18 Mar 1990
1,500	2:22.21	T. Kawai (Japan)	Seoul, South Korea	31 Mar 1991
3,000	5:04.24	Tatsuyoshi Ishihara (Japan)	Amsterdam, Netherlands	17 Mar 1985

WOMEN

Meters	min sec	Name (Country)	Place	Date
500	47.08	Zhang Vumei (China)	North Ryde, Australia	23 Mar 1991
1,000	1:39.00	Li Yan (China)	Calgary, Canada	25 Feb 1988
1,500	2:28.26	Eden Donatelli (Canada)	Seoul, South Korea	31 Mar 1991
3,000	5:18.33	Maria-Rosa Candido (Italy)	Budapest, Hungary	17 Jan 1988

originated in the 17th century, was held in the Netherlands from 1909–63, and again in 1985 and 1986, covering 200 km (124 miles 483 yd). As the weather does not permit an annual race in the Netherlands, alternative "Elfstedentocht" take place at suitable venues. These venues have included Lake Vesijärvi, near Lahti, Finland; Ottawa River, Canada; and Lake Weissenssee, Austria. The record time for 200 km is: (men), 5 hr 40 min 37 sec by Dries van Wijhe (Netherlands); and (women), 5 hr 48 min 8 sec by Alida Pasveer (Netherlands), both at Lake Weissensee (altitude 3,609 ft), Austria on 11 Feb 1989. Jan-Roelof Kruithof (Netherlands) won the race eight times—1974, 1976–77, 1979–83. An estimated 16,000 skaters took part in 1986.

Twenty-four hours Martinus Kuiper (Netherlands) skated 339.681 miles in 24 hr in Alkmaar, Netherlands on 12–13 Dec 1988.

Ice and Sand Yachting

Origins The sport originated in the Low Countries and along the Baltic coast in about 1600 (the year the earliest patent was granted). The earliest authentic record is Dutch, dating from 1768. Land or sand yachts of Dutch construction were first reported on beaches (now in Belgium) in 1595. The earliest international championship was staged in 1914.

Fastest speeds *Ice* The fastest speed officially recorded is 143 mph by John D. Buckstaff in a Class A stern-steerer on Lake Winnebago, WI in 1938. Such a speed is possible in a wind of 72 mph.

Sand The official world record for a sand yacht is 66.48 mph set by Christian-Yves Nau (France; b. 1944) in *Mobil* at Le Touquet, France on 22 Mar 1981, when the wind speed reached 75 mph. A speed of 88.4 mph was attained by Nord Embroden (USA) in *Midnight at the Oasis* at Superior Dry Lake, CA on 15 Apr 1976.

Jai Alai (Pelota Vasca)

Origins The game, which originated in Italy as *longue paume* and was introduced into France in the 13th century, is said to be the fastest of all ball games. The glove or *gant* was introduced *c.* 1840 and the *chistera* was invented by Jean "Gantchiki" Dithurbide of Ste Pée, France. The *grand chistera* was invented by Melchior Curuchague of Buenos Aires, Argentina in 1888. The world's largest *frontón* (enclosed stadium) is the Palm Beach Jai Alai, West Palm Beach, which has a seating capacity of 6,000 and covers three acres. The record attendance for a jai alai contest was 15,052

people at the World Jai Alai at Miami, FL, on 27 Dec 1975. The frontón, which is the oldest in the United States (1926), has seating capacity for only 3,884.

Jai alai was introduced in the United States at the St Louis World's Fair in 1903. The sport took root in Florida in 1924 in Miami.

World Championships The *Federacion Internacional de Pelota Vasca* stages World Championships every four years (the first in 1952). The most successful pair have been Roberto Elias and Juan Labat (Argentina), who won the *Trinquete Share* four times, 1952, 1958, 1962 and 1966. Labat won a record seven world titles in all. The most wins in the long court game *Cesta Punta* is three by Hamuy of Mexico, with two different partners, 1958, 1962 and 1966.

Fastest speed An electronically measured ball velocity of 188 mph was recorded by José Ramon Areitio at the Newport Jai Alai, RI on 3 Aug 1979.

Longest domination The longest domination as the world's No. 1 player was enjoyed by Chiquito de Cambo (ne Joseph Apesteguy [France]; 1881–1955) from the beginning of the century until succeeded in 1938 by Jean Urruty (France; b. 19 Oct 1913).

Judo

Origins Judo is a modern combat sport which developed out of an amalgam of several old Japanese martial arts, the most popular of which was ju-jitsu (jiu-jitsu), which is thought to be of Chinese origin. Judo has developed greatly since 1882, when it was first devised by Dr Jigoro Kano (1860–1938). The International Judo Federation was founded in 1951.

Most titles *World and Olympic* World Championships were inaugurated in Tokyo, Japan in 1956. Women's championships were first held in 1980 in New York. Yashiro Yamashita (b. 1 Jun 1957) won nine consecutive Japanese titles from 1977 to 1985; four world titles; Over 95 kg in 1979, 1981 and 1983; Open in 1981; and the Olympic Open category in 1984. He retired undefeated after 203 successive wins between 1977 and 1985. Two other men have won four world titles—Wilhelm Ruska (Netherlands; b. 29 Aug 1940), Over 93 kg 1967, 1971, and 1972 Olympic and Open titles; and Shozo Fujii (Japan; b. 12 May 1950), Under 80 kg 1971, 1973 and 1975, Under 75 kg 1979. The only men to have won two Olympic gold medals are Wilhelm Ruska (Netherlands), Over 93 kg and Open in 1972; Peter Seisenbacher (Austria; b. 25 Mar 1960), 86 kg 1984 and 1988; and Hitoshi Saito (Japan; b. 2 Jan 1961), Over 95 kg 1984 and 1988. Ingrid Berghmans (Belgium; b. 24 Aug 1961) has won a record six women's world titles (first held 1980): Open 1980, 1982, 1984 and 1986 and Under 72 kg in 1984 and 1989. She has also won three silver medals and a bronze. She also won the Olympic 72 kg title in 1988, when women's judo was introduced as a demonstration sport.

The only US judo players to win world titles have been Michael Swain (b. 21 Dec 1960), at men's 71 kg class in 1987, and Ann-Maria Bernadette Burns (b. 15 Aug 1958) at women's 56 kg in 1984.

Highest grades The efficiency grades in judo are divided into pupil (*kyu*) and master (*dan*) grades. The highest awarded is the extremely rare red belt *judan* (10th dan), given to only 13 men so far. The Judo protocol provides for an 11th dan (*juichidan*) who would also wear a red belt, a 12th dan (*junidan*) who would wear a white belt twice as wide as an ordinary belt, and the highest of all, *shihan* (ductor), but these have

■ **Most speed skating titles**
Karin Kania (nee Enke [East Germany]; b. 20 Jun 1961) has won a record five overall speed skating World Championships, in 1982, 1984, 1986–88. She has also won a record six overall titles at the World Sprint Championships, 1980–81, 1983–84, 1986–87. (Photo: All-Sport [USA]/Loubat)

Largest ice yacht
The largest ice yacht was *Icicle*, built for Commodore John E. Roosevelt for racing on the Hudson River, NY in 1869. It was 68 ft 11 in long and carried 1,070 ft^2 of canvas.

Judo throws
The brothers Carl and Peter Udry completed 18,779 judo throwing techniques in a ten-hour period at Hendra Sports Field, Truro, Great Britain on 29 Aug 1987.

Highest lacrosse score

The highest score in an international lacrosse match was the USA's 32–8 win over England at Toronto, Ontario, Canada in 1986.

Most international lacrosse appearances

The record number of international representations is 42, by Peter Daniel Roden (Great Britain; b. 8 Nov 1954) from 1976–90.

Microlighting endurance

Eve Jackson flew from Biggin Hill, Great Britain to Sydney, Australia from 26 Apr 1986 to 1 Aug 1987. The flight took 279 hr 55 min and covered 13,639 miles. From 1 Dec 1987 to 29 Jan 1988, Brian Milton (Great Britain) flew from London, Great Britain to Sydney with a flying time of 241 hr 20 min and covered 13,650 miles. Vijaypat Singhania (India) flew from Biggin Hill to Delhi, India, a distance of 5,420 miles, in 87 hr 55 min, from 18 Aug to 10 Sep 1988.

never been bestowed, except for the 12th dan, to the founder of the sport, Dr Jigoro Kano.

Jiu-Jitsu The World Council of Jiu-Jitsu Organization has staged World Championships biennially since 1984. The Canadian team has been the winner on each occasion.

Karate

Origins Based on techniques devised from the sixth century Chinese art of Shaolin boxing (kempo), karate was developed by an unarmed populace in Okinawa as a weapon against armed Japanese oppressors c. 1500. Transmitted to Japan in the 1920s by Funakoshi Gichin, this method of combat was refined into karate and organized into a sport with competitive rules. The five major styles of karate in Japan are: *shotokan, wado-ryu, goju-ryu, shito-ryu* and *kyokushinkai*, each of which places a different emphasis on speed, power, etc. Other styles include *sankukai, shotokai* and *Shukokai*. *Wu shu* is a comprehensive term embracing all Chinese martial arts. *Kung fu* is one aspect of these arts popularized by the movies.

World Championships Great Britain has won a record six world titles (instituted 1970) at the kumite team event, in 1975, 1982, 1984, 1986, 1988 and 1990. Two men's individual kumite titles have been won by: Pat McKay (Great Britain) at Under 80 kg, 1982 and 1984; Emmanuel Pinda (France) at Open, 1984, and Over 80 kg, in 1988; and Theirry Masci (France) at Under 70 kg, in 1986 and 1988. Four women's kumite titles have been won by Guus van Mourik (Netherlands) at Over 60 kg, in 1982, 1984, 1986 and 1988. Three individual kata titles have been won by: *men*: Tsuguo Sakumoto (Japan) in 1984, 1986 and 1988; *women*: Mie Nakayama (Japan) in 1982, 1984 and 1986.

Top exponents The leading exponents among karateka are a number of 10th dans in Japan.

Lacrosse

MEN

Origins The game is of Native American origin, derived from the inter-tribal game *baggataway*, and was played before 1492 by the Iroquois in lower Ontario, Canada and upper New York State. The French named it after their game of *chouler à la crosse*, known as far back as 1381.

Lacrosse was included in the Olympic Games of 1904 and 1908, and featured as an exhibition sport in the 1928, 1932 and 1948 Games.

The first college team in the United States was that of New York University

in 1877, and the US Amateur Lacrosse Association was founded in 1879.

Most titles *World* The USA has won five of the six World Championships, in 1967, 1974, 1982, 1986 and 1990. Canada won the other world title in 1978, beating the USA 17–16 after extra time; this was the first drawn international match.

United States National champions were determined by committee from 1936, and received the Wilson Wingate Trophy; since 1971 they have been decided by NCAA playoffs. Johns Hopkins University has the most wins overall: seven NCAA titles between 1974 and 1987, and six wins and five ties between 1941 and 1970.

Most points The record for most points in the NCAA lacrosse tournament is 25, by Eamon McEneaney (Cornell) in 1977 and Tim Goldstein (Cornell) in 1987. Both players played in 3 games.

Ed Mullen scored the most points in an NCAA championship game, with 12, for Maryland v Navy in the 1976 championship game.

WOMEN

The first reported playing of lacrosse by women was in 1886. The women's game has evolved separately from the men's game, so the rules now differ considerably.

World Championships/World Cup The first World Cup was held in 1982, and the USA has won twice, in 1982 and 1989.

Microlighting

The *Fédération Aéronautique Internationàle* has established two classes of aircraft for which records are accepted, C1 a/o and R 1-2-3, and the following are the overall best of the two classes (all in the C1 a/o class).

World records Distance in a straight line: *1,011.48 miles* Wilhelm Lischak (Austria), Volsau, Austria to Brest, France, 8 Jun 1988.

Altitude: *30,147 ft* Eric S. Winton (Australia), Tyagarah Aerodrome, New South Wales, Australia, 8 Apr 1989.

Distance in a closed circuit: *1,679.09 miles* Wilhelm Lischak (Austria), Wels, Austria, 18 Jun 1988.

Speed over a 100 km closed circuit: *185 mph* C.T. Andrews (USA), 3 Aug 1982.

Speed over a 500 km closed circuit: *182 mph* C.T. Andrews (USA), 3 Aug 1982.

Modern Pentathlon and Biathlon

Point scores in riding, fencing, cross country, and hence overall scores, have no comparative value between one competition and another. In shooting and swim-

ming (300 meters) the scores are of record significance.

The modern pentathlon (consisting of fencing, swimming, shooting, running and riding) was inaugurated at the Olympic Games in Stockholm in 1912. *L'Union Internationàle de Pentathlon Moderne* (UIPM) was founded at Aldershot, Great Britain on 3 Aug 1948. The administration of biathlon (consisting of cross-country skiing and shooting) was added in 1957, and the name modified accordingly, to *L'Union Internationàle de Pentathlon Moderne et Biathlon* (UIPMB). The first US national championship was held in 1955. The United States Modern Pentathlon and Biathlon Association was established in 1971, but this body was split to create the US Modern Pentathlon Association in 1978.

MODERN PENTATHLON

Most titles *World* András Balczó (Hungary; b. 16 Aug 1938) won the record number of world titles (instituted 1949), six individual and seven team. He won the world individual title in 1963, 1965–67 and 1969 and the Olympic title in 1972. His seven team titles (1960–70) comprised five world and two Olympic. The USSR has won a record 13 world and four Olympic team titles. Hungary has also won a record four Olympic team titles and ten world titles.

Women's World Championships were first held in 1981. Poland has won a record four women's world team titles: 1985, 1988, 1989 and 1990; Great Britain won three world titles and three World Cups, 1978–80, when this competition preceded the world championships. The only double individual champion has been Irina Kiselyeva (USSR), 1986–87.

The only US modern pentathletes to win world titles have been Robert Nieman (b. 21 Oct 1947), 1979, when the men's team also won, and Lori Norwood (women's) in 1989.

Olympic The greatest number of Olympic gold medals won is three, by András Balczó, a member of the winning team in 1960 and 1968 and the 1972 individual champion. Lars Hall (Sweden; b. 30 Apr 1927) has uniquely won two individual championships (1952 and 1956). Pavel Serafimovich Lednyev (USSR; b. 25 Mar 1943) won a record seven medals (two team gold, one team silver, one individual silver, three individual bronze), 1968–80.

The only US individual Olympic medalist has been Robert Lee Beck, who won the bronze in 1960.

Probably the greatest margin of victory was by William Oscar Guernsey Grut (Sweden; b. 17 Sep 1914) in the 1948 Games, when he won three events and placed fifth and eighth in the other two.

US National Championships The men's championship was inaugurated in 1955. Mike Burley has won a record four titles (1977, 1979, 1981, 1985). The women's championship was first held in

1977; Kim Dunlop (nee Arata) has won a record eight titles (1979–80, 1984–89).

BIATHLON

The biathlon, which combines cross-country skiing and rifle shooting, was first included in the Olympic Games in 1960, and World Championships were first held in 1958. Since 1984 there has been a women's World Championship, and women's biathlon will be contested at the 1992 Olympics.

Most titles *Olympic* Two Olympic individual titles have been won: by Magnar Solberg (Norway; b. 4 Feb 1937), in 1968 and 1972; and Franz-Peter Rötsch (East Germany; b. 19 Apr 1964) at both 10 km and 20 km in 1988. The USSR has won all six 4 × 7.5 km relay titles, from 1968 to 1988. Aleksandr Ivanovich Tikhonov (b. 2 Jan 1947), who was a member of the first four teams, also won a silver in the 1968 20 km.

World Frank Ullrich (East Germany; b. 24 Jan 1958) has won a record six individual world titles, four at 10 km, 1978–81, including the 1980 Olympics, and two at 20 km, 1982–83. Aleksandr Tikhonov was on ten winning USSR relay teams, 1968–80, and won four individual titles.

The Biathlon World Cup (instituted 1979) was won four times by Frank Ullrich in 1978 and 1980–82. He was second in 1979 and third in 1983.

Motorcycle Racing

Origins The first motorcycle race was held over a mile on an oval track at Sheen House, Richmond, Great Britain on 29 Nov 1897, won by Charles Jarrott (1877–1944) on a Fournier. The oldest continuous motorcycle races in the world are the Auto-Cycle Union Tourist Trophy (TT) series, first held on the 15.81 mile "Peel" (St John's) course in the Isle of Man, Great Britain on 28 May 1907, and still run in the island on the "Mountain" circuit.

Earliest race The first reported race in the United States was won by George Holden of Brooklyn, NY in 1903, recording 14 min 57.2 sec for 10 miles.

Fastest circuits The highest average lap speed attained on any closed circuit is 160.288 mph, by Yvon du Hamel (Canada; b. 1941) on a modified 903 cc four-cylinder Kawasaki Z1 at the 31-degree banked 2.5 mile Daytona International Speedway, FL in Mar 1973. His lap time was 56.149 sec.

The fastest road circuit used to be Francorchamps circuit near Spa, Belgium, then 8.74 miles in length. It was lapped in 3 min 50.3 sec (average speed 137.150 mph) by Barry Stephen Frank Sheene (Great Britain; b. 11 Sep 1950) on a 495 cc 4-cylinder Suzuki during the Belgian Grand Prix on 3 Jul 1977. On that occasion he set a record time for

this ten-lap (87.74 mile) race of 38 min 58.5 sec (average speed 135.068 mph).

Longest race The longest race was the Liège 24 hr, run on the old Francorchamps circuit. The greatest distance ever covered is 2,761.9 miles (average speed 115.08 mph) by Jean-Claude Chemarin and Christian Leon, both of France, on a 941 cc 4-cylinder Honda on the Francorchamps circuit on 14–15 Aug 1976.

Longest circuit The 37.73-mile "Mountain" circuit on the Isle of Man, Great Britain, over which the principal TT races have been run since 1911 (with minor amendments in 1920), has 264 curves and corners and is the longest used for any motorcycle race.

Most successful riders Angel Roldan Nieto (Spain; b. 25 Jan 1947) won a record seven 125 cc titles, 1971–72, 1979, 1981–84, and he also won

a record six titles at 50 cc, 1969–70, 1972, 1975–77. Klaus Enders (Germany; b. 1937) won six world sidecar titles, 1967, 1969–70, 1972–74.

Giacomo Agostini (Italy; b. 16 Jun 1942) won 122 races (68 at 500 cc, 54 at 350 cc) in the World Championship series between 24 Apr 1965 and 25 Sep 1977, including a record 19 in 1970, also achieved by Mike Hailwood (Great Britain) in 1966.

World Championships The most World Championship titles (instituted by the *Fédération Internationàle Motocycliste* in 1949) won is 15, by Giacomo Agostini, seven at 350 cc, 1968–74, and eight at 500 cc in 1966–72, 1975. He is the only man to have won two World Championships in five consecutive years (350 cc and 500 cc titles 1968–72).

In 1985 Freddie Burdette Spencer (USA;

Oldest mountain climber

Teiichi Igarashi (Japan; b. 21 Sep 1886) climbed Mt Fuji (Fujiyama) (12,388 ft) at the age of 99 years 302 days on 20 Jul 1986.

■ **Youngest motorcycle world champion** *The picture below shows the start of the 1990 British 125 cc Grand Prix at Donnington Park on 5 August. The race was won by Italian Loris Capirossi, the first of three wins during the season. His last win was at the Australian Grand Prix on 16 September when he was crowned world champion at the age of only 17 yr 165 days, the youngest ever in motorcycling. (Photo: All-Sport/P. Rondeau)*

b. 20 Dec 1961), riding for Honda, became the first man ever to win the 250 cc and 500 cc titles in the same year.

The most world titles won by an American motorcyclist is four, by Eddie Lawson (b. 11 Mar 1958), at 500 cc in 1984, 1986, 1988–89.

Most successful machines Japanese Yamaha machines won 40 World Championships between 1964 and 1990.

Moto-cross Joël Robert (Belgium; b. 11 Nov 1943) won six 250 cc Moto-cross World Championships (1964, 1968–72). Between 25 Apr 1964 and 18 Jun 1972 he won a record fifty 250 cc Grand Prix. The youngest moto-cross world champion was Dave Strijbos (Netherlands; b. 9 Nov 1968), who won the 125 cc title at the age of 18 yr 296 days on 31 Aug 1986. Eric Geboers (Belgium) has uniquely won all three categories of the Moto-Cross World Championships, at 125 cc in 1983, 250 cc in 1987 and 500 cc in 1988.

Youngest and oldest world champions Loris Capirossi (Italy; b. 4 Apr 1973) is the youngest to win a World Championship. He was 17 yr 165 days when he won the 125 cc title on 16 Sep 1990. The oldest was Hermann-Peter Müller (1909–76) of West Germany, who won the 250 cc title in 1955 at the age of 46.

Mountaineering

Although Bronze-Age artifacts have been found on the summit of the Riffelhorn, Switzerland (9,605 ft), mountaineering as a sport has a continuous history dating back only to 1854. Isolated instances of climbing for its own sake back to the 13th century. The Atacamenans built sacrificial platforms near the summit of Llullaillaco (22,057 ft) in late pre-Columbian times c. 1490.

Mount Everest Everest (29,078 ft) was first climbed at 11:30 A.M. on 29 May 1953, when the summit was reached by Edmund Percival Hillary (b. 20 Jul 1919), of New Zealand, and Sherpa Tenzing Norgay (1914–86, formerly called Tenzing Khumjung Bhutia). The successful expedition was led by Col. (later Hon. Brigadier) Henry Cecil John Hunt (b. 22 Jun 1910).

Most conquests Ang Rita Sherpa (b. 1947), with ascents in 1983, 1984, 1985, 1987, 1988 and 1990, has scaled Everest six times, and all without the use of bottled oxygen.

Solo Reinhold Messner (Italy; b. 17 Sep 1944) was the first to make the entire climb solo, on 20 Aug 1980. Also, Messner, with Peter Habeler (Austria; b. 22 Jul 1942), made the first entirely oxygenless ascent on 8 May 1978.

First woman Junko Tabei (Japan; b. 22 Sep 1939) reached the summit on 16 May 1975.

Oldest Richard Daniel Bass (USA; b. 21 Dec 1929) was age 55 yr 130 days when he reached the summit on 30 Apr 1985.

Most successful expedition The Mount Everest International Peace Climb, a team of American, Russian and Chinese climbers, led by James W. Whittaker (USA), in 1990 succeeded in putting the greatest number of people on the summit, 20, from 7–10 May 1990.

Sea level to summit Timothy John Macartney-Snape (Australia; b. 30 Apr 1963) traversed Everest's entire altitude from sea level to summit. He set off on foot from the Bay of Bengal near Calcutta, India on 5 Feb 1990 and reached the summit on 11 May, having walked approximately 745 miles.

All continents The first person to climb the highest mountain in each of the seven continents (Africa—Kilimanjaro, 19,340 ft; Antarctica—Vinson Massif, 16,863 ft; Asia—Everest, 29,078 ft; Europe—El'brus, 18,510 ft; North and Central America—McKinley, 20,320 ft; South America—Aconcagua, 22,834 ft; and Australasia—Carstensz Pyramid, 16,502 ft) was Patrick Morrow (Canada; b. 18 Oct 1952). He completed the last of the seven mountains with his successful conquest of Carstensz Pyramid on 7 May 1986.

Mountaineer Reinhold Messner was the first person to successfully scale all 14 of the world's mountains of over 26,250 ft, all without oxygen. With his ascent of Kanchenjunga in 1982, he became the first person to climb the world's three highest mountains, having earlier reached the summits of Everest and K2.

Greatest walls The highest final stage in any wall climb is the one on the south face of Annapurna I (26,545 ft). It was climbed by the British expedition led by Christian John Storey Bonington (b. 6 Aug 1934) when from 2 Apr to 27 May 1970, using 18,000 ft of rope, Donald Whillans (1933–85) and Dougal Haston scaled to the summit. The longest wall climb is on the Rupal-Flank from the base camp at 11,680 ft to the South Point 26,384 ft of Nanga Parbat—a vertical ascent of 14,704 ft. This was scaled by the Austro-German-Italian expedition led by Dr Karl Maria Herrligkoffer (b. 13 Jun 1916) in April 1970.

Europe's greatest wall is the 6,600 ft

north face of the Eigerwand (Ogre wall), first climbed by Heinrich Harrer and Fritz Kasparek of Austria and Andreas Heckmair and Wiggerl Vörg of Germany from 21–24 Jul 1938. The northeast face of the Eiger had been climbed on 20 Aug 1932 by Hans Lauper, Alfred Zurcher, Alexander Graven and Josef Knubel. The greatest Alpine solo climb was that of Walter Bonatti (Italy; b. 22 Jun 1930) of the southwest pillar of the Dru, Montenvers, now called the Bonatti Pillar, with five bivouacs in 126 hr 7 min from 17–22 Aug 1955.

The most demanding free climbs in the world are those rated at 5.13, the premier location for these being in the Yosemite Valley, CA.

Highest bivouac Four Nepalese summiters bivouacked at more than 28,870 ft in their descent from the summit of Everest on the night of 23 Apr 1990. They were Ang Rita Sherpa, on his record-breaking sixth ascent of Everest; Ang Kami Sherpa (b. 1952); Pasang Norbu Sherpa (b. 1963); and Top Bahadur Khatri (b. 1960).

MOUNTAIN RACING

Mount Cameroon Reginald Esuke (Cameroon) descended from the summit at 13,543 ft to Buea at 3,002 ft in 1 hr 2 min 15 sec on 24 Jan 1988, achieving a vertical rate of 167.5 ft per min. Timothy Leku Lekunze (Cameroon) set the record for the race to the summit and back of 3 hr 46 min 34 sec on 25 Jan 1987, when the temperature varied from 35° C to 0° C at the summit. The record time for the ascent is 2 hr 25 min 20 sec by Jack Maitland (Great Britain) in 1988. The women's record for the race is 4 hr 42 min 31 sec by Fabiola Rueda (Colombia; b. 26 Mar 1963) in 1989.

Netball

The game of netball was invented in the United States in 1891 and introduced into England in 1895 by Dr Toles.

Most titles *World* Australia has won the World Championships (instituted 1963) a record five times—1963, 1971, 1975, 1979 and 1983.

Highest scores The World Tournament record score was in Auckland, New Zealand in 1975 when England beat Papua New Guinea by 114 goals to 16. The record number of goals in the World Tournament is 402 by Judith Heath (England; b. 1942) in 1971.

Orienteering

Origins The first indications of orienteering as a competitive sport have been found in the Swedish army (1888) and the Norwegian army (1895). The first civilian competition seems to have been organized on 31 Oct 1897 (with eight participants) by the sport club Tjalve, outside Oslo, Norway. In spite of a number of other small events up to 1910, the sport died out in Norway, but in Sweden it survived World War I. On 25 Mar 1919, the first large competition with more than 200 participants was organized in the forest of Nacka, outside Stockholm. From there the sport spread rapidly throughout Sweden and later (about 1925) to Finland, Norway and (especially post-1945) to other countries in Europe and elsewhere. The initiator

was Major Ernst Killander, who is known as "The Father of Orienteering." World Championships were instituted in 1966. The United States Orienteering Federation was founded in 1971.

Most titles *World* The men's relay has been won a record seven times by Norway—1970, 1978, 1981, 1983, 1985, 1987 and 1989. Sweden has won the women's relay eight times—1966, 1970, 1974, 1976, 1981, 1983, 1985 and 1989. Three women's individual titles have been won by Annichen Kringstad-Svensson (Sweden; b. 15 Jul 1960), in 1981, 1983 and 1985. The men's title has been won twice by: Åge Hadler (Norway; b. 14 Aug 1944), in 1966 and 1972; Egil Johansen (Norway; b. 18 Aug 1954), in 1976 and 1978; and Øyvind Thon (Norway; b. 25 Mar 1958), in 1979 and 1981.

US National Championships This competition was first held on 17 Oct 1970. Sharon Crawford, New England Orienteering Club, has won a record 11 overall women's titles: 1977–82, 1984–87, 1989. Peter Gagarin, New England Orienteering Club, has won a record five overall men's titles: 1976–79, 1983.

Most competitors The most competitors at a one-day event is 38,000, in the Ruf des Herbstes held in Sibiu, Romanis in 1982. The largest event is the five-day Swedish O-Ring at Smaland, which attracted 120,000 competitors in 1983.

Ski orienteering Eight World Championships in ski orienteering have been held. Sweden has won the men's relay five times (1977, 1980, 1982, 1984 and 1990) and Finland has won the women's relay five times (1975, 1977, 1980, 1988 and 1990).

Rappeling
Wilmer Pérez and Luis Aulestia set a rappeling record of 3,376 ft by descending from above the Angel Falls in Venezuela down to its base on 24 Aug 1989. The descent took 1¼ hr.

The longest descent down the side of a skyscraper is one of 878 ft by David Griffiths and Phil Barber, who rappeled down the transmitting tower of National Transcommunications Ltd at Emley Moor, Great Britain in just over four minutes on 8 May 1991.

Human fly
The longest climb achieved on the vertical face of a building occurred on 26 Jun 1986 when Daniel Goodwin, 30, of California climbed a record 1,125 ft up the outside of the 1,815 ft 5 in CN Tower in Toronto, Ontario, Canada (the tallest self-supporting tower in the world) using neither climbing aids nor safety equipment.

TRACK AND FIELD RECORDS

MEN	min:sec	Name	Year
100 m	9.92	Carl Lewis (USA)	1988
200 m	19.75	Joe DeLoach (USA)	1988
400 m	† 43.86	Lee Evans (USA)	1968
800 m	1:43.00	Joaquim Cruz (Brazil)	1984
1,500 m	3:32.53	Sebastian Coe (Great Britain)	1984
5,000 m	13:05.59	Saïd Aouita (Morocco)	1984
10,000 m	27:21.46	Brahim Boutayeb (Morocco)	1988
Marathon	2:09:21.00	Carlos Lopes (Portugal)	1984
3,000 m Steeplechase	8:05.51	Julius Kariuki (Kenya)	1988
110 mh	12.98	Roger Kingdom (USA)	1988
400 mh	47.19	Andre Phillips (USA)	1988
4 × 100 m	37.83	USA	1984
4 × 400 m	2:56.16	USA	1968 † & 1988
20 km walk	1:19:57	Jozef Pribilinec (Czechoslovakia)	1988
50 km walk	3:38:29	Vyacheslav Ivanenko (USSR)	1988
	m		
High jump	2.38	Gennadiy Avdeyenko (USSR)	1988
Pole vault	5.90	Sergey Bubka (USSR)	1988
Long jump	† 8.90	Bob Beamon (USA)	1968
Triple jump	17.61	Khristo Markov (Bulgaria)	1988
Shot	22.47	Ulf Timmerman (East Germany)	1988
Discus	68.82	Jürgen Schult (East Germany)	1988
Hammer	84.80	Sergey Litvinov (USSR)	1988
Javelin	* 85.90	Jan Zelezny (Czechoslovakia)	1988
—old	94.58	Miklós Németh (Hungary)	1976
Decathlon	8,847 points	Daley Thompson (Great Britain)	1984
WOMEN	min:sec		
100 m	10.62	Florence Griffith-Joyner (USA)	1988
	‡ 10.56	Florence Griffith-Joyner (USA)	1988
200 m	21.34	Florence Griffith-Joyner (USA)	1988
400 m	48.65	Olga Bryzgina (USSR)	1988
800 m	1:53.43	Nadezhda Olizarenko (USSR)	1980
1,500 m	3:53.96	Paula Ivan (Romania)	1988
3,000 m	8:26.53	Tatyana Samolenko (USSR)	1988
10,000 m	31:05.21	Olga Bondarenko (USSR)	1988
Marathon	2:24:52	Joan Benoit (USA)	1984
100 m hurdles	12.38	Yodanka Donkova (Bulgaria)	1988
400 m hurdles	53.17	Debbie Flintoff-King (Australia)	1988
4 × 100 m	41.60	East Germany	1980
4 × 400 m	3:15.18	USSR	1988
	m		
High jump	2.03	Louise Ritter (USA)	1988
Long jump	7.40	Jackie Joyner-Kersee (USA)	1988
Shot	22.41	Ilona Slupianek (East Germany)	1980
Discus	72.30	Martina Hellman (East Germany)	1988
Javelin	74.68	Petra Felke (East Germany)	1988
Heptathlon	7,291 points	Jackie Joyner-Kersee (USA)	1988

* Performance made in qualifying round.
† At high altitude, Mexico City 2,240 m.
‡ Wind-assisted.

Olympic Games

These records include the Games, known as the Intercalated Games, held at Athens, Greece in 1906 to celebrate the tenth anniversary of the revival of the Olympics.

The earliest celebration of the ancient Olympic Games of which there is a definite record is that of July 776 B.C., when Coroibos, a cook from Elis, won the foot race, though their origin dates from perhaps as early as *c.* 1370 B.C. The ancient Games were terminated by an order issued in Milan in A.D. 393 by Theodosius I, "the Great" (*c.* 346–95), Emperor of Rome. At the instigation of Pierre de Fredi, Baron de Coubertin (1863–1937), the Olympic Games of the modern era were inaugurated in Athens on 6 Apr 1896. In 1992, the XVI Winter Games take place in Albertville, France from 8–23 February, and the XXV Summer Games take place in Barcelona, Spain from 25 July–9 August.

Best attendance Five countries have been represented at each of the 22 celebrations of the Summer Games: Australia, France, Greece, Great Britain and Switzerland (which only contested the equestrian events, held in Stockholm, Sweden, in 1956, and did not attend the Games in Melbourne, Australia). Of these only Great Britain has been present at all Winter celebrations as well.

Largest crowd The largest crowd at any Olympic site was 150,000 at the 1952 ski-jumping competition at the Holmenkollen, outside Oslo, Norway. Estimates of the number of spectators of the marathon race through Tokyo, Japan on 21 Oct 1964 ranged from 500,000 to 1.5 million. The total spectator attendance at Los Angeles in 1984 was given as 5,797,923 (see General Records).

Olympic torch relay The longest journey of the torch within one country was for the XV Olympic Winter Games in Canada in 1988. The torch arrived from Greece at St John's, Newfoundland on 17 Nov 1987 and was transported 11,222 miles (5,088 miles by foot, 4,419 miles by aircraft/ferry, 1,712 miles by snowmobile and 3 miles by dogsled) until its arrival at Calgary on 13 Feb 1988.

Most medals In ancient Olympic Games, victors were given a chaplet of wild olive leaves. Leonidas of Rhodos won 12 running titles 164–152 B.C. The most individual gold medals won by a male competitor in the modern Games is ten by Raymond Clarence Ewry (USA; 1874–1937) (see Track and Field). The female record is seven, by Vera Caslavska-Odlozil (Czechoslovakia) (see Gymnastics).

The most medals won by an American Olympian is 11, at shooting, by Carl Townsend Osburn (1884–1966) from 1912 to 1924—five gold, four silver, two bronze; and by Mark Andrew Spitz (b. 10 Feb 1950), at swimming, 1968–72—nine gold, one silver, one bronze.

The most gold medals won by an American woman is four, by Patricia Joan

SWIMMING RECORDS

MEN	min:sec		Year
50 m freestyle	22.14	Matt Biondi (USA)	1988
100 m freestyle	48.63	Matt Biondi (USA)	1988
200 m freestyle	1:47.25	Duncan Armstrong (Australia)	1988
400 m freestyle	3:46.95	Uwe Dassler (East Germany)	1988
1500 m freestyle	14:58.27	Vladimir Salnikov (USSR)	1980
4 × 100 m freestyle relay	3:16.53	USA	1988
4 × 200 m freestyle	7:12.51	USA	1988
100 m backstroke	54.51	David Berkoff (USA)	1988
200 m backstroke	1:58.99	Rick Carey (USA)	1984
100 m breaststroke	48.63	Steve Lunquist (USA)	1984
200 m breaststroke	2:13.34	Victor Davis (Canada)	1984
100 m butterfly	53.80	Anthony Nesty (Surinam)	1988
200 m butterfly	1:56.94	Michael Gross (West Germany)	1988
200 m individual medley	2:00.17	Tamás Darnyi (Hungary)	1988
400 m individual medley	4:14.75	Tamás Darnyi (Hungary)	1988
4 × 100 m medley relay	3:36.93	USA	1988
WOMEN			
50 m freestyle	25.49	Kristin Otto (East Germany)	1988
100 m freestyle	54.79	Barbara Krause (East Germany)	1980
200 m freestyle	1:57.65	Heike Freidrich (East Germany)	1988
400 m freestyle	4:03.85	Janet Evans (USA)	1988
800 m freestyle	8:20.20	Janet Evans (USA)	1988
4 × 100 m freestyle relay	3:40.63	East Germany	1988
100 m backstroke	1:00.86	Rica Reinisch (East Germany)	1980
200 m backstroke	2:09.99	Krisztina Egerszegi (Hungary)	1988
100 m breaststroke	1:07.95	Tania Dangalakova (Bulgaria)	1988
200 m breaststroke	2:26.71	Silke Hörner (East Germany)	1988
100 m butterfly	59.00	Kristin Otto (East Germany)	1988
200 m butterfly	2:06.90	Mary T. Meagher (USA)	1984
200 m individual medley	2:12.59	Daniela Hunger (East Germany)	1988
400 m individual medley	4:36.29	Petra Schneider (East Germany)	1980
4 × 100 m medley relay	4:03.74	East Germany	1988

McCormick (nee Keller, b. 12 May 1930), in both highboard and springboard diving, 1952 and 1956.

The most medals won by an American woman is eight, by swimmer Shirley Babashoff (b. 31 Jan 1957)—gold at 4 x 100 meters freestyle relay 1972 and 1976, and six silver medals 1972–76, a record for any competitor in Olympic history.

The only Olympian to win four consecutive individual titles in the same event has been Alfred Adolph Oerter (USA; b. 19 Sep 1936), who won the discus, in 1956–68. However, Raymond Clarence Ewry (USA) won both the standing long jump and the standing high jump at four games in succession, 1900, 1904, 1906 (the Intercalated Games) and 1908. Also, Paul B. Elvström (Denmark; b. 25 Feb 1928) won four successive gold medals at monotype yachting events, 1948–60, but there was a class change (1948 Firefly class, 1952–60 Finn class).

Swimmer Mark Andrew Spitz (USA) won a record seven golds at one celebration, at Munich in 1972, including three in relays. The most won in individual events at one celebration is five, by speed skater Eric Arthur Heiden (USA; b. 14 Jun 1958) at Lake Placid, NY in 1980.

The only man to win a gold medal in both the Summer and Winter Games is Edward Patrick Francis Eagan (USA; b. 1898–1967), who won the 1920 light-heavyweight boxing title and was a member of the winning four-man bob in 1932. Christa Luding (nee Rothenburger [East Germany]; b. 4 Dec 1959) became the first woman to win a medal at both the Summer and Winter Games when she won a silver in the cycling sprint event in 1988. She had previously won medals for speed skating—500 meter gold in 1984, and 1,000 meter gold and 500 meter silver in 1988.

Gymnast Larisa Latynina (USSR; b. 27 Dec 1934) won a record 18 medals, and the men's record is 15 by Nikolay Andrianov (see Gymnastics). The record at one celebration is eight, by gymnast Aleksandr Dityatin (USSR; b. 7 Aug 1957) in 1980.

Youngest and oldest gold medalist The youngest-ever winner was a French boy (whose name is not recorded) who coxed the Netherlands pair in rowing in 1900. He was 7–10 years years old and he substituted for Dr Hermanus Brockmann, who coxed in the heats but proved too heavy. The youngest female champion was Marjorie Gestring (USA; b. 18 Nov 1922, now Mrs Bowman), age 13 yr 268 days, in the 1936 women's springboard diving event. Oscar Swahn (Sweden) was on the winning Running Deer shooting team in 1912 at the age of 64 yr 258 days, and in this event was the oldest medalist—silver—at 72 yr 280 days in 1920.

The oldest American Olympic champion was retired minister Galen Carter Spencer (1840–1904), who assisted the Potomac Archers to an archery team medal two days after his 64th birthday in

1904. The oldest American medalist and Olympic participant was Samuel Harding Duvall (1836–1908), who was 68 yrs 194 days when he was a member of the Cincinnati Archers silver medal team in 1904.

The youngest American medalist and participant was Dorothy Poynton (b. 17 Jul 1915), who won the springboard diving bronze medal at 13 yr 23 days in 1928. She went on to win the highboard gold in 1932 and 1936 (by then Mrs Hill). The youngest American male medalist was Donald Wills Douglas, Jr. (b. 3 Jul 1917) with silver at 6-meter yachting in 1932, at 15 yr 40 days. He later became chief executive of the McDonnell-Douglas Corporation. The youngest American gold medalist was Jackie Fields, at 16 yrs 161 days (see Boxing).

Longest span The longest span of an Olympic competitor is 40 years, by: Dr Ivan Osiier (Denmark; 1888–1965) in fencing, 1908–32 and 1948; Magnus Konow (Norway; 1887–1972) in yachting, 1908–20, 1928 and 1936–48; Paul

MOST MEDALS

The total medals, by nation, for all Olympic events (including those now discontinued)

Summer Games (1896–1988)

Excludes medals won in Official Art competitions in 1912–48.

	G	S	B	Total
USA	752	569	481	1,802
USSR [1]	397	323	304	1,024
Great Britain	172	221	206	599
Germany [2]	153	206	208	567
France	153	170	175	498
Sweden	132	142	167	441
East Germany [3]	154	131	126	411
Italy	147	121	123	391
Hungary	125	112	137	374
Finland	97	75	110	282
Japan	87	75	82	244
Australia	71	67	87	225
Romania	55	64	82	201
Poland	40	56	95	191
Canada	39	62	73	174
Switzerland	41	63	58	162
Netherlands	43	46	65	154
Bulgaria	35	62	49	146
Czechoslovakia [4]	45	48	49	142
Denmark	25	50	49	124

Winter Games (1924–88)

USSR [1]	79	57	59	195
Norway	54	60	54	168
USA	42	46	35	123
East Germany [3]	39	36	35	110
Finland	33	43	34	110
Austria	28	38	32	98
Sweden	36	25	31	92
Germany [2]	26	26	23	75
Switzerland	23	25	25	73
Canada	14	12	18	44
Netherlands	13	17	12	42
France	13	10	16	39
Italy	14	10	9	33
Czechoslovakia [4]	2	8	13	23
Great Britain	7	4	10	21

[1] Includes Czarist Russia.
[2] Germany 1896–1964, West Germany 1968–88.
[3] East Germany, 1968–88.
[4] Includes Bohemia.

ARCHERY RECORDS

Double FITA rounds

Men	2616	Darrell Pace (USA)	1984
Women	2683	Kim Soo-nyung (South Korea)	1988

SHOOTING RECORDS

MEN

Small bore rifle—prone	599	Li Ho-jun (North Korea)	1972
		plus four other men	1976–84
Small bore rifle—3 positions	1181	Alister Allan (Great Britain)	1988
Air rifle	594	Goran Maksimovis (Yugoslavia)	1988
Free pistol	581	Aleksandr Melentyev (USSR)	1980
Rapid-fire pistol	598	Afanasiy Kuzmin (USSR)	1988
Air pistol	590	Eric Buljung (USA)	1988
Running game	591	Gennadiy Avramenko (USSR)	1988
		Tor Heiestad (Norway)	1988

WOMEN

Standard rifle—3 positions	590	Silvia Sperber (West Germany)	1988
Air rifle	395	Launi Meli (USA)	1988
		Irina Chilova (USSR)	1988
		Zhang Qiuping (China)	1988
Sport pistol	591	Nino Salukvadze (USSR)	1988
Air pistol	390	Nino Salukvadze (USSR)	1988

MIXED

Trap	199	Angelo Scalzone (Italy)	1972
Skeet	198	Yevgeniy Petrov (USSR)	1968
		plus seven other men	1968–88

SPEED SKATING RECORDS

MEN	min:sec		
500 m	36.45	Uwe-Jens Mey (East Germany)	1988
1,000 m	1:13.03	Nikolay Gulyayev (USSR)	1988
1,500 m	1:52.06	André Hoffman (East Germany)	1988
5,000 m	6:44.63	Tomas Gustafsson (Sweden)	1988
10,000 m	13:48.20	Tomas Gustafsson (Sweden)	1988
WOMEN			
500 m	39.10	Bonnie Blair (USA)	1988
1,000 m	1:17.65	Christa Rothenburger (East Germany)	1988
1,500 m	2:00.68	Yvonne van Gennip (Netherlands)	1988
3,000 m	4:11.94	Yvonne van Gennip (Netherlands)	1988
5,000 m	7:14.13	Yvonne van Gennip (Netherlands)	1988

Elvström (Denmark) in yachting, 1948–1960, 1968–72 and 1984–88; and Durward Randolph Knowles (Great Britain 1948, then Bahamas; b. 2 Nov 1917) in yachting, 1948–72 and 1988. Raimondo d'Inzeo (b. 8 Feb 1925) competed for Italy in equestrian events at a record eight celebrations from 1948–76, gaining one gold, two silver and three bronze medals. This was equaled by Paul Elvström and Durward Knowles in 1988. The longest span by a woman is 28 years by Anne Jessica Ransehousen (nee Newberry [USA]; b. 14 Oct 1938) in dressage, 1960, 1964 and 1988. Fencer Kerstin Palm (Sweden; b. 5 Feb 1946) competed in a women's record seven celebrations, 1964–88.

The US record for longest span of Olympic competition is 28 years, by fencer Norman Cudworth Armitage (ne Cohn, 1907–72), who competed in the six Games held between 1928 and 1956; he won a team bronze at saber in 1948. He was also selected for the Games of 1940, which were canceled. Four other Americans contested six games: Frank Davis Chapot (b. 24 Feb 1932), at show jumping 1956–76, winner of two team silver medals; Lt Col William Willard McMillan (b. 29 Jan 1929) at shooting, 1952–76, missing 1956, winning gold at rapid-fire pistol in 1960; Janice Lee York Romary (b. 6 Aug 1928), at fencing 1948–68; and John Michael Plumb (b. 28 Mar 1940) at three-day event, 1960–84, winner of a gold and four silver medals. Plumb was also named for the 1980 Games, which the US boycotted.

Most participants
The greatest number of competitors at a Summer Games celebration was 8,465 (6,279 men, 2,186 women), who represented a record 159 nations, at Seoul, South Korea in 1988. The greatest number at the Winter Games was 1,428 (1,113 men, 315 women) representing 57 countries, at Calgary, Canada in 1988.

■ **Most medals**
The most gold medals won at individual events at a single Olympic celebration is five by Eric Arthur Heiden (opposite page) (USA; b. 14 Jun 1958) when he won all the speed skating events at Lake Placid, NY in 1980. (Photo: All-Sport [USA]/Duffy)

Parachuting

Parachuting became a regulated sport with the institution of World Championships in 1951. A team title was introduced in 1954 and women's events were included in 1956.

Most titles *World* The USSR won the men's team title in 1954, 1958, 1960, 1966, 1972, 1976 and 1980, and the women's team title in 1956, 1958, 1966, 1968, 1972 and 1976. Nikolay Ushamyev (USSR) has won the individual title twice, 1974 and 1980.

Greatest accuracy At Yuma, AZ, in March 1978, Dwight Reynolds scored a record 105 daytime dead centers, and Bill Wenger and Phil Munden tied with 43 night-time dead centers, competing as members of the US Army Golden Knights. With electronic measuring, the official FAI record is 50 dead centers by Aleksandr Aasmiae (USSR) at Fergana, USSR in 1979 and by Linger Abdurakhmanov (USSR) at Fergana in 1988, when the women's record was set at 41 by Natalya Filinkova (USSR) in 1988.

The Men's Night Accuracy Landing record on an electronic score pad is 27 consecutive dead centers by Cliff Jones (USA) in 1981. Inessa Stepanova (USSR) had 21 at Fergana in 1988.

Parascending Andrew Wakelin (Great Britain) at Artesia Airport, NM on a Sorcerer 33 canopy on a 1,600 ft line on 1 Aug 1985 set records for distance: 23,950 ft, and height gain: 1,312 ft. The duration record is 21 min 8 sec by Pat Sugrue on a Paramount 9 in South Wales, Great Britain on 12 Apr 1986.

Nigel Horder scored four successive dead centers at the Dutch Open, Flevhof, Netherlands on 22 May 1983.

Pétanque

The origins of pétanque or boules can be traced back over 2,000 years, but it was not until 1945 that the *Fédération Française de Pétanque et Jeu Provençal* was formed, and subsequently the *Fédération Internationale* (FIPJP).

World Championships Winner of the most World Championships (instituted 1959) has been France, with ten titles to 1989. Women's World Championships were held in 1988 and 1990 and Thailand won on both occasions.

Polo

Origins Polo can be traced to origins in Manipur state, India *c.* 3100 B.C., when it was played as *sagol kangjei*. It is also claimed to be of Persian origin, having been played as *pulu c.* 525 B.C. The game was introduced to British officers at Cachar by the Manipur Maharaja, Sir Chandrakirti Singh, and the earliest club was the Cachar Club (founded in 1859) in Assam, India. The oldest club still in existence is the Calcutta Polo Club (1862).

The game was introduced into England from India in 1869 by the 10th Hussars at Aldershot, Great Britain, and the earliest match was one between the 9th Lancers and the 10th Hussars on Hounslow Heath, Great Britain in July 1871. The earliest international match between England and the USA was in 1886.

Polo was introduced to the United States by James Gordon Bennett in 1876, when he arranged for the first indoor game at Dickel's Riding Academy, NY. The first game played outdoors was held on 13 May 1876 at the Jerome Park Racetrack in Westchester County, NY. The oldest existing polo club in the United States is Meadow Brook Polo Club, Jericho, NY, founded in 1879. The United States Polo Association was formed on 20 Mar 1890. The United States Open Championship was inaugurated in 1904 and has been played continuously since then, with the exception of 1905–09, 1911, 1915, 1917–18 and 1942–45. The most wins is 28, by the Meadow Brook Polo Club, 1916, 1923–1941, 1946–51 and 1953.

World Championships The first World Championships were held in Berlin, Germany in 1989. The USA won the title, defeating Great Britain 7–6 in the final.

Highest handicap The highest handicap based on six 7½-min "chukkas" is ten goals introduced in the USA in 1891 and in Great Britain and in Argentina in 1910. A total of 55 players have received ten-goal handicaps.

A match of two 40-goal teams has been staged on three occasions—at Palermo, Buenos Aires, Argentina in 1975, in the USA in 1990, and in Australia in 1991.

Pool

Pool traces its ancestry to billiards, an English game introduced in Virginia in the late 17th century. During the 19th century the game evolved from a game in which a mace was used to push balls around the table, to a game of precise skill using a cue, with the aim of pocketing numbered balls. The original form of pool in the United States was known as pocket billiards, with the object being to pocket eight out of the 15 balls on the table. From this game evolved "61-pool"; each of the 15 balls was worth points equal to its numerical value, and the first player to score 61 points was the winner.

In 1878 the first world championship was staged under the rules of 61-pool. In 1910, Jerome Keogh suggested that the rules be adjusted to make the game faster and more attractive; he proposed that the last ball be left free on the table to be used as a target on the next rack; the result was 14.1 continuous pool (also known as American straight pool). This was adopted as the championship form of pool from 1912 onwards. In the last twenty years nine-ball pool and eight-ball pool have surpassed 14.1 in popularity. In 1990 the World Pool Billiard Authority inaugurated the nine-ball world championship.

14.1 CONTINUOUS POOL (AMERICAN STRAIGHT POOL) –

World Championship The two most dominant 14.1 players have been Ralph Greenleaf (USA; 1899–1950), who won the "world" professional title six times and defended it 13 times (1919–37), and William "Willie" Mosconi (USA; b. 27 Jun 1913), who dominated the game from 1941 to 1956, and also won the title six times and defended it 13 times.

Longest consecutive run The longest consecutive run in 14.1 recognized by the Billiard Congress of America (BCA) is 526 balls by Willie Mosconi in March 1954 during an exhibition in Springfield, OH. Michael Eufemia is reported to have pocketed 625 balls at Logan's Billiard Academy, Brooklyn, NY on 2 Feb 1960, but this run has never been ratified by the BCA.

Powerboat Racing

A gasoline engine was first installed in a boat by Jean Joseph Etienne Lenoir (1822–1900) on the River Seine, Paris, France in 1865. Actual powerboat racing started in about 1900, the first prominent race being from Calais, France to Dover, Great Britain in 1903. International racing was largely established by the presentation of a Challenge Trophy by Sir Alfred Harmsworth in 1903. Thereafter, racing developed mainly as a "circuit," or short, sheltered course type competition. Offshore or sea-passage races also developed, initially for displacement (non-planing) cruisers. Offshore events for fast (planing) cruisers began in 1958, with a 170-mile passage race from Miami, FL to Nassau, Bahamas. Outboard motor racing, i.e., the combined motor/transmission detachable propulsion unit type racing, began in the United States in about 1920. Both inboard and outboard motorboat engines are mainly gasoline fueled, but since 1950 diesel (compression ignition) engines have appeared and are widely used in offshore sport.

United States The American Power Boat Association (APBA) was founded on 22 Apr 1903 in New York City. In 1913 the APBA issued the "Racing Commission" rules, which created its powers for ruling the sport and sanctioning races in North America. In 1924 the APBA set rules for boats propelled by "Outboard Detachable Motors" and became the governing body for both inboard and outboard racing in North America.

APBA Gold Cup The American Power Boat Association (APBA) held its first Gold Cup race at the Columbia Yacht Club on the Hudson River, NY in 1904, when the winner was *Standard*, piloted by C.C. Riotto at an average speed of 23.6 mph. The most wins by a

■ **Powerboats**
Chip Hanauer with Miller American, *in which he won three of his record seven successive APBA Gold Cup races, 1982–88.*
(Photo: All-Sport [USA]/Levy)

pilot is eight by Bill Muncey, 1956–57, 1961–62, 1972, 1977–79. The most successful boat has been *Atlas Van Lines*, piloted by Muncey to victory in 1972, 1977–79 and by Chip Hanauer in 1982–84. Hanauer went on to complete a record seven successive victories to 1988.

Fastest speeds The fastest speed recorded by a propeller-driven boat is 229 mph, by *The Texan*, a Kurtis Top Fuel Hydro Drag boat, driven by Eddie Hill (USA) on 5 Sep 1982 at Chowchilla, CA. He also set a 440 yd elapsed time record of 5.16 sec in this boat at Firebird Lake, AZ on 13 Nov 1983. The official American Drag Boat Association record is 223.88 mph by *Final Effort*, a Blown Fuel Hydro boat driven by Robert T. Burns at Creve Coeur Lake, St Louis, MO on 15 Jul 1985 over a ¼ mile course.

The fastest speed recognized by the *Union Internationàle Motonautique* for an outboard-powered boat is in Class (e): 177.61 mph by P. R. Knight in a Chevrolet-engined Lautobach hull on Lake Ruataniwha, New Zealand in 1986. Robert F. Hering (USA) set the world Formula One record at 165.338 mph in *Second Effort* at Parker, AZ on 21 Apr 1986.

The fastest speed recognized for an offshore boat is 154.438 mph for one way and 148.238 mph for two runs on 8 Mar 1987 by Tom Gentry (USA), in his 49-ft catamaran *Gentry Turbo Eagle*, powered by four Gentry Turbo Eagle V8 Chevrolets on 8 Mar 1987.

The fastest speed recorded for a diesel (compression ignition) boat is 135.532 mph by the hydroplane *Iveco World Leader*, powered by an Aifo-Fiat engine, driven by Carlo Bonomi at Venice, Venice, Italy on 4 Apr 1985.

Fastest race speeds The fastest speed recorded in an offshore race is 103.29 mph, by Tony Garcia (USA) in a Class I powerboat at Key West, FL in Nov 1983.

Longest races The longest offshore race has been the Port Richborough London, Great Britain to Monte Carlo Marathon Offshore international event. The race extended over 2,947 miles in 14 stages from 10–25 Jun 1972. It was won by *H.T.S.* (Great Britain), driven by Mike Bellamy, Eddie Chater and Jim Brooker, in 71 hr 35 min 56 sec, for an average of 41.15 mph. The longest circuit race is the 24-hour race held annually since 1962 on the River Seine at Rouen, France.

Longest jetboat jumps The longest ramp jump achieved by a jetboat was 120 ft, by Peter Horak (USA) in a Glastron Carlson CVX 20 Jet Deluxe with a 460 Ford V8 engine (takeoff speed 55 mph), for a documentary TV film, at Salton Sea, CA on 26 Apr 1980. The longest leap onto land is 172 ft, by Norm Bagrie (New Zealand), from the Shotover River on 1 Jul 1982 in the 1½-ton jetboat *Valvolene*.

Projectiles

Throwing The longest independently authenticated throw of any inert object heavier than air is 1,257 ft, for a flying ring, by Scott Zimmerman on 8 Jul 1986 at Fort Funston, CA.

Greatest distances achieved with other miscellaneous objects:

Brick .... 146 ft 1 in
(standard 5-lb building brick)
Geoff Capes at Braybrook School, Orton, Great Britain on 19 Jul 1978.

Egg (fresh hen's) .... 317 ft 10 in
(without breaking it)
Risto Antikainen to Jyrki Korhonen at Siilinjarvi, Finland on 6 Sep 1981.

Rolling pin .... 175 ft 5 in
(2 lb)
Lori La Deane Adams, 21, at Iowa State Fair, IA on 21 Aug 1979.

Slingshot .... 1,434 ft 2 in
(51-in-long sling and a 2 oz stone)
Lawrence L. Bray at Loa, UT on 21 Aug 1981.

Rackets

There is a record of the sale of a racket court at Southernhay, Great Britain dated 12 Jan 1798. The game, which is of 17th-century origin, was played by debtors in the Fleet Prison, London, Great Britain in the middle of the 18th century, and an inmate, Robert Mackay, claimed the first "world" title in 1820. The first closed court champion was Francis Erwood at Woolwich, London, Great Britain in 1860.

World Championships Of the 22 world champions since 1820, the longest reign is by Geoffrey Willoughby Thomas Atkins (Great Britain; b. 20 Jan 1927), who held the title, after beating the professional James Dear (Great Britain; 1910–81) in 1954, until retiring, after defending it four times, in April 1972.

The first American to be world champion was Jock Souter, and he had the longest span as champion, 1913–28.

Racquetball

Racquetball, using a 40 ft x 20 ft court,

Boomerang throwing

The greatest number of consecutive two-handed catches is 801, by Stéphane Marguerite (France) on 26 Nov 1989 at Lyons, France.

The longest out-and-return distance is 440 ft 3 in by Jim Youngblood (USA) on 12 Jun 1989 at Gaithersburg, MD.

The longest flight duration (with self-catch) is one of 2 min 59.94 sec by Dennis Joyce (USA) at Bethlehem, PA on 25 Jun 1987.

John Flynn (USA) caught 70 boomerang throws in 5 min at Geneva, Switzerland on 20 Aug 1988.

The juggling record—the number of consecutive catches with two boomerangs, keeping at least one boomerang aloft at all times — is 136, also by John Flynn (USA) at Catskill, NY on 1 Sep 1990.

Cow chip tossing

The record distances in the country sport of throwing dried cow pats or "chips" depend on whether or not the projectile may be "molded into a spherical shape." The greatest distance achieved under the "non-sphericalization and 100 percent organic" rule (established in 1970) is 266 ft, by Steve Urner at the Mountain Festival, Tehachapi, CA on 14 Aug 1981.

The oldest of the surviving active real/royal tennis courts in Great Britain is the one at Falkland Palace, Fife, built by King James V of Scotland in 1539 and restored in the 1890s. The court at Falkland (bottom) is unique in that it has two instead of three penthouses and is the only court based on the jeu quarre *as opposed to the* jeu a dedans *court. The game is far more complex than lawn tennis, and as can be seen on the right, the racket is asymmetric.*

(Photo: All-Sport/J. Nicholson)

Flying disc throwing (formerly Frisbee)

The World Flying Disc Federation distance record is 623 ft 7 in, by Sam Ferrans (USA) on 2 Jul 1988 at La Habra, CA.

The throw, run and catch record is 303 ft 11 in, by Hiroshi Oshima (Japan) on 20 Jul 1988 at San Francisco, CA.

The 24-hour distance record for a pair is 362.4 miles, by Leonard Muise and Gabe Ontiveros (USA) on 21–22 Sep 1988 at Carson, CA.

The record for maximum time aloft is 16.72 sec, by Don Cain (USA) on 26 May 1984 at Philadelphia, PA.

was invented in 1950 by Joe Sobek at the Greenwich, CT YMCA. Sobek designed a "strung paddle racquet" and combined the rules of squash and handball to create the game of "paddle rackets." The International Racquetball Association (IRA) was founded in 1968 by Bob Kendler (USA), and renamed the American Amateur Racquetball Association (AARA) in 1979. The International Amateur Racquetball Federation (IARF) was founded in 1979 and staged its first world championships in 1981.

World Championships First held in 1981, the IARF world championships have been held biennially since 1984. The United States has won all five team titles, in 1981, 1984, 1986 (tie with Canada), 1988 and 1990. Egan Inoue (USA) has won the most men's singles titles with two, in 1986 and 1990. Two women have won the world singles championships twice: Cindy Baxter (USA) in 1981 and 1986; Heather Stupp (Canada) in 1988 and 1990.

US titles In 1968 championships were initiated by the AARA (the governing body for the sport in the United States). A record four men's open titles have been won by Ed Andrews of California, 1980–81 and 1985–86, and a record four women's open titles by Cindy Baxter of Pennsylvania, 1981, 1983, 1985–86.

Real/Royal Tennis

Origins The game originated as *jeu de paume* in French monasteries *c.* 1050. A tennis court is mentioned in the sale of the Hôtel de Nesle, Paris, France, bought by King Philippe IV of France in 1308. The oldest of the surviving active courts in Great Britain is the one at Falkland Palace, Fife, Scotland built by King James V of Scotland in 1539.

Most titles *World* The first recorded world tennis champion was Clerge (France), *c.* 1740. Jacques Edmond Barre (France; 1802–73) held the title for a record 33 yr from 1829 to 1862. Pierre Etchebaster (1893–1980), a Basque, holds the record for the greatest number of successful defenses of the title, with eight between 1928 and 1952.

The first two Women's World Championships in 1985 and 1987 were won by Judith Anne Clarke (Australia; b. 28 Dec 1954) .

United States Jay Gould, Jr. (1888 –1935) won his first US singles title in 1906, and retained the title until he retired from singles play in 1926. During his career he lost only one singles match. He also won 19 US doubles titles between 1909 and 1932.

Rodeo

Origins Rodeo, which developed from 18th-century *fiestas*, came into being in the early days of the North American cattle industry. The sport originated in

Mexico and spread from there into the cattle regions of the United States. Steer wrestling came in with Bill Pickett (1870–1932) of Texas in 1900, and a bronc-riding competition was held in Deer Trail, CO as early as 1869. There are many claims to the first paying rodeo spectators; The West of the Pecos Rodeo at Pecos, TX, first held in 1883, was the earliest documented, organized rodeo competition, and is now sanctioned by the Professional Rodeo Cowboys Association (PRCA), professional rodeo's largest organized association.

The largest rodeo in the world is the National Finals Rodeo, organized by the PRCA and Women's Professional Rodeo Association (WPRA). The top 15 money-earning cowboys in each of the six PRCA events and the top 15 WPRA barrel racers compete at the Finals. The event was first held at Dallas, TX in 1959, and was held at Oklahoma City, OK for 20 years before moving to Las Vegas, NV in 1985. The 1990 Finals had a paid attendance of 171,368 for ten performances. In 1989 a record $2.3 million in prize money was offered for the event, staged in Las Vegas.

Most world titles The record number of all-around titles (awarded to the leading money winner in a single season in two or more events) in the PRCA World Championships is six, by Larry Mahan (USA; b. 21 Nov 1943) in 1966–70 and 1973, and, consecutively, 1974–79 by Tom Ferguson (b. 20 Dec 1950). Jim Shoulders (b. 13 May 1928) of Henryetta, TX won a record 16 World Championships at four events between 1949 and 1959.

Earnings records Roy Cooper (b. 13 Nov 1955) holds the career earnings mark at $1,239,156 (1976–90). The single season record is $213,771 by Ty Murray in 1990. Lewis Feild (b. 28 Oct 1956) won a record $75,219 for one rodeo ($47,449 for saddle bronc-riding and $27,770 for bareback riding) at the 1987 National Finals Rodeo, Las Vegas, NV.

Youngest champions The youngest winner of a world title is Anne Lewis (b. 1 Sep 1958), who won the WPRA barrel racing title in 1968, at 10 years of age. Ty Murray (b. 11 Oct 1969) is the youngest cowboy to win the PRCA All-Around Champion title, at age 20, in 1989.

Time records Records for PRCA timed events, such as calf-roping and steer-wrestling, are not always comparable, because of the widely varying conditions due to the sizes of arenas and amount of start given the stock. The fastest time recorded for calf roping under the current PRCA rules is 6.7 sec by Joe Beaver (b. 13 Oct 1965) at West Jordan, UT in 1986, and the fastest time for steer wrestling is 2.4 sec by: James Bynum, at Marietta, OK in 1955; Carl Deaton at Tulsa, OK in 1976; and Gene Melton at Pecatonica, IL in 1976. The fastest team roping time is 3.7 sec, by Bob Harris and Tee Woolman at Spanish Fork, UT in 1986.

Bull riding Jim Sharp (b. 6 Oct 1965) of Kermit, TX became the first rider to ride all ten bulls at a National Finals Rodeo at Las Vegas in December 1988. This feat was matched by Norm Curry of Deberry, TX at the 1990 National Finals Rodeo.

The highest score in bull riding was 98 points out of a possible 100, by Denny Flynn on Red Lightning at Palestine, IL in 1979.

Saddle bronc-riding The highest scored saddle bronc ride is 95 out of a possible 100, by Doug Vold at Meadow Lake, Saskatchewan, Canada in 1979. Descent, a saddle bronc owned by Beutler Brothers and Cervi Rodeo Company, received a record six PRCA Saddle Bronc of the Year awards, 1966–69, 1971–72.

Bareback riding Joe Alexander of Cora, WY, scored 93 out of a possible 100 at Cheyenne, WY in 1974. Sippin' Velvet, owned by Bernis Johnson, has been awarded a record five PRCA Bareback Horse of the Year titles between 1978 and 1987.

Roller Skating

Origins The first roller skate was devised by Jean Joseph Merlin (1735–1803) of Huy, Belgium in 1760 and was demonstrated by him in London, Great Britain, but with disastrous results. James L. Plimpton of New York produced the present four-wheeled type and patented it in Jan 1863. The first indoor rink was opened in London, Great Britain in about 1824.

Most titles *Speed* The most world speed titles won is 18, by two women: Alberta Vianello (Italy), eight track and ten road 1953–65; and Annie Lambrechts (Belgium), one track and 17 road, 1964–81, at distances from 500 meters to 10,000 meters.

Figure The records for figure titles are: five by Karl Heinz Losch in 1958–59, 1961–62 and 1966; and four by Astrid Bader in 1965–68, both of West Germany. The most world pair titles is four by Dieter Fingerle (West Germany) in 1959, 1965–67, with two different partners, and by John Arishita and Tammy Jeru (USA) 1983–86.

Speed skating The fastest speed posted in an official world record is 26.85 mph, when Luca Antoniel (Italy; b. 12 Feb 1968) recorded 24.99 sec for 300 meters on a road at Gujan Mestras, France on 31 Jul 1987. The women's record is 25.04 mph by Marisa Canafoglia (Italy; b. 30 Sep 1965) for 300 meters on the road at Grenoble, France on 27 Aug 1987. The world records for 10,000 meters on a road or track are: *(men)* 14 min 55.64 sec, Giuseppe de Persio (Italy; b. 3 Jun 1959) at Gujan Mestras, France on 1 Aug 1988; *(women)* 15 min 58.022 sec, Marisa Canafogilia (Italy) at Grenoble, France on 30 Aug 1987.

Largest rink The largest indoor rink ever to operate was located in the Grand Hall, London, Great Britain. Opened in 1890 and closed in 1912, it had an actual skating area of 68,000 ft². The current largest is the main arena of 34,981 ft² at Guptill Roll-Arena, Boght Corner, NY. The total rink area is 41,380 ft².

Endurance Theodore James Coombs (b. 1954) of Hermosa Beach, CA skated 5,193 miles from Los Angeles, CA to New York and back as far as Yates Center, KS from 30 May to 14 Sep 1979.

Rowing

Origins The Sphinx Stela of Amenhotep (Amonophis) II (1450–1425 B.C.) records that he *stroked* a boat for some three miles. The earliest established sculling race is the Doggett's Coat and Badge, which was first rowed on 1 Aug 1716 from London Bridge to Chelsea as a race for apprentices, and is still contested annually. Although rowing regattas were held in Venice in 1300, the first English regatta probably took place on the river Thames, London, Great Britain by the Ranelagh Gardens, near Putney in 1775.

The first organized boat races in the United States were reported to be races staged between New York City boatsmen in New York harbor in the late 18th century. The first rowing club formed in the United States was the Castle Garden Amateur Boat Club Association, New York City in 1834. The oldest active club is the Detroit Boat Club, founded in 1839. The first and oldest collegiate boat club was formed at Yale University in 1843. The National Association of Amateur Oarsmen (NAAO) was formed in 1872 and merged with the National Women's Rowing Association in 1982 to form the United States Rowing Association.

Most Olympic medals Six oarsmen have won three gold medals: John Brendan Kelly (USA; 1889–1960), father of the late Princess Grace of Monaco, who won bronze at Single Sculls (1920) and Double Sculls (1920 and 1924); his son, John Brendan Kelly, Jr. (b. 24 May 1927), who won bronze at Single Sculls in 1956; his cousin, Paul Vincent Costello (USA; b. 27 Dec 1894), Double Sculls (1920, 1924 and 1928); Jack Beresford, Jr. (Great Britain; 1899–1977), Single Sculls (1924), Coxless Fours (1932) and Double Sculls (1936); Vyacheslav Nikolayevich Ivanov (USSR; b. 30 Jul 1938), Single Sculls (1956, 1960 and 1964); Siegfried Brietzke (East Germany; b. 12 Jun 1952), Coxless Pairs (1972) and Coxless Fours (1976, 1980); and Pertti Karppinen (Finland; b. 17 Feb 1953), Single Sculls (1976, 1980 and 1984).

World Championships World rowing championships distinct from the Olympic Games were first held in 1962, four times a year at first, but from 1974 annually, except in Olympic years.

The most gold medals won at World

Championships and Olympic Games is eight, at coxed pairs by the Italian brothers Giuseppe (b. 24 Jul 1959) and Carmine (b. 5 Jan 1962) Abbagnale, World 1981–82, 1985, 1987, 1989–90, Olympics 1984 and 1988. At women's events Jutta Behrendt (nee Hahn [East Germany]; b. 15 Nov 1960) has won a record six golds.

The most wins at Single Sculls is five, by Peter-Michael Kolbe (West Germany; b. 2 Aug 1953), 1975, 1978, 1981, 1983 and 1986; and by Pertti Karppinen, 1979 and 1985, and with his three Olympic wins (above); and in the women's events by Christine Hahn (nee Scheiblich [East Germany]; b. 31 Dec 1954), 1974–75, 1977–78 (and the 1976 Olympic title).

Collegiate Championships The first intercollegiate boat race in the United States was between Harvard and Yale in 1852. The Intercollegiate Rowing Association (IRA) was formed in 1895, and in 1898 inaugurated the Varsity Challenge Cup, which was recognized as the national championship. In 1982, the United States Rowing Assocation introduced the National Collegiate Championships, and this race now decides the national champion. Overall, Cornell University has won the most national championships, with 25 titles (all Varsity Cup wins). Since 1982, Harvard University has won 5 titles (1983, 1985, 1987–89).

The women's national championship was inaugurated in 1979. The University of Washington has won a record seven times (1981–85, 1987–88).

British University Boat Race The earliest University Boat Race, between Oxford University and Cambridge University, was from Hambledon Lock, to Henley Bridge, Great Britain, on 10 Jun 1829. Outrigged eights were first used in 1846. In the 137 races to 1991, Cambridge won 69 times, Oxford 67 times, and there was a dead heat on 24 Mar 1877.

Henley Royal Regatta The annual regatta at Henley-on-Thames, Great Britain was inaugurated on 26 Mar 1839. Since then the course, except in 1923, has been about 1 mile 550 yd, varying slightly according to the length of the boat. In 1967 the shorter craft were "drawn up" so all bows start level.

The most wins in the Diamond Challenge Sculls (instituted 1844) is six consecutively, by Stuart A. Mackenzie (Australia and Great Britain; b. 5 Apr 1937), 1957–62. The record time is 7 min 23 sec, by Vaclav Chalupa (Czechoslovakia; b. 7 Dec 1967) on 2 Jul 1989. The record time for the Grand Challenge Cup (instituted 1839) event is 5 min 58 sec, by Hansa Dortmund, West Germany on 2 Jul 1989.

Fastest speed The highest recorded speed on non-tidal water for 2,187 yd is by an American eight in 5 min 27.14 sec (13.68 mph) at Lucerne, Switzerland on 17 Jun 1984. A crew from Penn AC was timed in 5 min 18.8 sec (14.03 mph) in the FISA Championships on the River Meuse, Liège, Belgium on 17 Aug 1930.

Twenty-four hours The greatest distance rowed in 24 hours (upstream and downstream) by an eight is 130 miles, by members of the Renmark Rowing Club, South Australia on 20–21 Apr 1984.

Longest race The longest annual rowing race is the annual Tour du Lac Leman, Geneva, Switzerland for coxed fours (the five-man crew taking turns as cox) over 99 miles. The record winning time is 12 hr 52 min, by LAGA Delft, Netherlands on 3 Oct 1982.

International Dragon Boat Race Instituted in 1975 and held annually in Hong Kong, the fastest time achieved for the 700 yd course is 2 min 27.45 sec, by the Chinese Shun De team on 30 Jan 1985. Teams have 28 members—26 rowers, one steersman and one drummer.

Rugby

Records are determined in terms of present-day scoring values, i.e., a try at 4 points; a dropped goal, penalty or goal from a mark at 3 points; and a conversion at 2 points. The *actual* score, in accordance with whichever of the eight earlier systems was in force at the time, is also given, in parentheses.

Although there are records of a game with many similarities to rugby dating back to the Roman occupation of Britain, the game is traditionally said to have originated from a breach of the rules of soccer by William Webb Ellis (later the Rev.; *c.* 1807–72) in a match played at Rugby School in November 1823. This handling style of soccer evolved gradually and was known to have been played at Cambridge University, Great Britain in 1839. The Rugby Football Union was founded on 26 Jan 1871. The International Rugby Football Board (IRFB) was founded in 1886.

In competitions held at four Olympic Games from 1900 to 1924, the only double gold medalist was the United States, which won in 1920 and 1924, defeating France in the final on both occasions.

MOST INTERNATIONAL APPEARANCES IN RUGBY

FRANCE	85	Serge Blanco (b. 31 Aug 1958)	1980–91
IRELAND	69	Cameron Michael Henderson Gibson (b. 3 Dec 1942)	1964–79
NEW ZEALAND	55	Colin Earl Meads (b. 3 Jun 1936)	1957–71
WALES	55*	John Peter Rhys "JPR" Williams (b. 2 Mar 1949)	1969–81
AUSTRALIA	54	David Ian Campese (b. 21 Oct 1962)	1982–90
SCOTLAND	52	James Menzies "Jim" Renwick (b. 12 Feb 1952)	1972–84
	52	Colin Thomas Deans (b. 3 May 1955)	1978–87
ENGLAND	43	Anthony Neary (b. 25 Nov 1948)	1971–80
	43	Rory Underwood (b. 19 Jun 1963)	1984–91
SOUTH AFRICA	38	Frederick Christoffel Hendrick Du Preez (b. 28 Nov 1935)	1960–71
	38	Jan Hendrik Ellis (b. 5 Jan 1943)	1965–76

* Gareth Owen Edwards (b. 12 Jul 1947) made a record 53 consecutive international appearances, never missing a match throughout his career for Wales, 1967–78. Willie John McBride also had 53 consecutive appearances during his 63 games for Ireland.
Note: The criteria used to decide which games are classed as full internationals vary between countries.

WORLD CUP

The inaugural World Cup was contested in Australia and New Zealand by 16 national teams in 1987. The final in Auckland, New Zealand on 20 Jun 1987 was won by New Zealand, which beat France 29–9. The highest team score was New Zealand's 74–13 victory over Fiji at Christchurch, New Zealand on 27 May 1987. New Zealand scored 10 goals, 2 tries and 2 penalty goals. The individual match record was 30 (3 tries, 9 conversions), by Didier Camberabero (France; b. 9 Jan 1961) v Zimbabwe at Auckland on 2 Jun 1987. The leading scorer in the tournament was the New Zealand goal-kicker, Grant James Fox (b. 6 Jun 1962), with 126 points.

HIGHEST TEAM SCORES

Internationals The highest score in any full international was when New Zealand beat Japan by 106–4 at Tokyo, Japan on 1 Nov 1987. France beat Paraguay 106–12 at Asuncion, Paraguay on 28 Jun 1988.

HIGHEST INDIVIDUAL SCORES

Internationals Phil Bennett (Wales; b. 24 Oct 1948) scored 34 points (2 tries, 10 conversions, 2 penalty goals) for Wales v. Japan at Tokyo on 24 Sep 1975, when Wales won 82–6.

In all internationals, Michael Patrick Lynagh (b. 25 Oct 1963) scored a record 564 points in 43 matches for Australia, 1984–90.

Seven-a-sides Seven-a-side rugby dates from 28 Apr 1883, when Melrose RFC Borders (Scotland), in order to compensate for the poverty of a club in such a small town, staged a seven-a-side tournament. The idea was that of Ned Haig, the town's butcher.

Hong Kong Sevens This, the world's most prestigious international tournament for seven-a-side teams, was first held in 1976. The record of six wins is held by Fiji, 1977–78, 1980, 1984, 1990–91.

Shooting

The Lucerne Shooting Guild (Switzerland) was formed c. 1466 and the first recorded shooting match was at Zurich in 1472.

Most Olympic medals Carl Townsend Osburn (USA; 1884–1966) won 11 medals, in 1912, 1920 and 1924—five gold, four silver and two bronze. Six other marksmen have won five gold medals. Gudbrand Gudbrandsönn Skatteboe (Norway; 1875–1965) is the only marksman to win three individual gold medals, in 1906. Separate events for women were first held in 1984.

Six other marksmen have won five gold medals, including three Americans: Alfred P. Lane (b. 26 Sep 1891), 1912–20; Willis Augustus Lee, Jr. (1888–94), all in 1920; and Morris Fisher (1890–1968), 1920–24. In 1920 a record seven medals were won by both Willis Lee, who also won a silver and bronze, and Lloyd S. Spooner—four gold, a silver and two bronze.

The first US woman to win an Olympic medal was Margaret L. Murdock (nee Thompson; b. 25 Aug 1942), who took the silver at small-bore rifle (three positions) in mixed competition in 1976. The first to win an Olympic gold medal was Patricia Spurgin (b. 10 Aug 1965), at women's air rifle in 1984.

World record The first world record by a woman at any sport for a category in direct and measurable competition with men was by Margaret Murdock, who set a world record for small-bore rifle (kneeling position) of 391 in 1967.

Clay pigeon The most world titles have been won by Susan Nattrass

Bench rest shooting
The smallest area on record into which a group of shots have been fired at 1,000 yd is 4.375 in by Earl Chronister with a .30–378 Weatherby Mag at Williamsport, PA on 12 Jul 1987.

SHOOTING–INDIVIDUAL WORLD RECORDS

In 1986, the International Shooting Union (UIT) introduced new regulations for determining major championships and world records. Now the leading competitors undertake an additional round with a target subdivided to tenths of a point for rifle and pistol shooting, and an extra 25 shots for trap and skeet. Harder targets have since been introduced and the table below shows the world records, as recognized by the UIT on 1 Jan 1991, for the 13 Olympic shooting disciplines, giving in brackets the score for the number of shots specified plus the score in the additional round.

MEN

FREE RIFLE 50 m 3 × 40 shots	1,276.7	(1,179 + 97.7)	Rajmond Debevec (Yugoslavia)	Zürich, Switzerland	5 Jun 1990
FREE RIFLE 50 m 60 shots prone	702.9	(599 + 103.8)	Vari Zsolt (Hungary)	Munich, Germany	2 Jun 1990
AIR RIFLE 10 m 60 shots	699.4	(596 + 103.4)	Rajmond Debevec (Yugoslavia)	Zürich, Switzerland	8 Jun 1990
FREE PISTOL 50 m 60 shots	671	(579 + 92)	Sergey Pyzhyanov (USSR)	Munich, Germany	31 May 1990
	671	(577 + 94)	Spas Koprinkov (Bulgaria)	Moscow, USSR	9 Aug 1990
RAPID-FIRE PISTOL 25 m 60 shots	891	(594 + 297)	Ralf Schumann (West Germany)	Munich, Germany	3 Jun 1989
AIR PISTOL 10 m 60 shots	695.1	(593 + 102.1)	Sergey Pyzhyanov (USSR)	Munich, Germany	Oct 1989
RUNNING GAME TARGET 50 m 30 + 30 shots	678	(582 + 96)	Jan Kermiet (Czechoslovakia)	Munich, Germany	12 Oct 1990

WOMEN

STANDARD RIFLE 50 m 3 × 20 shots	684.4	(589 + 95.4)	Vessela Letcheva (Bulgaria)	Munich, Germany	1 Jun 1990
AIR RIFLE 10 m 40 shots	499.4	(397 + 102.4)	Valentina Cherkasova (USSR)	Suhl, Germany	30 May 1987
SPORT PISTOL 25 m 60 shots	693	(593 + 100)	Nino Salukvadse (USSR)	Zagreb, Yugoslavia	13 Jul 1989
AIR PISTOL 10 m 40 shots	492.4	(392 + 100.4)	Lieslotte Breker (West Germany)	Zagreb, Yugoslavia	18 May 1989

OPEN

TRAP 200 targets	224	(199 + 25)	Miloslav Bednarik (Czechoslovakia)	Suhl, Germany	14 Sep 1986
SKEET 200 targets	223	(198 + 25)	Valeriy Timokhin (USSR)	Tampere, Finland	15 Jun 1989
	223	(199 + 24)	Bruno Rosetti (Italy)	Zagreb, Yugoslavia	15 Jul 1989
	223	(199 + 24)	Ennio Falco (Italy)	Bologna, Italy	19 May 1990
	223	(198 + 25)	Ole Justesen (Denmark)	Suhl, Germany	27 May 1990

Snowshoeing
The United States Snowshoeing Association (USSA) record for covering 1 mile is 5 min 56.7 sec by Nick Akers of Edmonton, Alberta, Canada on 3 Feb 1991.

The 100 m record is 15.06 sec by Scott Hannay of Westerlo, NY on 25 Feb 1989.

Highest altitude
Jean Afanassieff and Nicolas Jaeger skied from 26,900 ft to 20,340 ft on the 1978 French expedition on Mt Everest.

Longest ski lift
The longest gondola ski lift is 3.88 miles long, at Grindelwald-Männlichen, Switzerland (in two sections, but one gondola). The longest chair lift in the world was the Alpine Way to Kosciusko Chalet lift above Thredbo, near the Snowy Mountains, New South Wales, Australia. It took from 45 to 75 min to ascend the 3.5 miles, depending on the weather. The chair lift has now collapsed. The highest is at Chacaltaya, Bolivia, rising to 16,500 ft.

(Canada; b. 5 Nov 1950) with six, 1974–75, 1977–79, 1981. The record number of clay birds shot in an hour is 3,172, by Dan Carlisle (USA) at Norco, CA on 20 May 1990.

The maximum 200/200 was achieved by Ricardo Ruiz Rumoroso at the Spanish Clay Pigeon Championships at Zaragossa on 12 Jun 1983.

Noel D. Townend achieved the maximum 200 consecutive down-the-line targets at Nottingham, Great Britain on 21 Aug 1983.

Highest score in 24 hours The Easingwold Rifle and Pistol Club (Yorkshire, Great Britain) team of John Smith, Edward Kendall, Phillip Kendall and Paul Duffield scored 120,242 points (averaging 95.66 per card) on 6–7 Aug 1983.

Skiing

The most ancient ski in existence was found well preserved in a peat bog at Hoting, Sweden, dating from c. 2500 B.C. The earliest recorded military use of skiing was at the Battle of Isen, near Oslo, Norway in 1200. The Trysil Shooting and Skiing Club, founded in Norway in 1861, claims it is the world's oldest. The oldest ski competitions are the Holmenkollen Nordic events, which were first held in 1866. The first downhill races were staged in Australia in the 1850s. The International Ski Federation (FIS) was founded on 2 Feb 1924, succeeding the International Skiing Commission, founded at Christiania (Oslo), Norway on 18 Feb 1910.

The first ski club in the United States was formed at Berlin, NH in January 1872, and later became known as the Nansen Ski Club. The US Ski Association was originally founded as the National Ski Association in 1905. In 1962 it was renamed the USA Ski Association, and was renamed US Skiing in May 1990.

Most titles *World/Olympic Championships—Alpine* The World Alpine

Championships were inaugurated at Mürren, Switzerland in 1931. The greatest number of titles won has been by Christel Cranz (b. 1 Jul 1914) of Germany, with seven individual—four slalom (1934, 1937–39) and three downhill (1935, 1937, 1939), and five combined (1934–35, 1937–39). She also won the gold medal for the combined in the 1936 Olympics. The most won by a man is seven, by Anton "Toni" Sailer (Austria; b. 17 Nov 1935), who won all four in 1956 (giant slalom, slalom, downhill and the non-Olympic Alpine combination) and the downhill, giant slalom and combined in 1958.

The only US skier to win two Olympic gold medals has been Andrea Mead-Lawrence (b. 19 Apr 1932), at slalom and giant slalom in 1952.

World/Olympic Championships—Nordic The first World Nordic Championships were those of the 1924 Winter Olympics in Chamonix, France. The greatest number of titles won is 11, by Gunde Svan (Sweden; b. 12 Jan 1962), seven individual—15 km 1989, 30km 1985 and 1991, 50 km 1985 and 1989, and Olympics, 15 km 1984, 50 km 1988; and four relays—4 × 10 km, 1987 and 1989, and Olympics, 1984 and 1988. The most titles won by a woman is nine, by Galina Alekseyevna Kulakova (USSR; b. 29 Apr 1942), in 1970–78. The most medals is 22, by Raisa Petrovna Smetanina (USSR; b. 29 Feb 1952), including six gold, 1974–91. Johann Grøttumsbraaten (1899–1942) of Norway also won six individual titles (two 18 km cross-country, four Nordic combined) in 1926–32. Ulrich Wehling (East Gremany) has also won four Nordic combined, winning the World Championship in 1974 and the Olympic title, 1972, 1976 and 1980—the first skier to win the same event at three successive Olympics. The record for a jumper is five, by Birger Ruud (b. 23 Aug 1911) of Norway, in 1931–32 and 1935–37. Ruud is the only person to win Olympic events in each of the dissimilar Alpine and Nordic disciplines. In 1936 he won the ski-jumping and the Alpine downhill (which was not then a separate event, but only a segment of the combined event).

World Cup The World Cup was introduced for Alpine events in 1967 and for

---

MOST WORLD CUP TITLES
ALPINE
MEN

OVERALL	4	Gustavo Thoeni (Italy)	1971–73, 1975
	4	Pirmin Zurbriggen (Switzerland)	1984, 1987–88, 1990
	4	Marc Giradelli (Luxembourg)	1985–86, 1989, 1991
DOWNHILL	5	Franz Klammer (Austria)	1975–78, 1983
SLALOM	8	Ingemar Stenmark (Sweden)	1975–81, 1983
GIANT SLALOM	7	Ingemar Stenmark	1975–76, 1978–81, 1984
SUPER GIANT SLALOM	4	Pirmin Zurbriggen	1987–90

Two men have won four titles in one year: Jean-Claude Killy (France; b. 30 Aug 1943) won all four possible disciplines (downhill, slalom, giant slalom and overall) in 1967; and Pirmin Zurbriggen (Switzerland; b. 4 Feb 1963) won four of the five possible disciplines (downhill, giant slalom, Super giant slalom [added 1986] and overall) in 1987.

WOMEN

OVERALL	6	Annemarie Moser (Austria)	1971–75, 1979
DOWNHILL	7	Annemarie Moser	1971–75, 1978–79
SLALOM	4	Erika Hess (Switzerland)	1981–83, 1985
GIANT SLALOM	4	Vreni Schneider (Switzerland)	1986, 1987 (tie), 1989, 1991
SUPER GIANT SLALOM	3	Carole Merle (France)	1989–91

NORDIC
MEN

JUMPING	4	Matti Nykänen (Finland)	1983, 1985–86, 1988
CROSS-COUNTRY	5	Gunde Svan (Sweden)	1984–86, 1988–89

WOMEN

CROSS-COUNTRY	3	Marjo Matikainen (Finland)	1986–88

MOST OLYMPIC SKIING TITLES
MEN

ALPINE	3	Anton "Toni" Sailer (Austria; b. 17 Nov 1935)	Downhill, slalom, giant slalom, 1956
	3	Jean-Claude Killy (France; b. 30 Aug 1943)	Downhill, slalom, giant slalom 1968
NORDIC	4[1]	Sixten Jernberg (Sweden; b. 6 Feb 1929)	50 km 1956; 30 km 1960; 50 km and 4 ×10 km 1964
	4	Gunde Svan (Sweden; b. 12 Mar 1962)	15 km and 4 × 10 km 1984; 50 km and 4 × 10 km 1988
	4	Thomas Wassberg (Sweden; b. 27 Mar 1956)	15 km 1980; 50 km 1984; 4 × 10 km 1984, 1988
Ski-jumping	4	Matti Nykänen (Finland; b. 17 Jul 1963)	70 m hill 1988; 90 m hill 1984, 1988; team 1988

WOMEN

ALPINE	2	Andrea Mead-Lawrence (USA; b. 19 Apr 1932)	Slalom, giant slalom 1952
	2	Marielle Goitschel (France; b. 28 Sep 1945)	Giant slalom 1964; slalom 1968
	2	Marie-Thérèse Nadig (Switzerland; b. 8 Mar 1954)	Downhill, giant slalom 1972
	2	Rosi Mittermaier (now Neureuther [West Germany]; b. 5 Aug 1950)	Downhill, slalom 1976
	2[2]	Hanni Wenzel (Liechtenstein; b. 14 Dec 1956)	Giant slalom, slalom 1980
	2	Vreni Schneider (Switzerland; b. 26 Nov 1964)	Giant slalom 1988
NORDIC (individual)	4	Galina Kulakova (USSR; b. 29 Apr 1942)	5 km, 10 km and 3 ×5 km relay 1972; 4 ×5 km relay 1976
	3	Marja-Liisa Hämäläinen (Finland; b. 10 Aug 1955)	5 km, 10 km and 20 km 1984

[1] **Most medals** 9, Sixten Jernberg, four golds, three silver and two bronze.
  9, Raisa Smetanina, three gold, five silver and one bronze at women's Nordic skiing 1976–88.
[2] *Wenzel won a silver in the 1980 downhill and a bronze in the 1976 slalom for a record four medals in Alpine skiing.*

Nordic events in 1981. The most individual event wins is 86 (46 giant slalom, 40 slalom from a total of 287 races) by Ingemar Stenmark (Sweden; b. 18 Mar 1956) in 1974–89, including a men's record 13 in one season in 1978/79, of which 10 were part of a record 14 successive giant slalom wins from 18 Mar 1978, his 22nd birthday, to 21 Jan 1980. Franz Klammer (Austria; b. 3 Dec 1953) won a record 25 downhill races, 1974–84. Annemarie Moser (nee Pröll [Austria]; b. 27 Mar 1953) won a women's record 62 individual event wins, 1970–79. She had a record 11 consecutive downhill wins from Dec 1972 to Jan 1974. Vreni Schneider (Switzerland; b. 26 Nov 1964). won a record 13 events and a combined including all seven slalom events in 1988/89.

The Nation's Cup, awarded on the combined results of the men and women in the World Cup, has been won a record 13 times by Austria—1969, 1973–82, 1990–91.

United States The most successful US skier has been Phillip Ferdinand Mahre (b. 10 May 1957), winner of the overall title three times, 1981–83, with two wins at giant slalom, and one at slalom. The most successful US woman has been Tamara McKinney (b. 16 Oct 1962), overall winner 1983, giant slalom 1981 and 1983, and slalom 1984.

The only American to win a Nordic skiing World Cup title has been William Koch (b. 7 Jun 1955), at cross-country in 1982.

Ski-jumping The longest ski-jump ever recorded is one of 636 ft, by Piotr Fijas (Poland) at Planica, Yugoslavia on 14 Mar 1987. The women's record is 361 ft, by Tiina Lehtola (Finland; b. 3 Aug 1962), at Ruka, Finland on 29 Mar 1981. The longest dry ski-jump is 302 ft, by Hubert Schwarz (West Germany) at Berchtesgarten, Germany on 30 Jun 1981.

Fastest speed The official world record, as recognized by the International Ski Federation for a skier, is 139.030 mph, by Michael Prufer (Monaco), and the fastest by a woman is 133.234 mph, by Tarja Mulari (Finland), both at Les Arcs, France on 16 Apr 1988. On the same occasion, Patrick Knaff (France) set a one-legged record of 115.309 mph.

The fastest average speed in the Olympic downhill race was 64.95 mph, by William D. Johnson (USA; b. 30 Mar 1960), at Sarajevo, Yugoslavia on 16 Feb 1984. The fastest in a World Cup downhill is 67.00 mph, by Harti Weirather (Austria; b. 25 Jan 1958), at Kitzbühel, Austria on 15 Jan 1982.

Fastest speed—cross-country Bill Koch (USA; b. 13 Apr 1943), on 26 Mar 1981 skied ten times around a 3.11 mile loop on Marlborough Pond, near Putney, VT. He completed the 50 km (31.07 mile) course in 1 hr 59 min 47 sec, an average speed of 15.57 mph. A race includes uphill and downhill sections; the record time for a race in World Championships or Olympic Games is

2 hr 3 min 31.6 sec, by Torgny Mogren (Sweden) in 1991, an average speed of 15.09 mph.

Closest verdict The narrowest winning margin in a championship ski race was one-hundredth of a second by Thomas Wassberg (Sweden) over Juha Mieto (Finland; b. 20 Nov 1949), in the Olympic 15-km cross-country race at Lake Placid, NY on 17 Feb 1980. His winning time was 41 min 57.63 sec.

Most competitors A total of 1,700 downhill skiers competed at Åre, Jämtland, Sweden on 30 Apr 1984.

Longest races The world's longest Nordic ski race is the Vasaloppet, which commemorates an event of 1521 when Gustav Vasa (1496–1560), later King Gustavus Eriksson, fled 53.3 miles from Mora to Sälen, Sweden. He was overtaken by loyal, speedy scouts on skis, who persuaded him to return eastwards to Mora to lead a rebellion and become the king of Sweden. The re-enactment of this return journey is now an annual event at 55.3 miles. There were a record 10,934 starters on 6 Mar 1977 and a record 10,633 finishers on 4 Mar 1979. The fastest time is 3 hr 48 min 55 sec, by Bengt Hassis (Sweden) on 2 Mar 1986.

The Finlandia Ski Race, 46.6 miles from Hämeenlinna to Lahti, on 26 Feb 1984, had a record 13,226 starters and 12,909 finishers.

The longest downhill race is the Inferno in Switzerland, 9.8 miles from the top of the Schilthorn to Lauterbrunnen. The record number of entries is 1,401 in 1981, and the record time was 15 min 26.44 sec, by Ueli Grossniklaus (Switzerland) in 1987.

Long-distance (Nordic) In 24 hours

Seppo-Juhani Savolainen covered 258.2 miles at Saariselkä, Finland on 8–9 Apr 1988. The women's 24 hr record is 205.05 miles, by Sisko Kainulaisen at Jyväskylä, Finland on 23–24 Mar 1985.

In 48 hours Bjørn Løkken (Norway; b. 27 Nov 1937) covered 319 miles 205 yd on 11–13 Mar 1982.

Ski-bob Origins The ski-bob was the invention of J. C. Stevenson of Hartford, CT in 1891, and patented (No. 47334) on 19 Apr 1892 as a "bicycle with ski-runners." The *Fédération Internationàle de Skibob* was founded on 14 Jan 1961 in Innsbruck, Austria, and the first World Championships were held at Bad Hofgastein, Austria in 1967.

The fastest speed attained is 103.4 mph, by Erich Brenter (Austria; b. 1940), at Cervinia, Italy in 1964.

World Championships The only ski-bobbers to retain a world championship are: (men) Alois Fischbauer (Austria; b. 6 Oct 1951), 1973 and 1975; Robert Mühlberger (West Germany), 1979 and 1981; (women) Gerhilde Schiffkorn (Austria; b. 22 Mar 1950), 1967 and 1969; Gertrude Geberth (Austria; b. 18 Oct 1951), 1971 and 1973.

Skipping Rope

Ten mile skip-run Vadivelu Karunakaren (India) skipped rope ten miles in 58 min at Madras, India, 1 Feb 1990.

Most turns Ten sec 128, by Albert Rayner (Great Britain; b. 19 Apr 1923), Stanford Sports, Birmingham, Great Britain, 19 Nov 1982.

One min 425, by Robert Commers (USA;

■ **All disciplines**
With a victory in a super-giant slalom event on 9 Dec 1990, Petra Kronberger (Austria) became the first woman to win World Cup races at all four disciplines. She is pictured at the World Championships at Saalbach, Austria in January 1991, when she won the downhill gold medal.

(Photo: All-Sport/Bob Martin)

Freestyle skiing
The first World Championships were held at Tignes, France in 1986, titles being awarded in ballet, moguls, aerials and combined. A record two titles have been won by Lloyd Langlois (Canada), aerials, 1986 and 1989; Jan Buchner (USA), ballet, 1986 and 1989; and Edgar Grospiron (France), moguls, 1989 and 1991. The three separate disciplines were included in the 1988 Olympics but only as demonstration events. Moguls will be contested with full status at the 1992 Olympics.

Longest ski run

The longest all-downhill ski run in the world is the Weissfluhjoch-Küblis Parsenn course, near Davos, Switzerland, which measures 7.6 miles. The run from the Aiguille du Midi top of the Chamonix lift (vertical lift 9,052 ft) across the Vallée Blanche is 13 miles.

Steepest descent

The steepest descents in Alpine skiing history have been by Sylvain Saudan. At the start of his descent from Mont Blanc on the northeast side down the Couloir Gervasutti from 13,937 ft, on 17 Oct 1967, he skied to gradients of *c.* 60°.

Grass skiing

Grass skis were first manufactured by Josef Kaiser (Germany) in 1963. World Championships (now awarded for Super G, giant slalom, slalom and combined) were first held in 1979. The most titles won is ten, by Ingrid Hirschhofer (Austria) 1979–89. The most by a man is seven, by Erwin Gansner (Switzerland) 1981–87.

The speed record is 53.99 mph by Erwin Gansner at Owen, Germany on 5 Sep 1982.

b. 15 May 1950) at The Holiday Inn, Jamestown, NY, 23 Feb 1990.

One hour 14,628, by Park Bong Tae (South Korea) at Pusan, South Korea, 2 Jul 1989. Robert Commers holds the US record, with 13,783, at Woodbridge, NJ, 13 May 1989.

On a single rope, team of 90 160, by students from the Nishigoshi Higashi Elementary School, Kumamoto, Japan, 27 Feb 1987.

On a tightrope 358 (consecutive), by Julian Albulet (USA) at Las Vegas, NV, 2 Jul 1990.

Most consecutive multiple turns
Double 10,709, by Frank Oliveri (USA) at Rochester, NY, 7 May 1988.

Double (with cross) 2,411, by Ken Solis (USA) at North Shore-Elite Fitness and Racquets Club, Glendale, WI, 29 Mar 1988.

Triple 423, by Shozo Hamada (Japan) at Saitama, Japan, 1 Jun 1987.

Quadruple 51, by Katsumi Suzuki (Japan) at Saitama, Japan, 29 May 1975.

Quintuple 6, by Hideyuki Tateda (Japan; b. 1968) at Aomori, Japan, 19 Jun 1982.

Most on a rope (minimum 12 turns obligatory) 220, by a team at the International Rope Skipping Competition, Greeley, CO, 28 Jun 1990.

Snooker

Origins Research shows that snooker was originated by Colonel Sir Neville Francis Fitzgerald Chamberlain (1856–1944) as a hybrid of pool and pyramids, in Jubbulpore, India in 1875. Chamberlain added a set of colored balls to the 15 red ones used in pyramids and devised a scoring system based on pocketing the balls in sequence: red, color, red, color until all the reds have been cleared, leaving the colored balls to be pocketed in numerical order. The modern scoring system (a red ball is worth one point, yellow—2, green—3, brown—4, blue—5, pink—6 and black—7) was adopted in England in 1891. The sequence of pocketing the balls is called a break, the maximum possible break being 147. The name *snooker* comes from the term coined for new recruits at the Woolwich Military Academy and was Chamberlain's label for anyone who lost at his game. Championships were not started until 1916. The World Professional Championship was instituted in 1927.

Most world titles The world professional title was won a record 15 times by Joe Davis, on the first 15 occasions it was contested, 1927–40 and 1946. The most wins in the Amateur Championships have been two—by Gary Owen (England) in 1963 and 1966; Ray Edmonds (England) 1972 and 1974; and Paul Mifsud (Malta) 1985–86.

Maureen Baynton (nee Barrett) won a record eight Women's Amateur Championships between 1954 and 1968, as well as seven at billiards.

Highest breaks Over 200 players have achieved the maximum break of 147. The first to do so was E.J. "Murt" O'Donoghue (b. New Zealand 1901) at Griffiths, New South Wales, Australia on 26 Sep 1934. The first officially ratified 147 was by Joe Davis against Willie Smith in London, Great Britain on 22 Jan 1955. Cliff Thorburn (Canada; b. 16 Jan 1948) has scored the only one in the World Professional Championship, on 23 Apr 1983.

The first century break by a woman in competitive play was 114, by Stacey Hillyard in a league match at Bournemouth, Great Britain on 15 Jan 1985. The highest break by a woman in competition is 116, by Allison Fisher in the British Open at Solihull, Great Britain on 7 Oct 1989.

Soccer

Origins A game called *Tsu chu* ("to kick a ball of stuffed leather") was played in China more than 2,500 years ago. However, the ancestry of the modern game is traced to England. In 1314, King Edward II prohibited the game because of excessive noise. Three subsequent monarchs also banned the game. Nevertheless, "football," the name by which soccer is known outside the USA, continued its development in England. In 1848, the first rules were drawn up at Cambridge University, Great Britain; in 1863, the Football Association (FA) was founded in England. The sport grew in popularity worldwide, and the *Fédération Internationale de Football Association* (FIFA), the world governing body, was formed in Paris, France in 1904. FIFA currently has more than 160 members.

THE FIFA WORLD CUP

FIFA, which was founded on 21 May 1904, instituted the first World Cup on 13 Jul 1930, in Montevideo, Uruguay. It is now held quadrennially. Three wins have been achieved by Brazil, in 1958, 1962 and 1970; Italy in 1934, 1938 and 1982; and West Germany, 1954, 1974 and 1990.

Team records *Most appearances* Brazil is the only country to qualify for all 14 World Cup tournaments.

Most goals The highest score by one team in a game is ten by Hungary in a 10–1 defeat of El Salvador at Elche, Spain on 15 Jun 1982. The most goals in tournament history is 148 (in 66 games) by Brazil.

Highest scoring game The highest scoring game took place on 26 Jun 1954 when Austria defeated Switzerland 7–5.

Individual records Most wins Pele

(Brazil) is the only player to have played on three winning teams. Mario Zagalo (Brazil) was the first man to play (in 1958 and 1962) and be manager (1970) of a World Cup winning team. Franz Beckenbauer emulated Zagalo when he managed the West German team to victory in 1990. He had previously captained the 1974 winning team. Beckenbauer is the only man to have both captained and managed a winning side.

Most goals The most goals scored in a final is three by Geoff Hurst for England *v* West Germany on 30 Jul 1966.

Most games played Two players have appeared in 21 games in the finals tournament: Uwe Seeler (West Germany; b. 5 Nov 1936) 1958–70; and Wladyslaw Zmuda (Poland; b. 6 Jun 1954) 1974–86.

Most goals scored The most goals scored by a player in a game is four; this has occurred nine times. The most goals scored in one tournament is 13 by Just Fontaine (France) in 1958, in six games. The most goals scored in a career is 14 by Gerd Muller (West Germany), ten goals in 1970 and four in 1974.

OLYMPIC GAMES

Soccer has been an official sport at the Olympics since 1908, except for 1932, when it was not staged in Los Angeles. The leading gold medal winner is Hungary with three wins (1952, 1964, 1968). The highest Olympic score is 17, by Denmark *v* France "A" (1) in 1908. A record 126 nations are taking part in qualifying for the 1992 tournament.

Largest crowds The top attendance for a soccer match in the USA was 101,799, for France's 2–0 Olympic final win over Brazil at the Rose Bowl, Pasadena on 11 Aug 1984.

NCAA DIVISION I CHAMPIONSHIPS

Men In this competition, first held in 1959, the University of St Louis has won the most Division I titles with ten victories, including one tie: 1959–60, 1962–63, 1965, 1967, 1969–70, 1972–73.

Women In this competition, first held in 1982, the University of North Carolina has won a record eight Division I titles. Its victories came in 1982–84, 1986–90.

MAJOR SOCCER LEAGUE (MSL)

The Major Soccer League (MSL) was founded in 1978 as the Major Indoor Soccer League (MISL), and renamed for the 1990/91 season.

Most championships The San Diego Sockers have won a record seven MSL championships, 1983, 1985–86, 1988–91.

Individual records Steve Zungul holds the career MSL records for the most goals scored, 652; most assists, 471; most power play goals, 89; most hat tricks, 99; and most points scored, 1,123. Zungul played 11 seasons for four teams: New York Arrows, 1978–83, Golden Bay Earthquakes 1983, San Diego Sockers

1984–86, Tacoma Stars 1986–88, San Diego Sockers 1989–90.

Andy Chapman has played the most games in MSL history, 444 in 11 seasons. Chapman has played for three teams: Wichita Wings, 1979–85; Cleveland Force, 1985–86; Baltimore Blast, 1986–88; Wichita Wings 1988–90.

Largest crowd The highest attendance for an MSL game was 21,728 at the Tacoma Dome on 20 Jun 1987 for the seventh game of the championship series. The Dallas Sidekicks defeated the Tacoma Stars 4–3 in overtime and won the title.

Most international appearances Bruce Murray has played a record 61 times for the United States in full international games as of July 1991.

Softball

Origins Softball, a derivative of baseball, was invented by George Hancock at the Farragut Boat Club of Chicago, IL in 1887. Rules were first codified in Minneapolis, MN in 1895 under the name kitten ball. The name softball was introduced by Walter Hakanson at a meeting of the National Recreation Congress in 1926. The name was adopted throughout the United States in 1930. Rules were formalized in 1933 by the International Joint Rules Committee for Softball and adopted by the Amateur Softball Association of America. The International Softball Federation was formed in 1950 as the governing body for both fast pitch and slow pitch. It was reorganized in 1965. Women's fast pitch softball has been added to the Olympic program for 1996.

Most titles The USA has won the men's World Championship (instituted 1966) five times, 1966, 1968, 1976 (shared), 1980 and 1988, and the women's title (instituted 1965) three times, in 1974, 1978 and 1986. The world's first slow pitch championships for men's teams were held in Oklahoma City in 1987, when the winner was the USA.

US National Championships The most wins in the fast pitch championships (first held in 1933) for men is 10, by the Clearwater (Florida) Bombers between 1950 and 1973, and for women is 21, by the Raybestos Brakettes of Stratford, CT, between 1958 and 1990.

Slow pitch championships have been staged annually since 1953 for men and since 1962 for women. Three wins for men have been achieved by Skip Hogan A.C. of Pittsburgh, 1962, 1964–65, and by Joe Gatliff Auto Sales of Newport, KY, 1956–57, 1963. At super slow pitch, four wins have been achieved by Steele's Silver Bullets, Grafton, OH, 1985–90. The Dots of Miami, FL have a record five women's titles, playing as the Converse Dots, 1969; Marks Brothers; North Miami Dots, 1974–75; and Bob Hoffman Dots, 1978–79.

Speedway

Motorcycle racing on large dirt track surfaces has been traced back to 1902 in the United States. The first fully documented motorcycle track races were at the Portman Road Ground, Ipswich, Great Britain on 2 Jul 1904. Two heats and a final were contested, F.E. Barker winning in 5 min 54.2 sec for three miles. Modern speedway has developed from the "short track" races held at the West Maitland Agricultural (New South Wales, Australia) Show on 22 Dec 1923, by Johnnie Hoskins (New Zealand; 1892–1987).

World Championships The World Speedway Championship was inaugurated at Wembley, London, Great Britain on 10 Sep 1936. The most wins have been six, by Ivan Gerald Mauger (New Zealand; b. 4 Oct 1939) in 1968–70, 1972, 1977 and 1979. Barry Briggs (New Zealand; b. 30 Dec 1934) made a record 18 appearances in the finals (1954–70, 1972) and won the world title in 1957–58, 1964 and 1966. He also scored a record 201 points in world championship competition in 87 races.

Ivan Mauger also won four World Team Cups (three for Great Britain), two World Pairs (including one unofficial) and three world long track titles. Ove Fundin (Sweden; b. 23 May 1933) won 12 world titles: five individual, one pairs, and six World Team Cup medals in 1956–70. In 1985 Erik Gundersen (Denmark) became the first man to hold world titles at individual, pairs, team and long-track events simultaneously.

The World Pairs Championships (instituted unofficially 1968, officially 1970) have been won a record seven times—by England/Great Britain, 1972, 1976–78, 1980 and 1983–84; and Denmark, 1979, 1985–90. The most successful individuals in the World Pairs have been Erik Gundersen (b. 8 Oct 1959) and Hans Hollen Nielsen (b. 26 Dec 1959) with five wins for Denmark. They won as a pair, 1986–89, and Gundersen also won with Tommy Knudsen in 1985 and Nielsen with Jan O. Pedersen in 1990. Maximum points (then 30) were scored in the World Pairs Championship by: Jerzy Szczakiel (b. 28 Jan 1949) and Andrzej Wyglenda (Poland) at Rybnik, Poland in 1971; and Arthur Dennis Sigalos (b. 16 Aug 1959) and Robert Benjamin ("Bobby") Schwartz (USA; b. 10 Aug 1956) at Liverpool, New South Wales, Australia on 11 Dec 1982.

The World Team Cup (instituted 1960) has been won a record nine times by England/Great Britain (Great Britain 1968, 1971–73; England 1974–75, 1977, 1980, 1989). Hans Nielsen (Denmark) has ridden in a record eight Team wins.

Squash

At Harrow School, London, from 1817 on, boys waiting to play racquets knocked a ball around a confined space adjoining the racquets court. Its small area necessitated the use of a softer and smaller ball—one which could be squashed—hence the name. There was no recognized champion of any country until John A. Miskey of Philadelphia, PA won the American Amateur Singles Championship in 1907.

The first organized game in the United States was held in 1882 at St Paul's School, Concord, NH.

World Championships Jahangir Khan (Pakistan; b. 10 Dec 1963) won six World Open (instituted 1976) titles, 1981–85 and 1988, and the ISRF world individual title (formerly World Amateur, instituted 1967) in 1979, 1983 and 1985. Geoffrey B. Hunt (Australia; b. 11 Mar 1947) won four World Open titles, 1976–77 and 1979–80, and three World Amateur, 1967, 1969 and 1971. The most women's World Open titles is three, by Susan Devoy (New Zealand; b. 4 Jan 1964), 1985, 1987 and 1990.

Pakistan (1977, 1981, 1983, 1985 and 1987) and Australia (1967, 1969, 1971, 1973 and 1989) have each won five men's world titles. England won the women's title in 1985, 1987, 1989 and 1990, following Great Britain's win in 1979.

Most titles *Open Championship* The most wins in the Open Championship held annually in Britain is ten by

■ **Most squash titles**
Jahangir Khan (Pakistan) takes time off during the British Open to sign autographs for some young admirers. Khan has dominated these championships since 1982, winning every year, for a record ten titles. (Photo: All-Sport/D. Smith)

Jahangir Khan, in successive years, 1982–91. Hashim Khan (Pakistan; b. 1915) won seven times, 1950–55 and 1957, and also won the Vintage title six times in 1978–83.

The most British Open women's titles is 16, by Heather Pamela McKay (nee Blundell [Australia]; b. 31 Jul 1941) from 1961 to 1977. She also won the World Open title in 1976 and 1979.

United States The US amateur squash championships were first held for men in 1907 and for women in 1928; the most singles wins is six, by Stanley W. Pearson, 1915–17 and 1921–23; G. Diehl Mateer won a record eleven men's doubles titles between 1949 and 1966 with five different partners. Sharif Khan (Pakistan) won a record 13 North American Open Championships (instituted 1953), 1969–74 and 1976–82. Alicia McConnell has won a record seven women's national champion- ships (1982–88).

Unbeaten sequences Heather McKay was unbeaten from 1962 to 1980. Jahangir Khan was unbeaten from his loss to Geoff Hunt at the British Open on 10 Apr 1981 until Ross Norman (New Zealand) ended his sequence in the World Open final on 11 Nov 1986.

Longest and shortest championship matches The longest recorded competitive match was one of 2 hr 45 min when Jahangir Khan beat Gamal Awad (Egypt; b. 8 Sep 1955) 9–10, 9–5, 9–7, 9–2, the first game lasting a record 1 hr 11 min, in the final of the Patrick International Festival at Chichester, Great Britain on 30 Mar 1983. Lucy Soutter (Great Britain) beat Hugolein van Hoorn (Netherlands) in just 7½ min (9–0, 9–0, 9–0) in the British Under-21 Open Championship at Lamb's Squash Club, London, Great Britain on 17 Jan 1988.

Surfing

The traditional Polynesian sport of surfing in a canoe (*ehorooe*) was recorded by Capt. James Cook (1728–79) on his first voyage to Tahiti in December 1771. Surfing on a board (*Amo Amo iluna ka lau oka nalu*) was first described as "most perilous and extraordinary... altogether astonishing and is scarcely to be credited" by Lt (later Capt.) James King, in March 1779 at Kealakekua Bay, Hawaii island. The first depiction of a surfer was by this voyage's official artist, John Webber. The sport was revived at Waikiki by 1900. Hollow boards were introduced in 1929 and the light plastic foam type in 1956.

Most titles World Amateur Championships were inaugurated in May 1964 at Sydney, Australia. The most titles is three, by Michael Novakov (Australia), who won the Kneeboard event in 1982, 1984 and 1986. A World Professional series was started in 1975. The men's title has been won five times, by Mark Richards (Australia), 1975 and from

1979 to 1982, and the women's title (instituted 1979) four times, by Freida Zamba (USA), 1984–86, 1988.

Longest ride About four to six times each year, ridable surfing waves break in Matanchen Bay near San Blas, Nayarit, Mexico, which makes rides of c. 5,700 ft possible.

Swimming

In Japan, swimming in schools was ordered by imperial edict of Emperor Go-Yozei (1586–1611) in 1603, but competition was known from 36 B.C. Seawater bathing was fashionable at Scarborough, Great Britain as early as 1660. The earliest pool was Pearless Pool, London, Great Britain, opened in 1743.

The first United States Swimming Championships were staged by the Amateur Athletic Union on 25 Aug 1888 in New York City. The international governing body for swimming, diving and water polo—the *Fédération Internationale de Natation Amateur* (FINA)—was founded in 1908.

Fastest swimmer In a 25-yd pool, Tom Jager (USA; b. 6 Oct 1964) achieved an average speed of 5.37 mph for 50 yards in 19.05 sec at Nashville, TN on 23 Mar 1990. The women's fastest is 4.48 mph by Yang Wenyi (China) in her 50 m world record (see World Record table).

US Championships Tracy Caulkins (b. 11 Jan 1963) won a record 48 US swimming titles and set 60 US records in her career, 1977–84. The men's record is 36 titles, by Johnny Weissmuller (ne Janos Weiszmuller; 1904–84), between 1921 and 1928.

Most world records Men: 32, Arne Borg (Sweden; 1901–87), 1921–29. Women: 42, Ragnhild Hveger (Denmark; b. 10 Dec 1920), 1936–42. For currently recognized events (only metric distances in 50 m pools) the most is 26 by Mark Andrew Spitz (USA; b. 10 Feb 1950), 1967–72, and 23 by Kornelia Ender (East Germany; b. 25 Oct 1958), 1973–76. The most by a US woman is 15, by Deborah "Debbie" Meyer (b. 14 Aug 1952), 1967–70.

The most world records set in a single pool is 86 in the North Sydney pool, Australia between 1955 and 1978. This total includes 48 imperial distance records, which ceased to be recognized in 1969. The pool, which was built in 1936, was originally 55 yards long but was shortened to 50 meters in 1964.

Most world titles In the World Championships (instituted 1973) the most medals won is 13, by Michael Gross (West Germany; b. 17 Jun 1964)—five gold, five silver and three bronze, 1982–90. The most medals won by a woman is ten, by Kornelia Ender, with eight gold and two silver in 1973 and 1975. The most gold medals won is six (two individual and four relay) by James Paul Montgomery (USA; b. 24 Jan 1955)

in 1973 and 1975. The most medals won at a single championship is seven, by Matthew Nicholas "Matt" Biondi (USA; b. 8 Oct 1965)—three gold, one silver, three bronze, in 1986.

The most gold medals by an American woman is five, by Tracy Caulkins, all in 1978, as well as a silver. The most medals is nine, by Mary Terstegge Meagher (b. 27 Oct 1964)—two gold, five silver, two bronze, 1978–82.

OLYMPIC RECORDS

Most medals *Men* The greatest number of Olympic gold medals won is nine, by Mark Spitz (USA): 100 m and 200 m freestyle, 1972; 100 m and 200 m butterfly, 1972; 4 × 100 m freestyle, 1968 and 1972; 4 × 200 m freestyle, 1968 and 1972; 4 × 100 m medley, 1972. All but one of these performances (the 4 × 200 m freestyle of 1968) were also new world records. He also won a silver (100 m butterfly) and a bronze (100 m freestyle) in 1968 for a record 11 medals. His record seven medals at one Games in 1972 was equaled by Matt Biondi (USA), who took five gold, a silver and a bronze in 1988.

Women The record number of gold medals won by a woman is six by Kristin Otto (East Germany; b. 7 Feb 1965) at Seoul in 1988: 100 m freestyle, backstroke and butterfly, 50 m freestyle, 4 × 100 m freestyle and 4 × 100 m medley. Dawn Fraser (Australia; b. 4 Sep 1937) is the only swimmer to win the same event, the 100 m freestyle, on three successive occasions (1956, 1960 and 1964). The most gold medals won by a US woman is three, by 14 swimmers.

The most medals won by a woman is eight, by: Dawn Fraser—four golds (100 m freestyle, 1956, 1960 and 1964, 4 × 100 m freestyle, 1956) and four silvers (400 m freestyle, 1956, 4 × 100 m freestyle, 1960 and 1964, 4 × 100 m medley 1960); by Kornelia Ender—four golds (100 m and 200 m freestyle, 100 m butterfly, and 4 × 100 m medley in 1976) and four silvers (200 m individual medley, 1972, 4 × 100 m medley, 1972, 4 × 100 m freestyle, 1972 and 1976); and by Shirley Babashoff (USA; b. 3 Jan 1957), who won two golds (4 × 100 m freestyle, 1972 and 1976) and six silvers (100 m freestyle, 1972, 200 m freestyle, 1972 and 1976, 400 m and 800 m freestyle, 1976, 4 × 100 m medley 1976).

Most individual gold medals The record number of individual gold medals won is four, by: Charles Meldrum Daniels (USA [1884–1973]; 100 m freestyle, 1906 and 1908, 220 yd freestyle 1904, 440 yd freestyle, 1904); Roland Matthes (East Germany; b. 17 Nov 1950) with 100 m and 200 m in backstroke 1968 and 1972; Mark Spitz and Kristin Otto; and the divers Pat McCormick and Greg Louganis (see Diving).

Closest verdict The closest verdict in the Olympic Games was in Los Angeles, CA on 29 Jul 1984, when Nancy Lynn Hogshead (b. 17 Apr 1962) and Carrie Lynne Steinseifer (b. 12 Feb 1968; both USA) dead-heated for the women's

■ **World record**
Matt Biondi and Troy Dalbey celebrate after the US team set a world record time of 7 min 12.51 sec for the 4 × 200 meter freestyle at the Olympic Games at Seoul, South Korea on 21 Sep 1988. (Photo: All-Sport [USA])

100 m freestyle gold medal in 55.92 sec. In the 1972 men's 400 m individual medley, Gunnar Larsson (Sweden; b. 12 May 1951) beat Aleksander Timothy McKee (USA; b. 14 Mar 1953) by just 2/1,000 th second, just 3 mm. Now timings are determined only to hundredths.

DIVING

Most Olympic medals The most medals won by a diver is five, by: Klaus Dibiasi (Austria; b. 6 Oct 1947 [Italy]; three gold, two silver), 1964–76; and Gregory Efthimios "Greg" Louganis (b. 29 Jan 1960; four golds, one silver), 1976, 1984–88. Dibiasi is the only diver to win the same event (highboard) at three successive Games (1968, 1972 and 1976). Two divers have won the highboard and springboard doubles at two Games: Patricia Joan McCormick (nee Keller; b. 12 May 1930), 1952 and 1956, and Greg Louganis, 1984 and 1988.

Most world titles Greg Louganis (USA) won a record five world titles—highboard in 1978, and both highboard and springboard in 1982 and 1986, as well as four Olympic gold medals, in 1984 and 1988. Three gold medals at one event have also been won by Philip George Boggs (USA; 1949–90), springboard, 1973, 1975 and 1978.

United States Championships The Amateur Athletic Union (AAU) organized the first national diving championships in 1909. Since 1981, United States Diving has been the governing body of the sport in this country, and thus responsible for the national championships.

Most titles Greg Louganis has won a record 47 national titles: 17 at 1-meter springboard; 17 at 3-meter springboard; 13 at platform. In women's competition Cynthia Potter has won a record 28 titles.

Highest scores Greg Louganis achieved record scores at the 1984 Olympic Games in Los Angeles, CA, with 754.41 points for the 11-dive springboard event and 710.91 for the highboard. At the world championships in Guayaquil, Ecuador in 1984 he was awarded a perfect score of 10.0 by all seven judges for his highboard inward 1 ½ somersault in the pike position.

The first diver to be awarded a score of 10.0 by all seven judges was Michael Holman Finneran (b. 21 Sep 1948) in the 1972 US Olympic Trials, in Chicago, IL, for a backward 1 ½ somersault, 2 ½ twist, from the 10 m board.

LONG-DISTANCE SWIMMING

Longest swims The greatest recorded distance ever swum is 1,826 miles down the Mississippi River between Ford Dam near Minneapolis, MN and Carrollton Ave, New Orleans, LA, by Fred P. Newton (b. 1903) of Clinton, OK from 6 Jul to 29 Dec 1930. He was in the water for 742 hr.

The greatest distance covered in a continuous swim is 299 miles, by Ricardo Hoffmann (b. 5 Oct 1941), from Corrientes to Santa Elena, Argentina in the River Paraná in 84 hr 37 min on 3–6 Mar 1981.

The longest ocean swim is one of

128.8 miles by Walter Poenisch, Sr. Havana, Cuba on 11 Jul 1978, and arrived at Little Duck Key, FL (in a shark cage and wearing flippers) 34 hr 15 min later on 13 July.

In 1966 Mihir Sen of Calcutta, India uniquely swam the Palk Strait from Sri Lanka to India (in 25 hr 36 min on 5–6 Apr); the Straits of Gibraltar (in 8 hr 1 min on 24 Aug); the length of the Dardanelles (in 13 hr 55 min on 12 Sep); the Bosphorus (in 4 hr on 21 Sep); and the length of the Panama Canal (in 34 hr 15 min on 29–31 Oct).

Twenty-four hours Anders Forvass (Sweden) swam 63.3 miles at the 25 meter Linköping public swimming pool, Sweden on 28–29 Oct 1989. In a 50 meter pool, Evan Barry (Australia) swam 60.08 miles, at the Valley Pool, Brisbane, Australia on 19–20 Dec 1987.

The women's record is 51.01 miles by Irene van der Laan (Netherlands) at Amersfoort, Netherlands on 20–21 Sep 1985. The longest distance swum by an American woman is 45.45 miles, by Jill Oviatt, of Madison, WI at the University of Michigan pool in Ann Arbor, MI on 24–25 Nov 1988.

Greatest lifetime distance Gustave Brickner (b. 10 Feb 1912) of Charleroi, PA in 59 years to November 1986 recorded 38,512 miles.

Long-distance relays The New Zealand national relay team of 20 swimmers swam a record 113.59 miles in Lower Hutt, New Zealand in 24 hours, passing 100 miles in 20 hr 47 min 13 sec on 9–10

Largest pools
The largest swimming pool in the world is the seawater Orthlieb Pool in Casablanca, Morocco. It is 1,574 ft long and 246 ft wide, and has an area of 8.9 acres. The largest land-locked swimming pool with heated water was the Fleishhacker Pool on Sloat Boulevard, near Great Highway, San Francisco, CA. It measured 1,000 × 150 ft and up to 14 ft deep and contained 7.5 million gal of heated water. It was opened on 2 May 1925 but has now been abandoned. The largest land-locked pool in current use is Willow Lake in Warren, OH. It measures 600 × 150 ft. The greatest spectator accommodation is 13,614 at Osaka, Japan.

High diving
The highest regularly performed head-first dives are those of professional divers from La Quebrada ("The Break in the Rocks") at Acapulco, Mexico, a height of 87½ ft. The base rocks, 21 ft out from the takeoff, necessitate a leap of 27 ft out. The water is 12 ft deep.

The world record high dive is 176 ft 10 in, by Olivier Favre (Switzerland) at Villers-le-Lac, France on 30 Aug 1987.

The women's record is 120 ft 9 in, by Lucy Wardle (USA) at Ocean Park, Hong Kong on 6 Apr 1985.

SWIMMING—WORLD RECORDS (set in 50 meter pools)

——— MEN ———

Event	Time	Name, country and date of birth	Place	Date	
FREESTYLE					
50 meters	21.81	Thomas Jager (USA; b. 6 Oct 1964)	Nashville, TN	24 Mar	1990
100 meters	48.42	Matthew Nicholas "Matt" Biondi (USA; b. 8 Oct 1965)	Austin, TX	10 Aug	1988
200 meters	1:46.69	Giorgio Lamberti (Italy; b. 28 Jan 1969)	Bonn, Germany	15 Aug	1989
400 meters	3:46.95	Uwe Dassler (East Germany; b. 11 Feb 1967)	Seoul, South Korea	23 Sep	1988
800 meters	7:50.64	Vladimir Salnikov (USSR; b. 21 May 1960)	Moscow, USSR	4 Jul	1986
1,500 meters	14:50.36	Jörg Hoffmann (Germany; b. 29 Jan 1970)	Perth, Australia	13 Jan	1991
4×100 meter relay	3:16.53	United States	Seoul, South Korea	23 Sep	1988
		(Christopher Jacobs, Troy Dalbey, Tom Jager, Matt Biondi)			
4×200 meter relay	7:12.51	United States	Seoul, South Korea	21 Sep	1988
		(Troy Dalbey, Matthew Cetlinski, Douglas Gjertsen, Matt Biondi)			
BREASTSTROKE					
100 meters	1:01.45	Norbert Rosza (Hungary)	Perth, Australia	7 Jan	1991
	1:01.45	Vasiliy Ivanov (USSR)	Moscow, USSR	11 Jun	1991
200 meters	2:11.23	Michael Ray Barrowman (USA; b. 4 Dec 1968)	Perth, Australia	11 Jan	1991
BUTTERFLY					
100 meters	52.84	Pedro Pablo Morales (USA; b. 5 Dec 1964)	Orlando, FL	23 Jun	1986
200 meters	1:55.69	Melvin Stewart (USA; b. 16 Nov 1968)	Perth, Australia	12 Jan	1991
BACKSTROKE					
100 meters	54.51	David Berkoff (USA; b. 30 Nov 1966)	Seoul, South Korea	24 Sep	1988
200 meters	1:58.14	Igor Polyanskiy (USSR; b. 20 Mar 1967)	Erfurt, Germany	3 Mar	1985
MEDLEY					
200 meters	1:59.36	Tamás Darnyi (Hungary; b. 3 Jun 1967)	Perth, Australia	13 Jan	1991
400 meters	4:12.36	Tamás Darnyi (Hungary)	Perth, Australia	8 Jan	1991
4×100 meter relay	3:36.93	United States	Seoul, South Korea	25 Sep	1988
		(David Berkoff, Richard Schroeder, Matt Biondi, Christopher Jacobs)			

——— WOMEN ———

Event	Time	Name, country and date of birth	Place	Date	
FREESTYLE					
50 meters	24.98	Yang Wenyi (China; b. 11 Jan 1972)	Guangzhou, China	11 Apr	1988
100 meters	54.73	Kristin Otto (East Germany; b. 7 Feb 1965)	Madrid, Spain (relay first leg)	19 Aug	1986
200 meters	1:57.55	Heike Friedrich (East Germany; b. 18 Apr 1970)	Berlin, Germany	18 Jun	1986
400 meters	4:03.85	Janet B. Evans (USA; b. 28 Aug 1971)	Seoul, South Korea	22 Sep	1988
800 meters	8:16.22	Janet B. Evans (USA)	Tokyo, Japan	20 Aug	1989
1,500 meters	15:52.10	Janet B. Evans (USA)	Orlando, FL	26 Mar	1988
4×100 meter relay	3:40.57	East Germany	Madrid, Spain	19 Aug	1986
		(Kristin Otto, Manuela Stellmach, Sabina Schulze, Heike Friedrich)			
4×200 meter relay	7:55.47	East Germany	Strasbourg, France	18 Aug	1987
		(Manuela Stellmach, Astrid Strauss, Anke Möhring, Heike Friedrich)			
BREASTSTROKE					
100 meters	1:07.91	Silke Hörner (East Germany; b. 12 Sep 1965)	Strasbourg, France	21 Aug	1987
200 meters	2:26.71	Silke Hörner (East Germany)	Seoul, South Korea	21 Sep	1988
BUTTERFLY					
100 meters	57.93	Mary Terstegge Meagher (USA; b. 27 Oct 1964)	Milwaukee, WI	16 Aug	1981
200 meters	2:05.96	Mary Terstegge Meagher (USA)	Milwaukee, WI	13 Aug	1981
BACKSTROKE					
100 meters	1:00.59	Ina Kleber (East Germany; b. 29 Sep 1964—relay first leg)	Moscow, USSR	24 Aug	1984
200 meters	2:08.60	Betsy Mitchell (USA; b. 15 Jan 1966)	Orlando, FL	27 Jun	1986
MEDLEY					
200 meters	2:11.73	Ute Geweniger (East Germany; b. 24 Feb 1964)	Berlin, Germany	4 Jul	1981
400 meters	4:36.10	Petra Schneider (East Germany; b. 11 Jan 1963)	Guayaquil, Ecuador	1 Aug	1982
4×100 meter relay	4:03.69	East Germany	Moscow, USSR	24 Aug	1984
		(Ina Kleber, Sylvia Gerasch, Ines Geissler, Birgit Meineke)			

Dec 1983. The 24-hour club record by a team of five is 96.27 miles, by the City of Newcastle ASC on 16–17 Dec 1986. A women's team from the club swam 88.93 miles on the same occasion. The most participants in a one-day swim relay is 2,135, each swimming a length, organized by the Syracuse YMCA in Syracuse, NY on 11 Apr 1986.

The longest-duration swim relay was 233 hr 15 min by a team of 15 from Maccabi Water Polo team at Sydney Football Stadium swimming pool, Sydney, Australia on 1–11 Dec 1988.

Underwater swimming Paul Cryne (Great Britain) and Samir Sawan al Awami of Qatar swam 49.04 miles in a 24-hr period from Doha, Qatar to Umm Said and back on 21–22 Feb 1985 using sub-aqua equipment. They were swimming under water for 95.5 percent of the time. A relay team of six swam 94.44 miles in a swimming pool at Olomouc, Czechoslovakia on 17–18 Oct 1987.

Manhattan swim The fastest swim around Manhattan Island in New York City was in 6 hr 12 min 29 sec, by Shelley Taylor (Australia; b. 1961) on 15 Oct 1985. Drury J. Gallagher set the men's record, 6 hr 41 min 35 sec, on 7 Sep 1983.

CHANNEL SWIMMING

The first to swim the English Channel from shore to shore (without a life jacket) was the Merchant Navy captain Matthew Webb (1848–83), who swam an estimated 38 miles to make the 21 mile crossing from Dover, Great Britain to Calais Sands, France, in 21 hr 45 min from 12:56 P.M. to 10:41 A.M., 24–25 Aug 1875. Paul Boyton (USA) had swum from

SWIMMING—US NATIONAL RECORDS (*set in 50 meter pools*)

MEN

Event	Time	Name and date of birth	Place	Date	
FREESTYLE					
50 meters	21.81	Thomas "Tom"Jager (b. 6 Oct 1964)	Nashville, TN	24 Mar	1990
100 meters	48.42	Matthew Nicholas "Matt" Biondi (b. 8 Oct 1965)	Austin, TX	10 Aug	1988
200 meters	1:47.72	Matt Biondi	Austin, TX	8 Aug	1988
400 meters	3:48.06	Matthew Cetlinski (b. 4 Oct 1964)	Austin, TX	11 Aug	1988
800 meters	7:52.45	Sean Killion (b. 24 Oct 1967)	Clovis, CA	27 Jul	1987
1,500 meters	15:01.51	George Thomas DiCarlo (b. 13 Jul 1963)	Indianapolis, IN	30 Jun	1984
4 × 100 meter relay	3:16.53	United States	Seoul, South Korea	23 Sep	1988
		(Christopher Jacobs, Troy Dalbey, Tom Jager, Matt Biondi)			
4 × 200 meter relay	7:12.51	United States	Seoul, South Korea	21 Sep	1988
		(Troy Dalbey, Matthew Cetlinski, Douglas Gjertsen, Matt Biondi)			
BREASTSTROKE					
100 meters	1:01.65	Steven K. Lundquist (b. 20 Feb 1961)	Los Angeles, CA	29 Jul	1984
200 meters	2:11.52	Michael Ray Barrowman (b. 4 Dec 1968)	Perth, Australia	11 Jan	1991
BUTTERFLY					
100 meters	52.84	Pedro Pablo Morales (b. 5 Dec 1964)	Orlando, FL	23 Jun	1986
200 meters	1:55.69	Melvin Stewart (b. 16 Nov 1968)	Perth, Australia	12 Jan	1991
BACKSTROKE					
100 meters	54.51	David Charles Berkoff (b. 30 Nov 1966)	Seoul, South Korea	24 Sep	1988
200 meters	1:58.86	Richard John "Rick" Carey (b. 13 Mar 1963)	Indianapolis, IN	27 Jun	1984
MEDLEY					
200 meters	2:00.11	David Wharton (b. 16 May 1969)	Tokyo, Japan	20 Aug	1989
400 meters	4:15.21	Eric Namesnik	Perth, Australia	8 Jan	1991
4 × 100 meter relay	3:36.93	United States	Seoul, South Korea	25 Sep	1988
		(David Berkoff, Richard Schroeder, Matt Biondi, Christopher Jacobs)			

WOMEN

Event	Time	Name and date of birth	Place	Date	
FREESTYLE					
50 meters	25.50	Leigh Ann Fetter (b. 23 May 1969)	Austin, TX	13 Aug	1988
100 meters	55.17	Nicole Haislett	Perth, Australia	7 Jan	1991
200 meters	1:58.23	Cynthia Woodhead (b. 7 Feb 1964)	Tokyo, Japan	3 Sep	1979
400 meters	4:03.85	Janet B. Evans (b. 28 Aug 1971)	Seoul, South Korea	22 Sep	1988
800 meters	8:16.22	Janet B. Evans	Tokyo, Japan	20 Aug	1989
1,500 meters	15:52.10	Janet B. Evans	Orlando, FL	26 Mar	1988
4 × 100 meter relay	3:43.26	United States World Championship Team	Perth, Australia	9 Jan	1991
		(Jenna Leigh Johnson, Carrie Steinseifer, Dara Torres, Nancy Lyn Hogshead)			
4 × 200 meter relay	8:02.12	United States	Madrid, Spain	17 Aug	1986
		(Betsy Mitchell, Mary Terstegge Meagher, Kim Brown, Mary Alice Wayte)			
BREASTSTROKE					
100 meters	1:08.91	Tracey McFarlane (b. 20 Jul 1966)	Austin, TX	11 Aug	1988
200 meters	2:27.08	Anita Hall	Federal Way, WA	4 Apr	1991
BUTTERFLY					
100 meters	57.93	Mary Terstegge Meagher (b. 27 Oct 1964)	Brown Deer, WI	16 Aug	1981
200 meters	2:05.96	Mary Terstegge Meagher	Brown Deer, WI	13 Aug	1981
BACKSTROKE					
100 meters	1:01.10	Janie Wagstaff	Federal Way, WA	4 Jun	1991
200 meters	2:08.60	Betsy Mitchell (b. 15 Jan 1966)	Orlando, FL	27 Jun	1986
MEDLEY					
200 meters	2:12.64	Tracy Anne Caulkins (b. 11 Jan 1963)	Los Angeles, CA	3 Aug	1984
400 meters	4:37.76	Janet B. Evans	Seoul, South Korea	19 Sep	1988
4 × 100 meter relay	4:06.94	United States	Seattle, WA	23 Jul	1990
		(Betsy Mitchell, Tracey McFarlane, Janel Jorgensen, Nicole Haislett)			

Cap Gris-Nez, France to the South Foreland, Great Britain in his life-saving suit in 23 hr 30 min on 28–29 May 1875. It is reported that Jean-Marie Saletti, a French soldier, escaped from a British prison hulk off Dover by swimming to Boulogne in July or August 1815.

The first woman to succeed was Gertrude Caroline Ederle (USA; b. 23 Oct 1906), who swam from Cap Gris-Nez, France to Deal, England on 6 Aug 1926, in the then-overall record time of 14 hr 39 min.

Fastest The official Channel Swimming Association (founded 1927) record is 7 hr 40 min by Penny Dean (b. 21 Mar 1955) of California, from Shakespeare Beach, Dover, Great Britain to Cap Gris-Nez, France on 29 Jul 1978.

T*able Tennis*

Origins The earliest evidence relating to a game resembling table tennis has been found in the catalogs of London, Great Britain sports goods manufac- turers in the 1880s. The old Ping Pong Association was formed in 1902, but the game proved only a temporary craze until resuscitated in 1921. The International Table Tennis Federation was founded in 1926 and the United States Table Tennis Association was established in 1933. Table tennis was included at the Olympic Games for the first time in 1988.

Most titles World G. Viktor Barna (1911–72; b. Hungary, Gyözö Braun) won a record five singles, 1930, 1932–35 and eight men's doubles, 1929–35, 1939

Counter hitting

The record number of hits in 60 sec is 172, by Thomas Busin and Stefan Renold, both of Switzerland, on 4 Nov 1989. The women's record is 168, by the sisters Lisa (b. 9 Mar 1967) and Jackie (b. 9 Sep 1964) Bellinger, at Crest Hotel, Luton, Great Britain on 14 Jul 1987. With a paddle in each hand, Gary D. Fisher of Olympia, WA completed 5,000 consecutive volleys over the net in 44 min 28 sec on 25 Jun 1979.

Fastest speed in table tennis

No conclusive measurements have been published, but in a lecture, M. Sklorz (Germany) stated that a smashed ball had been measured at speeds up to 105.6 mph.

Youngest table tennis player

The youngest-ever international contender was Joy Foster, who represented Jamaica in the West Indies Championships at Port of Spain, Trinidad in August 1958 at the age of 8.

in the World Championships (first held in 1926). Angelica Rozeanu (Romania; b. 15 Oct 1921) won a record six women's singles, 1950–55, and Maria Mednyanszky (Hungary; 1901–79) won seven women's doubles, 1928, 1930–35. With two more at mixed doubles, Viktor Barna won 15 world titles in all, while 18 have been won by Maria Mednyanszky.

With the staging of championships biennially, the breaking of the above records would now be very difficult.

The most men's team titles (Swaythling Cup) is 12, by Hungary, 1927–31, 1933–35, 1938, 1949, 1952 and 1979. The women's record (Marcel Corbillon Cup) is nine, by China, 1965 and eight successive from 1975 to 1989 (biennially).

United States The US won the Swaythling Cup in 1937 and the Corbillon Cup in 1937 and 1949. Ruth Aarons was the women's world champion in 1936 and 1937, sharing the title in the latter year. No American has won the men's world singles title, but James McClure won three men's doubles titles, with Robert Blattner in 1936–37 and with Sol Schiff in 1938.

English Open (instituted 1921) Richard Bergmann (Austria, then Great Britain; 1920–70) won a record six singles, 1939–40, 1948, 1950, 1952, 1954 and Viktor Barna won seven men's doubles titles, 1931, 1933–35, 1938–39, 1949. The women's singles record is six by Maria Alexandru (Romania; b. 1941), 1963–64, 1970–72, 1974, and Diane Rowe (Great Britain, now Scholer; b. 14 Apr 1933) won 12 women's doubles titles, 1950–56, 1960, 1962–65.

Viktor Barna won 20 titles in all and Diane Rowe won 17. Her twin Rosalind (now Mrs Cornett) has won nine (two in singles).

US Championships US national championships were first held in 1931. Leah Neuberger (nee Thall) won a record 21 titles between 1941 and 1961: 9 women's singles, 12 women's doubles. Richard Mills won a record ten men's singles titles between 1945 and 1962.

Taekwondo

Taekwondo is a martial art, with all activities based on defensive spirit, developed over 20 centuries in Korea. It was officially recognized as part of Korean tradition and culture on 11 Apr 1955. The first World Taekwondo Championships were organized by the Korean Taekwondo Association and were held at Seoul in 1973. The World Taekwondo Federation was then formed, and has organized biennial championships.

Most titles The most world titles won is four, by Chung Kook-hyun (South Korea), light-middleweight 1982–83, welterweight 1985, 1987. Taekwondo was included as a demonstration sport at the 1988 Olympic Games.

Three American women won gold medals at the 1988 Olympics, one of whom, Lynette Love (b. 21 Sep 1957), at heavyweight (over 70kg), was also world champion in 1987.

Tennis

Origins The modern game is generally agreed to have evolved as an outdoor form of the indoor game of tennis (see Real/Royal Tennis). "Field tennis" is mentioned in an English magazine—*Sporting Magazine*—of 29 Sep 1793. The earliest club for such a game, variously called pelota or lawn rackets, was the Leamington Club, founded in 1872 by Major Harry Gem. The earliest attempt to commercialize the game was by Major Walter Clopton Wingfield (1833–1912), who patented a form called "sphairistike" on 23 Feb 1874. It soon came to be called lawn tennis. Amateur players were permitted to play with and against professionals in "open" tournaments in 1968.

Grand Slam The grand slam for a tennis player is to hold all four of the world's major championship singles titles at the same time: the Australian Open, French Open, Wimbledon and US Open. The traditional slam is winning the four events in one year. The first man to have won all four was Frederick John Perry (Great Britain; b. 18 May 1909) when he won the French title in 1935. The first man to hold all four championships simultaneously, and thus achieve a grand slam, was John Donald "Don" Budge (USA; b. 13 Jun 1915) in 1938, and with Wimbledon and US in 1937, he won six successive grand slam tournaments. The first man to achieve the grand slam twice was Rodney George "Rod" Laver (Australia; b. 9 Aug 1938), as an amateur in 1962 and again in 1969, when the titles were open to professionals.

Four women have achieved the grand slam, and the first three won six successive grand slam tournaments: Maureen Catherine Connolly (USA; 1934–69), in 1953; Margaret Jean Court (nee Smith [Australia]; b. 16 Jul 1942) in 1970; and Martina Navratilova (USA; b. 18 Oct 1956) in 1983–84. The fourth was Stefanie Maria "Steffi" Graf (Germany; b. 14 Jun 1969) in 1988, when she also won the women's singles Olympic gold medal. Pamela Howard "Pam" Shriver (USA; b. 4 Jul 1962) with Navratilova won a record eight successive grand slam tournament women's doubles titles and 109 successive matches in all events from April 1983 to July 1985.

The first doubles pair to win the grand slam were the Australians Frank Allan Sedgeman (b. 29 Oct 1927) and Kenneth Bruce McGregor (b. 2 Jun 1929) in 1951.

The most singles championships won in grand slam tournaments is 24, by Margaret Court (11 Australian, 5 USA, 5 French, 3 Wimbledon), 1960–73. She also won the US Amateur in 1969 and 1970 when this was held, as well as the US Open. The men's record is 12, by Roy Stanley Emerson (Australia; b. 3 Nov 1936; 6 Australian, 2 each French, United States, Wimbledon), 1961–67.

The most grand slam tournament wins by a doubles partnership is 20, by Althea Louise Brough (USA; b. 11 Mar 1923) and Margaret Evelyn du Pont (nee Osborne; b. 4 Mar 1918: 12 USA, 5 Wimbledon, 3 French), 1942–57; and by Martina Navratilova and Pam Shriver (7 Australian, 5 Wimbledon, 4 French, 4 USA), 1981–89.

United States The most singles wins in grand slam tournaments by a US player is 19 by Helen Wills Moody (b. 6 Oct 1905: 8 Wimbledon, 7 US and 4 French). Martina Navratilova (formerly of Czechoslovakia) has won a total of 54 grand slam titles—18 singles, a world record 31 women's doubles and 5 mixed doubles. Billie Jean King has the most of US-born players with 39 titles—12 singles, 16 women's doubles and 11 mixed doubles.

WIMBLEDON CHAMPIONSHIPS

Most wins *Women* Billie Jean King (nee Moffitt; b. 22 Nov 1943) won a record 20 titles between 1961 and 1979—six singles, ten women's doubles and four mixed doubles. Elizabeth Montague Ryan (USA; 1892–1979) won a record 19 doubles (12 women's, 7 mixed) titles from 1914 to 1934.

Men The greatest number of titles by a man has been 13, by Hugh Laurence Doherty (Great Britain; 1875–1919) with five singles titles (1902–06) and a record eight men's doubles (1897–1901, 1903–05) partnered by his brother Reginald Frank (1872–1910).

The most titles won by a US man is seven, by John Patrick McEnroe (b. 16 Feb 1959), singles 1981, 1983 and 1984; men's doubles (all with Peter Fleming) 1979, 1981, 1983–84.

Singles Martina Navratilova won a record nine titles, 1978–79, 1982–87 and 1990. The most men's singles wins since the Challenge Round was abolished in 1922 is five consecutively, by Bjørn Borg (Sweden) in 1976–80. William Charles Renshaw (Great Britain; 1861–1904) won seven singles in 1881–86 and 1889.

Mixed doubles The male record is four titles shared by: Elias Victor "Vic" Seixas (USA; b. 30 Aug 1923), in 1953–56; Kenneth Norman Fletcher (Australia; b. 15 Jun 1940), in 1963, 1965–66, 1968; and Owen Keir Davidson (Australia; b. 4 Oct 1943) in 1967, 1971, 1973–74. The women's record is seven by Elizabeth Ryan (USA) between 1919 and 1932.

Most appearances Arthur William Charles "Wentworth" Gore (Great Britain; 1868–1928) made a record 36 appearances at Wimbledon between 1888 and 1927. In 1964, Jean Borotra (b. 13 Aug 1898) of France made his 35th appearance since 1922. In 1977 he appeared in the Veterans' Doubles at the age of 78.

Youngest champions The youngest

champion was Charlotte "Lottie" Dod (Great Britain; 1871–1960), who was 15 yr 285 days when she won in 1887. The youngest male champion was Boris Becker (West Germany; b. 22 Nov 1967), who won the men's singles title in 1985 at 17 yr 227 days. The youngest-ever player at Wimbledon was reputedly Mita Klima (Austria), who was 13 yr in the 1907 singles competition. The youngest seed was Jennifer Capriati (USA; b. 29 Mar 1976) at 14 yr 89 days at the time of her first match on 26 Jun 1990. She won this match, making her the youngest-ever winner at Wimbledon. The following year she became the youngest-ever semi finalist.

Oldest champions The oldest champion was Margaret Evelyn du Pont at 44 yr 125 days when she won the mixed doubles in 1962 with Neale Fraser (Australia). The oldest singles champion was Arthur Gore (Great Britain) in 1909 at 41 yr 182 days.

US OPEN CHAMPIONSHIPS

Most wins Margaret Evelyn du Pont won a record 25 titles between 1941 and 1960. She won a record 13 women's doubles (12 with Althea Louise Brough), nine mixed doubles and three singles. The men's record is 16 by William Tatem "Bill" Tilden (1893–1953), including seven men's singles, 1920–25, 1929—a record for singles shared with: Richard Dudley Sears (1861–1943), 1881–87; William A. Larned (1872 –1926), 1901–02, 1907–11; and at women's singles by: Molla Mallory (nee Bjurstedt; 1892–1959), 1915–16, 1918, 1920–22, 1926; and Helen Wills Moody, 1923–25, 1927–29, 1931.

Youngest and oldest The youngest champion was Vincent Richards (1903–59), who was 15 yr 139 days when he won the men's doubles with Bill Tilden in 1918. The youngest men's singles champion was Pete Sampras (USA; b. 12 Aug 1971), who was 19 yr 28 days when he won the 1990 title. The youngest singles champion was Tracy Ann Austin (b. 12 Dec 1962), who was 16 yr 271 days when she won the women's singles in 1979. The oldest champion was Margaret du Pont, who won the mixed doubles at age 42 yr 166 days in 1960. The oldest singles champion was William Larned at 38 yr 242 days in 1911.

FRENCH CHAMPIONSHIPS

Most wins (from international status 1925) Margaret Court won a record 13 titles—five singles, four women's doubles and four mixed doubles, 1962–73. The men's record is nine by Henri Cochet (France; 1901–87) —four singles, three men's doubles and two mixed doubles, 1926–30. The singles record is seven by Christine Marie "Chris" Evert (USA; b. 21 Dec 1954), 1974–75, 1979–80, 1983, 1985–86. Bjørn Borg won a record six men's singles, 1974–75, 1978–81.

Youngest and oldest The youngest doubles champions were the 1981 mixed doubles winners Andrea Jaeger (b. 4 Jun

1965), at 15 yr 339 days, and Jimmy Arias (b. 16 Aug 1964), at 16 yr 296 days. The youngest singles winners have been: Monica Seles (Yugoslavia; b. 2 Dec 1973), who won the 1990 women's title at 16 yr 169 days in 1990; and Michael Chang (USA; b. 22 Feb 1972), the men's at 17 yr 109 days in 1989. The oldest champion was Elizabeth Ryan, who won the 1934 women's doubles with Simone Mathieu (France) at 42 yr 88 days. The oldest singles champion was Andrés Gimeno (Spain; b. 3 Aug 1937) in 1972 at 34 yr 301 days.

AUSTRALIAN OPEN CHAMPIONSHIPS

Most wins Margaret Jean Court won the women's singles 11 times (1960–66, 1969–71 and 1973) as well as eight women's doubles and two mixed doubles, for a record total of 21 titles. A record six men's singles were won by Roy Stanley Emerson, 1961 and 1963–67. Thelma Dorothy Long (nee Coyne; b. 30 May 1918) won a record 12 women's doubles and four mixed doubles for a record total of 16 doubles titles. Adrian

Karl Quist (b. 4 Aug 1913) won ten consecutive men's doubles from 1936 to 1950 (the last eight with John Bromwich) and three men's singles.

Longest span, oldest and youngest Thelma Long won her first (1936) and last (1958) titles 22 years apart. Kenneth Robert "Ken" Rosewall (b. 2 Nov 1934) won the singles in 1953, and in 1972, 19 years later, at 37 yr 62 days, became the oldest singles winner. The oldest champion was (Sir) Norman Everard Brookes (1877–1968), who was 46 yr 2 months when he won the 1924 men's doubles. The youngest champions were Rodney W. Heath, age 17, when he won the men's singles in 1905, and Monica Seles (Yugoslavia), who won the women's singles at 17 yr 55 days in 1991.

ATP WORLD CHAMPIONSHIPS

The first Grand Prix Masters Championships were staged in Tokyo, Japan in 1970. They were held in New York City annually from 1977 to 1989, with qualification by relative success in the

"Golden set"
The only known example of a "Golden set" (winning a set 6–0 without dropping a single point, i.e., winning 24 consecutive points) in professional tennis was achieved by Bill Scanlon (USA) against Marcos Hocevar (Brazil) in the first round of the WCT Gold Coast Classic at Del Ray, FL on 22 Feb 1983. Scanlon won the match, 6–2, 6–0.

Fastest tennis service
The fastest service timed with modern equipment is 138 mph, by Steve Denton (USA; b. 5 Sep 1956) at Beaver Creek, CO on 29 Jul 1984. The fastest *ever* measured was one of 163.6 mph by Bill Tilden in 1931.

Greatest crowd
The record crowd for one day at Wimbledon was 39,813 on 26 Jun 1986. The record for the whole championship was 403,706 in 1989.

Longest career span

Duncan McLean (1884–1980) of Scotland set a world age (92) record of 100 m in 21.7 sec in Aug 1977, over 73 years after his best-ever sprint of 100 yd in 9.9 sec in South Africa in Feb 1904.

Most records in a day

Jesse Owens (USA; 1913–80) set six world records in 45 min at Ann Arbor, MI on 25 May 1935, with a 9.4 sec 100 yd at 3:15 P.M., a 26 ft 8¼ in long jump at 3:25 P.M., a 20.3 sec 220 yd (and 200 m) at 3:45 P.M. and a 22.6 sec 220 yd low hurdles (and 200 m) at 4 P.M.

Most international appearances

The greatest number of international matches contested for any nation is 89, by shot-putter Bjørn Bang Andersen (b. 14 Nov 1937) for Norway, 1960–81.

Backwards walking

The greatest-ever exponent of reverse pedestrianism has been Plennie L. Wingo (b. 24 Jan 1895), then of Abilene, TX, who completed his 8,000 mile transcontinental walk from Santa Monica, CA to Istanbul, Turkey from 15 Apr 1931 to 24 Oct 1932. The longest distance recorded for walking backwards in 24 hr is 84.0 miles by Anthony Thornton (USA) in Minneapolis, MN on 31 Dec 1985–1 Jan 1986.

preceding year's Grand Prix tournaments. The event was replaced from 1990 by the ATP Tour Championship, held in Frankfurt, Germany. A record five titles have been won by Ivan Lendl (Czechoslovakia; b. 7 Mar 1960), 1982–83, two in 1986 (January and December) and 1987, and he appeared in nine successive finals, 1980–88. Lendl has the highest earnings on the ATP Tour, with $16,772,078 through 1990. James Scott "Jimmy" Connors (USA; b. 2 Sep 1952) uniquely qualified for 14 consecutive years, 1972–85. He chose not to play in 1975, 1976 and 1985, and won in 1977. He qualified again in 1987 and 1988, but did not play in 1988. A record seven doubles titles were won by John McEnroe and Peter Fleming (USA; b. 21 Jan 1955), 1978–84.

OLYMPIC GAMES

Tennis was reintroduced to the Olympic Games in 1988, having originally been included from 1896 to 1924. It was also a demonstration sport in 1968 and 1984.

A record four gold medals, as well as a silver and a bronze, were won by Max Decugis (France; 1882–1978), 1900–20. A women's record five medals (one gold, two silver, two bronze) were won by Kitty McKane (later Mrs Godfree [Great Britain]; b. 7 May 1897) in 1920 and 1924.

United States Four US players have won two Olympic gold medals: Beals Coleman Wright (1879–1961) in 1904, Vincent Richards (1903–59) and Helen Wills Moody in 1924, all at both singles and doubles, and Hazel Virginia Hotchkiss Wightman (1886–1974), at ladies' and mixed doubles in 1924. Richards won a US record third medal, silver at mixed doubles (with Marion Jessup) in 1924.

INTERNATIONAL TEAM

Davis Cup (instituted 1900)

The most wins in the Davis Cup, the men's international team championship, has been 29, by the USA. The most appearances for Cup winners is eight, by Roy Emerson (Australia), 1959–62, 1964–67. Bill Tilden (USA) played in a record 28 matches in the final, winning a record 21–17 out of 22 singles and 4 out of 6 doubles. He was on seven winning sides, 1920–26, and then on four losing sides, 1927–30.

Nicola Pietrangeli (Italy; b. 11 Sep 1933) played a record 163 rubbers (66 ties), 1954 to 1972, winning 120. He played 109 singles (winning 78) and 54 doubles (winning 42).

Wightman Cup (instituted 1923)

The annual women's match was won 51 times by the United States and 10 times by Great Britain. The contest was suspended in 1990 after a series of wipeouts by the US team. Chris Evert won all 26 of her singles matches, from 1971 to 1985, and including doubles achieved a record 34 wins from 38 rubbers played. Virginia Wade (Great Britain; 10 Jul 1945) played in a record 21 ties and 56 rubbers, 1965–85. Jennifer Capriati became the youngest-ever Wightman Cup winner and player at 13 yr

168 days, when she beat Clare Wood (Great Britain) 6–0, 6–0 at Williamsburg, VA on 14 Sep 1989.

Federation Cup (instituted 1963)

The most wins in the Federation Cup, the women's international team championship, is 14, by the USA between 1963 and 1990. Virginia Wade (Great Britain) played each year from 1967 to 1983, in a record 57 ties, playing 100 rubbers, including 56 singles (winning 36) and 44 doubles (winning 30). Chris Evert won her first 29 singles matches, 1977–86. Her overall record, 1977–89, is 40 wins in 42 singles and 16 wins in 18 doubles matches.

Longest span as national champion

Keith Gledhill (b. 17 Feb 1911) won the US National Boys' Doubles Championship with Sidney Wood in Aug 1926. Sixty-one years later, at Goleta, CA in Aug 1987, he won the US National 75-and-over Men's Doubles Championship with Elbert Lewis.

Dorothy May Bundy-Cheney (USA; b. September 1916) won 180 US titles at various age groups from 1941 to March 1988.

International contest *Longest span* Jean Borotra (France; b. 13 Aug 1898) played in every one of the twice-yearly contests between the International Club of France and the International Club of Great Britain from the first in 1929 to his 100th match at Wimbledon on 1–3 Nov 1985. On that occasion he played mixed doubles against Kitty Godfree (Great Britain). Both were former Wimbledon singles champions, and were age 87 and 88 respectively.

Highest earnings Ivan Lendl won a men's season's record $2,344,367 in 1989 and had career earnings of $17,238,127 to 26 May 1991. The season's record for a woman is $2,173,556 in 1984 (including a $1 million Grand Slam bonus) by Martina Navratilova. Earnings from special restricted events and team tennis are not included. Navratilova's lifetime earnings by 9 Jul 1991 reached $17,048,143.

The greatest first-place prize money ever won is $2 million by Pete Sampras when he won the Grand Slam Cup in Munich, Germany on 16 Dec 1990. In the final he beat Brad Gilbert (USA; b. 9 Aug 1961) 6–3, 6–4, 6–2. Gilbert received $1 million, also well in excess of the previous record figure. The highest total prize money was $6,349,250 for the 1990 US Open Championships.

Largest crowd A record 30,472 people were at the Astrodome, Houston, TX on 20 Sep 1973, when Billie Jean King beat Robert Larimore "Bobby" Riggs (USA; b. 25 Feb 1918). The record for an orthodox tennis match is 25,578 at Sydney, New South Wales, Australia on 27 Dec 1954, in the Davis Cup Challenge Round (first day), Australia v USA.

Longest game The longest-known singles game was one of 37 deuces (80 points) between Anthony Fawcett (Rhodesia) and Keith Glass (Great Britain) in the first round of the Surrey

Championships at Surbiton, Great Britain on 26 May 1975. It lasted 31 min. Noëlle van Lottum and Sandra Begijn played a game lasting 52 min in the semifinals of the Dutch Indoor Championships at Ede, Gelderland on 12 Feb 1984.

The longest tiebreak was 26–24 for the fourth and decisive set of a first round men's doubles at the Wimbledon Championships on 1 Jul 1985. Jan Gunnarsson (Sweden) and Michael Mortensen (Denmark) defeated John Frawley (Australia) and Victor Pecci (Paraguay) 6–3, 6–4, 3–6, 7–6.

The longest rally in tournament play was one of 643 times over the net between Vicky Nelson and Jean Hepner at Richmond, VA in October 1984. The 6 hr 22 min match was won by Nelson 6–4, 7–6. It concluded with a 1 hr 47 min tiebreak, 13–11, for which one point took 29 minutes.

Will Duggan and Ron Kapp (both USA) performed a rally of 6,202 strokes, which took 3 hr 33 min, at Santa Barbara Municipal Stadium, CA on 12 Mar 1988.

Track and Field

The earliest evidence of organized running was at Memphis, Eygpt c. 3800 B.C. The earliest accurately dated Olympic Games was in July 776 B.C., when Coroibos won the foot race. The oldest surviving measurements are a long jump of 23 ft 1 ½ in by Chionis of Sparta in c. 656 B.C. and a discus throw of 100 cubits (about 152 ft) by Protesilaus.

Fastest speed An analysis of split times at each ten meters in the 1988 Olympic Games 100 m final in Seoul, South Korea on 24 Sep 1988, won by Ben Johnson (Canada) in 9.79 (average speed 22.85 mph but later disallowed as a world record due to his positive drug test for steroids) from Carl Lewis (USA) 9.92, showed that both Johnson and Lewis reached a peak speed (40 m–50 m and 80 m–90 m respectively) of 0.83 sec for 10 m, i.e., 26.95 mph. In the women's final, Florence Griffith Joyner was timed at 0.91 sec for each 10 m from 60 m–90 m, i.e., 24.58 mph.

Highest jump above own head The greatest height cleared above an athlete's own head is 23 ¼ in, by Franklin Jacobs (USA; b. 31 Dec 1957), 5 ft 8 in tall, who jumped 7 ft 7 ¼ in at New York City, on 27 Jan 1978. The greatest height cleared by a woman above her own head is 12 ¾ in, by Yolanda Henry (USA; b. 2 Dec 1964), 5 ft 6 in tall, who jumped 6 ft 6¾ in at Seville, Spain on 30 May 1990.

Most Olympic titles The most Olympic gold medals won is ten (an absolute Olympic record) by Raymond Clarence Ewry (USA; 1874–1937) in the standing high, long and triple jumps in 1900, 1904, 1906 and 1908.

Women The most gold medals won by a woman is four, shared by: Francina "Fanny" E. Blankers-Koen (Nether-

WORLD RECORDS MEN

World records for the men's events scheduled by the International Amateur Athletic Federation. Fully automatic electric timing is mandatory for events up to 400 meters.

RUNNING	min sec	Name and country	Place		Date
100 meters	9.90*	Leroy Russell Burrell (USA; b. 21 Feb 1967)	New York City	14 Jun	1991
200 meters	19.72†	Pietro Mennea (Italy; b. 28 Jun 1952)	Mexico City, Mexico	12 Sep	1979
400 meters	43.29	Harry Lee "Butch" Reynolds, Jr. (USA; b. 8 Aug 1964)	Zürich, Switzerland	17 Aug	1988
800 meters	1:41.73	Sebastian Newbold Coe (Great Britain; b. 29 Sep 1956)	Florence, Italy	10 Jun	1981
1,000 meters	2:12.18	Sebastian Newbold Coe (Great Britain)	Oslo, Norway	11 Jul	1981
1,500 meters	3:29.46	Saïd Aouita (Morocco; b. 2 Nov 1959)	Berlin, Germany	23 Aug	1985
I mile	3:46.32	Steven Cram (Great Britain; b. 14 Oct 1960)	Oslo, Norway	27 Jul	1985
2,000 meters	4:50.81	Saïd Aouita (Morocco)	Paris, France	16 Jul	1987
3,000 meters	7:29.45	Saïd Aouita (Morocco)	Köln, Germany	20 Aug	1989
5,000 meters	12:58.39	Saïd Aouita (Morocco)	Rome, Italy	22 Jul	1987
10,000 meters	27:08.23	Arturo Barrios (Mexico; b. 12 Dec 1963)	Berlin, Germany	18 Aug	1989
20,000 meters	56:55.6	Arturo Barrios (Mexico)	La Flèche, France	30 Mar	1991
25,000 meters	I hr 13:55.8	Toshihiko Seko (Japan; b. 15 Jul 1956)	Christchurch, New Zealand	22 Mar	1981
30,000 meters	I hr 29:18.8	Toshihiko Seko (Japan)	Christchurch, New Zealand	22 Mar	1981
I hour	13.111 miles	Arturo Barrios (Mexico)	La Flèche, France	30 May	1991

* Ben Johnson (Canada; b. 30 Dec 1961) ran 100 m in 9.79 sec at Seoul, South Korea on 24 Sep 1988, but was subsequently disqualified when he tested positive for steroids. He later admitted to having taken drugs over many years, and this also invalidated his 9.83 sec at Rome, Italy on 30 Aug 1987.
† This record was set at high altitude—Mexico City 7,349 ft. Best mark at low altitude: 200 m: 19.75 sec, Carl Lewis, Indianapolis, IN, 19 Jun 1983, and Joseph Nathaniel DeLoach (USA; b. 5 Jun 1967) at Seoul, South Korea on 28 Sep 1988.

HURDLING					
110 meters (3' 6")	12.92	Roger Kingdom (USA; b. 26 Aug 1962)	Zürich, Switzerland	16 Aug	1989
400 meters (3' 0")	47.02	Edwin Corley Moses (USA; b. 31 Aug 1955)	Koblenz, Germany	31 Aug	1983
3,000 meter steeplechase	8:05.35	Peter Koech (Kenya; b. 18 Feb 1958)	Stockholm, Sweden	4 Jul	1989

RELAYS					
4 × 100 meters	37.79	France	Split, Yugoslavia	I Sep	1990
		(Max Morinière, Daniel Sangouma, Jean-Charles Trouabal, Bruno Marie-Rose)			
4 × 200 meters	1:19.38	Santa Monica Track Club (USA)	Koblenz, Germany	23 Aug	1989
		(Daniel Everett, Leroy Russell Burrell, Floyd Wayne Heard, Carl Lewis)			
4 × 400 meters	2:56.16*	United States	Mexico City, Mexico	20 Oct	1968
		(Vincent Edward Matthews, Ronald John Freeman, II, George Lawrence James, Lee Edward Evans)			
	2:56.16	United States	Seoul, South Korea	I Oct	1988
		(Daniel Everett, Steven Earl Lewis, Kevin Bernard Robinzine, Butch Reynolds)			
4 × 800 meters	7:03.89	Great Britain	London, Great Britain	30 Aug	1982
		(Peter Elliott, Garry Peter Cook, Steven Cram, Sebastian Coe)			
4 × 1,500 meters	14:38.8	West Germany	Cologne, Germany	17 Aug	1977
		(Thomas Wessinghage, Harald Hudak, Michael Lederer, Karl Fleschen)			

FIELD EVENTS	m	ft in		Place		Date
High jump	2.44	8 0	Javier Sotomayor (Cuba; b. 13 Oct 1967)	San Juan, Puerto Rico	29 Jul	1989
Pole vault	6.09	19 11 ¾	Sergey Bubka (USSR; b. 4 Dec 1963)	Moscow, USSR	9 Jun	1991
Long jump	8.90*	29 2 ½	Robert Beamon (USA; b. 29 Aug 1946)	Formia, Italy	18 Oct	1968
Triple jump	17.97	58 11	William Augustus "Willie" Banks (USA; b. 11 Mar 1956)	Indianapolis, IN	16 Jun	1985
Shot 16 lb	23.12	75 10 ¼	Eric Randolph "Randy" Barnes (USA; b. 16 Jun 1966)	Los Angeles, CA	20 May	1990
Discus 4 lb 8 oz	74.08	243 0	Jürgen Schult (East Germany; b. 11 May 1960)	Neubrandenburg, Germany	6 Jun	1986
Hammer 16 lb	86.74	284 7	Yuriy Georgiyevich Sedykh (USSR; b. 11 Jun 1955)	Stuttgart, Germany	30 Aug	1986
Javelin	96.96 †	318 1	Seppo Räty (Finland; b. 27 Apr 1962)	Punkalaidun, Finland	2 Jun	1991

* Set at high altitude; the low altitude best: 28 ft 10 ¼ in, Carl Lewis at Indianapolis, IN on 19 Jun 1983.
† With the new javelin, which has the center of gravity moved back, introduced in 1986. The best performance with the old javelin was 343 ft 10 in by Uwe Hohn (East Germany; b. 16 Jul 1962) at Berlin, Germany on 20 Jul 1984.

DECATHLON

8,847 points	Francis Morgan "Daley" Thompson (Great Britain; b. 30 Jul 1958)	Los Angeles, CA	8–9 Aug 1984

(1st day: 100 m 10.44 sec, Long Jump 26' 3 ½",
Shot Put 51' 7", High Jump 6' 8",
400 m 46.97 sec)

(2nd day: 110 m hurdles 14.33 sec,
Discus 152' 9", Pole vault 16' 4 ¾",
Javelin 214' 0", 1,500 m 4:35.00 sec)

lands; b. 26 Apr 1918), with 100 m, 200 m, 80 m hurdles and 4 × 100 m relay, 1948; Betty Cuthbert (Australia; b. 20 Apr 1938), with 100 m, 200 m, 4 × 100 m relay, 1956 and 400 m, 1964; and Bärbel Wöckel (nee Eckert [East Germany]; b. 21 Mar 1955), with 200 m and 4 × 100 m relay in 1976 and 1980.

Most wins at one Games The most gold medals at one celebration is five by Paavo Johannes Nurmi (Finland; 1897–1973) in 1924; 1,500 m, 5,000 m, 10,000 m cross-country, 3,000 m team and cross-country team. The most at individual events is four, by Alvin Christian Kraenzlein (USA; 1876–1928) in 1900: 60 m, 110 m hurdles, 200 m hurdles and long jump.

Most Olympic medals The most medals won is 12 (nine gold and three silver) by Paavo Nurmi (Finland) in the Games of 1920, 1924 and 1928.

Women The most medals won by a woman athlete is seven by Shirley Barbara de la Hunty (nee Strickland [Australia]; b. 18 Jul 1925) with three gold, one silver and three bronze in the 1948, 1952 and 1956 Games. A reappraisal of the photo-finish indicates that she finished third, not fourth, in the 1948 200-meter event, thus unofficially increasing her medal haul to eight. Irena Szewinska (nee Kirszenstein [Poland]; b. 24 May 1946) won three gold, two silver and two bronze in 1964, 1968, 1972 and 1976, and is the only woman athlete to win a medal in four successive Games.

United States The most Olympic medals won is five, by Delorez Florence Griffith Joyner (b. 21 Dec 1959): 200 m silver in 1984, gold at 100 m, 200 m and 4 x 100 m relay, silver at 4 x 400 m relay in 1988. Wilma Glodean Rudolph (later Ward; b. 23 Jun 1940) won three gold medals: 100 m, 200 m and 4 x 100 m relay in 1960; by Wyomia Tyus (b. 29 Aug 1945): 100 m in 1968, 4 x 100 m relay

WORLD RECORDS WOMEN

World records for the women's events scheduled by the International Amateur Athletic Federation.

RUNNING	min sec	Name and country	Place	Date
100 meters	10.49	Delorez Florence Griffith Joyner (USA; b. 21 Dec 1959)	Indianapolis, IN	16 Jul 1988
200 meters	21.34	Delorez Florence Griffith Joyner (USA)	Seoul, South Korea	29 Sep 1988
400 meters	47.60	Marita Koch (East Germany; b. 18 Feb 1957)	Canberra, Australia	6 Oct 1985
800 meters	1:53.28	Jarmila Kratochvílová (Czechoslovakia; b. 26 Jan 1951)	Münich, Germany	26 Jul 1983
1,000 meters	2:30.6	Tatyana Providokhina (USSR; b. 26 Mar 1953)	Podolsk, USSR	20 Aug 1978
1,500 meters	3:52.47	Tatyana Kazankina (USSR; b. 17 Dec 1951)	Zürich, Switzerland	13 Aug 1980
1 mile	4:15.61	Paula Ivan (Romania; b. 20 Jul 1963)	Nice, France	10 Jul 1989
2,000 meters	5:28.69	Maricica Puică (Romania; b. 29 Jul 1950)	London, Great Britain	11 Jul 1986
3,000 meters	8:22.62	Tatyana Kazankina (USSR)	Leningrad, USSR	26 Aug 1984
5,000 meters	14:37.33	Ingrid Kristiansen (nee Christensen [Norway]; b. 21 Mar 1956)	Stockholm, Sweden	5 Aug 1986
10,000 meters	30:13.74	Ingrid Kristiansen (Norway)	Oslo, Norway	5 Jul 1986

HURDLING				
100 meters (2' 9")	12.21	Yordanka Donkova (Bulgaria; b. 28 Sep 1961)	Stara Zagora, Bulgaria	20 Aug 1988
400 meters (2' 6")	52.94	Marina Styepanova (nee Makeyeva [USSR]; b. 1 May 1950)	Tashkent, USSR	17 Sep 1986

RELAYS				
4 × 100 meters	41.37	East Germany	Canberra, Australia	6 Oct 1985
		(Silke Gladisch [now Möller], Sabine Rieger [now Günther], Ingrid Auerswald [nee Brestrich], Marlies Göhr [nee Oelsner])		
4 × 200 meters	1:28.15	East Germany	Jena, Germany	9 Aug 1980
		(Marlies Göhr [nee Oelsner], Romy Müller [nee Schneider], Bärbel Wöckel [nee Eckert], Marita Koch)		
4 × 400 meters	3:15.17	USSR	Seoul, South Korea	1 Oct 1988
		(Tatyana Ledovskaya, Olga Nazarova, Maria Pinigina [nee Kulchunova], Olga Bryzgina [nee Vladykina])		
4 × 800 meters	7:50.17	USSR	Moscow, USSR	5 Aug 1984
		(Nadezhda Olizarenko [nee Mushta], Lyubov Gurina, Lyudmila Borisova, Irina Podyalovskaya)		

FIELD EVENTS	m	ft in	Place	Date
High jump	2.09	6 10 1/4	Stefka Kostadinova (Bulgaria; b. 25 Mar 1965)	Rome, Italy ... 30 Aug 1987
Long jump	7.52	24 8 1/4	Galina Chistyakova (USSR; b. 26 Jul 1962)	Leningrad, USSR ... 11 Jun 1988
Triple jump	14.95	49 1	Inessa Kravets (USSR; b. 5 Oct 1966)	Moscow, USSR ... 10 Jun 1991
Shot 8 lb 13 oz	22.63	74 3	Natalya Lisovskaya (USSR; b. 16 Jul 1962)	Moscow, USSR ... 7 Jun 1987
Discus 2 lb 3 oz	76.80	252 0	Gabriele Reinsch (East Germany; b. 23 Sep 1963)	Neubrandenburg, Germany ... 9 Jul 1988
Javelin 24 lb 7 oz	80.00	262 5	Petra Felke (East Germany; b. 30 Jul 1959)	Potsdam, Germany ... 9 Sep 1988

HEPTATHLON				
7,291 points		Jacqueline Joyner-Kersee (USA; b. 3 Mar 1962)	Seoul, South Korea	23–24 Sep 1988

(100 m hurdles 12.69 sec; High jump 6 ft 1 1/4 in; Shot 51 ft 10 in; 200 m 22.56 sec; Long jump 23 ft 10 in; Javelin 149 ft 9 in; 800 m 2 min 08.51 sec)

One thousand hours

Ron Grant (Australia) ran 1.86 miles within an hour, every hour, for 1,000 consecutive hours at New Farm Park, Brisbane, Queensland, Australia from 6 Feb–20 Mar 1991.

Highest marathon

The highest start for a marathon is the biennially held Everest Marathon, first run on 27 Nov 1987. It begins at Gorak Shep at 17,100 ft and ends at Namche Bazar, 11,300 ft. The fastest time to complete this race is 3 hr 59 min 4 sec, by Jack Maitland in 1989.

in 1964 and 1968; and by Valerie Ann Brisco (b. 6 Jul 1960) at 200 m, 400 m and 4 x 400 m relay. Rudolph and Tyus also won one silver medal each. Four gold medals at one Games were won by Alvin Kraenzlein (see above). Jesse Owens (1913–80) in 1936 and Frederick Carleton "Carl" Lewis (b. 1 Jul 1961) in 1984 both won four gold medals at one Games, both at 100 m, 200 m, long jump and the 4 x 100 m relay. Lewis won two more gold medals in 1988.

Olympic champions Oldest and youngest The oldest athlete to win an Olympic title was Irish-born Patrick Joseph "Babe" McDonald (ne McDonnell; 1878–1954), who was age 42 yr 26 days when he won the 56 lb weight throw at Antwerp, Belgium on 21 Aug 1920. The oldest female champion was Lia Manoliu (Romania; b. 25 Apr 1932), age 36 yr 176 days when she won the discus at Mexico City on 18 Oct 1968. The youngest gold medalist was Barbara Pearl Jones (USA; b. 26 Mar 1937), who at 15 yr 123 days was a member of the winning 4 × 100 m relay team, at Helsinki, Finland on 27 Jul 1952. The youngest male champion was Robert Bruce "Bob" Mathias (USA; b. 17 Nov 1930), age 17 yr 263 days when he won the decathlon at the London Games on 5–6 Aug 1948.

The oldest Olympic medalist was Tebbs Lloyd Johnson (Great Britain; 1900–84), age 48 yr 115 days when he was third in the 1948 50,000 m walk. The oldest woman medalist was Dana Zátopková (Czechoslovakia; b. 19 Sep 1922), age 37 yr 348 days when she was 2nd in the javelin in 1960.

World Championships Quadrennial World Championships, distinct from the Olympic Games, were inaugurated in 1983, when they were held in Helsinki, Finland. The most medals won is six gold, by Carl Lewis (USA; b. 1 Jul 1961), at 100 m, long jump and 4 × 100 m relay in 1983 and the latter two also in 1987, when he added the 1987 100 m gold as Ben Johnson was stripped of his title by the IAAF in 1989 following his admission of drug taking. Lewis has also won six Olympic golds, four in 1984 and two in 1988.

World record breakers Oldest and youngest For the greatest age at which anyone has broken a world record under IAAF jurisdiction see General Records. The female record is 36 yr 139 days for Marina Styepanova (nee Makeyeva [USSR]; b. 1 May 1950) with 52.94 sec for the 400 m hurdles at Tashkent, USSR on

17 Sep 1986. The youngest individual record breaker is Wang Yan (China; b. 9 Apr 1971), who set a women's 5,000 m walk record at age 14 yr 334 days with 21 min 33.8 sec at Jian, China on 9 Mar 1986. The youngest male is Thomas Ray (Great Britain; 1862–1904) at 17 yrs 198 days when he pole-vaulted 11 ft 2¾ in on 19 Sep 1879 (prior to IAAF ratification).

US championships The most American national titles won at all events, indoors and out, is 65, by Ronald Owen Laird (b. 31 May 1938) at various walks events between 1958 and 1976. Excluding the walks, the record is 41, by Stella Walsh (nee Walasiewicz, 1911–80), who won women's events between 1930 and 1954—33 outdoors and 8 indoors.

The most wins outdoors at one event in AAU/TAC history is 11, by James Sarsfield Mitchel (1864–1921) at 56 lb weight in 1888, 1891–97, 1900, 1903, 1905; Stella Walsh, 220 y/200 m 1930–31, 1939–40, 1942–48 and long jump 1930, 1939–46, 1948 and 1951; Maren Seidler (b. 11 Jun 1951) in shot 1967–68, 1972–80; Dorothy Dodson (b. 28 Mar 1919) in javelin 1939–49.

Longest winning sequence Iolanda Balas (Romania; b. 12 Dec 1936) won a record 140 consecutive competitions at high jump from 1956 to 1967. The record at a track event is 122, at 400 meters hurdles, by Edwin Corley Moses (USA; b. 31 Jul 1955) between his loss to Harald Schmid (West Germany; b. 29 Sep 1957) at Berlin, Germany on 26 Aug 1977 and that to Danny Lee Harris (USA; b. 7 Sep 1965) at Madrid, Spain on 4 Jun 1987.

Longest running races The longest races ever staged were the 1928 (3,422 miles) and 1929 (3,665 miles) transcontinental races from New York City to Los Angeles, CA. The Finnish-born Johnny Salo (1893–1931) was the winner in 1929 in 79 days, from 31 Mar to 18 Jun. His elapsed time of 525 hr 57 min 20 sec (averaging 6.97 mph) left him only 2 min 47 sec ahead of Englishman Pietro "Peter" Gavuzzi (1905–81).

The longest race staged annually is Australia's Westfield Run from Paramatta, New South Wales to Doncaster, Victoria (Sydney to Melbourne). The distance run has varied slightly, but the record time is by Yiannis Kouros (Greece; b. 13 Feb 1956), 5 days 2 hr 27 min 27 sec in 1989, when the distance was 658 miles.

Longest runs The longest run by an individual is one of 11,134 miles around the United States, by Sarah Covington-Fulcher (USA; b. 14 Feb 1962), starting and finishing in Los Angeles, CA, 21 Jul 1987–2 Oct 1988. Robert J. Sweetgall (USA; b. 8 Dec 1947) ran 10,608 miles around the perimeter of the United States, starting and finishing in Washington, D.C., Oct 1982–15 Jul 1983. Ron Grant (Australia; b. 15 Feb 1943) ran around Australia, 8,316 miles in 217 days 3 hr 45 min, 28 Mar–31 Oct 1983. Max Telford (New Zealand; b. Hawick, Scotland 2 Feb 1955) ran 5,110 miles from Anchorage, AK to Halifax, Nova Scotia, in 106 days 18 hr 45 min from 25 Jul to 9 Nov 1977.

The fastest time for the cross-America run is 46 days 8 hr 36 min, by Frank Giannino, Jr. (USA; b. 1952) for the 3,100 miles from San Francisco to New York from 1 Sep–17 Oct 1980. The women's trans-America record is 69 days 2 hr 40 min, by Mavis Hutchinson (South Africa; b. 25 Nov 1942) from 12 Mar–21 May 1978.

Greatest mileage Douglas Alistair Gordon Pirie (Great Britain; b. 10 Feb 1931), who set five world records in the 1950s, estimated that he had run a total distance of 216,000 miles in 40 years up to 1981.

Dr Ron Hill (Great Britain; b. 21 Sep 1938), the 1969 European and 1970 Commonwealth marathon champion, has not missed a day's training since 20 Dec 1964. His meticulously compiled training log shows a total of 123,065 miles from 3 Sep 1956 to 17 May 1991. He has finished 114 marathons, all in less than 2:52, and has raced in 52 nations.

The greatest competitive distance run in a year is 5,502 miles by Malcolm Campbell (Great Britain; b. 17 Nov 1934) in 1985.

Mass relay records The record for 100 miles by 100 runners from one club is 7 hr 53 min 52.1 sec, by the Baltimore

Road Runners Club, Towson, MD on 17 May 1981. The women's record is 10 hr 47 min 9.3 sec on 3 Apr 1977, by the San Francisco Dolphins Southend Running Club. The record for 100 × 100 m is 19 min 14.19 sec by a team from Antwerp at Merksem, Belgium on 23 Sep 1989.

The longest relay ever run was 10,524 miles, by 2,660 runners at Trondheim, Norway from 26 Aug–20 Oct 1985. Twenty members of the Melbourne Fire Brigade ran 9,357 miles around Australia on Highway No. 1 in 43 days 23 hr 58 min, 10 Jul–23 Aug 1983. The most participants is 4,800—192 teams of 25—in the Batavierenrace, 103.89 miles from Nijmegen to Enschede, Netherlands on 23 Apr 1983. The greatest distance covered in 24 hr by a team of ten is 280.232 miles by Oxford Striders RC at East London, South Africa on 5–6 Oct 1990.

MARATHON

The marathon is run over a distance of 26 miles 385 yd. This distance was used for the race at the 1908 Olympic Games, run in Great Britain from Windsor to the White City Stadium, London, and became standard from 1924 on. The marathon (of 40 km) was introduced to the 1896 Olympic Games to commemorate the legendary run of Pheidippides (or Philippides) from the battlefield of Marathon to Athens in 490 B.C. The 1896 Olympic marathon was preceded by trial races that year. The first Boston Marathon, the world's longest-lasting major marathon, was held on 19 Apr 1897 at 24 miles 1,232 yd, and the first national marathon championship was that of Norway in 1897.

The first championship marathon for women was organized by the Road Runners Club of America on 27 Sep 1970.

Fastest There are as yet no official records for the marathon, and it should be noted that courses may vary in severity. The following are the best times recorded, all on courses whose distance has been verified:

Men: 2 hr 6 min 50 sec, by Belayneh Dinsamo (Ethiopia; b. 28 Jun 1965) at Rotterdam, Netherlands on 17 Apr 1988.
Women: 2 hr 21 min 6 sec by Ingrid Kristiansen (nee Christensen [Norway];

Pancake race record
Dominic M. Cuzzacrea (USA; b. 8 Jun 1960) of Lockport, NY ran the Buffalo, New York Nissan Marathon (26.2 miles) while flipping a pancake in a time of 3 hours 6 min and 22 sec on 6 May 1990.

Joggling
3 objects Owen Morse (USA), 100 m in 11.68 sec, 1989 and 400 m in 57.32 sec, 1990. Albert Lucas (USA), 110 m hurdles in 20.36 sec and 400 m hurdles in 1 min 10.37 sec, 1989. Owen Morse, Albert Lucas, Tuey Wilson and John Wee (all USA), 1 mile relay in 3 min 57.38 sec, 1990. Kirk Swenson (USA), 1 mile in 4 min 43 sec, 1986, and 3.1 miles in 16 min 55 sec, 1986. Ashrita Furman (USA), marathon—26 miles 385 yd—in 3 hr 22 min 32.5 sec, 1988 and 50 miles in 8 hr 52 min 7 sec, 1989.

5 objects Owen Morse (USA), 100 m in 13.8 sec, 1988. Bill Gillen (USA), 1 mile in 7 min 41.01 sec, 1989, and 3.1 miles in 28 min 11 sec, 1989. (See also Endurance and Endeavor, uggling.)

US NATIONAL RECORDS MEN

RUNNING

	min sec	Name	Place	Date
100 meters	9.90	Leroy Russell Burrell (b. 21 Feb 1967)	New York City	14 Jun 1991
200 meters	19.75	Frederick Carleton "Carl" Lewis (b. 1 Jul 1961)	Indianapolis, IN	19 Jun 1983
	19.75	Joseph Nathaniel "Joe" DeLoach (b. 5 Jun 1967)	Seoul, South Korea	28 Sep 1988
400 meters	43.29	Harry Lee "Butch" Reynolds, Jr. (b. 8 Aug 1964)	Zürich, Switzerland	17 Aug 1988
800 meters	1:42.60	John Lee "Johnny" Gray (b. 19 Jun 1960)	Koblenz, Germany	28 Aug 1985
1,000 meters	2:13.9	Richard Charles "Rick" Wohlhuter (b. 23 Dec 1948)	Oslo, Norway	30 Jul 1974
1,500 meters	3:29.77	Sydney Maree (b. 9 Sep 1956)	Köln, Germany	25 Aug 1985
1 mile	3:47.69	Steven Michael Scott (b. 5 May 1957)	Oslo, Norway	7 Jul 1982
2,000 meters	4:52.44	James C. "Jim" Spivey (b. 7 Mar 1960)	Lausanne, Switzerland	15 Sep 1987
3,000 meters	7:33.37	Sydney Maree ±	London, Great Britain	17 Jul 1982
	7:35.84	Douglas Floyd Padilla (b. 4 Oct 1956)	Oslo, Norway	9 Jul 1983
5,000 meters	13:01.15	Sydney Maree	Oslo, Norway	27 Jul 1985
10,000 meters	27:20.56	Marcus James Nenow (b. 16 Nov 1957)	Brussels, Belgium	5 Sep 1986
15,000 meters	43:39.8	William Henry "Bill" Rodgers (b. 23 Dec 1947)	Boston, MA	9 Aug 1977
20,000 meters	58:25.0	Bill Rodgers	Boston, MA	9 Aug 1977
25,000 meters	1 hr 14:11.8	Bill Rodgers	Saratoga, NY	21 Feb 1979
30,000 meters	1 hr 31:49	Bill Rodgers	Saratoga, NY	21 Feb 1979
1 hour	12 miles 135 yd	Bill Rodgers	Boston, MA	9 Aug 1977
Marathon	2 hr 08:52	Alberto Bauduy Salazar (b. 7 Aug 1958)	Boston, MA	19 Apr 1982

± Prior to obtaining US citizenship

HURDLING

		Name	Place	Date
110 meters	12.92	Roger Kingdom (b. 26 Aug 1962)	Zürich, Switzerland	16 Aug 1989
400 meters	47.02	Edwin Corley Moses (b. 31 Aug 1955)	Koblenz, Germany	31 Aug 1983
3,000 meter steeplechase	8:09.17	Henry Dinwoodey Marsh (b. 15 Mar 1954)	Koblenz, Germany	28 Aug 1985

RELAYS

		Name	Place	Date
4 × 100 meters	37.83	National Team (Samuel Louis Graddy, Ronald James Brown, Calvin Smith, Carl Lewis)	Los Angeles, CA	11 Aug 1984
4 × 200 meters	1:19.38	Santa Monica Track Club (Daniel Joe Everett, Leroy Russell Burrell, Floyd Heard, Carl Lewis)	Koblenz, Germany	23 Aug 1989
4 × 400 meters	2:56.16*	National Team (Vincent Edward Matthews, Ronald John Freeman, George Lawrence "Larry" James, Lee Edward Evans)	Mexico City, Mexico	20 Oct 1968
	2:56.16	National Team (Daniel Everett, Steven Earl Lewis, Kevin Bernard Robinzine, Harry Lee "Butch" Reynolds)	Seoul, South Korea	1 Oct 1988
4 × 800 meters	7:06.5	Santa Monica Track Club (James Robinson, David Mack, Earl Jones, Johnny Gray)	Walnut, CA	26 Apr 1986
4 × 1,500 meters	14:46.3	National Team	Bourges, France	24 Jun 1969

* Set at high altitude

FIELD EVENTS

	ft in	Name	Place	Date
High jump	7 10	Hollis Conway (b. 8 Jan 1967)	Norman, OK	30 Jul 1989
Pole vault	19 6 ½	Daniel Joe Dial (b. 26 Oct 1962)	Norman, OK	18 Jun 1987
Long jump	29 2 ½ *	Robert "Bob" Beamon (b. 29 Aug 1946)	Mexico City, Mexico	18 Oct 1968
Triple jump	58 11 ½	William Augustus "Willie" Banks (b. 11 Mar 1956)	Indianapolis, IN	16 Jun 1985
Shot	75 10 ¼	Earl Randolph "Randy" Barnes (b.16 Jun 1966)	Westwood, LA	20 May 1990
Discus	237 4**	Walter "Ben" Plunkett (b. 13 Apr 1953)	Stockholm, Sweden	7 Jul 1981
Hammer	268 8 †	Judson Campbell Logan (b. 19 Jul 1959)	University Park, PA	22 Apr 1988
Javelin	280 1 †	Thomas Alan Petranoff (b. 8 Apr 1958)	Helsinki, Finland	7 Jul 1986

* Set at high altitude; the low altitude best: 28 ft 10 ¼ in, Carl Lewis at Indianapolis, IN on 19 Jun 1983.
** Ratified despite the fact that it was achieved after a positive drug test.
† Petranoff has also thrown 292 ft 6 in at Potchefstroom, South Africa on 1 Mar 1991.

DECATHLON

		Name	Place	Date
8,634 points		William Bruce Jenner (b. 29 Oct 1949)	Montreal, Canada	29–30 Jul 1976

(1st day: 100 m 10.94 sec, Long jump 23 ft 8 ¼ in, Shot put 50 ft 4 ½ in, High jump 6 ft 8 in, 400 m 47.51 sec)   (2nd day: 110 m hurdles 14.84 sec, Discus 164 ft 2 in, Pole vault 15 ft 9 in, Javelin 224 ft 10 in, 1,500 m 4:12.61 sec)

TRACK WALKING WORLD RECORDS

The International Amateur Athletic Federation recognizes men's records at 20 km, 30 km, 50 km and 2 hours, and women's at 5 km and 10 km.

Event	hr:min:sec	Name, country and date of birth	Place	Date
MEN				
10 km	38:02.60	Jozef Pribilinec (Czechoslovakia; b. 6 Jul 1960)	Banská Bystrica, Czechoslovakia	30 Aug 1985
20 km	1:18:40.0	Ernesto Canto (Mexico; b. 18 Oct 1959)	Fana, Norway	5 May 1984
30 km	2:03:56.5	Thierry Toutain (France; b. 14 Feb 1962)	Héricourt, France	24 Mar 1991
50 km	3:41:38.4	Raul Gonzalez (Mexico; b. 29 Feb 1952)	Fana, Norway	25 May 1979
1 hour	15,447 m	Josef Pribilinec (Czechoslovakia)	Hildesheim, Germany	6 Sep 1986
2 hours	29,090 m	Thierry Toutain (France)	Héricourt, France	24 Mar 1991
WOMEN				
3 km	12:51.26	Kerry Ann Saxby (Australia; b. 2 Jun 1961)	Melbourne, Australia	7 Feb 1991
5 km	20:07.52	Beate Anders (East Germany; b. 4 Feb 1968)	Rostock, Germany	23 Jun 1990
10 km	41:56.23	Nadezhda Ryashkina (USSR; b. 2 Jan 1967)	Seattle, WA	24 Jul 1990

b. 21 Mar 1956) at London, Great Britain on 21 Apr 1985.

Boston Marathon First run by 15 men on 19 Apr 1897 over a distance of 24 miles 1,232 yards, the Boston Marathon is the world's oldest annual race. The full marathon distance was first run in 1927. It is run every year from Hopkinton to Boston on or about April 19, Patriot's Day, which honors the famed ride of Paul Revere through Boston.

The most wins is seven, by Clarence DeMar (1888–1958), in 1911, 1922–24, 1927–28 and 1930.

Kathy Switzer (USA) contested the race in 1967, although the race director tried

US NATIONAL RECORDS *WOMEN*

RUNNING	min sec	Name	Place	Date	
100 meters	10.49	Delorez Florence Griffith Joyner (b. 21 Dec 1959)	Indianapolis, IN	16 Jul	1988
200 meters	21.34	Florence Griffith Joyner	Seoul, South Korea	29 Sep	1988
400 meters	48.83	Valerie Ann Brisco (b. 6 Jul 1960)	Los Angeles, CA	6 Aug	1984
800 meters	1:56.90	Mary Thereza Slaney (nee Decker; b. 4 Aug 1958)	Berne, Switzerland	16 Aug	1985
1,000 meters	2:34.8	Mary Slaney	Eugene, OR	4 Jul	1985
1,500 meters	3:57.12	Mary Slaney	Stockholm, Sweden	26 Jul	1983
1 mile	4:16.71	Mary Slaney	Zürich, Switzerland	21 Aug	1985
2,000 meters	5:32.7	Mary Slaney	Eugene, OR	3 Aug	1984
3,000 meters	8:25.83	Mary Slaney	Rome, Italy	7 Sep	1985
5,000 meters	15:00.00	Patricia Susan "Patti-Sue" Plumer (b. 27 Apr 1962)	Stockholm, Sweden	3 Jul	1989
10,000 meters	31:28.92	Francie Larrieu-Smith (b. 23 Nov 1952)	Austin, TX	4 Apr	1991
Marathon	2 hr 21:21	Joan Samuelson (nee Benoit; b. 16 May 1957)	Chicago, IL	20 Oct	1985

HURDLING		Name	Place	Date	
100 meters	12.61	Yolanda Gail Devers (now Roberts; b. 19 Nov 1966)	Los Angeles, CA	21 May	1988
	12.61	Jacqueline Joyner-Kersee (b. 3 Mar 1962)	San Jose, CA	28 May	1988
400 meters	53.37	Sandra Marie Farmer-Patrick (b. 18 Aug 1962)	New York, NY	22 Jul	1989

RELAYS		Name	Place	Date	
4 × 100 meters	41.55	National Team (Alice Regina Brown, Diane Williams, Florence Griffith Joyner, Pam Marshall)	Berlin, Germany	21 Aug	1987
4 × 200 meters	1:32.57	Louisiana State University (Tananjalyn Stanley, Sylvia Brydson, Esther Jones, Dawn Sowell)	Des Moines, IA	28 Apr	1989
4 × 400 meters	3:15.51	National Team (Denean Howard, Diane Lynn Dixon, Valerie Brisco, Florence Griffith Joyner)	Seoul, South Korea	1 Oct	1988
4 × 800 meters	8:17.09	Athletics West (Susan Addison, Lee Arbogast, Mary Decker, Chris Mullen)	Walnut, CA	24 Apr	1983

FIELD EVENTS	ft in	Name	Place	Date	
High jump	6 8	Dorothy Louise Ritter (b. 18 Feb 1958)	Austin, TX	8 Jul	1988
	6 8	Louise Ritter	Seoul, South Korea	30 Sep	1988
Long jump	24 5 ½	Jacqueline Joyner-Kersee	Indianapolis, IN	13 Aug	1987
Triple jump	46 0 ¾	Sheila Hudson (b. 30 Jun 1967)	Durham, NC	2 Jun	1990
Shot	66 2 ½	Ramona Lu Pagel (nee Ebert; b. 10 Nov 1961)	San Diego, CA	25 Jun	1988
Discus	216 10	Carol Therese Cady (b. 6 Jun 1962)	San Jose, CA	31 May	1986
Javelin	227 5	Kathryn Joan "Kate" Schmidt (b. 29 Dec 1963)	Fürth, Germany	11 Sep	1977

HEPTATHLON		Name	Place	Date	
7,291 points		Jacqueline Joyner-Kersee	Seoul, South Korea	23–24 Sep	1988

(100 m hurdles 12.69 sec; High jump 6 ft 1 ¼ in; Shot 51 ft 10 in; 200 m 22.56 sec; Long jump 23 ft 10 in; Javelin 149 ft 9 in; 800 m 2 min 08.51 sec)

to prevent her, but pioneering efforts helped force the acceptance of women runners, and they were admitted officially for the first time in 1972. Rosa Mota (Portugal; b. 29 Jun 1958) has a record three wins, 1987–88 and 1990, in the women's competition.

The course record for men is 2 hr 8 min 19 sec, by Gelindo Bordin (Italy; b. 2 Apr 1959), and for women the record is 2 hr 22 min 43 sec, by Joan Benoit (USA; now Samuelson) in 1983.

New York City Marathon The race was run in Central Park each year from 1970 to 1976, when, to celebrate the US Bicentennial, the course was changed to a route through all five boroughs of the city. Since that year, when there were 2,090 runners, the race has become one of the world's great sporting occasions, and in 1989 reached a peak of 24,588 finishers. In 1990 there were 25,012 runners with 23,774 finishers.

William Henry "Bill" Rodgers (USA; b. 23 Dec 1947) had a record four wins—1976–79; and Grete Waitz (nee Andersen [Norway]; b. 1 Oct 1953) was the women's winner nine times—1978–80, 1982–86 and 1988.

The course record for men is 2 hr 8 min 1 sec by Juma Ikangaa (Tanzania; b. 19 Jul 1957), and for women it is 2 hr 25 min 30 sec by Ingrid Kristiansen (Norway; b. 21 Mar 1956) in 1990. On a course subsequently remeasured as about 170 yd short, Grete Waitz was the 1981 women's winner in 2 hr 25 min 29 sec.

Most competitors The record number of confirmed finishers in a marathon is 24,953 in the London Marathon, Great Britain on 22 Apr 1990. A record 105 men ran under 2 hr 20 min, and 46 ran under 2 hr 15 min in the World Cup Marathon at London on 21 Apr 1991, and a record six men ran under 2 hr 10 min at Fukuoka, Japan on 4 Dec 1983 and at London on 23 Apr 1989. A record nine women ran under 2 hr 30 min in the first Olympic marathon for women at Los Angeles on 5 Aug 1984.

Most run by an individual Thian K. "Sy" Mah (Canada; 1926–88) ran 524 marathons of 26 miles 385 yd or longer from 1967 to his death in 1988. He paced himself to take 3½ hr for each run.

Three in three days The fastest combined time for three marathons in three days is 8 hr 22 min 31 sec by Raymond Hubbard (Belfast, Northern Ireland: 2 hr 45 min 55 sec; London, Great Britain: 2 hr 48 min 45 sec; and Boston: 2 hr 47 min 51 sec) on 16–18 Apr 1988.

Oldest finishers The oldest man to complete a marathon was Dimitrion Yordanidis (Greece), age 98, in Athens, Greece on 10 Oct 1976. He finished in 7 hr 33 min. Thelma Pitt-Turner (New Zealand) set the women's age record in August 1985, completing the Hastings, New Zealand Marathon in 7 hr 58 min at the age of 82.

WALKING

Most Olympic medals Walking races have been included in the Olympic events since 1906. The only walker to win three gold medals has been Ugo Frigerio (Italy; 1901–68) with the 3,000 m in 1920, and 10,000 m in 1920 and 1924. He also holds the record for most medals, with four (he won the bronze medal at 50,000 m in 1932), a total shared with Vladimir Stepanovich Golubnichiy (USSR; b. 2 Jun 1936), who won gold medals for the 20,000 m in 1960 and 1968, the silver in 1972 and the bronze in 1964.

Most titles Four-time Olympian, Ronald Owen Laird (b. 31 May 1938) of the New York AC won a total of 65 US national titles from 1958 to 1976, plus four Canadian Championships.

Longest race The race from Paris to Colmar (until 1980 from Strasbourg to Paris) in France (instituted 1926 in the reverse direction), now about 325 miles, is the world's longest annual race walk.

Walking on hands The distance record for walking on hands is 871 miles, by Johann Hurlinger of Austria, who in 55 daily 10 hr stints averaged 1.58 mph from Vienna, Austria to Paris, France in 1900.

Shin Don-mok of South Korea completed a 54.68-yd inverted sprint in 17.44 sec at the Toda Sports Center, Saitama, Japan on 14 Nov 1986.

The four-man relay team of David Lutterman, Brendan Price, Philip Savage and Danny Scannell covered 1 mile in 24 min 48 sec on 15 Mar 1987 at Knoxville, TN. This compares with the record of 3 min 2 sec the right way up.

ULTRA LONG DISTANCE WORLD RECORDS

TRACK (Men)

Event	hr:min:sec	Name and country	Place	Date	
50 km	2:48:06	Jeff Norman (Great Britain)	Manchester, Great Britain	7 Jun	1980
50 miles	4:51:49	Don Ritchie (Great Britain)	London, Great Britain	12 Mar	1983
100 km	6:10:20	Don Ritchie (Great Britain)	London, Great Britain	28 Oct	1978
100 miles	11:30:51	Don Ritchie (Great Britain)	London, Great Britain	15 Oct	1977
200 km	15:11:10*	Yiannis Kouros (Greece)	Montauban, France	15–16 Mar	1985
200 miles	27:48:35	Yiannis Kouros (Greece)	Montauban, France	15–16 Mar	1985
500 km	60:23:00	Yiannis Kouros (Greece)	Colac, Australia	26–29 Nov	1984
500 miles	105:42:09	Yiannis Kouros (Greece)	Colac, Australia	26–30 Nov	1984
1,000 km	136:17:00	Yiannis Kouros (Greece)	Colac, Australia	26 Nov–1 Dec	1984
kilometers					
24 hours	283.600	Yiannis Kouros (Greece)	Montauban, France	15–16 Mar	1985
48 hours	452.270	Yiannis Kouros (Greece)	Montauban, France	15–17 Mar	1985
6 days	1,023.200	Yiannis Kouros (Greece)	Colac, Australia	26 Nov–1 Dec	1984

ROAD (Men)
Where superior to track bests and run on properly measured road courses

	hr:min:sec				
50 km	2:43:38	Thompson Magawana (S. Africa)	Claremont–Kirstenbosch, South Africa	12 Apr	1988
50 miles	4:50:21	Bruce Fordyce (S. Africa)	London–Brighton, Great Britain	25 Sep	1983
1,000 miles	10d 10hr 30min 35sec	Yiannis Kouros (Greece)	New York City	21–30 May	1988
kilometers					
24 hours	286.463	Yiannis Kouros (Greece)	New York City	28–29 Sep	1985
6 days	1,028.370	Yiannis Kouros (Greece)	New York City	21–26 May	1988

TRACK (Women)

	hr:min:sec				
15 km	49:44.0	Silvana Cruciata (Italy)	Rome, Italy	4 May	1981
20 km	1:06:55.5	Rosa Mota (Portugal)	Lisbon, Portugal	14 May	1983
25 km	1:29:30	Karolina Szabo (Hungary)	Budapest, Hungary	23 Apr	1988
30 km	1:47:06	Karolina Szabo (Hungary)	Budapest, Hungary	23 Apr	1988
50 km	3:36:58	Ann Franklin (Great Britain)	Barry, Great Britain	9 Mar	1986
50 miles	6:17:30*	Monika Kuno (West Germany)	Vogt, Germany	8–9 Jul	1983
100 km	8:01:01	Monika Kuno (West Germany)	Vogt, Germany	8–9 Jul	1983
100 miles	14:29:44	Ann Trason (USA)	Santa Rosa, CA	18–19 Mar	1989
200 km	19:28:48	Eleanor Adams (Great Britain)	Melbourne, Australia	19–20 Aug	1989
200 miles	39:09:03	Hilary Walker (Great Britain)	Blackpool, Great Britain	5–6 Nov	1988
500 km	77:53:46	Eleanor Adams (Great Britain)	Colac, Australia	13–15 Nov	1989
500 miles	134:01:59	Eleanor Adams (Great Britain)	Colac, Australia	13–19 Nov	1989
kilometers					
1 hour	18.084	Silvana Cruciata (Italy)	Rome, Italy	4 May	1981
24 hours	240.169	Eleanor Adams (Great Britain)	Melbourne, Australia	19–20 Aug	1989
48 hours	366.512	Hilary Walker (Great Britain)	Blackpool, Great Britain	5–7 Nov	1988
6 days	866.631	Sandra Barwick (New Zealand)	Campbelltown, Australia	18–24 Nov	1990

*Timed on one running watch only.

ROAD (Women)
Where run on properly measured road courses

	hr:min:sec				
30 km	1:38:27	Ingrid Kristiansen (Norway)	London, Great Britain	10 May	1987
50 km	3:08:13	Frith van der Merwe (S. Africa)	Claremont-Kirstenbosch, South Africa	25 Mar	1989
50 miles	5:40:18	Ann Trason (USA)	Houston, TX	23 Feb	1991
100 km	7:18:57	Birgit Lennartz (West Germany)	Hanua, Germany	28 Sep	1989
100 miles	13:55:02	Ann Trason (USA)	Queens, NY	16–17 Sep	1989
200 km	19:22:05	Ann Trason (USA)	Queens, NY	16–17 Sep	1989
(indoors)	19:00:31	Eleanor Adams (Great Britain)	Milton Keynes, Great Britain	3–4 Feb	1990
1,000 miles	14d 20hr 18min 24sec	Suprabha Schecter (USA)	New York City	20 Sep–5 Oct	1989

It should be noted that road times must be assessed with care as course conditions can vary considerably.

It should be noted that the severity of road race courses and the accuracy of their measurement may vary, sometimes making comparisons of times unreliable.

MEN

20 km: 1 hr 18 min 13 sec, Pavol Blazek (Czechoslovakia; b. 9 Jul 1958) at Hildesheim, Germany on 16 Sep 1990.

30 km: 2 hr 2 min 41 sec, Andrey Perlov (USSR; b. 12 Dec 1961) at Leningrad, USSR on 5 Aug 1989.

50 km: 3 hr 37 min 41 sec, Andrey Perlov (USSR) at Leningrad, USSR on 5 Aug 1989.

WOMEN

10 km: 41 min 30 sec, Kerry Ann Saxby (Australia; b. 2 Jun 1961) at Canberra, Australia on 27 Aug 1988.

20 km: 1 hr 29 min 40 sec, Kerry Saxby at Värnamo, Sweden on 13 May 1988.

---

lin, a springboard) dates from 1936, when the prototype "T" model trampoline was developed by George Nissen (USA).

World Championships World Championships were instituted in 1964. A record five titles were won by Judy Wills (USA; b. 1948) in the women's event, 1964–68. Five men have won two titles.

United States Championships The American Trampoline & Tumbling Association staged the first national individual trampoline championships in 1947. The inaugral event was open only to men; a women's event was introduced in 1961.

Most titles Stuart Ransom has won a record 12 national titles: 6, individual (1975–76, 1978–80, 1982); 3, synchronized (1975, 1979–80); and 3, double mini-tramp (1979–80, 1982). Leigh Hennessy has won a record 10 women's titles: 1, individual (1978); 8, synchronized (1972–73, 1976–78, 1980–82); and 1, double mini-tramp (1978).

Somersaults Christopher Gibson performed 3,025 consecutive somersaults at Shipley Park, Derbyshire, Great Britain on 17 Nov 1989.

The most complete somersaults in one minute is 75, by Richard Cobbing of Lightwater, Great Britain, at British Broadcasting Corporation Television Centre, London, Great Britain for the *Record Breakers* TV program on 8 Nov 1989. The most baranis in a minute is 78 by Zoe Finn of Chatham, Great Britain at British Broadcasting Corporation Television Centre, London, Great Britain on 25 Jan 1988.

---

50 km Road walk
Sandra Brown (Great Britain; b. 1 Apr 1949) was the first woman to walk 50 km in less than 5 hours. She completed the walk in 4 hrs 50 min 51 sec in Basildon, Great Britain on 13 Jul 1991.

The fastest performance is by Robert Pietquin (Belgium; b. 1938) who walked 315 miles in the 1980 race in 60 hr 1 min 10 sec (after deducting 4 hr compulsory stops). This represents an average speed of 5.25 mph. Roger Quémener (France) has won a record seven times, 1979, 1983, 1985–89. The first woman to complete the race was Annie van der Meer (Netherlands; b. 24 Feb 1947), who was 10th in 1983 in 82 hr 10 min.

Twenty-four hours The greatest distance walked in 24 hr is 140 miles 1,229 yd, by Paul Forthomme (Belgium)

on a road course at Woluwe, Belgium on 13–14 Oct 1984. The best by a woman is 125.7 miles by Annie van der Meer at Rouen, France on 30 Apr–1 May 1984 over a 1.185 km lap road course.

Trampolining

Trampolines were used in show business at least as early as "The Walloons" of the period 1910–12. The sport of trampolining (from the Spanish word *trampo-*

Triathlon

The triathlon combines long-distance swimming, cycling and running. Distances for each of the phases can vary, but for the best-established event, the

Walking on water
Wearing 11-ft water ski shoes, called Skijaks, and using a twin-bladed paddle, David Kiner walked 155 miles on the Hudson River from Albany, NY to Battery Park, New York City. His walk took him 57 hr, from 22–27 Jun 1987.

Rémy Bricka of Paris, France "walked" across the Atlantic Ocean on skis 13 ft 9 in long in 1988. Leaving Tenerife, Canary Islands on 2 Apr 1988, he covered 3,502 miles, arriving at Trinidad on 31 May 1988.

Hawaii Ironman (instituted 1978), competitors first swim 2.4 miles, then cycle 112 miles, and finally run a full marathon of 26 miles 385 yards. The fastest time recorded over the Ironman distances is 8 hr 1 min 32 sec, by Dave Scott at Lake Biwa, Japan on 20 Jul 1989.

World Championships After earlier abortive efforts, a world governing body, *L'Union Internationàle de Triathlon* (UIT), was founded at Avignon, France on 1 Apr 1989, staging the first official World Championships in August 1989.

A World Championship race has been held annually in Nice, France from 1982; the distances are 3,200 m, 120 km and 32 km respectively, with the swim increased to 4,000 m from 1988. Mark Allen (USA) has won eight times, 1982–86, 1989–91. Paula Newby-Fraser (Zimbabwe) has a record three women's wins 1989–91. The fastest times are: *(men)* 5 hr 46 min 10 sec in 1988, by Mark Allen; *(women)* 6 hr 27 min 6 sec in 1988, by Erin Baker (New Zealand).

Hawaii Ironman This is the first, and best known, of the triathlons. The first race, held on 18 Feb 1978, was contested by 15 athletes. The Ironman grew rapidly in popularity, and 1,000 athletes entered the 1984 race. Dave Scott (USA) has won the Ironman a record six times— 1980, 1982–84, 1986–87. Mark Allen (USA) holds the record for fastest time at 8 hr 9 min 16 sec on 15 Oct 1989. The women's event has been won a record three times by Paula Newby-Fraser (Zimbabwe) in 1986, 1988–89. Newby-Fraser holds the course record for women at 9 hr 0 min 56 sec on 15 Oct 1989.

Largest field The largest field in a triathlon race has been 3,888 finishers, in the Bud Lite US Triathlon race at Chicago, IL in 1987. This series encompasses races over 1,500 m, 40 km and 10 km for the three phases.

T*ug of War*

Origins Though ancient China and Egypt have been suggested as the originators of the sport, it is known that Neolithic flint miners in Great Britain practiced "rope-pulling." The first rules were those framed by the New York AC in 1879. Tug of War was an Olympic sport from 1900 until 1920. World Cham-

pionships have been held annually 1975–86 and biennially since, with a women's event introduced in 1986.

Most titles The most successful team at the World Championships has been England, which has won 15 of the 25 titles in all categories, 1975–88. Sweden has won both the 520 kg and the 560 kg category twice at the Womens' World Championships, in 1986 and 1988.

The Wood Treatment team (formerly the Bosley Farmers) of Cheshire, Great Britain won 20 consecutive AAA Catchweight Championships 1959–78, two world titles (1975–76) and ten European titles at 720 kg. Hilary Brown (b. 13 Apr 1934) was on every team. Trevor Brian Thomas (Great Britain; b. 1943) of British Aircraft Corporation Club is the only holder of three winners'

Tightrope walking

The greatest 19th-century tightrope walker was Jean-François Gravelet, alias Charles Blondin (1824–97), of France, who made the earliest crossing of Niagara Falls on a 3 in rope, 1,100 ft long, 160 ft above the falls on 30 Jun 1859.

The oldest tightrope walker was "Professor" William Ivy Baldwin (1866–1953), who crossed the South Boulder Canyon, CO on a 320 ft wire with a 125 ft drop on his 82nd birthday on 31 Jul 1948.

The world tightrope endurance record is 185 days, by Henri Rochatain (b. 1926) of France, on a wire 394 ft long, 82 ft above a supermarket in St Etienne, France from 28 Mar–29 Sep 1973. His ability to sleep on the wire has left doctors puzzled.

Ashley Brophy of Neilborough, Victoria, Australia walked 7.18 miles on a wire 147.64 ft long and 32.81 ft above the ground at the Adelaide Grand Prix, Australia on 1 Nov 1985 in 3½ hr.

Steve McPeak (b. 21 Apr 1945) of Las Vegas, NV ascended the 1.83-in-diameter Zugspitzbahn cable on the Zugspitze, Germany for a vertical height of 2,313 ft in three stages aggregating 5 hr 4 min on 24, 25 and 28 Jun 1981. The maximum gradient over the stretch of 7,485 ft was more than 30°.

The greatest drop over which anyone has walked on a tightrope is 10,335 ft, above the French countryside, by Michel Menin of Lons-le-Saunier, France, on 4 Aug 1989.

medals in the European Open club competitions and added a world gold medal in 1988.

Longest pulls *Duration* The longest recorded pull (prior to the introduction of AAA rules) is one of 2 hr 41 min when "H" Company beat "E" Company of the 2nd Battalion of the Sherwood Foresters (Derbyshire Regiment) at Jubbulpore, India on 12 Aug 1889. The longest recorded pull under AAA rules (in which lying on the ground or entrenching the feet is not permitted) is one of 24 min 45 sec for the first pull between the Republic of Ireland and England during the world championships (640 kg class) at Malmö, Sweden on 18 Sep 1988. The record time for "The Pull" (instituted 1898), across the Black River, between freshman and sophomore teams at Hope College, Holland, MI, is 3 hr 51 min on 23 Sep 1977, but the method of bracing the feet precludes this replacing the preceding records.

Distance The longest tug of war is the 1.616 mile Supertug across Little Traverse Bay, Lake Michigan. It has been contested annually since 1980 between two teams of 20 from Bay View Inn and Harbor Inn.

Volleyball

The game was invented as *mintonette* in 1895 by William G. Morgan at the YMCA gymnasium at Holyoke, MA. The *Fédération Internationale de Volleyball* (FIVB) was formed in Paris, France in April 1947 and is now based in Switzerland.

The United States Volleyball Association was founded in 1922 and remains the governing body for the sport in this country. The United States National Championships were inaugurated in 1928 for men and in 1949 for women.

Most world titles World Championships were instituted in 1949 for men and in 1952 for women. The USSR has won six men's titles (1949, 1952, 1960, 1962, 1978 and 1982) and five women's (1952, 1956, 1960, 1970 and 1990)

Most Olympic titles The sport was introduced to the Olympic Games for both men and women in 1964. The USSR has won a record three men's (1964, 1968 and 1980) and four women's (1968, 1972, 1980 and 1988) titles. The only player to win four medals is Inna Valeryevna Ryskal (USSR; b. 15 Jun 1944), who won women's silver medals in 1964 and 1976 and golds in 1968 and 1972. The record for men is held by Yuriy Mikhailovich Poyarkov (USSR; b. 10 Feb 1937), who won gold medals in 1964 and 1968 and a bronze in 1972; and by Katsutoshi Nekoda (Japan; b. 1 Feb 1944), who won gold in 1972, silver in 1968 and bronze in 1964.

The USA won the men's championship in 1984 and 1988. Three men played on each of the winning teams and on the only US teams to win the World Cup

(1985) and World Championships (1986): Craig Buck (b. 24 Aug 1958), Charles "Karch" Kiraly (b. 3 Nov 1960), and Stephen Timmons (b. 29 Nov 1958). David Saunders (b. 19 Oct 1960) was a reserve on the 1984 team and played on those of 1986 and 1988. "Karch" Kiraly is the only player to win an Olympic gold medal and the World Championship of Beach Volleyball.

Water Polo

Water polo was developed in England as "water soccer" in 1869 and first included in the Olympic Games in Paris, France in 1900.

Professor John Robinson, an Englishman hired as aquatics director of the Boston Athletic Association in 1888, is credited with introducing water polo to the United States. The first official game took place on 28 Jan 1890 in Providence, RI, with the Syndenham Swimming Club of Providence defeating Boston AA, 2–1. The Amateur Athletic Association served as the sport's governing body from 1897 to 1978; since 1978 U.S. Water Polo, Inc. has run the sport in the United States.

Most Olympic titles Hungary has won the Olympic tournament most often, with six wins, in 1932, 1936, 1952, 1956, 1964 and 1976.

Five players share the record of three gold medals: Britons George Wilkinson (1879–1946), in 1900, 1908, 1912; Paulo "Paul" Radmilovic (1886–1968), and Charles Sidney Smith (1879–1951), in 1908, 1912, 1920; and Hungarians Deszö Gyarmati (b. 23 Oct 1927) and György Kárpáti (b. 23 Jun 1935), in 1952, 1956, and 1964. Paul Radmilovic also won a gold medal for 4 × 200 m freestyle swimming in 1908.

US teams took all the medals in 1904, but there were no foreign contestants. Since then their best result has been silver in 1984.

World Championships This competition was first held at the World Swimming Championships in 1973. The most wins is two by the USSR, 1975 and 1982, and Yugoslavia, 1986 and 1991 (Yugoslavia has also won three Olympic titles, 1968, 1984 and 1988). A women's competition was introduced in 1986, when it was won by Australia. The Netherlands won the second women's world title in 1991.

Most goals The greatest number of goals scored by an individual in an international match is 13, by Debbie Handley for Australia (16) *v* Canada (10) at the World Championship in Guayaquil, Ecuador in 1982.

Most international appearances The greatest number of international appearances is 412, by Aleksey Stepanovich Barkalov (USSR; b. 18 Feb 1946), 1965–80.

US National Championships Inaugurated in 1891, the New York Athletic Club has won a record 24 men's championships: 1892–96, 1903–08, 1922, 1929–31, 1933–35, 1937–39, 1954, 1961, 1971. The women's championship was first held in 1926; the Industry Hills Athletic Club (California) has won a record seven titles: 1980–81, 1984–88.

Waterskiing

The origins of waterskiing derive from walking on planks and aquaplaning. A 19th-century treatise on sorcerers refers to Eliseo of Tarentum, who, in the 14th century, "walks and dances" on the water. The first report of aquaplaning was on America's Pacific Coast in the early 1900s. At Scarborough, Great Britain on 15 Jul 1914, a single plank-gliding contest was won by H. Storry.

The present-day sport of waterskiing was pioneered by Ralph W. Samuelson (1904–77) on Lake Pepin, MN, on two curved pine boards in the summer of 1922, although claims have been made for the birth of the sport on Lake Annecy (Haute-Savoie), France at about the same time. The first world organization, the *Union Internationale de Ski Nautique*, was formed in Geneva on 27 Jul 1946.

The American Water Ski Association was founded in 1939 and held the first national championships that year.

Most titles World Overall Championships (instituted 1949) have been won four times by Sammy Duvall (USA), in 1981, 1983, 1985 and 1987, and three times by two women, Willa McGuire (nee Worthington), of the USA in 1949–50 and 1955, and Elizabeth "Liz" Allan-Shetter (USA), in 1965, 1969 and 1975. Liz Allan-Shetter has won a record eight individual championship events and is the only person to win all four titles—slalom, jumping, tricks and overall in one year, at Copenhagen, Denmark in 1969. The USA has won the team championship on 17 successive occasions, 1957–89.

United States US national championships were first held at Marine Stadium, Jones Beach State Park, Long Island, NY on 22 Jul 1939. The most overall titles is eight, by Willa Worthington McGuire, 1946–51 and 1954–55, and by Liz Allan-Shetter, 1968–75. The men's record is six titles, by Chuck Stearns, 1957–58, 1960, 1962, 1965 and 1967.

Fastest speed The fastest waterskiing speed recorded is 143.08 mph, by Christopher Michael Massey (Australia) on the Hawkesbury River, Windsor, New South Wales, Australia on 6 Mar 1983. His drag boat driver was Stanley Charles Sainty. Donna Patterson Brice (b. 1953) set a women's record of 111.11 mph at Long Beach, CA on 21 Aug 1977.

Longest run The greatest distance traveled is 1,321.16 miles, by Steve Fontaine (USA) on 24–26 Oct 1988 at Jupiter Hills, FL.

WATERSKIING RECORDS

SLALOM
MEN: 3 buoys on a 10.25 m line, Andrew Mapple (Great Britain; b. 3 Nov 1958), at Lantana, FL on 29 Mar 1991.
WOMEN: 1 buoy on a 10.75 m line, Susi Graham (Canada) and Debra Mapple (nee Bush; USA) at West Palm Beach, FL on 13 Oct 1990.

TRICKS
MEN: 11,030 points, Tony Baggiaro (USA) at Destin, FL on 15 Sep 1990.
WOMEN: 8,460 points, Tawn Larsen (USA) at Sparta, NJ on 29 Aug 1988.

JUMPING
MEN: 205 ft, Sammy Duvall (USA) at Shreveport, FL on 24 Jul 1988.
WOMEN: 156 ft, Deena Mapple (nee Brush; USA) at Charlotte, NC on 9 Jul 1988.

Barefoot The first person to water-ski barefoot is reported to be Dick Pope, Jr. at Lake Eloise, FL on 6 Mar 1947. The barefoot duration record is 2 hr 42 min 39 sec, by Billy Nichols (USA; b. 1964) on Lake Weir, FL on 19 Nov 1978. The backward barefoot record is 39 min, by Paul McManus (Australia).

The official barefoot speed record is 135.74 mph by Scott Michael Pellaton (b. 8 Oct 1956) over a quarter-mile course at Chandler, AZ, in November 1989. The fastest by a woman is 73.67 mph by Karen Toms (Australia) on the Hawkesbury River, Windsor, New South Wales on 31 Mar 1984.

The fastest official speed backwards barefoot is 62 mph, by Robert Wing (Australia; b. 13 Aug 1957) on 3 Apr 1982.

The barefoot jump record is: *(men)* 76 ft 5 in, by Mike Seipel (USA) at Jacksonville, FL on 13 Oct 1990; and *(women)* 54 ft 1 in, by Debbie Pugh (Australia) in 1990.

Weightlifting

Competitions for lifting weights of stone were held in the ancient Olympic Games. The first championships entitled "world" were staged at the Café Monico, Piccadilly, London, Great Britain on 28 Mar 1891 and then in Vienna, Austria on 19–20 Jul 1898, subsequently recognized by the IWF. Prior to that time, weightlifting consisted of professional exhibitions in which some of the advertised poundages were open to doubt.

The *Fédération Internationàle Haltérophile et Culturiste*, now the International Weightlifting Federation (IWF), was established in 1905, and its first official championships were held in Tallinn, Estonia, USSR on 29–30 Apr 1922.

There are two standard lifts: the "snatch" and the "clean and jerk" (or "jerk"). Totals of the two lifts determine competition results. The "press," which was a standard lift, was abolished in 1972.

Most titles *World* The most world title wins, including Olympic Games, is eight, by: John Henry Davis (USA; 1921–84) in 1938, 1946–52; Tommy Kono (USA; b. 27 Jun 1930) in 1952–59; and Vasiliy Alekseiev (USSR; b. 7 Jan 1942), 1970–77.

United States The most US national titles won is 13, by Anthony Terlazzo (1911–66), at 137 lb, 1932 and 1936 and at 148 lb 1933, 1935, 1937–45.

The only American woman to win a world title has been Karyn Marshall, at 82 kg in 1987.

Youngest world record holder Naim Suleimanov (later Neum Shalamanov [Bulgaria]; b. 23 Jan 1967) (now Naim Suleymanoğlü of Turkey) set 56 kg world records for clean and jerk (160 kg) and total (285 kg), at 16 yr 62 days, at Allentown, NJ on 26 Mar 1983.

Heaviest lift to body weight The first man to clean and jerk more than three times his body weight was Stefan Topurov (Bulgaria), who lifted 396¾ lb

WOMEN'S WEIGHTLIFTING RECORDS

Official World records can only be set at World Championships, which were instituted in 1987. The venues have been: 1987, Daytona Beach, FL; 1988, Jakarta, Indonesia; 1989, Manchester, Great Britain; 1990, Sarajevo, Yugoslavia. However, this list includes superior marks (*), where applicable, made in the Asian Games.

Bodyweight	Lift	Weight kg	Weight lb	Name and country	
44 kg *97 lb*	Snatch	72.5	159¾	Xing Fen (China)	1989
	Jerk	95	209¼	Xing Fen (China) *	1990
	Total	165	363¾	Xing Fen (China)	1989
48 kg *105¾ lb*	Snatch	75	165¼	Huang Xiaoyu (China)	1987
	Jerk	97.5	215	Huang Xiaoyu (China)	1989
	Total	172.5	380¼	Huang Xiaoyu (China)	1989
52 kg *114½ lb*	Snatch	80	176¼	Peng Liping (China)	1988
	Jerk	107.5	237	Peng Liping (China)	1989
	Total	185	407¾	Peng Liping (China)	1989
56 kg *123¼ lb*	Snatch	85	187¼	Xing Liwei (China) *	1990
	Jerk	107.5	237	Wu Haiqing (China)	1990
	Total	190	418¾	Wu Haiqing (China)	1990
60 kg *132¼ lb*	Snatch	92.5	203¾	Ma Na (China) *	1990
	Jerk	115	253½	Ma Na (China)	1989
	Total	207.5	457¼	Ma Na (China) *	1990
67.5 kg *148¾ lb*	Snatch	100	220¼	Guo Qiuxiang (China) *	1990
	Jerk	122.5	270	Guo Qiuxiang (China)	1989
	Total	220	485	Guo Qiuxiang (China)	1989
75 kg *165¼ lb*	Snatch	102.5	226	Milena Trendafilova (Bulgaria)	1990
	Jerk	135	297½	Milena Trendafilova (Bulgaria)	1990
	Total	237.5	523½	Milena Trendafilova (Bulgaria)	1990
82.5 kg *181¾ lb*	Snatch	102.5	226	Li Hongling (China)	1989
	Jerk	137.5	303	Li Hongling (China)	1989
	Total	240	529	Li Hongling (China)	1989
+82.5 kg *242½ lb*	Snatch	112.5	248	Karyn Marshall (USA)	1990
	Jerk	142.5	314	Li Yajuan (China)	1990
	Total	245	540	Li Yajuan (China)	1990

■ **Most waterskiing titles**
The most World Overall Championships is four, by Sammy Duvall (USA) in 1981, 1983, 1985 and 1987. The overall title is decided on the combined results of the slalom, tricks, and jumping, and titles are also awarded for these individual disciplines. Duvall won two jumping titles, 1983 and 1987. (Photo: All-Sport [USA]/Tennent)

Most skiers towed by one boat
A record 100 waterskiers were towed on double skis over a nautical mile by the cruiser *Reef Cat* at Cairns, Queensland, Australia on 18 Oct 1986. This feat, organized by the Cairns and District Powerboat and Ski Club, was then replicated by 100 skiers on single skis.

MEN'S WEIGHTLIFTING RECORDS

Bodyweight class	Lift	Weight kg	lb	Name and country	Place	Date	
52 kg *114 1/2 lb* FLYWEIGHT	Snatch	120.0	264 1/2	Sevdalin Marinov (Bulgaria)	Seoul, South Korea	18 Sep	1988
	Jerk	155.0	341 3/4	Ivan Ivanov (Bulgaria)	Athens, Greece	16 Sep	1989
	Total	272.5	600 3/4	Ivan Ivanov (Bulgaria)	Athens, Greece	16 Sep	1989
56 kg *123 1/4 lb* BANTAMWEIGHT	Snatch	134.5	296 1/2	Liu Shoubin (China)	Kemerovo, USSR	1 Mar	1989
	Jerk	171.0	377	Neno Terziiski (Bulgaria)	Ostrava, Czechoslovakia	6 Sep	1987
	Total	300.0	661 1/4	Naim Suleimanov (Bulgaria)	Varna, Bulgaria	11 May	1984
60 kg *132 1/4 lb* FEATHERWEIGHT	Snatch	152.5	336	Naim Suleymanoğlü (Turkey)*	Seoul, South Korea	20 Sep	1988
	Jerk	190.0	418 3/4	Naim Suleymanoğlü (Turkey)*	Seoul, South Korea	20 Sep	1988
	Total	342.5	755	Naim Suleymanoğlü (Turkey)*	Seoul, South Korea	20 Sep	1988
67.5 kg *148 3/4 lb* † LIGHTWEIGHT	Snatch	160.0	352 3/4	Israil Militosyan (USSR)	Athens, Greece	18 Sep	1989
	Jerk	200.5	442	Mikhail Petrov (Bulgaria)	Ostrava, Czechoslovakia	8 Sep	1987
	Total	355.0	782 1/2	Mikhail Petrov (Bulgaria)	Seoul, South Korea	5 Dec	1987
75 kg *165 1/4 lb* MIDDLEWEIGHT	Snatch	170.0	374 3/4	Angel Guenchev (Bulgaria)	Miskolc, Hungary	11 Dec	1987
	Jerk	215.5	475	Aleksandr Varbanov (Bulgaria)	Seoul, South Korea	5 Dec	1987
	Total	382.5	843 1/4	Aleksandr Varbanov (Bulgaria)	Plovdiv, Bulgaria	20 Feb	1988
82.5 kg *181 3/4 lb* LIGHT-HEAVYWEIGHT	Snatch	183.0	403 1/4	Asen Zlatev (Bulgaria)	Melbourne, Australia	7 Dec	1986
	Jerk	225.0	496	Asen Zlatev (Bulgaria)	Sofia, Bulgaria	12 Nov	1986
	Total	405.0	892 3/4	Yurik Vardanyan (USSR)	Varna, Bulgaria	14 Sep	1984
90 kg *198 1/4 lb* MIDDLE-HEAVYWEIGHT	Snatch	195.5	431	Blagoi Blagoyev (Bulgaria)	Varna, Bulgaria	1 May	1983
	Jerk	235.0	518	Anatoliy Khrapatiy (USSR)	Cardiff, Great Britain	29 Apr	1988
	Total	422.5	931 1/4	Viktor Solodov (USSR)	Varna, Bulgaria	15 Sep	1984
100 kg *220 1/4 lb*	Snatch	200.5	442	Nicu Vlad (Romania)	Sofia, Bulgaria	14 Nov	1986
	Jerk	242.5	534 1/2	Aleksandr Popov (USSR)	Tallinn, USSR	5 Mar	1988
	Total	440.0	970	Yuriy Zakharevich (USSR)	Odessa, USSR	4 Mar	1983
110 kg *242 1/2 lb* HEAVYWEIGHT	Snatch	210.0	462 3/4	Yuriy Zakharevich (USSR)	Seoul, South Korea	27 Sep	1988
	Jerk	250.5	552 1/4	Yuriy Zakharevich (USSR)	Cardiff, Great Britain	30 Apr	1988
	Total	455.0	1003	Yuriy Zakharevich (USSR)	Seoul, South Korea	27 Sep	1988
Over 110 kg *242 1/2 lb* SUPER-HEAVYWEIGHT	Snatch	216.0	476	Antonio Krastev (Bulgaria)	Ostrava, Czechoslovakia	13 Sep	1987
	Jerk	266.0	586 1/4	Leonid Taranenko (USSR)	Canberra, Australia	26 Nov	1988
	Total	475.0	1,047	Leonid Taranenko (USSR)	Canberra, Australia	26 Nov	1988

* Formerly Naim Suleimanov or Neum Shalamanov of Bulgaria.

† Angel Guenchev (Bulgaria) achieved 160 kg snatch, 202.5 kg jerk for a 362.5 kg total at Seoul, South Korea on 21 Sep 1988 but was subsequently disqualified on a positive drugs test.

at Moscow, USSR on 24 Oct 1983. The first man to snatch two-and-a-half times his own body weight was Naim Suleymanoğlü (Turkey), who lifted 330 1/2 lb at Cardiff, Great Britain, on 27 Apr 1988. The first woman to clean and jerk more than two times her own body weight was Cheng Jinling (China), who lifted 198 lb in the class of the World Championships at Jakarta, Indonesia in December 1988.

Women's World Championships These are held annually, first at Daytona Beach, FL in October 1987. Women's world records have been ratified for the best marks at these championships. The heaviest lift for any of the nine weight categories has been the 142.5 kg (314 lb) jerk by Li Yajuan (China; b. 1971) for over 82.5 kg at Sarajevo in May 1990.

POWERLIFTING

The sport of powerlifting was first contested at a national level in Great Britain in 1958. The first US Championships were held in 1964. The International Powerlifting Federation was founded in 1972, a year after the first, unofficial world championships were held. Official championships have been held annually for men from 1973 and for women from 1980. The three standard lifts are squat, bench press and dead lift, the totals from the three lifts determining the results.

Most world titles *World* The winner of the most world titles is Hideaki Inaba (Japan) with 16, at 52 kg, 1974–83, 1985–90. Lamar Gant (USA) holds the record for an American with 15 titles, at 56 kg, 1975–77, 1979, 1982–84; and at 60 kg, 1978, 1980–81 and 1986–90. The most by a woman is six by Beverley Francis (Australia; b. 15 Feb 1955), at 75 kg 1980, 1982; 82.5 kg 1981, 1983–85.

Twenty-four-hr and one-hr lifts A

WORLD POWERLIFTING RECORDS
(All weights in kilograms)

Class	Squat		Bench Press		Deadlift		Total	
MEN								
52 kg	245.5	Magnus Karlsson (Sweden) 1990	146.5	Joe Cunha (USA) 1982	237.5	Hideaki Inaba (Japan) 1987	587.5	Hideaki Inaba (Japan) 1987
56 kg	242.5	Hideaki Inaba (Japan) 1988	160.5	Hiroyuki Isagawa (Japan) 1989	289.5	Lamar Gant (USA) 1982	625	Lamar Gant (USA) 1982
60 kg	295	Joe Bradley (USA) 1980	180	Joe Bradley (USA) 1980	310	Lamar Gant (USA) 1988	707.5	Joe Bradley (USA) 1982
67.5 kg	300	Jessie Jackson (USA) 1987	200	Kristoffer Hulecki (Sweden) 1985	315	Daniel Austin (USA) 1989	762.5	Daniel Austin (USA) 1989
75 kg	328	Ausby Alexander (USA) 1989	217.5	James Rouse (USA) 1980	333	Jarmo Virtanen (Finland) 1988	850	Rick Gaugler (USA) 1982
82.5 kg	379.5	Mike Bridges (USA) 1982	240	Mike Bridges (USA) 1981	357.5	Veli Kumpuniemi (Finland) 1980	952.5	Mike Bridges (USA) 1982
90 kg	375	Fred Hatfield (USA) 1980	255	Mike MacDonald (USA) 1980	372.5	Walter Thomas (USA) 1982	937.5	Mike Bridges (USA) 1980
100 kg	422.5	Ed Coan (USA) 1989	261.5	Mike MacDonald (USA) 1977	378	Ed Coan (USA) 1989	1,032.5	Ed Coan (USA) 1989
110 kg	393.5	Dan Wohleber (USA) 1981	270	Jeffrey Magruder (USA) 1982	395	John Kuc (USA) 1980	1,000	John Kuc (USA) 1980
125 kg	413	Kirk Karwoski (USA) 1990	278.5	Tom Hardman (USA) 1982	387.5	Lars Norén (Sweden) 1987	1,005	Ernie Hackett (USA) 1982
125 + kg	445	Dwayne Fely (USA) 1982	300	Bill Kazmaier (USA) 1981	406	Lars Norén (Sweden) 1988	1,100	Bill Kazmaier (USA) 1981
WOMEN								
44 kg	142.5	Delcy Palk (USA) 1988	75	Teri Hoyt (USA) 1982	165	Nancy Belliveau (USA) 1985	352.5	Marie-France Vassart (Bel) 1985
48 kg	150	Claudine Cognac (France) 1990	82.5	Michelle Evris (USA) 1981	182.5	Majik Jones (USA) 1984	390	Majik Jones (USA) 1984
52 kg	173.5	Sisi Dolman (Neth) 1989	95	Mary Ryan (USA) 1984	197.5	Diana Rowell (USA) 1984	427.5	Diana Rowell (USA) 1984
56 kg	191	Mary Jeffrey (nee Ryan; USA) 1989	115	Mary Jeffrey (USA) 1988	200.5	Joy Burt (Canada) 1989	485	Mary Jeffrey (USA) 1988
60 kg	200.5	Ruthi Shafer (USA) 1983	105.5	Judith Auerbach (USA) 1989	213	Ruthi Shafer (USA) 1983	502.5	Vicki Steenrod (USA) 1985
67.5 kg	230	Ruthi Shafer (USA) 1984	117.5	Vicki Steenrod (USA) 1989	244	Ruthi Shafer (USA) 1984	565	Ruthi Shafer (USA) 1984
75 kg	225	Sumita Laha (Ind) 1989	142.5	Liz Odendaal (Neth) 1989	230	Liz Odendaal (Neth) 1989	577.5	Liz Odendaal (Neth) 1989
82.5 kg	230	Juanita Trujillo (USA) 1986	150	Beverley Francis (Aus) 1981	230	Cathy Millen (NZ) 1990	577.5	Beverley Francis (Aus) 1983
90 kg	252.5	Lorraine Constanzo (USA) 1988	130	Lorraine Constanzo (USA) 1988	227.5	Lorraine Constanzo (USA) 1988	607.5	Lorraine Constanzo (USA) 1988
90 +kg	262.5	Lorraine Constanzo (USA) 1987	137.5	Myrtle Augee (GB) 1989	237.5	Lorraine Constanzo (USA) 1987	622.5	Lorraine Constanzo (USA) 1987

deadlifting record of 5,519,839 lb in 24 hr was set by a team of ten from Her Majesty's Prison, Wandsworth, London, Great Britain on 26–27 May 1990. The 24-hr deadlift record by an individual is 818,121 lb by Anthony Wright at Her Majesty's Prison, Featherstone, Wolverhampton, Great Britain, on 31 Aug–1 Sep 1990.

A bench press record of 8,529,699 lb was set by a nine-man team from the Hogarth Barbell Club, Chiswick, London, Great Britain on 18–19 Jul 1987. A squat record of 4,780,994 lb was set by a ten-man team from St Albans Weightlifting Club and Ware Boys Club, Hertfordshire, Great Britain on 20–21 Jul 1986. A record 133,380 arm-curling repetitions using three 48¼ lb weightlifting bars and dumbbells was achieved by a team of nine from Intrim Health and Fitness Club at Gosport, Great Britain on 4–5 Aug 1989.

Michael Williams achieved 1,438 repetitions of his body weight (147.7 lb) in one hour by bench presses at Don Styler's Gymnasium, Gosport, Great Britain on 17 Apr 1989.

Wrestling

The earliest depictions of wrestling holds and falls on wall plaques and a statue indicate that organized wrestling dates from c. 2750–2600 B.C. It was the most popular sport in the ancient Olympic Games, and victors were recorded from 708 B.C. The Greco-Roman style is of French origin, and arose about 1860. The International Amateur Wrestling Federation (FILA) was founded in 1912.

Most titles *Olympic* Three Olympic titles have been won by: Carl Westergren (Sweden; 1895–1958) in 1920, 1924 and 1932; Ivar Johansson (Sweden; 1903–79) in 1932 (two) and 1936; and Aleksandr Vasilyevich Medved (USSR; b. 16 Sep 1937) in 1964, 1968 and 1972. Four Olympic medals were won by: Eino Leino (Finland; b. 7 Apr 1891) at freestyle 1920–32; and by Imre Polyák (Hungary; b. 16 Apr 1932) at Greco-Roman in 1952–64.

The one US wrestler to win two Olympic freestyle titles was George Nicholas Mehnert (1881–1948), flyweight in 1904 and bantamweight in 1908. The first, and only, US men to win a Greco-Roman title were Steven Fraser (b. 23 Mar 1953) at light heavyweight and Jeffrey Blatnick (b. 27 Jul 1957) at super-heavyweight in 1984.

World The freestyler Aleksandr Medved (USSR) won a record ten World Championships, 1962–64, 1966–72 at three weight categories. The only wrestler to win the same title in seven successive years has been Valeriy Grigoryevich Rezantsev (USSR; b. 2 Feb 1947) in the Greco-Roman 90 kg class in 1970–76, including the Olympic Games of 1972 and 1976.

United States The most world titles won by a US wrestler is four (three world, one Olympic), by John Smith (b. 9 Aug 1965), featherweight 1987–90. Three world titles have been won by Leroy Kemp (b. 24 Dec 1956), welterweight, 1978–79 and 1982; and two world and one Olympic title have been won by Mark Schultz (b. 26 Oct 1960), middleweight, 1984, 1985 and 1987.

Most wins In international competition, Osamu Watanabe (Japan; b. 21 Oct 1940), the 1964 Olympic freestyle 63 kg champion, was unbeaten and unscored and unscored-upon in 189 consecutive matches. Outside of FILA sanctioned competition, Wade Schalles (USA) won 821 bouts from 1964 to 1984 with 530 of these victories by pin.

NCAA Division I Championship Oklahoma State University was the first unofficial national champion in 1928. Including five unofficial titles, Oklahoma State has won a record 29 NCAA titles, in 1928–31, 1933–35, 1937–1942, 1946, 1948–49, 1954–56, 1958–59, 1961–62, 1964, 1966, 1968, 1971, 1989–90. The University of Iowa has won the most consecutive titles, with nine championships from 1978–86.

SUMO WRESTLING

The sport's origins in Japan date from c. 23 B.C. The heaviest-ever *rikishi* is Samoan-American Salevaa Fuali Atisnoe of Hawaii, alias Konishiki, who in 1988 had a peak weight of 556 lb. He is also the first foreign *rikishi* to attain the second highest rank of *ozeki*, or champion. Weight is amassed by over-alimentation with a high-protein stew called *chankonabe*.

The most successful wrestlers have been *yokozuna* Sadaji Akiyoshi (b. 1912), alias Futabayama, winner of 69 consecutive bouts in the 1930s; *yokozuna* Koki Naya (b. 1940), alias Taiho ("Great Bird"), who won the Emperor's Cup 32 times up to his retirement in 1971; and the *ozeki* Tameemon Torokichi, alias Raiden (1767–1825), who in 21 years (1789–1810) won 254 bouts and lost only ten for the highest-ever winning percentage of 96.2. Taiho and Futabayama share the record of eight perfect tournaments without a single loss. The youngest of the 62 men to attain the rank of *yokozuna* (grand champion) was Toshimitsu Ogata (b. 16 May 1953), alias Kitanoumi, in July 1974 at the age of 21 years and two months. He set a record in 1978, winning 82 of the 90 bouts that top *rikishi* fight annually.

Yokozuna Mitsugu Akimoto (b. 1 Jun 1955), alias Chiyonofuji, set a record for domination of one of the six annual tournaments by winning the Kyushu Basho for eight successive years, 1981–88. He also holds the record for most career wins, 1,045, and *Makunouchi* (top division) wins, 807. He retired in May 1991 but remains in sumo as a training coach.

Hawaiian-born Jesse Kuhaulua (b. 16 Jun 1944), now a Japanese citizen named Daigoro Watanabe, alias Takamiyama, and a stablemaster in the Japan Sumo Association with the sumo elder (*toshiyori*) name

of Azumazeki Oyakaba, was the first non-Japanese to win an official top-division tournament, in July 1972, and in 1981 he set a record of 1,231 consecutive top-division bouts. He weighed in at 450 lb before his retirement in 1984.

Yukio Shoji (b. 14 Nov 1948), alias Aobajo, did not miss a single bout in his 22-year career, 1964–86, and contested a record 1,631 consecutive bouts. Kenji Hatano (b. 4 Jan 1948), alias Oshio, contested a record 1,891 nonconsecutive bouts in his 26-year career, 1962–88, the longest in modern sumo history.

Katsumi Yamanaka (b. 16 Mar 1967), alias Akinoshima, set a new *kinboshi* (gold star) record of 13 upsets over *yokozuna* by a *maegashira*. Chad Rowan (b. 8 May 1969), alias Akebono of Hawaii, scored a majority of wins for a record 18 consecutive tournaments, March 1988–March 1991.

Yachting

Sailing as a sport dates from the seventeenth century. Originating in the Netherlands, it was introduced to England by Charles II, who participated in a 23 mile race along the river Thames in 1661. The oldest yacht club in the world is the Royal Cork Yacht Club, which claims descent from the Cork Harbor Water Club, founded in Ireland in 1720. The oldest continuously existing yacht club in the United States is the New York Yacht Club, founded in 1844.

Olympic titles The first sportsman ever to win individual gold medals in four successive Olympic Games was Paul B. Elvstrøm (Denmark; b. 25 Feb 1928) in the Firefly class in 1948 and the Finn class in 1952, 1956 and 1960. He also won eight other world titles in a total of six classes. The lowest number of penalty points by the winner of any class in an Olympic regatta is three points (five wins, one disqualified and one second in seven starts) by *Superdocious* of the Flying Dutchman class (Lt Rodney Stuart Pattisson [b. 5 Aug 1943] and Iain Somerled Macdonald-Smith [b. 3 Jul 1945]), at Acapulco Bay, Mexico in Oct 1968.

United States The only US yachtsman to have won two gold medals is Herman Frasch Whiton (1904–67), at six-meter class, in 1948 and 1952.

Admiral's Cup and ocean racing The ocean racing series with the most participating nations (three boats allowed to each nation) is the Admiral's Cup, held by the Royal Ocean Racing Club. A record 19 nations competed in 1975, 1977 and 1979. Britain has a record nine wins.

Modern ocean racing (in moderate or small sailing yachts, rather than professionally manned sailing ships) began with a race from Brooklyn, NY to Bermuda, 630 nautical miles, organized by Thomas Fleming Day, editor of the magazine *The Rudder*, in June 1906. The

Backwards running
Anthony "Scott" Weiland, 27, ran the Detroit marathon backwards in 4 hr 7 min 54 sec on 13 Oct 1982. David Davis (USA; 10 Feb 1960) ran one mile backwards in 6 min 7.1 sec at the University of Hawaii on 21 Feb 1983. Ferdie Ato Adoboe (Ghana) ran 100 yd backwards in 12.8 sec at Amherst, MA on 28 Jul 1983. Arvind Pandya of India ran backwards from Los Angeles to New York in 107 days, from 18 Aug to 3 Dec 1984.

Powerlifting feats
Lamar Gant (USA) was the first man to deadlift five times his own body weight, lifting 661 lb when weighing 132 lb in 1985. The greatest powerlift by a woman is a squat of 628 lb by Lorraine Constanzo (USA) at Dayton, OH on 21 Nov 1987. Cammie Lynn Lusko (USA; b. 5 Apr 1958) became the first woman to lift more than her body weight with one arm, with 131 lb at a body weight of 128.5 lb, at Milwaukee, WI on 21 May 1983.

Most Olympic weightlifting medals
Norbert Schemansky (USA; b. 30 May 1924) won a record four Olympic medals: gold, middle heavyweight 1952; silver, heavyweight 1948; bronze, heavyweight 1960 and 1964. Three US lifters won two gold medals: John Henry Davis, Jr. (b. 12 Jan 1921), heavyweight 1948 and 1952; Tommy Tamio Kono (b. 27 Jun 1930), lightweight 1952, light heavyweight 1956; Charles Thomas "Chuck" Vinci, Jr. (b. 28 Feb 1933), bantamweight 1956 and 1960.

Heaviest heavyweight

The heaviest wrestler in Olympic history was Chris Taylor (1950–79), bronze medalist in the super-heavyweight class in 1972, who stood 6 ft 5 in tall and weighed over 420 lb. FILA introduced an upper weight limit of 286 lb for international competition in 1985.

Longest sailboard

The longest snake of sailboards was set by 70 windsurfers in a row at the Sailboard Show '89 event at Narrabeen Lakes, Manly, Australia on 21 Oct 1989.

The world's longest sailboard, 165 ft, was constructed at Fredrikstad, Norway, and first sailed on 28 Jun 1986.

race is still held today in every even-numbered year, though the course is now Newport, RI to Bermuda.

The oldest race for any type of craft and either kind of water (fresh or salt) still regularly held is the Chicago-to-Mackinac race on Lakes Michigan and Huron, first sailed in 1898. It was held again in 1904, then annually until the present day, except for 1917–20. The record for the course (333 nautical miles) is 1 day 1 hr 50 min (average speed 12.89 knots), by the sloop *Pied Piper*, owned by Dick Jennings (USA) in 1987.

The current record holder of the elapsed-time records for both the premier American and British ocean races (the Newport, RI, to Bermuda race and the Fastnet race) is the sloop *Nirvana*, owned by Marvin Green (USA). The record for the Bermuda race, 635 nautical miles, is 2 days 14 hr 29 min, in 1982; and for the Fastnet race, 605 nautical miles, the record is 2 days 12 hr 41 min, in 1985—an average speed of 10.16 knots and 9.97 knots respectively.

Longest race The world's longest sailing race is the Vendée Globe Challenge, the first of which started from Les Sables d'Olonne, France on 26 Nov 1989. The distance circumnavigated without stopping was 22,500 nautical miles . The race is for boats between 50–60 ft, sailed single-handedly. The record time on the course is 109 days 8 hr 48 min 50 sec by Titouan Lamazou (France; b. 1955) in the sloop *Ecureuil d'Aquitaine*, which finished at Les Sables on 19 Mar 1990.

The oldest regular sailing race around the world is the quadrennial Whitbread Round the World race (instituted Aug 1973) organized by the Royal Naval Sailing Association. It starts in England, and the course around the world and the number of legs with stops at specified ports are varied from race to race. The distance for 1989–90 was 32,000 nautical miles from Southampton,

Great Britain and return, with stops and restarts at Punta del Este, Uruguay; Fremantle, Australia; Auckland, New Zealand; Punta del Este, Uruguay; and Fort Lauderdale, FL.

America's Cup The America's Cup was originally won as an outright prize by the schooner *America* on 22 Aug 1851 at Cowes and was later offered by the New York Yacht Club as a challenge trophy. On 8 Aug 1870 J. Ashbury's *Cambria* (Great Britain) failed to capture the trophy from *Magic*, owned by F. Osgood (USA). The Cup has been challenged 27 times. The United States was undefeated, winning 77 races and only losing eight, until 1983, when *Australia II*, skippered by John Bertrand and owned by a Perth syndicate headed by Alan Bond, beat *Liberty* 4–3, the narrowest series victory, at Newport, RI.

Charlie Barr (USA; 1864–1911), who defended in 1899, 1901 and 1903, and Harold S. Vanderbilt (USA; 1884–1970) in 1930, 1934 and 1937, each steered the successful cup defender three times in succession. Dennis Walter Conner (USA; b. 16 Sep 1942) has been helmsman of American boats four times in succession: in 1980, when he successfully defended; in 1983, when he steered the defender, but lost; in 1987, when the American challenger regained the trophy; and in 1988, when he again successfully defended. He was also starting helmsman in 1974, with Ted Hood as skipper.

The largest yacht to have competed in the America's Cup was the 1903 defender, the gaff rigged cutter *Reliance*, with an overall length of 144 ft, a record sail area of 16,160 ft^2 and a rig 175 ft high.

Fastest speeds The fastest speed reached under sail on water by any craft over a 500-meter timed run is by Thierry Bielak (France) on a boardsailer at 44.66 knots at Saintes Maries-de-la-Mer

canal, Camargue, France on 27 Feb 1990. The women's record was set at the same location by Brigitte Gimenez (France; b. 6 Oct 1961), who achieved 39.45 knots in December 1990.

The American with the best time under sail over a 500 meter run is Jimmy Lewis, with 38.68 knots at Saintes Maries-de-la-Mer in Feb 1988.

Most competitors The most boats ever to start in a single race was 2,072 in the Round Zeeland (Denmark) race on 21 Jun 1984, over a course of 235 nautical miles.

The largest trans-oceanic race was the ARC (Atlantic Rally for Cruisers), when 204 boats of the 209 starters from 24 nations completed the race from Las Palmas de Gran Canaria (Canary Islands) to Barbados in 1989.

Highest The greatest altitude at which sailing has taken place is 16,109 ft on Laguna Huallatani, Bolivia, in *Mirror Dinghy 55448*, variously by Peter Williams, Gordon Siddeley, Keith Robinson and Brian Barrett, on 19 Nov 1977.

BOARDSAILING (Windsurfing) —

The British High Court ruled on 7 Apr 1982 that Peter Chilvers (when age 12) had devised a prototype of a boardsailer in 1958 in England. In 1968 Henry Hoyle Schweitzer and Jim Drake pioneered the sport, often termed windsurfing, in California. World Championships were first held in 1973 and the sport was added to the Olympic Games in 1984, when the winner was Stephan van den Berg (Netherlands; b. 20 Feb 1962), who also won five world titles 1979–83.

Highest altitude Richard Franklin of Liverpool, Great Britain boardsailed at a record height of 17,027 ft in an unnamed glacial meltwater near Cerro Wila Lloje, Bolivia in South America on 31 Jul 1988.

■ **Fastest speed**
The fastest speed reached under sail on water by a woman is by Brigitte Gimenez (France), who achieved 39.45 knots on the Saintes Maries-de-la-Mer canal, Camargue, France in December 1990. (Photo: All-Sport[USA]/J. Nicholson)

THE EARTH AND SPACE

Deepest caves by country (table, p. 16) The deepest cave in Mexico is the Cueva Cheve, with a depth of 4,547 ft.

Volcanoes, Largest active (p. 21) There was a minor eruption of Mauna Loa shortly after the total eclipse of the sun, which was clearly visible from Hawaii, on 11 Jul 1991.

THE LIVING WORLD

Largest toad (p. 42) The largest toad ever recorded was a marine toad (*Bufo marinus*) nicknamed Prinsen, owned by Håkan Forsberg of Åkers Styckebruk, Sweden. The toad weighed 5 lb 13½ oz and measured 15 in from snout-to-vent (21⅕ in when extended) in March 1991.

Mantle of bees (p. 46) Jed Shaner was covered in a mantle of an estimated 343,000 bees weighing 80 lb at Staunton, VA on 29 Jun 1991.

Largest apple (table, p. 55) *United States* In 1990 Justin and Richard Rothstein of Bingham Lake, MN grew the largest apple in the United States, which weighed 2 lb 10 oz and had a vertical circumference of 18¼ in.

Largest peanut (table, p. 55) Earl Adkins of Enfield, NC grew a peanut that was exactly 4 in in length in 1990.

THE HUMAN BEING

Earliest hominoid (p. 64) A hominoid jaw-bone with three molars, discovered in the Otavi Hills, Namibia on 4 Jun 1991 by Mark Pickford of the College de France, has been dated to 10–15 million years.

Oldest mother (p. 67) It was reported in the *British Medical Journal* (June 1991) that a mother gave birth at the age of 59 years.

Lightest single birth (p. 68) The lowest birth weight reported for a surviving infant is 9.9 oz in the case of a baby born at Loyola University Medical Center, Chicago, IL in June 1989.

Oldest siblings *United States* The oldest living siblings in the United States were Nellie Hardman Eby (b. 17 May 1881) and Katherine Hardman Davenport (31 Mar 1883), who on 17 May 1991 were 110 and 108 respectively.

Balancing on one foot (p. 77) The longest recorded duration for balancing on one foot is 45 hr 25 min by Leslie Silva at Negombo, Sri Lanka from 6–8 Apr 1991.

THE HUMAN WORLD

Largest elections (p. 90) For the Indian elections held on 20 May, 12 June and 15 June 1991, the electorate was around 520 million people, although details of votes cast are not yet available. As a result of the elections, P.V. Narasimha Rao of the Congress (I) Party became the country's new Prime Minister.

Death row (p. 94) *United States* Howard Virgil Lee Douglas spent 17½ years on death row, more than any other person in American penal history. On 15 May 1991 he was resentenced to life in prison.

Longest march (p. 97) A team of nine, representing II Squadron RAF Regiment from RAF Hullavington, Great Britain, each man carrying a 40-lb pack, including a rifle, completed the London Marathon in 4 hr 33 min 58 sec on 21 Apr 1991.

Most parade ribbons On 10 Jun 1991, at the massive "Operation Welcome Home" parade in New York City, 140 miles of waterproof yellow ribbon were donated by Berwick Industries, Inc. and New York's Operation Welcome Home committee.

SCIENCE AND TECHNOLOGY

Oil spills (p. 109) The worst single assault ever made on the environment was released on 19 Jan 1991 by the Iraqi president, Saddam Hussein, who ordered the pumping of Gulf crude oil from Kuwait's Sea Island terminal and from seven large tankers into the Persian Gulf. The best estimate of the outflow is 4–6 million barrels. On 17 February Hussein ordered the dynamiting and firing of 510 wellheads in the Burgan and five other Kuwaiti oil fields, thus raising oil and soot clouds to 22,000 ft, polluting the crops of southern Iran and carrying as far east as India and the snow fields of Pakistan.

Tallest timepiece The tallest clock in the world sits atop the Morton International Building in Chicago, IL. It is 580 ft above street level.

Longest pendulum (p. 114) The longest pendulum in the world is a reconstruction of Foucault's experiment. It swings from a cable 90 ft long and 23 ft above the heads of visitors to the Convention Center in Portland, OR and weighs 900 lb.

Longest manned space flight (p. 118) The most experience space traveler is the Soviet flight engineer Musa Manarov, who has clocked 541 days 31 min 10 sec on two spaceflights in 1987–88 and 1990–91.

Youngest astronaut (p. 117) The youngest American astronaut was astrophysicist Tamara Jernigan, who on 5 Jun 1991, at the age of 32 years, was launched aboard *STS 40 Columbia*.

BUILDINGS AND STRUCTURES

Office rentals (p. 120) The highest rentals in the world are still in Tokyo, Japan, but their rental value has dropped from $187 per ft² in January 1990 to $176.89 per ft² in December 1990. With added service charges and rates this is increased to $192.24 per ft².

Roller coasters (p. 123) *Longest* The longest roller coaster in the world is *The Ultimate* at Lightwater Valley, Ripon, Great Britain. The run is 1.42 miles.

Tallest The *Moonsault Scramble*, at the Fujikyu Highland Park near Kawaguchi Lake, Japan is 206.7 ft tall.

Wooden The tallest wooden roller coaster is the *Mean Streak* at Cedar Point Amusement Park in Sandusky, OH. At its highest point it is 161 ft, with a top speed of up to 65 mph.

Tallest tower (p. 124) On 10 Aug 1991 the Warszawa radio mast, the world's tallest structure, was reported to have fallen during renovation, causing over $20 million in damages.

Highest advertising signs (p. 128) The highest is the logo "I" at the top of the 73-story 1,017-ft-tall First Interstate World Center building, Los Angeles, CA.

Snow and ice constructions (p. 130) *Snowman* A snow structure 74 ft high and named "Yukichian, the Snow Girl" was built by villagers of Sumon and Niigata, Japan on 3 Mar 1991.

TRANSPORT

Highest mileage (p. 141) The highest recorded mileage for a car is 1,283,517 authenticated miles up to 11 Jul 1991 for a 1963 Volkswagen Beetle owned by Albert Klein of Pasadena, CA.

Longest fuel range (p. 142) The greatest distance driven without refueling on a single fuel fill in a standard vehicle (39.3 gal carried in factory optional twin fuel tanks) is 1,618.7 miles by a Tempo Trax diesel pick-up. Driven by Rajendra Singh and Lal Singh of India in 49 hr 24 min 25 sec from 17–19 Jun 1991, the fuel average was 41.2 mpg.

Two-wheel side driving (p. 143) Sven-Erik Söderman of Sweden drove a Daf2800 7.5-ton truck on two wheels for a distance of 6.73 miles at Mora Siljan airport, Delecarlia, Sweden on 19 May 1991.

Fastest camper (p. 144) The speed record for a camper is 126.76 mph by a Roadster camper towed by a 1990 Ford EA Falcon, driven by Charlie Kovacs, at Mangalore Airfield, Seymour, Victoria, Australia on 18 Apr 1991.

Biggest motorcycle pyramid (p. 145) The Dare Devils, the Corps of the Signals Indian Army, Motorcycle Display Team, established a world record with a pyramid of 40 men on 7 motorcycles. The pyramid, held together by muscle and determination only, with no straps, harnesses or any other aids, traveled a distance of 437 yd on 15 Feb 1991.

Motorcycling around the Americas Kurt Nerlich and Hans Schirmer traveled 67,000 miles (55,400 on a motorcycle) around the Americas (North, South and Central) in 27 months from July 1954 to September 1956. Travel to and through Central and South America was much more primitive at that time than it is today.

Longest driveable road (p. 146) The first all-land crossing of the gap known as the Tapon del Darién in

Panama and another at the Atrato Swamp, Colombia was achieved by Loren Lee Upton and Patricia Mercier in a 1966 CJ 5 Jeep. Their journey began at Yaviza, Republic of Panama on 22 Feb 1985 and ended on 4 Mar 1987 at Rio Suico, Colombia.

Parachuting (table, p. 153) On 8 Jun 1991 Don Kueller of Sugar Loaf, PA made his 15,000th parachute jump.

THE BUSINESS WORLD

Richest men (p. 158) Forbes magazine estimated in its issue of 22 Jul 1991 that Taikichiro Mori of Japan, aged 87, was the world's richest man, with assets of $15 billion. A former economics professor, he now owns some 80 offices.

Coin balancing (p. 160) The tallest single column of coins ever stacked on the edge of a coin was made up of 253 Indian one-rupee pieces on top of a vertical five-rupee coin, by Dipak Syal of Yamuna Nagar, India on 3 May 1991.

Coin snatching The greatest number of British 10p coins clean-caught from being flipped from the back of a forearm into the downward palm is 254, by Dean Gould of Felixstowe, Great Britain on 12 Jul 1991.

THE ARTS AND ENTERTAINMENT

Sand sculpture (p. 168) The longest sand sculpture ever made was the meticulously carved 86,535-ft-6-in-long masterpiece *The GTE Directories Ultimate Sand Castle*, built by more than 10,000 volunteers at Myrtle Beach, SC on 31 May 1991.

Antiques, Oldest auctioneers (p. 169) The oldest firm of art auctioneers in the world is the Stockholms Auktionsverk of Sweden, which was established on 27 Feb 1647.

Ancient sculpture (p. 170) The *Cycladic Marble Head of a Goddess*, from the early Bronze Age II, c. 2600–2500 B.C., was sold at Sotheby's, New York in December 1988 for $2,090,000.

Top-selling author (p. 176) Dame Barbara Cartland had completed her 543rd published title by 9 Jul 1991.

Largest guitar The largest (and possibly the loudest) playable guitar in the world is 38 ft 2 in tall, 16 ft wide and weighs 1,865 lb. Modeled on the Gibson "Flying V," it was made by students of Shakamak High School in Jasonville, IN. The instrument was unveiled on 17 May 1991 when, powered by six amplifiers, it was played simultaneously by six members of the school.

Stilt walking (p. 188) The fastest stilt-walker on record is Roy Luiking, who covered 328 ft on 1-ft-high stilts in 13.14 sec at Didam, Netherlands on 2 Jun 1991.

Largest television contracts (p. 194) Johnny Carson has announced that he will retire from presenting *The Tonight Show* on 22 May 1992. He first appeared as guest host in 1958 and became the established presenter on 1 Oct 1962.

HUMAN ACHIEVEMENTS

Dancing dragon (p. 185) The longest dancing dragon, created for the third International Abilympics in 1991, measured 3,034 ft from the end of its tongue to the tip of its tail and took four months to complete. A total of 1,024 people brought the dragon to life, making it dance for 2 minutes at the Happy Valley racecourse, Hong Kong on 11 Aug 1991.

Party giving (p. 198) The world's biggest birthday party was attended by 75,000 people at Buffalo, NY on 4 Jul 1991 as part of the 1991 Friendship Festival to celebrate the 215th birthday of the United States and Canada's 115th birthday.

Largest burrito Taco Tico of Nebraska, Inc created the world's largest burrito, 1,597 ft 9 in long, on 29 Jun 1991 in Newton, Kansas. The burrito was constructed from 2,557 tortillas, 607 lb of refried beans and 75.75 lb of shredded cheese.

Leapfrogging (p. 201) The greatest distance covered was 996.2 miles by 14 students from Trancos dormitory at Stanford University, CA. They started leapfrogging on 16 May 1991 and stopped 244 hr 43 min later on 26 May.

Needle threading (p. 201) The record number of times that a strand of cotton has been threaded through a number-13 needle (eye $\frac{1}{2} \times \frac{1}{16}$ in) in 2 hr is 8,927, set by Dipak Syal of Yamuna Nagar, India on 8 May 1991.

Largest cocktail (p. 202) The largest cocktail on record was one of 659.9 gal, made by Ettore Diana at Lazise, Italy on 4 Oct 1989 and named "Ciao."

United States The largest cocktail in the United States weighed 350 gal and was made by the Hyatt Regency's River Edge Cafe of Chicago, IL on 13 Jun 1991.

Popcorn (p. 204) The largest box of popcorn contained 5,438.16 ft^3 of popped corn. It measured 52 ft 7$\frac{1}{4}$ in × 10 ft 1$\frac{1}{2}$ in and was filled by Stanly County at Stanly Community College, Albemarle, NC from 6–8 Aug 1991. The average depth was 10 ft 2$\frac{1}{2}$ in.

Largest greeting card (p. 206) The Commerce Day Christmas card, made by students of University College, Dublin, Republic of Ireland and posted on 6 Dec 1990 to the city's Central Remedial Clinic for handicapped children, measured a world record 2,712.5 ft^2 (98.4 × 27.5 ft).

Jigsaw puzzles (p. 207) The world's largest jigsaw puzzle measures 11,302.2 ft^2 but consists of only 2,250 pieces. Assembled on 19 Mar 1991, it was devised by J.N. Nichols (Vimto) plc of Manchester, Great Britain, and designed and built by students from the Manchester Polytechnic school.

SPORTS AND GAMES

Auto Racing (p. 214) Formula One Grand Prix, most successful drivers After the Hungarian Grand Prix on 11 Aug 1991, Alain Prost had scored 686.5 points from 179 races, Ricardo Patrese has started 218 races and Ayrton Senna had achieved 57 pole positions from 120 races (31 wins).

Baseball (p. 218) Stolen bases Rickey Henderson, 973 bases to 11 Aug 1991.

Most strikeouts Nolan Ryan, 5,453 to 11 Aug 1991.

Billiards, Three cushion (p. 228) Most titles Raymond Ceulemans won a 20th world three-cushion championship in 1990.

Board games, solitare (p. 229) The shortest time taken to complete the game is 10 sec by Stephen Twigge in Scissett Baths, Great Britain on 2 Aug 1991.

Darts (p. 242) Highest 24-hour individual score is 518,060 by Davy Richardson-Page at Blucher Social Club, Newcastle, Great Britain on 6–7 Jul 1991.

Golf, British Open (p. 254) Lowest score Joseph Martin "Jodie" Mudd (USA; b. 23 Apr 1960) equaled the lowest score for any round of the British Open, shooting 63 in the final round at Royal Birkdale on 21 Jul 1991.

Gymnastics (table, p. 259) Push-ups (one arm)—5 hours: 7,683 by John Decker, at Congleton Cricket Club, Great Britain on 16 Jun 1991. Sit-ups (24 hours): 65,001 by Marc Scriven, at St John's Sports Centre, Worcester, Great Britain on 21–22 Jun 1991. Burpees (1 hour): 1,619 by Paddy Doyle at Birmingham International Convention Centre, Great Britain on 21 Jun 1991.

Judo, most titles (p. 268) Naoya Ogawa (Japan) won a record-equaling fourth world title at Barcelona on 28 Jun 1991, winning the Open category. He had previously won the Open in 1987 and 1989 and in the Over 95 kg category in 1989.

Netball (p. 271) Australia won a record 6th world title on 14 Jul 1991 in Sydney, defeating New Zealand 53–52. During the 1991 World Championships, the Cook Islands set a new highest team score when they defeated Vanuatu, 120–38 on 9 July.

Rappeling (p. 271) Recent research has shown that a team of eight men from the Code 4 Rescue unit rappeled 1,122 ft down the CN Tower, Toronto, Canada on 26 Jun 1985.

Rugby, Highest international scores (table, p. 279) David Campese has scored 40 tries in a record 57 international appearances for Australia and Michael Lynagh has scored a record 607 points in 45 matches, also for Australia.

Speedway (p. 283) World Championships Denmark won the World Pairs title for a record eighth time on 20 Jul 1991. Hans Nielsen was a member of the team for a record sixth time.

Swimming, Long-distance relay (p. 286) The most participants in a one-day swim relay is 2,145, each swimming a length, organized by Jeff D. Van-Buren and David W. Thompson at Hamilton College in Clinton, NY on 8 Apr 1989.

Track and Field (table, p. 291) World records Men, 4 × 100 m relay: USA (Mike Marsh, Dennis Mitchell, Leroy Burrell and Carl Lewis), 37.67 sec at Zürich, Switzerland on 7 Aug 1991. Pole vault: Sergey Bubka (USSR) 20 ft $\frac{1}{4}$ in at Malmö, Sweden on 5 Aug 1991.

Mass relay record The greatest distance covered by an American team of ten runners in 24 hr is 271.974 miles by students of Marcus High School in Texas from 17 May to 18 May 1991.

How To Use: Every index entry contains the page and column location (e.g., Aaron, Hank 175.3). The page is 175 and the column is 3. Asterisks * denote an updated record in Extra! Extra!

INDEX